OFFICIAL 2003 Men's

NCAA Basketball Records

NCAA

Individual and Team Records for all Divisions

Includes Single-Game, Season and Career Statistics

Coaching Records

Championship Results

2002 Statistical Leaders

All-Americans

Award Winners

Week-By-Week Polls

Attendance Records

2002 Conference Standings

Single-Game Highs

Rules History

THE NATIONAL COLLEGIATE ATHLETIC ASSOCIATION
P.O. Box 6222, Indianapolis, Indiana 46206-6222
317/917-6222
http://www.ncaa.org

October 2002

Compiled By:
Gary K. Johnson, *Senior Assistant Director of Statistics.*
Sean W. Straziscar, *Assistant Director of Statistics.*

Edited By:
Marty Benson, *Assistant Director of Communications.*

Production By:
Toi Davis, *Production Designer II.*

Cover Design By:
Wayne Davis, *Associate Director of Graphics.*

Cover Photography By:
Clarkson and Associates.

Distributed to sports information directors and conference publicity directors.

Contents

Name-Change Key

The following players changed their names after their collegiate careers ended. They are listed throughout the book by the names under which they played in college (those listed at the left). Their current names are listed below. In addition, various schools have changed their name. The current school name is listed along with other names by which the schools have been referred.

PLAYER name changes

Name as a collegian:	Changed to:
Lew Alcindor (UCLA)	Kareem Abdul-Jabbar
Walt Hazzard (UCLA)	Mahdi Abdul-Rahmad
Chris Jackson (LSU)	Mahmoud Abdul-Rauf
Akeem Olajuwon (Houston)	Hakeem Olajuwon
Keith Wilkes (UCLA)	Jamaal Wilkes
Jason Williams (Duke)	Jay Williams

SCHOOL name changes

Current school name:	Changed from:
Albertson	Col. of Idaho
Alcorn St.	Alcorn A&M
Alliant Int'l	U.S. Int'l; Cal Western
Arcadia	Beaver
Ark.-Pine Bluff	Arkansas AM&N
Armstrong Atlantic	Armstrong St.
Auburn	Alabama Poly
Augusta St.	Augusta
Bemidji St.	Bemidji Teachers
Benedictine (Ill.)	Ill. Benedictine
Bradley	Bradley Tech
UC Davis	California Aggies
Cal St. Fullerton	Orange County State College; Orange St.
Cal St. Northridge	San Fernando Valley St.
Case Reserve	Case Institute of Technology
Central Okla.	Central St. (Okla.)
Charleston So.	Baptist (S.C.)
Charleston (W.Va.)	Morris Harvey
Charlotte	UNC Charlotte
Chattanooga	Tenn.-Chatt.
Cleveland St.	Fenn
Colorado St.	Colorado A&M
Columbus St.	Columbus
Concordia (Calif.)	Christ College-Irvine
Concordia (Ill.)	Concordia Teachers
Crown	St. Paul Bible
DeSales	Allentown
Detroit	Detroit Mercy; Detroit Tech
Dist. of Columbia	D.C. Teachers; Federal City
Dominican	Rosary
Drexel	Drexel Tech
Duke	Trinity (N.C.)
Eastern Mich.	Michigan Normal
Emporia St.	Kansas St. Normal
FDU-Florham	FDU-Madison
Farmington St.	Maine-Farmington
Fresno St.	Fresno Pacific
Ga. Southern	Georgia Teachers
Ill.-Chicago	Ill.-Chicago Circle
Illinois St.	Illinois St. Normal; Illinois Normal
Indiana (Pa.)	Indiana St. (Pa.)
Indianapolis	Indiana Central
Iowa	State University of Iowa
Iowa St.	Ames
James Madison	Madison
Kansas St.	Kansas Aggies
Kent St.	Kent
La Sierra	Loma Linda
Lamar	Lamar Tech
Liberty	Lynchburg Baptist; Liberty Baptist
La.-Lafayette	Southwestern La.
La.-Monroe	Northeast La.
Loyola Marymount	Loyola U. of L.A.
Lynn	College of Boca Raton
Lyon	Arkansas College
Maritime (N.Y.)	N.Y. Maritime
Martin Luther	Northwestern (Wis.)
Marycrest Int'l	Teikyo Marycrest
Md.-East. Shore	Maryland St.
Massachusetts	Massachusetts St.; Massachusetts Agriculture Col.
Mass. Liberal Arts	North Adams St.
Mass.-Dartmouth	Southeastern Mass.
Mass.-Lowell	Lowell; Lowell St.; Lowell Tech

Current school name:	Changed from:
McDaniel	Western Md.
Memphis	Memphis St.
Minn. St. Mankato	Mankato Teachers; Mankato St.
Minn. St. Moorhead	Moorhead St.; Moorhead Teachers
Mont. St.-Billings	Eastern Montana
Montana St.-Northern	Northern Montana
Murray St.	Murray Teachers
Neb.-Kearney	Kearney St.
Neb.-Omaha	Omaha
New England U.	St. Francis (Me.)
Col. of New Jersey	Trenton St.
New Jersey City	Jersey City St.
N.J. Inst. of Tech.	Newark Engineering
New Mexico St.	New Mexico A&M
New Orleans	Louisiana St. (N.O.)
North Ala.	Florence St.
N.C. Central	North Caro. College
UNC Pembroke	Pembroke St.
North Central Texas	Cooke County
North Texas	North Tex. St.
Northeastern St.	Northeastern Okla. St.
Northern Ariz.	Arizona St.-Flagstaff; Flagstaff Teachers
Northern Colo.	Colorado St. College
Northern Iowa	Iowa Teachers
Oklahoma St.	Oklahoma A&M
Old Dominion	William & Mary (Norfolk)
Pepperdine	George Pepperdine
Philadelphia U.	Philadelphia Textile
Polytechnic (N.Y.)	New York Poly; Brooklyn Poly
Rhodes	Southwestern (Tenn.)
Rice	Rice Institute
Richard Stockton	Stockton St.
Rochester Inst.	Mechanics Institute
Rowan	Glassboro St.
Southern Ind.	Indiana St.-Evansville
Southern Me.	Maine Portland-Gorham; Gorham St. (Me.)
Southern N.H.	New Hamp. Col.
Southern U.	Southern B.R.
Taylor-Ft. Wayne	Summit Christian
Tex. A&M-Commerce	East Texas St.
Tex. A&M-Kingsville	Texas A&I
Tex.-Pan American	Pan American
Towson	Towson St.
Truman	Northeast Mo. St.; Truman St.
Tulsa	Henry Kendall
Washburn	Lincoln College
Washington St.	Washington Agricultural College
West Ala.	Livingston
West Tex. A&M	West Texas St.
Western Mich.	Western State Teachers
Western N. M.	New Mexico Western
Western Ore.	Oregon Tech; Oregon College of Education
Western St.	Colo. Western; Colorado Normal
Westmar	Western Union College; Teikyo Westmar
Wichita St.	Fairmount
Widener	Pennsylvania Military College
Wm. Paterson	Paterson St.
Wis.-Eau Claire	Eau Claire Teachers
Wis.-La Crosse	La Crosse Teachers
Wis.-River Falls	River Falls Teachers
Wis.-Superior	Superior Normal; Superior St. Teachers
Xavier	St. Xavier

SCHOOLS also known as

Current school name:	Also known as:
Air Force	U.S. Air Force Academy
Apprentice School	Newport News
Army	U.S. Military Academy; West Point
Baruch	Bernard M. Baruch
Case Reserve	Case Western Reserve
CCNY	City College of New York
Coast Guard	U.S. Coast Guard Academy
GC&SU	Georgia College & State
Hawthorne	Nathaniel Hawthorne
IPFW	Indiana/Purdue-Ft. Wayne
IUPUI	Indiana/Purdue-Indianapolis
Lehman	Herbert H. Lehman

Current school name:	Also known as:
Lipscomb	David Lipscomb
Long Island	LIU-Brooklyn
LSU	Louisiana St.
Merchant Marine	King's Point; U.S. Merchant Marine Academy
MIT	Massachusetts Institute of Technology
Navy	U.S. Naval Academy
NYCCT	New York City Tech
NYIT	New York Institute of Technology; New York Tech
Rochester Inst.	RIT
Sewanee	University of the South
TCU	Texas Christian
UAB	Ala.-Birmingham
UCF	Central Fla. (was Florida Tech)
UCLA	University of California, Los Angeles
UMBC	Md.-Balt. County
UMKC	Mo.-Kansas City
UNLV	Nevada-Las Vegas (was Nevada Southern)
UTEP	Texas-El Paso (was Texas Western)
VMI	Va. Military
WPI	Worcester Poly Inst.

Division I Records

Individual Records

Basketball records are confined to the "modern era," which began with the 1937-38 season, the first without the center jump after each goal scored. Except for the school's all-time won-lost record or coaches' records, only statistics achieved while an institution was an active member of the NCAA are included in team or individual categories. Official weekly statistics rankings in scoring and shooting began with the 1947-48 season; individual rebounds were added for the 1950-51 season, although team rebounds were not added until 1954-55. Assists were added in 1983-84, blocked shots and steals were added in 1985-86 and three-point field goals were added in 1986-87. Scoring, rebounding, assists, blocked shots and steals are ranked on total number and on per-game average; shooting, on percentage. In statistical rankings, the rounding of percentages and/or averages may indicate ties where none exist. In these cases, the numerical order of the rankings is accurate. In 1973, freshmen became eligible to compete on the varsity level.

Scoring

POINTS
Game
100—Frank Selvy, Furman vs. Newberry, Feb. 13, 1954 (41 FGs, 18 FTs)
Season
1,381—Pete Maravich, LSU, 1970 (522 FGs, 337 FTs, 31 games)
Career
3,667—Pete Maravich, LSU, 1968-70 (1,387 FGs, 893 FTs, 83 games)

POINTS VS. DIVISION I OPPONENT
Game
72—Kevin Bradshaw, U.S. Int'l vs. Loyola Marymount, Jan. 5, 1991

AVERAGE PER GAME
Season
44.5—Pete Maravich, LSU, 1970 (1,381 in 31)
Career
44.2—Pete Maravich, LSU, 1968-70 (3,667 in 83)

COMBINED POINTS, TWO TEAMMATES
Game
125—Frank Selvy (100) and Darrell Floyd (25), Furman vs. Newberry, Feb. 13, 1954

COMBINED POINTS, TWO TEAMMATES VS. DIVISION I OPPONENT
Game
92—Kevin Bradshaw (72) and Isaac Brown (20), U.S. Int'l vs. Loyola Marymount, Jan. 5, 1991

COMBINED POINTS, TWO OPPOSING PLAYERS ON DIVISION I TEAMS
Game
115—Pete Maravich (64), LSU and Dan Issel (51), Kentucky, Feb. 21, 1970

GAMES SCORING AT LEAST 50 POINTS
Season
10—Pete Maravich, LSU, 1970
Season—Consecutive Games
3—Pete Maravich, LSU, Feb. 10 to Feb. 15, 1969
Career
28—Pete Maravich, LSU, 1968-70

GAMES SCORING AT LEAST 40 POINTS
Career
56—Pete Maravich, LSU, 1968-70

GAMES SCORING IN DOUBLE FIGURES
Career
132—Danny Manning, Kansas, 1985-88

CONSECUTIVE GAMES SCORING IN DOUBLE FIGURES
Career
115—Lionel Simmons, La Salle, 1987-90

Field Goals

FIELD GOALS
Game
41—Frank Selvy, Furman vs. Newberry, Feb. 13, 1954 (66 attempts)
Season
522—Pete Maravich, LSU, 1970 (1,168 attempts)
Career
1,387—Pete Maravich, LSU, 1968-70 (3,166 attempts)

CONSECUTIVE FIELD GOALS
Game
16—Doug Grayson, Kent St. vs. North Carolina, Dec. 6, 1967 (18 of 19)
Season
25—Ray Voelkel, American, 1978 (during nine games, Nov. 24-Dec. 16)

FIELD-GOAL ATTEMPTS
Game
71—Jay Handlan, Wash. & Lee vs. Furman, Feb. 17, 1951 (30 made)
Season
1,168—Pete Maravich, LSU, 1970 (522 made)
Career
3,166—Pete Maravich, LSU, 1968-70 (1,387 made)

FIELD-GOAL PERCENTAGE
Game
(Min. 15 made) 100%—Clifford Rozier, Louisville vs. Eastern Ky., Dec. 11, 1993 (15 of 15)
(Min. 20 made) 95.5%—Bill Walton, UCLA vs. Memphis, March 26, 1973 (21 of 22)
***Season**
74.6%—Steve Johnson, Oregon St., 1981 (235 of 315)
*Based on qualifiers for national championship.
Career
(Min. 400 made and 4 made per game) 67.8%—Steve Johnson, Oregon St., 1976-81 (828 of 1,222)

Three-Point Field Goals

THREE-POINT FIELD GOALS
Game
15—Keith Veney, Marshall vs. Morehead St., Dec. 14, 1996 (25 attempts)
Season
158—Darrin Fitzgerald, Butler, 1987 (362 attempts)
Career
413—Curtis Staples, Virginia, 1995-98 (1,079 attempts)

THREE-POINT FIELD GOALS MADE PER GAME
Season
5.6—Darrin Fitzgerald, Butler, 1987 (158 in 28)
Career
(Min. 200 made) 4.6—Timothy Pollard, Mississippi Val., 1988-89 (256 in 56)

CONSECUTIVE THREE-POINT FIELD GOALS
Game
11—Gary Bossert, Niagara vs. Siena, Jan. 7, 1987
Season
15—Todd Leslie, Northwestern, 1990 (during four games, Dec. 15-28)

CONSECUTIVE GAMES MAKING A THREE-POINT FIELD GOAL
Season
38—Steve Kerr, Arizona, Nov. 27, 1987, to April 2, 1988
Career
88—Cory Bradford, Illinois, Nov. 10, 1998 to Feb. 10, 2001

THREE-POINT FIELD-GOAL ATTEMPTS
Game
27—Bruce Seals, Manhattan vs. Canisius, Jan. 31, 2000 (9 made)
Season
362—Darrin Fitzgerald, Butler, 1987 (158 made)
Career
1,079—Curtis Staples, Virginia, 1995-98 (413 made)

THREE-POINT FIELD-GOAL ATTEMPTS PER GAME
Game
12.9—Darrin Fitzgerald, Butler, 1987 (362 in 28)
Career
9.1—Keith Veney, Lamar & Marshall, 1993-94, 1996-97 (1,014 in 111)

THREE-POINT FIELD-GOAL PERCENTAGE
Game
(Min. 9 made) 100%—Mark Poag, Old Dominion vs. VMI, Nov. 25, 1997 (9 of 9); Markus Wilson, Evansville vs. Tenn.-Martin, Nov. 18, 1998 (9 of 9)
(Min. 12 made) 85.7%—Gary Bossert, Niagara vs. Siena, Jan. 7, 1987 (12 of 14)
Season
(Min. 50 made) 63.4%—Glenn Tropf, Holy Cross, 1988 (52 of 82)
(Min. 100 made) 57.3%—Steve Kerr, Arizona, 1988 (114 of 199)
Career
(Min. 200 made and 1.5 made per game) 49.7%—Tony Bennett, Wis.-Green Bay, 1989-92 (290 of 584)
(Min. 300 made) 45.5%—Shawn Respert, Michigan St., 1992-95 (331 of 728)

Free Throws

FREE THROWS
Game
30—Pete Maravich, LSU vs. Oregon St., Dec. 22, 1969 (31 attempts)
Season
355—Frank Selvy, Furman, 1954 (444 attempts)
Career
(3 yrs.) 893—Pete Maravich, LSU, 1968-70 (1,152 attempts)
(4 yrs.) 905—Dickie Hemric, Wake Forest, 1952-55 (1,359 attempts)

CONSECUTIVE FREE THROWS
Game
24—Arlen Clark, Oklahoma St. vs. Colorado, March 7, 1959 (24 of 24)
Season
73—Gary Buchanan, Villanova, 2000-01 (during 21 games, Nov. 17-Feb. 12)
Career
73—Gary Buchanan, Villanova, 2000-01 (during 21 games, Nov. 17-Feb. 12)

FREE-THROW ATTEMPTS
Game
36—Ed Tooley, Brown vs. Amherst, Dec. 4, 1954 (23 made)
Season
444—Frank Selvy, Furman, 1954 (355 made)
Career
(3 yrs.) 1,152—Pete Maravich, LSU, 1968-70 (893 made)
(4 yrs.) 1,359—Dickie Hemric, Wake Forest, 1952-55 (905 made)

FREE-THROW PERCENTAGE
Game
(Min. 24 made) 100%—Arlen Clark, Oklahoma St. vs. Colorado, March 7, 1959 (24 of 24)
***Season**
95.9%—Craig Collins, Penn St., 1985 (94 of 98)
*Based on qualifiers for national championship.
Career
(Min. 300 made and 2 made per game) 90.9%—Greg Starrick, Kentucky & Southern Ill., 1969, 1970-72 (341 of 375)
(Min. 600 made) 88.5%—Ron Perry, Holy Cross, 1976-80 (680 of 768)

(Min. 2.5 made per game) 92.3%—Dave Hildahl, Portland St., 1979-81 (131 of 142)

Rebounds

REBOUNDS
Game
51—Bill Chambers, William & Mary vs. Virginia, Feb. 14, 1953
(Since 1973) 35—Larry Abney, Fresno St. vs. Southern Methodist, Feb. 17, 2000
Season
734—Walt Dukes, Seton Hall, 1953 (33 games)
(Since 1973) 597—Marvin Barnes, Providence, 1974 (32 games)
Career
(3 yrs.) 1,751—Paul Silas, Creighton, 1962-64 (81 games)
(4 yrs.) 2,201—Tom Gola, La Salle, 1952-55 (118 games)
(Since 1973) 1,570—Tim Duncan, Wake Forest, 1994-97 (128 games)

AVERAGE PER GAME
Season
25.6—Charlie Slack, Marshall, 1955 (538 in 21)
(Since 1973) 20.4—Kermit Washington, American, 1973 (511 in 25)
Career
(Min. 800) 22.7—Artis Gilmore, Jacksonville, 1970-71 (1,224 in 54)
(4 yrs.) 21.8—Charlie Slack, Marshall, 1953-56 (1,916 in 88)
(Since 1973) 15.2—Glenn Mosley, Seton Hall, 1974-77 (1,263 in 83)

Assists

ASSISTS
Game
22—Tony Fairley, Charleston So. vs. Armstrong Atlantic, Feb. 9, 1987; Avery Johnson, Southern U. vs. Texas Southern, Jan. 25, 1988; Sherman Douglas, Syracuse vs. Providence, Jan. 28, 1989
Season
406—Mark Wade, UNLV, 1987 (38 games)
Career
1,076—Bobby Hurley, Duke, 1990-93 (140 games)

AVERAGE PER GAME
Season
13.3—Avery Johnson, Southern U., 1988 (399 in 30)

Career
(Min. 600) 12.0—Avery Johnson, Southern U., 1987-88 (732 in 61)
(4 yrs.) 8.4—Chris Corchiani, North Carolina St., 1988-91 (1,038 in 124)

Blocked Shots

BLOCKED SHOTS
Game
14—David Robinson, Navy vs. UNC Wilmington, Jan. 4, 1986; Shawn Bradley, Brigham Young vs. Eastern Ky., Dec. 7, 1990; Roy Rogers, Alabama vs. Georgia, Feb. 10, 1996; Loren Woods, Arizona vs. Oregon, Feb. 3, 2000
Season
207—David Robinson, Navy, 1986 (35 games)
Career
535—Wojciech Myrda, La.-Monroe, 1999-2002 (115 games)

AVERAGE PER GAME
Season
6.4—Adonal Foyle, Colgate, 1997 (180 in 28)
Career
(Min. 225) 5.9—Keith Closs, Central Conn. St., 1995-96 (317 in 54)
(4 yrs.) 4.7—Wojciech Myrda, La.-Monroe, 1999-2002 (535 in 115)

Steals

STEALS
Game
13—Mookie Blaylock, Oklahoma vs. Centenary (La.), Dec. 12, 1987; and vs. Loyola Marymount, Dec. 17, 1988
Season
160—Desmond Cambridge, Alabama A&M, 2002 (29 games)
Career
385—John Linehan, Providence, 1998-2002 (122 games)

AVERAGE PER GAME
Season
5.5—Desmond Cambridge, Alabama A&M, 2002 (160 in 29)
Career
(Min. 225) 3.9—Desmond Cambridge, Alabama A&M, 1999-2002 (330 in 84)

(4 yrs.) 3.2—Eric Murdock, Providence, 1988-91 (376 in 117)

Fouls

SHORTEST PLAYING TIME BEFORE BEING DISQUALIFIED
Game
1:38—Mike Pflugner, Butler vs. Ill.-Chicago, March 2, 1996

Games

GAMES PLAYED (Since 1947-48)
Season
40—Mark Alarie, Tommy Amaker, Johnny Dawkins, Danny Ferry and Billy King, Duke, 1986; Larry Johnson, UNLV, 1990; Anthony Epps, Jamaal Magloire, Ron Mercer and Wayne Turner, Kentucky, 1997
Career
151—Wayne Turner, Kentucky, 1996-99

General

ACHIEVED 2,000 POINTS AND 2,000 REBOUNDS
Career
Tom Gola, LaSalle, 1952-55 (2,462 points and 2,201 rebounds)
Joe Holup, George Washington, 1953-56 (2,226 points and 2,030 rebounds)

AVERAGED 20 POINTS AND 20 REBOUNDS
Career
Bill Russell, San Francisco, 1954-56 (20.7 points and 20.3 rebounds)
Paul Silas, Creighton, 1962-64 (20.5 points and 21.6 rebounds)
Julius Erving, Massachusetts, 1970-71 (26.3 points and 20.2 rebounds)
Artis Gilmore, Jacksonville, 1970-71 (24.3 points and 22.7 rebounds)
Kermit Washington, American, 1971-73 (20.1 points and 20.2 rebounds)

Team Records

Note: Where records involve both teams, each team must be an NCAA Division I member institution.

SINGLE-GAME RECORDS

Scoring

POINTS
186—Loyola Marymount vs. U.S. Int'l (140), Jan. 5, 1991

POINTS BY LOSING TEAM
150—U.S. Int'l vs. Loyola Marymount (181), Jan. 31, 1989

POINTS, BOTH TEAMS
331—Loyola Marymount (181) vs. U.S. Int'l (150), Jan. 31, 1989

MARGIN OF VICTORY
117—Long Island (179) vs. Medgar Evers (62), Nov. 26, 1997

MARGIN OF VICTORY VS. DIVISION I OPPONENT
91—Tulsa (141) vs. Prairie View (50), Dec. 7, 1995

POINTS IN A HALF
98—Long Island vs. Medgar Evers, Nov. 26, 1997 (2nd)

POINTS IN A HALF VS. DIVISION I OPPONENT
97—Oklahoma vs. U.S. Int'l, Nov. 29, 1989 (1st)

POINTS IN A HALF, BOTH TEAMS
172—Loyola Marymount (86) vs. Gonzaga (86), Feb. 18, 1989 (2nd)

LEAD BEFORE OPPONENT SCORES AT START OF A GAME
34-0—Seton Hall vs. Kean, Nov. 29, 1998

LEAD BEFORE DIVISION I OPPONENT SCORES AT START OF A GAME
32-0—Connecticut vs. New Hampshire, Dec. 12, 1990

DEFICIT OVERCOME TO WIN GAME
32—Duke (74) vs. Tulane (72), Dec. 30, 1950 (trailed 22-54 with 2:00 left in the first half)

SECOND-HALF DEFICIT OVERCOME TO WIN GAME
31—Duke (74) vs. Tulane (72), Dec. 30, 1950 (trailed 27-58 with 19:00 left in the second half); Kentucky (99) vs. LSU (95), Feb. 15, 1994 (trailed 37-68 with 15:34 left in the second half)

HALFTIME DEFICIT OVERCOME TO WIN GAME
29—Duke (74) vs. Tulane (72), Dec. 30, 1950 (trailed 27-56 at halftime)

DEFICIT BEFORE SCORING OVERCOME TO WIN GAME
28—New Mexico St. (117) vs. Bradley (109), Jan. 27, 1977 (trailed 0-28 with 13:49 left in first half)

FEWEST POINTS ALLOWED (Since 1938)
6—Tennessee (11) vs. Temple, Dec. 15, 1973; Kentucky (75) vs. Arkansas St., Jan. 8, 1945

FEWEST POINTS ALLOWED (Since 1986)
21—Coastal Caro. (61) vs. Georgia So., Jan. 2, 1997

FEWEST POINTS, BOTH TEAMS
(Since 1938)
17—Tennessee (11) vs. Temple (6), Dec. 15, 1973

Field Goals

FIELD GOALS
76—Long Island vs. Medgar Evers, Nov. 26, 1997 (124 attempts)

FIELD GOALS VS. DIVISION I OPPONENT
74—Houston vs. Valparaiso, Feb. 24, 1968 (112 attempts)

FIELD GOALS, BOTH TEAMS
130—Loyola Marymount (67) vs. U.S. Int'l (63), Jan. 31, 1989

FIELD GOALS IN A HALF
42—Oklahoma vs. U.S. Int'l, Nov. 29, 1989 (90 attempts) (1st)

FIELD-GOAL ATTEMPTS
147—Oklahoma vs. U.S. Int'l, Nov. 29, 1989 (70 made)

FIELD-GOAL ATTEMPTS, BOTH TEAMS
245—Loyola Marymount (124) vs. U.S. Int'l (121), Jan. 7, 1989

FIELD-GOAL ATTEMPTS IN A HALF
90—Oklahoma vs. U.S. Int'l, Nov. 29, 1989 (42 made) (1st)

FEWEST FIELD GOALS (Since 1938)
2—Duke vs. North Carolina St., March 8, 1968 (11 attempts); Arkansas St. vs. Kentucky, Jan. 8, 1945

FEWEST FIELD-GOAL ATTEMPTS (Since 1938)
9—Pittsburgh vs. Penn St., March 1, 1952 (3 made)

FIELD-GOAL PERCENTAGE
(Min. 15 made) 83.3%—Maryland vs. South Carolina, Jan. 9, 1971 (15 of 18)
(Min. 30 made) 81.4%—New Mexico vs. Oregon St., Nov. 30, 1985 (35 of 43)

FIELD-GOAL PERCENTAGE, HALF
94.1%—North Carolina vs. Virginia, Jan. 7, 1978 (16 of 17) (2nd)

Three-Point Field Goals

THREE-POINT FIELD GOALS
28—Troy St. vs. George Mason, Dec. 10, 1994 (74 attempts)

THREE-POINT FIELD GOALS, BOTH TEAMS
44—Troy St. (28) vs. George Mason (16), Dec. 10, 1994

CONSECUTIVE THREE-POINT FIELD GOALS MADE WITHOUT A MISS
11—Niagara vs. Siena, Jan. 7, 1987; Eastern Ky. vs. UNC Asheville, Jan. 14, 1987

THREE-POINT FIELD-GOAL ATTEMPTS WITHOUT MAKING ONE
22—Canisius vs. St. Bonaventure, Jan. 21, 1995

NUMBER OF DIFFERENT PLAYERS TO SCORE A THREE-POINT FIELD GOAL, ONE TEAM
9—Dartmouth vs. Boston College, Nov. 30, 1993

THREE-POINT FIELD-GOAL ATTEMPTS
74—Troy St. vs. George Mason, Dec. 10, 1994 (28 made)

THREE-POINT FIELD-GOAL ATTEMPTS, BOTH TEAMS
108—Troy St. (74) vs. George Mason (34), Dec. 10, 1994

THREE-POINT FIELD-GOAL PERCENTAGE
(Min. 10 made) 91.7%—Drexel vs. Delaware, Dec. 3, 2000 (11 of 12)
(Min. 15 made) 83.3%—Eastern Ky. vs. UNC Asheville, Jan. 14, 1987 (15 of 18)

THREE-POINT FIELD-GOAL PERCENTAGE, BOTH TEAMS
(Min. 10 made) 83.3%—Lafayette (7 of 8) vs. Marist (3 of 4), Dec. 6, 1986 (10 of 12)

(Min. 15 made) 76.2%—Florida (10 of 14) vs. California (6 of 7), Dec. 27, 1986 (16 of 21)
(Min. 20 made) 72.4%—Princeton (12 of 15) vs. Brown (9 of 14), Feb. 20, 1988 (21 of 29)

Free Throws

FREE THROWS MADE
56—TCU vs. Eastern Mich., Dec. 21, 1999 (70 attempts)

FREE THROWS MADE, BOTH TEAMS
88—Morehead St. (53) vs. Cincinnati (35), Feb. 11, 1956 (111 attempts)

FREE-THROW ATTEMPTS
79—Northern Ariz. vs. Arizona, Jan. 26, 1953 (46 made)

FREE-THROW ATTEMPTS, BOTH TEAMS
130—Northern Ariz. (79) vs. Arizona (51), Jan. 26, 1953 (78 made)

FEWEST FREE THROWS MADE
0—Many teams

FEWEST FREE-THROW ATTEMPTS
0—Many teams

FREE-THROW PERCENTAGE
(Min. 32 made) 100.0%—UC Irvine vs. Pacific (Cal.), Feb. 21, 1981 (34 of 34); Samford vs. UCF, Dec. 20, 1990 (34 of 34)
(Min. 35 made) 97.2%—Vanderbilt vs. Mississippi St., Feb. 26, 1986 (35 of 36); Butler vs. Dayton, Feb. 21, 1991 (35 of 36); Marquette vs. Memphis, Jan. 23, 1993 (35 of 36)
(Min. 40 made) 95.5%—UNLV vs. San Diego St., Dec. 11, 1976 (42 of 44)

FREE-THROW PERCENTAGE, BOTH TEAMS
100%—Purdue (25 of 25) vs. Wisconsin (22 of 22), Feb. 7, 1976 (47 of 47)

Rebounds

REBOUNDS
108—Kentucky vs. Mississippi, Feb. 8, 1964

REBOUNDS, BOTH TEAMS
152—Indiana (95) vs. Michigan (57), March 11, 1961

REBOUND MARGIN
84—Arizona (102) vs. Northern Ariz. (18), Jan. 6, 1951

Assists

ASSISTS (INCLUDING OVERTIMES)
44—Colorado vs. George Mason, Dec. 2, 1995 (ot)

ASSISTS (REGULATION)
41—North Carolina vs. Manhattan, Dec. 27, 1985; Weber St. vs. Northern Ariz., March 2, 1991

ASSISTS, BOTH TEAMS (INCLUDING OVERTIMES)
67—Colorado (44) vs. George Mason (23), Dec. 2, 1995 (ot)

ASSISTS, BOTH TEAMS (REGULATION)
65—Dayton (34) vs. UCF (31), Dec. 3, 1988

Blocked Shots

BLOCKED SHOTS
21—Georgetown vs. Southern (N.O.), Dec. 1, 1993

BLOCKED SHOTS, BOTH TEAMS
29—Rider (17) vs. Fairleigh Dickinson (12), Jan. 9, 1989

Steals

STEALS
39—Long Island vs. Medgar Evers, Nov. 26, 1997

STEALS VS. DIVISION I OPPONENT
34—Oklahoma vs. Centenary (La.), Dec. 12, 1987

STEALS, BOTH TEAMS
44—Oklahoma (34) vs. Centenary (La.) (10), Dec. 12, 1987

Fouls

FOULS
50—Arizona vs. Northern Ariz., Jan. 26, 1953

FOULS, BOTH TEAMS
84—Arizona (50) vs. Northern Ariz. (34), Jan. 26, 1953

PLAYERS DISQUALIFIED
8—St. Joseph's vs. Xavier, Jan. 10, 1976

PLAYERS DISQUALIFIED, BOTH TEAMS
12—UNLV (6) vs. Hawaii (6), Jan. 19, 1979 (ot); Arizona (7) vs. West Tex. A&M (5), Feb. 14, 1952

Overtimes

OVERTIME PERIODS
7—Cincinnati (75) vs. Bradley (73), Dec. 21, 1981

POINTS IN ONE OVERTIME PERIOD
26—Vermont vs. Hartford, Jan. 24, 1998

POINTS IN ONE OVERTIME PERIOD, BOTH TEAMS
45—Va. Commonwealth (23) vs. Texas A&M (22), Dec. 2, 2000

POINTS IN OVERTIME PERIODS
49—Middle Tenn. vs. Tennessee Tech, Feb. 12, 2000 (4 ot)

POINTS IN OVERTIME PERIODS, BOTH TEAMS
94—Middle Tenn. (49) vs. Tennessee Tech (45), Feb. 12, 2000 (4 ot)

WINNING MARGIN IN OVERTIME GAME
21—Nicholls St. (86) vs. Sam Houston St. (65), Feb. 4, 1999 (23-2 in the ot)

SEASON RECORDS

Scoring

POINTS
4,012—Oklahoma, 1988 (39 games)

POINTS PER GAME
122.4—Loyola Marymount, 1990 (3,918 in 32)

SCORING MARGIN AVERAGE
30.3—UCLA, 1972 (94.6 offense, 64.3 defense)

GAMES AT LEAST 100 POINTS
28—Loyola Marymount, 1990

CONSECUTIVE GAMES AT LEAST 100 POINTS
12—UNLV, 1977; Loyola Marymount, 1990

Field Goals

FIELD GOALS
1,533—Oklahoma, 1988 (3,094 attempts)

FIELD GOALS PER GAME
46.3—UNLV, 1976 (1,436 in 31)

FIELD-GOAL ATTEMPTS
3,094—Oklahoma, 1988 (1,533 made)

FIELD-GOAL ATTEMPTS PER GAME
98.5—Oral Roberts, 1973 (2,659 in 27)

FIELD-GOAL PERCENTAGE
57.2%—Missouri, 1980 (936 of 1,635)

Three-Point Field Goals

THREE-POINT FIELD GOALS
407—Duke, 2001 (1,057 attempts)

THREE-POINT FIELD GOALS PER GAME
11.1—Troy St., 1996 (300 in 27)

THREE-POINT FIELD-GOAL ATTEMPTS
1,057—Duke, 2001 (407 made)

THREE-POINT FIELD-GOAL ATTEMPTS PER GAME
34.0—Mississippi Val., 1997 (985 in 29)

THREE-POINT FIELD-GOAL PERCENTAGE
(Min. 100 made) 50.8%—Indiana, 1987 (130 of 256)
(Min. 150 made) 50.0%—Mississippi Val., 1987 (161 of 322)
(Min. 200 made) 49.2%—Princeton, 1988 (211 of 429)

CONSECUTIVE GAMES SCORING A THREE-POINT FIELD GOAL (Multiple Seasons)
505—UNLV, Nov. 26, 1986, to present; Vanderbilt, Nov. 28, 1986, to present

Free Throws

FREE THROWS
865—Bradley, 1954 (1,263 attempts)

FREE THROWS PER GAME
28.9—Morehead St., 1956 (838 in 29)

CONSECUTIVE FREE THROWS
49—Indiana St., 1991 (during two games, Feb. 13-18)

FREE-THROW ATTEMPTS
1,263—Bradley, 1954 (865 made)

FREE-THROW ATTEMPTS PER GAME
41.0—Bradley, 1953 (1,107 in 27)

FREE-THROW PERCENTAGE
82.2%—Harvard, 1984 (535 of 651)

Rebounds

REBOUNDS
2,109—Kentucky, 1951 (34 games)

REBOUNDS PER GAME
70.0—Connecticut, 1955 (1,751 in 25)

REBOUND MARGIN AVERAGE
25.0—Morehead St., 1957 (64.3 offense, 39.3 defense)
(Since 1973) 18.5—Manhattan, 1973 (56.5, 38.0)

Assists

ASSISTS
926—UNLV, 1990 (40 games)

ASSISTS PER GAME
24.7—UNLV, 1991 (863 in 35)

Blocked Shots

BLOCKED SHOTS
309—Georgetown, 1989 (34 games)

BLOCKED SHOTS PER GAME
9.1—Georgetown, 1989 (309 in 34)

Steals

STEALS
486—Oklahoma, 1988 (39 games)

STEALS PER GAME
14.9—Long Island, 1998 (478 in 32)

Fouls

FOULS
966—Providence, 1987 (34 games)

FOULS PER GAME
29.3—Indiana, 1952 (644 in 22)

FEWEST FOULS
253—Air Force, 1962 (23 games)

FEWEST FOULS PER GAME
11.0—Air Force, 1962 (253 in 23)

Defense

LOWEST SCORING AVERAGE PER GAME ALLOWED (Since 1982)
(Since 1938) 25.7—Oklahoma St., 1939 (693 in 27)
(Since 1948) 32.5—Oklahoma St., 1948 (1,006 in 31)
(Since 1965) 47.1—Fresno St., 1982 (1,412 in 30)

LOWEST FIELD-GOAL PERCENTAGE ALLOWED (Since 1978)
35.2—Stanford, 2000 (667 of 1,893)

Overtimes

OVERTIME GAMES
8—Western Ky., 1978 (won 5, lost 3); Portland, 1984 (won 4, lost 4); Valparaiso, 1993 (won 4, lost 4)

CONSECUTIVE OVERTIME GAMES
4—Jacksonville, 1982 (won 3, lost 1); Illinois St., 1985 (won 3, lost 1); Dayton, 1988 (won 1, lost 3)

OVERTIME WINS
6—Chattanooga, 1989 (6-0); Wake Forest, 1984 (6-1)

OVERTIME HOME WINS
5—Cincinnati, 1967 (5-0)

OVERTIME ROAD WINS
4—Delaware, 1973 (4-0); Arizona St., 1981 (4-0); Cal St. Fullerton, 1989 (4-0); New Mexico St., 1994 (4-0)

OVERTIME PERIODS
14—Bradley, 1982 (3-3)

CONSECUTIVE OVERTIME WINS—ALL-TIME
11—Louisville, Feb. 10, 1968-March 29, 1975; Massachusetts, March 21, 1991-Feb. 28, 1996; Virginia, Dec. 5, 1991-Feb. 8, 1996

General Records

GAMES IN A SEASON
45—Oregon, 1945 (30-15)

GAMES IN A SEASON (Since 1948)
40—Duke, 1986 (37-3); UNLV, 1990 (35-5); Kentucky, 1997 (35-5)

VICTORIES IN A SEASON
37—Duke, 1986 (37-3) & 1999 (37-2); UNLV, 1987 (37-2)

VICTORIES IN FIRST SEASON IN DIVISION I
29—Seattle, 1953 (29-4)

WON-LOST PERCENTAGE IN FIRST SEASON IN DIVISION I
.931—Md.-East. Shore, 1974 (27-2)

VICTORIES IN A PERFECT SEASON
32—North Carolina, 1957; Indiana, 1976

CONSECUTIVE VICTORIES IN A SEASON
34—UNLV, 1991 (34-1)

CONSECUTIVE VICTORIES
88—UCLA, from Jan. 30, 1971, through Jan. 17, 1974 (ended Jan. 19, 1974, at Notre Dame, 71-70; last UCLA defeat before streak also came at Notre Dame, 89-82)

CONSECUTIVE HOME-COURT VICTORIES
129—Kentucky, from Jan. 4, 1943, to Jan. 8, 1955 (ended by Georgia Tech, 59-58)

CONSECUTIVE REGULAR-SEASON VICTORIES (National Postseason Tournaments Not Included)
76—UCLA, 1971-74

DEFEATS IN A SEASON
28—Prairie View, 1992 (0-28)

CONSECUTIVE DEFEATS IN A SEASON
28—Prairie View, 1992 (0-28)

CONSECUTIVE DEFEATS
37—Citadel, from Jan. 16, 1954, to Dec. 12, 1955

CONSECUTIVE HOME-COURT DEFEATS
32—New Hampshire, from Feb. 9, 1988, to Feb. 2, 1991 (ended vs. Holy Cross, 72-56)

CONSECUTIVE ROAD DEFEATS (including only games at the opponents' home sites)
64—Tex.-Pan American, from Nov. 25, 1995, to Jan. 8, 2000 (ended vs. Oral Roberts, 79-62)

CONSECUTIVE NON-HOME DEFEATS (including games at the opponents' home sites and at neutral sites)
56—Sacramento St., from Nov. 22, 1991, to Jan. 5, 1995 [ended at Loyola (Ill.), 68-56]

CONSECUTIVE 30-WIN SEASONS
3—Kentucky, 1947-49 and 1996-98

CONSECUTIVE 25-WIN SEASONS
10—UCLA, 1967-76; UNLV, 1983-92

CONSECUTIVE 20-WIN SEASONS
31—North Carolina, 1971-2001

CONSECUTIVE WINNING SEASONS
54—UCLA, 1949-2002

CONSECUTIVE NON-LOSING SEASONS (Includes .500 Record)
60—Kentucky, 1928-52, 54-88# (2 .500 seasons)

#Kentucky did not play basketball during the 1953 season.

CONSECUTIVE NON-LOSING SEASONS (Includes .500 Record)-CURRENT
54—UCLA, 1949-2002

UNBEATEN TEAMS (Since 1938; Number Of Victories In Parentheses)
1939 Long Island (24)†
1940 Seton Hall (19)††
1944 Army (15)††
1954 Kentucky (25)††
1956 San Francisco (29)*
1957 North Carolina (32)*
1964 UCLA (30)*
1967 UCLA (30)*
1972 UCLA (30)*
1973 UCLA (30)*
1973 North Carolina St. (27)††
1976 Indiana (32)*

*NCAA champion; †NIT champion; ††not in either tournament

UNBEATEN IN REGULAR SEASON BUT LOST IN NCAA (*) OR NIT (†)
1939 Loyola (Ill.) (20; 21-1)†
1941 Seton Hall (19; 20-2)†
1951 Columbia (21; 21-1)*
1961 Ohio St. (24; 27-1)*
1968 Houston (28; 31-2)*
1968 St. Bonaventure (22; 23-2)*
1971 Marquette (26; 28-1)*
1971 Pennsylvania (26; 28-1)*
1975 Indiana (29; 31-1)*
1976 Rutgers (28; 31-2)*
1979 Indiana St. (27; 33-1)*
1979 Alcorn St. (25; 28-1)†
1991 UNLV (30; 34-1)*

30-GAME WINNERS (Since 1938)
37—Duke, 1986 & 1999; UNLV, 1987.
36—Kentucky, 1948.
35—Arizona, 1988; Duke, 2001; Georgetown, 1985; Kansas, 1986 & 1998; Kentucky, 1997 & 1998; Massachusetts, 1996; UNLV, 1990; Oklahoma, 1988.
34—Arkansas, 1991; Connecticut, 1999; Duke, 1992; Georgetown, 1984; Kansas, 1997; Kentucky, 1947 & 1996; UNLV, 1991; North Carolina, 1993 & 1998.

33—Indiana St., 1979; Louisville, 1980; Michigan St., 1999; UNLV, 1986.

32—Arkansas, 1978 & 1995; Bradley, 1950, 1951 & 1986; Connecticut, 1996 & 1998; Duke, 1991 & 1998; Houston, 1984; Indiana, 1976; Iowa St., 2000; Kentucky, 1949, 1951 & 1986; Louisville, 1983 & 1986; Marshall, 1947; Maryland, 2002; Michigan St., 2000; North Carolina, 1957, 1982 & 1987; Temple, 1987 & 1988; Tulsa, 2000.

31—Arkansas, 1994; Cincinnati, 2002; Connecticut, 1990; Duke, 2002; Houston, 1968 & 1983; Illinois, 1989; Indiana, 1975 & 1993; LSU, 1981; Memphis, 1985; Michigan, 1993; Minnesota, 1997; Oklahoma, 1985 & 2002; Oklahoma St., 1946; Rutgers, 1976; St. John's (N.Y.), 1985 & 1986; Seton Hall, 1953 & 1989; Stanford, 2001; Syracuse, 1987; UCLA, 1995; Wyoming, 1943.

30—Arizona, 1998; Arkansas, 1990; California,

1946; Georgetown, 1982; Indiana, 1987; Iowa, 1987; Kansas, 1990; Kentucky, 1978 & 1993; La Salle, 1990; Massachusetts, 1992; Michigan, 1989; Navy, 1986; North Carolina, 1946; North Carolina St., 1951 & 1974; Oklahoma, 1989; Oregon, 1945; Stanford 1998; Syracuse, 1989; Texas Tech, 1996; UCLA, 1964, 1967, 1972 & 1973; Utah, 1991 & 1998; Virginia, 1982; Western Ky., 1938.

All-Time Individual Leaders

Single-Game Records

SCORING HIGHS VS. DIVISION I OPPONENT

Pts.	Player, Team vs. Opponent	Date
72	Kevin Bradshaw, U.S. Int'l vs. Loyola Marymount	Jan. 5, 1991
69	Pete Maravich, LSU vs. Alabama	Feb. 7, 1970
68	Calvin Murphy, Niagara vs. Syracuse	Dec. 7, 1968
66	Jay Handlan, Wash. & Lee vs. Furman	Feb. 17, 1951
66	Pete Maravich, LSU vs. Tulane	Feb. 10, 1969
66	Anthony Roberts, Oral Roberts vs. N.C. A&T	Feb. 19, 1977
65	Anthony Roberts, Oral Roberts vs. Oregon	Mar. 9, 1977
65	Scott Haffner, Evansville vs. Dayton	Feb. 18, 1989
64	Pete Maravich, LSU vs. Kentucky	Feb. 21, 1970
63	Johnny Neumann, Mississippi vs. LSU	Jan. 30, 1971
63	Hersey Hawkins, Bradley vs. Detroit	Feb. 22, 1988
62	Darrell Floyd, Furman vs. Citadel	Jan. 14, 1956
62	Oscar Robertson, Cincinnati vs. North Texas	Feb. 6, 1960
62	Askia Jones, Kansas St. vs. Fresno St.	Mar. 24, 1994
61	Lew Alcindor, UCLA vs. Washington St.	Feb. 25, 1967
61	Pete Maravich, LSU vs. Vanderbilt	Dec. 11, 1969
61	Rick Mount, Purdue vs. Iowa	Feb. 28, 1970
61	Austin Carr, Notre Dame vs. Ohio	Mar. 7, 1970
61	Wayman Tisdale, Oklahoma vs. Texas-San Antonio	Dec. 28, 1983
61	Eddie House, Arizona St. vs. California (2 ot)	Jan. 8, 2000
60	Elgin Baylor, Seattle vs. Portland	Jan. 30, 1958
60	Billy McGill, Utah vs. Brigham Young	Feb. 24, 1962
60	John Mengelt, Auburn vs. Alabama	Feb. 14, 1970
60	Johnny Neumann, Mississippi vs. Baylor	Dec. 29, 1970
59	Pete Maravich, LSU vs. Alabama	Feb. 17, 1968
59	Ernie Fleming, Jacksonville vs. St. Peter's	Jan. 29, 1972
59	Kevin Bradshaw, U.S. Int'l vs. Florida Int'l	Jan. 14, 1991

SCORING HIGHS VS. NON-DIVISION I OPPONENT

Pts.	Player, Team vs. Opponent	Date
100	Frank Selvy, Furman vs. Newberry	Feb. 13, 1954
85	Paul Arizin, Villanova vs. Philadelphia NAMC	Feb. 12, 1949
81	Freeman Williams, Portland St. vs. Rocky Mountain	Feb. 3, 1978
73	Bill Mlkvy, Temple vs. Wilkes	Mar. 3, 1951
71	Freeman Williams, Portland St. vs. Southern Ore.	Feb. 9, 1977
67	Darrell Floyd, Furman vs. Morehead St.	Jan. 22, 1955

Oregon State's Steve Johnson set the record for single-season field-goal percentage in 1981.

Photo by Oregon State Sports Information

Pts.	Player, Team vs. Opponent	Date
66	Freeman Williams, Portland St. vs. George Fox	Jan. 13, 1978
65	Bob Zawoluk, St. John's (N.Y.) vs. St. Peter's	Mar. 30, 1950
63	Sherman White, Long Island vs. John Marshall	Feb. 1950
63	Frank Selvy, Furman vs. Mercer	Feb. 11, 1953
62	Elvin Hayes, Houston vs. Valparaiso	Feb. 24, 1968
61	Matt Teahan, Denver vs. Neb. Wesleyan	Feb. 26, 1979
60	Bob Pettit, LSU vs. Louisiana College	Dec. 7, 1953
60	Harry Kelly, Texas Southern vs. Jarvis Christian	Feb. 23, 1983
60	Dave Jamerson, Ohio vs. Col. of Charleston	Dec. 21, 1989
59	Rick Barry, Miami (Fla.) vs. Rollins	1965
58	Frank Selvy, Furman vs. Wofford	Feb. 23, 1954
57	David Thompson, North Carolina St. vs. Buffalo St.	Dec. 5, 1974
57	Calvin Murphy, Niagara vs. Villa Madonna	Dec. 6, 1967
56	Stan Davis, Appalachian St. vs. Carson-Newman	Jan. 24, 1974
56	Tim Roberts, Southern U. vs. Faith Baptist	Dec. 12, 1994
55	Rick Barry, Miami (Fla.) vs. Tampa	1965
55	Elvin Hayes, Houston vs. Southwest Tex. St.	Feb. 12, 1966
55	Wayman Tisdale, Oklahoma vs. Southwest Tex. St.	Dec. 10, 1984
54	Rick Barry, Miami (Fla.) vs. Florida Southern	1965

FIELD-GOAL PERCENTAGE
(Minimum 12 field goals made)

Pct.	Player, Team vs. Opponent (FG-FGA)	Date
100	Clifford Rozier, Louisville vs. Eastern Ky. (15 of 15)	Dec. 11, 1993
100	Dan Henderson, Arkansas St. vs. Ga. Southern (14 of 14)	Feb. 26, 1976
100	Cornelius Holden, Louisville vs. Southern Miss. (14 of 14)	Mar. 3, 1990
100	Dana Jones, Pepperdine vs. Boise St. (14 of 14)	Nov. 30, 1991
100	Ted Guzek, Butler vs. Michigan (13 of 13)	Dec. 15, 1956
100	Rick Dean, Syracuse vs. Colgate (13 of 13)	Feb. 14, 1966
100	Gary Lechman, Gonzaga vs. Portland St. (13 of 13)	Jan. 21, 1967
100	Kevin King, Charlotte vs. South Ala. (13 of 13)	Feb. 20, 1978
100	Vernon Smith, Texas A&M vs. Alas. Anchorage (13 of 13)	Nov. 26, 1978
100	Steve Johnson, Oregon St. vs. Hawaii-Hilo (13 of 13)	Dec. 5, 1979
100	Antoine Carr, Wichita St. vs. Abilene Christian (13 of 13)	Nov. 28, 1980
100	Doug Hashley, Montana St. vs. Idaho St. (13 of 13)	Feb. 5, 1982
100	Brad Daugherty, North Carolina vs. UCLA (13 of 13)	Nov. 24, 1985
100	Ricky Butler, UC Irvine vs. Cal St. Fullerton (13 of 13)	Feb. 21, 1991
100	Rafael Solis, Brooklyn vs. Wagner (13 of 13)	Dec. 11, 1991
100	Ben Handlogten, Western Mich. vs. Toledo (13 of 13)	Jan. 27, 1996
100	Mate Milisa, Long Beach St. vs. Cal St. Monterey (13 of 13)	Dec. 22, 1999
100	Leon Roberts, Northern Ill. vs. Rockford (13 of 13)	Dec. 6, 2000
100	George Faerber, Purdue vs. Iowa (12 of 12)	Mar. 13, 1971
100	Jeff Tropf, Central Mich. vs. Northern Ill. (12 of 12)	Jan. 4, 1978
100	Durand Macklin, LSU vs. Mississippi (12 of 12)	Jan. 5, 1980
100	Ron Charles, Michigan St. vs. Michigan (12 of 12)	Jan. 24, 1980
100	Ricky Frazier, Missouri vs. Oklahoma St. (12 of 12)	Feb. 26, 1980
100	Bryan Warrick, St. Joseph's vs. Charlotte (12 of 12)	Jan. 16, 1982
100	David Robinson, Navy vs. East Caro. (12 of 12)	Mar. 7, 1985
100	Michael Ansley, Alabama vs. New Mexico St. (12 of 12)	Nov. 27, 1987
100	Mike Doktorczyk, UC Irvine vs. Pacific (Cal.) (12 of 12)	Jan. 21, 1989
100	Brian Parker, Chicago St. vs. Eastern Ill. (12 of 12)	Jan. 30, 1989
100	Alan Ogg, UAB vs. Mo. Western St. (12 of 12)	Dec. 30, 1989
100	Samuel Hines, South Ala. vs. Auburn (12 of 12)	Dec. 21, 1991
100	Jarrell Evans, Mississippi vs. Abilene Christian (12 of 12)	Nov. 29, 1993
100	John Whorton, Kent St. vs. Akron (12 of 12)	Feb. 28, 1998
100	Anthony Glover, St. John's (N.Y.) vs. Hofstra (12 of 12)	Dec. 22, 1999
100	Tyson Patterson, Appalachian St. vs. Western Caro. (12 of 12)	Jan. 24, 2000
100	Mike Vukovich, UC Santa Barb. vs. Pacific (Cal.) (12 of 12)	Feb. 3, 2001

THREE-POINT FIELD GOALS MADE

3FG	Player, Team vs. Opponent	Date
15	Keith Veney, Marshall vs. Morehead St.	Dec. 14, 1996
14	Dave Jamerson, Ohio vs. Col. of Charleston	Dec. 21, 1989
14	Askia Jones, Kansas St. vs. Fresno St.	Mar. 24, 1994
14	Ronald Blackshear, Marshall vs. Akron	Mar. 1, 2002
12	Gary Bossert, Niagara vs. Siena	Jan. 7, 1987
12	Darrin Fitzgerald, Butler vs. Detroit	Feb. 9, 1987
12	Alex Dillard, Arkansas vs. Delaware St.	Dec. 11, 1993
12	Mitch Taylor, Southern U. vs. La. Christian	Dec. 1, 1994
12	David McMahan, Winthrop vs. Coastal Caro.	Jan. 15, 1996
12	Clarence Gilbert, Missouri vs. Colorado	Feb. 23, 2002

3FG	Player, Team vs. Opponent	Date
11	Jeff Hodson, Augusta St. vs. Armstrong Atlantic	Jan. 28, 1986
11	Dennis Scott, Georgia Tech vs. Houston	Dec. 28, 1988
11	Scott Haffner, Evansville vs. Dayton	Feb. 18, 1989
11	Bobby Phills, Southern U. vs. Alcorn St.	Feb. 3, 1990
11	Dave Jamerson, Ohio vs. Kent St.	Feb. 24, 1990
11	Jeff Fryer, Loyola Marymount vs. Michigan	Mar. 18, 1990
11	Doug Day, Radford vs. Central Conn. St.	Dec. 12, 1990
11	Brent Price, Oklahoma vs. Loyola Marymount	Dec. 15, 1990
11	Bobby Phills, Southern U. vs. Manhattan	Dec. 28, 1990
11	Terry Brown, Kansas vs. North Carolina St.	Jan. 5, 1991
11	Marc Rybczyk, Central Conn. St. vs. Long Island	Nov. 26, 1991
11	Mark Alberts, Akron vs. Wright St.	Feb. 8, 1992
11	Mike Alcorn, Youngstown St. vs. Pitt.-Bradford	Feb. 24, 1992
11	Doug Day, Radford vs. Morgan St.	Dec. 9, 1992
11	Lindsey Hunter, Jackson St. vs. Kansas	Dec. 27, 1992
11	Keith Veney, Lamar vs. Prairie View	Feb. 2, 1993
11	Keith Veney, Lamar vs. Ark.-Little Rock	Feb. 11, 1993
11	Scott Neely, Campbell vs. Coastal Caro.	Jan. 29, 1994
11	Chris Brown, UC Irvine vs. New Mexico St.	Mar. 13, 1994
11	Randy Rutherford, Oklahoma St. vs. Kansas	Mar. 5, 1995
11	Troy Hudson, Southern Ill. vs. Hawaii-Hilo	Dec. 29, 1995
11	Seth Chadwick, Wofford vs. Mercer	Feb. 15, 1997
11	Cory Schwab, Northern Ariz. vs. Cal Poly	Dec. 2, 2000
11	Ron Williamson, Howard vs. Georgetown	Dec. 16, 2000
11	T.J. Sorrentine, Vermont vs. Northeastern	Jan. 17, 2002

THREE-POINT FIELD-GOAL PERCENTAGE

(Minimum 7 three-point field goals made)

Pct.	Player, Team vs. Opponent (3FG-FGA)	Date
100	Mark Poag, Old Dominion vs. VMI (9 of 9)	Nov. 25, 1997
100	Marcus Wilson, Evansville vs. Tenn.-Martin (9 of 9)	Nov. 18, 1998
100	Tomas Thompson, San Francisco vs. Loyola Marymount (8 of 8)	Mar. 7, 1992
100	Shawn Haughn, Dayton vs. St. Louis (8 of 8)	Feb. 13, 1994
100	Kelvin Collins, Northeast La. vs. Nevada (7 of 7)	Dec. 30, 1986
100	Wally Lancaster, Virginia Tech vs. San Francisco St. (7 of 7)	Jan. 3, 1987
100	Ramon Trice, St. Louis vs. Butler (7 of 7)	Feb. 16, 1987
100	Juan Sanchez, Temple vs. Rhode Island (7 of 7)	Feb. 16, 1997
100	DeMar Moore, Bowling Green vs. Western Mich. (7 of 7)	Jan. 3, 1998
100	Senque Carey, Washington vs. Old Dominion (7 of 7)	Dec. 4, 1999
100	Okechi Egbe, Tenn.-Martin vs. Bethel (7 of 7)	Nov. 20, 2000
100	Justin Brown, Montana St. vs. Western Ill. (7 of 7)	Dec. 6, 2000
100	Lionel Armstead, West Virginia vs. Ark. Monticello (7 of 7)	Dec. 1, 2001
100	Bronski Dockery, St. Francis (N.Y.) vs. Central Conn. St. (7 of 7)	Dec. 3, 2001
100	Nick Moore, Toledo vs. Akron (7 of 7)	Feb. 13, 2002
90.0	Jarminca Resse, Air Force vs. Doane (9 of 10)	Nov. 22, 1997
90.0	Cory Schwab, Northern Ariz. vs. Southern Ore. (9 of 10)	Dec. 28, 1999
90.0	Aki Palmer, Colorado St. vs. Michigan (9 of 10)	Jan. 2, 2000
90.0	Eric Perry, Oral Roberts vs. Chicago St. (9 of 10)	Feb. 3, 2000
88.9	Delray Brooks, Providence vs. Villanova (8 of 9)	Jan. 10, 1987
88.9	Larry Jackson, Liberty vs. Cal Poly (8 of 9)	Nov. 29, 1996
88.9	Clayton Shields, New Mexico vs. TCU (8 of 9)	Jan. 5, 1998
88.9	Preston Murphy, Rhode Island vs. Temple (8 of 9)	Jan. 16, 1999
88.9	Demitrius Porter, Fresno St. vs. Rice (8 of 9)	Jan. 27, 2000
88.9	Rick Jones, Vanderbilt vs. Mississippi St. (8 of 9)	Mar. 9, 2000
88.9	Marcus Bullock, New Hampshire vs. Army (8 of 9)	Jan. 7, 2002

FREE-THROW PERCENTAGE

(Minimum 12 free throws made)

Pct.	Player, Team vs. Opponent (FT-FTA)	Date
100	Arlen Clark, Oklahoma St. vs. Colorado (24 of 24)	Mar. 7, 1959
100	York Larese, North Carolina vs. Duke (21 of 21)	Dec. 29, 1959
100	Steve Nash, Santa Clara vs. St. Mary's (Cal.) (21 of 21)	Jan. 7, 1995
100	Paul Renfro, Texas-Arlington vs. Lafayette (20 of 20)	Feb. 11, 1979
100	Anthony Peeler, Missouri vs. Iowa St. (20 of 20)	Jan. 31, 1990
100	Donyell Marshall, Connecticut vs. St. John's (N.Y.) (20 of 20)	Jan 15, 1994
100	Jeron Roberts, Wyoming vs. UTEP (20 of 20)	Feb. 7, 1998
100	Skip Chappelle, Maine vs. Massachusetts (19 of 19)	1961
100	Gene Phillips, Southern Methodist vs. Texas A&M (19 of 19)	Feb. 2, 1971
100	Jim Kennedy, Missouri vs. Hawaii (19 of 19)	Dec. 22, 1975
100	Kevin Smith, Michigan St. vs. Indiana (19 of 19)	Jan. 7, 1982
100	Sidney Goodman, Coppin St. vs. N.C. A&T (19 of 19)	Feb. 18, 1995
100	Geno Ford, Ohio vs. Eastern Mich. (19 of 19)	Feb. 12, 1997
100	Eddie Benton, Vermont vs. New Hampshire (19 of 19)	Feb. 18, 1993
100	Tommy Boyer, Arkansas vs. Texas Tech (18 of 18)	Feb. 19, 1963
100	Ted Kitchel, Indiana vs. Illinois (18 of 18)	Jan. 10, 1981
100	Eric Rhodes, Stephen F. Austin vs. Southwest Tex. St. (18 of 18)	Feb. 21, 1987
100	Todd Lichti, Stanford vs. UC Santa Barb. (18 of 18)	Dec. 28, 1987
100	Lionel Simmons, La Salle vs. American (18 of 18)	Feb. 2, 1988
100	Jeff Webster, Oklahoma vs. Southern Methodist (18 of 18)	Jan. 2, 1994
100	Anquell McCollum, Western Caro. vs. Marshall (18 of 18)	Feb. 5, 1996
100	Keith Van Horn, Utah vs. TCU (18 of 18)	Feb. 13, 1997
100	Edwin Young, Dayton vs. Northeast La. (18 of 18)	Dec. 18, 1997
100	Rayford Young, Texas Tech vs. Kansas (18 of 18)	Feb 13, 1993
100	Lynn Greer, Temple vs. St. Joseph's (18 of 18)	Feb. 2, 2002

REBOUNDS

Reb.	Player, Team vs. Opponent	Date
51	Bill Chambers, William & Mary vs. Virginia	Feb. 14, 1953
43	Charlie Slack, Marshall vs. Morris Harvey	Jan. 12, 1954
42	Tom Heinsohn, Holy Cross vs. Boston College	Mar. 1, 1955
40	Art Quimby, Connecticut vs. Boston U.	Jan. 11, 1955
39	Maurice Stokes, St. Francis (Pa.) vs. John Carroll	Jan. 28, 1955
39	Dave DeBusschere, Detroit vs. Central Mich.	Jan. 30, 1960
39	Keith Swagerty, Pacific (Cal.) vs. UC Santa Barb.	Mar. 5, 1965
38	Jerry Koch, St. Louis vs. Bradley	Mar. 5, 1954
38	Charlie Tyra, Louisville vs. Canisius	Dec. 10, 1955
38	Steve Hamilton, Morehead St. vs. Florida St.	Jan. 2, 1957
38	Paul Silas, Creighton vs. Centenary (La.)	Feb. 19, 1962
38	Tommy Woods, East Tenn. St. vs. Middle Tenn.	Mar. 1, 1965
36	Herb Neff, Tennessee vs. Georgia Tech	Jan. 26, 1952
36	Dickie Hemric, Wake Forest vs. Clemson	Feb. 4, 1955
36	Swede Halbrook, Oregon St. vs. Idaho	Feb. 15, 1955
36	Wilt Chamberlain, Kansas vs. Iowa St.	Feb. 15, 1958
36	Jim Barnes, UTEP vs. Western N.M.	Jan. 4, 1964
35	Ronnie Shavlik, North Carolina St. vs. Villanova	Jan. 29, 1955
35	Bill Ebben, Detroit vs. Brigham Young	Dec. 28, 1955
35	Larry Abney, Fresno St. vs. Southern Methodist	Feb. 17, 2000
34	Bob Burrow, Kentucky vs. Temple	Dec. 10, 1955
34	Ronnie Shavlik, North Carolina St. vs. South Carolina	Feb. 11, 1955
34	Fred Cohen, Temple vs. Connecticut	Mar. 16, 1956
34	Bailey Howell, Mississippi St. vs LSU	Feb. 1, 1957
34	David Vaughn, Oral Roberts vs. Brandeis	Jan. 8, 1973
33	Jerry Harper, Alabama vs. Louisiana College	Jan. 21, 1956
33	Walt Bellamy, Indiana vs. Michigan	Mar. 11, 1961

(Since 1973)

Reb.	Player, Team vs. Opponent	Date
35	Larry Abney, Fresno St. vs. Southern Methodist	Feb. 17, 2000
34	David Vaughn, Oral Roberts vs. Brandeis	Jan. 8, 1973
32	Durand Macklin, LSU vs. Tulane	Nov. 26, 1976
32	Jervaughn Scales, Southern U. vs. Grambling	Feb. 7, 1994
31	Jim Bradley, Northern Ill. vs. Wis.-Milwaukee	Feb. 19, 1973
31	Calvin Natt, Northeast La. vs. Ga. Southern	Dec. 29, 1976
30	Marvin Barnes, Providence vs. Assumption	Feb. 3, 1973
30	Brad Robinson, Kent St. vs. Central Mich.	Feb. 9, 1974
30	Monti Davis, Tennessee St. vs. Alabama St.	Feb. 8, 1979
29	Lionel Garrett, Southern U. vs. Bishop	Feb. 16, 1979
29	Donald Newman, Ark.-Little Rock vs. Centenary (La.)	Jan. 24, 1984
29	Hank Gathers, Loyola Marymount vs. U.S. Int'l	Jan. 31, 1989
28	Alvan Adams, Oklahoma vs. Indiana St.	Nov. 27, 1972
28	Cliff Robinson, Southern California vs. Portland St.	Jan. 20, 1978
28	Eric McArthur, UC Santa Barb. vs. New Mexico St.	Jan. 11, 1990
28	Marcus Mann, Mississippi Val. vs. Jackson St.	Mar. 9, 1996
28	David Bluthenthal, Southern California vs. Arizona St.	Jan. 20, 2000
27	Andy Hopson, Oklahoma St. vs. Missouri	Jan. 30, 1973
27	Henry Ray, McNeese St. vs. Texas-Arlington	1974
27	Bill Walton, UCLA vs. Loyola (Ill.)	Jan. 25, 1973
27	Bill Walton, UCLA vs. Maryland	Dec. 1, 1973
27	Rick Kelley, Stanford vs. Kentucky	Dec. 22, 1974
27	Kerry Davis, Cal St. Fullerton vs. Central Mich.	Dec. 15, 1975
27	Hank Gathers, Loyola Marymount vs. U.S. Int'l	Dec. 7, 1989
27	Dikembe Mutombo, Georgetown vs. Connecticut	Mar. 8, 1991
27	Reginald Slater, Wyoming vs. Troy St.	Dec. 14, 1991
27	Ervin Johnson, New Orleans vs. Lamar	Feb. 18, 1993
27	Willie Fisher, Jacksonville vs. Louisiana Tech	Dec. 4, 1993
27	Kareem Carpenter, Eastern Mich. vs. Western Mich.	Feb. 8, 1995
27	Amien Hicks, Morris Brown vs. Clark Atlanta	Jan. 14, 2002
27	Andre Brown, DePaul vs. TCU	Feb. 6, 2002

ASSISTS

Ast.	Player, Team vs. Opponent	Date
22	Tony Fairley, Charleston So. vs. Armstrong Atlantic	Feb. 9, 1987
22	Avery Johnson, Southern U. vs. Texas Southern	Jan. 25, 1988
22	Sherman Douglas, Syracuse vs. Providence	Jan. 28, 1989
21	Mark Wade, UNLV vs. Navy	Dec. 29, 1986
21	Kelvin Scarborough, New Mexico vs. Hawaii	Feb. 13, 1987
21	Anthony Manuel, Bradley vs. UC Irvine	Dec. 19, 1987
21	Avery Johnson, Southern U. vs. Alabama St.	Jan. 16, 1988
20	Grayson Marshall, Clemson vs. Md.-East. Shore	Nov. 25, 1985
20	James Johnson, Middle Tenn. vs. Freed-Hardeman	Jan. 2, 1986
20	Avery Johnson, Southern U. vs. Texas Southern	Mar. 6, 1987
20	Avery Johnson, Southern U. vs. Mississippi Val.	Feb. 8, 1988
20	Howard Evans, Temple vs. Villanova	Feb. 10, 1988
20	Jasper Walker, St. Peter's vs. Holy Cross	Feb. 11, 1989
20	Chris Corchiani, North Carolina St. vs. Maryland	Feb. 27, 1991
20	Drew Henderson, Fairfield vs. Loyola (Md.)	Jan. 25, 1992
20	Dana Harris, UMBC vs. St. Mary's	Dec. 12, 1992
20	Sam Crawford, New Mexico St. vs. Sam Houston St.	Dec. 21, 1992
20	Ray Washington, Nicholls St. vs. McNeese St.	Jan. 28, 1995

Ast.	Player, Team vs. Opponent	Date
20	Mateen Cleaves, Michigan St. vs. Michigan	Mar. 4, 2000
19	Frank Nardi, Wis.-Green Bay vs. Northern Iowa	Feb. 24, 1986
19	Avery Johnson, Southern U. vs. Tex. A&M-Kingsville	Dec. 6, 1986
19	Avery Johnson, Southern U. vs. Jackson St.	Jan. 16, 1987
19	Andre Van Drost, Wagner vs. Long Island	Feb. 25, 1987
19	Todd Lehmann, Drexel vs. Liberty	Feb. 5, 1990
19	Greg Anthony, UNLV vs. Pacific (Cal.)	Dec. 29, 1990
19	Keith Jennings, East Tenn. St. vs. Appalachian St.	Feb. 2, 1991
19	Nelson Haggerty, Baylor vs. Oral Roberts	Feb. 27, 1993

BLOCKED SHOTS

Blk.	Player, Team vs. Opponent	Date
14	David Robinson, Navy vs. UNC Wilmington	Jan. 4, 1986
14	Shawn Bradley, Brigham Young vs. Eastern Ky.	Dec. 7, 1990
14	Roy Rogers, Alabama vs. Georgia	Feb. 10, 1996
14	Loren Woods, Arizona vs. Oregon	Feb. 3, 2000
13	Kevin Roberson, Vermont vs. New Hampshire	Jan. 9, 1992
13	Jim McIlvaine, Marquette vs. Northeastern Ill.	Dec. 9, 1992
13	Keith Closs, Central Conn. St. vs. St. Francis (Pa.)	Dec. 21, 1994
13	D'or Fischer, Northwestern St. vs. Southwest Tex. St.	Jan. 22, 2001
13	Kyle Davis, Auburn vs. Miami (Fla.)	Mar. 14, 2001
13	Wojciech Myrda, La.-Monroe vs. Texas-San Antonio	Jan. 17, 2002
12	David Robinson, Navy vs. James Madison	Jan. 9, 1986
12	Derrick Lewis, Maryland vs. James Madison	Jan. 28, 1987
12	Rodney Blake, St. Joseph's vs. Cleveland St.	Dec. 2, 1987
12	Walter Palmer, Dartmouth vs. Harvard	Jan. 9, 1988
12	Alan Ogg, UAB vs. Florida A&M	Dec. 16, 1988
12	Dikembe Mutombo, Georgetown vs. St. John's (N.Y.)	Jan. 23, 1989
12	Shaquille O'Neal, LSU vs. Loyola Marymount	Feb. 3, 1990
12	Cedric Lewis, Maryland vs. South Fla.	Jan. 19, 1991
12	Ervin Johnson, New Orleans vs. Texas A&M	Dec. 29, 1992
12	Kurt Thomas, TCU vs. Texas A&M	Feb. 25, 1995
12	Keith Closs, Central Conn. St. vs. Troy St.	Jan. 20, 1996
12	Adonal Foyle, Colgate vs. Fairfield	Nov. 26, 1996
12	Adonal Foyle, Colgate vs. Navy	Feb. 5, 1997
12	Tarvis Williams, Hampton vs. N.C. A&T	Jan. 9, 1999
12	Darrick Davenport, TCU vs. Alas. Fairbanks	Nov. 20, 1999
12	Tarvis Williams, Hampton vs. Delaware St.	Jan. 13, 2001
12	D'or Fischer, Northwestern St. vs. Siena	Nov. 21, 2001

STEALS

Stl.	Player, Team vs. Opponent	Date
13	Mookie Blaylock, Oklahoma vs. Centenary (La.)	Dec. 12, 1987
13	Mookie Blaylock, Oklahoma vs. Loyola Marymount	Dec. 17, 1988
12	Kenny Robertson, Cleveland St. vs. Wagner	Dec. 3, 1988
12	Terry Evans, Oklahoma vs. Florida A&M	Jan. 27, 1993
12	Richard Duncan, Middle Tenn. vs. Eastern Ky.	Feb. 20, 1999
12	Greedy Daniels, TCU vs. Ark.-Pine Bluff	Dec. 30, 2000
12	Jehiel Lewis, Navy vs. Bucknell	Jan. 12, 2002
11	Darron Brittman, Chicago St. vs. McKendree	Jan. 24, 1986
11	Darron Brittman, Chicago St. vs. St. Xavier	Feb. 8, 1986
11	Marty Johnson, Towson vs. Bucknell	Feb. 17, 1988
11	Aldwin Ware, Florida A&M vs. Tuskegee	Feb. 24, 1988
11	Mark Macon, Temple vs. Notre Dame	Jan. 29, 1989
11	Carl Thomas, Eastern Mich. vs. Chicago St.	Feb. 20, 1991
11	Ron Arnold, St. Francis (N.Y.) vs. Mt. St. Mary's	Feb. 4, 1993
11	Tyus Edney, UCLA vs. George Mason	Dec. 22, 1995
11	Philip Huler, Fla. Atlantic vs. Campbell	Jan. 18, 1997
11	Ali Ton, Davidson vs. Tufts	Nov. 29, 1997
11	Chris Thomas, Notre Dame vs. New Hampshire	Nov. 16, 2001
11	Drew Schifino, West Virginia vs. Ark. Monticello	Dec. 1, 2001
11	John Linehan, Providence vs. Rutgers	Jan. 22, 2002
11	Travis Demanby, Fresno St. vs. Oklahoma St.	Feb. 10, 2002
10	28 tied	

Season Records

POINTS

Player, Team	Season	G	FG	3FG	FT	Pts.
Pete Maravich, LSU	†1970	31	522	—	337	1,381
Elvin Hayes, Houston	†1968	33	519	—	176	1,214
Frank Selvy, Furman	†1954	29	427	—	355	1,209
Pete Maravich, LSU	†1969	26	433	—	282	1,148
Pete Maravich, LSU	1968	26	432	—	274	1,138
Bo Kimble, Loyola Marymount	†1990	32	404	92	231	1,131
Hersey Hawkins, Bradley	†1988	31	377	87	284	1,125
Austin Carr, Notre Dame	1970	29	444	—	218	1,106
Austin Carr, Notre Dame	1971	29	430	—	241	1,101
Otis Birdsong, Houston	†1977	36	452	—	186	1,090
Dwight Lamar, La.-Lafayette	†1972	29	429	—	196	1,054
Kevin Bradshaw, U.S. Int'l	†1991	28	358	60	278	1,054

Player, Team	Season	G	FG	3FG	FT	Pts.
Glenn Robinson, Purdue	†1994	34	368	79	215	1,030
Hank Gathers, Loyola Marymount	†1989	31	419	0	177	1,015
Oscar Robertson, Cincinnati	†1960	30	369	—	273	1,011
Freeman Williams, Portland St.	1977	26	417	—	176	1,010
Billy McGill, Utah	†1962	26	394	—	221	1,009
Rich Fuqua, Oral Roberts	1972	28	423	—	160	1,006
Oscar Robertson, Cincinnati	†1958	28	352	—	280	984
Oscar Robertson, Cincinnati	†1959	30	331	—	316	978
Rick Barry, Miami (Fla.)	†1965	26	340	—	293	973
Larry Bird, Indiana St.	†1979	34	376	—	221	973
Dennis Scott, Georgia Tech	1990	35	336	137	161	970
Freeman Williams, Portland St.	†1978	27	410	—	149	969
Chris Jackson, LSU	1989	32	359	84	163	965

SCORING AVERAGE

Player, Team	Season	G	FG	3FG	FT	Pts.	Avg.
Pete Maravich, LSU	†1970	31	522	—	337	1,381	44.5
Pete Maravich, LSU	†1969	26	433	—	282	1,148	44.2
Pete Maravich, LSU	†1968	26	432	—	274	1,138	43.8
Frank Selvy, Furman	†1954	29	427	—	355	1,209	41.7
Johnny Neumann, Mississippi	†1971	23	366	—	191	923	40.1
Freeman Williams, Portland St.	†1977	26	417	—	176	1,010	38.8
Billy McGill, Utah	†1962	26	394	—	221	1,009	38.8
Calvin Murphy, Niagara	1968	24	337	—	242	916	38.2
Austin Carr, Notre Dame	1970	29	444	—	218	1,106	38.1
Austin Carr, Notre Dame	1971	29	430	—	241	1,101	38.0
Kevin Bradshaw, U.S. Int'l	†1991	28	358	60	278	1,054	37.6
Rick Barry, Miami (Fla.)	†1965	26	340	—	293	973	37.4
Elvin Hayes, Houston	1968	33	519	—	176	1,214	36.8
Marshall Rogers, Tex.-Pan American	†1976	25	361	—	197	919	36.8
Howard Komives, Bowling Green	†1964	23	292	—	260	844	36.7
Dwight Lamar, La.-Lafayette	†1972	29	429	—	196	1,054	36.3
Hersey Hawkins, Bradley	†1988	31	377	87	284	1,125	36.3
Darrell Floyd, Furman	†1955	25	344	—	209	897	35.9
Rich Fuqua, Oral Roberts	1972	28	423	—	160	1,006	35.9
Freeman Williams, Portland St.	†1978	27	410	—	149	969	35.9
Rick Mount, Purdue	1970	20	285	—	138	708	35.4
Bo Kimble, Loyola Marymount	†1990	32	404	92	231	1,131	35.3
Oscar Robertson, Cincinnati	†1958	28	352	—	280	984	35.1
Anthony Roberts, Oral Roberts	1977	28	402	—	147	951	34.0
Dan Issel, Kentucky	1970	28	369	—	210	948	33.9
William Averitt, Pepperdine	†1973	25	352	—	144	848	33.9

†national leader

FIELD-GOAL PERCENTAGE
(Based on qualifiers for annual championship)

Player, Team	Season	G	FG	FGA	Pct.
Steve Johnson, Oregon St.	†1981	28	235	315	74.6
Dwayne Davis, Florida	†1989	33	179	248	72.2
Keith Walker, Utica	†1985	27	154	216	71.3
Steve Johnson, Oregon St.	†1980	30	211	297	71.0
Adam Mark, Belmont	†2002	26	150	212	70.8
Oliver Miller, Arkansas	†1991	38	254	361	70.4
Alan Williams, Princeton	†1987	25	163	232	70.3
Mark McNamara, California	†1982	27	231	329	70.2
Warren Kidd, Middle Tenn.	1991	30	173	247	70.0
Pete Freeman, Akron	1991	28	175	250	70.0
Joe Senser, West Chester	†1977	25	130	186	69.9
Lee Campbell, Southwest Mo. St.	†1990	29	192	275	69.8
Stephen Scheffler, Purdue	1990	30	173	248	69.8
Brendan Haywood, North Carolina	†2000	36	191	274	69.7
Mike Atkinson, Long Beach St.	†1994	26	141	203	69.5
Lester James, St. Francis (N.Y.)	1991	29	149	215	69.3
Micheal Bradley, Villanova	†2001	31	254	367	69.2
Murray Brown, Florida St.	1979	29	237	343	69.1
Joe Senser, West Chester	†1978	25	135	197	68.5
Charles Outlaw, Houston	†1992	31	156	228	68.4
Shane Kline-Ruminski, Bowling Green	†1995	26	181	265	68.3
Marcus Kennedy, Eastern Mich.	1991	33	240	352	68.2
Felton Spencer, Louisville	1990	35	188	276	68.1
Tyrone Howard, Eastern Ky.	1987	30	156	230	67.8
Todd MacCulloch, Washington	†1997	28	163	241	67.6
Ron Charles, Michigan St.	1980	27	169	250	67.6

†national leader

THREE-POINT FIELD GOALS MADE

Player, Team	Season	G	3FG
Darrin Fitzgerald, Butler	†1987	28	158
Freddie Banks, UNLV	1987	39	152
Randy Rutherford, Oklahoma St.	†1995	37	146
Dennis Scott, Georgia Tech	†1990	35	137
Rashad Phillips, Detroit	†2001	35	136
Troy Hudson, Southern Ill.	†1997	30	134

Player, Team	Season	G	3FG
Timothy Pollard, Mississippi Val.	†1988	28	132
Jason Williams, Duke	2001	39	132
Dave Jamerson, Ohio	1990	28	131
Sydney Grider, La.-Lafayette	1990	29	131
Keith Veney, Marshall	1997	29	130
Curtis Staples, Virginia	†1998	30	130
Lazelle Durden, Cincinnati	1995	34	127
Jeff Fryer, Loyola Marymount	†1989	31	126
Timothy Pollard, Mississippi Val.	1989	28	124
Shane Battier, Duke	2001	39	124
Bobby Phills, Southern U.	†1991	28	123
Sydney Grider, La.-Lafayette	1989	29	122
Andy Kennedy, UAB	1989	34	122
Mark Alberts, Akron	1990	28	122
Chris Brown UC Irvine	†1994	26	122
Darren McLinton, James Madison	†1996	30	122
William Fourche, Southern U.	1997	27	122
Jeff Fryer, Loyola Marymount	1990	28	121
Randy Woods, La Salle	†1992	31	121

THREE-POINT FIELD GOALS MADE PER GAME
(Based on qualifiers for annual championship)

Player, Team	Season	G	3FG	Avg.
Darrin Fitzgerald, Butler	†1987	28	158	5.64
Timothy Pollard, Mississippi Val.	†1988	28	132	4.71
Chris Brown, UC Irvine	†1994	26	122	4.69
Dave Jamerson, Ohio	†1990	28	131	4.68
William Fourche, Southern U.	†1997	27	122	4.52
Sydney Grider, La.-Lafayette	1990	29	131	4.52
Keith Veney, Marshall	1997	29	130	4.48
Troy Hudson, Southern Ill.	1997	30	134	4.47
Timothy Pollard, Mississippi Val.	†1989	28	124	4.43
Keke Hicks, Coastal Caro.	1994	26	115	4.42
Bobby Phills, Southern U.	1991	28	123	4.39
Mitch Taylor, Southern U.	1995	25	109	4.36
Mark Alberts, Akron	1990	28	122	4.36
Curtis Staples, Virginia	†1998	30	130	4.33
Jeff Fryer, Loyola Marymount	1990	28	121	4.32
Shawn Respert, Michigan St.	1995	28	119	4.25
Sydney Grider, La.-Lafayette	1989	29	122	4.21
Bernard Haslett, Southern Miss.	†1993	26	109	4.19
Stevin Smith, Arizona St.	1993	27	113	4.19
Tim Roberts, Southern U.	1995	26	108	4.15
Dominick Young, Fresno St.	†1996	29	120	4.14
Mark Alberts, Akron	1993	26	107	4.12
Lazelle Durden, Cincinnati	1994	25	102	4.08
Brian Merriweather, Tex.-Pan American	†1999	27	110	4.07
Brian Merriweather, Tex.-Pan American	†2000	28	114	4.07
Darren McLinton, James Madison	1996	30	122	4.07

†national leader

THREE-POINT FIELD-GOAL PERCENTAGE
(Based on qualifiers for annual championship)

Player, Team	Season	G	3FG	3FGA	Pct.
Glenn Tropf, Holy Cross	†1988	29	52	82	63.4
Sean Wightman, Western Mich.	†1992	30	48	76	63.2
Keith Jennings, East Tenn. St.	†1991	33	84	142	59.2
Dave Calloway, Monmouth	†1989	28	48	82	58.5
Steve Kerr, Arizona	1988	38	114	199	57.3
Reginald Jones, Prairie View	†1987	28	64	112	57.1
Jim Cantamessa, Siena	†1998	29	66	117	56.4
Joel Tribelhorn, Colorado St.	1989	33	76	135	56.3
Mike Joseph, Bucknell	1988	28	65	116	56.0
Brian Jackson, Evansville	†1995	27	53	95	55.8
Amory Sanders, Southeast Mo. St.	†2001	24	53	95	55.8
Christian Laettner, Duke	1992	35	54	97	55.7
Reginald Jones, Prairie View	1988	27	85	155	54.8
Eric Rhodes, Stephen F. Austin	1987	30	58	106	54.7
Dave Orlandini, Princeton	1988	26	60	110	54.5
David Falknor, Akron	2001	22	47	87	54.0
Mike Joseph, Bucknell	1989	31	62	115	53.9
John Bays, Towson	1989	29	71	132	53.8
Jeff Anderson, Kent St.	†1993	26	44	82	53.7
Jay Edwards, Indiana	1988	23	59	110	53.6
Anthony Davis, George Mason	1987	27	45	84	53.6
Mark Anglavar, Marquette	1989	28	53	99	53.5
Scot Dimak, Stephen F. Austin	1987	30	46	86	53.5
Matt Lapin, Princeton	†1990	27	71	133	53.4
Michael Charles, UAB	1988	28	63	118	53.4
Tony Bennett, Wis.-Green Bay	1991	31	80	150	53.3
Roosevelt Moore, Sam Houston St.	1993	25	73	137	53.3

†national leader

FREE-THROW PERCENTAGE
(Based on qualifiers for annual championship)

Player, Team	Season	G	FT	FTA	Pct.
Craig Collins, Penn St.	†1985	27	94	98	95.9
Rod Foster, UCLA	†1982	27	95	100	95.0
Clay McKnight, Pacific (Cal.)	†2000	24	74	78	94.9
Carlos Gibson, Marshall	†1978	28	84	89	94.4
Danny Basile, Marist	†1994	27	84	89	94.4
Jim Barton, Dartmouth	†1986	26	65	69	94.2
Gary Buchanon, Villanova	†2001	31	97	103	94.2
Jack Moore, Nebraska	1982	27	123	131	93.9
Rob Robbins, New Mexico	†1990	34	101	108	93.5
Dandrea Evans, Troy St.	1994	27	72	77	93.5
Tommy Boyer, Arkansas	†1962	23	125	134	93.3
Damon Goodwin, Dayton	1986	30	95	102	93.1
Brent Jolly, Tennessee Tech	2001	29	95	102	93.1
Ryan Mendez, Stanford	2001	34	94	101	93.1
Brian Magid, George Washington	†1980	26	79	85	92.9
Mike Joseph, Bucknell	1990	29	144	155	92.9
Steve Kaplan, Rutgers	†1970	23	102	110	92.7
Dave Hildahl, Portland St.	†1981	21	76	82	92.7
Mike Dillard, Sam Houston St.	†1996	25	63	68	92.6
Casey Schmidt, Valparaiso	1994	25	75	81	92.6
Greg Starrick, Southern Ill.	†1972	26	148	160	92.5
Steve Henson, Kansas St.	†1988	34	111	120	92.5
Randy Nesbit, Citadel	1980	27	74	80	92.5
Robert Smith, UNLV	†1977	32	98	106	92.5
Matthew Hildebrand, Liberty	1994	30	149	161	92.5
Michael Smith, Brigham Young	†1989	29	160	173	92.5

†national leader

REBOUNDS

Player, Team	Ht.	Season	G	Reb.
Walt Dukes, Seton Hall	6-10	†1953	33	734
Leroy Wright, Pacific (Cal.)	6-8	†1959	26	652
Tom Gola, La Salle	6-6	†1954	30	652
Charlie Tyra, Louisville	6-8	†1956	29	645
Paul Silas, Creighton	6-7	1964	29	631
Elvin Hayes, Houston	6-8	†1968	33	624
Artis Gilmore, Jacksonville	7-2	†1970	28	621
Tom Gola, La Salle	6-6	†1955	31	618
Ed Conlin, Fordham	6-5	1953	26	612
Art Quimby, Connecticut	6-5	1955	25	611
Bill Russell, San Francisco	6-9	1956	29	609
Jim Ware, Oklahoma City	6-8	†1966	29	607
Joe Holup, George Washington	6-6	1956	26	604
Artis Gilmore, Jacksonville	7-2	†1971	26	603
Elton Tuttle, Creighton	6-5	1954	30	601
Marvin Barnes, Providence	6-9	†1974	32	597
Bill Russell, San Francisco	6-9	1955	29	594
Art Quimby, Connecticut	6-5	1954	26	588
Ed Conlin, Fordham	6-5	1955	27	578
Marvin Barnes, Providence	6-9	†1973	30	571
Bill Spivey, Kentucky	7-0	†1951	33	567
Bob Pelkington, Xavier	6-7	1964	26	567
Paul Silas, Creighton	6-7	†1962	25	563
Elgin Baylor, Seattle	6-6	1959	29	559
Paul Silas, Creighton	6-7	†1963	27	557

†national leader

(Since 1973)

Player, Team	Ht.	Season	G	Reb.
Marvin Barnes, Providence	6-9	†1974	32	597
Marvin Barnes, Providence	6-9	†1973	30	571
Kermit Washington, American	6-8	1973	25	511
Bill Walton, UCLA	6-11	1973	30	506
Larry Bird, Indiana St.	6-9	†1979	34	505
Larry Kenon, Memphis	6-9	1973	30	501
Akeem Olajuwon, Houston	7-0	†1984	37	500
Glenn Mosley, Seton Hall	6-8	†1977	29	473
Popeye Jones, Murray St.	6-8	†1991	33	469
Pete Padgett, Nevada	6-8	†1973	26	462
Xavier McDaniel, Wichita St.	6-8	†1985	31	460
Larry Johnson, UNLV	6-7	†1990	40	457
Tim Duncan, Wake Forest	6-11	†1997	31	457
Anthony Bonner, St. Louis	6-8	1990	33	456
Bill Cartwright, San Francisco	7-1	1979	29	455
David Robinson, Navy	6-11	†1986	35	455
Benoit Benjamin, Creighton	7-0	1985	32	451
Jerome Lane, Pittsburgh	6-6	†1987	33	444
Robert Elmore, Wichita St.	6-10	1977	28	441
John Irving, Hofstra	6-9	1977	27	440
Lionel Garrett, Southern U.	6-9	1979	28	433
Popeye Jones, Murray St.	6-8	†1992	30	431

Louisiana-Monroe's Wojciech Myrda blocked more shots than any other Division I player last season.

Photo by La. Monroe Sports Information

Player, Team	Ht.	Season	G	Reb.	Avg.
Robert Elmore, Wichita St.	6-10	1977	28	441	15.8
Bill Cartwright, San Francisco	7-1	1979	29	455	15.7
Bill Champion, Manhattan	6-10	1973	26	402	15.5
Bill Champion, Manhattan	6-10	1974	27	419	15.5
Lionel Garrett, Southern U.	6-9	1979	28	433	15.5
Dwayne Barnett, Samford	6-6	1976	23	354	15.4
John Irving, Hofstra	6-9	†1975	21	323	15.4
Cornelius Cash, Bowling Green	6-8	1973	26	396	15.2
Pete Padgett, Nevada	6-8	1974	26	395	15.2
Jimmie Baker, UNLV	6-9	1973	28	424	15.1
Larry Smith, Alcorn St.	6-8	†1980	26	392	15.1
Charles McKinney, Baylor	6-6	1974	25	375	15.0
Lewis Lloyd, Drake	6-6	1980	27	406	15.0

†*national leader*

ASSISTS

Player, Team	Season	G	Ast.
Mark Wade, UNLV	†1987	38	406
Avery Johnson, Southern U.	†1988	30	399
Anthony Manuel, Bradley	1988	31	373
Avery Johnson, Southern U.	1987	31	333
Mark Jackson, St. John's (N.Y.)	†1986	32	328
Sherman Douglas, Syracuse	†1989	38	326
Greg Anthony, UNLV	†1991	35	310
Sam Crawford, New Mexico St.	†1993	34	310
Reid Gettys, Houston	†1984	37	309
Carl Golston, Loyola (Ill.)	†1985	33	305
Craig Neal, Georgia Tech	1988	32	303
Keith Jennings, East Tenn. St.	1991	33	301
Doug Gottlieb, Oklahoma St.	†1999	34	299
Chris Corchiani, North Carolina St.	1991	31	299
Keith Jennings, East Tenn. St.	†1990	34	297
Howard Evans, Temple	1988	34	294
Ahlon Lewis, Arizona St.	†1998	32	294
Doug Gottlieb, Oklahoma St.	†2000	34	293
Danny Tarkanian, UNLV	1984	34	289
Sherman Douglas, Syracuse	1987	38	289
Bobby Hurley, Duke	1991	39	289
Greg Anthony, UNLV	1990	39	289
Sherman Douglas, Syracuse	1988	35	288
Bobby Hurley, Duke	1990	38	288
Marcus Carr, Cal St. Northridge	†2001	32	286
Steve Blake, Maryland	†2002	36	286

†*national leader*

ASSIST AVERAGE

Player, Team	Season	G	Ast.	Avg.
Avery Johnson, Southern U.	†1988	30	399	13.30
Anthony Manuel, Bradley	1988	31	373	12.03
Avery Johnson, Southern U.	†1987	31	333	10.74
Mark Wade, UNLV	1987	38	406	10.68
Nelson Haggerty, Baylor	†1995	28	284	10.14
Glenn Williams, Holy Cross	†1989	28	278	9.92
Chris Corchiani, North Carolina St.	†1991	31	299	9.65
Tony Fairley, Charleston So.	1987	28	270	9.64
Tyrone Bogues, Wake Forest	1987	29	276	9.52
Ron Weingard, Hofstra	†1985	24	228	9.50
Craig Neal, Georgia Tech	1988	32	303	9.47
Craig Lathan, Ill.-Chicago	†1984	29	274	9.45
Curtis McCants, George Mason	1995	27	251	9.30
Andre Van Drost, Wagner	1987	28	260	9.29
Todd Lehmann, Drexel	†1990	28	260	9.29
Danny Tirado, Jacksonville	1991	28	259	9.25
Carl Golston, Loyola (Ill.)	1985	33	305	9.24
Ahlon Lewis, Arizona St.	†1998	32	294	9.19
Terrell Lowery, Loyola Marymount	1991	31	283	9.13
Keith Jennings, East Tenn. St.	1991	33	301	9.12
Sam Crawford, New Mexico St.	†1993	34	310	9.12
Mark Jackson, St. John's (N.Y.)	†1986	36	328	9.11
Aaron Mitchell, La.-Lafayette	1990	29	264	9.10
Jason Kidd, California	†1994	30	272	9.07
Mark Dickel, UNLV	†2000	31	280	9.03

†*national leader*

BLOCKED SHOTS

Player, Team	Season	G	Blk.
David Robinson, Navy	†1986	35	207
Adonal Foyle, Colgate	†1997	28	180
Keith Closs, Central Conn. St.	†1996	28	178
Shawn Bradley, Brigham Young	1991	34	177
Wojciech Myrda, La.-Monroe	†2002	32	172
Alonzo Mourning, Georgetown	†1989	34	169

Player, Team	Ht.	Season	G	Reb.
Jim Bradley, Northern Ill.	6-10	1973	24	426
Hank Gathers, Loyola Marymount	6-7	†1989	31	426
Jimmie Baker, UNLV	6-9	1973	28	424

†*national leader*

REBOUND AVERAGE

Player, Team	Ht.	Season	G	Reb.	Avg.
Charlie Slack, Marshall	6-5	†1955	21	538	25.6
Leroy Wright, Pacific (Cal.)	6-8	†1959	26	652	25.1
Art Quimby, Connecticut	6-5	1955	25	611	24.4
Charlie Slack, Marshall	6-5	1956	22	520	23.6
Ed Conlin, Fordham	6-5	†1953	26	612	23.5
Joe Holup, George Washington	6-6	††1956	26	604	23.2
Artis Gilmore, Jacksonville	7-2	1971	26	603	23.2
Art Quimby, Connecticut	6-5	†1954	26	588	22.6
Paul Silas, Creighton	6-7	1962	25	563	22.5
Leroy Wright, Pacific (Cal.)	6-8	†1960	17	380	22.4
Walt Dukes, Seton Hall	6-10	1953	33	734	22.2
Charlie Tyra, Louisville	6-8	1956	29	645	22.2
Charlie Slack, Marshall	6-5	1954	21	466	22.2
Artis Gilmore, Jacksonville	7-2	†1970	28	621	22.2
Bill Chambers, William & Mary	6-4	1953	22	480	21.8
Bob Pelkington, Xavier	6-7	†1964	26	567	21.8
Dick Cunningham, Murray St.	6-10	†1967	22	479	21.8
Paul Silas, Creighton	6-7	1964	29	631	21.8
Tom Gola, La Salle	6-6	1954	30	652	21.7
Jerry Harper, Alabama	6-8	1956	24	517	21.5
Spencer Haywood, Detroit	6-8	†1969	22	472	21.5
Ed Conlin, Fordham	6-5	1955	27	578	21.4
Tom Heinsohn, Holy Cross	6-7	1956	26	549	21.1
Bill Russell, San Francisco	6-9	1956	29	609	21.0
Toby Kimball, Connecticut	6-8	†1965	23	483	21.0

†*national leader;* ††*From 1956 through 1962, individual champions were determined by percentage of all recoveries; Holup led in percentage of recoveries and Slack led in average in 1956.*

(Since 1973)

Player, Team	Ht.	Season	G	Reb.	Avg.
Kermit Washington, American	6-8	†1973	25	511	20.4
Marvin Barnes, Providence	6-9	1973	30	571	19.0
Marvin Barnes, Providence	6-9	†1974	32	597	18.7
Pete Padgett, Nevada	6-8	1973	26	462	17.8
Jim Bradley, Northern Ill.	6-10	1973	24	426	17.8
Bill Walton, UCLA	6-11	1973	30	506	16.9
Larry Kenon, Memphis	6-9	1973	30	501	16.7
Glenn Mosley, Seton Hall	6-8	†1977	29	473	16.3
John Irving, Hofstra	6-9	1977	27	440	16.3
Carlos McCullough, Tex.-Pan American	6-7	1974	22	358	16.3
Brad Robinson, Kent St.	6-7	1974	26	423	16.3
Monti Davis, Tennessee St.	6-7	†1979	26	421	16.2
Sam Pellom, Buffalo	6-8	†1976	26	420	16.2

Player, Team	Season	G	Blk.
Adonal Foyle, Colgate	1996	29	165
Ken Johnson, Ohio St.	†2000	30	161
Alonzo Mourning, Georgetown	†1992	32	160
Shaquille O'Neal, LSU	1992	30	157
Roy Rogers, Alabama	1996	32	156
Dikembe Mutombo, Georgetown	1991	32	151
Adonal Foyle, Colgate	†1995	30	147
Tarvis Williams, Hampton	†2001	32	147
Theo Ratliff, Wyoming	1995	28	144
David Robinson, Navy	†1987	32	144
Wojciech Myrda, La.-Monroe	2000	28	144
Cedric Lewis, Maryland	1991	28	143
Jim McIlvaine, Marquette	†1994	33	142
Alvin Jones, Georgia Tech	†1998	33	141
Shaquille O'Neal, LSU	1991	28	140
Calvin Booth, Penn St.	1998	32	140
Keith Closs, Central Conn. St.	1995	26	139
Kevin Roberson, Vermont	1992	28	139
Etan Thomas, Syracuse	1998	35	138
Emeka Okafor, Connecticut	2002	34	138

†national leader

BLOCKED-SHOT AVERAGE

Player, Team	Season	G	Blk.	Avg.
Adonal Foyle, Colgate	†1997	28	180	6.43
Keith Closs, Central Conn St.	†1996	28	178	6.36
David Robinson, Navy	†1986	35	207	5.91
Adonal Foyle, Colgate	1996	29	165	5.69
Wojciech Myrda, La.-Monroe	†2002	32	172	5.38
Ken Johnson, Ohio St.	†2000	30	161	5.37
Keith Closs, Central Conn. St.	1995	26	139	5.35
Shaquille O'Neal, LSU	†1992	30	157	5.23
Shawn Bradley, Brigham Young	†1991	34	177	5.21
Theo Ratliff, Wyoming	1995	28	144	5.14
Wojciech Myrda, La.-Monroe	2000	28	144	5.14
Cedric Lewis, Maryland	1991	28	143	5.11
Shaquille O'Neal, LSU	1991	28	140	5.00
Alonzo Mourning, Georgetown	1992	32	160	5.00
Tarvis Williams, Hampton	†1999	27	135	5.00
Alonzo Mourning, Georgetown	†1989	34	169	4.97
Kevin Roberson, Vermont	1992	28	139	4.96
Adonal Foyle, Colgate	1995	30	147	4.90
Roy Rogers, Alabama	1996	32	156	4.88
Lorenzo Coleman, Tennessee Tech	1997	28	134	4.79
Kenny Green, Rhode Island	†1990	26	124	4.77
Dikembe Mutombo, Georgetown	1991	32	151	4.72
Jerome James, Florida A&M	†1998	27	125	4.63
Tarvis Williams, Hampton	†2001	32	147	4.59
Pascal Fleury, UMBC	1995	27	124	4.59
Lorenzo Coleman, Tennessee Tech	1995	27	122	4.52

†national leader

STEALS

Player, Team	Season	G	Stl.
Desmond Cambridge, Alabama A&M	†2002	29	160
Mookie Blaylock, Oklahoma	†1988	39	150
Aldwin Ware, Florida A&M	1988	29	142
Darron Brittman, Chicago St.	†1986	28	139
John Linehan, Providence	2002	31	139
Nadav Henefeld, Connecticut	†1990	37	138
Mookie Blaylock, Oklahoma	†1989	35	131
Ronn McMahon, Eastern Wash.	1990	29	130
Marty Johnson, Towson	1988	30	124
Allen Iverson, Georgetown	†1996	37	124
Eric Coley, Tulsa	†2000	37	123
Jim Paguaga, St. Francis (N.Y.)	1986	28	120
Shawn Griggs, La.-Lafayette	†1994	30	120
Pointer Williams, McNeese St.	1996	27	118
Tony Fairley, Charleston So.	†1987	28	114
Scott Burrell, Connecticut	†1991	31	112
Kenny Robertson, Cleveland St.	1989	28	111
Lance Blanks, Texas	1989	34	111
Eric Murdock, Providence	1991	32	111
Jason Kidd, California	†1993	29	110
Johnny Rhodes, Maryland	1996	30	110
Robert Dowdell, Coastal Caro.	1990	29	109
Keith Jennings, East Tenn. St.	1991	33	109
Mark Woods, Wright St.	1993	30	109
Gerald Walker, San Francisco	1994	28	109

†national leader

STEAL AVERAGE

Player, Team	Season	G	Stl.	Avg.
Desmond Cambridge, Alabama A&M	†2002	29	160	5.52
Darron Brittman, Chicago St.	†1986	28	139	4.96
Aldwin Ware, Florida A&M	†1988	29	142	4.90
John Linehan, Providence	2002	31	139	4.48
Ronn McMahon, Eastern Wash.	†1990	29	130	4.48
Pointer Williams, McNeese St.	†1996	27	118	4.37
Greedy Daniels, TCU	†2001	25	108	4.32
Jim Paguaga, St. Francis (N.Y.)	1986	28	120	4.29
Marty Johnson, Towson	1988	30	124	4.13
Tony Fairley, Charleston So.	†1987	28	114	4.07
Shawn Griggs, La.-Lafayette	†1994	30	120	4.00
Kenny Robertson, Cleveland St.	†1989	28	111	3.96
Gerald Walker, San Francisco	1994	28	109	3.89
Mookie Blaylock, Oklahoma	1988	39	150	3.85
Carl Williams, Liberty	†2000	28	107	3.82
Desmond Cambridge, Alabama A&M	2001	28	107	3.82
Jason Kidd, California	†1993	29	110	3.79
Jay Goodman, Utah St.	1993	27	102	3.78
Andre Cradle, Long Island	1994	21	79	3.76
Robert Dowdell, Coastal Caro.	1990	29	109	3.76
Mookie Blaylock, Oklahoma	1989	35	131	3.74
Johnny Rhodes, Maryland	1996	30	110	3.67
Roderick Taylor, Jackson St.	1996	29	106	3.66
Mark Woods, Wright St.	1993	30	109	3.63
Mire Chatman, Tex.-Pan American	2002	29	105	3.62

†national leader

Top Season Performances by Class

SCORING AVERAGE

Class	Player, Team	Season	G	FG	3FG	FT	Pts.	Avg.
Senior	Pete Maravich, LSU	1970	31	522	—	337	1,381	44.5
Junior	Pete Maravich, LSU	1969	26	433	—	282	1,148	44.2
Sophomore	Pete Maravich, LSU	1968	26	432	—	274	1,138	43.8
Freshman	Chris Jackson, LSU	1989	32	359	84	163	965	30.2

FIELD-GOAL PERCENTAGE

Class	Player, Team	Season	G	FG	FGA	Pct.
Senior	Steve Johnson, Oregon St.	1981	28	235	315	74.6
Junior	Steve Johnson, Oregon St.	1980	30	211	297	71.0
Sophomore	Dwayne Davis, Florida	1989	33	179	248	72.2
Freshman	Sidney Moncrief, Arkansas	1976	28	149	224	66.5

THREE-POINT FIELD GOALS MADE PER GAME

Class	Player, Team	Season	G	3FG	Avg.
Senior	Darrin Fitzgerald, Butler	1987	28	158	5.64
Junior	Timothy Pollard, Mississippi Val.	1988	28	132	4.71
Sophomore	Mark Alberts, Akron	1990	28	122	4.36
Freshman	Keith Veney, Lamar	1993	27	106	3.93

THREE-POINT FIELD-GOAL PERCENTAGE

Class	Player, Team	Season	G	3FG	3FGA	Pct.
Senior	Keith Jennings, East Tenn. St.	1991	33	84	142	59.2
Junior	Glenn Tropf, Holy Cross	1988	29	52	82	63.4
Sophomore	Dave Calloway, Monmouth	1989	28	48	82	58.5
Freshman	Jay Edwards, Indiana	1988	23	59	110	53.6

FREE-THROW PERCENTAGE

Class	Player, Team	Season	G	FT	FTA	Pct.
Senior	Craig Collins, Penn St.	1985	27	94	98	95.9
Junior	Rod Foster, UCLA	1982	27	95	100	95.0
Sophomore	Danny Basile, Marist	1994	27	84	89	94.4
Freshman	Jim Barton, Dartmouth	1986	26	65	69	94.2

REBOUND AVERAGE

Class	Player, Team	Season	G	Reb.	Avg.
Senior	Art Quimby, Connecticut	1955	25	611	24.4
Junior	Charlie Slack, Marshall	1955	21	538	25.6
Sophomore	Ed Conlin, Fordham	1953	26	612	23.5
Freshman	Pete Padgett, Nevada	1973	26	462	17.8

ASSIST AVERAGE

Class	Player, Team	Season	G	Ast.	Avg.
Senior	Avery Johnson, Southern U.	1988	30	399	13.30
Junior	Anthony Manuel, Bradley	1988	31	373	12.03

Class	Player, Team	Season	G	Ast.	Avg.
Sophomore	Curtis McCants, George Mason	1995	27	251	9.30
Freshman	Omar Cook, St. John's (N.Y.)	2001	29	252	8.69

BLOCKED-SHOT AVERAGE

Class	Player, Team	Season	G	Blk.	Avg.
Senior	Wojciech Mydra, La.-Monroe	2002	32	172	5.38
Junior	Adonal Foyle, Colgate	1997	28	180	6.43
Sophomore	Keith Closs, Central Conn. St.	1996	28	178	6.36
Freshman	Keith Closs, Central Conn. St.	1995	26	139	5.35

STEAL AVERAGE

Class	Player, Team	Season	G	Stl.	Avg.
Senior	Desmond Cambridge, Alabama A&M	2002	29	160	5.52
Junior	Kenny Robertson, Cleveland St.	1989	28	111	3.96
Sophomore	Gerald Walker, San Francisco	1994	28	109	3.89
Freshman	Jason Kidd, California	1993	29	110	3.79

Top Season Performances by a Freshman

POINTS

Player, Team	Season	G	FG	3FG	FT	Pts.
Chris Jackson, LSU	1989	32	359	84	163	965
James Williams, Austin Peay	1973	29	360	—	134	854
Jason Conley, VMI	2002	28	285	79	171	820
Wayman Tisdale, Oklahoma	1983	33	338	—	134	810
Alphonso Ford, Mississippi Val.	1990	27	289	104	126	808

SCORING AVERAGE

Player, Team	Season	G	FG	3FG	FT	Pts.	Avg.
Chris Jackson, LSU	1989	32	359	84	163	965	30.2
Alphonso Ford, Mississippi Val.	1990	27	289	104	126	808	29.9
James Williams, Austin Peay	1973	29	360	—	134	854	29.4
Jason Conley, VMI	2002	28	285	79	171	820	29.3
Harry Kelly, Texas Southern	1980	26	313	—	127	753	29.0

FIELD-GOAL PERCENTAGE

Player, Team	Season	G	FG	FGA	Pct.
Sidney Moncrief, Arkansas	1976	28	149	224	66.5
Gary Trent, Ohio	1993	27	194	298	65.1
Ed Pinckney, Villanova	1982	32	169	264	64.0
David Harrison, Colorado	2002	27	139	218	63.8
Jimmy Lunsford, Alabama St.	1993	22	142	223	63.7

THREE-POINT FIELD GOALS MADE

Player, Team	Season	G	3FG
Keith Veney, Lamar	1993	27	106
Alphonso Ford, Mississippi Val.	1990	27	104
Tony Ross, San Diego St.	1987	28	104
Ronnie McCollum, Centenary (La.)	1998	30	101
Donnie Carr, La Salle	1997	27	99

THREE-POINT FIELD GOALS MADE PER GAME

Player, Team	Season	G	3FG	Avg.
Keith Veney, Lamar	1993	27	106	3.93
Alphonso Ford, Mississippi Val.	1990	27	104	3.85
Tony Ross, San Diego St.	1987	28	104	3.71
Donnie Carr, La Salle	1997	27	99	3.67
Troy Green, Southeastern La.	1996	27	98	3.63

THREE-POINT FIELD-GOAL PERCENTAGE

Player, Team	Season	G	3FG	3FGA	Pct.
Jay Edwards, Indiana	1988	23	59	110	53.6
Ross Richardson, Loyola Marymount	1991	25	61	116	52.6
Lance Barker, Valparaiso	1992	26	61	117	52.1
Ed Peterson, Yale	1989	28	53	104	51.0
Ross Land, Northern Ariz.	1997	28	64	126	50.8
Willie Brand, Texas-Arlington	1988	29	65	128	50.8

FREE-THROW PERCENTAGE

Player, Team	Season	G	FT	FTA	Pct.
Jim Barton, Dartmouth	1986	26	65	69	94.2
Steve Alford, Indiana	1984	31	137	150	91.3
Jay Edwards, Indiana	1988	23	69	76	90.8
LaBradford Smith, Louisville	1988	35	143	158	90.5
Salim Stoudamire, Arizona	2002	34	103	114	90.4

REBOUNDS

Player, Team	Season	G	Reb.
Pete Padgett, Nevada	1973	26	462
Kenny Miller, Loyola (Ill.)	1988	29	395
Shaquille O'Neal, LSU	1990	32	385
Ralph Sampson, Virginia	1980	34	381
Adonal Foyle, Colgate	1995	30	371

REBOUND AVERAGE

Player, Team	Season	G	Reb.	Avg.
Pete Padgett, Nevada	1973	26	462	17.8
Glenn Mosley, Seton Hall	1974	21	299	14.2
Ira Terrell, Southern Methodist	1973	25	352	14.1
Kenny Miller, Loyola (Ill.)	1988	29	395	13.6
Bob Stephens, Drexel	1976	23	307	13.3

ASSISTS

Player, Team	Season	G	Ast.
Bobby Hurley, Duke	1990	38	288
Kenny Anderson, Georgia Tech	1990	35	285
T.J. Ford, Texas	2002	33	273
Andre LaFleur, Northeastern	1984	32	252
Omar Cook, St. John's (N.Y.)	2001	29	252
Chris Thomas, Notre Dame	2002	33	252

ASSIST AVERAGE

Player, Team	Season	G	Ast.	Avg.
Omar Cook, St. John's (N.Y.)	2001	29	252	8.69
T.J. Ford, Texas	2002	33	273	8.27
Orlando Smart, San Francisco	1991	29	237	8.17
Kenny Anderson, Georgia Tech	1990	35	285	8.14
Taurence Chisholm, Delaware	1985	28	224	8.00

BLOCKED SHOTS

Player, Team	Season	G	Blk.
Shawn Bradley, Brigham Young	1991	34	177
Alonzo Mourning, Georgetown	1989	34	169
Adonal Foyle, Colgate	1995	30	147
Alvin Jones, Georgia Tech	1998	33	141
Keith Closs, Central Conn. St.	1995	26	139

BLOCKED-SHOT AVERAGE

Player, Team	Season	G	Blk.	Avg.
Keith Closs, Central Conn. St.	1995	26	139	5.35
Shawn Bradley, Brigham Young	1991	34	177	5.21
Alonzo Mourning, Georgetown	1989	34	169	4.97
Adonal Foyle, Colgate	1995	30	147	4.90
Richard Lugo, St. Francis (N.Y.)	1997	28	125	4.46

STEALS

Player, Team	Season	G	Stl.
Nadav Henefeld, Connecticut	1990	37	138
Jason Kidd, California	1993	29	110
Kellii Taylor, Pittsburgh	1997	32	101
Ben Larson, Cal Poly	1996	29	100
Five tied with 90			

STEAL AVERAGE

Player, Team	Season	G	Stl.	Avg.
Jason Kidd, California	1993	29	110	3.79
Nadav Henefeld, Connecticut	1990	37	138	3.73
Ben Larson, Cal Poly	1996	29	100	3.45
Eric Murdock, Providence	1988	28	90	3.21
Pat Baldwin, Northwestern	1991	28	90	3.21
Joel Hoover, Md.-East. Shore	1997	28	90	3.21

Career Records

POINTS

Player, Team	Ht.	Last Season	Yrs.	G	FG	3FG#	FT	Pts.
Pete Maravich, LSU	6-5	1970	3	83	1,387	—	893	3,667
Freeman Williams, Portland St.	6-4	1978	4	106	1,369	—	511	3,249
Lionel Simmons, La Salle	6-7	1990	4	131	1,244	56	673	3,217
Alphonso Ford, Mississippi Val.	6-2	1993	4	109	1,121	333	590	3,165
Harry Kelly, Texas Southern	6-7	1983	4	110	1,234	—	598	3,066
Hersey Hawkins, Bradley	6-3	1988	4	125	1,100	118	690	3,008
Oscar Robertson, Cincinnati	6-5	1960	3	88	1,052	—	869	2,973
Danny Manning, Kansas	6-10	1988	4	147	1,216	10	509	2,951
Alfredrick Hughes, Loyola (Ill.)	6-5	1985	4	120	1,226	—	462	2,914
Elvin Hayes, Houston	6-8	1968	3	93	1,215	—	454	2,884
Larry Bird, Indiana St.	6-9	1979	3	94	1,154	—	542	2,850

DIVISION I

Player, Team	Ht.	Season	Yrs.	G	FG	3FG#	FT	Pts.
Otis Birdsong, Houston	6-4	1977	4	116	1,176	—	480	2,832
Kevin Bradshaw, Bethune-Cookman & U.S. Int'l	6-6	1991	4	111	1,027	132	618	2,804
Allan Houston, Tennessee	6-5	1993	4	128	902	346	651	2,801
Hank Gathers, Southern California & Loyola Marymount	6-7	1990	4	117	1,127	0	469	2,723
Reggie Lewis, Northeastern	6-7	1987	4	122	1,043	30(1)	592	2,708
Daren Queenan, Lehigh	6-5	1988	4	118	1,024	29	626	2,703
Byron Larkin, Xavier	6-3	1988	4	121	1,022	51	601	2,696
David Robinson, Navy	7-1	1987	4	127	1,032	1	604	2,669
Wayman Tisdale, Oklahoma	6-9	1985	3	104	1,077	—	507	2,661
Michael Brooks, La Salle	6-7	1980	4	114	1,064	—	500	2,628
Calbert Cheaney, Indiana	6-6	1993	4	132	1,018	148	429	2,613
Mark Macon, Temple	6-5	1991	4	126	980	246	403	2,609
Don MacLean, UCLA	6-10	1992	4	127	943	11	711	2,608
Joe Dumars, McNeese St.	6-3	1985	4	116	941	(5)	723	2,605
Terrance Bailey, Wagner	6-2	1987	4	110	985	42	579	2,591
Dickie Hemric, Wake Forest	6-6	1955	4	104	841	—	905	2,587
Calvin Natt, Northeast La.	6-5	1979	4	108	1,017	—	547	2,581
Derrick Chievous, Missouri	6-7	1988	4	130	893	30	764	2,580
Skip Henderson, Marshall	6-2	1988	4	125	1,000	133	441	2,574
Austin Carr, Notre Dame	6-3	1971	3	74	1,017	—	526	2,560
Sean Elliott, Arizona	6-8	1989	4	133	896	140	623	2,555
Rodney Monroe, North Caro. St.	6-3	1991	4	124	885	322	459	2,551
Calvin Murphy, Niagara	5-10	1970	3	77	947	—	654	2,548
Keith Van Horn, Utah	6-9	1997	4	122	891	206	554	2,542
Frank Selvy, Furman	6-3	1954	3	78	922	—	694	2,538
Johnny Dawkins, Duke	6-2	1986	4	133	1,026	(19)	485	2,537
Willie Jackson, Centenary (La.)	6-6	1984	4	114	995	(18)	545	2,535
Steve Rogers, Alabama St.	6-5	1992	4	113	817	187	713	2,534
Steve Burtt, Iona	6-2	1984	4	121	1,003	—	528	2,534
Shawn Respert, Michigan St.	6-3	1995	4	118	866	331	468	2,531
Joe Jakubick, Akron	6-5	1984	4	108	973	(53)	584	2,530
Andrew Toney, La.-Lafayette	6-3	1980	4	107	996	—	534	2,526
Ron Perry, Holy Cross	6-2	1980	4	109	922	—	680	2,524
Ronnie McCollum, Centenary (La.)	6-4	2001	4	113	822	345	535	2,524
Mike Olliver, Lamar	6-1	1981	4	122	1,130	—	258	2,518
Bryant Stith, Virginia	6-5	1992	4	131	856	114	690	2,516
Bill Bradley, Princeton	6-5	1965	3	83	856	—	791	2,503
Jeff Grayer, Iowa St.	6-5	1988	4	125	974	27	527	2,502
Elgin Baylor, Albertson & Seattle	6-6	1958	3	80	956	—	588	2,500

#Listed is the number of three-pointers scored since it became the national rule in 1987; the number in the parenthesis is number scored before 1987—these counted as three points in the game but counted as two-pointers in the national rankings. The three-pointers in the parenthesis are not included in total points.

2,000-POINT SCORERS

A total of 384 players in Division I history have scored at least 2,000 points over their careers. The first was Jim Lacy, Loyola (Md.), with 2,154 over four seasons ending with 1949. The first to reach 2,000 in a three-season career was Furman's Frank Selvy, 2,538 through 1954. The 384 come from 202 different colleges. Duke leads with eight 2,000-pointers: Jim Spanarkel (last season was 1979), Mike Gminski (1980), Gene Banks (1981), Mark Alarie (1986), Johnny Dawkins (1986), Danny Ferry (1989), Christian Laettner (1992) and Jason Williams (2002). Next are Georgia Tech and La Salle with six, followed by Indiana, Michigan, Murray State, North Carolina, Notre Dame, Oklahoma, Tennessee, Villanova and Wake Forest with five apiece.

SCORING AVERAGE

Player, Team	Last Season	Yrs.	G	FG	3FG	FT	Pts.	Avg.
Pete Maravich, LSU	1968	3	83	1,387	—	893	3,667	44.2
Austin Carr, Notre Dame	1971	3	74	1,017	—	526	2,560	34.6
Oscar Robertson, Cincinnati	1960	3	88	1,052	—	869	2,973	33.8
Calvin Murphy, Niagara	1970	3	77	947	—	654	2,548	33.1
Dwight Lamar, La.-Lafayette	†1973	2	57	768	—	326	1,862	32.7
Frank Selvy, Furman	1954	3	78	922	—	694	2,538	32.5
Rick Mount, Purdue	1970	3	72	910	—	503	2,323	32.3
Darrell Floyd, Furman	1956	3	71	868	—	545	2,281	32.1
Nick Werkman, Seton Hall	1964	3	71	812	—	649	2,273	32.0
Willie Humes, Idaho St.	1971	2	48	565	—	380	1,510	31.5
William Averitt, Pepperdine	1973	2	49	615	—	311	1,541	31.4
Elgin Baylor, Albertson & Seattle	1958	3	80	956	—	588	2,500	31.3
Elvin Hayes, Houston	1968	3	93	1,215	—	454	2,884	31.0
Freeman Williams, Portland St.	1978	4	106	1,369	—	511	3,249	30.7
Larry Bird, Indiana St.	1979	3	94	1,154	—	542	2,850	30.3
Bill Bradley, Princeton	1965	3	83	856	—	791	2,503	30.2
Rich Fuqua, Oral Roberts	†1973	2	54	692	—	233	1,617	29.9
Wilt Chamberlain, Kansas	1958	2	48	503	—	427	1,433	29.9
Rick Barry, Miami (Fla.)	1965	3	77	816	—	666	2,298	29.8
Doug Collins, Illinois St.	1973	3	77	894	—	452	2,240	29.1
Alphonso Ford, Mississippi Val.	1993	4	109	1,121	333	590	3,165	29.0
Chris Jackson, LSU	1990	2	64	664	172	354	1,854	29.0
Dave Schellhase, Purdue	1966	3	74	746	—	582	2,074	28.8
Dick Wilkinson, Virginia	1955	3	78	783	—	665	2,233	28.6
James Williams, Austin Peay	1974	2	54	632	—	277	1,541	28.5

†Each played two years of non-Division I competition (Lamar—four years, 3,493 points and 31.2 average; Fuqua—four years, 3,004 points and 27.1 average).

FIELD-GOAL PERCENTAGE
(Minimum 400 field goals made and 4 field goals made per game)

Player, Team	Ht.	Last Season	Yrs.	G	FG	FGA	Pct.
Steve Johnson, Oregon St.	6-10	1981	4	116	828	1,222	67.8
Michael Bradley, Kentucky & Villanova	6-10	2001	3	100	441	651	67.7
Murray Brown, Florida St.	6-8	1980	4	106	566	847	66.8
Lee Campbell, Middle Tenn. & Southwest Mo. St.	6-7	1990	3	88	411	618	66.5
Warren Kidd, Middle Tenn.	6-9	1993	3	83	496	747	66.4
Todd MacCulloch, Washington	7-0	1999	4	115	702	1,058	66.4
Joe Senser, West Chester	6-5	1979	4	96	476	719	66.2
Kevin Magee, UC Irvine	6-8	1982	2	56	552	841	65.6
Orlando Phillips, Pepperdine	6-7	1983	2	58	404	618	65.4
Bill Walton, UCLA	6-11	1974	3	87	747	1,147	65.1
William Herndon, Massachusetts	6-3	1992	4	100	472	728	64.8
Larry Stewart, Coppin St.	6-8	1991	3	91	676	1,046	64.6
Larry Johnson, UNLV	6-7	1991	2	75	612	952	64.3
Dwayne Davis, Florida	6-7	1991	4	124	572	892	64.1
Lew Alcindor, UCLA	7-2	1969	3	88	943	1,476	63.9
Akeem Olajuwon, Houston	7-0	1984	3	100	532	833	63.9
Brendan Haywood, North Carolina	7-0	2001	4	141	541	849	63.7
Oliver Miller, Arkansas	6-9	1992	4	137	680	1,069	63.6
Mike Coleman, Liberty	6-7	1992	4	105	421	663	63.5
Jeff Ruland, Iona	6-10	1980	3	89	717	1,130	63.5
Mark McNamara, California	6-10	1982	4	107	709	1,119	63.4
Dan McClintock, Northern Ariz.	7-0	2000	4	115	542	858	63.2
Cherokee Rhone, Centenary (La.)	6-8	1982	3	63	421	667	63.1
Carlos Boozer, Duke	6-9	2002	3	101	554	878	63.1
Bobby Lee Hurt, Alabama	6-9	1985	4	126	646	1,024	63.1

THREE-POINT FIELD GOALS MADE

Player, Team	Ht.	Last Season	Yrs.	G	3FG
Curtis Staples, Virginia	6-3	1998	4	122	413
Keith Veney, Lamar & Marshall	6-3	1997	4	111	409
Doug Day, Radford	6-1	1993	4	117	401
Ronnie Schmitz, UMKC	6-3	1993	4	112	378
Mark Alberts, Akron	6-1	1993	4	107	375
Pat Bradley, Arkansas	6-2	1999	4	132	366
Bryce Drew, Valparaiso	6-3	1998	4	121	364
Jeff Fryer, Loyola Marymount	6-2	1990	4	112	363
Dennis Scott, Georgia Tech	6-8	1990	3	99	351
Rashad Phillips, Detroit	5-10	2001	4	129	348
Allan Houston, Tennessee	6-5	1993	4	128	346
Jobey Thomas, Charlotte	6-4	2002	4	130	346
Ronnie McCollum, Centenary (La.)	6-4	2001	4	113	345
Trajan Langdon, Duke	6-4	1999	4	136	342
Louis Bullock, Michigan	6-2	1999	4	132	339
Jeff Boschee, Kansas	6-3	2002	4	137	338
Alphonso Ford, Mississippi Val.	6-2	1993	4	109	333
Tim Gill, Oral Roberts	6-2	1998	4	112	333
Pete Lisicky, Penn St.	6-4	1998	4	118	332
Brian Merriweather, Tex.-Pan American	6-3	2001	3	84	332
Clarence Gilbert, Missouri	6-2	2002	4	128	332
Shawn Respert, Michigan St.	6-3	1995	4	118	331
Demond Mallet, McNeese St.	6-1	2001	5	117	331
Monty Mack, Massachusetts	6-3	2001	4	123	331
Andy Kennedy, North Carolina St. & UAB	6-8	1991	4	121	330

THREE-POINT FIELD GOALS MADE PER GAME
(Minimum 200 three-point field goals made)

Player, Team	Ht.	Last Season	Yrs.	G	3FG	Avg.
Timothy Pollard, Mississippi Val.	6-3	1989	2	56	256	4.57
Sydney Grider, La.-Lafayette	6-3	1990	2	58	253	4.36
Brian Merriweather, Tex.-Pan American	6-3	2001	3	84	332	3.95
Josh Heard, Tennessee Tech	6-2	2000	2	55	210	3.82
Kareem Townes, La Salle	6-3	1995	3	81	300	3.70
Keith Veney, Lamar & Marshall	6-3	1997	4	111	409	3.68
Dave Mooney, Coastal Caro.	6-4	1988	2	56	202	3.61
Dennis Scott, Georgia Tech	6-8	1990	3	99	351	3.55
Mark Alberts, Akron	6-1	1993	4	107	375	3.50
Doug Day, Radford	6-1	1993	4	117	401	3.43
Curtis Staples, Virginia	6-3	1998	4	122	413	3.39
Ronnie Schmitz, UMKC	6-3	1993	4	112	378	3.38
Jeff Fryer, Loyola Marymount	6-2	1990	4	112	363	3.24
Dana Barros, Boston College	5-11	1989	3	91	291	3.20
Tony Ross, San Diego St.	6-3	1989	3	85	270	3.18

Player, Team	Ht.	Last Season	Yrs.	G	3FG	Avg.
Randy Woods, La Salle	6-0	1992	3	88	278	3.16
Dominick Young, Fresno St.	5-10	1997	3	89	279	3.13
Wally Lancaster, Virginia Tech	6-5	1989	3	82	257	3.13
David Sivulich, St. Mary's (Cal.)	5-10	1998	3	76	238	3.13
Jim Barton, Dartmouth	6-4	1989	3	78	242	3.10
Alan Barkside, Colorado & Ark.-Little Rock	6-4	2001	4	86	264	3.07
Alphonso Ford, Mississippi Val.	6-2	1993	4	109	333	3.06
Ronnie McCollum, Centenary (La.)	6-4	2001	4	113	345	3.05
Charles Jones, Rutgers & Long Island	6-3	1998	4	108	329	3.05
Keke Hicks, Coastal Caro.	6-4	1995	4	93	282	3.03

THREE-POINT FIELD-GOAL PERCENTAGE

(Minimum 200 three-point field goals made and 2.0 three-point field goals made per game)

Player, Team	Ht.	Last Season	Yrs.	G	3FG	3FGA	Pct.
Tony Bennett, Wis.-Green Bay	6-0	1992	4	118	290	584	49.7
David Olson, Eastern Ill.	6-4	1992	4	111	262	562	46.6
Ross Land, Northern Ariz.	6-5	2000	4	117	308	664	46.4
Dan Dickau, Washington & Gonzaga	6-0	2002	4	97	215	465	46.2
Sean Jackson, Ohio & Princeton	5-11	1992	4	104	243	528	46.0
Barry Booker, Vanderbilt	6-3	1989	3	98	246	535	46.0
Kevin Booth, Mt. St. Mary's	6-0	1993	5	110	265	577	45.9
Dave Calloway, Monmouth	6-3	1991	4	115	260	567	45.9
Tony Ross, San Diego St.	6-3	1992	3	85	270	589	45.8
Jason Matthews, Pittsburgh	6-3	1991	4	123	259	567	45.7
Corey Reed, Radford	6-6	1998	4	104	232	510	45.5
Jim Barton, Dartmouth	6-4	1989	3	78	242	532	45.5
Shawn Respert, Michigan St.	6-3	1995	4	118	331	728	45.5
Carlton Becton, N.C. A&T	6-6	1989	3	84	209	462	45.2
Eric Channing, New Mexico St.	6-4	2002	4	124	283	627	45.1
Ray Allen, Connecticut	6-5	1996	3	101	233	520	44.8
Curtis Shelton, Southeast Mo. St.	5-9	1994	4	107	215	480	44.8
Jeff McCool, New Mexico St.	6-5	1989	3	92	201	450	44.7
Scott Neely, Campbell	6-3	1996	4	115	244	553	44.1
Wesley Person, Auburn	6-6	1994	4	108	262	594	44.1
Tim Gill, Oral Roberts	6-2	1998	4	112	333	757	44.0
Mark Alberts, Akron	6-1	1993	4	107	375	853	44.0
John Rillie, Gonzaga	6-5	1995	3	88	230	524	43.9
Scott Hartzell, UNC Greensboro	6-0	1996	4	113	309	704	43.9
Andy Kennedy, North Carolina St. & UAB	6-8	1991	4	121	330	752	43.9

FREE-THROW PERCENTAGE

(Minimum 300 free throws made and 2 free throws made per game)

Player, Team	Last Season	Yrs.	G	FT	FTA	Pct.
Greg Starrick, Kentucky & Southern Ill.	1972	4	72	341	375	90.9
Jack Moore, Nebraska	1982	4	105	446	495	90.1
Steve Henson, Kansas St.	1990	4	127	361	401	90.0
Steve Alford, Indiana	1987	4	125	535	596	89.8
Bob Lloyd, Rutgers	1967	3	77	543	605	89.8
Jim Barton, Dartmouth	1989	4	104	394	440	89.5
Tommy Boyer, Arkansas	1963	3	70	315	353	89.2
Rob Robbins, New Mexico	1991	4	133	309	348	88.8
Marcus Wilson, Evansville	1999	4	119	455	513	88.7
Sean Miller, Pittsburgh	1992	4	128	317	358	88.5
Joe Crispin, Penn St.	2001	4	127	448	506	88.5
Ron Perry, Holy Cross	1980	4	109	680	768	88.5
Joe Dykstra, Western Ill.	1983	4	117	587	663	88.5
Mike Joseph, Bucknell	1990	4	115	397	449	88.4
Kyle Macy, Purdue & Kentucky	1980	5	125	416	471	88.3
Matt Hildebrand, Liberty	1994	4	117	398	451	88.2
Jimmy England, Tennessee	1971	3	81	319	362	88.1
Rod Foster, UCLA	1983	4	113	309	351	88.0
Michael Smith, Brigham Young	1989	4	122	431	491	87.8
Jason Matthews, Pittsburgh	1991	4	123	481	548	87.8
Mike Iuzzolino, Penn St. & St. Francis (Pa.)	1991	4	112	402	458	87.7
Rick Suder, Duquesne	1986	4	105	342	390	87.7
Bill Bradley, Princeton	1965	3	83	791	903	87.6
William Lewis, Monmouth	1992	4	112	317	362	87.6
Rashad Phillips, Detroit	2001	4	129	541	618	87.5

REBOUNDS

Player, Team	Ht.	Last Season	Yrs.	G	Reb.
Tom Gola, La Salle	6-6	1955	4	118	2,201
Joe Holup, George Washington	6-6	1956	4	104	2,030
Charlie Slack, Marshall	6-5	1956	4	88	1,916
Ed Conlin, Fordham	6-5	1955	4	102	1,884
Dickie Hemric, Wake Forest	6-6	1955	4	104	1,802
Paul Silas, Creighton	6-7	1964	3	81	1,751
Art Quimby, Connecticut	6-5	1955	4	80	1,716

Player, Team	Ht.	Last Season	Yrs.	G	Reb.
Jerry Harper, Alabama	6-8	1956	4	93	1,688
Jeff Cohen, William & Mary	6-7	1961	4	103	1,679
Steve Hamilton, Morehead St.	6-7	1958	4	102	1,675
Charlie Tyra, Louisville	6-8	1957	4	95	1,617
Bill Russell, San Francisco	6-9	1956	3	79	1,606
Elvin Hayes, Houston	6-8	1968	3	93	1,602
Ron Shavlik, North Carolina St.	6-8	1956	3	95	1,598
Marvin Barnes, Providence	6-9	1974	3	89	1,592
Tim Duncan, Wake Forest	6-11	1997	4	128	1,570
Elgin Baylor, Albertson & Seattle	6-6	1958	3	80	1,559
Ernie Beck, Pennsylvania	6-4	1953	3	82	1,557
Dave DeBusschere, Detroit	6-5	1962	3	80	1,552
Wes Unseld, Louisville	6-8	1968	3	82	1,551
Derrick Coleman, Syracuse	6-9	1990	4	143	1,537
Malik Rose, Drexel	6-7	1996	4	120	1,514
Ralph Sampson, Virginia	7-4	1983	4	132	1,511
Chris Smith, Virginia Tech	6-6	1961	4	88	1,508
Keith Swagerty, Pacific (Cal.)	6-7	1967	3	82	1,505

(For careers beginning in 1973 or after)

Player, Team	Ht.	Last Season	Yrs.	G	Reb.
Tim Duncan, Wake Forest	6-11	1997	4	128	1,570
Derrick Coleman, Syracuse	6-9	1990	4	143	1,537
Malik Rose, Drexel	6-7	1996	4	120	1,514
Ralph Sampson, Virginia	7-4	1983	4	132	1,511
Pete Padgett, Nevada	6-8	1976	4	104	1,464
Lionel Simmons, La Salle	6-7	1990	4	131	1,429
Anthony Bonner, St. Louis	6-7	1990	4	133	1,424
Tyrone Hill, Xavier	6-9	1990	4	126	1,380
Popeye Jones, Murray St.	6-8	1992	4	123	1,374
Michael Brooks, La Salle	6-7	1980	4	114	1,372
Xavier McDaniel, Wichita St.	6-7	1985	4	117	1,359
John Irving, Arizona & Hofstra	6-9	1977	4	103	1,348
Sam Clancy, Pittsburgh	6-6	1981	4	116	1,342
Keith Lee, Memphis	6-10	1985	4	128	1,336
Larry Smith, Alcorn St.	6-8	1980	4	111	1,334
Clarence Weatherspoon, Southern Miss.	6-7	1992	4	117	1,320
Michael Cage, San Diego St.	6-9	1984	4	112	1,317
Bob Stephens, Drexel	6-7	1979	4	99	1,316
Patrick Ewing, Georgetown	7-0	1985	4	143	1,316
David Robinson, Navy	7-1	1987	4	127	1,314
Wayne Rollins, Clemson	7-1	1977	4	110	1,311
Bob Warner, Maine	6-6	1976	4	96	1,304
Ervin Johnson, New Orleans	6-11	1993	4	123	1,287
Calvin Natt, Northeast La.	6-5	1979	4	108	1,285
Leon Douglas, Alabama	6-10	1976	4	111	1,279
Reggie King, Alabama	6-6	1979	4	118	1,279

REBOUND AVERAGE

(Minimum 800 rebounds)

Player, Team	Ht.	Last Season	Yrs.	G	Reb.	Avg.
Artis Gilmore, Jacksonville	7-2	1971	2	54	1,224	22.7
Charlie Slack, Marshall	6-5	1956	4	88	1,916	21.8
Paul Silas, Creighton	6-7	1964	3	81	1,751	21.6
Leroy Wright, Pacific (Cal.)	6-8	1960	3	67	1,442	21.5
Art Quimby, Connecticut	6-5	1955	4	80	1,716	21.5
Walt Dukes, Seton Hall	6-10	1953	2	59	1,247	21.1
Bill Russell, San Francisco	6-9	1956	3	79	1,606	20.3
Kermit Washington, American	6-8	1973	3	73	1,478	20.2
Julius Erving, Massachusetts	6-6	1971	2	52	1,049	20.2
Joe Holup, George Washington	6-6	1956	4	104	2,030	19.5
Elgin Baylor, Albertson & Seattle	6-6	1958	3	80	1,559	19.5
Dave DeBusschere, Detroit	6-5	1962	3	80	1,552	19.4
Ernie Beck, Pennsylvania	6-4	1953	3	82	1,557	19.0
Wes Unseld, Louisville	6-8	1968	3	82	1,551	18.9
Tom Gola, La Salle	6-6	1955	4	118	2,201	18.7
Ed Conlin, Fordham	6-5	1955	4	102	1,884	18.5
Keith Swagerty, Pacific (Cal.)	6-7	1967	3	82	1,505	18.4
Wilt Chamberlain, Kansas	7-0	1958	2	48	877	18.3
Jerry Harper, Alabama	6-8	1956	4	93	1,688	18.2
Dick Cunningham, Murray St.	6-10	1968	3	71	1,292	18.2
Marvin Barnes, Providence	6-9	1974	3	89	1,592	17.9
Jim Barnes, UTEP	6-8	1964	2	54	965	17.9
Alex Ellis, Niagara	6-5	1958	3	77	1,376	17.9
Dickie Hemric, Wake Forest	6-6	1955	4	104	1,802	17.3
Elvin Hayes, Houston	6-8	1968	3	93	1,602	17.2

(For careers beginning in 1973 or after; minimum 800 rebounds)

Player, Team	Ht.	Last Season	Yrs.	G	Reb.	Avg.
Glenn Mosley, Seton Hall	6-8	1977	4	83	1,263	15.2
Bill Campion, Manhattan	6-10	1975	3	74	1,070	14.6
Pete Padgett, Nevada	6-8	1976	4	104	1,464	14.1

Player, Team	Ht.	Last Season	Yrs.	G	Reb.	Avg.
Bob Warner, Maine	6-6	1976	4	96	1,304	13.6
Shaquille O'Neal, LSU	7-1	1992	3	90	1,217	13.5
Cornelius Cash, Bowling Green	6-8	1975	3	79	1,068	13.5
Ira Terrell, Southern Methodist	6-8	1976	3	80	1,077	13.5
Bob Stephens, Drexel	6-7	1979	4	99	1,316	13.3
Larry Bird, Indiana St.	6-9	1979	3	94	1,247	13.3
Bernard King, Tennessee	6-7	1977	3	76	1,004	13.2
John Irving, Arizona & Hofstra	6-9	1977	4	103	1,348	13.1
Carey Scurry, Long Island	6-9	1985	3	79	1,013	12.8
Adonal Foyle, Colgate	6-10	1997	3	87	1,103	12.7
Warren Kidd, Middle Tenn.	6-6	1993	3	83	1,048	12.6
Malik Rose, Drexel	6-7	1996	4	120	1,514	12.6
Jervaughn Scales, Southern U.	6-6	1994	3	88	1,099	12.5
Tim Duncan, Wake Forest	6-11	1997	4	128	1,570	12.3
Michael Brooks, La Salle	6-7	1980	4	114	1,372	12.0
Larry Smith, Alcorn St.	6-8	1980	4	111	1,334	12.0
Wayne Rollins, Clemson	7-1	1977	4	110	1,311	11.9
Calvin Natt, Northeast La.	6-5	1979	4	108	1,285	11.9
Ed Lawrence, McNeese St.	7-0	1976	4	102	1,212	11.9
Michael Cage, San Diego St.	6-9	1984	4	112	1,317	11.8
Xavier McDaniel, Wichita St.	6-7	1985	4	117	1,359	11.6
John Rudd, McNeese St.	6-6	1978	4	102	1,181	11.6
Sam Clancy, Pittsburgh	6-6	1981	4	116	1,342	11.6
Larry Stewart, Coppin St.	6-6	1991	3	91	1,052	11.6
Reggie Jackson, Nicholls St.	6-6	1995	4	110	1,271	11.6

ASSISTS

Player, Team	Ht.	Last Season	Yrs.	G	Ast.
Bobby Hurley, Duke	6-0	1993	4	140	1,076
Chris Corchiani, North Carolina St.	6-1	1991	4	124	1,038
Ed Cota, North Carolina	6-2	2000	4	138	1,030
Keith Jennings, East Tenn. St.	5-7	1991	4	127	983
Sherman Douglas, Syracuse	6-0	1989	4	138	960
Tony Miller, Marquette	6-0	1995	4	123	956
Greg Anthony, Portland & UNLV	6-1	1991	4	138	950
Doug Gottlieb, Notre Dame & Oklahoma St.	6-1	2000	4	124	947
Gary Payton, Oregon St.	6-2	1990	4	120	939
Orlando Smart, San Francisco	6-0	1994	4	116	902
Andre LaFleur, Northeastern	6-3	1987	4	128	894
Chico Fletcher, Arkansas St.	5-6	2000	4	114	893
Jim Les, Bradley	5-11	1986	4	118	884
Frank Smith, Old Dominion	6-0	1988	4	120	883
Taurence Chisholm, Delaware	5-7	1988	4	110	877
Grayson Marshall, Clemson	6-2	1988	4	122	857
Anthony Manuel, Bradley	5-11	1989	4	108	855
Pooh Richardson, UCLA	6-1	1989	4	122	833
Butch Moore, Southern Methodist	5-10	1986	4	125	828
Mateen Cleaves, Michigan St.	6-3	2000	4	123	816
Drafton Davis, Marist	6-0	1988	4	115	804
Jacque Vaughn, Kansas	6-1	1997	4	126	804
Marc Brown, Siena	5-11	1991	4	123	796
Tyrone Bogues, Wake Forest	5-3	1987	4	119	781
Brevin Knight, Stanford	5-10	1997	4	115	780

ASSIST AVERAGE
(Minimum 550 assists)

Player, Team	Ht.	Last Season	Yrs.	G	Ast.	Avg.
Avery Johnson, Southern U.	5-11	1988	2	61	732	12.00
Sam Crawford, New Mexico St.	5-8	1993	2	67	592	8.84
Mark Wade, Oklahoma & UNLV	6-0	1987	3	79	693	8.77
Chris Corchiani, North Carolina St.	6-1	1991	4	124	1,038	8.37
Taurence Chisholm, Delaware	5-7	1988	4	110	877	7.97
Van Usher, Tennessee Tech	6-0	1992	3	85	676	7.95
Anthony Manuel, Bradley	5-11	1989	4	108	855	7.92
Chico Fletcher, Arkansas St.	5-6	2000	4	114	893	7.83
Gary Payton, Oregon St.	6-2	1990	4	120	938	7.82
Orlando Smart, San Francisco	6-0	1994	4	116	902	7.78
Tony Miller, Marquette	6-0	1995	4	123	956	7.77
Keith Jennings, East Tenn. St.	5-7	1991	4	127	983	7.74
Bobby Hurley, Duke	6-0	1993	4	140	1,076	7.69
Doub Gottlieb, Notre Dame & Oklahoma St.	6-1	2000	4	124	947	7.63
Chuck Evans, Old Dominion & Mississippi St.	5-11	1993	3	85	648	7.62
Jim Les, Bradley	5-11	1986	4	118	884	7.49
Ed Cota, North Carolina	6-2	2000	4	138	1,030	7.46
Curtis McCants, George Mason	6-0	1998	3	81	598	7.38
Frank Smith, Old Dominion	6-0	1988	4	120	883	7.36
Doug Wojcik, Navy	6-1	1987	3	99	714	7.21
Mark Woods, Wright St.	6-1	1993	4	113	811	7.18
Nelson Haggerty, Baylor	6-0	1995	4	98	699	7.13
Grayson Marshall, Clemson	6-2	1988	4	122	857	7.02
Drafton Davis, Marist	6-0	1988	4	115	804	6.99
Andre LaFleur, Northeastern	6-3	1987	4	128	894	6.98

BLOCKED SHOTS

Player, Team	Ht.	Last Season	Yrs.	G	Blk.
Wojciech Mydra, La.-Monroe	7-2	2002	4	115	535
Adonal Foyle, Colgate	6-10	1997	3	87	492
Tim Duncan, Wake Forest	6-11	1997	4	128	481
Alonzo Mourning, Georgetown	6-10	1992	4	120	453
Tarvis Williams, Hampton	6-9	2001	4	114	452
Ken Johnson, Ohio St.	6-11	2001	4	127	444
Lorenzo Coleman, Tennessee Tech	7-1	1997	4	113	437
Calvin Booth, Penn St.	6-11	1999	4	114	428
Theo Ratliff, Wyoming	6-10	1995	4	111	425
Troy Murphy, Notre Dame	6-9	2001	3	94	425
Etan Thomas, Syracuse	6-9	2000	4	122	424
Rodney Blake, St. Joseph's	6-8	1988	4	116	419
Shaquille O'Neal, LSU	7-1	1992	3	90	412
Kevin Roberson, Vermont	6-7	1992	4	112	409
Jim McIlvaine, Marquette	7-1	1994	4	118	399
Tim Perry, Temple	6-9	1988	4	130	392
Jason Lawson, Villanova	6-11	1997	4	131	375
Pervis Ellison, Louisville	6-9	1989	4	136	374
Peter Aluma, Liberty	6-10	1997	4	119	366
Acie Earl, Iowa	6-10	1993	4	116	365
Jerome James, Florida A&M	7-1	1998	3	81	363
Melvin Ely, Fresno St.	6-10	2002	4	124	361
Dikembe Mutombo, Georgetown	7-2	1991	3	96	354
David Robinson, Navy	6-11	1987	2	67	351
Charles Smith, Pittsburgh	6-10	1988	4	122	346
Brian Skinner, Baylor	6-10	1998	4	103	346

BLOCKED-SHOT AVERAGE
(Minimum 225 blocked shots)

Player, Team	Ht.	Last Season	Yrs.	G	Blk.	Avg.
Keith Closs, Central Conn. St.	7-2	1996	2	54	317	5.87
Adonal Foyle, Colgate	6-10	1997	3	87	492	5.66
David Robinson, Navy	6-11	1987	2	67	351	5.24
Wojciech Mydra, La.-Monroe	7-2	2002	4	115	535	4.65
Shaquille O'Neal, LSU	7-1	1992	3	90	412	4.58
Troy Murphy, Notre Dame	6-9	2001	3	94	425	4.52
Jerome James, Florida A&M	7-1	1998	3	81	363	4.48
Tarvis Williams, Hampton	6-9	2001	4	114	452	3.96
Lorenzo Coleman, Tennessee Tech	7-1	1997	4	113	437	3.87
Theo Ratliff, Wyoming	6-10	1995	4	111	425	3.83
Alonzo Mourning, Georgetown	6-10	1992	4	120	453	3.78
Tim Duncan, Wake Forest	6-11	1997	4	128	481	3.76
Calvin Booth, Penn St.	6-11	1999	4	114	428	3.75
Lorenzo Williams, Stetson	6-9	1991	2	63	234	3.71
Dikembe Mutombo, Georgetown	7-2	1991	3	96	354	3.69

John Linehan of Providence broke the record for career steals last season. Former Friars guard Eric Murdock set the previous mark in 1991.

Player, Team	Ht.	Last Season	Yrs.	G	Blk.	Avg.
Marcus Camby, Massachusetts	6-11	1996	3	92	336	3.65
Kevin Roberson, Vermont	6-7	1992	4	112	409	3.65
Rodney Blake, St. Joseph's	6-8	1988	4	116	419	3.61
Ken Johnson, Ohio St.	6-11	2001	4	127	444	3.50
Etan Thomas, Syracuse	6-9	2000	4	122	424	3.48
Kelvin Cato, South Ala. & Iowa St.	6-11	1997	3	79	274	3.47
Jim McIlvaine, Marquette	7-1	1994	4	118	399	3.38
Brian Skinner, Baylor	6-10	1998	4	103	346	3.36
Rik Smits, Marist	7-4	1988	4	107	345	3.22
Acie Earl, Iowa	6-10	1993	4	116	365	3.15

STEALS

Player, Team	Ht.	Last Season	Yrs.	G	Stl.
John Linehan, Providence	5-9	2002	5	122	385
Eric Murdock, Providence	6-2	1991	4	117	376
Pepe Sanchez, Temple	6-0	2000	4	116	365
Cookie Belcher, Nebraska	6-4	2001	5	131	353
Kevin Braswell, Georgetown	6-2	2002	4	128	349
Bonzi Wells, Ball St.	6-5	1998	4	116	347
Gerald Walker, San Francisco	6-1	1996	4	111	344
Johnny Rhodes, Maryland	6-6	1996	4	122	344
Michael Anderson, Drexel	5-11	1988	4	115	341
Kenny Robertson, Cleveland St.	6-0	1990	4	119	341
Keith Jennings, East Tenn. St.	5-7	1991	4	127	334
Juan Dixon, Maryland	6-3	2002	4	141	333
Desmond Cambridge, Alabama A&M	6-1	2002	3	84	330
Greg Anthony, Portland & UNLV	6-1	1991	4	138	329
Jason Hart, Syracuse	6-3	2000	4	132	329
Chris Corchiani, North Carolina St.	6-1	1991	4	124	328
Gary Payton, Oregon St.	6-2	1990	4	120	321
Chris Garner, Memphis	5-10	1997	4	123	321
Tim Winn, St. Bonaventure	5-10	2000	4	108	319
Mark Woods, Wright St.	6-1	1993	4	113	314
Pointer Williams, Tulane & McNeese St.	6-0	1996	4	115	314
Scott Burrell, Connecticut	6-7	1993	4	119	310
Clarence Ceasar, LSU	6-7	1995	4	112	310
Shawnta Rogers, George Washington	5-4	1999	4	114	310
Elliot Perry, Memphis	6-0	1991	4	126	304

STEAL AVERAGE
(Minimum 225 steals)

Player, Team	Ht.	Last Season	Yrs.	G	Stl.	Avg.
Desmond Cambridge, Alabama A&M	6-1	2002	3	84	330	3.93
Mookie Blaylock, Oklahoma	6-0	1989	2	74	281	3.80
Ronn McMahon, Eastern Wash.	5-9	1990	3	64	225	3.52
Eric Murdock, Providence	6-2	1991	4	117	376	3.21
Van Usher, Tennessee Tech	6-0	1992	3	85	270	3.18
John Linehan, Providence	5-9	2002	5	122	385	3.16
Pepe Sanchez, Temple	6-0	2000	4	116	365	3.15
Gerald Walker, San Francisco	6-1	1996	4	111	344	3.10
Bonzi Wells, Ball St.	6-5	1998	4	116	347	2.99
Michael Anderson, Drexel	5-11	1988	4	115	341	2.97
Tim Winn, St. Bonaventure	5-10	2000	4	108	319	2.95
Haywoode Workman, Oral Roberts	6-3	1989	3	85	250	2.94
Shawn Griggs, LSU & La.-Lafayette	6-6	1994	3	89	260	2.92
Morris Scott, Florida A&M	6-0	2001	4	87	252	2.90
Kenny Robertson, Cleveland St.	6-0	1990	4	119	341	2.87
Jason Rowe, Loyola (Md)	5-10	2000	4	95	272	2.86
Darnell Mee, Western Ky.	6-3	1993	3	91	259	2.85
Pat Baldwin, Northwestern	6-1	1994	4	96	272	2.83
Johnny Rhodes, Maryland	6-6	1996	4	122	344	2.82
Mark Woods, Wright St.	6-1	1993	4	113	314	2.78
Clarence Ceasar, LSU	6-7	1995	4	112	310	2.74
Aldwin Ware, Florida A&M	6-2	1988	4	110	301	2.74
Jarion Childs, American	6-0	2000	4	108	295	2.73
Pointer Williams, Tulane & McNeese St.	6-0	1996	4	115	314	2.73
Kevin Braswell, Georgetown	6-2	2002	4	128	349	2.73

GAMES PLAYED

Player, Team	Last Season	Yrs.	G
Wayne Turner, Kentucky	1999	4	151
Christian Laettner, Duke	1992	4	148
Danny Manning, Kansas	1988	4	147
Shane Battier, Duke	2001	4	146
Stacey Augmon, UNLV	1991	4	145
Jamaal Magloire, Kentucky	2000	4	145
Patrick Ewing, Georgetown	1985	4	143
Danny Ferry, Duke	1989	4	143
Derrick Coleman, Syracuse	1990	4	143
Jared Prickett, Kentucky	1997	4	143
Ryan Robertson, Kansas	1999	4	142
Brian Davis, Duke	1992	4	141

Player, Team	Last Season	Yrs.	G
Anthony Epps, Kentucky	1997	4	141
Brendan Haywood, North Carolina	2001	4	141
Juan Dixon, Maryland	2002	4	141
Kevin Freeman, Connecticut	2000	4	140
Charlie Bell, Michigan St.	2001	4	140
Ralph Beard, Kentucky	1949	4	139
Lee Mayberry, Arkansas	1992	4	139
Kevin Pritchard, Kansas	1990	4	139
Ademola Okulaja, North Carolina	1999	4	139
Eric Chenowith, Kansas	2001	4	139
Reggie Williams, Georgetown	1987	4	138
Sherman Douglas, Syracuse	1989	4	138
Doug West, Villanova	1989	4	138
Greg Anthony, Portland & UNLV	1991	4	138
Steve Woodberry, Kansas	1994	4	138
Ed Cota, North Carolina	2000	4	138
Jake Voskuhl, Connecticut	2000	4	138
Andre Huston, Michigan St.	2001	4	138
Lonny Baxter, Maryland	2002	4	138

2,000 POINTS & 1,000 REBOUNDS

Player, Team	Ht.	Last Season	Yrs.	G	Pts.	Reb.
Lionel Simmons, La Salle	6-7	1990	4	131	3,217	1,429
Harry Kelly, Texas Southern	6-7	1983	4	110	3,066	1,085
Oscar Robertson, Cincinnati	6-5	1960	3	88	2,973	1,338
Danny Manning, Kansas	6-10	1988	4	147	2,951	1,187
Elvin Hayes, Houston	6-8	1968	3	93	2,884	1,602
Larry Bird, Indiana St.	6-9	1979	3	94	2,850	1,247
Hank Gathers, Southern California & Loyola Marymount	6-7	1990	4	117	2,723	1,128
Daren Queenan, Lehigh	6-5	1988	4	118	2,703	1,013
David Robinson, Navy	7-1	1987	4	127	2,669	1,314
Wayman Tisdale, Oklahoma	6-9	1985	3	104	2,661	1,048
Michael Brooks, La Salle	6-7	1980	4	114	2,628	1,372
Dickie Hemric, Wake Forest	6-6	1955	4	104	2,587	1,802
Calvin Natt, Northeast La.	6-5	1979	4	108	2,581	1,285
Keith Van Horn, Utah	6-9	1997	4	122	2,542	1,074
Willie Jackson, Centenary (La.)	6-6	1984	4	114	2,535	1,013
Bill Bradley, Princeton	6-5	1965	3	83	2,503	1,008
Elgin Baylor, Albertson & Seattle	6-6	1958	3	80	2,500	1,559
Tom Gola, La Salle	6-6	1955	4	118	2,462	2,201
Christian Laettner, Duke	6-11	1992	4	148	2,460	1,149
Keith Lee, Memphis	6-11	1985	4	128	2,408	1,336
Phil Sellers, Rutgers	6-5	1976	4	114	2,399	1,115
Byron Houston, Oklahoma St.	6-7	1992	4	127	2,379	1,190
Ron Harper, Miami (Ohio)	6-6	1986	4	120	2,377	1,119
Bryant Reeves, Oklahoma St.	7-0	1995	4	136	2,367	1,152
Lew Alcindor, UCLA	7-2	1969	3	88	2,325	1,367
Mike Gminski, Duke	6-11	1980	4	122	2,323	1,242
Billy McGill, Utah	6-9	1962	3	86	2,321	1,106
Adam Keefe, Stanford	6-9	1992	4	125	2,319	1,119
Jerry West, West Virginia	6-3	1960	3	93	2,309	1,240
Tunji Awojobi, Boston U.	6-5	1997	4	114	2,308	1,237
Jonathan Moore, Furman	6-8	1980	4	117	2,299	1,242
Rick Barry, Miami (Fla.)	6-7	1965	3	77	2,298	1,274
Gary Winton, Army	6-6	1978	4	105	2,296	1,168
Kenneth Lyons, North Texas	6-7	1983	4	111	2,291	1,020
Tom Davis, Delaware St.	6-6	1991	4	95	2,274	1,013
Nick Werkman, Seton Hall	6-3	1964	3	71	2,273	1,036
Jim McDaniels, Western Ky.	7-0	1971	3	81	2,238	1,118
Joe Holup, George Washington	6-6	1956	4	104	2,226	2,030
Ralph Sampson, Virginia	7-4	1983	4	132	2,225	1,511
Doug Smith, Missouri	6-10	1991	4	128	2,184	1,054
Kenny Sanders, George Mason	6-5	1989	4	107	2,177	1,026
Joe Barry Carroll, Purdue	7-1	1980	4	123	2,175	1,148
Reggie King, Alabama	6-6	1979	4	118	2,168	1,279
Len Chappell, Wake Forest	6-8	1962	3	87	2,165	1,213
Danny Ferry, Duke	6-10	1989	4	143	2,155	1,003
Xavier McDaniel, Wichita St.	6-7	1985	4	117	2,152	1,359
Derrick Coleman, Syracuse	6-9	1990	4	143	2,143	1,537
Joe Binion, N.C. A&T	6-8	1984	4	116	2,143	1,194
Pervis Ellison, Louisville	6-9	1989	4	136	2,143	1,149
Dan Issel, Kentucky	6-9	1970	3	83	2,138	1,078
Jesse Arnelle, Penn St.	6-5	1955	4	102	2,138	1,238
Sam Perkins, North Carolina	6-10	1984	4	135	2,133	1,167
Bob Elliott, Arizona	6-10	1977	4	114	2,131	1,083
Clarence Weatherspoon, Southern Miss.	6-7	1992	4	117	2,130	1,320
Reggie Jackson, Nicholls St.	6-6	1995	4	110	2,124	1,270
Greg Grant, Utah St.	6-7	1986	4	115	2,124	1,003
John Wallace, Syracuse	6-8	1996	4	127	2,119	1,065
Tim Duncan, Wake Forest	6-11	1997	4	128	2,117	1,570

DIVISION I

Player, Team	Ht.	Last Season	Yrs.	G	Pts.	Reb.
Odell Hodge, Old Dominion	6-9	1997	5	128	2,117	1,086
Bill Cartwright, San Francisco	6-11	1979	4	111	2,116	1,137
Bob Harstad, Creighton	6-6	1991	4	128	2,110	1,126
Gary Trent, Ohio	6-8	1995	3	93	2,108	1,050
B.B. Davis, Lamar	6-8	1981	4	119	2,084	1,122
Durand Macklin, LSU	6-7	1981	5	123	2,080	1,276
Ralph Crosthwaite, Western Ky.	6-9	1959	4	103	2,076	1,309
Sidney Green, UNLV	6-9	1983	4	119	2,069	1,276
Bob Lanier, St. Bonaventure	6-11	1970	3	75	2,067	1,180
Raef LaFrentz, Kansas	6-11	1998	4	131	2,066	1,186
Fred West, Texas Southern	6-9	1990	4	118	2,066	1,136
Sidney Moncrief, Arkansas	6-4	1979	4	122	2,066	1,015
Popeye Jones, Murray St.	6-8	1992	4	123	2,057	1,374

Player, Team	Ht.	Last Season	Yrs.	G	Pts.	Reb.
Danya Abrams, Boston College	6-7	1997	4	122	2,053	1,029
Mark Acres, Oral Roberts	6-11	1985	4	110	2,038	1,051
Fred Hetzel, Davidson	6-8	1965	3	79	2,032	1,094
Bailey Howell, Mississippi St.	6-7	1959	3	75	2,030	1,277
Malik Rose, Drexel	6-7	1996	4	120	2,024	1,514
Larry Krystkowiak, Montana	6-9	1986	4	120	2,017	1,105
Greg Kelser, Michigan St.	6-7	1979	4	115	2,014	1,092
Herb Williams, Ohio St.	6-10	1981	4	114	2,011	1,111
Stacey Augmon, UNLV	6-8	1991	4	145	2,011	1,005
Jeff Cohen, William & Mary	6-7	1961	4	103	2,003	1,679
Tyrone Hill, Xavier	6-9	1990	4	126	2,003	1,380
Alonzo Mourning, Georgetown	6-10	1992	4	120	2,001	1,032
Josh Grant, Utah	6-9	1993	5	131	2,000	1,066

Annual Individual Champions

Scoring Average

Season	Player, Team	Ht.	Cl.	G	FG	FT	Pts.	Avg.
1948	Murray Wier, Iowa	5-9	Sr.	19	152	95	399	21.0
1949	Tony Lavelli, Yale	6-3	Sr.	30	228	215	671	22.4
1950	Paul Arizin, Villanova	6-3	Sr.	29	260	215	735	25.3
1951	Bill Mlkvy, Temple	6-4	Sr.	25	303	125	731	29.2
1952	Clyde Lovellette, Kansas	6-9	Sr.	28	315	165	795	28.4
1953	Frank Selvy, Furman	6-3	Jr.	25	272	194	738	29.5
1954	Frank Selvy, Furman	6-3	Sr.	29	427	*355	1,209	41.7
1955	Darrell Floyd, Furman	6-1	Jr.	25	344	209	897	35.9
1956	Darrell Floyd, Furman	6-1	Sr.	28	339	268	946	33.8
1957	Grady Wallace, South Carolina	6-4	Sr.	29	336	234	906	31.2
1958	Oscar Robertson, Cincinnati	6-5	So.	28	352	280	984	35.1
1959	Oscar Robertson, Cincinnati	6-5	Jr.	30	331	316	978	32.6
1960	Oscar Robertson, Cincinnati	6-5	Sr.	30	369	273	1,011	33.7
1961	Frank Burgess, Gonzaga	6-1	Sr.	26	304	234	842	32.4
1962	Billy McGill, Utah	6-9	Sr.	26	394	221	1,009	38.8
1963	Nick Werkman, Seton Hall	6-3	Jr.	22	221	208	650	29.5
1964	Howard Komives, Bowling Green	6-1	Sr.	23	292	260	844	36.7
1965	Rick Barry, Miami (Fla.)	6-7	Sr.	26	340	293	973	37.4
1966	Dave Schellhase, Purdue	6-4	Sr.	24	284	213	781	32.5
1967	Jim Walker, Providence	6-3	Sr.	28	323	205	851	30.4
1968	Pete Maravich, LSU	6-5	So.	26	432	274	1,138	43.8
1969	Pete Maravich, LSU	6-5	Jr.	26	433	282	1,148	44.2
1970	Pete Maravich, LSU	6-5	Sr.	31	*522	337	*1,381	*44.5
1971	Johnny Neumann, Mississippi	6-6	So.	23	366	191	923	40.1
1972	Dwight Lamar, La.-Lafayette	6-1	Jr.	29	429	196	1,054	36.3
1973	William Averitt, Pepperdine	6-1	Sr.	25	352	144	848	33.9
1974	Larry Fogle, Canisius	6-5	So.	25	326	183	835	33.4
1975	Bob McCurdy, Richmond	6-7	Sr.	26	321	213	855	32.9
1976	Marshall Rodgers, Tex.-Pan American	6-2	Sr.	25	361	197	919	36.8
1977	Freeman Williams, Portland St.	6-4	Jr.	26	417	176	1,010	38.8
1978	Freeman Williams, Portland St.	6-4	Sr.	27	410	149	969	35.9
1979	Lawrence Butler, Idaho St.	6-3	Sr.	27	310	192	812	30.1
1980	Tony Murphy, Southern U.	6-3	Sr.	29	377	178	932	32.1
1981	Zam Fredrick, South Carolina	6-2	Sr.	27	300	181	781	28.9
1982	Harry Kelly, Texas Southern	6-7	Jr.	29	336	190	862	29.7
1983	Harry Kelly, Texas Southern	6-7	Sr.	29	333	169	835	28.8
1984	Joe Jakubick, Akron	6-5	Sr.	27	304	206	814	30.1
1985	Xavier McDaniel, Wichita St.	6-8	Sr.	31	351	142	844	27.2
1986	Terrance Bailey, Wagner	6-2	Jr.	29	321	212	854	29.4

Season	Player, Team	Ht.	Cl.	G	FG	3FG	FT	Pts.	Avg.
1987	Kevin Houston, Army	5-11	Sr.	29	311	63	268	953	32.9
1988	Hersey Hawkins, Bradley	6-3	Sr.	31	377	87	284	1,125	36.3
1989	Hank Gathers, Loyola Marymount	6-7	Jr.	31	419	0	177	1,015	32.7
1990	Bo Kimble, Loyola Marymount	6-5	Sr.	32	404	92	231	1,131	35.3
1991	Kevin Bradshaw, U.S. Int'l	6-6	Sr.	28	358	60	278	1,054	37.6
1992	Brett Roberts, Morehead St.	6-8	Sr.	29	278	66	193	815	28.1
1993	Greg Guy, Tex.-Pan American	6-1	Jr.	19	189	67	111	556	29.3
1994	Glenn Robinson, Purdue	6-8	Jr.	34	368	79	215	1,030	30.3
1995	Kurt Thomas, TCU	6-9	Sr.	27	288	3	202	781	28.9
1996	Kevin Granger, Texas Southern	6-3	Sr.	24	194	30	230	648	27.0
1997	Charles Jones, Long Island	6-3	Jr.	30	338	109	118	903	30.1
1998	Charles Jones, Long Island	6-3	Sr.	30	326	116	101	869	29.0
1999	Alvin Young, Niagara	6-3	Sr.	29	253	65	157	728	25.1
2000	Courtney Alexander, Fresno St.	6-6	Sr.	27	252	58	107	669	24.8
2001	Ronnie McCollum, Centenary (La.)	6-4	Sr.	27	244	85	214	787	29.1
2002	Jason Conley, VMI	6-5	Fr.	28	285	79	171	820	29.3

*record

Field-Goal Percentage

Season	Player, Team	Cl.	G	FG	FGA	Pct.
1948	Alex Peterson, Oregon St.	Jr.	27	89	187	47.6
1949	Ed Macauley, St. Louis	Sr.	26	144	275	52.4
1950	Jim Moran, Niagara	Jr.	27	98	185	53.0
1951	Don Meineke, Dayton	Jr.	32	240	469	51.2
1952	Art Spoelstra, Western Ky.	So.	31	178	345	51.6
1953	Vernon Stokes, St. Francis (N.Y)	Sr.	24	147	247	59.5
1954	Joe Holup, George Washington	So.	26	179	313	57.2
1955	Ed O'Connor, Manhattan	Sr.	23	147	243	60.5
1956	Joe Holup, George Washington	Sr.	26	200	309	64.7
1957	Bailey Howell, Mississippi St.	So.	25	217	382	56.8
1958	Ralph Crosthwaite, Western Ky.	Jr.	25	202	331	61.0
1959	Ralph Crosthwaite, Western Ky.	Sr.	26	191	296	64.5
1960	Jerry Lucas, Ohio St.	So.	27	283	444	63.7
1961	Jerry Lucas, Ohio St.	Jr.	27	256	411	62.3
1962	Jerry Lucas, Ohio St.	Sr.	28	237	388	61.1
1963	Lyle Harger, Houston	Sr.	26	193	294	65.6
1964	Terry Holland, Davidson	Sr.	26	135	214	63.1
1965	Tim Kehoe, St. Peter's	Sr.	19	138	209	66.0
1966	Julian Hammond, Tulsa	Sr.	29	172	261	65.9
1967	Lew Alcindor, UCLA	So.	30	346	519	66.7
1968	Joe Allen, Bradley	Sr.	28	258	394	65.5
1969	Lew Alcindor, UCLA	Sr.	30	303	477	63.5
1970	Willie Williams, Florida St.	Sr.	26	185	291	63.6
1971	John Belcher, Arkansas St.	Jr.	24	174	275	63.3
1972	Kent Martens, Abilene Christian	Sr.	21	136	204	66.7
1973	Elton Hayes, Lamar	Sr.	24	146	222	65.8
1974	Al Fleming, Arizona	So.	26	136	204	66.7
1975	Bernard King, Tennessee	Fr.	25	273	439	62.2
1976	Sidney Moncrief, Arkansas	Fr.	28	149	224	66.5
1977	Joe Senser, West Chester	So.	25	130	186	69.9
1978	Joe Senser, West Chester	Jr.	25	135	197	68.5
1979	Murray Brown, Florida St.	Jr.	29	237	343	69.1
1980	Steve Johnson, Oregon St.	Jr.	30	211	297	*71.0
1981	Steve Johnson, Oregon St.	Sr.	28	235	315	*74.6
1982	Mark McNamara, California	Sr.	27	231	329	70.2
1983	Troy Lee Mikel, East Tenn. St.	Sr.	29	197	292	67.5
1984	Akeem Olajuwon, Houston	Jr.	37	249	369	67.5
1985	Keith Walker, Utica	Sr.	27	154	216	71.3
1986	Brad Daugherty, North Carolina	Sr.	34	284	438	64.8
1987	Alan Williams, Princeton	Sr.	25	163	232	70.3
1988	Arnell Jones, Boise St.	Sr.	30	187	283	66.1
1989	Dwayne Davis, Florida	So.	33	179	248	72.2
1990	Lee Campbell, Southwest Mo. St.	Sr.	29	192	275	69.8
1991	Oliver Miller, Arkansas	Jr.	38	254	361	70.4
1992	Charles Outlaw, Houston	Jr.	31	156	228	68.4
1993	Charles Outlaw, Houston	Sr.	30	196	298	65.8
1994	Mike Atkinson, Long Beach St.	Jr.	26	141	203	69.5
1995	Shane Kline-Ruminski, Bowling Green	Sr.	26	181	265	68.3
1996	Quadre Lollis, Montana St.	Sr.	30	212	314	67.5
1997	Todd MacCulloch, Washington	So.	28	163	241	67.6

Season	Player, Team	Cl.	G	FG	FGA	Pct.
1998	Todd MacCulloch, Washington	Jr.	30	225	346	65.0
1999	Todd MacCulloch, Washington	Sr.	29	210	317	66.2
2000	Brendan Haywood, North Carolina	Jr.	36	191	274	69.7
2001	Michael Bradley, Villanova	Jr.	31	254	367	69.2
2002	Adam Mark, Belmont	So.	26	150	212	70.8

*record

Three-Point Field Goals Made Per Game

Season	Player, Team	Cl.	G	3FG	Avg.
1987	Darrin Fitzgerald, Butler	Sr.	28	158	*5.64
1988	Timothy Pollard, Mississippi Val.	Jr.	28	132	4.71
1989	Timothy Pollard, Mississippi Val.	Sr.	28	124	4.43
1990	Dave Jamerson, Ohio	Sr.	28	131	4.68
1991	Bobby Phills, Southern U.	Sr.	28	123	4.39
1992	Doug Day, Radford	Jr.	29	117	4.03
1993	Bernard Haslett, Southern Miss.	Jr.	26	109	4.19
1994	Chris Brown, UC Irvine	Jr.	26	122	4.69
1995	Mitch Taylor, Southern U.	Jr.	25	109	4.36
1996	Dominick Young, Fresno St.	Jr.	29	120	4.14
1997	William Fourche, Southern U.	Sr.	27	122	4.52
1998	Curtis Staples, Virginia	Sr.	30	130	4.33
1999	Brian Merriweather, Tex.-Pan American	So.	27	110	4.07
2000	Brian Merriweather, Tex.-Pan American	Jr.	28	114	4.07
2001	DeWayne Jefferson, Mississippi Val.	Sr.	27	107	3.96
2002	Cain Doliboa, Wright St.	Sr.	28	104	3.71

*record

Three-Point Field-Goal Percentage

Season	Player, Team	Cl.	G	3FG	3FGA	Pct.
1987	Reginald Jones, Prairie View	Jr.	28	64	112	57.1
1988	Glenn Tropf, Holy Cross	Jr.	29	52	82	*63.4
1989	Dave Calloway, Monmouth	So.	28	48	82	58.5
1990	Matt Lapin, Princeton	Sr.	27	71	133	53.4
1991	Keith Jennings, East Tenn. St.	Sr.	33	84	142	59.2
1992	Sean Wightman, Western Mich.	Jr.	30	48	76	63.2
1993	Jeff Anderson, Kent St.	Jr.	26	44	82	53.7
1994	Brent Kell, Evansville	So.	29	62	123	50.4
1995	Brian Jackson, Evansville	Jr.	27	53	95	55.8
1996	Joe Stafford, Western Caro.	Jr.	30	58	110	52.7
1997	Kent McCausland, Iowa	So.	29	70	134	52.2
1998	Jim Cantamessa, Siena	So.	29	66	117	56.4
1999	Rodney Thomas, IUPUI	Jr.	26	59	113	52.2
2000	Jonathan Whitworth, Middle Tenn.	Jr.	28	50	99	50.5
2001	Amory Sanders, Southeast Mo. St.	Sr.	24	53	95	55.8
2002	Dante Swanson, Tulsa	Jr.	33	73	149	49.0

*record

Free-Throw Percentage

Season	Player, Team	Cl.	G	FT	FTA	Pct.
1948	Sam Urzetta, St. Bonaventure	So.	22	59	64	92.2
1949	Bill Schroer, Valparaiso	So.	24	59	68	86.8
1950	Sam Urzetta, St. Bonaventure	Sr.	22	54	61	88.5
1951	Jay Handlan, Wash. & Lee	Jr.	22	148	172	86.0
1952	Sy Chadroff, Miami (Fla.)	Sr.	22	99	123	80.5
1953	John Weber, Yale	Sr.	24	117	141	83.0
1954	Dick Daugherty, Arizona St.	Sr.	23	75	86	87.2
1955	Jim Scott, West Tex. A&M	Sr.	23	153	171	89.5
1956	Bill Von Weyhe, Rhode Island	Jr.	25	180	208	86.5
1957	Ernie Wiggins, Wake Forest	Sr.	28	93	106	87.7
1958	Semi Mintz, Davidson	Sr.	24	105	119	88.2
1959	Arlen Clark, Oklahoma St.	Sr.	25	201	236	85.2
1960	Jack Waters, Mississippi	Jr.	24	103	118	87.3
1961	Stew Sherard, Army	Jr.	24	135	154	87.7
1962	Tommy Boyer, Arkansas	Jr.	23	125	134	93.3
1963	Tommy Boyer, Arkansas	Sr.	24	147	161	91.3
1964	Rick Park, Tulsa	Jr.	25	121	134	90.3
1965	Bill Bradley, Princeton	Sr.	29	273	308	88.6
1966	Bill Blair, Providence	Sr.	27	101	112	90.2
1967	Bob Lloyd, Rutgers	Sr.	29	255	277	92.1
1968	Joe Heiser, Princeton	Sr.	26	117	130	90.0
1969	Bill Justus, Tennessee	Sr.	28	133	147	90.5
1970	Steve Kaplan, Rutgers	So.	23	102	110	92.7
1971	Greg Starrick, Southern Ill.	Jr.	23	119	132	90.2
1972	Greg Starrick, Southern Ill.	Sr.	26	148	160	92.5
1973	Don Smith, Dayton	Jr.	26	111	122	91.0
1974	Rickey Medlock, Arkansas	Jr.	26	87	95	91.6

Season	Player, Team	Cl.	G	FT	FTA	Pct.
1975	Frank Oleynick, Seattle	Sr.	26	135	152	88.8
1976	Tad Dufelmeier, Loyola (Ill.)	Jr.	25	71	80	88.8
1977	Robert Smith, UNLV	Sr.	32	98	106	92.5
1978	Carlos Gibson, Marshall	Jr.	28	84	89	94.4
1979	Darrell Mauldin, Campbell	Jr.	26	70	76	92.1
1980	Brian Magid, George Washington	Sr.	26	79	85	92.9
1981	Dave Hildahl, Portland St.	Sr.	21	76	82	92.7
1982	Rod Foster, UCLA	Jr.	27	95	100	95.0
1983	Rob Gonzalez, Colorado	Sr.	28	75	82	91.5
1984	Steve Alford, Indiana	Fr.	31	137	150	91.3
1985	Craig Collins, Penn St.	Sr.	27	94	98	*95.9
1986	Jim Barton, Dartmouth	Fr.	26	65	69	94.2
1987	Kevin Houston, Army	Sr.	29	268	294	91.2
1988	Steve Henson, Kansas St.	So.	34	111	120	92.5
1989	Michael Smith, Brigham Young	Sr.	29	160	173	92.5
1990	Rob Robbins, New Mexico	Jr.	34	101	108	93.5
1991	Darin Archbold, Butler	Jr.	29	187	205	91.2
1992	Don MacLean, UCLA	Sr.	32	197	214	92.1
1993	Josh Grant, Utah	Sr.	31	104	113	92.0
1994	Danny Basile, Marist	So.	27	84	89	94.4
1995	Greg Bibb, Tennessee Tech	Jr.	27	106	117	90.6
1996	Mike Dillard, Sam Houston St.	Jr.	25	63	68	92.6
1997	Aaron Zobrist, Bradley	Sr.	30	77	85	90.6
1998	Matt Sundblad, Lamar	Jr.	27	96	104	92.3
1999	Lonnie Cooper, Louisiana Tech	Sr.	25	70	76	92.1
2000	Clay McKnight, Pacific (Cal.)	Sr.	24	74	78	94.9
2001	Gary Buchanan, Villanova	So.	31	97	103	94.2
2002	Cary Cochran, Nebraska	Sr.	28	71	77	92.2

*record

Rebound Average

Season	Player, Team	Ht.	Cl.	G	Reb.	Avg.
1951	Ernie Beck, Pennsylvania	6-4	So.	27	556	20.6
1952	Bill Hannon, Army	6-3	So.	17	355	20.9
1953	Ed Conlin, Fordham	6-5	So.	26	612	23.5
1954	Art Quimby, Connecticut	6-5	Jr.	26	588	22.6
1955	Charlie Slack, Marshall	6-5	Jr.	21	538	*25.6
1956	Joe Holup, George Washington	6-6	Sr.	26	604	†.256
1957	Elgin Baylor, Seattle	6-6	Jr.	25	508	†.235
1958	Alex Ellis, Niagara	6-5	Sr.	25	536	†.262
1959	Leroy Wright, Pacific (Cal.)	6-8	Jr.	26	652	†.238
1960	Leroy Wright, Pacific (Cal.)	6-8	Sr.	17	380	†.234
1961	Jerry Lucas, Ohio St.	6-8	Jr.	27	470	†.198
1962	Jerry Lucas, Ohio St.	6-8	Sr.	28	499	†.211
1963	Paul Silas, Creighton	6-7	Sr.	27	557	20.6
1964	Bob Pelkington, Xavier	6-7	Sr.	26	567	21.8
1965	Toby Kimball, Connecticut	6-8	Sr.	23	483	21.0
1966	Jim Ware, Oklahoma City	6-8	Sr.	29	607	20.9
1967	Dick Cunningham, Murray St.	6-10	Jr.	22	479	21.8
1968	Neal Walk, Florida	6-10	Jr.	25	494	19.8
1969	Spencer Haywood, Detroit	6-8	So.	22	472	21.5
1970	Artis Gilmore, Jacksonville	7-2	Jr.	28	621	22.2
1971	Artis Gilmore, Jacksonville	7-2	Sr.	26	603	23.2
1972	Kermit Washington, American	6-8	Jr.	23	455	19.8
1973	Kermit Washington, American	6-8	Sr.	22	439	20.0
1974	Marvin Barnes, Providence	6-9	Sr.	32	597	18.7
1975	John Irving, Hofstra	6-9	So.	21	323	15.4
1976	Sam Pellom, Buffalo	6-8	So.	26	420	16.2
1977	Glenn Mosley, Seton Hall	6-8	Sr.	29	473	16.3
1978	Ken Williams, North Texas	6-7	Sr.	28	411	14.7
1979	Monti Davis, Tennessee St.	6-7	Jr.	26	421	16.2
1980	Larry Smith, Alcorn St.	6-8	Sr.	26	392	15.1
1981	Darryl Watson, Mississippi Val.	6-7	Sr.	27	379	14.0
1982	LaSalle Thompson, Texas	6-10	Jr.	27	365	13.5
1983	Xavier McDaniel, Wichita St.	6-7	So.	28	403	14.4
1984	Akeem Olajuwon, Houston	7-0	Jr.	37	500	13.5
1985	Xavier McDaniel, Wichita St.	6-8	Sr.	31	460	14.8
1986	David Robinson, Navy	6-11	Jr.	35	455	13.0
1987	Jerome Lane, Pittsburgh	6-6	So.	33	444	13.5
1988	Kenny Miller, Loyola (Ill.)	6-9	Fr.	29	395	13.6
1989	Hank Gathers, Loyola Marymount	6-7	Jr.	31	426	13.7
1990	Anthony Bonner, St. Louis	6-8	Sr.	33	456	13.8
1991	Shaquille O'Neal, LSU	7-1	So.	28	411	14.7
1992	Popeye Jones, Murray St.	6-8	Sr.	30	431	14.4
1993	Warren Kidd, Middle Tenn.	6-9	Sr.	26	386	14.8
1994	Jerome Lambert, Baylor	6-8	Jr.	24	355	14.8
1995	Kurt Thomas, TCU	6-9	Sr.	27	393	14.6
1996	Marcus Mann, Mississippi Val.	6-8	Sr.	29	394	13.6
1997	Tim Duncan, Wake Forest	6-11	Sr.	31	457	14.7
1998	Ryan Perryman, Dayton	6-7	Sr.	33	412	12.5
1999	Ian McGinnis, Dartmouth	6-8	So.	26	317	12.2
2000	Darren Phillip, Fairfield	6-7	Sr.	29	405	14.0

DIVISION I

Season	Player, Team	Ht.	Cl.	G	Reb.	Avg.
2001	Chris Marcus, Western Ky.	7-1	Jr.	31	374	12.1
2002	Jeremy Bishop, Quinnipiac	6-6	Jr.	29	347	12.0

*record; †From 1956 through 1962, championship was determined on highest individual recoveries out of total by both teams in all games.

Assist Average

Season	Player, Team	Cl.	G	Ast.	Avg.
1984	Craig Lathen, Ill.-Chicago	Jr.	29	274	9.45
1985	Rob Weingard, Hofstra	Sr.	24	228	9.50
1986	Mark Jackson, St. John's (N.Y.)	Jr.	36	328	9.11
1987	Avery Johnson, Southern U.	Jr.	31	333	10.74
1988	Avery Johnson, Southern U.	Sr.	30	399	*13.30
1989	Glenn Williams, Holy Cross	Sr.	28	278	9.93
1990	Todd Lehmann, Drexel	Sr.	28	260	9.29
1991	Chris Corchiani, North Carolina St.	Sr.	31	299	9.65
1992	Van Usher, Tennessee Tech	Sr.	29	254	8.76
1993	Sam Crawford, New Mexico St.	Sr.	34	310	9.12
1994	Jason Kidd, California	So.	30	272	9.07
1995	Nelson Haggerty, Baylor	Sr.	28	284	10.14
1996	Raimonds Miglinieks, UC Irvine	Sr.	27	230	8.52
1997	Kenny Mitchell, Dartmouth	Sr.	26	203	7.81
1998	Ahlon Lewis, Arizona St.	Sr.	32	294	9.19
1999	Doug Gottlieb, Oklahoma St.	Jr.	34	299	8.79
2000	Mark Dickel, UNLV	Sr.	31	280	9.03
2001	Markus Carr, Cal St. Northridge	Jr.	32	286	8.94
2002	T.J. Ford, Texas	Fr.	33	273	8.27

*record

Blocked-Shot Average

Season	Player, Team	Cl.	G	Blk.	Avg.
1986	David Robinson, Navy	Jr.	35	207	5.91
1987	David Robinson, Navy	Sr.	32	144	4.50
1988	Rodney Blake, St. Joseph's	Sr.	29	116	4.00
1989	Alonzo Mourning, Georgetown	Fr.	34	169	4.97

Season	Player, Team	Cl.	G	Blk.	Avg.
1990	Kenny Green, Rhode Island	Sr.	26	124	4.77
1991	Shawn Bradley, Brigham Young	Fr.	34	177	5.21
1992	Shaquille O'Neal, LSU	Jr.	30	157	5.23
1993	Theo Ratliff, Wyoming	Jr.	28	124	4.43
1994	Grady Livingston, Howard	Jr.	26	115	4.42
1995	Keith Closs, Central Conn. St.	Fr.	26	139	5.35
1996	Keith Closs, Central Conn. St.	So.	28	178	*6.36
1997	Adonal Foyle, Colgate	Jr.	28	180	6.43
1998	Jerome James, Florida A&M	Sr.	27	125	4.63
1999	Tarvis Williams, Hampton	So.	27	135	5.00
2000	Ken Johnson, Ohio St.	Sr.	30	161	5.37
2001	Tarvis Williams, Hampton	Sr.	32	147	4.59
2002	Wojciech Myrda, La.-Monroe	Sr.	32	172	5.38

*record

Steal Average

Season	Player, Team	Cl.	G	Stl.	Avg.
1986	Darron Brittman, Chicago St.	Sr.	28	139	*4.96
1987	Tony Fairley, Charleston So.	Sr.	28	114	4.07
1988	Aldwin Ware, Florida A&M	Sr.	29	142	4.90
1989	Kenny Robertson, Cleveland St.	Jr.	28	111	3.96
1990	Ronn McMahon, Eastern Wash.	Sr.	29	130	4.48
1991	Van Usher, Tennessee Tech	Jr.	28	104	3.71
1992	Victor Snipes, Northeastern Ill.	So.	25	86	3.44
1993	Jason Kidd, California	Fr.	29	110	3.79
1994	Shawn Griggs, La.-Lafayette	Sr.	30	120	4.00
1995	Roderick Anderson, Texas	Sr.	30	101	3.37
1996	Pointer Williams, McNeese St.	Sr.	27	118	4.37
1997	Joel Hoover, Md.-East. Shore	Fr.	28	90	3.21
1998	Bonzi Wells, Ball St.	Sr.	29	103	3.55
1999	Shawnta Rogers, George Washington	Sr.	29	103	3.55
2000	Carl Williams, Liberty	Sr.	28	107	3.82
2001	Greedy Daniels, TCU	Jr.	25	108	4.32
2002	Desmond Cambridge, Alabama A&M	Sr.	29	160	5.52

*record

All-Time Team Leaders

Single-Game Records

SCORING HIGHS

Pts.	Team vs. Opponent (Opp. Pts.)	Date
186	Loyola Marymount vs. U.S. Int'l (140)	Jan. 5, 1991
181	Loyola Marymount vs. U.S. Int'l (150)	Jan. 31, 1989
179	Long Island vs. Medgar Evers (62)	Nov. 26, 1997
173	Oklahoma vs. U.S. Int'l (101)	Nov. 29, 1989
172	Oklahoma vs. Loyola Marymount (112)	Dec. 15, 1990
166	Arkansas vs. U.S. Int'l (101)	Dec. 9, 1989
164	UNLV vs. Hawaii-Hilo (111)	Feb. 19, 1976
164	Loyola Marymount vs. Azusa-Pacific (138)	Nov. 28, 1988
162	Loyola Marymount vs. U.S. Int'l (144)	Jan. 7, 1989
162	Loyola Marymount vs. Chaminade (129)	Nov. 25, 1990
162	Oklahoma vs. Angelo St. (99)	Dec. 1, 1990
159	Southern U. vs. Texas College (65)	Dec. 6, 1990
159	LSU vs. Northern Ariz. (86)	Dec. 28, 1991
157	Loyola Marymount vs. San Francisco (115)	Feb. 5, 1990
156	Southern U. vs. Baptist Christian (91)	Dec. 14, 1992
156	South Ala. vs. Prairie View (114)	Dec. 2, 1994
155	Oral Roberts vs. Union (Tenn.) (113)	Feb. 24, 1972
155	Southern U. vs. Prairie View (91)	Feb. 22, 1993
154	Texas-Arlington vs. Huston-Tillotson (85)	Nov. 29, 1990
154	Southern U. vs. Patten (57)	Nov. 26, 1993
153	TCU vs. Tex.-Pan American (87)	Nov. 29, 1997
152	Jacksonville vs. St. Peter's (106)	Dec. 3, 1970
152	Oklahoma vs. Centenary (La.) (84)	Dec. 12, 1987
152	Oklahoma vs. Oral Roberts (122)	Dec. 10, 1988
152	Loyola Marymount vs. U.S. Int'l (137)	Dec. 7, 1989
152	Northeastern vs. Loyola Marymount (123)	Nov. 24, 1990

SCORING HIGHS BY LOSING TEAM

Pts.	Team vs. Opponent (Opp. Pts.)	Date
150	U.S. Int'l vs. Loyola Marymount (181)	Jan. 31, 1989
144	U.S. Int'l vs. Loyola Marymount (162)	Jan. 7, 1989

Pts.	Team vs. Opponent (Opp. Pts.)	Date
141	Loyola Marymount vs. LSU (148) (ot)	Feb. 3, 1990
140	Utah St. vs. UNLV (142) (3 ot)	Jan. 2, 1985
140	U.S. Int'l vs. Loyola Marymount (186)	Jan. 5, 1991
137	U.S. Int'l vs. Loyola Marymount (152)	Dec. 7, 1989
136	Gonzaga vs. Loyola Marymount (147)	Feb. 18, 1989
132	Troy St. vs. George Mason (148)	Dec. 10, 1994
127	Pepperdine vs. Loyola Marymount (142)	Feb. 20, 1988
127	Troy St. vs. George Mason (142)	Nov. 28, 1995
126	Western Mich. vs. Marshall (127)	Dec. 20, 1999
125	Nevada vs. Loyola Marymount (130)	Dec. 30, 1988
123	San Francisco vs. Loyola Marymount (137)	Feb. 9, 1990
123	Loyola Marymount vs. Pepperdine (148)	Feb. 17, 1990
123	Loyola Marymount vs. Northeastern (152)	Nov. 24, 1990
123	Sam Houston St. vs. Texas-Arlington (125)	Dec. 28, 1998
122	Oral Roberts vs. Oklahoma (152)	Dec. 10, 1988
121	Loyola Marymount vs. LSU (148) (ot)	Feb. 3, 1990
121	Loyola Marymount vs. Oklahoma (136)	Dec. 23, 1989

SCORING HIGHS BOTH TEAMS COMBINED

Pts.	Team (Pts.) vs. Team (Pts.)	Date
331	Loyola Marymount (181) vs. U.S. Int'l (150)	Jan. 31, 1989
326	Loyola Marymount (186) vs. U.S. Int'l (140)	Jan. 5, 1991
306	Loyola Marymount (162) vs. U.S. Int'l (144)	Jan. 7, 1989
289	Loyola Marymount (152) vs. U.S. Int'l (137)	Dec. 7, 1989
289	LSU (148) vs. Loyola Marymount (141) (ot)	Feb. 3, 1990
284	Oklahoma (172) vs. Loyola Marymount (112)	Dec. 15, 1990
283	Loyola Marymount (147) vs. Gonzaga (136)	Feb. 18, 1989
282	UNLV (142) vs. Utah St. (140) (3 ot)	Jan. 2, 1985
280	George Mason (148) vs. Troy St. (132)	Dec. 10, 1994
275	Northeastern (152) vs. Loyola Marymount (123)	Nov. 24, 1990
274	Oklahoma (152) vs. Oral Roberts (122)	Dec. 10, 1988
274	Oklahoma (173) vs. U.S. Int'l (101)	Nov. 29, 1989
272	Loyola Marymount (157) vs. San Francisco (115)	Feb. 4, 1990
269	Loyola Marymount (142) vs. Pepperdine (127)	Feb. 20, 1988
269	Loyola Marymount (150) vs. St. Mary's (Cal.) (119)	Feb. 1, 1990
269	George Mason (142) vs. Troy St. (127)	Nov. 28, 1995

MARGIN OF VICTORY

Pts.	Team (Pts.) vs. Opponent (Opp. Pts.)	Date
117	Long Island (179) vs. Medgar Evers (62)	Nov. 26, 1997
101	Texas (102) vs. San Marcos Baptist (1)	Jan. 10, 1916
97	Southern U. (154) vs. Patten (57)	Nov. 26, 1993
96	Purdue (112) vs. Indiana St. (6)	Jan. 10, 1911
96	Western Ky. (103) vs. Adairville Independents (7)	Jan. 10, 1923
95	Oklahoma (146) vs. Northeastern Ill. (51)	Dec. 2, 1989
94	Southern U. (159) vs. Texas College (65)	Dec. 6, 1990
93	Washington (100) vs. Puget Sound (7)	Jan. 14, 1921
92	Villanova (117) vs. Philadelphia NAMC (25)	Feb. 12, 1949
91	LSU (124) vs. Rhodes (33)	Dec. 8, 1952
91	Tennessee St. (148) vs. Fisk (57)	Dec. 6, 1993
91	Tulsa (141) vs. Prairie View (50)	Dec. 7, 1995
89	Northwestern La. vs. LeTourneau (51)	Jan. 20, 1992
89	Nicholls St. (140) vs. Faith Baptist (51)	Dec. 17, 1994
88	Southern U. (132) vs. Faith Baptist (44)	Dec. 12, 1994
88	Prairie View (129) vs. Oklahoma Baptist (41)	Jan. 21, 1997
87	Canisius (107) vs. St. Ann's (20)	Dec. 8, 1907
86	Ohio St. (88) vs. Ohio (2)	Feb. 6, 1903
84	Rhode Island (118) vs. Fort Varnum (34)	Nov. 20, 1943
83	Texas (89) vs. Southwest Tex. St. (6)	Feb. 11, 1919
82	Navy (126) vs. Western Md. (44)	Dec. 3, 1952
82	Morehead St. (130) vs. Asbury (48)	Nov. 30, 1996
81	Rhode Island (119) vs. Mass. Maritime (38)	1945
81	Oklahoma (146) vs. Florida A&M (65)	Jan. 27, 1993
80	Dayton (80) vs. Cedarville (0)	Jan. 23, 1907
80	Syracuse (106) vs. Oswego St. (26)	1945
80	Rhode Island (124) vs. Quonset Naval (44)	Dec. 12, 1946
80	Minnesota (80) vs. Alabama St. (34)	Dec. 23, 1996

MARGIN OF VICTORY VS. DIVISION I OPPONENT (SINCE 1938)

Pts.	Team (Pts.) vs. Opponent (Opp. Pts.)	Date
91	Tulsa (141) vs. Prairie View (50)	Dec. 7, 1995
81	Oklahoma (146) vs. Florida A&M (65)	Jan. 27, 1993
80	Minnesota (80) vs. Alabama St. (34)	Dec. 23, 1996
77	Kentucky (143) vs. Georgia (66)	Feb. 27, 1956
75	Maryland (132) vs. North Texas (57)	Dec. 23, 1998
74	Kentucky (124) vs. Tenn.-Martin (50)	Nov. 26, 1994
73	LSU (159) vs. Northern Ariz. (86)	Dec. 28, 1991
72	Oklahoma (173) vs. U.S. Int'l (101)	Nov. 29, 1989
72	Ohio St. (116) vs. Chicago St. (44)	Nov. 30, 1991
72	Missouri (117) vs. Chicago St. (45)	Dec. 2, 1995
72	Iowa (103) vs. Chicago (31)	Feb. 5, 1944
71	Ohio St. (109) vs. Delaware (38)	Jan. 11, 1960
71	New Mexico (71) vs. Dartmouth (36)	Dec. 29, 1972
71	Dayton (109) vs. Bowling Green (38)	Dec. 11, 1954
70	Massachusetts (108) vs. Maine (38)	Feb. 23, 1974
70	Kansas (115) vs. Brown (45)	Jan. 3, 1989
70	Connecticut (116) vs. Central Conn. St. (46)	Jan. 23, 1996
69	Kentucky (98) vs. Vanderbilt (29)	Feb. 27, 1947
69	Lamar (126) vs. Sam Houston St. (57)	Dec. 30, 1991
68	Oklahoma (152) vs. Centenary (La.) (84)	Dec. 12, 1987
68	Oklahoma (132) vs. Southern Utah St. (64)	Dec. 20, 1988
68	Connecticut (115) vs. Central Conn. St. (47)	Jan. 10, 1991
68	Kansas (140) vs. Oral Roberts (72)	Jan. 14, 1993
68	Southern Utah (140) vs. South Ala. (72)	Dec. 10, 1994

SCORING HIGHS IN A HALF

Pts.	Team vs. Opponent (Half)	Date
98	Long Island vs. Medgar Evers (2nd)	Nov. 26, 1997
97	Oklahoma vs. U.S. Int'l (1st)	Nov. 29, 1989
96	Southern U. vs. Texas College (2nd)	Dec. 6, 1990
94	Loyola Marymount vs. U.S. Int'l (1st)	Jan. 31, 1989
94	Oklahoma vs. Northeastern Ill. (2nd)	Dec. 2, 1989
94	Loyola Marymount vs. U.S. Int'l (1st)	Jan. 5, 1991
93	Loyola Marymount vs. U.S. Int'l (1st)	Jan. 7, 1989
93	Oklahoma vs. Loyola Marymount (2nd)	Dec. 15, 1990
92	Loyola Marymount vs. U.S. Int'l (2nd)	Jan. 5, 1991
92	Alabama St. vs. Grambling (2nd)	Jan. 21, 1991
91	Oklahoma vs. Angelo St. (2nd)	Dec. 1, 1990
87	Oklahoma vs. Oral Roberts (2nd)	Dec. 10, 1988
87	Loyola Marymount vs. U.S. Int'l (2nd)	Jan. 31, 1989
86	Jacksonville vs. St. Peter's (2nd)	Dec. 3, 1970
86	Lamar vs. Portland St. (2nd)	Jan. 12, 1980
86	Loyola Marymount vs. Gonzaga (2nd)	Feb. 18, 1989
86	Gonzaga vs. Loyola Marymount (2nd)	Feb. 18, 1989
86	Kentucky vs. LSU (1st)	Jan. 16, 1996

SCORING HIGHS IN A HALF BOTH TEAMS COMBINED

Pts.	Team (Pts.) vs. Team (Pts.) (Half)	Date
172	Loyola Marymount (86) vs. Gonzaga (86) (2nd)	Feb. 18, 1989
170	Loyola Marymount (94) vs. U.S. Int'l (76) (1st)	Jan. 31, 1989
164	Loyola Marymount (94) vs. U.S. Int'l (70) (1st)	Jan. 5, 1991
162	Loyola Marymount (92) vs. U.S. Int'l (70) (2nd)	Jan. 5, 1991
161	Loyola Marymount (93) vs. U.S. Int'l (68) (1st)	Jan. 7, 1989
161	Loyola Marymount (87) vs. U.S. Int'l (74) (2nd)	Jan. 31, 1989
160	Oklahoma (87) vs. Oral Roberts (73) (2nd)	Dec. 10, 1988

FEWEST POINTS SCORED IN A GAME SINCE 1938

Pts.	Team vs. Opponent (Opp. Pts.)	Date
6	Temple vs. Tennessee (11)	Dec. 15, 1974
9	Pittsburgh vs. Penn St. (24)	Mar. 1, 1952
10	Duke vs. North Carolina (12)	Mar. 8, 1968
11	Oklahoma vs. Oklahoma St. (14)	Feb. 19, 1944
11	Tennessee vs. Temple (6)	Dec. 15, 1974
11	Cincinnati vs. Kentucky (24)	Dec. 20, 1983
12	Marquette vs. Creighton (57)	Dec. 16, 1940
12	Pittsburgh vs. Penn St. (15)	Jan. 15, 1944
12	North Carolina St. vs. Duke (10)	Mar. 8, 1968
13	Pittsburgh vs. Penn St. (32)	Feb. 20, 1943
13	Illinois vs. Purdue (23)	Feb. 7, 1938
13	Virginia vs. Navy (36)	Jan. 12, 1938
14	Michigan St. vs. Michigan (42)	Dec. 7, 1940
14	Kansas St. vs. Missouri (38)	Mar. 4, 1944
14	Oklahoma St. vs. Oklahoma (11)	Feb. 19, 1944
14	Alabama vs. Tennessee (23)	1945
15	Alabama vs. Tennessee (37)	1942
15	Arkansas vs. Oklahoma St. (17)	Jan. 28, 1944
15	Penn St. vs. Pittsburgh (12)	Jan. 15, 1944
15	Creighton vs. Oklahoma St. (35)	Feb. 9, 1948
15	Charleston So. vs. Col. of Charleston (18)	Feb. 6, 1980
16	Vanderbilt vs. Tennessee Tech (21)	1938
16	Miami (Ohio) vs. Marshall (22)	Feb. 19, 1938
16	South Carolina vs. Clemson (38)	Feb. 10, 1939
16	South Carolina vs. Clemson (43)	Feb. 18, 1939
16	Stanford vs. Oregon St. (18)	Jan. 28, 1980

FEWEST POINTS SCORED IN A GAME SINCE 1986

Pts.	Team vs. Opponent (Opp. Pts.)	Date
21	Ga. Southern vs. Coastal Caro. (61)	Jan. 2, 1997
25	Texas-Pan American vs. North Carolina St. (75)	Jan. 7, 1997
25	Valparaiso vs. Wis.-Green Bay (69)	Mar. 2, 1992
26	UC Santa Barb. vs. Fresno St. (46)	Feb. 26, 1986
26	Northwestern vs. Evansville (48)	Nov. 26, 1999
27	New Hampshire vs. Providence (56)	Dec. 5, 1992
27	Yale vs. Princeton (55)	Jan. 11, 1991
27	Bucknell vs. Princeton (68)	Dec. 9, 1998
28	Dartmouth vs. Princeton (66)	Feb. 10, 1990
28	Wofford vs. North Carolina St. (57)	Dec. 3, 1996
28	Winthrop vs. North Carolina St. (57)	Dec. 3, 1996
29	Long Beach St. vs. UNLV (49)	Mar. 9, 1991
29	Texas-Pan American vs. Iowa (85)	Dec. 4, 1992
29	Loyola (Ill.) vs. Wisconsin (66)	Nov. 14, 1998
30	Columbia vs. Dartmouth (54)	Jan. 14, 1989
30	Akron vs. Northern Ill. (48)	Jan. 26, 1991
31	Tex.-Arlington vs. Southern Methodist (36)	Dec. 16, 1989
31	Cornell vs. Princeton (48)	Feb. 8, 1992
31	UMBC vs. Maryland (67)	Dec. 4, 1996
31	Jacksonville vs. South Ala. (52)	Jan. 29, 1998
32	Charleston So. vs. Alabama (63)	Dec. 18, 1989
32	New Hampshire vs. Connecticut (85)	Dec. 12, 1990
32	Appalachian St. vs. St. Bonaventure (76)	Jan. 7, 1995
32	Morehead St. vs. Kentucky (96)	Dec. 16, 1995
32	Lehigh vs. Miami (Fla.) (68)	Dec. 30, 1996
32	Brigham Young vs. New Mexico (74)	Feb. 3, 1997
32	Fordham vs. Virginia Tech (50)	Feb. 8, 1997
32	New Orleans vs. South Ala. (54)	Jan. 18, 1999

FIELD-GOAL PERCENTAGE

Pct.	Team (FG-FGA) vs. Opponent	Date
83.3	Maryland (15-18) vs. South Carolina	Jan. 9, 1971
81.4	New Mexico (35-43) vs. Oregon St.	Nov. 30, 1985
81.0	Fresno St. (34-42) vs. Portland St.	Dec. 3, 1977
81.0	St. Peter's (34-42) vs. Utica	Dec. 4, 1984
80.5	Fordham (33-41) vs. Fairfield	Feb. 27, 1984
80.0	Holy Cross (32-40) vs. Vermont	Nov. 30, 1981
80.0	Oklahoma St. (28-35) vs. Tulane	Mar. 22, 1992
80.0	Long Beach St. (56-70) vs. Cal St. Monterey	Dec. 22, 1999
79.4	Arkansas (27-34) vs. Texas Tech	Feb. 20, 1979
79.4	Columbia (27-34) vs. Dartmouth	Mar. 2, 1984
79.0	North Carolina (49-62) vs. Loyola Marymount	Mar. 19, 1988
78.6	Villanova (22-28) vs. Georgetown	Apr. 1, 1985
78.6	St. Peter's (22-28) vs. Army	Jan. 9, 1982
78.4	Western Ky. (29-37) vs. Dayton	Jan. 24, 1979
78.1	Army (25-32) vs. Manhattan	Jan. 20, 1979

Pct.	Team (FG-FGA) vs. Opponent	Date
77.8	Samford (35-45) vs. Loyola (La.)	Dec. 12, 1992
77.5	Nicholls St. (31-40) vs. Samford	Dec. 30, 1983
77.4	Richmond (24-31) vs. Citadel	Feb. 8, 1976
77.0	Purdue (47-61) vs. Long Island	Nov. 14, 1997

THREE-POINT FIELD GOALS

3FG	Team vs. Opponent	Date
28	Troy St. vs. George Mason	Dec. 10, 1994
24	Cincinnati vs. Oakland	Dec. 5, 1998
23	Lamar vs. Louisiana Tech	Feb. 28, 1993
23	Kansas St. vs. Fresno St.	Mar. 24, 1994
23	Troy St. vs. George Mason	Nov. 28, 1995
23	Sanford vs. Troy St.	Jan. 13, 2001
22	Gonzaga vs. San Francisco	Feb. 23, 1995
21	Kentucky vs. North Carolina	Dec. 27, 1989
21	Loyola Marymount vs. Michigan	Mar. 18, 1990
21	UNLV vs. Nevada	Dec. 8, 1990
21	Troy St. vs. Loyola (La.)	Dec. 22, 1993
21	Cal Poly vs. Cal Baptist	Dec. 3, 1996
21	Mississippi Val. vs. Troy St.	Dec. 6, 1996
21	Arkansas vs. Troy St.	Dec. 10, 1996
21	Long Island vs. Robert Morris	Feb. 3, 1997
20	Navy vs. Mt. St. Mary's	Nov. 26, 1990
20	Lamar vs. Prairie View	Feb. 3, 1993
20	Arkansas vs. Texas Southern	Dec. 29, 1993
20	Baylor vs. TCU	Feb. 14, 1995
20	Southern California vs. Oregon St.	Jan. 29, 2000
20	Northern Ariz. vs. Cal Poly	Dec. 2, 2000
20	Nicholls St. vs. Troy St.	Dec. 17, 2001
20	Missouri vs. Colorado	Feb. 23, 2002
19	17 tied	

THREE-POINT FIELD GOALS ATTEMPTED

3FGA	Team vs. Opponent	Date
74	Troy St. vs. George Mason	Dec 10, 1994
67	Mississippi Val. vs. Troy St.	Dec. 6, 1996
58	Cal Poly vs. Cal Baptist	Dec. 3, 1996
53	Kentucky vs. La.-Lafayette	Dec. 23, 1989
51	Texas-Arlington vs. New Mexico	Nov. 23, 1990
51	Arizona St. vs. Brigham Young	Dec. 1, 1992
50	Morehead St. vs. George Mason	Dec. 3, 1995
50	Cal Poly vs. Air Force	Dec. 5, 1997
48	Kentucky vs. North Carolina	Dec. 27, 1989
48	Cincinnati vs. Oakland	Dec. 5, 1998
47	Kentucky vs. Furman	Dec. 19, 1989
47	Charleston So. vs. Clemson	Dec. 1, 1993
47	Centenary (La.) vs. UCF	Jan. 11, 1993
46	UNLV vs. Nevada	Dec. 8, 1990
46	Georgetown vs. Boston College	Feb. 26, 1994
45	Loyola Marymount vs. LSU	Feb. 3, 1990
45	Houston vs. St. Louis	Dec. 15, 1990
45	Drake vs. Iowa	Nov. 29, 1994
45	Mississippi Valley vs. Loyola Marymount	Nov. 14, 2001
44	Cal St. Northridge vs. Colorado	Nov. 23, 1990
44	Central Conn. St. vs. Colorado	Dec. 8, 1990
44	Kentucky vs. LSU	Feb. 2, 1992
44	North Texas vs. Texas-Arlington	Jan. 9, 1993
44	Kentucky vs. LSU	Mar. 14, 1993
44	Samford vs. Mercer	Feb. 18, 1995
44	Fresno St. vs. Cal St. Northridge	Nov. 30, 1999
44	St. Bonaventure vs. Richmond	Mar. 7, 2002

THREE-POINT FIELD-GOAL PERCENTAGE
(Minimum 10-three point field goals made)

Pct.	Team (3FG-3FGA) vs. Opponent	Date
91.7	Drexel (11-12) vs. Delaware	Dec. 3, 2000
90.9	Duke (10-11) vs. Clemson	Feb. 1, 1988
90.9	Hofstra (10-11) vs. Rhode Island	Jan. 16, 1993
87.5	Stetson (14-16) vs. Centenary (La.)	Jan. 13, 1996
85.7	Western Ill. (12-14) vs. Valparaiso	Jan. 13, 1992
84.6	Murray St. (11-13) vs. Southeast Mo. St.	Jan. 16, 1993
83.3	Eastern Ky. (15-18) vs. UNC Asheville	Jan. 14, 1987
83.3	Princeton (10-12) vs. Pennsylvania	Jan. 6, 1990
83.3	Evansville (10-12) vs. Butler	Feb. 9, 1991
83.3	Southern Utah (10-12) vs. Cal St. Northridge	Mar. 1, 1991
83.3	Wis.-Milwaukee (10-12) vs. Eastern Mich.	Feb. 19, 1992
83.3	Purdue (10-12) vs. Michigan	Feb. 7, 1993
83.3	UNLV (10-12) vs. William & Mary	Feb. 11, 1995
83.3	Evansville (10-12) vs. Southern Ill.	Feb. 24, 1996
83.3	Wis.-Green Bay (10-12) vs. Miami (Ohio)	Dec. 5, 1998
81.3	Niagara (13-16) vs. Siena	Jan. 7, 1987
80.0	Marshall (12-15) vs. Wyoming	Dec. 7, 1991
80.0	Washington St. (12-15) vs. Princeton	Dec. 29, 1992

Pct.	Team (3FG-3FGA) vs. Opponent	Date
80.0	Princeton (12-15) vs. Columbia	Feb. 13, 1993
80.0	Niagara (12-15) vs. Iona	Feb. 17, 1995
80.0	Marquette (12-15) vs. Tulane	Jan. 27, 2001
78.9	Ohio (15-19) vs. Col. of Charleston	Dec. 21, 1989
78.9	San Francisco (15-19) vs. Gonzaga	Feb. 9, 2001
78.6	Toledo (11-14) vs. Akron	Jan. 20, 1993
78.6	UMBC (11-14) vs. Charleston So.	Jan. 23, 1993
78.6	Ohio (11-14) vs. Youngstown St.	Dec. 20, 1993
78.6	Ga. Southern (11-14) vs. Appalachian St.	Jan. 18, 1997
78.6	UCF (11-14) vs. South Carolina St.	Nov. 28, 1999

FREE-THROW PERCENTAGE
(Minimum 30 free throws made)

Pct.	Team (FT-FTA) vs. Opponent	Date
100	UC Irvine (34-34) vs. Pacific (Cal.)	Feb. 21, 1981
100	Samford (34-34) vs. UCF	Dec. 20, 1990
100	Marshall (31-31) vs. Davidson	Dec. 17, 1979
100	Indiana St. (31-31) vs. Wichita St.	Feb. 18, 1991
97.2	Vanderbilt (35-36) vs. Mississippi St.	Feb. 26, 1986
97.2	Butler (35-36) vs. Dayton	Feb. 21, 1991
97.2	Marquette (35-36) vs. Memphis	Jan. 23, 1993
97.0	Miami (Fla.) (32-33) vs. Creighton	Feb. 10, 1964
97.0	Toledo (32-33) vs. Old Dominion	Dec. 9, 1995
97.0	Hawaii (32-33) vs. New Mexico	Feb. 24, 1996
96.8	Oregon St. (30-31) vs. Memphis	Dec. 19, 1990
96.8	Niagara (30-31) vs. Fairfield	Jan. 31, 1998
95.5	UNLV (42-44) vs. San Diego St.	Dec. 11, 1976
94.7	Southwest Mo. St. (36-38) vs. Evansville	Dec. 30, 2001
94.6	TCU (35-37) vs. Tex.-Arlington	Dec. 23, 1996
94.4	Eastern Mich. (34-36) vs. Jackson St.	Dec. 20, 1994
93.8	North Carolina St. (30-32) vs. North Carolina	Feb. 21, 1998
93.8	Brigham Young (30-32) vs. Weber St.	Dec. 28, 2000
93.7	Mt. St. Mary's (30-32) vs. Robert Morris	Feb. 6, 1990

REBOUNDS

Reb.	Team vs. Opponent	Date
108	Kentucky vs. Mississippi	Feb. 8, 1964
103	Holy Cross vs. Boston College	Mar. 1, 1956
102	Arizona vs. Northern Ariz.	Jan. 6, 1951
101	Weber St. vs. Idaho St.	Jan. 22, 1966
100	William & Mary vs. Virginia	Feb. 14, 1954
95	Indiana vs. Michigan	Mar. 11, 1961
95	Murray St. vs. MacMurray	Jan. 2, 1967
92	Santa Clara vs. St. Mary's (Cal.)	Feb. 15, 1971
92	Oral Roberts vs. Brandeis	Jan. 8, 1973
91	Notre Dame vs. St. Norbert	Dec. 7, 1965
91	Southern Miss. vs. Tex.-Pan American	Feb. 9, 1970
91	Houston vs. Rice	Mar. 7, 1974
90	Vanderbilt vs. Sewanee	Dec. 4, 1954

ASSISTS

Ast.	Team vs. Opponent	Date
44	Colorado vs. George Mason (ot)	Dec. 2, 1995
43	TCU vs. Central Okla.	Dec. 12, 1998
41	North Carolina vs. Manhattan	Dec. 27, 1985
41	Weber St. vs. Northern Ariz.	Mar. 2, 1991
40	New Mexico vs. Texas-Arlington	Nov. 23, 1990
40	Loyola Marymount vs. U.S. Int'l	Jan. 5, 1991
40	Southern Utah vs. Texas Wesleyan	Jan. 25, 1992
40	Lamar vs. Prairie View	Feb. 2, 1993
40	TCU vs. North Texas	Dec. 1, 1998
39	Southern Miss. vs. Virginia Tech	Jan. 16, 1988
39	UNLV vs. Pacific (Cal.)	Feb. 8, 1990
39	UNLV vs. Rutgers	Feb. 3, 1991
39	Davidson vs. Warren Wilson	Dec. 9, 1991
39	TCU vs. Midwestern St.	Nov. 30, 1994
39	Arizona St. vs. Delaware St.	Dec. 1, 1997
39	TCU vs. Central Okla.	Dec. 9, 2000
38	New Mexico vs. U.S. Int'l	Dec. 3, 1985
38	Pepperdine vs. U.S. Int'l	Jan. 7, 1986
38	UCLA vs. Loyola Marymount	Dec. 2, 1990
38	Arizona vs. Northern Ariz.	Dec. 18, 1991
38	Tex.-Pan American vs. Concordia Lutheran	Dec. 4, 1993
38	LSU vs. George Mason	Dec. 3, 1994
38	Arizona vs. Morgan St.	Nov. 20, 1997
38	TCU vs. Ark.-Pine Bluff	Dec. 30, 2000
37	15 tied	

BLOCKED SHOTS

Blk.	Team vs. Opponent	Date
21	Georgetown vs. Southern (N.O.)	Dec. 1, 1993
20	Iona vs. Northern Ill.	Jan. 7, 1989
20	Georgia vs. Bethune-Cookman	Dec. 7, 1993

Blk.	Team vs. Opponent	Date
20	Massachusetts vs. West Virginia	Jan. 3, 1995
19	Seton Hall vs. Norfolk St.	Dec. 4, 2000
18	North Carolina vs. Stanford	Dec. 20, 1985
17	Maryland vs. Md.-East. Shore	Feb. 27, 1987
17	Rider vs. Fairleigh Dickinson	Jan. 9, 1989
17	Georgetown vs. Providence	Feb. 22, 1989
17	Georgetown vs. Hawaii-Loa	Nov. 23, 1990
17	Brigham Young vs. Eastern Ky.	Dec. 7, 1990
17	Northwestern St. vs. Oauchita Baptist	Nov. 30, 1991
17	New Orleans vs. Texas A&M	Dec. 29, 1992
17	Massachusetts vs. Hartford	Dec. 28, 1993
17	Louisville vs. Kentucky	Jan. 1, 1995
17	William & Mary vs. George Mason	Feb. 26, 1996
17	Miami (Fla.) vs. Hartford	Dec. 13, 1996
17	Fairleigh Dickinson vs. Hartford	Nov. 11, 1997
17	Kentucky vs. Morehead St.	Nov. 20, 1997
17	Duke vs. Virginia	Jan. 10, 1999
17	La.-Monroe vs. Lamar	Feb. 3, 2000
17	Georgetown vs. Southern-N.O.	Feb. 10, 2000
16	UTEP vs. Fort Lewis	Nov. 26, 1988
16	Maryland vs. Md.-East. Shore	Dec. 1, 1988
16	Oklahoma St. vs. Oklahoma	Feb. 14, 1989
16	Clemson vs. Radford	Dec. 9, 1989
16	Villanova vs. Drexel	Dec. 16, 1989
16	LSU vs. Texas	Jan. 2, 1990
16	UCLA vs. UC Irvine	Nov. 23, 1990
16	Kentucky vs. Georgia	Feb. 3, 1991
16	Rutgers vs. St. Bonaventure	Jan. 16, 1992
16	William & Mary vs. Marymount (Va.)	Nov. 29, 1995
16	Kentucky vs. Morehead St.	Dec. 16, 1995
16	Old Dominion vs. American	Jan 16, 1999
16	La.-Monroe vs. Ark.-Monticello	Dec. 4, 1999
16	TCU vs. Rice	Mar. 3, 2000
16	Seton Hall vs. St. Peter's	Nov. 27, 2000

STEALS

Stl.	Team vs. Opponent	Date
39	Long Island vs. Medgar Evers	Nov. 26, 1997
34	Oklahoma vs. Centenary (La.)	Dec. 12, 1987
34	Northwestern St. vs. LeTourneau	Jan. 20, 1992
33	Connecticut vs. Pittsburgh	Jan. 6, 1990
32	Manhattan vs. Lehman	Dec. 14, 1987
32	Oklahoma vs. Angelo St.	Dec. 1, 1990
32	Long Island vs. Medgar Evers	Nov. 29, 1994
32	La.-Lafayette vs. Baptist Christian	Nov. 25, 1995
30	Southern U. vs. Baptist Christian	Dec. 14, 1992
30	Cal Poly vs. Notre Dame (Cal.)	Nov. 25, 1995
30	TCU vs. Ark.-Pine Bluff	Dec. 30, 2000
29	Cleveland St. vs. Canisius	Dec. 28, 1986
29	Oklahoma vs. U.S. Int'l	Nov. 19, 1989
29	Centenary (La.) vs. East Texas Baptist	Dec. 12, 1992
29	TCU vs. Delaware St.	Dec. 3, 1997
28	Oklahoma vs. Morgan St.	Dec. 21, 1991
28	Memphis vs. Southeastern La.	Jan. 11, 1993
28	Oklahoma vs. Florida A&M	Jan. 27, 1993
27	Oregon St. vs. Hawaii-Loa	Dec. 22, 1985
27	Cal St. Fullerton vs. Lamar	Nov. 24, 1989
27	Texas-San Antonio vs. Samford	Jan. 19, 1991
27	Iowa St. vs. Bethune-Cookman	Dec. 31, 1992
27	San Francisco vs. Delaware St.	Nov. 27, 1993
27	Charleston So. vs. Warner Southern	Dec. 11, 1993
27	Georgetown vs. Southern (N.O.)	Feb. 13, 1999
27	TCU vs. Alabama St.	Nov. 20, 2000

Season Records

VICTORIES

Team	Season	Won	Lost	Pct.
UNLV	†1987	37	2	.949
Duke	†1999	37	2	.949
Duke	†1986	37	3	.925
Kentucky	†1948	36	3	.923
Massachusetts	†1996	35	2	.946
Georgetown	†1985	35	3	.921
Arizona	†1988	35	3	.921
Kansas	1986	35	4	.897
Oklahoma	†1988	35	4	.897
Kansas	†1998	35	4	.897
Kentucky	†1998	35	4	.897
Duke	†2001	35	4	.897

Team	Season	Won	Lost	Pct.
UNLV	†1990	35	5	.875
Kentucky	†1997	35	5	.875
UNLV	†1991	34	1	.971
Duke	†1992	34	2	.944
Kentucky	1996	34	2	.944
Kansas	1997	34	2	.944
Connecticut	1999	34	2	.944
Kentucky	†1947	34	3	.919
Georgetown	†1984	34	3	.919
Arkansas	†1991	34	4	.895
North Carolina	†1993	34	4	.895
North Carolina	1998	34	4	.895
Indiana St.	†1979	33	1	.971
Louisville	†1980	33	3	.917
Kansas	†2002	33	4	.892
UNLV	1986	33	5	.868
Michigan St.	1999	33	5	.868

VICTORIES IN FIRST SEASON IN DIVISION I

Team	Season	Won	Lost	Pct.
Seattle	1953	29	4	.879
Md.-East. Shore	1974	27	2	.931
Oral Roberts	1972	26	2	.929
Old Dominion	1977	25	4	.862
Long Beach St.	1970	24	5	.828
La.-Lafayette	1972	23	3	.885
Southern U.	1978	23	5	.821
Hawaii	1971	23	5	.821
Alabama St.	1983	22	6	.786
Alcorn St.	1978	22	7	.759
Stephen F. Austin	1987	22	8	.733
Idaho St.	1959	21	7	.750
McNeese St.	1974	20	5	.800
Memphis	1956	20	7	.741
Loyola (La.)	1952	20	14	.588
Jackson St.	1978	19	5	.792
Northeastern	1973	19	7	.731
Ga. Southern	1974	19	7	.731
Miami (Fla.)	1949	19	8	.704
Col. of Charleston	1992	19	8	.704
Morehead St.	1956	19	10	.655
New Mexico St.	1951	19	14	.576
New Orleans	1976	18	8	.692
Florida A&M	1979	18	9	.667
Alabama A&M	2000	18	10	.643

†national leader

WON-LOST PERCENTAGE

Team	Season	Won	Lost	Pct.
North Carolina	†1957	32	0	1.000
Indiana	†1976	32	0	1.000
UCLA	†1964	30	0	1.000
UCLA	†1967	30	0	1.000
UCLA	†1972	30	0	1.000
UCLA	†1973	30	0	1.000
San Francisco	†1956	29	0	1.000
North Carolina St.	1973	27	0	1.000
Kentucky	†1954	25	0	1.000
Long Island	†1939	24	0	1.000
Seton Hall	†1940	19	0	1.000
Army	†1944	15	0	1.000
UNLV	†1991	34	1	.971
Indiana St.	†1979	33	1	.971
Indiana	†1975	31	1	.969
North Carolina St.	†1974	30	1	.968
UCLA	†1968	29	1	.967
UCLA	†1969	29	1	.967
UCLA	†1971	29	1	.967
San Francisco	†1955	28	1	.966
UTEP	†1966	28	1	.966
Marquette	1971	28	1	.966
Pennsylvania	1971	28	1	.966
Alcorn St.	1979	28	1	.966
Ohio St.	†1961	27	1	.964

†national leader

WON-LOST PERCENTAGE IN FIRST SEASON IN DIVISION I

Team	Season	Won	Lost	Pct.
Md.-East. Shore	1974	27	2	.931
Oral Roberts	1972	26	2	.929
La.-Lafayette	1972	23	3	.885
Seattle	1953	29	4	.879
Old Dominion	1977	25	4	.862

Team	Season	Won	Lost	Pct.
Long Beach St.	1970	24	5	.828
Southern U.	1978	23	5	.821
Hawaii	1971	23	5	.821
McNeese St.	1974	20	5	.800
Jackson St.	1978	19	5	.792
Alabama St.	1983	22	6	.786
Alcorn St.	1978	22	7	.759
Idaho St.	1959	21	7	.750
Memphis	1956	20	7	.741
Air Force	1958	17	6	.739
Stephen F. Austin	1987	22	8	.733
Northeastern	1973	19	7	.731
Ga. Southern	1974	19	7	.731
Va. Commonwealth	1974	17	7	.708
Miami (Fla.)	1949	19	8	.704
Col. of Charleston	1992	19	8	.704
New Orleans	1976	18	8	.692
Weber St.	1964	17	8	.680
George Mason	1979	17	8	.680
Florida A&M	1979	18	9	.667
Mercer	1974	16	8	.667
Tennessee Tech	1956	14	7	.667
American	1967	16	8	.667
Fairfield	1965	14	7	.667

MOST-IMPROVED TEAMS

(Since 1974)

Team	Season	W-L Record	Previous Yr. W-L	Games Up
N.C. A&T	†1978	20-8	3-24	16½
Murray St.	†1980	23-8	4-22	16½
Liberty	†1992	22-7	5-23	16½
North Texas	†1976	22-4	6-20	16
Ohio State	†1999	27-9	8-22	16
Tulsa	†1981	26-7	8-19	15
Utah St.	†1983	20-9	4-23	15
Radford	†1991	22-7	7-22	15
Boston College	†2001	27-5	11-19	15
Western Mich.	1992	21-9	5-22	14½
Tennessee St.	†1993	19-10	4-24	14½
Central Mich.	2001	20-8	6-23	14½
Fresno St.	1978	21-6	7-20	14
James Madison	†1987	20-10	5-23	14
Loyola Marymount	†1988	28-4	12-16	14
Cal Poly	†1996	16-13	1-26	14
Northern Ariz.	†1997	21-7	6-20	14
McNeese St.	2001	22-9	6-21	14
Michigan St.	1978	25-5	10-17	13½
Loyola (Md.)	†1994	17-13	2-25	13½
Texas-San Antonio	†1998	16-11	3-25	13½
Iowa St.	†2000	32-5	15-15	13½
Ark.-Little Rock	2001	18-11	4-24	13½
Kansas	†1974	23-7	8-18	13
Wagner	†1979	21-7	7-19	13
Arizona	1988	35-3	18-12	13
Ball St.	†1989	29-3	14-14	13
Nebraska	1991	26-8	10-18	13
Wagner	1992	16-12	4-26	13
Winthrop	†1999	21-8	7-20	13

†national leader

POINTS

Team	Season	G	Pts.
Oklahoma	†1988	39	4,012
Loyola Marymount	†1990	32	3,918
Arkansas	1991	38	3,783
UNLV	1990	40	3,739
Oklahoma	†1989	36	3,680
UNLV	†1987	39	3,612
Duke	†1999	39	3,581
Duke	†2001	39	3,538
Loyola Marymount	1988	32	3,528
Loyola Marymount	1989	31	3,486
Houston	†1977	37	3,482
UNLV	†1976	31	3,426
UNLV	1977	32	3,426
Duke	1991	39	3,421
UNLV	1991	35	3,420
Arkansas	†1995	39	3,416
Syracuse	1989	38	3,410
Michigan	1989	37	3,393
Duke	1990	38	3,386
Kansas	†2002	37	3,365
Oklahoma	1991	35	3,363

Team	Season	G	Pts.
Arkansas	1990	35	3,345
North Carolina	1989	37	3,331
Oklahoma	†1985	37	3,328
Kentucky	†1997	40	3,325

†national leader

SCORING OFFENSE

Team	Season	G	Pts.	Avg.
Loyola Marymount	†1990	32	3,918	122.4
Loyola Marymount	†1989	31	3,486	112.5
UNLV	†1976	31	3,426	110.5
Loyola Marymount	†1988	32	3,528	110.3
UNLV	†1977	32	3,426	107.1
Oral Roberts	†1972	28	2,943	105.1
Southern U.	1991	28	2,924	104.4
Loyola Marymount	1991	31	3,211	103.6
Oklahoma	1988	39	4,012	102.9
Oklahoma	1989	36	3,680	102.2
Oklahoma	1990	32	3,243	101.3
Southern U.	†1994	27	2,727	101.0
Jacksonville	†1970	28	2,809	100.3
Jacksonville	†1971	26	2,598	99.9
Arkansas	1991	38	3,783	99.6
Southern U.	1990	31	3,078	99.3
Syracuse	†1966	28	2,773	99.0
Iowa	1970	25	2,467	98.7
Miami (Fla.)	†1965	26	2,558	98.4
Houston	1966	29	2,845	98.1
La.-Lafayette	1972	29	2,840	97.9
U.S. Int'l	1990	28	2,738	97.8
Houston	†1968	33	3,226	97.8
UNLV	1991	35	3,420	97.7
Md.-East. Shore	†1974	29	2,831	97.6
Troy St.	1994	27	2,634	97.6
Oklahoma City	1966	29	2,829	97.6

†national leader

SCORING DEFENSE

Team	Season	G	Pts.	Avg.
Oklahoma St.	†1948	31	1,006	32.5
Oklahoma St.	†1949	28	985	35.2
Oklahoma St.	†1950	27	1,059	39.2
Alabama	1948	27	1,070	39.6
Creighton	1948	23	925	40.2
Wyoming	1948	27	1,101	40.8
Wyoming	1950	36	1,491	41.4
Siena	1948	28	1,161	41.5
St. Bonaventure	1948	22	921	41.9
Siena	1949	29	1,215	41.9
Tulane	1948	26	1,102	42.4
Wyoming	1949	35	1,509	43.1
Texas	1948	25	1,079	43.2
Utah	1948	20	868	43.4
Minnesota	1949	21	912	43.4
Washington (Mo.)	1948	21	915	43.6
St. Bonaventure	1949	26	1,137	43.7
St. Louis	1948	27	1,183	43.8
Kentucky	1949	34	1,492	43.9
Washington St.	1949	30	1,317	43.9
Texas A&M	†1951	29	1,275	44.0
Kentucky	1948	39	1,730	44.4
Baylor	1949	24	1,068	44.5
Tulsa	1950	23	1,027	44.7
Hamline	1948	31	1,389	44.8

†national leader

(Since 1965)

Team	Season	G	Pts.	Avg.
Fresno St.	†1982	30	1,412	47.1
Princeton	†1999	30	1,581	52.7
Princeton	†1992	28	1,349	48.2
Princeton	†1991	27	1,320	48.9
North Carolina St.	1982	32	1,570	49.1
Princeton	1982	26	1,277	49.1
Princeton	†1984	28	1,403	50.1
St. Peter's	1980	31	1,563	50.4
Fresno St.	†1981	29	1,470	50.7
Princeton	†1990	27	1,378	51.0
Princeton	1981	28	1,438	51.4
Princeton	1998	29	1,491	51.4
St. Peter's	1981	26	1,338	51.5
Wyoming	1982	30	1,545	51.5
Princeton	†1977	26	1,343	51.7
Princeton	†1996	29	1,498	51.7
Princeton	†1983	29	1,507	52.0

Team	Season	G	Pts.	Avg.
James Madison	1982	30	1,559	52.0
Fresno St.	†1978	27	1,417	52.5
Princeton	†1999	30	1,581	52.7
Princeton	†1976	27	1,427	52.9
Columbia	1982	26	1,375	52.9
Princeton	†1989	27	1,430	53.0
Fresno St.	†1985	32	1,696	53.0
Princeton	†1997	28	1,496	53.4
UTEP	1982	28	1,497	53.5
Georgetown	1982	37	1,979	53.5
Army	†1969	28	1,498	53.5

†national leader

SCORING MARGIN

Team	Season	Off.	Def.	Mar.
UCLA	†1972	94.6	64.3	30.3
North Carolina St.	†1948	75.3	47.2	28.1
Kentucky	†1954	87.5	60.3	27.2
Kentucky	†1952	82.3	55.4	26.9
UNLV	†1991	97.7	71.0	26.7
UCLA	†1968	93.4	67.2	26.2
UCLA	†1967	89.6	63.7	25.9
Houston	1968	97.8	72.5	25.3
Duke	†1999	91.8	67.2	24.7
Kentucky	1948	69.0	44.4	24.6
Kentucky	†1949	68.2	43.9	24.3
Bowling Green	1948	70.5	46.7	23.8
Loyola (Ill.)	†1963	91.8	68.1	23.7
Charlotte	†1975	88.9	65.2	23.7
Arizona St.	†1962	90.1	67.6	22.5
St. Bonaventure	†1970	88.4	65.9	22.5
Kentucky	†1951	74.7	52.5	22.2
Indiana	1975	88.0	65.9	22.1
Kentucky	†1996	91.4	69.4	22.1
Cincinnati	†1960	86.7	64.7	22.0
Oklahoma	†1988	102.9	81.0	21.9
North Carolina St.	†1973	92.9	71.1	21.8
Jacksonville	1970	100.3	78.5	21.8
UNLV	†1976	110.5	89.0	21.5
Duke	†1998	85.6	64.1	21.5

†national leader

FIELD-GOAL PERCENTAGE

Team	Season	FG	FGA	Pct.
Missouri	†1980	936	1,635	57.2
Michigan	†1989	1,325	2,341	56.6
Oregon St.	†1981	862	1,528	56.4
UC Irvine	†1982	920	1,639	56.1
Michigan St.	†1986	1,043	1,860	56.1
North Carolina	1986	1,197	2,140	55.9
Kansas	1986	1,260	2,266	55.6
Kentucky	†1983	869	1,564	55.6
Notre Dame	1981	824	1,492	55.2
Houston Baptist	†1984	797	1,445	55.2
Maryland	1980	985	1,789	55.1
Idaho	1981	816	1,484	55.0
UC Irvine	1981	934	1,703	54.8
Navy	†1985	946	1,726	54.8
Stanford	1983	752	1,373	54.8
Maryland	†1975	1,049	1,918	54.7
New Orleans	1983	937	1,714	54.7
Georgia Tech	1986	1,008	1,846	54.6
Arkansas	†1978	1,060	1,943	54.6
Michigan	†1988	1,198	2,196	54.6
New Mexico	1989	992	1,819	54.5
Southern U.	1978	1,107	2,031	54.5
Arkansas	†1977	849	1,558	54.5
Arizona	1988	1,147	2,106	54.5
Pepperdine	1983	900	1,653	54.4
Oregon St.	1980	943	1,732	54.4
Ohio St.	†1970	831	1,527	54.4
UNC Wilmington	1977	816	1,500	54.4
Davidson	†1964	894	1,644	54.4

†national leader

FIELD-GOAL PERCENTAGE DEFENSE
(Since 1978)

Team	Season	FG	FGA	Pct.
Stanford	†2000	667	1,893	35.2
Marquette	†1994	750	2,097	35.8
Marquette	†1997	628	1,735	36.2
Temple	2000	633	1,747	36.2
Wake Forest	1997	667	1,832	36.4

Team	Season	FG	FGA	Pct.
UNLV	†1992	628	1,723	36.5
Wis.-Green Bay	1997	499	1,368	36.5
Georgetown	†1991	680	1,847	36.8
Temple	†1994	621	1,686	36.8
Princeton	2000	577	1,558	37.0
Kansas St.	†1999	729	1,963	37.1
Detroit	1999	590	1,583	37.3
Northwestern	1999	577	1,548	37.3
Southwest Tex. St.	1999	597	1,601	37.3
Wis.-Green Bay	1994	664	1,777	37.4
Va. Commonwealth	†2002	767	2,052	37.4
Cincinnati	2002	761	2,035	37.4
Alabama	†1995	771	2,048	37.6
Col. of Charleston	2002	663	1,762	37.6
Old Dominion	1999	797	2,116	37.7
Wisconsin	1997	502	1,329	37.8
Kansas	1995	768	2,032	37.8
Ohio St.	2000	654	1,730	37.8
Kansas	†2001	782	2,069	37.8
Navy	1999	575	1,519	37.9
Georgetown	1997	659	1,740	37.9
Rice	1999	606	1,599	37.9
Miami (Fla.)	†1998	634	1,672	37.9

†national leader

THREE-POINT FIELD GOALS MADE

Team	Season	G	3FG
Duke	†2001	39	407
Arkansas	†1995	39	361
Kentucky	†1993	34	340
Missouri	†2002	36	326
Kentucky	†1992	36	317
St. Bonaventure	2002	30	314
Samford	†2000	32	313
Long Island	†1998	32	310
Ball St.	2002	35	310
UNLV	†1987	39	309
Mississippi Val.	†1997	29	309
Charlotte	2001	33	305
Oregon	2002	35	304
East Tenn. St.	†1991	33	301
Arkansas	†1994	34	301
Kentucky	1994	34	301
Long Island	1997	30	301
New Mexico	1998	32	301
Duke	2002	35	301
New Mexico	1994	31	300
Troy St.	†1996	27	300
Loyola Marymount	†1990	32	298
Temple	2002	34	298
Georgia Tech	1996	36	296
Arkansas	†1999	34	296

†national leader

THREE-POINT FIELD GOALS MADE PER GAME

Team	Season	G	3FG	Avg.
Troy St.	†1996	27	300	11.11
Mississippi Val.	†1997	29	309	10.66
Troy St.	†1995	27	287	10.63
St. Bonaventure	2002	30	314	10.47
Duke	†2001	39	407	10.44
Samford	1995	27	279	10.33
Belmont	2001	28	288	10.29
Marshall	1996	28	284	10.14
Lamar	†1993	27	271	10.04
Kentucky	†1990	28	281	10.04
Long Island	1997	30	301	10.03
Kentucky	1993	34	340	10.00
Tennessee Tech	†2000	28	279	9.96
Vermont	1995	27	268	9.93
Florida	†1998	29	285	9.83
Samford	2001	29	284	9.79
Samford	2000	32	313	9.78
Belmont	2000	28	273	9.75
Dartmouth	2002	27	263	9.74
Troy St.	†1994	27	262	9.70
Long Island	1998	32	310	9.69
New Mexico	1994	31	300	9.68
Cal Poly	1997	30	290	9.67
North Texas	1998	26	250	9.62
Nebraska	2002	28	267	9.54

†national leader

DIVISION I

THREE-POINT FIELD-GOAL PERCENTAGE
(Minimum 100 three-point field goals made)

Team	Season	G	3FG	3FGA	Pct.
Indiana	†1987	34	130	256	50.8
Mississippi Val.	1987	28	161	322	50.0
Stephen F. Austin	1987	30	120	241	49.8
Princeton	†1988	26	211	429	49.2
Prairie View	1988	27	129	266	48.5
Kansas St.	1988	34	179	370	48.4
Arizona	1988	38	254	526	48.3
Indiana	†1989	35	121	256	47.3
Bucknell	1988	28	154	328	47.0
Holy Cross	1988	29	158	337	46.9
Michigan	1989	37	196	419	46.8
Wis.-Green Bay	†1992	30	204	437	46.7
Citadel	1989	28	153	328	46.6
Niagara	1987	31	128	275	46.5
Eastern Mich.	1987	29	144	310	46.5
Wis.-Green Bay	†1991	31	189	407	46.4
Colorado St.	1989	33	141	305	46.2
Bucknell	1989	31	160	347	46.1
Illinois	1987	31	112	243	46.1
Illinois St.	1987	32	110	240	45.8
Jacksonville	1987	30	188	412	45.6
Rider	1987	28	151	331	45.6
Davidson	1987	30	138	303	45.5
New Mexico St.	1988	32	143	314	45.5
Gonzaga	1989	28	119	262	45.4
Indiana	†1994	30	182	401	45.4

†national leader

FREE-THROW PERCENTAGE

Team	Season	FT	FTA	Pct.
Harvard	†1984	535	651	82.2
Brigham Young	†1989	527	647	81.5
Harvard	†1985	450	555	81.1
Ohio St.	†1970	452	559	80.9
Siena	†1998	574	715	80.3
Vanderbilt	†1974	477	595	80.2
Michigan St.	†1986	490	613	79.9
Butler	†1988	413	517	79.9
Miami (Fla.)	†1965	642	807	79.6
Tulane	†1963	390	492	79.3
Tennessee	†1971	538	679	79.2
Auburn	†1966	476	601	79.2
Oklahoma St.	†1958	488	617	79.1
Duke	†1978	665	841	79.1
Utah	†1993	476	602	79.1
Gonzaga	1989	485	614	79.0
Western Ky.	†1997	342	433	79.0
Montana St.	†2000	481	609	79.0
Oral Roberts	†1980	481	610	78.9
Marshall	1958	479	608	78.8
Bucknell	1989	590	749	78.8
Alabama	†1987	521	662	78.7
Siena	†1999	672	854	78.7
Butler	†1991	725	922	78.6
Western Ill.	†1982	·447	569	78.6

†national leader

REBOUNDS

Team	Season	G	Reb.
Kentucky	†1951	34	2,109
North Carolina St.	1951	37	2,091
Houston	†1968	33	2,074
Columbia	†1957	24	2,016
Fordham	†1953	27	1,879
North Carolina St.	†1955	32	1,864
Houston	†1967	31	1,862
Fordham	†1952	29	1,859
Kentucky	1952	32	1,817
West Virginia	†1959	34	1,810
Western Ky.	†1954	32	1,810
Creighton	†1964	29	1,803
North Carolina St.	1952	34	1,782
Dayton	1955	29	1,738
North Carolina St.	1954	35	1,735
Notre Dame	†1965	27	1,722
Dayton	†1956	29	1,713
New Mexico St.	1970	31	1,713
Seton Hall	1953	33	1,706
La Salle	1955	31	1,697
LSU	†1970	32	1,691

Team	Season	G	Reb.
Middle Tenn.	†1969	26	1,685
Kansas	†1998	39	1,682
Kentucky	1955	26	1,680
St. John's (N.Y.)	1952	31	1,678

†national leader

REBOUND MARGIN
(Since 1973)

Team	Season	Off.	Def.	Mar.
Manhattan	†1973	56.5	38.0	18.5
American	1973	56.7	40.3	16.4
Alcorn St.	†1978	52.3	36.0	16.3
Oral Roberts	1973	66.9	50.3	15.6
Alcorn St.	†1980	49.2	33.8	15.4
Michigan St.	†2001	42.5	27.1	15.4
UCLA	1973	49.0	33.9	15.1
Houston	1973	54.7	40.8	13.9
Massachusetts	†1974	44.5	30.7	13.8
Alcorn St.	†1979	50.1	36.3	13.8
Minnesota	1973	49.0	36.0	13.0
Va. Commonwealth	1974	55.1	42.1	13.0
Northeastern	†1981	44.9	32.0	12.9
Stetson	†1975	47.1	34.7	12.4
Notre Dame	†1976	46.3	34.1	12.2
Harvard	1973	53.5	41.3	12.2
Tennessee St.	1980	46.5	34.3	12.2
Tennessee St.	1979	49.7	37.9	11.8
Buffalo	1976	51.5	39.7	11.8
Southern U.	1978	43.1	31.4	11.7
Wyoming	1981	42.0	30.3	11.7
Michigan St.	†2000	39.0	27.3	11.7
Alabama	1973	50.9	39.3	11.6
Mississippi Val.	†1996	48.3	36.8	11.6
Iowa	†1987	43.1	31.5	11.5

†national leader

ASSISTS

Team	Season	G	Ast.
UNLV	†1990	40	926
UNLV	†1991	35	863
Oklahoma	†1988	39	862
UNLV	†1987	39	853
Oklahoma	†1985	37	828
Arkansas	1991	38	819
Kansas	†1986	39	814
North Carolina	1986	34	800
North Carolina	†1989	37	788
Southern Methodist	1988	35	786
Kentucky	†1996	36	783
North Carolina	1987	36	782
Kentucky	†1997	40	776
Kansas	†2002	37	767
Loyola Marymount	1990	32	763
Kansas	1990	35	762
Kansas	†1998	39	746
Oklahoma	1989	36	743
Arkansas	†1995	39	721
Maryland	2002	36	714
Duke	†2001	39	701
North Carolina	1991	35	699
North Carolina	1998	38	699
North Carolina	†1993	38	698
Maryland	2001	36	692

†national leader

ASSISTS PER GAME

Team	Season	G	Ast.	Avg.
UNLV	†1991	35	863	24.7
Loyola Marymount	†1990	32	762	23.8
North Carolina	†1986	34	800	23.5
UNLV	1990	40	926	23.2
Southern Methodist	†1987	29	655	22.6
Southern Methodist	†1988	35	786	22.5
Oklahoma	†1985	37	828	22.4
Oklahoma	1988	39	862	22.1
Northwestern St.	†1993	26	570	21.9
UNLV	1987	39	853	21.9
Kansas	1990	35	763	21.8
Kentucky	†1996	36	783	21.8
North Carolina	1987	36	782	21.7
Iowa St.	1988	32	694	21.7
Arkansas	1991	38	819	21.6
North Carolina	†1989	37	788	21.3

Marques Green of St. Bonaventure helped the Bonnies lead the nation in three-pointers made per game last season.

Photo by St. Bonaventure Sports Information

Team	Season	G	Ast.	Avg.
Georgia Tech	1988	32	680	21.3
Montana St.	1996	30	627	20.9
Montana St.	†1995	29	606	20.9
Montana St.	†1998	30	624	20.8
Kansas	†2002	37	767	20.7
TCU	1999	32	650	20.3
Arkansas	†1994	34	687	20.2
Fresno St.	1998	34	685	20.2
Montana St.	1999	29	583	20.1
UNLV	†2000	31	623	20.1

†national leader

BLOCKED SHOTS

Team	Season	G	Blk.
Georgetown	†1989	34	309
Massachusetts	†1995	34	273
UNLV	†1991	35	266
Old Dominion	†1999	34	248
Brigham Young	1991	34	246
Duke	1999	39	245
Kentucky	†1998	39	240
Seton Hall	†2001	31	236
Connecticut	†2002	34	236
Clemson	†1990	35	235
Georgetown	1991	32	235
Central Conn. St.	†1996	28	235
Maryland	†2000	35	235
Navy	†1986	35	233
Georgetown	1990	31	233
Old Dominion	†1997	33	233
Massachusetts	1996	37	232
Arkansas	1991	38	229
Syracuse	1999	33	229
Georgetown	2000	34	226
LSU	1990	32	225
Alabama	†1992	35	223
Cincinnati	2000	33	223
Kansas	1997	36	222
Kansas	1998	39	220
Iona	1999	30	220

†national leader

BLOCKED SHOTS PER GAME

Team	Season	G	Blk.	Avg.
Georgetown	†1989	34	309	9.09
Central Conn. St.	†1996	28	235	8.39
Massachusetts	†1995	34	273	8.03
Colgate	†1997	28	217	7.75
Seton Hall	†2001	31	236	7.61
UNLV	†1991	35	266	7.60
Georgetown	†1990	31	233	7.52
Central Conn. St.	1995	26	194	7.46
La.-Monroe	†2000	28	207	7.39
Georgetown	1991	32	235	7.34
Florida A&M	1996	27	198	7.33

Team	Season	G	Blk.	Avg.
Iona	†1999	30	220	7.33
Old Dominion	1999	34	248	7.29
Brigham Young	1991	34	246	7.24
Old Dominion	1997	33	233	7.06
LSU	1990	32	225	7.03
Iona	2000	31	216	6.97
Syracuse	1999	33	229	6.94
Connecticut	†2002	34	236	6.94
Rutgers	2002	31	215	6.94
Mississippi Val.	1999	27	187	6.93
Fairfield	2002	29	199	6.86
Vermont	†1992	29	198	6.83
Navy	2000	29	198	6.83
La.-Monroe	2002	32	217	6.78

†national leader

STEALS

Team	Season	G	Stl.
Oklahoma	†1988	39	486
Connecticut	†1990	37	484
Kentucky	†1997	40	480
Long Island	†1998	32	478
Cleveland St.	†1987	33	473
Arkansas	†1991	38	467
Texas	†1994	34	453
Loyola Marymount	1990	32	450
Arkansas	†1995	39	445
Cleveland St.	†1986	33	436
Kentucky	†1996	36	435
Tulsa	†2000	37	433
Georgetown	1996	37	431
Maryland	†1999	34	431
Texas-San Antonio	1991	29	430
Duke	†2001	39	411
West Virginia	1998	33	407
Oklahoma	†1993	32	405
UNLV	1991	35	399
Long Island	1997	30	396
Florida A&M	1988	30	395
Alabama A&M	†2002	27	395
Kentucky	1994	34	394
Syracuse	2002	36	394
Tulane	†1992	31	388

†national leader

STEALS PER GAME

Team	Season	G	Stl.	Avg.
Long Island	†1998	32	478	14.94
Texas-San Antonio	†1991	29	430	14.83
Cleveland St.	†1987	33	473	14.33
Centenary (La.)	†1993	27	380	14.07
Loyola Marymount	†1990	32	450	14.06
Alabama A&M	†2002	27	395	13.62
Liberty	†2000	28	376	13.43
Texas	†1994	34	453	13.32
Cleveland St.	†1986	33	436	13.21
Long Island	†1997	30	396	13.20
Florida A&M	†1988	30	395	13.17
Connecticut	1990	37	484	13.08
Alabama A&M	2000	28	366	13.07
Charlotte	1991	28	363	12.96
Northeastern Ill.	†1992	28	358	12.79
Maryland	†1999	34	431	12.68
Oklahoma	1993	32	405	12.66
Southern U.	1991	28	352	12.57
Cleveland St.	1988	30	376	12.53
Nicholls St.	†1995	30	376	12.53
Tulane	1992	31	388	12.52
Southern U.	1993	31	387	12.48
Drake	1994	27	337	12.48
West Virginia	1998	33	407	12.33
McNeese St.	†1996	27	330	12.22

†national leader

MOST GAMES PLAYED
(Since 1947-48)

Team	Season	W	L	G
Duke	†1986	37	3	40
UNLV	†1990	35	5	40

Team	Season	W	L	G
Kentucky	†1997	35	5	40
Kentucky	†1948	36	3	39
Kansas	†1986	35	4	39
Louisville	†1986	32	7	39
UNLV	†1987	37	2	39
LSU	†1987	24	15	39
Oklahoma	†1988	35	4	39
Duke	†1991	32	7	39
Arkansas	†1995	32	7	39
Kansas	†1998	35	4	39
Kentucky	†1998	35	4	39
Duke	†1999	37	2	39
Michigan St.	†2000	32	7	39
Duke	†2001	35	4	39
Georgetown	†1985	35	3	38
UNLV	1986	33	5	38
LSU	1986	26	12	38
Syracuse	1987	31	7	38
Western Ky.	1987	29	9	38
Kansas	1988	27	11	38
Arizona	1988	35	3	38
Seton Hall	†1989	31	7	38
Syracuse	†1989	30	8	38
Duke	1990	29	9	38
Arkansas	1991	34	4	38
North Carolina	†1993	34	4	38
Syracuse	†1996	29	9	38
North Carolina	1998	34	4	38
Michigan St.	1999	33	5	38

†national leader

Annual Team Champions

Won-Lost Percentage

Season	Team	Won	Lost	Pct.
1948	Western Ky.	28	2	.933
1949	Kentucky	32	2	.941
1950	Holy Cross	27	4	.871
1951	Columbia	21	1	.956
1952	Kansas	26	2	.929
1953	Seton Hall	31	2	.939
1954	Kentucky	25	0	1.000
1955	San Francisco	28	1	.966
1956	San Francisco	29	0	1.000
1957	North Carolina	32	0	1.000
1958	West Virginia	26	2	.929
1959	Mississippi St.	24	1	.960
1960	California	28	2	.933
	Cincinnati	28	2	.933
1961	Ohio St.	27	1	.964
1962	Mississippi St.	24	1	.960
1963	Loyola (Ill.)	29	2	.935
1964	UCLA	30	0	1.000
1965	UCLA	28	2	.933
1966	UTEP	28	1	.966
1967	UCLA	30	0	1.000
1968	UCLA	29	1	.967
1969	UCLA	29	1	.967
1970	UCLA	28	2	.933
1971	UCLA	29	1	.967
1972	UCLA	30	0	1.000
1973	UCLA	30	0	1.000
	North Carolina St.	27	0	1.000
1974	North Carolina St.	30	1	.968
1975	Indiana	31	1	.969
1976	Indiana	32	0	1.000
1977	San Francisco	29	2	.935
1978	Kentucky	30	2	.938
1979	Indiana St.	33	1	.971
1980	Alcorn St.	28	2	.933
1981	DePaul	27	2	.931
1982	North Carolina	32	2	.941
1983	Houston	31	3	.912
1984	Georgetown	34	3	.919
1985	Georgetown	35	3	.921
1986	Duke	37	3	.925
1987	UNLV	37	2	.949
1988	Temple	32	2	.941
1989	Ball St.	29	3	.906

Season	Team	Won	Lost	Pct.
1990	La Salle	30	2	.938
1991	UNLV	34	1	.971
1992	Duke	34	2	.944
1993	North Carolina	34	4	.895
1994	Arkansas	31	3	.912
1995	UCLA	31	2	.939
1996	Massachusetts	35	2	.946
1997	Kansas	34	2	.944
1998	Princeton	27	2	.931
1999	Duke	37	2	.949
2000	Cincinnnati	29	4	.879
2001	Stanford	31	3	.912
2002	Kansas	33	4	.892

Most-Improved Teams

Season	Team	W-L Record	Previous Yr. W-L	Games Up
1974	Kansas	23-7	8-18	13
1975	Holy Cross	20-8	8-18	11
1976	North Texas	22-4	6-20	16
1977	La.-Lafayette	21-8	7-19	12½
1978	N.C. A&T	20-8	3-24	16½
1979	Wagner	21-7	7-19	13
1980	Murray St.	23-8	4-22	16½
1981	Tulsa	26-7	8-19	15
1982	Cal St. Fullerton	18-14	4-23	11½
1983	Utah St.	20-9	4-23	15
1984	Northeastern	27-5	13-15	12
	Loyola (Md.)	16-12	4-24	12
1985	Cincinnati	17-14	3-25	12½
1986	Bradley	32-3	17-13	12½
1987	James Madison	20-10	5-23	14
1988	Loyola Marymount	28-4	12-16	14
1989	Ball St.	29-3	14-14	13
1990	South Fla.	20-11	7-21	11½
	George Washington	14-17	1-27	11½
1991	Radford	22-7	7-22	15
1992	Liberty	22-7	5-23	16½
1993	Tennessee St.	19-10	4-24	14½
1994	Loyola (Md.)	17-13	2-25	13½
1995	Western Ill.	20-8	7-20	12½
1996	Cal Poly	16-13	1-26	14
1997	Northern Ariz.	21-7	6-20	14
1998	Texas-San Antonio	16-11	3-25	13½
1999	Ohio St.	27-9	8-22	16
2000	Iowa St.	32-5	15-15	13½
2001	Boston College	27-5	11-19	15
2002	Fla. Atlantic	19-12	7-24	12
	Texas Tech	23-9	9-19	12

Scoring Offense

Season	Team	G	W-L	Pts.	Avg.
1948	Rhode Island	23	17-6	1,755	76.3
1949	Rhode Island	22	16-6	1,575	71.6
1950	Villanova	29	25-4	2,111	72.8
1951	Cincinnati	22	18-4	1,694	77.0
1952	Kentucky	32	29-3	2,635	82.3
1953	Furman	27	21-6	2,435	90.2
1954	Furman	29	20-9	2,658	91.7
1955	Furman	27	17-10	2,572	95.3
1956	Morehead St.	29	19-10	2,782	95.9
1957	Connecticut	25	17-8	2,183	87.3
1958	Marshall	24	17-7	2,113	88.0
1959	Miami (Fla.)	25	18-7	2,190	87.6
1960	Ohio St.	28	25-3	2,532	90.4
1961	St. Bonaventure	28	24-4	2,479	88.5
1962	Loyola (Ill.)	27	23-4	2,436	90.2
1963	Loyola (Ill.)	31	29-2	2,847	91.8
1964	Detroit	25	14-11	2,402	96.1
1965	Miami (Fla.)	26	22-4	2,558	98.4
1966	Syracuse	28	22-6	2,773	99.0
1967	Oklahoma City	26	16-10	2,496	96.0
1968	Houston	33	31-2	3,226	97.8
1969	Purdue	28	23-5	2,605	93.0
1970	Jacksonville	28	26-2	2,809	100.3
1971	Jacksonville	26	22-4	2,598	99.9
1972	Oral Roberts	28	26-2	2,943	105.1
1973	Oral Roberts	27	21-6	2,626	97.3
1974	Md.-East. Shore	29	27-2	2,831	97.6

Finger rolls from Nick Collison helped Kansas lead the country in field-goal percentage last year.

Photo by Rich Clarkson/NCAA Photos

Season	Team	G	W-L	Pts.	Avg.
1954	Oklahoma St.	29	24-5	1,539	53.1
1955	San Francisco	29	28-1	1,511	52.1
1956	San Francisco	29	29-0	1,514	52.2
1957	Oklahoma St.	26	17-9	1,420	54.6
1958	San Francisco	27	25-2	1,363	50.5
1959	California	29	25-4	1,480	51.0
1960	California	30	28-2	1,486	49.5
1961	Santa Clara	27	18-9	1,314	48.7
1962	Santa Clara	25	19-6	1,302	52.1
1963	Cincinnati	28	26-2	1,480	52.9
1964	San Jose St.	24	14-10	1,307	54.5
1965	Tennessee	25	20-5	1,391	55.6
1966	Oregon St.	28	21-7	1,527	54.5
1967	Tennessee	28	21-7	1,511	54.0
1968	Army	25	20-5	1,448	57.9
1969	Army	28	18-10	1,498	53.5
1970	Army	28	22-6	1,515	54.1
1971	Fairleigh Dickinson	23	16-7	1,236	53.7
1972	Minnesota	25	18-7	1,451	58.0
1973	UTEP	26	16-10	1,460	56.2
1974	UTEP	25	18-7	1,413	56.5
1975	UTEP	26	20-6	1,491	57.3
1976	Princeton	27	22-5	1,427	52.9
1977	Princeton	26	21-5	1,343	51.7
1978	Fresno St.	27	21-6	1,417	52.5
1979	Princeton	26	14-12	1,452	55.8
1980	St. Peter's	31	22-9	1,563	50.4
1981	Fresno St.	29	25-4	1,470	50.7
1982	Fresno St.	30	27-3	1,412	47.1
1983	Princeton	29	20-9	1,507	52.0
1984	Princeton	28	18-10	1,403	50.1
1985	Fresno St.	32	23-9	1,696	53.0
1986	Princeton	26	13-13	1,429	55.0
1987	Southwest Mo. St.	34	28-6	1,958	57.6
1988	Ga. Southern	31	24-7	1,725	55.6
1989	Princeton	27	19-8	1,430	53.0
1990	Princeton	27	20-7	1,378	51.0
1991	Princeton	27	24-3	1,320	48.9
1992	Princeton	28	22-6	1,349	48.2
1993	Princeton	26	15-11	1,421	54.7
1994	Princeton	26	18-8	1,361	52.3
1995	Princeton	26	16-10	1,501	57.7
1996	Princeton	29	22-7	1,498	51.7
1997	Princeton	28	24-4	1,496	53.4
1998	Princeton	29	27-2	1,491	51.4
1999	Princeton	30	22-8	1,581	52.7
2000	Princeton	30	19-11	1,637	54.6
2001	Wisconsin	29	18-11	1,641	56.6
2002	Columbia	28	11-17	1,596	57.0

* record

Season	Team	G	W-L	Pts.	Avg.
1975	South Ala.	26	19-7	2,412	92.8
1976	UNLV	31	29-2	3,426	110.5
1977	UNLV	32	29-3	3,426	107.1
1978	New Mexico	28	24-4	2,731	97.5
1979	UNLV	29	21-9	2,700	93.1
1980	Alcorn St.	30	28-2	2,729	92.0
1981	UC Irvine	27	17-10	2,332	86.4
1982	Long Island	30	20-10	2,605	86.8
1983	Boston College	32	25-7	2,697	84.3
1984	Tulsa	31	27-4	2,816	90.8
1985	Oklahoma	37	31-6	3,328	89.9
1986	U.S. Int'l	28	8-20	2,542	90.8
1987	UNLV	39	37-2	3,612	92.6
1988	Loyola Marymount	32	28-4	3,528	110.3
1989	Loyola Marymount	31	20-11	3,486	112.5
1990	Loyola Marymount	32	26-6	3,918	*122.4
1991	Southern U.	28	19-9	2,924	104.4
1992	Northwestern St.	28	15-13	2,660	95.0
1993	Southern U.	31	21-10	3,011	97.1
1994	Southern U.	27	16-11	2,727	101.0
1995	TCU	27	16-11	2,529	93.7
1996	Troy St.	27	11-16	2,551	94.5
1997	Long Island	30	21-9	2,746	91.5
1998	TCU	33	27-6	3,209	97.2
1999	Duke	39	37-2	3,581	91.8
2000	Duke	34	29-5	2,992	88.0
2001	TCU	31	20-11	2,902	93.6
2002	Kansas	37	33-4	3,365	90.9

* record

Scoring Defense

Season	Team	G	W-L	Pts.	Avg.
1948	Oklahoma St.	31	27-4	1,006	*32.5
1949	Oklahoma St.	28	23-5	985	35.2
1950	Oklahoma St.	27	18-9	1,059	39.2
1951	Texas A&M	29	17-12	1,275	44.0
1952	Oklahoma St.	27	19-8	1,228	45.5
1953	Oklahoma St.	30	23-7	1,614	53.8

Scoring Margin

Season	Team	Off.	Def.	Mar.
1949	Kentucky	68.2	43.9	24.3
1950	Holy Cross	72.6	55.4	17.2
1951	Kentucky	74.7	52.5	22.2
1952	Kentucky	82.3	55.4	26.9
1953	La Salle	80.1	61.8	18.3
1954	Kentucky	87.5	60.3	27.2
1955	Utah	79.0	59.9	19.1
1956	San Francisco	72.2	52.2	20.0
1957	Kentucky	84.2	69.4	14.8
1958	Cincinnati	86.5	65.9	20.6
1959	Idaho St.	74.2	53.7	20.5
1960	Cincinnati	86.7	64.7	22.0
1961	Memphis	85.0	64.2	20.8
1962	Arizona St.	90.1	67.6	22.5
1963	Loyola (Ill.)	91.8	68.1	23.7
1964	Davidson	89.3	70.5	18.8
1965	Connecticut	85.1	66.5	18.6
1966	Loyola (Ill.)	97.5	76.6	20.9
1967	UCLA	89.6	63.7	25.9
1968	UCLA	93.4	67.2	26.2
1969	UCLA	84.7	63.8	20.9
1970	St. Bonaventure	88.4	65.9	22.5
1971	Jacksonville	99.9	79.0	20.9
1972	UCLA	94.6	64.3	*30.3
1973	North Carolina St.	92.9	71.1	21.8
1974	Charlotte	90.2	69.4	20.8
1975	Charlotte	88.9	65.2	23.7
1976	UNLV	110.5	89.0	21.5
1977	UNLV	107.1	87.7	19.4

Scoring Margin

Season	Team	Off.	Def.	Mar.
1978	UCLA	85.3	67.4	17.9
1979	Syracuse	88.7	71.5	17.2
1980	Alcorn St.	91.0	73.6	17.4
1981	Wyoming	73.6	57.5	16.1
1982	Oregon St.	69.6	55.0	14.6
1983	Houston	82.4	64.9	17.4
1984	Georgetown	74.3	57.9	16.4
1985	Georgetown	74.3	57.3	17.1
1986	Cleveland St.	88.9	69.6	19.3
1987	UNLV	92.6	75.5	17.1
1988	Oklahoma	102.9	81.0	21.9
1989	St. Mary's (Cal.)	76.1	57.6	18.5
1990	Oklahoma	101.3	80.4	21.0
1991	UNLV	97.7	71.0	26.7
1992	Indiana	83.4	65.8	17.6
1993	North Carolina	86.1	68.3	17.8
1994	Arkansas	93.4	75.6	17.9
1995	Kentucky	87.4	69.0	18.4
1996	Kentucky	91.4	69.4	22.1
1997	Kentucky	83.1	62.8	20.3
1998	Duke	85.6	64.1	21.5
1999	Duke	91.8	67.2	24.7
2000	Stanford	78.9	59.7	19.3
2001	Duke	90.7	70.5	20.2
2002	Duke	88.9	69.2	19.7

*record

Field-Goal Percentage

Season	Team	FG	FGA	Pct.
1948	Oregon St.	668	1,818	36.7
1949	Muhlenberg	593	1,512	39.2
1950	TCU	476	1,191	40.0
1951	Maryland	481	1,210	39.8
1952	Boston College	787	1,893	41.6
1953	Furman	936	2,106	44.4
1954	George Washington	744	1,632	45.6
1955	George Washington	867	1,822	47.6
1956	George Washington	725	1,451	50.0
1957	Manhattan	679	1,489	45.6
1958	Fordham	693	1,440	48.1
1959	Auburn	593	1,216	48.8
1960	Auburn	532	1,022	52.1
1961	Ohio St.	939	1,886	49.8
1962	Florida St.	709	1,386	51.2
1963	Duke	984	1,926	51.1
1964	Davidson	894	1,644	54.4
1965	St. Peter's	579	1,089	53.2
1966	North Carolina	838	1,620	51.7
1967	UCLA	1,082	2,081	52.0
1968	Bradley	927	1,768	52.4
1969	UCLA	1,027	1,999	51.4
1970	Ohio St.	831	1,527	54.4
1971	Jacksonville	1,077	2,008	53.6
1972	North Carolina	1,031	1,954	52.8
1973	North Carolina	1,150	2,181	52.7
1974	Notre Dame	1,056	1,992	53.0
1975	Maryland	1,049	1,918	54.7
1976	Maryland	996	1,854	53.7
1977	Arkansas	849	1,558	54.5
1978	Arkansas	1,060	1,943	54.6
1979	UCLA	1,053	1,897	55.5
1980	Missouri	936	1,635	*57.2
1981	Oregon St.	862	1,528	56.4
1982	UC Irvine	920	1,639	56.1
1983	Kentucky	869	1,564	55.6
1984	Houston Baptist	797	1,445	55.2
1985	Navy	946	1,726	54.8
1986	Michigan St.	1,043	1,860	56.1
1987	Princeton	601	1,111	54.1
1988	Michigan	1,198	2,196	54.6
1989	Michigan	1,325	2,341	56.6
1990	Kansas	1,204	2,258	53.3
1991	UNLV	1,305	2,441	53.5
1992	Duke	1,108	2,069	53.6
1993	Indiana	1,076	2,062	52.2
1994	Auburn	854	1,689	50.6
1995	Washington St.	902	1,743	51.7
1996	UCLA	897	1,698	52.8
1997	UCLA	932	1,791	52.0
1998	North Carolina	1,131	2,184	51.8
1999	Northern Ariz.	783	1,497	52.3
2000	Samford	825	1,649	50.0

(continued)

Season	Team	FG	FGA	Pct.
2001	Stanford	953	1,865	51.1
2002	Kansas	1,259	2,487	50.6

*record

Field-Goal Percentage Defense

Season	Team	FG	FGA	Pct.
1977	Minnesota	766	1,886	40.6
1978	Delaware St.	733	1,802	40.7
1979	Illinois	738	1,828	40.4
1980	Penn St.	543	1,309	41.5
1981	Wyoming	637	1,589	40.1
1982	Wyoming	584	1,470	39.7
1983	Wyoming	599	1,441	41.6
1984	Georgetown	799	2,025	39.5
1985	Georgetown	833	2,064	40.4
1986	St. Peter's	574	1,395	41.1
1987	San Diego	660	1,645	40.1
1988	Temple	777	1,981	39.2
1989	Georgetown	795	1,993	39.9
1990	Georgetown	713	1,929	37.0
1991	Georgetown	680	1,847	36.8
1992	UNLV	628	1,723	36.4
1993	Marquette	634	1,613	39.3
1994	Marquette	750	2,097	*35.8
1995	Alabama	771	2,048	37.6
1996	Temple	670	1,741	38.5
1997	Marquette	628	1,735	36.2
1998	Miami (Fla.)	634	1,672	37.9
1999	Kansas St.	729	1,963	37.1
2000	Stanford	667	1,893	35.2
2001	Kansas	782	2,069	37.8
2002	Va. Commonwealth	767	2,052	37.4

*record

Three-Point Field Goals Made Per Game

Season	Team	G	3FG	Avg.
1987	Providence	34	280	8.24
1988	Princeton	26	211	8.12
1989	Loyola Marymount	31	287	9.26
1990	Kentucky	28	281	10.04
1991	Texas-Arlington	29	265	9.14
1992	La Salle	31	294	9.48
1993	Lamar	27	271	10.04
1994	Troy St.	27	262	9.70
1995	Troy St.	27	287	10.63
1996	Troy St.	27	300	*11.11
1997	Mississippi Val.	29	309	10.66
1998	Florida	29	285	9.83
1999	Cal Poly	27	255	9.44
2000	Tennessee Tech	28	279	9.96
2001	Duke	39	407	10.44
2002	St. Bonaventure	30	314	10.47

*record

Three-Point Field-Goal Percentage

Season	Team	G	3FG	3FGA	Pct.
1987	Indiana	34	130	256	*50.8
1988	Princeton	26	211	429	49.2
1989	Indiana	35	121	256	47.3
1990	Princeton	27	208	460	45.2
1991	Wis.-Green Bay	31	189	407	46.4
1992	Wis.-Green Bay	30	204	437	46.7
1993	Valparaiso	28	214	500	42.8
1994	Indiana	30	182	401	45.4
1995	Southern Utah	28	244	571	42.7
1996	Weber St.	30	245	577	42.5
1997	Northern Ariz.	28	221	527	41.9
1998	Northern Ariz.	29	254	591	43.0
1999	Northern Ariz.	29	243	546	44.5
2000	Colorado St.	30	255	579	44.0
2001	Akron	28	189	436	43.3
2002	Marshall	30	252	595	42.4

*record

Free-Throw Percentage

Season	Team	FT	FTA	Pct.
1948	Texas	351	481	73.0
1949	Davidson	347	489	71.0
1950	Temple	342	483	70.8
1951	Minnesota	287	401	71.6
1952	Kansas	491	707	69.4
1953	George Washington	502	696	72.1
1954	Wake Forest	734	1,010	72.7
1955	Wake Forest	709	938	75.6
1956	Southern Methodist	701	917	76.4
1957	Oklahoma St.	569	752	75.7
1958	Oklahoma St.	488	617	79.1
1959	Tulsa	446	586	76.1
1960	Auburn	424	549	77.2
1961	Tulane	459	604	76.0
1962	Southern Methodist	552	718	76.9
1963	Tulane	390	492	79.3
1964	Miami (Fla.)	593	780	76.0
1965	Miami (Fla.)	642	807	79.6
1966	Auburn	476	601	79.2
1967	West Tex. A&M	400	518	77.2
1968	Vanderbilt	527	684	77.0
1969	Jacksonville	574	733	78.3
1970	Ohio St.	452	559	80.9
1971	Tennessee	538	679	79.2
1972	Lafayette	656	844	77.7
1973	Duke	496	632	78.5
1974	Vanderbilt	477	595	80.2
1975	Vanderbilt	530	692	76.6
1976	Morehead St.	452	577	78.3
1977	Utah	499	638	78.2
1978	Duke	665	841	79.1
1979	St. Francis (Pa.)	350	446	78.5
1980	Oral Roberts	481	610	78.9
1981	Connecticut	487	623	78.2
1982	Western Ill.	447	569	78.6
1983	Western Ill.	526	679	77.5
1984	Harvard	535	651	*82.2
1985	Harvard	450	555	81.1
1986	Michigan St.	490	613	79.9
1987	Alabama	521	662	78.7
1988	Butler	413	517	79.9
1989	Brigham Young	527	647	81.5
1990	Lafayette	461	588	78.4
1991	Butler	725	922	78.6
1992	Northwestern	497	651	76.3
1993	Utah	476	602	79.1
1994	Colgate	511	665	76.8
1995	Brigham Young	617	798	77.3
1996	Utah	649	828	78.4
1997	Western Ky.	342	433	79.0
1998	Siena	574	715	80.3
1999	Siena	672	854	78.7
2000	Montana St.	481	609	79.0
2001	Brigham Young	651	835	78.0
2002	Morehead St.	485	619	78.4

*record

Rebounding

Season	Team	G	Reb.	Pct.
1955	Niagara	26	1,507	.624
1956	George Washington	26	1,451	.616
1957	Morehead St.	27	1,735	.621
1958	Manhattan	26	1,437	.591
1959	Mississippi St.	25	1,012	.589
1960	Iona	18	1,054	.607
1961	Bradley	26	1,330	.592
1962	Cornell	25	1,463	.590
1963	UTEP	26	1,167	.591
1964	Iona	20	1,071	.640
1965	Iona	23	1,191	.628
1966	UTEP	29	1,430	.577
1967	Florida	25	1,275	.600
1968	Houston	33	2,074	62.8
1969	Middle Tenn.	26	1,685	64.8
1970	Florida St.	26	1,451	55.8
1971	Pacific (Cal.)	28	1,643	58.7
1972	Oral Roberts	28	1,686	60.2
1973	Manhattan	56.5	38.0	*18.5
1974	Massachusetts	44.5	30.7	13.8
1975	Stetson	47.1	34.7	12.4
1976	Notre Dame	46.3	34.1	12.2
1977	Notre Dame	42.4	31.6	10.8

Season	Team	G	Reb.	Pct.
1978	Alcorn St.	52.3	36.0	16.3
1979	Alcorn St.	50.1	36.3	13.8
1980	Alcorn St.	49.2	33.8	15.4
1981	Northeastern	44.9	32.0	12.9
1982	Northeastern	41.2	30.8	10.4
1983	Wichita St.	42.4	33.6	8.8
1984	Northeastern	40.1	30.3	9.8
1985	Georgetown	39.6	30.5	9.1
1986	Notre Dame	36.4	27.8	8.6
1987	Iowa	43.1	31.5	11.5
1988	Notre Dame	36.0	26.2	9.9
1989	Iowa	41.4	31.8	9.6
1990	Georgetown	44.8	34.0	10.8
1991	New Orleans	41.7	32.4	9.3
1992	Delaware	42.1	33.8	8.3
1993	Massachusetts	43.9	32.8	11.2
1994	Utah St.	38.4	29.8	8.6
1995	Navy	40.6	29.6	11.0
1996	Mississippi Val.	48.3	36.8	11.6
1997	Utah St.	37.4	26.6	10.9
1998	Utah	37.0	27.1	10.0
1999	Navy	43.6	33.7	10.0
2000	Michigan St.	39.0	27.3	11.7
2001	Michigan St.	42.5	27.1	15.4
2002	Gonzaga	41.5	32.6	8.9

Note: From 1955 through 1967, the rebounding champion was determined by highest team recoveries out of the total by both teams in all games. From 1968 through 1972, the champion was determined by rebound average per game. Beginning with the 1973 season, the champion has been determined by rebounding margin.

*record

Assists

Season	Team	G	Ast.	Avg.
1984	Clemson	28	571	20.4
1985	Oklahoma	37	828	22.4
1986	North Carolina	34	800	23.5
1987	Southern Methodist	29	655	22.6
1988	Southern Methodist	35	786	22.5
1989	North Carolina	37	788	21.3
1990	Loyola Marymount	32	762	23.8
1991	UNLV	35	863	*24.7
1992	Arkansas	34	674	19.8
1993	Northwestern St.	26	570	21.9
1994	Arkansas	34	687	20.2
1995	Montana St.	29	606	20.9
1996	Kentucky	36	783	21.8
1997	Kentucky	40	776	19.4
1998	Montana St.	30	624	20.8
1999	TCU	32	650	20.3
2000	UNLV	31	623	20.1
2001	Kansas	33	641	19.4
2002	Kansas	37	767	20.7

*record

Blocked Shots

Season	Team	G	Blk.	Avg.
1986	Navy	35	233	6.66
1987	Siena	29	188	6.48
1988	Siena	29	193	6.66
1989	Georgetown	34	309	*9.09
1990	Georgetown	31	233	7.52
1991	UNLV	35	266	7.60
1992	Vermont	29	198	6.83
1993	Wyoming	28	184	6.57
1994	Howard	27	179	6.63
1995	Massachusetts	34	273	8.03
1996	Central Conn. St.	28	235	8.39
1997	Colgate	28	217	7.75
1998	Texas	31	203	6.55
1999	Iona	30	220	7.33
2000	La.-Monroe	28	207	7.39
2001	Seton Hall	31	236	7.61
2002	Connecticut	34	236	6.94

*record

Steals

Season	Team	G	Stl.	Avg.
1986	Cleveland St.	33	436	13.2
1987	Cleveland St.	33	473	14.3

Season	Team	G	Stl.	Avg.		Season	Team	G	Stl.	Avg.
1988	Florida A&M	30	395	13.2		1997	Long Island	30	396	13.2
1989	Arkansas	32	372	11.6		1998	Long Island	32	478	*14.9
1990	Loyola Marymount	32	450	14.1		1999	Maryland	34	431	12.7
1991	Texas-San Antonio	29	430	14.8		2000	Liberty	28	376	13.4
1992	Northeastern Ill.	28	358	12.8		2001	Alabama A&M	28	339	12.1
1993	Centenary (La.)	27	380	14.1		2002	Alabama A&M	29	395	13.6
1994	Texas	34	453	13.3		*record				
1995	Nicholls St.	30	376	12.5						
1996	McNeese St.	27	330	12.2						

Statistical Trends

Year	Teams	Games	FG Made	FG Att.	Pct.	FT Made	FT Att.	Pct.	PF	Pts.
1948	160	24.7	20.3	69.4	29.3	12.7	21.1	59.8	18.5	53.3
1949	148	25.3	20.7	67.4	30.8	13.4	21.7	61.6	19.4	54.8
1950	145	25.2	21.6	68.4	31.6	14.4	23.3	61.8	19.5	57.6
1951	153	26.0	22.8	68.9	33.1	15.1	24.1	62.8	21.4	60.7
1952	156	25.7	23.8	*70.3	33.7	15.8	25.3	62.6	*22.5	63.3
1953	158	23.8	24.0	69.1	34.7	21.1	*32.9	64.0	21.3	69.1
1954	160	24.6	24.4	67.8	35.4	21.0	32.2	65.2	21.0	69.0
1955	162	23.6	25.6	69.3	36.9	*21.6	32.4	66.5	19.0	72.7
1956	166	24.7	26.1	69.5	37.5	21.2	31.7	66.8	18.9	73.3
1957	167	24.6	25.8	67.6	38.2	20.4	30.3	67.3	18.3	72.0
1958	173	24.0	25.8	67.1	38.4	16.8	25.3	66.4	18.2	68.4
1959	174	24.3	25.9	66.2	39.1	17.0	25.4	67.1	18.2	68.7
1960	175	24.5	26.3	66.2	39.8	17.4	25.8	67.4	18.4	70.0
1961	173	24.5	26.7	65.6	40.7	17.4	25.5	68.2	18.2	70.7
1962	178	24.4	27.0	67.3	40.2	16.5	24.3	67.9	18.1	70.5
1963	178	23.5	26.6	63.8	41.7	16.3	23.9	68.2	18.2	69.5
1964	179	24.3	28.7	67.4	42.5	17.1	25.1	68.3	19.1	74.4
1965	182	24.8	29.2	67.7	43.1	17.4	25.2	69.0	19.3	75.7
1966	182	21.9	30.0	68.8	43.6	17.5	25.3	69.2	19.2	77.5
1967	185	24.9	28.9	66.0	43.8	17.2	24.9	69.0	19.2	74.9
1968	189	25.1	29.1	66.6	43.7	17.4	25.1	69.1	19.0	75.5
1969	193	25.3	29.1	66.4	43.8	17.4	25.4	68.4	19.0	75.6
1970	196	25.4	30.0	67.8	44.2	17.7	25.7	68.7	19.3	77.6
1971	203	25.8	30.1	67.8	44.4	17.5	25.7	68.1	19.3	*77.7
1972	210	25.7	30.1	67.2	44.8	17.5	25.6	68.6	19.2	*77.7
1973	216	25.8	31.2	69.6	44.8	13.1	19.2	68.4	19.2	75.5
1974	233	26.0	31.0	68.3	45.4	12.8	18.7	68.4	19.2	74.8
1975	235	26.2	*31.5	68.4	46.0	13.7	19.9	69.0	20.2	76.6
1976	235	26.6	31.0	66.3	46.7	13.8	19.9	69.2	20.2	75.7
1977	245	27.2	30.4	64.9	46.7	14.2	20.5	69.4	20.1	74.9
1978	254	27.2	30.1	63.6	47.3	14.3	20.7	69.2	20.2	74.5
1979	257	27.7	29.6	62.1	47.7	14.8	21.1	*69.7	20.6	74.0
1980	261	28.0	28.6	59.7	47.9	14.9	21.3	69.6	20.2	72.0
1981	264	28.1	27.8	58.0	48.0	14.5	21.0	68.9	20.1	70.1
1982	273	28.0	26.7	55.6	47.9	14.3	20.8	68.6	19.4	67.6
1983	274	29.0	27.2	57.0	47.7	14.5	21.2	68.5	19.9	69.3
1984	276	29.1	26.7	55.6	*48.1	14.8	21.4	68.9	20.0	68.2
1985	282	29.3	27.3	57.0	47.9	14.7	21.3	68.9	19.7	69.2
1986	283	29.5	27.4	57.3	47.7	14.7	21.3	69.1	19.6	69.4

Year	Teams	Games	FG Made	FG Att.	Pct.	3FG Made	3FG Att.	Pct.	FT Made	FT Att.	Pct.	PF	Pts.
1987	290	29.6	27.2	58.7	46.4	3.5	9.2	*38.4	14.9	21.5	69.1	19.7	72.8
1988	290	29.6	27.6	58.4	47.3	4.0	10.4	38.3	15.2	22.0	68.9	19.7	74.4
1989	293	29.6	28.1	59.4	47.3	4.4	11.8	37.8	15.6	22.6	69.1	20.1	76.2
1990	292	29.6	27.5	59.5	46.2	4.7	12.8	36.8	15.6	22.6	68.9	19.8	75.3
1991	295	29.6	27.9	60.6	46.1	5.0	13.8	36.2	15.9	23.2	68.6	19.6	76.7
1992	298	29.5	26.7	58.4	45.7	5.0	14.0	35.6	15.9	23.3	68.1	20.0	74.2
1993	298	28.6	26.5	58.6	45.2	5.3	14.9	35.4	15.4	22.8	67.7	19.6	73.6
1994	301	28.7	26.8	60.6	44.3	5.7	16.5	34.5	15.6	23.2	67.1	19.9	75.0
1995	302	28.7	26.5	59.7	44.4	5.9	17.2	34.5	15.3	22.6	67.6	19.7	74.2
1996	305	28.7	25.8	58.5	44.1	5.9	17.1	34.3	15.1	22.4	67.4	19.4	72.5
1997	305	28.8	25.0	57.3	43.7	5.8	17.1	34.1	14.8	21.9	67.4	19.3	70.6
1998	306	29.1	25.3	57.7	43.9	6.0	17.4	34.4	14.9	22.0	67.5	19.4	71.4
1999	310	29.1	24.8	57.0	43.6	5.9	17.4	34.2	14.7	21.6	68.1	19.0	70.3
2000	318	30.0	25.0	57.4	43.5	6.1	17.7	34.4	14.5	21.2	68.1	18.9	70.5
2001	318	29.8	25.0	56.8	44.0	6.1	17.7	34.6	15.4	22.4	68.5	19.9	71.4
2002	*321	*30.2	25.1	57.2	43.8	*6.3	*18.3	34.6	14.8	21.5	69.0	19.2	71.3

Year	Teams	Games	Reb.	Ast.	Blk.	St.	TO
1993	298	28.6	36.1	*14.5	3.2	7.6	15.8
1994	301	28.7	*37.8	*14.5	3.3	*7.8	15.9
1995	302	28.7	37.2	*14.5	3.3	7.5	15.9
1996	305	28.7	36.7	14.1	3.2	7.4	15.6
1997	305	28.8	36.1	13.9	3.2	7.5	15.7
1998	306	29.1	36.4	14.0	3.2	7.6	15.9
1999	310	29.1	36.1	13.9	*3.4	*7.8	*16.0
2000	318	30.0	36.3	14.0	*3.4	7.6	15.8
2001	318	29.8	35.9	13.9	3.3	7.1	15.2
2002	*321	*30.2	35.9	13.9	*3.4	7.3	15.1

*all-time high

All-Time Winningest Teams

Victories

(Minimum 25 years in Division I)

No.	Team	First Season	Yrs.	Won	Lost	Tied	Pct.
1.	Kentucky	1903	99	1,817	568	1	.762
2.	North Carolina	1911	92	1,789	650	0	.733
3.	Kansas	1899	104	1,771	745	0	.704
4.	Duke	1906	97	1,680	768	0	.686
5.	St. John's (N.Y.)	1908	95	1,641	750	0	.686
6.	Temple	1895	106	1,590	858	0	.650
7.	Syracuse	1901	101	1,572	732	0	.682
8.	Pennsylvania	1897	102	1,533	870	2	.638
9.	Indiana	1901	102	1,519	812	0	.652
10.	UCLA	1920	83	1,510	653	0	.698
11.	Notre Dame	1898	97	1,505	828	1	.645
12.	Oregon St.	1902	101	1,504	1,052	0	.588
13.	Utah	1909	94	1,467	767	0	.657
14.	Princeton	1901	102	1,459	885	0	.622
15.	Western Ky.	1915	83	1,442	714	0	.669
16.	Purdue	1897	104	1,434	838	0	.631
16.	Washington	1896	100	1,434	963	0	.598
18.	Illinois	1906	97	1,433	791	0	.644
19.	Cincinnati	1902	101	1,423	823	0	.634
20.	Arizona	1905	97	1,410	784	0	.643
21.	Louisville	1912	88	1,406	771	0	.646
22.	North Carolina St.	1913	90	1,401	833	0	.627
23.	West Virginia	1904	93	1,398	886	0	.612
24.	Bradley	1903	98	1,397	892	0	.610
25.	Texas	1906	96	1,386	874	0	.613
26.	Arkansas	1924	79	1,368	723	0	.654
27.	Fordham	1903	99	1,365	1,056	0	.564
28.	Ohio St.	1899	103	1,358	937	0	.592
29.	Montana St.	1902	100	1,349	1,034	0	.566
30.	Alabama	1913	89	1,348	811	1	.624
31.	Villanova	1921	82	1,346	772	0	.636
32.	Washington St.	1902	101	1,345	1,239	0	.521
33.	Iowa	1902	101	1,341	909	0	.596
34.	Oklahoma	1908	95	1,337	873	0	.605
35.	Southern California	1907	96	1,336	943	0	.586
36.	St. Joseph's	1910	93	1,330	890	0	.599
37.	Georgetown	1907	94	1,328	843	0	.612
38.	Missouri	1907	96	1,325	925	0	.589
39.	Connecticut	1901	99	1,318	783	0	.627
40.	Oklahoma St.	1908	93	1,317	952	0	.580
41.	Minnesota	1896	107	1,306	989	4	.569
42.	Kansas St.	1903	98	1,304	944	0	.580
43.	Tennessee	1909	93	1,299	841	2	.607
44.	Brigham Young	1918	85	1,295	866	0	.599
45.	Oregon	1903	97	1,292	1,149	0	.529
46.	Vanderbilt	1901	100	1,285	928	0	.581
47.	Michigan St.	1899	103	1,280	923	0	.581
48.	Dayton	1904	97	1,275	926	0	.579
49.	California	1908	93	1,270	964	0	.568
50.	Virginia	1906	97	1,267	975	1	.565

Percentage

(Minimum 25 years in Division I)

No.	Team	First Season	Yrs.	Won	Lost	Tied	Pct.
1.	Kentucky	1903	99	1,817	568	1	.762
2.	North Carolina	1911	92	1,789	650	0	.733
3.	UNLV	1959	44	907	352	0	.720
4.	Kansas	1899	104	1,771	745	0	.704
5.	UCLA	1920	83	1,510	653	0	.698
6.	St. John's (N.Y.)	1908	95	1,641	750	0	.686
7.	Duke	1906	97	1,680	768	0	.686
8.	Syracuse	1901	101	1,572	732	0	.682
9.	Western Ky.	1915	83	1,442	714	0	.669
10.	Utah	1909	94	1,467	767	0	.657
11.	Arkansas	1924	79	1,368	723	0	.654
12.	Indiana	1901	102	1,519	812	0	.652
13.	Temple	1895	106	1,590	858	0	.650
14.	Louisville	1912	88	1,406	771	0	.646
15.	Notre Dame	1898	97	1,505	828	1	.645
16.	Illinois	1906	97	1,433	791	0	.644
17.	Arizona	1905	97	1,410	784	0	.643
18.	Weber St.	1963	40	730	407	0	.642
19.	DePaul	1924	79	1,242	703	0	.639
20.	Pennsylvania	1897	102	1,533	870	2	.638

All-Time Won-Lost Records

(No Minimum Seasons of Competition)

Team	First Season	Yrs.	Won	Lost	Tied	Pct.
Villanova	1921	82	1,346	772	0	.636
Cincinnati	1902	101	1,423	823	0	.634
Murray St.	1926	77	1,257	732	0	.632
Purdue	1897	104	1,434	838	0	.631
Connecticut	1901	99	1,318	783	0	.627
North Carolina St.	1913	90	1,401	833	0	.627
Alabama	1913	89	1,348	811	1	.624
New Orleans	1970	33	587	354	0	.624
Princeton	1901	102	1,459	885	0	.622
Illinois St.	1972	31	566	344	0	.622
La Salle	1931	72	1,145	714	0	.616
Texas	1906	96	1,386	874	0	.613
UTEP	1947	56	930	589	0	.612
West Virginia	1904	93	1,398	886	0	.612
Georgetown	1907	94	1,328	843	0	.612
Navy	1907	96	1,190	758	0	.611
Bradley	1903	98	1,397	892	0	.610
Providence	1927	75	1,158	740	0	.610
Marquette	1917	85	1,263	808	0	.610
Houston	1946	57	967	625	0	.607
Tennessee	1909	93	1,299	841	2	.607
Va. Commonwealth	1969	34	576	373	0	.607
Old Dominion	1966	37	659	427	0	.607
Memphis	1921	81	1,165	760	0	.605
Oklahoma	1908	95	1,337	873	0	.605
San Francisco	1924	75	1,123	740	0	.603
Holy Cross	1901	83	1,138	751	0	.602
Brigham Young	1918	85	1,295	866	0	.599
St. Joseph's	1910	93	1,330	890	0	.599
Michigan	1909	86	1,238	829	0	.599

Numbered 21–50 in the right column (Villanova = 21 ... Michigan = 50).

Team	First Season	Yrs.	Won	Lost	Tied	Pct.
Air Force	1957	46	491	697	0	.413
Akron	1902	101	1,245	831	0	.600
Alabama	1913	89	1,348	811	1	.624
Alabama A&M	1987	16	345	131	0	.725
Alabama St.	1983	20	288	281	0	.506
UAB	1979	24	468	287	0	.620
Albany (N.Y.)	1910	93	988	688	0	.589
Alcorn St.	1978	25	375	346	0	.520
American	1927	76	941	872	0	.519
Appalachian St.	1920	77	979	855	0	.534
Arizona	1905	97	1,410	784	0	.643
Arizona St.	1912	86	1,056	944	0	.528
Arkansas	1924	79	1,368	723	0	.654
Arkansas St.	1971	32	476	420	0	.531
Ark.-Little Rock	1979	24	404	296	0	.577
Ark.-Pine Bluff	1996	7	36	147	0	.197
Army	1903	100	1,035	944	0	.523
Auburn	1906	94	1,072	921	1	.538
Austin Peay	1930	71	919	825	0	.527
Ball St.	1972	31	516	373	0	.580
Baylor	1907	96	1,018	1,151	0	.469
Belmont	1953	50	758	664	0	.533
Bethune-Cookman	1962	40	490	585	0	.456
Binghamton	1947	56	498	701	0	.415
Boise St.	1972	31	463	402	0	.535
Boston College	1905	69	914	736	0	.554
Boston U.	1902	93	885	896	0	.497
Bowling Green	1916	87	1,132	903	0	.556
Bradley	1903	98	1,397	892	0	.610
Brigham Young	1918	85	1,295	866	0	.599
Brown	1901	95	818	1,237	0	.398
Bucknell	1896	107	1,112	1,017	0	.522
Buffalo	1915	83	883	871	0	.503
Butler	1897	104	1,196	954	0	.556
California	1908	93	1,270	964	0	.568
UC Irvine	1966	37	500	531	0	.485
Cal Poly	1995	8	90	134	0	.402
UC Riverside	1955	48	778	570	0	.577
UC Santa Barb.	1938	62	849	783	0	.520
Cal St. Fullerton	1961	42	515	622	0	.453
Cal St. Northridge	1959	44	569	613	0	.481
Campbell	1978	25	293	396	0	.425
Canisius	1904	98	1,076	964	0	.527

DIVISION I

Team	First Season	Yrs.	Won	Lost	Tied	Pct.
Centenary (La.)	1946	52	672	750	0	.473
Central Conn. St.	1935	66	891	658	0	.575
UCF	1971	32	478	398	0	.546
Central Mich.	1974	29	348	443	0	.440
Col. of Charleston	1979	24	572	159	0	.782
Charleston So.	1966	37	424	569	0	.427
Charlotte	1966	37	586	463	0	.559
Chattanooga	1978	25	480	265	0	.644
Chicago St.	1985	18	128	367	0	.259
Cincinnati	1902	101	1,423	823	0	.634
Citadel	1913	89	827	1,014	0	.449
Clemson	1912	91	1,007	1,074	2	.484
Cleveland St.	1973	30	436	398	0	.523
Coastal Caro.	1975	28	375	417	0	.473
Colgate	1901	102	1,061	1,102	0	.491
Colorado	1902	99	1,013	962	0	.513
Colorado St.	1902	99	986	1,008	0	.494
Columbia	1901	102	1,074	1,042	0	.508
Connecticut	1901	99	1,318	783	0	.627
Coppin St.	1986	17	285	214	0	.571
Cornell	1899	104	1,034	1,178	0	.467
Creighton	1917	84	1,186	852	0	.582
Dartmouth	1901	101	1,142	1,184	0	.491
Davidson	1909	93	1,089	1,038	0	.512
Dayton	1904	97	1,275	926	0	.579
Delaware	1906	97	960	1,009	2	.488
Delaware St.	1974	29	309	486	0	.389
Denver	1904	99	1,037	1,057	0	.495
DePaul	1924	79	1,242	703	0	.639
Detroit	1906	95	1,175	942	0	.555
Drake	1907	96	995	1,190	0	.455
Drexel	1895	103	1,007	876	0	.535
Duke	1906	97	1,680	768	0	.686
Duquesne	1914	86	1,176	825	0	.588
East Caro.	1932	70	866	843	0	.507
East Tenn. St.	1928	72	939	786	0	.544
Eastern Ill.	1982	21	312	297	0	.512
Eastern Ky.	1926	76	906	865	1	.512
Eastern Mich.	1974	29	394	434	0	.476
Eastern Wash.	1984	19	192	326	0	.371
Elon	2000	3	35	51	0	.407
Evansville	1978	25	409	299	0	.578
Fairfield	1949	53	667	682	0	.494
Fairleigh Dickinson	1968	34	487	428	0	.532
Florida	1916	82	988	934	0	.514
Florida A&M	1979	24	275	406	0	.404
Fla. Atlantic	1989	14	140	253	0	.356
Florida Int'l	1982	21	264	325	0	.448
Florida St.	1948	55	863	638	0	.575
Fordham	1903	99	1,365	1,056	0	.564
Fresno St.	1922	80	1,109	884	0	.556
Furman	1946	57	762	783	0	.493
George Mason	1979	24	345	335	0	.507
George Washington	1907	85	1,051	899	0	.539
Georgetown	1907	94	1,328	843	0	.612
Georgia	1906	97	1,123	1,041	0	.519
Ga. Southern	1974	29	417	396	0	.513
Georgia St.	1964	39	351	679	0	.341
Georgia Tech	1906	86	1,093	966	0	.531
Gonzaga	1908	95	1,185	1,011	0	.540
Grambling	1978	25	281	418	0	.402
Hampton	1953	50	713	589	0	.548
Hartford	1958	45	548	600	0	.477
Harvard	1901	91	870	1,114	0	.439
Hawaii	1971	32	463	447	0	.509
High Point	1928	75	1,149	814	0	.585
Hofstra	1937	64	959	709	0	.575
Holy Cross	1901	83	1,138	751	0	.602
Houston	1946	57	967	625	0	.607
Howard	1974	29	371	440	0	.457
Idaho	1906	97	1,120	1,195	0	.484
Idaho St.	1927	75	986	898	0	.523
Illinois	1906	97	1,433	791	0	.644
Illinois St.	1972	31	566	344	0	.622
Ill.-Chicago	1948	55	624	682	0	.478
Indiana	1901	102	1,519	812	0	.652
Indiana St.	1924	79	1,102	856	0	.563
IUPUI	1973	30	418	458	0	.477
Iona	1941	59	878	627	0	.583
Iowa	1902	101	1,341	909	0	.596
Iowa St.	1908	95	1,046	1,092	0	.489
Jackson St.	1978	25	352	368	0	.489
Jacksonville	1958	45	622	589	0	.514
Jacksonville St.	1926	71	1,054	549	0	.658
James Madison	1970	33	541	372	0	.593
Kansas	1899	104	1,771	745	0	.704
Kansas St.	1903	98	1,304	944	0	.580
Kent St.	1914	86	869	1,039	0	.455
Kentucky	1903	99	1,817	568	1	.762
La Salle	1931	72	1,145	714	0	.616
Lafayette	1901	92	1,120	966	0	.537
Lamar	1952	51	754	621	0	.548
Lehigh	1902	101	808	1,188	0	.405
Liberty	1973	30	419	442	0	.487
Long Beach St.	1951	52	762	642	0	.543
Long Island	1929	68	1,012	703	2	.590
LSU	1909	94	1,243	954	0	.566
Louisiana Tech	1974	29	483	345	0	.583
La.-Lafayette	1912	86	1,158	858	0	.574
La.-Monroe	1952	51	794	578	0	.579
Louisville	1912	88	1,406	771	0	.646
Loyola (Ill.)	1914	84	1,067	896	1	.544
Loyola (Md.)	1909	91	1,059	1,015	0	.511
Loyola Marymount	1907	79	839	971	0	.464
Maine	1905	82	795	882	0	.474
Manhattan	1905	96	1,106	984	1	.529
Marist	1982	21	310	289	0	.518
Marquette	1917	85	1,263	808	0	.610
Marshall	1907	91	1,233	850	2	.592
Maryland	1924	79	1,185	812	0	.593
UMBC	1969	34	382	518	0	.424
Md.-East. Shore	1982	21	176	404	0	.303
Massachusetts	1902	92	1,017	902	0	.530
McNeese St.	1974	29	415	402	0	.508
Memphis	1921	81	1,165	760	0	.605
Mercer	1974	29	353	452	0	.439
Miami (Fla.)	1927	52	716	536	0	.572
Miami (Ohio)	1906	97	1,132	920	0	.552
Michigan	1909	86	1,238	829	0	.599
Michigan St.	1899	103	1,280	923	0	.581
Middle Tenn.	1914	79	901	858	0	.512
Minnesota	1896	107	1,306	989	4	.569
Mississippi	1909	92	991	1,078	0	.479
Mississippi St.	1909	90	1,096	966	0	.532
Mississippi Val.	1980	23	287	359	0	.444
Missouri	1907	96	1,325	925	0	.589
UMKC	1970	32	461	441	0	.511
Monmouth	1984	19	262	276	0	.487
Montana	1906	94	1,171	1,037	0	.530
Montana St.	1902	100	1,349	1,034	0	.566
Morehead St.	1930	73	893	852	0	.512
Morgan St.	1985	18	145	361	0	.287
Morris Brown	2002	1	4	25	0	.138
Mt. St. Mary's	1909	93	1,293	827	0	.610
Murray St.	1926	77	1,257	732	0	.632
Navy	1907	96	1,190	758	0	.611
Nebraska	1897	106	1,229	1,096	0	.529
Nevada	1913	89	982	991	0	.498
UNLV	1959	44	907	352	0	.720
New Hampshire	1903	98	735	1,169	0	.386
New Mexico	1900	99	1,179	919	0	.562
New Mexico St.	1905	93	1,173	891	2	.568
New Orleans	1970	33	587	354	0	.624
Niagara	1906	96	1,208	969	1	.555
Nicholls St.	1981	22	257	345	0	.427
Norfolk St.	1954	49	956	404	0	.703
North Carolina	1911	92	1,789	650	0	.733
N.C. A&T	1974	29	466	349	0	.572
North Carolina St.	1913	90	1,401	833	0	.627
UNC Asheville	1965	38	547	539	0	.504
UNC Greensboro	1968	35	401	481	0	.455
UNC Wilmington	1977	26	401	340	0	.541
North Texas	1917	84	888	1,061	0	.456
Northeastern	1921	81	914	877	0	.510
Northern Ariz.	1910	85	916	959	0	.489
Northern Ill.	1968	35	447	497	0	.474
Northern Iowa	1904	94	959	926	0	.509
Northwestern	1905	97	822	1,245	1	.398
Northwestern St.	1977	26	303	417	0	.421
Notre Dame	1898	97	1,505	828	1	.645
Oakland	1968	35	491	465	0	.514
Ohio	1908	95	1,213	915	0	.570
Ohio St.	1899	103	1,358	937	0	.592
Oklahoma	1908	95	1,337	873	0	.605
Oklahoma St.	1908	93	1,317	952	0	.580
Old Dominion	1966	37	659	427	0	.607

Team	First Season	Yrs.	Won	Lost	Tied	Pct.
Oral Roberts	1972	36	619	435	0	.587
Oregon	1903	97	1,292	1,149	0	.529
Oregon St.	1902	101	1,504	1,052	0	.588
Pacific (Cal.)	1911	92	998	1,020	0	.495
Penn St.	1897	106	1,228	888	1	.580
Pennsylvania	1897	102	1,533	870	2	.638
Pepperdine	1939	64	1,028	772	0	.571
Pittsburgh	1906	95	1,220	983	0	.554
Portland	1923	78	962	1,021	0	.485
Portland St.	1947	41	545	521	0	.511
Prairie View	1981	22	123	478	0	.205
Princeton	1901	102	1,459	885	0	.622
Providence	1927	75	1,158	740	0	.610
Purdue	1897	104	1,434	838	0	.631
Quinnipiac	1952	51	707	629	0	.529
Radford	1985	18	294	224	0	.568
Rhode Island	1907	94	1,196	889	0	.574
Rice	1917	86	846	1,100	0	.435
Richmond	1913	90	1,074	954	0	.530
Rider	1968	35	491	482	0	.505
Robert Morris	1977	26	318	412	0	.436
Rutgers	1907	90	1,018	916	0	.526
Sacramento St.	1949	54	592	824	0	.418
Sacred Heart	1966	37	632	418	0	.602
St. Bonaventure	1920	82	1,116	768	0	.592
St. Francis (N.Y.)	1902	83	995	984	0	.503
St. Francis (Pa.)	1946	57	744	718	1	.509
St. John's (N.Y.)	1908	95	1,641	750	0	.686
St. Joseph's	1910	93	1,330	890	0	.599
St. Louis	1916	86	1,127	960	0	.540
St. Mary's (Cal.)	1926	75	875	1,020	0	.462
St. Peter's	1931	69	866	784	0	.525
Sam Houston St.	1932	67	849	834	0	.504
Samford	1973	30	355	472	0	.429
San Diego	1956	47	655	611	0	.517
San Diego St.	1922	81	1,073	931	0	.535
San Francisco	1924	75	1,123	740	0	.603
San Jose St.	1910	88	996	1,021	0	.494
Santa Clara	1918	83	1,161	781	0	.598
Seton Hall	1904	90	1,203	845	2	.587
Siena	1939	61	842	694	0	.548
South Ala.	1969	34	549	404	0	.576
South Carolina	1909	94	1,131	997	1	.531
South Carolina St.	1958	45	716	512	0	.583
South Fla.	1972	31	435	441	0	.497
Southeast Mo. St.	1982	21	388	234	0	.624
Southeastern La.	1981	21	218	360	0	.377
Southern California	1907	96	1,336	943	0	.586
Southern Ill.	1968	35	552	448	0	.552
Southern Methodist	1917	86	1,044	975	0	.517
Southern Miss.	1913	83	976	818	1	.544
Southern U.	1978	25	420	292	0	.590
Southern Utah	1969	34	518	395	0	.567
Southwest Mo. St.	1909	90	1,373	740	0	.650
Southwest Tex. St.	1985	18	228	278	0	.451
Stanford	1914	87	1,190	937	0	.559
Stephen F. Austin	1925	76	1,123	765	0	.595
Stetson	1972	31	441	415	0	.515
Stony Brook	1961	42	537	474	0	.531
Syracuse	1901	101	1,572	732	0	.682
Temple	1895	106	1,590	858	0	.650
Tennessee	1909	93	1,299	841	2	.607
Tennessee St.	1978	25	304	382	0	.443
Tennessee Tech	1926	77	865	846	1	.506
Tenn.-Martin	1952	51	571	679	0	.457
Texas	1906	96	1,386	874	0	.613
Texas A&M	1913	90	1,085	1,058	0	.506
TCU	1914	89	970	1,082	0	.473
Texas Southern	1978	25	356	346	0	.507
Texas Tech	1926	77	1,118	850	0	.568
Texas-Arlington	1960	43	446	703	0	.388
UTEP	1947	56	930	589	0	.612
Tex.-Pan American	1969	34	422	491	0	.462
Texas-San Antonio	1982	21	324	271	0	.545
Toledo	1917	85	1,182	810	0	.593
Towson	1980	23	289	366	0	.441
Troy St.	1951	52	810	600	0	.574
Tulane	1913	83	946	949	0	.499
Tulsa	1908	91	1,140	923	0	.553
UCLA	1920	83	1,510	653	0	.698
Utah	1909	94	1,467	767	0	.657
Utah St.	1909	89	1,195	902	0	.570
Valparaiso	1918	85	1,039	998	0	.510
Vanderbilt	1901	100	1,285	928	0	.581
Vermont	1901	88	878	948	0	.481
Villanova	1921	82	1,346	772	0	.636
Virginia	1906	97	1,267	975	1	.565
Va. Commonwealth	1969	34	576	373	0	.607
VMI	1911	92	682	1,221	0	.358
Virginia Tech	1909	94	1,161	969	0	.545
Wagner	1977	26	308	412	0	.428
Wake Forest	1906	96	1,244	974	0	.561
Washington	1896	100	1,434	963	0	.598
Washington St.	1902	101	1,345	1,239	0	.521
Weber St.	1963	40	730	407	0	.642
West Virginia	1904	93	1,398	886	0	.612
Western Caro.	1977	26	320	404	0	.442
Western Ill.	1982	21	280	313	0	.472
Western Ky.	1915	83	1,442	714	0	.669
Western Mich.	1914	89	1,036	959	0	.519
Wichita St.	1906	95	1,174	1,034	0	.532
William & Mary	1906	97	996	1,116	0	.472
Winthrop	1979	24	364	353	0	.508
Wisconsin	1899	104	1,190	1,048	0	.532
Wis.-Green Bay	1974	29	502	344	0	.593
Wis.-Milwaukee	1897	105	1,068	1,016	0	.512
Wofford	1952	51	715	719	0	.499
Wright St.	1971	32	538	348	0	.607
Wyoming	1905	97	1,260	912	0	.580
Xavier	1920	81	1,086	825	0	.568
Yale	1896	107	1,204	1,253	0	.490
Youngstown St.	1928	72	910	830	0	.523

Winningest Teams by Decade

The 1930s

Rk.	Team	Won	Lost	Pct.
1.	Long Island	198	38	.839
2.	Kentucky	162	34	.827
3.	St. John's (N.Y.)	181	40	.819
4.	Kansas	153	37	.805
5.	Syracuse	143	37	.794
6.	Purdue	148	39	.791
7.	Western Ky.	197	52	.791
8.	Rhode Island	142	39	.785
9.	Notre Dame	170	49	.776
10.	CCNY	120	35	.774
11.	Washington	206	63	.766
12.	DePaul	142	44	.763
13.	Arkansas	167	57	.746
14.	Duquesne	143	50	.741
15.	Wyoming	147	52	.739
16.	Navy	108	40	.730
17.	North Carolina	163	61	.728
18.	George Washington	129	50	.721
19.	New York U.	124	49	.717
20.	Western Mich.	123	50	.711

The 1940s

Rk.	Team	Won	Lost	Pct.
1.	Kentucky	239	42	.851
2.	Oklahoma St.	237	55	.812
3.	Rhode Island	178	44	.802
4.	Eastern Ky.	145	40	.784
5.	Western Ky.	222	66	.771
6.	Tennessee	152	46	.768
7.	Bowling Green	204	66	.756
8.	Notre Dame	162	55	.747
9.	Toledo	176	65	.730
10.	St. John's (N.Y.)	162	60	.730
11.	North Carolina	196	75	.723
12.	West Virginia	157	59	.727
13.	Illinois	150	57	.725
14.	DePaul	180	69	.723
15.	Bradley	144	56	.720
16.	New York U.	150	60	.714
17.	Utah	159	68	.700
18.	Wyoming	163	70	.700
19.	Texas	168	73	.697
20.	CCNY	133	62	.682

Team	Won	Lost	Pct.
Played only seven seasons:			
Seton Hall	128	22	.853
Duquesne	118	32	.787
George Washington	117	47	.713

The 1950s

Rk.	Team	Won	Lost	Pct.
1.	Kentucky	224	33	.872
2.	North Carolina St.	240	65	.787
3.	Seattle	233	69	.772
4.	La Salle	209	65	.763
5.	Dayton	228	71	.763
6.	Holy Cross	199	65	.754
7.	Kansas St.	179	63	.740
8.	Connecticut	187	67	.736
9.	West Virginia	205	74	.735
10.	Louisville	202	77	.724
11.	Illinois	165	64	.721
12.	Western Ky.	205	82	.714
13.	UCLA	193	78	.712
14.	Duquesne	187	76	.711
15.	Kansas	171	74	.698
16.	St. John's (N.Y.)	176	77	.696
17.	Cincinnati	175	80	.686
18.	Oklahoma St.	192	88	.686
19.	Lafayette	171	81	.679
20.	St. Louis	185	88	.678

The 1960s

Rk.	Team	Won	Lost	Pct.
1.	UCLA	234	52	.818
2.	Cincinnati	214	63	.773
3.	Providence	204	64	.761
4.	Duke	213	67	.761
5.	Kentucky	197	69	.741
6.	Ohio St.	188	69	.732
7.	St. Joseph's	201	74	.731
8.	Dayton	207	77	.729
9.	Bradley	197	74	.727
10.	Princeton	188	71	.726
11.	Vanderbilt	182	69	.725
12.	North Carolina	184	72	.719
13.	St. Bonaventure	172	69	.714
14.	Villanova	193	79	.710
15.	Houston	198	82	.707
16.	St. John's (N.Y.)	185	79	.701
17.	Miami (Fla.)	183	82	.691
18.	West Virginia	197	89	.689
19.	Temple	183	83	.688
20.	UTEP	177	81	.686
Played only seven seasons:				
	Weber St.	147	36	.803

The 1970s

Rk.	Team	Won	Lost	Pct.
1.	UCLA	273	27	.910
2.	Marquette	251	41	.860
3.	Pennsylvania	223	56	.799
4.	North Carolina	239	65	.786
5.	Kentucky	223	69	.764
6.	Louisville	224	70	.762
7.	Syracuse	213	69	.755
8.	Long Beach St.	209	71	.746
9.	Indiana	208	75	.735
10.	Florida St.	201	74	.731
11.	UNLV	203	78	.722
12.	North Carolina St.	208	80	.722
13.	San Francisco	202	79	.719
14.	Houston	210	84	.714
15.	Providence	209	84	.713
16.	South Carolina	198	80	.712
17.	St. John's (N.Y.)	205	85	.707
18.	Maryland	199	85	.701
19.	Rutgers	193	84	.697
20.	Notre Dame	202	89	.694

Rk.	Team	Won	Lost	Pct.
	Played only eight seasons:			
	Oral Roberts	161	59	.732

The 1980s

Rk.	Team	Won	Lost	Pct.
1.	North Carolina	281	63	.817
2.	UNLV	271	65	.807
3.	Georgetown	269	69	.796
4.	DePaul	235	67	.778
5.	Temple	225	78	.743
6.	Syracuse	243	87	.736
7.	UTEP	227	82	.735
8.	Oklahoma	245	90	.731
9.	Kentucky	233	86	.730
10.	St. John's (N.Y.)	228	85	.728
11.	Indiana	228	86	.726
12.	Oregon St.	212	80	.726
13.	Louisville	250	96	.723
14.	Illinois	233	90	.721
15.	Memphis	225	89	.717
16.	Northeastern	213	86	.712
17.	Chattanooga	215	89	.707
18.	Arkansas	218	92	.703
19.	Missouri	227	99	.696
20.	West Virginia	217	95	.696

The 1990s

Rk.	Team	Won	Lost	Pct.
1.	Kansas	286	60	.827
2.	Kentucky	282	63	.817
3.	Arizona	256	67	.793
4.	Duke	271	78	.777
5.	North Carolina	270	78	.776
6.	Connecticut	259	75	.775
7.	Utah	250	76	.767
8.	Princeton	210	66	.761
9.	Arkansas	260	83	.758
10.	UCLA	240	79	.752
11.	Cincinnati	246	83	.748
12.	Xavier	217	86	.716
13.	Syracuse	232	92	.716
14.	Massachusetts	237	94	.716
15.	Murray St.	219	88	.713
16.	Indiana	229	94	.709
17.	New Mexico St.	219	91	.706
18.	Wis.-Green Bay	211	90	.701
19.	Purdue	222	96	.698
20.	New Mexico	224	97	.698
	Played only eight seasons:			
	Col. of Charleston	191	42	.820

The 2000s

Rk.	Team	Won	Lost	Pct.
1.	Duke	95	13	.880
2.	Cincinnati	85	18	.825
3.	Stanford	78	17	.821
4.	Oklahoma	84	19	.816
5.	Gonzaga	81	20	.802
6.	Kansas	83	21	.798
7.	Utah St.	79	20	.798
8.	Tulsa	85	23	.787
9.	Butler	73	22	.768
10.	Michigan St.	79	24	.767
11.	Maryland	82	25	.766
12.	Kent St.	77	24	.762
13.	Arizona	79	25	.760
14.	Florida	75	24	.758
15.	Col. of Charleston	67	22	.753
16.	Illinois	75	27	.735
17.	Oklahoma St.	70	26	.729
18.	Syracuse	74	28	.725
19.	Central Conn. St.	66	25	.725
20.	Hampton	68	26	.723

Winningest Teams Over Periods of Time

Victories Over a Two-Year Period

Team	First Year	Last Year	Won	Lost
Montana St.	1928	1929	72	4
Kentucky	1947	1948	70	6
UNLV	1986	1987	70	7
Kentucky	1997	1998	70	9
Georgetown	1984	1985	69	6
UNLV	1990	1991	69	6
Kansas	1997	1998	69	6
Duke	1998	1999	69	6
Kentucky	1996	1997	69	7
Kentucky	1948	1949	68	5
Connecticut	1998	1999	66	7
Duke	1999	2000	66	7
Duke	2001	2002	66	8
Montana St.	1927	1928	66	9
Duke	1991	1992	66	9
Oklahoma	1988	1989	65	10
Michigan St.	1999	2000	65	12
UNLV	1987	1988	65	8
Temple	1987	1988	64	6
Arizona	1988	1989	64	7
Massachusetts	1995	1996	64	7
Arkansas	1990	1991	64	9
Duke	2000	2001	64	9
Bradley	1950	1951	64	11
UNLV	1989	1990	64	13

Team	First Year	Last Year	Won	Lost
Montana St.	1927	1930	123	21
Duke	1989	1992	123	26
Georgetown	1984	1987	122	19
Duke	1997	2000	122	20
Montana St.	1926	1929	122	23
Kansas	1996	1999	121	21
Georgetown	1982	1985	121	23
Kentucky	1997	2000	121	28
Kentucky	1945	1948	120	12
Kentucky	1993	1996	119	18
Duke	1990	1993	119	26

Winning Percentage Over a Two-Year Period

(Minimum 40 games)

Team	First Year	Last Year	Won	Lost	Pct.
UCLA	1972	1973	60	0	1.000
Indiana	1975	1976	63	1	.984
UCLA	1967	1968	59	1	.983
UCLA	1971	1972	59	1	.983
North Carolina St.	1973	1974	57	1	.983
North Carolina	1923	1924	41	1	.976
UCLA	1964	1965	58	2	.967
UCLA	1968	1969	58	2	.967
Long Island	1935	1936	49	2	.961
St. John's (N.Y.)	1930	1931	46	2	.958
UNLV	1991	1992	60	3	.952
Seton Hall	1940	1941	39	2	.951
Arkansas	1928	1929	38	2	.950
Notre Dame	1926	1927	38	2	.950
UCLA	1969	1970	57	3	.950
UCLA	1970	1971	57	3	.950
Alcorn St.	1978	1979	56	3	.949
Montana St.	1928	1929	72	4	.947
Long Island	1936	1937	53	3	.946
Pennsylvania	1970	1971	53	3	.946
Ohio St.	1961	1962	53	3	.946
Long Island	1934	1935	50	3	.943
Kentucky	1954	1955	48	3	.941
St. John's (N.Y.)	1929	1930	46	3	.939
Pennsylvania	1920	1921	43	3	.935

Victories Over a Three-Year Period

Team	First Year	Last Year	Won	Lost
Kentucky	1996	1998	104	11
Kentucky	1947	1949	102	8
Montana St.	1927	1929	102	11
Duke	1999	2001	101	11
Kentucky	1946	1948	98	8
Kansas	1996	1998	98	11
Duke	1998	2000	98	11
UNLV	1985	1987	98	11
UNLV	1986	1988	98	13
UNLV	1989	1991	98	14
Kentucky	1997	1999	98	18
Kentucky	1995	1997	97	12
UNLV	1990	1992	95	8
Duke	2000	2002	95	13
Duke	1990	1992	95	18
UNLV	1987	1989	94	16
Kentucky	1948	1950	93	10
Montana St.	1928	1930	93	14
Georgetown	1984	1986	93	14
Duke	1997	1999	93	15
Michigan St.	1999	2001	93	17
Massachusetts	1994	1996	92	14
Oklahoma	1988	1990	92	15
Kansas	1997	1999	92	16
UNLV	1988	1990	92	19

Winning Percentage Over a Three-Year Period

(Minimum 60 games)

Team	First Year	Last Year	Won	Lost	Pct.
UCLA	1971	1973	89	1	.989
UCLA	1967	1969	88	2	.978
UCLA	1970	1972	87	3	.967
Long Island	1934	1936	75	3	.962
UCLA	1968	1970	86	4	.956
UCLA	1969	1971	86	4	.956
UCLA	1972	1974	86	4	.956
St. John's (N.Y.)	1929	1931	67	4	.944
Long Island	1935	1937	77	5	.939
Pennsylvania	1919	1921	58	4	.935
Indiana	1974	1976	86	6	.935
Ohio St.	1960	1962	78	6	.929
Pennsylvania	1970	1972	78	6	.929
Kentucky	1947	1949	102	8	.927
Kentucky	1946	1948	98	8	.925
Kentucky	1951	1953	61	5	.924
Cincinnati	1960	1962	84	7	.923
UCLA	1973	1975	84	7	.923
UNLV	1990	1992	95	8	.922
Pennsylvania	1970	1972	78	6	.929
Cincinnati	1961	1963	82	7	.921
North Carolina St.	1973	1975	79	7	.919
DePaul	1980	1982	79	7	.917
Arkansas	1926	1928	56	5	.918
Pennsylvania	1920	1922	67	6	.918
St. John's (N.Y.)	1930	1932	66	6	.917
Seton Hall	1940	1942	55	5	.917

Victories Over a Four-Year Period

Team	First Year	Last Year	Won	Lost
Duke	1998	2001	133	15
Duke	1999	2002	132	15
Kentucky	1995	1998	132	16
Kentucky	1996	1999	132	20
Kentucky	1946	1949	130	10
UNLV	1987	1990	129	21
Kentucky	1947	1950	127	13
UNLV	1984	1987	127	17
UNLV	1986	1989	127	21
UNLV	1985	1988	126	17
UNLV	1988	1991	126	20
Kentucky	1948	1951	125	12
UNLV	1989	1992	124	16
Kentucky	1994	1997	124	19
Kansas	1995	1998	123	17

Team	First Year	Last Year	Won	Lost	Pct.
Kentucky	1949	1951	89	9	.908
Marquette	1970	1972	79	8	.908
Kentucky	1996	1998	104	11	.904
Kentucky	1945	1947	84	9	.903

Team	First Year	Last Year	Won	Lost	Pct.
UCLA	1972	1975	114	7	.942
Kentucky	1946	1949	130	10	.929
Kentucky	1952	1955	77	6	.928
Pennsylvania	1918	1921	76	6	.927
Arkansas	1926	1929	75	6	.929
Long Island	1936	1939	99	8	.925
Cincinnati	1960	1963	110	9	.924
Pennsylvania	1919	1922	82	7	.921
St. John's (N.Y.)	1929	1932	89	8	.918
St. John's (N.Y.)	1928	1931	85	8	.914
UCLA	1964	1967	106	10	.914
UCLA	1966	1969	106	10	.914
Kentucky	1948	1951	125	12	.912
Long Island	1939	1942	92	9	.911
UCLA	1973	1976	112	11	.911
Long Island	1935	1938	100	10	.909
Kentucky	1945	1948	120	12	.909
Cincinnati	1959	1962	110	11	.909

Winning Percentage Over a Four-Year Period

(Minimum 80 games)

Team	First Year	Last Year	Won	Lost	Pct.
UCLA	1970	1973	117	3	.975
UCLA	1967	1970	116	4	.967
UCLA	1969	1972	116	4	.967
UCLA	1968	1971	115	5	.958
UCLA	1971	1974	115	5	.958
Kentucky	1951	1954	86	5	.945
Long Island	1934	1937	103	6	.945

Winning Streaks

Full Season

Wins	Team	Seasons	Ended By	Score
88	UCLA	1971-74	Notre Dame	71-70
60	San Francisco	1955-57	Illinois	62-33
47	UCLA	1966-68	Houston	71-69
45	UNLV	1990-91	Duke	79-77
44	Texas	1913-17	Rice	24-18
43	Seton Hall	1939-41	Long Island	49-26
43	Long Island	1935-37	Stanford	45-31
41	UCLA	1968-69	Southern California	46-44
39	Marquette	1970-71	Ohio St.	60-59
37	Cincinnati	1962-63	Wichita St.	65-64
37	North Carolina	1957-58	West Virginia	75-64
36	North Carolina St.	1974-75	Wake Forest	83-78
35	Arkansas	1927-29	Texas	26-25

Home Court

Wins	Team	Seasons	Ended By	Score
129	Kentucky	1943-55	Georgia Tech	59-58
99	St. Bonaventure	1948-61	Niagara	87-77
98	UCLA	1970-76	Oregon	65-45
86	Cincinnati	1957-64	Bradley	87-77
81	Arizona	1945-51	Kansas St.	76-57
81	Marquette	1967-73	Notre Dame	71-69
80	Lamar	1978-84	Louisiana Tech	68-65
75	Long Beach St.	1968-74	San Francisco	94-84
72	UNLV	1974-78	New Mexico	102-98
71	Arizona	1987-92	UCLA	89-87
68	Cincinnati	1972-78	Georgia Tech	59-56
67	Western Ky.	1949-55	Xavier	(ot) 82-80

Regular Season

(Does not include national postseason tournaments)

Wins	Team	Seasons	Ended By	Score
76	UCLA	1971-74	Notre Dame	71-70
57	Indiana	1975-77	Toledo	59-57
56	Marquette	1970-72	Detroit	70-49
54	Kentucky	1952-55	Georgia Tech	59-58
51	San Francisco	1955-57	Illinois	62-33
48	Pennsylvania	1970-72	Temple	57-52
47	Ohio St.	1960-62	Wisconsin	86-67
44	Texas	1913-17	Rice	24-18
43	UCLA	1966-68	Houston	71-69
43	Long Island	1935-37	Stanford	45-31
42	Seton Hall	1939-41	Long Island	49-26

Current Home Court

36	Brigham Young	16	La.-Monroe
29	Tennessee Tech	16	Marquette
26	Gonzaga	16	Oregon
23	McNeese St.	13	Kent St.
23	Western Ky.	12	Hawaii
22	Oklahoma	11	Valparaiso
20	Cincinnati	10	Central Conn. St.
19	Alabama	10	Vermont
18	Maryland	10	Xavier
16	Kansas		

Rivalries

Consecutive Years

Years	Opponents	First Year	Last Year
101	Columbia vs. Yale	1902	2002
101	Princeton vs. Yale	1902	2002
100	Pennsylvania vs. Princeton	1903	2002
99	Columbia vs. Pennsylvania	1904	2002
99	Cornell vs. Pennsylvania	1904	2002
98	Maine vs. New Hampshire	1905	2002
97	Idaho vs. Washington St.	1906	2002
96	Kansas vs. Kansas St.	1907	2002
96	Kansas vs. Missouri	1907	2002
95	Kansas St. vs. Nebraska	1908	2002

Games Played

Games	Opponents	First Year	Last Year
316	Oregon vs. Oregon St.	1903	2002
269	Oregon St. vs. Washington	1904	2002
269	Oregon vs. Washington	1904	2002
264	Oregon St. vs. Washington St.	1907	2002
259	Oregon vs. Washington St.	1908	2002
252	Washington vs. Washington St.	1910	2002
251	Kansas vs. Kansas St.	1907	2002
245	Kansas vs. Missouri	1907	2002
239	California vs. Stanford	1912	2002
230	Brigham Young vs. Utah	1909	2002

Victories for One Opponent

W-L	Opponents	First Year	Last Year
176-140	Oregon St. vs. Oregon	1903	2002
172- 96	Washington vs. Oregon	1904	2002
163- 88	Kansas vs. Kansas St.	1907	2002
162- 90	Washington vs. Washington St.	1910	2002
155- 90	Kansas vs. Missouri	1907	2002
155-109	Oregon St. vs. Washington St.	1909	2002
153- 56	Kansas vs. Iowa St.	1908	2002
151- 70	Kansas vs. Nebraska	1900	2002
150-106	Washington St. vs. Idaho	1906	2002
146- 59	North Carolina vs. Wake Forest	1911	2002

Consecutive Victories

Won	Opponents	First Year	Last Year
52	UCLA vs. California	1961	1985
41	Southern California vs. UCLA	1932	1943
39	Kentucky vs. Mississippi	1929	1972
39	Rhode Island vs. Maine	1924	1952
38	Providence vs. Brown	1959	1978
37	Syracuse vs. Cornell	1963	†2002
35	Connecticut vs. New Hampshire	1939	1961
35	South Carolina vs. Citadel	1945	1988
34	Marquette vs. Wis.-Milwaukee	1917	†1999
34	Arizona vs. Washington St.	1986	†2002

†active streak

Current Consecutive Victories

Won	Opponents	First Year	Last Year
37	Syracuse vs. Cornell	1963	2002
34	Marquette vs. Wis.-Milwaukee	1917	1999
34	Arizona vs. Washington St.	1986	2002
33	North Carolina vs. VMI	1922	1997
28	Kansas vs. Colorado	1991	2002
27	Syracuse vs. Cornell	1969	2002
26	Indiana vs. Northwestern	1988	2002
25	Kentucky vs. Xavier	1942	1968

Won	Opponents	First Year	Last Year
24	Kansas vs. Kansas St.	1994	2002
24	Ohio St. vs. Northwestern	1990	2002

Consecutive Home Victories

Won	Opponents	First Year	Last Year
52	Princeton vs. Brown	1929	†2002
48	North Carolina vs. Clemson	1926	†2002
46	UCLA vs. Washington St.	1950	†2002
41	Kentucky vs. Mississippi	1929	1996
37	Southern California vs. UCLA	1932	1944
34	Kentucky vs. Georgia	1930	1984
33	Rhode Island vs. Northeastern	1917	1988
32	Rhode Island vs. New Hampshire	1937	1973
32	UCLA vs. California	1961	1989
31	Marquette vs. Wis.-Milwaukee	1920	†1999
31	North Carolina vs. Virginia	1921	1972
31	Providence vs. Brown	1955	1978

†active streak

Current Consecutive Home Victories

Won	Opponents	First Year	Last Year
52	Princeton vs. Brown	1929	2002
48	North Carolina vs. Clemson	1926	2002
46	UCLA vs. Washington St.	1950	2002
31	Marquette vs. Wis.-Milwaukee	1920	1999
29	Indiana vs. Northwestern	1969	2002
28	Kentucky vs. Vanderbilt	1975	2002
20	Oklahoma St. vs. Drake	1931	1958

Victories for One Opponent in One Year

W-L	Opponents	Year
5-0	Kansas vs. Nebraska	1909
5-0	Kansas vs. Kansas St.	1935
4-0	by many	

A.P. Poll Records

Full Season At No. 1

1956, San Francisco, 14 weeks
1960, Cincinnati, 12 weeks
1961, Ohio St., 13 weeks
1962, Ohio St., 14 weeks
1963, Cincinnati, 16 weeks
1967, UCLA, 15 weeks
1969, UCLA, 15 weeks
1972, UCLA, 16 weeks
1973, UCLA, 16 weeks
1976, Indiana, 17 weeks
1991, UNLV, 17 weeks
1992, Duke, 18 weeks

Most Consecutive Weeks At No. 1

46, UCLA, Feb. 9, 1971 to Jan. 15, 1974
27, Ohio St., Dec. 13, 1960 to March 13, 1962
23, UCLA, Preseason Nov. 1966 to Jan. 16, 1968
19, San Francisco, Feb. 8, 1955 to March 6, 1956
18, Duke, Preseason Nov. 1991 to March 16, 1992
17, Indiana, Preseason Nov. 1975 to March 16, 1976
17, UNLV, Preseason Nov. 1990 to March 12, 1991
16, Cincinnati, Preseason Nov. 1962 to March 12, 1963
15, UCLA, Preseason Nov. 1968 to March 4, 1969
15, North Carolina, Dec. 6, 1983 to March 13, 1984
15, Kansas, Dec. 3, 1996 to March 11, 1997

Preseason No. 1 To Not Rank No. 1 The Rest of the Season

1970, South Carolina
1978, North Carolina
1981, Kentucky
1986, Georgia Tech
1988, Syracuse
1990, UNLV
2000, Connecticut

Biggest Jump To No. 1 From Previous Week

8th, West Virginia, Dec. 17 to Dec. 24, 1957
6th, Duke, Dec. 7 to Dec. 14, 1965
5th, Holy Cross, Jan. 10 to Jan. 17, 1950
5th, Kansas St., Dec. 23 to Dec. 30, 1952
5th, Indiana, Dec. 21 to Dec. 28, 1982
5th, UCLA, Jan. 11 to Jan. 18, 1983
5th, Temple, Feb. 2 to Feb. 9, 1988
5th, Oklahoma, Feb. 7 to Feb. 14, 1989
5th, Oklahoma, Feb. 27 to March 6, 1990
4th, 12 tied

Biggest Jump From Not Rated the Previous Week

(at least 20 rated)
4th, Kansas, Preseason to Nov. 27, 1989
5th, St. Louis, Dec. 26, 1950 to Jan. 3, 1951
5th, Cincinnati, Jan. 31 to Feb. 7, 1961
6th, Notre Dame, Jan. 12 to Jan. 19, 1954
6th, Missouri, Dec. 7 to Dec. 14, 1954
6th, Maryland, Dec. 10 to Dec. 17, 1957
6th, Oklahoma St., Jan. 21 to Jan. 28, 1958
7th, Bradley, Mar. 9 to Mar. 23, 1954
7th, Oklahoma City, Jan. 14 to Jan. 21, 1958
7th, Iowa, Dec. 27, 1960, to Jan. 3, 1961
7th, Wake Forest, Jan. 30 to Feb. 6, 1976
7th, North Carolina St., Preseason to Nov. 29, 1983

Biggest Jump From Not Rated the Previous Week

(at least 25 rated)
4th, Kansas, Preseason to Nov. 27, 1989
8th, Arizona, Preseason to Nov. 20, 2001
12th, Arizona St., Nov. 21 to Nov. 28, 1994
12th, Duke, Nov. 20 to Nov. 27, 1995
13th, Wake Forest, Jan. 25 to Feb. 1, 1993
13th, Oregon, Jan. 29 to Feb. 5, 2002
14th, Iowa, Jan. 9 to Jan. 16, 2001
14th, Pittsburgh, Feb. 5 to Feb. 12, 2002
15th, Minnesota, Nov. 21 to Nov. 28, 1994
15th, Ohio St., Jan. 19 to Jan. 26, 1999

Biggest Drop From No. 1 From Previous Week

9th, UNLV, Feb. 22 to Mar. 1, 1983
8th, UCLA, Dec. 7 to Dec. 14, 1965
8th, South Carolina, Preseason Nov. to Dec. 9, 1969
8th, Duke, Jan. 17 to Jan. 24, 1989
8th, Connecticut, Preseason Nov. to Nov. 16, 1999
7th, St. John (N.Y.), Dec. 18 to Dec. 26, 1951
7th, UCLA, Jan. 25 to Feb. 1, 1983
7th, Cincinnati, March 7 to March 14, 2000
6th, Michigan St., Jan. 9 to Jan. 16, 1979
6th, Memphis, Jan. 11 to Jan. 18, 1983
6th, UNLV, Preseason Nov. 1989 to Nov. 27, 1989
6th, Syracuse, Jan. 2 to Jan. 9, 1990
6th, Michigan, Nov. 30 to Dec. 7, 1992
6th, Kentucky, Nov. 29 to Dec. 6, 1993

Biggest Drop To Not Rated From The Previous Week

(at least 20 rated)
2nd, Louisville, Preseason to Dec. 2, 1986
4th, Indiana, Dec. 27, 1960, to Jan. 3, 1961
5th, Kansas, Dec. 8 to Dec. 15, 1953
6th, Iowa, Dec. 27, 1955, to Jan. 3, 1956
6th, Louisville, Preseason to Nov. 29, 1983
7th, Indiana, Dec. 14 to Dec. 21, 1954
7th, Missouri, Dec. 21 to Dec. 28, 1954
7th, Utah, Dec. 27, 1955, to Jan. 3, 1956
7th, Kansas, Dec. 9 to Dec. 16, 1958
7th, Duquesne, Dec. 9 to Dec. 16, 1969
7th, Ohio St., Dec. 16 to Dec. 23, 1980

Biggest Drop To Not Rated From The Previous Week

(at least 25 rated)
11th, Indiana, Dec. 21 to Dec. 28, 1994
15th, St. John's (N.Y.), Nov. 15 to Nov. 23, 1999
15th, UCLA, Nov. 21 to Nov. 28, 2000
15th, St. Joseph's, Dec. 18 to Dec. 25, 2001
16th, Oklahoma, Feb. 1 to Feb. 8, 1993
16th, Duke, Jan. 9 to Jan. 16, 1995
16th, Minnesota, Dec. 19 to Dec. 26, 1994
16th, Arkansas, Preseason to Nov. 20, 1995
16th, Temple, Dec. 8 to Dec. 15, 1998
17th, Eight tied

Lowest Ranking To Rise To No. 1 During The Season

(does not include 1962-69 when only 10 ranked)
NR, Indiana St., Dec. 5, 1978 to Feb. 13, 1979 (only 20 ranked)
20th, UNLV, Preseason Nov. 1982 to Feb. 15, 1983
19th, Indiana, Dec. 16, 1952 to March 3, 1953
19th, Houston, Jan. 4 to March 1, 1983
19th, Connecticut, Preseason Nov. 1994 to Feb. 13, 1995
18th, North Carolina, Jan. 4 to Feb. 1, 1983
18th, Duke, Nov. 16, 1999 to March 14, 2000
17th, San Francisco, Dec. 21, 1954 to Feb. 8, 1955
17th, Arizona, Preseason Nov. to Dec. 22, 1987
17th, Oklahoma, Nov. 27, 1989 to March 6, 1990
17th, UCLA, Jan. 24 to March 17, 1994

Lowest Ranking To Drop From No. 1 During The Season

(does not include 1962-69 when only 10 ranked)
NR, St. John's (N.Y.), Dec. 18, 1951 to Jan. 15, 1952 (only 20 ranked)
NR, Duke, Jan. 8 to Feb. 26, 1980 (only 20 ranked)
24th, Connecticut, Preseason Nov. 1999 to Feb, 29, 2000
21st, Arizona, Nov. 21, 2000 to Jan. 9, 2001
20th, Indiana, Dec. 11, 1979 to Feb. 5, 1980
17th, Memphis, Jan. 11 to March 1, 1983
17th, Syracuse, Preseason Nov. 1987 to Jan. 26, 1988
16th, North Carolina, Preseason Nov. 1977 to March 13, 1978
16th, North Carolina, Dec. 17, 1957 to Feb. 18, 1958
14th, Duke, Jan. 17 to Feb. 7, 1989
14th, UNLV, Preseason Nov. to Dec. 12, 1989
14th, UCLA, Nov. 22, 1993 to Jan. 24, 1994

Most Teams At No. 1 In One Season

7, 1983 (Houston, Indiana, Memphis, UNLV, North Carolina, UCLA and Virginia)
6, 1993 (Duke, Indiana, Kansas, Kentucky, Michigan and North Carolina)
6, 1994 (Arkansas, Duke, Kansas, Kentucky, North Carolina and UCLA)
6, 1995 (Arkansas, Connecticut, Kansas, Massachusetts, North Carolina and UCLA)
5, 1979 (Duke, Indiana, Michigan St., Notre Dame and UCLA)
5, 1990 (Kansas, Missouri, UNLV, Oklahoma and Syracuse)
5, 2001 (Arizona, Duke, Michigan St., North Carolina and Stanford)
4, eight tied

Most Consecutive Weeks With Different No. 1

7, Jan. 3 to Feb. 14, 1994 (in order: Arkansas, North Carolina, Kansas, UCLA, Duke, North Carolina and Arkansas)
5, Jan. 17 to Feb. 14, 1989 (in order: Duke, Illinois, Oklahoma, Arizona and Oklahoma)
5, Feb. 6 to March 6, 1990 (in order: Missouri, Kansas, Missouri, Kansas and Oklahoma)
5, Jan. 30 to Feb. 27, 1995 (in order: Massachusetts, North Carolina, Connecticut, Kansas and UCLA)
4, Dec. 11, 1951 to Jan. 2, 1952 (in order: Kentucky, St. John's (N.Y.), Kentucky and Kansas)
4, Feb. 17 to March 10, 1970 (in order: UCLA, Kentucky, UCLA and Kentucky)
4, Feb. 7 to Feb. 28, 1978 (in order: Kentucky, Arkansas, Marquette and Kentucky)
4, Feb. 6 to Feb. 27, 1979 (in order: Notre Dame, Indiana St., UCLA and Indiana St.)
4, Jan. 13 to Feb. 3, 1987 (in order: UNLV, Iowa, North Carolina and UNLV)

Most Weeks At No. 1 - All-Time

(Complete List)
128, UCLA, 1964-95
90, Duke, 1966-2002
84, North Carolina, 1957-2001
79, Kentucky, 1949-96
45, Cincinnati, 1959-2000
44, Indiana, 1953-93
39, Kansas, 1952-2002
32, UNLV, 1983-91
28, San Francisco, 1955-77
27, Ohio St., 1961-62
21, Michigan, 1965-93
16, Arizona, 1988-2001
16, Kansas St., 1952-59
15, DePaul, 1980-81
15, Massachusetts, 1995-96
13, North Carolina St., 1975

12, Arkansas, 1978-95
12, Connecticut, 1995-2000
12, Georgetown, 1985
12, Stanford, 2000-01
12, Virginia, 1981-83
11, Houston, 1968-83
8, St. John's (N.Y.), 1950-85
8, West Virginia, 1958
7, Syracuse, 1988-90
6, Missouri, 1982-90
6, Seton Hall, 1953
6, Temple, 1988
5, Bradley, 1950-51
5, Holy Cross, 1974-79
5, Notre Dame, 1974-79
5, Oklahoma, 1989-90

5, Oregon St., 1981
4, Indiana St., 1979
4, La Salle, 1953-55
4, Loyola (Ill.), 1964
4, Michigan St., 1979-2001
3, Marquette, 1971-78
2, Duquesne, 1954
2, Illinois, 1952-89
2, St. Louis, 1949
1, Georgia Tech, 1986
1, Iowa, 1987
1, Memphis, 1983
1, Oklahoma St., 1951
1, South Carolina, 1970
1, Wichita St., 1965

Week-by-Week A.P. Polls

REGULAR-SEASON POLLS

The Associated Press began its basketball poll on January 20, 1949. The following are those polls, year by year and week by week. Starting in the 1961-62 season, A.P. provided a preseason (PS) poll. A.P. did a post-tournament poll in 1953, 1954, 1974 and 1975.

1948-49

	January 18	25	February 1	8	15	22	March 1	8
Arkansas	-	-	-	-	-	-	20	-
Baylor	-	18	-	-	-	-	-	-
Bowling Green	15	-	14	14	10	9	9	10
Bradley	16	19	18	-	12	10	10	7
Butler	19	17	16	16	11	11	11	18
Cincinnati	13	-	-	-	-	-	-	-
DePaul	-	16	-	-	17	-	-	-
Duquesne	-	-	-	20	20	17	-	-
Eastern Ky.	-	-	20	-	-	-	-	-
Hamline	8	7	8	5	9	15	16	19
Holy Cross	14	20	19	15	-	-	-	-
Illinois	7	6	4	4	4	4	4	4
Kentucky	2	2	1	1	1	1	1	1
Loyola (Ill.)	12	13	13	11	13	12	14	16
Minnesota	4	5	5	7	6	5	5	6
North Carolina St.	-	15	17	-	18	-	15	13
New York U.	20	-	15	-	-	-	-	-
Ohio St.	-	-	-	18	-	18	19	20
Oklahoma	-	-	-	-	16	-	-	-
Oklahoma St.	5	3	3	3	3	3	2	2
San Francisco	6	9	10	9	8	8	8	8
Southern California	-	-	-	-	-	19	-	-
St. Louis	1	1	2	2	2	2	3	3
Stanford	17	11	9	10	20	-	-	-
Texas	-	-	-	-	-	20	-	-
Tulane	11	12	11	8	5	6	7	9
UCLA	-	-	-	-	-	-	-	15
Utah	10	10	12	12	14	16	13	12
Villanova	9	8	7	13	15	-	17	14
Western Ky.	3	4	6	6	7	7	6	5
Washington St.	18	14	-	17	-	-	-	-
Wyoming	-	-	-	19	19	14	12	17
Yale	-	-	-	-	20	13	18	11

1949-50

	January 5	10	17	24	31	February 7	14	21	28	March 7
Arizona	-	-	-	-	-	18	17	19	15	15
Bowling Green	19	-	-	-	-	-	-	-	-	-
Bradley	3	6	4	6	3	2	2	1	1	1
CCNY	14	7	7	8	10	14	13	20	-	-
Cincinnati	-	12	20	-	-	-	-	-	-	-
Duquesne	8	8	6	2	2	3	7	4	5	6
Hamline	-	-	-	-	-	20	-	-	-	-
Holy Cross	6	5	1	1	1	1	1	1	2	4
Illinois	16	-	-	20	-	-	-	-	-	-
Indiana	5	4	8	9	12	16	-	17	-	20
Kansas	-	-	-	-	-	-	-	-	-	19
Kansas St.	20	-	13	12	11	10	14	13	12	14
Kentucky	2	2	5	4	6	7	5	5	4	3
La Salle	18	13	10	7	8	9	11	12	9	10

1950-51

	December 19	26	3	January 9	16	23	30	F	February 13	20	27	March 7
Long Island	4	3	3	3	4	6	6	10	14			13
Louisville	-	-	19	-	15	13	-	-	-	-		
Minnesota	10	11	16	18	-	-	-	-	-	-		
Missouri	12	16	-	-	-	-	-	-	-	-		
Nebraska	-	-	-	-	-	-	-	-	16	-		
North Carolina St.	7	9	12	10	9	8	8	9	8			5
Notre Dame	-	-	-	-	16	-	-	-	-	-		
Ohio St.	-	15	11	13	7	4	3	3	2			2
Oklahoma	17	19	-	-	-	-	-	-	-	-		
Oklahoma St.	-	-	-	19	-	-	-	-	-	-		
St. John's (N.Y.)	1	1	2	5	5	4	4	6	10			9
St. Louis	11	-	-	-	-	19	18	15	-	-		
San Francisco	-	-	-	-	-	15	12	11	13			12
San Jose St.	-	-	-	-	-	-	-	18	19			17
Siena	-	18	-	-	-	-	-	-	-	-		
Southern California	-	-	-	-	-	-	19	16	-			
Tennessee	-	-	17	-	-	-	-	-	-	-		
Toledo	-	-	-	-	-	-	-	14	17			
Tulane	-	-	15	-	-	-	-	-	-	-		
UCLA	9	10	9	11	13	12	10	7	6			7
Vanderbilt	-	-	-	-	18	-	20	-	20			
Villanova	13	17	18	19	-	15	-	11	-			11
Washington	-	20	16	-	-	-	-	-	-	-		
Washington St.	-	-	-	-	-	17	16	-	-			18
Western Ky.	-	14	14	17	14	11	9	8	7			8
Wisconsin	15	-	-	15	-	17	-	-	-	-		16
Wyoming	-	-	14	-	20	-	-	18	-			

	December 19	26	3	January 9	16	23	30	F	February 13	20	27	March 7
Arizona	-	-	16	-	-	14	15	13	16	11	12	12
Beloit	-	-	-	-	-	-	-	-	18	20	16	-
Bradley	2	2	1	1	3	4	5	5	8	7	5	6
Brigham Young	15	-	-	19	12	14	12	12	11	11	11	
CCNY	6	11	-	-	-	-	-	-	-	-	-	-
Cincinnati	17	17	17	-	16	15	16	11	15	18	-	17
Columbia	-	8	14	8	7	7	6	6	4	3	3	3
Cornell	19	18	14	-	-	-	-	-	-	-	-	-
Dayton	-	-	-	-	-	-	-	18	17	14	14	13
Duquesne	-	-	13	15	20	-	-	-	-	-	-	-
Illinois	-	20	-	14	14	16	14	16	11	10	6	5
Indiana	4	5	6	6	5	3	3	4	4	7	7	
Kansas	11	10	20	17	-	17	20	-	-	-	-	
Kansas St.	20	-	9	9	10	9	7	4	3	5	4	4
Kentucky	1	1	3	3	2	1	1	1	1	1	1	1
La Salle	-	16	-	19	-	17	-	-	-	-	-	-
Long Island	7	4	4	4	4	2	4	12	19	16	-	-
Louisville	-	-	-	-	-	-	-	17	14	-	-	
Missouri	8	9	-	-	-	-	-	-	-	-	-	-
Murray St.	-	-	-	-	-	-	-	-	-	20	16	
North Carolina St.	3	6	7	7	9	8	10	9	9	8	8	
Notre Dame	14	-	-	-	-	-	-	-	-	-	-	
Oklahoma	16	-	-	-	18	18	-	17	-	-	-	
Oklahoma St.	5	3	2	2	1	3	2	2	2	2	2	2
Princeton	-	18	20	-	-	-	-	-	-	-	-	
St. Bonaventure	-	-	-	17	-	-	-	-	-	-	-	
St. John's (N.Y.)	13	12	11	11	5	6	9	7	7	8	9	9

	December		January					February				March
	19	26	3	9	16	23	30	F	13	20	27	7
St. Louis	-	-	5	5	8	10	10	8	5	6	10	10
Seattle	-	-	-	-	-	-	-	-	20	-	-	-
Siena	-	-	-	-	18	13	-	19	-	-	-	18
Southern California	-	-	-	13	19	12	13	15	13	13	18	19
Toledo	10	13	19	18	12	-	20	-	-	-	13	14
UCLA	9	-	-	-	-	-	19	-	-	-	17	-
Villanova	18	7	8	16	11	11	11	9	10	15	15	20
Washington	12	15	12	12	15	-	-	-	-	19	19	15
West Virginia	-	19	-	-	-	-	-	-	-	-	-	-
Wyoming	-	14	10	10	13	20	-	-	-	-	-	-

1951-52

	December			January					February				March
	11	18	26	2	8	15	22	29	5	12	19	26	4
Dayton	-	-	-	-	20	19	16	14	11	11	11	11	11
DePaul	-	-	-	-	-	-	-	19	-	18	-	-	-
Duke	12	19	-	-	-	-	-	-	-	-	-	15	12
Duquesne	-	-	-	-	16	7	10	7	5	3	3	4	4
Eastern Ky.	19	-	-	-	-	-	-	-	-	-	-	-	-
Fordham	-	-	-	-	-	-	-	20	-	-	-	-	-
Holy Cross	-	17	-	-	-	20	11	17	-	19	17	17	13
Illinois	3	3	2	2	2	2	1	3	3	6	5	2	2
Indiana	11	6	5	5	4	14	20	13	18	20	-	-	-
Iowa	-	-	-	12	10	4	4	8	9	5	4	7	7
Kansas	8	7	4	1	1	1	2	4	6	9	7	8	8
Kansas St.	5	5	8	9	7	9	7	2	2	2	2	3	3
Kentucky	1	2	1	4	3	3	3	1	1	1	1	1	1
La Salle	9	12	17	13	-	15	18	-	19	-	20	-	-
Louisville	17	-	-	-	15	13	14	12	13	15	15	13	17
Michigan St.	-	-	-	20	19	-	-	-	-	-	-	-	-
Minnesota	-	15	-	-	-	-	-	-	-	-	-	-	-
Murray St.	-	-	18	16	-	-	-	-	-	-	-	-	-
North Carolina St.	10	9	19	17	-	17	-	-	-	-	-	-	-
Notre Dame	14	20	9	14	-	-	-	-	-	-	-	-	-
New York U.	20	11	6	6	13	-	-	-	-	-	-	-	-
Oklahoma St.	13	13	-	-	-	-	-	-	16	-	-	-	-
Oklahoma City	-	-	-	15	18	18	-	16	15	13	-	-	-
Penn St.	-	-	-	-	-	-	-	-	14	17	13	-	-
St. Bonaventure	-	-	-	10	8	6	5	5	4	4	10	12	15
St. John's (N.Y.)	2	1	7	8	12	-	15	15	10	10	8	9	10
St. Louis	4	4	12	7	5	5	8	6	7	7	9	5	5
Seattle	-	-	-	-	-	-	-	-	-	-	16	-	18
Seton Hall	7	10	10	11	9	12	13	11	17	12	14	14	14
Siena	-	-	-	-	17	11	19	18	-	16	18	20	-
Stanford	16	-	13	-	-	-	-	-	-	-	-	-	-
Southwest Tex. St.	-	-	-	-	-	-	-	-	-	-	-	-	20
Syracuse	-	-	20	19	14	-	-	-	-	-	-	-	-
TCU	-	-	-	-	-	15	12	-	-	-	-	-	-
UCLA	-	-	16	-	-	-	-	-	-	-	-	-	19
Utah	-	-	15	18	-	-	17	-	-	-	-	-	-
Vanderbilt	18	-	-	-	-	-	-	-	-	-	-	-	-
Villanova	15	18	14	-	-	-	-	-	-	-	-	19	-
Washington	6	8	3	3	6	8	6	9	8	8	6	6	6
West Virginia	-	-	-	-	11	10	9	10	12	14	12	10	9
Western Ky.	-	16	11	-	-	-	-	-	20	-	-	18	-
Wyoming	-	14	-	-	-	-	-	-	-	-	19	16	16

1952-53

	December			January				February				March		
	16	23	30	6	13	20	27	3	10	17	24	3	10	24
California	18	-	-	20	-	14	-	14	19	19	-	-	-	-
Colorado	-	18	-	-	-	-	-	-	-	-	-	-	-	-
DePaul	-	-	14	-	-	-	10	7	7	14	15	-	-	19
Duke	-	-	-	-	-	-	-	-	-	18	-	-	-	-
Duquesne	-	-	-	-	-	-	-	-	-	-	19	18	11	9
Eastern Ky.	-	-	-	-	-	18	15	-	-	-	20	17	-	-
Fordham	-	-	-	8	7	10	7	13	16	-	-	-	-	-
Georgetown	-	-	-	-	20	-	-	-	-	-	-	-	-	-
Holy Cross	8	4	6	14	17	-	-	17	-	-	-	20	-	13
Idaho	-	20	-	18	-	-	-	-	-	-	-	-	-	-
Illinois	3	2	4	4	4	6	6	6	5	5	10	10	13	11
Indiana	19	15	12	7	6	2	2	2	2	2	2	1	1	1
Kansas	20	-	-	-	15	9	14	18	14	10	5	6	5	3
Kansas St.	2	5	1	1	1	4	5	5	10	8	9	8	8	12
La Salle	1	1	3	3	3	5	4	4	4	4	4	2	3	6
LSU	10	8	17	11	14	14	11	10	8	6	6	5	7	5
Louisville	-	-	-	-	-	-	-	-	17	16	18	14	14	-
Manhattan	-	-	-	-	-	20	19	19	15	13	16	-	20	-
Miami (Ohio)	-	-	-	-	-	-	-	-	-	-	12	16	-	-
Minnesota	16	17	9	19	-	19	-	-	-	-	-	-	-	-
Murray St.	-	-	-	-	-	-	-	-	-	17	-	-	-	-
Navy	20	13	-	15	-	-	16	-	-	-	-	18	19	-
Niagara	-	-	-	-	-	-	-	20	17	-	-	-	-	-
North Carolina	-	-	-	-	-	-	18	12	-	-	-	-	-	-
North Carolina St.	6	6	11	9	8	8	12	15	12	15	13	12	18	18
Notre Dame	7	11	19	13	11	16	17	-	-	-	17	13	17	10
Oklahoma St.	5	9	7	5	9	7	8	9	6	7	7	7	6	8
Oklahoma City	13	19	16	-	18	17	-	16	13	12	11	11	10	-
St. Bonaventure	14	12	15	-	-	-	-	-	-	-	-	-	-	-
St. John's (N.Y.)	-	-	-	-	-	-	-	-	-	-	-	-	20	7
St. Louis	17	-	-	-	-	-	-	-	-	-	-	-	-	-
Santa Clara	-	-	-	-	-	-	-	-	-	-	-	-	-	16
Seattle	-	15	13	16	16	13	13	11	11	11	14	15	14	14
Seton Hall	4	3	2	2	2	1	1	1	1	1	1	3	4	2
Southern California	-	-	-	12	12	-	-	-	-	-	-	-	-	-
Southwest Mo. St.	-	-	-	-	-	-	-	-	-	-	-	-	-	20
Toledo	-	-	18	-	-	-	-	-	-	-	-	-	-	-
Tulsa	15	14	8	17	13	11	20	-	19	-	-	-	-	-
UCLA	12	20	-	-	19	-	-	-	-	-	-	-	-	-
Villanova	-	-	-	-	-	-	-	-	-	19	-	-	-	-
Wake Forest	-	-	-	-	-	-	-	-	-	-	-	-	12	15
Washington	9	7	5	6	5	3	3	3	3	3	3	4	2	4
Wayne St. (Mich.)	-	-	20	-	-	-	-	-	-	-	-	-	-	-
Western Ky.	11	10	10	10	10	12	9	8	9	9	8	9	9	17
Wyoming	-	-	-	-	-	-	-	-	-	-	-	-	16	-

1953-54

	December				January				February				March		
	8	15	22	29	5	12	19	26	2	9	16	23	2	9	23
Bradley	-	-	-	-	-	-	-	-	18	-	-	-	-	-	7
Brigham Young	-	-	-	19	-	-	-	-	-	-	-	-	-	-	-
California	17	15	-	-	-	-	15	14	15	14	-	-	-	-	-
Colorado A&M	-	-	-	-	-	18	-	-	-	-	19	18	-	19	-
Connecticut	-	-	-	-	-	-	-	18	-	-	-	-	19	-	-
Dayton	15	-	16	-	14	17	-	18	-	-	17	16	14	15	-
Duke	-	13	-	-	8	9	13	20	8	15	14	10	11	18	15
Duquesne	3	3	3	2	2	2	2	2	2	2	1	1	4	3	5
Fordham	-	9	7	10	-	-	-	-	-	-	-	-	-	-	-
George Washington	-	-	-	-	12	7	10	10	11	10	8	8	9	7	12
Holy Cross	19	14	10	12	7	6	8	7	10	9	9	7	13	9	3
Idaho	-	-	20	17	-	20	-	-	-	-	-	-	-	-	-
Illinois	9	4	4	8	15	19	20	-	-	-	-	20	-	-	19
Indiana	1	1	1	3	3	3	3	3	3	3	3	3	2	2	4
Iowa	-	-	-	-	-	-	-	-	-	-	10	20	16	16	13
Kansas	5	-	-	-	16	11	17	17	19	20	-	17	15	13	18
Kansas St.	8	-	-	-	-	-	-	-	-	-	-	-	-	-	-
Kentucky	2	2	2	1	1	1	1	1	1	1	2	2	1	1	1
La Salle	6	20	16	13	-	-	19	12	9	7	12	13	8	12	2
LSU	10	5	14	18	-	16	12	14	17	17	13	12	7	8	14
Louisville	-	-	-	-	-	-	-	-	20	-	-	-	20	-	-
Maryland	-	-	-	-	-	-	14	13	13	11	11	11	17	14	20
Minnesota	12	6	8	6	6	10	9	8	12	12	18	-	-	-	-
Navy	-	-	-	-	18	-	-	-	-	16	20	-	-	-	-
Niagara	-	18	-	-	12	13	18	-	-	-	-	-	-	-	16
North Carolina St.	7	8	9	9	20	-	-	-	-	19	-	-	18	10	-
Notre Dame	-	16	19	-	-	-	6	6	7	6	6	6	5	6	6
Oklahoma St.	4	7	5	5	4	4	5	4	5	4	5	5	6	5	10
Oklahoma City	19	12	15	11	9	8	7	9	16	13	16	15	-	-	-
Oregon St.	13	11	12	4	10	-	-	-	-	-	-	-	-	16	-
Penn St.	-	-	-	-	-	-	-	-	-	-	-	-	-	-	9
Rice	-	-	11	16	11	15	-	-	-	-	-	-	-	-	-
St. Louis	18	-	-	-	-	-	-	-	-	-	-	-	-	-	-
Santa Clara	16	-	-	-	-	-	-	-	-	-	-	-	-	-	-
Seattle	-	-	-	15	16	14	16	11	6	8	7	9	10	11	17
Siena	-	19	-	-	-	-	-	-	-	-	-	-	-	-	-
Southern California	-	-	-	-	-	-	-	-	-	-	-	-	-	-	11
UCLA	-	17	13	14	-	-	-	-	-	-	-	19	-	-	-
Vanderbilt	-	-	20	20	19	-	-	-	-	-	-	-	-	-	-
Western Ky.	11	10	6	7	5	5	4	4	4	5	4	4	3	4	8
Wichita St.	-	-	-	-	-	11	11	16	14	18	15	14	12	20	-
Wisconsin	-	-	18	-	-	-	-	-	-	-	-	-	-	-	-
Wyoming	14	-	-	20	-	-	-	-	-	-	-	-	-	-	-

1954-55

	December				January				February				March	
	7	14	21	28	4	11	18	25	1	8	15	22	1	8
Alabama	-	-	19	12	20	16	12	14	13	13	17	12	11	12
Auburn	-	-	-	-	-	20	-	-	-	-	-	-	-	-
Cincinnati	-	-	-	-	-	-	-	-	-	17	12	17	-	-
Colorado	-	-	-	-	-	-	-	-	-	-	-	-	-	15
Dayton	7	5	6	4	10	12	18	15	15	16	13	11	10	9
Duke	17	-	-	18	17	-	-	-	-	-	-	-	-	-
Duquesne	3	9	9	8	2	3	5	4	4	4	4	4	8	6
George Washington	-	11	8	9	6	8	9	6	7	6	5	10	13	14
Holy Cross	5	19	-	-	-	-	16	13	14	-	-	-	-	-
Illinois	14	3	3	6	12	7	7	10	10	10	14	13	17	18
Indiana	6	7	-	-	-	-	-	-	-	-	-	-	-	-
Iowa	4	13	20	19	14	19	19	19	-	15	15	16	12	5
Kansas	-	-	20	16	-	-	-	-	-	-	-	-	-	-
Kentucky	2	2	1	1	1	1	1	1	1	2	2	2	2	2

1954-55

Team	Dec 7	14	21	28	Jan 4	11	18	25	Feb 1	8	15	22	Mar 1	8
La Salle	1	1	4	3	4	4	4	5	3	3	3	3	3	3
Louisville	-	12	14	13	16	20	-	-	-	-	-	-	-	-
Marquette	-	-	-	-	-	-	15	11	9	9	6	5	4	8
Maryland	-	-	-	-	11	11	6	8	12	11	11	17	18	-
Memphis	-	-	-	-	-	-	-	-	-	-	-	15	19	-
Minnesota	-	-	-	11	13	14	14	-	11	12	8	7	6	11
Missouri	-	6	7	-	9	6	8	12	17	14	-	20	20	-
Niagara	8	10	10	10	15	15	20	20	16	-	-	-	-	-
North Carolina St.	10	4	5	2	3	2	2	3	6	7	7	6	5	4
Northwestern	-	-	-	-	-	-	-	16	-	-	-	-	-	-
Notre Dame	9	20	-	-	20	-	-	-	-	-	-	-	-	-
Ohio St.	-	14	11	20	-	-	-	-	-	-	-	-	-	-
Oklahoma St.	11	-	-	-	-	-	-	-	-	-	-	-	-	-
Oregon St.	-	-	-	-	-	-	-	-	19	18	16	-	14	10
Penn St.	19	-	-	-	-	-	-	-	-	-	-	-	-	-
Pennsylvania	-	-	16	17	19	-	-	-	-	-	-	-	-	-
Purdue	-	-	-	-	-	17	-	-	-	-	-	-	-	-
Richmond	-	-	-	-	-	13	13	17	-	-	-	-	-	-
St. John's (N.Y.)	-	16	-	-	-	-	-	-	-	-	-	-	-	-
St. Louis	12	-	-	-	-	-	-	-	-	-	-	-	-	20
San Francisco	-	-	17	5	5	5	3	2	2	1	1	1	1	1
Seton Hall	-	-	-	-	-	20	-	-	-	-	-	-	-	-
Southern California	-	-	13	14	-	18	-	-	-	-	-	-	-	-
Tennessee	-	-	-	-	-	-	-	-	-	-	-	18	-	-
TCU	-	-	-	-	-	-	20	-	-	-	-	-	-	-
Tulsa	-	-	-	-	-	-	-	-	-	-	19	19	15	16
UCLA	13	8	17	15	7	10	10	9	8	8	9	9	9	13
Utah	16	15	2	7	8	9	10	7	5	5	10	8	7	7
Vanderbilt	-	-	-	-	-	-	17	18	20	20	20	14	16	17
Villanova	-	-	-	-	-	17	-	-	17	19	-	-	-	-
Wake Forest	17	17	-	-	-	-	-	-	-	-	-	-	-	-
West Virginia	-	-	12	-	-	-	-	-	-	-	-	-	-	19
Western Ky.	20	-	-	-	-	-	-	-	-	-	-	-	-	-
Wichita St.	15	17	14	-	-	-	-	-	-	-	-	-	-	-

1955-56

Team	Dec 6	13	20	27	Jan 3	10	17	24	31	Feb 7	14	21	28	Mar 6
Alabama	6	5	16	19	17	19	13	12	12	10	8	7	4	4
Brigham Young	10	8	5	20	-	-	-	-	-	-	-	-	-	-
Cincinnati	-	14	-	-	20	-	-	14	-	20	-	-	-	-
Dayton	7	7	4	2	3	2	2	2	2	2	2	4	3	3
Duke	-	-	14	8	11	6	7	10	10	8	11	11	11	19
Duquesne	9	6	20	-	-	-	-	-	-	-	-	-	-	-
George Washington	13	13	11	12	7	14	-	-	-	19	-	19	-	-
Holy Cross	11	10	7	14	14	11	12	11	14	13	16	17	15	12
Houston	-	-	-	-	-	-	-	-	-	-	18	14	18	17
Illinois	8	-	17	9	9	8	6	5	6	6	3	2	2	7
Indiana	-	19	18	-	13	12	-	-	-	-	-	-	-	-
Iowa	4	4	10	6	-	-	20	13	19	17	15	13	10	5
Iowa St.	-	-	-	-	8	15	-	-	-	-	-	20	-	-
Kansas	-	18	-	-	-	-	-	-	-	-	-	-	-	-
Kansas St.	-	-	-	-	-	-	-	-	-	-	-	-	17	-
Kentucky	2	12	9	13	6	5	4	3	8	7	7	8	12	9
La Salle	18	-	-	-	-	-	-	-	-	-	-	-	-	-
Louisville	-	-	-	11	-	13	10	9	5	5	4	3	6	6
Marquette	14	-	13	-	-	-	-	-	-	-	-	-	-	-
Marshall	-	-	-	-	-	-	-	-	18	-	-	-	-	-
Memphis	-	-	18	-	12	17	15	19	16	-	19	-	-	-
Michigan St.	-	-	-	16	20	-	-	-	-	-	-	-	-	-
Minnesota	20	-	-	-	-	-	-	-	-	-	-	-	-	-
North Carolina	-	16	6	4	5	9	9	8	9	12	10	9	8	15
North Carolina St.	3	2	2	3	2	3	3	4	4	4	5	6	5	2
Ohio St.	16	-	-	15	10	7	11	-	-	-	-	-	-	-
Oklahoma St.	-	-	-	-	-	20	-	20	-	-	-	-	-	-
Oklahoma City	12	20	15	10	-	16	14	16	15	14	14	18	16	16
Rice	-	-	-	17	18	-	-	-	-	-	-	-	-	-
St. Francis (N.Y.)	-	-	-	-	-	-	-	15	13	16	13	16	-	-
St. Louis	-	17	-	-	-	-	17	17	11	11	17	-	19	-
San Francisco	1	1	1	1	1	1	1	1	1	1	1	1	1	1
Southern Methodist	-	-	-	-	-	-	19	18	17	15	12	12	9	8
Stanford	19	-	-	-	-	-	-	-	-	-	-	-	-	-
Temple	-	11	12	17	16	10	8	6	7	9	9	10	14	13
Tulsa	-	-	-	-	15	-	-	-	-	-	-	-	-	-
UCLA	16	-	-	-	-	-	-	18	-	18	20	15	13	10
Utah	5	3	3	7	-	20	16	-	-	-	-	-	-	20
Vanderbilt	-	9	8	5	4	4	5	7	3	3	6	5	7	11
Wake Forest	-	-	-	-	-	-	-	18	-	-	-	-	20	18
West Virginia	14	15	-	-	-	19	-	-	-	-	-	-	-	14

1956-57

Team	Dec 11	18	26	Jan 2	8	15	22	29	Feb 5	12	19	26	Mar 5	12
Alabama	9	17	-	-	-	-	-	-	-	-	-	-	-	-
Bradley	-	-	-	-	-	12	10	10	8	5	5	7	13	19
California	-	-	-	-	-	19	19	15	19	12	15	-	14	13
Canisius	10	18	17	15	14	14	14	12	14	14	-	-	-	20
Dayton	15	-	-	-	-	-	-	-	-	-	-	-	-	-
Duke	-	13	9	-	15	16	15	19	-	17	16	-	-	-
Idaho St.	-	-	20	-	-	-	17	-	20	-	-	15	15	16
Illinois	7	5	6	5	10	8	9	7	15	16	-	-	-	-
Indiana	-	-	-	-	-	-	-	-	18	11	10	-	-	-
Iowa St.	17	14	14	7	7	9	3	8	9	9	9	16	17	-
Kansas	1	1	1	1	1	1	2	2	2	2	2	2	2	2
Kansas St.	14	10	-	-	-	-	-	-	-	17	12	-	-	-
Kentucky	3	7	3	3	3	4	5	4	3	3	3	3	3	3
Louisville	4	6	8	6	5	5	4	3	6	8	7	8	6	6
Manhattan	-	-	-	13	-	-	-	-	-	-	-	-	-	-
Memphis	-	-	-	20	-	-	-	-	16	-	20	19	19	12
Michigan St.	-	-	-	-	-	-	-	-	-	-	-	-	8	11
Minnesota	-	-	-	-	-	19	-	-	-	-	-	-	-	-
Mississippi St.	-	-	-	-	-	-	-	-	-	-	19	20	18	15
Niagara	16	-	-	-	-	-	-	-	-	-	-	-	-	-
North Carolina	6	3	2	2	2	2	1	1	1	1	1	1	1	1
North Carolina St.	8	19	-	-	-	-	-	-	-	-	-	-	-	-
Notre Dame	-	-	-	-	-	-	-	-	-	-	-	-	-	17
Ohio St.	11	11	-	-	-	17	12	11	12	-	-	-	-	-
Oklahoma City	18	15	11	17	11	13	16	16	13	13	13	18	10	9
Oklahoma St.	19	12	10	11	12	19	-	20	-	-	17	-	16	20
Purdue	-	-	-	-	-	-	-	-	17	-	-	-	-	-
St. John's (N.Y.)	-	15	-	-	-	-	-	-	-	-	-	-	-	-
St. Louis	-	9	5	16	17	-	-	-	-	20	-	14	12	10
San Francisco	2	2	19	-	-	-	-	-	-	-	-	-	-	-
Seattle	20	-	18	10	9	7	8	9	7	4	4	5	5	5
Southern Methodist	5	4	7	4	4	3	6	6	4	6	4	4	4	4
Tennessee	-	-	12	12	16	-	-	-	-	-	-	-	-	-
Tulane	-	-	16	-	-	-	18	14	-	-	-	-	-	-
UCLA	-	-	-	8	8	6	5	7	5	7	8	6	7	14
Vanderbilt	-	-	12	9	6	10	13	-	18	18	10	9	9	8
Wake Forest	-	-	-	18	13	11	11	13	10	11	12	13	20	18
West Virginia	13	8	4	19	18	15	17	18	11	10	14	11	11	7
West Va. Tech	-	-	-	-	-	-	-	-	-	-	15	18	-	-
Western Ky.	12	20	15	14	20	18	20	-	-	-	-	-	-	-

1957-58

Team	Dec 10	17	24	31	Jan 7	14	21	28	Feb 4	11	18	25	Mar 4	11
Arkansas	-	-	-	-	-	-	20	17	18	-	-	-	-	-
Auburn	-	-	-	-	-	-	-	-	-	-	-	20	16	16
Bradley	4	11	11	12	10	10	10	12	11	13	15	14	11	14
California	-	-	19	-	-	-	-	-	-	-	-	19	-	-
Cincinnati	19	4	5	5	7	5	4	3	3	3	2	3	3	2
Dartmouth	-	-	-	-	-	19	18	19	20	-	19	-	-	-
Dayton	-	-	-	-	-	17	16	-	14	14	11	10	8	11
Duke	-	-	-	-	-	-	-	-	13	8	7	6	6	10
Georgia Tech	-	-	-	-	-	-	-	-	19	-	-	-	-	-
Illinois	-	-	-	-	17	-	-	-	-	-	-	-	-	-
Indiana	-	-	-	-	-	-	-	-	-	-	-	-	-	12
Iowa St.	-	20	-	-	-	-	-	-	-	-	-	-	-	-
Kansas	2	2	2	2	3	2	2	2	2	4	4	7	10	7
Kansas St.	5	3	3	3	4	2	3	4	1	1	1	1	1	3
Kentucky	3	5	9	10	9	9	9	8	12	12	13	12	9	9
La Salle	-	-	-	20	-	-	-	-	-	-	-	-	-	-
Maryland	-	6	6	7	11	8	6	9	8	9	14	17	17	6
Memphis	20	-	-	-	18	-	-	-	-	-	-	-	-	-
Michigan St.	7	9	8	8	14	18	15	15	15	19	12	15	12	17
Minnesota	11	10	-	-	-	-	-	-	-	-	-	-	-	-
Mississippi St.	-	18	10	9	5	11	14	14	17	18	18	16	15	15
North Carolina	1	1	4	4	3	6	8	7	7	11	16	9	13	13
North Carolina St.	12	20	13	11	13	20	12	10	9	10	9	11	14	20
Notre Dame	15	-	-	-	-	-	-	-	-	17	10	8	7	8
Oklahoma	-	-	-	-	-	-	14	-	-	20	-	-	-	-
Oklahoma St.	18	16	14	14	8	7	7	6	6	6	8	13	18	19
Oregon St.	-	17	-	18	15	16	-	20	-	-	-	-	-	-
Rice	16	14	-	-	-	-	-	-	-	-	-	-	-	-
Richmond	-	19	17	-	-	-	-	-	-	-	-	-	-	-
St. Bonaventure	-	-	-	-	-	-	-	-	-	-	-	-	20	-
St. John's (N.Y.)	-	-	19	17	16	15	13	13	-	-	-	-	-	-
St. Louis	9	-	18	-	-	-	-	-	-	-	-	-	-	-
San Francisco	6	7	7	6	6	4	5	5	5	5	5	4	4	4
Seattle	14	12	15	-	20	-	-	-	16	16	17	18	19	18
Syracuse	17	-	-	-	-	-	-	-	-	-	-	-	-	-
Temple	10	-	13	-	12	12	11	11	10	7	6	5	5	5

1957-58 (continued)

	Dec 10	17	24	31	Jan 7	14	21	28	Feb 4	11	18	25	Mar 4	11
Tennessee	-	-	-	-	-	13	16	-	-	15	20	-	-	-
TCU	-	-	-	16	-	-	-	-	-	-	-	-	-	-
UCLA	13	13	-	-	-	-	-	-	-	-	-	-	-	-
Utah	-	15	12	15	19	-	-	-	-	-	-	-	-	-
West Virginia	8	8	1	1	1	1	1	1	1	2	3	2	2	1
Western Ky.	-	-	16	-	-	-	-	-	-	-	-	-	-	-
Wichita St.	-	-	-	-	20	17	19	18	-	-	-	-	-	-

1958-59

	Dec 9	16	23	30	Jan 6	13	20	27	Feb 3	10	17	24	Mar 2	9
Auburn	12	13	8	9	6	5	5	4	4	4	2	6	7	8
Bradley	-	11	13	10	9	7	9	9	8	7	10	9	9	4
California	-	15	14	20	-	20	-	20	19	18	15	12	11	11
Cincinnati	1	1	2	2	7	6	6	5	5	5	6	4	3	5
Dayton	-	-	20	-	-	-	-	-	-	-	-	-	-	-
Illinois	-	-	-	-	20	-	18	-	-	-	-	-	-	-
Indiana	19	-	-	-	-	19	-	-	-	15	19	-	-	-
Kansas	7	-	-	-	-	-	-	-	-	-	-	-	-	-
Kansas St.	3	3	4	3	4	4	3	3	3	3	4	2	2	1
Kentucky	2	2	1	1	1	2	1	1	1	1	3	1	1	2
Louisville	-	-	-	-	-	-	-	17	-	-	-	-	-	-
Marquette	17	-	17	15	15	13	12	12	12	11	13	13	13	20
Memphis	-	-	-	18	-	-	-	-	-	-	-	-	-	-
Michigan St.	15	11	9	7	5	8	8	8	7	12	9	8	6	7
Mississippi St.	8	8	7	8	12	12	11	11	11	10	5	5	4	3
North Carolina	13	10	3	4	3	3	2	2	2	2	1	3	5	9
North Carolina St.	5	4	6	5	2	1	4	6	6	6	6	7	10	6
Northwestern	10	6	12	6	8	11	18	-	-	-	-	-	-	-
Notre Dame	11	-	-	-	-	-	-	-	-	-	-	-	-	-
Oklahoma City	-	-	-	17	13	17	15	14	13	14	18	15	14	17
Oklahoma St.	20	-	-	-	-	-	-	-	-	-	-	-	-	-
Pittsburgh	-	18	-	-	-	-	-	-	-	-	-	-	-	-
Portland	-	-	-	-	-	18	17	-	-	-	-	19	-	-
Purdue	-	-	-	18	-	-	-	-	-	20	20	-	-	-
St. Bonaventure	-	-	-	-	-	14	13	16	18	-	14	18	19	19
St. John's (N.Y.)	20	-	13	-	10	9	7	7	15	19	-	17	18	-
St. Joseph's	-	14	-	12	-	-	-	-	20	-	-	-	20	14
St. Louis	9	17	16	16	14	15	14	15	9	8	8	11	12	12
St. Mary's (Cal.)	14	-	-	-	-	-	-	-	-	-	-	20	17	15
Seattle	-	16	-	-	16	16	16	13	14	13	12	16	-	13
Southern Methodist	18	20	-	-	-	-	-	-	-	-	-	-	-	-
Tennessee	6	5	11	14	17	-	-	-	-	-	-	-	-	-
Texas A&M	-	-	-	-	19	-	-	-	-	-	-	-	-	-
TCU	-	-	-	19	-	-	-	19	17	16	16	14	15	16
UCLA	-	19	-	-	-	-	-	-	-	-	-	-	-	-
Utah	-	-	-	-	-	-	-	20	16	17	17	-	16	18
Villanova	-	-	15	-	18	-	19	-	-	-	-	-	-	-
Washington	-	19	-	-	-	-	-	-	-	-	-	-	-	-
West Virginia	4	7	5	11	11	10	10	10	10	9	11	8	8	10
Xavier	16	9	10	-	-	-	-	-	-	-	-	-	-	-

1959-60

	Dec 22	29	Jan 5	12	19	26	Feb 2	9	16	23	Mar 1	8
Auburn	-	-	-	-	-	-	-	17	17	13	11	11
Bradley	5	9	4	4	2	2	2	2	3	4	4	4
California	4	3	2	2	3	3	3	3	3	4	3	2
Cincinnati	1	1	1	1	1	1	1	1	1	1	1	1
Dayton	-	-	-	-	19	19	13	15	-	-	-	-
DePaul	-	20	-	-	-	-	-	-	-	-	-	-
Detroit	17	11	15	20	20	14	14	19	-	-	-	-
Duke	16	18	-	-	-	-	-	-	-	-	-	18
Georgia Tech	8	10	6	6	6	6	6	6	6	6	7	13
Holy Cross	-	-	-	-	-	-	-	16	13	17	20	16
Illinois	10	8	9	14	13	-	19	20	20	-	-	-
Indiana	9	7	11	-	-	-	-	-	-	20	12	7
Iowa	19	14	-	15	-	-	-	-	-	-	-	-
Kansas St.	-	-	-	-	-	-	15	-	-	-	-	-
Kentucky	13	13	-	17	16	15	-	-	-	-	-	-
La Salle	14	-	-	19	-	-	-	-	-	-	-	-
Miami (Fla.)	-	15	14	15	11	11	11	10	10	9	8	10
Michigan St.	11	-	-	-	-	-	-	-	-	-	-	-
New York U.	12	12	-	-	-	-	-	-	-	14	14	12
North Carolina	-	-	-	19	16	12	12	17	13	19	16	-
Ohio	-	-	-	-	-	-	-	-	18	-	-	-
Ohio St.	3	5	7	5	5	5	4	4	4	2	2	3
Providence	-	-	-	-	-	20	16	14	16	15	15	14
St. Bonaventure	-	-	-	-	-	-	19	-	14	10	9	9
St. John's (N.Y.)	-	-	-	-	-	-	-	-	15	11	19	20
St. Louis	7	6	12	11	18	16	18	18	-	16	13	15
Southern California	20	-	10	10	14	18	-	-	-	-	-	-
Texas A&M	18	-	13	8	10	10	10	12	11	12	-	-
Toledo	-	16	20	18	17	13	19	11	12	19	-	-

1959-60 (continued)

	Dec 22	29	Jan 5	12	19	26	Feb 2	9	16	23	Mar 1	8
Utah	6	4	5	7	7	7	9	7	7	8	6	6
Utah St.	-	-	17	12	9	9	9	7	7	8	10	8
Villanova	15	17	16	9	8	8	8	8	9	12	17	17
Virginia Tech	-	-	-	-	-	-	-	17	-	-	-	-
Wake Forest	-	19	8	13	-	20	-	-	-	-	18	19
West Virginia	2	2	3	3	4	4	5	5	5	7	5	5
Western Ky.	-	-	18	-	-	-	-	-	-	-	-	-

1960-61

	Dec 13	20	27	Jan 3	10	17	24	31	Feb 7	14	21	28	Mar 7
Auburn	11	9	9	10	-	-	-	-	-	-	-	-	-
Bradley	2	2	2	2	2	3	3	4	4	5	4	4	6
Cincinnati	-	-	-	-	-	-	-	5	4	3	3	3	2
Colorado	-	15	-	-	-	-	-	-	-	-	-	-	-
Dayton	20	-	-	-	-	-	-	-	-	-	-	-	-
DePaul	-	-	-	-	7	-	-	-	-	-	-	-	-
Detroit	3	8	13	-	-	-	-	-	-	-	-	-	-
Drake	-	20	14	-	-	-	-	-	-	-	-	-	-
Duke	8	7	6	8	8	8	5	4	3	3	6	9	10
Georgia Tech	15	-	-	-	-	-	-	-	-	-	-	-	-
Illinois	19	-	-	-	-	-	-	-	-	-	-	-	-
Indiana	4	4	4	-	-	-	-	-	-	-	-	-	-
Iowa	-	-	-	-	7	6	4	6	6	9	5	6	8
Kansas	16	20	-	-	-	-	-	-	-	-	-	-	-
Kansas St.	20	12	12	-	9	10	-	10	7	6	8	7	4
Kentucky	20	-	19	-	-	-	-	-	-	-	-	-	-
Louisville	9	5	5	4	4	5	8	10	-	-	-	-	-
Maryland	12	-	-	-	-	-	-	-	-	-	-	-	-
Memphis	-	-	19	-	-	-	-	-	-	-	-	-	-
North Carolina	5	10	11	6	7	6	4	5	6	7	7	5	5
North Carolina St.	10	10	10	-	-	-	-	-	-	-	-	-	-
Ohio St.	1	1	1	1	1	1	1	1	1	1	1	1	1
Providence	-	13	15	-	-	-	-	-	-	-	-	-	-
Purdue	-	-	-	-	-	-	-	10	-	-	-	-	-
St. Bonaventure	6	3	3	3	3	2	2	2	2	2	2	2	3
St. John's (N.Y.)	7	6	7	5	5	9	7	7	-	-	-	-	-
St. Louis	-	16	8	-	-	-	-	-	-	-	-	-	-
Southern California	-	-	-	-	-	-	9	9	8	8	10	10	7
UCLA	13	14	16	9	10	-	-	-	-	-	-	-	-
Utah	18	18	-	-	-	-	-	-	-	-	-	-	-
Utah St.	14	-	-	-	-	-	-	-	-	-	-	-	-
Vanderbilt	-	17	16	-	-	-	-	-	-	-	-	-	-
Wake Forest	-	19	-	-	-	-	-	-	-	-	-	-	-
West Virginia	-	-	-	-	-	-	-	10	9	8	-	-	9
Wichita St.	16	-	18	-	-	-	-	-	-	-	-	-	-

1961-62

	PS	Dec 19	26	Jan 2	9	16	23	30	Feb 6	13	20	27	Mar 6	13
Arizona St.	-	10	-	-	-	-	-	-	-	-	-	-	-	-
Bowling Green	-	-	-	10	9	8	8	8	10	7	7	8	8	8
Bradley	-	-	-	-	9	9	9	7	5	6	6	6	5	-
Cincinnati	2	2	2	2	2	3	3	3	3	2	2	2	2	-
Colorado	-	-	-	-	-	-	-	-	9	9	-	-	9	-
Duke	7	-	10	8	10	7	7	6	5	7	8	8	9	10
Duquesne	-	-	-	7	3	7	8	5	6	7	6	9	-	-
Kansas St.	8	4	5	4	5	4	4	4	4	4	3	3	6	-
Kentucky	-	-	6	3	3	2	2	2	2	3	4	4	3	-
Loyola (Ill.)	-	-	-	-	-	-	-	-	-	-	10	-	-	-
Mississippi St.	-	-	-	9	7	10	10	10	-	-	-	-	-	-
Ohio St.	1	-	-	1	1	1	1	1	1	1	1	1	1	-
Oregon St.	-	-	-	-	-	-	-	-	10	6	10	-	-	-
Providence	5	3	-	-	-	-	-	-	-	-	-	-	-	-
Purdue	6	8	9	-	-	-	-	-	-	-	-	-	-	-
St. Bonaventure	-	9	-	-	-	-	-	-	-	-	-	-	-	-
St. John's (N.Y.)	9	-	-	-	-	-	-	-	-	-	-	-	-	-
Seattle	10	10	-	-	-	-	-	-	-	-	-	-	-	-
Southern California	4	6	4	6	4	6	5	5	-	-	-	-	-	-
Utah	-	-	-	-	-	-	-	-	-	-	-	10	7	7
Villanova	-	-	-	5	6	-	-	-	-	-	-	-	-	-
Wake Forest	3	-	-	-	-	-	-	-	-	-	-	-	-	-
West Virginia	-	5	7	-	-	-	-	-	-	-	-	-	-	-
Wichita St.	-	8	-	-	-	-	-	-	-	-	-	-	-	-

1962-63

	PS	Dec 4	11	18	25	Jan 1	8	15	22	29	Feb 5	12	19	26	Mar 5	12
Arizona St.	-	-	-	6	4	3	4	5	5	5	5	4	4	4	4
Auburn	-	-	-	-	10	-	-	-	-	-	9	-	-	-	-
Cincinnati	1	1	1	1	1	1	1	1	1	1	1	1	1	1	1
Colorado	-	-	8	6	-	-	-	-	-	8	7	7	-	-	10
Duke	2	2	2	2	7	6	5	4	3	3	3	2	2	2	2
Georgia Tech	-	-	-	-	-	7	6	7	6	6	10	-	10	-	8
Illinois	8	-	10	8	4	3	4	5	3	4	4	6	6	8	8

	PS	December 4	11	18	25	January 1	8	15	22	29	February 5	12	19	26	March 5	12
Indiana	-	8	-	-	-	-	-	-	-	-	-	-	-	-	-	-
Kentucky	3	9	-	9	5	6	-	-	-	-	-	-	-	-	-	-
Loyola (Ill.)	4	4	4	4	3	2	2	2	2	2	2	2	3	3	5	3
Mississippi St.	6	5	5	5	10	-	-	9	9	-	8	6	8	7	7	6
New York U.	-	-	-	-	-	-	-	-	-	-	-	-	10	9	-	9
North Carolina	-	-	-	-	-	-	10	-	-	-	-	-	-	-	-	-
Ohio St.	-	-	3	3	2	5	4	8	-	-	-	9	5	5	3	7
Oregon St.	7	7	9	-	-	-	-	10	-	9	-	-	-	-	-	-
Providence	-	-	-	-	-	-	-	-	-	-	-	-	-	-	10	-
St. Bonaventure	9	-	-	-	-	-	-	-	-	-	-	-	-	-	-	-
Seattle	-	-	-	10	-	-	-	-	-	-	-	-	-	-	-	-
Southern California	-	-	-	-	7	-	-	-	-	-	-	-	-	-	-	-
Stanford	-	-	-	-	9	-	-	-	10	7	10	8	-	-	9	-
UCLA	-	-	-	-	-	9	-	-	-	-	-	-	-	-	-	-
West Virginia	5	3	6	7	-	-	9	-	6	-	-	-	-	-	-	-
Wichita St.	-	10	-	-	-	8	8	7	8	10	9	-	7	8	6	5
Wisconsin	10	6	7	-	-	-	-	-	-	-	-	-	-	-	-	-

1963-64

	PS	December 10	17	24	31	January 7	14	21	28	February 4	11	18	25	March 3	10
Arizona St.	6	4	-	-	-	-	-	-	-	-	-	-	-	-	-
Cincinnati	3	6	4	5	4	8	8	-	-	-	-	-	-	-	-
Davidson	-	-	10	7	7	5	5	4	3	5	4	8	7	10	10
DePaul	-	-	-	-	-	-	-	9	9	10	10	9	9	8	9
Drake	-	-	-	-	-	-	-	-	-	-	-	10	-	-	-
Duke	4	3	5	8	9	9	10	8	8	7	5	4	4	4	3
Kansas	-	10	-	-	-	-	-	-	-	-	-	-	-	-	-
Kentucky	9	5	2	2	1	2	4	5	4	3	3	3	2	3	4
Loyola (Ill.)	1	1	1	1	3	3	2	3	10	9	-	-	10	9	8
Michigan	8	7	3	3	5	4	3	2	2	2	2	2	3	2	2
New York U.	2	2	7	10	-	-	-	-	-	-	-	-	-	-	-
Ohio St.	7	8	-	-	-	-	-	-	-	-	-	-	-	-	-
Oregon St.	10	9	-	9	8	6	7	10	-	-	9	7	6	6	6
Toledo	-	-	9	-	-	-	-	-	-	-	-	-	-	-	-
UCLA	-	-	6	4	2	1	1	1	1	1	1	1	1	1	1
Vanderbilt	-	-	8	6	6	7	6	6	5	8	7	-	-	-	-
Villanova	-	-	-	-	10	10	9	7	6	6	8	5	8	7	7
Wichita St.	5	-	-	-	-	-	-	10	7	4	6	6	5	5	5

1964-65

	PS	December 8	15	22	29	January 5	12	19	26	February 2	9	16	23	March 2	9
Bradley	14	-	-	-	-	-	-	-	-	-	-	-	-	-	-
Brigham Young	19	-	-	-	-	-	-	-	-	-	-	-	-	10	9
Davidson	4	-	-	10	-	10	8	7	6	5	5	5	6	7	6
DePaul	20	-	-	-	-	-	-	-	-	-	-	-	-	-	-
Duke	5	8	6	6	8	6	10	10	10	6	6	6	5	8	10
Illinois	-	-	-	7	6	-	-	-	-	-	10	-	-	-	-
Indiana	-	-	-	8	7	2	5	5	9	7	8	7	7	-	-
Kansas	18	-	-	-	-	-	-	-	-	-	-	-	-	-	-
Kansas St.	8	-	-	-	-	-	-	-	-	-	-	-	-	-	-
Kentucky	11	9	8	-	-	-	-	-	-	-	-	-	-	-	-
Michigan	1	1	2	1	1	3	2	2	2	1	1	1	1	1	1
Minnesota	11	6	4	3	3	-	-	-	-	-	-	9	8	6	7
New Mexico	-	-	-	-	-	-	-	-	-	-	-	-	10	-	-
North Carolina	13	-	-	-	-	-	-	-	-	-	-	-	-	-	-
Notre Dame	17	-	-	-	-	-	-	-	-	-	-	-	-	-	-
Providence	-	-	-	-	-	9	6	6	4	4	4	4	4	4	4
St. John's (N.Y.)	10	10	7	-	-	7	7	8	7	-	-	-	-	-	-
St. Joseph's	-	-	-	-	10	4	4	3	3	3	3	3	3	3	3
St. Louis	-	4	10	9	9	-	-	-	-	-	-	-	-	-	-
San Francisco	9	5	3	5	5	8	9	9	8	10	-	-	-	-	-
Seattle	15	-	-	-	-	-	-	-	-	-	-	-	-	-	-
Syracuse	7	-	-	-	-	-	-	-	-	-	-	-	-	-	-
Tennessee	-	-	-	-	-	-	-	-	-	-	-	8	-	-	-
UCLA	2	7	5	4	4	1	1	1	1	2	2	2	2	2	2
Vanderbilt	6	3	9	-	-	-	-	-	-	9	7	-	9	5	5
Villanova	16	-	-	-	-	-	-	-	-	-	-	-	-	9	8
Wichita St.	3	2	1	2	2	5	3	4	5	8	9	10	-	-	-

1965-66

	PS	December 7	14	21	28	January 4	11	18	25	February 1	8	15	22	March 1	8
Bradley	9	9	9	5	3	5	5	7	-	-	-	-	-	-	-
Brigham Young	-	-	-	-	6	8	7	-	-	-	-	-	-	-	-
Cincinnati	-	-	-	-	-	-	-	-	8	10	-	-	-	10	7
Duke	3	6	1	1	1	1	1	1	1	1	2	2	2	3	2
Iowa	-	-	-	9	4	7	-	-	-	-	-	-	-	-	-
Kansas	8	7	4	-	-	-	10	6	9	7	7	7	6	6	4
Kansas St.	10	-	-	-	-	-	-	-	-	-	-	-	-	-	-
Kentucky	-	-	-	10	5	2	2	2	2	2	1	1	1	1	1
Loyola (Ill.)	-	-	-	-	-	-	-	9	7	5	3	4	4	4	6
Michigan	2	2	3	3	7	-	-	-	-	9	10	10	10	-	9
Minnesota	7	5	6	6	9	-	-	-	-	-	-	-	-	-	-
Nebraska	-	-	-	-	-	-	-	-	-	-	9	9	8	9	-
Providence	6	8	7	7	10	6	6	4	3	4	6	6	9	8	-
St. Joseph's	4	3	2	2	8	4	4	3	5	8	8	8	7	7	5
South Carolina	-	10	-	-	-	-	-	-	-	-	-	-	-	-	-
UTEP	-	-	-	-	-	9	8	8	6	6	4	3	3	2	3
UCLA	1	1	8	-	-	10	9	10	10	-	-	-	-	-	-
Vanderbilt	5	4	5	4	2	3	3	5	4	3	5	5	5	5	8
Western Ky.	-	-	-	-	-	-	-	-	-	-	-	-	-	-	10
Wichita St.	-	-	10	8	-	-	-	-	-	-	-	-	-	-	-

1966-67

	PS	December 6	13	20	27	January 3	10	17	24	31	February 7	14	21	28	March 7
Boston College	-	-	-	-	-	-	-	-	-	-	10	-	-	10	9
Bradley	-	-	-	-	-	10	-	-	-	-	-	-	-	-	-
Brigham Young	-	9	7	-	-	-	-	-	-	-	-	-	-	-	-
Cincinnati	10	10	10	7	7	8	-	-	-	-	-	-	-	-	-
Duke	4	7	-	-	-	-	-	-	-	-	-	-	-	-	-
Florida	-	-	-	-	-	-	10	8	-	-	-	-	-	-	-
Houston	7	5	9	8	6	5	4	3	3	6	5	7	7	7	7
Kansas	-	-	-	9	-	9	8	7	7	7	7	6	4	4	3
Kentucky	3	3	4	-	-	-	-	-	-	-	-	-	-	-	-
Louisville	5	4	3	2	2	2	2	2	4	3	3	2	2	2	2
Michigan St.	-	-	8	5	10	-	-	-	-	-	-	-	-	-	-
Mississippi St.	-	-	-	-	-	10	-	-	-	-	-	-	-	-	-
New Mexico	6	6	5	6	5	4	3	9	-	-	-	-	-	-	-
North Carolina	9	8	6	3	3	3	5	4	2	2	2	4	5	3	4
Princeton	-	-	-	-	-	-	7	5	5	5	4	3	6	5	5
Providence	-	-	-	-	-	7	9	10	10	10	9	-	-	-	-
St. John's (N.Y.)	-	-	-	-	8	-	-	-	-	-	-	-	-	-	-
Syracuse	-	-	-	-	-	-	-	-	-	-	-	10	8	-	-
Tennessee	-	-	-	-	-	-	-	-	-	-	-	-	9	8	8
UTEP	2	2	2	4	4	6	6	6	6	4	8	8	10	9	10
UCLA	1	1	1	1	1	1	1	1	1	1	1	1	1	1	1
Vanderbilt	-	-	-	10	9	-	-	-	9	9	-	9	-	-	-
Western Ky.	8	-	-	-	-	-	-	-	8	8	6	5	3	6	6

1967-68

	PS	December 5	12	19	26	January 2	9	16	23	30	February 6	13	20	27	March 5	12
Boston College	7	10	6	8	10	-	-	-	-	-	-	-	-	-	-	-
Bradley	-	-	-	10	-	-	-	-	-	-	-	-	-	-	-	-
Columbia	-	-	-	-	-	-	10	10	8	8	7	6	6	6	8	7
Davidson	10	-	8	6	8	-	-	-	-	-	-	-	-	-	10	8
Dayton	6	6	-	-	-	-	-	-	-	-	-	-	-	-	-	-
Duke	-	-	-	-	-	-	-	-	-	9	-	10	8	10	6	10
Houston	2	2	2	2	2	2	2	2	1	1	1	1	1	1	1	1
Indiana	-	-	9	5	3	-	-	-	-	-	-	-	-	-	-	-
Kansas	5	4	-	-	-	-	-	-	-	-	-	-	-	-	-	-
Kentucky	-	9	4	7	6	5	4	8	9	10	8	8	5	5	4	5
Louisville	3	3	5	-	-	-	-	-	-	-	-	-	-	9	9	9
Marquette	-	-	-	-	-	-	-	-	-	-	-	-	10	8	-	-
New Mexico	-	-	-	-	-	10	9	6	4	4	6	5	7	7	7	6
New Mexico St.	-	-	-	-	-	-	-	-	-	-	10	-	-	-	-	-
North Carolina	4	5	7	4	5	3	3	3	3	3	3	3	3	3	5	4
Oklahoma City	-	-	-	-	-	8	-	-	-	-	-	-	-	-	-	-
Princeton	8	-	10	-	-	-	-	-	-	-	-	-	-	-	-	-
Purdue	-	7	-	-	-	-	-	-	-	-	-	-	-	-	-	-
St. Bonaventure	-	-	-	-	-	9	7	7	5	5	4	4	4	4	3	3
Tennessee	-	-	-	9	4	6	5	4	6	6	5	7	-	-	-	-
UCLA	1	1	1	1	1	1	1	1	2	2	2	2	2	2	2	2
Utah	-	-	-	-	7	7	6	5	10	-	-	-	-	-	-	-
Vanderbilt	9	8	3	3	9	4	8	9	7	7	9	9	9	-	-	-

1968-69

	PS	December 3	10	17	24	31	January 7	14	21	28	February 4	11	18	25	March 4
Baylor	-	-	-	-	-	-	-	18	-	-	-	19	-	-	-
Boston College	-	-	-	-	-	-	-	-	-	-	-	-	-	20	16
California	-	19	18	15	-	-	-	-	-	-	-	-	-	-	-
Cincinnati	14	9	6	6	10	10	19	19	-	-	-	-	-	-	-
Colorado	-	-	-	-	-	-	-	20	17	17	20	14	18	-	18
Columbia	-	-	-	-	-	-	-	-	19	18	14	-	-	-	-
Davidson	6	6	3	3	3	2	6	4	4	4	6	6	5	5	5
Dayton	-	-	-	-	-	-	-	-	20	20	19	17	-	-	-
Detroit	18	15	14	13	11	7	13	-	-	-	-	-	-	-	-
Drake	-	-	-	-	-	-	18	-	-	-	-	-	-	-	11
Duke	17	16	9	-	-	-	-	-	-	-	-	-	-	-	-
Duquesne	-	-	-	-	-	15	15	12	10	11	15	13	8	10	9
Florida	19	-	-	-	-	-	-	-	-	-	-	-	-	-	-
Houston	8	6	12	20	-	-	-	-	-	-	-	-	-	-	-
Illinois	-	-	-	-	12	8	4	8	8	7	10	10	19	15	20
Iowa	-	20	19	-	-	-	-	-	-	-	-	-	-	-	-
Kansas	5	4	11	11	8	5	5	10	13	15	13	12	16	13	19
Kentucky	3	3	4	4	4	3	7	5	5	5	4	4	6	6	7
La Salle	-	-	20	16	17	11	11	11	9	9	7	5	4	3	2

WEEK-BY-WEEK A.P. POLLS—1968-69 51

DIVISION I

		December					January				February				March
	PS	3	10	17	24	31	7	14	21	28	4	11	18	25	4
Louisville	-	-	-	19	14	14	14	-	-	-	-	20	13	11	15
Marquette	15	20	-	-	-	-	20	15	16	16	17	18	20	18	14
New Mexico	9	8	5	5	6	18	-	-	-	-	18	-	-	-	-
New Mexico St.	-	-	-	14	15	12	10	7	7	8	16	15	15	16	12
North Carolina	2	2	2	2	2	4	2	2	2	2	2	2	3	2	4
Northwestern	-	-	-	-	-	19	12	17	-	-	-	-	-	-	-
Notre Dame	4	5	7	7	7	16	17	16	15	-	-	-	-	-	17
Ohio St.	12	13	17	17	16	13	16	13	12	12	12	16	10	14	-
Purdue	10	14	13	12	18	-	-	-	18	14	9	8	9	9	6
St. Bonaventure	7	11	10	9	13	20	-	-	-	-	-	-	-	-	-
St. John's (N.Y.)	-	-	-	-	-	17	8	6	6	6	5	9	7	7	8
Santa Clara	-	18	16	10	9	6	3	3	3	3	3	3	2	4	3
South Carolina	-	-	-	-	-	-	-	-	-	19	-	-	12	8	13
Tennessee	20	20	-	-	20	-	-	-	-	-	-	-	17	17	-
Tulsa	-	-	-	-	-	-	-	14	14	13	11	7	14	19	-
UCLA	1	1	1	1	1	1	1	1	1	1	1	1	1	1	1
Vanderbilt	13	12	-	-	-	-	-	-	-	-	-	-	-	-	-
Villanova	11	10	8	8	5	9	9	9	11	10	8	11	11	12	10
Western Ky.	16	17	15	18	-	-	-	-	-	-	-	-	-	-	-
Wyoming	-	-	-	-	19	-	-	-	-	-	-	-	-	-	-

1969-70

		December				January				February				March	
	PS	9	16	23	30	6	13	20	27	3	10	17	24	3	10
Cincinnati	-	-	-	-	-	-	-	-	-	-	-	-	-	19	-
Colorado	10	17	16	-	20	-	-	-	-	-	-	-	-	-	-
Columbia	-	-	-	-	15	17	13	-	17	17	19	-	18	-	-
Davidson	5	4	4	9	11	8	8	11	11	15	13	9	11	10	15
Drake	19	-	-	-	-	-	-	-	16	13	11	17	16	14	14
Duke	-	-	-	-	-	19	19	16	-	-	-	-	-	-	-
Duquesne	11	7	-	-	-	-	-	-	-	-	-	-	-	-	-
Florida St.	-	-	-	-	-	-	-	-	18	12	9	8	10	11	11
Georgia	-	-	-	-	-	-	-	-	-	-	20	-	-	-	-
Houston	20	-	19	8	8	11	9	7	12	16	15	15	15	13	12
Illinois	-	-	-	15	-	-	17	12	10	14	-	-	-	-	-
Iowa	-	-	-	-	-	-	-	18	20	20	14	11	9	8	7
Jacksonville	-	18	18	13	10	7	6	6	6	8	7	6	6	6	4
Kansas	-	-	-	16	-	-	-	-	-	-	-	-	-	-	-
Kansas St.	-	-	-	-	-	-	-	17	19	18	-	18	17	16	-
Kentucky	2	1	1	1	1	2	2	2	2	3	3	2	1	2	1
Long Beach St.	-	-	-	-	-	-	-	-	-	-	-	-	-	-	19
Louisville	15	11	14	14	-	20	18	18	-	-	-	19	-	-	-
LSU	-	-	15	-	-	-	-	-	-	-	-	-	-	-	-
Marquette	8	12	17	-	18	13	10	8	7	9	12	10	8	9	8
New Mexico St.	6	3	3	7	7	6	5	5	5	6	6	5	5	5	5
Niagara	-	-	-	-	-	15	12	-	-	-	-	-	-	-	17
North Carolina	7	5	7	4	4	4	7	9	9	7	10	13	19	-	-
North Carolina St.	-	-	-	-	15	10	11	10	8	5	5	12	14	19	10
Notre Dame	13	10	6	11	13	-	-	20	-	-	16	14	13	15	9
Ohio St.	18	16	-	-	-	-	-	-	-	-	-	-	-	-	-
Ohio	-	19	10	5	5	9	14	13	13	-	-	-	-	17	-
Oklahoma	-	-	-	-	-	16	-	-	-	-	-	-	-	-	-
Pennsylvania	-	-	-	17	14	18	15	14	14	10	8	7	7	7	13
Purdue	3	14	12	18	17	-	-	-	-	-	-	-	-	-	-
St. Bonaventure	17	20	-	19	12	5	4	4	3	4	4	3	3	4	3
St. John's (N.Y.)	14	-	-	-	-	-	-	-	-	-	-	-	-	-	-
Santa Clara	12	15	11	-	-	-	-	-	-	-	-	20	-	-	-
South Carolina	1	8	5	3	3	3	3	3	4	2	2	4	4	3	6
Southern California	16	6	13	12	19	-	20	15	15	11	18	-	-	-	20
Tennessee	-	9	8	6	6	12	-	-	-	-	-	-	-	-	-
UCLA	4	2	2	2	2	1	1	1	1	1	1	1	2	1	2
Utah St.	-	-	-	-	-	-	-	-	-	-	-	-	20	18	16
Villanova	9	12	9	20	-	-	-	-	-	19	-	-	-	-	-
Western Ky.	-	-	-	-	-	-	-	-	-	-	17	16	12	12	18
Washington	-	-	20	10	9	14	15	-	-	-	-	-	-	-	-

1970-71

		December				January				February				March		
	PS	8	15	22	29	5	12	19	26	2	9	16	23	2	9	16
Army	-	14	-	-	-	-	-	-	-	-	-	-	-	-	-	-
Brigham Young	-	-	-	-	-	-	-	-	-	-	-	-	-	-	-	20
Drake	10	7	9	9	7	16	-	-	-	-	-	-	-	-	-	18
Duke	13	-	-	-	-	-	-	-	-	-	-	-	-	-	19	-
Duquesne	-	-	-	-	-	-	-	-	17	14	12	10	8	11	11	15
Florida St.	-	-	17	-	-	-	-	-	-	-	-	-	-	-	-	-
Fordham	-	-	-	-	-	18	14	17	-	-	20	18	11	10	10	9
Houston	17	-	-	-	-	-	-	-	-	18	15	-	-	15	18	14
Illinois	-	-	-	-	-	-	-	-	18	15	-	-	-	-	-	-
Indiana	16	11	13	11	14	12	11	18	-	-	-	-	-	18	-	-
Jacksonville	4	3	5	4	9	7	7	6	6	6	6	6	6	9	9	11
Kansas	14	11	12	8	12	8	8	5	5	5	5	5	5	4	5	4
Kentucky	3	5	3	7	8	11	10	12	11	8	8	12	10	8	8	8
La Salle	-	-	-	-	-	-	-	15	14	10	13	11	14	19	-	-
Long Beach St.	18	-	-	-	-	-	-	-	-	-	-	-	20	17	17	16
LSU	-	-	-	-	18	-	-	-	-	-	-	-	-	-	-	-
Louisville	-	20	-	-	17	13	16	-	-	-	-	19	15	-	-	-
Marquette	6	4	4	3	3	3	2	2	1	1	2	2	2	2	2	2
Memphis	-	-	-	-	-	-	19	-	-	-	-	-	-	-	-	-
Miami (Ohio)	-	-	-	-	-	-	-	-	-	-	-	-	-	-	20	-
Michigan	-	-	-	-	-	-	-	-	-	20	16	16	12	-	-	-
Murray St.	-	-	-	-	-	-	-	-	19	19	17	17	-	-	-	-
New Mexico St.	15	15	17	20	-	-	-	-	-	-	-	-	-	-	-	-
North Carolina	-	-	20	17	-	20	15	20	20	16	11	8	13	12	13	13
North Caro. St.	19	-	-	-	-	-	-	-	-	-	-	-	-	-	-	-
Notre Dame	5	6	7	14	15	9	9	9	7	12	9	14	19	16	14	12
Ohio St.	-	-	-	-	-	-	-	-	-	-	-	20	18	13	12	10
Oregon	-	18	16	17	16	-	-	16	13	-	-	-	-	-	-	-
Oregon St.	-	-	-	-	-	-	20	-	-	-	-	-	-	-	-	-
Pennsylvania	11	8	6	5	6	5	4	4	4	4	4	4	4	5	4	3
Purdue	-	-	-	16	20	19	-	-	-	-	-	-	-	-	-	-
St. Bonaventure	-	19	19	15	13	10	12	10	-	-	-	-	-	-	-	-
St. John's (N.Y.)	-	-	-	19	-	-	-	-	-	-	-	-	-	-	-	-
Southern California	7	9	8	6	4	4	3	3	3	2	3	3	3	3	3	5
South Carolina	2	2	2	2	2	2	6	11	10	7	10	7	7	6	6	6
Tennessee	-	17	14	12	10	17	18	8	8	11	14	13	17	14	15	17
UCLA	1	1	1	1	1	1	1	1	2	3	1	1	1	1	1	1
Utah St.	12	16	15	-	19	15	17	12	9	13	19	15	16	20	16	-
Villanova	8	10	10	13	11	14	13	14	16	17	18	-	-	-	-	19
Virginia	-	-	-	-	-	-	-	19	15	-	-	-	-	-	-	-
Western Ky.	9	13	11	10	5	6	5	7	12	9	7	9	9	7	7	7

1971-72

		December				January					February				March	
	PS	7	14	21	28	4	11	18	25	1	8	15	22	29	7	14
Arizona St.	-	17	-	-	-	-	-	-	-	-	-	-	-	-	-	-
Brigham Young	19	15	6	7	8	18	14	13	13	10	10	11	7	7	8	9
Duquesne	-	-	-	-	-	-	-	-	-	-	20	-	-	-	-	-
Florida St.	-	18	9	14	-	20	12	11	10	12	14	14	11	10	14	10
Hawaii	-	-	-	-	18	16	19	18	15	14	18	16	17	15	12	-
Houston	7	12	20	-	-	-	-	-	-	-	-	-	16	13	19	-
Illinois	-	-	-	-	-	-	16	-	-	-	-	-	-	-	-	-
Indiana	-	-	12	8	7	5	17	-	-	-	-	-	-	-	20	17
Jacksonville	11	8	14	16	-	-	-	-	-	17	16	-	-	-	-	-
Kansas	14	-	-	-	-	-	-	-	-	-	-	-	-	-	-	-
Kentucky	10	7	7	11	12	19	15	-	-	-	-	17	18	-	-	18
Long Beach St.	8	6	13	9	10	8	7	4	5	5	8	9	6	6	5	5
Louisville	9	16	17	19	15	7	5	6	4	3	4	4	3	2	4	4
La.-Lafayette	-	-	16	12	13	15	13	12	12	13	13	12	10	11	9	8
Marquette	4	2	2	2	2	2	2	2	2	2	2	2	2	5	7	7
Marshall	-	-	-	20	17	13	20	16	14	11	11	10	8	9	10	12
Maryland	6	5	15	15	16	12	-	-	18	-	-	19	12	18	13	14
Memphis	-	-	-	-	-	-	-	-	-	-	15	18	19	20	11	13
Michigan	13	9	-	-	-	-	-	-	-	20	-	-	-	16	-	-
Minnesota	-	-	-	-	-	-	-	17	16	19	19	-	-	-	16	11
Missouri	-	-	-	-	-	-	18	-	20	15	17	15	14	19	18	-
New Mexico	16	-	-	-	-	-	-	-	-	-	-	-	-	-	-	-
North Carolina	2	3	4	4	4	3	3	3	3	4	3	3	5	3	3	2
North Caro. St.	-	20	-	-	-	-	-	-	-	-	-	-	-	-	-	-
Northern Ill.	-	-	-	-	-	-	-	20	19	-	-	-	-	-	-	-
Ohio	-	-	-	17	-	-	-	-	-	-	-	-	-	-	-	-
Ohio St.	5	4	10	6	6	10	9	7	6	9	7	8	15	14	-	19
Oklahoma	20	-	-	-	-	-	-	-	-	-	-	-	-	-	-	-
Oral Roberts	-	-	-	-	-	-	-	-	-	-	-	-	20	17	17	16
Pennsylvania	15	10	5	13	14	6	6	10	9	6	5	5	4	4	2	3
Princeton	-	-	18	-	-	-	-	14	17	-	-	-	-	-	-	-
Providence	-	-	-	-	-	-	-	-	-	16	12	13	-	-	-	-
St. John's (N.Y.)	17	14	8	10	9	17	-	-	-	-	-	-	-	-	-	-
South Carolina	12	11	3	3	3	4	4	5	11	8	9	7	9	8	6	6
Southern California	3	13	10	5	5	11	10	8	7	18	-	-	-	-	-	-
Tennessee	-	-	-	-	20	-	-	19	-	-	-	20	-	-	-	-
UCLA	1	1	1	1	1	1	1	1	1	1	1	1	1	1	1	1
Villanova	18	18	-	-	-	14	11	15	-	-	-	-	-	-	-	15
Virginia	-	-	19	18	11	9	8	9	8	7	6	6	13	12	15	20
West Virginia	-	-	-	-	19	-	-	-	-	-	-	-	-	-	-	-

1972-73

		December				January					February				March	
	PS	5	12	19	26	2	9	16	23	30	6	13	20	27	6	13
Alabama	-	-	-	-	18	14	14	11	9	6	10	17	18	-	-	-
Arizona St.	-	-	-	-	-	-	-	-	-	-	-	-	-	-	-	16
Austin Peay	-	-	-	-	-	-	-	-	-	-	-	-	-	-	-	19
Brigham Young	12	-	17	15	14	15	-	-	-	-	-	20	-	-	-	-
Florida St.	2	2	2	7	12	19	18	19	-	-	-	-	-	-	-	-
Houston	15	20	16	14	13	10	10	12	11	11	11	7	9	8	7	13
Indiana	-	-	15	9	15	20	16	16	6	5	4	11	10	12	9	6
Jacksonville	-	-	-	-	-	-	15	15	13	15	16	13	20	18	16	-
Kansas St.	17	16	20	17	16	18	17	14	18	18	18	15	13	16	11	9
Kentucky	13	8	-	-	-	-	-	-	-	-	-	-	-	-	19	17
Long Beach St.	6	7	7	6	6	5	6	5	5	4	3	3	3	4	4	3

		December				January					February				March	
	PS	5	12	19	26	2	9	16	23	30	6	13	20	27	6	13
La.-Lafayette	7	10	8	8	9	8	13	13	12	13	13	14	12	11	14	7
Louisville	20	-	-	-	-	-	20	20	-	-	-	-	-	-	-	-
Marquette	5	5	4	3	3	3	4	7	10	10	7	5	5	5	6	5
Maryland	3	3	3	2	2	2	2	3	4	3	9	10	8	9	10	8
Memphis	11	11	19	-	-	-	-	-	17	17	15	16	14	10	15	12
Michigan	19	18	18	-	-	-	-	-	-	-	-	-	-	-	-	-
Minnesota	4	4	5	5	5	6	8	6	8	9	5	4	4	3	3	10
Missouri	-	-	12	10	7	7	5	8	7	7	8	12	16	13	12	15
New Mexico	-	-	-	-	-	16	-	-	19	-	20	18	15	15	-	-
North Carolina	-	13	11	13	11	9	7	4	3	8	6	6	6	7	8	11
North Carolina St.	8	6	6	4	4	4	3	2	2	2	2	2	2	2	2	2
Ohio St.	10	15	-	-	-	-	-	-	-	-	-	-	-	-	-	-
Oklahoma	-	-	-	19	19	-	-	-	-	-	-	-	-	-	-	-
Oral Roberts	18	12	10	16	-	-	-	-	-	19	19	-	-	-	-	-
Pennsylvania	9	9	9	11	8	17	-	-	-	-	-	-	-	-	-	18
Providence	-	19	14	18	17	13	11	9	14	12	12	8	7	6	5	4
Purdue	-	-	-	-	-	-	-	-	20	-	-	-	17	20	-	-
St. John's (N.Y.)	-	-	-	-	-	-	18	17	15	14	14	9	11	17	17	-
St. Joseph's	-	-	-	-	-	-	-	-	-	-	-	-	-	-	18	-
San Francisco	-	-	-	-	20	12	12	10	16	16	17	-	-	-	19	20
Santa Clara	-	-	-	20	-	-	-	-	-	-	-	-	-	-	-	-
South Carolina	16	-	-	-	-	-	-	-	-	-	-	-	-	19	-	-
Southern California	20	17	-	-	-	-	-	-	-	20	-	-	-	-	-	-
Syracuse	-	-	-	-	-	-	-	-	-	-	-	-	-	14	13	14
Tennessee	14	14	-	-	-	-	-	-	-	-	-	-	-	-	-	-
UCLA	1	1	1	1	1	1	1	1	1	1	1	1	1	1	1	1
Vanderbilt	-	-	13	12	10	11	9	18	-	-	-	-	-	-	-	-
Virginia Tech	-	-	-	-	-	-	-	-	-	-	-	19	19	-	-	-

1973-74

		December				January					February				March			
	PS	4	11	18	25	2	8	15	22	29	5	12	19	26	5	12	19	27
Alabama	18	18	13	10	13	7	12	10	9	8	8	8	8	7	12	11	13	14
Arizona	15	15	14	14	12	15	-	-	-	-	-	20	-	18	-	-	-	-
Arizona St.	-	-	-	-	-	-	-	-	20	-	-	-	-	-	-	-	-	-
Austin Peay	-	-	-	-	20	20	-	-	-	-	-	-	-	-	-	-	-	-
Centenary (La.)	-	-	-	-	-	-	-	-	18	-	-	-	-	-	-	-	-	-
Cincinnati	-	-	-	20	-	-	-	20	-	-	-	-	-	-	-	-	-	-
Creighton	-	-	-	-	-	-	-	-	-	-	-	17	15	16	19	19	-	-
Dayton	-	-	-	-	-	-	-	-	-	-	-	-	-	-	-	20	16	20
Hawaii	-	-	-	-	-	-	20	-	-	-	-	-	-	-	-	-	-	-
Houston	14	14	-	-	-	-	-	-	-	-	-	-	-	-	-	-	-	-
Indiana	3	3	3	7	7	8	13	12	11	12	12	12	10	9	13	10	11	9
Jacksonville	17	17	19	19	-	-	-	-	-	-	-	-	-	-	-	-	-	-
Kansas	13	-	-	-	-	-	-	-	-	18	17	16	16	15	15	14	6	7
Kansas St.	-	13	15	13	18	-	-	-	-	-	-	-	18	-				
Kentucky	10	10	-	-	-	-	-	-	-	-	-	-	-	-	-	-	-	-
Long Beach St.	12	12	12	11	10	9	9	9	10	10	9	10	13	13	9	9	9	10
Louisville	9	9	9	8	8	13	11	16	14	15	15	18	20	20	18	16	-	-
Marquette	7	7	7	6	6	6	7	6	6	5	6	9	9	8	11	7	3	3
Maryland	4	4	4	2	2	3	3	4	5	6	7	6	5	5	4	4	4	4
Md.-East. Shore	-	-	-	-	-	-	-	-	-	-	20	-	-	-	-	-	-	-
Memphis	20	10	12	16	18	19	-	-	-	-	-	-	-	-	-	-	-	-
Michigan	-	-	-	-	-	-	18	14	15	20	16	15	19	17	16	12	7	6
Missouri	-	-	-	-	-	-	-	18	-	-	-	-	-	-	-	-	-	-
UNLV	19	19	-	-	19	15	16	-	-	-	-	-	-	-	-	-	-	-
New Mexico	-	-	-	-	17	12	8	15	19	17	-	-	-	19	17	17	20	-
North Carolina	5	5	5	4	4	4	5	5	4	4	4	4	6	4	6	8	10	12
North Carolina St.	2	2	2	5	5	5	4	3	3	2	2	2	1	1	1	1	1	1
Notre Dame	8	8	6	3	3	2	2	2	1	3	3	3	2	2	2	3	5	5
Oral Roberts	-	-	-	-	-	-	-	-	-	19	19	-	-	-	20	-	18	18
Penn	16	16	11	-	-	-	-	-	-	-	-	-	-	-	-	-	-	-
Pittsburgh	-	-	-	-	-	-	-	17	16	13	10	7	7	11	14	13	15	16
Providence	6	6	8	9	9	14	10	7	8	9	11	11	11	12	8	5	8	8
Purdue	-	-	-	-	-	-	-	-	-	-	-	-	-	-	-	-	18	11
San Francisco	11	11	17	-	-	-	-	-	-	-	-	-	-	-	-	-	-	-
South Carolina	-	-	16	15	-	-	15	11	13	14	13	14	14	14	10	18	17	19
Southern California	-	-	20	16	14	11	17	13	12	11	14	13	12	10	7	15	14	17
Syracuse	-	-	18	18	15	19	-	-	-	-	-	-	-	-	-	-	-	-
UTEP	-	-	-	-	-	-	-	-	18	-	-	-	-	-	-	-	-	-
UCLA	1	1	1	1	1	1	1	1	2	1	1	1	3	3	3	2	2	2
Utah	-	-	-	-	-	-	-	-	-	-	-	19	17	-	-	-	-	15
Vanderbilt	-	-	-	17	11	10	6	8	7	7	5	5	4	6	5	6	11	13
Wisconsin	-	-	-	-	-	17	13	19	17	16	-	-	-	-	-	-	-	-

1974-75

		December					January				February				March				April
	PS	3	10	17	24	31	7	14	21	28	4	11	18	25	4	11	18	25	2
Alabama	9	11	10	8	7	6	8	7	6	9	7	7	5	8	7	10	11	11	10
Arizona	19	18	17	13	10	14	10	13	13	15	17	19	15	19	19	-	-	-	-
Arizona St.	-	-	-	-	-	16	12	9	10	12	10	8	8	9	9	8	7	7	8
Auburn	-	-	-	-	-	-	-	-	20	14	-	-	-	-	-	-	-	-	-
Centenary (La.)	-	-	-	-	-	-	-	-	-	-	-	-	18	-	-	17	19	18	-
Cincinnati	-	-	-	-	-	-	-	-	-	-	-	-	-	-	-	17	12	12	13
Clemson	-	-	-	-	-	-	-	-	-	-	16	18	16	11	14	14	-	-	-
Creighton	-	-	-	-	-	-	-	-	-	-	18	20	14	13	13	-	-	-	-
Drake	-	-	-	-	-	-	-	-	-	-	-	-	-	-	-	-	14	16	16
Houston	-	20	-	-	-	-	-	-	-	-	-	-	-	-	-	-	-	-	-
Indiana	3	3	3	2	2	2	1	1	1	1	1	1	1	1	1	1	1	3	3
Kansas	6	7	9	18	-	-	-	-	18	20	-	-	-	-	-	-	-	-	-
Kansas St.	-	-	-	-	-	-	-	-	-	-	-	-	-	-	-	-	17	15	15
Kentucky	16	15	-	20	17	9	7	10	11	5	5	4	7	4	6	6	5	2	2
La Salle	-	-	-	-	-	-	14	11	9	7	13	12	17	-	-	-	-	-	-
Louisville	8	6	4	4	4	4	3	3	2	3	3	6	6	3	3	3	3	4	4
Marquette	5	8	7	6	14	13	13	12	12	13	11	9	9	6	5	5	10	10	11
Maryland	4	4	5	5	5	7	5	5	3	8	4	3	3	2	2	4	4	5	5
Memphis	15	16	14	11	16	19	-	-	-	-	-	-	-	-	-	-	-	-	-
Michigan	17	19	16	-	-	17	11	19	-	-	-	-	-	-	-	-	-	19	19
Minnesota	18	-	-	-	-	-	17	16	17	-	-	-	-	-	-	-	-	-	-
UNLV	-	-	-	-	-	-	-	-	-	-	-	-	-	-	-	-	16	20	17
North Carolina	11	9	8	10	8	8	15	14	14	10	12	11	13	14	12	7	6	9	9
North Carolina St.	1	1	1	1	1	1	4	4	5	2	6	5	4	7	8	9	8	8	7
Notre Dame	12	13	11	12	13	19	-	-	-	16	14	16	11	16	16	12	9	14	14
Oklahoma	-	-	19	17	18	-	-	-	-	-	-	-	-	-	-	-	-	-	-
Oregon	-	-	18	19	19	11	9	8	8	11	9	13	-	-	-	-	-	-	-
Oregon St.	-	-	-	-	-	-	-	-	-	-	-	17	20	17	15	15	13	-	18
Penn	20	14	12	9	9	12	-	-	-	-	20	14	12	10	10	11	15	17	-
Princeton	-	-	-	-	-	-	-	-	-	-	-	-	-	-	-	-	-	13	12
Providence	14	17	20	16	12	10	19	15	16	-	-	-	-	-	-	-	-	-	20
Purdue	13	12	15	15	15	18	-	-	20	-	-	-	-	-	-	-	-	-	-
Rutgers	-	-	-	-	20	-	-	17	19	-	19	-	-	-	20	16	-	-	-
South Carolina	7	5	13	14	11	15	16	20	-	19	-	-	-	-	-	-	-	-	-
Southern California	10	10	6	7	6	5	6	6	7	6	8	10	10	12	11	13	18	-	-
Stanford	-	-	-	-	-	-	-	-	15	17	-	-	-	-	-	-	-	-	-
Syracuse	-	-	-	-	-	-	-	-	-	-	-	-	-	-	-	-	20	6	6
Tennessee	-	-	-	-	-	-	18	18	-	18	15	-	-	-	-	-	-	-	-
UTEP	-	-	-	-	-	-	-	-	-	-	-	-	-	15	18	17	-	-	-
Tex.-Pan American	-	-	-	-	-	-	-	-	-	-	-	15	19	18	17	20	-	-	-
UCLA	2	2	2	3	3	3	2	2	4	4	2	2	2	5	4	2	2	1	1
Wake Forest	-	-	-	-	-	-	19	-	-	-	-	-	-	-	-	-	-	-	-
Washington	-	-	-	-	-	-	-	-	-	-	-	-	-	20	-	-	-	-	-

1975-76

		December					January				February				March		
	PS	2	9	16	23	30	6	13	20	27	3	10	17	24	2	9	16
Alabama	12	14	11	8	8	8	10	11	12	11	14	11	10	7	16	8	6
Arizona	11	11	10	-	-	-	-	-	-	-	-	-	-	-	-	18	15
Arizona St.	18	19	19	19	-	-	-	-	-	-	-	-	-	-	-	-	-
Auburn	-	17	17	17	-	-	-	-	-	-	-	-	-	-	-	-	-
Centenary (La.)	-	-	-	-	19	18	-	18	-	19	18	19	20	19	20	20	19
Charlotte	19	-	-	-	-	-	-	-	-	-	-	-	-	-	-	18	17
Cincinnati	10	10	9	7	6	7	15	14	16	18	16	13	13	18	13	15	12
DePaul	-	-	-	-	-	-	-	-	-	-	-	-	-	-	-	-	17
Florida St.	-	-	-	-	-	-	-	-	-	-	-	-	-	-	18	-	-
Indiana	1	1	1	1	1	1	1	1	1	1	1	1	1	1	1	1	1
Kansas St.	14	18	-	-	-	-	-	-	-	-	-	-	-	-	-	-	-
Kentucky	6	7	14	20	18	-	-	-	-	-	-	-	-	-	-	-	-
La Salle	-	-	-	-	-	20	-	-	-	-	-	-	-	-	-	-	-
Louisville	8	6	6	10	11	11	16	-	-	-	-	-	19	-	-	-	-
Marquette	4	3	3	3	7	6	4	3	3	2	2	2	2	2	2	2	2
Maryland	3	2	2	2	2	2	2	2	2	7	5	4	7	10	9	12	11
Memphis	19	-	-	-	-	-	-	-	-	-	-	-	-	-	-	-	-
Michigan	16	16	18	16	16	17	19	16	17	15	16	16	15	13	11	14	9
Minnesota	-	-	-	-	20	16	17	-	-	-	-	-	-	-	-	-	-
Missouri	-	-	20	-	-	-	-	20	-	13	13	14	14	12	15	10	14
UNLV	-	-	16	13	12	10	5	4	4	3	3	7	6	5	5	4	3
North Carolina	5	4	4	4	3	3	6	7	5	4	4	3	3	4	4	5	8
North Carolina St.	13	13	13	9	9	9	11	13	11	8	10	12	12	15	17	-	-
North Texas	-	-	-	-	-	-	-	-	-	-	20	20	-	-	-	-	-
Notre Dame	7	9	8	5	5	5	13	15	15	10	11	10	8	6	8	7	7
Oregon	-	-	-	-	-	-	-	-	-	-	-	-	-	17	-	-	-
Oregon St.	-	-	-	-	-	-	-	17	13	16	-	-	-	-	-	-	-
Pepperdine	-	-	-	-	-	-	-	-	-	-	-	-	-	-	-	-	20
Princeton	-	-	-	-	-	-	-	-	-	17	15	-	-	-	-	-	-
Providence	17	15	-	-	-	-	-	-	-	-	-	-	-	-	-	-	-
Rutgers	-	-	-	15	15	14	12	10	7	5	7	5	4	3	3	3	4
St. John's (N.Y.)	-	-	-	18	17	15	14	12	9	14	12	17	16	14	16	17	-
San Francisco	15	12	12	14	14	19	20	-	-	-	-	-	-	-	-	-	-
Southern California	-	-	-	-	-	-	18	-	-	-	-	-	-	-	-	-	-
Syracuse	20	-	-	-	-	-	-	-	-	-	-	-	-	-	-	-	-
Tennessee	9	8	7	11	10	12	9	9	10	9	8	8	9	11	12	9	13
Texas A&M	-	-	-	-	-	-	-	-	-	-	-	-	-	20	19	-	-
Texas Tech	-	-	-	-	-	-	-	-	-	-	-	-	-	-	-	19	16
UCLA	2	5	5	6	4	4	3	8	6	12	9	6	5	9	7	6	5
Virginia	-	-	-	-	-	-	-	-	-	-	-	-	-	-	-	13	18
Virginia Tech	-	-	-	-	-	-	-	-	-	-	19	18	18	-	-	-	-
VMI	-	-	-	-	-	-	-	-	20	-	-	-	-	-	-	-	-
Wake Forest	-	-	-	-	-	-	7	5	14	-	-	-	-	-	-	-	-
Washington	-	20	15	12	13	13	8	6	8	6	6	9	11	8	10	11	-

		December					January				February				March		
	PS	2	9	16	23	30	6	13	20	27	3	10	17	24	2	9	16
West Tex. A&M..	-	-	-	-	-	-	-	19	19	20	-	-	-	-	-	-	-
Western Mich. ..	-	-	-	-	-	-	-	-	-	-	17	15	17	16	14	16	10
Wisconsin..........	-	-	-	-	-	-	-	-	18	-	-	-	-	-	-	-	-

1976-77

		Nov.	December				January				February				March		
	PS	30	7	14	21	28	4	11	18	25	1	8	15	22	1	8	15
Alabama............	13	13	10	7	5	4	4	4	3	3	8	7	4	8	12	12	11
Arizona	10	11	9	8	14	13	11	10	16	16	19	18	17	20	17	20	-
Arkansas............	-	-	-	19	18	17	18	16	17	15	14	13	11	6	7	8	18
Auburn	-	-	-	-	-	20	-	-	-	-	-	-	-	-	-	-	-
Charlotte............	19	-	-	-	-	-	-	-	-	-	-	-	-	-	-	18	17
Cincinnati	12	12	8	6	4	5	2	3	2	12	12	12	10	14	14	11	-
Clemson.............	-	-	16	13	11	10	16	17	-	19	16	15	18	19	18	-	-
DePaul...............	18	18	19	-	-	-	-	-	-	-	-	-	-	-	-	-	-
Detroit...............	-	-	-	-	-	-	-	-	-	-	20	19	15	16	15	17	12
Indiana	5	4	13	16	-	-	-	-	-	-	-	-	-	-	-	-	-
Kansas St.	-	-	-	-	-	-	-	-	-	-	-	-	-	-	-	-	16
Kentucky	6	5	4	3	7	6	3	2	6	6	3	3	2	2	2	6	3
Louisville	9	7	14	17	13	14	14	13	12	11	9	6	8	10	10	14	19
Marquette	2	2	2	2	6	12	12	11	8	9	6	9	9	18	19	16	7
Maryland...........	8	16	17	14	15	16	15	14	13	-	-	-	-	-	-	-	-
Memphis............	-	-	-	-	-	-	20	18	18	20	-	-	-	-	-	-	-
Michigan	1	1	1	1	1	1	5	6	5	2	7	5	5	3	3	1	1
Minnesota..........	-	-	-	-	20	15	13	9	11	13	10	8	12	13	9	9	13
Missouri.............	20	-	-	-	-	-	-	-	-	-	-	-	-	-	-	-	-
UNLV	7	6	5	12	12	11	9	8	7	5	4	10	6	4	5	5	4
North Carolina ..	3	9	12	11	10	9	6	5	4	4	13	14	13	9	6	4	5
North Carolina St.	15	-	-	-	-	-	-	-	-	-	-	-	-	-	-	-	-
Notre Dame.......	14	8	7	4	2	2	8	19	-	-	-	-	-	-	-	-	-
Oregon..............	-	-	-	-	-	-	-	20	-	-	-	-	-	17	-	-	-
Providence	-	-	-	-	-	-	17	15	15	14	15	16	16	12	8	13	-
Purdue	-	-	-	-	-	-	-	-	19	18	18	-	-	-	-	-	-
Rutgers...............	17	19	-	-	-	-	-	-	-	-	-	-	-	-	-	-	-
St. John's (N.Y.)..	-	-	-	20	-	-	-	-	-	-	-	-	-	-	-	-	-
San Francisco.....	11	10	6	5	3	3	1	1	1	1	1	1	1	1	1	3	8
Southern Ill.	-	17	18	18	-	-	-	-	-	-	-	-	-	-	-	-	-
Syracuse	-	-	20	15	17	18	19	-	20	17	17	17	20	15	13	10	6
Tennessee	16	15	15	-	19	-	-	-	14	7	11	11	14	7	11	7	15
UCLA	4	3	3	9	8	8	7	12	10	8	2	2	3	5	4	2	2
Utah	-	-	-	-	16	19	-	-	-	-	-	-	-	-	20	19	14
VMI...................	-	-	-	-	-	-	-	-	-	-	-	20	19	-	-	-	20
Wake Forest.......	-	14	11	10	9	7	10	7	9	10	5	4	7	11	16	-	9

1977-78

		Nov.	December				January					February				March	
	PS	29	6	13	20	27	3	10	17	24	31	7	14	21	28	6	13
Alabama............	15	15	-	-	18	-	-	-	-	-	-	-	-	-	-	-	-
Arkansas............	7	7	6	4	4	3	3	3	6	4	2	2	1	4	4	7	5
Cincinnati	9	8	7	6	12	11	12	19	-	-	-	-	-	-	-	-	-
DePaul...............	-	-	-	-	-	-	-	20	18	19	13	11	8	7	6	4	3
Detroit...............	19	19	17	16	15	20	-	-	-	-	-	17	19	16	16	19	18
Duke..................	-	-	-	-	-	-	-	-	17	11	17	-	20	13	15	8	7
Florida St.	-	-	-	-	-	18	-	-	-	17	15	16	14	12	11	13	15
Georgetown.......	-	-	-	-	-	-	20	17	19	16	14	-	18	18	17	-	-
Holy Cross	18	17	15	13	12	16	13	14	-	-	-	-	-	-	-	-	-
Houston	-	-	-	-	-	-	-	-	-	-	-	-	-	-	-	14	-
Illinois St.	-	-	-	-	-	-	-	-	-	20	19	15	15	15	13	17	-
Indiana	-	-	-	-	-	15	11	18	-	-	-	-	-	-	-	-	13
Indiana St.	-	-	11	7	6	6	6	6	4	13	-	-	-	-	-	-	-
Kansas...............	-	-	19	20	16	17	14	10	8	8	8	8	6	6	5	9	10
Kansas St.	-	-	-	19	-	-	-	-	-	-	-	-	-	-	-	-	-
Kentucky	2	1	1	1	1	1	1	1	1	1	1	1	3	2	1	1	1
Louisville	10	9	16	10	8	7	10	9	9	12	9	9	9	20	20	12	9
Marquette	3	4	4	3	2	5	4	4	2	2	3	3	2	1	3	3	8
Maryland...........	14	14	12	18	20	14	15	-	-	-	-	-	-	-	-	-	-
Miami (Ohio)	-	-	-	-	-	-	-	-	-	-	-	-	-	-	-	-	19
Michigan	13	13	9	15	-	-	-	-	-	-	-	-	-	-	-	-	-
Michigan St.	-	-	-	-	-	-	18	12	10	7	7	10	10	10	9	6	4
Minnesota..........	16	-	-	-	-	-	-	-	-	-	-	-	-	19	-	-	-
Nebraska...........	-	-	-	-	-	-	-	-	-	-	-	19	-	-	-	-	-
UNLV	8	10	10	9	9	9	9	11	16	-	-	-	-	-	-	-	-
New Mexico	-	-	-	-	-	-	-	-	20	14	10	6	5	5	8	5	12
North Carolina ..	1	2	2	5	3	2	2	2	5	3	6	7	11	8	10	11	16
North Carolina St.	-	-	-	-	-	-	-	16	-	-	-	-	-	-	-	-	-
Notre Dame.......	4	3	3	2	5	4	5	5	7	5	4	4	7	9	7	10	6
Pennsylvania	-	-	-	-	-	-	-	-	-	-	-	-	-	-	-	-	20
Providence	-	-	20	14	14	13	17	14	12	9	16	20	13	11	18	-	-
Purdue	12	11	-	17	-	-	-	-	-	-	-	-	-	-	-	-	-
St. John's (N.Y.)..	20	16	13	-	-	-	-	-	-	-	-	-	-	-	-	-	-
San Francisco.....	5	5	8	11	11	19	19	-	-	-	20	-	-	-	-	20	11
Syracuse	11	12	18	12	10	10	8	8	11	10	18	18	16	17	14	18	-
Texas.................	-	-	-	-	-	-	-	-	15	15	12	12	12	14	12	16	17
UCLA	6	6	5	8	7	8	7	7	3	6	5	5	4	3	2	2	2
Utah	-	20	14	-	17	-	-	-	-	-	-	-	-	-	19	15	14
Virginia.............	-	-	-	-	19	16	13	15	13	18	11	13	17	-	-	-	-
Wake Forest.......	17	18	-	-	-	-	-	-	-	-	-	14	-	-	-	-	-

1978-79

		Nov.	December				January					February				March	
	PS	28	5	12	19	26	3	9	16	23	30	6	13	20	27	6	13
Alabama............	19	-	-	-	-	-	-	-	18	18	15	16	20	-	-	-	-
Arkansas............	-	-	-	-	-	20	14	10	11	15	14	14	11	10	9	7	5
DePaul...............	-	-	-	-	-	-	-	-	-	-	-	-	-	20	15	8	6
Detroit...............	-	-	-	-	-	-	-	-	-	-	-	-	18	16	18	17	-
Duke..................	1	1	1	1	1	1	5	7	8	7	3	3	5	6	5	6	11
Georgetown.......	-	-	20	16	14	15	12	14	10	11	17	18	16	17	16	11	-
Illinois	-	-	-	18	15	6	4	4	4	8	19	20	-	-	-	-	-
Indiana	10	20	-	-	-	-	-	-	-	-	-	-	-	-	-	-	-
Indiana St.	-	-	-	20	16	11	11	9	5	3	2	2	1	2	1	1	1
Iowa..................	-	-	-	-	-	-	-	-	-	-	18	15	14	12	11	14	20
Kansas..............	5	4	5	8	7	18	19	15	20	-	-	-	-	-	-	-	-
Kentucky	11	10	10	6	11	13	9	17	-	-	-	-	-	-	-	-	-
Long Beach St. ..	-	-	-	-	-	17	15	19	-	-	-	-	-	-	-	-	-
LSU....................	14	11	12	11	10	7	7	5	9	9	9	8	6	5	8	9	7
Louisville	4	5	7	4	12	10	16	12	7	5	5	5	9	13	13	18	13
Marquette	18	17	16	14	13	16	17	13	13	13	10	9	13	9	10	12	10
Maryland...........	-	19	19	-	-	-	20	-	19	-	-	-	-	-	-	-	-
Michigan	8	8	6	9	9	8	13	16	-	-	-	-	-	-	-	-	-
Michigan St.	7	7	4	3	5	4	1	1	6	4	4	10	8	7	4	4	3
Mississippi St.	-	-	-	-	-	-	18	-	-	-	-	-	-	-	-	-	-
UNLV	20	18	15	15	18	14	-	-	-	-	-	-	-	-	-	-	-
North Carolina ..	16	14	14	13	6	5	3	3	2	2	7	6	4	4	7	3	9
North Carolina St.	12	6	8	7	4	9	8	8	14	20	-	-	-	-	-	-	-
Notre Dame.......	3	3	3	2	2	2	2	2	1	1	1	1	3	3	2	5	4
Ohio St.	-	-	-	-	-	-	-	-	16	10	13	13	17	14	17	-	-
Oklahoma..........	-	-	-	-	-	-	-	-	-	-	-	-	-	-	-	-	16
Pennsylvania	-	-	-	-	-	-	-	-	-	-	-	-	-	-	-	-	14
Purdue	-	-	-	-	-	-	-	-	-	-	-	-	13	18	19	16	15
Rutgers...............	15	16	18	-	-	-	-	-	-	-	-	-	-	-	-	-	18
St. John's (N.Y.)..	-	-	-	-	-	-	-	-	-	-	-	-	-	-	-	-	17
San Francisco.....	17	15	17	19	-	-	-	-	-	-	-	-	-	-	20	19	12
Southern California	13	12	11	12	20	-	-	-	-	-	-	-	-	-	-	-	-
Syracuse	9	9	9	10	8	19	-	20	12	12	8	7	7	8	6	10	8
Temple..............	-	-	-	-	-	-	-	18	17	16	20	19	15	15	12	13	-
Tennessee	-	-	-	-	-	-	-	-	-	-	-	-	-	-	-	20	-
Texas.................	6	13	13	17	19	-	-	-	-	17	11	12	12	11	14	15	-
Texas A&M........	-	-	-	-	17	12	10	11	15	14	12	11	-	-	-	-	-
Toledo	-	-	-	-	-	-	-	-	-	-	-	-	-	-	-	-	19
UCLA	2	2	2	5	3	3	6	6	3	6	6	4	2	1	3	2	2
Vanderbilt..........	-	-	-	-	-	-	-	-	-	19	16	17	19	19	-	-	-

1979-80

		December				January					February				March
	PS	4	11	18	26	2	8	15	22	29	5	12	19	26	4
Arizona St.	-	-	-	-	-	-	-	-	-	-	19	18	18	15	18
Arkansas	-	-	20	20	19	-	-	-	-	-	-	-	-	-	-
Brigham Young ...	15	18	18	18	20	19	17	18	20	19	14	13	14	12	12
Clemson	-	-	-	-	-	-	18	17	12	16	16	10	12	17	-
DePaul...............	9	10	11	6	4	3	2	1	1	1	1	1	1	1	1
Duke	3	2	2	1	1	1	1	5	3	5	10	16	17	-	14
Georgetown........	19	17	16	17	17	18	20	-	-	-	-	-	-	20	11
Illinois................	-	-	-	-	-	20	-	-	-	-	-	-	-	-	-
Indiana..............	1	1	1	5	10	11	19	19	16	18	20	-	19	13	7
Iona	-	-	-	-	-	-	-	-	-	-	-	-	-	-	19
Iowa..................	-	20	17	13	11	10	12	13	-	-	-	20	-	-	-
Kansas	20	19	-	-	-	-	-	-	-	-	-	-	-	-	-
Kansas St.	-	-	-	-	-	-	-	-	-	20	-	19	-	-	-
Kentucky............	2	5	5	3	2	2	4	6	5	3	6	5	3	2	4
LSU	7	6	6	7	5	4	6	14	11	10	7	6	5	5	3
Louisville	10	14	12	11	12	15	11	7	7	7	3	3	2	4	2
Marquette...........	18	16	-	-	-	-	-	-	-	-	-	-	-	-	-
Maryland...........	-	-	-	-	-	-	-	-	15	12	5	8	9	7	8
Missouri.............	-	-	19	16	13	12	13	15	10	14	15	14	13	11	16
North Carolina ...	6	8	8	8	6	6	15	9	13	11	11	11	8	10	15
North Carolina St.	-	-	-	-	-	-	-	16	-	-	-	-	-	19	-
Notre Dame........	5	4	4	4	3	7	7	8	8	8	9	12	10	14	9
Ohio St.	4	3	3	2	7	5	3	2	4	6	13	9	11	9	10
Oregon St.	17	15	14	19	18	14	9	4	2	2	4	4	6	6	5
Purdue...............	11	12	9	9	8	8	10	11	14	17	12	15	15	18	20
St. John's (N.Y.) ..	16	9	15	15	15	17	14	10	9	9	8	7	7	8	13
Syracuse............	12	11	10	10	9	9	5	3	6	4	2	2	4	3	6
Tennessee	-	-	-	-	-	-	-	20	19	-	-	-	-	-	-
Texas A&M.........	14	-	-	-	-	-	-	-	-	-	-	-	-	-	-
UCLA	8	7	7	14	16	16	16	-	-	-	-	-	-	-	-
Virginia	13	13	13	12	14	13	8	12	17	13	18	-	-	-	-
Washington St. ..	-	-	-	-	-	-	-	-	-	-	-	-	20	-	-
Weber St.	-	-	-	-	-	-	-	-	18	15	17	17	16	16	17

1980-81

		December					January				February				March	
	PS	2	9	16	23	30	6	13	20	27	3	10	17	24	3	10
Arizona St.	-	-	15	14	11	13	14	12	7	5	5	5	7	5	5	3
Arkansas	20	11	17	19	17	-	-	-	-	-	-	-	-	18	15	20
Brigham Young	18	19	19	18	20	19	17	15	18	15	16	15	17	15	18	16
Clemson	-	-	-	-	-	-	20	19	19	-	-	-	-	-	-	-
Connecticut	-	-	-	-	-	-	-	-	20	20	-	-	-	-	-	-
DePaul	2	1	1	1	1	1	1	4	T3	3	3	3	3	4	2	1
Georgetown	16	19	-	-	-	-	-	-	-	-	-	-	-	-	-	-
Illinois	-	-	-	17	18	16	12	18	15	-	18	17	15	14	16	19
Indiana	5	5	7	11	15	15	-	-	-	-	17	20	16	16	14	9
Iowa	14	12	16	16	14	14	11	14	9	13	15	14	12	8	8	13
Kansas	-	-	-	-	-	-	-	-	-	18	-	-	-	-	-	-
Kentucky	1	2	2	2	2	5	4	3	6	7	6	11	10	9	7	8
Lamar	-	-	-	-	-	-	-	-	-	-	-	-	19	-	-	-
LSU	12	15	11	10	10	10	9	6	5	4	4	4	4	2	3	4
Louisville	3	8	-	20	-	-	-	-	-	-	-	-	-	20	17	12
Maryland	4	4	4	9	9	9	8	10	10	14	13	19	20	17	20	18
Michigan	-	-	18	15	13	12	10	9	16	17	14	13	18	-	-	-
Minnesota	-	-	-	-	-	-	19	20	-	19	-	-	-	-	-	-
Missouri	11	17	14	-	-	-	-	-	-	-	-	-	-	-	-	-
North Carolina	13	10	10	8	6	6	16	17	17	12	11	10	13	11	12	6
Notre Dame	10	13	9	6	8	4	5	7	13	8	9	12	11	6	6	7
Ohio St.	9	9	8	7	-	-	-	-	-	-	-	-	-	-	-	-
Oregon St.	7	6	5	4	4	2	2	1	1	T1	2	2	2	1	1	2
St. John's (N.Y.)	17	16	-	-	-	-	-	-	-	-	-	-	-	-	-	-
South Ala.	-	-	-	-	16	17	15	13	11	16	20	18	-	-	-	-
Syracuse	19	18	20	-	-	-	-	-	-	-	-	-	-	-	-	-
Tennessee	-	-	-	-	-	18	13	11	8	11	10	9	8	10	10	15
Texas A&M	15	14	12	13	12	11	-	-	-	-	-	-	-	-	-	-
UCLA	6	3	3	3	3	7	7	8	12	10	12	8	6	13	13	10
Utah	-	-	-	-	19	20	18	16	14	9	7	6	9	7	9	14
Virginia	8	7	6	5	5	3	3	2	2	T1	1	1	1	3	4	5
Wake Forest	-	-	13	12	7	8	6	5	T3	6	8	7	5	12	11	11
Wichita St.	-	-	-	-	-	-	-	-	-	-	19	16	14	19	-	-
Wyoming	-	-	-	-	-	-	-	-	-	-	-	-	-	-	19	17

1981-82

		December					January				February				March	
	PS	1	8	15	22	29	5	12	19	26	2	9	16	23	2	9
Alabama	20	17	16	14	12	12	16	13	16	13	8	10	19	17	18	13
UAB	14	11	9	16	19	-	-	-	-	-	-	-	-	-	20	17
Arkansas	18	13	11	9	6	5	11	9	15	12	14	8	17	15	14	12
Brigham Young	-	15	-	-	-	-	-	-	-	-	-	-	-	-	-	-
DePaul	8	7	7	7	13	8	5	4	4	4	4	3	3	3	2	2
Fresno St.	-	-	-	-	-	-	-	-	-	19	17	18	15	14	12	11
Georgetown	5	20	20	19	17	17	13	8	13	-	-	20	13	12	8	6
Georgia	16	-	-	-	-	-	-	-	-	-	-	-	-	-	-	-
Houston	-	-	-	-	18	18	14	10	19	-	-	-	-	-	-	-
Idaho	-	-	-	-	-	-	18	14	8	11	15	13	11	9	6	8
Indiana	12	12	10	13	11	11	-	-	-	-	-	-	20	-	-	-
Iowa	9	6	6	6	10	10	7	5	6	6	5	5	7	11	11	16
Kansas St.	-	-	-	-	-	-	-	-	18	14	T19	15	18	-	17	-
Kentucky	3	2	2	2	2	4	3	6	9	7	9	12	10	7	15	15
LSU	17	-	-	-	-	-	-	-	-	-	-	-	-	-	-	-
La.-Lafayette	-	-	18	15	-	-	-	-	-	-	-	-	-	-	-	-
Louisville	4	3	3	3	8	14	12	17	17	-	-	-	-	-	-	20
Memphis	-	-	-	-	-	-	-	-	-	-	T19	14	12	10	13	9
Minnesota	10	10	8	8	5	9	6	11	5	10	6	9	8	13	7	7
Missouri	15	16	13	11	9	7	4	2	2	1	1	4	4	5	5	5
UNLV	-	18	15	-	-	-	-	-	-	-	-	-	-	-	-	-
North Carolina	1	1	1	1	1	1	1	1	1	2	2	2	2	2	1	1
North Carolina St.	-	-	-	-	-	20	15	12	14	17	-	-	-	-	-	-
Notre Dame	19	-	-	-	-	-	-	-	-	-	-	-	-	-	-	-
Oregon St.	-	-	19	20	16	15	17	15	12	8	10	6	5	4	4	4
St. John's (N.Y.)	-	-	-	-	-	-	20	-	-	-	-	-	-	-	-	-
San Francisco	-	14	12	10	7	6	8	7	11	9	7	17	16	16	-	-
Tennessee	-	-	-	-	-	-	-	-	20	15	16	-	-	19	-	-
Texas	-	-	-	-	-	-	-	19	7	5	12	-	-	-	-	-
Tulsa	11	9	14	12	14	13	10	18	10	16	11	7	6	8	10	10
UCLA	2	8	17	17	15	16	19	-	-	-	-	-	-	20	19	19
Villanova	-	-	-	18	20	19	-	-	-	20	-	-	-	-	-	-
Virginia	7	5	5	5	4	3	2	3	3	3	3	1	1	1	3	3
Virginia Tech	-	-	-	-	-	-	-	20	-	-	-	-	-	-	-	-
Wake Forest	13	-	-	-	-	-	-	-	-	18	13	16	14	18	16	18
Washington	-	-	-	-	-	-	-	-	-	-	-	19	-	-	-	-
West Virginia	-	-	-	-	-	-	-	-	-	-	18	11	9	6	9	14
Wichita St.	6	4	4	4	3	2	9	16	-	-	-	-	-	-	-	-

1982-83

		Nov.	December				January				February				March		
	PS	30	7	14	21	28	4	11	18	25	1	8	15	22	1	8	15
Alabama	12	13	11	10	8	6	5	10	-	-	-	-	-	-	-	-	-
Arkansas	17	16	15	13	12	11	10	7	4	12	9	8	7	6	5	6	9
Auburn	-	-	-	-	-	-	-	-	20	-	-	-	-	-	-	-	-
Boston College	-	-	-	-	-	-	-	-	-	-	-	-	18	19	15	14	11
Chattanooga	-	-	-	-	-	-	-	-	-	-	-	-	-	-	19	18	15
Georgetown	2	2	3	T5	11	10	17	-	19	15	14	14	14	18	16	15	20
Georgia	-	-	-	-	-	-	-	-	-	-	19	-	-	-	-	-	18
Houston	14	11	9	14	19	18	19	16	14	9	8	6	4	2	1	1	1
Illinois St.	-	-	-	-	-	-	-	-	-	17	16	17	-	-	-	-	-
Indiana	9	8	6	T5	5	1	1	4	2	2	6	4	2	4	11	7	5
Iowa	11	10	7	7	10	9	8	12	10	14	13	20	16	17	-	-	-
Kentucky	4	3	2	2	2	3	3	6	11	10	15	13	11	10	7	10	12
Louisville	8	7	13	12	14	13	13	9	9	8	12	11	9	5	3	3	2
Marquette	18	17	16	-	-	-	-	-	-	-	-	-	-	-	-	-	-
Memphis	6	5	4	3	4	2	2	1	6	5	4	9	13	14	17	17	17
Minnesota	-	-	-	-	-	-	-	17	16	16	17	19	-	-	-	-	-
Missouri	15	9	8	8	6	12	15	14	12	13	10	10	12	T15	13	12	10
UNLV	T20	19	18	18	17	15	11	8	5	4	2	2	1	1	9	9	6
North Carolina	3	15	17	17	-	-	18	11	3	3	1	1	3	11	8	5	8
North Carolina St.	16	18	18	15	15	17	16	19	-	-	-	-	-	-	-	-	16
Ohio St.	-	-	-	-	-	-	-	20	-	-	-	-	20	T15	14	16	-
Oklahoma	T20	-	-	-	-	-	-	-	-	-	-	-	19	-	-	19	-
Oklahoma St.	-	-	-	-	-	-	-	-	18	20	-	-	-	-	-	-	19
Oregon St.	10	19	-	-	-	-	-	-	-	-	-	-	-	-	-	-	-
Purdue	-	-	20	-	-	-	20	-	-	-	-	18	-	-	20	-	-
St. John's (N.Y.)	19	12	12	9	7	7	7	3	8	7	5	7	6	9	10	8	3
Syracuse	-	-	-	16	13	14	9	13	15	18	20	15	17	13	18	20	-
Tennessee	13	14	14	11	9	8	12	18	-	-	-	-	-	20	-	-	-
Tulsa	-	-	-	-	20	19	-	-	-	-	-	-	-	-	-	-	-
UCLA	7	6	5	4	3	5	6	5	1	1	7	5	10	8	6	4	7
Villanova	5	4	10	19	18	16	14	15	13	11	11	12	8	7	4	13	13
Virginia	1	1	1	1	1	4	4	2	7	6	3	3	5	3	2	2	4
Virginia Tech	-	-	-	-	-	-	-	-	17	-	-	-	-	-	-	-	-
Wake Forest	-	-	-	-	-	-	-	-	-	19	-	-	-	-	-	-	-
Washington St.	-	-	-	-	-	-	-	-	-	-	18	-	-	-	-	-	-
West Virginia	-	-	-	20	16	20	-	-	-	-	-	-	-	-	-	-	-
Wichita St.	-	-	-	-	-	-	-	-	-	-	-	16	15	12	12	11	14

1983-84

		Nov.	December				January					February				March	
	PS	29	6	13	20	27	3	10	17	24	31	7	14	21	28	6	13
Arkansas	14	14	15	-	-	-	-	-	-	16	-	-	14	11	12	8	8
Auburn	-	-	-	-	-	-	-	-	-	-	19	16	-	19	-	-	-
Boston College	15	15	12	8	6	12	17	18	16	-	-	-	-	-	-	-	-
DePaul	18	16	13	4	4	4	3	3	2	2	2	2	3	5	5	4	4
Duke	-	-	-	-	-	-	-	-	-	-	-	-	19	14	15	16	14
Fresno St.	13	17	20	-	-	-	16	13	17	-	-	-	-	-	-	-	-
Georgetown	4	3	3	5	5	5	4	4	6	4	4	3	2	2	4	2	2
Georgia	16	13	10	12	14	11	11	15	-	18	-	-	-	-	-	-	-
Georgia Tech	-	-	-	-	-	-	-	-	-	-	18	18	-	-	-	-	-
Houston	3	8	6	3	3	3	7	7	4	7	6	5	4	3	2	5	5
Illinois	-	-	-	-	-	20	14	9	10	9	8	8	7	6	10	7	6
Indiana	19	-	-	-	-	-	-	-	-	-	-	-	T17	-	-	-	-
Iowa	7	5	5	18	19	-	-	-	-	-	-	-	-	-	-	-	-
Kansas	17	-	-	-	-	-	-	-	-	-	-	-	-	-	-	-	-
Kentucky	2	1	2	2	2	2	2	2	3	3	3	6	6	4	3	3	3
LSU	11	12	9	10	11	9	9	11	15	10	14	20	T17	-	-	-	-
Louisville	6	-	-	16	10	14	-	-	-	14	17	15	-	-	-	18	-
Maryland	8	6	11	9	8	6	5	5	7	5	10	13	-	-	19	14	11
Memphis	5	4	4	T6	16	17	19	19	18	13	9	9	8	12	14	17	16
Michigan	-	-	-	-	20	15	-	-	-	-	-	-	-	-	-	-	-
Michigan St.	12	11	17	17	-	-	-	-	-	-	-	-	-	-	-	-	-
UNLV	-	-	-	-	-	-	18	14	8	6	5	4	5	7	7	10	13
North Carolina	1	2	1	1	1	1	1	1	1	1	1	1	1	1	1	1	1
North Carolina St.	-	7	8	T6	13	13	12	-	-	-	-	-	-	-	-	-	-
Oklahoma	20	-	-	-	-	-	-	17	20	11	12	10	9	8	6	6	7
Oregon St.	10	10	18	14	15	19	15	16	11	-	-	-	-	20	20	20	17
Purdue	-	-	19	11	7	18	-	-	19	-	16	11	11	13	11	11	10
St. John's (N.Y.)	-	19	16	13	12	8	13	10	14	-	-	-	-	-	-	-	-
Syracuse	-	-	-	-	-	-	-	-	-	20	13	19	16	16	16	-	18
Temple	-	-	-	-	-	-	-	-	-	-	-	-	20	17	18	15	20
UTEP	-	-	-	20	18	16	10	8	5	8	7	7	10	9	8	9	9
Tulsa	-	-	-	-	-	-	-	20	13	12	11	12	12	10	9	12	12
UCLA	9	9	7	15	9	7	6	6	9	15	20	-	-	-	-	-	-
Virginia	-	-	-	-	-	-	20	-	-	19	-	-	-	-	-	-	-
Va. C'wealth	-	20	-	-	-	-	-	-	-	-	-	-	-	-	-	-	-
Wake Forest	-	-	-	19	17	10	8	12	12	17	15	14	13	15	17	19	19
Washington	-	-	-	-	-	-	-	-	-	-	-	17	15	18	13	13	15
Wichita St.	-	18	14	-	-	-	-	-	-	-	-	-	-	-	-	-	-

1984-85

		Nov.	December				January					February				March	
	PS	27	4	11	18	25	1	8	15	22	29	5	12	19	26	5	12
UAB	-	13	18	17	-	-	-	-	-	-	20	-	19	-	-	-	-
Arizona	-	-	-	-	-	-	-	-	-	-	-	-	-	-	19	-	-
Arkansas	16	17	-	-	-	-	-	-	-	-	-	-	-	-	-	-	-
Boston College	-	-	-	-	-	-	-	12	15	-	-	-	-	20	-	-	-
DePaul	3	2	2	2	5	9	10	13	10	7	13	18	-	-	-	-	-

WEEK-BY-WEEK A.P. POLLS—1984-85

55

DIVISION I

	PS	Nov. 27	Dec. 4	11	18	25	Jan. 1	8	15	22	29	Feb. 5	12	19	26	March 5	12
Duke	6	4	4	3	2	2	2	2	2	5	6	5	7	6	5	7	10
Georgetown	1	1	1	1	1	1	1	1	1	1	2	2	2	2	2	1	1
Georgia	-	-	-	-	-	-	-	-	-	-	-	-	-	18	14	17	19
Georgia Tech	20	18	15	12	13	10	8	9	17	16	8	10	6	8	10	9	6
Illinois	2	7	7	6	4	8	6	15	11	6	5	9	17	16	18	14	12
Indiana	4	12	11	16	16	15	12	11	8	13	-	-	-	-	-	-	-
Iowa	-	-	-	-	-	-	-	19	-	-	-	12	11	14	-	-	-
Kansas	19	t20	19	18	15	12	11	10	9	15	19	13	10	15	11	10	13
Kentucky	18	-	-	-	-	-	-	-	-	-	-	-	-	-	-	-	-
LSU	14	16	13	19	19	18	14	-	-	-	-	-	-	-	-	19	20
Louisiana Tech	-	-	-	-	20	19	18	14	12	12	15	14	12	10	7	8	8
Louisville	17	6	6	14	12	20	-	-	-	-	-	-	-	-	-	-	-
Loyola (Ill.)	-	-	-	-	-	-	-	-	-	-	-	-	-	-	20	16	14
Maryland	-	-	-	-	-	-	19	-	-	-	17	20	20	-	-	-	-
Memphis	8	5	5	5	3	3	3	6	5	4	3	3	5	4	4	5	5
Michigan	-	-	-	20	18	13	16	-	-	18	10	8	3	3	3	3	2
Michigan St.	-	-	-	-	-	-	-	17	19	-	-	-	-	-	-	-	-
UNLV	11	t20	20	-	-	-	-	-	-	20	16	11	14	11	9	11	9
North Carolina	-	19	16	13	10	7	9	5	6	8	11	15	13	13	8	6	7
North Carolina St.	13	11	10	9	14	14	17	-	-	-	-	-	-	-	16	18	16
Oklahoma	5	10	17	15	11	17	13	8	13	9	7	7	4	5	6	4	4
Oregon St.	-	-	-	-	-	-	-	20	14	10	14	16	18	19	-	-	-
Southern Methodist		10	9	8	7	6	4	7	4	3	2	4	4	9	9	13	20
St. John's (N.Y.)	7	3	3	4	8	5	4	3	4	3	1	1	1	1	1	2	3
Syracuse	12	14	12	10	9	6	5	7	7	11	9	6	8	7	12	13	15
Texas Tech	-	-	-	-	-	-	-	-	-	-	-	-	-	-	-	-	17
Tulsa	-	-	-	-	-	-	-	-	20	17	12	17	15	12	15	15	18
Va. C'wealth	-	-	-	-	-	-	20	18	16	19	-	-	-	17	17	12	11
Virginia Tech	15	15	14	11	17	16	-	-	-	-	-	-	-	-	-	-	-
Villanova	-	-	-	-	-	-	-	16	18	14	18	19	16	-	-	-	-
Washington	9	8	9	8	7	11	15	-	-	-	-	-	-	-	-	-	-

1985-86

	PS	Nov. 26	Dec. 3	10	17	24	31	Jan. 7	14	21	28	Feb. 4	11	18	25	March 4	11
Alabama	-	-	-	-	-	-	-	-	-	-	-	20	18	-	-	-	-
UAB	16	20	17	16	14	14	16	14	12	18	-	-	-	-	-	-	-
Auburn	10	19	t19	-	-	-	-	-	-	-	-	-	-	-	-	-	-
Bradley	-	-	-	-	-	-	-	-	20	17	13	13	13	12	11	9	14
DePaul	-	-	-	19	18	20	-	-	-	-	-	-	-	-	-	-	-
Duke	6	6	3	3	3	3	3	3	3	2	5	4	2	2	1	1	1
Georgetown	8	8	6	t5	5	5	11	13	15	12	12	11	9	13	15	14	13
Georgia Tech	1	2	5	t5	7	7	6	5	5	4	3	2	5	5	4	6	6
Illinois	7	7	12	10	15	16	14	18	-	-	-	-	-	-	-	19	19
Indiana	-	-	t19	18	17	17	15	-	-	-	15	18	16	15	16	16	16
Iowa	-	-	18	-	-	-	-	-	-	-	-	-	-	-	-	-	-
Kansas	5	5	7	7	6	6	5	9	8	7	4	6	3	3	2	2	2
Kentucky	11	10	9	9	13	13	12	11	11	11	8	12	11	8	5	3	3
LSU	14	12	11	11	9	9	8	8	14	14	17	-	-	-	-	-	-
Louisville	9	9	16	15	16	15	18	17	18	13	18	16	19	16	13	11	7
Maryland	t19	17	-	-	-	-	-	-	-	-	-	-	-	-	-	-	-
Memphis	15	14	13	12	10	10	9	6	6	3	2	3	4	4	7	10	12
Michigan	3	3	2	2	2	2	2	2	2	6	9	7	10	7	10	7	5
Michigan St.	-	-	-	-	-	-	-	-	-	-	-	-	-	19	17	17	18
Navy	t19	-	-	-	-	-	-	-	-	-	-	-	-	17	19	18	17
UNLV	18	16	14	13	12	12	13	12	10	10	10	9	6	11	9	13	11
North Carolina	2	1	1	1	1	1	1	1	1	1	1	1	1	1	3	4	8
North Carolina St.	17	15	-	-	-	-	-	-	-	-	-	-	17	20	18	20	-
Notre Dame	12	11	10	17	19	18	17	16	13	16	14	14	14	14	12	12	10
Ohio St.	-	-	-	20	-	-	-	-	-	-	-	-	-	-	-	-	-
Oklahoma	13	13	8	8	8	8	7	7	7	5	6	5	8	10	14	15	15
Purdue	-	-	-	-	-	-	-	20	19	15	-	-	-	-	20	-	-
Richmond	-	-	-	-	-	-	-	-	-	-	20	-	-	-	-	-	-
St. John's (N.Y.)	-	18	15	14	11	11	10	10	9	8	7	10	7	6	8	5	4
Syracuse	4	4	4	4	4	4	4	4	4	9	11	8	12	9	6	8	9
UTEP	-	-	-	-	-	-	19	15	17	19	19	17	15	-	-	-	20
Virginia Tech	-	-	-	-	20	19	20	19	16	20	16	15	20	18	-	-	-
Western Ky.	-	-	-	-	-	-	-	-	-	-	-	19	-	-	-	-	-

1986-87

	PS	Dec. 2	9	16	23	30	Jan. 6	13	20	27	Feb. 3	10	17	24	March 3	10
Alabama	13	8	18	-	-	-	-	15	13	9	9	14	12	10	9	9
Arizona	19	20	-	-	-	-	-	-	-	-	-	-	-	-	-	-
Arkansas	-	-	20	-	-	-	-	-	-	-	-	-	-	-	-	-
Auburn	12	7	7	6	5	5	13	10	17	18	20	-	-	-	-	-
Clemson	-	-	-	-	-	-	20	12	10	14	12	12	10	13	13	13
Cleveland St.	20	-	-	-	-	-	-	-	-	-	-	-	-	-	-	-
DePaul	-	-	-	19	17	15	7	7	6	8	5	5	4	4	5	5
Duke	-	-	-	-	-	20	17	14	12	13	16	15	17	17	14	17
Florida	-	-	-	-	20	-	-	-	-	19	-	19	18	18	-	-
Georgetown	18	16	13	10	10	8	16	9	15	11	10	13	11	8	7	4
Georgia Tech	6	15	16	16	19	18	-	-	-	-	-	-	-	-	-	-
Illinois	14	9	6	5	9	16	12	8	9	12	14	11	14	14	12	11
Indiana	3	3	2	8	8	6	4	4	3	t4	2	2	2	3	4	3
Iowa	10	5	4	3	3	3	2	2	1	2	4	4	7	7	6	6
Kansas	8	6	14	13	13	12	19	20	-	20	18	17	15	16	-	20
Kentucky	11	13	19	18	18	11	9	-	-	-	-	-	-	-	-	-
Louisville	2	-	-	-	-	-	-	-	-	-	-	-	-	-	-	-
Missouri	-	-	-	-	-	-	-	-	-	-	-	-	-	-	19	14
Navy	9	10	10	11	12	9	15	19	18	-	-	-	-	-	-	-
UNLV	5	2	1	1	1	1	1	1	4	3	1	1	1	1	1	1
New Orleans	-	-	-	-	-	-	-	-	-	-	-	-	-	19	16	16
North Carolina	1	1	5	4	4	4	3	3	2	1	3	3	3	2	2	2
North Carolina St.	17	18	15	12	11	19	18	17	20	-	-	-	-	-	-	-
Northeastern	-	19	-	-	-	-	-	-	-	-	-	-	-	-	-	-
Notre Dame	-	-	-	-	-	-	-	-	-	-	-	-	-	-	20	18
Oklahoma	7	11	9	7	6	13	11	16	11	10	8	8	13	12	17	-
Pittsburgh	16	12	17	14	14	17	14	18	16	17	13	10	8	9	11	12
Providence	-	-	-	-	-	-	-	-	-	-	17	20	19	20	-	-
Purdue	4	4	3	2	2	2	6	6	5	t4	7	7	6	6	3	7
St. John's (N.Y.)	-	-	-	15	15	10	10	13	14	15	19	16	20	-	-	-
Syracuse	15	17	12	9	7	7	5	5	7	6	11	9	9	11	10	10
Temple	-	-	-	20	16	14	8	11	8	7	6	6	5	5	8	8
TCU	-	-	-	-	-	-	-	-	19	16	15	18	16	15	15	19
UCLA	-	-	11	17	-	-	-	-	-	-	-	-	-	-	18	15
Western Ky.	-	14	8	-	-	-	-	-	-	-	-	-	-	-	-	-

1987-88

	PS	Dec. 1	8	15	22	29	Jan. 5	12	19	26	Feb. 2	9	16	23	March 1	8	15
Arizona	17	9	4	2	1	1	3	1	1	1	1	3	3	3	3	3	2
Auburn	-	-	-	-	-	-	-	19	-	-	-	-	-	-	-	-	-
Bradley	-	-	-	-	-	-	-	-	-	-	18	15	17	14	14	12	11
Brigham Young	-	-	-	-	-	-	-	-	12	7	4	t8	7	11	15	17	19
DePaul	20	-	-	-	-	-	-	-	-	-	-	-	-	-	-	-	-
Duke	15	13	10	10	9	9	9	7	9	5	3	t8	6	5	9	8	5
Florida	14	7	12	11	8	8	15	-	-	14	19	-	-	-	-	-	-
Georgia Tech	18	-	-	-	-	-	-	-	-	-	-	-	-	20	13	18	-
Georgetown	16	17	14	18	19	18	14	11	15	15	14	-	-	-	-	-	-
Illinois	-	-	-	-	-	-	19	20	13	13	17	-	-	-	-	19	16
Indiana	6	5	6	5	13	13	12	15	-	-	-	19	-	-	-	-	-
Iowa	11	6	3	7	14	14	16	17	19	16	13	13	13	13	11	15	17
Iowa St.	-	-	-	20	16	16	17	14	10	12	16	-	-	-	-	-	-
Kansas	7	16	18	17	18	17	18	16	16	-	-	-	-	-	-	-	-
Kansas St.	-	-	-	-	-	-	-	-	-	-	-	14	-	-	-	-	20
Kentucky	5	2	1	1	2	2	1	5	4	9	10	10	9	12	8	6	6
Louisville	13	14	-	-	-	20	-	-	-	-	-	-	-	-	-	-	-
Loyola Marymount	-	-	-	-	-	-	-	-	-	-	-	-	20	19	18	16	15
Memphis	-	20	20	19	20	19	-	-	-	-	-	-	-	-	-	-	-
Michigan	9	15	15	13	11	12	11	10	7	8	11	12	10	7	10	10	10
Missouri	8	8	9	16	17	-	-	-	-	-	-	-	15	15	-	-	-
UNLV	-	19	17	15	15	15	13	13	8	4	2	7	11	8	5	7	12
New Mexico	-	-	-	-	-	-	-	18	-	-	-	-	-	-	-	-	-
North Carolina	3	1	5	4	4	4	4	2	2	3	8	6	5	9	6	9	7
North Carolina St.	-	-	-	-	-	-	-	-	20	-	-	-	-	-	16	11	14
Notre Dame	-	-	19	-	-	-	-	-	-	-	-	-	-	-	-	-	-
Oklahoma	19	18	16	14	12	10	8	3	11	10	7	4	4	4	4	4	4
Pittsburgh	4	4	2	3	3	3	2	6	6	11	9	5	8	6	7	5	8
Purdue	2	11	13	12	10	11	10	8	5	2	6	2	2	2	2	2	3
St. John's (N.Y.)	-	-	-	-	-	-	20	-	-	-	20	-	-	-	-	-	-
Southern Miss.	-	-	-	-	-	-	-	-	-	20	-	16	14	18	-	-	-
Syracuse	1	3	8	9	7	7	7	9	14	17	12	11	12	10	12	13	9
Temple	12	12	11	8	6	6	6	4	3	6	5	1	1	1	1	1	1
UTEP	-	-	-	-	-	-	-	-	18	18	-	-	-	-	-	-	-
Vanderbilt	-	-	-	-	-	-	-	-	-	-	15	17	16	17	19	-	-
Villanova	-	-	-	-	-	-	-	-	-	19	-	20	-	-	-	-	-
Wyoming	10	10	7	6	5	5	5	12	17	-	-	18	19	16	17	14	13
Xavier	-	-	-	-	-	-	-	-	-	-	-	-	-	-	20	20	18

1988-89

	PS	Nov. 22	29	Dec. 6	13	20	27	Jan. 3	10	17	24	31	Feb. 7	14	21	28	March 7	14
Alabama	-	-	-	-	-	-	-	-	-	-	-	-	-	-	-	-	-	20
Arizona	11	10	11	10	9	9	8	8	12	9	6	4	1	2	2	1	1	1
Ball St.	-	-	-	-	-	-	-	-	-	-	-	-	-	-	20	19	19	18
Connecticut	-	-	-	-	18	-	-	-	-	-	-	-	-	-	-	-	-	-
Duke	1	1	1	1	1	1	1	1	1	1	8	12	14	11	9	9	7	9
Florida	15	15	19	-	-	-	-	-	-	-	-	-	-	-	-	-	-	-
Florida St.	16	17	14	13	12	11	10	15	14	14	11	8	12	7	12	16	14	16
Georgia Tech	13	14	12	12	11	16	17	19	19	-	-	-	20	-	-	-	-	-
Georgetown	2	2	3	4	5	6	5	5	7	3	2	6	2	4	3	2	3	2
Georgia	-	-	-	-	-	-	-	-	20	-	-	-	-	-	-	-	-	-
Illinois	9	9	7	7	6	5	4	3	2	2	1	2	7	5	10	8	4	3
Indiana	-	20	-	-	-	-	-	-	-	19	16	17	13	9	4	3	6	8
Iowa	7	7	6	5	4	4	9	9	5	7	12	9	8	15	14	11	15	14
Kansas	-	-	-	-	-	-	20	20	18	16	17	18	-	-	-	-	-	-
LSU	-	-	-	-	-	-	-	-	-	-	-	-	19	-	20	-	-	-
Louisville	4	12	13	15	15	14	14	13	9	4	3	7	4	10	8	14	16	12

		Nov.		December				January					February				March	
	PS	**22**	**29**	**6**	**13**	**20**	**27**	**3**	**10**	**17**	**24**	**31**	**7**	**14**	**21**	**28**	**7**	**14**
Michigan	3	3	2	2	2	2	2	7	6	6	10	11	10	13	13	10	8	10
Missouri	14	13	8	11	10	10	11	11	10	8	5	5	3	3	7	7	10	6
UNLV	10	8	9	9	13	13	12	12	11	10	13	16	19	18	18	18	18	15
North Carolina St.	18	18	16	19	18	17	18	16	15	15	15	13	17	19	17	20	17	19
North Carolina	6	5	10	8	8	8	7	6	8	13	7	3	6	8	5	5	9	5
Notre Dame	-	-	-	-	-	19	-	-	-	-	-	-	-	-	-	-	-	-
Ohio St.	17	16	15	14	14	12	15	14	18	16	17	17	16	16	-	-	-	-
Oklahoma	5	4	5	6	7	7	6	4	3	5	4	1	5	1	1	4	2	4
Providence	-	-	-	-	-	-	-	-	-	20	-	20	-	-	-	-	-	-
St. Mary's (Cal.)	-	-	-	-	-	-	-	-	-	-	-	-	-	-	-	19	17	20
Seton Hall	-	-	-	20	17	15	13	10	13	12	9	10	11	12	15	12	11	11
South Carolina	-	-	-	-	-	-	18	16	-	-	-	-	-	-	-	-	-	-
Stanford	20	-	-	-	-	-	-	-	-	20	19	20	18	17	16	13	12	13
Syracuse	8	6	4	3	3	3	3	2	4	11	14	14	9	6	6	6	5	7
Temple	19	19	17	-	-	-	-	-	-	-	-	-	-	-	-	-	-	-
Tennessee	-	-	-	20	16	16	19	19	17	17	18	-	-	-	-	-	-	-
UCLA	-	-	-	-	-	20	-	-	-	-	-	-	-	-	-	-	-	-
Villanova	12	11	18	17	-	-	-	-	-	-	-	-	-	-	-	-	-	-
West Virginia	-	-	-	-	-	-	-	-	-	-	-	18	15	14	11	15	13	17

1989-90

		Nov.	December				January					February				March	
	PS	**27**	**5**	**12**	**19**	**26**	**2**	**9**	**16**	**23**	**30**	**6**	**13**	**20**	**27**	**6**	**13**
Alabama	-	-	21	19	20	22	22	24	25	24	-	-	-	-	-	-	23
Arizona	6	2	20	20	22	21	19	18	23	19	24	22	20	21	23	15	14
Arkansas	9	11	10	7	10	11	14	12	12	6	3	3	8	13	12	9	7
Clemson	-	-	-	-	-	-	-	-	-	-	-	-	-	23	20	17	17
Connecticut	-	-	-	-	-	-	-	-	-	20	13	8	10	6	4	8	4
Duke	10	7	6	12	12	13	13	10	8	8	5	4	6	3	t5	12	15
Florida	23	24	25	24	-	-	-	-	-	-	-	-	-	-	-	-	-
Georgetown	5	3	3	3	3	3	3	2	2	3	6	5	3	5	7	5	8
Georgia	-	-	-	-	-	-	-	-	-	-	-	-	-	-	25	25	-
Georgia Tech	22	21	18	15	14	14	12	9	11	13	17	16	13	8	11	14	9
Illinois	8	8	7	5	5	4	4	8	7	10	11	12	15	t19	18	20	18
Indiana	14	14	14	11	11	10	9	13	14	12	22	25	-	25	-	-	-
Iowa	-	-	-	21	16	18	20	-	-	-	-	-	-	-	-	-	-
Kansas	-	4	2	2	2	2	2	1	1	2	2	2	1	2	1	2	5
La Salle	-	-	-	-	23	20	17	21	17	18	15	14	14	14	13	11	12
LSU	2	9	9	9	8	9	11	14	13	16	14	11	9	12	15	16	19
Louisville	12	13	11	10	9	8	8	11	10	4	10	15	18	16	21	18	16
Loyola Marymount	-	-	-	-	-	-	25	23	21	22	20	20	19	22	22	21	21
Memphis	24	22	16	17	17	15	21	20	-	-	-	-	-	-	-	-	-
Michigan	4	10	8	6	6	5	5	3	6	7	4	7	5	7	8	13	13
Michigan St.	-	-	-	25	25	-	-	-	-	-	-	23	21	15	14	7	3
Minnesota	20	-	-	-	-	25	24	16	22	21	19	17	17	18	17	19	20
Missouri	11	5	4	4	4	7	7	5	4	1	1	1	2	1	3	6	11
UNLV	1	6	5	14	13	12	10	7	9	5	12	9	7	4	2	3	2
New Mexico St.	-	-	-	-	-	-	-	-	-	-	-	-	25	24	24	23	24
North Carolina	7	12	17	-	-	24	-	-	-	-	25	-	-	-	-	-	-
North Carolina St.	19	25	19	16	15	19	18	17	19	-	-	-	-	-	-	-	-
Notre Dame	17	19	-	-	-	-	-	-	-	-	-	-	-	-	-	-	-
Oklahoma St.	21	23	-	22	24	-	-	-	-	-	-	-	-	-	-	-	-
Oklahoma	16	17	12	8	7	6	6	4	3	9	9	13	11	10	t5	1	1
Oregon St.	-	-	24	23	21	23	23	22	18	17	21	18	16	17	16	22	22
Pittsburgh	18	18	22	-	-	-	-	-	-	-	-	-	-	-	-	-	-
Purdue	-	-	-	-	-	-	-	-	24	13	8	10	12	9	9	10	10
St. John's (N.Y.)	25	20	15	18	19	17	16	15	15	15	18	24	24	-	-	-	-
Syracuse	3	1	1	1	1	1	1	6	5	11	7	6	4	11	10	4	6
Temple	15	16	23	-	-	-	-	-	-	-	-	-	-	-	-	-	-
UCLA	13	15	13	13	18	16	15	19	16	23	16	19	23	-	-	-	-
Xavier	-	-	-	-	-	-	-	25	20	25	23	21	22	t19	19	24	25

1990-91

		Nov.	December				January					February				March	
	PS	**27**	**4**	**11**	**18**	**25**	**1**	**8**	**15**	**22**	**29**	**5**	**12**	**19**	**26**	**5**	**12**
Alabama	7	6	12	20	-	-	-	-	-	-	-	-	-	24	-	24	19
Arizona	3	2	2	4	4	4	4	6	6	5	6	5	6	9	7	9	8
Arkansas	2	3	3	2	2	2	2	2	2	2	2	2	3	3	3	5	2
Connecticut	17	15	14	16	15	13	12	9	13	19	-	-	-	-	-	-	-
DePaul	-	-	-	-	-	-	-	-	-	-	-	-	-	-	-	25	24
Duke	6	8	5	10	9	8	8	14	12	9	7	6	5	7	8	6	6
East Tenn. St.	-	-	-	24	21	20	17	16	15	12	16	13	10	13	19	15	17
Georgetown	9	9	6	5	12	16	15	15	19	21	18	20	18	25	-	-	-
Georgia	21	17	13	11	17	17	-	-	-	-	-	-	-	-	-	-	-
Georgia Tech	16	14	20	23	-	-	24	24	-	-	23	-	-	-	-	-	-
Indiana	8	10	7	7	6	5	5	3	3	3	4	4	4	4	5	3	3
Iowa	-	-	-	-	-	23	22	22	24	-	-	-	-	-	-	-	-
Kansas	-	-	-	-	-	-	-	-	-	-	24	18	11	8	10	12	12
Kentucky	-	-	25	18	18	18	16	11	9	8	10	10	16	12	13	10	9
LSU	14	20	18	12	10	15	14	20	20	16	14	19	20	19	18	16	22
Louisville	23	25	-	-	-	-	-	-	-	-	-	-	-	-	-	-	-
Michigan St.	4	5	19	21	24	25	25	-	-	22	-	25	-	-	-	-	-
Mississippi St.	-	-	-	-	-	-	-	-	-	-	-	-	23	21	23	18	21
Missouri	20	23	-	-	-	-	-	-	-	-	-	-	-	-	-	-	-
Nebraska	-	-	-	-	22	22	19	18	17	14	11	15	17	14	15	13	11
UNLV	1	1	1	1	1	1	1	1	1	1	1	1	1	1	1	1	1
New Mexico St.	-	-	-	-	-	24	23	23	21	23	20	16	12	15	11	11	15
New Orleans	-	-	-	-	-	-	-	-	-	24	22	21	-	-	-	-	-
North Carolina	5	4	10	9	8	7	7	5	5	7	9	9	8	6	4	7	4
Ohio St.	10	11	9	8	7	6	6	4	4	4	3	3	2	2	2	2	5
Oklahoma	15	18	16	13	11	14	13	12	11	13	21	23	-	-	-	-	-
Oklahoma St.	-	-	-	-	-	-	-	-	-	-	-	22	21	16	12	12	14
Pittsburgh	12	13	11	15	14	11	11	17	16	17	19	24	22	23	22	-	-
Princeton	-	-	-	-	25	-	-	-	-	-	-	-	25	23	21	19	18
Seton Hall	-	-	-	-	-	-	-	-	25	-	25	-	-	24	20	21	13
South Carolina	-	-	t21	17	16	12	20	21	22	25	-	-	-	-	-	-	-
Southern Miss.	24	19	15	22	20	21	21	19	18	15	17	12	9	11	14	22	25
St. John's (N.Y.)	25	21	17	14	13	9	9	10	10	10	5	8	13	18	17	20	20
Syracuse	13	7	4	3	3	3	3	8	8	6	8	7	7	5	6	4	7
Temple	19	-	24	-	-	-	-	-	-	-	-	-	-	-	-	-	-
Texas	22	22	23	25	23	-	-	-	-	-	-	-	24	-	-	23	23
UTEP	-	-	-	-	-	-	-	25	-	-	-	-	-	-	-	-	-
UCLA	11	12	8	6	5	10	10	7	7	11	12	14	15	17	16	17	16
Utah	-	-	-	-	-	-	-	-	23	20	13	17	14	10	9	8	10
Villanova	-	24	-	-	-	-	-	-	-	-	-	-	-	-	-	-	-
Virginia	18	16	t21	19	19	19	18	13	14	18	15	11	19	20	25	-	-

1991-92

		Nov.	December					January				February				March		
	PS	**25**	**2**	**9**	**16**	**23**	**30**	**6**	**13**	**20**	**27**	**3**	**10**	**17**	**24**	**2**	**9**	**16**
Alabama	17	16	15	20	20	20	19	16	9	15	22	18	16	14	16	20	17	13
Arizona St.	24	25	-	-	-	-	-	-	-	-	-	-	-	-	-	-	-	-
Arizona	5	3	3	2	2	6	6	6	7	11	9	7	7	5	5	4	2	10
Arkansas	3	2	11	19	19	15	16	13	12	9	7	5	11	10	9	7	6	9
Charlotte	-	-	-	24	24	25	21	22	18	19	17	20	22	-	-	-	-	-
Cincinnati	-	-	-	-	-	-	-	-	-	-	-	-	24	19	19	14	12	12
Connecticut	15	15	12	8	7	5	5	5	8	7	6	10	18	21	24	-	-	-
DePaul	18	20	20	-	-	-	-	-	-	-	-	-	-	-	21	15	19	24
Duke	1	1	1	1	1	1	1	1	1	1	1	1	1	1	1	1	1	1
Florida St.	-	-	-	-	-	-	-	-	-	-	23	23	23	16	22	19	18	20
Georgetown	16	17	18	23	23	24	22	-	22	-	-	-	-	25	18	17	21	22
Georgia Tech	23	18	17	t13	13	13	15	14	16	18	20	24	-	-	-	-	-	-
Indiana	2	10	9	t13	14	10	10	10	5	4	4	6	4	7	2	2	4	5
Iowa	21	21	21	16	22	23	-	-	-	-	-	-	-	-	-	-	-	-
Iowa St.	-	-	-	-	-	-	-	-	24	-	-	-	-	23	-	-	-	-
Kansas	12	12	10	7	6	4	4	4	6	5	5	3	4	3	3	3	3	2
Kentucky	4	13	14	9	8	17	17	15	10	8	14	19	19	13	11	10	9	6
LSU	6	9	16	25	-	-	-	-	-	-	-	22	20	-	-	23	23	25
Louisville	25	-	-	-	25	21	24	-	25	20	24	-	-	-	-	-	-	-
Massachusetts	-	-	-	-	-	-	-	25	-	-	-	-	-	-	-	25	22	17
Michigan	20	23	25	18	15	11	11	11	15	16	15	15	17	20	17	18	14	15
Michigan St.	-	-	22	t13	12	9	9	9	11	14	13	11	12	11	12	13	16	14
Missouri	-	-	-	21	17	16	13	12	13	12	8	12	9	9	6	11	13	16
Nebraska	-	-	-	-	-	-	-	-	-	-	-	-	-	-	25	-	-	-
UNLV	-	-	24	-	-	-	-	-	-	25	21	17	15	12	7	6	7	7
North Carolina	8	6	5	5	9	8	8	8	14	10	11	9	6	4	10	16	20	18
Ohio St.	7	5	4	4	4	7	7	7	4	6	10	8	8	6	8	5	5	3
Oklahoma	19	19	19	17	16	14	14	21	23	17	18	21	-	-	-	-	24	23
Oklahoma St.	13	11	8	6	5	3	3	3	3	3	3	2	2	8	14	12	11	11
Pittsburgh	-	24	-	-	-	-	-	-	-	-	-	-	-	-	-	-	-	-
St. John's (N.Y.)	10	8	7	11	10	18	18	17	17	22	-	-	-	24	20	-	25	-
Seton Hall	9	7	6	12	11	12	12	18	21	-	-	-	25	22	-	22	15	19
Southern California	-	-	-	-	-	-	25	23	-	-	25	16	13	15	13	8	10	8
Stanford	-	-	-	-	-	-	-	-	-	24	-	-	-	-	-	-	-	-
Syracuse	-	-	-	-	-	-	23	20	20	13	12	13	10	17	22	24	-	21
UTEP	-	-	-	-	-	-	-	-	-	23	19	25	21	-	-	-	-	-
Tulane	-	-	-	-	-	-	-	24	19	21	16	14	14	18	15	21	-	-
UCLA	11	4	2	3	3	2	2	2	2	2	2	4	3	2	4	9	8	4
Utah	14	14	13	10	18	19	-	-	-	-	-	-	-	-	-	-	-	-
Wake Forest	22	22	23	22	21	22	20	19	-	-	-	-	-	-	-	-	-	-

1992-93

		Nov.		December				January				February				March		
	PS	**23**	**30**	**7**	**14**	**21**	**28**	**4**	**11**	**18**	**25**	**1**	**8**	**15**	**22**	**1**	**8**	**15**
Arizona	10	10	9	14	15	14	22	20	12	11	8	8	5	4	4	3	6	5
Arkansas	-	-	-	16	12	10	9	13	9	8	16	17	14	13	15	13	14	12
Boston College	-	-	-	-	-	-	-	-	22	-	-	-	21	-	-	-	-	-
Brigham Young	-	-	-	-	-	-	25	-	-	-	-	-	-	-	23	21	25	-
California	-	-	-	-	25	21	19	-	-	-	-	-	-	-	-	-	-	-
Cincinnati	21	23	22	19	19	23	21	16	11	9	6	4	8	8	10	12	11	7
Connecticut	16	16	25	-	24	22	23	19	15	17	22	-	-	-	-	-	-	-
Duke	3	3	4	1	1	1	1	1	3	6	7	5	3	7	9	6	8	10
Florida St.	9	7	11	10	10	18	18	23	-	-	19	12	10	9	6	11	10	11
Georgia Tech	14	14	13	17	17	16	14	10	8	16	18	22	-	-	-	-	-	18
Georgetown	12	13	14	t11	11	11	10	17	20	18	21	23	-	-	-	-	-	-
Houston	-	-	-	-	-	-	-	-	-	-	25	-	-	-	-	-	-	-
Indiana	4	4	2	4	4	4	4	5	6	2	2	1	1	1	1	2	2	1
Iowa	11	11	10	8	8	8	8	8	13	14	11	9	13	20	18	15	17	13
Iowa St.	19	24	-	-	-	-	-	-	-	-	-	-	-	-	-	-	-	-

	PS	Nov. 23	Nov. 30	Dec. 7	Dec. 14	Dec. 21	Dec. 28	Jan. 4	Jan. 11	Jan. 18	Jan. 25	Feb. 1	Feb. 8	Feb. 15	Feb. 22	Mar. 1	Mar. 8	Mar. 15
Kansas	2	2	3	2	2	2	2	4	4	1	1	3	7	6	7	8	7	9
Kansas St.	-	-	-	-	-	-	-	-	-	-	-	-	23	-	-	-	-	-
Kentucky	5	5	5	3	3	3	3	2	1	4	4	2	2	2	2	5	4	2
Long Beach St.	-	-	-	-	-	-	-	-	-	25	-	-	-	-	-	-	-	-
Louisville	13	12	12	9	21	-	-	-	-	-	-	-	-	22	-	22	16	15
Marquette	-	-	-	-	-	-	-	-	-	-	24	20	15	24	20	-	-	-
Massachusetts	23	20	19	23	-	-	-	22	-	-	-	-	22	19	21	23	20	14
Memphis	8	9	8	21	-	-	-	-	-	-	-	-	-	-	-	-	-	-
Michigan	1	1	1	6	6	6	6	3	2	5	5	7	4	5	5	4	3	3
Michigan St.	20	18	18	24	23	20	17	14	23	21	-	25	-	-	-	-	-	-
Minnesota	-	-	-	-	-	-	-	-	19	-	-	-	-	-	-	-	-	-
Nebraska	25	25	-	25	20	17	20	-	-	-	-	-	-	-	-	-	-	-
UNLV	22	22	23	22	22	19	16	12	18	15	10	10	12	15	13	16	19	25
New Mexico	-	-	-	-	-	-	-	-	-	-	-	-	-	-	-	-	-	21
New Mexico St.	-	-	21	-	-	-	-	-	-	-	-	-	-	-	-	-	24	24
New Orleans	-	-	-	-	-	-	-	-	-	-	-	-	25	21	19	17	13	17
North Carolina	7	8	7	5	5	5	5	6	5	3	3	6	6	3	3	1	1	4
Ohio St.	-	-	-	-	-	-	-	-	21	24	-	-	-	-	-	-	-	-
Oklahoma	15	15	15	t11	9	9	15	11	10	12	20	16	-	-	-	-	-	-
Oklahoma St.	-	-	-	-	-	-	-	-	-	-	-	-	-	-	-	19	21	23
Pittsburgh	-	-	-	-	-	-	-	24	-	20	13	15	17	17	25	-	-	-
Purdue	-	-	24	18	16	15	13	9	17	13	14	19	18	14	17	24	18	22
Seton Hall	6	6	6	7	7	7	7	7	7	10	9	14	19	16	14	10	9	6
St. John's (N.Y.)	-	-	-	-	-	-	-	-	-	-	-	-	-	25	-	25	-	-
Syracuse	18	17	17	15	14	13	12	21	24	-	-	-	-	-	-	-	-	-
Tulane	17	19	20	20	18	24	-	-	-	-	23	18	20	18	16	20	23	-
UCLA	24	21	16	13	13	12	11	15	16	23	-	-	-	-	-	-	-	-
Utah	-	-	-	-	-	-	-	-	25	22	17	21	16	12	11	9	15	19
Vanderbilt	-	-	-	-	-	25	24	18	-	19	11	11	11	11	8	7	5	8
Virginia	-	-	-	-	-	-	-	25	14	7	15	24	24	23	22	-	-	-
Western Ky.	-	-	-	-	-	-	-	-	-	-	-	-	-	-	-	-	-	20
Wake Forest	-	-	-	-	-	-	-	-	-	-	-	13	9	10	12	14	12	16
Xavier	-	-	-	-	-	-	-	-	-	-	-	-	-	-	24	18	22	-

1993-94

	PS	Nov. 22	Nov. 29	Dec. 6	Dec. 13	Dec. 20	Dec. 27	Jan. 3	Jan. 10	Jan. 17	Jan. 24	Jan. 31	Feb. 7	Feb. 14	Feb. 21	Feb. 28	Mar. 7	Mar. 14
UAB	-	-	-	-	-	-	-	-	22	18	20	17	19	21	-	24	22	-
Arizona	18	19	19	14	13	13	12	9	6	9	13	12	16	15	9	8	7	9
Arkansas	3	3	2	1	1	1	1	1	4	3	5	6	3	1	1	1	1	2
Boston College	-	-	-	-	20	18	23	20	20	-	-	-	-	-	21	23	-	-
California	6	12	13	25	-	-	-	24	19	21	-	19	18	19	17	20	16	16
Cincinnati	19	22	23	20	17	20	18	17	21	19	-	25	-	23	-	-	-	25
Connecticut	-	-	-	21	16	15	14	16	14	10	6	5	6	3	5	4	2	4
Duke	4	4	6	4	3	3	3	3	2	5	2	1	2	6	2	2	5	6
Florida	-	-	-	-	-	-	-	-	-	-	-	24	20	17	16	19	17	14
Florida St.	25	-	-	-	-	-	-	-	-	-	-	-	-	-	-	-	-	-
Geo. Washington	24	23	22	24	23	23	21	23	-	-	-	-	-	-	-	-	-	-
Georgetown	15	15	25	-	-	-	-	-	-	-	-	-	-	-	-	-	-	-
Georgia Tech	14	13	17	18	14	14	15	12	17	17	21	-	-	25	23	-	-	-
Illinois	17	17	16	16	19	19	22	21	-	-	-	-	24	-	-	-	-	-
Indiana	12	11	21	12	12	12	13	14	11	8	11	14	12	16	12	17	18	18
Kansas	9	6	3	7	6	6	6	5	3	1	3	3	5	4	10	13	11	13
Kentucky	2	2	1	6	5	5	5	4	8	7	9	7	4	11	7	7	10	7
LSU	-	-	-	-	25	-	-	-	-	-	-	-	-	-	-	-	-	-
Louisville	7	7	11	10	10	11	11	11	15	13	12	9	7	5	13	10	14	10
Marquette	-	-	-	-	-	24	24	25	-	-	22	-	22	22	22	22	19	21
Maryland	-	-	-	-	-	-	-	-	-	25	18	21	-	-	-	-	-	-
Massachusetts	22	18	9	8	8	8	9	8	7	6	8	11	13	10	11	11	9	8
Michigan	5	5	5	3	7	7	7	13	10	15	15	13	11	7	3	3	8	11
Minnesota	10	9	15	17	15	16	16	19	18	20	17	22	23	20	20	18	20	23
Missouri	-	-	-	-	-	-	-	-	t25	-	24	20	15	12	6	6	3	5
Nebraska	-	-	-	-	-	-	-	-	-	-	-	-	-	-	-	-	-	22
New Mexico St.	-	-	-	-	-	-	-	-	-	-	25	23	-	-	25	-	-	-
North Carolina	1	1	4	2	2	2	2	2	1	4	4	2	1	2	4	5	4	1
Oklahoma St.	11	10	8	15	22	22	20	-	-	-	-	-	-	-	24	21	23	19
Pennsylvania	-	-	-	-	-	-	-	-	-	-	-	-	-	-	-	25	24	-
Purdue	21	21	14	11	11	10	10	10	9	12	7	8	10	9	14	9	6	3
St. Louis	-	-	-	-	-	-	-	-	-	23	23	18	17	18	19	16	21	24
Syracuse	20	20	18	13	21	21	19	18	16	16	14	15	14	14	18	14	13	15
Temple	8	8	7	5	4	4	4	7	13	11	10	10	8	13	8	12	12	12
Texas	-	-	-	-	-	-	-	-	-	-	-	-	-	-	-	-	25	20
UCLA	13	14	10	9	9	9	8	6	5	2	1	4	9	8	15	15	15	17
Vanderbilt	23	24	20	23	24	-	-	22	24	-	-	-	-	-				
Virginia	16	16	12	22	-	-	-	-	-	-	-	-	-	-	-	-	-	-
West Virginia	-	-	-	-	-	-	-	-	23	24	19	-	-	-	-	-	-	-
Western Ky.	-	-	-	-	-	25	25	-	-	-	-	-	-	-	-	-	-	-
Wisconsin	-	25	24	19	18	17	17	15	12	14	16	16	21	24	-	-	-	-
Xavier	-	-	-	-	-	-	-	-	t25	22	-	-	25	-	-	-	-	-

1994-95

Team	PS	Nov. 21	Nov. 28	Dec. 5	Dec. 12	Dec. 19	Dec. 26	Jan. 2	Jan. 9	Jan. 16	Jan. 23	Jan. 30	Feb. 6	Feb. 13	Feb. 20	Feb. 27	Mar. 6	Mar. 13
Alabama	18	25	-	-	-	-	-	-	-	-	-	20	23	18	20	21	20	20
Arizona	5	5	9	8	7	6	10	9	13	11	12	12	9	12	13	12	12	15
Arizona St.	-	-	12	16	13	15	16	15	12	13	13	16	14	13	15	15	18	16
Arkansas	1	1	4	3	4	3	3	3	5	9	9	8	12	10	8	7	5	6
California	-	-	-	-	-	24	14	17	20	-	-	-	-	-	-	-	-	-
Cincinnati	13	12	10	13	17	13	20	-	-	23	19	23	-	-	-	-	-	-
Clemson	-	-	-	-	-	-	-	-	18	-	-	-	-	-	-	-	-	-
Connecticut	19	16	16	10	10	10	8	6	2	2	2	4	3	1	4	4	6	8
Duke	8	8	6	9	9	9	7	11	16	-	-	-	-	-	-	-	-	-
Florida	10	10	8	6	8	8	13	13	15	24	23	25	-	-	-	-	-	-
Georgetown	15	14	19	18	15	12	12	12	10	10	14	13	20	-	-	23	24	22
Georgia Tech	23	22	20	17	14	18	17	24	22	22	21	21	18	20	24	-	-	-
Illinois	25	-	-	-	-	23	-	-	-	20	-	-	-	-	-	-	-	-
Indiana	9	11	-	-	-	-	24	21	-	-	-	-	-	-	-	-	-	-
Iowa	-	-	-	-	-	-	-	22	19	-	-	-	-	-	-	-	-	-
Iowa St.	-	-	-	-	-	25	21	16	23	14	11	11	19	21	23	24	-	24
Kansas	11	9	7	4	3	7	6	5	3	7	7	3	2	3	1	3	2	5
Kentucky	4	4	3	7	6	5	5	8	7	5	5	6	5	4	6	5	3	2
Maryland	7	7	11	11	12	11	9	7	9	8	8	5	8	7	7	6	10	10
Massachusetts	3	3	1	5	5	4	4	4	1	1	1	1	4	5	5	8	8	7
Michigan	16	13	17	23	25	-	-	-	-	-	-	-	-	-	-	-	-	-
Michigan St.	20	17	18	15	18	17	15	14	11	12	10	9	7	8	12	10	9	11
Minnesota	-	-	15	12	11	16	-	-	-	-	-	-	-	24	22	-	-	-
Mississippi St.	-	-	-	-	-	-	-	-	-	-	-	-	21	23	16	14	15	18
Missouri	-	-	-	-	-	-	-	-	17	16	20	18	13	9	14	19	17	23
Nebraska	-	-	-	-	-	-	23	19	-	-	-	-	-	-	-	-	-	-
New Mexico St.	-	-	25	22	24	21	22	20	24	19	24	-	-	-	-	-	-	-
North Carolina	2	2	2	1	1	1	1	1	4	3	3	2	1	2	3	2	4	4
Ohio	-	23	14	21	19	-	-	-	-	-	-	-	-	-	-	-	-	-
Oklahoma	-	-	-	-	-	-	-	-	-	-	25	24	-	-	25	16	16	17
Oklahoma St.	21	19	-	-	-	-	-	-	-	-	-	-	24	22	18	18	19	14
Oregon	-	-	-	-	-	-	-	-	25	17	18	22	22	19	-	-	25	-
Pennsylvania	-	-	-	-	-	-	-	25	21	25	-	-	-	-	-	-	-	-
Purdue	-	-	-	-	-	-	-	-	-	-	-	-	25	25	21	17	14	12
St. John's (N.Y.)	-	-	-	-	-	-	25	-	-	-	-	-	-	-	-	-	-	-
Stanford	-	-	-	-	-	-	-	23	-	21	17	17	15	17	19	20	-	-
Syracuse	12	18	22	19	16	14	11	10	8	6	6	10	10	11	17	22	21	25
UCLA	6	6	5	2	2	2	2	2	6	4	4	7	6	6	2	1	1	1
Utah	-	-	-	-	-	-	-	-	-	-	-	-	-	-	-	-	22	19
Villanova	22	21	24	24	22	-	-	-	-	-	22	19	16	15	9	11	13	9
Virginia	14	20	23	20	23	22	-	-	-	18	15	15	17	16	11	13	11	13
Wake Forest	24	24	21	25	21	19	18	18	14	15	16	14	11	14	10	9	7	3
Western Ky.	-	-	-	-	-	-	-	-	-	-	-	-	-	-	-	-	23	21
Wisconsin	17	15	13	14	20	20	19	-	-	-	-	-	-	-	-	-	-	-
Xavier	-	-	-	-	-	-	-	-	-	-	-	-	-	-	-	25	-	-

1995-96

Team	PS	Nov. 20	Nov. 27	Dec. 4	Dec. 11	Dec. 18	Dec. 26	Jan. 2	Jan. 8	Jan. 15	Jan. 22	Jan. 29	Feb. 5	Feb. 12	Feb. 19	Feb. 26	Mar. 5	Mar. 12
Arizona	19	4	4	4	3	9	9	18	18	13	14	16	13	13	13	11	11	11
Arkansas	16	-	25	-	-	-	-	-	-	-	-	-	-	-	-	-	-	-
Auburn	-	-	-	-	-	-	-	-	-	23	21	22	-	-	-	-	-	-
Boston College	-	-	-	-	-	-	-	24	-	24	20	21	22	21	20	-	-	-
California	25	-	-	-	-	24	-	-	-	-	25	-	-	-	-	-	-	-
Cincinnati	21	21	21	17	12	9	5	5	4	3	5	5	5	6	6	7	8	7
Clemson	-	-	-	-	-	-	24	22	16	19	18	24	-	-	-	-	-	-
Connecticut	6	6	9	9	8	8	7	7	6	5	4	4	4	3	3	4	3	3
Duke	-	-	12	18	21	20	20	19	-	-	-	-	-	-	-	-	-	-
Eastern Mich.	-	-	-	-	-	-	-	-	-	-	-	23	24	23	-	-	-	-
Geo. Washington	-	-	-	-	-	-	-	-	-	-	-	-	-	-	-	24	-	-
Georgetown	5	5	6	6	7	6	6	6	5	8	6	9	8	14	11	8	6	4
Georgia	-	-	-	-	-	18	16	14	19	22	-	-	-	-	-	-	-	-
Georgia Tech	-	25	20	16	19	21	-	-	-	-	-	25	-	-	23	18	18	13
Illinois	-	-	-	21	16	14	12	13	21	-	-	-	-	-	-	-	-	-
Indiana	23	23	-	-	-	-	-	-	-	-	-	-	-	-	-	-	-	-
Iowa	8	10	11	12	9	10	10	10	11	16	T22	16	19	19	18	20	19	21
Iowa St.	-	-	-	-	-	-	-	-	-	-	-	-	21	22	22	23	23	17
Kansas	2	2	2	1	1	1	4	4	3	4	3	3	3	5	5	3	5	6
Kentucky	1	1	1	5	5	4	2	2	2	2	2	2	2	2	2	1	1	2
Louisville	12	13	18	23	20	25	-	-	-	-	-	-	20	24	21	21	22	24
Marquette	-	-	-	-	-	-	-	-	-	-	24	-	-	-	-	-	21	20
Maryland	15	14	19	20	-	-	-	-	-	-	-	-	-	-	-	-	-	-
Massachusetts	7	7	5	3	3	2	1	1	1	1	1	1	1	1	1	2	2	1
Memphis	13	12	7	7	6	5	3	3	9	9	12	11	15	15	19	14	14	16
Michigan	17	16	24	22	18	17	19	21	23	20	16	20	23	-	-	-	-	-
Mississippi St.	9	9	8	8	15	16	17	17	12	21	-	-	-	25	-	-	-	-
Missouri	14	15	13	11	14	15	18	-	-	-	-	-	-	-	-	-	-	-
New Mexico	-	-	-	-	-	-	-	25	25	-	-	-	-	-	-	-	-	23
North Carolina	20	20	17	13	10	11	11	16	10	10	11	8	12	17	17	19	20	25
Penn St.	-	-	-	-	-	-	-	-	20	14	14	10	10	9	14	12	16	18
Purdue	24	24	-	-	-	-	-	-	22	17	19	17	14	11	7	5	4	5
Santa Clara	-	-	-	25	22	-	-	-	-	-	-	-	-	-	-	-	-	-
Stanford	18	18	16	24	-	-	-	-	24	-	-	-	25	20	24	25	-	-
Syracuse	-	-	-	-	25	19	13	11	14	12	17	18	18	16	15	15	13	15

Team	PS	Nov. 20	27	Dec. 4	11	18	26	Jan. 2	8	15	22	29	Feb. 5	12	19	26	Mar. 5	12
Texas	-	-	-	-	-	-	-	23	-	-	-	-	-	-	-	-	-	-
Texas Tech	-	-	-	-	-	-	-	-	-	25T	22	15	13	12	9	9	7	8
Tulsa	-	-	-	-	-	-	25	-	-	-	-	-	-	-	-	-	-	-
UCLA	4	4	23	-	24	-	23	20	17	13	15	19	17	18	16	17	17	14
Utah	10	8	14	14	13	13	15	15	13	15	10	7	7	7	8	10	10	12
Villanova	3	3	3	2	2	7	8	8	7	7	7	6	6	4	4	6	9	10
Virginia	19	17	15	15	23	23	22	-	-	-	-	-	-	-	-	-	-	-
Virginia Tech	22	22	22	19	17	22	21	18	15	11	8	13	11	10	12	16	15	22
Wake Forest	11	11	10	10	11	12	14	12	8	6	9	12	9	8	10	13	12	9
Wis.-Green Bay	-	-	-	-	-	-	-	-	-	-	-	-	-	-	25	22	24	-

1996-97

Team	PS	Nov. 19	26	Dec. 3	10	17	24	31	Jan. 7	14	21	28	Feb. 4	11	18	25	Mar. 4	11
Alabama	-	-	-	-	24	20	19	-	-	-	-	-	-	-	-	-	-	-
Arizona	19	19	11	15	8	6	9	9	7	6	11	10	14	11	13	15	12	15
Arkansas	13	16	16	22	20	19	22	22	-	-	-	-	-	-	-	-	-	-
Boston College	21	21	23	20	25	-	25	25	23	19	22	-	-	-	-	-	-	23
California	-	-	-	-	-	-	-	-	-	-	-	-	-	-	25	-	-	-
Col. of Charleston	-	-	-	-	-	-	-	-	-	-	-	-	-	25	22	20	17	16
Cincinnati	1	1	1	4	7	7	7	6	6	4	9	8	12	8	11	9	10	10
Clemson	20	12	10	12	10	8	6	5	5	3	2	7	10	7	8	12	13	14
Colorado	-	-	-	-	-	-	-	-	-	-	18	18	15	15	21	19	18	24
Duke	10	10	6	10	14	11	12	13	10	13	10	12	8	6	6	7	7	8
Fresno St.	14	14	15	13	16	21	-	-	-	-	-	-	-	-	-	-	-	-
Geo. Washington	24	24	25	-	-	-	-	-	-	-	-	-	-	-	-	-	-	-
Georgia	-	-	-	-	-	-	-	-	24	21	-	-	-	-	-	-	24	17
Illinois	-	-	-	-	-	-	-	24	25	-	-	-	-	20	23	21	15	19
Indiana	-	22	20	8	12	13	13	12	15	17	21	17	24	-	24	22	25	-
Iowa	23	25	-	-	-	-	-	-	-	-	-	-	25	-	-	-	-	-
Iowa St.	11	11	9	9	6	5	5	4	4	8	14	11	6	9	7	13	16	18
Kansas	2	2	2	1	1	1	1	1	1	1	1	1	1	1	1	1	1	1
Kentucky	3	8	8	6	3	3	3	3	3	5	3	3	3	4	3	3	6	5
Louisville	-	-	-	-	22	18	16	14	14	10	6	9	11	17	15	17	20	25
Marquette	25	-	-	-	-	-	-	-	-	-	25	24	-	-	-	-	-	-
Maryland	-	-	-	-	-	25	21	19	19	11	7	5	7	10	14	16	22	22
Massachusetts	15	15	17	-	-	-	-	-	-	-	-	-	-	-	-	-	-	-
Michigan	9	9	7	7	5	4	4	8	16	18	13	16	13	14	18	24	-	-
Minnesota	22	23	24	16	17	16	15	15	11	7	8	6	4	3	2	2	2	3
Mississippi	-	-	-	-	-	-	-	-	-	20	-	-	-	-	-	-	-	-
New Mexico	17	18	19	11	15	15	14	16	18	12	15	13	9	13	10	11	14	11
North Carolina	8	7	14	14	11	12	11	11	13	22	19	19	20	16	12	8	5	4
Oregon	-	-	-	-	-	-	24	20	17	24	-	-	-	-	-	-	-	-
St. Joseph's	-	-	-	-	-	-	-	-	-	-	-	-	-	-	-	23	19	12
South Carolina	-	-	-	-	-	-	-	-	-	-	-	25	19	12	9	6	4	6
Stanford	18	20	21	24	21	22	23	21	21	15	17	15	18	22	20	25	23	21
Syracuse	12	13	12	19	-	-	-	-	-	-	-	-	-	-	-	-	-	-
Texas	16	17	18	18	13	14	18	18	22	23	23	23	-	-	-	-	-	-
Texas Tech	-	-	-	-	18	23	-	23	20	25	20	22	23	21	-	-	-	-
Tulane	-	-	-	-	-	-	-	-	-	-	-	-	21	23	-	-	-	-
Tulsa	-	-	22	21	-	-	-	-	-	-	24	21	22	-	-	-	-	-
UCLA	5	5	13	17	23	24	-	-	-	-	-	-	-	24	17	10	9	7
Utah	6	4	4	3	9	9	8	7	9	9	5	4	5	5	5	4	3	2
Villanova	7	6	5	5	4	10	10	10	8	16	12	14	16	18	19	18	21	20
Virginia	-	-	-	25	-	-	-	-	-	-	-	-	-	-	-	-	-	-
Wake Forest	4	3	3	2	2	2	2	2	2	2	4	2	2	2	4	5	8	9
Xavier	-	-	-	23	19	17	17	17	12	14	16	20	17	19	16	14	11	13

PS=preseason

1997-98

Team	PS	Nov. 18	25	Dec. 2	9	16	23	30	Jan. 6	13	20	27	Feb. 3	10	17	24	Mar. 3	10
Arizona	1	1	1	4	6	5	5	8	5	5	6	6	4	3	3	2	2	4
Arkansas	-	-	-	18	15	13	12	23	22	22	18	15	14	12	16	12	16	17
Charlotte	18	17	25	-	-	-	-	-	-	-	-	-	-	-	-	-	-	-
Cincinnati	-	-	-	-	-	-	-	-	-	-	21	18	20	19	17	17	14	9
Clemson	5	5	13	17	17	-	21	21	24	-	25	-	-	-	-	-	-	-
Connecticut	12	12	11	13	13	12	11	10	8	10	8	9	7	6	7	6	6	6
Duke	3	3	3	1	1	3	3	3	2	2	1	1	1	2	2	1	1	3
Florida St.	-	-	-	19	16	17	17	15	13	17	20	-	-	-	-	-	-	-
Fresno St.	13	13	12	16	18	-	-	-	-	-	-	-	-	-	-	-	-	-
Geo. Washington	-	-	-	-	-	-	-	-	-	-	-	-	22	17	24	-	-	-
Georgia	19	25	22	21	23	20	-	-	-	-	-	-	-	-	-	-	-	-
Georgia Tech	-	-	-	22	24	-	-	-	-	-	-	-	-	-	-	-	-	-
Hawaii	-	-	-	-	-	-	-	-	21	24	24	-	-	-	-	-	-	-
Illinois	-	-	-	-	-	-	-	-	-	-	-	-	-	-	23	22	18	22
Illinois St.	-	24	-	-	-	-	-	-	-	-	-	-	-	-	-	-	-	-
Indiana	17	23	21	-	-	-	-	-	-	-	-	25	-	-	-	-	-	-
Iowa	15	14	14	10	10	15	15	14	11	13	10	16	24	-	-	-	-	-
Kansas	2	2	2	2	3	2	2	2	4	3	3	5	3	4	4	4	4	2
Kentucky	8	9	8	7	4	4	4	6	6	6	7	7	8	7	8	7	7	5
Louisville	25	22	19	-	-	-	-	-	-	-	-	-	-	-	-	-	-	-
Marquette	-	-	-	-	-	-	-	25	20	23	-	-	-	-	-	-	-	-
Maryland	-	-	24	23	19	22	20	20	-	-	-	23	25	24	25	-	21	20
Massachusetts	-	-	-	-	-	-	-	-	-	-	-	-	23	20	18	20	-	-
Michigan	-	-	-	-	-	21	-	18	17	19	16	19	18	21	22	21	17	12
Michigan St.	-	-	-	-	-	-	-	-	-	-	-	22	16	13	14	10	12	16
Mississippi	23	21	17	14	21	18	16	16	14	11	13	12	17	18	15	13	10	13
Murray St.	-	-	-	-	-	-	-	-	-	-	-	-	-	-	-	-	-	25
New Mexico	11	11	10	8	14	14	14	12	12T	15	17	14	12	11	11	16	20	18
North Carolina	4	4	4	3	2	1	1	1	1	1	2	2	2	1	1	3	4	1
Oklahoma	20	19	18	-	-	-	-	-	-	-	-	-	-	-	-	-	-	-
Oklahoma St.	-	-	-	-	-	-	-	-	-	25	-	-	-	-	-	25	25	-
Princeton	-	-	-	25	22	19	18	17	15	12	11	11	11	10	9	9	8	8
Purdue	9	8	6	6	8	8	7	5	9	9	12	10	10	8	5	11	9	11
Rhode Island	21	20	23	-	-	-	22	24	23	20	22	21	-	25	-	-	-	-
South Carolina	7	6	5	5	5	6	10	11	16	14	14	13	13	15	13	14	15	14
Stanford	14	15	15	12	11	9	8	7	7	7	5	4	9	14	10	8	11	10
Syracuse	-	-	-	-	-	25	19	19	18T	15	15	20	19	23	21	23	22	21
Temple	24	18	20	20	20	16	24	-	-	-	-	-	-	-	-	24	24	24
Texas	22	-	-	-	-	-	-	-	-	-	-	-	-	-	-	-	-	-
TCU	-	-	-	-	-	24	25	-	-	-	-	-	-	22	19	15	13	15
UCLA	6	7	7	15	12	11	9	9	10	8	9	8	6	9	12	18	19	19
Utah	16	16	16	11	9	7	6	4	3	4	4	3	5	5	6	5	5	7
Wake Forest	-	-	-	24	25	23	-	-	-	-	-	-	-	-	-	-	-	-
West Virginia	-	-	-	-	-	-	23	22	25	21	23	17	15	16	20	19	23	-
Xavier	10	10	9	9	7	10	13	13	19	18	19	24	21	-	-	-	-	23

PS=Preseason

1998-99

Team	PS	Nov. 17	24	Dec. 1	8	15	22	29	Jan. 5	12	19	26	Feb. 2	9	16	23	Mar. 2	9
Arizona	18	12	11	13	8	T8	8	6	11	7	9	13	10	10	8	7	13	12
Arkansas	19	19	21	19	23	20	19	20	18	24	22	21	23	-	-	-	22	17
Auburn	-	-	-	-	-	19	18	17	14	8	6	7	6	3	3	2	4	4
Charlotte	-	-	-	-	-	-	-	-	-	-	-	-	-	-	-	-	-	24
Col. of Charleston	-	-	-	-	-	-	-	-	-	-	-	-	22	20	18	17	16	16
Cincinnati	15	17	15	6	4	4	4	3	3	3	5	5	3	4	9	9	7	11
Clemson	-	24	22	24	17	16	16	14	20	25	-	-	-	-	-	-	-	-
Connecticut	2	2	2	1	1	1	1	1	1	1	1	1	1	2	2	4	3	3
Duke	1	1	1	4	3	2	2	2	2	2	2	2	2	1	1	1	1	1
Florida	-	-	-	-	-	-	-	-	-	-	-	25	-	23	23	19	21	23
Indiana	22	21	17	16	11	10	10	8	13	23	18	20	21	17	19	20	17	19
Iowa	-	-	-	-	-	25	21	21	19	12	14	16	14	19	20	18	20	21
Kansas	8	8	8	7	10	13	13	18	16	15	19	22	-	24	-	-	-	22
Kentucky	4	4	4	8	5	3	3	7	5	6	7	6	5	8	6	13	14	8
Louisville	-	-	-	-	-	-	-	-	-	-	24	-	-	-	-	-	-	-
Maryland	6	6	5	2	2	5	5	4	6	5	4	4	7	7	5	5	5	5
Massachusetts	24	23	-	-	-	-	-	-	-	-	-	-	-	-	-	-	-	-
Miami (Fla.)	-	-	-	-	-	-	-	-	-	-	25	23	25	16	15	11	9	10
Miami (Ohio)	-	-	24	22	-	-	-	-	-	-	-	-	-	-	25	-	-	-
Michigan St.	5	5	7	9	14	14	15	13	12	14	11	8	8	5	4	3	2	2
Minnesota	-	-	-	-	24	17	17	16	17	19	17	19T	18	22	-	-	23	-
Missouri	-	-	-	-	-	-	-	-	-	-	-	-	24	-	22	-	24	-
New Mexico	T20	20	20	17	12	11	11	15	15	16	12	18	17	25	24	21	25	25
North Carolina	11	10	9	3	7	7	7	9	10	9	10	10	12	12	14	14	15	13
Ohio St.	-	-	-	-	-	-	-	-	25	21	-	15	15	13	11	10	11	14
Oklahoma	-	-	-	-	-	24	23	-	-	-	-	-	-	-	-	-	-	-
Oklahoma St.	13	13	12	11	19	18	25	25	22	22	23	-	-	-	-	-	-	-
Pittsburgh	-	-	-	20	20	22	24	23	-	-	-	-	-	-	-	-	-	-
Purdue	16	15	14	14	9	T8	9	11	7	13	16	14T	18	21	17	23	-	-
Rhode Island	23	25	-	-	-	-	-	-	-	-	-	-	-	-	-	-	-	-
St. John's (N.Y.)	-	-	23	25	18	15	14	12	9	11	8	9	9	11	10	8	10	9
Stanford	3	3	3	5	6	6	6	5	4	4	3	3	4	6	7	6	6	7
Syracuse	T20	22	19	12	13	21	22	22	21	18	20	17	16	18	21	T24	-	-
Temple	7	7	6	10	16	-	-	-	-	-	-	-	-	-	-	T24	-	-
Tennessee	9	18	25	-	21	-	-	-	-	-	-	-	-	-	-	-	18	20
Texas	-	-	-	-	-	-	-	-	-	-	-	-	-	-	22	-	-	-
TCU	25	-	-	-	-	-	-	24	24	20	21	24	-	-	-	-	-	-
UCLA	12	11	10	18	15	12	12	10	8	10	13	11	13	9	16	15	12	15
Utah	10	9	18	21	25	-	-	-	-	-	-	-	20	14	12	12	8	6
Washington	14	14	16	15	22	-	-	-	-	-	-	-	-	-	-	-	-	-
Wisconsin	-	-	-	-	-	23	20	19	23	17	15	12	11	15	13	16	19	18
Xavier	17	16	13	23	-	-	-	-	-	-	-	-	-	-	-	-	-	-

PS=preseason

1999-2000

Team	PS	Nov. 16	23	30	Dec. 7	14	21	28	Jan. 4	11	18	25	Feb. 1	8	15	22	29	Mar. 7	14
Arizona	9	10	8	4	2	4	3	5	5	2	2	5	9	7	4	4	3	9	4
Auburn	4	3	2	7	8	6	7	4	4	4	4	7	10	9	12	11	19	-	24
Cincinnati	2	1	1	1	1	1	4	3	3	1	1	1	1	1	1	3	2	1	7
Connecticut	1	8	7	5	6	3	2	2	2	5	8	6	7	13	18	22	24	21	20
DePaul	20	20	18	22	20	19	24	24	23	21	23	-	-	-	-	-	-	-	-
Duke	10	18	16	17	14	11	10	9	8	6	5	3	3	3	3	2	4	3	1
Florida	8	7	6	11	9	9	8	6	6	10	9	10	12	12	11	9	8	11	13
Gonzaga	24	25	25	25	24	22	22	-	-	-	-	-	-	-	-	-	-	-	-
Illinois	16	17	15	16	22	20	15	20	19	22	-	-	-	-	-	-	25	25	21
Indiana	-	-	-	23	15	21	20	12	10	9	11	14	11	10	10	16	14	18	22

DIVISION I

1999-2000 (continued)

Team	PS	Nov 16	23	30	Dec 7	14	21	28	Jan 4	11	18	25	Feb 1	8	15	22	29	Mar 7	14
Iowa	-	22	23	-	-	-	-	-	-	-	-	-	-	-	-	-	-	-	-
Iowa St.	-	-	-	-	-	-	-	-	-	-	-	-	20	17	14	17	10	7	6
Kansas	-	11	11	10	6	5	8	12	10	9	8	7	12	15	20	24	23	23	24
Kentucky	14	14	11	13	23	-	-	25	20	18	16	14	11	19	18	22	16	19	-
LSU	-	-	-	-	-	-	21	24	-	-	22	25	16	15	12	-	-	10	10
Louisville	-	-	-	-	-	-	-	-	25	-	-	-	-	-	-	-	-	-	-
Maryland	-	24	24	21	16	17	14	12	18	24	22	25	23	22	19	17	-	20	17
Miami (Fla.)	25	-	-	-	-	-	-	-	-	-	-	-	-	-	-	-	-	23	23
Michigan St.	3	2	3	8	4	5	5	8	11	11	10	9	8	6	6	5	7	5	2
North Carolina	6	5	4	2	7	6	13	14	13	21	-	-	-	-	-	-	-	-	-
North Carolina St.	-	-	-	-	25	-	-	21	-	-	-	-	-	-	-	-	-	-	-
Ohio St.	5	4	12	15	13	12	16	15	13	17	13	8	5	5	7	6	6	4	8
Oklahoma	-	-	-	-	-	23	21	22	20	16	17	18	18	16	20	20	21	15	12
Oklahoma St.	22	23	21	21	17	14	13	11	16	14	12	15	13	14	8	10	13	17	14
Oregon	-	-	-	-	-	-	-	-	-	23	24	-	-	-	-	-	-	-	-
Purdue	23	24	22	19	25	24	-	-	-	-	-	-	-	25	21	20	22	25	-
St. John's (N.Y.)	18	15	-	-	-	-	-	-	-	-	-	-	19	25	-	-	18	19	9
Seton Hall	-	-	-	-	-	-	-	-	-	-	-	-	-	-	-	23	-	-	-
Southern California	-	-	-	-	-	-	-	-	-	-	23	-	-	-	-	-	-	-	-
Stanford	13	9	9	3	3	2	1	1	3	3	2	2	2	1	1	2	3	-	-
Syracuse	17	13	14	14	12	10	9	7	7	7	6	4	4	4	9	13	9	12	16
Temple	-	7	6	5	10	19	17	19	17	-	23	-	23	21	19	15	8	5	6
Tennessee	19	19	17	18	16	13	11	16	15	12	16	11	6	8	5	7	11	8	11
Texas	21	21	20	-	-	-	-	-	-	-	18	19	10	15	14	18	16	13	15
Tulsa	-	-	-	-	-	25	22	19	15	13	17	15	13	12	15	-	-	14	18
UCLA	12	12	13	12	11	18	18	23	24	-	25	-	-	-	-	-	-	-	-
Utah	15	16	19	20	-	-	21	18	-	22	19	19	21	21	25	-	-	-	-
Vanderbilt	-	-	-	-	-	-	-	-	-	-	-	-	20	20	24	22	-	24	-
Wake Forest	-	-	-	18	25	23	19	-	-	-	-	-	-	-	-	-	-	-	-

2000-01

Team	PS	Nov 14	21	28	Dec 5	12	19	26	Jan 2	9	16	23	30	Feb 6	13	20	27	Mar 6	13
Alabama	-	-	-	-	23	18	17	20	18	16	T15	18	17	18	21	14	20	-	-
Arizona	1	1	1	5	5	7	10	12	16	21	17	12	7	11	8	8	9	8	5
Arkansas	T15	15	24	25	21	25	25	-	-	-	-	-	-	-	-	-	-	-	-
Boston College	-	-	-	-	-	-	-	-	-	24	25	23	20	17	9	10	11	10	7
Cincinnati	18	17	16	22	18	17	22	19	25	-	-	-	-	-	-	-	-	-	-
Connecticut	14	13	12	16	15	11	11	10	10	13	T15	24	-	-	-	-	-	-	-
Dayton	-	-	-	-	-	-	-	24	-	-	-	-	-	-	-	-	-	-	-
DePaul	21	22	21	-	-	-	-	-	-	-	-	-	-	-	-	-	-	-	-
Duke	2	2	2	1	1	1	1	3	3	2	2	2	2	3	3	4	2	3	1
Florida	11	11	11	10	8	8	7	5	5	8	7	14	13	8	11	7	6	5	8
Fresno St.	-	-	-	-	-	-	-	-	-	-	22	19	23	20	-	25	-	-	-
Georgetown	-	-	-	-	24	23	21	19	12	9	10	14	15	18	21	21	18	21	-
Georgia	-	-	-	-	-	-	-	-	-	-	-	-	25	-	-	-	-	-	-
Illinois	8	8	8	9	9	5	5	9	9	7	11	7	6	7	4	3	5	4	4
Indiana	-	-	-	-	-	-	-	-	-	-	-	-	-	-	-	-	-	-	20
Iowa	-	-	-	-	22	19	23	-	-	14	21	18	14	25	-	-	24	-	-
Iowa St.	25	-	-	25	-	25	23	18	23	17	15	12	7	6	8	7	10	7	10
Kansas	7	4	3	2	3	10	9	7	7	5	5	4	3	5	6	11	10	9	12
Kentucky	12	20	22	-	-	-	-	-	-	-	-	-	-	22	13	15	15	9	-
Maryland	5	6	6	13	19	20	20	18	17	14	12	8	9	13	17	20	16	11	11
Michigan St.	3	3	4	3	2	2	2	1	1	3	3	3	5	4	5	5	3	2	3
Mississippi	-	-	-	-	-	23	24	24	22	20	21	19	-	25	16	12	14	14	14
Missouri	-	-	-	-	-	-	-	-	-	-	-	20	-	-	-	-	-	-	-
North Carolina	6	7	7	6	14	15	15	14	13	9	6	5	4	1	1	2	4	6	6
Notre Dame	T15	16	14	11	10	21	21	22	21	25	-	23	20	14	18	13	19	19	-
Ohio St.	-	-	-	-	-	-	-	-	-	-	-	-	-	-	-	-	-	24	-
Oklahoma	22	21	19	14	20	19	18	17	15	22	22	-	24	21	13	16	17	16	13
Providence	-	-	-	-	-	-	-	-	-	-	-	-	-	-	-	-	25	-	-
St. John's (N.Y.)	-	24	23	19	24	-	-	-	-	-	-	-	-	-	-	-	-	-	-
St. Joseph's	-	-	-	-	-	-	-	-	-	-	-	-	-	-	-	23	18	21	22
Seton Hall	10	10	10	8	7	9	8	11	11	15	18	16	22	-	-	-	-	-	-
Southern Cal	23	23	20	15	-	12	13	13	16	20	19	24	25	21	22	-	-	-	-
Stanford	4	5	5	4	3	3	2	2	1	1	1	1	2	1	1	1	2	1	2
Syracuse	-	-	20	13	12	12	15	14	11	8	11	12	9	10	17	19	17	17	-
Temple	-	-	-	17	-	-	-	-	-	-	-	-	-	-	-	-	-	-	-
Tennessee	9	9	9	7	6	4	4	6	4	4	6	8	10	15	22	-	-	-	-
Texas	-	-	-	-	-	-	24	23	-	20	-	-	-	-	-	-	24	20	18
UCLA	17	14	15	-	-	-	-	-	-	-	-	-	-	24	15	12	-	13	15
Utah	13	12	13	18	22	-	-	-	-	-	-	-	-	-	-	-	-	-	-
Virginia	24	25	25	21	16	14	14	8	8	10	13	13	11	6	12	9	7	12	6
Wake Forest	20	18	17	12	11	6	6	4	4	6	10	9	16	19	23	24	23	22	23
Wisconsin	19	19	18	23	17	16	16	13	12	17	19	15	10	16	19	19	22	23	25
Xavier	-	-	-	-	-	-	-	-	-	-	-	-	-	24	-	25	-	-	-

2001-02

Team	PS	Nov 20	27	Dec 4	11	18	25	Jan 1	8	15	22	29	Feb 5	12	19	26	Mar 5	12
Alabama	24	22	21	16	22	23	21	18	T14	16	14	11	4	7	5	6	8	8
Arizona	-	8	4	7	6	11	14	15	20	15	10	19	11	9	14	14	15	7
Ball St.	-	-	16	15	20	21	-	-	-	-	-	-	-	-	-	-	-	-
Boston College	17	17	15	13	11	10	11	11	16	22	-	-	-	-	-	-	-	-
Butler	-	-	-	-	-	23	20	24	-	-	-	-	-	-	-	-	-	-
California	-	-	-	-	-	-	-	-	-	-	-	-	-	-	21	25	-	-
Cincinnati	-	-	-	25	17	13	10	7	4	4	6	5	4	4	5	5	-	-
Connecticut	-	-	-	-	-	-	-	-	-	25	17	-	-	23	19	10	-	-
Duke	1	1	1	1	1	1	1	1	2	1	1	1	1	1	3	3	3	1
Florida	6	7	6	6	5	4	3	3	2	5	5	8	6	8	8	11	15	-
Fresno St.	-	23	24	21	-	-	-	-	-	-	-	-	-	-	-	-	-	-
Georgetown	14	16	18	19	18	16	20	24	-	-	-	-	-	-	-	-	-	-
Georgia	-	-	-	-	-	-	-	-	-	20	15	16	17	21	18	16	17	23
Gonzaga	-	-	-	-	25	24	22	22	18	13	16	11	9	8	7	7	6	-
Hawaii	-	-	-	-	-	-	-	-	-	-	-	-	-	-	-	-	-	25
Illinois	3	2	2	5	10	9	7	7	9	11	9	12	21	18	16	15	10	13
Indiana	22	20	-	-	21	-	-	-	-	-	-	-	22	23	25	23	-	-
Iowa	9	9	7	12	15	12	9	9	13	17	-	-	-	-	-	-	-	-
Kansas	7	4	8	4	3	2	2	1	4	2	2	2	2	1	1	1	2	-
Kentucky	4	10	13	11	9	7	6	6	8	12	8	10	7	10	12	11	12	16
Marquette	-	-	23	17	14	14	19	25	-	-	-	18	11	9	9	13	12	-
Maryland	2	6	5	3	3	2	8	8	4	3	3	3	3	2	2	2	4	-
Memphis	12	12	20	22	-	-	-	-	-	-	-	-	-	-	-	-	-	-
Miami (Fla.)	-	-	-	-	-	24	21	21	24	22	15	12	13	17	22	20	21	-
Michigan St.	15	13	22	24	23	17	13	19	25	-	-	-	-	-	-	-	-	-
Mississippi St.	-	-	-	-	-	-	-	22	-	-	-	-	17	-	-	-	-	-
Missouri	8	5	3	2	2	8	10	17	17	21	18	22	22	-	-	-	-	-
North Carolina	19	-	-	-	-	-	-	-	-	-	-	-	-	-	-	-	-	-
North Caro. St.	-	-	-	-	-	-	-	-	-	-	-	-	-	24	-	-	-	-
Ohio St.	-	-	-	-	-	-	-	-	-	25	16	23	19	18	21	14	-	-
Oklahoma	25	-	-	24	22	12	10	5	5	6	4	4	6	5	4	3	-	-
Oklahoma St.	18	15	14	10	8	6	5	5	6	11	9	14	16	13	12	14	20	-
Oregon	-	-	-	-	-	-	-	-	-	23	19	-	21	-	13	17	15	13
Pittsburgh	-	-	-	-	-	-	-	-	23	-	21	-	14	11	10	7	9	-
St. Joseph's	10	19	19	18	16	15	-	-	-	-	-	-	-	-	-	-	-	-
Southern Cal	20	24	-	-	-	-	-	-	18	23	23	25	25	T20	19	22	18	-
Stanford	13	14	11	14	12	13	16	12	T14	19	17	18	20	12	10	17	16	24
Syracuse	21	18	12	9	13	18	18	16	12	8	12	14	23	-	-	-	-	-
Temple	16	25	-	-	-	-	-	-	-	-	-	-	-	-	-	-	-	-
Texas	23	-	-	-	-	-	-	-	-	-	-	24	-	-	-	-	-	-
Texas Tech	-	-	-	-	-	-	-	-	-	-	-	-	20	24	-	-	-	-
UCLA	5	3	10	20	17	19	15	14	11	9	13	13	15	20	25	-	-	-
Virginia	11	11	9	8	7	5	4	7	10	7	8	10	15	22	-	-	-	-
Wake Forest	-	-	25	23	19	20	25	23	19	14	21	24	19	19	T20	24	-	-
Western Ky.	-	21	17	25	-	-	-	-	-	-	-	-	-	-	-	24	20	18	19
Xavier	-	-	-	-	-	-	-	-	-	-	-	-	-	-	-	24	22	-

PS=preseason
(Note: AP does not do a post-tournament poll)

Final Season Polls

Final Regular-Season Polls

The Helms Foundation of Los Angeles selected the national college men's basketball champions from 1942-82 and researched retroactive picks from 1901-41. The Helms winners are listed in this section to the time The Associated Press (AP) poll started in 1949. The AP is the writers' poll, while the UPI and USA Today/CNN and USA Today/NABC polls are the coaches' polls.

HELMS

1901 Yale	1913 Navy	1925 Princeton	1937 Stanford
1902 Minnesota	1914 Wisconsin	1926 Syracuse	1938 Temple
1903 Yale	1915 Illinois	1927 Notre Dame	1939 LIU-Brooklyn
1904 Columbia	1916 Wisconsin	1928 Pittsburgh	1940 Southern California
1905 Columbia	1917 Washington St.	1929 Montana St.	1941 Wisconsin
1906 Dartmouth	1918 Syracuse	1930 Pittsburgh	1942 Stanford
1907 Chicago	1919 Minnesota	1931 Northwestern	1943 Wyoming
1908 Chicago	1920 Pennsylvania	1932 Purdue	1944 Army
1909 Chicago	1921 Pennsylvania	1933 Kentucky	1945 Oklahoma St.
1910 Columbia	1922 Kansas	1934 Wyoming	1946 Oklahoma St.
1911 St. John's (N.Y.)	1923 Kansas	1935 New York U.	1947 Holy Cross
1912 Wisconsin	1924 North Carolina	1936 Notre Dame	1948 Kentucky

1949
AP
1. Kentucky
2. Oklahoma St.
3. St. Louis
4. Illinois
5. Western Ky.
6. Minnesota
7. Bradley
8. San Francisco
9. Tulane
10. Bowling Green
11. Yale
12. Utah
13. North Carolina St.
14. Villanova
15. UCLA
16. Loyola (Ill.)
17. Wyoming
18. Butler
19. Hamline
20. Ohio St.

1950
AP
1. Bradley
2. Ohio St.
3. Kentucky
4. Holy Cross
5. North Carolina St.
6. Duquesne
7. UCLA
8. Western Ky.
9. St. John's (N.Y.)
10. La Salle
11. Villanova
12. San Francisco
13. Long Island
14. Kansas St.
15. Arizona
16. Wisconsin
17. San Jose St.
18. Washington St.
19. Kansas
20. Indiana

1951
AP
1. Kentucky
2. Oklahoma St.
3. Columbia
4. Kansas St.
5. Illinois
6. Bradley
7. Indiana
8. North Carolina St.
9. St. John's (N.Y.)
10. St. Louis
11. Brigham Young
12. Arizona
13. Dayton
14. Toledo
15. Washington
16. Murray St.
17. Cincinnati
18. Siena
19. Southern California
20. Villanova

UPI
1. Kentucky
2. Oklahoma St.
3. Kansas St.
4. Illinois
5. Columbia
6. Bradley
7. North Carolina St.
8. Indiana
9. St. John's (N.Y.)
10. Brigham Young
11. St. Louis
12. Arizona
13. Washington
14. Beloit
14. Villanova
16. UCLA
17. Cincinnati
18. Dayton
18. St. Bonaventure
18. Seton Hall
18. Texas A&M

1952
AP
1. Kentucky
2. Illinois
3. Kansas St.
4. Duquesne
5. St. Louis
6. Washington
7. Iowa
8. Kansas
9. West Virginia
10. St. John's (N.Y.)
11. Dayton
12. Duke
13. Holy Cross
14. Seton Hall
15. St. Bonaventure
16. Wyoming
17. Louisville
18. Seattle
19. UCLA
20. Southwest Tex. St.

UPI
1. Kentucky
2. Illinois
3. Kansas
4. Duquesne
5. Washington
6. Kansas St.
7. St. Louis
8. Iowa
9. St. John's (N.Y.)
10. Wyoming
11. St. Bonaventure
12. Seton Hall
13. TCU
14. West Virginia
15. Holy Cross
16. Western Ky.
17. La Salle
18. Dayton
19. Louisville
20. UCLA
20. Indiana

1953
AP
1. Indiana
2. Seton Hall
3. Kansas
4. Washington
5. LSU
6. La Salle
7. St. John's (N.Y.)
8. Oklahoma St.
9. Duquesne
10. Notre Dame
11. Illinois
12. Kansas St.
13. Holy Cross
14. Seattle
15. Wake Forest
16. Santa Clara
17. Western Ky.
18. North Carolina St.
19. DePaul
20. Southwest Mo. St.

UPI
1. Indiana
2. Seton Hall
3. Washington
4. La Salle
5. Kansas
6. LSU
7. Oklahoma St.
8. North Carolina St.
9. Kansas St.
10. Illinois
11. Western Ky.
12. California
13. Notre Dame
14. DePaul
14. Wyoming
16. St. Louis
17. Holy Cross
18. Oklahoma City
19. Brigham Young
20. Duquesne

1954
AP
1. Kentucky
2. La Salle
3. Holy Cross
4. Indiana
5. Duquesne
6. Notre Dame
7. Bradley
8. Western Ky.
9. Penn St.
10. Oklahoma St.
11. Southern California
12. George Washington
13. Iowa
14. LSU
15. Duke
16. Niagara
17. Seattle
18. Kansas
19. Illinois
20. Maryland

UPI
1. Indiana
2. Kentucky
3. Duquesne
4. Oklahoma St.
5. Notre Dame
6. Western Ky.
7. Kansas
8. LSU
9. Holy Cross
10. Iowa
11. La Salle
12. Illinois
13. Colorado St.
14. North Carolina St.
14. Southern California
16. Oregon St.
17. Seattle
17. Dayton
19. Rice
20. Duke

1955
AP
1. San Francisco
2. Kentucky
3. La Salle
4. North Carolina St.
5. Iowa
6. Duquesne
7. Utah
8. Marquette
9. Dayton
10. Oregon St.
11. Minnesota
12. Alabama
13. UCLA
14. George Washington
15. Colorado
16. Tulsa
17. Vanderbilt
18. Illinois
19. West Virginia
20. St. Louis

UPI
1. San Francisco
2. Kentucky
3. La Salle
4. Utah
5. Iowa
6. North Carolina St.
7. Duquesne
8. Oregon St.
9. Marquette
10. Dayton
11. Colorado
12. UCLA
13. Minnesota
14. Tulsa
15. George Washington
16. Illinois
17. Niagara
18. St. Louis
19. Holy Cross
20. Cincinnati

1956

AP
1. San Francisco
2. North Carolina St.
3. Dayton
4. Iowa
5. Alabama
6. Louisville
7. Southern Methodist
8. UCLA
9. Kentucky
10. Illinois
11. Oklahoma City
12. Vanderbilt
13. North Carolina
14. Holy Cross
15. Temple
16. Wake Forest
17. Duke
18. Utah
19. Oklahoma St.
20. West Virginia

UPI
1. San Francisco
2. North Carolina St.
3. Dayton
4. Iowa
5. Alabama
6. Southern Methodist
7. Louisville
8. Illinois
9. UCLA
10. Vanderbilt
11. North Carolina
12. Kentucky
13. Utah
14. Temple
15. Holy Cross
16. Oklahoma St.
16. St. Louis
18. Seattle
18. Duke
18. Canisius

1957

AP
1. North Carolina
2. Kansas
3. Kentucky
4. Southern Methodist
5. Seattle
6. Louisville
7. West Virginia
8. Vanderbilt
9. Oklahoma City
10. St. Louis
11. Michigan St.
12. Memphis
13. California
14. UCLA
15. Mississippi St.
16. Idaho St.
17. Notre Dame
18. Wake Forest
19. Canisius
19. Oklahoma St.

UPI
1. North Carolina
2. Kansas
3. Kentucky
4. Southern Methodist
5. Seattle
6. California
7. Michigan St.
8. Louisville
9. UCLA
10. St. Louis
11. West Virginia
12. Dayton
13. Bradley
14. Brigham Young
15. Indiana
16. Vanderbilt
16. Xavier
16. Oklahoma City
19. Notre Dame
20. Kansas St.

1958

AP
1. West Virginia
2. Cincinnati
3. Kansas St.
4. San Francisco
5. Temple
6. Maryland
7. Kansas
8. Notre Dame
9. Kentucky
10. Duke
11. Dayton
12. Indiana
13. North Carolina
14. Bradley
15. Mississippi St.
16. Auburn
17. Michigan St.
18. Seattle
19. Oklahoma St.
20. North Carolina St.

UPI
1. West Virginia
2. Cincinnati
3. San Francisco
4. Kansas St.
5. Temple
6. Maryland
7. Notre Dame
8. Kansas
9. Dayton
10. Indiana
11. Bradley
12. North Carolina
13. Duke
14. Kentucky
15. Oklahoma St.
16. Oregon St.
16. North Carolina St.
18. St. Bonaventure
19. Michigan St.
19. Wyoming
19. Seattle

1959

AP
1. Kansas St.
2. Kentucky
3. Mississippi St.
4. Bradley
5. Cincinnati
6. North Carolina St.
7. Michigan St.
8. Auburn
9. North Carolina
10. West Virginia
11. California
12. St. Louis
13. Seattle
14. St. Joseph's
15. St. Mary's (Cal.)
16. TCU
17. Oklahoma City
18. Utah
19. St. Bonaventure
20. Marquette

UPI
1. Kansas St.
2. Kentucky
3. Michigan St.
4. Cincinnati
5. North Carolina St.
6. North Carolina
7. Mississippi St.
8. Bradley
9. California
10. Auburn
11. West Virginia
12. TCU
13. St. Louis
14. Utah
15. Marquette
16. Tennessee Tech
17. St. John's (N.Y.)
18. Navy
18. St. Mary's (Cal.)
20. St. Joseph's

1960

AP
1. Cincinnati
2. California
3. Ohio St.
4. Bradley
5. West Virginia
6. Utah
7. Indiana
8. Utah St.
9. St. Bonaventure
10. Miami (Fla.)
11. Auburn
12. New York U.
13. Georgia Tech
14. Providence
15. St. Louis
16. Holy Cross
17. Villanova
18. Duke
19. Wake Forest
20. St. John's (N.Y.)

UPI
1. California
2. Cincinnati
3. Ohio St.
4. Bradley
5. Utah
6. West Virginia
7. Utah St.
8. Georgia Tech
9. Villanova
10. Indiana
11. St. Bonaventure
12. New York U.
13. Texas
14. North Carolina
15. Duke
16. Kansas St.
17. Auburn
18. Providence
19. St. Louis
20. Dayton

1961

AP
1. Ohio St.
2. Cincinnati
3. St. Bonaventure
4. Kansas St.
5. North Carolina
6. Bradley
7. Southern California
8. Iowa
9. West Virginia
10. Duke
11. Utah
12. Texas Tech
13. Niagara
14. Memphis
15. Wake Forest
16. St. John's (N.Y.)
17. St. Joseph's
18. Drake
19. Holy Cross
20. Kentucky

UPI
1. Ohio St.
2. Cincinnati
3. St. Bonaventure
4. Kansas St.
5. Southern California
6. North Carolina
7. Bradley
8. St. John's (N.Y.)
9. Duke
10. Wake Forest
11. Iowa
12. West Virginia
13. Utah
14. St. Louis
15. Louisville
16. St. Joseph's
17. Dayton
18. Kentucky
18. Texas Tech
20. Memphis

1962

AP
1. Ohio St.
2. Cincinnati
3. Kentucky
4. Mississippi St.
5. Bradley
6. Kansas St.
7. Utah
8. Bowling Green
9. Colorado
10. Duke
11. Loyola (Ill.)
12. St. John's (N.Y.)
13. Wake Forest
14. Oregon St.
15. West Virginia
16. Arizona St.
17. Duquesne
18. Utah St.
19. UCLA
20. Villanova

UPI
1. Ohio St.
2. Cincinnati
3. Kentucky
4. Mississippi St.
5. Kansas St.
6. Bradley
7. Wake Forest
8. Colorado
9. Bowling Green
10. Utah
11. Oregon St.
12. St. John's (N.Y.)
13. Duke
13. Loyola (Ill.)
15. Arizona St.
16. West Virginia
17. UCLA
18. Duquesne
19. Utah St.
20. Villanova

1963

AP
1. Cincinnati
2. Duke
3. Loyola (Ill.)
4. Arizona St.
5. Wichita St.
6. Mississippi St.
7. Ohio St.
8. Illinois
9. New York U.
10. Colorado

UPI
1. Cincinnati
2. Duke
3. Arizona St.
4. Loyola (Ill.)
5. Illinois
6. Wichita St.
7. Mississippi St.
8. Ohio St.
9. Colorado
10. Stanford
11. New York U.
12. Texas
13. Providence
14. Oregon St.
15. UCLA
16. St. Joseph's
16. West Virginia
18. Bowling Green
19. Kansas St.
19. Seattle

1964

AP
1. UCLA
2. Michigan
3. Duke
4. Kentucky
5. Wichita St.
6. Oregon St.
7. Villanova
8. Loyola (Ill.)
9. DePaul
10. Davidson

UPI
1. UCLA
2. Michigan
3. Kentucky
4. Duke
5. Oregon St.
6. Wichita St.
7. Villanova
8. Loyola (Ill.)
9. UTEP
10. Davidson
11. DePaul
12. Kansas St.
13. Drake
13. San Francisco
15. Utah St.
16. Ohio St.
16. New Mexico
18. Texas A&M
19. Arizona St.
19. Providence

1965

AP
1. Michigan
2. UCLA
3. St. Joseph's
4. Providence
5. Vanderbilt
6. Davidson
7. Minnesota
8. Villanova
9. Brigham Young
10. Duke

UPI
1. Michigan
2. UCLA
3. St. Joseph's
4. Providence
5. Vanderbilt
6. Brigham Young
7. Davidson
8. Minnesota
9. Duke
10. San Francisco
11. Villanova
12. North Carolina St.
13. Oklahoma St.
14. Wichita St.
15. Connecticut
16. Illinois
17. Tennessee
18. Indiana
19. Miami (Fla.)
20. Dayton

1966

AP
1. Kentucky
2. Duke
3. UTEP
4. Kansas
5. St. Joseph's
6. Loyola (Ill.)
7. Cincinnati
8. Vanderbilt
9. Michigan
10. Western Ky.

UPI
1. Kentucky
2. Duke
3. UTEP
4. Kansas
5. Loyola (Ill.)
6. St. Joseph's
7. Michigan
8. Vanderbilt
9. Cincinnati
10. Providence
11. Nebraska
12. Utah
13. Oklahoma City
14. Houston
15. Oregon St.
16. Syracuse
17. Pacific (Cal.)
18. Davidson
19. Brigham Young
19. Dayton

1967

AP
1. UCLA
2. Louisville
3. Kansas
4. North Carolina
5. Princeton
6. Western Ky.
7. Houston
8. Tennessee
9. Boston College
10. UTEP

UPI
1. UCLA
2. Louisville
3. North Carolina
4. Kansas
5. Princeton
6. Houston
7. Western Ky.
8. UTEP
9. Tennessee
10. Boston College
11. Toledo
12. St. John's (N.Y.)
13. Tulsa
13. Vanderbilt
14. Utah St.
16. Pacific (Cal.)
17. Providence
18. New Mexico
19. Duke
20. Florida

1968

AP
1. Houston
2. UCLA
3. St. Bonaventure
4. North Carolina
5. Kentucky
6. New Mexico
7. Columbia
8. Davidson
9. Louisville
10. Duke

UPI
1. Houston
2. UCLA
3. St. Bonaventure
4. North Carolina
5. Kentucky
6. Columbia
7. New Mexico
8. Louisville
9. Davidson
10. Marquette
11. Duke
12. New Mexico St.
13. Vanderbilt
14. Kansas St.
15. Princeton
16. Army
17. Santa Clara
18. Utah
19. Bradley
20. Iowa

1969

AP
1. UCLA
2. La Salle
3. Santa Clara
4. North Carolina
5. Davidson
6. Purdue
7. Kentucky
8. St. John's (N.Y.)
9. Duquesne
10. Villanova
11. Drake
12. New Mexico St.
13. South Carolina
14. Marquette
15. Louisville
16. Boston College
17. Notre Dame
18. Colorado
19. Kansas
20. Illinois

UPI
1. UCLA
2. North Carolina
3. Davidson
4. Santa Clara
5. Kentucky
6. La Salle
7. Purdue
8. St. John's (N.Y.)
9. New Mexico St.
10. Duquesne
11. Drake
12. Colorado
13. Louisville
14. Marquette
15. Villanova
15. Boston College
17. Weber St.
17. Wyoming
19. Colorado St.
20. South Carolina
20. Kansas

1970

AP
1. Kentucky
2. UCLA
3. St. Bonaventure
4. Jacksonville
5. New Mexico St.
6. South Carolina
7. Iowa
8. Marquette
9. Notre Dame
10. North Carolina St.
11. Florida St.
12. Houston
13. Pennsylvania
14. Drake
15. Davidson
16. Utah St.
17. Niagara
18. Western Ky.
19. Long Beach St.
20. Southern California

UPI
1. Kentucky
2. UCLA
3. St. Bonaventure
4. New Mexico St.
5. Jacksonville
6. South Carolina
7. Iowa
8. Notre Dame
9. Drake
10. Marquette
11. Houston
12. North Carolina St.
13. Pennsylvania
14. Florida St.
15. Villanova
15. Long Beach St.
17. Western Ky.
17. Utah St.
17. Niagara
20. Cincinnati
20. UTEP

1971

AP
1. UCLA
2. Marquette
3. Pennsylvania
4. Kansas
5. Southern California
6. South Carolina
7. Western Ky.
8. Kentucky
9. Fordham
10. Ohio St.
11. Jacksonville
12. Notre Dame
13. North Carolina
14. Houston
15. Duquesne
16. Long Beach St.
17. Tennessee
18. Villanova
19. Drake
20. Brigham Young

UPI
1. UCLA
2. Marquette
3. Pennsylvania
4. Kansas
5. Southern California
6. South Carolina
7. Western Ky.
8. Kentucky
9. Fordham
10. Ohio St.
11. Jacksonville
11. Brigham Young
13. North Carolina
14. Notre Dame
14. Long Beach St.
16. Drake
17. Villanova
18. Duquesne
19. Houston
20. Weber St.

1972

AP
1. UCLA
2. North Carolina
3. Pennsylvania
4. Louisville
5. Long Beach St.
6. South Carolina
7. Marquette
8. La.-Lafayette
9. Brigham Young
10. Florida St.
11. Minnesota
12. Marshall
13. Memphis
14. Maryland
15. Villanova
16. Oral Roberts
17. Indiana
18. Kentucky
19. Ohio St.
20. Virginia

UPI
1. UCLA
2. North Carolina
3. Pennsylvania
4. Louisville
5. South Carolina
6. Long Beach St.
7. Marquette
8. La.-Lafayette
9. Brigham Young
10. Florida St.
11. Maryland
12. Minnesota
13. Memphis
14. Kentucky
15. Villanova
16. Kansas St.
17. UTEP
18. Marshall
19. Missouri
19. Weber St.

1973

AP
1. UCLA
2. North Carolina St.
3. Long Beach St.
4. Providence
5. Marquette
6. Indiana
7. La.-Lafayette
8. Maryland
9. Kansas St.
10. Minnesota
11. North Carolina
12. Memphis
13. Houston
14. Syracuse
15. Missouri
16. Arizona St.
17. Kentucky
18. Pennsylvania
19. Austin Peay
20. San Francisco

UPI
1. UCLA
2. North Carolina St.
3. Long Beach St.
4. Marquette
5. Providence
6. Indiana
7. La.-Lafayette
8. Kansas St.
9. Minnesota
10. Maryland
11. Memphis
12. North Carolina
13. Arizona St.
14. Syracuse
15. Kentucky
16. South Carolina
17. Missouri
18. Weber St.
19. Houston
20. Pennsylvania

1974

AP
1. North Carolina St.
2. UCLA
3. Marquette
4. Maryland
5. Notre Dame
6. Michigan
7. Kansas
8. Providence
9. Indiana
10. Long Beach St.
11. Purdue
12. North Carolina
13. Vanderbilt
14. Alabama
15. Utah
16. Pittsburgh
17. Southern California
18. Oral Roberts
19. South Carolina
20. Dayton

UPI
1. North Carolina St.
2. UCLA
3. Notre Dame
4. Maryland
5. Marquette
6. Providence
7. Vanderbilt
8. North Carolina
9. Indiana
10. Kansas
11. Long Beach St.
12. Michigan
13. Southern California
14. Pittsburgh
15. Louisville
16. South Carolina
17. Creighton
18. New Mexico
19. Alabama
19. Dayton

1975

AP
1. UCLA
2. Kentucky
3. Indiana
4. Louisville
5. Maryland
6. Syracuse
7. North Carolina St.
8. Arizona St.
9. North Carolina
10. Alabama
11. Marquette
12. Princeton
13. Cincinnati
14. Notre Dame
15. Kansas St.
16. Drake
17. UNLV
18. Oregon St.
19. Michigan
20. Pennsylvania

UPI
1. Indiana
2. UCLA
3. Louisville
4. Kentucky
5. Maryland
6. Marquette
7. Arizona St.
8. Alabama
9. North Carolina St.
10. North Carolina
11. Pennsylvania
12. Southern California
13. Utah St.
14. UNLV
14. Notre Dame
16. Creighton
17. Arizona
18. New Mexico St.
19. Clemson
20. UTEP

1976

AP
1. Indiana
2. Marquette
3. UNLV
4. Rutgers
5. UCLA
6. Alabama
7. Notre Dame
8. North Carolina
9. Michigan
10. Western Mich.
11. Maryland
12. Cincinnati
13. Tennessee
14. Missouri
15. Arizona
16. Texas Tech
17. DePaul
18. Virginia
19. Centenary (La.)
20. Pepperdine

UPI
1. Indiana
2. Marquette
3. Rutgers
4. UNLV
5. UCLA
6. North Carolina
7. Alabama
8. Notre Dame
9. Michigan
10. Washington
11. Missouri
12. Arizona
13. Maryland
14. Tennessee
15. Virginia
16. Cincinnati
17. Florida St.
18. St. John's (N.Y.)
19. Western Mich.
19. Princeton

1977

AP
1. Michigan
2. UCLA
3. Kentucky
4. UNLV
5. North Carolina
6. Syracuse
7. Marquette
8. San Francisco
9. Wake Forest
10. Notre Dame
11. Alabama
12. Detroit
13. Minnesota
14. Utah
15. Tennessee
16. Kansas St.
17. Charlotte
18. Arkansas
19. Louisville
20. VMI

UPI
1. Michigan
2. San Francisco
3. North Carolina
4. UCLA
5. Kentucky
6. UNLV
7. Arkansas
8. Tennessee
9. Syracuse
10. Utah
11. Kansas St.
12. Cincinnati
13. Louisville
14. Marquette
15. Providence
16. Indiana St.
17. Minnesota
18. Alabama
19. Detroit
20. Purdue

1978

AP
1. Kentucky
2. UCLA
3. DePaul
4. Michigan St.
5. Arkansas
6. Notre Dame
7. Duke
8. Marquette
9. Louisville
10. Kansas
11. San Francisco
12. New Mexico
13. Indiana
14. Utah
15. Florida St.
16. North Carolina
17. Texas
18. Detroit
19. Miami (Ohio)
20. Pennsylvania

UPI
1. Kentucky
2. UCLA
3. Marquette
4. New Mexico
5. Michigan St.
6. Arkansas
7. DePaul
8. Kansas
9. Duke
10. North Carolina
11. Notre Dame
12. Florida St.
13. San Francisco
14. Louisville
15. Indiana
16. Houston
17. Utah St.
18. Utah
19. Texas
20. Georgetown

1979

AP
1. Indiana St.
2. UCLA
3. Michigan St.
4. Notre Dame
5. Arkansas
6. DePaul
7. LSU
8. Syracuse
9. North Carolina
10. Marquette
11. Duke
12. San Francisco
13. Louisville
14. Pennsylvania
15. Purdue
16. Oklahoma
17. St. John's (N.Y.)
18. Rutgers
19. Toledo
20. Iowa

UPI
1. Indiana St.
2. UCLA
3. North Carolina
4. Michigan St.
5. Notre Dame
6. Arkansas
7. Duke
8. DePaul
9. LSU
10. Syracuse
11. Iowa
12. Georgetown
13. Marquette
14. Purdue
15. Texas
16. Temple
17. San Francisco
18. Tennessee
19. Louisville
20. Detroit

1980

AP
1. DePaul
2. Louisville
3. LSU
4. Kentucky
5. Oregon St.
6. Syracuse
7. Indiana
8. Maryland
9. Notre Dame
10. Ohio St.
11. Georgetown
12. Brigham Young
13. St. John's (N.Y.)
14. Duke
15. North Carolina
16. Missouri
17. Weber St.
18. Arizona St.
19. Iona
20. Purdue

UPI
1. DePaul
2. LSU
3. Kentucky
4. Louisville
5. Oregon St.
6. Syracuse
7. Indiana
8. Maryland
9. Ohio St.
10. Georgetown
11. Notre Dame
12. Brigham Young
13. St. John's (N.Y.)
14. Missouri
15. North Carolina
16. Duke
17. Weber St.
18. Texas A&M
19. Arizona St.
20. Kansas St.

1981

AP
1. DePaul
2. Oregon St.
3. Arizona St.
4. LSU
5. Virginia
6. North Carolina
7. Notre Dame
8. Kentucky
9. Indiana
10. UCLA
11. Wake Forest
12. Louisville
13. Iowa
14. Utah
15. Tennessee
16. Brigham Young
17. Wyoming
18. Maryland
19. Illinois
20. Arkansas

UPI
1. DePaul
2. Oregon St.
3. Virginia
4. LSU
5. Arizona St.
6. North Carolina
7. Indiana
8. Kentucky
9. Notre Dame
10. Utah
11. UCLA
12. Iowa
13. Louisville
14. Wake Forest
15. Tennessee
16. Wyoming
17. Brigham Young
18. Illinois
19. Kansas
20. Maryland

1982

AP
1. North Carolina
2. DePaul
3. Virginia
4. Oregon St.
5. Missouri
6. Georgetown
7. Minnesota
8. Idaho
9. Memphis
10. Tulsa
11. Fresno St.
12. Arkansas
13. Alabama
14. West Virginia
15. Kentucky
16. Iowa
17. UAB
18. Wake Forest
19. UCLA
20. Louisville

UPI
1. North Carolina
2. DePaul
3. Virginia
4. Oregon St.
5. Missouri
6. Minnesota
7. Georgetown
8. Idaho
9. Memphis
10. Fresno St.
11. Tulsa
12. Alabama
13. Arkansas
14. Kentucky
15. Wyoming
16. Iowa
17. West Virginia
18. Kansas St.
19. Wake Forest
20. Louisville

1983

AP
1. Houston
2. Louisville
3. St. John's (N.Y.)
4. Virginia
5. Indiana
6. UNLV
7. UCLA
8. North Carolina
9. Arkansas
10. Missouri
11. Boston College
12. Kentucky
13. Villanova
14. Wichita St.
15. Chattanooga
16. North Carolina St.
17. Memphis
18. Georgia
19. Oklahoma St.
20. Georgetown

UPI
1. Houston
2. Louisville
3. St. John's (N.Y.)
4. Virginia
5. Indiana
6. UNLV
7. UCLA
8. North Carolina
9. Arkansas
10. Kentucky
11. Villanova
12. Missouri
13. Boston College
14. North Carolina St.
15. Georgia
16. Chattanooga
17. Memphis
18. Illinois St.
19. Oklahoma St.
20. Georgetown

1984

AP
1. North Carolina
2. Georgetown
3. Kentucky
4. DePaul
5. Houston
6. Illinois
7. Oklahoma
8. Arkansas
9. UTEP
10. Purdue
11. Maryland
12. Tulsa
13. UNLV
14. Duke
15. Washington
16. Memphis
17. Oregon St.
18. Syracuse
19. Wake Forest
20. Temple

UPI
1. North Carolina
2. Georgetown
3. Kentucky
4. DePaul
5. Houston
6. Illinois
7. Arkansas
8. Oklahoma
9. UTEP
10. Maryland
11. Purdue
12. Tulsa
13. UNLV
14. Duke
15. Washington
16. Memphis
17. Syracuse
18. Indiana
19. Auburn
20. Oregon St.

1985

AP
1. Georgetown
2. Michigan
3. St. John's (N.Y.)
4. Oklahoma
5. Memphis
6. Georgia Tech
7. North Carolina
8. Louisiana Tech
9. UNLV
10. Duke
11. Va. Commonwealth
12. Illinois
13. Kansas
14. Loyola (Ill.)
15. Syracuse
16. North Carolina St.
17. Texas Tech
18. Tulsa
19. Georgia
20. LSU

UPI
1. Georgetown
2. Michigan
3. St. John's (N.Y.)
4. Memphis
5. Oklahoma
6. Georgia Tech
7. North Carolina
8. Louisiana Tech
9. UNLV
10. Illinois
11. Va. Commonwealth
12. Duke
13. Kansas
14. Tulsa
15. Syracuse
16. Texas Tech
17. Loyola (Ill.)
18. North Carolina St.
19. LSU
20. Michigan St.

1986

AP
1. Duke
2. Kansas
3. Kentucky
4. St. John's (N.Y.)
5. Michigan
6. Georgia Tech
7. Louisville
8. North Carolina
9. Syracuse
10. Notre Dame
11. UNLV
12. Memphis
13. Georgetown
14. Bradley
15. Oklahoma
16. Indiana
17. Navy
18. Michigan St.
19. Illinois
20. UTEP

UPI
1. Duke
2. Kansas
3. St. John's (N.Y.)
4. Kentucky
5. Michigan
6. Georgia Tech
7. Louisville
8. North Carolina
9. Syracuse
10. UNLV
11. Notre Dame
12. Memphis
13. Bradley
14. Indiana
15. Georgetown
16. UTEP
17. Oklahoma
18. Michigan St.
19. Alabama
20. Illinois

1987

AP
1. UNLV
2. North Carolina
3. Indiana
4. Georgetown
5. DePaul
6. Iowa
7. Purdue
8. Temple
9. Alabama
10. Syracuse
11. Illinois
12. Pittsburgh
13. Clemson
14. Missouri
15. UCLA
16. New Orleans
17. Duke
18. Notre Dame
19. TCU
20. Kansas

UPI
1. UNLV
2. Indiana
3. North Carolina
4. Georgetown
5. DePaul
6. Purdue
7. Iowa
8. Temple
9. Alabama
10. Syracuse
11. Illinois
12. Pittsburgh
13. UCLA
14. Missouri
15. Clemson
16. TCU
17. Wyoming
18. Notre Dame
19. New Orleans
19. Oklahoma
19. UTEP

1988

AP
1. Temple
2. Arizona
3. Purdue
4. Oklahoma
5. Duke
6. Kentucky
7. North Carolina
8. Pittsburgh
9. Syracuse
10. Michigan
11. Bradley
12. UNLV
13. Wyoming
14. North Carolina St.
15. Loyola Marymount
16. Illinois
17. Iowa
18. Xavier
19. Brigham Young
20. Kansas St.

UPI
1. Temple
2. Arizona
3. Purdue
4. Oklahoma
5. Duke
6. Kentucky
7. Pittsburgh
8. North Carolina
9. Syracuse
10. Michigan
11. UNLV
12. Bradley
13. North Carolina St.
14. Wyoming
15. Illinois
16. Loyola Marymount
17. Brigham Young
18. Iowa
19. Indiana
20. Kansas St.

1989

AP
1. Arizona
2. Georgetown
3. Illinois
4. Oklahoma
5. North Carolina
6. Missouri
7. Syracuse
8. Indiana
9. Duke
10. Michigan
11. Seton Hall
12. Louisville
13. Stanford
14. Iowa
15. UNLV
16. Florida St.
17. West Virginia
18. Ball St.
19. North Carolina St.
20. Alabama

UPI
1. Arizona
2. Georgetown
3. Illinois
4. North Carolina
5. Oklahoma
6. Indiana
7. Duke
8. Missouri
9. Syracuse
10. Michigan
11. Seton Hall
12. Stanford
13. Louisville
14. UNLV
15. Iowa
16. Florida St.
17. Arkansas
18. North Carolina St.
19. West Virginia
20. Alabama

1990

AP
1. Oklahoma
2. UNLV
3. Connecticut
4. Michigan St.
5. Kansas
6. Syracuse
7. Arkansas
8. Georgetown
9. Georgia Tech
10. Purdue
11. Missouri
12. La Salle
13. Michigan
14. Arizona
15. Duke
16. Louisville
17. Clemson
18. Illinois
19. LSU
20. Minnesota
21. Loyola Marymount
22. Oregon St.
23. Alabama
24. New Mexico St.
25. Xavier

UPI
1. Oklahoma
2. UNLV
3. Connecticut
4. Michigan St.
5. Kansas
6. Syracuse
7. Georgia Tech
8. Arkansas
9. Georgetown
10. Purdue
11. Missouri
12. Arizona
13. La Salle
14. Duke
15. Michigan
16. Louisville
17. Clemson
18. Illinois
19. Alabama
20. New Mexico St.

1991

AP
1. UNLV
2. Arkansas
3. Indiana
4. North Carolina
5. Ohio St.
6. Duke
7. Syracuse
8. Arizona
9. Kentucky
10. Utah
11. Nebraska
12. Kansas
13. Seton Hall
14. Oklahoma St.
15. New Mexico St.
16. UCLA
17. East Tenn. St.
18. Princeton
19. Alabama
20. St. John's (N.Y.)
21. Mississippi St.
22. LSU
23. Texas
24. DePaul
25. Southern Miss.

UPI
1. UNLV
2. Arkansas
3. Indiana
4. North Carolina
5. Ohio St.
6. Duke
7. Arizona
8. Syracuse
9. Nebraska
10. Utah
11. Seton Hall

12. Kansas
13. Oklahoma St.
14. UCLA
15. East Tenn. St.
16. Alabama
17. New Mexico St.
18. Mississippi St.
19. St. John's (N.Y.)
20. Princeton
21. LSU
22. Michigan St.
23. Georgetown
24. North Carolina St.
25. Texas

1992
AP
1. Duke
2. Kansas
3. Ohio St.
4. UCLA
5. Indiana
6. Kentucky
7. UNLV
8. Southern California
9. Arkansas
10. Arizona
11. Oklahoma St.
12. Cincinnati
13. Alabama
14. Michigan St.
15. Michigan
16. Missouri
17. Massachusetts
18. North Carolina
19. Seton Hall
20. Florida St.
21. Syracuse
22. Georgetown
23. Oklahoma
24. DePaul
25. LSU

UPI
1. Duke
2. Kansas
3. UCLA
4. Ohio St.
5. Arizona
6. Indiana
7. Southern California
8. Arkansas
9. Kentucky
10. Oklahoma St.
11. Michigan St.
12. Missouri
13. Alabama
14. Cincinnati
15. North Carolina
16. Florida St.
17. Michigan
18. Seton Hall
19. Georgetown
20. Syracuse
21. Massachusetts
22. Oklahoma
23. DePaul
24. St. John's (N.Y.)
25. Tulane

1993
AP
1. Indiana
2. Kentucky
3. Michigan
4. North Carolina
5. Arizona
6. Seton Hall
7. Cincinnati
8. Vanderbilt
9. Kansas
10. Duke
11. Florida St.
12. Arkansas
13. Iowa
14. Massachusetts
15. Louisville
16. Wake Forest
17. New Orleans
18. Georgia Tech
19. Utah
20. Western Ky.
21. New Mexico
22. Purdue
23. Oklahoma St.
24. New Mexico St.
25. UNLV

USA TODAY/CNN
1. Indiana
2. North Carolina
3. Kentucky
4. Michigan
5. Arizona
6. Seton Hall
7. Cincinnati
8. Kansas
9. Vanderbilt
10. Duke
11. Florida St.
12. Arkansas
13. Iowa
14. Louisville
15. Wake Forest
16. Utah
17. Massachusetts
18. New Orleans
19. UNLV
20. Georgia Tech
21. Purdue
22. Virginia
23. Oklahoma St.
24. New Mexico St.
25. Western Ky.

1994
AP
1. North Carolina
2. Arkansas
3. Purdue
4. Connecticut
5. Missouri
6. Duke
7. Kentucky
8. Massachusetts
9. Arizona
10. Louisville
11. Michigan
12. Temple
13. Kansas
14. Florida
15. Syracuse
16. California
17. UCLA
18. Indiana
19. Oklahoma St.
20. Texas
21. Marquette
22. Nebraska
23. Minnesota
24. St. Louis
25. Cincinnati

USA TODAY/CNN
1. Arkansas
2. North Carolina
3. Connecticut
4. Purdue
5. Missouri
6. Duke
7. Massachusetts
8. Kentucky
9. Louisville
10. Arizona
11. Michigan
12. Temple
13. Kansas
14. Syracuse
15. Florida
16. UCLA
17. California
18. Indiana
19. Oklahoma St.
20. Minnesota
21. St. Louis
22. Marquette
23. UAB
24. Texas
25. Cincinnati

1995
AP
1. UCLA
2. Kentucky
3. Wake Forest
4. North Carolina
5. Kansas
6. Arkansas
7. Massachusetts
8. Connecticut
9. Villanova
10. Maryland
11. Michigan St.
12. Purdue
13. Virginia
14. Oklahoma St.
15. Arizona
16. Arizona St.
17. Oklahoma
18. Mississippi St.
19. Utah
20. Alabama
21. Western Ky.
22. Georgetown
23. Missouri
24. Iowa St.
25. Syracuse

USA TODAY/NABC
1. UCLA
2. Kentucky
3. Wake Forest
4. Kansas
5. North Carolina
6. Arkansas
7. Massachusetts
8. Connecticut
9. Michigan St.
10. Maryland
11. Purdue
12. Villanova
13. Arizona
14. Oklahoma St.
15. Virginia
16. Arizona St.
17. Utah
18. Iowa St.
19. Mississippi St.
20. Oklahoma
21. Alabama
22. Syracuse
23. Missouri
24. Oregon
25. Stanford

1996
AP
1. Massachusetts
2. Kentucky
3. Connecticut
4. Georgetown
5. Kansas
6. Purdue
7. Cincinnati
8. Texas Tech
9. Wake Forest
10. Villanova
11. Arizona
12. Utah
13. Georgia Tech
14. UCLA
15. Syracuse
16. Memphis
17. Iowa St.
18. Penn St.
19. Mississippi St.
20. Marquette
21. Iowa
22. Virginia Tech
23. New Mexico
24. Louisville
25. North Carolina

USA TODAY/NABC
1. Massachusetts
2. Kentucky
3. Connecticut
4. Purdue
5. Georgetown
6. Cincinnati
7. Texas Tech
8. Kansas
9. Wake Forest
10. Utah
11. Arizona
12. Villanova
13. UCLA
14. Syracuse
15. Georgia Tech
16. Iowa St.
17. Memphis
18. Penn St.
19. Iowa
20. Mississippi St.
21. Virginia Tech
22. Marquette
23. Louisville
24. North Carolina
25. Stanford

1997
AP
1. Kansas
2. Utah
3. Minnesota
4. North Carolina
5. Kentucky
6. South Carolina
7. UCLA
8. Duke
9. Wake Forest
10. Cincinnati
11. New Mexico
12. St. Joseph's
13. Xavier
14. Clemson
15. Arizona
16. Col. of Charleston
17. Georgia
18. Iowa St.
19. Illinois
20. Villanova
21. Stanford
22. Maryland
23. Boston College
24. Colorado
25. Louisville

USA TODAY/NABC
1. Kansas
2. Utah
3. Minnesota
4. Kentucky
5. North Carolina
6. South Carolina
7. UCLA
8. Duke
9. Wake Forest
10. Cincinnati
11. New Mexico
12. Clemson
13. Arizona
14. Xavier
15. St. Joseph's
16. Villanova
17. Iowa St.
18. Col. of Charleston
19. Maryland
20. Boston College
21. Stanford
22. Georgia
23. Colorado
24. Illinois
25. Louisville

1998
AP
1. North Carolina
2. Kansas
3. Duke
4. Arizona
5. Kentucky
6. Connecticut
7. Utah
8. Princeton
9. Cincinnati
10. Stanford
11. Purdue
12. Michigan
13. Mississippi
14. South Carolina
15. TCU
16. Michigan St.
17. Arkansas
18. New Mexico
19. UCLA
20. Maryland
21. Syracuse
22. Illinois
23. Xavier
24. Temple
25. Murray St.

USA TODAY/NABC
1. North Carolina
2. Kansas
3. Duke
4. Arizona
5. Connecticut
6. Kentucky
7. Utah
8. Princeton
9. Purdue
10. Stanford
11. Cincinnati
12. Michigan
13. South Carolina
14. Mississippi
15. Michigan St.
16. TCU
17. Arkansas
18. New Mexico
19. Syracuse
20. UCLA
21. Xavier
22. Maryland
23. Illinois
24. Temple
25. Oklahoma

1999
AP
1. Duke
2. Michigan St.
3. Connecticut
4. Auburn
5. Maryland
6. Utah
7. Stanford
8. Kentucky
9. St. John's (N.Y.)
10. Miami (Fla.)
11. Cincinnati
12. Arizona
13. North Carolina
14. Ohio St.
15. UCLA
16. Col. of Charleston
17. Arkansas
18. Wisconson
19. Indiana
20. Texas
21. Iowa
22. Kansas
23. Florida
24. Charlotte
25. New Mexico

USA TODAY/NABC
1. Duke
2. Michigan St.
3. Connecticut
4. Auburn
5. Maryland
6. Utah
7. Stanford
8. St. John's (N.Y.)
9. Cincinnati
10. Arizona
11. Kentucky
12. Miami (Fla.)
13. North Carolina
14. Ohio St.
15. UCLA
16. Col. of Charleston
17. Wisconsin
18. Indiana
19. Arkansas
20. Iowa
21. Syracuse
22. Kansas
23. Texas
24. New Mexico
25. Florida

2000
AP
1. Duke
2. Michigan St.
3. Stanford
4. Arizona
5. Temple
6. Iowa St.
7. Cincinnati
8. Ohio St.
9. St. John's (N.Y.)
10. LSU
11. Tennessee
12. Oklahoma
13. Florida
14. Oklahoma St.
15. Texas
16. Syracuse
17. Maryland
18. Tulsa
19. Kentucky
20. Connecticut
21. Illinois
22. Indiana
23. Miami (Fla.)
24. Auburn
25. Purdue

USA TODAY/NABC
1. Duke
2. Michigan St.
3. Stanford
4. Arizona
5. Temple
6. Cincinnati
7. Iowa St.
8. Ohio St.
9. LSU
10. Tennessee
11. Florida
12. St. John's (N.Y.)
13. Oklahoma
14. Syracuse
15. Oklahoma St.
16. Maryland
17. Indiana
18. Texas
19. Tulsa
20. Kentucky
21. Connecticut
22. Auburn
23. Illinois
24. Purdue
25. Miami (Fla.)

2001

AP
1. Duke
2. Stanford
3. Michigan St.
4. Illinois
5. Arizona
6. North Carolina
7. Boston College
8. Florida
9. Kentucky
10. Iowa St.
11. Maryland
12. Kansas
13. Oklahoma
14. Mississippi
15. UCLA
16. Virginia
17. Syracuse
18. Texas
19. Notre Dame
20. Indiana
21. Georgetown
22. St. Joseph's
23. Wake Forest
24. Iowa
25. Wisconsin

USA TODAY/NABC
1. Duke
2. Stanford
3. Michigan St.
4. Arizona
5. North Carolina
6. Illinois
7. Boston College
8. Florida
9. Iowa St.
10. Kentucky
11. Maryland
12. Kansas
13. Mississippi
14. Oklahoma
15. Virginia
16. Syracuse
17. Texas
18. UCLA
19. Notre Dame
20. Georgetown
21. Indiana
22. Wake Forest
23. St. Joseph's
24. Wisconsin
25. Iowa

2002

AP
1. Duke
2. Kansas
3. Oklahoma
4. Maryland
5. Cincinnati
6. Gonzaga
7. Arizona
8. Alabama
9. Pittsburgh
10. Connecticut
11. Oregon
12. Marquette
13. Illinois
14. Ohio St.
15. Florida
16. Kentucky
17. Mississippi St.
18. Southern California
19. Western Ky.
20. Oklahoma St.
21. Miami (Fla.)
22. Xavier
23. Georgia
24. Stanford
25. Hawaii

USA TODAY/ESPN
1. Duke
2. Kansas
3. Oklahoma
4. Maryland
5. Cincinnati
6. Gonzaga
7. Pittsburgh
8. Alabama
9. Arizona
10. Marquette
11. Oregon
12. Ohio St.
13. Connecticut
14. Florida
15. Kentucky
16. Illinois
16. Southern California
18. Mississippi St.
19. Xavier
20. Western Ky.
21. Miami (Fla.)
22. Oklahoma St.
23. Stanford
24. Hawaii
25. North Carolina St.

Final Post-Tournament Polls

1994

USA TODAY/CNN
1. Arkansas
2. Duke
3. Arizona
4. Florida
5. Purdue
6. Missouri
7. Connecticut
8. Michigan
9. North Carolina
10. Louisville
11. Boston College
12. Kansas
13. Kentucky
14. Syracuse
15. Massachusetts
16. Indiana
17. Marquette
18. Temple
19. Tulsa
20. Maryland
21. Oklahoma St.
22. UCLA
23. Minnesota
24. Texas
25. Pennsylvania

1995

USA TODAY/NABC
1. UCLA
2. Arkansas
3. North Carolina
4. Oklahoma St.
5. Kentucky
6. Connecticut
7. Massachusetts
8. Virginia
9. Wake Forest
10. Kansas
11. Maryland
12. Mississippi St.
13. Arizona St.
14. Memphis
15. Tulsa
16. Georgetown
17. Syracuse
18. Missouri
19. Purdue
20. Michigan St.
21. Alabama
22. Utah

23. Villanova
24. Texas
25. Arizona

1996

USA TODAY/NABC
1. Kentucky
2. Massachusetts
3. Syracuse
4. Mississippi St.
5. Kansas
6. Cincinnati
7. Georgetown
8. Connecticut
9. Wake Forest
10. Texas Tech
11. Arizona
12. Utah
13. Georgia Tech
14. Louisville
15. Purdue
16. Georgia
17. Villanova
18. Arkansas
19. UCLA
20. Iowa St.
21. Virginia Tech
22. Iowa
23. Marquette
24. North Carolina
25. New Mexico

1997

USA TODAY/NABC
1. Arizona
2. Kentucky
3. Minnesota
4. North Carolina
5. Kansas
6. Utah
7. UCLA
8. Clemson
9. Wake Forest
10. Louisville
11. Duke
12. Stanford
13. Iowa St.
14. South Carolina
15. Providence
16. Cincinnati
17. St. Joseph's
18. California

19. New Mexico
20. Texas
21. Col. of Charleston
22. Xavier
23. Boston College
24. Michigan
25. Colorado

1998

USA TODAY/NABC
1. Kentucky
2. Utah
3. North Carolina
4. Stanford
5. Duke
6. Arizona
7. Connecticut
8. Kansas
9. Purdue
10. Michigan St.
11. Rhode Island
12. UCLA
13. Syracuse
14. Cincinnati
15. Maryland
16. Princeton
17. Michigan
18. West Virginia
19. South Carolina
20. Mississippi
21. New Mexico
22. Arkansas
23. Valparaiso
24. Washington
25. TCU

1999

USA TODAY/NABC
1. Connecticut
2. Duke
3. Michigan St.
4. Ohio St.
5. Kentucky
5. St. John's (N.Y.)
7. Auburn
8. Maryland
9. Stanford
10. Utah
11. Cincinnati
12. Gonzaga
12. Miami (Fla.)
14. Temple
15. Iowa
16. Arizona
17. Florida
18. North Carolina
19. Oklahoma
20. Miami (Ohio)

21. UCLA
22. Purdue
23. Kansas
24. Southwest Mo. St.
25. Arkansas

2000

USA TODAY/NABC
1. Michigan St.
2. Florida
3. Iowa St.
4. Duke
5. Stanford
5. Oklahoma St.
7. Cincinnati
8. Arizona
9. Tulsa
10. Temple
11. North Carolina
12. Syracuse
12. LSU
14. Tennessee
15. Purdue
16. Wisconsin
17. Ohio St.
18. St. John's (N.Y.)
19. Oklahoma
20. Miami (Fla.)
21. Texas
22. Kentucky
23. UCLA
24. Gonzaga
25. Maryland

2001

USA TODAY/NABC
1. Duke
2. Arizona
3. Michigan St.
4. Maryland
5. Stanford
6. Illinois
7. Kansas
8. Kentucky
9. Mississippi
10. North Carolina
11. Boston College
12. UCLA
13. Florida
14. Southern California
15. Iowa St.
16. Temple
17. Georgetown
18. Syracuse
19. Oklahoma
20. Gonzaga
21. Virginia
22. Cincinnati

23. Notre Dame
24. St. Joseph's
25. Penn St.

2002

USA/ESPN
1. Maryland
2. Kansas
3. Indiana
4. Oklahoma
5. Duke
6. Connecticut
7. Oregon
8. Cincinnati
9. Pittsburgh
10. Arizona
11. Illinois
12. Kent St.
13. Kentucky
14. Alabama
15. Missouri
16. Gonzaga
17. Ohio St.
18. Marquette
18. Texas
20. UCLA
21. Mississippi St.
22. Southern Ill.
23. Florida
24. Xavier
25. North Carolina St.

American Sports Wire Poll

The following poll ranks the top historically black institutions of the NCAA as selected by American Sports Wire and compiled by Dick Simpson.

Year	Team	Coach	Won	Lost
1992	Howard	Butch Beard	17	14
1993	Jackson St.	Andy Stoglin	25	9
1994	Texas Southern	Robert Moreland	19	11
1995	Texas Southern	Robert Moreland	22	7
1996	South Carolina St.	Cy Alexander	22	8
1997	Coppin St.	Fang Mitchell	22	9
1998	South Carolina St.	Cy Alexander	22	8
1999	Alcorn St.	Davey L. Whitney	23	7
2000	South Carolina	Cy Alexander	20	14
2001	Hampton	Steve Merfeld	25	7
2002	Hampton	Steve Merfeld	25	7

No. 1 vs. No. 2

Date	No. 1, Score	W-L	No. 2, Score	Site
Mar. 26, 1949	Kentucky 46	W	Oklahoma St. 36	Seattle (NCAA final)
Dec. 17, 1951	Kentucky 81	W	St. John's (N.Y.) 40	Lexington, KY
Dec. 21, 1954	Kentucky 70	W	Utah 65	Lexington, KY
Mar. 23, 1957	North Carolina 54	W	Kansas 53	Kansas City, MO (NCAA final)
Mar. 18, 1960	Cincinnati 69	L	California 77	San Francisco (NCAA semis)
Mar. 25, 1961	Ohio St. 65	L (ot)	Cincinnati 70	Kansas City, MO (NCAA final)
Dec. 14, 1964	Wichita St. 85	L	Michigan 87	Detroit
Mar. 20, 1965	Michigan 80	L	UCLA 91	Portland, OR (NCAA final)
Mar. 18, 1966	Kentucky 83	W	Duke 79	College Park, MD (NCAA semis)
Jan. 20, 1968	UCLA 69	L	Houston 71	Houston
Mar. 22, 1968	Houston 69	L	UCLA 101	Los Angeles (NCAA semis)
Dec. 15, 1973	UCLA 84	W	North Carolina St. 66	St. Louis
Jan. 19, 1974	UCLA 70	L	Notre Dame 71	South Bend, IN
Jan. 26, 1974	Notre Dame 75	L	UCLA 94	Los Angeles
Mar. 25, 1974	North Carolina St. 80	W	UCLA 77	Greensboro, NC (NCAA semis)
Mar. 31, 1975	UCLA 92	W	Kentucky 85	San Diego (NCAA final)
Nov. 29, 1975	Indiana 84	W	UCLA 64	St. Louis
Mar. 22, 1976	Indiana 65	W	Marquette 56	Baton Rouge, LA
Dec. 26, 1981	North Carolina 82	W	Kentucky 69	East Rutherford, NJ
Jan. 9, 1982	North Carolina 65	W	Virginia 60	Chapel Hill, NC
April 2, 1983	Houston 94	W	Louisville 81	Albuquerque, NM (NCAA semis)
Dec. 15, 1984	Georgetown 77	W	DePaul 57	Landover, MD
Feb. 27, 1985	St. John's (N.Y.) 69	L	Georgetown 85	New York
Mar. 9, 1985	Georgetown 92	W	St. John's (N.Y.) 80	New York
Feb. 4, 1986	North Carolina 78	W (ot)	Georgia Tech 77	Atlanta
Mar. 29, 1986	Duke 71	W	Kansas 67	Dallas (NCAA semis)
Feb. 13, 1990	Kansas 71	L	Missouri 77	Lawrence, KS
Mar. 10, 1990	Oklahoma 95	W	Kansas 77	Kansas City, MO
Feb. 10, 1991	UNLV 112	W	Arkansas 105	Fayetteville, AR
Feb. 3, 1994	Duke 78	L	North Carolina 89	Chapel Hill, NC
Mar. 30, 1996	Massachusetts 74	L	Kentucky 81	East Rutherford, NJ (NCAA semis)
Feb. 5, 1998	Duke 73	L	North Carolina 97	Chapel Hill, NC

Division II Records

Individual Records

Basketball records are confined to the "modern era," which began with the 1937-38 season, the first without the center jump after each goal scored. Official weekly statistics rankings in scoring and shooting began with the 1947-48 season. Individual rebounds were added for the 1950-51 season, while team rebounds were added for the 1959-60 season. Assists were added for the 1988-89 season. Blocked shots and steals were added for the 1992-93 season. Scoring and rebounding are ranked on per-game average; shooting, on percentage. Beginning with the 1967-68 season, Division II rankings were limited only to NCAA members. The 1973-74 season was the first under a three-division reorganization plan adopted by the special NCAA Convention of August 1973. In statistical rankings, the rounding of percentages and/or averages may indicate ties where none exist. In these cases, the numerical order of the rankings is accurate.

Scoring

POINTS
Game
113—Clarence "Bevo" Francis, Rio Grande vs. Hillsdale, Feb. 2, 1954
Season
1,329—Earl Monroe, Winston-Salem, 1967 (32 games)
Career
4,045—Travis Grant, Kentucky St., 1969-72 (121 games)

AVERAGE PER GAME
Season
†46.5—Clarence "Bevo" Francis, Rio Grande, 1954 (1,255 in 27)
Career
(Min. 1,400) 33.4—Travis Grant, Kentucky St., 1969-72 (4,045 in 121)
†Season and career figures for Francis limited only to his 39 games (27 in 1954) against four-year colleges.

GAMES SCORING AT LEAST 50 POINTS
Season
†8—Clarence "Bevo" Francis, Rio Grande, 1954
Career
†14—Clarence "Bevo" Francis, Rio Grande, 1953-54
†Season and career figures for Francis limited only to his 39 games (27 in 1954) against four-year colleges.

MOST GAMES SCORING IN DOUBLE FIGURES
Career
130—Lambert Shell, Bridgeport, 1989-92

Field Goals

FIELD GOALS
Game
38—Clarence "Bevo" Francis, Rio Grande vs. Alliance, Jan. 16, 1954 (71 attempts) and vs. Hillsdale, Feb. 2, 1954 (70 attempts)
Season
539—Travis Grant, Kentucky St., 1972 (869 attempts)
Career
1,760—Travis Grant, Kentucky St., 1969-72 (2,759 attempts)

CONSECUTIVE FIELD GOALS
Game
20—Lance Berwald, North Dakota St. vs. Augustana (S.D.), Feb. 17, 1984
Season
28—Don McAllister, Hartwick, 1980 (during six games, Jan. 26-Feb. 9); Lance Berwald, North Dakota St., 1984 (during three games, Feb. 13-18)

FIELD-GOAL ATTEMPTS
Game
71—Clarence "Bevo" Francis, Rio Grande vs. Alliance, Jan. 16, 1954 (38 made)
Season
925—Jim Toombs, Stillman, 1965 (388 made)
Career
3,309—Bob Hopkins, Grambling, 1953-56 (1,403 made)

FIELD-GOAL PERCENTAGE
Game
(Min. 20 made) 100%—Lance Berwald, North Dakota St. vs. Augustana (S.D.), Feb. 17, 1984 (20 of 20)
*Season
75.2%—Todd Linder, Tampa, 1987 (282 of 375)
*based on qualifiers for annual championship
Career
(Min. 400 made) 70.8%—Todd Linder, Tampa, 1984-87 (909 of 1,284)

Three-Point Field Goals

THREE-POINT FIELD GOALS
Game
16—Markus Hallgrimson, Mont. St.-Billings vs. Western N.M., Feb. 12, 2000 (28 attempts)
Season
167—Alex Williams, Sacramento St., 1988 (369 attempts)
Career
442—Steve Moyer, Gannon, 1996-99 (1,026 attempts)

THREE-POINT FIELD GOALS MADE PER GAME
Season
6.2—Markus Hallgrimson, Mont. St.-Billings, 2000 (160 in 26)
Career
4.7—Antonio Harris, LeMoyne-Owen, 1998-99 (245 in 52)

CONSECUTIVE THREE-POINT FIELD GOALS
Game
10—Duane Huddleston, Mo.-Rolla vs. Truman, Jan. 23, 1988
Season
18—Dan Drews, Le Moyne (during 11 games, Dec. 11, 1993 to Feb. 2, 1994)

CONSECUTIVE GAMES MAKING A THREE-POINT FIELD GOAL
Season
34—Roger Powers, St. Rose, Nov. 8, 1996 to March 8, 1997
Career
93—Daniel Parke, Rollins, Jan. 26, 1994, to Feb. 28, 1997

THREE-POINT FIELD-GOAL ATTEMPTS
Game
34—Markus Hallgrimson, Mont. St.-Billings vs. Western N.M., Feb. 26, 2000 (13 made)
Season
382—Markus Hallgrimson, Mont. St.-Billings, 2000 (160 made)
Career
1,047—Tony Smith, Pfeiffer, 1989-92 (431 made)

THREE-POINT FIELD-GOAL ATTEMPTS PER GAME
Season
14.7—Markus Hallgrimson, Mont. St.-Billings, 2000 (382 in 26)
Career
11.3—Markus Hallgrimson, Mont. St.-Billings, 1997-00 (927 in 82)

THREE-POINT FIELD-GOAL PERCENTAGE
Game
(Min. 9 made) 100%—Steve Divine, Ky. Wesleyan vs. Wayne St. (Mich.), March 14, 1992 (9 of 9)
*Season
(Min. 35 made) 65.0%—Ray Lee, Hampton, 1988 (39 of 60)

(Min. 50 made) 60.3%—Aaron Fehler, Oakland City, 1995 (73 of 121)
(Min. 100 made) 56.7%—Scott Martin, Rollins, 1991 (114 of 201)
(Min. 150 made) 45.3%—Alex Williams, Sacramento St., 1988 (167 of 369)
*based on qualifiers for annual championship
Career
(Min. 200 made) 51.3%—Scott Martin, Rollins, 1988-91 (236 of 460)

Free Throws

FREE THROWS
Game
37—Clarence "Bevo" Francis, Rio Grande vs. Hillsdale, Feb. 2, 1954 (45 attempts)
Season
401—Joe Miller, Alderson-Broaddus, 1957 (496 attempts)
Career
1,130—Joe Miller, Alderson-Broaddus, 1954-57 (1,460 attempts)

CONSECUTIVE FREE THROWS
Game
23—Carl Hartman, Alderson-Broaddus vs. Salem, Dec. 6, 1954
Season
94—Paul Cluxton, Northern Ky., 1997 (during 34 games, Nov. 8-Mar. 20)

FREE-THROW ATTEMPTS
Game
45—Clarence "Bevo" Francis, Rio Grande vs. Hillsdale, Feb. 2, 1954 (37 made)
Season
†510—Clarence "Bevo" Francis, Rio Grande, 1954 (367 made)
Career
1,460—Joe Miller, Alderson-Broaddus, 1954-57 (1,130 made)
†Season figure for Francis limited to 27 games against four-year colleges.

FREE-THROW PERCENTAGE
Game
(Min. 20 made) 100%—Milosh Pujo, Lewis vs. Mt. St. Clare, Dec. 30, 1997 (20 of 20); Forrest "Butch" Meyeraan, Minn. St.-Mankato vs. Wis.-River Falls, Feb. 21, 1961 (20 of 20)
*Season
100%—Paul Cluxton, Northern Ky., 1997 (94 of 94)
*based on qualifiers for annual championship
Career
(Min. 250 made) 93.5%—Paul Cluxton, Northern Ky., 1994-97 (272 of 291)
(Min. 500 made) 87.9%—Steve Nisenson, Hofstra, 1963-65 (602 of 685)

Rebounds

REBOUNDS
Game
46—Tom Hart, Middlebury vs. Trinity (Conn.), Feb. 5, 1955, and vs. Clarkson, Feb. 12, 1955
Season
799—Elmore Smith, Kentucky St., 1971 (33 games)
Career
2,334—Jim Smith, Steubenville, 1955-58 (112 games)

AVERAGE PER GAME
Season
29.5—Tom Hart, Middlebury, 1956 (620 in 21)
Career
(Min. 900) 27.6—Tom Hart, Middlebury, 1953, 55-56 (1,738 in 63)

Assists

ASSISTS
Game
25—Ali Baaqar, Morris Brown vs. Albany St. (Ga.), Jan. 26, 1991; Adrian Hutt, Metro St. vs. Sacramento St., Feb. 9, 1991
Season
400—Steve Ray, Bridgeport, 1989 (32 games)
Career
1,044—Demetri Beekman, Assumption, 1990-93 (119 games)

AVERAGE PER GAME
Season
12.5—Steve Ray, Bridgeport, 1989 (400 in 32)
Career
(Min. 550) 12.1—Steve Ray, Bridgeport, 1989-90 (785 in 65)

Blocked Shots

BLOCKED SHOTS
Game
15—Mark Hensel, Pitt.-Johnstown vs. Slippery Rock, Jan. 22, 1994
Season
157—James Doyle, Concord, 1998 (30 games)
Career
416—James Doyle, Concord, 1995-98 (120 games)

AVERAGE PER GAME
Season
5.3—Antonio Harvey, Pfeiffer, 1993 (155 in 29)
Career
4.00—Derek Moore, S.C.-Aiken, 1996-99 (408 in 102)

Steals

STEALS
Game
17—Antonio Walls, Alabama A&M vs. Albany St. (Ga.), Jan. 5, 1998

Season
139—J.R. Gamble, Queens (N.C.), 2001 (32 games)
Career
383—Eddin Santiago, Mo. Southern St., 1999-02, (117 games)

AVERAGE PER GAME
Season
5.0—Wayne Copeland, Lynn, 2000 (129 in 26)
Career
4.46—Wayne Copeland, Lynn, 1999-00 (254 in 57)

Games

GAMES PLAYED
Season
37—Michael Alcock, Lee Barlow, John Bynun, Rashawn Fulcher, Kane Oakley, Metro St., 2000; Antonio Garcia, Dana Williams, Patrick Critchelow, Leroy John, Chris Haskin, and Adam Mattingly, Ky. Wesleyan, 1999
Career
133—Gino Bartolone, Ky. Wesleyan, 1998-01; Pat Morris, Bridgeport, 1989-92

Team Records

Note: Where records involve both teams, each team must be an NCAA Division II member institution.

SINGLE-GAME RECORDS

Scoring

POINTS
258—Troy St. vs. DeVry (Ga.) (141), Jan. 12, 1992

POINTS VS. DIVISION II TEAM
169—Stillman vs. Miles (123), Feb. 17, 1966

POINTS BY LOSING TEAM
146—Mississippi Col. vs. West Ala. (160), Dec. 2, 1969

POINTS, BOTH TEAMS
306—West Ala. (160) and Mississippi Col. (146), Dec. 2, 1969

POINTS IN A HALF
135—Troy St. vs. DeVry (Ga.), Jan. 12, 1992

FEWEST POINTS ALLOWED (Since 1938)
4—Albion (76) vs. Adrian, Dec. 12, 1938; Tennessee St. (7) vs. Oglethorpe, Feb. 16, 1971

FEWEST POINTS, BOTH TEAMS (Since 1938)
11—Tennessee St. (7) and Oglethorpe (4), Feb. 16, 1971

WIDEST MARGIN OF VICTORY
118—Mississippi Col. (168) vs. Dallas Bible (50), Dec. 9, 1971

Field Goals

FIELD GOALS
102—Troy St. vs. DeVry (Ga.), Jan. 12, 1992 (190 attempts)

FIELD-GOAL ATTEMPTS
190—Troy St. vs. DeVry (Ga.), Jan. 12, 1992 (102 made)

FEWEST FIELD GOALS (Since 1938)
0—Adrian vs. Albion, Dec. 12, 1938 (28 attempts)

FEWEST FIELD-GOAL ATTEMPTS
7—Mansfield vs. West Chester, Dec. 8, 1984 (4 made)

FIELD-GOAL PERCENTAGE
81.6%—Youngstown St. vs. Northern Iowa, Jan. 26, 1980 (31 of 38)

FIELD-GOAL PERCENTAGE, HALF
95.0%—Abilene Christian vs. Cameron, Jan. 21, 1989 (19 of 20)

Three-Point Field Goals

THREE-POINT FIELD GOALS
51—Troy St. vs. DeVry (Ga.), Jan. 12, 1992 (109 attempts)

THREE-POINT FIELD GOALS, BOTH TEAMS
39—Columbus St. (22) vs. Troy St. (17), Feb. 14, 1991

CONSECUTIVE THREE-POINT FIELD GOALS MADE WITHOUT A MISS
12—Southwest St. vs. Bemidji St., Jan. 22, 2000; Catawba vs. Wingate, Feb. 28, 1998; Pace vs. Medgar Evers, Nov. 27, 1991

NUMBER OF DIFFERENT PLAYERS TO SCORE A THREE-POINT FIELD GOAL, ONE TEAM
10—Troy St. vs. DeVry (Ga.), Jan. 12, 1992

THREE-POINT FIELD-GOAL ATTEMPTS
109—Troy St. vs. DeVry (Ga.), Jan. 12, 1992 (51 made)

THREE-POINT FIELD-GOAL ATTEMPTS, BOTH TEAMS
95—Columbus St. (52) vs. Troy St. (43), Feb. 14, 1991

THREE-POINT FIELD-GOAL PERCENTAGE
(Min. 10 made) 90.9%—Philadelphia U. vs. Spring Garden, Nov. 24, 1987 (10 of 11); Armstrong Atlantic vs. Columbus St., Feb. 24, 1990 (10 of 11); Norfolk St. vs. Clark Atlanta, Dec. 26, 1992 (10 of 11)

HIGHEST THREE-POINT FIELD-GOAL PERCENTAGE, BOTH TEAMS
(Min. 10 made) 83.3%—Tampa (9 of 10) vs. St. Leo (1 of 2), Jan. 21, 1987 (10 of 12)
(Min. 20 made) 75.9%—Indiana (Pa.) (11 of 15) vs. Cheyney (11 of 14), Jan. 26, 1987 (22 of 29)

Free Throws

FREE THROWS
64—Wayne St. (Mich.) vs. Grand Valley St., Feb. 13, 1993 (79 attempts); Baltimore vs. Washington (Md.), Feb. 9, 1955 (84 attempts)

FREE THROWS, BOTH TEAMS
89—Southern Ind. (50) vs. Northern St. (39), Nov. 15, 1997 (3ot); Baltimore (64) and Washington (Md.) (25), Feb. 9, 1955

FREE-THROW ATTEMPTS
84—Baltimore vs. Washington (Md.), Feb. 9, 1955 (64 made)

FREE-THROW ATTEMPTS, BOTH TEAMS
142—Southern Ind. (80) vs. Northern St. (62), Nov. 15, 1997 (3 ot) (89 made)

FREE-THROW PERCENTAGE
(Min. 31 made) 100%—Dowling vs. Southampton, Feb. 6, 1985 (31 of 31)

FREE-THROW PERCENTAGE, BOTH TEAMS
(Min. 30 made) 97.0%—Hartford (17 of 17) vs. Bentley (15 of 16), Feb. 22, 1983 (32 of 33)

Rebounds

REBOUNDS
111—Central Mich. vs. Alma, Dec. 7, 1963

REBOUNDS, BOTH TEAMS
141—Loyola (Md.) (75) vs. Western Md. (66), Dec. 6, 1961; Concordia (Ill.) (72) vs. Concordia (Neb.) (69), Feb. 26, 1965

REBOUND MARGIN
65—Moravian (100) vs. Drew (35), Feb. 18, 1969

Assists

ASSISTS
65—Troy St. vs. DeVry (Ga.), Jan. 12, 1992

ASSISTS, BOTH TEAMS
65—Central Okla. (34) vs. Stonehill (31), Dec. 29, 1990

Personal Fouls

PERSONAL FOULS
51—Northern St. vs. Southern Ind., Nov. 15, 1997 (3 ot)

PERSONAL FOULS, BOTH TEAMS (Including Overtimes)
91—Northern St. (51) vs. Southern Ind. (40), Nov. 15, 1997 (3 ot)

PERSONAL FOULS, BOTH TEAMS (Regulation Time)
74—Bentley (36) vs. Mass.-Boston (38), Jan. 23, 1971

PLAYERS DISQUALIFIED
7—Northern St. vs. Southern Ind., Nov. 15, 1997 (3 ot); Illinois Col. vs. Illinois Tech, Dec. 13, 1952; Steubenville vs. West Liberty, 1952; Washington (Md.) vs. Baltimore, Feb. 9, 1955; Southern Colo. vs. Air Force, Jan. 12, 1972; Edinboro vs. Calif. (Pa.) (5 ot), Feb. 4, 1989

PLAYERS DISQUALIFIED, BOTH TEAMS
12—Alfred (6) and Rensselaer (6), Jan. 9, 1971

Overtimes

OVERTIME PERIODS
7—Yankton (79) vs. Black Hills (80), Feb. 18, 1956

POINTS IN ONE OVERTIME PERIOD
27—Southern Ind. vs. Central Mo. St., Jan. 5, 1985

POINTS IN ONE OVERTIME PERIOD, BOTH TEAMS
46—North Dakota St. (25) vs. St. Cloud St. (21), Jan. 16, 1999; North Dakota St. (25) vs. South Dakota (21), Jan. 9, 1999

POINTS IN OVERTIME PERIODS
60—Calif. (Pa.) vs. Edinboro (5 ot), Feb. 4, 1989

POINTS IN OVERTIME PERIODS, BOTH TEAMS
114—Calif. (Pa.) (60) vs. Edinboro (54) (5 ot), Feb. 4, 1989

WINNING MARGIN IN OVERTIME GAME
22—Pfeiffer (72) vs. Belmont Abbey (50), Dec. 8, 1960

SEASON RECORDS

Scoring

POINTS
3,566—Troy St., 1993 (32 games); Central Okla., 1992 (32 games)

AVERAGE PER GAME
121.1—Troy St., 1992 (3,513 in 29)

AVERAGE SCORING MARGIN
31.4—Bryan, 1961 (93.8 offense, 62.4 defense)

GAMES AT LEAST 100 POINTS
25—Troy St., 1993 (32-game season)

CONSECUTIVE GAMES AT LEAST 100 POINTS
17—Norfolk St., 1970

Field Goals

FIELD GOALS
1,455—Kentucky St., 1971 (2,605 attempts)

FIELD GOALS PER GAME
46.9—Lincoln (Mo.), 1967 (1,267 in 27)

FIELD-GOAL ATTEMPTS
2,853—Ark.-Pine Bluff, 1967 (1,306 made)

FIELD-GOAL ATTEMPTS PER GAME
108.2—Stillman, 1968 (2,814 in 26)

FIELD-GOAL PERCENTAGE
62.4%—Kentucky St., 1976 (1,093 of 1,753)

Three-Point Field Goals

THREE-POINT FIELD GOALS
444—Troy St., 1992 (1,303 attempts)

THREE-POINT FIELD GOALS PER GAME
15.3—Troy St., 1992 (444 in 29)

THREE-POINT FIELD-GOAL ATTEMPTS
1,303—Troy St., 1992 (444 made)

THREE-POINT FIELD-GOAL ATTEMPTS PER GAME
44.9—Troy St., 1992 (1,303 in 29)

THREE-POINT FIELD-GOAL PERCENTAGE
(Min. 90 made) 53.8%—Winston-Salem, 1988 (98 of 182)
(Min. 200 made) 50.2%—Oakland City, 1992 (244 of 486)

CONSECUTIVE GAMES SCORING A THREE-POINT FIELD GOAL (Multiple Seasons)
502—Ky. Wesleyan, Nov. 22, 1986-Present

Free Throws

FREE THROWS
896—Ouachita, 1965 (1,226 attempts)

FREE THROWS PER GAME
36.1—Baltimore, 1955 (686 in 19)

FREE-THROW ATTEMPTS
1,226—Ouachita, 1965 (896 made)

FREE-THROW ATTEMPTS PER GAME
49.6—Baltimore, 1955 (943 in 19)

FREE-THROW PERCENTAGE
82.5%—Gannon, 1998 (473 of 573)

Rebounds

REBOUNDS
1,667—Norfolk St., 1973 (31 games)

AVERAGE PER GAME
65.8—Bentley, 1964 (1,513 in 23)

AVERAGE REBOUND MARGIN
24.4—Mississippi Val., 1976 (63.9 offense, 39.5 defense)

Assists

ASSISTS
736—New Hamp. Col., 1993 (33 games)

AVERAGE PER GAME
25.6—Quincy, 1994 (716 in 28)

Personal Fouls

PERSONAL FOULS
947—Seattle, 1952 (37 games)

PERSONAL FOULS PER GAME
29.9—Shaw, 1987 (748 in 25)

FEWEST PERSONAL FOULS
184—Sewanee, 1962 (17 games)

FEWEST PERSONAL FOULS PER GAME
10.0—Ashland, 1969 (301 in 30)

Defense

LOWEST POINTS PER GAME ALLOWED
20.2—Alcorn St., 1941 (323 in 16)

LOWEST POINTS PER GAME ALLOWED (Since 1948)
29.1—Miss. Industrial, 1948 (436 in 15)

LOWEST FIELD-GOAL PERCENTAGE ALLOWED (Since 1978)
35.8—Tarleton St., 2002 (657 of 1,837)

Overtimes

MOST OVERTIME GAMES
8—Belmont Abbey, 1983 (won 4, lost 4)

MOST CONSECUTIVE OVERTIME GAMES
3—10 times, most recent: Pace, 1996 (won 3, lost 0)

MOST MULTIPLE-OVERTIME GAMES
5—Cal St. Dom. Hills, 1987 (four 2 ot, one 3 ot; won 2, lost 3)

General Records

GAMES IN A SEASON
39—Regis (Colo.), 1949 (36-3)

VICTORIES IN A SEASON
36—Regis (Colo.), 1949 (36-3)

VICTORIES IN A PERFECT SEASON
34—Fort Hays St., 1996

CONSECUTIVE VICTORIES
52—Langston (from 1943-44 opener through fifth game of 1945-46 season)

CONSECUTIVE 30-WIN SEASONS
4—Ky. Wesleyan, 1998 (30); 1999 (35); 2000 (31); 2001 (31)

CONSECUTIVE HOME-COURT VICTORIES
80—Philadelphia U. (from Jan. 8, 1991 to Nov. 21, 1995)

CONSECUTIVE REGULAR-SEASON VICTORIES (Postseason Tournaments Not Included)
52—Langston (from 1943-44 opener through fifth game of 1945-46 season)

DEFEATS IN A SEASON
27—Colorado Mines, 1992 (0-27); Bowie St., 1985 (1-27)

CONSECUTIVE DEFEATS IN A SEASON
27—Colorado Mines, 1992 (0-27)

CONSECUTIVE DEFEATS
46—Olivet, Feb. 21, 1959, to Dec. 4, 1961; Southwest St. (Minn.), Dec. 11, 1971, to Dec. 1, 1973

CONSECUTIVE WINNING SEASONS
35—Norfolk St., 1963-97

CONSECUTIVE NON-LOSING SEASONS
35—Norfolk St., 1963-97

††UNBEATEN TEAMS (Since 1938; Number Of Victories In Parentheses)
1938 Glenville St. (28)
1941 Milwaukee St. (16)
1942 Indianapolis (16)
1942 Rochester (16)
1944 Langston (23)
1945 Langston (24)
1948 West Virginia St. (23)
1949 Tennessee St. (24)
1956 Rochester Inst. (17)
1959 Grand Canyon (20)
1961 Calvin (20)
1964 Bethany (W. Va.) (18)
1965 Central St. (Ohio) (30)
1965 Evansville (29)#
1993 Cal St. Bakersfield (33)#
1996 Fort Hays St. (34)#

††at least 15 victories; #NCAA Division II champion

All-Time Individual Leaders

Single-Game Records

SCORING HIGHS

Pts.	Player, Team vs. Opponent	Season
113	Clarence "Bevo" Francis, Rio Grande vs. Hillsdale	1954
84	Clarence "Bevo" Francis, Rio Grande vs. Alliance	1954
82	Clarence "Bevo" Francis, Rio Grande vs. Bluffton	1954
80	Paul Crissman, Southern California Col. vs. Pacific Christian	1966
77	William English, Winston-Salem vs. Fayetteville St.	1968
75	Travis Grant, Kentucky St. vs. Northwood	1970
72	Nate DeLong, Wis.-River Falls vs. Winona St.	1948
72	Lloyd Brown, Aquinas vs. Cleary	1953
72	Clarence "Bevo" Francis, Rio Grande vs. Calif. (Pa.)	1953
72	John McElroy, Youngstown St. vs. Wayne St. (Mich.)	1969
71	Clayborn Jones, L.A. Pacific vs. L.A. Baptist	1965
70	Paul Wilcox, Davis & Elkins vs. Glenville St.	1959
70	Bo Clark, UCF vs. Fla. Memorial	1977

Season Records

SCORING AVERAGE

Player, Team	Season	G	FG	FT	Pts.	Avg.
Clarence "Bevo" Francis, Rio Grande	†1954	27	444	367	1,255	*46.5
Earl Glass, Miss. Industrial	†1963	19	322	171	815	42.9
Earl Monroe, Winston-Salem	†1967	32	509	311	*1,329	41.5
John Rinka, Kenyon	†1970	23	354	234	942	41.0
Willie Shaw, Lane	†1964	18	303	121	727	40.4
Travis Grant, Kentucky St.	†1972	33	*539	226	1,304	39.5
Thales McReynolds, Miles	†1965	18	294	118	706	39.2
Bob Johnson, Fitchburg St.	1963	18	213	277	703	39.1
Roger Kuss, Wis.-River Falls	†1953	21	291	235	817	38.9
Florindo Vieira, Quinnipiac	1954	14	191	138	520	37.1

†national champion; *record

FIELD-GOAL PERCENTAGE
(Based on qualifiers for annual championship)

Player, Team	Season	G	FG	FGA	Pct.
Todd Linder, Tampa	†1987	32	282	375	*75.2
Maurice Stafford, North Ala.	†1984	34	198	264	75.0
Matthew Cornegay, Tuskegee	†1982	29	208	278	74.8
Brian Moten, West Ga.	†1992	26	141	192	73.4
Ed Phillips, Alabama A&M	†1968	22	154	210	73.3
Ray Strozier, Central Mo. St.	†1980	28	142	195	72.8
Harold Booker, Cheyney	†1965	24	144	198	72.7
Chad Scott, Calif. (Pa.)	†1994	30	178	245	72.7
Tom Schurfranz, Bellarmine	†1991	30	245	339	72.3
Marv Lewis, Southampton	†1969	24	271	375	72.3
Louis Newsome, North Ala.	†1988	29	192	266	72.2
Ed Phillips, Alabama A&M	†1971	24	159	221	71.9
Gregg Northington, Alabama St.	1971	26	324	451	71.8

†national champion; *record

THREE-POINT FIELD GOALS MADE

Player, Team	Season	G	3FG
Alex Williams, Sacramento St.	1988	30	167
Markus Hallgrimson, Mont. St.-Billings	2000	26	160
Eric Kline, Northern St.	1995	30	148
Eric Kline, Northern St.	1994	33	148
Shawn Pughsley, Central Okla.	1998	32	139
Reece Gliko, Mont. St.-Billings	1997	28	135
Ray Gutierrez, Calif. (Pa.)	1993	27	135
Jason Garrow, Augustana (S.D.)	1992	27	135
Markus Hallgrimson, Mont. St.-Billings	1999	28	133
Shawn Williams, Central Okla.	1991	29	129
Robert Martin, Sacramento St.	1988	30	128
Steve Brown, West Ala.	2000	26	126
Antonio Harris, LeMoyne-Owen	1999	26	126
Tommie Spearman, Columbus	1995	29	126
Kwame Morton, Clarion	1994	26	126
Damien Blair, West Chester	1994	28	125
Steve Moyer, Gannon	1999	28	124
John Boyd, LeMoyne-Owen	1992	26	123
Roger Powers, St. Rose	1997	34	121
Danny Phillips, Mont. St.-Billings	2002	28	120
Jeff McBroom Seattle Pacific	1999	31	120
Stephen Hamrick, Eastern N.M.	1994	27	120

THREE-POINT FIELD GOALS MADE PER GAME

Player, Team	Season	G	3FG	Avg.
Markus Hallgrimson, Mont. St.-Billings	†2000	26	160	*6.2
Alex Williams, Sacramento St.	†1988	30	*167	5.6
Jason Garrow, Augustana (S.D.)	†1992	27	135	5.0
Eric Kline, Northern St.	†1995	30	148	4.9
Ray Gutierrez, Calif. (Pa.)	†1993	29	142	4.9
Steve Brown, West Ala.	2000	26	126	4.8
Antonio Harris, LeMoyne-Owen	†1999	26	126	4.8
Kwame Morton, Clarion	†1994	26	126	4.8
Reece Gliko, Mont. St.-Billings	†1997	28	135	4.8
Markus Hallgrimson, Mont. St.-Billings	1999	28	133	4.8
John Boyd, LeMoyne-Owen	1992	26	123	4.7
Duane Huddleston, Mo.-Rolla	1988	25	118	4.7
Antonio Harris, LeMoyne-Owen	†1998	26	119	4.6
Ricardo Watkins, Tuskegee	2000	24	110	4.6
Eric Kline, Northern St.	1994	33	148	4.5
Robbie Waldrop, Lees-McRae	2001	25	112	4.5
Damien Blair, West Chester	1994	28	125	4.5
Eric Carpenter, Cal St. San B'dino	1994	26	116	4.5
Shawn Williams, Central Okla.	†1991	29	129	4.4
Stephen Hamrick, Eastern N.M.	1994	27	120	4.4
Steve Moyer, Gannon	1999	28	124	4.4

†national champion; *record

THREE-POINT FIELD-GOAL PERCENTAGE
(Based on qualifiers for annual championship)

Player, Team	Season	G	3FG	3FGA	Pct.
Ray Lee, Hampton	†1988	24	39	60	*65.0
Steve Hood, Winston-Salem	1988	28	42	67	62.7
Mark Willey, Fort Hays St.	1990	29	49	81	60.5
Aaron Fehler, Oakland City	†1995	26	73	121	60.3
Aaron Baker, Mississippi Col.	†1989	27	69	117	59.0
Walter Hurd, Johnson Smith	1989	27	49	84	58.3
Matt Hopson, Oakland City	†1996	31	84	145	57.9
Jon Bryant, St. Cloud St.	1996	27	54	94	57.4
Adam Harness, Oakland City	†1997	26	39	68	57.4
Scott Martin, Rollins	†1991	28	114	201	56.7
Charles Byrd, West Tex. A&M	†1987	31	95	168	56.5
Aaron Buckoski, Michigan Tech	1997	26	39	69	56.5
Jay Nolan, Bowie St.	1987	27	70	124	56.5
Kris Kidwell, Oakland City	1996	28	44	78	56.4
Tony Harris, Dist. Columbia	1987	30	79	141	56.0
Rickey Barrett, Ala.-Huntsville	1987	26	63	113	55.8
Quinn Murphy, Drury	1995	27	45	81	55.6
Erik Fisher, San Fran. St.	1991	28	80	144	55.6
Mike Doyle, Philadelphia U.	1988	30	82	149	55.0

†national champion; *record

FREE-THROW PERCENTAGE
(Based on qualifiers for annual championship)

Player, Team	Season	G	FT	FTA	Pct.
Paul Cluxton, Northern Ky.	†1997	35	94	94	*100.0
Tomas Rimkus, Pace	1997	25	65	68	95.6
C. J. Cowgill, Chaminade	†2001	22	113	119	95.0
Billy Newton, Morgan St.	†1976	28	85	90	94.4
Kent Andrews, McNeese St.	†1968	24	85	90	94.4
Mike Sanders, Northern Colo.	†1987	28	82	87	94.3
Curtis Small, Southampton	†2002	29	109	116	94.0
Brent Mason, St. Joseph's (Ind.)	2001	31	125	133	94.0
Travis Starns, Colorado Mines	†1999	26	87	93	93.5
Jay Harrie, Mont. St.-Billings	†1994	26	86	92	93.5
Joe Cullen, Hartwick	†1969	18	96	103	93.2
Dan Shanks, Coker	1997	27	119	128	93.0
Charles Byrd, West Tex. A&M	†1988	29	92	99	92.9
Jeremy Kudera, South Dakota	2001	28	78	84	92.9
Brian Koephick, Minn. St.-Mankato	1988	28	104	112	92.9
Jon Hagen, Minn. St.-Mankato	†1963	25	76	82	92.7
Paul Cluxton, Northern Ky.	†1996	32	100	108	92.6
Jim Borodawka, Mass.-Lowell	†1995	27	74	80	92.5
Carl Gonder, Augustana (S.D.)	†1982	27	86	93	92.5
Hal McManus, Lander	†1992	28	110	119	92.4
John Palosi, Texas Lutheran	2001	20	61	66	92.4
Troy Nesmith, Gannon	†1998	27	146	158	92.4
Terry Gill, New Orleans	†1974	30	97	105	92.4
Emery Sammons, Philadelphia U.	†1977	28	145	157	92.4

†national champion; *record

DIVISION II

REBOUND AVERAGE

Player, Team	Season	G	Reb.	Avg.
Tom Hart, Middlebury	†1956	21	620	*29.5
Tom Hart, Middlebury	†1955	22	649	29.5
Frank Stronczek, American Int'l	†1966	26	717	27.6
R.C. Owens, Albertson	†1954	25	677	27.1
Maurice Stokes, St. Francis (Pa.)	1954	26	689	26.5
Roman Turmon, Clark Atlanta	1954	23	602	26.2
Pat Callahan, Lewis	1955	20	523	26.2
Hank Brown, Mass.-Lowell	1966	19	496	26.1
Maurice Stokes, St. Francis (Pa.)	1955	28	726	25.9

†national champion; *record

ASSISTS

Player, Team	Season	G	Ast.
Steve Ray, Bridgeport	†1989	32	*400
Steve Ray, Bridgeport	†1990	33	385
Tony Smith, Pfeiffer	†1992	35	349
Rob Paternostro, New Hamp. Col.	1995	33	309
Jim Ferrer, Bentley	1989	31	309
Brian Gregory, Oakland	1989	28	300
Charles Jordan, Erskine	1992	34	298
Ernest Jenkins, N.M. Highlands	†1995	27	291
Pat Chambers, Philadelphia U.	1994	30	290
Craig Lottie, Alabama A&M	1995	32	287
Adrian Hutt, Metro St.	†1991	28	285
Javar Cheatham, Gannon	†2001	30	283
Patrick Boen, Stonehill	1989	32	278
Ernest Jenkins, N.M. Highlands	†1994	27	277
Adam Kaufman, Edinboro	1998	34	273
Darnell White, Calif. (Pa.)	1994	30	273
Demetri Beekman, Assumption	1992	32	271
Tyrone Tate, Southern Ind.	1994	32	270
Gallagher Driscoll, St. Rose	1991	29	267

†national champion; *record

ASSIST AVERAGE

Player, Team	Season	G	Ast.	Avg.
Steve Ray, Bridgeport	†1989	32	*400	*12.5
Steve Ray, Bridgeport	†1990	33	385	11.7
Demetri Beekman, Assumption	†1993	23	264	11.5
Ernest Jenkins, N.M. Highlands	†1995	27	291	10.8
Brian Gregory, Oakland	1989	28	300	10.7
Brent Schremp, Slippery Rock	1995	25	259	10.4
Ernest Jenkins, N.M. Highlands	†1994	27	277	10.3
Adrian Hutt, Metro St.	†1991	28	285	10.2
Tony Smith, Pfeiffer	†1992	35	349	10.0
Jim Ferrer, Bentley	1989	31	309	10.0
Todd Chappell, Texas Wesleyan	†2000	27	263	9.7
Pat Chambers, Philadelphia U.	1994	30	290	9.7
Marcus Talbert, Colo. Christian	1994	27	261	9.7
Paul Beaty, Miles	1992	26	248	9.5
Lawrence Jordan, IPFW	1990	28	266	9.5
Hal Chambers, Columbus St.	1993	24	227	9.5
Javar Cheatham, Gannon	†2001	30	283	9.4
Rob Paternostro, New Hamp. Col.	1995	33	309	9.4
Gallagher Driscoll, St. Rose	1991	29	267	9.2
David Daniels, Colo. Christian	1993	29	264	9.1
Darnell White, Calif. (Pa.)	1994	30	273	9.1

†national champion; *record

BLOCKED SHOTS

Player, Team	Season	G	Blk.
James Doyle, Concord	†1998	30	*157
Antonio Harvey, Pfeiffer	†1993	29	155
John Burke, Southampton	†1996	28	142
Vonzell McGrew, Mo. Western St.	†1995	31	132
Colin Ducharme, Longwood	2001	31	130
Corey Johnson, Pace	1995	30	130
Derek Moore, S.C.-Aiken	1998	30	129
Johnny Tyson, Central Okla.	†1994	27	126
Garth Joseph, St. Rose	†1997	34	124
Kino Outlaw, Mount Olive	1995	28	124
Kino Outlaw, Mount Olive	1996	27	117
Ben Wallace, Virginia Union	1996	31	114
Mark Hensel, Pitt.-Johnstown	1994	27	113
Ben Wallace, Virginia Union	1995	31	111
Elwood Vines, Bloomsburg	1993	27	107
Horacio Llamas, Grand Canyon	1996	29	106
Coata Malone, Alabama A&M	1995	32	106
Eugene Haith, Philadelphia U.	1993	31	105

†national champion; *record

BLOCKED-SHOT AVERAGE

Player, Team	Season	G	Blk.	Avg.
Antonio Harvey, Pfeiffer	†1993	29	155	*5.34
James Doyle, Concord	†1998	30	*157	5.23
John Burke, Southampton	†1996	28	142	5.07
Johnny Tyson, Central Okla.	†1994	27	126	4.66
Kino Outlaw, Mount Olive	†1995	28	124	4.43
Kino Outlaw, Mount Olive	1996	27	117	4.33
Corey Johnson, Pace	1995	30	130	4.33
Derek Moore, S.C.-Aiken	1998	30	129	4.30
Vonzell McGrew, Mo. Western St.	1995	31	132	4.26
Jason Roseto, Edinboro	†2001	23	97	4.2
Colin Ducharme, Longwood	2001	31	130	4.2
Mark Hensel, Pitt.-Johnstown	1994	27	113	4.19
Victorius Payne, Lane	1996	25	101	4.04
Elwood Vines, Bloomsburg	1993	27	107	3.96
George Bailey, Lock Haven	†2002	20	79	3.95
Lawrence Williams, San Fran. St.	1995	27	103	3.81
Derek Moore, S.C.-Aiken	1996	26	97	3.73
Ben Wallace, Virginia Union	1996	31	114	3.68
Horacio Llamas, Grand Canyon	1996	29	106	3.66
Garth Joseph, St. Rose	†1997	34	124	3.65

†national champion; *record

STEALS

Player, Team	Season	G	Stl.
J.R. Gamble, Queens (N.C.)	†2001	32	*139
Wayne Copeland, Lynn	†2000	26	129
Wayne Copeland, Lynn	†1999	31	125
Terrance Gist, S.C.-Spartanburg	†1998	29	122
Devlin Herring, Pitt.-Johnstown	†1997	27	122
Oronn Brown, Clarion	1997	29	120
Devlin Herring, Pitt.-Johnstown	1998	29	118
David Clark, Bluefield St.	†1996	31	118
Tyrone McDaniel, Lenoir-Rhyne	†1993	32	116
Ken Francis, Molloy	†1994	27	116
Darnell White, Calif. (Pa.)	1994	30	115
Eddin Santiago, Mo. Southern St.	2001	30	114
Tracy Gross, High Point	1997	29	114
Robert Campbell, Armstrong Atlantic	2001	33	113
Joe Newton, Central Okla.	1993	32	110
Peron Austin, Southern Colo.	1997	28	110
Marcus Stubblefield, Queens (N.C.)	1993	28	110
Shannon Holmes, New York Tech	†1995	30	110
Terrence Baxter, Pfeiffer	2000	31	109
Terryl Woolery, Cal Poly Pomona	1997	27	109

†national champion; *record

STEAL AVERAGE

Player, Team	Season	G	Stl.	Avg.
Wayne Copeland, Lynn	†2000	26	129	*4.96
John Morris, Bluefield St.	1994	23	104	4.52
Devlin Herring, Pitt.-Johnstown	†1997	27	122	4.52
J.R. Gamble, Queens (N.C.)	†2001	32	*139	4.34
Ken Francis, Molloy	†1994	27	116	4.29
Terrance Gist, S.C.-Spartanburg	†1998	29	122	4.21
Oronn Brown, Clarion	1997	29	120	4.14
Devlin Herring, Pitt.-Johnstown	1998	29	118	4.07
Michael Dean, Cal St. Hayward	1998	26	105	4.04
Terryl Woolery, Cal Poly Pomona	1997	27	109	4.04
Wayne Copeland, Lynn	†1999	31	125	4.03
Kevin Nichols, Bemidji St.	1994	26	104	4.00
Tracy Gross, High Point	1997	29	114	3.93
Peron Austin, Southern Colo.	1997	28	110	3.93
Marcus Stubblefield, Queens (N.C.)	1993	28	110	3.93
Demetri Beekman, Assumption	1993	23	89	3.87
Darnell White, Calif. (Pa.)	1994	30	115	3.83
J.R. Gamble, Queens (N.C.)	2000	28	107	3.82
David Clark, Bluefield St.	†1996	31	118	3.81
Eddien Santiago, Mo. Southern St.	2001	30	114	3.80

†national champion; *record

Career Records

POINTS

Player, Team	Seasons	Pts.
Travis Grant, Kentucky St.	1969-72	*4,045
Bob Hopkins, Grambling	1953-56	3,759
Tony Smith, Pfeiffer	1989-92	3,350
Earnest Lee, Clark Atlanta	1984-87	3,298

Player, Team	Seasons	Pts.
Joe Miller, Alderson-Broaddus	1954-57	3,294
Henry Logan, Western Caro.	1965-68	3,290
John Rinka, Kenyon	1967-70	3,251
Dick Barnett, Tennessee St.	1956-59	3,209
Willie Scott, Alabama St.	1966-69	3,155
Johnnie Allen, Bethune-Cookman	1966-69	3,058
Bennie Swain, Texas Southern	1955-58	3,008
Lambert Shell, Bridgeport	1989-92	3,001
Carl Hartman, Alderson-Broaddus	1952-55	2,959
Earl Monroe, Winston-Salem	1964-67	2,935

*record

SCORING AVERAGE
(Minimum 1,400 points)

Player, Team	Seasons	G	FG	3FG	FT	Pts.	Avg.
Travis Grant, Kentucky St.	1969-72	121	*1,760	—	525	*4,045	*33.4
John Rinka, Kenyon	1967-70	99	1,261	—	729	3,251	32.8
Florindo Vieira, Quinnipiac	1954-57	69	761	—	741	2,263	32.8
Willie Shaw, Lane	1961-64	76	960	—	459	2,379	31.3
Mike Davis, Virginia Union	1966-69	89	1,014	—	730	2,758	31.0
Henry Logan, Western Caro.	1965-68	107	1,263	—	764	3,290	30.7
Willie Scott, Alabama St.	1966-69	103	1,277	—	601	3,155	30.6
Carlos Knox, IUPUI	1995-98	85	832	208	684	2,556	30.1
George Gilmore, Chaminade	1991-92	51	485	174	387	1,531	30.0
Brett Beeson, Moorhead St.	1995-96	54	551	92	421	1,615	29.9
Bob Hopkins, Grambling	1953-56	126	1,403	—	953	3,759	29.8
Rod Butler, Western New Eng.	1968-72	59	697	—	331	1,725	29.2
Gregg Northington, Alabama St.	1970-72	75	894	—	403	2,191	29.2
Isaiah Wilson, Baltimore	1969-71	67	731	—	471	1,933	28.9

*record

FIELD-GOAL PERCENTAGE
(Minimum 400 field goals made)

Player, Team	Seasons	G	FG	FGA	Pct.
Todd Linder, Tampa	1984-87	122	909	1,284	*70.8
Tom Schurfranz, Bellarmine	1987-88, 91-92	112	742	1,057	70.2
Chad Scott, Calif. (Pa.)	1991-94	115	465	664	70.0
Ed Phillips, Alabama A&M	1968-71	95	610	885	68.9
Ulysses Hackett, S.C.-Spartanburg	1990-92	90	824	1,213	67.9
Larry Tucker, Lewis	1981-83	84	677	999	67.8
Otis Evans, Wayne St. (Mich.)	1989-92	106	472	697	67.7
Matthew Cornegay, Tuskegee	1979-82	105	524	783	66.9
Ray Strozier, Central Mo. St.	1978-81	110	563	843	66.8
Dennis Edwards, Fort Hays St.	1994-95	59	666	998	66.7
James Morris, Central Okla.	1990-93	76	532	798	66.7
Lance Berwald, North Dakota St.	1983-84	58	475	717	66.2
Harold Booker, Cheyney	1965-67, 69	108	662	1,002	66.1

*record

THREE-POINT FIELD GOALS MADE

Player, Team	Seasons	G	3FG
Steve Moyer, Gannon	1996-99	112	*442
Tony Smith, Pfeiffer	1989-92	126	431
Kwame Morton, Clarion	1991-94	105	411
Gary Duda, Merrimack	1989-92	122	389
Markus Hallgrimson, Mont. St.-Billings	1998-00	82	371
Columbus Parker, Johnson Smith	1990-93	115	354
Gary Paul, Indianapolis	1987-90	111	354
Matt Miller, Drury	1999-02	106	351
Travis Tuttle, North Dakota	1994-97	108	350
Mike Ziegler, Colorado Mines	1987-90	118	344
Chris Brown, Tuskegee	1993-96	104	339
Stephen Hamrick, Eastern N.M.	1993-96	107	339
Mike Kuhens, Queens (N.Y.)	1995-98	104	334
Jesse Ogden, Edinboro	1995-98	110	334
Brent Kincaid, Calif. (Pa.)	1993-96	115	325
Damien Blair, West Chester	1992-95	109	317
Matt Van Leeuwen, Merrimack	1998-01	112	312
Cliff DuBois, Barry	1996-99	112	311
Brad Joens, Wayne St. (Neb.)	1998-01	117	310
Michael Shue, Lock Haven	1994-97	92	308
Jon Cronin, Stonehill	1989-92	117	308
Wil Pierce, Western St.	1993-96	114	307
Roger Powers, St. Rose	1994-97	123	305

*record

THREE-POINT FIELD GOALS MADE PER GAME
(Minimum 200 three-point field goals made)

Player, Team	Seasons	G	3FG	Avg.
Antonio Harris, LeMoyne-Owen	1998-99	52	245	*4.71
Markus Hallgrimson, Mont. St.-Billings	1998-00	82	371	4.52
Alex Williams, Sacramento St.	1987-88	58	247	4.26
Tommie Spearman, Columbus St.	1994-95	56	233	4.16
Reece Gliko, Mont. St.-Billings	1996-97	56	231	4.13
Danny Phillips, Mont. St.-Billings	2001-02	55	222	4.03
Steve Moyer, Gannon	1996-99	112	*442	3.95
Kwame Morton, Clarion	1991-94	105	411	3.91
Zoderick Green, Central Okla.	1993-95	57	212	3.72
Shawn Williams, Central Okla.	1989-91	57	212	3.72
Mike Sinclair, Bowie St.	1987-89	82	299	3.65
Nate Allen, Western St.	1996-97	57	205	3.60
Robert Martin, Sacramento St.	1987-89	85	294	3.46
Tony Smith, Pfeiffer	1989-92	126	431	3.42
Michael Shue, Lock Haven	1994-97	92	308	3.35
Matt Miller, Drury	1999-02	106	351	3.31
Chris Brown, Tuskegee	1993-96	104	339	3.26
Travis Tuttle, North Dakota	1994-97	108	350	3.24
Mike Kuhens, Queens (N.Y.)	1995-98	104	334	3.21
Gary Paul, Indianapolis	1987-90	111	354	3.19
Gary Duda, Merrimack	1989-92	122	389	3.19
Stephen Hamrick, Eastern N.M.	1993-96	107	339	3.17
Rod Harris, Southampton	1987-89	78	241	3.09

*record

THREE-POINT FIELD-GOAL PERCENTAGE
(Minimum 200 three-point field goals made)

Player, Team	Seasons	G	3FG	3FGA	Pct.
Scott Martin, Rollins	1988-91	104	236	460	*51.3
Todd Woelfle, Oakland City	1995-98	103	210	412	51.0
Matt Markle, Shippensburg	1989-92	101	202	408	49.5
Paul Cluxton, Northern Ky.	1994-97	122	303	619	48.9
Lance Gelnett, Millersville	1989-92	109	266	547	48.6
Antonio Harris, LeMoyne-Owen	1998-99	52	245	510	48.0
Mark Willey, Fort Hays St.	1989-92	117	224	478	46.9
Todd Bowden, Randolph-Macon	1987-89	84	229	491	46.6
Gary Paul, Indianapolis	1987-90	111	354	768	46.1
Matt Ripaldi, New Hamp. Col.	1993-96	123	277	604	45.9
Alex Williams, Sacramento St.	1987-88	58	247	541	45.7
Jason Bullock, Indiana (Pa.)	1993-96	119	287	637	45.1
Boyd Printy, Truman	1990-92	77	201	447	45.0
Lance Luitjens, Northern St.	1994-96	95	275	614	44.8
Buck Williams, North Ala.	1987-89	84	238	535	44.5

*record

FREE-THROW PERCENTAGE
(Minimum 250 free throws made)

Player, Team	Seasons	G	FT	FTA	Pct.
Paul Cluxton, Northern Ky.	1994-97	122	272	291	*93.5
Kent Andrews, McNeese St.	1967-69	67	252	275	91.6
Jon Hagen, Minn. St.-Mankato	1963-65	73	252	280	90.0
Dave Reynolds, Davis & Elkins	1986-89	107	383	429	89.3
Michael Shue, Lock Haven	1994-97	92	354	400	88.5
Tony Budzik, Mansfield	1989-92	107	367	416	88.2
Terry Gill, New Orleans	1972-74	79	261	296	88.2
Bryan Vacca, Randolph-Macon	1980-83	94	262	298	87.9
Steve Nisenson, Hofstra	1963-65	83	602	685	87.9
Jeff Gore, St. Rose	1991-93	91	333	379	87.9
Jack Sparks, Bentley	1976-80	99	253	288	87.8
Dan Shanks, Coker	1994-97	102	467	533	87.6
Troy Nesmith, Gannon	1997-98	54	274	313	87.5
Wayne Profitt, Lynchburg	1965-67	57	482	551	87.5
Clyde Briley, McNeese St.	1962-65	101	561	642	87.4
Jason Sempsrott, South Dakota St.	1994-97	110	462	529	87.3
Foy Ballance, Armstrong Atlantic	1978-81	108	351	402	87.3
Jehu Brabham, Mississippi Col.	1969-71	72	452	518	87.3
Pete Chambers, West Chester	1966-68	67	267	306	87.3

*record

REBOUND AVERAGE
(Minimum 900 rebounds)

Player, Team	Seasons	G	Reb.	Avg.
Tom Hart, Middlebury	1953, 55-56	63	1,738	*27.6
Maurice Stokes, St. Francis (Pa.)	1953-55	72	1,812	25.2
Frank Stronczek, American Int'l	1965-67	62	1,549	25.0
Bill Thieben, Hofstra	1954-56	76	1,837	24.2
Hank Brown, Mass.-Lowell	1965-67	49	1,129	23.0
Elmore Smith, Kentucky St.	1969-71	85	1,917	22.6
Charles Wrinn, Trinity (Conn.)	1951-53	53	1,176	22.2
Roman Turmon, Clark Atlanta	1952-54	60	1,312	21.9
Tony Missere, Pratt	1966-68	62	1,348	21.7
Ron Horton, Delaware St.	1966-68	64	1,384	21.6

*record

DIVISION II

ASSISTS

Player, Team	Seasons	G	Ast.
Demetri Beekman, Assumption	1990-93	119	*1,044
Adam Kaufman, Edinboro	1998-01	116	936
Rob Paternostro, New Hamp. Col.	1992-95	129	919
Gallagher Driscoll, St. Rose	1989-92	121	878
Tony Smith, Pfeiffer	1989-92	126	828
Jamie Stevens, Mont. St.-Billings	1996-99	110	805
Steve Ray, Bridgeport	1989-90	65	785
Dan Ward, St. Cloud St.	1992-95	100	774
Jordan Canfield, Washburn	1994-97	126	756
Charles Jordan, Erskine	1989-92	119	727
Donald Johnson, Franklin Pierce	1998-01	114	722
Patrick Chambers, Philadelphia U.	1991-94	123	709
Lamont Jones, Bridgeport	1992-95	119	708
Ernest Jenkins, N.M. Highlands	1992-95	84	699
Antoine Campbell, Ashland	1995-98	113	697
Pat Madden, Jacksonville St.	1989-91	88	688
Nate Tibbetts, South Dakota	1998-01	112	678
Candice Pickens, Calif. (Pa.)	1993-96	121	675
Mark Benson, Tex. A&M-Kingsville	1989-91	86	674
Craig Lottie, Alabama A&M	1992-95	93	673

*record

ASSIST AVERAGE
(Minimum 550 assists)

Player, Team	Seasons	G	Ast.	Avg.
Steve Ray, Bridgeport	1989-90	65	785	*12.1
Demetri Beekman, Assumption	1990-93	119	*1,044	8.8
Ernest Jenkins, N.M. Highlands	1992-95	84	699	8.3
Adam Kaufman, Edinboro	1998-01	116	936	8.1
Mark Benson, Tex. A&M-Kingsville	1989-91	86	674	7.8
Pat Madden, Jacksonville St.	1989-91	88	688	7.8
Dan Ward, St. Cloud St.	1992-95	100	774	7.7
Jamie Stevens, Mont. St.-Billings	1996-99	110	805	7.3
Gallagher Driscoll, St. Rose	1989-92	121	878	7.3
Craig Lottie, Alabama A&M	1992-95	93	673	7.2
Rob Paternostro, New Hamp. Col.	1992-95	129	919	7.1
Eddin Santiago, Mo. Southern St.	1999-02	117	804	6.9
Tony Smith, Pfeiffer	1989-92	126	828	6.6
Donald Johnson, Franklin Pierce	1998-01	114	722	6.3
Mike Buscetto, Quinnipiac	1990-93	99	624	6.3
Patrick Herron, Winston-Salem	1992-95	97	604	6.2
Pat Delaney, St. Anselm	1999-02	118	731	6.2
Antoine Campbell, Ashland	1995-98	113	697	6.2
Charles Jordan, Erskine	1989-92	119	727	6.1
Nate Tibbetts, South Dakota	1998-01	112	678	6.1

*record

BLOCKED SHOTS

Player, Team	Seasons	G	Blk.
James Doyle, Concord	1995-98	120	*416
Derek Moore, S.C.-Aiken	1996-99	102	408
Rich Edwards, Adelphi	1999-02	123	305

Eddin Santiago (right) of Missouri Southern State set a new career steals record last season.

Photo by Mo. Southern St. Sports Information

Player, Team	Seasons	G	Blk.
Kino Outlaw, Mount Olive	1994-96	81	305
Garth Joseph, St. Rose	1995-97	89	300
Sylvere Bryan, Tampa	1999-02	116	294
Kerwin Thompson, Eckerd	1993-96	116	284
Eugene Haith, Philadelphia U.	1993-95	86	267
John Tomsich, Le Moyne	1996-99	114	264
Chandar Bingham, Virginia Union	1997-00	106	261
Coata Malone, Alabama A&M	1994-96	90	243
Alonzo Goldston, Fort Hays St.	1995-97	96	240
Damon Reed, St. Rose	1997-00	128	236
Ben Wallace, Virginia Union	1995-96	62	225
Antwain Smith, St. Paul's	1996-99	105	222
Eric Watson, Calif. (Pa.)	1996-99	119	214
Vonzell McGrew, Mo. Western St.	1993-95	57	211
Corey Johnson, Pace	1993-95	58	210
John Burke, Southampton	1995-96	54	205
Adrian Machado, Stonehill	1993-96	108	196
Steve Schutz, Fort Lewis	1994-97	96	195
Allen Wilson, Francis Marion/S.C.-Aiken	1995,97-99	110	194

*record

BLOCKED-SHOT AVERAGE
(Minimum 175 blocked shots)

Player, Team	Seasons	G	Blk.	Avg.
Derek Moore, S.C.-Aiken	1996-99	102	408	4.00
John Burke, Southampton	1995-96	54	205	3.80
Kino Outlaw, Mount Olive	1994-96	81	305	3.77
Vonzell McGrew, Mo. Western St.	1993-95	57	211	3.70
Tihomir Juric, Wis.-Parkside	1993-94	53	193	3.64
Ben Wallace, Virginia Union	1995-96	62	225	3.63
Corey Johnson, Pace	1993-95	58	210	3.62
James Doyle, Concord	1995-98	120	*416	3.47
Mark Hensel, Pitt.-Johnstown	1993-95	53	180	3.40
Garth Joseph, St. Rose	1995-97	89	300	3.37
Eugene Haith, Philadelphia U.	1993-95	86	267	3.10
Coata Malone, Alabama A&M	1994-96	90	243	2.70
Sylvere Bryan, Tampa	1999-02	116	294	2.53
Alonzo Goldston, Fort Hays St.	1995-97	96	240	2.50
Rich Edwards, Adelphi	1999-02	123	305	2.48
Chandar Bingham, Virginia Union	1997-00	106	261	2.46
Kerwin Thompson, Eckerd	1993-96	116	284	2.45
Merriel Jenkins, Hawaii-Hilo	1997-99	77	188	2.44
John Tomsich, Le Moyne	1996-99	114	264	2.32
Lawrence Williams, San Fran. St.	1993-95	79	176	2.23

*record

STEALS

Player, Team	Seasons	G	Stl.
Eddin Santiago, Mo. Southern St.	1999-02	117	383
Oronn Brown, Clarion	1994-97	106	361
Robert Campbell, Armstrong Atlantic	1998-01	118	357
Marcus Best, Winston-Salem	1999-02	119	345
Devlin Herring, Pitt.-Johnstown	1995-98	106	333
Rolondo Hall, Davis & Elkins	1998-01	106	314
Terrence Baxter, Pfeiffer	1998-01	108	281
David Clark, Bluefield St.	1994-96	83	278
Terrance Gist, S.C.-Spartanburg	1994-97	112	276
Omar Kasi, Molloy	1997-00	109	272
DeMarcos Anzures, Metro St.	1997-00	125	271
Mike Hancock, Neb.-Kearney	1995-98	121	271
Lorinza Harrington, Wingate	1999-02	121	263
Patrick Herron, Winston-Salem	1993-95	78	263
Ken Francis, Molloy	1993-95	81	260
Brandon Hughes, Newberry	1997-00	88	259
Lamont Jones, Bridgeport	1993-95	84	256
Deartrus Goodmon, Alabama A&M	1993-96	126	255
Wayne Copeland, Lynn	1999-00	57	254
J.R. Gamble, Queens (N.C.)	2000-01	60	246
Donald Johnson, Franklin Pierce	1998-01	114	243
Keith Linson, Central Mo. St.	1994-97	116	241

*record

STEAL AVERAGE
(Minimum 150 steals)

Player, Team	Seasons	G	Stl.	Avg.
Wayne Copeland, Lynn	1999-00	57	254	4.46
J.R. Gamble, Queens (N.C.)	2000-01	60	246	4.10
John Morris, Bluefield St.	1994-95	50	185	3.70
Oronn Brown, Clarion	1994-97	106	*361	3.41
Patrick Herron, Winston-Salem	1993-95	78	263	3.37
David Clark, Bluefield St.	1994-96	83	278	3.35
Peron Austin, Southern Colo.	1997-98	58	190	3.28

Player, Team	Seasons	G	Stl.	Avg.
Eddin Santiago, Mo. Southern St.	1999-02	117	*383	3.27
Darnell White, Calif. (Pa.)	1993-94	59	192	3.25
Rudy Berry, Cal St. Stanislaus	1993-94	51	164	3.21
Ken Francis, Molloy	1993-95	81	260	3.21
Bob Cunningham, New York Tech	1995-96	55	175	3.18
Devlin Herring, Pitt.-Johnstown	1995-98	106	333	3.14
Craig Fergeson, Columbus St.	1995-96	61	191	3.13
Bryan Heaps, Abilene Christian	1993-94	56	171	3.05
Lamont Jones, Bridgeport	1993-95	84	256	3.05
Kelly Mann, Concord	1997-98	62	185	2.98

Player, Team	Seasons	G	Stl.	Avg.
Javar Cheatham, Gannon	2000-01	58	172	2.97
Rolondo Hall, Davis & Elkins	1998-01	106	314	2.96
Brandon Hughes, Newberry	1997-00	88	259	2.94
Malcolm Turner, Sonoma St.	1995-96	52	152	2.92
Tullius Pate, Coker	1994-95	55	158	2.87
Aaron Johnson, C.W. Post	1993-94	56	160	2.86
Steve St. Martin, Assumption	1995-98	72	205	2.85

*record

Annual Individual Champions

Scoring Average

Season	Player, Team	G	FG	FT	Pts.	Avg.
1948	Nate DeLong, Wis.-River Falls	22	206	206	618	28.1
1949	George King, Charleston (W.Va.)	26	289	179	757	29.1
1950	George King, Charleston (W.Va.)	31	354	259	967	31.2
1951	Scott Seagall, Millikin	31	314	260	888	28.6
1952	Harold Wolfe, Findlay	22	285	101	671	30.5
1953	Roger Kuss, Wis.-River Falls	21	291	235	817	38.9
1954	Clarence "Bevo" Francis, Rio Grande	27	444	367	1,255	*46.5
1955	Bill Warden, North Central	13	162	127	451	34.7
1956	Bill Reigel, McNeese St.	36	425	370	1,220	33.9
1957	Ken Hammond, West Va. Tech	27	334	274	942	34.9
1958	John Lee Butcher, Pikeville	27	330	210	870	32.2
1959	Paul Wilcox, Davis & Elkins	23	289	195	773	33.6
1960	Don Perrelli, Southern Conn. St.	22	263	168	694	31.5
1961	Lebron Bell, Bryan	14	174	114	462	33.0
1962	Willie Shaw, Lane	18	239	115	593	32.9
1963	Earl Glass, Miss. Industrial	19	322	171	815	42.9
1964	Willie Shaw, Lane	18	303	121	727	40.4
1965	Thales McReynolds, Miles	18	294	118	706	39.2
1966	Paul Crissman, Southern Cal College	23	373	90	836	36.3
1967	Earl Monroe, Winston-Salem	32	509	311	*1,329	41.5
1968	Mike Davis, Virginia Union	25	351	206	908	36.3
1969	John Rinka, Kenyon	26	340	202	882	33.9
1970	John Rinka, Kenyon	23	354	234	942	41.0
1971	Bo Lamar, La.-Lafayette	29	424	196	1,044	36.0
1972	Travis Grant, Kentucky St.	33	*539	226	1,304	39.5
1973	Claude White, Elmhurst	18	248	101	597	33.2
1974	Aaron James, Grambling	27	366	137	869	32.2
1975	Ron Barrow, Southern U.	23	296	115	707	30.7
1976	Ron Barrow, Southern U.	27	318	136	772	28.6
1977	Ed Murphy, Merrimack	28	369	158	896	32.0
1978	Harold Robertson, Lincoln (Mo.)	28	408	149	965	34.5
1979	Bo Clark, UCF	23	315	97	727	31.6
1980	Bill Fennelly, Central Mo. St.	28	337	189	863	30.8
1981	Gregory Jackson, St. Paul's	26	267	183	717	27.6
1982	John Ebeling, Fla. Southern	32	286	284	856	26.8
1983	Danny Dixon, Alabama A&M	27	379	152	910	33.7
1984	Earl Jones, Dist. Columbia	22	215	200	630	28.6
1985	Earnest Lee, Clark Atlanta	29	380	230	990	34.1
1986	Earnest Lee, Clark Atlanta	28	314	191	819	29.3

Season	Player, Team	G	FG	3FG	FT	Pts.	Avg.
1987	Earnest Lee, Clark Atlanta	29	326	35	174	861	29.7
1988	Daryl Cambrelen, Southampton	25	242	32	170	686	27.4
1989	Steve deLaveaga, Cal Lutheran	28	278	79	151	786	28.1
1990	A.J. English, Virginia Union	30	333	65	270	1,001	33.4
1991	Gary Mattison, St. Augustine's	26	277	53	159	766	29.5
1992	George Gilmore, Chaminade	28	280	82	238	880	31.4
1993	Darrin Robinson, Sacred Heart	26	313	75	130	831	32.0
1994	Kwame Mortin, Clarion	26	264	126	191	845	32.5
1995	Carlos Knox, IUPUI	29	284	39	218	825	28.4
1996	Brett Beeson, Moorhead St.	27	305	58	232	900	33.3
1997	Dan Sancomb, Wheeling Jesuit	27	295	11	125	726	26.9
1998	Carlos Knox, IUPUI	26	238	96	209	781	30.0
1999	Eddie Robinson, Central Okla.	26	305	24	95	729	28.0
2000	David Evans, BYU-Hawaii	28	300	48	134	782	27.9
2001	Marlon Dawson, Central Okla.	26	206	101	155	668	25.7
2002	Angel Figueroa, Dowling	25	216	79	143	654	26.2

*record

Field-Goal Percentage

Season	Player, Team	G	FG	FGA	Pct.
1949	Vern Mikkelson, Hamline	30	203	377	53.8
1950	Nate DeLong, Wis.-River Falls	29	287	492	58.3
1951	Johnny O'Brien, Seattle	33	248	434	57.1
1952	Forrest Hamilton, Southwest Mo. St.	30	147	246	59.8
1953	Bob Buis, Carleton	21	149	246	60.6
1954	Paul Lauritzen, Augustana (Ill.)	19	158	251	62.9
1955	Jim O'Hara, UC Santa Barb.	24	140	214	65.4
1956	Logan Gipe, Ky. Wesleyan	22	134	224	59.8
1957	John Wilfred, Winston-Salem	30	229	381	60.1
1958	Bennie Swain, Texas Southern	35	363	587	61.8
1959	Dick O'Meara, Babson	18	144	225	64.0
1960	Edwin Cox, Howard Payne	26	126	194	64.9
1961	Tony Solomon, St. Paul's	20	94	149	63.1
1962	Tom Morris, St. Paul's	17	108	168	64.3
1963	Howard Trice, Howard Payne	26	168	237	70.9
1964	Robert Springer, Howard Payne	24	119	174	68.4
1965	Harold Booker, Cheyney	24	144	198	72.7
1966	Harold Booker, Cheyney	27	170	240	70.8
1967	John Dickson, Arkansas St.	24	214	308	69.5
1968	Edward Phillips, Alabama A&M	22	154	210	73.3
1969	Marvin Lewis, Southampton	24	271	375	72.3
1970	Travis Grant, Kentucky St.	31	482	688	70.1
1971	Edward Phillips, Alabama A&M	24	159	221	71.9
1972	Don Manley, Otterbein	23	146	207	70.5
1973	Glynn Berry, Southampton	26	191	302	63.2
1974	Kirby Thurston, Western Caro.	25	242	367	65.9
1975	Gerald Cunningham, Kentucky St.	29	280	411	68.1
1976	Thomas Blue, Elizabeth City St.	24	270	388	69.6
1977	Kelvin Hicks, New York Tech	24	161	232	69.4
1978	Ron Ripley, Wis.-Green Bay	32	162	239	67.8
1979	Carl Bailey, Tuskegee	27	210	307	68.4
1980	Ray Strozier, Central Mo. St.	28	142	195	72.8
1981	Matthew Cornegay, Tuskegee	26	177	247	71.7
1982	Matthew Cornegay, Tuskegee	29	208	278	74.8
1983	Rudy Burton, Elizabeth City St.	24	142	201	70.6
1984	Maurice Stafford, North Ala.	34	198	264	75.0
1985	Todd Linder, Tampa	31	219	306	71.6
1986	Todd Linder, Tampa	28	204	291	70.1
1987	Todd Linder, Tampa	32	282	375	*75.2
1988	Louis Newsome, North Ala.	29	192	266	72.2
1989	Tom Schurfranz, Bellarmine	28	164	240	68.2
1990	Ulysses Hackett, S.C.-Spartanburg	32	301	426	70.7
1991	Tom Schurfranz, Bellarmine	30	245	339	72.3
1992	Brian Moten, West Ga.	26	141	192	73.4
1993	Chad Scott, Calif. (Pa.)	28	173	245	70.6
1994	Chad Scott, Calif. (Pa.)	30	178	245	72.7
1995	John Pruett, SIU-Edwardsville	26	138	193	71.5
1996	Kyle Kirby, IPFW	26	133	195	68.2
1997	Andy Robertson, Fla. Southern	32	183	269	68.0
1998	Anthony Russell, West Fla.	28	191	284	67.3
1999	DaVonn Harp, Kutztown St.	27	140	205	68.3
2000	Shaun Bass, Drury	28	156	237	65.8
2001	Charles Ward, St. Augustine's	27	159	243	65.4
2002	Brett Barnard, Le Moyne	27	141	211	66.8

*record

DIVISION II

Three-Point Field Goals Made Per Game

Season	Player, Team	G	3FG	Avg.
1987	Bill Harris, Northern Mich.	27	117	4.3
1988	Alex Williams, Sacramento St.	30	*167	5.6
1989	Robert Martin, Sacramento St.	28	118	4.2
1990	Gary Paul, Indianapolis	28	110	3.9
1991	Shawn Williams, Central Okla.	29	129	4.4
1992	Jason Garrow, Augustana (S.D.)	27	135	5.0
1993	Ray Gutierrez, Calif. (Pa.)	29	142	4.9
1994	Kwame Morton, Clarion	26	126	4.8
1995	Eric Kline, Northern St.	30	148	4.9
1996	Daren Alix, Merrimack	28	114	4.1
1997	Reece Gliko, Mont. St.-Billings	28	135	4.8
1998	Antonio Harris, LeMoyne-Owen	26	119	4.6
1999	Antonio Harris, LeMoyne-Owen	26	126	4.8
2000	Markus Hallgrimson, Mont. St.-Billings	26	160	*6.2
2001	Blake Johnson, Edinboro	28	111	4.0
2002	Danny Phillips, Mont. St.-Billings	28	120	4.3

*record

Three-Point Field-Goal Percentage

Season	Player, Team	G	3FG	3FGA	Pct.
1987	Charles Byrd, West Tex. A&M	31	95	168	56.5
1988	Ray Lee, Hampton	24	39	60	*65.0
1989	Aaron Baker, Mississippi Col.	27	69	117	59.0
1990	Mark Willey, Fort Hays St.	29	49	81	60.5
1991	Scott Martin, Rollins	28	114	201	56.7
1992	Jeff Duvall, Oakland City	30	49	91	53.8
1993	Greg Wilkinson, Oakland City	32	82	152	53.9
1994	Todd Jones, Southern Ind.	29	56	105	53.3
1995	Aaron Fehler, Oakland City	26	73	121	60.3
1996	Matt Hopson, Oakland City	31	84	145	57.9
1997	Adam Harness, Oakland City	26	39	68	57.4
1998	Todd Woelfe, Oakland City	27	87	162	53.7
1999	John Cabanilla, Oakland City	29	46	85	54.1
2000	Jasen Gast, Incarnate Word	26	39	72	54.2
2001	Bobby Hoegh, Southwest Baptist	23	72	147	49.0
2002	Jared Ramirez, Northern Colo.	27	60	115	52.2

*record

Free-Throw Percentage

Season	Player, Team	G	FT	FTA	Pct.
1948	Frank Cochran, Delta St.	22	36	43	83.7
1949	Jim Walsh, Spring Hill	25	62	75	82.7
1950	Dean Ehlers, Central Methodist	33	186	213	87.3
1951	Jim Hoverder, Central Mo. St.	23	75	85	88.2
1952	Jim Fenton, Akron	24	104	121	86.0
1953	Dick Parfitt, Central Mich.	22	93	105	88.6
1954	Bill Parrott, David Lipscomb	24	174	198	87.9
1955	Pete Kovacs, Monmouth (Ill.)	20	175	199	87.9
1956	Fred May, Loras	22	127	146	87.0
1957	Jim Sutton, South Dakota St.	22	127	138	92.0
1958	Arnold Smith, Allen	22	103	113	91.2
1959	Bill Reece, Lenoir-Rhyne	27	84	92	91.3
1960	Ron Slaymaker, Emporia St.	20	80	88	90.9
1961	Harvey Rosen, Wilkes	22	105	115	91.3
1962	Wayne Mahone, Stephen F. Austin	26	76	84	90.5
1963	Jon Hagen, Minn. St.-Mankato	25	76	82	92.7
1964	Steve Nisenson, Hofstra	28	230	252	91.3
1965	Jon Hagen, Minn. St.-Mankato	23	103	112	92.0
1966	Jack Cryan, Rider	25	182	198	91.9
1967	Kent Andrews, McNeese St.	22	101	110	91.8
1968	Kent Andrews, McNeese St.	24	85	90	94.4
1969	Joe Cullen, Hartwick	18	96	103	93.2
1970	John Rinka, Kenyon	23	234	263	89.0
1971	Ed Roeth, Defiance	26	138	152	90.8
1972	Jeff Kuntz, St. Norbert	25	142	155	91.6
1973	Bob Kronisch, Brooklyn	30	93	105	88.6
1974	Terry Gill, New Orleans	30	97	105	92.4
1975	Clarence Rand, Alabama St.	29	91	101	90.1
1976	Billy Newton, Morgan St.	28	85	90	94.4
1977	Emery Sammons, Philadelphia U.	28	145	157	92.4
1978	Dana Skinner, Merrimack	28	142	154	92.2
1979	Jack Sparks, Bentley	28	76	84	90.5
1980	Grey Giovanine, Central Mo. St.	28	75	83	90.4
1981	Ted Smith, SIU-Edwardsville	26	67	73	91.8
1982	Carl Gonder, Augustana (S.D.)	27	86	93	92.5

Season	Player, Team	G	FT	FTA	Pct.
1983	Joe Sclafani, New Haven	28	86	98	87.8
1984	Darrell Johnston, New Hamp. Col.	29	74	81	91.4
1985	Tom McDonald, South Dakota St.	33	88	97	90.7
1986	Todd Mezzulo, Alas. Fairbanks	27	114	125	91.2
1987	Mike Sanders, Northern Colo.	28	82	87	94.3
1988	Charles Byrd, West Tex. A&M	29	92	99	92.8
1989	Mike Boschee, North Dakota	28	71	77	92.2
1990	Mike Morris, Ala.-Huntsville	28	114	125	91.2
1991	Ryun Williams, South Dakota	30	114	125	91.2
1992	Hal McManus, Lander	28	110	119	92.4
1993	Jason Williams, New Haven	27	115	125	92.0
1994	Jay Harrie, Mont. St.-Billings	26	86	92	93.5
1995	Jim Borodawka, Mass.-Lowell	27	74	80	92.5
1996	Paul Cluxton, Northern Ky.	32	100	108	92.6
1997	Paul Cluxton, Northern Ky.	35	94	94	*100.0
1998	Troy Nesmith, Gannon	27	146	158	92.4
1999	Travis Starns, Colorado Mines	26	87	93	93.5
2000	Jason Kreider, Michigan Tech	31	84	91	92.3
2001	C.J. Cowgill, Chaminade	22	113	119	95.0
2002	Curtis Small, Southampton	29	109	116	94.0

*record

Rebound Average

Season	Player, Team	G	Reb.	Avg.
1951	Walter Lenz, Frank. & Marsh.	17	338	19.9
1952	Charley Wrinn, Trinity (Conn.)	19	486	25.6
1953	Ellerbe Neal, Wofford	23	609	26.5
1954	R.C. Owens, Albertson	25	677	27.1
1955	Tom Hart, Middlebury	22	649	29.5
1956	Tom Hart, Middlebury	21	620	*29.5
1957	Jim Smith, Steubenville	26	651	25.0
1958	Marv Becker, Widener	18	450	25.0
1959	Jim Davis, King's (Pa.)	17	384	22.6
1960	Jackie Jackson, Virginia Union	19	424	†.241
1961	Jackie Jackson, Virginia Union	26	641	24.7
1962	Jim Ahrens, Buena Vista	28	682	24.4
1963	Gerry Govan, St. Mary's (Kan.)	18	445	24.7
1964	Ernie Brock, Virginia St.	24	597	24.9
1965	Dean Sandifer, Lakeland	23	592	25.7
1966	Frank Stronczek, American Int'l	26	717	27.6
1967	Frank Stronczek, American Int'l	25	602	24.1
1968	Ron Horton, Delaware St.	23	543	23.6
1969	Wilbert Jones, Albany St. (Ga.)	28	670	23.9
1970	Russell Jackson, Southern U.	22	544	24.7
1971	Tony Williams, St. Francis (Me.)	24	599	25.0
1972	No rankings			
1973	No rankings			
1974	Larry Johnson, Prairie View	23	519	22.6
1975	Major Jones, Albany St. (Ga.)	27	608	22.5
1976	Major Jones, Albany St. (Ga.)	24	475	19.8
1977	Andre Means, Sacred Heart	32	516	16.1
1978	Scott Mountz, Calif. (Pa.)	24	431	18.0
1979	Keith Smith, Shaw	20	329	16.5
1980	Ricky Mahorn, Hampton	31	490	15.8
1981	Earl Jones, Dist. Columbia	25	333	13.3
1982	Donnie Carter, Tuskegee	29	372	12.8
1983	David Binion, N.C. Central	25	400	16.0
1984	Jerome Kersey, Longwood	27	383	14.2
1985	Charles Oakley, Virginia Union	31	535	17.3
1986	Raheem Muhammad, Wayne St. (Mich.)	31	428	13.8
1987	Andre Porter, Southampton	23	309	13.4
1988	Anthony Ikeobi, Clark Atlanta	27	380	14.1
1989	Toby Barber, Winston-Salem	24	327	13.6
1990	Leroy Gasque, Morris Brown	24	375	15.6
1991	Sheldon Owens, Shaw	27	325	12.0
1992	David Allen, Wayne St. (Neb.)	28	362	12.9
1993	James Hector, American Int'l	28	389	13.9
1994	Pat Armour, Jacksonville St.	25	363	14.5
1995	Lorenzo Poole, Albany St. (Ga.)	26	417	16.0
1996	J.J. Sims, West Ga.	28	374	13.4
1997	Kebu Stewart, Cal St. Bakersfield	33	442	13.4
1998	Antonio Garcia, Ky. Wesleyan	33	457	13.8
1999	Antonio Garcia, Ky. Wesleyan	37	540	14.6
2000	Howard Jackson, Lincoln Memorial	24	321	13.4
2001	Colin Duchacme, Longwood	31	490	15.8
2002	Danny Jones, Tarleton St.	33	416	13.0

*record; †Championship determined by highest individual recoveries out of total by both teams in all games.

Assist Average

Season	Player, Team	G	Ast.	Avg.
1989	Steve Ray, Bridgeport	32	*400	*12.5
1990	Steve Ray, Bridgeport	33	385	11.7
1991	Adrian Hutt, Metro St.	28	285	10.2
1992	Tony Smith, Pfeiffer	35	349	10.0
1993	Demetri Beekman, Assumption	23	264	11.5
1994	Ernest Jenkins, N.M. Highlands	27	277	10.3
1995	Ernest Jenkins, N.M. Highlands	27	291	10.8
1996	Bobby Banks, Metro St.	27	244	9.0
1997	Emanuel Richardson, Pitt.-Johnstown	27	235	8.7
1998	Emanuel Richardson, Pitt.-Johnstown	29	260	9.0
1999	Shawn Brown, Merrimack	27	223	8.3
2000	Todd Chappell, Texas Wesleyan	27	263	9.7
2001	Javar Cheatham, Gannon	30	283	9.4
2002	Pat Delany, St. Anselm	30	234	7.8

*record

Blocked-Shot Average

Season	Player, Team	G	Blk.	Avg.
1993	Antonio Harvey, Pfeiffer	29	155	*5.3
1994	Johnny Tyson, Central Okla.	27	126	4.7
1995	Kino Outlaw, Mount Olive	28	124	4.4
1996	John Burke, Southampton	28	142	5.1
1997	Garth Joseph, St. Rose	34	124	3.6
1998	James Doyle, Concord	30	*157	5.2
1999	Chandar Bingham, Virginia Union	27	95	3.5
2000	Josh Stanhiser, Columbia Union	25	87	3.5
2001	Jason Roseto, Edinboro	23	97	4.2
2002	George Bailey, Lock Haven	20	79	4.0

*record

Steal Average

Season	Player, Team	G	Stl.	Avg.
1993	Marcus Stubblefield, Queens (N.C.)	28	110	3.9
1994	Ken Francis, Molloy	27	116	4.3
1995	Shannon Holmes, New York Tech	30	110	3.7
1996	David Clark, Bluefield St.	31	118	3.8
1997	Devlin Herring, Pitt.-Johnstown	27	122	4.5
1998	Terrance Gist, S.C.-Spartanburg	29	122	4.2
1999	Wayne Copeland, Lynn	31	125	4.0
2000	Wayne Copeland, Lynn	26	*129	*5.0
2001	J.R. Gamble, Queens (N.C.)	32	139	4.3
2002	Shahar Golan, Assumption	30	106	3.5

*record

Annual Team Champions

Won-Lost Percentage

Season	Team	Won	Lost	Pct.
1968	Monmouth	27	2	.931
1969	Alcorn St.	26	1	.963
1970	Central Wash.	31	2	.939
1971	Kentucky St.	31	2	.939
1972	Olivet	22	1	.957
1973	Coe	24	1	.960
1974	West Ga.	29	4	.879
1975	Bentley	23	2	.920
1976	Philadelphia U.	25	3	.893
1977	Clarion	27	3	.900
	Kentucky St.	27	3	.900
	Towson	27	3	.900
1978	Wis.-Green Bay	30	2	.938
1979	Roanoke	25	3	.893
1980	Alabama St.	32	2	.941
1981	Mt. St. Mary's	28	3	.903
1982	Cheyney	28	3	.903
1983	Dist. Columbia	29	3	.906
1984	Norfolk St.	29	2	.935
1985	Jacksonville St.	31	1	.969
	Virginia Union	31	1	.969
1986	Wright St.	28	3	.903
1987	Norfolk St.	28	3	.903
1988	Fla. Southern	31	3	.912
1989	UC Riverside	30	4	.882
1990	Ky. Wesleyan	31	2	.939
1991	Southwest Baptist	29	3	.906
1992	Calif. (Pa.)	31	2	.939
1993	Cal St. Bakersfield	33	0	1.000
1994	Philadelphia U.	29	2	.935
1995	Jacksonville St.	24	1	.960
1996	Fort Hays St.	34	0	1.000
1997	Fort Hays St.	29	2	.935
1998	UC Davis	31	2	.939
1999	Ky. Wesleyan	35	2	.946
2000	Fla. Southern	32	2	.941
2001	Adelphi	31	1	.969
2002	Cal St. San B'dino	28	2	.933
	Northeastern St.	28	2	.933

Scoring Offense

Season	Team	G	W-L	Pts.	Avg.
1948	St. Anselm	19	12-7	1,329	69.9
1949	Charleston (W.Va.)	26	18-8	2,023	77.8
1950	Charleston (W.Va.)	31	22-9	2,477	79.9
1951	Beloit	23	18-5	1,961	85.3
1952	Lambuth	22	17-5	1,985	90.2
1953	Arkansas Tech	21	20-1	1,976	94.1
1954	Montclair St.	22	18-4	2,128	96.7
1955	West Va. Tech	20	15-5	2,150	107.5
1956	West Va. Tech	22	16-6	2,210	100.5
1957	West Va. Tech	29	26-3	2,976	102.6
1958	West Va. Tech	29	24-5	2,941	101.4
1959	Grambling	29	28-1	2,764	95.3
1960	Mississippi Col.	19	15-4	2,169	114.2
1961	Lawrence Tech	25	19-6	2,409	96.4
1962	Troy St.	25	20-5	2,402	96.1
1963	Miles	21	17-4	2,011	95.8
1964	Benedict	27	19-8	2,730	101.1
1965	Ark.-Pine Bluff	26	22-4	2,655	102.1
1966	Southern Cal College	23	15-8	2,480	107.8
1967	Lincoln (Mo.)	27	24-3	2,925	108.3
1968	Stillman	26	17-9	2,898	111.5
1969	Norfolk St.	25	21-4	2,653	106.1
1970	Norfolk St.	26	19-7	2,796	107.5
1971	Savannah St.	29	18-11	3,051	105.2
1972	Florida A&M	28	18-10	2,869	102.5
1973	Md.-East. Shore	31	26-5	2,974	95.9
1974	Texas Southern	28	15-13	2,884	103.0
1975	Prairie View	26	16-10	2,774	106.7
1976	Southern U.	27	13-14	2,637	97.7
1977	Virginia Union	30	25-5	2,966	98.9
1978	Merrimack	28	22-6	2,606	93.1
1979	Armstrong Atlantic	27	21-6	2,626	97.3
1980	Ashland	27	11-16	2,514	93.1
1981	Virginia Union	31	20-11	2,761	89.1
1982	Alabama St.	28	22-6	2,429	86.8
1983	Virginia St.	29	19-10	2,802	96.6
1984	New Hamp. Col.	29	18-11	2,564	88.4
1985	Alabama A&M	31	21-10	2,881	92.9
1986	Alabama A&M	32	23-9	2,897	90.5
1987	Alabama A&M	30	23-7	2,826	94.2
1988	Oakland	28	19-9	2,685	95.9
1989	Stonehill	32	23-9	3,244	101.4
1990	Jacksonville St.	29	24-5	2,872	99.0
1991	Troy St.	30	22-8	3,259	108.6
1992	Troy St.	29	23-6	3,513	*121.1
1993	Central Okla.	29	23-6	3,293	113.6
1994	Central Okla.	27	17-10	2,782	103.0
1995	Central Okla.	30	23-7	3,219	107.3
1996	Central Okla.	29	19-10	2,933	101.1
1997	Mont. St.-Billings	28	22-6	2,904	103.7
1998	Mont. St.-Billings	28	21-7	2,945	105.2
1999	Central Okla.	27	16-11	2,657	98.4
2000	Mont. St.-Billings	26	17.9	2,460	94.6
2001	Mont. St.-Billings	27	18-9	2,648	98.1
2002	Mont. St.-Billings	28	21-7	2,559	91.4

*record

DIVISION II

Scoring Defense

Season	Team	G	W-L	Pts.	Avg.
1948	Miss. Industrial	15	13-2	436	‡29.1
1949	Gordon	20	16-4	655	32.8
1950	Tex. A&M-Corp. Chris.	26	25-1	1,030	39.6
1951	St. Martin's	24	11-13	1,137	47.4
1952	Truman	19	12-7	876	46.1
1953	Sacramento St.	26	18-8	1,381	53.1
1954	Sacramento St.	18	9-9	883	49.1
1955	Amherst	22	16-6	1,233	56.0
1956	Amherst	22	16-6	1,277	58.0
1957	Stephen F. Austin	26	23-3	1,337	51.4
1958	McNeese St.	23	19-4	1,068	46.4
1959	Humboldt St.	23	14-9	1,166	50.7
1960	Wittenberg	24	22-2	1,122	46.8
1961	Wittenberg	29	25-4	1,270	43.8
1962	Wittenberg	26	21-5	1,089	41.9
1963	Wittenberg	28	26-2	1,285	45.9
1964	Wittenberg	23	18-5	1,186	51.6
1965	Cheyney	25	24-1	1,393	55.7
1966	Chicago	16	12-4	894	55.9
1967	Ashland	24	21-3	1,025	42.7
1968	Ashland	30	23-7	1,164	38.8
1969	Ashland	30	26-4	1,017	33.9
1970	Ashland	27	23-4	1,118	41.4
1971	Ashland	28	25-3	1,523	54.4
1972	Chicago	20	16-4	1,132	56.6
1973	Steubenville	29	22-7	1,271	43.8
1974	Steubenville	26	14-12	1,336	51.4
1975	Cal Poly	26	15-11	1,590	61.2
1976	Wis.-Green Bay	29	21-8	1,768	61.0
1977	Wis.-Green Bay	29	26-3	1,682	58.0
1978	Wis.-Green Bay	32	30-2	1,682	52.6
1979	Wis.-Green Bay	32	24-8	1,612	50.4
1980	Wis.-Green Bay	27	15-12	1,577	58.4
1981	San Fran. St.	26	17-9	1,463	56.3
1982	Cal Poly	29	23-6	1,537	53.0
1983	Cal Poly	28	18-10	1,553	55.5
1984	Cal Poly	28	20-8	1,458	52.1
1985	Cal Poly	27	16-11	1,430	53.0
1986	Lewis	30	24-6	1,702	56.7
1987	Denver	29	20-9	1,844	63.6
1988	N.C. Central	29	26-3	1,683	58.0
1989	N.C. Central	32	28-4	1,791	56.0
1990	Humboldt St.	31	20-11	1,831	59.1
1991	Minn.-Duluth	32	27-5	1,899	59.3
1992	Pace	30	23-7	1,517	50.6
1993	Philadelphia U.	32	30-2	1,898	59.3
1994	Pace	29	19-10	1,715	59.1
1995	Armstrong Atlantic	31	20-11	1,929	62.2
1996	Coker	26	16-10	1,592	61.2
1997	Fort Hays St.	31	29-2	1,837	59.3
1998	Presbyterian	28	16-12	1,704	60.9
1999	Incarnate Word	30	28-2	1,727	57.6
2000	Wingate	30	26-4	1,775	59.2
2001	Henderson St.	32	22-10	1,919	60.0
2002	Tusculum	28	15-13	1,600	57.1

‡ record since 1948

Scoring Margin

Season	Team	Off.	Def.	Mar.
1950	Montana	77.4	57.7	19.7
1951	Eastern Ill.	84.7	57.9	26.8
1952	Southwest Tex. St.	77.4	48.9	28.5
1953	Arkansas Tech	94.7	74.3	20.4
1954	Texas Southern	89.2	63.3	25.9
1955	Mt. St. Mary's	95.2	73.3	21.9
1956	Western Ill.	92.5	72.1	20.4
1957	West Va. Tech	102.6	77.2	25.4
1958	Tennessee St.	88.7	64.1	24.6
1959	Grambling	95.3	73.3	22.0
1960	Mississippi Col.	114.2	92.9	21.3
1961	Bryan	93.8	62.4	*31.4
1962	Mansfield	87.6	64.7	22.9
1963	Gorham St.	94.7	69.7	25.0
1964	Central Conn. St.	94.5	67.7	26.8
1965	Cheyney	80.7	55.7	25.0
1966	Cheyney	90.0	64.4	25.6
1967	Lincoln (Mo.)	108.3	82.2	26.1
1968	Western New Eng.	104.7	76.8	27.9
1969	Indiana (Pa.)	88.6	64.5	24.1

Season	Team	Off.	Def.	Mar.
1970	Husson	106.1	79.0	27.1
1971	Kentucky St.	103.5	78.2	25.3
1972	Brockport St.	93.8	70.3	23.5
1973	Wis.-Green Bay	71.2	52.1	19.1
1974	Alcorn St.	96.9	79.8	17.1
1975	Bentley	95.2	78.7	16.5
1976	UCF	94.8	78.4	16.4
1977	Texas Southern	88.4	71.9	16.5
1978	Wis.-Green Bay	68.8	52.6	16.2
1979	Roanoke	77.8	60.8	17.0
1980	UCF	91.7	72.1	19.6
1981	West Ga.	88.5	70.2	18.3
1982	Minn.-Duluth	81.7	64.8	16.9
1983	Minn.-Duluth	84.8	69.8	15.0
1984	Chicago St.	85.9	70.2	15.7
1985	Virginia Union	87.6	67.8	19.8
1986	Mt. St. Mary's	80.0	65.7	14.3
1987	Ky. Wesleyan	92.4	72.9	19.8
1988	Fla. Southern	89.6	70.5	19.1
1989	Virginia Union	88.2	69.6	18.6
1990	Ky. Wesleyan	97.3	76.8	20.5
1991	Ashland	99.8	78.2	21.6
1992	Oakland City	99.5	77.1	22.4
1993	Philadelphia U.	78.8	59.3	19.4
1994	Oakland City	87.8	65.5	22.3
1995	Jacksonville St.	101.2	77.6	23.6
1996	Fort Hays St.	92.1	70.2	21.9
1997	Fort Hays St.	84.1	59.3	24.8
1998	Oakland City	85.8	64.1	21.7
1999	Incarnate Word	78.5	57.6	21.0
2000	Metro St.	87.0	67.9	19.1
2001	Adelphi	85.3	65.7	19.7
2002	Ky. Wesleyan	91.3	72.7	18.6

*record

Field-Goal Percentage

Season	Team	FG	FGA	Pct.
1948	Tex. A&M-Commerce	445	1,119	39.8
1949	Southwest Mo. St.	482	1,106	43.6
1950	Tex. A&M-Corp. Chris.	555	1,290	43.0
1951	Beloit	773	1,734	44.6
1952	Southwest Mo. St.	890	1,903	46.8
1953	Lebanon Valley	637	1,349	47.2
1954	San Diego St.	675	1,502	44.9
1955	UC Santa Barb.	672	1,383	48.6
1956	UC Santa Barb.	552	1,142	48.3
1957	Alderson-Broaddus	1,006	2,094	48.0
1958	N.C. A&T	552	1,072	51.5
1959	Grambling	1,048	2,048	51.2
1960	William Carey	708	1,372	51.6
1961	Virginia Union	908	1,735	52.3
1962	West Va. Tech	871	1,575	55.3
1963	Lenoir-Rhyne	869	1,647	52.8
1964	LeMoyne-Owen	844	1,520	55.5
1965	Southern U.	1,036	1,915	54.1
1966	Howard Payne	932	1,710	54.5
1967	Alabama St.	874	1,555	56.2
1968	South Carolina St.	588	1,010	58.2
1969	Southampton	846	1,588	53.3
1970	Savannah St.	1,145	1,969	58.2
1971	Alabama St.	1,196	2,100	57.0
1972	Florida A&M	1,194	2,143	55.7
1973	Wis.-Green Bay	929	1,700	54.6
1974	Kentucky St.	1,252	2,266	55.3
1975	Kentucky St.	1,121	1,979	56.6
1976	Kentucky St.	1,093	1,753	*62.4
1977	Merrimack	1,120	2,008	55.8
1978	Wis.-Green Bay	840	1,509	55.7
1979	Morris Brown	980	1,763	55.6
1980	UNC Pembroke	849	1,544	55.0
1981	Bellarmine	851	1,561	54.5
1982	Fla. Southern	943	1,644	57.4
1983	Lewis	807	1,448	55.7
1984	Lewis	851	1,494	57.0
1985	Virginia Union	1,132	1,967	57.5
1986	Tampa	856	1,546	55.4
1987	Johnson Smith	995	1,817	54.8
1988	Fla. Southern	1,118	2,026	55.2
1989	Millersville	1,119	2,079	53.8
1990	S.C.-Spartanburg	954	1,745	54.7
1991	S.C.-Spartanburg	923	1,631	56.6
1992	S.C.-Spartanburg	898	1,664	54.0

Season	Team	FG	FGA	Pct.
1993	Cal St. Bakersfield	1,002	1,849	54.2
1994	Southern Ind.	1,171	2,142	54.7
1995	High Point	862	1,603	53.8
1996	Fort Hays St.	1,158	2,145	54.0
1997	Oakland City	961	1,821	52.8
1998	West Tex. A&M	953	1,841	51.8
1999	South Dakota	835	1,631	51.2
2000	Mo. Western St.	845	1,621	52.1
2001	Southern Ind.	1,014	1,937	52.3
2002	Neb.-Kearney	899	1,762	51.0

*record

Field-Goal Percentage Defense

Season	Team	FG	FGA	Pct.
1978	Wis.-Green Bay	681	1,830	37.2
1979	Wis.-Green Bay	639	1,709	37.4
1980	Wis.-Parkside	688	1,666	41.3
1981	Central St. (Ohio)	675	1,724	39.2
1982	Minn. St.-Mankato	699	1,735	40.3
1983	Central Mo. St.	746	1,838	40.6
1984	Norfolk St.	812	1,910	42.5
1985	Central Mo. St.	683	1,660	41.1
1986	Norfolk St.	782	1,925	40.6
1987	Denver	691	1,709	40.4
1988	Minn.-Duluth	702	1,691	41.5
1989	N.C. Central	633	1,642	38.6
1990	Central Mo. St.	696	1,757	39.6
1991	Southwest Baptist	758	1,942	39.0
1992	Virginia Union	766	2,069	37.0
1993	Pfeiffer	767	2,028	37.8
1994	Virginia Union	705	1,966	35.9
1995	Virginia Union	723	1,973	36.6
1996	Virginia Union	718	1,944	36.9
1997	St. Rose	887	2,409	36.8
1998	Delta St.	705	1,930	36.5
1999	Delta St.	610	1,652	36.9
2000	Fla. Southern	702	1,887	37.2
2001	Tampa	631	1,723	36.6
2002	Tarleton St.	657	1,837	*35.8

*record

Three-Point Field Goals Made Per Game

Season	Team	G	3FG	Avg.
1987	Northern Mich.	27	187	6.9
1988	Sacramento St.	30	303	10.1
1989	Central Okla.	27	280	10.4
1990	Stonehill	27	259	9.6
1991	Hillsdale	27	318	11.8
1992	Troy St.	29	*444	*15.3
1993	Hillsdale	28	366	13.1
1994	Hillsdale	25	315	12.6
1995	Hillsdale	29	330	11.4
1996	Mont. St.-Billings	28	304	10.9
1997	Mont. St.-Billings	28	394	14.1
1998	Mont. St.-Billings	28	375	13.4
1999	Mont. St.-Billings	28	355	12.7
2000	Mont. St.-Billings	26	294	11.3
2001	Mont. St.-Billings	27	284	10.5
2002	St. Anselm	30	301	10.0

*record

Three-Point Field-Goal Percentage

Season	Team	G	3FG	3FGA	Pct.
1987	St. Anselm	30	97	189	51.3
1988	Winston-Salem	28	98	182	*53.8
1989	Mississippi Col.	27	144	276	52.2
1990	Shaw	27	74	143	51.7
1991	Rollins	28	278	585	47.5
1992	Oakland City	30	244	486	50.2
1993	Oakland City	32	215	465	46.2
1994	Oakland City	28	225	495	45.5
1995	Oakland City	30	256	561	45.6
1996	Oakland City	31	260	537	48.4
1997	Oakland City	30	311	651	47.8
1998	Michigan Tech	31	267	613	43.6
1999	South Dakota	29	258	577	44.7
2000	Eckerd	28	156	366	42.6
2001	Mesa St.	27	152	346	43.9
2002	Michigan Tech	30	216	499	43.3

*record

Free-Throw Percentage

Season	Team	FT	FTA	Pct.
1948	Charleston (W.Va.)	446	659	67.7
1949	Linfield	276	402	68.7
1950	Jacksonville St.	452	613	73.7
1951	Millikin	603	846	71.3
1952	Eastern Ill.	521	688	75.7
1953	Upsala	513	69	74.0
1954	Central Mich.	376	509	73.9
1955	Mississippi Col.	559	733	76.3
1956	Wheaton (Ill.)	625	842	74.2
1957	Wheaton (Ill.)	689	936	73.6
1958	Wheaton (Ill.)	517	689	75.0
1959	Wabash	418	545	76.7
1960	Allen	225	297	75.8
1961	Southwest Mo. St.	453	605	74.9
1962	Lenoir-Rhyne	477	599	79.6
1963	Hampden-Sydney	442	559	79.1
1964	Western Caro.	492	621	79.2
1965	Mississippi Col.	529	663	79.8
1966	Athens St.	631	802	78.7
1967	Northwestern St.	528	678	77.9
1968	Kenyon	684	858	79.7
1969	Kenyon	583	727	80.2
1970	Wooster	571	714	80.0
1971	South Ala.	422	518	81.5
1972	Clark Atlanta	409	520	78.7
1973	Rockford (Ill.)	367	481	76.3
1974	New Orleans	537	701	76.6
1975	Alabama St.	456	565	80.7
1976	Alabama St.	451	576	78.3
1977	Puget Sound	495	637	77.7
1978	Merrimack	508	636	79.9
1979	Bentley	506	652	77.6
1980	Philadelphia U.	436	549	79.4
1981	Coppin St.	401	514	78.0
1982	Fla. Southern	726	936	77.6
1983	Transylvania	463	606	76.4
1984	Transylvania	491	639	76.8
1985	Minn. St.-Mankato	349	445	78.4
1986	New Hamp. Col.	507	672	75.4
1987	Columbus St.	339	433	78.3
1988	Rollins	631	795	79.4
1989	Rollins	477	607	78.6
1990	Rollins	449	582	77.1
1991	Lenoir-Rhyne	441	564	78.2
1992	Adams St.	397	512	77.5
1993	Philadelphia U.	491	630	77.9
1994	West Liberty St.	473	602	78.6
1995	Western St.	469	603	77.8
1996	South Dakota	501	648	77.3
1997	Hawaii-Hilo	471	606	77.7
1998	Gannon	473	573	*82.5
1999	Minn.-Duluth	430	547	78.6
2000	Bemidji St.	386	492	78.5
2001	Morningside	383	485	79.0
2002	St. Cloud St.	461	587	78.5

*record

Rebound Margin

Season	Team	Off.	Def.	Mar.
1976	Mississippi Val.	63.9	39.5	*24.4
1977	Philadelphia U.	38.7	24.1	14.6
1978	Mass.-Lowell	49.0	37.5	11.5
1979	Dowling	48.2	32.6	15.6
1980	Ark.-Pine Bluff	40.3	25.9	14.4
1981	Wis.-Green Bay	40.6	26.5	14.1
1982	Central St. (Ohio)	48.0	37.2	10.8
1983	Hampton	50.2	38.5	11.8
1984	Calif. (Pa.)	46.4	33.1	13.3
1985	Virginia Union	44.1	32.0	12.1
1986	Tampa	39.9	28.0	11.8
1987	Millersville	44.7	33.8	10.9
1988	Clark Atlanta	44.7	32.5	12.1

Season	Team	Off.	Def.	Mar.
1989	Hampton	46.7	36.3	10.3
1990	Fla. Atlantic	41.0	29.4	11.6
1991	Calif. (Pa.)	44.6	32.0	12.6
1992	Oakland City	43.4	31.8	11.6
1993	Metro St.	45.5	32.0	13.5
1994	Oakland City	44.0	33.7	10.3
1995	Jacksonville St.	47.7	35.2	12.5
1996	Virginia Union	48.0	36.1	11.9

Season	Team	Off.	Def.	Mar.
1997	Southern Conn. St.	41.6	32.3	9.3
1998	South Dakota St.	46.5	35.9	10.6
1999	Ky. Wesleyan	44.8	32.6	12.2
2000	Salem Int'l	44.2	32.1	12.1
2001	Salem Int'l	42.6	31.3	11.4
2002	Tarleton St.	43.0	32.0	11.1

*record

2002 Most-Improved Teams

School (Coach)	2002	2001	Games Improved
1. Lincoln (Mo.) (Bill Pope)	20-7	2-24	17½
2. Longwood (Michael Leeder)	23-8	4-22	16½
3. Humboldt St. (Tom Wood)	20-8	6-20	13
4. Bowie St. (Luke D'Alessio)	19-9	7-21	12
5. Concordia (N.Y.) (John Dwindell)	11-16	0-26	10½
5. Mercy (Steve Kelly)	10-15	0-26	10½
7. Catawba (Jim Baker)	25-4	14-14	10
7. Johnson Smith (Steve Joyner)	27-5	16-13	9½
9. Ark.-Monticello (Charlie Schaef)	20-8	10-16	9

School (Coach)	2002	2001	Games Improved
9. Central Ark. (Charles Hervey)	13-13	4-22	9
11. Barry (Cesar Odio)	18-11	9-19	8½
11. Westminster (Pa.) (Jim Dafler)	19-6	11-15	8½
13. Queens (N.C.) (Bart Lundy)	26-6	16-12	8
13. Shaw (Joel Hopkins)	15-10	8-19	8
13. Western Wash. (Brad Jackson)	27-4	17-10	8

To determine games improved, add the difference in victories between the two seasons to the difference in losses, then divide by two.

All-Time Winningest Teams

Includes records as a senior college only; minimum 10 seasons of competition. Postseason games are included.

Percentage

Team	Yrs.	Won	Lost	Pct.
1. Cal St. Bakersfield	31	636	259	.711
2. Philadelphia U.	78	1,099	474	.699
3. Cheyney	39	746	336	.689
4. Virginia Union	77	1,233	585	.678
5. LeMoyne-Owen	43	800	384	.676
6. Southern N.H.	39	743	358	.675
7. Queens (N.C.)	13	252	124	.670
8. Fla. Southern	46	869	431	.668
9. Ky. Wesleyan	91	*1,347	673	.667
10. Metro St.	18	349	178	.662
11. Fort Hays St.	84	1,202	635	.654
12. St. Rose	28	530	288	.648
13. Incarnate Word	19	357	194	.648
14. Gannon	58	961	536	.642
15. Northern St.	83	1,209	684	.639
16. Carson-Newman	44	850	483	.638
17. Southern Ind.	33	583	333	.636
18. Fairmont St.	79	1,273	732	.635
19. Grand Canyon	54	898	521	.633
20. Bentley	39	649	386	.627
21. Bloomsburg	99	1,153	690	.626
22. Alas. Anchorage	25	454	274	.624
23. Central Ark.	80	1,279	775	.623
24. North Dakota	97	1,328	808	.622
25. West Tex. A&M	81	1,234	763	.618
26. Central Mo. St.	97	1,335	832	.616
27. Drury	93	1,265	790	.616
28. Indiana (Pa.)	72	975	612	.614
29. C.W. Post	46	717	452	.613
30. Millersville	72	990	628	.612

*Includes one tie.

Victories

Team	Yrs.	Won	Lost	Pct.
1. Ky. Wesleyan	91	*1,347	673	.667
2. Central Mo. St.	97	1,335	832	.616
3. North Dakota	97	1,328	808	.622
4. Washburn	96	1,317	950	.581
5. North Dakota St.	104	1,300	929	.583
6. Central Ark.	80	1,279	775	.623

Team	Yrs.	Won	Lost	Pct.
7. Fairmont St.	79	1,273	732	.635
8. Drury	93	1,265	790	.616
9. West Tex. A&M	81	1,234	763	.618
10. Virginia Union	77	1,233	585	.678
11. Northern St.	83	1,209	684	.639
12. Fort Hays St.	84	1,202	635	.654
13. South Dakota St.	94	1,191	803	.597
14. Pittsburg St.	91	1,181	961	.551
15. Emporia St.	96	1,158	958	.547
16. Bloomsburg	99	1,153	690	.626
17. Cal St. Chico	89	1,124	983	.533
18. Neb.-Kearney	94	1,114	793	.584
19. East Central	75	1,099	726	.602
19. Lenoir-Rhyne	81	1,099	878	.556
19. Philadelphia U.	78	1,099	474	.699
22. Indianapolis	77	1,091	754	.591
23. Northwest Mo. St.	86	1,085	818	.570
24. Tex. A&M-Commerce	87	1,075	877	.551
25. Northern Mich.	96	1,069	732	.594
26. Catawba	76	1,060	892	.543
27. St. Cloud St.	79	1,045	681	.605
27. Wayne St. (Neb.)	87	1,045	884	.542
29. Arkansas Tech	79	1,039	815	.560
30. Henderson St.	87	1,038	806	.563

All-Time Won-Lost Records

(No Minimum Seasons of Competition)

Team	First Year	Yrs.	Won	Lost	Pct.
Abilene Christian	1920	79	970	874	.526
Adelphi	1946	55	825	638	.564
Ala.-Huntsville	1974	29	392	434	.475
Alas. Anchorage	1978	25	454	274	.624
Alas. Fairbanks	1953	46	466	578	.446
Alderson-Broaddus	1936	64	949	836	.532
American Int'l	1934	68	806	799	.502
Anderson (S.C.)	1999	4	47	39	.547
Angelo St.	1966	37	512	495	.508
Arkansas Tech	1914	79	1039	815	.560
Armstrong Atlantic	1967	36	541	464	.538
Ashland	1922	81	957	823	.538
Assumption	1924	73	934	730	.561
Augusta St.	1966	37	549	476	.536
Augustana (S.D.)	1928	72	782	878	.471
Barry	1985	18	227	265	.461
Bellarmine	1952	52	449	391	.535
Bemidji St.	1922	76	761	855	.471

Team	First Year	Yrs.	Won	Lost	Pct.
Bentley	1964	39	649	386	.627
Bloomsburg	1902	99	1153	690	.626
Bryant	1963	40	507	547	.481
UC Davis	1910	90	863	1014	.460
UC San Diego	1966	27	480	464	.508
Cal Poly Pomona	1948	55	737	737	.500
Cal St. Bakersfield	1972	31	636	259	.711
Cal St. Chico	1914	89	1124	983	.533
Cal St. Dom. Hills	1978	25	340	328	.509
Cal St. Los Angles	1949	54	687	711	.491
Cal St. San B'dino	1985	18	277	201	.579
Cal St. Stanislaus	1967	36	393	479	.451
Carson-Newman	1959	44	850	483	.638
Catawba	1927	76	1060	892	.543
Central Ark.	1921	80	1279	775	.623
Central Mo. St.	1906	97	1335	832	.616
Central Okla.	1921	75	1004	821	.550
Chadron St.	1922	77	922	873	.514
Chaminade	1977	26	408	328	.554
Cheyney	1964	39	746	336	.689
Clayton St.	1990	13	159	180	.469
Colorado Mines	1910	93	603	1100	.354
Columbus St.	1967	35	542	397	.577
C.W. Post	1956	46	717	452	.613
Delta St.	1928	72	1012	669	.602
Drury	1909	93	1265	790	.616
East Central	1928	75	1099	726	.602
East Stroudsburg	1927	75	795	845	.485
Eckerd	1964	39	531	435	.550
Edinboro	1929	72	887	640	.581
Emporia St.	1902	96	1158	958	.547
Erskine	1914	77	927	833	.527
Fairmont St.	1917	79	1273	732	.635
Ferris St.	1926	73	849	790	.518
Fla. Southern	1957	46	869	431	.668
Florida Tech	1965	38	405	577	.412
Fort Hays St.	1917	84	1202	635	.654
Fort Lewis	1963	40	464	567	.450
Francis Marion	1970	32	421	468	.474
Franklin Pierce	1964	39	622	395	.612
Gannon	1945	58	961	536	.642
GC&SU	1970	33	452	436	.509
Grand Canyon	1949	54	898	521	.633
Grand Valley St.	1967	36	581	406	.589
Hawaii-Hilo	1977	26	453	329	.579
Henderson St.	1911	87	1038	806	.563
Humboldt St.	1924	79	607	816	.427
Incarnate Word	1984	19	357	194	.648
Indiana (Pa.)	1927	72	975	612	.614
Indianapolis	1923	77	1091	754	.591
Johnson Smith	1929	62	896	639	.584
Kennesaw St.	1986	17	260	226	.535
Ky. Wesleyan	1908	91	1347	673	.667
Lake Superior St.	1947	55	767	592	.564
Lander	1969	34	577	437	.569
Le Moyne	1949	54	752	574	.567
LeMoyne-Owen	1960	43	800	384	.676
Lenoir-Rhyne	1920	81	1099	878	.556
Lewis	1949	53	845	564	.600
Lincoln Memorial	1981	22	380	265	.589
Longwood	1977	26	379	320	.542
Lynn	1994	9	185	73	.717
Mansfield	1918	75	797	678	.540
Mass.-Lowell	1976	27	370	380	.493
Mercyhurst	1972	31	422	419	.502
Merrimack	1950	53	666	655	.504
Metro St.	1985	18	349	178	.662
Michigan Tech	1920	80	672	853	.441
Midwestern St.	1947	56	1032	677	.604
Millersville	1929	72	990	628	.612
Minn.-Duluth	1930	71	1015	663	.605
Minn. St.-Mankato	1921	77	951	723	.568
Mo.-Rolla	1910	90	691	1003	.408
Mo.-St. Louis	1967	36	459	480	.489
Mo. Southern St.	1969	34	532	452	.541
Mo. Western St.	1970	33	589	384	.605
Mont. St.-Billings	1927	73	870	728	.544
Morehouse	1911	91	970	892	.521
Morningside	1902	101	870	967	.474
Neb.-Kearney	1906	94	1114	793	.584
Neb.-Omaha	1911	87	888	949	.483
New Haven	1962	39	569	471	.547
N.J. Inst. Of Tech	1954	49	640	483	.570
N.M. Highlands	1924	76	786	889	.469
New York Tech	1959	41	554	438	.558
Newberry	1913	87	874	1097	.443
North Ala.	1949	54	865	701	.552
N.C. Central	1928	68	945	717	.569
UNC-Pembroke	1940	63	814	730	.527
North Dakota	1905	97	1328	808	.622
North Dakota St.	1898	104	1300	929	.583
North Fla.	1993	10	109	161	.404
Northern Colo.	1902	101	937	971	.491
Northern Ky.	1972	31	510	362	.585
Northern Mich.	1906	96	1069	732	.594
Northern St.	1920	83	1209	684	.639
Northwest Mo. St.	1917	86	1085	818	.570
Oakland City	1923	61	741	666	.527
Pace	1948	54	676	663	.505
Philadelphia U.	1920	78	1099	474	.699
Pittsburg St.	1912	91	1181	961	.551
Pitt.-Johnstown	1970	33	386	447	.463
Presbyterian	1914	89	1003	973	.508
Queens (N.C.)	1990	13	252	124	.670
Quincy	1940	63	922	696	.570
Regis (Colo.)	1945	55	779	665	.539
Saginaw Valley	1970	33	480	435	.525
St. Anselm	1935	68	859	648	.570
St. Cloud St.	1923	79	1045	681	.605
St. Joseph's (Ind.)	1906	90	906	852	.515
St. Leo	1966	37	387	560	.409
St. Michael's	1921	82	946	836	.531
St. Rose	1974	28	530	288	.648
Seattle Pacific	1943	58	867	649	.572
Shepherd	1950	53	693	661	.512
Slippery Rock	1926	72	796	781	.505
Sonoma St.	1964	33	349	481	.420
S.C.-Aiken	1991	12	165	169	.494
S.C.-Spartanburg	1975	28	474	328	.591
South Dakota	1908	92	1006	891	.530
South Dakota St.	1906	94	1191	803	.597
Southern Colo.	1964	39	656	418	.61
Southern Conn. St.	1968	35	472	427	.525
SIU-Edwardsville	1968	35	441	448	.496
Southern Ind.	1970	33	583	333	.636
Southern N.H.	1964	39	743	358	.675
Southwest Baptist	1966	37	532	462	.535
Southwest St.	1967	36	379	565	.401
Stonehill	1949	53	750	595	.558
Tampa	1950	40	624	464	.574
Tex. A&M-Commerce	1916	87	1075	877	.551
Tex. A&M-Kingsville	1926	73	766	932	.451
Truman	1920	83	989	857	.536
Valdosta St.	1955	52	661	501	.569
Virginia Union	1926	77	1233	585	.678
Washburn	1905	96	1317	950	.581
Wayne St. (Mich.)	1942	61	802	927	.464
Wayne St. (Neb.)	1912	87	1045	884	.542
West Ala.	1957	45	524	613	.461
West Chester	1928	75	867	797	.521
West Fla.	1968	18	269	210	.562
West Ga.	1957	45	672	494	.576
West Tex. A&M	1921	81	1234	763	.618
Wheeling Jesuit	1958	46	559	613	.477
Winona St.	1916	87	813	969	.456

Division III Records

Individual Records

Division III men's basketball records are based on the performances of Division III teams since the three-division re-organization plan was adopted by the special NCAA Convention in August 1973. Assists were added for the 1988-89 season; blocked shots and steals were added for the 1992-93 season. In statistical rankings, the rounding of percentages and/or averages may indicate ties where none exist. In these cases, the numerical order of the rankings is accurate.

Scoring

POINTS
Game
77—Jeff Clement, Grinnell vs. Illinois Col., Feb. 18, 1998
Season
1,044—Greg Grant, Col. of New Jersey, 1989 (32 games)
Career
2,940—Andre Foreman, Salisbury, 1988-89, 91-92 (109 games)

AVERAGE PER GAME
Season
37.3—Steve Diekmann, Grinnell, 1995 (745 in 20)
Career
(Min. 1,400) 32.8—Dwain Govan, Bishop, 1974-75 (1,805 in 55)

POINTS SCORED WITH NO TIME ELAPSING
Game
24—Rob Rittgers, UC San Diego vs. Menlo, Jan. 16, 1988 (made 24 consecutive free throws due to 12 bench technical fouls)

CONSECUTIVE POINTS SCORED
Game
25—Andy Panko, Lebanon Valley vs. Frank. & Marsh., Jan. 19, 1998

GAMES SCORING AT LEAST 50 POINTS
Season
3—Jeff Clement, Grinnell, 1998
Career
4—Jeff Clement, Grinnell, 1996-99; Steve Diekmann, Grinnell, 1993-95

GAMES SCORING IN DOUBLE FIGURES
Career
116—Lamont Strothers, Chris. Newport, 1988-91

CONSECUTIVE GAMES SCORING IN DOUBLE FIGURES
Career
116—Lamont Strothers, Chris. Newport, from Nov. 20, 1987, to March 8, 1991

Field Goals

FIELD GOALS
Game
29—Shannon Lilly, Bishop vs. Southwest Assembly of God, Jan. 31, 1983 (36 attempts)
Season
394—Dave Russell, Shepherd, 1975 (687 attempts)
Career
1,140—Andre Foreman, Salisbury, 1988-89, 91-92 (2,125 attempts)

CONSECUTIVE FIELD GOALS
Game
18—Jason Light, Emory & Henry vs. King (Tenn.), Dec. 2, 1995
Season
24—Todd Richards, Mount Union, 2000 (during five games)

FIELD-GOAL ATTEMPTS
Game
68—Jeff Clement, Grinnell vs. Illinois Col., Feb. 18, 1998 (26 made)
Season
742—Greg Grant, Col. of New Jersey, 1989 (387 made)
Career
2,149—Lamont Strothers, Chris. Newport, 1988-91 (1,016 made)

FIELD-GOAL PERCENTAGE
Game
(Min. 18 made) 100%—Jason Light, Emory & Henry vs. King (Tenn.), Dec. 2, 1995 (18 of 18)
*Season
76.6—Travis Weiss, St. John's (Minn.), 1994 (160 of 209)
*Based on qualifiers for annual championship.
Career
(Min. 400 made) 73.6—Tony Rychlec, Mass. Maritime, 1981-83 (509 of 692)

Three-Point Field Goals

THREE-POINT FIELD GOALS
Game
19—Jeff Clement, Grinnell vs. Illinois Col., Feb. 18, 1998
Season
186—Jeff Clement, Grinnell, 1998 (511 attempts)
Career
516—Jeff Clement, Grinnell, 1996-99 (1,532 attempts)

THREE-POINT FIELD GOALS MADE PER GAME
Season
8.5—Jeff Clement, Grinnell, 1998 (186 in 22)
Career
5.7—Jeff Clement, Grinnell, 1996-99 (516 in 91)

CONSECUTIVE THREE-POINT FIELD GOALS
Game
10—Brad Block, Aurora vs. Rockford, Feb. 20, 1988; Jim Berrigan, Framingham St. vs. Western New Eng., Feb. 27, 1988
Season
16—John Richards, Sewanee (during five games, Feb. 10 to Feb. 25, 1990)

CONSECUTIVE GAMES MAKING A THREE-POINT FIELD GOAL
Season
31—Troy Greenlee, DePauw, Nov. 17, 1989, to March 17, 1990
Career
75—Chris Carideo, Widener, 1992-95

THREE-POINT FIELD-GOAL ATTEMPTS
Game
52—Jeff Clement, Grinnell vs. Illinois Col., Feb. 18, 1998 (19 made)
Season
511—Jeff Clement, Grinnell, 1998 (186 made)
Career
1,532—Jeff Clement, Grinnell, 1996-99 (516 made)

THREE-POINT FIELD-GOAL ATTEMPTS PER GAME
Season
23.2—Jeff Clement, Grinnell, 1998 (511 in 22)
Career
16.8—Jeff Clement, Grinnell, 1996-99 (1,532 in 91)

THREE-POINT FIELD-GOAL PERCENTAGE
Game
(Min. 11 made) 100%—Joe Goldin, Randolph-Macon vs. Emory & Henry, Feb. 16, 1997 (11 of 11)
Season
(Min. 40 made) 67.0%—Reggie James, N.J. Inst. of Tech., 1989 (59 of 88)
(Min. 90 made) 56.9%—Eric Harris, Bishop, 1987 (91 of 160)
Career
(Min. 200 made) 51.3%—Jeff Seifriz, Wis.-Whitewater, 1987-89 (217 of 432)

Free Throws

FREE THROWS
Game
30—Rob Rittgers, UC San Diego vs. Menlo, Jan. 16, 1988 (30 attempts)
Season
249—Dave Russell, Shepherd, 1975 (293 attempts)
Career
792—Matt Hancock, Colby, 1987-90 (928 attempts)

CONSECUTIVE FREE THROWS
Game
30—Rob Rittgers, UC San Diego vs. Menlo, Jan. 16, 1988
Season
59—Mike Michelson, Coast Guard (during 13 games, Jan. 16 to Feb. 27, 1990)
Career
70—Korey Coon, Ill. Wesleyan (12 games, Feb. 13, 1998 to Dec. 4, 1999)

FREE-THROW ATTEMPTS
Game
30—Rob Rittgers, UC San Diego vs. Menlo, Jan. 16, 1988 (30 made)
Season
326—Moses Jean-Pierre, Plymouth St., 1994 (243 made)
Career
928—Matt Hancock, Colby, 1987-90 (792 made)

FREE-THROW PERCENTAGE
Game
(Min. 30 made) 100%—Rob Rittgers, UC San Diego vs. Menlo, Jan. 16, 1988 (30 of 30)
*Season
96.3%—Korey Coon, Ill. Wesleyan, 2000 (157 of 163)
*based on qualifiers for annual championship
Career
(Min. 250 made) 92.5%—Andy Enfield, Johns Hopkins, 1988-91 (431 of 466)
(Min. 500 made) 86.2%—Brad Clark, Wis.-Oshkosh, 1997-00 (535 of 621)

Rebounds

REBOUNDS
Game
36—Mark Veenstra, Calvin vs. Southern Colo., Feb. 3, 1976; Clinton Montford, Methodist vs. Warren Wilson, Jan. 21, 1989
Season
579—Joe Manley, Bowie St., 1976 (29 games)
Career
1,628—Michael Smith, Hamilton, 1989-92 (107 games)

AVERAGE PER GAME
Season
20.0—Joe Manley, Bowie St., 1976 (579 in 29)
Career
(Min. 900) 17.4—Larry Parker, Plattsburgh St., 1975-78 (1,482 in 85)

Assists

ASSISTS
Game
26—Robert James, Kean vs. N.J. Inst. of Tech., March 11, 1989
Season
391—Robert James, Kean, 1989 (29 games)
Career
909—Steve Artis, Chris. Newport, 1990-93 (112 games)

AVERAGE PER GAME
Season
13.5—Robert James, Kean, 1989 (391 in 29)

Career
(Min. 550) 8.6—Phil Dixon, Shenandoah, 1993-96 (889 in 103)

Blocked Shots

BLOCKED SHOTS
Game
16—Tory Black, N.J. Inst. of Tech. vs. Polytechnic (N.Y.), Feb. 5, 1997
Season
198—Tory Black, N.J. Inst. of Tech., 1997 (26 games)
Career
576—Ira Nicholson, Mt. St. Vincent, 1994-97 (100 games)

AVERAGE PER GAME
Season
7.6—Tory Black, N.J. Inst. of Tech., 1997 (198 in 26)

Career
6.1—Neil Edwards, York (N.Y.), 1998-00 (337 in 55)

Steals

STEALS
Game
17—Matt Newton, Principia vs. Harris-Stowe, Jan. 4, 1994
Season
189—Moses Jean-Pierre, Plymouth St., 1994 (30 games)
Career
413—John Gallogly, Salve Regina, 1995-98 (98 games)

AVERAGE PER GAME
Season
6.3—Moses Jean-Pierre, Plymouth St., 1994 (189 in 30)

Career
5.5—Moses Jean-Pierre, Plymouth St., 1993-94 (303 in 55 games)

Games

GAMES PLAYED
Season
34—Thane Anderson, Matt Benedict, Tim Blair, Lanse Carter, Mike Johnson, Todd Oehrlein, Mike Prasher and Derrick Shelton, Wis.-Eau Claire, 1990
Career
119—Steve Honderd, Calvin, 1990-93; Chris Finch, Frank. & Marsh., 1989-92; Chris Fite, Rochester, 1989-92; Jim Clausen, North Park, 1978-81

Team Records

Note: Where records involve both teams, each team must be an NCAA Division III member institution.

SINGLE-GAME RECORDS

Scoring

POINTS
168—Bishop vs. Southwest Assembly of God (76), Jan. 31, 1983
POINTS BY LOSING TEAM
149—Grinnell vs. Illinois Col. (157), Feb. 18, 1994
POINTS, BOTH TEAMS
315—Simpson (167) vs. Grinnell (148), Nov. 19, 1994
POINTS IN A HALF
92—Wis.-Platteville vs. Mt. St. Clare, Dec. 14, 1989 (first)
POINTS SCORED WITH NO TIME ELAPSING OFF OF THE CLOCK
24—UC San Diego vs. Menlo, Jan. 16, 1988 (made 24 consecutive free throws due to 12 bench technical fouls)
FEWEST POINTS ALLOWED
6—Dickinson (15) vs. Muhlenberg, Feb. 3, 1982
FEWEST POINTS ALLOWED IN A HALF
0—Dickinson (2) vs. Muhlenberg (first), Feb. 3, 1982
FEWEST POINTS, BOTH TEAMS
21—Dickinson (15) vs. Muhlenberg (6), Feb. 3, 1982
FEWEST POINTS, HALF, BOTH TEAMS
2—Dickinson (2) vs. Muhlenberg (0) (first), Feb. 3, 1982
MARGIN OF VICTORY
112—Eureka (149) vs. Barat (37), Nov. 29, 1989

Field Goals

FIELD GOALS
78—Bishop vs. Southwest Assembly of God, Jan. 31, 1983 (103 attempts)
FIELD-GOAL ATTEMPTS
135—Grinnell vs. Simpson, Nov. 25, 1995 (52 made)
FEWEST FIELD GOALS
3—Muhlenberg vs. Dickinson, Feb. 3, 1982 (11 attempts)
FEWEST FIELD-GOAL ATTEMPTS
11—Muhlenberg vs. Dickinson, Feb. 3, 1982 (3 made)

FIELD-GOAL PERCENTAGE
89.8%—St. Norbert vs. Grinnell, Jan. 28, 2000
FIELD-GOAL PERCENTAGE, HALF
95.7—Beloit vs. Grinnell, Jan. 27, 2001 (22 of 23)

Three-Point Field Goals

THREE-POINT FIELD GOALS
32—Grinnell vs. Clarke, Dec. 3, 1997 (78 attempts)
THREE-POINT FIELD GOALS, BOTH TEAMS
35—Grinnell (30) vs. Colorado Col. (5), Nov. 17, 1995; Manhattanville (25) vs. St. Joseph's (N.Y.) (10), Dec. 10, 1994; Beloit (21) vs. Carthage (14), Nov. 23, 1993
CONSECUTIVE THREE-POINT FIELD GOALS MADE WITHOUT A MISS
11—Willamette vs. Western Baptist, Jan. 8, 1987
NUMBER OF DIFFERENT PLAYERS TO SCORE A THREE-POINT FIELD GOAL, ONE TEAM
13—Grinnell vs. Monmouth (Ill.), Feb. 14, 1998
THREE-POINT FIELD-GOAL ATTEMPTS
86—Grinnell vs. Pillsbury, Dec. 7, 1999 (31 made)
THREE-POINT FIELD-GOAL ATTEMPTS, BOTH TEAMS
97—Grinnell (79) vs. Colorado Col. (18), Nov. 17, 1995
THREE-POINT FIELD-GOAL PERCENTAGE
(Min. 10 made) 100%—Willamette vs. Western Baptist, Jan. 8, 1987 (11 of 11); Kean vs. Ramapo, Feb. 11, 1987 (10 of 10)
(Min. 15 made) 83.3%—Rockford vs. Trinity (Ill.), Jan. 21, 1989 (15 of 18)
THREE-POINT FIELD-GOAL PERCENTAGE, BOTH TEAMS
(Min. 10 made) 92.9%—Luther (8 of 8) vs. Wartburg (5 of 6), Feb. 14, 1987 (13 of 14)
(Min. 15 made) 75.0%—Anna Maria (4 of 6) vs. Nichols (11 of 14), Feb. 10, 1987 (15 of 20)
(Min. 20 made) 62.2%—Beloit (13 of 23) vs. Rockford (10 of 14), Jan. 18, 1988 (23 of 37)

Free Throws

FREE THROWS
53—UC San Diego vs. Menlo, Jan. 16, 1988 (59 attempts)
FREE THROWS, BOTH TEAMS
93—Grinnell (50) vs. Beloit (43), Jan. 10, 1998

FREE-THROW ATTEMPTS
71—Earlham vs. Oberlin, Dec. 5, 1992 (46 made)
FREE-THROW ATTEMPTS, BOTH TEAMS
105—Earlham (71) vs. Oberlin (34), Dec. 5, 1992
FEWEST FREE THROWS
0—Many teams
FEWEST FREE-THROW ATTEMPTS
0—Many teams
FREE-THROW PERCENTAGE
(Min. 28 made) 100.0%—Albany (N.Y.) vs. Potsdam St., Feb. 19, 1994 (28 of 28)
(Min. 30 made) 97.1%—Rochester Inst. vs. Rensselaer, Feb. 16, 1980 (34 of 35)
(Min. 45 made) 92.6%—Grinnell vs. Beloit, Jan. 10, 1998 (50 of 54)
FREE-THROW PERCENTAGE, BOTH TEAMS
(Min. 20 made) 95.5%—Baldwin-Wallace (13 of 13) vs. Muskingum (8 of 9), Dec. 29, 1977 (21 of 22)
(Min. 30 made) 94.9%—Muskingum (30 of 31) vs. Ohio Wesleyan (7 of 8), Jan. 10, 1981 (37 of 39)

Rebounds

REBOUNDS
98—Alma vs. Marion, Dec. 28, 1973
REBOUNDS, BOTH TEAMS
124—Ill. Wesleyan (62) vs. North Central (62), Feb. 8, 1977; Rochester Inst. (72) vs. Thiel (52), Nov. 18, 1988
REBOUND MARGIN
56—MIT (74) vs. Emerson-MCA (18), Feb. 21, 1990

Assists

ASSISTS
53—Simpson vs. Grinnell, Nov. 25, 1995
ASSISTS, BOTH TEAMS
79—Simpson (53) vs. Grinnell (26), Nov. 25, 1995

Personal Fouls

PERSONAL FOULS
47—Concordia (Ill.) vs. Trinity Christian, Feb. 26, 1988

DIVISION III

PERSONAL FOULS, BOTH TEAMS
80—Grinnell (46) vs. St. Norbert (34), Jan. 28, 2000

PLAYERS DISQUALIFIED
6—Thomas More vs. Franklin, Feb.2, 2002; Union (N.Y.) vs. Rochester, Feb. 15, 1985; Haverford vs. Drew, Jan. 10, 1990; Manhattanville vs. Drew, Jan. 11, 1992; Roger Williams vs Curry, Jan. 14, 1995

PLAYERS DISQUALIFIED, BOTH TEAMS
11—Union (N.Y.) (6) vs. Rochester (5), Feb. 15, 1985

Overtimes

OVERTIME PERIODS
5—1,373-(115) vs. Wheaton (Mass.)(107), Feb. 18, 1999; Capital (86) vs. Muskingum (89), Jan. 5, 1980; Carnegie Mellon (81) vs. Allegheny (76), Feb. 12, 1983; Rochester (99) vs. Union (N.Y.) (98), Feb. 15, 1985

POINTS IN ONE OVERTIME PERIOD
31—Marymount (Va.) vs. Catholic, Jan. 30, 1999

POINTS IN ONE OVERTIME PERIOD, BOTH TEAMS
51—Wash. & Lee (28) vs. Mary Washington (23), Jan. 9, 1995

POINTS IN OVERTIME PERIODS
50—Babson (50) vs. Wheaton (Mass.) (5 ot), Feb. 18, 1999

POINTS IN OVERTIME PERIODS, BOTH TEAMS
92—Babson (50) vs. Wheaton (Mass.) (42) (5 ot), Feb. 18, 1999

SEASON RECORDS

Scoring

POINTS
3,073—Franklin Pierce, 1980 (31 games)

AVERAGE PER GAME
124.9—Grinnell, 2002 (2,997 in 24)

AVERAGE SCORING MARGIN
31.1—Husson, 1976 (98.7 offense, 67.6 defense)

GAMES AT LEAST 100 POINTS
23—Grinnell, 2002 (24-game season)

CONSECUTIVE GAMES AT LEAST 100 POINTS
15—Grinnell, from Nov. 18, 2000, to Jan. 27, 2001

CONSECUTIVE GAMES AT LEAST 100 POINTS (Multiple Seasons)
15—Grinnell, from Nov. 18, 2000, to Jan. 27, 2001; Grinnell, from Feb. 11, 1994, to Jan. 13, 1995

Field Goals

FIELD GOALS
1,323—Shepherd, 1975 (2,644 attempts)

FIELD GOALS PER GAME
42.5—Mercy, 1977 (1,062 in 25)

FIELD-GOAL ATTEMPTS
2,644—Shepherd, 1975 (1,323 made)

FIELD-GOAL ATTEMPTS PER GAME
98.4—Grinnell, 2002 (2,361 in 24)

FIELD-GOAL PERCENTAGE
60.0—Stony Brook, 1978 (1,033 of 1,721)

Three-Point Field Goals

THREE-POINT FIELD GOALS
490—Grinnell, 2002 (1,410 attempts)

THREE-POINT FIELD GOALS PER GAME
20.4—Grinnell, 2002 (490 in 24)

THREE-POINT FIELD-GOAL ATTEMPTS
1,410—Grinnell, 2002 (490 made)

THREE-POINT FIELD-GOAL ATTEMPTS PER GAME
62.4—Grinnell, 1999 (1,373 in 22)

THREE-POINT FIELD-GOAL PERCENTAGE
(Min. 100 made) 62.0%—N.J. Inst. of Tech., 1989 (124 of 200)
(Min. 150 made) 49.1%—Eureka, 1994 (317 of 646)

CONSECUTIVE GAMES SCORING A THREE-POINT FIELD GOAL
398—Salisbury, Nov. 25, 1986-Present

Free Throws

FREE THROWS
698—Ohio Wesleyan, 1988 (888 attempts)

FREE THROWS PER GAME
23.7—Grinnell, 1995 (498 in 21)

FREE-THROW ATTEMPTS
930—Queens (N.Y.), 1981 (636 made)

FREE-THROW ATTEMPTS PER GAME
33.2—Grinnell, 1995 (698 in 21)

FREE-THROW PERCENTAGE
81.8%—Wis.-Oshkosh, 1998 (516 of 631)

Rebounds

REBOUNDS
1,616—Keene St., 1976 (29 games)

AVERAGE PER GAME
56.3—Mercy, 1977 (1,408 in 25)

AVERAGE REBOUND MARGIN
17.0—Hamilton, 1991 (49.6 offense, 32.5 defense)

Assists

ASSISTS
861—Salisbury, 1991 (29 games)

AVERAGE PER GAME
31.2—Me.-Farmington, 1991 (748 in 24)

Fouls

FOULS
801—McMurry, 2001 (28 games)

FOULS PER GAME
30.9—Grinnell, 1998 (679 in 22)

FEWEST FOULS
177—Caltech, 1997 (20 games)

FEWEST FOULS PER GAME
8.9—Caltech, 1997 (177 in 20)

Defense

FEWEST POINTS PER GAME ALLOWED
47.5—Wis.-Platteville, 1997 (1,283 in 27)

LOWEST FIELD-GOAL PERCENTAGE ALLOWED (Since 1978)
36.3—Grove City, 1999 (533 of 1,469)

Overtimes

OVERTIME GAMES
7—Albany (N.Y.), 1981 (won 5, lost 2); Col. of New Jersey, 1982 (won 6, lost 1); St. John's (Minn.), 1983 (won 4, lost 3); New Jersey City, 1994 (won 4, lost 3)

CONSECUTIVE OVERTIME GAMES
3—Albright, 1997 (won 3, lost 0); Buffalo St., 1997 (won 2, lost 1); Ferrum, 1997 (won 1, lost 2); Ithaca, 1987 (won 3, lost 0); Cortland St., 1989 (won 1, lost 2); Oberlin, 1989 (won 1, lost 2); Susquehanna, 1989 (won 3, lost 0)

General Records

GAMES PLAYED IN A SEASON
34—LeMoyne-Owen, 1980 (26-8); Wis.-Eau Claire, 1990 (30-4)

VICTORIES IN A SEASON
32—Potsdam St., 1986 (32-0)

CONSECUTIVE VICTORIES
60—Potsdam St. (from first game of 1985-86 season to March 14, 1987)

CONSECUTIVE HOME-COURT VICTORIES
62—North Park (from Feb. 8, 1984, to Feb. 3, 1988)

CONSECUTIVE REGULAR SEASON VICTORIES
59—Potsdam St. (from Nov. 22, 1985, to Dec. 12, 1987)

DEFEATS IN A SEASON
26—Otterbein, 1988 (1-26); Maryville (Mo.), 1991 (0-26)

CONSECUTIVE DEFEATS IN A SEASON
26—Maryville (Mo.), 1991 (0-26)

CONSECUTIVE DEFEATS
117—Rutgers-Camden (from Jan. 22, 1992, to Jan. 3, 1997; ended with 77-72 win vs. Bloomfield on Jan. 7, 1997)

CONSECUTIVE WINNING SEASONS
33—Wis.-Eau Claire, 1969-01; Wittenberg, 1969-01

MOST CONSECUTIVE NON-LOSING SEASONS
40—Albany (N.Y.), 1956-1995

UNBEATEN TEAMS (NUMBER OF VICTORIES IN PARENTHESES)
1986 Potsdam St. (32); 1995 Wis.-Platteville (31); 1998 Wis.-Platteville (30)

All-Time Individual Leaders

Single-Game Records

SCORING HIGHS

Pts.	Player, Team vs. Opponent	Season
77	Jeff Clement, Grinnell vs. Illinois Col.	1998
69	Steve Diekmann, Grinnell vs. Simpson	1995
63	Joe DeRoche, Thomas vs. St. Joseph's (Me.)	1988
62	Shannon Lilly, Bishop vs. Southwest Assembly of God	1983
61	Josh Metzger, Wis.-Lutheran vs. Grinnell	2001
61	Steve Honderd, Calvin vs. Kalamazoo	1993
61	Dana Wilson, Husson vs. Ricker	1974
60	Ed Brands, Grinnell vs. Ripon	1996
60	Steve Diekmann, Grinnell vs. Coe	1994
59	Ed Brands, Grinnell vs. Chicago	1996
59	Steve Diekmann, Grinnell vs. Monmouth (Ill.)	1995
58	Andy Panko, Lebanon Valley vs. Juniata	1999
58	Jeff Clement, Grinnell vs. Clarke	1998
57	David Otte, Simpson vs. Grinnell	1995
56	Scott Wilson, Grinnell vs. Martin Luther	1998
56	Steve Diekmann, Grinnell vs. Illinois Col.	1994
56	Kyle Price, Illinois Col. vs. Grinnell	1994
56	Shay DeLaney, Coe vs. Grinnell	1994
56	Mark Veenstra, Calvin vs. Adrian	1976
55	Jeff Clement, Grinnell vs. Lawrence	1998
55	Eric Ochel, Sewanee vs. Emory	1995
55	Dwain Govan, Bishop vs. Texas Southern	1975

Season Records

SCORING AVERAGE

Player, Team	Season	G	FG	3FG	FT	Pts.	Avg.
Steve Diekmann, Grinnell	†1995	20	223	137	162	745	*37.3
Rickey Sutton, Lyndon St.	†1976	14	207	—	93	507	36.2
Shannon Lilly, Bishop	†1983	26	345	—	218	908	34.9
Dana Wilson, Husson	†1974	20	288	—	122	698	34.9
Rickey Sutton, Lyndon St.	†1977	16	223	—	112	558	34.9
Steve Diekmann, Grinnell	†1994	21	250	117	106	723	34.4
Ed Brands, Grinnell	†1996	24	260	158	136	814	33.9
Jeff Clement, Grinnell	†1998	22	238	*186	84	746	33.9
Dwain Govan, Bishop	†1975	29	392	—	179	963	33.2
Clarence Caldwell, Greensboro	1976	22	306	—	111	723	32.8
Jeff Clement, Grinnell	†1999	22	217	166	121	721	32.8
Greg Grant, Col. of New Jersey	†1989	32	387	76	194	*1,044	32.6
Dave Russell, Shepherd	1975	32	*394	—	*249	1,037	32.4
Dwain Govan, Bishop	1974	26	358	—	126	842	32.4
Ron Stewart, Otterbein	1983	24	297	—	166	760	31.7

*†national champion; *record*

FIELD-GOAL PERCENTAGE
(Based on qualifiers for annual championship)

Player, Team	Season	G	FG	FGA	Pct.
Travis Weiss, St. John's (Minn.)	†1994	26	160	209	*76.6
Pete Metzelaars, Wabash	†1982	28	271	360	75.3
Tony Rychlec, Mass. Maritime	†1981	25	233	311	74.9
Tony Rychlec, Mass. Maritime	1982	20	193	264	73.1
Russ Newnan, Menlo	1991	26	130	178	73.0
Ed Owens, Hampden-Sydney	†1979	24	140	192	72.9
Scott Baxter, Capital	†1991	26	164	226	72.6
Maurice Woods, Potsdam St.	1982	30	203	280	72.5
Earl Keith, Stony Brook	1979	24	164	227	72.2
Pete Metzelaars, Wabash	1981	25	204	283	72.1
Jon Rosner, Yeshiva	1991	22	141	196	71.9
Pete Metzelaars, Wabash	1979	24	122	170	71.8
Anthony Farley, Miles	1982	26	168	235	71.5

*†national champion; *record*

THREE-POINT FIELD GOALS MADE

Player, Team	Season	G	3FG
Jeff Clement, Grinnell	1998	22	*186
Jeff Clement, Grinnell	1999	22	166
Ed Brands, Grinnell	1996	24	158
Chris Peterson, Eureka	1994	31	145
Steve Nordlund, Grinnell	2002	24	137
Steve Diekmann, Grinnell	1995	20	137
Chris Jans, Loras	1991	25	133
Eric Burdette, Wis.-Whitewater	1996	28	130
Ed Brands, Grinnell	1995	20	129
Tommy Doyle, Salem St.	1996	28	124
Everett Foxx, Ferrum	1992	29	124
Kirk Anderson, Augustana (Ill.)	1993	30	123
Jeff deLaveaga, Cal Lutheran	1992	28	122
Dave Stantial, Keene St.	2002	27	120
David Bailey, Concordia (Ill.)	1994	24	120
Woody Piirto, Grinnell	1999	22	117
Steve Matthews, Emerson	1999	25	117
Steve Diekmann, Grinnell	1994	21	117
Jeff Seifriz, Wis.-Whitewater	1989	31	114
Steve Matthews, Emerson	2000	27	113
Jeff Clement, Grinnell	1997	22	113
Chris Carideo, Widener	1995	27	113

**record*

THREE-POINT FIELD GOALS MADE PER GAME

Player, Team	Season	G	3FG	Avg.
Jeff Clement, Grinnell	†1998	22	*186	*8.5
Jeff Clement, Grinnell	†1999	22	166	7.5
Steve Diekmann, Grinnell	†1995	20	137	6.9
Ed Brands, Grinnell	†1996	24	158	6.6
Ed Brands, Grinnell	1995	29	129	6.5
Steve Nordlund, Grinnell	†2002	24	137	5.7
Steve Diekmann, Grinnell	†1994	21	117	5.6
Chris Jans, Loras	†1991	25	133	5.3
Woody Piirto, Grinnell	1999	22	117	5.3
Jeff Clement, Grinnell	†1997	22	113	5.1
Mark Bedell, Fisk	1997	19	97	5.1
David Bailey, Concordia (Ill.)	1994	24	120	5.0
Steve Matthews, Emerson	1999	25	117	4.7
Chris Peterson, Eureka	1994	31	145	4.7
Eric Burdette, Wis.-Whitewater	1996	28	130	4.6
Chris Geruschat, Bethany (W.Va.)	1991	24	111	4.6
Chris Carideo, Widener	1994	24	110	4.6
Luke Madsen, Wis.-River Falls	1996	22	98	4.5
Dave Stantial, Keene St.	2002	27	120	4.4
Tommy Doyle, Salem St.	1996	28	124	4.4
Mark Van Winkle, Eureka	1998	25	110	4.4
Ernie Bray, UC Santa Cruz	1994	24	105	4.4
Jeff deLaveaga, Cal Lutheran	†1992	28	122	4.4

*†national champion; *record*

THREE-POINT FIELD-GOAL PERCENTAGE
(Based on qualifiers for annual championship)

Player, Team	Season	G	3FG	3FGA	Pct.
Reggie James, N.J. Inst. of Tech.	†1989	29	59	88	*67.0
Chris Miles, N.J. Inst. of Tech.	†1987	26	41	65	63.1
Chris Miles, N.J. Inst. of Tech.	1989	29	46	75	61.3
Matt Miota, Lawrence	†1990	22	33	54	61.1
Mike Bachman, Alma	†1991	26	46	76	60.5
Ray Magee, Richard Stockton	†1988	26	41	71	57.7
Keith Orchard, Whitman	1988	26	42	73	57.5
Brian O'Donnell, Rutgers-Camden	1988	24	65	114	57.0
Eric Harris, Bishop	1987	26	91	160	56.9
Rick Brown, Muskingum	1988	30	71	125	56.8
Jamie Eichel, Fredonia St.	1989	24	51	90	56.7

*†national champion; *record*

FREE-THROW PERCENTAGE
(Based on qualifiers for annual championship)

Player, Team	Season	G	FT	FTA	Pct.
Korey Coon, Ill. Wesleyan	†2000	25	157	163	*96.3
Chanse Young, Manchester	†1998	25	65	68	95.6
Andy Enfield, Johns Hopkins	†1991	29	123	129	95.3
Chris Carideo, Widener	†1992	26	80	84	95.2
Yudi Teichman, Yeshiva	†1989	21	119	125	95.2
Brett Davis, Wis.-Oshkosh	1998	27	72	76	94.7
Mark Giovino, Babson	†1997	28	86	91	94.5
Mike Scheib, Susquehanna	†1977	22	80	85	94.1
Jason Prenevost, Middlebury	†1994	22	60	64	93.8
Derrick Rogers, Averett	†2001	27	72	77	93.5
Jerry Prestier, Baldwin-Wallace	†1978	25	125	134	93.3
Charlie Nanick, Scranton	†1996	25	96	103	93.2
Jeff Bowers, Southern Me.	†1988	29	95	102	93.1
Eric Jacobs, Scranton	1986	29	81	87	93.1
Jim Durrell, Colby-Sawyer	†1993	25	67	72	93.1
Joe Purcell, King's (Pa.)	†1979	26	66	71	93.0
Todd Reinhardt, Wartburg	†1990	26	91	98	92.9
Reiner Kolodinski, Occidental	1979	24	65	70	92.9

Player, Team	Season	G	FT	FTA	Pct.
Shannon Lilly, Bishop	†1982	22	142	153	92.8
Matt Freesemann, Wartburg	†1995	24	128	138	92.8

†national champion; *record

REBOUND AVERAGE

Player, Team	Season	G	Reb.	Avg.
Joe Manley, Bowie St.	†1976	29	*579	*20.0
Fred Petty, New Hamp. Col.	†1974	22	436	19.8
Larry Williams, Pratt	†1977	24	457	19.0
Charles Greer, Thomas	1977	17	318	18.7
Larry Parker, Plattsburgh St.	†1975	23	430	18.7
John Jordan, Southern Me.	†1978	29	536	18.5
Keith Woolfolk, Upper Iowa	1978	26	479	18.4
Michael Stubbs, Trinity (Conn.)	†1990	22	398	18.1
Mike Taylor, Pratt	1978	23	414	18.0
Walt Edwards, Husson	1976	26	467	18.0
Dave Kufeld, Yeshiva	†1979	20	355	17.8

†national champion; *record

ASSISTS

Player, Team	Season	G	Ast.
Robert James, Kean	†1989	29	*391
Tennyson Whitted, Ramapo	†2002	29	319
Ricky Spicer, Wis.-Whitewater	1989	31	295
Joe Marcotte, N.J. Inst. of Tech.	†1995	30	292
Andre Bolton, Chris. Newport	†1996	30	289
Ron Torgalski, Hamilton	1989	26	275
Albert Kirchner, Mt. St. Vincent	†1990	24	267
Steve Artis, Chris. Newport	1991	29	262
Phil Dixon, Shenandoah	1996	27	258
Phil Dixon, Shenandoah	†1994	26	253
Steve Artis, Chris. Newport	1990	28	251
David Genovese, Mt. St. Vincent	1994	27	248
Russell Springman, Salisbury	1990	27	246
Tom Genco, Manhattanville	1990	26	244
Andre Bolton, Chris. Newport	1995	28	243
Mark Cottom, Ferrum	1991	25	242
Tim Lawrence, Maryville (Tenn.)	1992	29	241

†national champion; *record

ASSIST AVERAGE

Player, Team	Season	G	Ast.	Avg.
Robert James, Kean	†1989	29	*391	*13.5
Albert Kirchner, Mt. St. Vincent	†1990	24	267	11.1
Tennyson Whitted, Ramapo	†2002	29	319	11.0
Ron Torgalski, Hamilton	1989	26	275	10.6
Louis Adams, Rust	1989	22	227	10.3
Eric Johnson, Coe	†1991	24	238	9.9
Joe Marcotte, N.J. Inst. of Tech.	†1995	30	292	9.7
Phil Dixon, Shenandoah	†1994	26	253	9.7
Mark Cottom, Ferrum	1991	25	242	9.7
Andre Bolton, Chris. Newport	†1996	30	289	9.6
Phil Dixon, Shenandoah	1996	27	258	9.6
Ricky Spicer, Wis.-Whitewater	1989	31	295	9.5
David Rubin, Hobart	†1998	25	237	9.5
Pat Heldman, Maryville (Tenn.)	1989	25	236	9.4
Deshone Bond, Stillman	†1997	25	235	9.4
Tom Genco, Manhattanville	1990	26	244	9.4
Justin Culhane, Suffolk	1992	24	225	9.4

†national champion; *record

BLOCKED SHOTS

Player, Team	Season	G	Blk.
Tory Black, N.J. Inst. of Tech.	†1997	26	*198
Neil Edwards, York (N.Y.)	†2000	26	193
Ira Nicholson, Mt. St. Vincent	†1995	28	188
Ira Nicholson, Mt. St. Vincent	†1996	27	163
Ira Nicholson, Mt. St. Vincent	1997	24	151
Antoine Hyman, Keuka	1997	26	148
Matt Cusano, Scranton	†1993	29	145
Neil Edwards, York (N.Y.)	†1999	26	144
Johnny Woods, Wesley	2000	24	132
Antoine Hyman, Keuka	1996	25	131
Andrew South, N.J. Inst. of Tech.	†1994	27	128
Mike Mientus, Allentown	1995	27	118
Roy Woods, Fontbonne	1995	25	117
Erik Lidecis, Maritime (N.Y.)	1994	26	116
Antonio Ramos, Clarke	2001	25	114
Joe Henderson, Hunter	1999	22	112
Mike Mientus, Allentown	1997	26	112
Andrew South, N.J. Inst. of Tech.	1993	26	111

Player, Team	Season	G	Blk.
Jeremy Putman, Dubuque	1995	25	110
Robert Clyburn, Kean	1995	27	108

†national champion; *record

BLOCKED-SHOT AVERAGE

Player, Team	Season	G	Blk.	Avg.
Tory Black, N.J. Inst. of Tech.	†1997	26	*198	*7.62
Neil Edwards, York (N.Y.)	†2000	26	193	7.42
Ira Nicholson, Mt. St. Vincent	†1995	28	188	6.71
Ira Nicholson, Mt. St. Vincent	1997	24	151	6.29
Ira Nicholson, Mt. St. Vincent	†1996	27	163	6.04
Antoine Hyman, Keuka	1997	26	148	5.69
Neil Edwards, York (N.Y.)	†1999	26	144	5.54
Johnny Woods, Wesley	2000	24	132	5.50
Antoine Hyman, Keuka	1996	25	131	5.24
Joe Henderson, Hunter	1999	22	112	5.09
Matt Cusano, Scranton	†1993	29	145	5.00
Andrew South, N.J. Inst. of Tech.	†1994	27	128	4.74
Roy Woods, Fontbonne	1995	25	117	4.68
Johnny Woods, Wesley	†2001	22	101	4.59
Antonio Ramos, Clarke	2001	25	114	4.56
Erik Lidecis, Maritime (N.Y.)	1994	26	116	4.46
Jeremy Putman, Dubuque	1995	25	110	4.40
Mike Mientus, Allentown	1995	27	118	4.37
Mike Mientus, Allentown	1997	26	112	4.31
Kyle McNamar, Curry	†2002	25	107	4.28

†national champion; *record

STEALS

Player, Team	Season	G	Stl.
Moses Jean-Pierre, Plymouth St.	†1994	30	*189
Daniel Martinez, McMurry	†2000	29	178
Purvis Presha, Stillman	†1996	25	144
Tennyson Whitted, Ramapo	†2002	29	138
Matt Newton, Principia	1994	25	138
John Gallogly, Salve Regina	†1997	24	137
Greg Dean, Concordia-M'head	1997	23	126
Scott Clarke, Utica	†1995	24	126
Deron Black, Allegheny	1996	27	123
David Brown, Westfield St.	1994	25	122
Ricky Hollis, Brockport St.	2000	27	121
John Gallogly, Salve Regina	†1998	23	121
Barry Aranoff, Yeshiva	1995	22	121
Horace Jenkins, Wm. Paterson	2001	31	120
Brian Meehan, Salve Regina	1995	28	120
Scott Clarke, Utica	1996	26	118
Darrel Lewis, Lincoln (Pa.)	1997	26	115
Mario Thompson, Occidental	†1999	24	114
Moses Jean-Pierre, Plymouth St.	†1993	25	114
Keith Darden, Concordia-Austin	†2001	24	111
Shawn McCartney, Hunter	1995	28	111
Gerald Garlic, Goucher	1995	29	111

†national champion; *record

STEAL AVERAGE

Player, Team	Season	G	Stl.	Avg.
Moses Jean-Pierre, Plymouth St.	†1994	30	*189	*6.30
Daniel Martinez, McMurry	†2000	29	178	6.14
Purvis Presha, Stillman	†1996	25	144	5.76
John Gallogly, Salve Regina	†1997	24	137	5.71
Matt Newton, Principia	1994	25	138	5.52
Barry Aranoff, Yeshiva	†1995	22	121	5.50
Greg Dean, Concordia-M'head	1997	23	126	5.48
John Gallogly, Salve Regina	†1998	23	121	5.26
Scott Clarke, Utica	1995	24	126	5.25
Joel Heckendorf, Martin Luther	1996	17	84	4.94
David Brown, Westfield St.	1994	25	122	4.88
Ivo Moyano, Polytechnic (N.Y.)	1994	19	91	4.78
Tennyson Whitted, Ramapo	†2002	29	138	4.76
Mario Thompson, Occidental	†1999	24	114	4.75
Keith Darden, Concordia-Austin	†2001	24	111	4.63
Moses Jean-Pierre, Plymouth St.	†1993	25	114	4.56
Deron Black, Allegheny	1996	27	123	4.55
Scott Clarke, Utica	1996	26	118	4.54
Ricky Hollis, Brockport St.	2000	27	121	4.48
Darrel Lewis, Lincoln (Pa.)	1997	26	115	4.42

†national champion; *record

Career Records

POINTS

Player, Team	Seasons	Pts.
Andre Foreman, Salisbury	1988-89, 91-92	*2,940
Lamont Strothers, Chris. Newport	1988-91	2,709
Matt Hancock, Colby	1987-90	2,678
Scott Fitch, Geneseo St.	1990-91, 93-94	2,634
Greg Grant, Col. of New Jersey	1987-89	2,611
Rick Hughes, Thomas More	1993-96	2,605
Wil Peterson, St. Andrews	1980-83	2,553
Ron Stewart, Otterbein	1980-83	2,549
Andy Panko, Lebanon Valley	1996-99	2,515
Scott Tedder, Ohio Wesleyan	1985-88	2,501
Moses Jean-Pierre, Plymouth St.	1991-94	2,483
Steve Honderd, Calvin	1990-93	2,469
Herman Alston, Kean	1988-91	2,457
Dick Hempy, Otterbein	1984-87	2,439
John Patraitis, Anna Maria	1995-98	2,434
Kevin Moran, Curry	1983-86	2,415
Alex Butler, Rhode Island Col.	1994-97	2,398
Rickey Sutton, Lyndon St.	1976-79	2,379
Frank Wachlarowicz, St. John's (Minn.)	1975-79	2,357
Henry Shannon, Maryville (Mo.)	1996-99	2,352
Cedric Oliver, Hamilton	1976-79	2,349
Dana Janssen, Neb. Wesleyan	1983-86	2,333
Kevin Brown, Emory & Henry	1984-87	2,322

*record

SCORING AVERAGE
(Minimum 1,400 points)

Player, Team	Seasons	G	FG	3FG	FT	Pts.	Avg.
Dwain Govan, Bishop	1974-75	55	750	—	305	1,805	*32.8
Dave Russell, Shepherd	1974-75	60	710	—	413	1,833	30.6
Rickey Sutton, Lyndon St.	1976-79	80	960	—	459	2,379	29.7
John Atkins, Knoxville	1976-78	70	845	—	322	2,012	28.7
Steve Peknik, Windham	1974-77	76	816	—	467	2,099	27.6
Andre Foreman, Salisbury	1988-89, 91-92	109	1,140	68	592	*2,940	27.0
Darrel Lewis, Lincoln (Pa.)	1996-99	86	796	265	409	2,267	26.4
Matt Hancock, Colby	1987-90	102	844	198	*792	2,678	26.3
Terrence Dupree, Polytechnic (N.Y.)	1990-92	70	700	22	407	1,829	26.1
Steve Diekmann, Grinnell	1992-95	85	741	371	365	2,218	26.1
Rick Hughes, Thomas More	1993-96	101	1,039	13	514	2,605	25.8
Mark Veenstra, Calvin	1974-77	89	960	—	341	2,261	25.4
Ron Swartz, Hiram	1984-87	90	883	78	408	2,252	25.0
Clarence Caldwell, Greensboro	1974-77	93	971	—	363	2,309	24.8
James Rehnquist, Amherst	1975-77	61	614	—	284	1,512	24.8

*record

FIELD-GOAL PERCENTAGE
(Minimum 400 field goals made)

Player, Team	Seasons	G	FG	FGA	Pct.
Tony Rychlec, Mass. Maritime	1981-83	55	509	692	*73.6
Pete Metzelaars, Wabash	1979-82	103	784	1,083	72.4
Maurice Woods, Potsdam St.	1980-82	93	559	829	67.4
Earl Keith, Stony Brook	1975-76, 78-79	94	777	1,161	66.9
Dan Rush, Bridgewater (Va.)	1992-95	102	712	1,069	66.6
Wade Gugino, Hope	1989-92	97	664	1,010	65.7
David Otte, Simpson	1992-95	76	549	840	65.4
Rick Batt, UC San Diego	1989-92	106	558	855	65.2
Kevin Ryan, Col. of New Jersey	1987-90	102	619	955	64.8
Greg Kemp, Aurora	1991-94	102	680	1,051	64.7
Scott Baxter, Capital	1988-91	104	505	782	64.6
Paul Rich, Geneseo St.	1978-81	88	452	700	64.6
Nate Thomas, Neb. Wesleyan	1995-98	98	497	772	64.4
Tod Hart, Ithaca	1980-83	97	726	1,133	64.1
Tony Seay, Averett	1989-90	55	465	726	64.0
John Ellenwood, Wooster	1997-00	98	442	692	63.9
Jeff Gibbs, Otterbein	1999-02	109	758	1,188	63.8
Dick Hempy, Otterbein	1984-87	112	923	1,447	63.8
John Wassenbergh, St. Joseph's (Me.)	1993-96	108	815	1,281	63.6
Jason Nickerson, Va. Wesleyan	1996-99	79	614	967	63.5
Mike Johnson, Wis.-Eau Claire	1989-91	89	402	636	63.2

*record

THREE-POINT FIELD GOALS MADE

Player, Team	Seasons	G	3FG
Jeff Clement, Grinnell	1996-99	91	*516
Chris Carideo, Widener	1992-95	103	402
Steve Diekmann, Grinnell	1992-95	85	371
Matt Garvey, Bates	1994-97	95	361
Ray Wilson, UC Santa Cruz	1989-92	100	354
Ed Brands, Grinnell	1993-96	78	347
Chris Hamilton, Blackburn	1988-91	101	334
Scott Fitch, Geneseo St.	1990-91, 93-94	109	332
Billy Collins, Nichols	1992-95	92	331
John Estelle, Wabash	1997-00	109	328
Mark Bedell, Fisk	1994-97	94	321
Jason Valant, Colorado Col.	1990-93	103	315
Everett Foxx, Ferrum	1989-92	104	315
Nevada Smith, Bethany (W.Va.)	1999-02	105	313
Aaron Lee, Mass.-Dartmouth	1992-95	115	313
Steve Chase, St. Joseph's (Me.)	1990-93	119	311
Jim Durrell, Colby-Sawyer	1991-94	100	308
Chris Geruschat, Bethany (W.Va.)	1989-92	89	307
Tommy Doyle, Salem St.	1993-96	110	304
Ryan Knuppel, Elmhurst	1998-01	102	303
Burt Paddock, Manchester	1994-97	109	302

*record

THREE-POINT FIELD GOALS MADE PER GAME
(Minimum 200 three-point field goals made)

Player, Team	Seasons	G	3FG	Avg.
Jeff Clement, Grinnell	1996-99	91	*516	*5.67
Ed Brands, Grinnell	1993-96	78	347	4.45
Steve Diekmann, Grinnell	1992-95	85	371	4.36
Chris Carideo, Widener	1992-95	103	402	3.90
Matt Garvey, Bates	1994-97	95	361	3.80
Billy Collins, Nichols	1992-95	92	331	3.60
Ray Wilson, UC Santa Cruz	1989-92	100	354	3.54
Chris Geruschat, Bethany (W.Va.)	1989-92	89	307	3.45
Mark Bedell, Fisk	1994-97	94	321	3.41
Chris Hamilton, Blackburn	1988-91	101	334	3.31
Jeff Jones, Lycoming	1987-89	71	232	3.27
Darrel Lewis, Lincoln (Pa.)	1996-99	86	265	3.08
Jim Durrell, Colby-Sawyer	1991-94	100	308	3.08
Jason Valant, Colorado Col.	1990-93	103	315	3.06
Scott Fitch, Geneseo St.	1990-91, 93-94	109	332	3.05
Everett Foxx, Ferrum	1989-92	104	315	3.03
Josh Estelle, Wabash	1997-00	109	328	3.01
Nevada Smith, Bethany (W.Va.)	1999-02	105	313	2.98
Ryan Knuppel, Elmhurst	1998-01	102	303	2.97
Perry Junius, Allegheny	1988-91	93	275	2.96
David Bailey, Concordia (Ill.)	1992-95	94	277	2.95

*record

THREE-POINT FIELD-GOAL PERCENTAGE
(Minimum 200 three-point field goals made)

Player, Team	Seasons	G	3FG	3FGA	Pct.
Jeff Seifriz, Wis.-Whitewater	1987-89	85	217	423	*51.3
Chris Peterson, Eureka	1991-94	78	215	421	51.1
Everett Foxx, Ferrum	1989-92	104	315	630	50.0
Brad Alberts, Ripon	1989-92	95	277	563	49.2
Jeff Jones, Lycoming	1987-89	71	232	472	49.2
Troy Greenlee, DePauw	1988-91	106	232	473	49.0

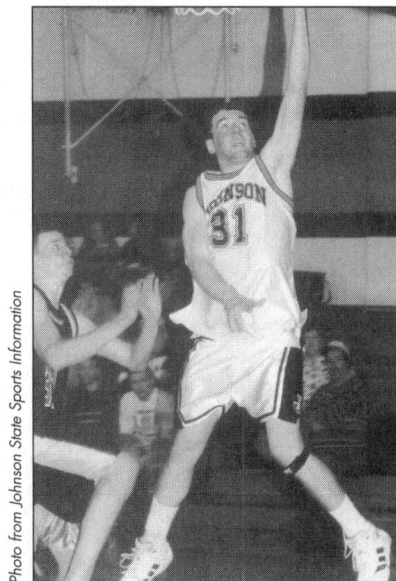

Patrick Glover of Johnson State led Division III in scoring last season.

Photo from Johnson State Sports Information

DIVISION III

Player, Team	Seasons	G	3FG	3FGA	Pct.
David Todd, Pomona-Pitzer	1987-90	84	212	439	48.3
Al Callejas, Scranton	1998-01	90	225	466	48.3

*record

FREE-THROW PERCENTAGE
(Minimum 250 free throws made)

Player, Team	Seasons	G	FT	FTA	Pct.
Andy Enfield, Johns Hopkins	1988-91	108	431	466	*92.5
Korey Coon, Ill. Wesleyan	1997-00	109	449	492	91.3
Ryan Knuppel, Elmhurst	1998-01	102	288	317	90.9
Doug Brown, Elizabethtown	1976-80	96	252	279	90.3
Al Callejas, Scranton	1998-01	90	333	372	89.5
Tim McGraw, Hartwick	1985-88	107	330	371	88.9
Eric Jacobs, Wilkes & Scranton	1984-87	106	303	343	88.3
John Luisi, Suffolk	1999-02	105	265	300	88.3
Charles Nenick, Scranton	1994-97	98	259	294	88.1
Todd Reinhardt, Wartburg	1988-91	105	283	322	87.9
Jeff Thomas, King's (Pa.)	1989-92	110	466	532	87.6
Brian Andrews, Alfred	1984-87	101	306	350	87.4
Matt Freesemann, Wartburg	1994-96	73	297	340	87.4
Dave Jannuzzi, Wilkes	1997-99, 2001	112	425	487	87.3
Eric Elliott, Hope	1988-91	103	350	403	86.8
Chad Onofrio, Tufts	1993-96	100	329	379	86.8
Pat Pruitt, Albright	1989-92	87	261	301	86.7
Ryan Billet, Elizabethtown	1995-98	98	434	501	86.6
Mike Johnson, Wis.-Eau Claire	1989-91	89	421	486	86.6
Ron Barczak, Kalamazoo	1988-91	98	360	416	86.5
Scott Smith, Salisbury	1981-85	106	290	336	86.3
Brad Howe, Capital	1997-00	100	239	277	86.3
Rick Alspach, North Park	1997-00	100	283	328	86.3

*record

REBOUND AVERAGE
(Minimum 900 rebounds)

Player, Team	Seasons	G	Reb.	Avg.
Larry Parker, Plattsburgh St.	1975-78	85	1,482	*17.4
Charles Greer, Thomas	1975-77	58	926	16.0
Willie Parr, LeMoyne-Owen	1974-76	76	1,182	15.6
Michael Smith, Hamilton	1989-92	107	*1,628	15.2
Dave Kufeld, Yeshiva	1977-80	81	1,222	15.1
Ed Owens, Hampden-Sydney	1977-80	77	1,160	15.1
Kevin Clark, Clark (Mass.)	1978-81	101	1,450	14.4
Mark Veenstra, Calvin	1974-77	89	1,260	14.2

*record

ASSISTS

Player, Team	Seasons	G	Ast.
Steve Artis, Chris. Newport	1990-93	112	*909
Phil Dixon, Shenandoah	1993-96	103	889
David Genovese, Mt. St. Vincent	1992-95	107	800
Andre Bolton, Chris. Newport	1993-96	109	737
Matt Lucero, Austin	1998-01	99	677
Brian Nigro, Mt. St. Vincent	1997-00	99	674
Greg Dunne, Nazareth	1996-99	106	671
Moses Jean-Pierre, Plymouth St.	1991-94	109	669
Mike Rhoades, Lebanon Valley	1992-95	114	668
Tennyson Whitted, Ramapo#	2000-02	78	664
Lance Andrews, N.J. Inst. of Tech.	1990-93	113	664
Dennis Jacobi, Bowdoin	1989-92	93	662
Tim Lawrence, Maryville (Tenn.)	1989-92	106	660
Pat Skerry, Tufts	1989-92	95	650
Eric Prendeville, Salisbury	1996-99	107	641
Eric Johnson, Coe	1989-92	90	637
John Snyder, King's (Pa.)	1989-92	107	631
Jason Saurbaugh, York (Pa.)	1997-00	101	624
Sammy Briggs, Catholic	1994-97	103	621
Anthony Robinson, Wittenberg	1993-96	117	618
Jerry Dennis, Otterbein	1989-92	118	613

*record, #active player

ASSIST AVERAGE
(Minimum 550 assists)

Player, Team	Seasons	G	Ast.	Avg.
Phil Dixon, Shenandoah	1993-96	103	889	*8.6
Steve Artis, Chris. Newport	1990-93	112	909	8.1
David Genovese, Mt. St. Vincent	1992-95	107	800	7.5
Kevin Root, Eureka	1989-91	81	579	7.1
Dennis Jacobi, Bowdoin	1989-92	93	662	7.1
Eric Johnson, Coe	1989-92	90	637	7.1
Nathan Reeves, York (N.Y.)	1994-97	81	572	7.1
Pat Skerry, Tufts	1989-92	95	650	6.8

Player, Team	Seasons	G	Ast.	Avg.
Matt Lucero, Austin	1998-01	99	677	6.8
Brian Nigro, Mt. St. Vincent	1997-00	99	674	6.8
Andre Bolton, Chris. Newport	1993-96	109	737	6.8
Tony Wyzzard, Emerson-MCA	1992-95	90	604	6.7
Greg Dunne, Nazareth	1996-99	106	671	6.3
Tim Lawrence, Maryville (Tenn.)	1989-92	106	660	6.2
Jason Saurbaugh, York (Pa.)	1997-00	101	624	6.2
Kevin Clipperton, Upper Iowa	1994-97	99	610	6.2
Moses Jean-Pierre, Plymouth St.	1991-94	109	669	6.1
Paul Ferrell, Guilford	1991-94	99	607	6.1
Eric Prendeville, Salisbury	1996-99	107	641	6.0
Sammy Briggs, Catholic	1994-97	103	621	6.0

*record

BLOCKED SHOTS

Player, Team	Seasons	G	Blk.
Ira Nicholson, Mt. St. Vincent	1994-97	100	*576
Antoine Hyman, Keuka	1994-97	101	440
Andrew South, N.J. Inst. of Tech.	1993-95	80	344
Neil Edwards, York (N.Y.)	1998-00	55	337
Mike Mientus, Allentown	1994-97	87	324
Johnny Woods, Wesley #	1999-02	78	319
Jason Alexander, Catholic	1995-98	107	283
Jeremy Putman, Dubuque	1993-96	99	274
Terry Thomas, Chris. Newport	1993-96	113	271
Ken LaFlamme, Emerson-MCA	1994-97	91	269
David Apple, Averett	1998-00	76	268
Tory Black, N.J. Inst. of Tech.	1995-96	53	261
Kris Silveria, Salem St.	1995-98	112	254
Ryan Gorman, Wooster	1996-99	112	253
Tyrone Bennett, Methodist.	1994-97	101	253
Michael Lynch, Roger Williams	1998-01	106	248
Jon Wallenfelsz, Wis.-Eau Claire	1997-00	104	242
John Garber, Millsaps	1994-97	102	229
Kris Merritt, Hope	1995-98	96	217
Terry Gray, Chris. Newport#	2000-02	75	214
Jarriot Rook, Washington (Mo.)	1999-02	79	214
David Kline, Widener	1994-97	103	212

*record, #active player

BLOCKED-SHOT AVERAGE
(Minimum 175 blocked shots)

Player, Team	Seasons	G	Blk.	Avg.
Neil Edwards, York (N.Y.)	1998-00	55	337	*6.13
Ira Nicholson, Mt. St. Vincent	1994-97	100	576	5.76
Tory Black, N.J. Inst. of Tech.	1995-96	53	261	4.92
Antoine Hyman, Keuka	1994-97	101	440	4.36
Andrew South, N.J. Inst. of Tech.	1993-95	80	344	4.30
Antonio Ramos, Clarke	2001-02	50	212	4.24
Johnny Woods, Wesley	1999-02	78	319	4.09
Mike Mientus, Allentown	1994-97	87	324	3.72
Steve Butler, Chris. Newport	1997-98	55	196	3.56
David Apple, Averett	1998-00	76	268	3.53
Ken LaFlamme, Emerson-MCA	1994-97	91	269	2.96
Jeremy Putman, Dubuque	1993-96	99	274	2.77
Mike Brown, Clark (Mass.)	1997-00	71	195	2.75
Jason Alexander, Catholic	1995-98	107	283	2.64
Robert Clyburn, Kean	1993-95	77	201	2.61
Tyrone Bennett, Methodist.	1994-97	101	253	2.50
Jeff Manning, Curry	1993-95	74	184	2.49
Terry Thomas, Chris. Newport	1993-96	113	271	2.40

*record

STEALS

Player, Team	Seasons	G	Stl.
John Gallogly, Salve Regina	1995-98	98	*413
Daniel Martinez, McMurry	1998-00	76	380
Ivo Moyano, Polytechnic (N.Y.)	1994-97	87	368
Eric Bell, New Paltz St.	1993-96	94	355
Scott Clarke, Utica	1993-96	96	346
Tennyson Whitted, Ramapo#	2000-02	78	330
Ricky Hollis, Brockport St.	1999-02	90	322
Greg Dean, Concordia-M'head	1995-97	75	307
Tom Roeder, St. Joseph's (N.Y.)	1999-02	98	303
Moses Jean-Pierre, Plymouth St.	1993-94	55	303
Joel Holstege, Hope	1995-98	118	301
Mario Thompson, Occidental	1999-01	71	300
Darrell Lewis, Lincoln (Pa.)	1996-99	86	298
Henry Shannon, Maryville (Mo.)	1996-99	106	292
B.J. Reilly, Montclair St.	1997-00	101	287
Damien Hunter, Alvernia	1995-98	110	287
Keith Poppor, Amherst	1993-96	98	283
Carl Cochran, Richard Stockton	1994-97	113	281

Player, Team	Seasons	G	Stl.
Kevin Weakly, Otterbein	1996-99	104	277
Terrence Stewart, Rowan	1993-96	113	277
Clarence Pierce, N.J. Inst. of Tech.	1993-96	102	273
Ben Hoffmann, Wis.-Platteville	1995-98	109	270
Dave Eshaya, Aurora	1995-98	101	265

*record; #active player

STEAL AVERAGE
(Minimum 175 steals)

Player, Team	Seasons	G	Stl.	Avg.
Moses Jean-Pierre, Plymouth St.	1993-94	55	303	*5.51
Daniel Martinez, McMurry	1998-00	76	380	5.00
Ivo Moyano, Polytechnic (N.Y.)	1994-97	87	368	4.23
Mario Thompson, Occidental	1999-01	71	300	4.23
John Gallogly, Salve Regina	1995-98	98	*413	4.21
Greg Dean, Concordia-M'head	1995-97	75	307	4.09

Player, Team	Seasons	G	Stl.	Avg.
Rodney Lusain, UC San Diego	1993-94	50	193	3.86
Eric Bell, New Paltz St.	1993-96	94	355	3.78
David Brown, Westfield St.	1993-95	53	193	3.64
Scott Clarke, Utica	1993-96	96	346	3.60
Ricky Hollis, Brockport St.	1999-02	90	322	3.58
Gerald Garlic, Goucher	1993-95	70	244	3.49
Darrel Lewis, Lincoln (Pa.)	1996-99	86	298	3.47
Shuron Woodyard, Villa Julie	1995-97	73	238	3.26
Shawn McCarthy, Hunter	1993-95	81	261	3.22
Carl Small, Cornell College	1993-95	69	222	3.22
Horace Jenkins, Wm. Paterson	1998-01	82	263	3.21
Tom Roeder, St. Joseph's (N.Y.)	1999-02	98	303	3.09
Deron Black, Allegheny	1993-96	78	240	3.08
Reuben Reyes, Salve Regina	1993-95	74	226	3.05
Ernie Peavy, Wis.-Platteville	1993-95	87	264	3.03

*record

Annual Individual Champions

Scoring Average

Season	Player, Team	G	FG	FT	Pts.	Avg.
1974	Dana Wilson, Husson	20	288	122	698	34.9
1975	Dwain Govan, Bishop	29	392	179	963	33.2
1976	Rickey Sutton, Lyndon St.	14	207	93	507	36.2
1977	Rickey Sutton, Lyndon St.	16	223	112	558	34.9
1978	John Atkins, Knoxville	25	340	103	783	31.3
1979	Scott Rogers, Kenyon	24	289	109	687	28.6
1980	Ray Buckland, Mass.-Boston	25	271	153	695	27.8
1981	Gerald Reece, William Penn	27	306	145	757	28.0
1982	Ashley Cooper, Ripon	22	256	89	601	27.3
1983	Shannon Lilly, Bishop	26	345	218	908	34.9
1984	Mark Van Valkenburg, Framingham St.	25	312	133	757	30.3
1985	Adam St. John, Maine Maritime	18	193	135	521	28.9
1986	John Saintignon, UC Santa Cruz	22	291	104	686	31.2

Season	Player, Team	G	FG	3FG	FT	Pts.	Avg.
1987	Rod Swartz, Hiram	23	232	78	133	675	29.3
1988	Matt Hancock, Colby	27	275	56	247	853	31.6
1989	Greg Grant, Col. of New Jersey	32	387	76	194	*1,044	32.6
1990	Grant Glover, Rust	23	235	1	164	635	27.6
1991	Andre Foreman, Salisbury	29	350	39	175	914	31.5
1992	Jeff deLaveaga, Cal Lutheran	28	258	122	187	825	29.5
1993	Dave Shaw, Drew	23	210	74	169	663	28.8
1994	Steve Diekmann, Grinnell	21	250	117	106	723	34.4
1995	Steve Diekmann, Grinnell	20	223	137	162	745	*37.3
1996	Ed Brands, Grinnell	24	260	158	136	814	33.9
1997	Mark Bedell, Fisk	19	177	97	88	539	28.4
1998	Jeff Clement, Grinnell	22	238	*186	84	746	33.9
1999	Jeff Clement, Grinnell	22	217	166	121	721	32.8
2000	Willie Chandler, Misericordia	27	249	92	114	704	26.1
2001	Willie Chandler, Misericordia	26	271	96	125	763	29.3
2002	Patrick Glover, Johnson St.	24	237	28	147	649	27.0

*record

Field-Goal Percentage

Season	Player, Team	G	FG	FGA	Pct.
1974	Fred Waldstein, Wartburg	28	163	248	65.7
1975	Dan Woodard, Elizabethtown	23	190	299	63.5
1976	Paul Merlis, Yeshiva	21	145	217	66.8
1977	Brent Cawelti, Trinity (Conn.)	20	107	164	65.2
1978	Earl Keith, Stony Brook	29	228	322	70.8
1979	Ed Owens, Hampden-Sydney	24	140	192	72.9
1980	E.D. Schechterley, Lynchburg	25	184	259	71.0
1981	Tony Rychlec, Mass. Maritime	25	233	311	74.9
1982	Pete Metzelaars, Wabash	28	271	360	75.3
1983	Mike Johnson, Drew	23	138	205	67.3
1984	Mark Van Valkenburg, Framingham St.	25	312	467	66.8
1985	Reinout Brugman, Muhlenberg	26	176	266	66.2
1986	Oliver Kyler, Frostburg St.	28	183	266	68.8
1987	Tim Ervin, Albion	21	127	194	65.5
1988	Matt Strong, Hope	27	163	232	70.3
1989	Kevin Ryan, Col. of New Jersey	32	246	345	71.3
1990	Bill Triplett, N.J. Inst. of Tech.	28	169	237	71.3
1991	Scott Baxter, Capital	26	164	226	72.6

Season	Player, Team	G	FG	FGA	Pct.
1992	Brett Grebing, Redlands	23	125	176	71.0
1993	Jim Leibel, St. Thomas (Minn.)	28	141	202	69.8
1994	Travis Weiss, St. John's (Minn.)	26	160	209	*76.6
1995	Justin Wilkins, Neb. Wesleyan	28	163	237	68.8
1996	Jason Light, Emory & Henry	25	207	294	70.4
1997	Jason Hayes, Marietta	25	184	271	67.9
1998	Lonnie Walker, Alvernia	27	165	237	69.6
1999	Jason Nickerson, Va. Wesleyan	26	242	363	66.7
2000	Jack Jirak, Hampden-Sydney	28	147	220	66.8
2001	John Thomas, Fontbonne	22	157	223	70.4
2002	Omar Warthen, Neumann	27	135	202	66.8

*record

Three-Point Field Goals Made Per Game

Season	Player, Team	G	3FG	Avg.
1987	Scott Fearrin, MacMurray	25	96	3.8
1988	Jeff Jones, Lycoming	23	97	4.2
1989	Brad Block, Aurora	26	112	4.3
1990	Chris Hamilton, Blackburn	24	109	4.5
1991	Chris Jans, Loras	25	133	5.3
1992	Jeff deLaveaga, Cal Lutheran	28	122	4.4
1993	Mike Connelly, Catholic	27	111	4.1
1994	Steve Diekmann, Grinnell	21	117	5.6
1995	Steve Diekmann, Grinnell	20	137	6.8
1996	Ed Brands, Grinnell	24	158	6.6
1997	Jeff Clement, Grinnell	22	113	5.1
1998	Jeff Clement, Grinnell	22	*186	*8.5
1999	Jeff Clement, Grinnell	22	166	7.5
2000	Woody Piirto, Grinnell	20	87	4.3
2001	Nevada Smith, Bethany (W.Va.)	26	101	3.9
2002	Steve Nordlund, Grinnell	24	137	5.7

*record

Three-Point Field-Goal Percentage

Season	Player, Team	G	3FG	3FGA	Pct.
1987	Chris Miles, N.J. Inst. of Tech.	26	41	65	63.1
1988	Ray Magee, Richard Stockton	26	41	71	57.7
1989	Reggie James, N.J. Inst. of Tech.	29	59	88	*67.0
1990	Matt Miota, Lawrence	22	33	54	61.1
1991	Mike Bachman, Alma	26	46	76	60.5
1992	John Kmack, Plattsburgh St.	26	44	84	52.4
1993	Brad Apple, Greensboro	26	49	91	53.8
1994	Trever George, Coast Guard	23	38	72	52.8
1995	Tony Frieden, Manchester	32	58	107	54.2
1996	Joey Bigler, John Carroll	27	54	111	48.6
1997	Andy Strommen, Chicago	27	49	93	52.7
1998	Pat Maloney, Catholic	29	59	114	51.8
1999	Al Callejas, Scranton	26	66	122	54.1
2000	Brett Lively, Mary Washington	20	40	78	51.3
2001	Bryan Bertola, Lake Forest	23	58	110	52.7
2002	Doug Schneider, Pitt.-Bradford	28	78	143	54.5

*record

DIVISION III

Free-Throw Percentage

Season	Player, Team	G	FT	FTA	Pct.
1974	Bruce Johnson, Plymouth St.	17	73	81	90.1
1975	Harold Howard, Austin	24	83	92	90.2
1976	Tim Mieure, Hamline	25	88	95	92.6
1977	Mike Scheib, Susquehanna	22	80	85	94.1
1978	Jerry Prestier, Baldwin-Wallace	25	125	134	93.3
1979	Joe Purcell, King's (Pa.)	26	66	71	93.0
1980	David Whiteside, UNC Greensboro	28	120	132	90.9
1981	Jim Cooney, Elmhurst	26	65	72	90.3
1982	Shannon Lilly, Bishop	22	142	153	92.8
1983	Mike Sain, Eureka	26	66	72	91.7
1984	Chris Genian, Redlands	24	71	78	91.0
1985	Bob Possehl, Coe	22	59	65	90.8
1986	Eric Jacobs, Scranton	29	81	87	93.1
1987	Chris Miles, N.J. Inst. of Tech.	26	70	76	92.1
1988	Jeff Bowers, Southern Me.	29	95	102	93.1
1989	Yudi Teichman, Yeshiva	21	119	125	95.2
1990	Todd Reinhardt, Wartburg	26	91	98	92.9
1991	Andy Enfield, Johns Hopkins	29	123	129	95.3
1992	Chris Carideo, Widener	26	80	84	95.2
1993	Jim Durrell, Colby-Sawyer	25	67	72	93.1
1994	Jason Prenevost, Middlebury	22	60	64	93.8
1995	Matt Freesemann, Wartburg	24	128	138	92.8
1996	Charlie Nanick, Scranton	25	96	103	93.2
1997	Mark Giovino, Babson	28	86	91	94.5
1998	Chanse Young, Manchester	25	65	68	95.6
1999	Ryan Eklund, Wis.-La Crosse	26	80	87	92.0
2000	Korey Coon, Ill. Wesleyan	25	157	163	*96.3
2001	Derrick Rogers, Averett	27	72	77	93.5
2002	Jason Luisi, Suffolk	28	87	94	92.6

*record

Rebound Average

Season	Player, Team	G	Reb.	Avg.
1974	Fred Petty, New Hamp. Col.	22	436	19.8
1975	Larry Parker, Plattsburgh St.	23	430	18.7
1976	Joe Manley, Bowie St.	29	*579	*20.0
1977	Larry Williams, Pratt	24	457	19.0
1978	John Jordan, Southern Me.	29	536	18.5
1979	Dave Kufeld, Yeshiva	20	355	17.8
1980	Dave Kufeld, Yeshiva	20	353	17.7
1981	Kevin Clark, Clark (Mass.)	27	465	17.2
1982	Len Washington, Mass.-Boston	23	361	15.7
1983	Luis Frias, Anna Maria	23	320	13.9
1984	Joe Weber, Aurora	27	370	13.7
1985	Albert Wells, Rust	22	326	14.8
1986	Russell Thompson, Westfield St.	22	338	15.4
1987	Randy Gorniak, Penn St.-Behrend	25	410	16.4
1988	Mike Nelson, Hamilton	26	349	13.4
1989	Clinton Montford, Methodist	27	459	17.0
1990	Michael Stubbs, Trinity (Conn.)	22	398	18.1
1991	Mike Smith, Hamilton	27	435	16.1
1992	Jeff Black, Fitchburg St.	22	363	16.5
1993	Steve Lemmer, Hamilton	27	404	15.0
1994	Chris Sullivan, St. John Fisher	23	319	13.9
1995	Scott Suhr, Milwaukee Engr.	25	349	14.0
1996	Craig Jones, Rochester Inst.	26	363	14.0

Season	Player, Team	G	Reb.	Avg.
1997	Lonnie Walker, Alvernia	32	430	13.4
1998	Adam Doll, Simpson	25	366	14.6
1999	Anthony Peeples, Montclair St.	24	345	14.4
2000	Jeff Gibbs, Otterbein	23	307	13.3
2001	Jeff Gibbs, Otterbein	25	390	15.6
2002	Jeff Gibbs, Otterbein	32	523	16.3

*record

Assist Average

Season	Player, Team	G	Ast.	Avg.
1989	Robert James, Kean	27	*391	*13.5
1990	Albert Kirchner, Mt. St. Vincent	24	267	11.1
1991	Eric Johnson, Coe	24	238	9.9
1992	Edgar Loera, La Verne	23	202	8.8
1993	David Genovese, Mt. St. Vincent	27	237	8.8
1994	Phil Dixon, Shenandoah	26	253	9.7
1995	Joe Marcotte, N.J. Inst. of Tech	30	292	9.7
1996	Andre Bolton, Chris. Newport	30	289	9.6
1997	Deshone Bond, Stillman	25	235	9.4
1998	David Rubin, Hobart	25	237	9.5
1999	Tim Kelly, Pacific Lutheran	25	214	8.6
2000	Daniel Martinez, McMurry	29	229	7.9
2001	Jimmy Driggs, Hamilton	25	213	8.5
2002	Tennyson Whitted, Ramapo	29	319	11.0

*record

Blocked-Shot Average

Season	Player, Team	G	Stl.	Avg.
1993	Matt Cusano, Scranton	29	145	5.0
1994	Andrew South, N.J. Inst. of Tech.	27	128	4.7
1995	Ira Nicholson, Mt. St. Vincent	28	188	6.7
1996	Ira Nicholson, Mt. St. Vincent	27	163	6.0
1997	Tory Black, N.J. Inst. of Tech.	26	*198	*7.6
1998	Tony Seehase, Upper Iowa	23	89	3.9
1999	Neil Edwards, York (N.Y.)	26	144	5.5
2000	Neil Edwards, York (N.Y.)	26	193	7.4
2001	Johnny Woods, Wesley	22	101	4.6
2002	Kyle McNamar, Curry	25	107	4.3

*record

Steal Average

Season	Player, Team	G	Stl.	Avg.
1993	Moses Jean-Pierre, Plymouth St.	25	114	4.6
1994	Moses Jean-Pierre, Plymouth St.	30	*189	*6.3
1995	Barry Aranoff, Yeshiva	22	121	5.5
1996	Purvis Presha, Stillman	25	144	5.8
1997	John Gallogly, Salve Regina	24	137	5.7
1998	John Gallogly, Salve Regina	23	121	5.3
1999	Mario Thompson, Occidental	24	114	4.8
2000	Daniel Martinez, McMurry	29	178	6.1
2001	Keith Darden, Concordia-Austin	24	111	4.6
2002	Tennyson Whitted, Ramapo	29	138	4.8

*record

Annual Team Champions

Won-Lost Percentage

Season	Team	Won	Lost	Pct.
1974	Calvin	21	2	.913
1975	Calvin	22	1	.957
1976	Husson	25	1	.961
1977	Mass.-Boston	25	3	.893
1978	North Park	29	2	.935
1979	Stony Brook	24	3	.889
1980	Franklin Pierce	29	2	.935
1981	Potsdam St.	30	2	.938
1982	St. Andrews	27	3	.900
1983	Roanoke	31	2	.939
1984	Roanoke	27	2	.931

Season	Team	Won	Lost	Pct.
1985	Colby	22	3	.880
1986	Potsdam St.	32	0	1.000
1987	Potsdam St.	28	1	.966
1988	Scranton	29	3	.906
1989	Col. of New Jersey	30	2	.938
1990	Colby	26	1	.963
1991	Hamilton	26	1	.963
1992	Calvin	31	1	.969
1993	Rowan	29	2	.935
1994	Wittenberg	30	2	.938
1995	Wis.-Platteville	31	0	1.000
1996	Wilkes	28	2	.933
1997	Ill. Wesleyan	29	2	.935
1998	Wis.-Platteville	30	0	1.000

Season	Team	Won	Lost	Pct.
1999	Connecticut Col.	28	1	.966
2000	Calvin	30	2	.938
2001	Mass.-Dartmouth	25	3	.893
2002	Carthage	28	2	.933

Scoring Offense

Season	Team	G	W-L	Pts.	Avg.
1974	Bishop	26	14-12	2,527	97.2
1975	Bishop	29	25-4	2,932	101.1
1976	Husson	26	25-1	2,567	98.7
1977	Mercy	25	16-9	2,587	103.5
1978	Mercy	26	16-10	2,602	100.1
1979	Ashland	25	14-11	2,375	95.0
1980	Franklin Pierce	31	29-2	*3,073	99.1
1981	Husson	23	20-3	2,173	94.5
1982	Husson	26	19-7	2,279	87.7
1983	Bishop	26	18-8	2,529	97.3
1984	St. Joseph's (Me.)	29	24-5	2,666	91.9
1985	St. Joseph's (Me.)	30	22-8	2,752	91.7
1986	St. Joseph's (Me.)	30	26-4	2,837	94.6
1987	Bishop	26	13-13	2,534	97.5
1988	St. Joseph's (Me.)	29	20-9	2,785	96.0
1989	Redlands	25	15-10	2,507	100.3
1990	Salisbury	27	14-13	2,822	104.5
1991	Redlands	26	15-11	2,726	104.8
1992	Redlands	25	18-7	2,510	100.4
1993	Salisbury	26	18-8	2,551	98.1
1994	Grinnell	21	13-8	2,297	109.4
1995	Grinnell	21	14-7	2,422	115.3
1996	Grinnell	25	17-8	2,587	103.5
1997	Grinnell	22	10-12	2,254	102.5
1998	Grinnell	22	10-12	2,434	110.6
1999	Grinnell	22	11-11	2,509	114.0
2000	Grinnell	21	6-15	2,175	103.6
2001	Grinnell	24	16-8	2,837	118.2
2002	Grinnell	24	12-12	2,997	*124.9

*record

Scoring Defense

Season	Team	G	W-L	Pts.	Avg.
1974	Fredonia St.	22	13-9	1,049	47.7
1975	Chicago	15	9-6	790	52.7
1976	Fredonia St.	23	10-13	1,223	53.2
1977	Hamline	30	22-8	1,560	52.0
1978	Widener	31	26-5	1,693	54.6
1979	Coast Guard	24	21-3	1,160	48.3
1980	John Jay	27	10-17	1,411	52.3
1981	Wis.-Stevens Point	26	19-7	1,394	53.6
1982	Wis.-Stevens Point	28	22-6	1,491	53.3
1983	Ohio Northern	26	18-8	1,379	53.0
1984	Wis.-Stevens Point	32	28-4	1,559	48.7
1985	Wis.-Stevens Point	30	25-3	1,438	47.9
1986	Widener	27	15-12	1,356	50.2
1987	Muskingum	27	16-11	1,454	53.9
1988	Ohio Northern	30	21-9	1,734	57.8
1989	Wooster	28	21-7	1,600	57.1
1990	Randolph-Macon	29	24-5	1,646	56.8
1991	Ohio Northern	27	14-13	1,508	55.9
1992	Wittenberg	29	23-6	1,651	56.9
1993	St. Thomas (Minn.)	28	19-9	1,599	57.1
1994	Yeshiva	22	12-10	1,308	59.5
1995	Johnson St.	26	15-11	1,559	60.0
1996	Upper Iowa	26	21-5	1,500	57.7
1997	Wis.-Platteville	27	24-3	1,283	*47.5
1998	Wis.-Platteville	30	30-0	1,552	51.7
1999	Rowan	27	25-2	1,549	57.4
2000	Baruch	28	19-9	1,639	58.5
2001	Cortland St.	28	21-7	1,678	59.9
2002	Babson	30	25-5	1,693	56.4

*record

Scoring Margin

Season	Team	Off.	Def.	Mar.
1974	Fisk	83.3	65.7	17.6
1975	Monmouth (Ill.)	83.9	66.0	17.9
1976	Husson	98.7	67.6	*31.1

Season	Team	Off.	Def.	Mar.
1977	Husson	101.2	78.6	22.6
1978	Stony Brook	86.6	68.7	17.9
1979	North Park	84.4	67.3	17.1
1980	Franklin Pierce	99.1	76.5	22.6
1981	Husson	94.5	70.1	24.4
1982	Hope	83.9	70.0	13.8
1983	Trinity (Conn.)	79.8	61.4	18.4
1984	Wis.-Stevens Point	68.4	48.7	19.7
1985	Hope	85.4	66.0	19.4
1986	Potsdam St.	81.5	57.3	24.2
1987	N.J. Inst. of Tech.	90.8	63.9	26.9
1988	Cal St. San B'dino	89.4	69.4	20.0
1989	Col. of New Jersey	92.3	68.5	23.8
1990	Colby	94.7	71.9	22.8
1991	Hamilton	89.8	66.2	23.6
1992	N.J. Inst. of Tech.	95.0	73.4	21.6
1993	N.J. Inst. of Tech.	90.4	65.7	24.7
1994	Rowan	89.6	64.4	25.3
1995	Colby-Sawyer	94.4	71.7	22.6
1996	Cabrini	89.4	67.6	21.8
1997	Williams	83.6	62.5	21.0
1998	Wis.-Platteville	73.9	51.7	22.2
1999	Hampden-Sydney	84.2	62.3	21.9
2000	Hampden-Sydney	88.2	66.4	21.8
2001	Chapman	81.2	63.4	17.9
2002	Brockport St.	84.5	64.9	19.6

*record

Field-Goal Percentage

Season	Team	FG	FGA	Pct.
1974	Muskingum	560	1,056	53.0
1975	Savannah St.	1,072	1,978	54.2
1976	Stony Brook	778	1,401	55.5
1977	Stony Brook	842	1,455	57.9
1978	Stony Brook	1,033	1,721	*60.0
1979	Stony Brook	980	1,651	59.4
1980	Framingham St.	924	1,613	57.3
1981	Averett	845	1,447	58.4
1982	Lebanon Valley	608	1,098	55.4
1983	Bishop	1,037	1,775	58.4
1984	Framingham St.	849	1,446	58.7
1985	Me.-Farmington	751	1,347	55.8
1986	Frostburg St.	971	1,747	55.6
1987	N.J. Inst. of Tech.	969	1,799	53.9
1988	Rust	878	1,493	58.8
1989	Bridgewater (Va.)	650	1,181	55.0
1990	Wartburg	792	1,474	53.7
1991	Otterbein	1,104	2,050	53.9
1992	Bridgewater (Va.)	706	1,315	53.7
1993	St. John's (Minn.)	744	1,415	52.6
1994	Oglethorpe	774	1,491	51.9
1995	Simpson	892	1,627	54.8
1996	Simpson	946	1,749	54.1
1997	Neb. Wesleyan	968	1,834	52.8
1998	Ill. Wesleyan	843	1,546	54.5
1999	Lebanon Valley	751	1,445	52.0
2000	Franklin	814	1,577	51.6
2001	St. John's (Minn.)	772	1,471	52.5
2002	Wis.-Oshkosh	784	1,500	52.3

*record

Field-Goal Percentage Defense

Season	Team	FG	FGA	Pct.
1978	Grove City	589	1,477	39.9
1979	Coast Guard	464	1,172	39.6
1980	Calvin	552	1,364	40.5
1981	Wittenberg	670	1,651	40.6
1982	Tufts	622	1,505	41.3
1983	Trinity (Conn.)	580	1,408	41.2
1984	Widener	617	1,557	39.6
1985	Colby	679	1,712	39.7
1986	Widener	531	1,344	39.5
1987	Widener	608	1,636	37.2
1988	Rust	603	1,499	40.2
1989	Wooster	595	1,563	38.1
1990	Rochester	760	1,990	38.2
1991	Hamilton	679	1,771	38.3
1992	Scranton	589	1,547	38.1

DIVISION III

Season	Team	FG	FGA	Pct.
1993	Scranton	659	1,806	36.5
1994	Lebanon Valley	708	1,925	36.8
1995	New Jersey City	702	1,897	37.0
1996	Bowdoin	569	1,482	38.4
1997	N.J. Inst. of Tech.	572	1,565	36.5
1998	Rhodes	552	1,488	37.1
1999	Grove City	533	1,469	36.3
2000	Baruch	608	1,689	*36.0
2001	Endicott	575	1,569	36.6
2002	Rowan	503	1,377	36.5

*record

Three-Point Field Goals Made Per Game

Season	Team	G	3FG	Avg.
1987	Grinnell	22	166	7.5
1988	Southern Me.	29	233	8.0
1989	Redlands	25	261	10.4
1990	Augsburg	25	266	10.6
1991	Redlands	26	307	11.8
1992	Catholic	26	335	12.9
1993	Anna Maria	27	302	11.2
1994	Grinnell	21	297	14.1
1995	Grinnell	21	368	17.5
1996	Grinnell	25	415	16.6
1997	Grinnell	22	367	16.7
1998	Grinnell	22	406	18.5
1999	Grinnell	22	436	19.8
2000	Grinnell	21	353	16.8
2001	Grinnell	24	443	18.5
2002	Grinnell	24	*490	*20.4

*record

Three-Point Field-Goal Percentage

Season	Team	G	3FG	3FGA	Pct.
1987	Mass.-Dartmouth	28	102	198	51.5
1988	Richard Stockton	26	122	211	57.8
1989	N.J. Inst. of Tech.	29	124	200	*62.0
1990	Western New Eng.	26	85	167	50.9
1991	Ripon	26	154	331	46.5
1992	Dickinson	27	126	267	47.2
1993	DePauw	26	191	419	45.6
1994	Eureka	31	317	646	49.1
1995	Manchester	32	222	487	45.6
1996	John Carroll	27	169	388	43.6
1997	Williams	30	235	507	46.4
1998	Franklin	29	168	390	43.1
1999	Union (N.Y.)	25	233	512	45.5
2000	Franklin	28	195	467	41.8
2001	Albion	25	192	417	46.0
2002	Gordon	27	262	590	44.4

*record

Free-Throw Percentage

Season	Team	FT	FTA	Pct.
1974	Lake Superior St.	369	461	80.0
1975	Muskingum	298	379	78.6
1976	Case Reserve	266	343	77.6

Season	Team	FT	FTA	Pct.
1977	Hamilton	491	640	76.7
1978	Case Reserve	278	351	79.2
1979	Marietta	364	460	79.1
1980	Denison	377	478	78.9
1981	Ripon	378	494	76.5
1982	Otterbein	458	589	77.8
1983	DePauw	368	475	77.5
1984	Redlands	426	534	79.8
1985	Wis.-Stevens Point	363	455	79.8
1986	Heidelberg	375	489	76.7
1987	Denison	442	560	78.9
1988	Capital	377	473	79.7
1989	Colby	464	585	79.3
1990	Colby	485	605	80.2
1991	Wartburg	565	711	79.5
1992	Thiel	393	491	80.0
1993	Colby	391	506	77.3
1994	Wheaton (Ill.)	455	572	79.5
1995	Baldwin-Wallace	454	582	78.0
1996	Anderson	454	592	76.7
1997	Ill. Wesleyan	616	790	78.0
1998	Wis.-Oshkosh	516	631	*81.8
1999	Carleton	423	540	78.3
2000	Ill. Wesleyan	426	543	78.5
2001	Franklin	570	713	79.9
2002	Moravian	407	512	79.5

*record

Rebound Margin

Season	Team	Off.	Def.	Mar.
1976	Bowie St.	54.0	37.5	16.5
1977	Husson	51.6	35.0	16.7
1978	Gallaudet	46.3	33.0	13.3
1979	St. Lawrence	43.2	28.7	14.5
1980	Elmira	41.4	28.7	12.7
1981	Clark (Mass.)	40.0	25.0	15.0
1982	Maryville (Mo.)	41.0	26.7	14.4
1983	Framingham St.	38.0	22.2	15.8
1984	New England Col.	43.3	29.3	14.0
1985	Bethel (Minn.)	45.0	32.2	12.8
1986	St. Joseph's (Me.)	43.7	29.5	14.2
1987	Elmira	40.6	29.3	11.3
1988	Cal St. San B'dino	46.6	29.7	16.9
1989	Yeshiva	49.8	34.6	15.2
1990	Bethel (Minn.)	42.2	30.3	12.0
1991	Hamilton	49.6	32.5	*17.0
1992	Bethel (Minn.)	42.3	31.0	11.3
1993	Eureka	33.9	22.2	11.7
1994	Maritime (N.Y.)	46.3	32.3	14.1
1995	Wittenberg	43.1	29.2	13.9
1996	Cabrini	47.9	34.7	13.1
1997	Rochester Inst.	42.8	31.9	10.8
1998	Chris. Newport	47.5	33.7	13.9
1999	Rensselaer	41.5	29.8	11.7
2000	Albright	41.3	29.6	11.7
2001	Wittenberg	44.7	30.7	14.0
2002	Wittenberg	42.5	30.1	12.4

*record

2002 Most-Improved Teams

School (Coach)	2002	2001	*Games Improved
1. Otterbein (Dick Reynolds)	30-3	13-12	13
2. Southern Vt. (Ryan Marks)	15-12	3-22	11
3. Clarkson (Tobin Anderson)	19-10	7-18	10
4. Colorado Col. (Mike McCubbin)	9-15	1-24	8½
4. Concordia (Wis.) (Pete Gnan)	16-12	6-19	8½
4. Johnson St. (Charles Mason)	14-11	5-19	8½
4. Sul Ross St. (Roger Grant)	12-13	3-21	8½
8. St. Norbert (Paul DeNoble)	21-5	11-11	8

School (Coach)	2002	2001	*Games Improved
9. Claremont-M-S (Ken Scalmanini)	21-5	13-12	7½
9. Plattsburgh St. (Ed Jones)	16-11	7-17	7½
9. Ramapo (Chuck McBreen)	21-8	11-13	7½
9. Rochester (Mike Neer)	24-6	14-11	7½
9. Rutgers-Camden (Jim Flynn)	14-11	6-18	7½

* To determine games improved, add the difference in victories between the two seasons to the difference in losses, then divide by two.

All-Time Winningest Teams

Includes records as a senior college only; minimum 10 seasons of competition. Postseason games are included.

Percentage

	Team	Yrs.	Won	Lost	Pct.
1.	Wittenberg	91	1,438	594	.708
2.	Cabrini	22	435	182	.705
3.	Colby-Sawyer	13	218	99	.688
4.	New Jersey City	67	735	354	.675
5.	St. Joseph's (Me.)	31	552	269	.672
6.	Calvin	82	1,106	541	.672
7.	Hope	96	1,257	644	.661
8.	Defiance	55	917	476	.658
9.	Wis.-Eau Claire	86	*1,206	634	.655
10.	Richard Stockton	30	520	275	.654
11.	Chris. Newport	35	600	318	.654
12.	Staten Island	25	453	243	.651
13.	Williams	101	1,174	647	.645
14.	Wooster	101	1,312	725	.644
15.	Roanoke	89	1,177	667	.638
16.	Ill. Wesleyan	92	1,331	764	.635
17.	St. Thomas (Minn.)	85	1,312	767	.631
18.	New York U.	84	1,058	631	.626
19.	Mass.-Dartmouth	36	582	354	.622
20.	St. John Fisher	39	585	364	.616
21.	Augsburg	43	672	420	.615
22.	Wartburg	66	967	607	.614
23.	Hartwick	72	930	588	.613
24.	Springfield	93	1,237	789	.611
25.	Colby	63	890	571	.609
26.	Beloit	95	1,083	704	.606
27.	Wis.-Stevens Point	103	1,145	747	.605
28.	Buffalo St.	73	935	622	.601
29.	Neb. Wesleyan	97	1,253	836	.600
30.	Augustana (Ill.)	97	1,179	787	.600

*Includes one tie.

Victories

	Team	Yrs.	Won	Lost	Pct.
1.	Wittenberg	91	1,438	594	.708
2.	Ill. Wesleyan	92	1,331	764	.635
3.	Wooster	101	1,312	725	.644
3.	St. Thomas (Minn.)	85	1,312	767	.631
5.	Hope	96	1,257	644	.661
6.	Neb. Wesleyan	97	1,253	836	.600
7.	Springfield	93	1,237	789	.611
8.	Wis.-Eau Claire	86	*1,206	634	.655
9.	Randolph-Macon	89	1,184	808	.594
9.	Scranton	85	1,184	810	.594
11.	Gust. Adolphus	91	1,180	850	.581
12.	Augustana (Ill.)	97	1,179	787	.600
13.	Roanoke	89	1,177	667	.638
14.	Williams	101	1,174	647	.645
15.	Wheaton (Ill.)	102	1,156	923	.556
16.	Wis.-Stevens Point	103	1,145	747	.605
17.	Willamette	78	1,127	852	.569
18.	Hamline	92	1,126	839	.573
19.	Muskingum	98	1,118	834	.573
20.	Loras	94	1,113	882	.558
21.	Calvin	82	1,106	541	.672
22.	Frank. & Marsh.	98	1,099	794	.581
23.	Mount Union	105	1,098	927	.542
24.	DePauw	96	**1,092	859	.560
25.	Capital	96	1,089	745	.594
26.	Albright	95	1,086	952	.533
27.	Beloit	95	1,083	704	.606
27.	Millikin	95	1,083	903	.545
29.	Rochester	101	1,082	819	.569
30.	Ohio Wesleyan	97	1,080	979	.525

*Includes one tie.   **Includes two ties.

All-Time Won-Lost Records

(No Minimum Seasons of Competition)

Team	First Year	Yrs.	Won	Lost	Pct.
Albion	1898	91	922	830	.526
Albright	1901	95	1086	952	.533
Alfred	1921	80	698	901	.437
Allegheny	1896	107	1000	842	.543
Alma	1911	91	834	929	.473
Alvernia	1976	27	421	324	.565
Amherst	1902	101	924	668	.580
Anderson (Ind.)	1931	71	855	845	.503
Augsburg	1960	43	672	420	.615
Augustana (Ill.)	1901	97	1179	787	.600
Aurora	1928	72	741	797	.482
Baldwin-Wallace	1907	95	966	977	.497
Beloit	1906	95	1083	704	.606
Benedictine (Ill.)	1966	36	499	413	.547
Bethany (W.Va.)	1905	94	719	1003	.418
Bethel (Minn.)	1947	56	621	669	.481
Bluffton	1915	87	724	1040	.410
Bridgewater St.	1907	97	733	784	.483
Bridgewater (Va.)	1903	81	743	898	.453
Brockport St.	1929	70	769	672	.534
Buffalo St.	1926	73	935	622	.601
Cabrini	1981	22	435	182	.705
Cal Lutheran	1962	41	489	616	.443
Caltech	1919	83	302	1123	.212
Calvin	1920	82	1106	541	.672
Capital	1907	96	1089	745	.594
Carleton	1909	93	1009	803	.557
Carnegie Mellon	1907	95	753	1144	.397
Carroll (Wis.)	1956	47	437	673	.394
Carthage	1907	94	897	1029	.466
Case Reserve	1902	101	1046	844	.553
Catholic	1910	91	1006	968	.510
Central (Iowa)	1924	79	834	820	.504
Chicago	1903	98	993	973	.505
Chris. Newport	1968	35	600	318	.654
CCNY	1905	97	948	903	.512
Claremont-M-S	1959	44	571	537	.515
Clarkson	1930	73	581	890	.395
Coast Guard	1926	77	643	838	.434
Colby	1938	63	890	571	.609
Colby-Sawyer	1991	12	218	99	.688
Colorado Col.	1915	88	725	942	.435
Concordia (Ill.)	1924	79	760	882	.463
Connecticut Col.	1970	33	348	323	.519
Cornell College	1910	93	848	892	.487
Cortland St.	1926	77	802	706	.532
Curry	1967	37	308	557	.356
Dallas	1917	29	170	416	.290
Defiance	1948	55	917	476	.658
Delaware Valley	1949	53	365	792	.315
DePauw	1904	96	1092	859	.560
DeSales	1969	34	367	457	.445
Dickinson	1900	92	797	904	.469
Drew	1930	71	533	836	.389
Dubuque	1915	88	813	888	.478
Eastern Conn. St.	1941	62	643	629	.506
East. Mennonite	1967	36	306	556	.355
Edgewood	1972	27	387	285	.576
Elizabethtown	1927	74	811	826	.495
Elmhurst	1925	78	672	929	.420
Elmira	1971	32	418	382	.523
Emory	1987	16	181	220	.451
Emory & Henry	1927	71	742	817	.476
Eureka	1920	81	913	801	.533
FDU-Madison	1959	44	491	508	.491
Franklin	1907	96	1027	896	.534
Frank. & Marsh.	1900	98	1099	794	.581
Fredonia St.	1935	64	627	722	.465
Frostburg St.	1936	60	653	698	.483
Gallaudet	1904	99	511	1251	.290
Geneseo St.	1915	84	713	756	.485
Gettysburg	1901	99	1044	948	.524
Goucher	1991	12	172	141	.550
Grove City	1898	98	1069	859	.554
Guilford	1906	88	779	940	.453

DIVISION III

Team	First Year	Yrs.	Won	Lost	Pct.
Gust. Adolphus	1904	91	1180	850	.581
Gwynedd-Mercy	1993	10	89	133	.401
Hamilton	1899	90	873	664	.568
Hamline	1910	92	1126	839	.573
Hampden-Sydney	1909	91	1074	838	.562
Hanover	1901	97	1003	860	.538
Hartwick	1928	72	930	588	.613
Heidelberg	1903	96	827	982	.457
Hobart	1902	92	627	955	.396
Hope	1901	96	1257	644	.661
Hunter	1953	48	591	541	.522
Ill. Wesleyan	1910	92	1331	764	.635
Ithaca	1930	72	884	635	.582
John Carroll	1920	81	803	841	.488
Johns Hopkins	1920	77	692	846	.450
Johnson & Wales	1996	7	56	124	.311
Juniata	1905	98	721	1077	.401
Kalamazoo	1907	95	1013	861	.541
Kean	1930	64	669	779	.462
Keene St.	1926	74	636	792	.445
King's (Pa.)	1947	56	717	626	.534
Knox	1909	93	844	824	.506
Lake Erie	1988	15	75	300	.200
Lakeland	1934	69	1011	775	.566
Lawrence	1904	99	741	913	.448
Lebanon Valley	1904	99	895	871	.507
Loras	1909	94	1113	882	.558
Luther	1905	98	553	438	.558
Lycoming	1949	54	579	631	.479
Lynchburg	1957	46	478	664	.419
Manhattanville	1976	27	359	347	.508
Marian (Wis.)	1973	30	405	355	.533
Marietta	1902	98	904	991	.477
Mary Washington	1975	28	273	427	.390
Marymount (Va.)	1988	15	181	209	.464
Maryville (Tenn.)	1903	99	1014	849	.544
Maryville (Mo.)	1977	26	284	394	.419
Mass.-Boston	1981	22	228	331	.408
Mass.-Dartmouth	1967	36	582	354	.622
McMurry	1923	77	896	861	.510
Merchant Marine	1946	57	579	751	.435
Messiah	1962	41	438	500	.467
Millikin	1904	95	1083	903	.545
Millsaps	1912	91	763	1097	.410
Mississippi Col.	1909	90	1000	843	.543
Monmouth (Ill.)	1900	102	1072	809	.570
Montclair St.	1928	73	922	738	.555
Moravian	1936	61	720	694	.509
Mount Union	1896	105	1098	927	.542
Muhlenberg	1901	95	1068	927	.535
Muskingum	1903	98	1118	834	.573
Nazareth	1978	25	376	265	.587
Neb. Wesleyan	1906	97	1253	836	.600
New Jersey City	1935	67	735	354	.675
New York U.	1906	84	1058	631	.626
Nichols	1959	44	382	614	.384
N.C. Wesleyan	1964	39	444	478	.482
North Central	1948	55	516	804	.391
North Park	1959	44	665	447	.598
Oberlin	1903	99	708	1005	.413
Occidental	1981	22	266	293	.476
Ohio Northern	1911	90	1061	808	.568
Ohio Wesleyan	1906	97	1080	979	.525
Otterbein	1903	99	1051	850	.553
Pacific (Ore.)	1911	92	789	1152	.406
Pacific Lutheran	1939	62	931	680	.578
Pitt.-Bradford	1980	23	304	305	.499
Plattsburgh St.	1926	73	599	605	.498

Team	First Year	Yrs.	Won	Lost	Pct.
Plymouth St.	1948	55	684	544	.557
Randolph-Macon	1910	89	1184	808	.594
Redlands	1917	85	916	786	.538
Rensselaer	1897	105	852	889	.489
Richard Stockton	1973	30	520	275	.654
Ripon	1898	104	1022	775	.569
Roanoke	1911	89	1177	667	.638
Rochester	1902	101	1082	819	.569
Rochester Inst.	1916	82	868	777	.528
Roger Williams	1973	29	217	327	.399
Rose-Hulman	1901	80	823	764	.519
Rowan	1923	60	818	579	.586
St. John Fisher	1964	39	585	364	.616
St. John's (Minn.)	1903	100	964	959	.501
St. Joseph's (Me.)	1972	31	552	269	.672
St. Mary's (Md.)	1967	36	393	517	.432
St. Norbert	1917	84	816	743	.523
St. Thomas (Minn.)	1905	98	1312	767	.631
Salisbury	1963	40	491	495	.498
Salve Regina	1975	28	255	345	.425
Scranton	1917	85	1184	810	.594
Sewanee	1927	76	648	823	.441
Shenandoah	1975	28	312	401	.438
Simpson	1901	100	1023	974	.512
Southern Me.	1923	85	766	632	.548
Springfield	1906	93	1237	789	.611
Staten Island	1978	25	453	243	.651
Stevens Tech	1917	86	649	725	.472
Susquehanna	1902	100	827	993	.454
Swarthmore	1902	101	727	1065	.406
Thiel	1917	85	495	1061	.318
Trinity (Conn.)	1914	89	892	692	.563
Tufts	1912	91	930	851	.522
Upper Iowa	1916	87	786	855	.479
Wabash	1897	106	1046	922	.532
Wartburg	1936	66	967	607	.614
Washington (Md.)	1914	90	950	861	.525
Washington (Mo.)	1905	96	947	840	.530
Wash. & Jeff.	1913	90	851	777	.523
Wash. & Lee	1907	84	1002	958	.511
Wentworth Inst.	1984	18	169	281	.376
Wesleyan (Conn.)	1902	101	927	831	.527
Western Conn. St.	1947	56	619	610	.504
Western Md.	1922	80	651	1039	.385
Western New Eng.	1966	34	435	458	.487
Westfield St.	1951	52	567	615	.480
Westminster (Mo.)	1909	87	850	937	.476
Wheaton (Ill.)	1901	102	1156	923	.556
Wheaton (Mass.)	1989	14	156	175	.471
Widener	1906	94	1001	747	.573
Wilkes	1947	56	662	645	.507
Willamette	1925	78	1127	852	.569
Wm. Paterson	1939	61	770	705	.522
Williams	1901	101	1174	647	.645
Wilmington (Ohio)	1917	85	756	1015	.427
Wis.-Eau Claire	1917	86	1206	634	.655
Wis.-Oshkosh	1899	104	988	887	.527
Wis.-Platteville	1905	91	1060	720	.596
Wis.-Stevens Point	1897	103	1145	747	.605
Wis.-Stout	1907	96	843	905	.482
Wis.-Whitewater	1902	92	960	792	.548
Wittenberg	1912	91	1438	594	.708
Wooster	1901	101	1312	725	.644
Worcester St.	1950	52	576	617	.483
Worcester Tech	1903	92	754	900	.456
Yeshiva	1936	66	584	719	.448
York (Pa.)	1970	33	378	459	.452

*Includes one tie. **Includes two ties.

Individual Collegiate Records

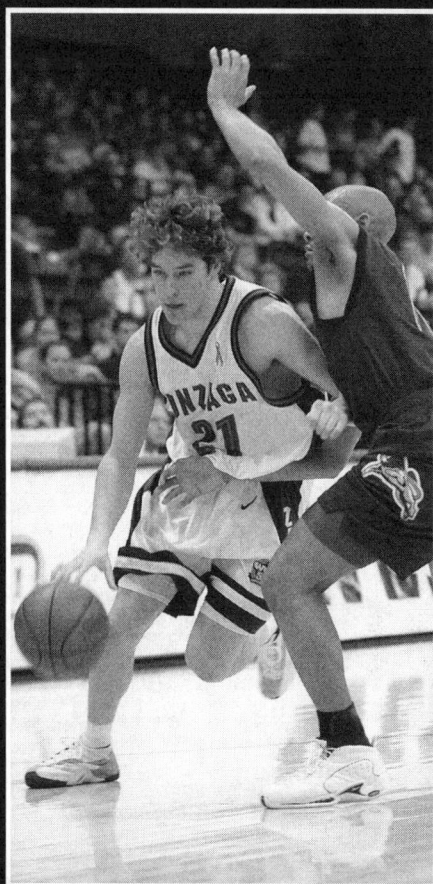

Individual Collegiate Records

Individual collegiate leaders are determined by comparing the best records in all three divisions in equivalent categories. Included are players whose careers were split between two divisions (e.g., Dwight Lamar of Louisiana-Lafayette or Howard Shockley of Salisbury).

Single-Game Records

POINTS

Pts.	Div.	Player, Team vs. Opponent	Date
113	II	Clarence "Bevo" Francis, Rio Grande vs. Hillsdale	Feb. 2, 1954
100	I	Frank Selvy, Furman vs. Newberry	Feb. 13, 1954
85	I	Paul Arizin, Villanova vs. Philadelphia NAMC	Feb. 12, 1949
84	II	Clarence "Bevo" Francis, Rio Grande vs. Alliance	1954
82	II	Clarence "Bevo" Francis, Rio Grande vs. Bluffton	1954
81	I	Freeman Williams, Portland St. vs. Rocky Mountain	Feb. 3, 1978
80	II	Paul Crissman, Southern Cal Col. vs. Pacific Christian	Feb. 18, 1966
77	III	Jeff Clement, Grinnell vs. Illinois Col.	Feb. 18, 1998
77	II	William English, Winston-Salem vs. Fayetteville St.	Feb. 19, 1968
75	II	Travis Grant, Kentucky St. vs. Northwood	1970
73	I	Bill Mlkvy, Temple vs. Wilkes	Mar. 3, 1951
72	II	Nate DeLong, Wis.-River Falls vs. Winona St.	Feb. 24, 1948
72	II	Lloyd Brown, Aquinas vs. Cleary	1953
72	II	Clarence "Bevo" Francis, Rio Grande vs. Calif. (Pa.)	1953
72	II	John McElroy, Youngstown St. vs. Wayne St. (Mich.)	Feb. 26, 1969
72	I	Kevin Bradshaw, U.S. Int'l vs. Loyola Marymount	Jan. 5, 1991
71	II	Clayborn Jones, L.A. Pacific vs. L.A. Baptist	Jan. 30, 1965
71	I	Freeman Williams, Portland St. vs. Southern Ore.	Feb. 9, 1977
70	II	Paul Wilcox, Davis & Elkins vs. Glenville St.	1959
70	II	Bo Clark, UCF vs. Fla. Memorial	Jan. 31, 1977
69	II	Clarence "Bevo" Francis, Rio Grande vs. Wilberforce	1953
69	II	Clarence Burks, St. Augustine's vs. St. Paul's	1955
69	I	Pete Maravich, LSU vs. Alabama	Feb. 7, 1970
69	II	John Rinka, Kenyon vs. Wooster	Dec. 9, 1969
69	III	Steve Diekmann, Grinnell vs. Simpson	Nov. 19, 1994
68	II	Florindo Vieira, Quinnipiac vs. Brooklyn Poly	Feb. 13, 1957
68	II	Wayne Proffitt, Lynchburg vs. Charlotte	Feb. 5, 1966
68	II	Earl Monroe, Winston-Salem vs. Fayetteville St.	Jan. 6, 1967
68	I	Calvin Murphy, Niagara vs. Syracuse	Dec. 7, 1968

Photo by Justin Kase Conder/Fresno State Sports Information

Fresno State's Larry Abney is the only player to grab more than 30 rebounds in a game this century.

FIELD-GOAL PERCENTAGE
(Minimum 13 field goals made)

Pct.	Div.	Player, Team vs. Opponent (FG-FGA)	Date
100	II	Lance Berwald, North Dakota St. vs. Augustana (S.D.) (20 of 20)	Feb. 17, 1984
100	III	Jason Light, Emory & Henry vs. King (Tenn.) (18 of 18)	Dec. 2, 1995
100	I	Clifford Rozier, Louisville vs. Eastern Ky. (15 of 15)	Dec. 11, 1993
100	II	Derrick Scott, Calif. (Pa.) vs. Columbia Union (14 of 14)	Dec. 6, 1995
100	I	Dan Henderson, Arkansas St. vs. Ga. Southern (14 of 14)	Feb. 26, 1976
100	I	Cornelius Holden, Louisville vs. Southern Miss. (14 of 14)	Mar. 3, 1990
100	I	Dana Jones, Pepperdine vs. Boise St. (14 of 14)	Nov. 30, 1991
100	III	Waverly Yates, Clark (Mass.) vs. Suffolk (14 of 14)	Feb. 10, 1993
100	II	Derrick Freeman, Indiana (Pa.) vs. Clarion (13 of 13)	Feb. 17, 1996
100	I	Ben Handlogten, Western Mich. vs. Toledo (13 of 13)	Jan. 27, 1996
100	II	Ralfs Jansons, St. Rose vs. Concordia (N.Y.) (13 of 13)	Jan. 13, 1996
100	I	Ted Guzek, Butler vs. Michigan (13 of 13)	Dec. 15, 1956
100	I	Rick Dean, Syracuse vs. Colgate (13 of 13)	Feb. 14, 1966
100	I	Gary Lechman, Gonzaga vs. Portland St. (13 of 13)	Jan. 21, 1967
100	I	Kevin King, Charlotte vs. South Ala. (13 of 13)	Feb. 20, 1978
100	I	Vernon Smith, Texas A&M vs. Alas. Anchorage (13 of 13)	Nov. 26, 1978
100	I	Steve Johnson, Oregon St. vs. Hawaii-Hilo (13 of 13)	Dec. 5, 1979
100	I	Antoine Carr, Wichita St. vs. Abilene Christian (13 of 13)	Nov. 28, 1980
100	III	Rich Lengieza, Nichols vs. Mass.-Dartmouth (13 of 13)	Feb. 22, 1981
100	I	Doug Hashley, Montana St. vs. Idaho St. (13 of 13)	Feb. 5, 1982
100	I	Brad Daugherty, North Carolina vs. UCLA (13 of 13)	Nov. 24, 1985
100	III	Bruce Merklinger, Susquehanna vs. Drew (13 of 13)	Jan. 22, 1986
100	III	Antonio Randolph, Averett vs. Methodist (13 of 13)	Jan. 26, 1991
100	III	Pat Holland, Randolph-Macon vs. East. Mennonite (13 of 13)	Feb. 9, 1991
100	I	Ricky Butler, UC Irvine vs. Cal St. Fullerton (13 of 13)	Feb. 21, 1991
100	I	Rafael Solis, Brooklyn vs. Wagner (13 of 13)	Dec. 11, 1991
100	III	Todd Seifferlein, DePauw vs. Franklin (13 of 13)	Jan. 18, 1992
100	II	Mate Milisa, Long Beach St. vs. Cal St. Monterey (13 of 13)	Dec. 22, 1999
100	I	Nathan Blessen, South Dakota vs. Neb.-Omaha (13 of 13)	Jan. 9, 2000

THREE-POINT FIELD GOALS MADE

3FG	Div.	Player, Team vs. Opponent	Date
19	III	Jeff Clement, Grinnell vs. Illinois Col.	Feb. 18, 1998
17	III	Jeff Clement, Grinnell vs. Clarke	Dec. 3, 1997
16	II	Markus Hallgrimson, Mont. St.-Billings vs. Western N.M.	Feb. 9, 2000
16	III	Jeff Clement, Grinnell vs. Lawrence	Feb. 21, 1998
16	III	Jeff Clement, Grinnell vs. Monmouth (Ill.)	Feb. 8, 1997
15	I	Keith Veney, Marshall vs. Morehead St.	Dec. 14, 1996
14	I	Ronald Blackshear, Marshall vs. Akron	Mar. 1, 2002
14	II	Antonio Harris, LeMoyne-Owen vs. Savannah St.	Feb. 6, 1999
14	III	Ed Brands, Grinnell vs. Ripon	Feb. 24, 1996
14	I	Dave Jamerson, Ohio vs. Col. of Charleston	Dec. 21, 1989
14	I	Askia Jones, Kansas St. vs. Fresno St.	Mar. 24, 1994
14	II	Andy Schmidtmann, Wis.-Parkside vs. Lakeland	Feb. 14, 1989
14	II	Steve Diekmann, Grinnell vs. Illinois Col.	Feb. 18, 1994
14	III	Steve Diekmann, Grinnell vs. Simpson	Nov. 19, 1994
13	II	Markus Hallgrimson, Mont. St.-Billings vs. Western N.M.	Feb. 26, 2000
13	II	Markus Hallgrimson, Mont. St.-Billings vs. Chaminade	Feb. 5, 2000
13	II	Rodney Thomas, IUPUI vs. Wilberforce	Feb. 24, 1997
13	II	Danny Lewis, Wayne St. (Mich.) vs. Michigan Tech	Feb. 20, 1993
13	III	Eric Ochel, Sewanee vs. Emory	Feb. 22, 1995

REBOUNDS

Reb.	Div.	Player, Team vs. Opponent	Date
51	I	Bill Chambers, William & Mary vs. Virginia	Feb. 14, 1953
46	II	Tom Hart, Middlebury vs. Trinity (Conn.)	Feb. 5, 1955
46	II	Tom Hart, Middlebury vs. Clarkson	Feb. 12, 1955
45	II	William Henrikson, Windham vs. New England Col.	Feb. 4, 1970
44	II	Charles McCullough, Loyola (Md.) vs. McDaniel	Feb. 17, 1955
44	II	Norman Rokeach, Long Island vs. Brooklyn Poly	Dec. 28, 1963
43	I	Charlie Slack, Marshall vs. Morris Harvey	Jan. 12, 1954
43	II	Bob Bessoir, Scranton vs. King's (Pa.)	Mar. 5, 1955
42	I	Tom Heinsohn, Holy Cross vs. Boston College	Mar. 1, 1955
42	II	Larry Gooding, St. Augustine's vs. Shaw	Jan. 12, 1974
41	II	Richard Kross, American Int'l vs. Springfield	Feb. 19, 1958
40	II	Ellerbe Neal, Wofford vs. Presbyterian	Jan. 3, 1953
40	I	Art Quimby, Connecticut vs. Boston U.	Jan. 11, 1955
40	II	Donnie Fowler, Wofford vs. Mercer	Jan. 22, 1955
40	II	Charlie Harrison, N.C. A&T vs. Johnson Smith	Feb. 8, 1958

Reb.	Div.	Player, Team vs. Opponent	Date
40	II	Anthony Romano, Willimantic St. vs. Fitchburg St.	Jan. 5, 1963
40	II	Ed Halicki, Monmouth vs. Southeastern	Dec. 4, 1970
39	II	Maurice Stokes, St. Francis (Pa.) vs. John Carroll	Jan. 28, 1955
39	II	Roger Lotchin, Millikin vs. Lake Forest	Feb. 11, 1956
39	II	Joe Cole, Southwest Tex. St. vs. Tex. Lutheran	Dec. 10, 1956
39	I	Dave DeBusschere, Detroit vs. Central Mich.	Jan. 30, 1960
39	I	Keith Swagerty, Pacific (Cal.) vs. UC Santa Barb.	Mar. 5, 1965
39	II	Curtis Pritchett, St. Augustine vs. St. Paul's	Jan. 24, 1970
38		14 tied	

(Since 1973)

Reb.	Div.	Player, Team vs. Opponent	Date
42	II	Larry Gooding, St. Augustine's vs. Shaw	Jan. 12, 1974
36	III	Mark Veenstra, Calvin vs. Southern Colo.	Feb. 3, 1976
36	III	Clinton Montford, Methodist vs. Warren Wilson	Jan. 21, 1989
35	I	Larry Abney, Fresno St. vs. Southern Methodist	Feb. 17, 2000
35	III	Ayal Hod, Yeshiva vs. Vassar	Feb. 22, 1989
34	I	David Vaughn, Oral Roberts vs. Brandeis	Jan. 8, 1973
34	II	Major Jones, Albany St. (Ga.) vs. Valdosta St.	Jan. 23, 1975
34	II	Herman Harris, Mississippi Val. vs. Texas Southern	Jan. 12, 1976
34	III	Walt Edwards, Husson vs. Me.-Farmington	Feb. 24, 1976
33	II	Joe Dombrowski, St. Anselm vs. New Hampshire	Dec. 8, 1974
33	II	Lee Roy Williams, Cal Poly Pomona vs. Wheaton (Ill.)	Dec. 15, 1973
33	III	Willie Parr, LeMoyne-Owen vs. Southern U.	Jan. 10, 1976
33	III	Larry Williams, Pratt vs. Mercy	Jan. 22, 1977
32	II	Marvin Webster, Morgan St. vs. South Carolina St.	Dec. 8, 1973
32	II	Earl Williams, Winston-Salem vs. N.C. Central	Dec. 13, 1973
32	III	Fred Petty, New Hamp. College vs. Curry	Jan. 28, 1974
32	II	George Wilson, Union (Ky.) vs. Southwestern	1974
32	II	Tony DuCros, Regis vs. Neb. Wesleyan	Feb. 28, 1975
32	I	Durand Macklin, LSU vs. Tulane	Nov. 26, 1976
32	II	Robert Clements, Jacksonville vs. Shorter	Jan. 12, 1977
32	I	Jervaughn Scales, Southern U. vs. Grambling St.	Feb. 7, 1994
31	I	Pete Harris, Stephen F. Austin vs. Texas A&M	Jan. 22, 1973
31	I	Jim Bradley, Northern Ill. vs. Wis.-Milwaukee	Feb. 19, 1973
31	III	John Humphrie, Swarthmore vs. Ursinus	Dec. 8, 1973
31	II	Roy Smith, Kentucky St. vs. Union (Ky.)	Feb. 10, 1975
31	I	Larry Parker, Plattsburgh St. vs. Clarkson	Jan. 19, 1976
31	I	Calvin Natt, Northeast La. vs. Ga. Southern	Dec. 29, 1976
31	II	Charles Wode, Mississippi Val. vs. Miss. Industrial	Dec. 10, 1977
31	III	Jon Ford, Norwich vs. Johnson St.	Feb. 16, 1982

ASSISTS

Ast.	Div.	Player, Team vs. Opponent	Date
26	III	Robert James, Kean vs. N.J. Inst. of Tech.	Mar. 11, 1989
25	II	Ali Baqqar, Morris Brown vs. Albany St. (Ga.)	Jan. 26, 1991
25	II	Adrian Hutt, Metro St. vs. Sacramento St.	Feb. 9, 1991
24	II	Steve Ray, Bridgeport vs. Sacred Heart	Jan. 25, 1989
24	II	Steve Ray, Bridgeport vs. New Haven	Feb. 8, 1989
24	III	Adam Dzierzynski, Chapman vs. Amer. Indian Bible	Feb. 9, 1995
23	II	Todd Chappell, Texas Wesleyan vs. Texas Lutheran	Feb. 12, 2000
23	II	Steve Ray, Bridgeport vs. St. Anselm	Nov. 26, 1989
23	II	Jeff Duvall, Oakland City vs. St. Meinrad	Dec. 3, 1991
22	I	Tony Fairley, Charleston So. vs. Armstrong Atlantic	Feb. 9, 1987
22	I	Avery Johnson, Southern U. vs. Texas Southern	Jan. 25, 1988
22	I	Sherman Douglas, Syracuse vs. Providence	Jan. 28, 1989
22	II	Antonio Whitley, St. Augustine's vs. Shaw	Feb. 1, 1992
22	II	Ernest Jenkins, N.M. Highlands vs. Panhandle St.	Jan. 29, 1994
21	I	Mark Wade, UNLV vs. Navy	Dec. 29, 1986
21	I	Kelvin Scarborough, New Mexico vs. Hawaii	Feb. 13, 1987
21	I	Anthony Manuel, Bradley vs. UC Irvine	Dec. 19, 1987
21	I	Avery Johnson, Southern U. vs. Alabama St.	Jan. 16, 1988
21	III	Ron Torgalski, Hamilton vs. Vassar	Jan. 28, 1989
21	III	Mark Cottom, Ferrum vs. Concord	Dec. 15, 1990
21	II	Candice Pickens, Calif. (Pa.) vs. Slippery Rock	Feb. 8, 1995

BLOCKED SHOTS

Blk.	Div.	Player, Team vs. Opponent	Date
16	III	Tory Black, N.J. Inst. of Tech. vs. Polytechnic (N.Y.)	Feb. 5, 1997
15	III	Johnny Woods, Wesley vs. Salisbury	Feb. 14, 2000
15	III	Antoine Hyman, Keuka vs. Hobart	Feb. 21, 1996
15	III	Erick Lidecis, Maritime (N.Y.) vs. Stevens Tech	Nov. 30, 1993
15	II	Mark Hensel, Pitt.-Johnstown vs. Slippery Rock	Jan. 22, 1994
15	III	Roy Woods, Fontbonne vs. MacMurray	Jan. 26, 1995
15	III	Ira Nicholson, Mt. St. Vincent vs. Stevens Tech	Nov. 27, 1994
14	III	Johnny Woods, Wesley vs. Eastern	Jan. 17, 2001
14	III	Neil Edwards, York (N.Y.) vs. Lehman	Feb. 12, 2000
14	I	Loren Woods, Arizona vs. Oregon	Feb. 3, 2000
14	I	Roy Rogers, Alabama vs. Georgia	Feb. 10, 1996
14	II	Victorlus Payne, Lane vs. Talladega	Jan. 26, 1996
14	I	David Robinson, Navy vs. UNC Wilmington	Jan. 4, 1986
14	I	Shawn Bradley, Brigham Young vs. Eastern Ky.	Dec. 7, 1990
14	II	Maurice Barnett, Elizabeth City St. vs. Bowie St.	Feb. 3, 1994
14	III	Andrew South, N.J. Inst. of Tech. vs. Stevens Tech	Feb. 14, 1994

Blk.	Div.	Player, Team vs. Opponent	Date
13	I	Wojciech Myrda, La.-Monroe vs. Texas-San Antonio	Jan. 17, 2002
13	I	Kyle Davis, Auburn vs. Miami (Fla.)	Mar. 14, 2001
13	I	D'or Fischer, Northwestern St. vs. Southwest Tex. St.	Jan. 22, 2001
13	III	Neil Edwards, York (N.Y.) vs. Brooklyn	Feb. 22, 2000
13	III	Antoine Hyman, Keuka vs. Hobart	Jan. 8, 1997
13	III	Damon Avinger, CCNY vs. St. Joseph's (N.Y.)	Jan. 7, 1996
13	I	Kevin Roberson, Vermont vs. New Hampshire	Jan. 9, 1992
13	I	Jim McIlvaine, Marquette vs. Northeastern Ill.	Dec. 9, 1992
13	II	Mark Hensel, Pitt.-Johnstown vs. Wheeling Jesuit	Jan. 31, 1994
13	I	Keith Closs, Central Conn. St. vs. St. Francis (Pa.)	Dec. 21, 1994

STEALS

Stl.	Div.	Player, Team vs. Opponent	Date
17	II	Antonio Walls, Alabama A&M vs. Albany St. (Ga.)	Jan. 5, 1998
17	II	Matt Newton, Principia vs. Harris-Stowe	Jan. 4, 1994
14	III	Moses Jean-Pierre, Plymouth St. vs. Rivier	Dec. 7, 1993
13	III	Daniel Martinez, McMurry vs. Concordia (Tex.)	Feb. 3, 2000
13	III	Todd Lange, Pomona-Pitzer vs. LaSierra	Jan. 7, 1999
13	III	John Gallogly, Salve Regina vs. Roger Williams	Feb. 10, 1997
13	I	Mookie Blaylock, Oklahoma vs. Centenary (La.)	Dec. 12, 1987
13	I	Mookie Blaylock, Oklahoma vs. Loyola Marymount	Dec. 17, 1988
12	I	Jehiel Lewis, Navy vs. Bucknell	Jan. 12, 2002
12	I	Greedy Daniels, TCU vs. Ark.-Pine Bluff	Dec. 30, 2000
12	II	Terrence Baxter, Pfeiffer vs. Livingstone	Nov. 22, 2000
12	III	Greg Brown, Albertus Magnus vs. Rivier	Feb. 3, 2000
12	III	Daniel Martinez, McMurry vs. Ozarks (Ark.)	Dec. 2, 1999
12	I	Richard Duncan, Middle Tenn. vs. Eastern Ky.	Feb. 20, 1999
12	II	Derrick Brown, Davis & Elkins vs. Ohio Valley	Feb. 9, 1999
12	II	Marche' Bearad, Ark.-Monticello vs. Christian Bros.	Feb. 8, 1999
12	II	Freddy Conyers, Mass.-Boston vs. Westfield St.	Dec. 10, 1998
12	III	Mario Thompson, Occidental vs. LIFE Bible	Nov. 21, 1998
12	III	Deron Black, Allegheny vs. Case Reserve	Jan. 17, 1996
12	III	Jamal Elliott, Haverford vs. Gwynedd Mercy	Jan. 15, 1996
12	I	Kenny Robertson, Cleveland St. vs. Wagner	Dec. 3, 1988
12	III	Moses Jean-Pierre, Plymouth St. vs. Rhode Island Col.	Jan. 23, 1993
12	I	Terry Evans, Oklahoma vs. Florida A&M	Jan. 27, 1993
12	III	David Brown, Westfield St. vs. Albertus Magnus	Jan. 8, 1994
12	III	Barry Aranoff, Yeshiva vs. Purchase St.	Feb. 13, 1995

Season Records

(Based on qualifiers for annual statistical championship)

POINTS

Player, Team (Division)	Season	G	FG	3FG	FT	Pts.
Pete Maravich, LSU (I)	1970	31	522	—	337	1,381
Earl Monroe, Winston-Salem (II)	1967	32	509	—	311	1,329
Travis Grant, Kentucky St. (II)	1972	33	539	—	226	1,304
Clarence "Bevo" Francis, Rio Grande (II)	1954	27	444	—	367	1,255
Bill Reigel, McNeese St. (II)	1956	36	425	—	370	1,220
Elvin Hayes, Houston (I)	1968	33	519	—	176	1,214
Frank Selvy, Furman (I)	1954	29	427	—	355	1,209
Pete Maravich, LSU (I)	1969	26	433	—	282	1,148
Pete Maravich, LSU (I)	1968	26	432	—	274	1,138
Bo Kimble, Loyola Marymount (I)	1990	32	404	92	231	1,131
Hersey Hawkins, Bradley (I)	1988	31	377	87	284	1,125
Austin Carr, Notre Dame (I)	1970	29	444	—	218	1,106
Austin Carr, Notre Dame (I)	1971	29	430	—	241	1,101
Otis Birdsong, Houston (I)	1977	36	452	—	186	1,090
Dwight Lamar, La.-Lafayette (I)	1972	29	429	—	196	1,054
Kevin Bradshaw, U.S. Int'l (I)	1991	28	358	60	278	1,054
Dwight Lamar, La.-Lafayette (II)	1971	29	424	—	196	1,044
Greg Grant, Col. of New Jersey (III)	1989	32	387	76	194	1,044
Dave Russell, Shepherd (II)	1975	32	394	—	249	1,037
Glenn Robinson, Purdue (I)	1994	34	368	79	215	1,030
Oscar Robertson, Cincinnati (I)	1958	28	352	—	280	984
Oscar Robertson, Cincinnati (I)	1959	30	331	—	316	978
Rick Barry, Miami (Fla.) (I)	1965	26	340	—	221	973
Larry Bird, Indiana St. (I)	1979	34	376	—	221	973
Dennis Scott, Georgia Tech (I)	1990	35	336	137	161	970

SCORING AVERAGE

Player, Team (Division)	Season	G	FG	3FG	FT	Pts.	Avg.
Clarence "Bevo" Francis, Rio Grande (II)	1954	27	444	—	367	1,255	46.5
Pete Maravich, LSU (I)	1970	31	522	—	337	1,381	44.5
Pete Maravich, LSU (I)	1969	26	433	—	282	1,148	44.2
Pete Maravich, LSU (I)	1968	26	432	—	274	1,138	43.8
Earl Glass, Miss. Industrial (II)	1963	19	322	—	171	815	42.9
Frank Selvy, Furman (I)	1954	29	427	—	355	1,209	41.7
Earl Monroe, Winston-Salem (II)	1967	32	509	—	311	1,329	41.5
John Rinka, Kenyon (II)	1970	23	354	—	234	942	41.0

Player, Team (Division)	Season	G	FG	3FG	FT	Pts.	Avg.
Willie Shaw, Lane (II)	1964	18	303	—	121	727	40.4
Johnny Neumann, Mississippi (I)	1971	23	366	—	191	923	40.1
Travis Grant, Kentucky St. (II)	1972	33	539	—	226	1,304	39.5
Thales McReynolds, Miles (II)	1965	18	294	—	118	706	39.2
Bob Johnson, Fitchburg St. (II)	1963	18	213	—	277	703	39.1
Roger Kuss, Wis.-River Falls (II)	1953	21	291	—	235	817	38.9
Freeman Williams, Portland St. (I)	1977	26	417	—	176	1,010	38.8
Billy McGill, Utah (I)	1962	26	394	—	221	1,009	38.8
Calvin Murphy, Niagara (I)	1968	24	337	—	242	916	38.2
Austin Carr, Notre Dame (I)	1970	29	444	—	218	1,106	38.1
Austin Carr, Notre Dame (I)	1971	29	430	—	241	1,101	38.0
Kevin Bradshaw, U.S. Int'l (I)	1991	28	358	60	278	1,054	37.6
Rick Barry, Miami (Fla.) (I)	1965	26	340	—	221	973	37.4
Steve Diekmann, Grinnell (III)	1995	20	223	137	162	745	37.3
Florindo Vieira, Quinnipiac (II)	1954	14	191	—	138	520	37.1
Elvin Hayes, Houston (I)	1968	33	519	—	176	1,214	36.8
Marshall Rogers, Tex.-Pan American (I)	1976	25	361	—	197	919	36.8

FIELD-GOAL PERCENTAGE

Player, Team (Division)	Season	G	FG	FGA	Pct.
Travis Weiss, St. John's (Minn.) (III)	1994	26	160	209	76.6
Pete Metzelaars, Wabash (III)	1982	28	271	360	75.3
Todd Linder, Tampa (II)	1987	32	282	375	75.2
Maurice Stafford, North Ala. (II)	1984	34	198	264	75.0
Tony Rychlec, Mass. Maritime (III)	1981	25	233	311	74.9
Matthew Cornegay, Tuskegee (II)	1982	29	208	278	74.8
Steve Johnson, Oregon St. (I)	1981	28	235	315	74.6
Brian Moten, West Ga. (II)	1992	26	141	192	73.4
Ed Phillips, Alabama A&M (II)	1968	22	154	210	73.3
Tony Rychlec, Mass. Maritime (III)	1982	20	193	264	73.1
Russ Newman, Menlo (III)	1991	26	130	178	73.0
Ed Owens, Hampden-Sydney (III)	1979	24	140	192	72.9
Ray Strozier, Central Mo. St. (II)	1980	28	142	195	72.8
Harold Booker, Cheyney (II)	1965	24	144	198	72.7
Chad Scott, Calif. (Pa.) (II)	1994	30	178	245	72.7
Scott Baxter, Capital (III)	1991	26	164	226	72.6
Maurice Woods, Potsdam St. (III)	1982	30	203	280	72.5
Tom Schurfranz, Bellarmine (II)	1991	30	245	339	72.3
Marv Lewis, Southampton (II)	1969	24	271	375	72.3
Earl Keith, Stony Brook (III)	1979	24	164	227	72.2
Louis Newsome, North Ala. (II)	1988	29	192	266	72.2
Pete Metzelaars, Wabash (III)	1981	25	204	283	72.1
Ed Phillips, Alabama A&M (II)	1971	24	159	221	71.9
Jon Rosner, Yeshiva (III)	1991	22	141	196	71.9
Gregg Northington, Alabama St. (II)	1971	26	324	451	71.8
Pete Metzelaars, Wabash (III)	1979	24	122	170	71.8

THREE-POINT FIELD GOALS MADE

Player, Team (Division)	Season	G	3FG
Jeff Clement, Grinnell (III)	1998	22	186
Alex Williams, Sacramento St. (II)	1988	30	167
Jeff Clement, Grinnell (III)	1999	22	166
Markus Hallgrimson, Mont. St.-Billings (II)	2000	26	160
Ed Brands, Grinnell (III)	1996	24	158
Darrin Fitzgerald, Butler (I)	1987	28	158
Freddie Banks, UNLV (I)	1987	39	152
Eric Kline, Northern St. (II)	1994	33	148
Eric Kline, Northern St. (II)	1995	30	148
Randy Rutherford, Oklahoma St. (I)	1995	37	146
Chris Peterson, Eureka (III)	1994	31	145
Shawn Pughsley, Central Okla. (II)	1998	32	139
Dennis Scott, Georgia Tech (I)	1990	35	137
Steve Diekmann, Grinnell (III)	1995	20	137
Steve Nordlund, Grinnell (III)	2002	24	137
Rashad Phillips, Detroit (I)	2001	35	136
Reece Gliko, Mont. St.-Billings (II)	1997	28	135
Ray Gutierrez, Calif. (Pa.) (II)	1993	27	135
Jason Garrow, Augustana (S.D.) (II)	1992	27	135
Troy Hudson, Southern Ill. (I)	1997	30	134
Markus Hallgrimson, Mont. St.-Billings (II)	1999	28	133
Chris Jans, Loras (III)	1991	25	133
Jason Williams, Duke (I)	2001	39	132
Timothy Pollard, Mississippi Val. (I)	1988	28	132
Dave Jamerson, Ohio (I)	1990	28	131
Sydney Grider, La.-Lafayette (I)	1990	29	131

THREE-POINT FIELD GOALS MADE PER GAME

Player, Team (Division)	Season	G	3FG	Avg.
Jeff Clement, Grinnell (III)	1998	22	186	8.45
Jeff Clement, Grinnell (III)	1999	22	166	7.55
Steve Diekmann, Grinnell (III)	1995	20	137	6.85

Player, Team (Division)	Season	G	3FG	Avg.
Ed Brands, Grinnell (III)	1996	24	158	6.58
Ed Brands, Grinnell (III)	1995	20	129	6.45
Markus Hallgrimson, Mont. St.-Billings (II)	2000	26	160	6.15
Steve Nordlund, Grinnell (III)	2002	24	137	5.71
Darrin Fitzgerald, Butler (I)	1987	28	158	5.64
Steve Diekmann, Grinnell (III)	1994	21	117	5.57
Alex Williams, Sacramento St. (II)	1988	30	167	5.57
Chris Jans, Loras (III)	1991	25	133	5.32
Woody Piirto, Grinnell (III)	1999	22	117	5.32
Jeff Clement, Grinnell (III)	1997	22	113	5.14
Mark Bedell, Fisk (III)	1997	19	97	5.11
Jason Garrow, Augustana (S.D.) (II)	1992	27	135	5.00
David Bailey, Concordia (Ill.) (III)	1994	24	120	5.00
Eric Kline, Northern St. (II)	1995	30	148	4.93
Ray Gutierrez, Calif. (Pa.) (II)	1993	29	142	4.90
Steve Brown, West Ala. (II)	2000	26	126	4.85
Antonio Harris, LeMoyne-Owen (II)	1999	26	126	4.85
Kwame Morton, Clarion (II)	1994	26	126	4.85
Reece Gliko, Mont. St.-Billings (II)	1997	28	135	4.82
Markus Hallgrimson, Mont. St.-Billings (II)	1999	28	133	4.75
John Boyd, LeMoyne-Owen (II)	1992	26	123	4.73
Duane Huddleston, Mo.-Rolla (II)	1988	25	118	4.72

THREE-POINT FIELD-GOAL PERCENTAGE

Player, Team (Division)	Season	G	3FG	3FGA	Pct.
Reggie James, N.J. Inst. of Tech (III)	1989	29	59	88	67.0
Ray Lee, Hampton (II)	1988	24	39	60	65.0
Glenn Tropf, Holy Cross (I)	1988	29	52	82	63.4
Sean Wightman, Western Mich. (I)	1992	30	48	76	63.2
Chris Miles, N.J. Inst. of Tech (III)	1987	26	41	65	63.1
Steve Hood, Winston-Salem (II)	1988	28	42	67	62.7
Chris Miles, N.J. Inst. of Tech (III)	1989	29	46	75	61.3
Matt Miota, Lawrence (III)	1990	22	33	54	61.1
Mike Bachman, Alma (III)	1991	26	46	76	60.5
Mark Wiley, Fort Hays St. (II)	1990	29	49	81	60.5
Aaron Fehler, Oakland City (II)	1995	26	73	121	60.3
Keith Jennings, East Tenn. St. (I)	1991	33	84	142	59.2
Aaron Baker, Mississippi Col. (II)	1989	27	69	117	59.0
Dave Calloway, Monmouth (I)	1989	28	48	82	58.5
Walter Hurd, Johnson Smith (II)	1989	27	49	84	58.3
Matt Hopson, Oakland City (II)	1996	31	84	145	57.9
Ray Magee, Richard Stockton (III)	1988	26	41	71	57.7
Keith Orchard, Whitman (III)	1988	26	42	73	57.5
Jon Bryant, St. Cloud St. (II)	1996	27	54	94	57.4
Adam Harness, Oakland City (II)	1997	26	39	68	57.4
Steve Kerr, Arizona (I)	1988	38	114	199	57.3
Reginald Jones, Prairie View (I)	1987	28	64	112	57.1
Brian O'Donnell, Rutgers-Camden (III)	1988	24	65	114	57.0
Eric Harris, Bishop (III)	1987	26	91	160	56.9
Rick Brown, Muskingum (III)	1988	30	71	125	56.8

FREE-THROW PERCENTAGE

Player, Team (Division)	Season	G	FT	FTA	Pct.
Paul Cluxton, Northern Ky. (II)	1997	35	94	94	100.0
Korey Coon, Ill. Wesleyan (III)	2000	25	157	163	96.3
Craig Collins, Penn St. (I)	1985	27	94	98	95.9
Chanse Young, Manchester (III)	1998	25	65	68	95.6
Tomas Rimkus, Pace (II)	1997	25	65	68	95.6
Andy Enfield, Johns Hopkins (III)	1991	29	123	129	95.3
Chris Carideo, Eureka (III)	1992	26	80	84	95.2
Yudi Teichman, Yeshiva (III)	1989	21	119	125	95.2
Rod Foster, UCLA (I)	1982	27	95	100	95.0
C.J. Cowgill, Chaminade (II)	2001	22	113	119	95.0
Clay McKnight, Pacific (Cal.) (I)	2000	24	74	78	94.9
Brett Davis, Wis.-Oshkosh (III)	1998	27	72	76	94.7
Mark Giovino, Babson (III)	1997	28	86	91	94.5
Kent Andrews, McNeese St. (II)	1968	24	85	90	94.4
Billy Newton, Morgan St. (II)	1976	28	85	90	94.4
Carlos Gibson, Marshall (I)	1978	28	84	89	94.4
Danny Basile, Marist (I)	1994	27	84	89	94.4
Mike Sanders, Northern Colo. (II)	1987	28	82	87	94.3
Jim Barton, Dartmouth (I)	1986	26	65	69	94.2
Gary Buchanan, Villanova (I)	2001	31	97	103	94.2
Mike Scheib, Susquehanna (III)	1977	22	80	85	94.1
Curtis Small, Southampton (II)	2002	29	109	116	94.0
Jack Moore, Nebraska (I)	1982	27	123	131	93.9
Jason Prenevost, Middlebury (III)	1994	22	60	64	93.8
Travis Starns, Colorado Mines (II)	1999	26	87	93	93.5
Rob Robbins, New Mexico (I)	1990	34	101	108	93.5
Derrick Rogers, Averett (III)	2001	27	72	77	93.5
Dandrea Evans, Troy St. (I)	1994	27	72	77	93.5
Jay Harrie, Mont. St.-Billings (II)	1994	26	86	92	93.5

REBOUNDS

Player, Team (Division)	Season	G	Reb.
Elmore Smith, Kentucky St. (II)	1972	33	799
Marvin Webster, Morgan St. (II)	1974	33	740
Walt Dukes, Seton Hall (I)	1953	33	734
Maurice Stokes, St. Francis (Pa.) (II)	1955	28	726
Frank Stronczek, American Int'l (II)	1966	26	717
Maurice Stokes, St. Francis (Pa.) (II)	1954	26	689
Jim Ahrens, Buena Vista (II)	1962	28	682
Elmore Smith, Kentucky St. (II)	1970	30	682
R.C. Owens, Col. Idaho (II)	1954	25	677
Wilbert Jones, Albany St. (Ga.) (II)	1969	28	670
Leroy Wright, Pacific (Cal.) (I)	1959	26	652
Tom Gola, La Salle (I)	1954	30	652
Jim Smith, Steubenville (II)	1957	26	651
Marvin Webster, Morgan St. (II)	1973	28	650
Tom Hart, Middlebury (II)	1955	22	649
Charlie Tyra, Louisville (I)	1956	29	645
Jackie Jackson, Virginia Union (II)	1961	26	641
Vincent White, Savannah St. (II)	1972	29	633
Paul Silas, Creighton (I)	1964	29	631
Bill Thieben, Hofstra (II)	1955	26	627
Lucious Jackson, Tex.-Pan American (II)	1963	32	626
Elvin Hayes, Houston (I)	1968	33	624
Vincent White, Savannah St. (II)	1970	27	624
Artis Gilmore, Jacksonville (I)	1970	28	621
Bill Thieben, Hofstra (II)	1954	24	620
Tom Hart, Middlebury (II)	1956	21	620

(Since 1973)

Player, Team (Division)	Season	G	Reb.
Marvin Webster, Morgan St. (II)	1974	33	740
Marvin Webster, Morgan St. (II)	1973	28	650
Major Jones, Albany St. (Ga.) (II)	1975	27	608
Marvin Barnes, Providence (I)	1974	32	597
Joe Manley, Bowie St. (III)	1976	29	579
Marvin Barnes, Providence (I)	1973	30	571
Earl Williams, Winston-Salem (II)	1974	26	553
John Jordan, Southern Me. (III)	1978	29	536
Charles Oakley, Virginia Union (III)	1985	31	535
Lawrence Johnson, Prairie View (II)	1974	23	519
Andre Means, Sacred Heart (II)	1977	32	516
Major Jones, Albany St. (Ga.) (II)	1975	25	513
Kermit Washington, American (I)	1973	25	511
Bill Walton, UCLA (I)	1973	30	506
Larry Bird, Indiana St. (I)	1979	34	505
Harvey Jones, Alabama St. (II)	1974	28	503
Larry Kenon, Memphis (I)	1973	30	501
Akeem Olajuwon, Houston (I)	1984	37	500
Andre Means, Sacred Heart (II)	1978	30	493
Ricky Mahorn, Hampton (II)	1980	31	490
Rob Roesch, Staten Island (II)	1989	31	482
Howard Shockley, Salisbury (III)	1974	27	482
Keith Woolfolk, Upper Iowa (III)	1978	26	479
Leonard Robinson, Tennessee St. (II)	1974	28	478
Major Jones, Albany St. (Ga.) (II)	1976	24	475

REBOUND AVERAGE

Player, Team (Division)	Season	G	Reb.	Avg.
Tom Hart, Middlebury (II)	1956	21	620	29.5
Tom Hart, Middlebury (II)	1955	22	649	29.5
Frank Stronczek, American Int'l (II)	1966	26	717	27.6
R.C. Owens, Col. Idaho (II)	1954	25	677	27.1
Maurice Stokes, St. Francis (Pa.) (II)	1954	26	689	26.5
Ellerbe Neal, Wofford (II)	1953	23	609	26.5
Roman Turmon, Clark Atlanta (II)	1954	23	602	26.2
Pat Callahan, Lewis (II)	1955	20	523	26.2
Hank Brown, Mass.-Lowell (II)	1966	19	496	26.1
Maurice Stokes, St. Francis (Pa.) (II)	1955	28	726	25.9
Bill Thieben, Hofstra (II)	1954	24	620	25.8
Dean Sandifer, Lakeland (II)	1965	23	592	25.7
Charlie Slack, Marshall (I)	1955	21	538	25.6
Charles Wrinn, Trinity (Conn.) (II)	1952	19	486	25.6
Leroy Wright, Pacific (Cal.) (I)	1959	26	652	25.1
Jim Smith, Steubenville (II)	1957	26	651	25.0
Marv Becker, Widener (II)	1958	18	450	25.0
Tony Williams, St. Francis (Me.) (II)	1971	24	599	25.0
Ernie Brock, Virginia St. (II)	1964	24	597	24.9
Russell Jackson, Southern U. (II)	1970	22	544	24.7
Gerry Govan, St. Mary's (Kan.) (II)	1963	18	445	24.7
Merv Shorr, CCNY (II)	1954	18	444	24.7
Art Quimby, Connecticut (I)	1955	25	611	24.4
Charlie Slack, Marshall (I)	1956	22	520	23.6
Ed Conlin, Fordham (I)	1953	26	612	23.5

(Since 1973)

Player, Team (Division)	Season	G	Reb.	Avg.
Marvin Webster, Morgan St. (II)	1973	28	650	23.2
Lawrence Johnson, Prairie View (II)	1974	23	519	22.6
Major Jones, Albany St. (Ga.) (II)	1975	27	608	22.5
Marvin Webster, Morgan St. (II)	1974	33	740	22.4
Earl Williams, Winston-Salem (II)	1974	26	553	21.3
Major Jones, Albany St. (Ga.) (II)	1975	25	513	20.5
Kermit Washington, American (I)	1973	25	511	20.4
Larry Gooding, St. Augustine's (II)	1974	22	443	20.1
Joe Manley, Bowie St. (III)	1976	29	579	20.0
Fred Petty, New Hamp. Col. (II)	1974	22	436	19.8
Major Jones, Albany St. (Ga.) (II)	1976	24	475	19.8
Larry Williams, Pratt (III)	1977	24	457	19.0
Marvin Barnes, Providence (I)	1973	30	571	19.0
Calvin Robinson, Mississippi Val. (II)	1976	23	432	18.8
Larry Williams, Pratt (III)	1977	17	318	18.7
Larry Parker, Plattsburgh St. (III)	1975	23	430	18.7
Marvin Barnes, Providence (I)	1974	32	597	18.7
Charles Greer, Thomas (III)	1977	17	318	18.7
John Jordan, Southern Me. (III)	1978	29	536	18.5
Keith Woolfolk, Upper Iowa (III)	1978	26	479	18.4
Michael Stubbs, Trinity (Conn.) (III)	1990	22	398	18.1
Mike Taylor, Pratt (III)	1978	23	414	18.0
Harvey Jones, Alabama St. (II)	1974	28	503	18.0
Walt Edwards, Husson (III)	1976	26	467	18.0
Scott Mountz, Calif. (Pa.) (II)	1978	24	431	18.0

ASSISTS

Player, Team (Division)	Season	G	Ast.
Mark Wade, UNLV (I)	1987	38	406
Steve Ray, Bridgeport (II)	1989	32	400
Avery Johnson, Southern U. (I)	1988	30	399
Robert James, Kean (III)	1989	29	391
Steve Ray, Bridgeport (II)	1990	33	385
Anthony Manuel, Bradley (I)	1988	31	373
Tony Smith, Pfeiffer (II)	1992	35	349
Avery Johnson, Southern U. (I)	1987	31	333
Mark Jackson, St. John's (N.Y.) (I)	1986	32	328
Sherman Douglas, Syracuse (I)	1989	38	326
Tennyson Whitted, Ramapo (III)	2002	29	319
Greg Anthony, UNLV (I)	1991	35	310
Sam Crawford, New Mexico St. (I)	1993	34	310
Reid Gettys, Houston (I)	1984	37	309
Jim Ferrer, Bentley (II)	1989	31	309
Rob Paternostro, New Hamp. Col. (II)	1995	33	309
Carl Golson, Loyola (Ill.) (I)	1985	33	305
Craig Neal, Georgia Tech (I)	1988	32	303
Keith Jennings, East Tenn. St. (I)	1991	33	301
Brian Gregory, Oakland (II)	1989	28	300
Doug Gottlieb, Oklahoma St. (I)	1999	34	299
Chris Corchiani, North Carolina St. (I)	1991	31	299
Charles Jordan, Erskine (II)	1992	34	298
Keith Jennings, East Tenn. St. (I)	1990	34	297
Ricky Spicer, Wis.-Whitewater (III)	1989	31	295

ASSIST AVERAGE

Player, Team (Division)	Season	G	Ast.	Avg.
Robert James, Kean (III)	1989	29	391	13.48
Avery Johnson, Southern U. (I)	1988	30	399	13.30
Steve Ray, Bridgeport (II)	1989	32	400	12.50
Anthony Manuel, Bradley (I)	1988	31	373	12.03
Steve Ray, Bridgeport (II)	1990	33	385	11.66
Demetri Beekman, Assumption (II)	1993	23	264	11.47
Albert Kirchner, Mt. St. Vincent (III)	1990	24	267	11.12
Tennyson Whitted, Ramapo (III)	2002	29	319	11.00
Ernest Jenkins, N.M. Highlands (II)	1995	27	291	10.78
Avery Johnson, Southern U. (I)	1987	31	333	10.74
Brian Gregory, Oakland (II)	1989	28	300	10.71
Mark Wade, UNLV (I)	1987	38	406	10.68
Ron Torgalski, Hamilton (III)	1989	26	275	10.57
Brent Schremp, Slippery Rock (II)	1995	25	259	10.36
Louis Adams, Rust (III)	1989	22	227	10.31
Ernest Jenkins, N.M. Highlands (II)	1994	27	277	10.31
Adrian Hutt, Metro St. (II)	1991	28	285	10.17
Nelson Haggerty, Baylor (I)	1995	28	284	10.14
Tony Smith, Pfeiffer (II)	1992	35	349	9.97
Jim Ferrer, Bentley (II)	1989	31	309	9.96
Glenn Williams, Holy Cross (I)	1989	28	278	9.92
Eric Johnson, Coe (III)	1991	24	238	9.91
Todd Chappell, Texas Wesleyan (II)	2000	27	263	9.74
Joe Marcotte, N.J. Inst. of Tech (III)	1995	30	292	9.73
Phil Dixon, Shenandoah (III)	1994	26	253	9.73

BLOCKED SHOTS

Player, Team (Division)	Season	G	Blk.
David Robinson, Navy (I)	1986	35	207
Tory Black, N.J. Inst. of Tech. (III)	1997	26	198
Neil Edwards, York (N.Y.) (III)	2000	26	193
Ira Nicholson, Mt. St. Vincent (III)	1995	28	188
Adonal Foyle, Colgate (I)	1997	28	180
Keith Closs, Central Conn. St. (I)	1996	28	178
Shawn Bradley, Brigham Young (I)	1991	34	177
Wojciech Mydra, La.-Monroe (I)	2002	32	172
Alonzo Mourning, Georgetown (I)	1989	34	169
Adonal Foyle, Colgate (I)	1996	29	165
Ira Nicholson, Mt. St. Vincent (III)	1996	27	163
Ken Johnson, Ohio St. (I)	2000	30	161
Alonzo Mourning, Georgetown (I)	1992	32	160
James Doyle, Concord (II)	1998	30	157
Shaquille O'Neal, LSU (I)	1992	30	157
Roy Rogers, Alabama (I)	1996	32	156
Antonio Harvey, Pfeiffer (II)	1993	29	155
Ira Nicholson, Mt. St. Vincent (III)	1997	24	151
Dikembe Mutombo, Georgetown (I)	1991	32	151
Antoine Hyman, Keuka (III)	1997	26	148
Tarvis Williams, Hampton (I)	2001	32	147
Adonal Foyle, Colgate (I)	1995	30	147
Matt Cusano, Scranton (III)	1993	29	145
Wojciech Mydra, La.-Monroe (I)	2000	28	144
Neil Edwards, York (N.Y.) (III)	1999	26	144
David Robinson, Navy (I)	1987	32	144
Theo Ratliff, Wyoming (I)	1995	28	144

BLOCKED-SHOT AVERAGE

Player, Team (Division)	Season	G	Blk.	Avg.
Tory Black, N.J. Inst. of Tech. (III)	1997	26	198	7.62
Neil Edwards, York (N.Y.) (III)	2000	26	193	7.42
Ira Nicholson, Mt. St. Vincent (III)	1995	28	188	6.71
Adonal Foyle, Colgate (I)	1997	28	180	6.43
Keith Closs, Central Conn. St. (I)	1996	28	178	6.36
Ira Nicholson, Mt. St. Vincent (III)	1997	24	151	6.29
Ira Nicholson, Mt. St. Vincent (III)	1996	27	163	6.04
David Robinson, Navy (I)	1986	35	207	5.91
Antoine Hyman, Keuka (III)	1997	26	148	5.69
Adonal Foyle, Colgate (I)	1996	29	165	5.69
Neil Edwards, York (N.Y.) (III)	1999	26	144	5.54
Johnny Woods, Wesley (III)	2000	24	132	5.50
Wojciech Mydra, La.-Monroe (I)	2002	32	172	5.38
Ken Johnson, Ohio St. (I)	2000	30	161	5.37
Keith Closs, Central Conn. St. (I)	1995	26	139	5.35
Antonio Harvey, Pfeiffer (II)	1993	29	155	5.34
Antoine Hyman, Keuka (III)	1996	25	131	5.24
James Doyle, Concord (II)	1998	30	157	5.23
Shaquille O'Neal, LSU (I)	1992	30	157	5.23
Shawn Bradley, Brigham Young (I)	1991	34	177	5.21
Wojciech Mydra, La.-Monroe (I)	2000	28	144	5.14
Theo Ratliff, Wyoming (I)	1995	28	144	5.14
Cedric Lewis, Maryland (I)	1991	28	143	5.11
Joe Henderson, Hunter (III)	1999	22	112	5.09
John Burke, Southampton (II)	1996	28	142	5.07

STEALS

Player, Team (Division)	Season	G	Stl.
Moses Jean-Pierre, Plymouth St. (III)	1994	30	189
Daniel Martinez, McMurry (III)	2000	29	178
Desmond Cambridge, Alabama A&M (I)	2002	29	160
Mookie Blaylock, Oklahoma (I)	1988	39	150
Purvis Presha, Stillman (III)	1996	25	144
Aldwin Ware, Florida A&M (I)	1988	29	142
John Linehan, Providence (I)	2002	31	139
J.R. Gamble, Queens (N.C.) (II)	2001	32	139
Darron Brittman, Chicago St. (I)	1986	28	139
Tennyson Whitted, Ramapo (III)	2002	29	138
Nadav Henefeld, Connecticut (I)	1990	37	138
Matt Newton, Principia (III)	1994	25	138
John Gallogly, Salve Regina (III)	1997	24	137
Mookie Blaylock, Oklahoma (I)	1989	35	131
Ronn McMahon, Eastern Wash. (I)	1990	29	130
Wayne Copeland, Lynn (II)	2000	26	129
Greg Dean, Concordia-M'head (III)	1997	23	126
Scott Clarke, Utica (III)	1995	24	126
Wayne Copeland, Lynn (II)	1999	31	125
Allen Iverson, Georgetown (I)	1996	37	124
Marty Johnson, Towson (I)	1988	30	124
Eric Coley, Tulsa (I)	2000	37	123
Deron Black, Allegheny (III)	1996	27	123
Terrance Gist, S.C.-Spartanburg (II)	1998	29	122
Devlin Herring, Pitt.-Johnstown (II)	1997	27	122
David Brown, Westfield St. (III)	1994	25	122

STEAL AVERAGE

Player, Team (Division)	Season	G	Stl.	Avg.
Moses Jean-Pierre, Plymouth St. (III)	1994	30	189	6.30
Daniel Martinez, McMurry (III)	2000	29	178	6.14
Purvis Presha, Stillman (III)	1996	25	144	5.76
John Gallogly, Salve Regina (III)	1997	24	137	5.71
Matt Newton, Principia (III)	1994	25	138	5.52
Desmond Cambridge, Alabama A&M (I)	2002	29	160	5.52
Barry Aranoff, Yeshiva (III)	1995	22	121	5.50
Greg Dean, Concordia-M'head (III)	1997	23	126	5.48
John Gallogly, Salve Regina (III)	1998	23	121	5.26
Scott Clarke, Utica (III)	1995	24	126	5.25
Darron Brittman, Chicago St. (I)	1986	28	139	4.96
Wayne Copeland, Lynn (II)	2000	26	129	4.96
Joel Heckendorf, Martin Luther (III)	1996	17	84	4.94
Aldwin Ware, Florida A&M (I)	1988	29	142	4.90
David Brown, Westfield St. (III)	1994	25	122	4.88
Ivo Moyano, Polytechnic (N.Y.) (III)	1994	19	91	4.78
Tennyson Whitted, Ramapo (III)	2002	29	138	4.76
Mario Thompson, Occidental (III)	1999	24	114	4.75
Keith Darden, Concordia-Austin (III)	2001	24	111	4.63
Moses Jean-Pierre, Plymouth St. (III)	1993	25	114	4.56
Deron Black, Allegheny (III)	1996	27	123	4.56
Scott Clark, Utica (III)	1996	26	118	4.54
John Morris, Bluefield St. (II)	1994	23	104	4.52
Devlin Herring, Pitt.-Johnstown (II)	1997	27	122	4.52
John Linehan, Providence (I)	2002	31	139	4.48
Ronn McMahon, Eastern Wash. (I)	1990	29	130	4.48
Ricky Hollis, Brockport St. (III)	2000	27	121	4.48

Career Records

POINTS

Player, Team (Division)	Last Season	Yrs.	G	FG	3FG	FT	Pts.
Travis Grant, Kentucky St. (II)	1972	4	121	1,760	—	525	4,045
Bob Hopkins, Grambling (II)	1956	4	126	1,403	—	953	3,759
Pete Maravich, LSU (I)	1970	3	83	1,387	—	893	3,667
Dwight Lamar, La.-Lafayette (II & I)	1973	4	112	1,445	—	603	3,493
Tony Smith, Pfeiffer (II)	1992	4	126	1,150	431	619	3,350
Earnest Lee, Clark Atlanta (II)	1987	4	115	1,270	35	723	3,298
Joe Miller, Alderson-Broaddus (II)	1957	4	129	1,082	—	1,130	3,294
Henry Logan, Western Caro. (II)	1968	4	107	1,263	—	764	3,290
John Rinka, Kenyon (II)	1970	4	99	1,261	—	729	3,251
Freeman Williams, Portland St. (I)	1978	4	106	1,369	—	511	3,249
Lionel Simmons, La Salle (I)	1990	4	131	1,244	56	673	3,217
Dick Barnett, Tennessee St. (II)	1959	4	136	1,312	—	585	3,209
Alphonso Ford, Mississippi Val. (I)	1993	4	109	1,121	333	590	3,165
Willie Scott, Alabama St. (II)	1969	4	103	1,277	—	601	3,155
Harry Kelly, Texas Southern (I)	1983	4	110	1,234	—	598	3,066
Johnnie Allen, Bethune-Cookman (II)	1969	4	111	1,306	—	446	3,058
Bennie Swain, Texas Southern (II)	1958	4	137	1,157	—	694	3,008
Hersey Hawkins, Bradley (I)	1988	4	125	1,100	118	690	3,008
Rich Fuqua, Oral Roberts (II & I)	1973	4	111	1,273	—	458	3,004
Lambert Shell, Bridgeport (II)	1992	4	132	1,102	22	775	3,001
Oscar Robertson, Cincinnati (I)	1960	3	88	1,052	—	869	2,973
Carl Hartman, Alderson-Broaddus (II)	1955	4	118	1,124	—	711	2,959
Danny Manning, Kansas (I)	1988	4	147	1,216	10	509	2,951
Andre Foreman, Salisbury (II)	1992	5	109	1,141	68	592	2,940
Earl Monroe, Winston-Salem (II)	1967	4	110	1,158	—	619	2,935

SCORING AVERAGE
(Minimum 1,500 points)

Player, Team (Division)	Last Season	Yrs.	G	FG	3FG	FT	Pts.	Avg.
Pete Maravich, LSU (I)	1970	3	83	1,387	—	893	3,667	44.2
Austin Carr, Notre Dame (I)	1971	3	74	1,017	—	526	2,560	34.6
Oscar Robertson, Cincinnati (I)	1960	3	88	1,052	—	869	2,973	33.8
Travis Grant, Kentucky St. (II)	1972	4	121	1,760	—	525	4,045	33.4
Calvin Murphy, Niagara (I)	1970	3	77	947	—	654	2,548	33.1
John Rinka, Kenyon (II)	1970	4	99	1,261	—	729	3,251	32.8
Dwain Govan, Bishop (III)	1975	2	55	750	—	305	1,805	32.8
Florindo Vieira, Quinnipiac (II)	1957	4	69	761	—	741	2,263	32.8
Dwight Lamar, La.-Lafayette (I)	1973	2	57	768	—	326	1,862	32.7
Frank Selvy, Furman (I)	1954	3	78	922	—	694	2,538	32.5
Rick Mount, Purdue (I)	1970	3	72	910	—	503	2,323	32.3
Darrell Floyd, Furman (I)	1956	3	71	868	—	545	2,281	32.1
Nick Werkman, Seton Hall (I)	1964	3	71	812	—	649	2,273	32.0
Willie Humes, Idaho St. (I)	1971	2	48	565	—	380	1,510	31.5

Player, Team (Division)	Last Season	Yrs.	G	FG	3FG	FT	Pts.	Avg.
William Averitt, Pepperdine (I)	1973	2	48	615	—	311	1,541	31.4
Elgin Baylor, Albertson & Seattle (I)	1958	3	80	956	—	588	2,500	31.3
Willie Shaw, Lane (II)	1964	4	76	960	—	459	2,379	31.3
Mike Davis, Virginia Union (II)	1969	4	89	1,014	—	730	2,758	31.0
Elvin Hayes, Houston (I)	1968	3	93	1,215	—	454	2,884	31.0
Freeman Williams, Portland St. (I)	1978	4	106	1,369	—	511	3,249	30.7
Henry Logan, Western Caro. (II)	1968	4	107	1,263	—	764	3,290	30.7
Willie Scott, Alabama St. (II)	1969	4	103	1,277	—	601	3,155	30.6
Dave Russell, Shepherd (III)	1975	2	60	710	—	413	1,833	30.6
Larry Bird, Indiana St. (I)	1979	3	94	1,154	—	542	2,850	30.3
Carlos Knox, IUPUI (II)	1998	4	85	832	208	684	2,556	30.1

FIELD-GOAL PERCENTAGE
(Minimum 400 field goals made)

Player, Team (Division)	Last Season	Yrs.	G	FG	FGA	Pct.
Tony Rychlec, Mass. Maritime (III)	1983	3	55	509	692	73.6
Pete Metzelaars, Wabash (III)	1982	4	103	784	1,083	72.4
Todd Linder, Tampa (II)	1987	4	122	909	1,284	70.8
Tom Schurfranz, Bellarmine (II)	1992	4	112	742	1,057	70.2
Chad Scott, Calif. (Pa.) (II)	1994	4	115	465	664	70.0
Ricky Nedd, Appalachian St. (I)	1994	4	113	412	597	69.0
Ed Phillips, Alabama A&M (II)	1971	4	95	610	885	68.9
Stephen Scheffler, Purdue (I)	1990	4	110	408	596	68.5
Ulysses Hackett, S.C.-Spartanburg (II)	1992	3	90	824	1,213	67.9
Larry Tucker, Lewis (II)	1983	3	84	677	994	67.8
Steve Johnson, Oregon St. (I)	1981	4	116	828	1,222	67.8
Michael Bradley, Kentucky & Villanova (I)	2001	4	100	441	651	67.7
Otis Evans, Wayne St. (Mich.) (II)	1992	4	106	472	697	67.7
Maurice Woods, Potsdam St. (III)	1982	3	93	559	829	67.4
Matthew Cornegay, Tuskegee (II)	1982	4	105	524	783	66.9
Earl Keith, Stony Brook (III)	1979	4	94	777	1,161	66.9
Murray Brown, Florida St. (I)	1980	4	106	566	847	66.8
Ray Strozier, Central Mo. St. (II)	1981	4	110	563	843	66.8
Dennis Edwards, Fort Hays St. (II)	1995	2	59	666	998	66.7
James Morris, Central Okla. (II)	1993	4	76	532	798	66.7
Dan Rush, Bridgewater (Va.) (III)	1995	4	102	712	1,069	66.6
Lee Campbell, Middle Tenn. & Southwest Mo. St. (I)	1990	3	88	411	618	66.5
Warren Kidd, Middle Tenn. (I)	1993	3	83	496	747	66.4
Todd MacCulloch, Washington (I)	1999	4	115	702	1,058	66.4
Joe Senser, West Chester (I)	1979	4	96	476	719	66.2
Lance Berwald, North Dakota St. (II)	1984	2	58	475	717	66.2

THREE-POINT FIELD GOALS MADE

Player, Team (Division)	Last Season	Yrs.	G	3FG
Jeff Clement, Grinnell (III)	1999	4	91	516
Steve Moyer, Gannon (II)	1999	4	112	442
Tony Smith, Pfeiffer (II)	1992	4	126	431
Curtis Staples, Virginia (I)	1998	4	122	413
Kwame Morton, Clarion (II)	1994	4	105	411
Keith Veney, Lamar & Marshall (I)	1997	4	111	409
Chris Carideo, Widener (III)	1995	4	103	402
Doug Day, Radford (I)	1993	4	117	401
Gary Duda, Merrimack (II)	1992	4	122	389
Ronnie Schmitz, UMKC (I)	1993	4	112	378
Mark Alberts, Akron (I)	1993	4	107	375
Markus Hallgrimson, Mont. St.-Billings (II)	2000	3	82	371
Steve Diekmann, Grinnell (III)	1995	4	85	371
Pat Bradley, Arkansas (I)	1999	4	132	366
Bryce Drew, Valparaiso (I)	1998	4	121	364
Jeff Fryer, Loyola Marymount (I)	1990	4	112	363
Matt Garvey, Bates (III)	1997	4	95	361
Columbus Parker, Johnson Smith (II)	1993	4	115	354
Gary Paul, Indianapolis (II)	1990	4	111	354
Ray Wilson, UC Santa Cruz (III)	1992	4	100	354
Matt Miller, Drury (II)	2002	4	106	351
Dennis Scott, Georgia Tech (I)	1990	3	99	351
Travis Tuttle, North Dakota (II)	1997	4	108	350
Rashad Phillips, Detroit (I)	2001	4	129	348
Ed Brands, Grinnell (III)	1996	4	78	347

THREE-POINT FIELD GOALS MADE PER GAME
(Minimum 200 three-point field goals made)

Player, Team (Division)	Last Season	Yrs.	G	3FG	Avg.
Jeff Clement, Grinnell (III)	1999	4	91	516	5.67
Antonio Harris, LeMoyne-Owen (II)	1999	2	52	245	4.71
Timothy Pollard, Mississippi Val. (I)	1989	2	56	256	4.57
Markus Hallgrimson, Mont. St.-Billings (II)	2000	3	82	371	4.52
Ed Brands, Grinnell (III)	1996	4	78	347	4.45
Steve Diekmann, Grinnell (III)	1995	4	85	371	4.36

Lynn's Wayne Copeland holds the Division II career record for steals per game average.

Player, Team (Division)	Last Season	Yrs.	G	3FG	Avg.
Sydney Grider, La.-Lafayette (I)	1990	2	58	253	4.36
Alex Williams, Sacramento St. (II)	1988	2	58	247	4.26
Tommie Spearman, Columbus St. (II)	1995	2	56	233	4.16
Reece Gliko, Mont. St.-Billings (II)	1997	2	56	231	4.13
Danny Phillips, Mont. St.-Billings (II)	2002	2	55	222	4.03
Brian Merriweather, Tex.-Pan American (I)	2001	3	84	332	3.95
Steve Moyer, Gannon (II)	1999	4	112	442	3.95
Kwame Morton, Clarion (II)	1994	4	105	411	3.91
Chris Carideo, Widener (III)	1995	4	103	402	3.90
Josh Heard, Tennessee Tech (I)	2000	2	55	210	3.82
Matt Garvey, Bates (III)	1997	4	95	361	3.80
Shawn Williams, Central Okla. (II)	1991	3	57	212	3.72
Zoderick Green, Central Okla. (II)	1995	3	57	212	3.72
Kareem Townes, La Salle (I)	1995	3	81	300	3.70
Keith Veney, Lamar & Marshall (I)	1997	4	111	409	3.68
Mike Sinclair, Bowie St. (II)	1989	3	82	299	3.65
Dave Mooney, Coastal Caro. (I)	1988	2	56	202	3.61
Billy Collins, Nichols (III)	1995	4	92	331	3.60
Nate Allen, Western St. (II)	1997	2	57	205	3.60

THREE-POINT FIELD-GOAL PERCENTAGE
(Minimum 200 three-point field goals made)

Player, Team (Division)	Last Season	Yrs.	G	3FG	3FGA	Pct.
Scott Martin, Rollins (II)	1991	4	104	236	460	51.3
Jeff Seifriz, Wis.-Whitewater (III)	1989	3	85	217	423	51.3
Chris Peterson, Eureka (III)	1994	4	78	215	421	51.1
Todd Woelfle, Oakland City (II)	1998	4	103	210	412	51.0
Everett Foxx, Ferrum (III)	1992	4	104	315	630	50.0
Tony Bennett, Wis.-Green Bay (I)	1992	4	118	290	584	49.7
Matt Markle, Shippensburg (II)	1992	4	101	202	408	49.5
Keith Jennings, East Tenn. St. (I)	1991	4	127	223	452	49.3
Brad Alberts, Ripon (III)	1992	4	95	277	563	49.2
Jeff Jones, Lycoming (III)	1989	3	71	232	472	49.2
Troy Greenlee, DePauw (III)	1991	4	106	232	473	49.0
Paul Cluxton, Northern Ky. (II)	1997	4	122	303	619	48.9
Lance Gelnett, Millersville (II)	1992	4	109	266	547	48.6
David Todd, Pomona-Pitzer (III)	1990	4	84	212	439	48.3
Al Callejas, Scranton (III)	2001	4	90	225	466	48.3

Player, Team (Division)	Last Season	Yrs.	G	3FG	3FGA	Pct.
Antonio Harris, LeMoyne-Owen (II)	1999	2	52	245	510	48.0
Jason Bullock, Indiana (Pa.) (II)	1995	4	88	235	491	47.9
Matt Ripaldi, New Hamp. Col. (II)	1995	4	95	205	431	47.6
Kirk Manns, Michigan St. (I)	1990	4	120	212	446	47.5
Tim Locum, Wisconsin (I)	1991	4	118	227	481	47.2
Mark Willey, Fort Hays St. (II)	1992	4	117	224	478	46.9
David Olson, Eastern Ill. (II)	1992	4	111	262	562	46.6
Todd Bowden, Randolph-Macon (III)	1989	3	84	229	491	46.6
Ross Land, Northern Ariz. (I)	2000	4	117	308	664	46.4
Dan Dickau, Washington (I) & Gonzaga (I)	2002	4	97	215	465	46.2

FREE-THROW PERCENTAGE
(Minimum 300 free throws made)

Player, Team (Division)	Last Season	Yrs.	G	FT	FTA	Pct.
Andy Enfield, Johns Hopkins (III)	1991	4	108	431	466	92.5
Korey Coon, Ill. Wesleyan (III)	2000	4	109	449	492	91.3
Greg Starrick, Kentucky & Southern Ill. (I)	1972	4	72	341	375	90.9
Ryan Knuppel, Elmhurst (III)	2001	4	102	288	317	90.9
Jack Moore, Nebraska (I)	1982	4	105	446	495	90.1
Steve Henson, Kansas St. (I)	1990	4	127	361	401	90.0
Steve Alford, Indiana (I)	1987	4	125	535	596	89.8
Bob Lloyd, Rutgers (I)	1967	3	77	543	605	89.8
Jim Barton, Dartmouth (I)	1989	4	104	394	440	89.5
Al Callejas, Scranton (III)	2001	4	90	333	372	89.5
Dave Reynolds, Davis & Elkins (II)	1989	4	107	383	429	89.3
Tommy Boyer, Arkansas (I)	1963	3	70	315	353	89.2
Tim McGraw, Hartwick (III)	1988	4	107	330	371	88.9
Rob Robbins, New Mexico (I)	1991	4	133	309	348	88.8
Marcus Wilson, Evansville (I)	1999	4	119	455	513	88.7
Sean Miller, Pittsburgh (I)	1992	4	128	317	358	88.5
Ron Perry, Holy Cross (I)	1980	4	109	680	768	88.5
Joe Crispin, Penn. St. (I)	2001	4	127	448	506	88.5
Joe Dykstra, Western Ill. (I)	1983	4	117	587	663	88.5
Michael Shue, Lock Haven (II)	1997	4	92	354	400	88.5
Mike Joseph, Bucknell (I)	1990	4	115	397	449	88.4
Kyle Macy, Purdue & Kentucky (I)	1980	5	125	416	471	88.3
Eric Jacobs, Wilkes & Scranton (III)	1987	4	106	303	343	88.3
Matt Hildebrand, Liberty (I)	1994	4	117	398	451	88.2
Tony Budzik, Mansfield (II)	1992	4	107	367	416	88.2

REBOUNDS

Player, Team (Division)	Last Season	Yrs.	G	Reb.
Jim Smith, Steubenville (II)	1958	4	112	2,334
Marvin Webster, Morgan St. (II)	1975	4	114	2,267
Tom Gola, La Salle (I)	1955	4	118	2,201
Major Jones, Albany St. (Ga.) (II)	1976	4	105	2,052
Joe Holup, George Washington (I)	1956	4	104	2,030
Charles Hardnett, Grambling (II)	1962	4	117	1,983
Jim Ahrens, Buena Vista (II)	1962	4	95	1,977
Elmore Smith, Kentucky St. (II)	1971	3	85	1,917
Charlie Slack, Marshall (I)	1956	4	88	1,916
Zelmo Beaty, Prairie View (II)	1962	4	97	1,916
Ed Conlin, Fordham (I)	1955	4	102	1,884
Hal Booker, Cheyney (II)	1969	4	103	1,882
Bill Thieben, Hofstra (II)	1956	3	76	1,837
Maurice Stokes, St. Francis (Pa.) (II)	1955	3	72	1,812
Dickie Hemric, Wake Forest (I)	1955	4	104	1,802
Paul Silas, Creighton (I)	1964	3	81	1,751
James Morgan, Md.-Eastern Shore (II)	1970	4	95	1,747
Tom Hart, Middlebury (III)	1956	3	63	1,738
Joe Casey, Boston St. (II)	1969	4	102	1,733
Art Quimby, Connecticut (I)	1955	4	80	1,716
Jerry Harper, Alabama (I)	1956	4	93	1,688
Jeff Cohen, William & Mary (I)	1961	4	103	1,679
Steve Hamilton, Morehead St. (I)	1958	4	102	1,675
Herb Lake, Youngstown St. (II)	1959	4	95	1,638
Jim Fay, St. Ambrose (II)	1953	4	95	1,633

(For careers beginning in 1973 or after)

Player, Team (Division)	Last Season	Yrs.	G	Reb.
Major Jones, Albany St. (Ga.) (II)	1976	4	105	2,052
Michael Smith, Hamilton (III)	1992	4	107	1,628
Tim Duncan, Wake Forest (I)	1997	4	128	1,570
Derrick Coleman, Syracuse (I)	1990	4	143	1,537
Malik Rose, Drexel (I)	1996	4	120	1,514
Ralph Sampson, Virginia (I)	1983	4	132	1,511
John Jordan, Southern Me. (III)	1981	4	105	1,504
Clemon Johnson, Florida A&M (II)	1978	4	109	1,494
Larry Parker, Plattsburgh St. (III)	1978	4	85	1,482
Carlos Terry, Winston-Salem (II)	1978	4	117	1,467
Pete Padgett, Nevada (I)	1976	4	104	1,464
Kevin Clark, Clark (Mass.) (III)	1981	4	101	1,450
Lionel Simmons, La Salle (I)	1990	4	131	1,429
Anthony Bonner, St. Louis (I)	1990	4	133	1,424

Player, Team (Division)	Last Season	Yrs.	G	Reb.
E.D. Schecterly, Lynchburg (III)	1980	4	104	1,404
Jeff Covington, Youngstown St. (II)	1978	4	106	1,381
Tyrone Hill, Xavier (I)	1990	4	126	1,380
Larry Sheets, East. Mennonite (III)	1983	4	105	1,378
Popeye Jones, Murray St. (I)	1992	4	123	1,374
Michael Brooks, La Salle (I)	1980	4	114	1,372
Xavier McDaniel, Wichita St. (I)	1985	4	117	1,359
John Irving, Arizona & Hofstra (I)	1977	4	103	1,348
Sam Clancy, Pittsburgh (I)	1981	4	116	1,342
Keith Lee, Memphis (I)	1985	4	128	1,336
Larry Smith, Alcorn St. (I)	1980	4	111	1,334

REBOUND AVERAGE
(Minimum 800 rebounds)

Player, Team (Division)	Last Season	Yrs.	G	Reb.	Avg.
Tom Hart, Middlebury (III)	1956	3	63	1,738	27.6
Maurice Stokes, St. Francis (Pa.) (II)	1955	3	72	1,812	25.2
Frank Stronczek, American Int'l (II)	1967	3	62	1,549	25.0
Bill Thieben, Hofstra (II)	1956	3	76	1,837	24.2
Hank Brown, Mass.-Lowell (II)	1967	3	49	1,129	23.0
Artis Gilmore, Jacksonville (I)	1970	2	54	1,224	22.7
Elmore Smith, Kentucky St. (II)	1971	3	85	1,917	22.6
Charles Wrinn, Trinity (Conn.) (II)	1953	3	53	1,176	22.2
Roman Turmon, Clark Atlanta (II)	1954	3	60	1,312	21.9
Charlie Slack, Marshall (I)	1956	4	88	1,916	21.8
Tony Missere, Pratt (II)	1968	3	62	1,348	21.7
Ron Horton, Delaware St. (II)	1968	3	64	1,384	21.6
Paul Silas, Creighton (I)	1964	3	81	1,751	21.6
Leroy Wright, Pacific (Cal.) (I)	1960	3	67	1,442	21.5
Art Quimby, Connecticut (I)	1955	4	80	1,716	21.5
Walt Dukes, Seton Hall (I)	1953	2	59	1,247	21.1
Jim Smith, Steubenville (II)	1958	4	112	2,334	20.8
Jim Ahrens, Buena Vista (II)	1962	4	95	1,977	20.8
Bob Brandes, Upsala (II)	1962	3	74	1,520	20.5
Jackie Jackson, Virginia Union (II)	1961	3	66	1,351	20.5
Bill Russell, San Francisco (I)	1956	3	79	1,606	20.3
Kermit Washington, American (I)	1973	3	73	1,478	20.2
Julius Erving, Massachusetts (I)	1971	2	52	1,049	20.2
Frank Hunter, Northland (III)	1962	4	79	1,581	20.0
Marvin Webster, Morgan St. (II)	1975	4	114	2,267	19.9

(For careers beginning in 1973 or after)

Player, Team (Division)	Last Season	Yrs.	G	Reb.	Avg.
Major Jones, Albany St. (Ga.) (II)	1976	4	105	2,052	19.5
Larry Parker, Plattsburgh St. (III)	1978	4	85	1,482	17.4
Howard Shockley, Salisbury (III & II)	1976	3	76	1,299	17.1
Andre Means, Sacred Heart (II)	1978	2	62	1,009	16.3
Charles Greer, Thomas (III)	1977	3	58	926	16.0
Willie Parr, LeMoyne-Owen (III)	1976	3	76	1,182	15.6
Glenn Mosley, Seton Hall (I)	1977	4	83	1,263	15.2
Michael Smith, Hamilton (III)	1992	4	107	1,628	15.2
Dave Kufeld, Yeshiva (III)	1980	4	81	1,222	15.1
Ed Owens, Hampden-Sydney (III)	1980	4	77	1,160	15.1
Tony Rychlec, Mass. Maritime (III)	1983	3	55	812	14.8
Bill Campion, Manhattan (I)	1975	3	74	1,070	14.5
John Jordan, Southern Me. (III)	1981	4	105	1,504	14.4
Kevin Clark, Clark (Mass.) (III)	1981	4	101	1,450	14.4
Antonio Garcia, Ky. Wesleyan (II)	1999	2	70	997	14.2
Mark Veenstra, Calvin (III)	1977	4	89	1,260	14.2
Pete Padgett, Nevada (I)	1976	4	104	1,464	14.1
Rob Roesch, Staten Island (III)	1989	2	61	850	13.9
Clemon Johnson, Florida A&M (II)	1978	4	109	1,494	13.7
Larry Johnson, Ark.-Little Rock (II)	1978	3	69	944	13.7
Carlo DeTommaso, Rhode Island Col. (III)	1976	3	72	984	13.7
Bob Warner, Maine (I)	1976	4	96	1,304	13.6
Shaquille O'Neal, LSU (I)	1992	3	90	1,217	13.5
Cornelius Cash, Bowling Green (I)	1975	3	79	1,068	13.5
E.D. Schecterly, Lynchburg (III)	1980	4	104	1,404	13.5
Ira Terrell, Southern Methodist (I)	1976	3	80	1,077	13.5

ASSISTS

Player, Team (Division)	Last Season	Yrs.	G	Ast.
Bobby Hurley, Duke (I)	1993	4	140	1,076
Demetri Beekman, Assumption (II)	1993	4	119	1,044
Chris Corchiani, North Carolina St. (I)	1991	4	124	1,038
Ed Cota, North Carolina (I)	2000	4	138	1,030
Keith Jennings, East Tenn. St. (I)	1991	4	127	983
Sherman Douglas, Syracuse (I)	1989	4	138	960
Tony Miller, Marquette (I)	1995	4	123	956
Greg Anthony, Portland/UNLV (I)	1991	4	138	950
Doug Gottlieb, Notre Dame & Oklahoma St. (I)	2000	4	124	947
Gary Payton, Oregon St. (I)	1990	4	120	938
Adam Kaufman, Edinboro (II)	2001	4	116	936
Rob Paternostro, New Hamp. Col. (II)	1995	4	129	919

Player, Team (Division)	Last Season	Yrs.	G	Ast.
Steve Artis, Chris. Newport (III)	1993	4	112	909
Orlando Smart, San Francisco (I)	1994	4	116	902
Andre LaFleur, Northeastern (I)	1987	4	128	894
Chico Fletcher, Arkansas St. (I)	2000	4	114	893
Phil Dixon, Shenandoah (III)	1996	4	103	889
Jim Les, Bradley (I)	1986	4	118	884
Frank Smith, Old Dominion (I)	1988	4	120	883
Gallagher Driscoll, St. Rose (II)	1992	4	121	878
Taurence Chisholm, Delaware (I)	1988	4	110	877
Grayson Marshall, Clemson (I)	1988	4	122	857
Anthony Manuel, Bradley (I)	1989	4	108	855
Pooh Richardson, UCLA (I)	1989	4	122	833
Butch Moore, Southern Methodist (I)	1986	4	125	828
Tony Smith, Pfeiffer (II)	1992	4	126	828

ASSIST AVERAGE
(Minimum 550 assists)

Player, Team (Division)	Last Season	Yrs.	G	Ast.	Avg.
Steve Ray, Bridgeport (II)	1990	2	65	785	12.08
Avery Johnson, Southern U. (I)	1988	2	61	732	12.00
Sam Crawford, New Mexico St. (I)	1993	2	67	592	8.84
Mark Wade, Oklahoma & UNLV (I)	1987	3	79	693	8.77
Demetri Beekman, Assumption (II)	1993	4	119	1,044	8.77
Phil Dixon, Shenandoah (III)	1996	4	103	889	8.63
Chris Corchiani, North Carolina St. (I)	1991	4	124	1,038	8.37
Ernest Jenkins, N.M. Highlands (II)	1995	4	84	699	8.32
Steve Artis, Chris. Newport (III)	1993	4	112	909	8.12
Adam Kaufman, Edinboro (II)	2001	4	116	936	8.07
Taurence Chisholm, Delaware (I)	1988	4	110	877	7.97
Van Usher, Tennessee Tech (I)	1992	3	85	676	7.95
Anthony Manuel, Bradley (I)	1989	4	108	855	7.92
Mark Benson, Tex. A&M-Kingsville (II)	1991	3	86	674	7.84
Chico Fletcher, Arkansas St. (I)	2000	4	114	893	7.83
Pat Madden, Jacksonville St. (II)	1991	3	88	688	7.82
Gary Payton, Oregon St. (I)	1990	4	120	938	7.82
Orlando Smart, San Francisco (I)	1994	4	116	902	7.78
Tony Miller, Marquette (I)	1995	4	123	956	7.77
Keith Jennings, East Tenn. St. (I)	1991	4	127	983	7.74
Dan Ward, St. Cloud St. (II)	1995	4	100	774	7.74
Bobby Hurley, Duke (I)	1993	4	140	1,076	7.69
Doug Gottlieb, Notre Dame & Oklahoma St. (I)	2000	4	124	947	7.63
Chuck Evans, Old Dominion & Mississippi St. (I)	1993	3	85	648	7.62
Jim Les, Bradley (I)	1986	4	118	884	7.49

BLOCKED SHOTS

Player, Team (Division)	Last Season	Yrs.	G	Blk.
Ira Nicholson, Mt. St. Vincent (III)	1997	4	100	576
Wojciech Mydra, La.-Monroe (I)	2002	4	115	535
Adonal Foyle, Colgate (I)	1997	3	87	492
Tim Duncan, Wake Forest (I)	1997	4	128	481
Alonzo Mourning, Georgetown (I)	1992	4	120	453
Tarvis Williams, Hampton (II)	2001	4	114	452
Ken Johnson, Ohio St. (I)	2001	4	127	444
Antoine Hyman, Keuka (III)	1997	4	101	440
Lorenzo Coleman, Tennessee Tech (I)	1997	4	113	437
Calvin Booth, Penn St. (I)	1999	4	114	428
Troy Murphy, Notre Dame (I)	2001	3	94	425
Theo Ratliff, Wyoming (I)	1995	4	111	425
Etan Thomas, Syracuse (I)	2000	4	122	424
Rodney Blake, St. Joseph's (I)	1988	4	116	419
James Doyle, Concord (II)	1998	4	120	416
Shaquille O'Neal, LSU (I)	1992	3	90	412
Kevin Roberson, Vermont (I)	1992	4	112	409
Derek Moore, S.C.-Aiken (II)	1999	4	102	408
Jim McIlvaine, Marquette (I)	1994	4	118	399
Tim Perry, Temple (I)	1988	4	130	392
Jason Lawson, Villanova (I)	1997	4	131	375
Pervis Ellison, Louisville (I)	1989	4	136	374
Peter Aluma, Liberty (I)	1997	4	119	366
Acie Earl, Iowa (I)	1993	3	116	365
Jerome James, Florida A&M (I)	1998	3	81	363

BLOCKED-SHOT AVERAGE
(Minimum 200 blocked shots)

Player, Team (Division)	Last Season	Yrs.	G	Blk.	Avg.
Neil Edwards, York (N.Y.) (III)	2000	3	55	337	6.13
Ira Nicholson, Mt. St. Vincent (III)	1997	4	100	576	5.76
Adonal Foyle, Colgate (I)	1997	3	87	492	5.66
David Robinson, Navy (I)	1987	2	67	351	5.24
Wojciech Mydra, La.-Monroe (I)	2002	4	115	535	4.65

Player, Team (Division)	Last Season	Yrs.	G	Blk.	Avg.
Shaquille O'Neal, LSU (I)	1992	3	90	412	4.58
Troy Murphy, Notre Dame (I)	2001	3	94	425	4.52
Jerome James, Florida A&M (I)	1998	3	81	363	4.48
Antoine Hyman, Keuka (III)	1997	4	101	440	4.36
Andrew South, N.J. Inst. of Tech. (III)	1995	3	80	344	4.30
Antonio Ramos, Clarke (III)	2002	2	50	212	4.24
Johnny Woods, Wesley (III)	2002	4	78	319	4.09
Derek Moore, S.C.-Aiken (II)	1999	4	102	408	4.00
Tarvis Williams, Hampton (II)	2001	4	114	452	3.96
Lorenzo Coleman, Tennessee Tech (I)	1997	4	113	437	3.87
Theo Ratliff, Wyoming (I)	1995	4	111	425	3.83
John Burke, Southampton (II)	1996	2	54	205	3.80
Alonzo Mourning, Georgetown (I)	1992	4	120	453	3.78
Kino Outlaw, Mount Olive (II)	1996	3	81	305	3.77
Calvin Booth, Penn St. (I)	1999	4	114	428	3.75
Mike Mientus, Allentown (III)	1997	4	87	324	3.72
Tarvis Williams, Hampton (II)	2000	3	82	305	3.72
Lorenzo Williams, Stetson (I)	1991	2	63	234	3.71
Vonzell McGrew, Mo. Western St. (II)	1995	3	57	211	3.70
Dikembe Mutombo, Georgetown (I)	1991	3	96	354	3.69

STEALS

Player, Team (Division)	Last Season	Yrs.	G	Stl.
John Gallogly, Salve Regina (III)	1998	4	98	413
John Linehan, Providence (I)	2002	5	122	385
Eddin Santiago, Mo. Southern St. (II)	2002	4	117	383
Daniel Martinez, McMurry (III)	2000	3	76	380
Eric Murdock, Providence (I)	1991	4	117	376
Ivo Moyano, Polytechnic (N.Y.) (III)	1997	4	87	368
Pepe Sanchez, Temple (I)	2000	4	116	365
Oronn Brown, Clarion (II)	1997	4	106	361
Robert Campbell, Armstrong Atlantic (II)	2001	4	118	357
Eric Bell, New Paltz St. (III)	1996	4	94	355
Cookie Belcher, Nebraska (I)	2001	5	131	353
Kevin Braswell, Georgetown (I)	2002	4	128	349
Bonzi Wells, Ball St. (I)	1998	4	116	347
Scott Clarke, Utica (III)	1996	4	96	346
Marcus Best, Winston-Salem (II)	2002	4	119	345
Gerald Walker, San Francisco (I)	1996	4	111	344
Johnny Rhodes, Maryland (I)	1996	4	122	344
Michael Anderson, Drexel (I)	1988	4	115	341
Kenny Robertson, Cleveland St. (I)	1990	4	119	341
Keith Jennings, East Tenn. St. (I)	1991	4	127	334
Juan Dixon, Maryland (I)	2002	4	141	333
Devlin Herring, Pitt.-Johnstown (II)	1998	4	106	333
Tennyson Whitted, Ramapo (III)#	2002	3	78	330
Desmond Cambridge, Alabama A&M (I)	2002	3	84	330
Jason Hart, Syracuse (I)	2000	4	132	329
Greg Anthony, Portland & UNLV (I)	1991	4	138	329

#-active player

STEAL AVERAGE
(Minimum 200 steals)

Player, Team (Division)	Last Season	Yrs.	G	Stl.	Avg.
Moses Jean-Pierre, Plymouth St. (III)	1994	2	55	303	5.51
Daniel Martinez, McMurry (III)	2000	3	76	380	5.00
Wayne Copeland, Lynn (II)	2000	2	57	254	4.46
Ivo Moyano, Polytechnic (N.Y.) (III)	1997	4	87	368	4.23
Mario Thompson, Occidental (III)	2001	3	71	300	4.23
John Gallogly, Salve Regina (III)	1998	4	98	413	4.21
Greg Dean, Concordia-M'head (III)	1997	3	75	307	4.09
Desmond Cambridge, Alabama A&M (I)	2002	3	84	330	3.93
Mookie Blaylock, Oklahoma (I)	1989	2	74	281	3.80
Eric Bell, New Paltz St. (III)	1996	4	94	355	3.78
Scott Clarke, Utica (III)	1996	4	96	346	3.60
Ricky Hollis, Brockport St. (III)	2002	4	90	322	3.58
Ronn McMahon, Eastern Wash. (I)	1990	3	64	225	3.52
Gerald Garlic, Goucher (III)	1995	3	70	244	3.49
Darrel Lewis, Lincoln (Pa.) (III)	1999	4	86	298	3.47
Oronn Brown, Clarion (II)	1997	4	106	361	3.41
Patrick Herron, Winston-Salem (II)	1995	3	78	263	3.37
David Clark, Bluefield St. (II)	1996	3	83	278	3.35
Eddin Santiago, Mo. Southern St. (II)	2002	4	117	383	3.27
Shuron Woodyard, Villa Julie (III)	1997	3	73	238	3.26
Shawn McCartney, Hunter (III)	1995	3	81	261	3.22
Carl Small, Cornell College (III)	1995	3	69	222	3.22
Eric Murdock, Providence (I)	1991	4	117	376	3.21
Ken Francis, Molloy (II)	1995	3	81	260	3.21
Van Usher, Tennessee Tech (I)	1992	3	85	270	3.18

Award Winners

Division I Consensus All-America Selections

By Season

1929
Charley Hyatt, Pittsburgh; Joe Schaaf, Pennsylvania; Charles Murphy, Purdue; Vern Corbin, California; Thomas Churchill, Oklahoma; John Thompson, Montana St.

1930
Charley Hyatt, Pittsburgh; Charles Murphy, Purdue; Branch McCracken, Indiana; John Thompson, Montana St.; Frank Ward, Montana St.; John Wooden, Purdue.

1931
John Wooden, Purdue; Joe Reiff, Northwestern; George Gregory, Columbia; Wes Fesler, Ohio St.; Elwood Romney, Brigham Young.

1932
Forest Sale, Kentucky; Ed Krause, Notre Dame; John Wooden, Purdue; Louis Berger, Maryland; Les Witte, Wyoming.

1933
Forest Sale, Kentucky; Don Smith, Pittsburgh; Elliott Loughlin, Navy; Joe Reiff, Northwestern; Ed Krause, Notre Dame; Jerry Nemer, Southern California

1934
Claire Cribbs, Pittsburgh; Ed Krause, Notre Dame; Les Witte, Wyoming; Hal Lee, Washington; Norman Cottom, Purdue.

1935
Jack Gray, Texas; Lee Guttero, Southern California; Claire Cribbs, Pittsburgh; Bud Browning, Oklahoma; Leroy Edwards, Kentucky.

1936
Bob Kessler, Purdue; Paul Nowak, Notre Dame; Hank Luisetti, Stanford; Vern Huffman, Indiana; John Moir, Notre Dame; Ike Poole, Arkansas; Bill Kinner, Utah.

1937
Hank Luisetti, Stanford; Paul Nowak, Notre Dame; Jules Bender, Long Island; John Moir, Notre Dame; Jewell Young, Purdue.

1938
Hank Luisetti, Stanford; John Moir, Notre Dame; Fred Pralle, Kansas; Jewell Young, Purdue; Paul Nowak, Notre Dame; Meyer Bloom, Temple.

1939
First Team—Irving Torgoff, Long Island; Urgel Wintermute, Oregon; Chet Jaworski, Rhode Island; Ernie Andres, Indiana; Jimmy Hull, Ohio St.

Second Team—Bob Calihan, Detroit; Michael Novak, Loyola (Ill.); Bernard Opper, Kentucky; Robert Anet, Oregon; Bob Hassmiller, Fordham.

1940
First Team—Ralph Vaughn, Southern California; John Dick, Oregon; Bill Hapac, Illinois; George Glamack, North Carolina; Gus Broberg, Dartmouth.

Second Team—Jack Harvey, Colorado; Marvin Huffman, Indiana; James McNatt, Oklahoma; Jesse Renick, Oklahoma St.

1941
First Team—Gus Broberg, Dartmouth; John Adams, Arkansas; Howard Engleman, Kansas; George Glamack, North Carolina; Gene Englund, Wisconsin.

Second Team—Frank Baumholtz, Ohio; Paul Lindeman, Washington St.; Oscar Schechtman, Long Island; Robert Kinney, Rice; Stan Modzelewski, Rhode Island.

1942
First Team—John Kotz, Wisconsin; Price Brookfield, West Tex. A&M; Bob Kinney, Rice; Andrew Phillip, Illinois; Robert Davies, Seton Hall.

Second Team—Robert Doll, Colorado; Wilfred Doerner, Evansville; Donald Burness, Stanford; George Munroe, Dartmouth; Stan Modzelewski, Rhode Island; John Mandic, Oregon St.

1943
First Team—Andrew Phillip, Illinois; George Senesky, St. Joseph's; Ken Sailors, Wyoming; Harry Boykoff, St. John's (N.Y.); Charles Black, Kansas; Ed Beisser, Creighton; William Closs, Rice.

Second Team—Gerald Tucker, Oklahoma; Bob Rensberger, Notre Dame; Gene Rock, Southern California; John Kotz, Wisconsin; Otto Graham, Northwestern; Gale Bishop, Washington St.

1944
First Team—George Mikan, DePaul; Audley Brindley, Dartmouth; Otto Graham, Northwestern; Robert Brannum, Kentucky; Alva Paine, Oklahoma; Robert Kurland, Oklahoma St.; Leo Klier, Notre Dame.

Second Team—Arnold Ferrin, Utah; Dale Hall, Army; Don Grate, Ohio St.; Bob Dille, Valparaiso; William Henry, Rice; Dick Triptow, DePaul.

1945
First Team—George Mikan, DePaul; Robert Kurland, Oklahoma St.; Arnold Ferrin, Utah; Walton Kirk, Illinois; William Hassett, Notre Dame; William Henry, Rice; Howard Dallmar, Pennsylvania; Wyndol Gray, Bowling Green.

Second Team—Richard Ives, Iowa; Vince Hanson, Washington St.; Dale Hall, Army; Max Norris, Northwestern; Don Grate, Ohio St.; Herb Wilkinson, Iowa.

1946
First Team—George Mikan, DePaul; Robert Kurland, Oklahoma St.; Leo Klier, Notre Dame; Max Norris, Northwestern; Sid Tanenbaum, New York U.

Second Team—Jack Parkinson, Kentucky; John Dillon, North Carolina; Ken Sailors, Wyoming; Charles Black, Kansas; Tony Lavelli, Yale; William Hassett, Notre Dame.

1947
First Team—Ralph Beard, Kentucky; Gerald Tucker, Oklahoma; Alex Groza, Kentucky; Sid Tanenbaum, New York U.; Ralph Hamilton, Indiana.

Second Team—George Kaftan, Holy Cross; John Hargis, Texas; Don Barksdale, UCLA; Arnold Ferrin, Utah; Andrew Phillip, Illinois; Ed Koffenberger, Duke; Vern Gardner, Utah.

1948
First Team—Murray Wier, Iowa, 5-9, Muscatine, Iowa; Ed Macauley, St. Louis, 6-8, St. Louis; Jim McIntyre, Minnesota, 6-10, Minneapolis; Kevin O'Shea, Notre Dame, 6-1, San Francisco; Ralph Beard, Kentucky, 5-10, Louisville, Ky.

Second Team—Dick Dickey, North Carolina St.; Arnold Ferrin, Utah; Alex Groza, Kentucky; Harold Haskins, Hamline; George Kaftan, Holy Cross; Duane Klueh, Indiana St.; Tony Lavelli, Yale; Jack Nichols, Washington; Andy Wolfe, California.

1949
First Team—Tony Lavelli, Yale, 6-3, Somerville, Mass.; Vince Boryla, Denver, 6-5, East Chicago, Ind.; Ed Macauley, St. Louis, 6-8, St. Louis; Alex Groza, Kentucky, 6-7, Martin's Ferry, Ohio; Ralph Beard, Kentucky, 5-10, Louisville, Ky.

Second Team—Bill Erickson, Illinois; Vern Gardner, Utah; Wallace Jones, Kentucky; Jim McIntyre, Minnesota; Ernie Vandeweghe, Colgate.

1950
First Team—Dick Schnittker, Ohio St., 6-5, Sandusky, Ohio; Bob Cousy, Holy Cross, 6-1, St. Albans, N.Y.; Paul Arizin, Villanova, 6-3, Philadelphia; Paul Unruh, Bradley, 6-4, Toulon, Ill.; Bill Sharman, Southern California, 6-2, Porterville, Calif.

Second Team—Charles Cooper, Duquesne; Don Lofgran, San Francisco; Kevin O'Shea, Notre Dame; Don Rehfeldt, Wisconsin; Sherman White, Long Island.

1951
First Team—Bill Mlkvy, Temple, 6-4, Palmerton, Pa.; Sam Ranzino, North Carolina St., 6-1, Gary, Ind.; Bill Spivey, Kentucky, 7-0, Macon, Ga.; Clyde Lovellette, Kansas, 6-9, Terre Haute, Ind.; Gene Melchiorre, Bradley, 5-8, Highland Park, Ill.

Second Team—Ernie Barrett, Kansas St.; Bill Garrett, Indiana; Dick Groat, Duke; Mel Hutchins, Brigham Young; Gale McArthur, Oklahoma St.

1952
First Team—Cliff Hagan, Kentucky, 6-4, Owensboro, Ky.; Rod Fletcher, Illinois, 6-4, Champaign, Ill.; Chuck Darling, Iowa, 6-8, Denver; Clyde Lovellette, Kansas, 6-9, Terre Haute, Ind.; Dick Groat, Duke, 6-0, Swissvale, Pa.

Second Team—Bob Houbregs, Washington; Don Meineke, Dayton; Johnny O'Brien, Seattle; Mark Workman, West Virginia; Bob Zawoluk, St. John's (N.Y.).

1953
First Team—Ernie Beck, Pennsylvania, 6-4, Philadelphia; Bob Houbregs, Washington, 6-7, Seattle; Walt Dukes, Seton Hall, 6-11, Rochester, N.Y.; Tom Gola, La Salle, 6-6, Philadelphia; Johnny O'Brien, Seattle, 5-8, South Amboy, N.J.

Second Team—Dick Knostman, Kansas St.; Bob Pettit, LSU; Joe Richey, Brigham Young; Don Schlundt, Indiana; Frank Selvy, Furman.

1954
First Team—Frank Selvy, Furman, 6-3, Corbin, Ky.; Tom Gola, La Salle, 6-6, Philadelphia; Don Schlundt, Indiana, 6-10, South Bend, Ind.; Bob Pettit, LSU, 6-9, Baton Rouge, La.; Cliff Hagan, Kentucky, 6-4, Owensboro, Ky.

Second Team—Bob Leonard, Indiana; Tom Marshall, Western Ky.; Bob Mattick, Oklahoma St.; Frank Ramsey, Kentucky; Dick Ricketts, Duquesne.

1955
First Team—Tom Gola, La Salle, 6-6, Philadelphia; Dick Ricketts, Duquesne, 6-8, Pottstown, Pa.; Bill Russell, San Francisco, 6-9, Oakland, Calif.; Si Green, Duquesne, 6-3, Brooklyn, N.Y.; Dick Garmaker, Minnesota, 6-3, Hibbing, Minn.

Second Team—Darrell Floyd, Furman; Robin Freeman, Ohio St.; Dickie Hemric, Wake Forest; Don Schlundt, Indiana; Ron Shavlik, North Carolina St.

1956
First Team—Tom Heinsohn, Holy Cross, 6-7, Union City, N.J.; Ron Shavlik, North Carolina St., 6-9, Denver; Bill Russell, San Francisco, 6-9, Oakland, Calif.; Si Green, Duquesne, 6-3, Brooklyn, N.Y.; Robin Freeman, Ohio St., 5-11, Cincinnati.

Second Team—Bob Burrow, Kentucky; Darrell Floyd, Furman; Rod Hundley, West Virginia; K.C. Jones, San Francisco; Willie Naulls, UCLA; Bill Uhl, Dayton.

1957
First Team—Rod Hundley, West Virginia, 6-4, Charleston, W. Va.; Lenny Rosenbluth, North Carolina, 6-5, New York; Jim Krebs, Southern Methodist, 6-8, Webster Groves, Mo.; Wilt Chamberlain, Kansas, 7-0, Philadelphia; Charlie Tyra, Louisville, 6-8, Louisville, Ky.; Chet Forte, Columbia, 5-9, Hackensack, N.J.

Second Team—Elgin Baylor, Seattle; Frank Howard, Ohio St.; Guy Rodgers, Temple; Gary Thompson, Iowa St.; Grady Wallace, South Carolina

1958

First Team—Bob Boozer, Kansas St., 6-8, Omaha, Neb.; Elgin Baylor, Seattle, 6-6, Washington, D.C.; Wilt Chamberlain, Kansas, 7-0, Philadelphia; Oscar Robertson, Cincinnati, 6-5, Indianapolis; Guy Rodgers, Temple, 6-0, Philadelphia; Don Hennon, Pittsburgh, 5-9, Wampum, Pa.

Second Team—Pete Brennan, North Carolina; Archie Dees, Indiana; Dave Gambee, Oregon St.; Mike Farmer, San Francisco; Bailey Howell, Mississippi St.

1959

First Team—Bailey Howell, Mississippi St., 6-7, Middleton, Tenn.; Bob Boozer, Kansas St., 6-8, Omaha, Neb.; Oscar Robertson, Cincinnati, 6-5, Indianapolis; Jerry West, West Virginia, 6-3, Cabin Creek, W.Va.; Johnny Cox, Kentucky, 6-4, Hazard, Ky.

Second Team—Leo Byrd, Marshall; Johnny Green, Michigan St.; Tom Hawkins, Notre Dame; Don Hennon, Pittsburgh; Alan Seiden, St. John's (N.Y.).

1960

First Team—Oscar Robertson, Cincinnati, 6-5, Indianapolis; Jerry West, West Virginia, 6-3, Cabin Creek, W.Va.; Jerry Lucas, Ohio St., 6-8, Middletown, Ohio; Darrall Imhoff, California, 6-10, Alhambra, Calif.; Tom Stith, St. Bonaventure, 6-5, Brooklyn, N.Y.

Second Team—Terry Dischinger, Purdue; Tony Jackson, St. John's (N.Y.); Roger Kaiser, Georgia Tech; Lee Shaffer, North Carolina; Len Wilkens, Providence.

1961

First Team—Jerry Lucas, Ohio St., 6-8, Middletown, Ohio; Tom Stith, St. Bonaventure, 6-5, Brooklyn, N.Y.; Terry Dischinger, Purdue, 6-7, Terre Haute, Ind.; Roger Kaiser, Georgia Tech, 6-1, Dale, Ind.; Chet Walker, Bradley, 6-6, Benton Harbor, Mich.

Second Team—Walt Bellamy, Indiana; Frank Burgess, Gonzaga; Tony Jackson, St. John's (N.Y.); Billy McGill, Utah; Larry Siegfried, Ohio St.

1962

First Team—Jerry Lucas, Ohio St., 6-8, Middletown, Ohio; Len Chappell, Wake Forest, 6-8, Portage Area, Pa.; Billy McGill, Utah, 6-9, Los Angeles; Terry Dischinger, Purdue, 6-7, Terre Haute, Ind.; Chet Walker, Bradley, 6-6, Benton Harbor, Mich.

Second Team—Jack Foley, Holy Cross; John Havlicek, Ohio St.; Art Heyman, Duke; Cotton Nash, Kentucky; John Rudometkin, Southern California; Rod Thorn, West Virginia

1963

First Team—Art Heyman, Duke, 6-5, Rockville Center, N.Y.; Ron Bonham, Cincinnati, 6-5, Muncie, Ind.; Barry Kramer, New York U., 6-4, Schenectady, N.Y.; Jerry Harkness, Loyola (Ill.), 6-3, New York; Tom Thacker, Cincinnati, 6-2, Covington, Ky.

Second Team—Gary Bradds, Ohio St.; Bill Green, Colorado St.; Cotton Nash, Kentucky; Rod Thorn, West Virginia; Nate Thurmond, Bowling Green.

1964

First Team—Bill Bradley, Princeton, 6-5, Crystal City, Mo.; Dave Stallworth, Wichita St., 6-7, Dallas; Gary Bradds, Ohio St., 6-8, Jamestown, Ohio; Walt Hazzard, UCLA, 6-2, Philadelphia; Cotton Nash, Kentucky, 6-5, Leominster, Mass.

Second Team—Ron Bonham, Cincinnati; Mel Counts, Oregon St.; Fred Hetzel, Davidson; Jeff Mullins, Duke; Cazzie Russell, Michigan.

1965

First Team—Bill Bradley, Princeton, 6-5, Crystal City, Mo.; Rick Barry, Miami (Fla.), 6-7, Roselle Park, N.J.; Fred Hetzel, Davidson, 6-8, Washington, D.C.; Cazzie Russell, Michigan, 6-5, Chicago; Gail Goodrich, UCLA, 6-1, North Hollywood, Calif.

Second Team—Bill Buntin, Michigan; Wayne Estes, Utah St.; Clyde Lee, Vanderbilt; Dave Schellhase, Purdue; Dave Stallworth, Wichita St.

1966

First Team—Dave Bing, Syracuse, 6-3, Washington, D.C.; Dave Schellhase, Purdue, 6-4, Evansville, Ind.; Clyde Lee, Vanderbilt, 6-9, Nashville, Tenn.; Cazzie Russell, Michigan, 6-5, Chicago; Jim Walker, Providence, 6-3, Boston.

Second Team—Lou Dampier, Kentucky; Matt Guokas, St. Joseph's; Jack Marin, Duke; Dick Snyder, Davidson; Bob Verga, Duke; Walt Wesley, Kansas.

1967

First Team—Lew Alcindor, UCLA, 7-2, New York; Elvin Hayes, Houston, 6-8, Rayville, La.; Wes Unseld, Louisville, 6-8, Louisville, Ky.; Jim Walker, Providence, 6-3, Boston; Clem Haskins, Western Ky., 6-3, Campbellsville, Ky.; Bob Lloyd, Rutgers, 6-1, Upper Darby, Pa.; Bob Verga, Duke, 6-0, Sea Girt, N.J.

Second Team—Mel Daniels, New Mexico; Sonny Dove, St. John's (N.Y.); Larry Miller, North Carolina; Don May, Dayton; Lou Dampier, Kentucky.

1968

First Team—Wes Unseld, Louisville, 6-8, Louisville, Ky.; Elvin Hayes, Houston, 6-8, Rayville, La.; Lew Alcindor, UCLA, 7-2, New York; Pete Maravich, LSU, 6-5, Raleigh, N.C.; Larry Miller, North Carolina, 6-4, Catasauga, Pa.

Second Team—Lucius Allen, UCLA; Bob Lanier, St. Bonaventure; Don May, Dayton; Calvin Murphy, Niagara; Jo Jo White, Kansas.

1969

First Team—Lew Alcindor, UCLA, 7-2, New York; Spencer Haywood, Detroit, 6-8, Detroit; Pete Maravich, LSU, 6-5, Raleigh, N.C.; Rick Mount, Purdue, 6-4, Lebanon, Ind.; Calvin Murphy, Niagara, 5-10, Norwalk, Conn.

Second Team—Dan Issel, Kentucky; Mike Maloy, Davidson; Bud Ogden, Santa Clara; Charlie Scott, North Carolina; Jo Jo White, Kansas.

1970

First Team—Pete Maravich, LSU, 6-5, Raleigh, N.C.; Rick Mount, Purdue, 6-4, Lebanon, Ind.; Bob Lanier, St. Bonaventure, 6-11, Buffalo, N.Y.; Dan Issel, Kentucky, 6-9, Batavia, Ill.; Calvin Murphy, Niagara, 5-10, Norwalk, Conn.

Second Team—Austin Carr, Notre Dame; Jim Collins, New Mexico St.; John Roche, South Carolina; Charlie Scott, North Carolina; Sidney Wicks, UCLA.

1971

First Team—Austin Carr, Notre Dame, 6-3, Washington, D.C.; Sidney Wicks, UCLA, 6-8, Los Angeles; Artis Gilmore, Jacksonville, 7-2, Dothan, Ala.; Dean Meminger, Marquette, 6-1, New York; Jim McDaniels, Western Ky., 7-0, Scottsville, Ky.

Second Team—John Roche, South Carolina; Johnny Neumann, Mississippi; Ken Durrett, La Salle; Howard Porter, Villanova; Curtis Rowe, UCLA.

1972

First Team—Bill Walton, UCLA, 6-11, La Mesa, Calif.; Dwight Lamar, La.-Lafayette, 6-1, Columbus, Ohio; Ed Ratleff, Long Beach St., 6-6, Columbus, Ohio; Bob McAdoo, North Carolina, 6-8, Greensboro, N.C.; Tom Riker, South Carolina, 6-10, Oyster Bay, N.Y.; Jim Chones, Marquette, 6-11, Racine, Wis.; Henry Bibby, UCLA, 6-1, Franklinton, N.C.

Second Team—Barry Parkhill, Virginia; Jim Price, Louisville; Bud Stallworth, Kansas; Henry Willmore, Michigan; Rich Fuqua, Oral Roberts.

1973

First Team—Doug Collins, Illinois St., 6-6, Benton, Ill.; Ed Ratleff, Long Beach St., 6-6, Columbus, Ohio; Dwight Lamar, La.-Lafayette, 6-1, Columbus, Ohio; Bill Walton, UCLA, 6-11, La Mesa, Calif.; Ernie DiGregorio, Providence, 6-0, North Providence, R.I.; David Thompson, North Carolina St., 6-4, Shelby, N.C.; Keith Wilkes, UCLA, 6-6, Santa Barbara, Calif.

Second Team—Jim Brewer, Minnesota; Kevin Joyce, South Carolina; Kermit Washington, American; Tom Burleson, North Carolina St.; Larry Finch, Memphis; Tom McMillen, Maryland.

1974

First Team—Keith Wilkes, UCLA, 6-6, Santa Barbara, Calif.; John Shumate, Notre Dame, 6-9, Elizabeth, N.J.; Bill Walton, UCLA, 6-11, La Mesa, Calif.; David Thompson, North Carolina St., 6-4, Shelby, N.C.; Marvin Barnes, Providence, 6-9, Providence, R.I.

Second Team—Len Elmore, Maryland; Bobby Jones, North Carolina; Bill Knight, Pittsburgh; Larry Fogle, Canisius; Campy Russell, Michigan.

1975

First Team—David Thompson, North Carolina St., 6-4, Shelby, N.C.; Adrian Dantley, Notre Dame, 6-5, Washington, D.C.; Scott May, Indiana, 6-7, Sandusky, Ohio; John Lucas, Maryland, 6-4, Durham, N.C.; Dave Meyers, UCLA, 6-8, La Habra, Calif.

Second Team—Luther Burden, Utah; Kevin Grevey, Kentucky; Leon Douglas, Alabama; Gus Williams, Southern California; Ron Lee, Oregon.

1976

First Team—Scott May, Indiana, 6-7, Sandusky, Ohio; Richard Washington, UCLA, 6-10, Portland, Ore.; John Lucas, Maryland, 6-4, Durham, N.C.; Kent Benson, Indiana, 6-11, New Castle, Ind.; Adrian Dantley, Notre Dame, 6-5, Washington, D.C.

Second Team—Mitch Kupchak, North Carolina; Phil Sellers, Rutgers; Phil Ford, North Carolina; Earl Tatum, Marquette; Bernard King, Tennessee.

1977

First Team—Otis Birdsong, Houston, 6-4, Winter Haven, Fla.; Marques Johnson, UCLA, 6-7, Los Angeles; Kent Benson, Indiana, 6-11, New Castle, Ind.; Rickey Green, Michigan, 6-2, Chicago; Phil Ford, North Carolina, 6-2, Rocky Mount, N.C.; Bernard King, Tennessee, 6-7, Brooklyn, N.Y.

Second Team—Phil Hubbard, Michigan; Mychal Thompson, Minnesota; Ernie Grunfeld, Tennessee; Greg Ballard, Oregon; Rod Griffin, Wake Forest; Butch Lee, Marquette; Bill Cartwright, San Francisco.

1978

First Team—Phil Ford, North Carolina, 6-2, Rocky Mount, N.C.; Butch Lee, Marquette, 6-2, Bronx, N.Y.; David Greenwood, UCLA, 6-9, Los Angeles; Mychal Thompson, Minnesota, 6-10, Nassau, Bahamas; Larry Bird, Indiana St., 6-9, French Lick, Ind.

Second Team—Jack Givens, Kentucky; Freeman Williams, Portland St.; Rick Robey, Kentucky; Ron Brewer, Arkansas; Rod Griffin, Wake Forest.

1979

First Team—Larry Bird, Indiana St., 6-9, French Lick, Ind.; David Greenwood, UCLA, 6-9, Los Angeles; Earvin Johnson, Michigan St., 6-8, Lansing, Mich.; Sidney Moncrief, Arkansas, 6-4, Little Rock, Ark.; Mike Gminski, Duke, 6-11, Monroe, Conn.

Second Team—Bill Cartwright, San Francisco; Calvin Natt, Northeast La.; Kelly Tripucka, Notre Dame; Mike O'Koren, North Carolina; Jim Spanarkel, Duke; Jim Paxson, Dayton; Sly Williams, Rhode Island.

1980

First Team—Mark Aguirre, DePaul, 6-7, Chicago; Michael Brooks, La Salle, 6-7, Philadelphia; Joe Barry Carroll, Purdue, 7-1, Denver; Kyle Macy, Kentucky, 6-3, Peru, Ind.; Darrell Griffith, Louisville, 6-4, Louisville, Ky.

Second Team—Albert King, Maryland; Mike Gminski, Duke; Mike O'Koren, North Carolina; Sam Worthen, Marquette; Kelvin Ransey, Ohio St.

1981

First Team—Mark Aguirre, DePaul, 6-7, Chicago; Danny Ainge, Brigham Young, 6-5, Eugene, Ore.; Steve Johnson, Oregon St., 6-11, San Bernardino, Calif.; Ralph

Sampson, Virginia, 7-4, Harrisonburg, Va.; Isiah Thomas, Indiana, 6-1, Chicago.

Second Team—Sam Bowie, Kentucky; Jeff Lamp, Virginia; Durand Macklin, LSU; Kelly Tripucka, Notre Dame; Danny Vranes, Utah; Al Wood, North Carolina

1982

First Team—Terry Cummings, DePaul, 6-9, Chicago; Quintin Dailey, San Francisco, 6-4, Baltimore; Eric Floyd, Georgetown, 6-3, Gastonia, N.C.; Ralph Sampson, Virginia, 7-4, Harrisonburg, Va.; James Worthy, North Carolina, 6-9, Gastonia, N.C.

Second Team—Dale Ellis, Tennessee; Kevin Magee, UC Irvine; John Paxson, Notre Dame; Sam Perkins, North Carolina; Paul Pressey, Tulsa.

1983

First Team—Dale Ellis, Tennessee, 6-7, Marietta, Ga.; Patrick Ewing, Georgetown, 7-0, Cambridge, Mass.; Michael Jordan, North Carolina, 6-6, Wilmington, N.C.; Sam Perkins, North Carolina, 6-9, Latham, N.Y.; Ralph Sampson, Virginia, 7-4, Harrisonburg, Va.; Wayman Tisdale, Oklahoma, 6-9, Tulsa, Okla.; Keith Lee, Memphis, 6-9, West Memphis, Ark.

Second Team—Clyde Drexler, Houston; John Paxson, Notre Dame; Steve Stipanovich, Missouri; Jon Sundvold, Missouri; Darrell Walker, Arkansas; Sidney Green, UNLV; Randy Wittman, Indiana.

1984

First Team—Wayman Tisdale, Oklahoma, 6-9, Tulsa, Okla.; Sam Perkins, North Carolina, 6-10, Latham, N.Y.; Patrick Ewing, Georgetown, 7-0, Cambridge, Mass.; Akeem Olajuwon, Houston, 7-0, Lagos, Nigeria; Michael Jordan, North Carolina, 6-5, Wilmington, N.C.

Second Team—Chris Mullin, St. John's (N.Y.); Devin Durrant, Brigham Young; Leon Wood, Cal St. Fullerton; Keith Lee, Memphis; Melvin Turpin, Kentucky; Michael Cage, San Diego St.

1985

First Team—Wayman Tisdale, Oklahoma, 6-9, Tulsa, Okla.; Patrick Ewing, Georgetown, 7-0, Cambridge, Mass.; Keith Lee, Memphis, 6-10, West Memphis, Ark.; Chris Mullin, St. John's (N.Y.), 6-6, Brooklyn, N.Y.; Xavier McDaniel, Wichita St., 6-7, Columbia, S.C.; Johnny Dawkins, Duke, 6-2, Washington, D.C.

Second Team—Kenny Walker, Kentucky; Jon Koncak, Southern Methodist; Len Bias, Maryland; Mark Price, Georgia Tech; Dwayne Washington, Syracuse.

1986

First Team—Len Bias, Maryland, 6-8, Landover, Md.; Kenny Walker, Kentucky, 6-8, Roberta, Ga.; Walter Berry, St. John's (N.Y.), 6-8, Bronx, N.Y.; Johnny Dawkins, Duke, 6-2, Washington, D.C.; Steve Alford, Indiana, 6-2, New Castle, Ind.

Second Team—Dell Curry, Virginia Tech; Brad Daugherty, North Carolina; Danny Manning, Kansas; Ron Harper, Miami (Ohio); Scott Skiles, Michigan St.; David Robinson, Navy.

1987

First Team—David Robinson, Navy, 7-1, Woodbridge, Va.; Danny Manning, Kansas, 6-11, Lawrence, Kan.; Reggie Williams, Georgetown, 6-7, Baltimore; Steve Alford, Indiana, 6-2, New Castle, Ind.; Kenny Smith, North Carolina, 6-3, Queens, N.Y.

Second Team—Armon Gilliam, UNLV; Dennis Hopson, Ohio St.; Mark Jackson, St. John's (N.Y.); Ken Norman, Illinois; Horace Grant, Clemson.

1988

First Team—Gary Grant, Michigan, 6-3, Canton, Ohio; Hersey Hawkins, Bradley, 6-3, Chicago; J.R. Reid, North Carolina, 6-9, Virginia Beach, Va.; Sean Elliott, Arizona, 6-8, Tucson, Ariz.; Danny Manning, Kansas, 6-11, Lawrence, Kan.

Second Team—Mark Macon, Temple; Rony Seikaly, Syracuse; Danny Ferry, Duke; Jerome Lane, Pittsburgh; Mitch Richmond, Kansas St.; Michael Smith, Brigham Young.

1989

First Team—Sean Elliott, Arizona, 6-8, Sr., Tucson, Ariz.; Pervis Ellison, Louisville, 6-9, Sr., Savannah, Ga.; Danny Ferry, Duke, 6-10, Sr., Bowie, Md.; Chris Jackson, LSU, 6-1, Fr., Gulfport, Miss.; Stacey King, Oklahoma, 6-11, Sr., Lawton, Okla.

Second Team—Mookie Blaylock, Oklahoma, 6-1, Sr.; Sherman Douglas, Syracuse, 6-0, Sr.; Jay Edwards, Indiana, 6-4, So.; Todd Lichti, Stanford, 6-4, Sr.; Glen Rice, Michigan, 6-7, Sr.; Lionel Simmons, La Salle, 6-6, Jr.

1990

First Team—Derrick Coleman, Syracuse, 6-10, Sr., Detroit; Chris Jackson, LSU, 6-1, So., Gulfport, Miss.; Larry Johnson, UNLV, 6-7, Jr., Dallas; Gary Payton, Oregon St., 6-3, Sr., Oakland, Calif.; Lionel Simmons, La Salle, 6-6, Sr., Philadelphia.

Second Team—Hank Gathers, Loyola Marymount, 6-7, Sr.; Kendall Gill, Illinois, 6-5, Sr.; Bo Kimble, Loyola Marymount, 6-5, Sr.; Alonzo Mourning, Georgetown, 6-10, So.; Rumeal Robinson, Michigan, 6-2, Sr.; Dennis Scott, Georgia Tech, 6-8, Jr.; Doug Smith, Missouri, 6-10, Jr.

1991

First Team—Kenny Anderson, Georgia Tech, 6-2, So., Rego Park, N.Y.; Jim Jackson, Ohio St., 6-6, So., Toledo, Ohio; Larry Johnson, UNLV, 6-7, Sr., Dallas; Shaquille O'Neal, LSU, 7-1, So., San Antonio, Texas; Billy Owens, Syracuse, 6-9, Jr., Carlisle, Pa.

Second Team—Stacey Augmon, UNLV, 6-8, Sr.; Keith Jennings, East Tenn. St., 5-7, Sr.; Christian Laettner, Duke, 6-11, Jr.; Eric Murdock, Providence, 6-2, Sr.; Steve Smith, Michigan St., 6-6, Sr.

1992

First Team—Jim Jackson, Ohio St., 6-6, Jr., Toledo, Ohio; Christian Laettner, Duke, 6-11, Sr., Angola, N.Y.; Harold Miner, Southern California, 6-5, Jr., Inglewood, Calif.; Alonzo Mourning, Georgetown, 6-10, Sr., Chesapeake, Va.; Shaquille O'Neal, LSU, 7-1, Jr., San Antonio, Texas.

Second Team—Byron Houston, Oklahoma St., 6-7, Sr.; Don MacLean, UCLA, 6-10, Sr.; Anthony Peeler, Missouri, 6-4, Sr.; Malik Sealy, St. John's (N.Y.), 6-7, Sr.; Walt Williams, Maryland, 6-8, Sr.

1993

First Team—Calbert Cheaney, Indiana, 6-7, Sr., Evansville, Ind.; Anfernee Hardaway, Memphis, 6-7, Jr., Memphis, Tenn.; Bobby Hurley, Duke, 6-0, Sr., Jersey City, N.J.; Jamal Mashburn, Kentucky, 6-8, Jr., New York; Chris Webber, Michigan, 6-9, So., Detroit.

Second Team—Terry Dehere, Seton Hall, 6-3, Sr.; Grant Hill, Duke, 6-7, Jr.; Billy McCaffrey, Vanderbilt, 6-3, Jr.; Eric Montross, North Carolina, 7-0, Jr.; J.R. Rider, UNLV, 6-7, Sr.; Glenn Robinson, Purdue, 6-9, So.; Rodney Rogers, Wake Forest, 6-8, Jr.

1994

First Team—Grant Hill, Duke, 6-8, Sr., Reston, Va.; Jason Kidd, California, 6-4, So., Oakland, Calif.; Donyell Marshall, Connecticut, 6-9, Jr., Reading, Pa.; Glenn Robinson, Purdue, 6-8, Jr., Gary, Ind.; Clifford Rozier, Louisville, 6-9, Jr., Bradenton, Fla.

Second Team—Melvin Booker, Missouri, 6-2, Sr.; Eric Montross, North Carolina, 7-0, Sr.; Lamond Murray, California, 6-7, Jr.; Khalid Reeves, Arizona, 6-2, Sr.; Jalen Rose, Michigan, 6-8, Jr.; Corliss Williamson, Arkansas, 6-7, So.

1995

First Team—Ed O'Bannon, UCLA, 6-8, Sr., Lakewood, Calif.; Shawn Respert, Michigan St., 6-3, Sr., Detroit; Joe

Smith, Maryland, 6-10, So., Norfolk, Va.; Jerry Stackhouse, North Carolina, 6-6, So., Kingston, N.C.; Damon Stoudamire, Arizona, 6-10, Sr., Portland, Ore.

Second Team—Randolph Childress, Wake Forest, 6-2, Sr.; Kerry Kittles, Villanova, 6-5, Jr.; Lou Roe, Massachusetts, 6-7, Sr.; Rasheed Wallace, North Carolina, 6-10, So.; Corliss Williamson, Arkansas, 6-7, Jr.

1996

First Team—Ray Allen, Connecticut, 6-5, Jr., Dalzell, S.C.; Marcus Camby, Massachusetts, 6-11, Jr., Hartford, Conn.; Tony Delk, Kentucky, 6-1, Sr., Brownsville, Tenn.; Tim Duncan, Wake Forest, 6-10, Jr., St. Croix, Virgin Islands; Allen Iverson, Georgetown, 6-1, So., Hampton, Va.; Kerry Kittles, Villanova, 6-5, Sr., New Orleans.

Second Team—Danny Fortson, Cincinnati, 6-7, So.; Keith Van Horn, Utah, 6-9, Jr.; Jacque Vaughn, Kansas, 6-1, Jr.; John Wallace, Syracuse, 6-8, Sr.; Lorenzen Wright, Memphis, 6-11, So.

1997

First Team—Tim Duncan, Wake Forest, 6-10, Sr., St. Croix, Virgin Islands; Danny Fortson, Cincinnati, 6-7, Jr., Pittsburgh; Raef LaFrentz, Kansas, 6-11, Jr., Monona, Ia.; Ron Mercer, Kentucky, 6-7, So., Nashville, Tenn.; Keith Van Horn, Utah, 6-9, Sr., Diamond Bar, Calif.

Second Team—Chauncey Billups, Colorado, 6-3, So.; Bobby Jackson, Minnesota, 6-1, Sr.; Antawn Jamison, North Carolina, 6-9, So.; Brevin Knight, Stanford, 5-10, Sr.; Jacque Vaughn, Kansas, 6-1, Sr.

1998

First Team—Mike Bibby, Arizona, 6-2, So., Phoenix, Ariz.; Antawn Jamison, North Carolina, 6-9, Jr., Charlotte, N.C.; Raef LaFrentz, Kansas, 6-11, Sr., Monona, Ia.; Paul Pierce, Kansas, 6-7, Jr., Inglewood, Calif.; Miles Simon, Arizona, 6-5, Sr., Fullerton, Calif.

Second Team—Vince Carter, North Carolina, 6-6, Jr.; Mateen Cleaves, Michigan St., 6-2, So.; Pat Garrity, Notre Dame, 6-9, Sr.; Richard Hamilton, Connecticut, 6-6, So.; Ansu Sesay, Mississippi, 6-9, Sr.

1999

First Team—Elton Brand, Duke, 6-8, So., Peekskill, N.Y.; Mateen Cleaves, Michigan St., 6-2, Jr., Flint, Mich.; Richard Hamilton, Connecticut, 6-6, Jr., Coatesville, Pa.; Andre Miller, Utah, 6-2, Sr., Los Angeles; Jason Terry, Arizona, 6-2, Sr., Seattle.

Second Team—Evan Eschmeyer, Northwestern, 6-11, Sr.; Steve Francis, Maryland, 6-3, Jr.; Trajan Langdon, Duke, 6-3, Sr.; Chris Porter, Auburn, 6-7, Jr.; Wally Szczerbiak, Miami (Ohio), 6-8, Sr.

2000

First Team—Chris Carrawell, Duke, 6-6, Sr., St. Louis; Marcus Fizer, Iowa St., Jr., Arcadia, La.; A.J. Guyton, Indiana, 6-1, Sr., Peoria, Ill.; Kenyon Martin, Cincinnati, 6-9, Sr., Dallas, Tex.; Chris Mihm, Texas, 7-0, Jr., Austin, Tex.; Troy Murphy, Notre Dame, 6-10, So., Morristown, N.J.

Second Team—Courtney Alexander, Fresno St., 6-6, Sr.; Shane Battier, Duke, 6-8, Jr.; Mateen Cleaves, Michigan St., 6-2, Sr.; Scoonie Penn, Ohio St., 5-10, Sr.; Morrison Peterson, Michigan St., 6-6, Sr.; Stromile Swift, LSU, 6-9, So.

2001

First Team—Shane Battier, Duke, 6-8, Sr., Birmingham, Mich.; Joseph Forte, North Carolina, 6-4, So., Greenbelt, Md.; Casey Jacobsen, Stanford, 6-6, So., Glendora, Calif.; Troy Murphy, Notre Dame, 6-10, Jr., Morristown, N.J.; Jason Williams, Duke, 6-2, So., Plainfield, N.J.

Second Team—Troy Bell, Boston College, 6-1, So.; Michael Bradley, Villanova, 6-10, Jr.; Tayshaun Prince, Kentucky, 6-9, Jr.; Jason Richardson, Michigan St., 6-6, So.; Jamaal Tinsley, Iowa St., 6-3 Sr.

2002

First Team—Juan Dixon, Maryland, 6-3, Sr., Baltimore, Md.; Dan Dickau, Gonzaga, 6-1, Sr., Vancouver, Wash.; Drew Gooden, Kansas, 6-10, Jr., Richmond, Calif.; Steve Logan, Cincinnati, 6-1, Sr., Cleveland, Ohio; Jason Williams, Duke, 6-2, Jr., Plainfield, N.J.

Second Team—Sam Clancy, Southern California, 6-7, Sr.; Mike Dunleavy, Duke, 6-9, Jr.; Casey Jacobsen, Stanford, 6-6, Jr.; Jared Jeffries, Indiana, 6-10, So.; David West, Xavier, 6-8, Jr.

Teams used for consensus selections:

Helms Foundation—1929-48
Converse Yearbook—1932-48
College Humor Magazine—1929-33, 1936
Christy Walsh Syndicate—1929-30
Literary Digest Magazine—1934
Madison Square Garden—1937-42
Omaha World Newspaper—1937
Newspaper Enterprises Assn.—1938, 1953-63
Colliers (Basketball Coaches)—1939, 1949-56
Pic Magazine—1942-44
Argosy Magazine—1945

True Magazine—1946-47
International News Service—1950-58
Look Magazine—1949-63
United Press International—1949-96
Sporting News—1943-46, 1997-2002
The Associated Press—1948-2002
National Association of Basketball Coaches—1957-2002
U.S. Basketball Writers Association—1960-2002

Consensus First-Team All-Americans By Team

ARIZONA
1988—Sean Elliott
1989—Sean Elliott
1995—Damon Stoudamire
1998—Mike Bibby
        Miles Simon
1999—Jason Terry

ARKANSAS
1936—Ike Poole
1941—John Adams
1979—Sidney Moncrief

BOWLING GREEN
1945—Wyndol Gray

BRADLEY
1950—Paul Unruh
1951—Gene Melchiorre
1961—Chet Walker
1962—Chet Walker
1988—Hersey Hawkins

BRIGHAM YOUNG
1931—Elwood Romney
1981—Danny Ainge

CALIFORNIA
1929—Vern Corbin
1960—Darrall Imhoff
1994—Jason Kidd

CINCINNATI
1958—Oscar Robertson
1959—Oscar Robertson
1960—Oscar Robertson
1963—Ron Bonham
        Tom Thacker
1997—Danny Fortson
2000—Kenyon Martin
2002—Steve Logan

COLUMBIA
1931—George Gregory
1957—Chet Forte

CONNECTICUT
1994—Donyell Marshall
1996—Ray Allen
1999—Richard Hamilton

CREIGHTON
1943—Ed Beisser

DARTMOUTH
1940—Gus Broberg
1941—Gus Broberg
1944—Audley Brindley

DAVIDSON
1965—Fred Hetzel

DENVER
1949—Vince Boryla

DEPAUL
1944—George Mikan
1945—George Mikan
1946—George Mikan
1980—Mark Aguirre

1981—Mark Aguirre
1982—Terry Cummings

DETROIT
1969—Spencer Haywood

DUKE
1952—Dick Groat
1963—Art Heyman
1967—Bob Verga
1979—Mike Gminski
1985—Johnny Dawkins
1986—Johnny Dawkins
1989—Danny Ferry
1992—Christian Laettner
1993—Bobby Hurley
1994—Grant Hill
1999—Elton Brand
2000—Chris Carrawell
2001—Shane Battier
        Jason Williams
2002—Jason Williams

DUQUESNE
1955—Dick Ricketts
        Si Green
1956—Si Green

FURMAN
1954—Frank Selvy

GEORGETOWN
1982—Eric Floyd
1983—Patrick Ewing
1984—Patrick Ewing
1985—Patrick Ewing
1987—Reggie Williams
1992—Alonzo Mourning
1996—Allen Iverson

GEORGIA TECH
1961—Roger Kaiser
1991—Kenny Anderson

GONZAGA
2002—Dan Dickau

HOLY CROSS
1950—Bob Cousy
1956—Tom Heinsohn

HOUSTON
1967—Elvin Hayes
1968—Elvin Hayes
1977—Otis Birdsong
1984—Akeem Olajuwon

ILLINOIS
1940—Bill Hapac
1942—Andrew Phillip
1943—Andrew Phillip
1945—Walton Kirk
1952—Rod Fletcher

ILLINOIS ST.
1973—Doug Collins

INDIANA
1930—Branch McCracken
1936—Vern Huffman
1939—Ernie Andres
1947—Ralph Hamilton
1954—Don Schlundt
1975—Scott May
1976—Scott May
        Kent Benson
1977—Kent Benson

1981—Isiah Thomas
1986—Steve Alford
1987—Steve Alford
1993—Calbert Cheaney
2000—A.J. Guyton

INDIANA ST.
1978—Larry Bird
1979—Larry Bird

IOWA
1948—Murray Wier
1952—Chuck Darling

IOWA ST.
2000—Marcus Fizer

JACKSONVILLE
1971—Artis Gilmore

KANSAS
1938—Fred Pralle
1941—Howard Engleman
1943—Charles Black
1951—Clyde Lovellette
1952—Clyde Lovellette
1957—Wilt Chamberlain
1958—Wilt Chamberlain
1987—Danny Manning
1988—Danny Manning
1997—Raef LaFrentz
1998—Raef LaFrentz
        Paul Pierce
2002—Drew Gooden

KANSAS ST.
1958—Bob Boozer
1959—Bob Boozer

KENTUCKY
1932—Forest Sale
1933—Forest Sale
1935—Leroy Edwards
1944—Robert Brannum
1947—Ralph Beard
        Alex Groza
1948—Ralph Beard
1949—Ralph Beard
        Alex Groza
1951—Bill Spivey
1952—Cliff Hagan
1954—Cliff Hagan
1959—Johnny Cox
1964—Cotton Nash
1970—Dan Issel
1980—Kyle Macy
1986—Kenny Walker
1993—Jamal Mashburn
1996—Tony Delk
1997—Ron Mercer

LA.-LAFAYETTE
1972—Dwight Lamar
1973—Dwight Lamar

LA SALLE
1953—Tom Gola
1954—Tom Gola
1955—Tom Gola
1980—Michael Brooks
1990—Lionel Simmons

LONG BEACH ST.
1972—Ed Ratleff
1973—Ed Ratleff

LONG ISLAND
1937—Jules Bender
1939—Irving Torgoff

LSU
1954—Bob Pettit
1968—Pete Maravich
1969—Pete Maravich
1970—Pete Maravich
1989—Chris Jackson
1990—Chris Jackson
1991—Shaquille O'Neal
1992—Shaquille O'Neal

LOUISVILLE
1957—Charlie Tyra
1967—Wes Unseld
1968—Wes Unseld
1980—Darrell Griffith
1989—Pervis Ellison
1994—Clifford Rozier

LOYOLA (ILL.)
1963—Jerry Harkness

MARQUETTE
1971—Dean Meminger
1972—Jim Chones
1978—Butch Lee

MARYLAND
1932—Louis Berger
1975—John Lucas
1976—John Lucas
1986—Len Bias
1995—Joe Smith
2002—Juan Dixon

MASSACHUSETTS
1996—Marcus Camby

MEMPHIS
1983—Keith Lee
1985—Keith Lee
1993—Anfernee Hardaway

MIAMI (FLA.)
1965—Rick Barry

MICHIGAN
1965—Cazzie Russell
1966—Cazzie Russell
1977—Rickey Green
1988—Gary Grant
1993—Chris Webber

MICHIGAN ST.
1979—Earvin Johnson
1995—Shawn Respert
1999—Mateen Cleaves

MINNESOTA
1948—Jim McIntyre
1955—Dick Garmaker
1978—Mychal Thompson

MISSISSIPPI ST.
1959—Bailey Howell

MONTANA ST.
1929—John Thompson
1930—John Thompson
        Frank Ward

NAVY
1933—Elliott Loughlin
1987—David Robinson

UNLV
1990—Larry Johnson
1991—Larry Johnson

NEW YORK U.
1946—Sid Tanenbaum
1947—Sid Tanenbaum
1963—Barry Kramer

NIAGARA
1969—Calvin Murphy
1970—Calvin Murphy

NORTH CAROLINA
1940—George Glamack
1941—George Glamack
1957—Lenny Rosenbluth
1968—Larry Miller
1972—Bob McAdoo
1977—Phil Ford
1978—Phil Ford
1982—James Worthy
1983—Michael Jordan
      Sam Perkins
1984—Michael Jordan
      Sam Perkins
1987—Kenny Smith
1988—J.R. Reid
1995—Jerry Stackhouse
1998—Antawn Jamison
2001—Joseph Forte

NORTH CAROLINA ST.
1951—Sam Ranzino
1956—Ron Shavlik
1973—David Thompson
1974—David Thompson
1975—David Thompson

NORTHWESTERN
1931—Joe Reiff
1933—Joe Reiff
1944—Otto Graham
1946—Max Norris

NOTRE DAME
1932—Ed Krause
1933—Ed Krause
1934—Ed Krause
1936—Paul Nowak
      John Moir
1937—Paul Nowak
      John Moir
1938—Paul Nowak
      John Moir
1944—Leo Klier
1945—William Hassett
1946—Leo Klier
1948—Kevin O'Shea
1971—Austin Carr
1974—John Shumate
1975—Adrian Dantley
1976—Adrian Dantley
2000—Troy Murphy
2001—Troy Murphy

OHIO ST.
1931—Wes Fesler
1939—Jimmy Hull
1950—Dick Schnittker
1956—Robin Freeman
1960—Jerry Lucas
1961—Jerry Lucas
1962—Jerry Lucas
1964—Gary Bradds
1991—Jim Jackson
1992—Jim Jackson

OKLAHOMA
1929—Thomas Churchill
1935—Bud Browning

1944—Alva Paine
1947—Gerald Tucker
1983—Wayman Tisdale
1984—Wayman Tisdale
1985—Wayman Tisdale
1989—Stacey King

OKLAHOMA ST.
1944—Robert Kurland
1945—Robert Kurland
1946—Robert Kurland

OREGON
1939—Urgel Wintermute
1940—John Dick

OREGON ST.
1981—Steve Johnson
1990—Gary Payton

PENNSYLVANIA
1929—Joe Schaaf
1945—Howard Dallmar
1953—Ernie Beck

PITTSBURGH
1929—Charley Hyatt
1930—Charley Hyatt
1933—Don Smith
1934—Claire Cribbs
1935—Claire Cribbs
1958—Don Hennon

PRINCETON
1964—Bill Bradley
1965—Bill Bradley

PROVIDENCE
1966—Jim Walker
1967—Jim Walker
1973—Ernie DiGregorio
1974—Marvin Barnes

PURDUE
1929—Charles Murphy
1930—Charles Murphy
      John Wooden
1931—John Wooden
1932—John Wooden
1934—Norman Cottom
1936—Bob Kessler
1937—Jewell Young
1938—Jewell Young
1961—Terry Dischinger
1962—Terry Dischinger
1966—Dave Schellhase
1969—Rick Mount
1970—Rick Mount
1980—Joe Barry Carroll
1994—Glenn Robinson

RHODE ISLAND
1939—Chet Jaworski

RICE
1942—Bob Kinney
1943—William Closs
1945—William Henry

RUTGERS
1967—Bob Lloyd

ST. BONAVENTURE
1960—Tom Stith
1961—Tom Stith
1970—Bob Lanier

ST. JOHN'S (N.Y.)
1943—Harry Boykoff
1985—Chris Mullin
1986—Walter Berry

ST. JOSEPH'S
1943—George Senesky

ST. LOUIS
1948—Ed Macauley
1949—Ed Macauley

SAN FRANCISCO
1955—Bill Russell
1956—Bill Russell
1982—Quintin Dailey

SEATTLE
1953—Johnny O'Brien
1958—Elgin Baylor

SETON HALL
1942—Robert Davies
1953—Walt Dukes

SOUTH CAROLINA
1972—Tom Riker

SOUTHERN CALIFORNIA
1933—Jerry Nemer
1935—Lee Guttero
1940—Ralph Vaughn
1950—Bill Sharman
1992—Harold Miner

SOUTHERN METHODIST
1957—Jim Krebs

STANFORD
1936—Hank Luisetti
1937—Hank Luisetti
1938—Hank Luisetti
2001—Casey Jacobsen

SYRACUSE
1966—Dave Bing
1990—Derrick Coleman
1991—Billy Owens

TEMPLE
1938—Meyer Bloom
1951—Bill Mlkvy
1958—Guy Rodgers

TENNESSEE
1977—Bernard King
1983—Dale Ellis

TEXAS
1935—Jack Gray
2000—Chris Mihm

UCLA
1964—Walt Hazzard
1965—Gail Goodrich
1967—Lew Alcindor
1968—Lew Alcindor
1969—Lew Alcindor
1971—Sidney Wicks
1972—Bill Walton
      Henry Bibby
1973—Bill Walton
      Keith Wilkes
1974—Bill Walton
      Keith Wilkes
1975—Dave Meyers
1976—Richard Washington
1977—Marques Johnson
1978—David Greenwood
1979—David Greenwood
1995—Ed O'Bannon

UTAH
1936—Bill Kinner
1945—Arnold Ferrin
1962—Billy McGill
1997—Keith Van Horn
1999—Andre Miller

VANDERBILT
1966—Clyde Lee

VILLANOVA
1950—Paul Arizin
1996—Kerry Kittles

VIRGINIA
1981—Ralph Sampson
1982—Ralph Sampson
1983—Ralph Sampson

WAKE FOREST
1962—Len Chappell
1996—Tim Duncan
1997—Tim Duncan

WASHINGTON
1934—Hal Lee
1953—Bob Houbregs

WEST TEX. A&M
1942—Price Brookfield

WEST VIRGINIA
1957—Rod Hundley
1959—Jerry West
1960—Jerry West

WESTERN KY.
1967—Clem Haskins
1971—Jim McDaniels

WICHITA ST.
1964—Dave Stallworth
1985—Xavier McDaniel

WISCONSIN
1941—Gene Englund
1942—John Kotz

WYOMING
1932—Les Witte
1934—Les Witte
1943—Ken Sailors

YALE
1949—Tony Lavelli

Team Leaders In Consensus First-Team All-Americans

(Ranked on total number of selections)

Team	No.	Players
Kentucky	20	15
Notre Dame	19	10
UCLA	18	12
North Carolina	17	13
Purdue	16	10
Duke	15	12
Indiana	14	11
Kansas	13	9
Ohio St.	10	7
Cincinnati	8	6
Oklahoma	8	6
LSU	8	4
Georgetown	7	5
Arizona	6	5
Louisville	6	5
Maryland	6	5
Pittsburgh	6	4
DePaul	6	3
Southern California	5	5
Utah	5	5
Bradley	5	4
Illinois	5	4
La Salle	5	3
Michigan	5	3
North Carolina St.	5	3

Division I Academic All-Americans By Team

AIR FORCE
1968—Cliff Parsons
1970—Jim Cooper
1978—Tom Schneeberger

AMERICAN
1972—Kermit Washington
1973—Kermit Washington
1987—Patrick Witting

ARIZONA
1976—Bob Elliott
1977—Bob Elliott

ARIZONA ST.
1964—Art Becker
1999—Bobby Lazor

ARKANSAS
1978—Jim Counce

ARMY
1964—Mike Silliman

BALL ST.
2002—Patrick Jackson

BAYLOR
1996—Doug Brandt
1997—Doug Brandt

BELMONT
2002—Wes Burtner

BOSTON COLLEGE
1968—Terry Driscoll

BRIGHAM YOUNG
1980—Danny Ainge
1981—Danny Ainge
1983—Devin Durrant
1984—Devin Durrant
1987—Michael Smith
1988—Michael Smith
1989—Michael Smith
1990—Andy Toolson

BROWN
1986—Jim Turner

BUCKNELL
1999—Valter Karavanic

CALIFORNIA
1987—David Butler

CENTRAL MICH.
1993—Sander Scott

COL. OF CHARLESTON
2000—Jody Lumpkin
2001—Jody Lumpkin

CINCINNATI
1967—Mike Rolf

CLEVELAND ST.
1973—Pat Lyons

COLGATE
1997—Adonal Foyle

CONNECTICUT
1967—Wes Bialosuknia

CREIGHTON
1964—Paul Silas
1978—Rick Apke

DARTMOUTH
1984—Paul Anderson
1996—Seamus Lonergan

DAVIDSON
1988—Derek Rucker

DAYTON
1979—Jim Paxson
1981—Mike Kanieski
1982—Mike Kanieski

DEPAUL
1991—Stephen Howard
1992—Stephen Howard

DUKE
1963—Jay Buckley
1964—Jay Buckley

1971—Dick DeVenzio
1972—Gary Melchionni
1975—Bob Fleischer
1978—Mike Gminski
        Jim Spanarkel
1979—Mike Gminski
        Jim Spanarkel
1980—Mike Gminski
2000—Shane Battier
2001—Shane Battier

DUQUESNE
1969—Bill Zopf
1970—Bill Zopf

EVANSVILLE
1989—Scott Haffner

FAIRLEIGH DICKINSON
1978—John Jorgensen

FLORIDA
2002—Matt Bonner

FORDHAM
1975—Darryl Brown

GEORGE WASHINGTON
1976—Pat Tallent
1986—Steve Frick

GEORGIA
1988—Alec Kessler
1989—Alec Kessler
1990—Alec Kessler

GEORGIA TECH
1964—Jim Caldwell
1969—Rich Yunkus
1970—Rich Yunkus
1971—Rich Yunkus
1998—Matt Harpring

GONZAGA
1984—Bryce McPhee
        John Stockton
1985—Bryce McPhee
1992—Jarrod Davis
1993—Jeff Brown
1994—Jeff Brown
2002—Dan Dickau

HARVARD
1985—Joe Carrabino
1987—Arne Duncan

HOLY CROSS
1969—Ed Siudut
1978—Ronnie Perry
1979—Ronnie Perry
1980—Ronnie Perry
1991—Jim Nairus,

ILLINOIS
1968—Dave Scholz
1969—Dave Scholz
1971—Rich Howatt
1974—Rick Schmidt
1975—Rick Schmidt

ILLINOIS ST.
1973—Doug Collins

INDIANA
1964—Dick Van Arsdale
1965—Dick Van Arsdale
1965—Tom Van Arsdale
1973—John Ritter
1974—Steve Green
1975—Steve Green
1976—Kent Benson
1977—Kent Benson
1978—Wayne Radford
1982—Randy Wittman
1983—Randy Wittman
1985—Uwe Blab
1989—Joe Hillman

IOWA ST.
1995—Fred Hoiberg

JACKSONVILLE
1971—Vaughan Wedeking
1983—Maurice Roulhac

KANSAS
1971—Bud Stallworth
1974—Tom Kivisto
1977—Ken Koenigs
        Chris Barnthouse
1978—Ken Koenigs
1979—Darnell Valentine
1980—Darnell Valentine
1981—Darnell Valentine
1982—David Magley
1996—Jacque Vaughn
1997—Jerod Haase
        Jacque Vaughn
1999—Ryan Robertson

KANSAS ST.
1968—Earl Seyfert
1982—Tim Jankovich
        Ed Nealy

KENTUCKY
1966—Lou Dampier
1967—Lou Dampier
1969—Larry Conley
1970—Dan Issel
        Dan Pratt
1971—Mike Casey
1975—Bob Guyette
        Jimmy Dan Conner
1979—Kyle Macy

LA SALLE
1977—Tony DiLeo
1988—Tim Legler
1992—Jack Hurd

LAMAR
1999—Matt Sundblad

LEWIS
1989—Jamie Martin

LOUISVILLE
1976—Phil Bond

LOYOLA MARYMOUNT
1973—Steve Smith

MANHATTAN
1990—Peter Runge

MARQUETTE
1982—Marc Marotta
1983—Marc Marotta
1984—Marc Marotta

MARSHALL
1972—Mike D'Antoni
1973—Mike D'Antoni

MARYLAND
1972—Tom McMillen
1973—Tom McMillen
1974—Tom McMillen
1991—Matt Roe

MIAMI (OHIO)
1993—Craig Michaelis

MICHIGAN
1976—Steve Grote
1981—Marty Bodnar

MICHIGAN ST.
1970—Ralph Simpson
1979—Greg Kelser

MISSISSIPPI
1975—Dave Shepherd

MISSOURI
1983—Steve Stipanovich

MONTANA
1981—Craig Zanon
1985—Larry Krystkowiak
1986—Larry Krystkowiak

MURRAY ST.
1985—Mike Lahm

NEBRASKA
1984—John Matzke

UNLV
1983—Danny Tarkanian
1984—Danny Tarkanian

NEW MEXICO
1969—Ron Becker
1970—Ron Becker

NEW MEXICO ST.
2001—Eric Channing
2002—Eric Channing

NORTH CAROLINA
1965—Billy Cunningham
1970—Charlie Scott
1972—Dennis Wuycik
        Steve Previs
1976—Tommy LaGarde
1986—Steve Hale
1994—Eric Montross

UNC GREENSBORO
2001—Nathan Jameson

NORTH CAROLINA ST.
1984—Terry Gannon
1985—Terry Gannon
1995—Todd Fuller
1996—Todd Fuller

NORTHEASTERN
1977—David Caligaris
1978—David Caligaris

NORTHERN ILL.
1984—Tim Dillion
1998—T.J. Lux
2000—T.J. Lux

NORTHERN IOWA
1984—Randy Kraayenbrink

NORTHWESTERN
1967—Jim Burns
1980—Mike Campbell
1987—Shon Morris
1988—Shon Morris

NOTRE DAME
1967—Bob Arnzen
1968—Bob Arnzen
1969—Bob Arnzen
1974—Gary Novak
1979—Kelly Tripucka
1980—Rich Branning
1982—John Paxson
1983—John Paxson
1997—Pat Garrity
1998—Pat Garrity

OHIO
1971—Craig Love
1977—Steve Skaggs
1990—Dave Jamerson

OHIO ST.
1968—Bill Hosket

OKLAHOMA
1974—Alvan Adams
1975—Alvan Adams
1980—Terry Stotts

OKLAHOMA ST.
1964—Gary Hassmann
1969—Joe Smith

PACIFIC (CAL.)
1967—Keith Swagerty

PENNSYLVANIA
1972—Robert Morse

PENN ST.
1994—John Amaechi
1995—John Amaechi

PRINCETON
1965—Bill Bradley
1991—Kit Mueller

PURDUE
1965—Dave Schellhase
1966—Dave Schellhase
1972—Robert Ford
1981—Brian Walker
1982—Keith Edmonson
1983—Steve Reid
1985—Steve Reid

RADFORD
1998—Corey Reed

RICE
1994—Adam Peakes

ST. FRANCIS (PA.)
1990—Michael Iuzzolino
1991—Michael Iuzzolino

ST. LOUIS
1968—Rich Niemann
1994—Scott Highmark
1995—Scott Highmark

SAN DIEGO ST.
1976—Steve Copp

SANTA CLARA
1968—Dennis Awtrey
1969—Dennis Awtrey
1970—Dennis Awtrey

SIENA
1985—Doug Peotzch
1992—Bruce Schroeder

SOUTH CAROLINA
1970—John Roche
1971—John Roche

SOUTHERN ILL.
1976—Mike Glenn
1977—Mike Glenn

SOUTHERN METHODIST
1977—Pete Lodwick

STANFORD
2000—Mark Madsen

SYRACUSE
1981—Dan Schayes

TENNESSEE
1968—Bill Justus
1993—Lang Wiseman

TEXAS
1979—Jim Krivacs

TEXAS A&M
1964—Bill Robinette

UTEP
2000—Brandon Wolfram
2001—Brandon Wolfram

TULSA
1999—Michael Ruffin

UCLA
1967—Mike Warren
1969—Kenny Heitz
1971—Sidney Wicks
1972—Bill Walton
        Keith Wilkes
        Greg Lee
1973—Bill Walton
        Keith Wilkes
        Greg Lee

1974—Bill Walton
        Keith Wilkes
        Greg Lee
1975—Ralph Drollinger
1977—Marques Johnson
1979—Kiki Vandeweghe
1980—Kiki Vandeweghe
1995—George Zidek

UTAH
1970—Mike Newlin
1971—Mike Newlin
1977—Jeff Jonas
1998—Michael Doleac

UTAH ST.
1964—Gary Watts
1980—Dean Hunger
1982—Larry Bergeson
1996—Eric Franson

VANDERBILT
1975—Jeff Fosnes
1976—Jeff Fosnes
1993—Bruce Elder

VILLANOVA
1973—Tom Inglesby
1982—John Pinone
1983—John Pinone
1986—Harold Jensen
1987—Harold Jensen

VIRGINIA
1976—Wally Walker
1981—Jeff Lamp
        Lee Raker

VMI
1980—Andy Kolesar
1981—Andy Kolesar

WASHINGTON
1982—Dave Henley

WASHINGTON ST.
1989—Brian Quinnett

WEBER ST.
1985—Randy Worster

WICHITA ST.
1967—Jamie Thompson
1969—Ron Mendell

WILLIAM & MARY
1985—Keith Cieplicki

WISCONSIN
1974—Dan Anderson

WIS.-GREEN BAY
1992—Tony Bennett

Division I Player Of The Year

Season	United Press International	The Associated Press	U.S. Basketball Writers Assn.	Wooden Award	Nat'l Assn. of Basketball Coaches	Naismith Award	Frances Pomeroy Naismith Award
1955	Tom Gola La Salle						
1956	Bill Russell San Francisco						
1957	Chet Forte Columbia						
1958	Oscar Robertson Cincinnati						
1959	Oscar Robertson Cincinnati		Oscar Robertson Cincinnati				
1960	Oscar Robertson Cincinnati		Oscar Robertson Cincinnati				
1961	Jerry Lucas Ohio St.	Jerry Lucas Ohio St.	Jerry Lucas Ohio St.				
1962	Jerry Lucas Ohio St.	Jerry Lucas Ohio St.	Jerry Lucas Ohio St.				
1963	Art Heyman Duke	Art Heyman Duke	Art Heyman Duke				
1964	Gary Bradds Ohio St.	Gary Bradds Ohio St.	Walt Hazzard UCLA				
1965	Bill Bradley Princeton	Bill Bradley Princeton	Bill Bradley Princeton				
1966	Cazzie Russell Michigan	Cazzie Russell Michigan	Cazzie Russell Michigan				
1967	Lew Alcindor UCLA	Lew Alcindor UCLA	Lew Alcindor UCLA				
1968	Elvin Hayes Houston	Elvin Hayes Houston	Elvin Hayes Houston				
1969	Lew Alcindor UCLA	Lew Alcindor UCLA	Lew Alcindor UCLA			Lew Alcindor UCLA	Billy Keller Purdue
1970	Pete Maravich LSU	Pete Maravich LSU	Pete Maravich LSU			Pete Maravich LSU	John Rinka Kenyon

Season	United Press International	The Associated Press	U.S. Basketball Writers Assn.	Wooden Award	Nat'l Assn. of Basketball Coaches	Naismith Award	Frances Pomeroy Naismith Award
1971	Austin Carr Notre Dame	Austin Carr Notre Dame	Sidney Wicks UCLA			Austin Carr Notre Dame	Charlie Johnson California
1972	Bill Walton UCLA	Bill Walton UCLA	Bill Walton UCLA			Bill Walton UCLA	Scott Martin Oklahoma
1973	Bill Walton UCLA	Bill Walton UCLA	Bill Walton UCLA			Bill Walton UCLA	Bobby Sherwin Army
1974	Bill Walton UCLA	David Thompson North Carolina St.	Bill Walton UCLA			Bill Walton UCLA	Mike Robinson Michigan St.
1975	David Thompson North Carolina St.	David Thompson North Carolina St.	David Thompson North Carolina St.		David Thompson North Carolina St.	David Thompson North Carolina St.	Monty Towe North Carolina St.
1976	Scott May Indiana	Scott May Indiana	Adrian Dantley Notre Dame		Scott May Indiana	Scott May Indiana	Frank Algia St. John's (N.Y.)
1977	Marques Johnson UCLA	Marques Johnson UCLA	Marques Johnson UCLA	Marques Johnson UCLA	Marques Johnson UCLA	Marques Johnson UCLA	Jeff Jonas Utah
1978	Butch Lee Marquette	Butch Lee Marquette	Phil Ford North Carolina	Phil Ford North Carolina	Phil Ford North Carolina	Butch Lee Marquette	Mike Schib Susquehanna
1979	Larry Bird Indiana St.	Larry Bird Indiana St.	Larry Bird Indiana St.	Larry Bird Indiana St.	Larry Bird Indiana St.	Larry Bird Indiana St.	Alton Byrd Columbia
1980	Mark Aguirre DePaul	Mark Aguirre DePaul	Mark Aguirre DePaul	Darrell Griffith Louisville	Michael Brooks La Salle	Mark Aguirre DePaul	Jim Sweeney Boston College
1981	Ralph Sampson Virginia	Ralph Sampson Virginia	Ralph Sampson Virginia	Danny Ainge Brigham Young	Danny Ainge Brigham Young	Ralph Sampson Virginia	Terry Adolph West Tex. A&M
1982	Ralph Sampson Virginia	Ralph Sampson Virginia	Ralph Sampson Virginia	Ralph Sampson Virginia	Ralph Sampson Virginia	Ralph Sampson Virginia	Jack Moore Nebraska
1983	Ralph Sampson Virginia	Ralph Sampson Virginia	Ralph Sampson Virginia	Ralph Sampson Virginia	Ralph Sampson Virginia	Ralph Sampson Virginia	Ray McCallum Ball St.
1984	Michael Jordan North Carolina	Michael Jordan North Carolina	Michael Jordan North Carolina	Michael Jordan North Carolina	Michael Jordan North Carolina	Michael Jordan North Carolina	Ricky Stokes Virginia
1985	Chris Mullin St. John's (N.Y.)	Patrick Ewing Georgetown	Chris Mullin St. John's (N.Y.)	Chris Mullin St. John's (N.Y.)	Patrick Ewing Georgetown	Patrick Ewing Georgetown	Bubba Jennings Texas Tech
1986	Walter Berry St. John's (N.Y.)	Walter Berry St. John's (N.Y.)	Walter Berry St. John's (N.Y.)	Walter Berry St. John's (N.Y.)	Walter Berry St. John's (N.Y.)	Johnny Dawkins Duke	Jim Les Bradley
1987	David Robinson Navy	David Robinson Navy	David Robinson Navy	David Robinson Navy	David Robinson Navy	David Robinson Navy	Tyrone Bogues Wake Forest
1988	Hersey Hawkins Bradley	Hersey Hawkins Bradley	Hersey Hawkins Bradley	Danny Manning Kansas	Danny Manning Kansas	Danny Manning Kansas	Jerry Johnson Fla. Southern
1989	Danny Ferry Duke	Sean Elliott Arizona	Danny Ferry Duke	Sean Elliott Arizona	Sean Elliott Arizona	Danny Ferry Duke	Tim Hardaway UTEP
1990	Lionel Simmons La Salle	Lionel Simmons La Salle	Lionel Simmons La Salle	Lionel Simmons La Salle	Lionel Simmons La Salle	Lionel Simmons La Salle	Boo Harvey St. John's (N.Y.)
1991	Shaquille O'Neal LSU	Shaquille O'Neal LSU	Larry Johnson UNLV	Larry Johnson UNLV	Larry Johnson UNLV	Larry Johnson UNLV	Keith Jennings East Tenn. St.
1992	Jim Jackson Ohio St.	Christian Laettner Duke	Christian Laettner Duke	Christian Laettner Duke	Christian Laettner Duke	Christian Laettner Duke	Tony Bennett Wis.-Green Bay
1993	Calbert Cheaney Indiana	Calbert Cheaney Indiana	Calbert Cheaney Indiana	Calbert Cheaney Indiana	Calbert Cheaney Indiana	Calbert Cheaney Indiana	Sam Crawford New Mexico S.
1994	Glenn Robinson Purdue	Glenn Robinson Purdue	Glenn Robinson Purdue	Glenn Robinson Purdue	Glenn Robinson Purdue	Glenn Robinson Purdue	Greg Brown Evansville
1995	Joe Smith Maryland	Joe Smith Maryland	Ed O'Bannon UCLA	Ed O'Bannon UCLA	Shawn Respert Michigan St.	Joe Smith Maryland	Tyus Edney UCLA
1996	Marcus Camby Massachusetts	Marcus Camby Massachusetts	Marcus Camby Massachusetts	Marcus Camby Massachusetts	Marcus Camby Massachusetts	Marcus Camby Massachusetts	Eddie Benton Vermont
1997		Tim Duncan Wake Forest	Tim Duncan Wake Forest	Tim Duncan Wake Forest	Tim Duncan Wake Forest	Tim Duncan Wake Forest	Kent McCausland Iowa
1998		Antawn Jamison North Carolina	Antawn Jamison North Carolina	Antawn Jamison North Carolina	Antawn Jamison North Carolina	Antawn Jamison North Carolina	Earl Boykins Eastern Mich.
1999		Elton Brand Duke	Elton Brand Duke	Elton Brand Duke	Elton Brand Duke	Elton Brand Duke	Shawnta Rogers George Washington
2000		Kenyon Martin Cincinnati	Kenyon Martin Cincinnati	Kenyon Martin Cincinnati	Kenyon Martin Cincinnati	Kenyon Martin Cincinnati	Scoonie Penn Ohio St.
2001		Shane Battier Duke	Shane Battier Duke	Shane Battier Duke	Jason Williams Duke	Shane Battier Duke	Rashad Phillips Detriot
2002		Jason Williams Duke	Jason Williams Duke	Jason Williams Duke	Jason Williams Duke / Drew Gooden Kansas	Jason Williams Duke	Steve Logan Cincinnati

Note: The Francis Pomeroy Naismith Award is given to the top player who is less than 6 feet tall.

Basketball Times Player of the Year: 1982-Ralph Sampson, Virginia; 1983-Ralph Sampson, Virginia; 1984-Akeem Olajuwon, Houston; 1985-Patrick Ewing, Georgetown; 1986-Scott Skiles, Michigan St.; 1987-Kenny Smith, North Carolina; 1988-Hersey Hawkins, Bradley; 1989-Sean Elliot, Arizona; 1990-Derrick Coleman, Syracuse; 1991-Larry Johnson, UNLV; 1992-Christian Laettner, Duke; 1993-Jamaal Mashburn, Kentucky; 1994-Glenn Robinson, Purdue; 1995-Ed O'Bannon, UCLA; 1996-Marcus Camby, Massachusetts; 1997-Tim Duncan, Wake Forest; 1998-Antawn Jamison, North Carolina; 1999-Jason Terry, Arizona; 2000-Kenyon Martin, Cincinnati; 2001-Shane Battier, Duke; 2002-Jason Williams, Duke.

Defensive Player of the Year: 1987-Tommy Amaker, Duke; 1988-Billy King, Duke; 1989-Stacey Augmon, UNLV; 1990-Stacey Augmon, UNLV; 1991-Stacey Augmon, UNLV; 1992-Alonzo Mourning, Georgetown; 1993-Grant Hill, Duke; 1994-Jim McIlvaine, Marquette; 1995-Tim Duncan, Wake Forest; 1996-Tim Duncan, Wake Forest; 1997-Tim Duncan, Wake Forest; 1998-Steve Wojciechowski, Duke; 1999-Shane Battier, Duke; 2000-Kenyon Martin, Cincinnati & Shane Battier, Duke; 2001-Shane Battier, Duke; 2002-John Linehan, Providence.

Divisions II and III First-Team All-Americans By Team

Current Division I member denoted by (*). Non-NCAA member denoted by (†).

ABILENE CHRISTIAN
1968—John Godfrey

ADELPHI
2001—Ryan McCormack

AKRON*
1967—Bill Turner
1972—Len Paul

ALA.-HUNTSVILLE
1978—Tony Vann

ALAS. ANCHORAGE
1987—Jesse Jackson
1987—Hansi Gnad
1989—Michael Johnson
1990—Todd Fisher

ALBANY ST. (GA.)
1975—Major Jones

ALCORN ST.*
1976—John McGill

ALFRED
2001—Devon Downing

AMERICAN*
1960—Willie Jones

AMERICAN INT'L
1969—Greg Hill
1970—Greg Hill
2002—Malik Moore

AMHERST
1970—Dave Auten
1971—James Rehnquist

ARKANSAS ST.*
1965—Jerry Rook

ARMSTRONG ATLANTIC
1975—Ike Williams

ASSUMPTION
1970—Jake Jones
1971—Jake Jones
1973—Mike Boylan
1974—John Grochowalski
1975—John Grochowalski
1976—Bill Wurm

AUGUSTANA (ILL.)
1973—John Laing

BABSON
1992—Jim Pierrakos

BENTLEY
1974—Brian Hammel
1975—Brian Hammel

BISHOP
1983—Shannon Lilly

BRIDGEPORT
1969—Gary Baum
1976—Lee Hollerbach
1985—Manute Bol
1991—Lambert Shell
1992—Lambert Shell
1995—Lamont Jones

BRIDGEWATER (VA.)
1995—Dan Rush
2002—Kyle Williford

BYU-HAWAII
2000—David Evans

BROCKPORT ST.
2002—Mike Medbury

BRYANT
1981—Ernie DeWitt

CALIF. (PA.)
1993—Ray Gutierrez

UC RIVERSIDE
1989—Maurice Pullum

CAL ST. BAKERSFIELD
1996—Kebu Stewart
1997—Kebu Stewart

CALVIN
1993—Steve Honderd
2000—Aaron Winkle

CAMERON
1974—Jerry Davenport

CARLETON
1993—Gerrick Monroe

CARTHAGE
2002—Antoine McDaniel

CENTENARY (LA.)*
1957—Milt Williams

CENTRAL CONN. ST.*
1969—Howie Dickenman

UCF*
1979—Bo Clark
1980—Bo Clark

CENTRAL MO. ST.
1981—Bill Fennelly
1985—Ron Nunnelly
1991—Armando Becker

CENTRAL OKLA.
1993—Alex Wright
1997—Tyrone Hopkins
1998—Joe Newton
1999—Eddie Robinson

CENTRAL WASHINGTON
1967—Mel Cox

CHARLESTON (W.VA.)
2000—Ajamu Gaines

CHATTANOOGA*
1977—Wayne Golden

CHEYNEY
1979—Andrew Fields
1981—George Melton
1982—George Melton

CHRIS. NEWPORT
1991—Lamont Strothers
2001—Antoine Sinclair

CLAREMONT-M-S
1992—Chris Greene

CLARION
1994—Kwame Morton

CLARK (MASS.)
1980—Kevin Clark
1981—Kevin Clark
1988—Kermit Sharp

COLBY
1977—Paul Harvey
1978—Paul Harvey
1989—Matt Hancock
1990—Matt Hancock

CORTLAND ST.
2000—Tom Williams

DAVID LIPSCOMB†
1988—Phillip Hutcheson
1989—Phillip Hutcheson
1990—Phillip Hutcheson
1992—John Pierce

DAVIS & ELKINS
1959—Paul Wilcox

DELTA ST.
1969—Sammy Little

DEPAUW
1987—David Galle

DIST. COLUMBIA
1982—Earl Jones
1983—Earl Jones
    Michael Britt
1984—Earl Jones

EASTERN MICH.*
1971—Ken McIntosh
1972—George Gervin

EDINBORO
1996—Tyrone Mason
2002—Kenny Tate

ELMHURST
2001—Ryan Knuppel

EMORY
1990—Tim Garrett

EVANSVILLE*
1959—Hugh Ahlering
1960—Ed Smallwood
1965—Jerry Sloan
    Larry Humes
1966—Larry Humes

FLA. SOUTHERN
1981—John Ebeling
1982—John Ebeling
1988—Jerry Johnson
    Kris Kearney
1989—Kris Kearney
1990—Donolly Tyrell

FORT HAYS ST.
1997—Alonzo Goldston

FRAMINGHAM ST.
1984—Mark Van Valkenburg

FRANKLIN
1999—Jason Sibley

FRANK. & MARSH.
1992—Will Lasky
1996—Jeremiah Henry
2000—Alex Kraft

GANNON
1985—Butch Warner
1998—Troy Nesmith

GENESEO ST.
1994—Scott Fitch

GEORGETOWN (KY.)†
1964—Cecil Tuttle

GRAMBLING*
1961—Charles Hardnett
1962—Charles Hardnett
1964—Willis Reed
1966—Johnny Comeaux
1976—Larry Wright

GRAND CANYON
1976—Bayard Forest

GRAND VALLEY ST.
1997—Joe Modderman

GUILFORD
1968—Bob Kauffman
1975—Lloyd Free

HAMILTON
1977—Cedric Oliver
1978—Cedric Oliver
1979—Cedric Oliver
1987—John Cavanaugh
1998—Mike Schantz
1999—Michael Schantz

HAMPDEN-SYDNEY
1992—Russell Turner
2000—T.J. Grimes

HANOVER
1996—David Benter

HARTFORD*
1979—Mark Noon

HARTWICK
1977—Dana Gahres
1983—Tim O'Brien

HAVERFORD
1977—Dick Vioth

HENDERSON ST.
2002—Niki Arinze

HOPE
1984—Chip Henry
1998—Joel Holstege

ILLINOIS ST.*
1968—Jerry McGreal

ILL. WESLEYAN
1977—Jack Sikma
1989—Jeff Kuehl
1995—Chris Simich
1997—Bryan Crabtree
1998—Brent Niebrugge
2000—Korey Coon

INDIANA (PA.)
1995—Derrick Freeman

IUPUI*
1996—Carlos Knox

INDIANA ST.*
1968—Jerry Newsome

ITHACA
2000—Pat Britton

JACKSON ST.*
1974—Eugene Short
1975—Eugene Short
1977—Purvis Short

JACKSONVILLE*
1962—Roger Strickland
1963—Roger Strickland

JOHNSON SMITH
2001—Wyle Perry

KEAN
1993—Fred Drains

KEENE ST.
2001—Chris Coates

KENTUCKY ST.
1971—Travis Grant
    Elmore Smith
1972—Travis Grant
1975—Gerald Cunningham
1977—Gerald Cunningham

KY. WESLEYAN
1957—Mason Cope
1967—Sam Smith
1968—Dallas Thornton
1969—George Tinsley
1984—Rod Drake
    Dwight Higgs
1988—J.B. Brown
1990—Corey Crowder
1991—Corey Crowder
1995—Willis Cheaney
1998—Antonio Garcia
1999—Antonio Garcia
    Dana Williams
2000—LeRoy John
2001—Lorico Duncan
2002—Ronald Evans

KENYON
1969—John Rinka
1970—John Rinka
1979—Scott Rogers
1980—Scott Rogers

LEBANON VALLEY
1995—Mike Rhodes
1997—Andy Panko
1998—Andy Panko
1999—Andy Panko

LEWIS & CLARK†
1963—Jim Boutin
1964—Jim Boutin
1999—Andy Panko

LINCOLN (MO.)
1978—Harold Robertson

LONG ISLAND*
1968—Luther Green
    Larry Newbold

LONGWOOD
1984—Jerome Kersey
2001—Colin Ducharme

LOUISIANA COLLEGE†
1979—Paul Poe

LOUISIANA TECH*
1973—Mike Green

LA.-LAFAYETTE*
1965—Dean Church
1970—Marvin Winkler
1971—Dwight Lamar

MAINE*
1961—Tom Chappelle

MASS.-DARTMOUTH
1993—Steve Haynes

MASS.-LOWELL
1989—Leo Parent

MERCHANT MARINE
1990—Kevin D'Arcy

MERRIMACK
1977—Ed Murphy
1978—Ed Murphy
         Dana Skinner
1983—Joe Dickson

METHODIST
1997—Jason Childers

MINN. DULUTH
1977—Bob Bone

MO.-ST. LOUIS
1977—Bob Bone

MONTCLAIR ST.
1999—Anthony Peoples

MORGAN ST.
1974—Marvin Webster
1975—Marvin Webster
1999—Tim West

MT. ST. MARY'S*
1957—Jack Sullivan

MOUNT UNION
1997—Aaron Shipp

MUHLENBERG
2002—Mark Lesko

MUSKINGUM
1992—Andy Moore

NEB.-OMAHA
1992—Phil Cartwright

NEB. WESLEYAN
1986—Dana Janssen

NEW HAVEN
1988—Herb Watkins

N.J. INST. OF TECH.
1996—Clarence Pierce

COL. OF NEW JERSEY
1988—Greg Grant
1989—Greg Grant

NEW JERSEY CITY
1979—Brett Wyatt

NEW ORLEANS*
1971—Xavier Webster

NEW YORK TECH
1980—Kelvin Hicks

NICHOLLS ST.*
1978—Larry Wilson

NORFOLK ST.
1979—Ken Evans
1984—David Pope
1987—Ralph Talley
1995—Corey Williams

NORTH ALA.
1980—Otis Boddie

N.C. WESLEYAN
1999—Marquis McDougald

NORTH DAKOTA
1966—Phil Jackson
1967—Phil Jackson

1991—Dave Vonesh
1993—Scott Guldseth

NORTH DAKOTA ST.
1960—Marvin Bachmeier

NORTH PARK
1979—Mike Harper
1980—Mike Harper
1981—Mike Thomas

NORTHERN MICH.
1987—Bill Harris
2000—Cory Brathol

NORTHWOOD
1973—Fred Smile

OHIO NORTHERN
1982—Stan Mories
1995—D'Artis Jones
2001—Kris Oberdick

OHIO WESLEYAN
1987—Scott Tedder
1988—Scott Tedder

OKLAHOMA CITY†
1992—Eric Manuel

OLD DOMINION*
1972—Dave Twardzik
1974—Joel Copeland
1976—Wilson Washington

OTTERBEIN
1966—Don Carlos
1982—Ron Stewart
1983—Ron Stewart
1985—Dick Hempy
1986—Dick Hempy
1987—Dick Hempy
1991—James Bradley
1994—Nick Gutman
1999—Kevin Weakley
2002—Jeff Gibbs

PACIFIC LUTHERAN†
1959—Chuck Curtis

PFEIFFER
1992—Tony Smith

PHILADELPHIA U.
1976—Emory Sammons
1977—Emory Sammons

PLYMOUTH ST.
1994—Moses Jean-Pierre
1999—Adam DeChristopher

POTSDAM ST.
1980—Derrick Rowland
1981—Derrick Rowland
1982—Maurice Woods
1983—Leroy Witherspoon
1984—Leroy Witherspoon
1986—Roosevelt Bullock
1986—Brendan Mitchell
1987—Brendan Mitchell
1988—Steve Babiarz
1989—Steve Babiarz

PRAIRIE VIEW*
1962—Zelmo Beaty

PUGET SOUND
1979—Joe Leonard

QUEENS (N.C.)
1998—Soce Faye

RANDOLPH-MACON
1983—Bryan Vacca

RICHARD STOCKTON
1997—Carl Cochrane

ROANOKE
1972—Hal Johnston
1973—Jay Piccola
1974—Jay Piccola
1983—Gerald Holmes
1984—Reggie Thomas
1985—Reggie Thomas
1994—Hilliary Scott

ROCHESTER
1991—Chris Fite
1992—Chris Fite

ROCHESTER INST.
1996—Craig Jones
1997—Craig Jones

ROWAN
1998—Rob Scott

RUTGERS-CAMDEN
2002—Brian Turner

SACRED HEART*
1972—Ed Czernota
1978—Hector Olivencia
         Andre Means
1982—Keith Bennett
1983—Keith Bennett
1986—Roger Younger
1993—Darrin Robinson

ST. CLOUD ST.
1957—Vern Baggenstoss
1986—Kevin Catron

ST. JOSEPH'S (IND.)
1960—Bobby Williams

ST. MICHAEL'S
1965—Richie Tarrant

ST. NORBERT
1963—Mike Wisneski

SALEM (W.VA.)†
1976—Archie Talley

SALEM ST.
2000—Tishaun Jenkins

SALISBURY
1991—Andre Foreman
1992—Andre Foreman

SAM HOUSTON ST.
1973—James Lister

SCRANTON
1963—Bill Witaconis
1977—Irvin Johnson
1978—Irvin Johnson
1984—Bill Bessoir
1985—Bill Bessoir
1993—Matt Cusano

SEWANEE
1998—Ryan Harrigan

SHAW
2002—Ronald Murray

SHENANDOAH
1996—Phil Dixon

SLIPPERY ROCK
1991—Myron Brown

SOUTH DAKOTA
1958—Jim Daniels

SOUTH DAKOTA ST.
1961—Don Jacobsen
1964—Tom Black

SE OKLAHOMA†
1957—Jim Spivey

SOUTHERN ILL.*
1966—George McNeil
1967—Walt Frazier

SOUTHERN IND.
1995—Stan Gouard
1996—Stan Gouard

SOUTHWEST TEX. ST.*
1959—Charles Sharp
1960—Charles Sharp

SPRINGFIELD
1970—Dennis Clark
1986—Ivan Olivares

STEPHEN F. AUSTIN*
1970—Surry Oliver

STETSON*
1970—Ernie Killum

STEUBENVILLE†
1958—Jim Smith

STONEHILL
1979—Bill Zolga
1980—Bill Zolga
1982—Bob Reitz

STONY BROOK*
1979—Earl Keith

SUSQUEHANNA
1986—Dan Harnum

TAMPA
1985—Todd Linder
1986—Todd Linder
1987—Todd Linder
1994—DeCarlo Deveaux

TENNESSEE ST.*
1958—Dick Barnett
1959—Dick Barnett
1971—Ted McClain
1972—Lloyd Neal
1974—Leonard Robinson

TEX.-PAN AMERICAN*
1964—Lucious Jackson
1968—Otto Moore

TEXAS SOUTHERN*
1958—Bennie Swain
1977—Alonzo Bradley

THOMAS MORE
1996—Rick Hughes

TRINITY (TEX.)
1968—Larry Jeffries
1969—Larry Jeffries
2002—Colin Tabb

TROY ST.*
1993—Terry McCord

TUFTS
1995—Chris McMahon

UPSALA
1981—Steve Keenan
1982—Steve Keenan

VIRGINIA UNION
1985—Charles Oakley
1990—A.J. English
1994—Derrick Johnson
         Warren Peebles
1996—Ben Wallace
1998—Marquise Newbie

WABASH
1982—Pete Metzelaars

WASHBURN
1994—Clarence Tyson
1997—Dan Buie
2001—Ewan Auguste

WASH. & LEE
1978—Pat Dennis

WAYNE ST. (NEB.)
1999—Tyler Johnson

WEST GA.
1974—Clarence Walker

WESTERN CARO.*
1968—Henry Logan

WESTMINSTER (PA.)†
1962—Ron Galbreath

WESTMINSTER (UTAH)†
1969—Ken Hall

WHEATON (ILL.)
1958—Mel Peterson

WIDENER
1978—Dennis James
1988—Lou Stevens

WILKES
2001—Dave Jannuzzi

WM. PATERSON
2000—Horace Jenkins
2001—Horace Jenkins

WILLIAMS
1961—Bob Mahland
1962—Bob Mahland
1996—Mike Nogelo
1997—Mike Nogelo
1998—Mike Nogelo

WINSTON-SALEM
1967—Earl Monroe
1980—Reginald Gaines

WIS.-EAU CLAIRE
1972—Mike Ratliff

WIS.-GREEN BAY*
1978—Tom Anderson
1979—Ron Ripley

WIS.-OSHKOSH
1996—Dennis Ruedinger
2002—Tim Dworak

WIS.-PARKSIDE
1976—Gary Cole

WIS.-PLATTEVILLE
1992—T.J. Van Wie

1998—Ben Hoffmann
1999—Merrill Brunson

WIS.-STEVENS POINT
1985—Terry Porter
2000—Brant Bailey

WIS.-SUPERIOR
2001—Vince Thomas

WIS.-WHITEWATER
1990—Ricky Spicer
1994—Ty Evans
1997—James Stewart

WITTENBERG
1961—George Fisher
1963—Al Thrasher
1980—Brian Agler
1981—Tyrone Curtis
1985—Tim Casey
1989—Steve Allison
1990—Brad Baldridge
1991—Brad Baldridge

WRIGHT ST.
1981—Rodney Benson
1986—Mark Vest

XAVIER (LA.)†
1973—Bruce Seals

YOUNGSTOWN ST.*
1977—Jeff Covington
1978—Jeff Covington

Teams used for selections:
AP Little All-America—1957-79
NABC College Division—1967-76
NABC Divisions II, III—1977-2002

Divisions II and III Academic All-Americans By Team

ABILENE CHRISTIAN
1999—Jared Mosley

AKRON
1972—Wil Schwarzinger

ALBANY (N.Y.)
1988—John Carmello

ALBION
1979—John Nibert

ALDERSON-BROADDUS
2002—Kevyn McBride

ARKANSAS TECH
1990—Gray Townsend
1994—David Bevis
1995—David Bevis

ASHLAND
1967—Jim Basista
1970—Jay Franson

ASSUMPTION
1967—George Ridick

AUGUSTANA (ILL.)
1973—Bruce Hamming
1974—Bruce Hamming
1975—Bruce Hamming
1979—Glen Heiden

AUGUSTANA (S.D.)
1974—John Ritterbusch
1975—John Ritterbusch

BALDWIN-WALLACE
1985—Bob Scelza

BARRINGTON
1982—Shawn Smith

BATES
1983—Herb Taylor
1984—Herb Taylor

BEMIDJI ST.
1976—Steve Vogel
1977—Steve Vogel
1978—Steve Vogel

BENTLEY
1980—Joe Betley

BETHEL (MINN.)
1994—Jason Mekelburg

BLOOMSBURG
1978—Steve Bright

BRANDEIS
1978—John Martin

BRIAR CLIFF
1989—Chad Neubrand

BRIDGEWATER (VA.)
1985—Sean O'Connell

BRYAN
1981—Dean Ropp

C.W. POST
1973—Ed Fields

CALIF. (PA.)
1993—Raymond Guttierez

CAL LUTHERAN
1983—Bill Burgess

UC DAVIS
1970—Tom Cupps
1983—Preston Neumayr

UC RIVERSIDE
1971—Kirby Gordon

CALVIN
1992—Steve Honderd
1993—Steve Honderd
1994—Chris Knoester

CAPITAL
1973—Charles Gashill

CARNEGIE MELLON
1973—Mike Wegener
1979—Larry Hufnagel
1980—Larry Hufnagel

CASE RESERVE
1996—Jim Fox
1997—Jim Fox

CASTLETON ST.
1985—Bryan DeLoatch

CATHOLIC
1997—Jeremy Borys

UCF
1982—Jimmie Farrell

CENTRAL MICH.
1967—John Berends
1971—Mike Hackett

CENTRAL ST. (OHIO)
1971—Sterling Quant

CHADRON ST.
1992—Josh Robinson

CLAREMONT-M-S
2002—Bob Donlan

COAST GUARD
1971—Ken Bicknell

COLORADO MINES
1991—Daniel McKeon
1991—Hank Prey

CORNELL COLLEGE
1974—Randy Kuhlman
1977—Dick Grant
1978—Robert Wisco
1979—Robert Wisco
1987—Jeff Fleming

DAVID LIPSCOMB
1989—Phil Hutcheson
1990—Phil Hutcheson
1992—Jerry Meyer

DELTA ST.
1972—Larry MaGee

DENISON
1967—Bill Druckemiller
1970—Charles Claggett
1987—Kevin Locke

1988—Kevin Locke
1997—Casey Chroust

DENVER
1987—Joe Fisher

DEPAUW
1970—Richard Tharp
1973—Gordon Pittenger
1987—David Galle

DICKINSON
1971—Lloyd Bonner
1981—David Freysinger
1982—David Freysinger

DREXEL
1967—Joe Hertrich

ELMHURST
2001—Ryan Knuppel

ELON
1988—Brian Branson
1988—Steve Page
1998—Christopher Kiger

EMBRY-RIDDLE
2001—Kyle Mas

EMORY
2000—Neil Bhutta

FORT HAYS ST.
1978—Mike Pauls

FORT LEWIS
1998—Ryan Ostrom

FRANK. & MARSH.
2000—Jerome Maiatico

GETTYSBURG
1975—Jeffrey Clark

GRINNELL
1976—John Haigh
1994—Steve Diekmann
1995—Steve Diekmann
1996—Ed Brands

GROVE CITY
1979—Mike Donahoe
1984—Curt Silverling
1985—Curt Silverling

GUST. ADOLPHUS
1983—Mark Hanson

HAMILTON
1978—John Klauberg

HAMLINE
1986—Paul Westling
1989—John Banovetz

HAMPDEN-SYDNEY
1992—Russell Turner

HARDING
1985—Kenneth Collins
1986—Kenneth Collins

HOWARD PAYNE
1973—Garland Bullock
1974—Garland Bullock

ILL. WESLEYAN
1972—Dean Gravlin

Christopher Unton of Rose-Hulman was a Division III Academic All-American last season.

1973—Dean Gravlin
1975—Jack Sikma
    Bob Spear
1976—Jack Sikma
    Bob Spear
1977—Jack Sikma
    Bob Spear
1979—Al Black
1981—Greg Yess
1982—Greg Yess
1987—Brian Coderre
1999—Korey Coon
2000—Korey Coon

INCARNATE WORD
1993—Randy Henderson

JAMES MADISON
1976—Sherman Dillard

JAMESTOWN
1980—Pete Anderson
1981—Pete Anderson

JOHN CARROLL
1999—Mark Heidorf

JOHNS HOPKINS
1991—Andy Enfield

KENYON
1970—John Rinka
1977—Tim Appleton
1985—Chris Coe Russell

LAGRANGE
1980—Todd Whitsitt

LIBERTY
1980—Karl Hess

LUTHER
1981—Doug Kintzinger
1982—Doug Kintzinger

MACMURRAY
1970—Tom Peters

MARIAN
2002—Scott Jaeger

MARIETTA
1982—Rick Clark
1983—Rick Clark

MASS.-LOWELL
1970—Alfred Spinell
1984—John Paganetti

MIT
1980—Ray Nagem
1991—David Tomlinson

MCDANIEL
1983—Douglas Pinto
1985—David Malin

MCGILL
1983—Willie Hinz

MCNEESE ST.
1972—David Wallace

MERRIMACK
1983—Joseph Dickson
1984—Joseph Dickson

MICHIGAN TECH
1981—Russ VanDuine
1985—Wayne Helmila

MILLIKIN
1977—Roy Mosser
    Dale Wills
1978—Gregg Finigan
1979—Rich Rames
    Gary Jackson
1980—Gary Jackson
1981—Gary Jackson
1989—Brian Horst

MILWAUKEE ENGR.
1983—Jeffrey Brezovar

MINN. ST.-MANKATO
1997—David Kruse

MO.-ROLLA
1984—Todd Wentz

MO.-ST. LOUIS
1975—Bobby Bone
1976—Bobby Bone
1977—Bobby Bone

MONMOUTH (ILL.)
1990—S. Juan Mitchell

MOORHEAD ST.
1996—Brett Beeson

MOUNT UNION
1971—Jim Howell

MUHLENBERG
1979—Greg Campisi
1981—Dan Barletta

NEB.-KEARNEY
1974—Tom Kropp
1975—Tom Kropp

NEB.-OMAHA
1981—Jim Gregory

NEB. WESLEYAN
1984—Kevin Cook
1986—Kevin Cook
1995—Justin Wilkins
1997—Kipp Kissinger
1998—Kipp Kissinger

UNC ASHEVILLE
1974—Randy Pallas

NORTHERN COLO.
1967—Dennis Colson

OBERLIN
1971—Vic Guerrieri
1972—Vic Guerrieri

OHIO NORTHERN
2001—Kris Oberdick

OHIO WESLEYAN
1990—Mark Slayman
1998—John Camillus

OLD DOMINION
1974—Gray Eubank
1975—Gray Eubank

OTTERBEIN
1980—Mike Cochran

PACIFIC LUTHERAN
1967—Doug Leeland

POINT PARK
1986—Richard Condo

RIPON
1999—Bret Van Dyken

ROCHESTER
1984—Joe Augustine

ROCKFORD
1976—John Morrissey
1977—John Morrissey

ROSE-HULMAN
2002—Christopher Unton

ST. JOHN'S (MINN.)
1995—Joe Deignan

ST. JOSEPH'S (IND.)
1975—James Thordsen

ST. LEO
1977—Ralph Nelson

ST. THOMAS (FLA.)
1976—Arthur Collins
1977—Mike LaPrete

ST. THOMAS (MINN.)
1967—Dan Hansard
1978—Terry Fleming

SCRANTON
1983—Michael Banas
1984—Michael Banas
1985—Dan Polacheck
1993—Matt Cusano

SHIPPENSBURG
1979—John Whitmer
1981—Brian Cozzens
1982—Brian Cozzens

SIMPSON
2002—Jesse Harris

SLIPPERY ROCK
1971—Robert Wiegand
1979—Mike Hardy
1983—John Samsa
1995—Mark Metzka

SOUTH DAKOTA
1970—Bill Hamer
1975—Rick Nissen
1976—Rick Nissen
1978—Jeff Nannen
1980—Jeff Nannen
1985—Rob Swanhorst

SOUTH DAKOTA ST.
1971—Jim Higgins
1972—Jim Higgins

SOUTHERN COLO.
1972—Jim Von Loh

SUSQUEHANNA
1986—Donald Harnum
1994—Tres Wolf

TENNESSEE TEMPLE
1977—Dan Smith
1978—Dan Smith

TRINITY (CONN.)
1996—Keith Wolff

TRUMAN
1984—Mark Campbell
1999—Jason Reinberg
2000—Jason Reinberg

UNION (N.Y.)
1970—Jim Tedisco

VIRGINIA TECH
1968—Ted Ware

WABASH
1973—Joe Haklin

WARTBURG
1971—Dave Platte
1972—Dave Platte
1974—Fred Waldstein
1990—Dan Nettleton
1991—Dan Nettleton

WASHBURN
2001—Ewan Auguste

WASHINGTON (MO.)
1988—Paul Jackson

WASH. & JEFF.
1980—David Damico

WENTWORTH INST.
2000—Kevin Hanlon

WESLEYAN (CONN.)
1972—James Akin
1974—Rich Fairbrother
1982—Steven Maizes

WESTERN ST. (COLO.)
1970—Michael Adams
1973—Rod Smith

WESTMINSTER (PA.)
1967—John Fontanella

WILKES
2001—Dave Jannuzzi

WM. PATERSON
2001—Horace Jenkins

WIS.-EAU CLAIRE
1972—Steven Johnson
1975—Ken Kaiser
1976—Ken Kaiser

WIS.-GREEN BAY
1974—Tom Jones

WIS.-OSHKOSH
1998—Joe Imhoff

WIS.-PLATTEVILLE
1992—T.J. Van Wie
1993—T.J. Van Wie

WIS.-SUPERIOR
2001—Vince Thomas

WITTENBERG
1967—Jim Appleby

WORCESTER TECH
1996—James Naughton

NCAA Postgraduate Scholarship Winners By Team

ABILENE CHRISTIAN
1999—Jared Mosley

AIR FORCE
1970—James Cooper
1973—Thomas Blase
1974—Richard Nickelson
1978—Thomas Schneeberger
1992—Brent Roberts
1993—Brad Boyer

UAB
1999—Damon Cobb

ALBANY (N.Y.)
1988—John Carmello

ALLEGHENY
1976—Robert Del Greco

ALLENTOWN
1985—George Bilicic Jr.

ALMA
1976—Stuart TenHoor

AMERICAN
1973—Kermit Washington
1998—Nathan Smith

ARIZONA
1988—Steve Kerr
1991—Matt Muehlebach

ARIZONA ST.
1965—Dennis Dairman

ARKANSAS ST.
1975—J.H. Williams

ARMY
1965—John Ritch III
1972—Edward Mueller
1973—Robert Sherwin Jr.
1985—Randall Cozzens
1994—David Ardayfio

ASSUMPTION
1975—Paul Brennan
1977—William Wurm

AUBURN
1976—Gary Redding

AUGUSTANA (ILL.)
1975—Bruce Hamming

AUGUSTANA (S.D.)
1975—Neil Klutman
1992—Jason Garrow

BALL ST.
1989—Richard Hall

BATES
1984—Herbert Taylor

BAYLOR
1997—Doug Brandt

BELLARMINE
1992—Tom Schurfranz
2001—Ronald Brooks

BENTLEY
1980—Joseph Betley

BOSTON COLLEGE
1967—William Wolters
1970—Thomas Veronneau
1972—James Phelan
1980—James Sweeney
1995—Marc Molinsky

BOWDOIN
1966—Howard Pease

BOWLING GREEN
1965—Robert Dwors

BRANDEIS
1972—Donald Fishman
1978—John Martin

BRIDGEWATER (VA.)
1970—Frederick Wampler

BRIGHAM YOUNG
1966—Richard Nemelka
1983—Gregory Kite
1984—Devin Durrant
1987—Brent Stephenson
1989—Michael Smith
1990—Andy Toolson
1991—Steve Schreiner

BYU-HAWAII
2000—David Evans

BROWN
1972—Arnold Berman
1997—Jade Newburn

BUENA VISTA
2000—Landon Roth

BUTLER
1977—Wayne Burris
1991—John Karaffa

CALIFORNIA
1987—David Butler

UC DAVIS
1970—Thomas Cupps
1977—Mark Ford
1983—Preston Neumayr
1991—Matt Cordova

UC IRVINE
1975—Carl Baker

UC RIVERSIDE
1975—Randy Burnett

UC SAN DIEGO
1997—Matt Aune

UC SANTA BARB.
1973—Robert Schachter
1993—Michael Meyer

CALIF. (PA.)
1984—William Belko

CAL POLY POMONA
1978—Thomas Ispas

CAL ST. DOM. HILLS
1987—John Nojima

CAL ST. STANISLAUS
1983—Richard Thompson

CALTECH
1966—Alden Holford
1967—James Pearson
1968—James Stanley
1971—Thomas Heinz

CALVIN
1977—Mark Veenstra
1993—Steve Honderd

CARLETON
1969—Thomas Weaver
1982—James Tolf
1999—Joshua Wilhelm

CARNEGIE MELLON
1980—Lawrence Hufnagel

CASE RESERVE
1971—Mark Estes

CATHOLIC
1972—Joseph Good
1997—Jeremy Borys

CENTRAL (IOWA)
1973—Dana Snoap
1980—Jeffrey Verhoef

CENTRAL MICH.
1993—Sander Scott

CENTRE
1985—Thomas Cowens

CHAPMAN
1970—Anthony Mason

CHICAGO
1969—Dennis Waldon
1974—Gerald Clark
1985—Keith Libert

CINCINNATI
1977—Gary Yoder

CLAREMONT-M-S
1972—Jeffrey Naslund

CLARION
1973—Joseph Sebestyen

CLEMSON
1967—James Sutherland
1980—Robert Conrad Jr.
1999—Tom Wideman

COE
1965—Gary Schlarbaum

COLBY
1972—Matthew Zweig

COLGATE
1999—Ben Wandtke

COLORADO
1966—Charles Gardner
1985—Alex Stivrins

COLORADO MINES
1991—Hank Prey
1994—Todd Kenyon

COLORADO ST.
1986—Richard Strong Jr.

COLUMBIA
1968—William Ames

CORNELL COLLEGE
1967—David Crow
1979—Robert Wisco
1981—Eric Reitan
1987—Jefferson Fleming
1994—Abram Tubbs
       Chad Reed

CREIGHTON
1971—Dennis Bresnahan Jr.
1978—Richard Apke

DARTMOUTH
1968—Joseph Colgan
1976—William Healey
1984—Paul Anderson
1997—Sea Lonergan

DAVIDSON
1969—Wayne Huckel
1983—Clifford Tribus

DAYTON
1979—Jim Paxson
1985—Larry Schellenberg

DELAWARE
1978—Brian Downie

DENISON
1968—William Druckemiller Jr.
1988—Kevin Locke
1993—Kevin Frye
1997—Casey Chroust
1999—John Rusnak

DENVER
1968—Richard Callahan
2000—Tyler Church

DEPAUL
1992—Stephen Howard

DEPAUW
1969—Thomas McCormick
1970—Richard Tharp
1973—Gordon Pittenger
1986—Phillip Wendel

DICKINSON
1982—David Freysinger
1987—Michael Erdos

DREW
1989—Joe Novak

DUKE
1975—Robert Fleischer

EASTERN WASH.
2000—Ryan Hansen

ELON
1998—Christopher Kiger

EMORY
1993—Kevin Felner
1999—Lewis Satterwhite
2000—Neil Bhutta

EVANSVILLE
1989—Scott Haffner

FAIRLEIGH DICKINSON
1978—John Jorgensen
1993—Kevin Conway

FLORIDA
1970—Andrew Owens Jr.
1973—Anthony Miller

FLA. SOUTHERN
1969—Richard Lewis
1979—Larry Tucker
1989—Kris Kearney

FORT LEWIS
1998—Ryan Ostrom

FRANKLIN
1994—David Dunkle

FRANK. & MARSH.
2000—Jerome Maiatico

GEORGE WASHINGTON
1976—Pat Tallent
1987—Steve Frick

GEORGETOWN
1968—Bruce Stinebrickner

GEORGIA
1965—McCarthy Crenshaw Jr.
1987—Chad Kessler
1990—Alec Kessler

GEORGIA TECH
1998—Matt Harping

GONZAGA
1992—Jarrod Davis
1994—Jeff Brown
1996—Jon Kinloch

GRAMBLING
1983—William Hobdy

GRINNELL
1968—James Schwartz
1976—John Haigh

HAMILTON
1969—Brooks McCuen
1978—John Klauberg

HAMLINE
1989—John Banovetz

HAMPDEN-SYDNEY
1983—Christopher Kelly
1999—David Hobbs

HARVARD
1979—Glenn Fine

HAVERFORD
1966—Hunter Rawlings III
1967—Michael Bratman
1977—Richard Voith

HIRAM
1977—Edwin Niehaus

HOLY CROSS
1969—Edward Siudut
1977—William Doran Jr.
1979—John O'Connor
1980—Ronnie Perry

HOUSTON BAPTIST
1985—Albert Almanza

IDAHO
1967—Michael Wicks

IDAHO ST.
1993—Corey Bruce

ILLINOIS
1971—Rich Howat

ILLINOIS ST.
1988—Jeffrey Harris
1998—Dan Muller

ILLINOIS TECH
1969—Eric Wilson

ILL. WESLEYAN
1988—Brian Coderre
2000—Korey Coon

INDIANA
1975—Steven Green
1982—Randy Wittman
1985—Uwe Blab

INDIANA ST.
1972—Danny Bush
1981—Steven Reed

IOWA
1966—Dennis Pauling
1976—G. Scott Thompson
1981—Steven Waite
1998—Jess Settles

IOWA ST.
1989—Marc Urquhart

ITHACA
1973—David Hollowell

JACKSONVILLE
1971—Vaughn Wedeking
1983—Maurice Roulhac
1986—Thomas Terrell

JAMES MADISON
1978—Sherman Dillard

JAMESTOWN
1981—Peter Anderson

JOHNS HOPKINS
1965—Robert Smith
1975—Andrew Schreiber
1991—Andy Enfield
1992—Jay Gangemi
1997—Matt Gorman
1998—Greg Roehrig

KALAMAZOO
1965—Thomas Nicolai
1973—James Van Sweden
1979—David Dame
1982—John Schelske
1996—Jeremy Cole

KANSAS
1974—Thomas Kivisto
1978—Kenneth Koenigs

1997—Jerod Haase
1999—Ryan Robertson
    T.J. Pugh

KANSAS ST.
1968—Earl Seyfert

KENT ST.
1994—Rodney Koch
2002—Demetric Shaw

KENTUCKY
1975—Robert Guyette
1996—Mark Pope

KENYON
1995—Jamie Harless

KING'S (PA.)
1981—James Shea

KNOX
1965—James Jepson

LA SALLE
1992—John Hurd

LA VERNE
2001—Kevin Gustafson

LAFAYETTE
1972—Joseph Mottola
1980—Robert Falconiero
1991—Bruce Stankavage
1994—Keith Brazzo

LAKE FOREST
1968—Frederick Broda

LAMAR
1970—James Nicholson
1999—Matt Sundblad

LEWIS
1989—James Martin

LONG BEACH ST.
1990—Tyrone Mitchell

LORAS
1971—Patrick Lillis
1972—John Buri

LOUISVILLE
1977—Phillip Bond

LOYOLA MARYMOUNT
1973—Stephen Smith

LOYOLA (MD.)
1979—John Vogt

LUTHER
1968—David Mueller
1974—Timothy O'Neill
1982—Douglas Kintzinger
1986—Scott Sawyer

MAINE
1990—Dean Smith

MARQUETTE
1984—Marc Marotta

MARSHALL
1973—Michael D'Antoni
1997—John Brannen

MARYLAND
1974—Tom McMillen
1981—Gregory Manning
1991—Matt Roe

MASS.-LOWELL
1970—Alfred Spinell Jr.

MIT
1966—John Mazola
1967—Robert Hardt
1968—David Jansson
1971—Bruce Wheeler
1991—David Tomlinson

MCNEESE ST.
1978—John Rudd

MIAMI (OHIO)
1982—George Sweigert

MICHIGAN
1981—Martin Bodnar
1993—Rob Pelinka

MICHIGAN TECH
1978—Michael Trewhella
1981—Russell Van Duine

MIDDLEBURY
1975—David Pentkowski
1982—Paul Righi

MINNESOTA
1970—Michael Regenfuss

MINN.-MORRIS
1997—Todd Hanson

MINN. ST.-MANKATO
1997—David Kruse

MISSISSIPPI ST.
1976—Richard Knarr

MISSOURI
1972—Gregory Flaker

MO.-ROLLA
1977—Ross Klie

MO.-ST. LOUIS
1977—Robert Bone

MONMOUTH (ILL.)
1992—Steve Swanson

MONTANA
1968—Gregory Hanson
1981—Craig Zanon
1986—Larry Krystkowiak
1992—Daren Engellant
1995—Jeremy Lake

MONTANA ST.
1988—Ray Willis Jr.
1996—Nico Harrison

MOORHEAD ST.
1980—Kevin Mulder
1996—Brett Beeson

MORNINGSIDE
1986—John Kelzenberg

MT. ST. MARY'S
1976—Richard Kidwell

MUHLENBERG
1976—Glenn Salo

MUSKINGUM
1974—Gary Ferber
1983—Myron Dulkoski Jr.

NAVY
1979—Kevin Sinnett
1984—Clifford Maurer
1995—Wesley Cooper

NEBRASKA
1972—Alan Nissen
1986—John Matzke
1987—William Jackman
1991—Beau Reid

NEB.-OMAHA
1981—James Gregory

NEB. WESLEYAN
1995—Justin Wilkins
1998—Kipp Kissinger

UNLV
1984—Danny Tarkanian

NEW MEXICO
1973—Breck Roberts

NEW YORK POLY
1968—Charles Privalsky

NEW YORK U.
1996—Greg Belinfanti

NORTH CAROLINA
1966—Robert Bennett Jr.
1974—John O'Donnell
1977—Bruce Buckley
1986—Steve Hale
1995—Pearce Landry

UNC GREENSBORO
2001—Nathan Jameson

UNC WILMINGTON
1997—Bill Mayew

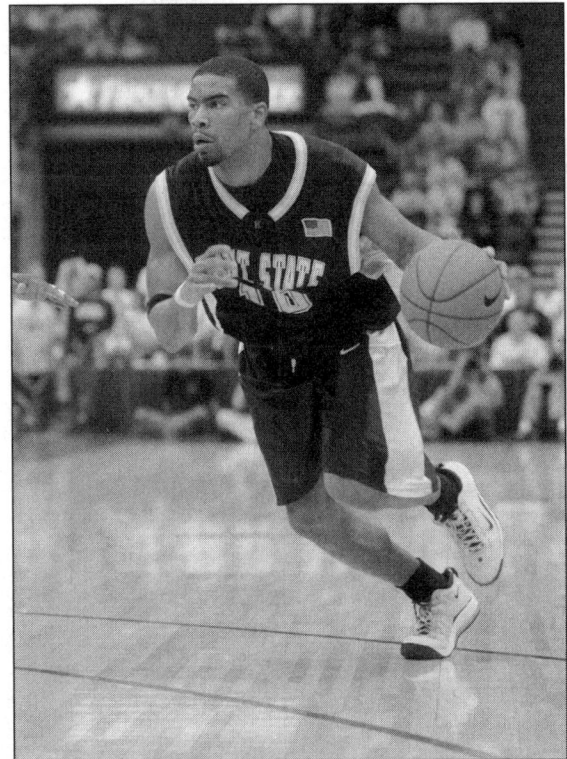

Kent State's Demetric Shaw earned a postgraduate scholarship last season.

NORTH CAROLINA ST.
1966—Peter Coker
1985—Terrence Gannon
1996—Todd Fuller

NORTH DAKOTA ST.
1989—Joe Regnier
2000—Jason Retzlaff

NORTHEASTERN
1978—David Caligaris

NORTHERN ARIZ.
1979—Troy Hudson

NORTHERN COLO.
1968—Dennis Colson
1990—Toby Moser

NORTHERN ILL.
1984—Timothy Dillion
2000—A.J. Lux

NORTHERN IOWA
1979—Michael Kemp

NORTHERN KY.
2000—Kevin Listerman

NORTHWEST MO. ST.
1989—Robert Sundell

NORTHWESTERN
1973—Richard Sund
1980—Michael Campbell
1990—Walker Lambiotte
1994—Kevin Rankin

NORTHWOOD
1999—Jeremy Piggott

NOTRE DAME
1969—Robert Arnzen
1974—Gary Novak
1983—John Paxson
1998—Pat Garrity

OAKLAND
1990—Brian Gregory

OBERLIN
1972—Victor Guerrieri

OCCIDENTAL
1973—Douglas McAdam
1981—Miles Glidden
1996—John Pike

OGLETHORPE
1992—David Fischer

OHIO
1967—John Hamilton
1968—Wayne Young
1979—Steven Skaggs

OHIO ST.
1968—Wilmer Hosket

OKLAHOMA
1972—Scott Martin
1975—Robert Pritchard
1980—Terry Stotts
1988—Dave Sieger

OKLAHOMA CITY
1967—Gary Gray

OKLAHOMA ST.
1965—Gary Hassmann
1969—Joseph Smith

OLD DOMINION
1975—Gray Eubank

OLIVET
1999—Jeff Bell

OREGON
1971—William Drozdiak
1988—Keith Balderston
2000—Adrian Smith

OREGON ST.
1967—Edward Fredenburg

PACIFIC (CAL.)
1967—Bruce Parsons Jr.
1979—Terence Carney
1986—Richard Anema
1992—Delano Demps

PENNSYLVANIA
1972—Robert Morse

PENN ST.
1982—Michael Edelman
1995—John Amaechi

PITTSBURGH
1976—Thomas Richards
1986—Joseph David
1992—Darren Morningstar

POMONA-PITZER
1966—Gordon Schloming
1970—Douglas Covey
1986—David Di Cesaris

PORTLAND ST.
1966—John Nelson

PRINCETON
1969—Christopher Thomforde
1997—Sydney Johnson

PRINCIPIA
1979—William Kelsey

PUGET SOUND
1974—Richard Brown

PURDUE
1971—George Faerber
1981—Brian Walker

RADFORD
1998—Corey Reed

REDLANDS
1990—Robert Stone

REGIS (COLO.)
1988—John Nilles
1994—Pat Holloway

RENSSELAER
1967—Kurt Hollasch

RHODES
1994—Greg Gonda
1996—Scott Brown

RICE
1995—Adam Peakes
2001—Michael Wilks

RICHMOND
1986—John Davis Jr.

RIPON
1978—Ludwig Wurtz
1999—Bret Van Dyken

ROANOKE
2000—Paris Butler

ROLLINS
1993—David Wolf

RUTGERS
1985—Stephen Perry

ST. ANSELM
1980—Sean Canning

ST. FRANCIS (PA.)
1997—Eric Shaner

ST. JOHN FISHER
1997—Eric Shaner

ST. JOHN'S (N.Y.)
1981—Frank Gilroy

ST. JOSEPH'S (IND.)
1975—James Thordsen

ST. JOSEPH'S
1966—Charles McKenna

ST. LAWRENCE
1969—Philip McWhorter

ST. LEO
1981—Kevin McDonald

ST. LOUIS
1967—John Kilo
1995—Scott Highmark

ST. MARY'S (CAL.)
1980—Calvin Wood
1999—Eric Schraeder

ST. NORBERT
1987—Andris Arians

ST. OLAF
1966—Eric Grimsrud
1971—David Finholt

ST. THOMAS (MINN.)
1967—Daniel Hansard
1995—John Tauer

SAN DIEGO
1978—Michael Strode

SAN DIEGO ST.
1976—Steven Copp

SAN FRANCISCO
1990—Joel DeBortoli

SANTA CLARA
1994—Peter Eisenrich

SCRANTON
1974—Joseph Cantafio
1984—Michael Banas
1985—Daniel Polacheck
1988—John Andrejko
1993—Matt Cusano

SEATTLE PACIFIC
1997—Geoffrey Ping

SETON HALL
1969—John Suminski

SEWANEE
1967—Thomas Ward Jr.
1976—Henry Hoffman Jr.
1982—James Sherman
1998—Ryan Harrigan

SIENA
1992—Bruce Schroeder

SIMPSON
1980—John Hines
1995—David Otte

SLIPPERY ROCK
1975—Clyde Long

SOUTH ALA.
1998—Toby Madison

SOUTH DAKOTA
1976—Rick Nissen
2001—Jeremy Kudera

SOUTH DAKOTA ST.
1973—David Thomas
1997—Jason Sempsrott
2000—Casey Estling

SOUTH FLA.
1992—Radenko Dobras

SOUTHERN CALIFORNIA
1974—Daniel Anderson
1975—John Lambert

SOUTHERN ILL.
1977—Michael Glenn

SOUTHERN METHODIST
1977—Peter Lodwick

SOUTHERN UTAH
1991—Peter Johnson
1993—Richard Barton

SOUTHWEST MO. ST.
1971—Tillman Williams

STANFORD
1976—Edward Schweitzer
1980—Kimberly Belton
2000—Mark Madsen

SUSQUEHANNA
1986—Donald Harnum
1994—Lloyd Wolf

SWARTHMORE
1965—Cavin Wright
1987—Michael Dell

SYRACUSE
1981—Dan Schayes
1998—Marius Janulis

TENNESSEE
1993—Lang Wiseman

TENN.-MARTIN
1976—Michael Baker

TEXAS
1974—Harry Larrabee
1979—Jim Krivacs

TEXAS A&M
1970—James Heitmann

TEXAS-ARLINGTON
1980—Paul Renfor

TCU
1970—Jeffrey Harp
1981—Larry Frevert

TEX.-PAN AMERICAN
1976—Jesus Guerra Jr.

TEXAS TECH
1985—Brooks Jennings Jr.
1986—Tobin Doda

TOLEDO
1967—William Backensto
1980—Timothy Selgo

TRANSYLVANIA
1972—Robert Jobe Jr.
1980—Lawrence Kopczyk

TRINITY (CONN.)
1971—Howard Greenblatt
1996—Keith Wolff

TRINITY (TEX.)
1975—Phillip Miller

TRUMAN
2000—Jason Reinberg

TUFTS
1981—Scott Brown

TULSA
1999—Michael Ruffin

UCLA
1969—Kenneth Heitz
1971—George Schofield
1980—Kiki Vandeweghe
1995—George Zidek

UTAH
1968—Lyndon MacKay
1971—Michael Newlin
1977—Jeffrey Jonas
1998—Drew Hansen

UTAH ST.
1996—Eric Franson

VANDERBILT
1976—Jeffrey Fosnes

VILLANOVA
1983—John Pinone

VIRGINIA
1973—James Hobgood

VMI
1969—John Mitchell
1971—Jan Essenburg
1977—William Bynum III
1981—Andrew Kolesar
1987—Gay Elmore Jr.
1996—Bobby Prince

VIRGINIA TECH
1972—Robert McNeer

WABASH
1976—Len Fulkerson

WAKE FOREST
1969—Jerry Montgomery
1994—Marcus Blucas
1996—Rusty LaRue

WARTBURG
1972—David Platte
1974—Fred Waldstein
1991—Dan Nettleton

WASHINGTON
1970—Vincent Stone
1974—Raymond Price
1987—Rodney Ripley

WASHINGTON (MD.)
1979—Joseph Wilson
1990—Tim Keehan
1998—Bradd Burkhart

WASHINGTON (MO.)
1991—Jed Bargen

WASH. & JEFF.
1970—Terry Evans
1981—David Damico

WASH. & LEE
1983—Brian Hanson
1984—John Graves

WEBER ST.
1980—Mark Mattos
1985—Kent Hagan

WESLEYAN (CONN.)
1973—Brad Rogers
1974—Richard Fairbrother
1977—Steve Malinowski
1982—Steven Maizes
1985—Gregory Porydzy

WESTERN CARO.
1982—Gregory Dennis
1987—Richard Rogers

WESTERN ILL.
1984—Todd Hutcheson

WESTERN MD.
1983—Douglas Pinto

WESTMINSTER (PA.)
1967—John Fontanella

WHEATON (ILL.)
1995—Nathan Frank

WHITTIER
1977—Rodney Snook

WICHITA ST.
1969—Ronald Mendell
1991—Paul Guffrovich

WIDENER
1983—Louis DeRogatis

WILLIAM & MARY
1985—Keith Cieplicki

WILLIAMS
1965—Edgar Coolidge III
1986—Timothy Walsh

WISCONSIN
1987—Rodney Ripley

WIS.-OSHKOSH
1998—Joe Imhoff

WIS.-PLATTEVILLE
1993—T. J. Van Wie

WIS.-STEVENS POINT
1983—John Mack

WITTENBERG
1984—Jay Ferguson
1996—Scott Schwartz

WOOSTER
1995—Scott Meech

WRIGHT ST.
1978—Alan McGee

XAVIER
1975—Peter Accetta
8191—Gary Massa

YALE
1967—Richard Johnson
1968—Robert McCallum Jr.

Coaching Records

All-Division Coaching Records

Some of the won-lost records included in this coaches' section have been adjusted because of action by the NCAA Council or the NCAA Executive Committee to forfeit particular regular-season games or vacate particular NCAA Tournament games.

Coaches With At Least 500 Career Wins

(This list includes all coaches who have won at least 500 games regardless of classification with a minimum 10 head coaching seasons at NCAA schools.)

Coach (Alma Mater), Teams Coached, Tenure	Yrs.	Won	Lost	Pct.
1. Dean Smith (Kansas 1953) North Carolina 1962-97	36	879	254	.776
2. Adolph Rupp (Kansas 1923) Kentucky 1931-52, 54-72	41	876	190	.822
3. Clarence "Big House" Gaines (Morgan St. 1945) Winston-Salem 1947-93	47	828	447	.649
4. Jim Phelan (La Salle 1951) Mt. St. Mary's 1955-2002*	48	819	508	.617
5. Jerry Johnson (Fayetteville St. 1951) LeMoyne-Owen 1959-2002*	44	798	386	.674
6. Bob Knight (Ohio St. 1962) Army 1966-71, Indiana 72-2000, Texas Tech 02*	36	787	298	.725
7. Lefty Driesell (Duke 1954) Davidson 1961-69, Maryland 70-86, James Madison 89-97, Georgia St. 98-2002*	40	782	388	.668
8. Jerry Tarkanian (Fresno St. 1956) Long Beach St. 1969-73, UNLV 74-92, Fresno St. 96-2002	31	778	202	.794
9. Henry Iba (Northwest Mo. St. 1928) Northwest Mo. St. 1930-33, Colorado 34, Oklahoma St. 35-70	41	767	338	.694
10. Ed Diddle (Centre 1921) Western Ky. 1923-64	42	759	302	.715
11. Phog Allen (Kansas 1906) Baker 1906-08, Kansas 08-09, Haskell 09, Central Mo. St. 13-19, Kansas 20-56	48	746	264	.739
12. Lou Henson (New Mexico St. 1956) Hardin-Simmons 1963-66, Illinois 76-96, New Mexico St. 67-75, 99-2002*	38	742	377	.663
13. Norm Stewart (Missouri 1956) Northern Iowa 1962-67, Missouri 68-99	38	731	375	.661
14. Herb Magee (Philadelphia U. 1963) Philadelphia U. 1968-2002*	35	730	277	.725
15. Ray Meyer (Notre Dame 1938) DePaul 1943-84	42	724	354	.672
16. Don Haskins (Oklahoma St. 1953) UTEP 1962-99	38	719	353	.671
17. Eddie Sutton (Oklahoma St. 1958) Creighton 1970-74, Arkansas 75-85, Kentucky 86-89, Oklahoma St. 91-2002*	32	702	278	.716
17. Dick Sauers (Slippery Rock 1951) Albany (N.Y.) 1956-87, 89-97	41	702	330	.680
19. John Chaney (Bethune-Cookman 1955) Cheyney 1973-82, Temple 1983-2002*	30	675	253	.727
19. Denny Crum (UCLA 1958) Louisville 1972-2001	30	675	295	.696
21. Dennis Bridges (Ill. Wesleyan 1961) Ill. Wesleyan 1966-2001	36	666	320	.675
22. Ed Messbarger (Northwest Mo. St. 1956) Benedictine Heights 1957-60, Dallas 61-63, St. Mary's (Tex.) 63-78, Angelo St. 79-98	41	665	515	.564
23. John Wooden (Purdue 1932) Indiana St. 1947-48, UCLA 49-75	29	664	162	.804
24. Lute Olson (Augsburg 1956) Long Beach St. 1974, Iowa 75-83, Arizona 85-2002*	29	662	236	.737
25. Ralph Miller (Kansas 1942) Wichita St. 1952-64, Iowa 65-70, Oregon St. 71-89	38	657	382	.632
26. Marv Harshman (Pacific Lutheran 1942) Pacific Lutheran 1946-58, Washington St. 59-71, Washington 72-85	40	654	449	.593
27. Gene Bartow (Truman 1953) Central Mo. St. 1962-64, Valparaiso 65-70, Memphis 71-74, Illinois 75, UCLA 76-77, UAB 79-96	34	647	353	.647
28. Ed Adams (Tuskegee 1933) N.C. Central 1935-36, Tuskegee 37-49, Texas Southern 50-58	24	645	153	.808
29. John Lance (Pittsburg St. 1918) Southwestern Okla. 1919-22, Pittsburg St. 23-63	45	643	345	.651
30. Mike Krzyzewski (Army 1969) Army 1976-80, Duke 81-2002*	27	637	227	.737
31. Ken Anderson (Wis.-Eau Claire 1955) Wis.-Eau Claire 1969-95	27	631	152	.806
32. Cam Henderson (Salem [W.Va.] 1917) Muskingum 1920-23, Davis & Elkins 24-35, Marshall 36-55	35	630	243	.722
33. Jim Calhoun (American Int'l 1968) Northeastern 1973-86, Connecticut 87-2002*	30	624	286	.686
33. Norm Sloan (North Carolina St. 1951) Presbyterian 1952-55, Citadel 57-60, Florida 61-66, North Carolina St. 67-80, Florida 81-89	37	624	393	.614
35. Jim Boeheim (Syracuse 1966) Syracuse 1977-2002*	26	623	221	.738
36. Glenn Robinson (West Chester 1967) Frank. & Marsh. 1972-2002*	31	623	226	.734
37. Dean Nicholson (Central Wash. 1950) Central Wash. 1965-90	26	609	219	.736
38. Jim Smith (Marquette 1956) St. John's (Minn.) 1965-2002*	38	606	397	.604
39. Jerry Steele (Wake Forest 1961) Guilford 1963-70, High Point 73-2002*	38	602	466	.564
40. Slats Gill (Oregon St. 1925) Oregon St. 1929-64	36	599	392	.604
41. Abe Lemons (Oklahoma City 1949) Oklahoma City 1956-73, Tex.-Pan American 74-76, Texas 77-82, Oklahoma City 84-90	34	597	344	.634
42. John Thompson (Providence 1964) Georgetown 1973-99	27	596	239	.714
43. Billy Tubbs (Lamar 1958) Southwestern (Tex.) 1972-73, Lamar 77-80, Oklahoma 81-94, TCU 95-2002	28	595	297	.667
44. Guy Lewis (Houston 1947) Houston 1957-86	30	592	279	.680
45. Dom Rosselli (Geneva 1959) Youngstown St. 1941-42 & 47-82	38	591	384	.606
45. Hugh Durham (Florida St. 1959) Florida St. 1967-78, Georgia 79-95, Jacksonville 98-2002*	34	591	385	.606
47. Joe Hutton (Carleton 1924) Hamline 1931-65	35	590	208	.739
48. Dan McCarrell (North Park 1961) North Park 1968-84, Minn. St.-Mankato 85-2001	34	579	347	.625
49. Fred Hobdy (Grambling 1949) Grambling 1957-86	30	571	287	.666
50. Eldon Miller (Wittenberg 1961) Wittenberg 1963-70, Western Mich. 71-76, Ohio St. 77-86, Northern Iowa 87-98	36	568	419	.575
51. Dave Robbins (Catawba 1966) Va. Union 1979-2002*	24	565	156	.784
51. Gale Catlett (West Virginia 1963) Cincinnati 1973-78, West Virginia 79-2002*	30	565	325	.635
53. Gary Colson (David Lipscomb 1956) Valdosta St. 1959-68, Pepperdine 69-79, New Mexico 81-88, Fresno St. 91-95	34	563	385	.594
54. John Kresse [St. John's (N.Y.) 1964] Col. of Charleston 1980-2002	23	560	143	.797
54. Tom Murphy (Springfield 1962) Hamilton 1971-2002*	32	560	248	.693
56. Charles Chronister (East Stroudsburg 1963) Bloomsburg 1972-2002	31	559	288	.660
57. Tony Hinkle (Chicago 1921) Butler 1927-42 & 46-70	41	557	393	.586
58. Bill Knapton (Wis.-La Crosse 1952) Beloit 1958-97	40	555	344	.617
59. Bob Bessoir (Scranton 1955) Scranton 1973-2001	29	554	263	.678
60. Davey L. Whitney (Kentucky St. 1953) Texas Southern 1965-69, Alcorn St. 70-2002*	31	551	337	.620
60. Glenn Wilkes (Mercer 1950) Stetson 1958-93	36	551	436	.558
62. Frank McGuire [St. John's (N.Y.) 1936] St. John's (N.Y.) 1948-52, North Carolina 53-61, South Carolina 65-80	30	549	236	.699
62. Bruce Webster (Rutgers 1959) Bridgeport 1966-99	34	549	405	.575
64. Jim Gudger (Western Caro. 1942) Western Caro. 1951-69, Tex. A&M-Commerce 70-83	33	547	365	.600
64. Rudy Marisa (Penn St. 1956) Waynesburg 1970-2002*	33	547	291	.653
66. Tom Davis (Wis.-Platteville 1960) Lafayette 1972-77, Boston College 78-82, Stanford 83-86, Iowa 87-99	28	543	290	.652
67. Dick Whitmore (Bowdoin 1965) Colby 1971-2002*	32	535	250	.682
67. C. Alan Rowe (Villanova 1953) Widener 1966-98	33	535	325	.622
69. Harry Miller (Eastern N.M. 1951) Western St. (Colo.) 1953-58, Fresno St. 61-65, Eastern N.M. 66-70, North Tex. St. 71, Wichita St. 72-78, Stephen F. Austin 79-88	34	534	374	.588
70. Bob Chipman (Kansas St. 1973) Washburn 1980-2002*	23	533	186	.741
71. Bill Foster (Carson-Newman 1958) Shorter 1963-67, Charlotte 71-75, Clemson 76-84, Miami (Fla.) 86-90, Virginia Tech 92-97	30	532	325	.621
72. Tom Penders (Connecticut 1967) Tufts 1972-74, Columbia 75-78, Fordham 79-86, Rhode Island 87-88, Texas 89-98, George Washington 99-2001	30	527	361	.593
73. Lou Carnesecca [St. John's (N.Y.) 1946] St. John's (N.Y.) 1966-70, 74-92	24	526	200	.725
74. Pete Carril (Lafayette 1952) Lehigh 1967, Princeton 68-96	30	525	273	.658
74. Gene Mehaffey (Southern Methodist 1954) Carson-Newman 1968-78, Ohio Wesleyan 80-99	31	525	384	.578
76. Tom Young (Maryland 1958) Catholic 1959-67, American 70-73, Rutgers 74-85, Old Dominion 86-91	31	524	328	.615
77. John McLendon Jr. (Kansas 1936) N.C. Central 1941-52, Hampton 53-54, Tennessee St. 55-59, Kentucky St. 64-66, Cleveland St. 67-69	25	523	165	.760
78. Fred Enke (Minnesota 1921) Louisville 1924-25, Arizona 26-61	38	522	344	.603
79. Arad McCutchan (Evansville 1934) Evansville 1947-77	31	514	314	.621
79. Arthur McAfee (Wichita St. 1951) Lane 1961, Mississippi Val. 62, Lincoln (Mo.) 63, Bishop 64-65, Morehouse 66-2000	40	514	512	.501
81. Dave Bliss (Cornell 1965) Oklahoma 1976-80, Southern Methodist 89-99, Baylor 2000-02*	27	512	314	.620
81. Ben Jobe (Fisk 1956) Talladega 1965-67, Alabama St. 68, South Carolina St. 69-73, Denver 79-80, Alabama A&M 83-86, Tuskegee 97-2000, Southern U. 1987-96, 2002*	30	512	318	.617

Coach (Alma Mater), Teams Coached, Tenure	Yrs.	Won	Lost	Pct.
83. Paul Webb (William & Mary 1951) Randolph-Macon 1957-75, Old Dominion 76-85	29	511	257	.665
84. Lewis Levick (Drake 1950) Wartburg 1966-93	28	510	225	.694
84. Aubrey Bonham (Northern Iowa 1927) Whittier 1938-43 & 46-68	29	510	285	.642
84. Dick Reynolds (Otterbein 1965) Otterbein 1973-2002*	30	510	303	.627
87. Nolan Richardson (UTEP 1965) Tulsa 1981-85, Arkansas 86-2002	22	509	207	.711
87. Larry Hunter (Ohio 1971) Wittenberg 1977-89, Ohio 90-2001	25	509	224	.694
89. Hec Edmundson (Idaho 1909) Idaho 1917-18, Washington 21-47	29	508	204	.713
90. Rollie Massimino (Vermont 1956) Stony Brook 1970-71, Villanova 74-92, UNLV 93-94, Cleveland St. 97-2002*	29	507	369	.579
91. Leo Nicholson (Washington 1925) Central Wash. 1930-43 & 46-64	33	505	281	.642

Coach (Alma Mater), Teams Coached, Tenure	Yrs.	Won	Lost	Pct.
91. Homer Drew (William Jewell 1966) Bethel (Ind.) 1977-87, Ind.-South Bend 88, Valparaiso 89-2002	26	505	306	.623
93. Harold Anderson (Otterbein 1924) Toledo 1935-42, Bowling Green 43-63	29	504	226	.690
94. Jerry Welsh (Ithaca 1958) Potsdam St. 1969-91, Iona 92-95	26	502	205	.710
94. Jim Burson (Muskingum 1963) Muskingum 1968-2002	35	502	385	.566
96. Ed Martin (N.C. A&T 1951) South Carolina 1956-68, Tennessee St. 69-85	30	501	253	.664
96. Robert Vaughan (Virginia St. 1948) Elizabeth City St. 1952-86	34	501	363	.580
98. Bob Huggins (West Virginia 1977) Walsh 1981-83, Akron 85-89, Cincinnati 90-2002*	21	500	172	.744

*active

Division I Coaching Records

Winningest Active Coaches

(Minimum five years as a Division I head coach; includes record at four-year U.S. colleges only.)

BY PERCENTAGE

No.	Coach	Team	Yrs.	Won	Lost	Pct.
1.	Roy Williams	Kansas	14	388	93	.807
2.	Bob Huggins	Cincinnati	21	500	172	.744
3.	Rick Majerus	Utah	18	382	134	.740
4.	Jim Boeheim	Syracuse	26	623	221	.738
5.	Mike Krzyzewski	Duke	27	637	227	.737
6.	Lute Olson	Arizona	29	662	236	.737
7.	Rick Pitino	Louisville	16	371	137	.730
8.	John Chaney	Temple	30	675	253	.727
9.	Bob Knight	Texas Tech	36	787	298	.725
10.	Tom Izzo	Michigan St.	7	167	65	.720
11.	Eddie Sutton	Oklahoma St.	32	702	278	.716
12.	John Calipari	Memphis	10	237	94	.716
13.	Tubby Smith	Kentucky	11	256	105	.709
14.	Pat Douglass	UC Irvine	21	451	187	.707
15.	Steve Lavin	UCLA	6	135	59	.696
16.	Jim Calhoun	Connecticut	30	624	286	.686
17.	Mike Montgomery	Stanford	24	493	233	.679
18.	John Giannini	Maine	13	259	123	.678
19.	Bill Carmody	Northwestern	6	119	57	.676
20.	Skip Prosser	Wake Forest	9	186	91	.671
21.	Mark Gottfried	Alabama	7	150	74	.670
22.	Lefty Driesell	Georgia St.	40	782	388	.668
23.	Jim Harrick	Georgia	22	452	226	.667
24.	Lou Henson	New Mexico St.	38	742	377	.663
25.	Pete Gillen	Virginia	17	344	177	.660
26.	Mike Brey	Notre Dame	7	141	73	.659
27.	Blaine Taylor	Old Dominion	8	154	82	.653
28.	Gene Keady	Purdue	24	488	260	.652
29.	Billy Donovan	Florida	8	159	85	.652
30.	Charles Spoonhour	UNLV	17	340	182	.651
31.	Bill Self	Illinois	9	182	98	.650
32.	Larry Eustachy	Iowa St.	12	243	131	.650
33.	Mike Jarvis	St. John's (N.Y.)	17	340	185	.648
34.	Stew Morrill	Utah St.	16	312	171	.646
35.	Buzz Peterson	Tennessee	6	120	66	.645
36.	Tic Price	McNeese St.	6	114	63	.644
37.	Fran Dunphy	Pennsylvania	13	231	129	.642
38.	Gary Williams	Maryland	24	481	271	.640
39.	Steve Alford	Iowa	11	212	121	.637
40.	Royce Waltman	Indiana St.	15	269	154	.636
41.	Perry Watson	Detroit	9	176	101	.635
42.	Steve Fisher	San Diego St.	12	225	130	.634
43.	John Beilein	West Virginia	20	372	215	.634
44.	Bill Herrion	East Caro.	11	203	121	.627
45.	Kevin Stallings	Vanderbilt	9	174	104	.626
46.	Rick Barnes	Texas	15	292	177	.623
47.	Kelvin Sampson	Oklahoma	19	364	221	.622
48.	Tim Welsh	Providence	7	133	81	.621
49.	Davey L. Whitney	Alcorn St.	31	551	337	.620
50.	Dave Bliss	Baylor	27	512	314	.620
51.	Jim Phelan	Mt. St. Mary's	48	819	508	.617

No.	Coach	Team	Yrs.	Won	Lost	Pct.
52.	Ben Jobe	Southern U.	30	512	318	.617
53.	Cliff Ellis	Auburn	27	498	311	.616
54.	Mike Deane	Lamar	18	329	206	.615
55.	Dave Odom	South Carolina	16	300	189	.613
56.	Herb Sendek	North Carolina St.	9	172	111	.608
57.	Hugh Durham	Jacksonville	34	591	385	.606
58.	Jim Boone	Eastern Mich.	16	281	186	.602
59.	Gary Waters	Rutgers	6	110	73	.601

(Coaches with fewer than five years as a Division I head coach; includes record at four-year U.S. colleges only.)

No.	Coach	Team	Yrs.	Won	Lost	Pct.
1.	Bruce Pearl	Wis.-Milwaukee	10	247	59	.807
2.	Bo Ryan	Wisconsin	18	402	116	.776
3.	Danny Kaspar	Stephen F. Austin	11	241	84	.742
4.	L. Vann Pettaway	Alabama A&M	16	345	131	.725
5.	Bob Hoffman	Tex.-Pan American	12	286	123	.699
6.	Jeff Price	Ga. Southern	9	181	83	.686
7.	John Masi	UC Riverside	23	434	222	.662
8.	Greg Jackson	Delaware St.	11	201	106	.655
9.	Bob Lutz	Charlotte	13	260	139	.652
10.	Greg McDermott	Northern Iowa	8	145	79	.647
11.	Brad Soderberg	St. Louis	8	131	73	.642
12.	Rick Byrd	Belmont	21	421	236	.641
13.	Dale Layer	Colorado St.	11	195	119	.621
14.	Rick Scruggs	Gardner-Webb	16	304	188	.618
15.	Bob Williams	UC Santa Barb.	14	247	154	.616

BY VICTORIES

No.	Coach, Team	Won
1.	Jim Phelan, Mt. St. Mary's	819
2.	Bob Knight, Texas Tech	787
3.	Lefty Driesell, Georgia St.	782
4.	Lou Henson, New Mexico St.	742
5.	Eddie Sutton, Oklahoma St.	702
6.	John Chaney, Temple	675
7.	Lute Olson, Arizona	662
8.	Mike Krzyzewski, Duke	637
9.	Jim Calhoun, Connecticut	624
10.	Jim Boeheim, Syracuse	623
11.	Hugh Durham, Jacksonville	591
12.	Davey L. Whitney, Alcorn St.	551
13.	Dave Bliss, Baylor	512
13.	Ben Jobe, Southern U.	512
15.	Rollie Massimino, Cleveland St.	507
16.	Bob Huggins, Cincinnati	500
17.	Don DeVoe, Navy	499
18.	Cliff Ellis, Auburn	498
19.	Mike Montgomery, Stanford	493
20.	Gene Keady, Purdue	488
21.	Gary Williams, Maryland	481
22.	Jim Harrick, Georgia	452
23.	Pat Douglass, UC Irvine	451
23.	Ben Braun, California	451
25.	Pat Kennedy, Montana	393
26.	Roy Williams, Kansas	388
27.	Rick Majerus, Utah	382
28.	Danny Nee, Duquesne	377

No.	Coach, Team	Won
29.	John Beilein, West Virginia	372
30.	Rick Pitino, Louisville	371
31.	Mike Vining, La.-Monroe	369
32.	Kelvin Sampson, Oklahoma	364
33.	Pete Gillen, Virginia	344
34.	Charles Spoonhour, UNLV	340
34.	Mike Jarvis, St. John's (N.Y.)	340
36.	Nick Macarchuk, Stony Brook	339
37.	Jim O'Brien, Ohio St.	337
38.	Billy Lee, Campbell	332
39.	Don Maestri, Troy St.	331
40.	Mike Deane, Lamar	329
40.	Gary Garner, Southeast Mo. St.	329
42.	Rick Samuels, Eastern Ill.	328
43.	Stew Morrill, Utah St.	312
44.	Tom Green, Fairleigh Dickinson	306
45.	Dave Odom, South Carolina	300
46.	Jim Crews, Army	294
46.	Dave Magarity, Marist	294
48.	Rick Barnes, Texas	292
49.	Jim Boone, Eastern Mich.	281
49.	Jim Larranaga, George Mason	281
51.	Ron Mitchell, Coppin St.	275
51.	Bob Thomason, Pacific (Cal.)	275
53.	Royce Waltman, Indiana St.	269
54.	John Giannini, Maine	259
54.	Kurt Kanaskie, Drake	259

No.	Coach, Team	Won
56.	Riley Wallace, Hawaii	258
56.	Rob Spivery, Alabama St.	258
58.	Cy Alexander, South Carolina St.	257
58.	Dave Loos, Austin Peay	257
58.	Steve Aggers, Loyola Marymount	257
61.	Tubby Smith, Kentucky	256
61.	Lafayette Stribling, Mississippi Val.	256
63.	Jim Wooldridge, Kansas St.	252
64.	Tom Brennan, Vermont	248
65.	Tom Sullivan, UMBC	245
66.	Larry Eustachy, Iowa St.	243

No.	Coach, Team	Won
66.	Steve Lappas, Massachusetts	243
68.	Frank Sullivan, Harvard	239
69.	John Calipari, Memphis	237
70.	Mike Dement, Southern Methodist	233
71.	Oliver Purnell, Dayton	232
72.	Fran Dunphy, Pennsylvania	231
73.	Dana Altman, Creighton	229
74.	Steve Fisher, San Diego St.	225
74.	Perry Clark, Miami (Fla.)	225
76.	Barry Collier, Nebraska	223
77.	Greg White, Marshall	220
78.	Andy Stoglin, Jackson St.	219
79.	Al Skinner, Boston College	217

No.	Coach, Team	Won
80.	Pat Flannery, Bucknell	215
81.	Jim Baron, Rhode Island	214
82.	Steve Alford, Iowa	212
83.	Dan Hipsher, Akron	211
84.	Bob McKillop, Davidson	205
85.	Bill Herrion, East Caro.	203
86.	Leonard Hamilton, Florida St.	200

(Coaches with fewer than five years as a Division I head coach; includes record at four-year U.S. colleges only.)

No.	Coach, Team	Won
1.	Jerry Steele, High Point	602
2.	John Masi, UC Riverside	434

No.	Coach, Team	Won
3.	Rick Byrd, Belmont	421
4.	Bo Ryan, Wisconsin	402
5.	Dave Bike, Sacred Heart	392
6.	L. Vann Pettaway, Alabama A&M	345
7.	Rick Scruggs, Gardner-Webb	304
7.	Greg Kampe, Oakland	304
9.	Bob Hoffman, Tex.-Pan American	286
10.	Bob Lutz, Charlotte	260
11.	Bruce Pearl, Wis.-Milwaukee	247
11.	Bob Williams, UC Santa Barb.	247
13.	Danny Kaspar, Stephen F. Austin	241
14.	Greg Jackson, Delaware St.	201

Winningest Coaches All-Time

(Minimum 10 head coaching seasons in Division I)

	Coach, team coached & tenure	Yrs.	Won	Lost	Pct.
1.	Clair Bee, Rider 1929-31, Long Island 32-45 & 46-51.	21	412	87	.826
2.	Adolph Rupp, Kentucky 1931-72	41	876	190	.822
3.	Roy Williams, Kansas 1989-2002*	14	388	93	.807
4.	John Wooden, Indiana St. 1947-48, UCLA 49-75	29	664	162	.804
5.	John Kresse, Col. of Charleston 1980-2002	23	560	143	.797
6.	Jerry Tarkanian, Long Beach St. 1969-73, UNLV 74-92, Fresno St. 96-2002	31	778	202	.794
7.	Dean Smith, North Carolina 1962-97	36	879	254	.776
8.	Harry Fisher, Columbia 1907-16, Army 22-23, 25	13	147	44	.770
9.	Frank Keaney, Rhode Island 1921-48	27	387	117	.768
10.	George Keogan, St. Louis 1916, Allegheny 19, Valparaiso 20-21, Notre Dame 24-43	24	385	117	.767
11.	Jack Ramsay, St. Joseph's 1956-66	11	231	71	.765
12.	Vic Bubas, Duke 1960-69	10	213	67	.761
13.	Chick Davies, Duquesne 1925-43 & 47-48	21	314	106	.748
14.	Ray Mears, Wittenberg 1957-62, Tennessee 63-77	21	399	135	.747
15.	Bob Huggins, Walsh 1981-83, Akron 85-89, Cincinnati 90-2002*	21	500	172	.744
16.	Rick Majerus, Marquette 1984-86, Ball St. 88-89, Utah 90-2002*	18	382	134	.740
17.	Al McGuire, Belmont Abbey 1958-64, Marquette 65-77	20	405	143	.739
18.	Everett Case, North Carolina St. 1947-64	18	376	133	.739
19.	Phog Allen, Baker 1906-08, Kansas 08-09, Haskell 09, Central Mo. St. 13-19, Kansas 20-56	48	746	264	.739
20.	Jim Boeheim, Syracuse 1977-2002*	26	623	221	.738
21.	Mike Krzyzewski, Army 1976-80, Duke 81-2002*	27	637	227	.737
22.	Lute Olson, Long Beach St. 1974, Iowa 75-83, Arizona 84-2002*	29	662	236	.737
23.	Walter Meanwell, Wisconsin 1912-17 & 21-34, Missouri 18, 20	22	280	101	.735
24.	Rick Pitino, Boston U. 1979-83, Providence 1986-87, Kentucky 90-97, Louisville 2002*	16	371	137	.730
25.	John Chaney, Cheyney 1973-82, Temple 83-2002*	30	675	253	.727
26.	Lew Andreas, Syracuse 1925-43 & 45-50	25	355	134	.726
27.	Bob Knight, Army 1966-71, Indiana 72-2000, Texas Tech 02*	36	787	298	.725
28.	Lou Carnesecca, St. John's (N.Y.) 1966-70 & 74-92	24	526	200	.725
29.	Fred Schaus, West Virginia 1955-60, Purdue 73-78	12	251	96	.723
30.	Cam Henderson, Muskingum 1920-23, Davis & Elkins 24-35, Marshall 36-55	35	630	243	.722
31.	Hugh Greer, Connecticut 1947-63	17	290	112	.721
32.	Joe Lapchick, St. John's (N.Y.) 1937-47 & 57-65	20	335	130	.720
33.	Eddie Sutton, Creighton 1970-74, Arkansas 75-85, Kentucky 86-89, Oklahoma St. 91-2002*	32	702	278	.716
34.	Dudey Moore, Duquesne 1949-58, La Salle 59-63	15	270	107	.716
35.	Ed Diddle, Western Ky. 1923-64	42	759	302	.715
36.	Tom Blackburn, Dayton 1948-64	17	352	141	.714
37.	John Lawther, Westminster 1927-36, Penn St. 37-49	23	317	127	.714
38.	John Thompson, Georgetown 1973-99	27	596	239	.714
39.	Hec Edmundson, Idaho 1917-18, Washington 21-47	29	508	204	.713
40.	Nolan Richardson, Tulsa 1981-85, Arkansas 86-2002*	22	509	207	.711
41.	Pat Page, Chicago 1913-20, Butler 21-26	14	242	99	.710
42.	Piggy Lambert, Purdue 1917 & 19-45	29	371	152	.709
43.	Tubby Smith, Tulsa 1992-95, Georgia 96-97, Kentucky 98-2002*	11	256	105	.709
44.	Peck Hickman, Louisville 1945-67	23	443	183	.708
45.	Lee Rose, Transylvania 1965-75, Charlotte 76-78, Purdue 79-80, South Fla. 1981-86	19	388	162	.705

	Coach, team coached & tenure	Yrs.	Won	Lost	Pct.
46.	Joe B. Hall, Regis (Colo.) 1960-64, Central Mo. St. 65, Kentucky 73-85	19	373	156	.705
47.	Frank McGuire, St. John's (N.Y.) 1948-52, North Carolina 53-61, South Carolina 65-80	30	549	236	.699
48.	Boyd Grant, Fresno St. 1978-86, Colorado St. 88-91	13	275	120	.696
49.	Denny Crum, Louisville 1972-2001	30	675	295	.696
50.	Doug Mills, Illinois 1937-47	11	151	66	.696
51.	Larry Hunter, Wittenberg 1977-89, Ohio 1990-2001	25	509	224	.694
52.	Henry Iba, Northwest Mo. St. 1930-33, Colorado 34, Oklahoma St. 35-70	41	767	338	.694
53.	Honey Russell, Seton Hall 1937-43 & 50-60, Manhattan 46	19	308	137	.692
54.	Larry Weise, St. Bonaventure 1962-73	12	202	90	.692
55.	Gene Smithson, Illinois St. 1976-78, Wichita St. 79-86	11	221	99	.691
56.	Harold Anderson, Toledo 1935-42, Bowling Green 42-63	29	504	226	.690
57.	Nat Holman, CCNY 1920-52, 55-56 & 59-60	37	423	190	.690
58.	Jim Calhoun, Northeastern 1973-86, Connecticut 87-2002*	30	624	286	.686
59.	Dana Kirk, Tampa 1967-71, Va. Commonwealth 77-79, Memphis 80-86	15	281	131	.682
60.	Ozzie Cowles, Carleton 1925-30, Wis.-River Falls 34-36, Dartmouth 37-43 & 45-46, Michigan 47-48, Minnesota 49-59	31	421	198	.680
61.	Guy Lewis, Houston 1957-86	30	592	279	.680
62.	Mike Montgomery, Montana 1979-86, Stanford 87-2002*	24	493	233	.679
63.	Johnny Oldham, Tennessee Tech 1956-64, Western Ky. 65-71	16	260	123	.679
64.	Harry Combes, Illinois 1948-67	20	316	150	.678
65.	Digger Phelps, Fordham 1971, Notre Dame 72-91	21	419	200	.677
66.	Bob King, New Mexico 1963-72, Indiana St. 76-78	13	236	113	.676
67.	Jack Gardner, Kansas St. 1940-42 & 47-53, Utah 54-71	28	486	235	.674
68.	Roy Skinner, Vanderbilt 1959 & 62-76	16	278	135	.673
69.	Alex Severance, Villanova 1937-61	25	413	201	.673
70.	Ray Meyer, DePaul 1943-84	42	724	354	.672
71.	Herbert Read, Western Mich. 1923-49	27	351	172	.671
72.	Don Haskins, UTEP 1962-99	38	719	353	.671
73.	Neil McCarthy, Weber St. 1976-85, New Mexico St. 86-97	22	448	221	.670
74.	Don Corbett, Lincoln (Mo.) 1972-79, N.C. A&T 80-93	22	413	204	.669
75.	Lefty Driesell, Davidson 1961-69, Maryland 70-86, James Madison 89-97, Georgia St. 98-2002*	40	782	388	.668
76.	Billy Tubbs, Southwestern (Tex.) 1972-73, Lamar 77-80, Oklahoma 81-94, TCU 95-2002	28	595	297	.667
77.	Joel Eaves, Auburn 50-64	15	224	112	.667
77.	Jack Gray, Texas 1937-42 & 46-51	12	194	97	.667
77.	Dutch Hermann, Penn St. 1916-17 & 20-32	15	148	74	.667
77.	Charles Moir, Roanoke 1968-73, Tulane 74-76, Virginia Tech 77-87	20	392	196	.667
77.	Jim Harrick, Pepperdine 1980-88, UCLA 89-96, Rhode Island 98-99, Georgia 2000-02*	22	452	226	.667
82.	Harold Bradley, Hartwick 1948-50, Duke 51-59, Texas 60-67	20	337	169	.666
83.	Wimp Sanderson, Alabama 1981-92, Ark.-Little Rock 95-99	17	350	176	.665
84.	Lou Henson, Hardin-Simmons 1963-66, Illinois 76-96, New Mexico St. 67-75, 99-2002*	38	742	377	.663
85.	Norm Stewart, Northern Iowa 1962-67, Missouri 68-99	38	731	375	.661
86.	Branch McCracken, Ball St. 1930-37, Indiana 39-43 & 47-65	32	450	231	.661
87.	Pete Gillen, Xavier 1986-94, Providence 96-98, Virginia 99-2002*	17	344	177	.660

	Coach, team coached & tenure	Yrs.	Won	Lost	Pct.
88.	Dave Gavitt, Dartmouth 1968-69, Providence 70-79	12	227	117	.660
89.	Terry Holland, Davidson 1970-74, Virginia 75-90	21	418	216	.659
90.	Harry Litwack, Temple 1953-73	21	373	193	.659
91.	Pete Carril, Lehigh 1967, Princeton 68-96	30	525	273	.658
92.	Pete Newell, San Francisco 1947-50, Michigan St. 51-54, California 55-60	14	234	123	.655
93.	Dick Tarrant, Richmond 1982-93	12	239	126	.655
94.	Jack Kraft, Villanova 1962-73, Rhode Island 74-81	20	361	191	.654
95.	Paul Evans, St. Lawrence 1974-80, Navy 81-86, Pittsburgh 87-94	21	392	208	.653
96.	Jack Hartman, Southern Ill. 1963-70, Kansas St. 71-86	24	439	233	.653
97.	Eddie Hickey, Creighton 1936-43 & 47, St. Louis 48-58, Marquette 59-64	26	435	231	.653
98.	Fred Taylor, Ohio St. 1959-76	18	297	158	.653
99.	Gene Keady, Western Ky. 1979-80, Purdue 81-2002*	24	488	260	.652
100.	George King, Col. of Charleston 1957, West Virginia 61-65, Purdue 66-72	13	223	119	.652
101.	Tom Davis, Lafayette 1972-77, Boston College 78-82, Stanford 83-86, Iowa 87-99	28	543	290	.652
102.	Tim Floyd, Idaho 1987-88, New Orleans 89-94, Iowa St. 95-98	12	243	130	.651
103.	Charlie Spoonhour, Southwest Mo. St. 1984-92, St. Louis 93-99, UNLV 2002*	17	340	182	.651
104.	Larry Eustachy, Idaho 199-193, Utah St. 94-98, Iowa St. 99-2002*	12	243	131	.650

*active

BY VICTORIES

(Minimum 10 head coaching seasons in Division I)

Coach	Wins
1. Dean Smith	879
2. Adolph Rupp	876
3. Jim Phelan, Mt. St. Mary's 1955-2002*	819
4. Bob Knight*	787
5. Lefty Driesell*	782
6. Jerry Tarkanian	778
7. Henry Iba	767
8. Ed Diddle	759
9. Phog Allen	746
10. Lou Henson*	742
11. Norm Stewart	731
12. Ray Meyer	724
13. Don Haskins	719
14. Eddie Sutton*	702
15. John Chaney*	675
15. Denny Crum	675
17. John Wooden	664
18. Lute Olson*	662
19. Ralph Miller, Wichita St. 1952-64, Iowa 65-70, Oregon St. 71-89	657
20. Marv Harshman, Pacific Lutheran 1946-58, Washington St. 59-71, Washington 72-85	654
21. Gene Bartow	647
22. Mike Krzyzewski*	637
23. Cam Henderson	630
24. Norm Sloan, Presbyterian 1952-55, Citadel 57-60, North Carolina St. 67-80, Florida 61-66, 81-89	627
25. Jim Calhoun*	624
26. Jim Boeheim*	623
27. Slats Gill, Oregon St. 1929-64	599
28. Abe Lemons, Oklahoma City 1956-73, 84-90, Tex.-Pan American 74-76, Texas 77-82	597
29. John Thompson	596
30. Billy Tubbs	595
31. Guy Lewis	592
32. Hugh Durham, Florida St. 1967-78, Georgia 79-95, Jacksonville 99-2002*	591
33. Eldon Miller, Wittenberg 1963-70, Western Mich. 71-76, Ohio St. 77-86, Northern Iowa 87-98	568
34. Gale Catlett, Cincinnati 1973-78, West Virginia 79-2002*	565
35. Gary Colson, Valdosta St. 1959-68, Pepperdine 69-79, New Mexico 81-88, Fresno St. 91-95	563
36. John Kresse	560
37. Tony Hinkle, Butler 1927-43, 46-70	557
38. Davey L. Whitney, Texas Southern 1965-69, Alcorn St. 70-89, 97-2002*	551
38. Glenn Wilkes, Stetson 1958-93	551
40. Frank McGuire	549
41. Tom Davis	543
42. Harry Miller, Western St. 1953-58, Fresno St. 61-65, Eastern N.M. 66-70, North Texas 71, Wichita St. 72-78, Stephen F. Austin 79-88	534
43. Bill Foster, Shorter 1963-67, Charlotte 71-75, Clemson 76-84, Miami (Fla.) 86-90, Virginia Tech 92-97	532
44. Tom Penders, Tufts 1972-74, Columbia 75-78, Fordham 79-86, Rhode Island 87-88, Texas 89-98, George Washington 99-2001	527
45. Lou Carnesecca	526
46. Pete Carril	525

Coach	Wins
47. Tom Young, Catholic 1959-67, American 70-73, Rutgers 74-85, Old Dominion 86-91	524
48. Fred Enke, Louisville 1924-25, Arizona 27-61	522
49. Dave Bliss, Oklahoma 1976-80, Southern Methodist 81-88, New Mexico 89-99, Baylor 2000-02*	512
49. Ben Jobe, Talladega 1965-73, Alabama St. 68, South Carolina St. 69-73, Denver 79-80, Alabama A&M 83-86, Tuskegee 97-2000, Southern U. 1987-96, 2002*	512
51. Larry Hunter	509
51. C.M. Newton, Transylvania 1956-68, Alabama 69-80, Vanderbilt 82-89	509
51. Nolan Richardson	509
54. Hec Edmundson	508
55. Rollie Massimino, Stony Brook 1970-71, Villanova 74-92, UNLV 93-94, Cleveland St. 97-2002*	507
56. Homer Drew, Bethel (Ind.) 1977-87, Ind.-South Bend 88, Valparaiso 89-2002	505
57. Harold Anderson	504
58. Bob Huggins*	500
59. Don DeVoe, Virginia Tech 1972-76, Wyoming 77-78, Tennessee 79-89, Florida 90, Navy 93-2002*	499
60. Cliff Ellis, South Ala. 1976-84, Clemson 85-94, Auburn 95-2002*	498
61. Ned Wulk, Xavier 1952-57, Arizona St. 58-82	495
62. Jack Friel, Washington St. 1929-58	494
62. Calvin Luther, DePauw 1955-58, Murray St. 59-73, Longwood 82-90, Tenn.-Martin 91-99	494
62. Everett Shelton, Phillips 1924-26, Wyoming 40-59, Sacramento St. 60-68	494
65. Mike Montgomery*	493
66. Gene Keady*	488
67. Jack Gardner	486
68. Bob Hallberg, St. Xavier (Ill.) 1972-77, Chicago St. 78-87, Ill.-Chicago 88-96	484
69. Butch van Breda Kolff, Lafayette 1952-55, 85-88, Hofstra 56-62, 89-94, Princeton 63-67, New Orleans 78-79	482
70. Gary Williams, American 1979-82, Boston College 83-86, Ohio St. 87-89, Maryland 90-2002*	481
71. Bill E. Foster, Bloomsburg 1961-63, Rutgers 64-71, Utah 72-74, Duke 75-80, South Carolina 81-86, Northwestern 87-93	467
72. Johnny Orr, Massachusetts 1964-66, Michigan 69-80, Iowa St. 81-94	466
73. Taps Gallagher, Niagara 1932-65	465
74. Bill Reinhart, Oregon 1924-35, George Washington 36-66	464
75. Clarence "Nibs" Price, California 1925-54	463
76. George Blaney, Stonehill 1968-69, Dartmouth 70-72, Holy Cross 73-94, Seton Hall 95-97	459

Arizona coach Lute Olson celebrates the 1997 championship with wife Bobbi, who passed away two seasons ago.

COACHING RECORDS

Coach	Wins
77. Dick Bennett, Wis.-Stevens Point 1981-85, Wis.-Green Bay 86-95, Wisconsin 96-2001	455
78. Bobby Cremins, Appalachian St. 1976-81, Georgia Tech 82-2000	454
78. Tex Winter, Marquette 1952-53, Kansas St. 54-68, Washington 69-71, Northwestern 74-78, Long Beach St. 79-83	454
80. Jim Harrick*	452
81. Ben Braun, Siena Heights 1978-85, Eastern Mich. 86-96, California 97-2002*	451
82. Branch McCracken	450
83. Dale Brown, LSU 1973-97	448
83. Neil McCarthy	448
85. Peck Hickman	443
85. Shelby Metcalf, Texas A&M 1964-90	443
87. Jack Hartman	439
88. Don Donoher, Dayton 1965-89	437
89. Eddie Hickey	435
90. Nat Holman	423
91. Ozzie Cowles	421
92. Richard "Digger" Phelps	419
93. Terry Holland	418
94. Jud Heathcote, Montana 1972-76, Michigan St. 77-95	417
95. Don Corbett	413
95. Alex Severance	413
97. Clair Bee	412
98. Howard Cann, New York U. 1924-58	409
99. Murray Arnold, Birmingham-So. 1971-78, Chattanooga 80-85, Western Ky. 87-90, Stetson 98-2001	407
100. Al McGuire	405
101. Howard Hobson, Southern Ore. 1933-35, Oregon 36-48, Yale 49-56	401

*active

All Active Coaches Listed by School

Coach	School	Yr	W	L	Pct.
Joe Scott	Air Force	2	17	40	.298
Dan Hipsher	Akron	13	211	153	.580
Mark Gottfried	Alabama	7	150	74	.670
Vann Pettaway	Alabama A&M	16	345	131	.725
Rob Spivery	Alabama St.	16	258	236	.522
Mike Anderson	UAB	0	0	0	.000
Will Brown	Albany (N.Y.)	1	7	13	.350
Davey L. Whitney	Alcorn St.	31	551	337	.620
Jeff Jones	American	10	171	136	.557
Houston Fancher	Appalachian St.	2	21	38	.356
Lute Olson	Arizona	29	662	236	.737
Rob Evans	Arizona St.	10	146	141	.509
open	Ark.-Pine Bluff				
Stan Heath	Arkansas	1	30	6	.833
Dickey Nutt	Arkansas St.	7	104	98	.515
Porter Moser	Ark.-Little Rock	2	36	22	.621
Jim Crews	Army	17	294	209	.584
Cliff Ellis	Auburn	27	498	311	.616
Dave Loos	Austin Peay	16	257	226	.532
Tim Buckley	Ball St.	2	41	24	.631
Dave Bliss	Baylor	27	512	314	.620
Rick Byrd	Belmont	21	421	236	.641
Clifford Reed Jr.	Bethune-Cookman	1	6	4	.600
Al Walker	Binghamton	14	165	204	.447
Greg Graham	Boise St.	1	18	5	.783
Al Skinner	Boston College	14	217	199	.522
Dennis Wolff	Boston U.	10	159	125	.560
Dan Dakich	Bowling Green	5	89	57	.610
Jim Les	Bradley	0	0	0	.000
Steve Cleveland	Brigham Young	5	85	69	.552
Glen Miller	Brown	9	135	99	.577
Pat Flannery	Bucknell	13	215	149	.591
Reggie Witherspoon	Buffalo	3	19	62	.235
Todd Lickliter	Butler	1	26	6	.813
Kevin Bromley	Cal Poly	2	19	24	.442
Ben Braun	California	25	451	305	.597
Pat Douglass	UC Irvine	21	451	187	.707
John Masi	UC Riverside	23	434	222	.662
Bob Williams	UC Santa Barb.	14	247	154	.616
Donny Daniels	Cal St. Fullerton	2	10	45	.182
Bobby Braswell	Cal St. Northridge	6	97	79	.551
Billy Lee	Campbell	24	332	352	.485
Mike MacDonald	Canisius	5	68	77	.469
Kevin Johnson	Centenary (La.)	3	32	50	.390
Howie Dickenman	Central Conn. St.	6	97	79	.551
Kirk Speraw	UCF	9	125	137	.477
Jay Smith	Central Mich.	6	73	93	.440
Tom Herrion	Col. of Charleston	0	0	0	.000
Jim Platt	Charleston So.	6	77	96	.445

Coach	School	Yr	W	L	Pct.
Bob Lutz	Charlotte	13	260	139	.652
Jeff Lebo	Chattanooga	4	75	43	.636
Bo Ellis	Chicago St.	4	20	91	.180
Bob Huggins	Cincinnati	21	500	172	.744
Pat Dennis	Citadel	10	121	154	.440
Larry Shyatt	Clemson	5	74	80	.481
Rollie Massimino	Cleveland St.	29	507	369	.579
Pete Strickland	Coastal Caro.	4	33	78	.297
Emmett Davis	Colgate	4	57	56	.504
Ricardo Patton	Colorado	7	105	91	.536
Dale Layer	Colorado St.	11	195	119	.621
Armond Hill	Columbia	7	70	116	.376
Jim Calhoun	Connecticut	30	624	286	.686
Ron Mitchell	Coppin St.	16	275	197	.583
Steve Donahue	Cornell	2	12	42	.222
Dana Altman	Creighton	13	229	162	.586
Dave Faucher	Dartmouth	11	125	164	.433
Bob McKillop	Davidson	13	205	171	.545
Oliver Purnell	Dayton	14	232	185	.556
David Henderson	Delaware	2	34	26	.567
Greg Jackson	Delaware St.	11	201	106	.655
Terry Carroll	Denver	1	8	20	.286
Dave Leitao	DePaul	2	22	35	.386
Perry Watson	Detroit	9	176	101	.635
Kurt Kanaskie	Drake	17	259	223	.537
Bruiser Flint	Drexel	6	100	86	.538
Mike Krzyzewski	Duke	27	637	227	.737
Danny Nee	Duquesne	22	377	298	.559
Bill Herrion	East Caro.	11	203	121	.627
Ed DeChellis	East Tenn. St.	6	85	82	.509
Rick Samuels	Eastern Ill.	22	328	308	.516
Travis Ford	Eastern Ky.	5	72	79	.477
Jim Boone	Eastern Mich.	16	281	186	.602
Ray Giacoletti	Eastern Wash.	5	82	57	.590
Mark Simons	Elon	16	192	256	.429
Steve Merfeld	Evansville	5	90	57	.612
Tim O'Toole	Fairfield	4	50	63	.442
Tom Green	Fairleigh Dickinson	19	306	241	.559
Billy Donovan	Florida	8	159	85	.652
Mike Gillespie	Florida A&M	1	9	19	.321
Sidney Green	Fla. Atlantic	7	77	124	.383
Donnie Marsh	Florida Int'l	7	93	95	.495
Leonard Hamilton	Florida St.	14	200	210	.488
Bob Hill	Fordham	3	34	52	.395
Ray Lopes	Fresno St.	0	0	0	.000
Larry Davis	Furman	5	62	84	.425
Rick Scruggs	Gardner-Webb	16	304	188	.618
Jim Larranaga	George Mason	18	281	232	.548
Karl Hobbs	George Washington	1	12	16	.429
Craig Esherick	Georgetown	4	71	44	.617
Jim Harrick	Georgia	22	452	226	.667
Jeff Price	Ga. Southern	9	181	83	.686
Lefty Driesell	Georgia St.	40	782	388	.668
Paul Hewitt	Georgia Tech	5	98	56	.636
Mark Few	Gonzaga	3	81	20	.802
Larry Wright	Grambling	3	18	67	.212
Bobby Collins	Hampton	0	0	0	.000
Larry Harrison	Hartford	2	18	42	.300
Frank Sullivan	Harvard	18	239	248	.491
Riley Wallace	Hawaii	17	258	231	.528
Jerry Steele	High Point	38	602	466	.564
Tom Pecora	Hofstra	1	12	20	.375
Ralph Willard	Holy Cross	12	194	165	.540
Ray McCallum	Houston	9	153	111	.580
Frankie Allen	Howard	15	199	232	.462
Leonard Perry	Idaho	1	9	19	.321
Doug Oliver	Idaho St.	4	38	70	.352
Bill Self	Illinois	9	182	98	.650
Tom Richardson	Illinois St.	3	48	43	.527
Jimmy Collins	Ill.-Chicago	6	86	92	.483
Mike Davis	Indiana	2	46	25	.648
Royce Waltman	Indiana St.	15	269	154	.636
Doug Noll	IPFW	10	157	167	.485
Ron Hunter	IUPUI	8	115	110	.511
Jeff Ruland	Iona	4	71	53	.573
Steve Alford	Iowa	11	212	121	.637
Larry Eustachy	Iowa St.	12	243	131	.650
Andy Stoglin	Jackson St.	15	219	224	.494
Hugh Durham	Jacksonville	34	591	385	.606
Mike LaPlante	Jacksonville St.	2	22	35	.386
Sherman Dillard	James Madison	8	102	119	.462
Roy Williams	Kansas	14	388	93	.807
Jim Wooldridge	Kansas St.	15	252	182	.581
Jim Christian	Kent St.	0	0	0	.000

Coach	School	Yr	W	L	Pct.
Tubby Smith	Kentucky	11	256	105	.709
Billy Hahn	La Salle	1	15	17	.469
Fran O'Hanlon	Lafayette	7	110	91	.547
Mike Deane	Lamar	18	329	206	.615
Billy Taylor	Lehigh	15	176	242	.421
Randy Dunton	Liberty	1	11	17	.393
Larry Reynolds	Long Beach St.	5	110	35	.759
Jim Ferry	Long Island	4	104	19	.846
John Brady	LSU	11	170	147	.536
Keith Richard	Louisiana Tech	4	79	39	.669
Jessie Evans	La.-Lafayette	5	92	62	.597
Mike Vining	La.-Monroe	21	369	249	.597
Rick Pitino	Louisville	16	371	137	.730
Larry Farmer	Loyola (Ill.)	10	142	143	.498
Scott Hicks	Loyola (Md.)	10	142	137	.509
Steve Aggers	Loyola Marymount	18	257	271	.487
John Giannini	Maine	13	259	123	.678
Bobby Gonzalez	Manhattan	3	46	39	.541
Dave Magarity	Marist	21	294	297	.497
Tom Crean	Marquette	3	56	35	.615
Greg White	Marshall	16	220	222	.498
Gary Williams	Maryland	24	481	271	.640
Tom Sullivan	UMBC	17	245	230	.516
Thomas C. Trotter	Md.-East. Shore	2	23	34	.404
Steve Lappas	Massachusetts	14	243	188	.564
Tic Price	McNeese St.	6	114	63	.644
John Calipari	Memphis	10	237	94	.716
Mark Slonaker	Mercer	6	45	122	.269
Perry Clark	Miami (Fla.)	13	225	166	.575
Charlie Coles	Miami (Ohio)	12	199	162	.551
Tommy Amaker	Michigan	5	79	73	.520
Tom Izzo	Michigan St.	7	167	65	.720
Kermit Davis Jr.	Middle Tenn.	4	71	50	.587
Dan Monson	Minnesota	5	100	60	.625
Rod Barnes	Mississippi	4	86	46	.652
Rick Stansbury	Mississippi St.	4	79	50	.612
Lafayette Stribling	Mississippi Val.	19	256	282	.476
Quin Snyder	Missouri	3	62	38	.620
Rich Zvosec	UMKC	10	118	159	.426
Dave Calloway	Monmouth	5	59	69	.461
Pat Kennedy	Montana	22	393	276	.587
Mick Durham	Montana St.	12	192	155	.553
Kyle Macy	Morehead St.	5	55	83	.399
Butch Beard	Morgan St.	5	48	94	.338
Derek Thompson	Morris Brown	2	10	48	.172
Jim Phelan	Mt. St. Mary's	48	819	508	.617
Tevester Anderson	Murray St.	4	86	40	.683
Don DeVoe	Navy	29	499	346	.591
Barry Collier	Nebraska	13	223	163	.578
Trent Johnson	Nevada	3	36	51	.414
Charles Spoonhour	UNLV	17	340	182	.651
Phil Rowe	New Hampshire	16	193	220	.467
Ritchie McKay	New Mexico	6	83	89	.483
Lou Henson	New Mexico St.	38	742	377	.663
Monte Towe	New Orleans	1	15	14	.517
Joe Mihalich	Niagara	4	67	51	.568
Ricky Blanton	Nicholls St.	0	0	0	.000
Dwight Freeman	Norfolk St.	4	46	65	.414
Eddie Biedenbach	UNC Asheville	9	116	135	.462
Brad Brownell	UNC Wilmington	0	0	0	.000
Matt Doherty	North Carolina	3	56	42	.571
Curtis Hunter	N.C. A&T	3	38	49	.437
Fran McCaffery	UNC Greensboro	6	103	75	.579
Herb Sendek	North Carolina St.	9	172	111	.608
Johnny Jones	North Texas	2	30	30	.500
Ron Everhart	Northeastern	8	99	125	.442
Mike Adras	Northern Ariz.	3	49	39	.557
Rob Judson	Northern Ill.	1	12	16	.429
Greg McDermott	Northern Iowa	8	145	79	.647
Bill Carmody	Northwestern	6	119	57	.676
Mike McConathy	Northwestern St.	3	49	44	.527
Mike Brey	Notre Dame	7	141	73	.659
Greg Kampe	Oakland	18	304	211	.590
Tim O'Shea	Ohio	1	17	11	.607
Jim O'Brien	Ohio St.	20	337	274	.552
Kelvin Sampson	Oklahoma	19	364	221	.622
Eddie Sutton	Oklahoma St.	32	702	278	.716
Blaine Taylor	Old Dominion	8	154	82	.653
Scott Sutton	Oral Roberts	3	40	50	.444
Ernie Kent	Oregon	11	184	138	.571
Jay John	Oregon St.	0	0	0	.000
Bob Thomason	Pacific (Cal.)	17	275	211	.566
Jerry Dunn	Penn St.	7	110	100	.524
Fran Dunphy	Pennsylvania	13	231	129	.642

Coach	School	Yr	W	L	Pct.
Paul Westphal	Pepperdine	4	106	36	.746
Ben Howland	Pittsburgh	8	140	94	.598
Michael Holton	Portland	1	6	24	.200
Heath Schroyer	Portland St.	0	0	0	.000
Jerry Francis	Prairie View	0	0	0	.000
John Thompson III	Princeton	2	32	23	.582
Tim Welsh	Providence	7	133	81	.621
Gene Keady	Purdue	24	488	260	.652
Joe DeSantis	Quinnipiac	6	56	108	.341
Byron Samuels	Radford	2	17	36	.321
Jim Baron	Rhode Island	15	214	222	.491
Willis Wilson	Rice	10	127	155	.450
Jerry Wainwright	Richmond	8	136	103	.569
Don Harnum	Rider	5	79	63	.556
Mark Schmidt	Robert Morris	1	12	18	.400
Gary Waters	Rutgers	6	110	73	.601
Jerome Jenkins	Sacramento St.	2	14	41	.255
Dave Bike	Sacred Heart	24	392	311	.558
Jan van Breda Kolff	St. Bonaventure	11	191	141	.575
Ron Ganulin	St. Francis (NY)	13	172	186	.480
Bobby Jones	St. Francis (Pa.)	3	25	57	.305
Mike Jarvis	St. John's (N.Y.)	17	340	185	.648
Phil Martelli	St. Joseph's	7	126	90	.583
Brad Soderberg	St. Louis	8	131	73	.642
Radny Bennett	St. Mary's (Cal.)	1	9	20	.310
Bob Leckie	St. Peter's	2	8	48	.143
Bob Marlin	Sam Houston St.	4	62	50	.554
Jimmy Tillette	Samford	5	89	58	.605
Brad Holland	San Diego	10	149	130	.534
Steve Fisher	San Diego St.	12	225	130	.634
Philip Mathews	San Francisco	7	107	95	.530
Phil Johnson	San Jose St.	1	12	16	.429
Dick Davey	Santa Clara	10	173	117	.597
open	Savannah St.				
Louis Orr	Seton Hall	2	32	29	.525
Rob Lanier	Siena	1	17	19	.472
John Pelphrey	South Ala.	0	0	0	.000
Dave Odom	South Carolina	16	300	189	.613
Cy Alexander	South Carolina St.	15	257	191	.574
Seth Greenberg	South Fla.	12	198	156	.559
Gary Garner	Southeast Mo. St.	19	329	227	.592
Billy Kennedy	Southeastern La.	5	49	92	.348
Henry Bibby	Southern California	7	104	85	.550
Bruce Weber	Southern Ill.	4	79	47	.627
Mike Dement	Southern Methodist	16	233	215	.520
James Green	Southern Miss.	6	97	80	.548
Ben Jobe	Southern U.	30	512	318	.617
Bill Evans	Southern Utah	11	149	139	.517
Barry Hinson	Southwest Mo. St.	5	89	65	.578
Dennis Nutt	Southwest Tex. St.	2	25	31	.446
Mike Montgomery	Stanford	24	493	233	.679
Danny Kaspar	Stephen F. Austin	11	241	84	.742
Derek Waugh	Stetson	2	23	24	.489
Nick Macarchuk	Stony Brook	25	339	376	.474
Jim Boeheim	Syracuse	26	623	221	.738
John Chaney	Temple	30	675	253	.727
Buzz Peterson	Tennessee	6	120	66	.645
Nolan Richardson III	Tennessee St.	2	21	36	.368
Mike Sutton	Tennessee Tech	0	0	0	.000
Bret Campbell	Tenn.-Martin	3	35	51	.407
Rick Barnes	Texas	15	292	177	.623
Melvin Watkins	Texas A&M	6	81	97	.455
Ronnie Arrow	Tex. A&M-C.C.	11	153	135	.531
Neil Dougherty	TCU	0	0	0	.000
Ronnie Courtney	Texas Southern	1	11	17	.393
Bob Knight	Texas Tech	36	787	298	.725
Eddie McCarter	Texas-Arlington	10	119	155	.434
Jason Rabedeaux	UTEP	3	46	46	.500
Bob Hoffman	Tex.-Pan American	12	286	123	.699
Tim Carter	Texas-San Antonio	8	116	107	.520
Stan Joplin	Toledo	6	103	73	.585
Michael Hunt	Towson	1	11	18	.379
Don Maestri	Troy St.	20	331	235	.585
Shawn Finney	Tulane	2	23	36	.390
John Phillips	Tulsa	1	27	7	.794
Steve Lavin	UCLA	6	135	59	.696
Rick Majerus	Utah	18	382	134	.740
Stew Morrill	Utah St.	16	312	171	.646
Scott Drew	Valparaiso	0	0	0	.000
Kevin Stallings	Vanderbilt	9	174	104	.626
Tom Brennan	Vermont	21	248	324	.434
Jay Wright	Villanova	8	141	98	.590
Pete Gillen	Virginia	17	344	177	.660

Coach	School	Yr	W	L	Pct.
Jeff Capel III	Va. Commonwealth	0	0	0	.000
Bart Bellairs	VMI	10	112	158	.415
Ricky Stokes	Virginia Tech	3	34	52	.395
Dereck Whittenburg	Wagner	3	46	39	.541
Skip Prosser	Wake Forest	9	186	91	.671
Lorenzo Romar	Washington	6	93	88	.514
Paul Graham	Washington St.	3	24	59	.289
Joe Cravens	Weber St.	7	105	88	.544
John Beilein	West Virginia	20	372	215	.634
Steve Shurina	Western Caro.	2	18	41	.305
Jim Kerwin	Western Ill.	10	127	154	.452
Dennis Felton	Western Ky.	4	76	45	.628
Robert McCullum	Western Mich.	2	24	34	.414
Mark Turgeon	Wichita St.	4	49	63	.438
Rick Boyages	William & Mary	2	21	36	.368
Gregg Marshall	Winthrop	4	79	42	.653
Bo Ryan	Wisconsin	18	402	116	.776
Tod Kowalczyk	Wis.-Green Bay	0	0	0	.000
Bruce Pearl	Wis.-Milwaukee	10	247	59	.807
Mike Young	Wofford	0	0	0	.000
Ed Schilling	Wright St.	5	65	75	.464
Steve McClain	Wyoming	4	79	41	.658
Thad Matta	Xavier	2	50	14	.781
James Jones	Yale	3	38	48	.442
John Robic	Youngstown St.	3	36	50	.419

Fastest To Milestone Wins

(Head coaches with at least half their seasons at Division I.)

FASTEST TO 100 WINS

Rk. Name, School	Games	Won	Lost	Pct.	Season	Year
1. Doc Meanwell, Wisconsin & Missouri	109	100	9	.917	7th	1918
2. Buck Freeman, St. John's (N.Y.)	110	100	10	.909	5th	1932
3. Adolph Rupp, Kentucky	116	100	16	.862	6th	1936
4. Jim Boeheim, Syracuse	117	100	17	.855	4th	1980
4. Jerry Tarkanian, Long Beach St.	117	100	17	.855	5th	1973
6. Everett Case, North Carolina St.	120	100	20	.833	4th	1950
6. Fred Taylor, Ohio St.	120	100	20	.833	5th	1963
7. Lew Andreas, Syracuse	122	100	22	.820	7th	1931
7. Denny Crum, Louisville	122	100	22	.820	5th	1976
7. Everett Dean, Carleton & Indiana	122	100	22	.820	7th	1929
11. Clair Bee, Rider & Long Island	123	100	23	.813	5th	1934
12. Don Haskins, UTEP	125	100	25	.800	5th	1966
12. Nat Holman, CCNY	125	100	25	.800	10th	1929
12. Buster Sheary, Holy Cross	125	100	25	.800	5th	1953
15. Tony Hinkle, Butler	126	100	26	.794	7th	1933
15. Ray Meyer, DePaul	126	100	26	.794	6th	1948
17. Harry Combes, Illinois	127	100	27	.787	6th	1953
17. Peck Hickman, Louisville	127	100	27	.787	6th	1949
19. Vic Bubas, Duke	128	100	28	.781	5th	1964
20. Hugh Greer, Connecticut	129	100	29	.775	6th	1952
20. Roy Williams, Kansas	129	100	29	.775	4th	1992
22. Speedy Morris, La Salle	130	100	30	.769	4th	1990
22. Fred Schaus, West Virginia	130	100	30	.769	5th	1959
22. Clifford Wells, Tulane	130	100	30	.769	6th	1951
25. Harry Fisher, Columbia	131	100	31	.763	10th	1916
25. Joseph Lapchick, St. John's (N.Y.)	131	100	31	.763	7th	1943
25. Nolan Richardson, Tulsa	131	100	31	.763	5th	1985
28. Gale Catlett, Cincinnati	132	100	32	.758	5th	1977
28. Jack Ramsay, St. Joseph's	132	100	32	.758	5th	1960
28. Bruce Stewart, West Virginia Wesleyan & Middle Tenn.	132	100	32	.758	4th	1986
31. Lou Carnesecca, St. John's (N.Y.)	134	100	34	.746	5th	1970
31. Frank McGuire, St. John's (N.Y.)	134	100	34	.746	5th	1952
31. Dudey Moore, Duquesne	134	100	34	.746	5th	1953
34. Ben Carnevale, North Carolina & Navy	135	100	35	.741	6th	1950
34. John Wooden, Indiana St. & UCLA	135	100	35	.741	5th	1951

FASTEST TO 200 WINS

Rk. Name, School	Games	Won	Lost	Pct.	Season	Year
1. Clair Bee, Rider & Long Island	231	200	31	.866	12th	1938
2. Jerry Tarkanian, Long Beach St. & UNLV	234	200	34	.855	9th	1977
3. Everett Case, North Carolina St.	250	200	50	.800	9th	1954
4. Harold Anderson, Toledo & Bowling Green	251	200	51	.797	10th	1945
4. Lew Andreas, Syracuse	251	200	51	.797	14th	1939
4. Nat Holman, CCNY	251	200	51	.797	18th	1937
4. Adolph Rupp, Kentucky	251	200	51	.797	13th	1943
8. Henry Iba, Northwest Mo. St., Colorado & Oklahoma St.	252	200	52	.794	10th	1939
8. Roy Williams, Kansas	252	200	52	.794	8th	1996
10. Vic Bubas, Duke	254	200	54	.787	10th	1969
10. Denny Crum, Louisville	254	200	54	.787	9th	1980
10. Doc Meanwell, Missouri & Wisconsin	254	200	54	.787	15th	1927
13. Hec Edmundson, Washington	261	200	61	.766	13th	1931
13. Hugh Greer, Connecticut	261	200	61	.766	11th	1957
15. George Keogan, Wis.-Superior, St. Louis, St. Thomas (Minn.), Allegheny, Valparaiso & Notre Dame	263	200	63	.760	14th	1930
15. Joseph Lapchick, St. John's (N.Y.)	263	200	63	.760	13th	1958
17. Jack Ramsay, St. Joseph's	264	200	64	.758	10th	1965
18. Peck Hickman, Louisville	265	200	65	.755	10th	1954
19. Jim Boeheim, Syracuse	266	200	66	.752	9th	1985
19. Fred Schaus, West Virginia & Purdue	266	200	66	.752	10th	1976
21. Don Haskins, UTEP	269	200	69	.743	11th	1972
22. Bob Knight, Army & Indiana	270	200	70	.741	11th	1976
23. Lou Carnesecca, St. John's (N.Y.)	271	200	71	.738	10th	1978
23. Harry Combes, Illinois	271	200	71	.738	12th	1959
23. Arthur Schabinger, Ottawa, Emporia St. & Creighton	271	200	71	.738	16th	1932
26. Dudey Moore, Duquesne	272	200	72	.735	11th	1959
27. Pete Gillen, Xavier	273	200	73	.733	9th	1994
28. Tom Blackburn, Dayton	274	200	74	.730	11th	1957
29. Chick Davies, Duquesne	275	200	75	.727	15th	1939
29. Boyd Grant, Fresno St. & Colorado St.	275	200	75	.727	10th	1988

FASTEST TO 300 WINS

Rk. Name, School	Games	Won	Lost	Pct.	Season	Year
1. Clair Bee, Rider & Long Island	344	300	44	.872	15th	1943
2. Adolph Rupp, Kentucky	366	300	66	.820	17th	1947
3. Jerry Tarkanian, Long Beach St. & UNLV	370	300	70	.811	13th	1982
3. Roy Williams, Kansas	370	300	70	.811	11th	1999
5. Everett Case, North Carolina St.	377	300	77	.796	13th	1959
6. Harold Anderson, Toledo & Bowling Green	378	300	78	.794	14th	1949
7. Denny Crum, Louisville	382	300	82	.785	13th	1984
7. Henry Iba, Northwest Mo. St., Colorado & Oklahoma St.	382	300	82	.785	15th	1944
9. Hec Edmundson, Washington	392	300	92	.765	18th	1936
10. Jim Boeheim, Syracuse	393	300	93	.763	13th	1989
10. Frank Keaney, Rhode Island	393	300	93	.763	24th	1944
12. George Keogan, Wis.-Superior, St. Louis, St. Thomas (Minn.), Allegheny, Valparaiso & Notre Dame	394	300	94	.761	20th	1936
13. Ray Mears, Wittenberg & Tennessee	395	300	95	.759	16th	1972
14. Piggy Lambert, Purdue	397	300	97	.756	23rd	1940
15. Lew Andreas, Syracuse	400	300	100	.750	23rd	1947
15. Chick Davies, Duquesne	400	300	100	.750	21st	1948
17. John Lawther, Westminster (Pa.) & Penn St.	402	300	102	.746	21st	1947
18. Nolan Richardson, Tulsa & Arkansas	404	300	104	.743	13th	1993
19. Peck Hickman, Louisville	405	300	105	.741	15th	1959
20. Dean Smith, North Carolina	406	300	106	.739	15th	1976
20. Eddie Sutton, Creighton & Arkansas	406	300	106	.739	15th	1984
22. Bob Knight, Army & Indiana	407	300	107	.737	15th	1980
22. John Thompson, Georgetown	407	300	107	.737	14th	1986
24. Nat Holman, CCNY	408	300	108	.735	27th	1946
25. Rick Majerus, Marquette, Ball St. & Utah	409	300	109	.733	14th	1998

FASTEST TO 400 WINS

Rk. Name, School	Games	Won	Lost	Pct.	Season	Year
1. Adolph Rupp, Kentucky	477	400	77	.839	20th	1950
2. Clair Bee, Rider & Long Island	483	400	83	.828	21st	1951
3. Jerry Tarkanian, Long Beach St. & UNLV	492	400	92	.813	17th	1985
4. Henry Iba, Northwest Mo. St., Colorado & Oklahoma St.	500	400	100	.800	19th	1948
5. Frank Keaney, Rhode Island	521	400	121	.768	28th	1948
6. Phog Allen, Baker, Haskell, Central Mo. St. & Kansas	522	400	122	.766	29th	1935
6. George Keogan, Wis.-Superior, St. Louis, St. Thomas (Minn.), Allegheny, Valparaiso & Notre Dame	522	400	122	.766	26th	1942

Rk. Name, School	Games	Won	Lost	Pct.	Season	Year
8. Jim Boeheim, Syracuse	527	400	127	.759	17th	1993
9. Dean Smith, North Carolina	531	400	131	.753	19th	1980
10. Lou Carnesecca, St. John's (N.Y.)	535	400	135	.748	18th	1986
10. John Thompson, Georgetown	535	400	135	.748	18th	1990
12. Denny Crum, Louisville	536	400	136	.746	17th	1988
12. Ed Diddle, Western Ky.	536	400	136	.746	24th	1946
12. Nolan Richardson, Tulsa & Arkansas	536	400	136	.746	17th	1997
15. Nat Holman, CCNY	539	400	139	.742	32nd	1952
16. Eddie Sutton, Creighton, Arkansas & Kentucky	541	400	141	.739	19th	1988
17. Al McGuire, Belmont Abbey & Marquette	542	400	142	.738	20th	1977
18. Bob Knight, Army & Indiana	545	400	145	.734	20th	1985
19. Bob Huggins, Walsh, Akron & Cincinnati	548	400	148	.730	19th	1999
19. John Wooden, Indiana St. & UCLA	548	400	148	.730	20th	1966

FASTEST TO 500 WINS

Rk. Name, School	Games	Won	Lost	Pct.	Season	Year
1. Adolph Rupp, Kentucky	583	500	83	.858	23rd	1955
2. Jerry Tarkanian, Long Beach St. & UNLV	604	500	104	.828	20th	1988
3. Henry Iba, Northwest Mo. St., Colorado & Oklahoma St.	631	500	131	.792	23rd	1952
4. Phog Allen, Baker, Haskell, Central Mo. St. & Kansas	646	500	146	.774	34th	1940
5. John Wooden, Indiana St. & UCLA	652	500	152	.767	24th	1970
6. Dean Smith, North Carolina	653	500	153	.766	23rd	1984
7. John Chaney, Cheyney & Temple	662	500	162	.755	22nd	1994
8. Ed Diddle, Western Ky.	667	500	167	.750	28th	1950
9. Jim Boeheim, Syracuse	669	500	169	.747	21st	1997
10. Bob Huggins, Walsh, Akron & Cincinnati	671	500	171	.745	21st	2002
11. Lou Carnesecca, St. John's (N.Y.)	683	500	183	.732	23rd	1991
11. Bob Knight, Army & Indiana	683	500	183	.732	24th	1989
13. Eddie Sutton, Creighton, Arkansas, Kentucky & Oklahoma St.	685	500	185	.730	23rd	1993
13. John Thompson, Georgetown	685	500	185	.730	22nd	1994
15. Denny Crum, Louisville	687	500	187	.728	22nd	1993
16. Lute Olson, Long Beach St., Iowa & Arizona	690	500	190	.725	23rd	1996
17. Nolan Richardson, Tulsa & Arkansas	695	500	195	.719	22nd	2002
18. Frank McGuire, St. John's (N.Y.)	699	500	199	.715	27th	1977

FASTEST TO 600 WINS

Rk. Name, School	Games	Won	Lost	Pct.	Season	Year
1. Adolph Rupp, Kentucky	704	600	104	.852	27th	1959
2. Jerry Tarkanian, Long Beach St. & UNLV	720	600	120	.833	24th	1992
3. John Wooden, Indiana St. & UCLA	755	600	155	.795	27th	1973
4. Dean Smith, North Carolina	773	600	173	.776	26th	1987
5. Henry Iba, Northwest Mo. St., Colorado & Oklahoma St.	775	600	175	.774	29th	1958
6. Phog Allen, Baker, Haskell, Central Mo. St. & Kansas	780	600	180	.769	41st	1947
7. Ed Diddle, Western Ky.	790	600	190	.759	32nd	1954
8. Jim Boeheim, Syracuse	807	600	207	.743	25th	2001
9. Bob Knight, Army & Indiana	812	600	212	.739	27th	1993
10. Lute Olson, Long Beach St., Iowa & Arizona	815	600	215	.736	27th	2000
11. John Chaney, Cheyney & Temple	816	600	216	.735	27th	1999
12. Mike Krzyzewski, Army & Duke	823	600	223	.729	26th	2001
13. Denny Crum, Louisville	825	600	225	.727	26th	1997
14. Cam Henderson, Muskingum, Davis & Elkins & Marshall	830	600	230	.723	34th	1953
15. Eddie Sutton, Creighton, Arkansas, Kentucky & Oklahoma St.	837	600	237	.717	28th	1998

FASTEST TO 700 WINS

Rk. Name, School	Games	Won	Lost	Pct.	Season	Year
1. Adolph Rupp, Kentucky	836	700	136	.837	32nd	1964
2. Jerry Tarkanian, Long Beach St., UNLV & Fresno St.	864	700	164	.810	28th	1999
3. Dean Smith, North Carolina	904	700	204	.774	30th	1991
4. Phog Allen, Baker, Haskell, Central Mo. St. & Kansas	938	700	238	.746	47th	1953
5. Ed Diddle, Western Ky.	946	700	246	.740	28th	1960
6. Henry Iba, Northwest Mo. St., Colorado & Oklahoma St.	951	700	251	.736	35th	1964
7. Bob Knight, Army & Indiana	956	700	256	.732	32nd	1997
8. Eddie Sutton, Creighton, Arkansas, Kentucky & Oklahoma St.	975	700	275	.718	32nd	2002
9. Don Haskins, UTEP	1,029	700	329	.680	37th	1998

Rk. Name, School	Games	Won	Lost	Pct.	Season	Year
10. Lou Henson, Hardin-Simmons, Illinois & New Mexico St.	1,046	700	346	.669	36th	2000
11. Lefty Driesell, Davidson, Maryland, James Madison & Georgia St.	1,048	700	348	.668	37th	1999
12. Ray Meyer, DePaul	1,051	700	351	.666	52nd	1984
13. Norm Stewart, Northern Iowa & Missouri	1,055	700	355	.664	36th	1998

FASTEST TO 800 WINS

Rk. Name, School	Games	Won	Lost	Pct.	Season	Year
1. Adolph Rupp, Kentucky	972	800	172	.823	37th	1969
2. Dean Smith, North Carolina	1,029	800	229	.777	33rd	1994

Top 10 Best Career Starts By Percentage

(Head coaches with at least half their seasons at Division I)

1 SEASON

Coach, Team	Season	W	L	Pct.
Norman Shepard, North Carolina	1924	23	0	1.000
Bill Hodges, Indiana St.	1979	33	1	.970
Tom Gola, La Salle	1969	23	1	.958
Lou Rossini, Columbia	1951	21	1	.955
Earl Brown, Dartmouth	1944	19	2	.905
Phil Johnson, Weber St.	1969	27	3	.900
Bill Guthridge, North Carolina	1998	34	4	.895
Gary Cunningham, UCLA	1978	25	3	.893
Bob Davies, Seton Hall	1947	24	3	.889
Jerry Tarkanian, Long Beach St.	1969	23	3	.885

2 SEASONS

Coach, Team	Seasons	W	L	Pct.
Lew Andreas, Syracuse	1925-26	33	3	.917
Bill Carmody, Princeton	1997-98	51	6	.895
Everett Case, North Carolina St.	1947-48	55	8	.873
Buck Freeman, St. John's (N.Y.)	1928-29	41	6	.872
Gary Cunningham, UCLA	1978-79	50	8	.862
Nibs Price, California	1925-26	25	4	.862
Denny Crum, Louisville	1972-73	49	8	.860
Adolph Rupp, Kentucky	1931-32	30	5	.857
Jerry Tarkanian, Long Beach St.	1969-70	47	8	.855
John Castellani, Seattle	1957-58	45	9	.833

3 SEASONS

Coach, Team	Seasons	W	L	Pct.
Nibs Price, California	1925-27	38	4	.905
Buck Freeman, St. John's (N.Y.)	1928-30	64	7	.901
Lew Andreas, Syracuse	1925-27	48	7	.873
Adolph Rupp, Kentucky	1931-33	51	8	.864
Jerry Tarkanian, Long Beach St.	1969-71	71	13	.845
Jim Boeheim, Syracuse	1977-79	74	14	.841
Bill Carmody, Princeton	1997-99	73	14	.841
Everett Case, North Carolina St.	1947-49	80	16	.833
Ben Carnevale, North Carolina & Navy	1945-47	68	14	.829
Phil Johnson, Weber St.	1969-71	68	16	.810

4 SEASONS

Coach, Team	Seasons	W	L	Pct.
Buck Freeman, St. John's (N.Y.)	1928-31	85	8	.914
Adolph Rupp, Kentucky	1931-34	67	9	.882
Jerry Tarkanian, Long Beach St.	1969-72	96	17	.850
Jim Boeheim, Syracuse	1977-80	100	18	.847
Fred Taylor, Ohio St.	1959-62	89	17	.840
Everett Case, North Carolina St.	1947-50	107	22	.829
Nibs Price, California	1925-28	47	10	.825
Nat Holman, CCNY	1920-23	46	10	.821
Denny Crum, Louisville	1972-75	98	22	.817
Lew Andreas, Syracuse	1925-28	58	13	.817

5 SEASONS

Coach, Team	Seasons	W	L	Pct.
Buck Freeman, St. John's (N.Y.)	1928-32	107	12	.899
Adolph Rupp, Kentucky	1931-35	86	11	.887
Jerry Tarkanian, Long Beach St. & UNLV	1969-73	122	20	.859
Nat Holman, CCNY	1920-24	58	11	.841
Fred Taylor, Ohio St.	1959-63	109	21	.838
Nibs Price, California	1925-29	64	13	.831
Everett Case, North Carolina St.	1947-51	137	29	.825
Buster Sheary, Holy Cross	1949-53	110	27	.803
Jim Boeheim, Syracuse	1977-81	122	30	.803
Lew Andreas, Syracuse	1925-29	69	17	.802

COACHING RECORDS

6 SEASONS

Coach, Team	Seasons	W	L	Pct.
Buck Freeman, St. John's (N.Y.)	1928-33	130	16	.890
Adolph Rupp, Kentucky	1931-36	101	17	.856
Jerry Tarkanian, Long Beach St. & UNLV	1969-74	142	26	.845
Nat Holman, CCNY	1920-25	70	13	.843
Buster Sheary, Holy Cross	1949-54	136	29	.824
Lew Andreas, Syracuse	1925-30	87	19	.821
Everett Dean, Carleton & Indiana	1922-27	82	18	.820
Clair Bee, Rider & Long Island	1929-34	101	23	.815
Fred Taylor, Ohio St.	1959-64	125	29	.812
Everett Case, North Carolina St.	1947-52	161	39	.805

7 SEASONS

Coach, Team	Seasons	W	L	Pct.
Buck Freeman, St. John's (N.Y.)	1928-34	146	19	.885
Jerry Tarkanian, Long Beach St. & UNLV	1969-75	166	31	.843
Adolph Rupp, Kentucky	1931-37	118	22	.843
Clair Bee, Rider & Long Island	1929-35	125	25	.833
Everett Dean, Carleton & Indiana	1922-28	97	20	.829
Lew Andreas, Syracuse	1925-31	103	23	.817
Nat Holman, CCNY	1920-26	79	18	.814
Buster Sheary, Holy Cross	1949-55	155	36	.812
Everett Case, North Carolina St.	1947-53	187	45	.806
Vic Bubas, Duke	1960-66	158	39	.802

8 SEASONS

Coach, Team	Seasons	W	L	Pct.
Clair Bee, Rider & Long Island	1929-36	150	25	.857
Buck Freeman, St. John's (N.Y.)	1928-35	159	27	.855
Jerry Tarkanian, Long Beach St. & UNLV	1969-76	195	33	.855
Adolph Rupp, Kentucky	1931-38	131	27	.829
Nat Holman, CCNY	1920-27	88	21	.807
Everett Case, North Carolina St.	1947-54	213	52	.804
Hugh Greer, Connecticut	1947-54	151	38	.799
Lew Andreas, Syracuse	1925-32	116	30	.795
Roy Williams, Kansas	1989-96	213	56	.792
Henry Iba, Northwest Mo. St., Colorado & Oklahoma St.	1930-37	157	42	.789

9 SEASONS

Coach, Team	Seasons	W	L	Pct.
Clair Bee, Rider & Long Island	1929-37	177	28	.863
Jerry Tarkanian, Long Beach St. & UNLV	1969-77	224	36	.862
Buck Freeman, St. John's (N.Y.)	1928-36	177	31	.851
Adolph Rupp, Kentucky	1931-39	147	31	.826
Everett Case, North Carolina St.	1947-55	241	56	.811
Roy Williams, Kansas	1989-97	247	58	.810
Lew Andreas, Syracuse	1925-33	130	32	.802
Henry Iba, Northwest Mo. St., Colorado & Oklahoma St.	1930-38	182	45	.802
Denny Crum, Louisville	1972-80	219	55	.799
Hugh Greer, Connecticut	1947-55	171	43	.799

10 SEASONS

Coach, Team	Seasons	W	L	Pct.
Clair Bee, Rider & Long Island	1929-38	200	32	.862
Jerry Tarkanian, Long Beach St. & UNLV	1969-78	244	44	.847
Roy Williams, Kansas	1989-98	282	62	.820
Everett Case, North Carolina St.	1947-56	265	60	.815
Adolph Rupp, Kentucky	1931-40	162	37	.814
Lew Andreas, Syracuse	1925-34	145	34	.810
Henry Iba, Northwest Mo. St., Colorado & Oklahoma St.	1930-39	201	53	.791
Denny Crum, Louisville	1972-81	240	64	.789
Harold Anderson, Toledo & Bowling Green	1935-44	182	50	.784
Nat Holman, CCNY	1920-29	108	30	.783

11 SEASONS

Coach, Team	Seasons	W	L	Pct.
Clair Bee, Rider & Long Island	1929-39	223	32	.875
Jerry Tarkanian, Long Beach St. & UNLV	1969-79	259	49	.841
Lew Andreas, Syracuse	1925-35	160	36	.816
Roy Williams, Kansas	1989-99	305	72	.809
Henry Iba, Northwest Mo. St., Colorado & Oklahoma St.	1930-40	227	56	.802
Adolph Rupp, Kentucky	1931-41	179	45	.799
Everett Case, North Carolina St.	1947-57	280	71	.798
Harold Anderson, Toledo & Bowling Green	1935-45	206	54	.792
Nat Holman, CCNY	1920-30	119	33	.783
Denny Crum, Louisville	1972-82	263	74	.780

12 SEASONS

Coach, Team	Seasons	W	L	Pct.
Clair Bee, Rider & Long Island	1929-40	242	36	.871
Jerry Tarkanian, Long Beach St. & UNLV	1969-80	282	58	.829
Lew Andreas, Syracuse	1925-36	172	41	.806
Roy Williams, Kansas	1989-2000	329	82	.800
Harold Anderson, Toledo & Bowling Green	1935-46	233	59	.798
Henry Iba, Northwest Mo. St., Colorado & Oklahoma St.	1930-41	245	63	.795
Adolph Rupp, Kentucky	1931-42	198	51	.795
Everett Case, North Carolina St.	1947-58	298	77	.795
Denny Crum, Louisville	1972-83	295	78	.791
Joe Mullaney, Norwich & Providence	1955-66	243	68	.781

13 SEASONS

Coach, Team	Seasons	W	L	Pct.
Clair Bee, Rider & Long Island	1929-41	267	38	.875
Jerry Tarkanian, Long Beach St. & UNLV	1969-81	298	70	.810
Lew Andreas, Syracuse	1925-37	185	45	.804
Roy Williams, Kansas	1989-2001	355	89	.800
Harold Anderson, Toledo & Bowling Green	1935-47	261	66	.798
Everett Case, North Carolina St.	1947-59	320	81	.798
Nat Holman, CCNY	1920-32	147	38	.795
Henry Iba, Northwest Mo. St., Colorado & Oklahoma St.	1930-42	265	69	.793
Adolph Rupp, Kentucky	1931-43	215	57	.790
Denny Crum, Louisville	1972-84	319	89	.782

14 SEASONS

Coach, Team	Seasons	W	L	Pct.
Clair Bee, Rider & Long Island	1929-42	291	41	.877
Roy Williams, Kansas	1989-2002	388	93	.807
Nat Holman, CCNY	1920-33	160	39	.804
Harold Anderson, Toledo & Bowling Green	1935-48	288	72	.800
Jerry Tarkanian, Long Beach St. & UNLV	1969-82	318	80	.799
Adolph Rupp, Kentucky	1931-44	234	59	.799
Lew Andreas, Syracuse	1925-38	198	50	.798
Henry Iba, Northwest Mo. St., Colorado & Oklahoma St.	1930-43	279	79	.779
Everett Case, North Carolina St.	1947-60	331	96	.775
Jim Boeheim, Syracuse	1977-90	343	108	.761

15 SEASONS

Coach, Team	Seasons	W	L	Pct.
Clair Bee, Rider & Long Island	1929-43	304	47	.866
Nat Holman, CCNY	1920-34	174	40	.813
Jerry Tarkanian, Long Beach St. & UNLV	1969-83	346	83	.807
Adolph Rupp, Kentucky	1931-45	256	63	.803
Harold Anderson, Toledo & Bowling Green	1935-49	312	79	.798
Lew Andreas, Syracuse	1925-39	212	54	.797
Henry Iba, Northwest Mo. St., Colorado & Oklahoma St.	1930-44	306	85	.783
Everett Case, North Carolina St.	1947-61	347	105	.768
Denny Crum, Louisville	1972-86	370	114	.764
Jim Boeheim, Syracuse	1977-91	369	114	.764

16 SEASONS

Coach, Team	Seasons	W	L	Pct.
Clair Bee, Rider & Long Island	1929-43, 46	318	56	.850
Adolph Rupp, Kentucky	1931-46	284	65	.814
Jerry Tarkanian, Long Beach St. & UNLV	1969-84	375	89	.808
Nat Holman, CCNY	1920-35	184	46	.800
Henry Iba, Northwest Mo. St., Colorado & Oklahoma St.	1930-45	333	89	.789
Harold Anderson, Toledo & Bowling Green	1935-50	331	90	.786
Lew Andreas, Syracuse	1925-40	222	62	.782
Everett Case, North Carolina St.	1947-62	358	111	.763
Ray Mears, Wittenberg & Tennessee	1957-72	306	97	.759
Jim Boeheim, Syracuse	1977-92	391	124	.759

17 SEASONS

Coach, Team	Seasons	W	L	Pct.
Clair Bee, Rider & Long Island	1929-43, 46-47	335	61	.850
Adolph Rupp, Kentucky	1931-47	318	68	.824
Jerry Tarkanian, Long Beach St. & UNLV	1969-85	403	93	.813
Henry Iba, Northwest Mo. St., Colorado & Oklahoma St.	1930-46	364	91	.800
Nat Holman, CCNY	1920-36	194	50	.795
Harold Anderson, Toledo & Bowling Green	1935-51	341	94	.784
Lew Andreas, Syracuse	1925-41	236	67	.779
Jim Boeheim, Syracuse	1977-93	411	133	.756
Joseph Lapchick, St. John's (N.Y.)	1937-47, 57-62	291	95	.754
Ray Mears, Wittenberg & Tennessee	1957-73	321	106	.752

18 SEASONS

Coach, Team	Seasons	W	L	Pct.
Clair Bee, Rider & Long Island	1929-43, 46-48	352	65	.844
Adolph Rupp, Kentucky	1931-48	354	71	.833
Jerry Tarkanian, Long Beach St. & UNLV	1969-86	436	98	.816
Henry Iba, Northwest Mo. St., Colorado & Oklahoma St.	1930-47	388	99	.797
Nat Holman, CCNY	1920-37	204	56	.785
Harold Anderson, Toledo & Bowling Green	1935-52	358	104	.775
Lew Andreas, Syracuse	1925-42	251	73	.775
Jim Boeheim, Syracuse	1977-94	434	140	.756
Dean Smith, North Carolina	1962-79	386	127	.752
John Thompson, Georgetown	1973-90	423	142	.749

19 SEASONS

Coach, Team	Seasons	W	L	Pct.
Adolph Rupp, Kentucky	1931-49	386	73	.841
Clair Bee, Rider & Long Island	1929-43, 46-49	370	77	.828
Jerry Tarkanian, Long Beach St. & UNLV	1969-87	473	100	.825
Henry Iba, Northwest Mo. St., Colorado & Oklahoma St.	1930-48	415	103	.801
Nat Holman, CCNY	1920-38	217	59	.786
Lew Andreas, Syracuse	1925-43	259	83	.757
Harold Anderson, Toledo & Bowling Green	1935-53	370	119	.757
Jim Boeheim, Syracuse	1977-95	454	150	.752
Dean Smith, North Carolina	1962-80	407	135	.751
Frank Keaney, Rhode Island	1922-40	244	82	.748
Denny Crum, Louisville	1972-90	463	156	.748

20 SEASONS

Coach, Team	Seasons	W	L	Pct.
Adolph Rupp, Kentucky	1931-50	411	78	.840
Clair Bee, Rider & Long Island	1929-43, 46-50	390	82	.826
Jerry Tarkanian, Long Beach St. & UNLV	1969-88	501	106	.825
Henry Iba, Northwest Mo. St., Colorado & Oklahoma St.	1930-49	438	108	.802
Phog Allen, Baker, Kansas, Haskell, Central Mo. St. & Kansas	1906-09, 13-28	325	89	.785
Nat Holman, CCNY	1920-39	228	65	.778
John Chaney, Cheyney & Temple	1973-92	458	143	.762
Frank Keaney, Rhode Island	1922-41	265	86	.755
Harold Anderson, Toledo & Bowling Green	1935-54	387	126	.754
Dean Smith, North Carolina	1962-81	436	143	.753

21 SEASONS

Coach, Team	Seasons	W	L	Pct.
Adolph Rupp, Kentucky	1931-51	443	80	.847
Clair Bee, Rider & Long Island	1929-43, 46-51	410	86	.827
Jerry Tarkanian, Long Beach St. & UNLV	1969-89	530	114	.823
Henry Iba, Northwest Mo. St., Colorado & Oklahoma St.	1930-50	456	117	.796
Nat Holman, CCNY	1920-40	236	73	.764
Dean Smith, North Carolina	1962-82	468	145	.763
Phog Allen, Baker, Kansas, Haskell, Central Mo. St. & Kansas	1906-09, 13-29	328	104	.759
Frank Keaney, Rhode Island	1922-42	283	90	.759
John Chaney, Cheyney & Temple	1973-93	478	156	.754
Chick Davies, Duquesne	1925-40, 47-48	314	106	.748

22 SEASONS

Coach, Team	Seasons	W	L	Pct.
Adolph Rupp, Kentucky	1931-52	472	83	.850
Jerry Tarkanian, Long Beach St. & UNLV	1969-90	565	119	.826
Henry Iba, Northwest Mo. St., Colorado & Oklahoma St.	1930-51	485	123	.798
Nat Holman, CCNY	1920-41	253	78	.764
Dean Smith, North Carolina	1962-83	496	153	.764
Frank Keaney, Rhode Island	1922-43	299	93	.763
Phog Allen, Baker, Kansas, Haskell, Central Mo. St. & Kansas	1906-09, 13-30	342	108	.760
John Wooden, Indiana St. & UCLA	1947-68	464	151	.754
John Chaney, Cheyney & Temple	1973-94	501	164	.753
Lew Andreas, Syracuse	1925-47	308	105	.746

23 SEASONS

Coach, Team	Seasons	W	L	Pct.
Adolph Rupp, Kentucky	1931-52, 54	497	83	.857
Jerry Tarkanian, Long Beach St. & UNLV	1969-91	599	120	.833
Henry Iba, Northwest Mo. St., Colorado & Oklahoma St.	1930-52	504	131	.794
Dean Smith, North Carolina	1962-84	524	156	.771
Nat Holman, CCNY	1920-42	269	81	.769
John Wooden, Indiana St. & UCLA	1947-69	493	152	.764
Phog Allen, Baker, Kansas, Haskell, Central Mo. St. & Kansas	1906-09, 13-31	357	111	.763
Frank Keaney, Rhode Island	1922-44	313	99	.760
John Chaney, Cheyney & Temple	1973-95	520	175	.748
Ed Diddle, Western Ky.	1923-45	395	134	.747

24 SEASONS

Coach, Team	Seasons	W	L	Pct.
Adolph Rupp, Kentucky	1931-52, 54-55	520	86	.858
Jerry Tarkanian, Long Beach St. & UNLV	1969-92	625	122	.837
Henry Iba, Northwest Mo. St., Colorado & Oklahoma St.	1930-53	527	138	.792
John Wooden, Indiana St. & UCLA	1947-70	521	154	.772
Dean Smith, North Carolina	1962-85	551	165	.770
Frank Keaney, Rhode Island	1922-45	333	104	.762
Phog Allen, Baker, Kansas, Haskell, Central Mo. St. & Kansas	1906-09, 13-32	370	116	.761
Nat Holman, CCNY	1920-43	277	91	.753
Jim Boeheim, Syracuse	1977-2000	575	199	.743
Bob Knight, Army & Indiana	1966-89	514	187	.733

25 SEASONS

Coach, Team	Seasons	W	L	Pct.
Adolph Rupp, Kentucky	1931-52, 54-56	540	92	.854
Jerry Tarkanian, Long Beach St., UNLV & Fresno St.	1969-92, 96	647	133	.829
Henry Iba, Northwest Mo. St., Colorado & Oklahoma St.	1930-54	551	143	.794
John Wooden, Indiana St. & UCLA	1947-71	550	155	.780
Dean Smith, North Carolina	1962-86	579	171	.772
Frank Keaney, Rhode Island	1922-46	354	107	.768
Phog Allen, Baker, Kansas, Haskell, Central Mo. St. & Kansas	1906-09, 13-33	383	120	.761
Jim Boeheim, Syracuse	1977-2001	600	208	.743
John Chaney, Cheyney & Temple	1973-97	560	199	.738
Nat Holman, CCNY	1920-44	283	102	.735
Ed Diddle, Western Ky.	1923-47	435	157	.735

26 SEASONS

Coach, Team	Seasons	W	L	Pct.
Adolph Rupp, Kentucky	1931-52, 54-57	563	97	.853
Jerry Tarkanian, Long Beach St., UNLV & Fresno St.	1969-92, 96-97	667	145	.821
John Wooden, Indiana St. & UCLA	1947-72	580	155	.789
Henry Iba, Northwest Mo. St., Colorado & Oklahoma St.	1930-55	563	156	.783
Dean Smith, North Carolina	1962-87	611	175	.777
Frank Keaney, Rhode Island	1922-47	371	110	.771
Phog Allen, Baker, Kansas, Haskell, Central Mo. St. & Kansas	1906-09, 13-34	399	121	.767
Ed Diddle, Western Ky.	1923-48	463	159	.744

Dean Smith posted a record 879 career wins before retiring from North Carolina after the 1996-97 season.

Photo by Rich Clarkson/NCAA Photos

COACHING RECORDS

Coach, Team	Seasons	W	L	Pct.
Jim Boeheim, Syracuse	1977-2002	623	221	.738
John Chaney, Cheyney & Temple	1973-98	581	208	.736
Nat Holman, CCNY	1920-45	295	106	.736

27 SEASONS

Coach, Team	Seasons	W	L	Pct.
Adolph Rupp, Kentucky	1931-52, 54-58	586	103	.851
Jerry Tarkanian, Long Beach St., UNLV & Fresno St.	1969-92, 96-98	688	158	.813
John Wooden, Indiana St. & UCLA	1947-73	610	155	.797
Henry Iba, Northwest Mo. St., Colorado & Oklahoma St.	1930-56	581	165	.779
Dean Smith, North Carolina	1962-88	638	182	.778
Frank Keaney, Rhode Island	1922-48	387	117	.768
Phog Allen, Baker, Kansas, Haskell, Central Mo. St. & Kansas	1906-09, 13-35	414	126	.767
Ed Diddle, Western Ky.	1923-49	488	163	.750
Nat Holman, CCNY	1920-46	309	110	.737
Bob Knight, Army & Indiana	1966-92	588	210	.737

28 SEASONS

Coach, Team	Seasons	W	L	Pct.
Adolph Rupp, Kentucky	1931-52, 54-59	610	106	.852
Jerry Tarkanian, Long Beach St., UNLV & Fresno St.	1969-92, 96-99	709	170	.807
John Wooden, Indiana St. & UCLA	1947-74	636	159	.800
Dean Smith, North Carolina	1962-89	667	190	.778
Henry Iba, Northwest Mo. St., Colorado & Oklahoma St.	1930-57	598	174	.775
Phog Allen, Baker, Kansas, Haskell, Central Mo. St. & Kansas	1906-09, 13-36	435	128	.773
Ed Diddle, Western Ky.	1923-50	513	169	.752
Bob Knight, Army & Indiana	1966-93	619	214	.743
Lute Olson, Long Beach St., Iowa & Arizona	1974-2001	638	226	.738
Nat Holman, CCNY	1920-47	326	116	.738

29 SEASONS

Coach, Team	Seasons	W	L	Pct.
Adolph Rupp, Kentucky	1931-52, 54-60	628	113	.848
John Wooden, Indiana St. & UCLA	1947-75	664	162	.804
Phog Allen, Baker, Kansas, Haskell, Central Mo. St. & Kansas	1906-09, 13-37	450	132	.773
Henry Iba, Northwest Mo. St., Colorado & Oklahoma St.	1930-58	619	182	.773
Dean Smith, North Carolina	1962-90	688	203	.772
Ed Diddle, Western Ky.	1923-51	532	179	.748
Nat Holman, CCNY	1920-48	344	119	.743
Bob Knight, Army & Indiana	1966-94	640	223	.742
John Chaney, Cheyney & Temple	1973-2001	656	238	.734
Lute Olson, Long Beach St., Iowa & Arizona	1974-2002	662	236	.737

30 SEASONS

Coach, Team	Seasons	W	L	Pct.
Adolph Rupp, Kentucky	1931-52, 54-61	647	122	.841
Jerry Tarkanian, Long Beach St., UNLV & Fresno St.	1969-92, 96-2001	759	187	.802
Phog Allen, Baker, Kansas, Haskell, Central Mo. St. & Kansas	1906-09, 13-38	468	134	.777
Dean Smith, North Carolina	1962-91	717	209	.774
Henry Iba, Northwest Mo. St., Colorado & Oklahoma St.	1930-59	630	196	.763
Ed Diddle, Western Ky.	1923-52	558	184	.752
Nat Holman, CCNY	1920-49	361	127	.740
Bob Knight, Army & Indiana	1966-95	659	235	.737
John Chaney, Cheyney & Temple	1973-2002	675	253	.727
Eddie Sutton, Creighton, Arkansas, Kentucky & Oklahoma St.	1970-89, 91-2000	659	259	.718

31 SEASONS

Coach, Team	Seasons	W	L	Pct.
Adolph Rupp, Kentucky	1931-52, 54-62	670	125	.843
Phog Allen, Baker, Kansas, Haskell, Central Mo. St. & Kansas	1906-09, 13-39	481	141	.773
Dean Smith, North Carolina	1962-92	740	219	.772
Ed Diddle, Western Ky.	1923-53	583	190	.754
Henry Iba, Northwest Mo. St., Colorado & Oklahoma St.	1930-60	640	211	.752
Nat Holman, CCNY	1920-50	385	132	.745
Bob Knight, Army & Indiana	1966-96	678	247	.733
Eddie Sutton, Creighton, Arkansas, Kentucky & Oklahoma St.	1970-89, 91-2001	679	269	.716
Don Haskins, UTEP	1962-92	606	263	.697
Lefty Driesell, Davidson, Maryland & James Madison	1961-86, 89-93	621	279	.690

32 SEASONS

Coach, Team	Seasons	W	L	Pct.
Adolph Rupp, Kentucky	1931-52, 54-63	686	134	.837
Dean Smith, North Carolina	1962-93	774	223	.776
Phog Allen, Baker, Kansas, Haskell, Central Mo. St. & Kansas	1906-09, 13-40	500	147	.773
Ed Diddle, Western Ky.	1923-54	612	193	.760
Henry Iba, Northwest Mo. St., Colorado & Oklahoma St.	1930-61	655	221	.748
Nat Holman, CCNY	1920-51	397	139	.741
Bob Knight, Army & Indiana	1966-97	700	258	.731
Eddie Sutton, Creighton, Arkansas, Kentucky & Oklahoma St.	1970-89, 91-2002	702	278	.716
Don Haskins, UTEP	1962-93	627	276	.694
Lefty Driesell, Davidson, Maryland & James Madison	1961-86, 89-94	641	289	.689

33 SEASONS

Coach, Team	Seasons	W	L	Pct.
Adolph Rupp, Kentucky	1931-52, 54-64	707	140	.835
Dean Smith, North Carolina	1962-94	802	230	.777
Phog Allen, Baker, Kansas, Haskell, Central Mo. St. & Kansas	1906-09, 13-41	512	153	.770
Ed Diddle, Western Ky.	1923-55	630	203	.756
Henry Iba, Northwest Mo. St., Colorado & Oklahoma St.	1930-62	669	232	.743
Nat Holman, CCNY	1920-52	405	150	.730
Bob Knight, Army & Indiana	1966-98	720	270	.727
Don Haskins, UTEP	1962-94	645	288	.691
Lefty Driesell, Davidson, Maryland & James Madison	1961-86, 89-95	657	302	.685
Norm Stewart, Northern Iowa & Missouri	1962-94	640	310	.674

34 SEASONS

Coach, Team	Seasons	W	L	Pct.
Adolph Rupp, Kentucky	1931-52, 54-65	722	150	.828
Dean Smith, North Carolina	1962-95	830	236	.779
Phog Allen, Baker, Kansas, Haskell, Central Mo. St. & Kansas	1906-09, 13-42	529	158	.770
Ed Diddle, Western Ky.	1923-56	646	215	.750
Henry Iba, Northwest Mo. St., Colorado & Oklahoma St.	1930-63	685	241	.740
Bob Knight, Army & Indiana	1966-99	743	281	.726
Nat Holman, CCNY	1920-52, 55	413	160	.721
Don Haskins, UTEP	1962-95	665	298	.691
Lefty Driesell, Davidson, Maryland & James Madison	1961-86, 89-96	667	322	.674
Norm Stewart, Northern Iowa & Missouri	1962-95	660	319	.674

35 SEASONS

Coach, Team	Seasons	W	L	Pct.
Adolph Rupp, Kentucky	1931-52, 54-66	749	152	.831
Dean Smith, North Carolina	1962-96	851	247	.775
Phog Allen, Baker, Kansas, Haskell, Central Mo. St. & Kansas	1906-09, 13-43	551	164	.771
Ed Diddle, Western Ky.	1923-57	663	224	.747
Henry Iba, Northwest Mo. St., Colorado & Oklahoma St.	1930-64	700	251	.736
Bob Knight, Army & Indiana	1966-2000	764	289	.726
Nat Holman, CCNY	1920-52, 55-56	417	174	.706
Don Haskins, UTEP	1962-96	678	313	.684
Lefty Driesell, Davidson, Maryland & James Madison	1961-86, 89-97	683	335	.671
Norm Stewart, Northern Iowa & Missouri	1962-96	678	334	.670

36 SEASONS

Coach, Team	Seasons	W	L	Pct.
Adolph Rupp, Kentucky	1931-52, 54-67	762	165	.822
Dean Smith, North Carolina	1962-97	879	254	.776
Phog Allen, Baker, Kansas, Haskell, Central Mo. St. & Kansas	1906-09, 13-44	568	173	.767
Ed Diddle, Western Ky.	1923-58	677	235	.742
Henry Iba, Northwest Mo. St., Colorado & Oklahoma St.	1930-65	720	258	.736
Bob Knight, Army, Indiana & Texas Tech	1966-2000, 02	787	298	.725
Nat Holman, CCNY	1920-52, 55-56, 59	423	186	.695
Don Haskins, UTEP	1962-97	691	351	.679
Lou Henson, Hardin-Simmons, New Mexico St., Illinois & New Mexico St.	1963-96, 99-2000	708	351	.669
Lefty Driesell, Davidson, Maryland, James Madison & Georgia St.	1961-86, 89-98	699	347	.668

37 SEASONS

Coach, Team	Seasons	W	L	Pct.
Adolph Rupp, Kentucky	1931-52, 54-68	784	170	.822
Phog Allen, Baker, Kansas, Haskell, Central Mo. St. & Kansas	1906-09, 13-45	580	178	.765
Ed Diddle, Western Ky.	1923-59	693	245	.739
Henry Iba, Northwest Mo. St., Colorado & Oklahoma St.	1930-66	724	279	.722
Nat Holman, CCNY	1920-52, 55-56, 59-60	423	190	.690
Don Haskins, UTEP	1962-98	703	341	.673
Lefty Driesell, Davidson, Maryland, James Madison & Georgia St.	1961-86, 89-99	716	360	.665
Lou Henson, Hardin-Simmons, New Mexico St., Illinois & New Mexico St.	1963-96, 99-2001	722	365	.664
Norm Stewart, Northern Iowa & Missouri	1962-98	711	366	.660
Ray Meyer, DePaul	1943-79	597	333	.642

38 SEASONS

Coach, Team	Seasons	W	L	Pct.
Adolph Rupp, Kentucky	1931-52, 54-69	807	175	.822
Phog Allen, Baker, Kansas, Haskell, Central Mo. St. & Kansas	1906-09, 13-46	599	180	.769
Ed Diddle, Western Ky.	1923-60	714	252	.739
Henry Iba, Northwest Mo. St., Colorado & Oklahoma St.	1930-67	731	297	.711
Don Haskins, UTEP	1962-99	719	353	.671
Lefty Driesell, Davidson, Maryland, James Madison & Georgia St.	1961-86, 89-2000	733	372	.663
Lou Henson, Hardin-Simmons, New Mexico St., Illinois & New Mexico St.	1963-96, 99-2002	742	377	.663
Norm Stewart, Northern Iowa & Missouri	1962-99	731	375	.661
Ray Meyer, DePaul	1943-80	623	335	.650
Ralph Miller, Wichita St., Iowa & Oregon St.	1952-89	657	382	.632

39 SEASONS

Coach, Team	Seasons	W	L	Pct.
Adolph Rupp, Kentucky	1931-52, 54-70	833	177	.825
Phog Allen, Baker, Kansas, Haskell, Central Mo. St. & Kansas	1906-09, 13-47	607	185	.766
Ed Diddle, Western Ky.	1923-61	732	260	.740
Henry Iba, Northwest Mo. St., Colorado & Oklahoma St.	1930-68	741	313	.703
Lefty Driesell, Davidson, Maryland, James Madison & Georgia St.	1961-86, 89-2001	762	377	.669
Ray Meyer, DePaul	1943-81	650	337	.659
Tony Hinkle, Butler	1927-42, 46-68	531	367	.591
Marv Harshman, Pacific Lutheran, Washington St. & Washington	1946-84	632	439	.590

40 SEASONS

Coach, Team	Seasons	W	L	Pct.
Adolph Rupp, Kentucky	1931-52, 54-71	855	183	.824
Phog Allen, Baker, Kansas, Haskell, Central Mo. St. & Kansas	1906-09, 13-48	616	200	.755
Ed Diddle, Western Ky.	1923-62	749	270	.735
Henry Iba, Northwest Mo. St., Colorado & Oklahoma St.	1930-69	753	326	.698
Lefty Driesell, Davidson, Maryland, James Madison & Georgia St.	1961-86, 89-2002	782	388	.668
Ray Meyer, DePaul	1943-82	676	339	.666
Marv Harshman, Pacific Lutheran, Washington St. & Washington	1946-85	654	449	.593
Tony Hinkle, Butler	1927-42, 46-69	542	382	.587

41 SEASONS

Coach, Team	Seasons	W	L	Pct.
Adolph Rupp, Kentucky	1931-52, 54-72	876	190	.822
Phog Allen, Baker, Kansas, Haskell, Central Mo. St. & Kansas	1906-09, 13-49	628	212	.748
Ed Diddle, Western Ky.	1923-63	754	286	.725
Henry Iba, Northwest Mo. St., Colorado & Oklahoma St.	1930-70	767	338	.694
Ray Meyer, DePaul	1943-83	697	351	.665
Tony Hinkle, Butler	1927-42, 46-70	557	393	.586

42 SEASONS

Coach, Team	Seasons	W	L	Pct.
Phog Allen, Baker, Kansas, Haskell, Central Mo. St. & Kansas	1906-09, 13-50	642	223	.742
Ed Diddle, Western Ky.	1923-64	759	302	.715
Ray Meyer, DePaul	1943-84	724	354	.672

Top 10 Best Career Starts By Wins

(Head coaches with at least half their seasons at Division I)

1 SEASON

Coach, Team	Season	W	L	Pct.
Bill Guthridge, North Carolina	1998	34	4	.895
Bill Hodges, Indiana St.	1979	33	1	.970
Stan Heath, Kent St.	2002	30	6	.833
John Warren, Oregon	1945	30	13	.698
Phil Johnson, Weber St.	1969	27	3	.900
Blaine Taylor, Montana	1992	27	4	.871
Tevester Anderson, Murray St.	1999	27	6	.818
John Phillips, Tulsa	2002	27	7	.794
Jim Boeheim, Syracuse	1977	26	4	.867
Everett Case, North Carolina St.	1947	26	5	.839
Denny Crum, Louisville	1972	26	5	.839
Pete Herrmann, Navy	1987	26	6	.813
Todd Lickliter, Butler	2002	26	6	.813
Nolan Richardson, Tulsa	1981	26	7	.788
Dick Hunsaker, Ball St.	1990	26	7	.788
Larry Finch, Memphis	1987	26	8	.765
Mark Few, Gonzaga	2000	26	9	.743

2 SEASONS

Coach, Team	Seasons	W	L	Pct.
Bill Guthridge, North Carolina	1998-99	58	14	.806
Everett Case, North Carolina St.	1947-48	55	8	.873
Ben Carnevale, North Carolina	1945-46	52	11	.825
Mark Few, Gonzaga	2000-01	52	16	.765
Don Monson, Gonzaga	1998-99	52	17	.754
Bill Carmody, Princeton	1997-98	51	6	.895
Gary Cunningham, UCLA	1978-79	50	8	.862
Kermit Davis Jr., Idaho	1989-90	50	12	.806
Nolan Richardson, Tulsa	1981-82	50	13	.794
Thad Matta, Butler & Xavier	2001-02	50	14	.781
Tevester Anderson, Murray St.	1999-2000	50	15	.769
Stan Watts, Brigham Young	1950-51	50	21	.704

3 SEASONS

Coach, Team	Seasons	W	L	Pct.
Mark Few, Gonzaga	2000-02	81	20	.802
Everett Case, North Carolina St.	1947-49	80	16	.833
Bill Guthridge, North Carolina	1998-2000	80	28	.741
Roy Williams, Kansas	1989-91	76	25	.752
Jim Boeheim, Syracuse	1977-79	74	14	.841
Bill Carmody, Princeton	1997-99	73	14	.839
Jerry Tarkanian, Long Beach St.	1969-71	71	13	.845
Dick Hunsaker, Ball St.	1990-92	71	26	.732
Denny Crum, Louisville	1972-74	70	19	.787
Don Donoher, Dayton	1965-67	70	19	.787
Pat Foster, Lamar	1981-83	70	20	.777
Pete Gillen, Xavier	1986-88	70	22	.761
Tim Welsh, Iona	1996-98	70	22	.761
Randy Ayers, Ohio St.	1990-92	70	23	.753
Steve Lavin, UCLA	1997-99	70	26	.729
Speedy Morris, La Salle	1987-89	70	29	.707

4 SEASONS

Coach, Team	Seasons	W	L	Pct.
Everett Case, North Carolina St.	1947-50	107	22	.829
Bruce Stewart, West Va. Wesleyan & Middle Tenn.	1983-86	104	34	.754
Roy Williams, Kansas	1989-92	103	30	.774
Jim Boeheim, Syracuse	1977-80	100	18	.847
Speedy Morris, La Salle	1987-90	100	31	.763
Denny Crum, Louisville	1972-75	98	22	.817
Dick Hunsaker, Ball St.	1990-93	97	34	.740
Jerry Tarkanian, Long Beach St.	1969-72	96	17	.850
Pat Foster, Lamar	1981-84	96	25	.793
Nolan Richardson, Tulsa	1981-84	96	29	.768

5 SEASONS

Coach, Team	Seasons	W	L	Pct.
Everett Case, North Carolina St.	1947-51	137	29	.825
Roy Williams, Kansas	1989-93	132	37	.781
Bruce Stewart, West Va. Wesleyan & Middle Tenn.	1983-87	126	41	.754
Forddy Anderson, Drake & Bradley	1947-51	123	42	.745
Jerry Tarkanian, Long Beach St. & UNLV	1969-73	122	20	.859
Jim Boeheim, Syracuse	1977-81	122	30	.803
Fred Schaus, West Virginia	1955-59	120	32	.789

Coach, Team	Seasons	W	L	Pct.
Larry Brown, UCLA & Kansas	1980-81, 84-86	120	38	.759
Tom Izzo, Michigan St.	1996-2000	120	48	.714
Nolan Richardson, Tulsa	1981-85	119	37	.763
Speedy Morris, La Salle	1987-91	119	41	.744
Pete Gillen, Xavier	1986-90	119	39	.753

6 SEASONS

Coach, Team	Seasons	W	L	Pct.
Everett Case, North Carolina St.	1947-52	161	39	.805
Roy Williams, Kansas	1989-94	159	45	.779
Bruce Stewart, West Va. Wesleyan & Middle Tenn.	1983-88	149	52	.741
Tom Izzo, Michigan St.	1996-2001	148	53	.736
Fred Schaus, West Virginia	1955-60	146	37	.798
Larry Brown, UCLA & Kansas	1980-81, 84-87	145	49	.747
Jerry Tarkanian, Long Beach St. & UNLV	1969-74	142	26	.845
Pete Gillen, Xavier	1986-91	141	49	.742
Forddy Anderson, Drake & Bradley	1947-52	140	54	.722
Denny Crum, Louisville	1972-77	139	37	.790
Speedy Morris, La Salle	1987-92	139	52	.728

7 SEASONS

Coach, Team	Seasons	W	L	Pct.
Everett Case, North Carolina St.	1947-53	187	45	.806
Roy Williams, Kansas	1989-95	184	51	.783
Larry Brown, UCLA & Kansas	1980-81, 84-88	172	60	.741
Bruce Stewart, West Va. Wesleyan & Middle Tenn.	1983-89	172	60	.741
Tom Izzo, Michigan St.	1996-2002	167	65	.720
Jerry Tarkanian, Long Beach St. & UNLV	1969-75	166	31	.843
Denny Crum, Louisville	1972-78	162	44	.786
Howard Hobson, Southern Ore. & Oregon	1933-39	162	48	.771
Fred Schaus, West Virginia & Purdue	1955-60, 73	161	46	.778
Jim Boeheim, Syracuse	1977-83	159	53	.750
Tubby Smith, Tulsa, Georgia & Kentucky	1992-98	159	66	.707

8 SEASONS

Coach, Team	Seasons	W	L	Pct.
Everett Case, North Carolina St.	1947-54	213	52	.804
Roy Williams, Kansas	1989-96	213	56	.792
Jerry Tarkanian, Long Beach St. & UNLV	1969-76	195	33	.855
Tubby Smith, Tulsa, Georgia & Kentucky	1992-99	187	75	.714
Denny Crum, Louisville	1972-79	186	52	.782
Bruce Stewart, West Va. Wesleyan & Middle Tenn.	1983-90	184	75	.710
Fred Schaus, West Virginia & Purdue	1955-60, 73-74	182	55	.768
Jim Boeheim, Syracuse	1977-84	182	62	.745
Howard Hobson, Southern Ore. & Oregon	1933-40	181	60	.751
John Calipari, Massachusetts	1989-96	189	70	.730

9 SEASONS

Coach, Team	Seasons	W	L	Pct.
Roy Williams, Kansas	1989-97	247	58	.810
Everett Case, North Carolina St.	1947-55	241	56	.811
Jerry Tarkanian, Long Beach St. & UNLV	1969-77	224	36	.862
Denny Crum, Louisville	1972-80	219	55	.799
John Calipari, Massachusetts & Memphis	1989-96, 2001	210	85	.712
Tubby Smith, Tulsa, Georgia & Kentucky	1992-2000	210	85	.712
Jim Boeheim, Syracuse	1977-85	204	71	.742
Fred Schaus, West Virginia & Purdue	1955-60, 73-75	199	66	.751
Howard Hobson, Southern Ore. & Oregon	1933-41	199	78	.718
Vic Bubas, Duke	1960-68	198	54	.786
Tom Blackburn, Dayton	1948-56	198	74	.728

10 SEASONS

Coach, Team	Seasons	W	L	Pct.
Roy Williams, Kansas	1989-98	282	62	.820
Everett Case, North Carolina St.	1947-56	265	60	.815
Jerry Tarkanian, Long Beach St. & UNLV	1969-78	244	44	.847
Denny Crum, Louisville	1972-81	240	64	.789
John Calipari, Massachusetts & Memphis	1989-96, 2001-02	237	94	.716
Tubby Smith, Tulsa, Georgia & Kentucky	1992-2001	234	95	.711

Coach, Team	Seasons	W	L	Pct.
Jim Boeheim, Syracuse	1977-86	230	77	.749
Nolan Richardson, Tulsa & Arkansas	1981-90	226	88	.720
Pete Gillen, Xavier & Providence	1986-95	219	88	.713
Tom Blackburn, Dayton	1948-57	217	83	.723

11 SEASONS

Coach, Team	Seasons	W	L	Pct.
Roy Williams, Kansas	1989-99	305	72	.809
Everett Case, North Carolina St.	1947-57	280	71	.798
Denny Crum, Louisville	1972-82	263	74	.780
Jim Boeheim, Syracuse	1977-87	261	84	.757
Nolan Richardson, Tulsa & Arkansas	1981-91	260	92	.739
Jerry Tarkanian, Long Beach St. & UNLV	1969-79	259	49	.841
Tubby Smith, Tulsa, Georgia & Kentucky	1992-2002	256	105	.709
Tom Blackburn, Dayton	1948-58	242	87	.736
Boyd Grant, Fresno St. & Colorado St.	1978-86, 88-89	239	97	.711
Wimp Sanderson, Alabama	1981-91	239	109	.687

12 SEASONS

Coach, Team	Seasons	W	L	Pct.
Roy Williams, Kansas	1989-2000	329	82	.800
Everett Case, North Carolina St.	1947-58	298	77	.795
Denny Crum, Louisville	1972-83	295	78	.791
Jim Boeheim, Syracuse	1977-88	287	93	.755
Nolan Richardson, Tulsa & Arkansas	1981-92	286	100	.741
Jerry Tarkanian, Long Beach St. & UNLV	1969-80	282	58	.829
Wimp Sanderson, Alabama	1981-92	265	118	.692
John Thompson, Georgetown	1973-84	262	104	.716
Bob Huggins, Walsh, Akron & Cincinnati	1981-93	262	108	.708
Pete Gillen, Xavier & Providence	1986-97	261	112	.700

13 SEASONS

Coach, Team	Seasons	W	L	Pct.
Roy Williams, Kansas	1989-2001	355	89	.800
Everett Case, North Carolina St.	1947-59	320	81	.798
Denny Crum, Louisville	1972-84	319	89	.782
Jim Boeheim, Syracuse	1977-89	317	101	.758
Nolan Richardson, Tulsa & Arkansas	1981-93	308	109	.739
Jerry Tarkanian, Long Beach St. & UNLV	1969-81	298	70	.810
John Thompson, Georgetown	1973-85	297	107	.735
Bob Huggins, Walsh, Akron & Cincinnati	1981-94	284	118	.706
Rick Pitino, Boston U., Providence & Kentucky	1979-83, 86-87, 90-95	283	117	.708
Wimp Sanderson, Alabama & Ark.-Little Rock	1981-92, 95	282	130	.684
Rick Majerus, Marquette, Ball St. & Utah	1984-86, 88-97	279	107	.723

14 SEASONS

Coach, Team	Seasons	W	L	Pct.
Roy Williams, Kansas	1989-2002	388	93	.807
Jim Boeheim, Syracuse	1977-90	343	108	.761
Nolan Richardson, Tulsa & Arkansas	1981-94	339	112	.752
Denny Crum, Louisville	1972-85	338	107	.760
Everett Case, North Carolina St.	1947-60	331	96	.775
John Thompson, Georgetown	1973-86	321	115	.736
Jerry Tarkanian, Long Beach St. & UNLV	1969-82	318	80	.799
Rick Pitino, Boston U., Providence & Kentucky	1979-83, 86-87, 90-96	317	119	.727
Rick Majerus, Marquette, Ball St. & Utah	1984-86, 88-98	309	111	.736
Bob Huggins, Walsh, Akron & Cincinnati	1981-95	307	129	.704

15 SEASONS

Coach, Team	Seasons	W	L	Pct.
Nolan Richardson, Tulsa & Arkansas	1981-95	371	119	.757
Denny Crum, Louisville	1972-86	370	114	.764
Jim Boeheim, Syracuse	1977-91	369	114	.764
Rick Pitino, Boston U., Providence & Kentucky	1979-83, 86-87, 90-97	352	124	.739
John Thompson, Georgetown	1973-87	350	120	.745
Everett Case, North Carolina St.	1947-61	347	105	.768
Jerry Tarkanian, Long Beach St. & UNLV	1969-83	346	83	.807
Rick Majerus, Marquette, Ball St. & Utah	1984-86, 88-99	337	116	.744
Billy Tubbs, Southwest Tex. St., Lamar & Oklahoma	1972-73, 77-89	336	148	.694
Bob Huggins, Walsh, Akron & Cincinnati	1981-96	335	134	.714
Wimp Sanderson, Alabama & Ark.-Little Rock	1981-92, 95-97	323	148	.686

16 SEASONS

Coach, Team	Seasons	W	L	Pct.
Jim Boeheim, Syracuse	1977-92	391	124	.759
Nolan Richardson, Tulsa & Arkansas	1981-96	391	132	.748

Coach, Team	Seasons	W	L	Pct.
Denny Crum, Louisville	1972-87	388	128	.752
Jerry Tarkanian, Long Beach St. & UNLV	1969-84	375	89	.808
Rick Pitino, Boston U., Providence, Kentucky & Louisville	1979-83, 86-87, 90-97, 2002	371	137	.730
John Thompson, Georgetown	1973-88	370	130	.740
Billy Tubbs, Southwest Tex. St., Lamar & Oklahoma	1972-73, 77-90	363	153	.703
Bob Huggins, Walsh, Akron & Cincinnati	1981-97	361	142	.718
Rick Majerus, Marquette, Ball St. & Utah	1984-86, 88-2000	360	125	.742
Everett Case, North Carolina St.	1947-62	358	111	.763

17 SEASONS

Coach, Team	Seasons	W	L	Pct.
Denny Crum, Louisville	1972-88	412	139	.748
Jim Boeheim, Syracuse	1977-93	411	133	.756
Nolan Richardson, Tulsa & Arkansas	1981-97	409	146	.737
Jerry Tarkanian, Long Beach St. & UNLV	1969-85	403	93	.813
John Thompson, Georgetown	1973-89	399	135	.747
Bob Huggins, Walsh, Akron & Cincinnati	1981-98	388	148	.724
Billy Tubbs, Southwest Tex. St., Lamar & Oklahoma	1972-73, 77-91	383	168	.695
Eddie Sutton, Creighton, Arkansas & Kentucky	1970-86	374	129	.744
Lou Carnesecca, St. John's (N.Y.)	1966-70, 74-85	371	131	.739
Mike Krzyzewski, Army & Duke	1976-92	370	169	.686

18 SEASONS

Coach, Team	Seasons	W	L	Pct.
Jerry Tarkanian, Long Beach St. & UNLV	1969-86	436	98	.816
Denny Crum, Louisville	1972-89	436	148	.747
Jim Boeheim, Syracuse	1977-94	434	140	.756
Nolan Richardson, Tulsa & Arkansas	1981-98	433	155	.736
John Thompson, Georgetown	1973-90	423	142	.749
Bob Huggins, Walsh, Akron & Cincinnati	1981-99	415	154	.729
Billy Tubbs, Southwest Tex. St., Lamar & Oklahoma	1972-73, 77-92	404	177	.695
Lou Carnesecca, St. John's (N.Y.)	1966-70, 74-86	402	136	.747
Mike Krzyzewski, Army & Duke	1976-93	394	177	.690
Eddie Sutton, Creighton, Arkansas & Kentucky	1970-87	392	140	.740

19 SEASONS

Coach, Team	Seasons	W	L	Pct.
Jerry Tarkanian, Long Beach St. & UNLV	1969-87	473	100	.825
Denny Crum, Louisville	1972-90	463	156	.748
Nolan Richardson, Tulsa & Arkansas	1981-99	456	166	.733
Jim Boeheim, Syracuse	1977-95	454	150	.752
Bob Huggins, Walsh, Akron & Cincinnati	1981-2000	444	158	.738
John Thompson, Georgetown	1973-91	442	155	.740
Billy Tubbs, Southwest Tex. St., Lamar & Oklahoma	1972-73, 77-93	424	189	.692
Lou Carnesecca, St. John's (N.Y.)	1966-70, 74-87	423	145	.745
Mike Krzyzewski, Army & Duke	1976-94	422	183	.698
Eddie Sutton, Creighton, Arkansas & Kentucky	1970-88	417	145	.742

20 SEASONS

Coach, Team	Seasons	W	L	Pct.
Jerry Tarkanian, Long Beach St. & UNLV	1969-88	501	106	.825
Jim Boeheim, Syracuse	1977-96	483	159	.752
Denny Crum, Louisville	1972-91	477	172	.735
Nolan Richardson, Tulsa & Arkansas	1981-2000	475	181	.724
Bob Huggins, Walsh, Akron & Cincinnati	1981-2001	469	168	.736
John Thompson, Georgetown	1973-92	464	165	.738
John Chaney, Cheyney & Temple	1973-92	458	143	.762
Lou Carnesecca, St. John's (N.Y.)	1966-70, 74-88	440	157	.737
Billy Tubbs, Southwest Tex. St., Lamar & Oklahoma	1972-73, 77-94	439	202	.685
Henry Iba, Northwest Mo. St., Colorado & Oklahoma St.	1930-49	438	108	.802

21 SEASONS

Coach, Team	Seasons	W	L	Pct.
Jerry Tarkanian, Long Beach St. & UNLV	1969-89	530	114	.823
Jim Boeheim, Syracuse	1977-97	502	172	.745
Bob Huggins, Walsh, Akron & Cincinnati	1981-2002	500	172	.744
Denny Crum, Louisville	1972-92	496	183	.730
Nolan Richardson, Tulsa & Arkansas	1981-2001	495	192	.721
John Thompson, Georgetown	1973-93	484	178	.731
John Chaney, Cheyney & Temple	1973-93	478	156	.754
Dean Smith, North Carolina	1962-82	468	145	.763
Lou Carnesecca, St. John's (N.Y.)	1966-70, 74-89	460	170	.730
Lute Olson, Long Beach St., Iowa & Arizona	1974-94	458	179	.719

22 SEASONS

Coach, Team	Seasons	W	L	Pct.
Jerry Tarkanian, Long Beach St. & UNLV	1969-90	565	119	.826
Jim Boeheim, Syracuse	1977-98	528	181	.745
Denny Crum, Louisville	1972-93	518	192	.730
John Thompson, Georgetown	1973-94	503	190	.726
John Chaney, Cheyney & Temple	1973-94	501	164	.753
Dean Smith, North Carolina	1962-83	496	153	.764
Henry Iba, Northwest Mo. St., Colorado & Oklahoma St.	1930-51	485	123	.798
Lou Carnesecca, St. John's (N.Y.)	1966-70, 74-90	484	180	.729
Eddie Sutton, Creighton, Arkansas, Kentucky & Oklahoma St.	1970-89, 91-92	482	180	.728
Lute Olson, Long Beach St., Iowa & Arizona	1974-95	482	186	.722

23 SEASONS

Coach, Team	Seasons	W	L	Pct.
Jerry Tarkanian, Long Beach St. & UNLV	1969-91	599	120	.833
Jim Boeheim, Syracuse	1977-99	549	193	.740
Denny Crum, Louisville	1972-94	524	198	.734
Dean Smith, North Carolina	1962-84	524	156	.771
John Thompson, Georgetown	1973-95	524	200	.724
John Chaney, Cheyney & Temple	1973-95	520	175	.748
Lute Olson, Long Beach St., Iowa & Arizona	1974-96	509	192	.726
Lou Carnesecca, St. John's (N.Y.)	1966-70, 74-91	507	189	.728
Mike Krzyzewski, Army & Duke	1976-98	505	212	.704
Henry Iba, Northwest Mo. St., Colorado & Oklahoma St.	1930-52	504	131	.794

24 SEASONS

Coach, Team	Seasons	W	L	Pct.
Jerry Tarkanian, Long Beach St. & UNLV	1969-92	625	122	.837
Jim Boeheim, Syracuse	1977-2000	575	199	.743
Denny Crum, Louisville	1972-95	565	212	.727
John Thompson, Georgetown	1973-96	553	208	.727
Dean Smith, North Carolina	1962-85	551	165	.770
Mike Krzyzewski, Army & Duke	1976-99	542	214	.717
John Chaney, Cheyney & Temple	1973-96	540	188	.742
Lute Olson, Long Beach St., Iowa & Arizona	1974-97	534	201	.718
Henry Iba, Northwest Mo. St., Colorado & Oklahoma St.	1930-53	527	138	.792
Eddie Sutton, Creighton, Arkansas, Kentucky & Oklahoma St.	1970-89, 91-94	526	199	.726
Lou Carnesecca, St. John's (N.Y.)	1966-70, 74-92	526	200	.725

25 SEASONS

Coach, Team	Seasons	W	L	Pct.
Jerry Tarkanian, Long Beach St., UNLV & Fresno St.	1969-92, 96	647	133	.829
Jim Boeheim, Syracuse	1977-2001	600	208	.743
Denny Crum, Louisville	1972-96	587	224	.724
Dean Smith, North Carolina	1962-86	579	171	.772
John Thompson, Georgetown	1973-97	573	218	.724
Mike Krzyzewski, Army & Duke	1976-2000	571	219	.723
Lute Olson, Long Beach St., Iowa & Arizona	1974-98	564	206	.732
John Chaney, Cheyney & Temple	1973-97	560	199	.738
Eddie Sutton, Creighton, Arkansas, Kentucky & Oklahoma St.	1970-89, 91-95	553	209	.726
Henry Iba, Northwest Mo. St., Colorado & Oklahoma St.	1930-54	551	143	.794

26 SEASONS

Coach, Team	Seasons	W	L	Pct.
Jerry Tarkanian, Long Beach St., UNLV & Fresno St.	1969-92, 96-97	667	145	.821
Jim Boeheim, Syracuse	1977-2002	623	221	.738
Denny Crum, Louisville	1972-97	613	233	.725
Dean Smith, North Carolina	1962-87	611	175	.777
Mike Krzyzewski, Army & Duke	1976-2001	606	223	.731
John Thompson, Georgetown	1973-98	589	233	.717
Lute Olson, Long Beach St., Iowa & Arizona	1974-99	586	213	.733
John Chaney, Cheyney & Temple	1973-98	581	208	.736
John Wooden, Indiana St. & UCLA	1947-72	580	155	.789
Eddie Sutton, Creighton, Arkansas, Kentucky & Oklahoma St.	1970-89, 91-96	570	219	.722

27 SEASONS

Coach, Team	Seasons	W	L	Pct.
Jerry Tarkanian, Long Beach St., UNLV & Fresno St.	1969-92, 96-98	688	158	.813
Dean Smith, North Carolina	1962-88	638	182	.778
Mike Krzyzewski, Army & Duke	1976-2002	637	227	.737
Denny Crum, Louisville	1972-98	625	253	.712
Lute Olson, Long Beach St., Iowa & Arizona	1974-2000	613	220	.736
John Wooden, Indiana St. & UCLA	1947-73	610	155	.797

Coach, Team	Seasons	W	L	Pct.
John Chaney, Cheyney & Temple	1973-99	605	219	.734
John Thompson, Georgetown	1973-99	596	239	.714
Bob Knight, Army & Indiana	1966-92	588	210	.737
Eddie Sutton, Creighton, Arkansas, Kentucky & Oklahoma St.	1970-89, 91-97	587	234	.715

28 SEASONS

Coach, Team	Seasons	W	L	Pct.
Jerry Tarkanian, Long Beach St.,UNLV & Fresno St.	1969-92, 96-99	709	170	.807
Dean Smith, North Carolina	1962-89	667	190	.778
Denny Crum, Louisville	1972-99	644	264	.709
Lute Olson, Long Beach St., Iowa & Arizona	1974-2001	638	226	.738
John Wooden, Indiana St. & UCLA	1947-74	636	159	.800
John Chaney, Cheyney & Temple	1973-2000	632	225	.737
Bob Knight, Army & Indiana	1966-93	619	214	.743
Adolph Rupp, Kentucky	1931-52, 54-59	610	106	.852
Eddie Sutton, Creighton, Arkansas, Kentucky & Oklahoma St.	1970-89, 91-98	609	241	.716
Henry Iba, Northwest Mo. St., Colorado & Oklahoma St.	1930-57	598	174	.775

29 SEASONS

Coach, Team	Seasons	W	L	Pct.
Jerry Tarkanian, Long Beach St., UNLV & Fresno St.	1969-92, 96-2000	733	180	.803
Dean Smith, North Carolina	1962-90	688	203	.772
John Wooden, Indiana St. & UCLA	1947-75	664	162	.804
Denny Crum, Louisville	1972-2000	663	276	.706
Lute Olson, Long Beach St., Iowa & Arizona	1974-2002	662	236	.737
John Chaney, Cheyney & Temple	1973-2001	656	238	.734
Bob Knight, Army & Indiana	1966-94	640	223	.742
Eddie Sutton, Creighton, Arkansas, Kentucky & Oklahoma St.	1970-89, 91-99	632	252	.715
Adolph Rupp, Kentucky	1931-52, 54-60	628	113	.848
Henry Iba, Northwest Mo. St., Colorado & Oklahoma St.	1930-58	619	182	.773

30 SEASONS

Coach, Team	Seasons	W	L	Pct.
Jerry Tarkanian, Long Beach St., UNLV & Fresno St.	1969-92, 96-2001	759	187	.802
Dean Smith, North Carolina	1962-91	717	209	.774
John Chaney, Cheyney & Temple	1973-2002	675	253	.727
Denny Crum, Louisville	1972-2001	675	295	.696
Bob Knight, Army & Indiana	1966-95	659	235	.737
Eddie Sutton, Creighton, Arkansas, Kentucky & Oklahoma St.	1970-89, 91-2000	659	259	.718
Adolph Rupp, Kentucky	1931-52, 54-61	647	122	.841
Henry Iba, Northwest Mo. St., Colorado & Oklahoma St.	1930-59	630	196	.763
Jim Calhoun, Northeastern & Connecticut	1973-2002	624	286	.686
Lefty Driesell, Davidson, Maryland & James Madison	1961-86, 89-92	600	270	.690

31 SEASONS

Coach, Team	Seasons	W	L	Pct.
Dean Smith, North Carolina	1962-92	740	219	.772
Bob Knight, Army & Indiana	1966-96	679	246	.734
Eddie Sutton, Creighton, Arkansas, Kentucky & Oklahoma St.	1970-89, 91-2001	679	269	.716
Adolph Rupp, Kentucky	1931-52, 54-62	670	125	.843
Henry Iba, Northwest Mo. St., Colorado & Oklahoma St.	1930-60	640	211	.752
Lefty Driesell, Davidson, Maryland & James Madison	1961-86, 89-93	621	279	.690
Lou Henson, Hardin-Simmons, New Mexico St. & Illinois	1963-93	609	295	.674
Don Haskins, UTEP	1962-92	606	263	.697
Gene Bartow, Central Mo. St., Valparaiso, Memphis, Illinois, UCLA, & UAB	1962-77, 78-93	595	315	.654
Norm Stewart, Northern Iowa & Missouri	1962-92	593	292	.670

32 SEASONS

Coach, Team	Seasons	W	L	Pct.
Dean Smith, North Carolina	1962-93	774	223	.776
Eddie Sutton, Creighton, Arkansas, Kentucky & Oklahoma St.	1970-89, 91-2002	702	278	.716
Bob Knight, Army & Indiana	1966-97	701	257	.732
Adolph Rupp, Kentucky	1931-52, 54-63	686	134	.837
Henry Iba, Northwest Mo. St., Colorado & Oklahoma St.	1930-61	655	221	.748
Lefty Driesell, Davidson, Maryland & James Madison	1961-86, 89-94	641	289	.689
Don Haskins, UTEP	1962-93	627	276	.694

Coach, Team	Seasons	W	L	Pct.
Lou Henson, Hardin-Simmons, New Mexico St. & Illinois	1963-94	626	306	.672
Gene Bartow, Central Mo. St., Valparaiso, Memphis, Illinois, UCLA, & UAB	1962-77, 78-94	617	323	.656
Ed Diddle, Western Ky.	1923-54	612	193	.760
Norm Stewart, Northern Iowa & Missouri	1962-93	612	306	.667

33 SEASONS

Coach, Team	Seasons	W	L	Pct.
Dean Smith, North Carolina	1962-94	802	230	.777
Bob Knight, Army & Indiana	1966-98	721	269	.728
Adolph Rupp, Kentucky	1931-52, 54-64	707	140	.835
Henry Iba, Northwest Mo. St., Colorado & Oklahoma St.	1930-62	669	232	.743
Lefty Driesell, Davidson, Maryland & James Madison	1961-86, 89-95	657	302	.685
Don Haskins, UTEP	1962-94	645	288	.691
Lou Henson, Hardin-Simmons, New Mexico St. & Illinois	1963-95	645	318	.670
Norm Stewart, Northern Iowa & Missouri	1962-94	640	310	.674
Gene Bartow, Central Mo. St., Valparaiso, Memphis, Illinois, UCLA, & UAB	1962-77, 78-95	631	339	.651
Ed Diddle, Western Ky.	1923-55	630	203	.756

34 SEASONS

Coach, Team	Seasons	W	L	Pct.
Dean Smith, North Carolina	1962-95	830	236	.779
Bob Knight, Army & Indiana	1966-99	744	280	.727
Adolph Rupp, Kentucky	1931-52, 54-65	722	150	.828
Henry Iba, Northwest Mo. St., Colorado & Oklahoma St.	1930-63	685	241	.740
Lefty Driesell, Davidson, Maryland & James Madison	1961-86, 89-96	667	322	.674
Don Haskins, UTEP	1962-95	665	298	.691
Lou Henson, Hardin-Simmons, New Mexico St. & Illinois	1963-96	663	331	.667
Norm Stewart, Northern Iowa & Missouri	1962-95	660	319	.674
Ed Diddle, Western Ky.	1923-56	646	215	.750
Abe Lemons, Oklahoma City, Tex.-Pan American, Texas & Oklahoma City	1956-82, 84-90	597	344	.634

35 SEASONS

Coach, Team	Seasons	W	L	Pct.
Dean Smith, North Carolina	1962-96	851	247	.775
Bob Knight, Army & Indiana	1966-2000	764	289	.726
Adolph Rupp, Kentucky	1931-52, 54-66	749	152	.831
Henry Iba, Northwest Mo. St., Colorado & Oklahoma St.	1930-64	700	251	.736
Lou Henson, Hardin-Simmons, New Mexico St., Illinois & New Mexico St.	1963-96, 99	686	341	.668
Lefty Driesell, Davidson, Maryland & James Madison	1961-86, 89-97	683	335	.671
Don Haskins, UTEP	1962-96	678	313	.684
Norm Stewart, Northern Iowa & Missouri	1962-96	678	334	.670
Ed Diddle, Western Ky.	1923-57	663	224	.747
Ralph Miller, Wichita St., Iowa & Oregon St.	1952-86	596	352	.629
Norm Sloan, Presbyterian, Citadel, Florida, North Carolina St. & Florida	1952-55, 57-87	583	370	.612

36 SEASONS

Coach, Team	Seasons	W	L	Pct.
Dean Smith, North Carolina	1962-97	879	254	.776
Bob Knight, Army, Indiana & Texas Tech	1966-2000, 02	787	298	.725
Adolph Rupp, Kentucky	1931-52, 54-67	762	165	.822
Henry Iba, Northwest Mo. St., Colorado & Oklahoma St.	1930-65	720	258	.736
Lou Henson, Hardin-Simmons, New Mexico St., Illinois & New Mexico St.	1963-96, 99-2000	708	351	.669
Lefty Driesell, Davidson, Maryland, James Madison & Georgia St.	1961-86, 89-98	699	347	.668
Norm Stewart, Northern Iowa & Missouri	1962-97	694	351	.664
Don Haskins, UTEP	1962-97	691	327	.679
Ed Diddle, Western Ky.	1923-58	677	235	.742
Ralph Miller, Wichita St., Iowa & Oregon St.	1952-87	615	363	.629

37 SEASONS

Coach, Team	Seasons	W	L	Pct.
Adolph Rupp, Kentucky	1931-52, 54-68	784	170	.822
Henry Iba, Northwest Mo. St., Colorado & Oklahoma St.	1930-66	724	279	.722

Coach, Team	Seasons	W	L	Pct.
Lou Henson, Hardin-Simmons, New Mexico St., Illinois & New Mexico St.	1963-96, 99-2001	722	365	.664
Lefty Driesell, Davidson, Maryland, James Madison & Georgia St.	1961-86, 89-99	716	360	.665
Norm Stewart, Northern Iowa & Missouri	1962-98	711	366	.660
Don Haskins, UTEP	1962-98	703	341	.673
Ed Diddle, Western Ky.	1923-59	693	245	.739
Ralph Miller, Wichita St., Iowa & Oregon St.	1952-88	635	374	.629
Norm Sloan, Presbyterian, Citadel, Florida, North Carolina St. & Florida	1952-55, 57-89	627	395	.614
Ray Meyer, DePaul	1943-79	597	333	.642

38 SEASONS

Coach, Team	Seasons	W	L	Pct.
Adolph Rupp, Kentucky	1931-52, 54-69	807	175	.822
Lou Henson, Hardin-Simmons, New Mexico St., Illinois & New Mexico St.	1963-96, 99-2002	742	377	.663
Lefty Driesell, Davidson, Maryland, James Madison & Georgia St.	1961-86, 89-2000	733	372	.663
Henry Iba, Northwest Mo. St., Colorado & Oklahoma St.	1930-67	731	297	.711
Norm Stewart, Northern Iowa & Missouri	1962-99	731	375	.661
Don Haskins, UTEP	1962-99	719	353	.671
Ed Diddle, Western Ky.	1923-60	714	252	.739
Ralph Miller, Wichita St., Iowa & Oregon St.	1952-89	657	382	.632
Ray Meyer, DePaul	1943-80	623	335	.650
Marv Harshman, Pacific Lutheran, Washington St. & Washington	1946-83	608	432	.585

39 SEASONS

Coach, Team	Seasons	W	L	Pct.
Adolph Rupp, Kentucky	1931-52, 54-70	833	177	.825
Lefty Driesell, Davidson, Maryland, James Madison & Georgia St.	1961-86, 89-2001	762	377	.669
Henry Iba, Northwest Mo. St., Colorado & Oklahoma St.	1930-68	741	313	.703
Ed Diddle, Western Ky.	1923-61	732	260	.740
Ray Meyer, DePaul	1943-81	650	337	.659
Marv Harshman, Pacific Lutheran, Washington St. & Washington	1946-84	632	439	.590
Phog Allen, Baker, Kansas, Haskell, Central Mo. St. & Kansas	1906-09, 13-47	607	185	.766
Tony Hinkle, Butler	1927-42, 46-68	531	367	.591

40 SEASONS

Coach, Team	Seasons	W	L	Pct.
Adolph Rupp, Kentucky	1931-52, 54-71	855	183	.824
Lefty Driesell, Davidson, Maryland, James Madison & Georgia St.	1961-86, 89-2002	782	388	.668
Henry Iba, Northwest Mo. St., Colorado & Oklahoma St.	1930-69	753	326	.698
Ed Diddle, Western Ky.	1923-62	749	270	.735
Ray Meyer, DePaul	1943-82	676	339	.666
Marv Harshman, Pacific Lutheran, Washington St. & Washington	1946-85	654	449	.593
Phog Allen, Baker, Kansas, Haskell, Central Mo. St. & Kansas	1906-09, 13-40	616	200	.755
Tony Hinkle, Butler	1927-42, 46-69	542	382	.587

41 SEASONS

Coach, Team	Seasons	W	L	Pct.
Adolph Rupp, Kentucky	1931-52, 54-72	876	190	.822
Henry Iba, Northwest Mo. St., Colorado & Oklahoma St.	1930-70	767	338	.694
Ed Diddle, Western Ky.	1923-63	754	286	.725
Ray Meyer, DePaul	1943-83	697	351	.665
Phog Allen, Baker, Kansas, Haskell, Central Mo. St. & Kansas	1906-09, 13-49	628	212	.748
Tony Hinkle, Butler	1927-42, 46-70	557	393	.586

42 SEASONS

Coach, Team	Seasons	W	L	Pct.
Ed Diddle, Western Ky.	1923-64	759	302	.715
Ray Meyer, DePaul	1943-84	724	354	.672
Phog Allen, Baker, Kansas, Haskell, Central Mo. St. & Kansas	1906-09, 13-50	642	223	.742

Active Coaching Longevity Records

(Minimum five years as a Division I head coach)

MOST GAMES

No.	Coach, Team and Seasons
1,327	James Phelan, Mt. St. Mary's 1955-2002
1,170	Lefty Driesell, Davidson 1961-69, Maryland 70-86, James Madison 89-97, Georgia St. 98-2002
1,119	Lou Henson, Hardin-Simmons 1963-66, Illinois 76-96, New Mexico St. 67-75, 99-2002
1,085	Bob Knight, Army 1966-71, Indiana 72-2000, Texas Tech 02
980	Eddie Sutton, Creighton 1970-74, Arkansas 75-85, Kentucky 86-89, Oklahoma St. 91-2002
976	Hugh Durham, Florida St. 1967-78, Georgia 79-95, Jacksonville 98-2002
928	John Chaney, Cheyney 1973-82, Temple 83-2002
910	Jim Calhoun, Northeastern 1973-86, Connecticut 87-2002
898	Lute Olson, Long Beach St. 1974, Iowa 75-83, Arizona 84-2002
888	Davey L. Whitney, Texas Southern 1965-69, Alcorn St. 70-89, 97-2002
876	Rollie Massimino, Stony Brook 1970-71, Villanova 74-92, UNLV 93-94, Cleveland St. 97-2002
864	Mike Krzyzewski, Army 1976-80, Duke 81-2002
845	Don DeVoe, Virginia Tech 1972-76, Wyoming 77-78, Tennessee 79-89, Florida 90, Navy 93-2002
844	Jim Boeheim, Syracuse 1977-2002
830	Ben Jobe, Talladega 1965-67, Alabama St. 68, South Carolina St. 69-73, Denver 79-80, Alabama A&M 83-86, Tuskegee 97-2000, Southern U. 1987-96, 2002
826	Dave Bliss, Oklahoma 1976-80, Southern Methodist 81-88, New Mexico 89-99, Baylor 2000-02
809	Cliff Ellis, South Ala. 1976-84, Clemson 85-94, Auburn 95-2002
756	Ben Braun, Siena Heights 1978-85, Eastern Mich. 86-96, California 97-2002
752	Gary Williams, American 1979-82, Boston College 83-86, Ohio St. 87-89, Maryland 91-2002
748	Gene Keady, Western Ky. 1979-80, Purdue 81-2002

MOST SEASONS

No.	Coach, Team and Seasons
48	James Phelan, Mt. St. Mary's 1955-2002
40	Lefty Driesell, Davidson 1961-69, Maryland 70-86, James Madison 89-97, Georgia St. 98-2002
38	Lou Henson, Hardin-Simmons 1963-66, Illinois 76-96, New Mexico St. 67-75, 99-2002
36	Bob Knight, Army 1966-71, Indiana 72-2000, Texas Tech 02
34	Hugh Durham, Florida St. 1967-78, Georgia 79-95, Jacksonville 99-2002
32	Eddie Sutton, Creighton 1970-74, Arkansas 75-85, Kentucky 86-89, Oklahoma St. 91-2002
31	Davey L. Whitney, Texas Southern 1965-69, Alcorn St. 70-89, 97-2002
30	Jim Calhoun, Northeastern 1973-86, Connecticut 87-2002
30	John Chaney, Cheyney 1973-82, Temple 83-2002
30	Ben Jobe, Talladega 1965-67, Alabama St. 68, South Carolina St. 69-73, Denver 79-80, Alabama A&M 83-86, Tuskegee 97-2000, Southern U. 1987-96, 2002
29	Don DeVoe, Virginia Tech 1972-76, Wyoming 77-78, Tennessee 79-89, Florida 90, Navy 93-2002
29	Rollie Massimino, Stony Brook 1970-71, Villanova 74-92, UNLV 93-94, Cleveland St. 97-2002
29	Lute Olson, Long Beach St. 1974, Iowa 75-83, Arizona 84-2002
27	Dave Bliss, Oklahoma 1976-80, Southern Methodist 81-88, New Mexico 89-99, Baylor 2000-02
27	Cliff Ellis, South Ala. 1976-84, Clemson 85-94, Auburn 95-2002
27	Mike Krzyzewski, Army 1976-80, Duke 81-2002
26	Jim Boeheim, Syracuse 1977-2002
25	Ben Braun, Siena Heights 1978-85, Eastern Mich. 86-96, California 97-2002
25	Nick Macarchuk, Canisius 1978-87, Fordham 88-99, Stony Brook 2000-02
24	Gene Keady, Western Ky. 1979-80, Purdue 81-2002
24	Billy Lee, UNC Pembroke 1979-85, Campbell 86-2002
24	Mike Montgomery, Montana 1979-86, Stanford 87-2002
24	Gary Williams, American 1979-82, Boston College 83-86, Ohio St. 87-89, Maryland 91-2002

MOST SEASONS WITH CURRENT SCHOOL

No.	Coach, Team and Seasons
48	James Phelan, #Mt. St. Mary's 1955-2002
30	Jerry Steele, High Point 1973-2002 (fewer than 5 DI)

COACHING RECORDS

No.	Coach, Team and Seasons
26	Jim Boeheim, #Syracuse 1977-2002
26	Davey L. Whitney, Alcorn St. 1970-89, 97-2002
24	Dave Bike, #Sacred Heart 1979-2002 (fewer than 5 DI)
22	Gene Keady, Purdue 1981-2002
22	Mike Krzyzewski, Duke 1981-2002
22	Rick Samuels, #Eastern Ill. 1981-2002
21	Mike Vining, #La.-Monroe 1982-2002
20	John Chaney, Temple 1983-2002
20	Don Meastri, #Troy St. 1983-2002
19	Tom Green, #Fairleigh Dickinson 1984-2002
19	Lute Olson, Arizona 1984-2002
19	Lafayette Stribling, #Mississippi Val. 1984-2002
18	Greg Kampe, #Oakland 1985-2002 (fewer than 5 DI)
17	Jim Crews, #Evansville 1986-2002
17	Billy Lee, Campbell 1986-2002
16	Tom Brennan, Vermont 87-2002
16	Rick Byrd, Belmont 87-2002 (fewer than 5 DI)
16	Jim Calhoun, Connecticut 87-2002
16	Dave Magarity, Marist 1987-2002
16	Ron Mitchell, #Coppin St. 1987-2002
16	Mike Montgomery, Stanford 1987-2002
16	L. Vann Pettaway, #Alabama A&M 1987-2002 (fewer than 5 DI)

#has coached only at this school

MOST DIVISION I 20-WIN SEASONS

No.	Coach, Team and Seasons
24	Jim Boeheim, Syracuse 1977-2002
24	Bob Knight, Army 1966-71, Indiana 72-2000, Texas Tech 02
24	Lute Olson, Long Beach St. 1974, Iowa 75-83, Arizona 84-2002
22	Lefty Driesell, Davidson 1961-69, Maryland 70-86, James Madison 89-97, Georgia St. 98-2002
22	Eddie Sutton, Creighton 1970-74, Arkansas 75-85, Kentucky 86-89, Oklahoma St. 91-2002
19	Lou Henson, Hardin-Simmons 1963, 65-66, Illinois 76-96, New Mexico St. 67-75, 99-2002
19	Mike Krzyzewski, Army 1976-80, Duke 81-2002
17	Jim Calhoun, Northeastern 1973-86, Connecticut 87-2002
16	Bob Huggins, Akron 85-89, Cincinnati 90-2002
15	John Chaney, Temple 83-2002
15	Jim Harrick, Pepperdine 1980-88, UCLA 1989-96, Rhode Island 98-99, Georgia 2000-02
15	Mike Montgomery, Montana 1979-86, Stanford 87-2002
14	Dave Bliss, Oklahoma 1976-80, Southern Methodist 81-88, New Mexico 89-99, Baylor 2000-02
14	Gene Keady, Western Ky. 1979-80, Purdue 81-2002
13	Gary Williams, American 1979-82, Boston College 83-86, Ohio St. 87-89, Maryland 91-2002
13	Roy Williams, Kansas 1989-2002
12	Don DeVoe, Virginia Tech 1972-76, Wyoming 77-78, Tennessee 79-89, Florida 90, Navy 93-2002
12	Rick Majerus, Marquette 1984-86, Ball St. 88-89, Utah 90-2002
11	Danny Nee, Ohio 1981-86, Nebraska 87-2000, Robert Morris 01, Duquesne 02
11	Charles Spoonhour, Southwest Mo. St. 1984-92, St. Louis 93-99, UNLV 2002

MOST TEAMS

No.	Coach, Team and Seasons
7	Ben Jobe, Talladega 1965-67, Alabama St. 68, South Carolina St. 69-73, Denver 79-80, Alabama A&M 83-86, Tuskegee 97-2000, Southern U. 1987-96, 2002
5	John Beilein, Nazareth 1983, Le Moyne 84-92, Canisius 93-97, Richmond 99-2002, West Virginia
5	Don DeVoe, Virginia Tech 1972-76, Wyoming 77-78, Tennessee 79-89, Florida 90, Navy 93-2002
4	Steve Aggers, Great Falls 1980-85, Wayne St. (Neb.) 86-90, Eastern Wash. 96-2000, Loyola Marymount 01-02
4	Rick Barnes, George Mason 1988, Providence 89-94, Clemson 95-98, Texas 99-2002
4	Dave Bliss, Oklahoma 1976-80, Southern Methodist 81-88, New Mexico 89-99, Baylor 2002
4	Mike Deane, Oswego St. 1981-82, Siena 87-94, Marquette 95-99, Lamar 2000-02
4	Lefty Driesell, Davidson 1961-69, Maryland 70-86, James Madison 89-97, Georgia St. 98-2002
4	Gary Garner, Mo. Southern St. 1977, Drake 82-88, Fort Hays St. 92-97, Southeast Mo. St. 98-2002
4	Jim Harrick, Pepperdine 1980-88, UCLA 1989-96, Rhode Island 98-99, Georgia 2000-02
4	Pat Kennedy, Iona 1981-86, Florida St. 87-97, DePaul 99-2002, Montana
4	Rollie Massimino, Stony Brook 1970-71, Villanova 74-92, UNLV 93-94, Cleveland St. 97-2002
4	Ritchie McKay, Portland St. 1997-98, Colorado St. 99-2000, Oregon St. 01-02, New Mexico
4	Danny Nee, Ohio 1981-86, Nebraska 87-2000, Robert Morris 01, Duquesne 02

No.	Coach, Team and Seasons
4	Rick Pitino, Boston U. 1979-83, Providence 86-87, Kentucky 90-97, Louisville 2002
4	Brad Soderberg, Loras 1989-93, South Dakota St. 94-95, Wisconsin 2001, St. Louis
4	Eddie Sutton, Creighton 1970-74, Arkansas 75-85, Kentucky 86-89, Oklahoma St. 91-2002
4	Jan van Breda Kolff, Cornell 1992-93, Vanderbilt 94-99, Pepperdine 2000-01, St. Bonaventure 02
4	Gary Williams, American 1979-82, Boston College 83-86, Ohio St. 87-89, Maryland 91-2002
4	Rich Zvosec, St. Francis (N.Y.) 1989-91, North Fla. 93-97, Millersville 98, UMKC 2002

All-Time Coaching Longevity Records

(Minimum 10 years as a Division I head coach)

MOST GAMES

No.	Coach, Team and Seasons
1,327	James Phelan, Mt. St. Mary's 1955-2002*
1,170	Lefty Driesell, Davidson 1961-69, Maryland 70-86, James Madison 89-97, Georgia St. 98-2002*
1,133	Dean Smith, North Carolina 1962-97
1,119	Lou Henson, Hardin-Simmons 1963-66, Illinois 76-96, New Mexico St. 67-75, 99-2002*
1,106	Norm Stewart, Northern Iowa 1962-67, Missouri 68-99
1,105	Henry Iba, Northwest Mo. St. 1930-33, Colorado 34, Oklahoma St. 35-70
1,090	Marv Harshman, Pacific Lutheran 1946-58, Washington St. 59-71, Washington 72-85
1,085	Bob Knight, Army 1966-71, Indiana 72-2000, Texas Tech 02*
1,078	Ray Meyer, DePaul 1943-84
1,072	Don Haskins, UTEP 1962-99
1,066	Adolph Rupp, Kentucky 1931-72
1,061	Ed Diddle, Western Ky. 1923-64
1,039	Ralph Miller, Wichita St. 1952-64, Iowa 65-70, Oregon St. 71-89
1,017	Norm Sloan, Presbyterian 1952-55, Citadel 57-60, Florida 61-66, North Carolina St. 67-80, Florida 81-89
1,010	Phog Allen, Baker 1906-08, Kansas 08-09, Haskell 09, Central Mo. St. 13-19, Kansas 20-56
1,000	Gene Bartow, Central Mo. St. 1962-64, Valparaiso 65-70, Memphis 71-74, Illinois 75, UCLA 76-77, UAB 79-96
991	Slats Gill, Oregon St. 1929-64
987	Eldon Miller, Wittenberg 1963-70, Western Mich. 71-76, Ohio St. 77-86, Northern Iowa 87-98
987	Glenn Wilkes, Stetson 1958-93
980	Eddie Sutton, Creighton 1970-74, Arkansas 75-85, Kentucky 86-89, Oklahoma St. 1991-2002*
980	Jerry Tarkanian, Long Beach St. 1969-73, UNLV 74-92, Fresno St. 96-2002

*active

MOST SEASONS

No.	Coach, Team and Seasons
48	Phog Allen, Baker 1906-08, Kansas 08-09, Haskell 09, Central Mo. St. 13-19, Kansas 20-56
48	James Phelan, Mt. St. Mary's 1955-2002*
42	Ed Diddle, Western Ky. 23-64
42	Ray Meyer, DePaul 1943-84
41	Tony Hinkle, Butler 1927-42, 46-70
41	Henry Iba, Northwest Mo. St. 1930-33, Colorado 34, Oklahoma St. 35-70
41	Adolph Rupp, Kentucky 1931-72
40	Lefty Driesell, Davidson 1961-69, Maryland 70-86, James Madison 89-97, Georgia St. 98-2002*
40	Marv Harshman, Pacific Lutheran 1946-58, Washington St. 59-71, Washington 72-85
38	Fred Enke, Louisville 1924-25, Arizona 26-61
38	Don Haskins, UTEP 1962-99
38	Lou Henson, Hardin-Simmons 1963-66, Illinois 76-96, New Mexico St. 67-75, 99-2002*
38	Calvin Luther, DePauw 1955-58, Murray St. 59-73, Longwood 82-90, Tenn.-Martin 91-99
38	Ralph Miller, Wichita St. 1952-64, Iowa 65-70, Oregon St. 71-89
38	Norm Stewart, Northern Iowa 1962-67, Missouri 68-99
37	Nat Holman, CCNY 1920-52 and 55-56 and 59-60
37	Norm Sloan, Presbyterian 1952-55, Citadel 57-60, Florida 61-66, North Carolina St. 67-80, Florida 81-89
36	Slats Gill, Oregon St. 1929-64
36	Bob Knight, Army 1966-71, Indiana 72-2000, Texas Tech 02*
36	Eldon Miller, Wittenberg 1963-70, Western Mich. 71-76, Ohio St. 77-86, Northern Iowa 87-98
36	William Reinhart, Oregon 1924-35, George Washington 36-42 and 50-66
36	Dean Smith, North Carolina 1962-97
36	Glenn Wilkes, Stetson 1958-93

*active

MOST SEASONS AT ONE SCHOOL

No.	Coach, Team and Seasons
48	James Phelan, Mt. St. Mary's 1955-2002*
42	Ed Diddle, #Western Ky. 1923-64
42	Ray Meyer, #DePaul 1943-84
41	Tony Hinkle, #Butler 1927-42, 46-70
41	Adolph Rupp, #Kentucky 1931-72
39	Phog Allen, Kansas 1908-09 and 20-56
38	Don Haskins, #UTEP 1962-99
37	Nat Holman, #CCNY 1920-52 and 55-56 and 59-60
36	Fred Enke, Arizona 1926-61
36	Slats Gill, #Oregon St. 1929-64
36	Henry Iba, Oklahoma St. 1935-70
36	Dean Smith, #North Carolina 1962-97
36	Glenn Wilkes, #Stetson 1958-93
32	Norm Stewart, Missouri 1968-99
31	Taps Gallagher, #Niagara 1932-43 and 47-65
31	Cy McClairen, #Bethune-Cookman 1962-66 and 68-93
30	Denny Crum, #Louisville 1972-2001
30	Jack Friel, #Washington St. 1929-58
30	Guy Lewis, #Houston 1957-86
30	Nibs Price, #California 1925-54
29	Pete Carril, Princeton 1968-96
29	Denny Crum, #Louisville 1972-2000*
29	Bob Knight, Indiana 1972-00
29	Piggy Lambert, #Purdue 1917 and 19-46
29	Harry Rabenhorst, #LSU 1926-42 and 46-57
28	Frank Keaney, #Rhode Island 1921-48

*active; #has coached only at this school

MOST DIVISION I 20-WIN SEASONS

No.	Coach, Team and Seasons
30	Dean Smith, North Carolina 1962-97
29	Jerry Tarkanian, Long Beach St. 1969-73, UNLV 74-92, Fresno St. 96-2002*
24	Jim Boeheim, Syracuse 1977-2002*
24	Bob Knight, Army 1966-71, Indiana 72-2000, Texas Tech 02*
24	Lute Olson, Long Beach St. 1974, Iowa 75-83, Arizona 84-2002*
23	Adolph Rupp, Kentucky 1931-72
22	Lefty Driesell, Davidson 1961-69, Maryland 70-86, James Madison 89-97, Georgia St. 98-2002*
22	Eddie Sutton, Creighton 1970-74, Arkansas 75-85, Kentucky 86-89, Oklahoma St. 1991-2002*
21	Denny Crum, Louisville 1972-2001
19	Lou Henson, Hardin-Simmons 1963, 65-66, Illinois 76-96, New Mexico St. 67-75, 99-2002*
19	Mike Krzyzewski, Army 1976-80, Duke 81-2002*
19	John Thompson, Georgetown 1973-99
18	Lou Carnesecca, St. John's (N.Y.) 1966-70 and 74-92
18	Ed Diddle, Western Ky. 1923-64
18	Don Haskins, UTEP 1962-99
18	Henry Iba, Northwest Mo. St. 1930-33, Colorado 34, Okla. St. 35-70
18	Norm Stewart, Northern Iowa 1962-67, Missouri 68-99

No.	Coach, Team and Seasons
18	Billy Tubbs, Lamar 77-80, Oklahoma 81-94, TCU 95-2002*
18	John Wooden, Indiana St. 1947-48, UCLA 49-75
17	Jim Calhoun, Northeastern 1973-86, Connecticut 87-2002*

*active

MOST TEAMS

No.	Coach, Team and Seasons
7	Ben Jobe, Talladega 1965-67, Alabama St. 68, South Carolina St. 69-73, Denver 79-80, Alabama A&M 83-86, Tuskegee 97-2000, Southern U. 1987-96, 2002*
7	Elmer Ripley, Wagner 1923-25, Georgetown 28-29, 39-43 and 47-49, Yale 30-35, Columbia 44-45, Notre Dame 46, John Carroll 50-51, Army 52-53
7	Bob Vanatta, Central Methodist 1943 and 48-50, Southwest Mo. St. 51-53, Army 54, Bradley 55-56, Memphis 57-62, Missouri 63-67, Delta St. 73
6	J.D. Barnett, Lenoir Rhyne 1970, High Point 71, Louisiana Tech 78-79, Va. Commonwealth 80-85, Tulsa 86-91, Northwestern St. 95-99
6	Gene Bartow, Central Mo. St. 1962-64, Valparaiso 65-70, Memphis 71-74, Illinois 75, UCLA 76-77, UAB 79-96
6	Bill E. Foster, Bloomsburg 1961-63, Rutgers 64-71, Utah 72-74, Duke 75-80, South Carolina 81-86, Northwestern 87-93
6	Robert Hopkins, Prairie View 1965, Alcorn St. 67-69, Xavier (La.) 70-74, Southern U. 85-86, Grambling 87-89, Md.-East. Shore 91-92
6	Press Maravich, West Va. Wesleyan 1950, Davis & Elkins 51-52; Clemson 57-62, North Carolina St. 65-66, LSU 1967-72, Appalachian St. 73-75
6	Harry Miller, Western St. 1953-58, Fresno St. 61-65, Eastern N.M. 66-70, North Texas 71, Wichita St. 72-78, Stephen F. Austin 79-88
6	Tom Penders, Tufts 1972-74, Columbia 75-78, Fordham 79-86, Rhode Island 87-88, Texas 89-98, George Washington 99-2001
6	Hal Wissel, Col. of New Jersey 1965-67, Lafayette 68-71, Fordham 72-76, Fla. Southern 78-82, Charlotte 83-85, Springfield 87-90
5	John Beilein, Nazareth 1983, Le Moyne 84-92, Canisius 93-97, Richmond 99-2002, West Virginia*
5	Ozzie Cowles, Carleton 1925-30, Wis.-River Falls 34-36, Dartmouth 37-43 and 45-46, Michigan 47-48, Minnesota 49-59
5	Don DeVoe, Virginia Tech 1972-76, Wyoming 77-78, Tennessee 79-89, Florida 90, Navy 93-2002*
5	Bill C. Foster, Shorter 1963-67, Charlotte 71-75, Clemson 76-84, Miami (Fla.) 86-90, Virginia Tech 92-97
5	Ron Greene, Loyola (La.) 1968-69, New Orleans 70-77, Mississippi St. 78, Murray St. 79-85, Indiana St. 86-89
5	Blair Gullion, Earlham 1928-35, Tennessee 36-38, Cornell 39-42, Connecticut 46-47, Washington (Mo.) 48-59
5	Tates Locke, Army 1964-65, Miami (Ohio) 67-70, Clemson 71-75, Jacksonville 79-81, Indiana St. 91-94
5	John Mauer, Kentucky 1928-30, Miami (Ohio) 31-38, Tennessee 39-47, Army 48-51, Florida 52-60
5	Gordon Stauffer, Washburn 1967, Indiana St. 68-75, IPFW 76-79, Geneva 80-81, Nicholls 82-90
5	Tex Winter, Marquette 1952-53, Kansas St. 54-68, Washington 69-71, Northwestern 74-78, Long Beach St. 79-83

*active

Division I Head Coaching Changes

Year	Teams	Chngs.	Pct.	1st Yr.	Year	Teams	Chngs.	Pct.	1st Yr.
1950	145	22	15.2	11	1961	173	15	8.7	11
1951	153	28	18.3	15	1962	178	15	8.4	14
1952	156	23	14.7	18	1963	178	24	13.5	15
1953	158	20	12.7	13	1964	179	23	12.8	17
1954	160	12	7.5	7	1965	182	15	8.2	8
1955	162	21	13.0	9	1966	182	24	13.2	20
1956	166	18	10.8	12	1967	185	33	17.8	18
1957	167	18	10.8	9	1968	189	26	13.8	16
1958	173	14	8.1	8	1969	193	29	15.0	19
1959	174	20	11.5	10	1970	196	29	14.8	17
1960	175	23	13.1	15	1971	203	30	14.8	17

Year	Teams	Chngs.	Pct.	1st Yr.	Year	Teams	Chngs.	Pct.	1st Yr.
1972	210	37	17.6	21	1988	290	39	13.4	16
1973	216	38	17.6	24	1989	293	42	14.3	24
1974	233	41	17.6	23	1990	292	54	18.5	29
1975	235	44	18.7	30	1991	295	41	13.9	16
1976	235	34	14.5	20	1992	298	39	13.1	15
1977	245	39	15.9	21	1993	298	34	11.4	15
1978	254	39	15.4	24	1994	301	33	11.0	17
1979	257	53	20.6	28	1995	302	58	19.2	28
1980	261	43	16.5	23	1996	305	42	13.8	31
1981	264	42	15.9	21	1997	305	52	17.0	29
1982	273	37	13.6	20	1998	306	63	20.6	31
1983	274	37	13.5	18	1999	310	45	14.5	30
1984	276	38	13.8	21	2000	318	55	17.3	27
1985	282	26	9.2	15	2001	318	53	16.7	31
1986	283	56	19.8	21	2002	321	47	14.6	22
1987	290	66	22.8	35					

COACHING RECORDS

Division I Coach of the Year

Season	United Press International	The Associated Press	U.S. Basketball Writers Assn.	National Assn. of Basketball Coaches	Naismith	The Sporting News	CBS/Chevrolet
1955	Phil Woolpert, San Francisco						
1956	Phil Woolpert, San Francisco						
1957	Frank McGuire, North Carolina						
1958	Tex Winter, Kansas St.						
1959	Adolph Rupp, Kentucky		Eddie Hickey, Marquette				
1960	Pete Newell, California		Pete Newell, California				
1961	Fred Taylor, Ohio St.		Fred Taylor, Ohio St.				
1962	Fred Taylor, Ohio St.		Fred Taylor, Ohio St.				
1963	Ed Jucker, Cincinnati		Ed Jucker, Cincinnati				
1964	John Wooden, UCLA		John Wooden, UCLA			John Wooden, UCLA	
1965	Dave Strack, Michigan		Bill van Breda Kolff, Princeton				
1966	Adolph Rupp, Kentucky		Adolph Rupp, Kentucky			Adolph Rupp, Kentucky	
1967	John Wooden, UCLA	John Wooden, UCLA	John Wooden, UCLA			Jack Hartman, Southern Ill.	
1968	Guy Lewis, Houston	Guy Lewis, Houston	Guy Lewis, Houston			Guy Lewis, Houston	
1969	John Wooden, UCLA	John Wooden, UCLA	Maury John, Drake	John Wooden, UCLA		John Wooden, UCLA	
1970	John Wooden, UCLA	John Wooden, UCLA	John Wooden, UCLA	John Wooden, UCLA		Adolph Rupp, Kentucky	
1971	Al McGuire, Marquette	Al McGuire, Marquette	Al McGuire, Marquette	Jack Kraft, Villanova		Al McGuire, Marquette	
1972	John Wooden, UCLA	John Wooden, UCLA	John Wooden, UCLA	John Wooden, UCLA		John Wooden, UCLA	
1973	John Wooden, UCLA	John Wooden, UCLA	John Wooden, UCLA	Gene Bartow, Memphis		John Wooden, UCLA	
1974	Digger Phelps, Notre Dame	Norm Sloan, North Carolina St.	Norm Sloan, North Carolina St.	Al McGuire, Marquette		Digger Phelps, Notre Dame	
1975	Bob Knight, Indiana	Bob Knight, Indiana	Bob Knight, Indiana	Bob Knight, Indiana		Bob Knight, Indiana	
1976	Tom Young, Rutgers	Bob Knight, Indiana	Bob Knight, Indiana	Johnny Orr, Michigan		Tom Young, Rutgers	
1977	Bob Gaillard, San Francisco	Bob Gaillard, San Francisco	Eddie Sutton, Arkansas	Dean Smith, North Carolina		Lee Rose, Charlotte	
1978	Eddie Sutton, Arkansas	Eddie Sutton, Arkansas	Ray Meyer, DePaul	Bill Foster, Duke; Abe Lemons, Texas		Bill Foster, Duke	
1979	Bill Hodges, Indiana St.	Bill Hodges, Indiana St.	Dean Smith, North Carolina	Ray Meyer, DePaul		Bill Hodges, Indiana St.	
1980	Ray Meyer, DePaul	Ray Meyer, DePaul	Ray Meyer, DePaul	Lute Olson, Iowa		Lute Olson, Iowa	
1981	Ralph Miller, Oregon St.	Ralph Miller, Oregon St.	Ralph Miller, Oregon St.	Ralph Miller, Oregon St.; Jack Hartman, Kansas St.		Dale Brown, LSU	Dale Brown, LSU
1982	Norm Stewart, Missouri	Ralph Miller, Oregon St.	John Thompson, Georgetown	Don Monson, Idaho		Ralph Miller, Oregon St.	Gene Keady, Purdue
1983	Jerry Tarkanian, UNLV	Guy Lewis, Houston	Lou Carnesecca, St. John's (N.Y.)	Lou Carnesecca, St. John's (N.Y.)		Denny Crum, Louisville	Lou Carnesecca, St. John's (N.Y)
1984	Ray Meyer, DePaul	Ray Meyer, DePaul	Gene Keady, Purdue	Marv Harshman, Washington		John Thompson, Georgetown	Gene Keady, Purdue
1985	Lou Carnesecca, St. John's (N.Y.)	Bill Frieder, Michigan	Lou Carnesecca, St. John's (N.Y.)	John Thompson, Georgetown		Lou Carnesecca, St. John's (N.Y.)	Dale Brown, LSU
1986	Mike Krzyzewski, Duke	Eddie Sutton, Kentucky	Dick Versace, Bradley	Eddie Sutton, Kentucky		Denny Crum, Louisville	Mike Krzyzewski, Duke
1987	John Thompson, Georgetown	Tom Davis, Iowa	John Chaney, Temple	Rick Pitino, Providence	Bob Knight, Indiana	Rick Pitino, Providence	Joey Meyer, DePaul
1988	John Chaney, Temple	John Chaney, Temple	John Chaney, Temple	John Chaney, Temple	Larry Brown, Kansas	John Chaney, Temple	John Chaney, Temple
1989	Bob Knight, Indiana	Bob Knight, Indiana	Bob Knight, Indiana	P.J. Carlesimo, Seton Hall	Mike Krzyzewski, Duke	P.J. Carlesimo, Seton Hall	Lute Olson, Arizona
1990	Jim Calhoun, Connecticut	Jim Calhoun, Connecticut	Roy Williams, Kansas	Jud Heathcote, Michigan St.	Bobby Cremins, Georgia Tech	Jim Calhoun, Connecticut	Jim Calhoun, Connecticut

Season	United Press International	The Associated Press	U.S. Basketball Writers Assn.	National Assn. of Basketball Coaches	Naismith	The Sporting News	CBS/Chevrolet
1991	Rick Majerus Utah	Randy Ayers Ohio St.	Randy Ayers Ohio St.	Mike Krzyzewski Duke	Randy Ayers Ohio St.	Rick Pitino Kentucky	Randy Ayers Ohio St.
1992	Perry Clark Tulane	Roy Williams Kansas	Perry Clark Tulane	George Raveling Southern California	Mike Krzyzewski Duke	Mike Krzyzewski Duke	George Raveling Southern California
1993	Eddie Fogler Vanderbilt	Eddie Fogler Vanderbilt	Eddie Fogler Vanderbilt	Eddie Fogler Vanderbilt	Dean Smith North Carolina	Eddie Fogler Vanderbilt	Eddie Fogler Vanderbilt
1994	Norm Stewart Missouri	Norm Stewart Missouri	Charlie Spoonhour St. Louis	Nolan Richardson Arkansas Gene Keady Purdue	Nolan Richardson Arkansas	Norm Stewart Missouri	Nolan Richardson Arkansas
1995	Leonard Hamilton Miami (Fla.)	Kelvin Sampson Oklahoma	Kelvin Sampson Oklahoma	Jim Harrick UCLA	Jim Harrick UCLA	Jud Heathcote Michigan St.	Gene Keady Purdue
1996	Gene Keady Purdue	Gene Keady Purdue	Gene Keady Purdue	John Calipari Massachusetts	John Calipari Massachusetts	John Calipari Massachusetts	Gene Keady Purdue
1997		Clem Haskins Minnesota	Clem Haskins Minnesota	Clem Haskins Minnesota	Roy Williams Kansas	Roy Williams Kansas	Clem Haskins Minnesota
1998		Tom Izzo Michigan St.	Tom Izzo Michigan St.	Bill Guthridge North Carolina	Bill Guthridge North Carolina	Bill Guthridge North Carolina	Bill Guthridge North Carolina
1999		Cliff Ellis Auburn	Cliff Ellis Auburn	Mike Krzyzewski Duke	Mike Krzyzewski Duke	Cliff Ellis Auburn	Cliff Ellis Auburn
2000		Larry Eustachy Iowa St.	Larry Eustachy Iowa St.	Gene Keady Purdue	Mike Montgomery Stanford	Bob Huggins Cincinnati Bill Self Tulsa	Mike Krzyzewski Duke
2001		Matt Doherty North Carolina	Al Skinner Boston College	Tom Izzo Michigan St.	Rod Barnes Mississippi	Al Skinner Boston College	Al Skinner Boston College
2002		Ben Howland Pittsburgh	Bob Howland Pittsburgh	Kelvin Sampson Oklahoma	Ben Howland Pittsburgh	Ben Howland Pittsburgh	Kelvin Sampson Oklahoma

Basketball Times Coach of the Year: 1982-Gale Catlett, West Virginia; 1983-Lou Carnesecca, St. John's (N.Y.); 1984-Jerry Tarkanian, UNLV; 1985-Bobby Cremins, Georgia Tech; 1986-Mike Krzyzewski, Duke; 1987-Wimp Sanderson, Alabama; 1988-Lute Olson, Arizona; 1989-Bob Knight, Indiana; 1990-Rick Pitino, Kentucky; 1991-Rick Majerus, Utah; 1992-Steve Fisher, Michigan; 1993-Dean Smith, North Carolina; 1994-Norm Stewart, Missouri; 1995-Eddie Sutton, Oklahoma St.; 1996-John Calipari, Massachusetts; 1997-Mike Krzyzewski, Duke; 1998-Bob Huggins, Cincinnati; 1999-Tom Izzo, Michigan St.; 2000-Mike Montgomery, Stanford; 2001-Al Skinner, Boston College; 2002-Bob Knight, Texas Tech.

Legends of Coaching Award: 1999-Dean Smith, North Carolina; 2000-Mike Krzyzewski, Duke; 2001-Lute Olson, Arizona; 2002-Denny Crum, Louisville.

COACHING RECORDS

Oklahoma coach Kelvin Sampson collected coach of the year honors from two different organizations for leading the Sooners to the Final Four.

Division II Coaching Records

Winningest Active Coaches

(Minimum five years as a head coach; includes record at four-year colleges only.)

BY PERCENTAGE

Coach, Team	Years	Won	Lost	Pct.
1. Ray Harper, Ky. Wesleyan	6	179	22	.891
2. Dave Robbins, Virginia Union	24	565	156	.784
3. Gordon Gibbons, Clayton St.	11	265	74	.782
4. Scott Nagy, South Dakota St.	7	159	45	.779
5. Jayson Gee, Charleston (W.Va.)	6	139	45	.755
6. Henry Clark, Cal St. Bakersfield	5	104	36	.743
7. Bob Chipman, Washburn	23	533	186	.741
8. Brian Beaury, St. Rose	16	366	132	.735
9. Herb Magee, Philadelphia	35	730	277	.725
10. Mike Dunlap, Metro St.	10	218	83	.724
11. Rick Cooper, West Tex. A&M	15	330	128	.721
12. Butch Haswell, Fairmont St.	9	189	74	.719
13. Richard Schmidt, Tampa	21	445	178	.714
14. Stan Spirou, Southern N.H.	17	362	150	.707
15. Tom Kropp, Neb.-Kearney	12	245	105	.700
16. Dave Boots, South Dakota	20	390	170	.696
17. Jim Baker, Catawba	8	155	71	.686
18. Ed Douma, Hillsdale	27	490	230	.681
19. Jerry Johnson, LeMoyne-Owen	44	798	386	.674
20. Kevin Schlagel, St. Cloud St.	5	95	46	.674
21. Brett Vincent, Alderson-Broaddus	6	114	57	.667
22. Steve Rives, Delta St.	17	322	163	.664
23. Craig Carse, Mont. St.-Billings	11	209	106	.664
24. Tom O'Shea, St. Michael's	5	99	51	.660
25. Greg Walcavich, Edinboro	21	390	201	.660
26. Keith Dickson, St. Anselm	16	314	162	.660
27. Gary Stanfield, Drury	11	204	106	.658
28. Kevin Luke, Michigan Tech	8	151	81	.651
29. Dick DeLaney, West Chester	15	269	145	.650
30. Jerry Slocum, Gannon	27	520	284	.647
31. Steve Tappmeyer, Northwest Mo. St.	14	256	140	.647
32. Lonn Reisman, Tarleton St.	14	264	146	.644
33. Art Luptowski, American Int'l	13	242	134	.644
34. Tom Galeazzi, C.W. Post	21	389	216	.643
35. Ken Shields, Northern Ky.	14	265	149	.640
36. Jim Heaps, Mesa St.	6	105	60	.636
37. Herbert Greene, Columbus St.	23	415	238	.636
38. Terry Sellers, GC&SU	9	159	93	.631
39. Rich Glas, North Dakota	24	423	251	.628
40. Charlie Bruns, Alas. Anchorage	9	154	94	.621
41. Tim Miles, North Dakota St.	7	124	76	.620
42. Stephen Joyner, Johnson Smith	15	267	165	.618
43. Gary Tuell, Augusta St.	15	280	177	.613
44. Ron Spry, Paine	22	415	265	.610
45. Barry Hamler, Elizabeth City St.	7	117	75	.609
46. Jim Harter, Pace	5	78	50	.609
47. Tom Smith, Mo. Western St.	27	467	303	.607
48. Ed Murphy, West Ga.	23	397	259	.605
49. Ron Righter, Clarion	16	254	167	.603
50. Andy Russo, Lynn	20	344	227	.603
51. Joe Folda, Southern Colo.	18	307	204	.601
52. Leighton McCrary, Grand Canyon	12	204	136	.600
53. Jay Lawson, Bentley	11	186	124	.600
54. Roger Lyons, Ashland	9	148	99	.599
55. Tom Klusman, Rollins	22	367	246	.599
56. Chipper Bagwell, Lander	5	86	58	.597
57. Lonnie Porter, Regis (Colo.)	25	415	280	.597
58. Bill Brown, Calif. (Pa.)	16	252	171	.596
59. Jeff Morgan, Harding	10	163	114	.588
60. Gregg Nibert, Presbyterian	13	221	155	.588
61. Tom Ryan, Eckerd	6	98	69	.587
62. Gary Elliott, North Ala.	17	274	195	.584
63. Bob Taylor, Northwood	5	80	57	.584
64. Perry Ford, Augustana (S.D.)	17	283	203	.582
65. Gene Iba, Pittsburg St.	22	366	267	.578
66. Dean Ellis, Northern Mich.	16	260	190	.578
67. Don Hogan, West Fla.	9	143	105	.577
68. Gary Edwards, Indiana (Pa.)	18	303	223	.576
69. Griff Mills, Tusculum	11	176	132	.571
70. Dan Schmotzer, Coker	15	228	172	.570

BY VICTORIES

(Minimum five years as a head coach; includes record at four-year colleges only.)

Coach, Team	Years	Won	Lost	Pct.
1. Jerry Johnson, LeMoyne-Owen	44	798	386	.674
2. Herb Magee, Philadelphia	35	730	277	.725
3. Dave Robbins, Virginia Union	24	565	156	.784
4. Bob Chipman, Washburn	23	533	186	.741
5. Jerry Slocum, Gannon	27	520	284	.647
6. Ed Douma, Hillsdale	27	490	230	.681
7. Tom Smith, Mo. Western St.	27	467	303	.607
8. Richard Schmidt, Tampa	21	445	178	.714
9. Oliver Jones, Tuskegee	30	433	394	.524
10. Rich Glas, North Dakota	24	423	251	.628
11. Herbert Greene, Columbus St.	23	415	238	.636
11. Ron Spry, Paine	22	415	265	.610
11. Lonnie Porter, Regis (Colo.)	25	415	280	.597
14. Ed Murphy, West Ga.	23	397	259	.605
15. Dave Boots, South Dakota	20	390	170	.696
15. Greg Walcavich, Edinboro	21	390	201	.660
17. Tom Galeazzi, C.W. Post	21	389	216	.643
18. Dave Yanai, Cal St. Los Angeles	25	382	292	.567
19. Tom Klusman, Rollins	22	367	246	.599
20. Brian Beaury, St. Rose	16	366	132	.735
20. Gene Iba, Pittsburg St.	22	366	267	.578
22. Stan Spirou, Southern N.H.	17	362	150	.707
23. Art Leary, Southern Conn. St.	24	348	333	.511
24. Andy Russo, Lynn	20	344	227	.603
25. Rick Cooper, West Tex. A&M	15	330	128	.721
26. Steve Rives, Delta St.	17	322	163	.664
26. Bert Hammel, Merrimack	22	322	301	.517
28. Keith Dickson, St. Anselm	16	314	162	.660
29. Terry Brown, Bluefield St.	23	308	355	.465
30. Joe Folda, Southern Colo.	18	307	204	.601
31. Gary Edwards, Indiana (Pa.)	18	303	223	.576
32. Tom Wood, Humboldt St.	21	291	285	.505
33. John Lentz, Lenoir-Rhyne	19	285	245	.538
34. Perry Ford, Augustana (S.D.)	17	283	203	.582
35. Gary Tuell, Augusta St.	15	280	177	.613
36. Gary Elliott, North Ala.	17	274	195	.584
37. Dick DeLaney, West Chester	15	269	145	.650
38. Stephen Joyner, Johnson Smith	15	267	165	.618
39. Gordon Gibbons, Clayton St.	11	265	74	.772
39. Ken Shields, Northern Ky.	14	265	149	.640
41. Lonn Reisman, Tarleton St.	14	264	146	.644
42. Dean Ellis, Northern Mich.	16	260	190	.578
43. Karl Fogel, Mercyhurst	18	258	234	.524
44. Steve Tappmeyer, Northwest Mo. St.	14	256	140	.647
45. Ron Righter, Clarion	16	254	167	.603
46. Bill Brown, Calif. (Pa.)	16	252	171	.596
47. Tom Kropp, Neb.-Kearney	12	245	105	.700
48. Art Luptowski, American Int'l	13	242	134	.644
49. Jim Whitesell, Lewis	15	231	179	.563
50. Dan Schmotzer, Coker	15	228	172	.570
51. Rick Reedy, West Ala.	18	226	254	.471
52. Gregg Nibert, Presbyterian	13	221	155	.588
53. Mike Dunlap, Metro St.	10	218	83	.724
54. Prescott Smith, Cal St. Chico	15	211	207	.505
54. Steve Cox, Concord	13	211	168	.557
56. Bob Hofman, Fort Lewis	14	211	182	.537
57. Craig Carse, Mont St.-Billings	11	209	106	.664
58. Al Sokaitis, Alas. Fairbanks	15	208	187	.527
58. Jay DeFruscio, Wheeling Jesuit	13	208	167	.555
58. Dale Clayton, Carson-Newman	14	208	188	.525
61. Tom Ackerman, Assumption	17	206	255	.447
62. Gary Stanfield, Drury	11	204	106	.658
62. Leighton McCrary, Grand Canyon	12	204	136	.600
62. Robert Corn, Mo. Southern St.	13	204	161	.559
65. Bob Rukavina, Pitt.-Johnstown	13	195	152	.562
66. Charlie Miller, West Va. Wesleyan	21	191	317	.376
67. Butch Haswell, Fairmont St.	9	189	74	.719
68. Jay Lawson, Bentley	11	186	124	.600
69. Lennie Acuff, Ala.-Huntsville	11	185	147	.557
69. Dale Martin, Mo.-Rolla	15	185	213	.465

Winningest Coaches All-Time

(Minimum 10 head coaching seasons in Division II)

BY PERCENTAGE

Coach (Team coached, tenure)	Years	Won	Lost	Pct.
1. Walter Harris (Philadelphia 1954-65, 67)	13	240	56	.811
2. Dolph Stanley (Beloit 1946-57)	12	238	56	.810
3. Ed Adams (N.C. Central 1935-36, Tuskegee 37-49, Texas Southern 50-58)	24	645	153	.808
4. Harry Good (Indianapolis 1929-43)	15	194	53	.785
5. Dave Robbins (Virginia Union 1979-02)*	24	565	156	.784
6. Gordon Gibbons (Fla. Southern 1991-00, Clayton St. 2002)*	11	265	74	.782
7. Charles Christian (Norfolk St. 1974-90)	14	318	95	.770
8. John McLendon Jr. (N.C. Central 1941-52, Hampton 53-54, Tennessee St. 55-59, Kentucky St. 64-66, Cleveland St. 67-69)	25	523	165	.760
9. Lucias Mitchell (Alabama St. 1964-67, Kentucky St. 68-75, Norfolk St. 79-81)	15	325	103	.759
10. John Kochan (Millersville 1984-96)	13	285	96	.748
11. Rock Oglesby (Florida A&M 1950-70, 72)	22	386	132	.745
12. Bob Chipman (Washburn 1980-02)*	23	533	186	.741
13. Joe Hutton (Hamline 1931-65)	35	590	208	.739
14. Dean Nicholson (Central Wash. 1965-90)	26	609	219	.736
15. Brian Beaury (St. Rose 1987-02)*	16	366	132	.735
16. Calvin Irvin (Johnson Smith 1948-51, North Caro. A&T 55-72)	22	397	144	.734
17. Garland Pinholster (Oglethorpe 1957-66)	10	180	68	.726
18. Herb Magee (Philadelphia 1968-02)*	35	730	277	.725
19. L. Vann Pettaway (Alabama A&M 1987-02)*	16	345	131	.725
20. Richard Schmidt (Vanderbilt 1980-81, Tampa 84-02)*	21	445	178	.714
21. Ed Jucker (Merchant Marine 1946-47, Rensselaer 49-53, Cincinnati 61-65, Rollins 73-77)	17	266	109	.709
22. Stan Spirou (Southern N.H. 1986-02)*	17	362	150	.707
23. Pat Douglass (Mont. St.-Billings 1982-87, Cal St. Bakersfield 88-97, UC Irvine 99-02)*	21	451	187	.707
24. Al Shields (Bentley 1964-78)	15	257	107	.706
25. Lou D'Allesandro (New Hamp. Col. 1964-75)	10	183	77	.704
26. Bill Boylan (Monmouth 1957-77)	21	368	155	.704
27. Tom Kropp (Neb.-Kearney 1991-02)*	12	245	105	.700
28. Beryl Shipley (La.-Lafayette 1958-73)	16	296	129	.696
29. Dave Boots (Augsburg 1983-88, South Dakota 89-02)*	20	390	170	.696
30. Ernest Hole (Wooster 1927-58)	32	412	181	.695
31. Sam Cozen (Drexel 1953-68)	16	213	94	.694
32. Barney Steen (Calvin 1954-66)	13	189	84	.692
33. Ken Bone (Cal St. Stanislaus 1985, Seattle Pacific 91-02)	13	257	118	.685
34. Robert Rainey [Albany St. (Ga.) 1961-72]	12	243	112	.685
35. Danny Rose (Central Mich. 1938-53)	13	163	76	.682
36. Bill Jones (Florence St. 1973, North Ala. 74, Jacksonville St. 75-98)	26	477	226	.679
37. Jerry Johnson (LeMoyne-Owen 1959-02)*	44	798	386	.674
38. Dale Race (Milton 1975-79, Minn.-Duluth 85-98)	18	363	177	.672
39. Russell Beichly (Akron 1941-59)	19	288	141	.671
40. Jim McDonald (Edinboro 1963-71, 73-75)	12	179	89	.668
41. William Lucas (Central St. 1961-74)	14	241	120	.668
42. Roger Kaiser (West Ga. 1971-90)	20	379	189	.667
43. Fred Hobdy (Grambling 1957-86)	30	571	287	.666
44. Paul Webb (Randolph-Macon 1957-75, Old Dominion 76-85)	29	511	257	.665
45. Ed Martin (South Carolina St. 1956-68, Tennessee St. 69-85)	30	501	253	.664
46. Steve Rives (Louisiana Col. 1986, Delta St. 87-02)*	17	322	163	.664
47. Marlowe Severson (St. Cloud St. 1959-69, Minn. St.-Mankato 70-73)	15	250	127	.663
48. Don Zech (Puget Sound 1969-89)	21	386	197	.662
49. Malcolm Eiken (Buffalo 1947-56)	10	141	72	.662
50. John Masi (UC Riverside 1980-02)*	23	434	222	.662
51. Dave Buss (Wis.-Green Bay 1970-82, Long Beach St. 84, St. Olaf 88-94)	21	381	195	.661
52. Charles Chronister (Bloomsburg 1972-02)	31	559	288	.660
53. Greg Walcavich (Birmingham-So. 1979-83, Rice 87, West Va. Wesleyan 88-89, Edinboro 90-02)*	21	390	201	.660
54. Keith Dickson (St. Anselm 1987-02)*	16	314	162	.660
55. Donald Feeley (Sacred Heart 1966-78, FDU-Florham 81-83)	16	285	148	.658
56. Gary Stanfield (Drury 1992-02)*	11	204	106	.658
57. Michael Bernard (N.C. Central 1986-91, Norfolk St. 92-98, Fayetteville St. 99-02)	17	321	167	.658
58. John Lance (Southwestern Okla. 1919-22, Pittsburg St. 23-63)	45	669	353	.655
59. Boyd King (Truman 1947-71)	25	377	199	.655
60. Ernie Wheeler (Cal Poly 1973-86, Mont. St.-Billings 89-91)	17	314	166	.654
61. Scotty Robertson (Louisiana Tech 1965-74)	10	162	86	.653
62. Jim Wink (Ferris St. 1960-81)	21	337	179	.653
63. Joseph O'Brien (Assumption 1968-85)	18	322	172	.652
64. Ed Steitz (Springfield 1957-66)	10	160	86	.650
65. Dick DeLaney (West Chester 1988-02)*	15	269	145	.650
66. LeRoy Moore (Prairie View 1954-66)	13	191	103	.650

*Active coaches

BY VICTORIES

(Minimum 10 head coaching seasons in Division II)

Coach	Wins
1. Clarence "Big House" Gaines (Winston-Salem 1947-93)	828
2. Jerry Johnson (LeMoyne-Owen 1959-02)*	798
3. Herb Magee (Philadelphia 1968-02)*	730
4. John Lance (Southwestern Okla. 1919-22, Pittsburg St. 23-63)	669
5. Ed Messbarger [Benedictine Heights 1957-60, Dallas 61-63, St. Mary's (Tex.) 63-78, Angelo St. 79-98]	665
6. Ed Adams (N.C. Central 1935-36, Tuskegee 37-49, Texas Southern 50-58)	645
7. Dean Nicholson (Central Wash. 1965-90)	609
8. Dom Rosselli (Youngstown St. 1941-42 & 47-82)	591
9. Joe Hutton (Hamline 1931-65)	590
10. Dan McCarrell, (North Park 1968-84, Minn. St.-Mankato 85-01)	579
11. Fred Hobdy (Grambling 1957-86)	571
12. Dave Robbins (Virginia Union 1979-02)*	565
13. Charles Chronister (Bloomsburg 1972-02)	559
14. Bruce Webster (Bridgeport 1966-99)	549
15. Jim Gudger (Western Caro. 1951-69, Tex. A&M-Commerce 70-83)	547
16. Harry Miller (Western St. 1953-58, Fresno St. 61-65, Eastern N.M. 66-70, North Tex. St. 71, Wichita St. 72-78, Stephen F. Austin St. 79-88)	534
17. Bob Chipman (Washburn 1980-02)*	533
18. John McLendon Jr. (N.C. Central 1941-52, Hampton 53-54, Tennessee St. 55-59, Kentucky St. 64-66, Cleveland St. 67-69)	523
19. Arthur McAfee (Lane 1961, Mississippi Val. 62, Lincoln (Mo.) 63, Bishop 64-65, Morehouse 66-00]	514
19. Arad McCutchan (Evansville 1947-77)	514
21. Paul Webb (Randolph-Macon 1957-75, Old Dominion 76-85)	511
22. Aubrey Bonham (Whittier 1938-43 & 46-68)	510
23. Leo Nicholson (Central Wash. 1930-43 & 46-64)	505
24. Ed Martin (South Carolina St. 1956-68, Tennessee St. 69-85)	501
24. Robert Vaughan (Elizabeth City St. 1952-86)	501
26. Angus Nicoson (Indianapolis 1948-77)	483
27. Bill Jones (Florence St. 1973, North Ala. 74, Jacksonville St. 75-98)	477
28. Dave Gunther [Wayne St. (Neb.) 1968-70, North Dakota 1971-88, Buena Vista 94-95, Bemidji St. 96-01]	476
28. Bill Detrick (Central Conn. St. 1960-88, Coast Guard 90)	476
30. Tom Smith (Central Mo. St. 1976-80, Valparaiso 81-88, Mo. Western St. 89-02)*	467
31. Hamlet Peterson (Luther 1923-65)	465
32. Richard Meckfessel [Charleston (S.C.) 1966-79, Mo.-St. Louis 83-99]	459
32. Burt Kahn (Quinnipiac 1962-91)	459
34. Jim Seward [Wayne St. (Neb.) 1975-78, Ashland 79-83, Kansas Newman 84-88, Central Okla. 89-02]	455
35. Pat Douglass (Mont. St.-Billings 1982-87, Cal St. Bakersfield 88-97, UC Irvine (99-01)*	451
36. Butch Raymond (Augsburg 1971-73, Mankato St. 74-84, St. Cloud St. 85-97)	447
37. Richard Schmidt (Vanderbilt 1980-81, Tampa 84-02)*	445
37. J.B. Scearce (North Ga. 1942-43, Cumberland 47, Ga. Southern 48-80)	445
38. Tom Villemure (Detroit Business 1967, Grand Valley St. 73-96)	437
39. James Dominey (Valdosta St. 1972-00)	436
40. John Masi (UC Riverside 1980-02)*	434
41. Oliver Jones [Albany St. (Ga.) 1973-00, Tuskegee 01-02]*	433
42. Hal Nunnally (Randolph-Macon 1976-99)	431
42. Leonidas Epps (Clark Atlanta 1950-78)	431
44. Rich Glas (Minn.-Morris 1975-79, Willamette 80-85, North Dakota 89-02)*	423
45. Jim Harley (Eckerd 1956-96)	420
46. Irvin Peterson (Neb. Wesleyan 1949-80)	419
47. Tom Feely [St. Thomas (Minn.) 1955-80]	417
48. Herbert Greene (Auburn-Montgomery 1976-77, Columbus St. 82-02]*	415
48. Ron Spry (Paine 1987-02)*	415
48. Lonnie Porter [Regis (Colo.) 1978-02]*	415
51. Ernest Hole (Wooster 1927-58)	412

*Active coaches

COACHING RECORDS

Division III Coaching Records

Winningest Active Coaches

(Minimum five years as a head coach; includes record at four-year colleges only.)

BY PERCENTAGE

Coach, Team	Years	Won	Lost	Pct.
1. Brian Meehan, Salem St.	6	137	33	.806
2. Jerry Rickrode, Wilkes	10	214	60	.781
3. Brian VanHaaften, Buena Vista	6	123	39	.759
3. Joe Cassidy, Rowan	6	123	39	.759
5. Joe Campoli, Ohio Northern	10	207	68	.753
6. Mike Jones, Mississippi Col.	14	284	95	.749
7. Bill Foti, Colby-Sawyer	10	199	68	.745
8. Glenn Van Wieren, Hope	25	477	169	.738
9. Tony Shaver, Hampden-Sydney	16	330	117	.738
10. Glenn Robinson, Frank. & Marsh.	31	623	226	.734
11. Brian Baptiste, Mass.-Dartmouth	19	383	139	.734
12. Bob Campbell, Western Conn. St.	18	358	131	.732
13. Steve Moore, Wooster	21	416	154	.730
14. Jack Bennett, Wis.-Stevens Point	6	118	44	.728
15. Mike Lonergan, Catholic	10	203	77	.725
16. C.J. Woollum, Chris. Newport	18	367	140	.724
17. Mark Hanson, Gust. Adolphus	12	236	91	.722
18. Rick Simonds, St. Joseph's (Me.)	22	443	171	.721
19. Bob Gillespie, Ripon	22	378	147	.720
20. Bosko Djurickovic, Carthage	16	313	122	.720
21. Gerry Matthews, Richard Stockton	16	320	125	.719
22. Stan Ogrodnik, Trinity (Conn.)	21	353	147	.706
23. Todd Raridon, Neb. Wesleyan	13	243	102	.704
24. John Dzik, Cabrini	22	425	182	.700
25. Richard Bihr, Buffalo St.	22	407	175	.699
26. Charles Brown, New Jersey City	20	390	169	.698
27. Tom Murphy, Hamilton	32	560	248	.693
28. Joe Nesci, New York U.	14	248	111	.691
29. Page Moir, Roanoke	13	241	112	.683
30. Dick Whitmore, Colby	32	535	250	.682
31. Jose Rebimas, Wm. Paterson	8	146	69	.679
32. Randy Lambert, Maryville (Tenn.)	22	391	188	.675
33. David Hixon, Amherst	25	415	204	.670
34. Steve Fritz, St. Thomas (Minn.)	22	390	195	.667
35. Ron Holmes, McMurry	12	211	106	.666
36. Bill Harris, Wheaton (Ill.)	17	312	157	.665
37. John McCloskey, Alvernia	10	185	95	.661
38. Brad McAlester, Lebanon Valley	8	143	75	.656
39. Cazzie Russell, Savannah A&D	6	97	51	.655
40. James Lancaster, Aurora	8	132	70	.653
41. Rudy Marisa, Waynesburg	33	547	291	.653
42. Dick Reynolds, Otterbein	30	531	289	.648
43. Dick Peth, Wartburg	17	308	168	.647
44. Kevin Vande Streek, Calvin	12	218	119	.647
45. Keith Bunkenburg, Benedictine (Ill.)	7	115	63	.646
46. Dave Niland, Penn St.-Behrend	8	138	76	.645
47. Jim Shaw, Rose-Hulman	8	133	74	.643
48. Ted Van Dellen, Wis.-Oshkosh	12	203	113	.642
49. Will Biggs, Cal St. Hayward	5	88	49	.642
50. Bill Brown, Wittenberg	15	266	150	.639
51. Mark Scherer, Elmhurst	6	97	55	.638
52. Steven Larson, Edgewood	16	301	171	.638
53. Chris Downs, St. Lawrence	5	86	49	.637
54. Bill Nelson, Johns Hopkins	22	364	208	.636
55. Mark Edwards, Washington (Mo.)	21	345	198	.635
56. Paul Phillips, Clark (Mass.)	16	272	157	.634
57. Terry Glasgow, Monmouth (Ill.)	30	424	247	.632
58. Bill Fenlon, DePauw	17	274	160	.631
59. Gordie James, Willamette	15	260	152	.631
60. Tom Spanbauer, Cortland St.	8	139	82	.629
61. David Paulsen, Williams	8	135	80	.628
62. Mike Bokosky, Chapman	10	155	93	.625
63. Herb Hilgeman, Rhodes	26	396	240	.623
64. Mike Moran, John Carroll	10	166	101	.622
65. Robert Sheldon, Tufts	14	214	133	.617
66. Mike Beitzel, Hanover	22	374	234	.615
67. Charles Katsiaficas, Pomona-Pitzer	15	236	149	.613
68. Steve Brennan, Babson	7	116	74	.611
69. John Stroud, Millsaps	12	188	120	.610
70. Dave Duda, Widener	6	94	60	.610

BY VICTORIES

(Minimum five years as a head coach; includes record at four-year colleges only.)

Coach, Team	Years	Won	Lost	Pct.
1. Glenn Robinson, Frank. & Marsh.	31	623	226	.734
2. Jim Smith, St. John's (Minn.)	38	606	397	.604
3. Tom Murphy, Hamilton	32	560	248	.693
4. Rudy Marisa, Waynesburg	33	547	291	.653
5. Dick Whitmore, Colby	32	535	250	.682
6. Dick Reynolds, Otterbein	30	531	289	.648
7. Jim Burson, Muskingum	35	502	385	.566
8. Glenn Van Wieren, Hope	25	477	169	.738
9. Cliff Garrsion, Hendrix	30	456	359	.560
10. Rick Simonds, St. Joseph's (Me.)	22	443	171	.721
11. Jon Davison, Clarke	33	428	413	.509
12. John Dzik, Cabrini	22	425	182	.700
13. Terry Glasgow, Monmouth (Ill.)	30	424	247	.632
14. Steve Moore, Wooster	21	416	154	.730
15. David Hixon, Amherst	25	415	204	.670
16. Mike Turner, Albion	28	410	276	.598
17. Richard Bihr, Buffalo St.	22	407	175	.699
18. Lee McKinney, Fontbonne	24	405	279	.592
19. Mac Petty, Wabash	29	405	316	.562
20. Mike Neer, Rochester	26	403	273	.596
21. Herb Hilgeman, Rhodes	26	396	240	.623
22. Randy Lambert, Maryville (Tenn.)	22	391	188	.675
23. Charles Brown, New Jersey City	20	390	169	.698
23. Steve Fritz, St. Thomas (Minn.)	22	390	195	.667
25. Gary Smith, Redlands	31	386	408	.486
26. Brian Baptiste, Mass.-Dartmouth	19	383	139	.734
27. Bob Gillespie, Ripon	22	378	147	.720
28. Mike Beitzel, Hanover	22	374	234	.615
29. Rees Johnson, North Park	26	372	347	.517
30. C.J. Woollum, Chris. Newport	18	367	140	.724
31. Joe Ramsey, Blackburn	27	366	325	.530
32. Bill Nelson, Johns Hopkins	22	364	208	.636
33. Bob Campbell, Western Conn. St.	18	358	131	.732
34. Stan Ogrodnik, Trinity (Conn.)	21	353	147	.706
35. Mark Edwards, Washington (Mo.)	21	345	198	.635
36. Bob McVean, Rochester Inst.	24	341	262	.566
37. Tony Shaver, Hampden-Sydney	16	330	117	.738
38. Peter Barry, Coast Guard	20	321	226	.587
39. Gerry Matthews, Richard Stockton	16	320	125	.719
40. Chuck Mancuso, Mt. St. Vincent	21	319	217	.595
41. Jeff Gamber, York (Pa.)	25	318	326	.494
42. Bob Gay, MacMurray	27	317	372	.460
43. Jim Walker, Moravian	23	315	262	.546
44. Steve Bankston, Baldwin-Wallace	22	313	270	.537
44. Bosko Djurickovic, Carthage	16	313	122	.720
46. Bill Harris, Wheaton (Ill.)	17	312	157	.665
47. Kerry Prather, Franklin	19	311	201	.607
48. Dick Peth, Wartburg	17	308	168	.647
49. Charlie Brock, Springfield	22	305	266	.534
50. Bob Johnson, Emory & Henry	22	302	272	.526
50. Roger Kindel, FDU-Florham	25	302	310	.493
52. Steven Larson, Edgewood	16	301	171	.638
53. Jonathon Halpert, Yeshiva	30	297	365	.449
54. Charlie Titus, Mass.-Boston	26	291	354	.451
55. Mike Jones, Mississippi Col.	14	284	95	.749
56. Mike Griffin, Rensselaer	25	282	343	.451
57. Bill Fenlon, DePauw	17	274	160	.631
58. Paul Phillips, Clark (Mass.)	16	272	157	.634
59. Rich Rider, Cal Lutheran	17	266	173	.606
60. Bill Brown, Wittenberg	15	266	150	.639
61. Gordie James, Willamette	15	260	152	.631
62. Bill Leatherman, Bridgewater (Va.)	17	259	179	.591
63. Bruce Wilson, Simpson	17	252	186	.575
64. Joe Nesci, New York U.	14	248	111	.691
65. Todd Raridon, Neb. Wesleyan	13	243	102	.704
66. Page Moir, Roanoke	13	241	112	.683
67. Ray Rankis, Baruch	19	238	256	.482
68. Mark Hanson, Gust. Adolphus	12	236	91	.722
68. Charles Katsiaficas, Pomona-Pitzer	15	236	149	.613
70. Dave Madeira, Muhlenburg	15	231	150	.606

Winningest Coaches All-Time

(Minimum 10 head coaching seasons in Division III)

BY PERCENTAGE

Coach (Team coached, tenure)	Years	Won	Lost	Pct.
1. Ken Anderson (Wis.-Eau Claire 1969-95)	27	631	152	.806
2. Jerry Rickrode (Wilkes 1993-02)*	10	˙214	60	.781
3. Bo Ryan (Wis.-Platteville 1985-99, Wis.-Milwaukee 00-01, Wisconsin 02)*	18	402	116	.776
4. Jim Borcherding [Augustana (Ill.) 1970-84]	15	313	100	.758
5. Harry Sheehy (Williams 1984-00)	17	324	104	.757
6. Joe Campoli (Ohio Northern 1993-02)*	10	207	68	.753
7. Bill Foti (Colby-Sawyer 1993-02)*	10	199	68	.745
8. Glenn Van Wieren (Hope 1978-02)*	25	477	169	.738
9. Tony Shaver (Hampden-Sydney 1987-02)*	16	330	117	.738
10. Glenn Robinson (Frank. & Marsh. 1972-02)*	31	623	226	.734
11. Brian Baptiste (Mass.-Dartmouth 1984-02)*	19	383	139	.734
12. Bob Campbell (Western Conn. St. 1985-02)*	18	358	131	.732
13. Steve Moore (Muhlenberg 1982-87, Wooster 88-02)*	21	416	154	.730
14. Mike Longeran (Catholic 1993-02)*	10	203	77	.725
15. C.J. Woollum (Chris. Newport 85-02)*	18	367	140	.724
16. Mark Hanson (Gust. Adolphus 1991-02)*	12	236	91	.722
17. Rick Simonds [St. Joseph's (Me.) 1980-02]*	22	443	171	.721
18. Bob Gillespie (Ripon 1981-02)*	22	378	147	.720
19. Bosko Djurickovic (North Park 1985-94, Carthage 1997-02)*	16	313	122	.720
20. Gerry Mathews (Richard Stockton 1987-02)*	16	320	125	.719
21. Dave Darnall (Eureka 1975-94)	20	383	150	.719
22. Bob Ward (St. John Fisher 1988-01)	14	261	106	.711
23. Jerry Welsh (Potsdam St. 1969-91, Iona 92-95)	26	502	205	.710
24. James Catalano (N.J. Inst. of Tech 1980-01)	22	431	177	.709
25. Dave Vander Meulen (Wis.-Whitewater 1981-01)	23	440	182	.707
26. Stan Ogrodnik [Trinity (Conn.) 1982-02]*	21	353	147	.706
27. Todd Raridon (Neb. Wesleyan 1990-02)*	13	243	102	.704
28. John Dzik (Cabrini 1981-02)*	22	425	182	.700
29. Richard Bihr (Buffalo St. 1980-02)*	22	407	175	.699
30. Charles Brown (New Jersey City 1983-02)*	20	390	169	.698
31. John Reynders (Allegheny 1980-89)	10	180	78	.698
32. Lewis Levick (Wartburg 1966-93)	28	510	225	.694
33. Tom Murphy (Hamilton 1971-02)*	32	560	248	.693
34. Joe Nesci (New York U. 1989-02)*	14	248	111	.691
35. Page Moir (Roanoke 1990-02)*	13	241	112	.683
36. Dick Whitmore (Colby 1971-02)*	32	535	250	.682
37. Ed Douma (Alma 1974, Lake Superior St. 75-78, Kent 79-82, UNC Greensboro 83-85, Calvin 85-96, Hillsdale 99-02)*	27	490	230	.681
38. Bob Bessoir (Scranton 1973-01)	29	554	263	.678
39. Dennie Bridges (Ill. Wesleyan 1966-01)	36	666	320	.675
40. Randy Lambert [Maryville (Tenn.) 1981-02]*	22	391	188	.675

Coach (Team coached, tenure)	Years	Won	Lost	Pct.
41. David Hixon (Amherst 1978-02)*	25	415	204	.670
42. Steve Fritz [St. Thomas (Minn.) 1981-02]*	22	390	195	.667
42. Naylond Hayes (Rust 1970-88)	18	338	169	.667
44. Bill Harris [Wheaton (Ill.) 1986-02]*	17	312	157	.665
45. Rudy Marisa (Waynesburg 1970-02)*	33	547	291	.653

BY VICTORIES

(Minimum 10 head coaching seasons in Division III)

Coach, Team	Wins
1. Dick Sauers [Albany (N.Y.) 1957-97]	702
2. Dennie Bridges (Ill. Wesleyan 1966-01)	666
3. Ken Anderson (Wis.-Eau Claire 1969-95)	631
4. Glenn Robinson (Frank. & Marsh. 1972-02)*	623
5. Jim Smith [St. John's (Minn.) 1965-02]*	606
6. Tom Murphy (Hamilton 1971-02)*	560
7. Bill Knapton (Beloit 1958-97)	555
8. Bob Bessoir (Scranton 1973-01)	554
9. Rudy Marisa (Waynesburg 1970-02)*	547
10. C. Alan Rowe (Widener 1966-98)	536
11. Dick Whitmore (Colby 1971-02)*	535
12. Dick Reynolds (Otterbein 1973-02)*	531
13. Gene Mehaffey (Carson-Newman 1968-78, Ohio Wesleyan 80-99)	525
14. Lewis Levick (Wartburg 1966-93)	510
15. Larry Hunter (Wittenberg 1977-89, Ohio 90-01)	509
16. Jim Burson (Muskingum 1968-02)*	502
16. Jerry Welsh (Potsdam St. 1969-91, Iona 92-95)	502
18. Will Renken (Bloomfield 1948-52, Albright 56-88)	497
19. Ed Douma(Alma 1974, Lake Superior St. 75-78, Kent St. 79-82, UNC Greensboro 83-85, Calvin 85-96, Hillsdale 99-02)*	490
20. Glenn Van Wieren (Hope 1978-02)*	477
21. Verne Canfield (Wash. & Lee 1965-95)	460
22. Leon Richardson (1956, Dubuque 58-59, Drury 60-65, William Penn 75-01)	444
23. Rick Simonds [St. Joseph's (Me.) 1980-02]*	443
24. Dave Vander Meulen (Wis.-Whitewater 1979-01)	440
25. Ward Lambert (Salisbury 1974-00)	432
26. James Catalano (N.J. Inst. Of Tech 1980-01)	431
27. Ollie Gelston (New Jersey City 1960-67, Montclair St. 1968-91)	429
28. John Dzik (Cabrini 1981-02)*	425
29. Terry Glasgow [Monmouth (Ill.) 1973-02]*	424
30. Steve Moore (Muhlenberg 1982-87, Wooster 88-02)*	416
31. David Hixon (Amherst 1978-02)*	415
32. Don Smith (Elizabethtown 1955-64 & 73-88, Bucknell 65-72)	413
33. Mike Turner (Albion 1975-02)*	410
34. Richard Bihr (Buffalo St. 1980-02)*	407
35. Lee McKinney (Mo. Baptist 1979-88, Fontbonne 89-02)*	405
35. Mac Petty (Sewanee 1974-76, Wabash 77-02)*	405
37. Mike Neer (Rochester 1977-02)*	403

* Active coaches.

COACHING RECORDS

Championships

Division I Championship

2002 Results

OPENING ROUND

Siena 81, Alcorn St. 77

FIRST ROUND

Duke 84, Winthrop 37
Notre Dame 82, Charlotte 63
Indiana 75, Utah 56
UNC Wilmington 93, Southern California 89 (ot)
California 82, Pennsylvania 75
Pittsburgh 71, Central Conn. St. 54
Kent St. 69, Oklahoma St. 61
Alabama 86, Fla. Atlantic 78
Cincinnati 90, Boston U. 52
UCLA 80, Mississippi 58
Missouri 93, Miami (Fla.) 80
Ohio St. 69, Davidson 64
Wyoming 73, Gonzaga 66
Arizona 86, UC Santa Barb. 81
Xavier 70, Hawaii 58
Oklahoma 71, Ill.-Chicago 63
Maryland 85, Siena 70
Wisconsin 80, St. John's (N.Y.) 70
Tulsa 71, Marquette 69
Kentucky 83, Valparaiso 68
Southern Ill. 76, Texas Tech 68
Georgia 85, Murray St. 68
North Carolina St. 69, Michigan St. 58
Connecticut 78, Hampton 67
Kansas 70, Holy Cross 59
Stanford 84, Western Ky. 68
Creighton 83, Florida 82 (2 ot)
Illinois 93, San Diego St. 64
Texas 70, Boston College 57
Mississippi St. 70, McNeese St. 58
Wake Forest 83, Pepperdine 74
Oregon 81, Montana 62

SECOND ROUND

Duke 84, Notre Dame 77
Indiana 76, UNC Wilmington 67
Pittsburgh 63, California 50
Kent St. 71, Alabama 58

Maryland's high-flying Chris Wilcox produced numerous championship game highlights.

UCLA 105, Cincinnati 101 (2 ot)
Missouri 83, Ohio St. 67
Arizona 68, Wyoming 60
Oklahoma, 78, Xavier 65
Maryland 87, Wisconsin 57
Kentucky 87, Tulsa 82
Southern Ill. 77, Georgia 75
Connecticut 77, North Carolina St. 74
Kansas 86, Stanford 63
Illinois 72, Creighton 60
Texas 68, Mississippi St. 64
Oregon 92, Wake Forest 87

REGIONAL SEMIFINALS

Indiana 74, Duke 73
Kent St. 78, Pittsburgh 73 (ot)
Missouri 82, UCLA 73
Oklahoma 88, Arizona 67
Maryland 78, Kentucky 68
Connecticut 71, Southern Ill. 59
Kansas 73, Illinois 69
Oregon 72, Texas 70

REGIONAL FINALS

Indiana 81, Kent St. 69
Oklahoma 81, Missouri 75
Kansas 104, Oregon 86
Maryland 90, Connecticut 82

SEMIFINALS

Indiana 73, Oklahoma 64
Maryland 97, Kansas 88

CHAMPIONSHIP

Maryland 64, Indiana 52

Final Four Box Scores

SEMIFINALS
MARCH 30
AT ATLANTA
Indiana 73, Oklahoma 64

Indiana	FG-FGA	FT-FTA	RB	PF	TP
Jared Jeffries	2-5	3-4	8	3	8
Kyle Hornsby	2-4	1-2	2	2	7
Jarrad Odle	5-10	0-0	1	2	11
Tom Coverdale	1-5	0-1	4	3	3
Dane Fife	1-4	0-0	1	2	3
A.J. Moye	4-6	0-0	3	2	9
George Leach	1-1	1-3	2	1	3
Donald Perry	2-3	5-6	4	0	10
Jeff Newton	7-10	5-8	6	2	19
Team			1		
TOTALS	25-48	15-24	32	17	73

Oklahoma	FG-FGA	FT-FTA	RB	PF	TP
Aaron McGhee	8-15	6-7	8	5	22
Jabahri Brown	4-5	1-2	6	3	9
Ebi Ere	7-12	0-0	5	2	15
Quannas White	0-5	0-0	1	3	0
Hollis Price	1-11	3-4	3	3	6
Jason Detrick	1-6	4-4	3	2	6
Blake Johnston	1-1	0-0	0	0	2
Daryan Selvy	2-10	0-1	8	4	4
Jozsef Szendrei	0-1	0-0	2	0	0
Team			4		
TOTALS	24-66	14-18	40	22	64

Halftime: Oklahoma 34, Indiana 30. Three-point field goals: Indiana 8-13 (Jeffries 1-1, Hornsby 2-4, Odle 1-1, Coverdale 1-3, Fife 1-2, Moye 1-1, Perry 1-1); Oklahoma 2-18 (McGhee 0-1, Ere 1-5, White 0-1, Price 1-7, Detrick 0-2, Selvy 0-2). Officials: Mike Kitts, David Libbey, Duke Edsall. Attendance: 53,378.

Maryland 97, Kansas 88

Kansas	FG-FGA	FT-FTA	RB	PF	TP
Nick Collison	9-14	3-4	10	3	21
Drew Gooden	5-12	3-5	9	4	15
Kirk Hinrich	4-8	1-2	4	5	11
Aaron Miles	1-7	10-12	3	4	12
Jeff Boschee	6-16	0-0	3	3	17
Brett Ballard	0-0	0-0	0	1	0
Keith Langford	2-6	4-8	5	4	8
Jeff Carey	0-1	0-0	0	1	0
Wayne Simien	2-3	0-0	5	2	4
Team			5		
TOTALS	29-67	21-31	44	27	88

Maryland	FG-FGA	FT-FTA	RB	PF	TP
Byron Mouton	4-9	4-4	6	2	12
Chris Wilcox	8-15	2-3	9	4	18
Lonny Baxter	2-4	0-0	7	5	4
Juan Dixon	10-18	8-11	3	2	33
Steve Blake	1-7	5-9	3	4	8
Drew Nicholas	2-9	2-2	2	2	7
Ryan Randle	1-3	0-1	2	1	2
Tahj Holden	4-5	5-5	5	4	13
Team			3		
TOTALS	32-70	26-35	40	24	97

Halftime: Maryland 44, Kansas 37. Three-point field goals: Kansas 9-23 (Gooden 2-2, Hinrich 2-3, Miles 0-4, Boschee 5-13, Langford 0-1); Maryland 7-21 (Dixon 5-11, Blake 1-4, Nicholas 1-5, Holden 0-1). Officials: Tim Higgins, Ed Hightower, Ed Corbett. Attendance: 53,378.

NATIONAL CHAMPIONSHIP
APRIL 1
AT ATLANTA
Maryland 64, Indiana 52

Indiana	FG-FGA	FT-FTA	RB	PF	TP
Jared Jeffries	4-11	0-1	7	4	8
Kyle Hornsby	5-12	0-1	5	4	14
Jarrad Odle	0-4	0-3	4	2	0
Tom Coverdale	3-11	0-0	4	2	8
Dane Fife	4-9	0-0	5	3	11
A.J. Moye	1-1	0-0	1	2	2
George Leach	0-0	0-0	0	0	0
Donald Perry	1-3	0-0	1	1	3
Jeff Newton	2-7	2-2	5	3	6
Team			0		
TOTALS	20-58	2-7	31	20	52

Maryland	FG-FGA	FT-FTA	RB	PF	TP
Byron Mouton	1-5	2-2	4	2	4
Chris Wilcox	4-8	2-4	7	3	10
Lonny Baxter	6-15	3-8	14	1	15
Juan Dixon	6-9	4-4	3	1	18
Steve Blake	2-6	2-2	6	2	6
Drew Nicholas	1-2	5-6	3	0	7
Ryan Randle	1-1	0-0	0	1	2
Tahj Holden	0-2	2-2	3	3	2
Team			0		
TOTALS	21-48	20-28	42	13	64

Halftime: Maryland 31, Indiana 25. Three-point field goals: Indiana 10-23 (Jeffries 0-1, Hornsby 4-8, Coverdale 2-7, Fife 3-6, Perry 1-1); Maryland 2-9 (Dixon 2-4, Blake 0-3, Nicholas 0-1, Holden 0-1). Officials: Jim Burr, Richard Cartmell, Tony Greene. Attendance: 53,406.

Photo by Rich Clarkson/NCAA photos

Year-by-Year Results

Season	Champion	Score	Runner-Up	Third Place	Fourth Place
1939	Oregon	46-33	Ohio St.	+Oklahoma	+Villanova
1940	Indiana	60-42	Kansas	+Duquesne	+Southern California
1941	Wisconsin	39-34	Washington St.	+Pittsburgh	+Arkansas
1942	Stanford	53-38	Dartmouth	+Colorado	+Kentucky
1943	Wyoming	46-34	Georgetown	+Texas	+DePaul
1944	Utah	42-40 (ot)	Dartmouth	+Iowa St.	+Ohio St.
1945	Oklahoma St.	49-45	New York U.	+Arkansas	+Ohio St.
1946	Oklahoma St.	43-40	North Carolina	Ohio St.	California
1947	Holy Cross	58-47	Oklahoma	Texas	CCNY
1948	Kentucky	58-42	Baylor	Holy Cross	Kansas St.
1949	Kentucky	46-36	Oklahoma St.	Illinois	Oregon St.
1950	CCNY	71-68	Bradley	North Carolina St.	Baylor
1951	Kentucky	68-58	Kansas St.	Illinois	Oklahoma St.
1952	Kansas	80-63	St. John's (N.Y.)	Illinois	Santa Clara
1953	Indiana	69-68	Kansas	Washington	LSU
1954	La Salle	92-76	Bradley	Penn St.	Southern California
1955	San Francisco	77-63	La Salle	Colorado	Iowa
1956	San Francisco	83-71	Iowa	Temple	Southern Methodist
1957	North Carolina	54-53 (3ot)	Kansas	San Francisco	Michigan St.
1958	Kentucky	84-72	Seattle	Temple	Kansas St.
1959	California	71-70	West Virginia	Cincinnati	Louisville
1960	Ohio St.	75-55	California	Cincinnati	New York U.
1961	Cincinnati	70-65 (ot)	Ohio St.	* St. Joseph's	Utah
1962	Cincinnati	71-59	Ohio St.	Wake Forest	UCLA
1963	Loyola (Ill.)	60-58 (ot)	Cincinnati	Duke	Oregon St.
1964	UCLA	98-83	Duke	Michigan	Kansas St.
1965	UCLA	91-80	Michigan	Princeton	Wichita St.
1966	UTEP	72-65	Kentucky	Duke	Utah
1967	UCLA	79-64	Dayton	Houston	North Carolina
1968	UCLA	78-55	North Carolina	Ohio St.	Houston
1969	UCLA	92-72	Purdue	Drake	North Carolina
1970	UCLA	80-69	Jacksonville	New Mexico St.	St. Bonaventure
1971	UCLA	68-62	*Villanova	* Western Ky.	Kansas
1972	UCLA	81-76	Florida St.	North Carolina	Louisville
1973	UCLA	87-66	Memphis	Indiana	Providence
1974	North Carolina St.	76-64	Marquette	UCLA	Kansas
1975	UCLA	92-85	Kentucky	Louisville	Syracuse
1976	Indiana	86-68	Michigan	UCLA	Rutgers
1977	Marquette	67-59	North Carolina	UNLV	Charlotte
1978	Kentucky	94-88	Duke	Arkansas	Notre Dame
1979	Michigan St.	75-64	Indiana St.	DePaul	Pennsylvania
1980	Louisville	59-54	*UCLA	Purdue	Iowa
1981	Indiana	63-50	North Carolina	Virginia	LSU
1982	North Carolina	63-62	Georgetown	+Houston	+Louisville
1983	North Carolina St.	54-52	Houston	+Georgia	+Louisville
1984	Georgetown	84-75	Houston	+Kentucky	+Virginia
1985	Villanova	66-64	Georgetown	+ St. John's (N.Y.)	+*Memphis
1986	Louisville	72-69	Duke	+Kansas	+LSU
1987	Indiana	74-73	Syracuse	+UNLV	+Providence
1988	Kansas	83-79	Oklahoma	+Arizona	+Duke
1989	Michigan	80-79 (ot)	Seton Hall	+Duke	+Illinois
1990	UNLV	103-73	Duke	+Arkansas	+Georgia Tech
1991	Duke	72-65	Kansas	+UNLV	+North Carolina
1992	Duke	71-51	Michigan	+Cincinnati	+Indiana
1993	North Carolina	77-71	Michigan	+Kansas	+Kentucky
1994	Arkansas	76-72	Duke	+Arizona	+Florida
1995	UCLA	89-78	Arkansas	+North Carolina	+Oklahoma St.
1996	Kentucky	76-67	Syracuse	+Massachusetts	+Mississippi St.
1997	Arizona	84-79 (ot)	Kentucky	+Minnesota	+North Carolina
1998	Kentucky	78-69	Utah	+North Carolina	+Stanford
1999	Connecticut	77-74	Duke	+Michigan St.	+Ohio St.
2000	Michigan St.	89-76	Florida	+North Carolina	+Wisconsin
2001	Duke	82-72	Arizona	+Maryland	+Michigan St.
2002	Maryland	64-52	Indiana	+Kansas	+Oklahoma

+tied for third place; *later vacated

Maryland's Lonny Baxter rejects a Jared Jeffries shot in the championship game.

Season	Site of Finals	Coach of Champion	Outstanding Player Award
1939	Evanston, Ill.	Howard Hobson, Oregon	Jimmy Hull, Ohio St.
1940	Kansas City, Mo.	Branch McCracken, Indiana	Marvin Huffman, Indiana
1941	Kansas City, Mo.	Harold Foster, Wisconsin	John Kotz, Wisconsin
1942	Kansas City, Mo.	Everett Dean, Stanford	Howard Dallmar, Stanford
1943	New York City	Everett Shelton, Wyoming	Ken Sailors, Wyoming
1944	New York City	Vadal Peterson, Utah	Arnold Ferrin, Utah
1945	New York City	Henry Iba, Oklahoma St.	Bob Kurland, Oklahoma St.
1946	New York City	Henry Iba, Oklahoma St.	Bob Kurland, Oklahoma St.
1947	New York City	Alvin Julian, Holy Cross	George Kaftan, Holy Cross
1948	New York City	Adolph Rupp, Kentucky	Alex Groza, Kentucky
1949	Seattle	Adolph Rupp, Kentucky	Alex Groza, Kentucky
1950	New York City	Nat Holman, CCNY	Irwin Dambrot, CCNY
1951	Minneapolis	Adolph Rupp, Kentucky	Bill Spivey, Kentucky
1952	Seattle	Forrest Allen, Kansas	Clyde Lovellette, Kansas

CHAMPIONSHIPS

Maryland's Juan Dixon scored 33 points in the title game and was named most outstanding player.

Photo by Rich Clarkson/NCAA photos

Season	Site of Finals	Coach of Champion	Outstanding Player Award
1953	Kansas City, Mo.	Branch McCracken, Indiana	B.H. Born, Kansas
1954	Kansas City, Mo.	Kenneth Loeffler, La Salle	Tom Gola, La Salle
1955	Kansas City, Mo.	Phil Woolpert, San Francisco	Bill Russell, San Francisco
1956	Evanston, Ill.	Phil Woolpert, San Francisco	Hal Lear, Temple
1957	Kansas City, Mo.	Frank McGuire, North Carolina	Wilt Chamberlain, Kansas
1958	Louisville, Ky.	Adolph Rupp, Kentucky	Elgin Baylor, Seattle
1959	Louisville, Ky.	Pete Newell, California	Jerry West, West Virginia
1960	San Francisco	Fred Taylor, Ohio St.	Jerry Lucas, Ohio St.
1961	Kansas City, Mo.	Edwin Jucker, Cincinnati	Jerry Lucas, Ohio St.
1962	Louisville, Ky.	Edwin Jucker, Cincinnati	Paul Hogue, Cincinnati
1963	Louisville, Ky.	George Ireland, Loyola (Ill.)	Art Heyman, Duke
1964	Kansas City, Mo.	John Wooden, UCLA	Walt Hazzard, UCLA
1965	Portland, Ore.	John Wooden, UCLA	Bill Bradley, Princeton
1966	College Park, Md.	Don Haskins, UTEP	Jerry Chambers, Utah
1967	Louisville, Ky.	John Wooden, UCLA	Lew Alcindor, UCLA
1968	Los Angeles	John Wooden, UCLA	Lew Alcindor, UCLA
1969	Louisville, Ky.	John Wooden, UCLA	Lew Alcindor, UCLA
1970	College Park, Md.	John Wooden, UCLA	Sidney Wicks, UCLA
1971	Houston	John Wooden, UCLA	*Howard Porter, Villanova
1972	Los Angeles	John Wooden, UCLA	Bill Walton, UCLA
1973	St. Louis	John Wooden, UCLA	Bill Walton, UCLA
1974	Greensboro, N.C.	Norm Sloan, North Carolina St.	David Thompson, North Carolina St.
1975	San Diego	John Wooden, UCLA	Richard Washington, UCLA
1976	Philadelphia	Bob Knight, Indiana	Kent Benson, Indiana
1977	Atlanta	Al McGuire, Marquette	Butch Lee, Marquette
1978	St. Louis	Joe B. Hall, Kentucky	Jack Givens, Kentucky
1979	Salt Lake City	Jud Heathcote, Michigan St.	Earvin Johnson, Michigan St.
1980	Indianapolis	Denny Crum, Louisville	Darrell Griffith, Louisville
1981	Philadelphia	Bob Knight, Indiana	Isiah Thomas, Indiana
1982	New Orleans	Dean Smith, North Carolina	James Worthy, North Carolina
1983	Albuquerque, N.M.	Jim Valvano, North Carolina St.	Akeem Olajuwon, Houston
1984	Seattle	John Thompson, Georgetown	Patrick Ewing, Georgetown
1985	Lexington, Ky.	Rollie Massimino, Villanova	Ed Pinckney, Villanova
1986	Dallas	Denny Crum, Louisville	Pervis Ellison, Louisville
1987	New Orleans	Bob Knight, Indiana	Keith Smart, Indiana
1988	Kansas City, Mo.	Larry Brown, Kansas	Danny Manning, Kansas
1989	Seattle	Steve Fisher, Michigan	Glen Rice, Michigan
1990	Denver	Jerry Tarkanian, UNLV	Anderson Hunt, UNLV
1991	Indianapolis	Mike Krzyzewski, Duke	Christian Laettner, Duke
1992	Minneapolis	Mike Krzyzewski, Duke	Bobby Hurley, Duke
1993	New Orleans	Dean Smith, North Carolina	Donald Williams, North Carolina
1994	Charlotte, N.C.	Nolan Richardson, Arkansas	Corliss Williamson, Arkansas
1995	Seattle	Jim Harrick, UCLA	Ed O'Bannon, UCLA
1996	East Rutherford, N.J.	Rick Pitino, Kentucky	Tony Delk, Kentucky
1997	Indianapolis	Lute Olson, Arizona	Miles Simon, Arizona
1998	San Antonio	Tubby Smith, Kentucky	Jeff Sheppard, Kentucky
1999	St. Petersburg, Fla.	Jim Calhoun, Connecticut	Richard Hamilton, Connecticut
2000	Indianapolis	Tom Izzo, Michigan St.	Mateen Cleaves, Michigan St.
2001	Minneapolis	Mike Krzyzewski, Duke	Shane Battier, Duke
2002	Atlanta	Gary Williams, Maryland	Juan Dixon, Maryland

*later vacated

LEADING SCORER

Season	Player, Team	G	FG	FT	Pts.	Avg.
1939	Jim Hull, Ohio St.	3	22	14	58	19.3
1940	Howard Engleman, Kansas	3	18	3	39	13.0
1941	John Adams, Arkansas	2	21	6	48	24.0
1942	Jim Pollard, Stanford	2	19	5	43	21.5
	Chet Palmer, Rice	2	20	3	43	21.5
1943	John Hargis, Texas	2	21	17	59	29.5
1944	Aud Brindley, Dartmouth	3	24	4	52	17.3
1945	Bob Kurland, Oklahoma St.	3	30	5	65	21.7
1946	Bob Kurland, Oklahoma St.	3	28	16	72	24.0
1947	George Kaftan, Holy Cross	3	25	13	63	21.0
1948	Alex Groza, Kentucky	3	23	8	54	18.0
1949	Alex Groza, Kentucky	3	31	20	82	27.3
1950	Sam Ranzino, North Carolina St.	3	25	25	75	25.0
1951	Don Sunderlage, Illinois	4	28	27	83	20.8
1952	Clyde Lovellette, Kansas	4	53	35	141	35.3
1953	Bob Houbregs, Washington	4	57	25	139	34.8
1954	Tom Gola, La Salle	5	38	38	114	22.8
1955	Bill Russell, San Francisco	5	49	20	118	23.6
1956	Hal Lear, Temple	5	63	34	160	32.0
1957	Len Rosenbluth, North Carolina	5	53	34	140	28.0
1958	Elgin Baylor, Seattle	5	48	39	135	27.0
1959	Jerry West, West Virginia	5	57	46	160	32.0
1960	Oscar Robertson, Cincinnati	4	47	28	122	30.5
1961	Billy McGill, Utah	4	49	21	119	29.8
1962	Len Chappell, Wake Forest	5	45	44	134	26.8
1963	Mel Counts, Oregon St.	5	50	23	123	24.6
1964	Jeff Mullins, Duke	4	50	16	116	29.0
1965	Bill Bradley, Princeton	5	65	47	177	35.4
1966	Jerry Chambers, Utah	4	55	33	143	35.8
1967	Elvin Hayes, Houston	5	57	14	128	25.6
1968	Elvin Hayes, Houston	5	70	27	167	33.4
1969	Rick Mount, Purdue	4	49	24	122	30.5
1970	Austin Carr, Notre Dame	3	68	22	158	52.7
1971	*Jim McDaniels, Western Ky.	5	61	25	147	29.4
	Austin Carr, Notre Dame	3	48	29	125	41.7
1972	Jim Price, Louisville	4	41	21	103	25.8
1973	Ernie DiGregorio, Providence	5	59	10	128	25.6
1974	David Thompson, North Carolina St.	4	38	21	97	24.3
1975	Jim Lee, Syracuse	5	51	17	119	23.8
1976	Scott May, Indiana	5	45	23	113	22.6
1977	Cedric Maxwell, Charlotte	5	39	45	123	24.6
1978	Mike Gminski, Duke	5	45	19	109	21.8
1979	Tony Price, Pennsylvania	6	58	26	142	23.7
1980	Joe Barry Carroll, Purdue	6	63	32	158	26.4
1981	Al Wood, North Carolina	5	44	21	109	21.8
1982	Rob Williams, Houston	5	30	28	88	17.6
1983	Dereck Whittenburg, North Carolina St.	6	47	26	120	20.0
1984	Roosevelt Chapman, Dayton	4	35	35	105	26.3
1985	Chris Mullin, St. John's (N.Y.)	5	39	32	110	22.0
1986	Johnny Dawkins, Duke	6	66	21	153	25.5

Season	Player, Team	G	FG	3FG	FT	Pts.	Avg.
1987	Steve Alford, Indiana	6	42	21	33	138	23.0
	Rony Seikaly, Syracuse	6	87	0	32	138	23.0
1988	Danny Manning, Kansas	6	69	2	23	163	27.2
1989	Glen Rice, Michigan	6	75	27	7	184	30.7
1990	Dennis Scott, Georgia Tech	5	51	24	27	153	30.6
1991	Christian Laettner, Duke	6	37	2	49	125	20.8
1992	Christian Laettner, Duke	6	39	7	30	115	19.2
1993	Donald Williams, North Carolina	6	40	22	16	118	19.7
1994	Khalid Reeves, Arizona	5	45	8	39	137	27.4
1995	Corliss Williamson, Arkansas	6	49	0	27	125	20.8
1996	John Wallace, Syracuse	6	47	7	30	131	21.8
1997	Miles Simon, Arizona	6	42	10	38	132	22.0
1998	Michael Doleac, Utah	6	34	2	45	115	19.2
1999	Richard Hamilton, Connecticut	6	56	7	26	145	24.2
2000	Morris Peterson, Michigan St.	6	35	15	20	105	17.5
2001	Jason Williams, Duke	6	52	23	27	154	25.7
2002	Juan Dixon, Maryland	6	52	22	29	155	25.8

*later vacated

SCORING AVERAGE

(Minimum: 50% of maximum tournament games)

Season	Player, Team	G	FG	FT	Pts.	Avg.
1939	Jim Hull, Ohio St.	3	22	14	58	19.3
1940	Howard Engleman, Kansas	3	18	3	39	13.0
	Bob Kinney, Rice	2	12	2	26	13.0
1941	John Adams, Arkansas	2	21	6	48	24.0
1942	Chet Palmer, Rice	2	19	5	43	21.5
	Jim Pollard, Stanford	2	20	3	43	21.5
1943	John Hargis, Texas	2	21	17	59	29.5
1944	Nick Bozolich, Pepperdine	2	17	11	45	22.5
1945	Dick Wilkins, Oregon	2	19	6	44	22.0
1946	Bob Kurland, Oklahoma St.	3	28	16	72	24.0
1947	George Kaftan, Holy Cross	3	25	13	63	21.0
1948	Jack Nichols, Washington	2	13	13	39	19.5
1949	Alex Groza, Kentucky	3	31	20	82	27.3
1950	Sam Ranzino, North Carolina St.	3	25	25	75	25.0
1951	William Kukoy, North Carolina St.	3	25	19	69	23.0
1952	Clyde Lovellette, Kansas	4	53	35	141	35.3
1953	Bob Houbregs, Washington	4	57	25	139	34.8
1954	John Clune, Navy	3	30	19	79	26.3
1955	Terry Rand, Marquette	3	31	11	73	24.3
1956	Hal Lear, Temple	5	63	34	160	32.0
1957	Wilt Chamberlain, Kansas	4	40	41	121	30.3
1958	Wayne Embry, Miami (Ohio)	3	32	19	83	27.7
1959	Jerry West, West Virginia	5	57	46	160	32.0
1960	Jerry West, West Virginia	3	35	35	105	35.0
1961	Billy McGill, Utah	4	49	21	119	29.8
1962	Len Chappell, Wake Forest	5	45	44	134	26.8
1963	Barry Kramer, New York U.	3	31	28	100	33.3
1964	Jeff Mullins, Duke	4	50	16	116	29.0
1965	Bill Bradley, Princeton	5	65	47	147	35.4
1966	Jerry Chambers, Utah	4	55	33	143	35.8
1967	Lew Alcindor, UCLA	4	39	28	106	26.5
1968	Elvin Hayes, Houston	5	70	27	167	33.4
1969	Rick Mount, Purdue	4	49	24	122	30.5
1970	Austin Carr, Notre Dame	3	68	22	158	52.7
1971	Austin Carr, Notre Dame	3	48	29	125	41.7
1972	*Dwight Lamar, La.-Lafayette	4	41	18	100	33.3
	Jim Price, Louisville	4	41	21	103	25.8
1973	Larry Finch, Memphis	4	34	39	107	26.8
1974	John Shumate, Notre Dame	3	35	16	86	28.7
1975	Adrian Dantley, Notre Dame	3	29	34	92	30.7
1976	Willie Smith, Missouri	3	38	18	94	31.3
1977	Cedric Maxwell, Charlotte	5	39	45	123	24.6
1978	Dave Corzine, DePaul	3	33	16	82	27.3
1979	Larry Bird, Indiana St.	5	52	32	136	27.2
1980	Joe Barry Carroll, Purdue	6	63	32	158	26.3
1981	Al Wood, North Carolina	5	44	21	109	21.8
1982	Oliver Robinson, UAB	3	27	12	66	22.0
1983	Greg Stokes, Iowa	3	24	13	61	20.3
1984	Roosevelt Chapman, Dayton	4	35	35	105	26.3
1985	Kenny Walker, Kentucky	3	28	19	75	25.0
1986	David Robinson, Navy	4	35	40	110	27.5

Season	Player, Team	G	FG	3FG	FT	Pts.	Avg.
1987	Fennis Dembo, Wyoming	3	25	11	23	84	28.0
1988	Danny Manning, Kansas	6	69	2	23	163	27.2
1989	Glen Rice, Michigan	6	75	27	7	184	30.7
1990	Bo Kimble, Loyola Marymount	4	51	15	26	143	35.8
1991	Terry Dehere, Seton Hall	4	34	12	17	97	24.3
1992	Jamal Mashburn, Kentucky	4	34	6	22	96	24.0
1993	Calbert Cheaney, Indiana	4	40	3	23	106	26.5
1994	Gary Collier, Tulsa	3	30	13	21	94	31.3
1995	Darryl Wilson, Mississippi St.	3	21	9	22	73	24.3
1996	Allen Iverson, Georgetown	4	38	12	23	111	27.8

Season	Player, Team	G	FG	3FG	FT	Pts.	Avg.
1997	Dedric Willoughby, Iowa St.	3	24	12	14	74	24.7
1998	Khalid El-Amin, Connecticut	4	30	10	23	93	23.3
1999	Wally Szczerbiak, Miami (Ohio)	3	32	11	15	90	30.0
2000	Marcus Fizer, Iowa St.	4	32	2	14	80	20.0
2001	Jason Williams, Duke	6	52	23	27	154	25.7
2002	Caron Butler, Connecticut	4	32	8	34	106	26.5

*later vacated

CAREER SCORING

Player, Team (Seasons Competed)	G	FG	3FG	FT	Pts.	Avg.
Christian Laettner, Duke (1989-92)	23	128	9	142	407	17.7
Elvin Hayes, Houston (1966-68)	13	152	—	54	358	27.5
Danny Manning, Kansas (1985-88)	16	140	2	46	328	20.5
Oscar Robertson, Cincinnati (1958-60)	10	117	—	90	324	32.4
Glen Rice, Michigan (1986-89)	13	128	35	17	308	23.7
Lew Alcindor, UCLA (1967-69)	12	115	—	74	304	25.3
Bill Bradley, Princeton (1963-65)	9	108	—	87	303	33.7
Corliss Williamson, Arkansas (1993-95)	15	123	0	57	303	20.2
Juan Dixon, Maryland (1999-2002)	16	99	38	58	294	18.4
Austin Carr, Notre Dame (1969-71)	7	117	—	55	289	41.3

SINGLE-GAME SCORING PERFORMANCES

Player, Team vs. Opponent, Season	Round	FG	3FG	FT	Pts.
Austin Carr, Notre Dame vs. Ohio, 1970	1st	25	—	11	61
Bill Bradley, Princeton vs. Wichita St., 1965	N3d	22	—	14	58
Oscar Robertson, Cincinnati vs. Arkansas, 1958	R3d	21	—	14	56
Austin Carr, Notre Dame vs. Kentucky, 1970	RSF	22	—	8	52
Austin Carr, Notre Dame vs. TCU, 1971	1st	20	—	12	52
David Robinson, Navy vs. Michigan, 1987	1st	22	0	6	50
Elvin Hayes, Houston vs. Loyola (Ill.), 1968	1st	20	—	9	49
Hal Lear, Temple vs. Southern Methodist, 1956	N3d	17	—	14	48
Austin Carr, Notre Dame vs. Houston, 1971	R3d	17	—	13	47
Dave Corzine, DePaul vs. Louisville, 1978	RSF	18	—	10	46

[Key: 1st—first round; 2nd—second round; RSF—regional semifinal; RF—regional final; R3d—regional third place; N3d—national third place; CH—national championship.]

LEADING REBOUNDER

Season	Player, Team	G	Reb.	Avg.
1951	Bill Spivey, Kentucky	4	65	16.3
1957	John Green, Michigan St.	4	77	19.3
1958	Elgin Baylor, Seattle	5	91	18.2
1959	Jerry West, West Virginia	5	73	14.6
1960	Tom Sanders, New York U.	5	83	16.6
1961	Jerry Lucas, Ohio St.	4	73	18.3
1962	Len Chappell, Wake Forest	5	86	17.2
1963	Nate Thurmond, Bowling Green	3	70	23.3
	Vic Rouse, Loyola (Ill.)	5	70	14.0
1964	Paul Silas, Creighton	3	57	19.0
1965	Bill Bradley, Princeton	5	57	11.4
1966	Jerry Chambers, Utah	4	56	14.0
1967	Don May, Dayton	5	82	16.4
1968	Elvin Hayes, Houston	5	97	19.4
1969	Lew Alcindor, UCLA	4	64	16.0
1970	Artis Gilmore, Jacksonville	5	93	18.6
1971	*Clarence Glover, Western Ky.	5	89	17.8
	Sidney Wicks, UCLA	4	52	13.0
1972	Bill Walton, UCLA	4	64	16.0
1973	Bill Walton, UCLA	4	58	14.5
1974	Tom Burleson, North Carolina St.	4	61	15.3
1975	Richard Washington, UCLA	5	60	12.0
1976	Phil Hubbard, Michigan	5	61	12.2
1977	Cedric Maxwell, Charlotte	5	64	12.8
1978	Eugene Banks, Duke	5	50	10.0
1979	Larry Bird, Indiana St.	5	67	13.4
1980	Mike Sanders, UCLA	6	60	10.0
1981	Cliff Levingston, Wichita St.	4	53	13.3
1982	Clyde Drexler, Houston	5	42	8.4
1983	Akeem Olajuwon, Houston	5	65	13.0
1984	Akeem Olajuwon, Houston	5	57	11.4
1985	Ed Pinckney, Villanova	6	48	8.0
1986	Pervis Ellison, Louisville	6	57	9.5
1987	Derrick Coleman, Syracuse	6	73	12.2
1988	Danny Manning, Kansas	6	56	9.3
1989	Daryll Walker, Seton Hall	6	58	9.7
1990	Larry Johnson, UNLV	6	75	12.5
1991	Larry Johnson, UNLV	5	51	10.2
1992	Chris Webber, Michigan	6	58	9.7
1993	Chris Webber, Michigan	6	68	11.3
1994	Cherokee Parks, Duke	6	55	9.2
1995	Ed O'Bannon, UCLA	6	54	9.0
1996	Tim Duncan, Wake Forest	4	52	13.0
1997	A. J. Bramlett, Arizona	6	62	10.3
1998	Antawn Jamison, North Carolina	5	63	12.6
1999	Elton Brand, Duke	6	55	9.2

Season	Player, Team	G	Reb.	Avg.
2000	Brendan Haywood, North Carolina	5	48	9.6
2001	Shane Battier, Duke	6	61	10.2
2002	Drew Gooden, Kansas	5	61	12.2

*later vacated

REBOUNDING AVERAGE

Season	Player, Team	G	Reb.	Avg.
1951	Bill Spivey, Kentucky	4	65	16.3
1957	John Green, Michigan St.	4	77	19.3
1958	Elgin Baylor, Seattle	5	91	18.2
1959	Oscar Robertson, Cincinnati	4	63	15.8
1960	Howard Jolliff, Ohio	3	64	21.3
1961	Jerry Lucas, Ohio St.	4	73	18.3
1962	Mel Counts, Oregon St.	3	53	17.7
1963	Nate Thurmond, Bowling Green	3	70	23.3
1964	Paul Silas, Creighton	3	57	19.0
1965	James Ware, Oklahoma City	3	55	18.3
1966	Elvin Hayes, Houston	3	50	16.7
1967	Don May, Dayton	5	82	16.4
1968	Elvin Hayes, Houston	5	97	19.4
1969	Lew Alcindor, UCLA	4	64	16.0
1970	Artis Gilmore, Jacksonville	5	93	18.6
1971	*Clarence Glover, Western Ky.	5	89	17.8
	Collis Jones, Notre Dame	3	49	16.3
1972	Bill Walton, UCLA	4	64	16.0
1973	Bill Walton, UCLA	4	58	14.5
1974	Marvin Barnes, Providence	3	51	17.0
1975	Mike Franklin, Cincinnati	3	49	16.3
1976	Al Fleming, Arizona	3	39	13.0
1977	Phil Hubbard, Michigan	3	45	15.0
1978	Greg Kelser, Michigan St.	3	37	12.3
1979	Larry Bird, Indiana St.	5	67	13.4
1980	Durand Macklin, LSU	3	31	10.3
1981	Cliff Levingston, Wichita St.	4	53	13.3
1982	Ed Pinckney, Villanova	3	30	10.0
1983	Akeem Olajuwon, Houston	5	65	13.0
1984	*Keith Lee, Memphis	3	37	12.3
	Akeem Olajuwon, Houston	5	57	11.4
1985	Karl Malone, Louisiana Tech	3	40	13.3
1986	David Robinson, Navy	4	47	11.8
1987	Derrick Coleman, Syracuse	6	73	12.2
1988	Pervis Ellison, Louisville	3	33	11.0
1989	Pervis Ellison, Louisville	3	31	10.3
	Stacey King, Oklahoma	3	31	10.3
1990	Dale Davis, Clemson	3	44	14.7
1991	Byron Houston, Oklahoma St.	3	36	12.0
1992	Doug Edwards, Florida St.	3	32	10.7
1993	Chris Webber, Michigan	6	68	11.3
1994	Juwan Howard, Michigan	6	51	12.8
1995	Tim Duncan, Wake Forest	3	43	14.3
1996	Tim Duncan, Wake Forest	4	52	13.0
1997	Paul Pierce, Kansas	3	36	12.0
1998	Antawn Jamison, North Carolina	5	63	12.6
1999	Eduardo Najera, Oklahoma	3	35	11.7
2000	Eric Coley, Tulsa	4	43	10.8
2001	Eric Coley, Tulsa	4	43	10.8
2002	Drew Gooden, Kansas	5	61	12.2

*later vacated

CAREER REBOUNDING

Player, Team (Seasons Competed)	G	Reb.	Avg.
Elvin Hayes, Houston (1966-68)	13	222	17.1
Lew Alcindor, UCLA (1967-69)	12	201	16.8
Jerry Lucas, Ohio St. (1960-62)	12	197	16.4
Bill Walton, UCLA (1972-74)	12	176	14.7
Christian Laettner, Duke (1989-92)	23	169	7.3
Tim Duncan, Wake Forest (1994-97)	11	165	15.0
Paul Hogue, Cincinnati (1960-62)	12	160	13.3
Sam Lacey, New Mexico St. (1968-70)	11	157	14.3
Derrick Coleman, Syracuse (1987-90)	14	155	11.1
Akeem Olajuwon, Houston (1982-84)	15	153	10.2

SINGLE-GAME REBOUNDING PERFORMANCES

Player, Team vs. Opponent, Season	Round	Reb.
Fred Cohen, Temple vs. Connecticut, 1956	RSF	34
Nate Thurmond, Bowling Green vs. Mississippi St., 1963	R3d	31
Jerry Lucas, Ohio St. vs. Kentucky, 1961	RF	30
Toby Kimball, Connecticut vs. St. Joseph's, 1965	1st	29
Elvin Hayes, Houston vs. Pacific (Cal.), 1966	R3d	28
Bill Russell, San Francisco vs. Iowa, 1956	CH	27
John Green, Michigan St. vs. Notre Dame, 1957	2nd	27
Paul Silas, Creighton vs. Oklahoma City, 1964	1st	27
Elvin Hayes, Houston vs. Loyola (Ill.), 1968	1st	27
Howard Jolliff, Ohio vs. Georgia Tech, 1960	RSF	26
Phil Hubbard, Michigan vs. Detroit, 1977	RSF	26

[Key: 1st—first round; 2nd—second round; RSF—regional semifinal; RF—regional final; R3d—regional third place; NSF—national semifinal; CH—national championship.]

INDIVIDUAL RECORDS

Single Game

POINTS
61—Austin Carr, Notre Dame vs. Ohio, SE 1st, 1970

POINTS BY TWO TEAMMATES
85—Austin Carr (61) and Collis Jones (24), Notre Dame vs. Ohio, SE 1st, 1970

POINTS BY TWO OPPOSING PLAYERS
96—Austin Carr (52), Notre Dame, and Dan Issel (44), Kentucky, SE RSF, 1970

FIELD GOALS
25—Austin Carr, Notre Dame vs. Ohio, SE 1st, 1970

FIELD GOALS ATTEMPTED
44—Austin Carr, Notre Dame vs. Ohio, SE 1st, 1970

FIELD-GOAL PERCENTAGE (Minimum 11 Made)
100% (11-11)—Kenny Walker, Kentucky vs. Western Ky., SE 2nd, 1986

THREE-POINT FIELD GOALS
11—Jeff Fryer, Loyola Marymount vs. Michigan, West 2nd, 1990

THREE-POINT FIELD GOALS ATTEMPTED
22—Jeff Fryer, Loyola Marymount vs. Arkansas, MW 1st, 1989

THREE-POINT FIELD-GOAL PERCENTAGE (Minimum 7 Made)
100% (7-7)—Sam Cassell, Florida St. vs. Tulane, SE 2nd, 1993

FREE THROWS MADE
23—Bob Carney, Bradley vs. Colorado, MW RSF, 1954; Travis Mays, Texas vs. Georgia, MW 1st, 1990

FREE THROWS ATTEMPTED
27—David Robinson, Navy vs. Syracuse, East 2nd, 1986; Travis Mays, Texas vs. Georgia, MW 1st, 1990

FREE-THROW PERCENTAGE (Minimum 16 Made)
100% (16-16)—Bill Bradley, Princeton vs. St. Joseph's, East 1st, 1963; Fennis Dembo, Wyoming vs. UCLA, West 2nd, 1987

REBOUNDS
34—Fred Cohen, Temple vs. Connecticut, East RSF, 1956

ASSISTS
18—Mark Wade, UNLV vs. Indiana, NSF, 1987

BLOCKED SHOTS
11—Shaquille O'Neal, LSU vs. Brigham Young, West 1st, 1992

STEALS
8—Darrell Hawkins, Arkansas vs. Holy Cross, East 1st, 1993; Grant Hill, Duke vs. California, MW 2nd, 1993; Duane Clemens, Ball St. vs. UCLA, MW 1st, 2000

Series

(Three-game minimum for averages and percentages)

POINTS
184—Glen Rice, Michigan, 1989 (6 games)

SCORING AVERAGE
52.7—Austin Carr, Notre Dame, 1970 (158 points in 3 games)

FIELD GOALS
75—Glen Rice, Michigan, 1989 (6 games)

FIELD GOALS ATTEMPTED
138—*Jim McDaniels, Western Ky., 1971 (5 games)
137—Elvin Hayes, Houston, 1968 (5 games)

FIELD-GOAL PERCENTAGE (Minimum 5 Made Per Game)
78.8% (26-33)—Christian Laettner, Duke, 1989 (5 games)

THREE-POINT FIELD GOALS
27—Glen Rice, Michigan, 1989 (6 games)

THREE-POINT FIELD GOALS ATTEMPTED
66—Jason Williams, Duke, 2001 (6 games)

THREE-POINT FIELD-GOAL PERCENTAGE (Minimum 1.5 Made Per Game)
100% (6-6)—Ranzino Smith, North Carolina, 1987 (4 games)

FREE THROWS MADE
55—Bob Carney, Bradley, 1954 (5 games)

FREE THROWS ATTEMPTED
71—Jerry West, West Virginia, 1959 (5 games)

PERFECT FREE-THROW PERCENTAGE (Minimum 2.5 Made Per Game)
100% (35-35)—Arthur Lee, Stanford, 1998 (5 games)

REBOUNDS
97—Elvin Hayes, Houston, 1968 (5 games)

REBOUND AVERAGE
23.3—Nate Thurmond, Bowling Green, 1963 (70 rebounds in 3 games)

ASSISTS
61—Mark Wade, UNLV, 1987 (5 games)

BLOCKED SHOTS
24—Loren Woods, Arizona, 2001 (6 games)

STEALS
23—Mookie Blaylock, Oklahoma, 1988 (6 games)

Career

(Two-year minimum for averages and percentages)

POINTS
407—Christian Laettner, Duke, 1989-92 (23 games)

SCORING AVERAGE (Minimum 6 Games)
41.3—Austin Carr, Notre Dame, 1969-71 (289 points in 7 games)

FIELD GOALS
152—Elvin Hayes, Houston, 1966-68

FIELD GOALS ATTEMPTED
310—Elvin Hayes, Houston, 1966-68

FIELD-GOAL PERCENTAGE (Minimum 70 Made)
68.6% (109-159)—Bill Walton, UCLA, 1972-74

THREE-POINT FIELD GOALS
42—Bobby Hurley, Duke, 1990-93 (20 games)

THREE-POINT FIELD GOALS ATTEMPTED
112—Jason Williams, Duke, 2000-02 (12 games)

THREE-POINT FIELD-GOAL PERCENTAGE
(Minimum 30 made)
56.5% (35-62)—Glen Rice, Michigan, 1986-89 (13 games)
(Minimum 20 made)
65.0% (26-40)—William Scott, Kansas St., 1987-88 (5 games)

FREE THROWS MADE
142—Christian Laettner, Duke, 1989-92 (23 games)

FREE THROWS ATTEMPTED
167—Christian Laettner, Duke, 1989-92 (23 games)

FREE-THROW PERCENTAGE
(Minimum 50 made)
93.5% (58-62)—Arthur Lee, Stanford, 1996-99 (12 games)
(Minimum 30 made)
97.7% (42-43), Keith Van Horn, Utah, 1995-97 (8 games)

REBOUNDS
222—Elvin Hayes, Houston, 1966-68 (13 games)

REBOUNDING AVERAGE (Minimum 6 Games)
19.7—John Green, Michigan St., 1957-59 (118 rebounds in 6 games)

ASSISTS
145—Bobby Hurley, Duke, 1990-93 (20 games)

BLOCKED SHOTS
50—Tim Duncan, Wake Forest, 1994-97 (11 games)

STEALS
39—Grant Hill, Duke, 1991-94 (20 games)

GAMES PLAYED
23—Christian Laettner, Duke, 1989-92

TEAM RECORDS

Single Game

POINTS
149—Loyola Marymount vs. Michigan, West 2nd, 1990

FEWEST POINTS
20—North Carolina vs. Pittsburgh (26), East RF, 1941

WINNING MARGIN
69—Loyola (Ill.) (111) vs. Tennessee Tech (42), SE 1st, 1963

SMALLEST WINNING MARGIN
1—140 tied (most recent: three in 2001)

POINTS SCORED BY LOSING TEAM
120—Utah vs. *St. Joseph's (127), N3d, 1961 (4 ot)

FIELD GOALS
52—Iowa vs. Notre Dame, SE R3d, 1970

FEWEST FIELD GOALS
8—Springfield vs. Indiana, East 1st, 1940

FIELD GOALS ATTEMPTED
112—Marshall vs. La.-Lafayette, MW 1st, 1972

FIELD-GOAL PERCENTAGE
80.0% (28-35)—Oklahoma St. vs. Tulane, SE 2nd, 1992

LOWEST FIELD-GOAL PERCENTAGE
12.7% (8-63)—Springfield vs. Indiana, East RSF, 1940

THREE-POINT FIELD GOALS
21—Loyola Marymount vs. Michigan, West 2nd, 1990

THREE-POINT FIELD GOALS ATTEMPTED
43—St. Joseph's vs. Boston College, West 2nd, 1997 (ot)

THREE-POINT FIELD-GOAL PERCENTAGE (Minimum 7 Made)
88.9% (8-9)—Kansas St. vs. Georgia, West 1st, 1987

FREE THROWS MADE
43—Arizona vs. Illinois, MW RF, 2001

FREE THROWS ATTEMPTED
56—Arizona vs. Illinois, MW RF, 2001

HIGHEST FREE-THROW PERCENTAGE (Minimum 22 Made)
100% (22-22)—Fordham vs. South Carolina, East R3d, 1971

MOST REBOUNDS
86—Notre Dame vs. Tennessee Tech, SE 1st, 1958

LARGEST REBOUND MARGIN
42—Notre Dame (86) vs. Tennessee Tech (44), SE 1st, 1958

MOST ASSISTS
36—North Carolina vs. Loyola Marymount, West 2nd, 1988

MOST BLOCKED SHOTS
14—Kentucky vs. UCLA, South RSF, 1998

MOST STEALS
19—Providence vs. Austin Peay, SE 2nd, 1987; Connecticut vs. Boston U., East 1st, 1990

MOST PERSONAL FOULS
41—Dayton vs. Illinois, East RSF, 1952

MOST PLAYERS DISQUALIFIED
6—Kansas vs. Notre Dame, MW 1st, 1975; Illinois vs. Arizona, MW RF, 2001

Single Game, Both Teams

POINTS
264—Loyola Marymount (149) vs. Michigan (115), West 2nd, 1990

FEWEST POINTS
46—Pittsburgh (26) vs. North Carolina (20), East RF, 1941

FIELD GOALS
97—Iowa (52) vs. Notre Dame (45), SE R3d, 1970

FIELD GOALS ATTEMPTED
204—Utah (103) vs. *St. Joseph's (101), N3d, 1961 (4 ot)

THREE-POINT FIELD GOALS
28—Seton Hall (15) vs. Temple (13), East 2nd, 2000 (ot)

THREE-POINT FIELD GOALS IN REGULATION GAME
27—Wisconsin (15) vs. Missouri (12), West 2nd, 1994

THREE-POINT FIELD GOALS ATTEMPTED
66—UCLA (36) vs. Cincinnati (30), West 2nd, 2002

FREE THROWS MADE
69—Morehead St. (37) vs. Pittsburgh (32), SE 1st, 1957

FREE THROWS ATTEMPTED
105—Iowa (52) vs. Morehead St. (53), MW RSF, 1956

REBOUNDS
134—Marshall (68) vs. *La.-Lafayette (66), MW 1st, 1972

ASSISTS
58—UNLV (35) vs. Loyola Marymount (23), West RF, 1990

BLOCKED SHOTS
20—Kentucky (14) vs. UCLA (6), South RSF, 1998

STEALS
28—N.C. A&T (16) vs. Arkansas (12), MW 1st, 1994; Purdue (16) vs. Delaware (12), MW 1st, 1998; TCU (16) vs. Florida St. (12), MW 1st, 1998; Florida (15) vs. Weber St. (13), West 2nd, 1999

PERSONAL FOULS
68—Iowa (35) vs. Morehead St. (33), South RSF, 1956

Series

(Three-game minimum for averages and percentages)

POINTS
571—UNLV, 1990 (6 games)

SCORING AVERAGE
105.8—Loyola Marymount, 1990 (423 points in 4 games)

FIELD GOALS
218—UNLV, 1977 (5 games)

FIELD GOALS ATTEMPTED
442—*Western Ky., 1971 (5 games)
441—UNLV, 1977 (6 games)

FIELD-GOAL PERCENTAGE
60.4% (113-187)—North Carolina, 1975 (3 games)

THREE-POINT FIELD GOALS
60—Arkansas, 1995 (6 games); Duke, 2001 (6 games)

THREE-POINT FIELD GOALS ATTEMPTED
175—Duke, 2001 (6 games)

THREE-POINT FIELD-GOAL PERCENTAGE
(Minimum 30 made)
51.9% (40-77)—Kansas, 1993 (5 games)
(Minimum 12 made)
60.9% (14-23)—Indiana, 1995 (3 games)

FREE THROWS MADE
146—Bradley, 1954 (5 games)

FREE THROWS ATTEMPTED
194—Bradley, 1954 (5 games)

FREE-THROW PERCENTAGE
87.0% (47-54)—St. John's (N.Y.), 1969 (3 games)

REBOUNDS
306—Houston, 1968 (5 games)

ASSISTS
143—Kentucky, 1996 (6 games)

BLOCKED SHOTS
48—Kentucky, 1998 (6 games)

STEALS
72—Oklahoma, 1988 (6 games)

PERSONAL FOULS
150—Pennsylvania, 1979 (6 games)

CH-National championship game
NSF-National semifinal game
N3d-National third-place game
RF-Regional final game
RSF-Regional semifinal game
R3d-Regional third-place game
2nd-Second-round game
1st-First-round game
Op-Opening-round game
East-East region
SE-Southeast/Mideast region
MW-Midwest region
West-West/Far West region

later vacated

CHAMPIONSHIPS

All-Time Division I Tournament Records

RECORD OF EACH TEAM COACH BY COACH
(281 Teams)

	Yrs.	Won	Lost	CH	2D	3d%	4th	RR
AIR FORCE								
Bob Spear (DePauw 1941) 1960, 62	2	0	2	0	0	0	0	0
TOTAL	2	0	2	0	0	0	0	0
AKRON								
Bob Huggins (West Virginia 1977) 1986	1	0	1	0	0	0	0	0
TOTAL	1	0	1	0	0	0	0	0
ALABAMA*								
C.M. Newton (Kentucky 1952) 1975, 76	2	1	2	0	0	0	0	0
Wimp Sanderson (North Ala. 1959) 1982, 83,84, 85, 86, 87, 89, 90, 91,92	10	12	10	0	0	0	0	0
David Hobbs (Va. Commonwealth 1971) 1994,95	2	2	2	0	0	0	0	0
Mark Gottfried (Alabama 1987) 2002	1	1	1	0	0	0	0	0
TOTAL	15	16	15	0	0	0	0	0
ALABAMA ST.								
Rob Spivery (Ashland 1972) 2001	1	0	1	0	0	0	0	0
TOTAL	1	0	1	0	0	0	0	0
UAB								
Gene Bartow (Truman 1953) 1981, 82RR, 83,84, 85, 86, 87, 90, 94	9	6	9	0	0	0	0	1
Murry Bartow (UAB 1985) 1999	1	0	1	0	0	0	0	0
TOTAL	10	6	10	0	0	0	0	1
ALCORN ST.								
Davey L. Whitney (Kentucky St. 1953) 1980, 82, 83, 84, 99, 2002	6	3	6	0	0	0	0	0
TOTAL	6	3	6	0	0	0	0	0
APPALACHIAN ST.								
Bobby Cremins (South Carolina 1970) 1979	1	0	1	0	0	0	0	0
Buzz Peterson (North Carolina 1986) 2000	1	0	1	0	0	0	0	0
TOTAL	2	0	2	0	0	0	0	0
ARIZONA *								
Fred Enke (Minnesota 1921) 1951	1	0	1	0	0	0	0	0
Fred Snowden [Wayne St. (Mich.) 1958] 1976RR, 77	2	2	2	0	0	0	0	1
Luther "Lute" Olson (Augsburg 1957) 1985, 86, 87, 88-T3d, 89, 90, 91, 92, 93, 94-T3d, 95, 96, 97-CH, 98RR, 99, 2000, 01-2d, 02	18	32	17	1	1	2	0	1
TOTAL	21	34	20	1	1	2	0	2
ARIZONA ST. *								
Ned Wulk (Wis.-La Crosse 1942) 1958, 61RR, 62, 63RR, 64, 73, 75RR, 80, 81	9	8	10	0	0	0	0	3
Bill Frieder (Michigan 1964) 1991, 95	2	3	2	0	0	0	0	0
TOTAL	11	11	12	0	0	0	0	3
ARKANSAS								
Eugene Lambert (Arkansas 1929) 1945-T3d, 49RR	2	2	2	0	0	1	0	1
Glen Rose (Arkansas 1928) 1941-T3d, 58	2	1	3	0	0	1	0	0
Eddie Sutton (Oklahoma St. 1958) 1977, 78-3d, 79RR,80, 81, 82, 83, 84, 85	9	10	9	0	0	1	0	1
Nolan Richardson (UTEP 1965) 1988, 89, 90-T3d, 91RR, 92, 93, 94-CH, 95-2d, 96, 98, 99, 2000, 01	13	26	12	1	1	1	0	1
TOTAL	26	39	26	1	1	4	0	3
ARKANSAS ST.								
Dickey Nutt (Oklahoma St. 1982) 1999	1	0	1	0	0	0	0	0
TOTAL	1	0	1	0	0	0	0	0
ARK.-LITTLE ROCK								
Mike Newell (Sam Houston St. 1973) 1986, 89, 90	3	1	3	0	0	0	0	0
TOTAL	3	1	3	0	0	0	0	0
AUBURN								
Sonny Smith (Milligan 1958) 1984, 85, 86RR, 87, 88	5	7	5	0	0	0	0	1
Cliff Ellis (Florida St. 1968) 1999, 2000	2	3	2	0	0	0	0	0
TOTAL	7	10	7	0	0	0	0	1
AUSTIN PEAY*								
Lake Kelly (Ga. Tech 1956) 1973, 74, 87	3	2	4	0	0	0	0	0
Dave Loos (Memphis 1970) 1996	1	0	1	0	0	0	0	0
TOTAL	4	2	5	0	0	0	0	0
BALL ST.								
Steve Yoder (Ill. Wesleyan 1962) 1981	1	0	1	0	0	0	0	0
Al Brown (Purdue 1964) 1986	1	0	1	0	0	0	0	0
Rick Majerus (Marquette 1970) 1989	1	1	1	0	0	0	0	0
Dick Hunsaker (Weber St. 1977) 1990, 93	2	2	2	0	0	0	0	0
Ray McCallum (Ball St. 1983) 1995, 2000	2	0	2	0	0	0	0	0
TOTAL	7	3	7	0	0	0	0	0
BAYLOR								
R.E. "Bill" Henderson (Howard Payne 1925) 1946RR, 48-2d, 50-4th	3	3	5	0	1	0	1	1
Gene Iba (Tulsa 1963) 1988	1	0	1	0	0	0	0	0
TOTAL	4	3	6	0	1	0	1	1
BOISE ST.								
Doran "Bus" Connor (Idaho St. 1955) 1976	1	0	1	0	0	0	0	0
Bob Dye (Idaho St. 1962) 1988, 93, 94	3	0	3	0	0	0	0	0
TOTAL	4	0	4	0	0	0	0	0
BOSTON COLLEGE								
Donald Martin (Georgetown 1941) 1958	1	0	1	0	0	0	0	0
Bob Cousy (Holy Cross 1948) 1967RR, 68	2	2	2	0	0	0	0	1
Bob Zuffelato (Central Conn. St. 1959) 1975	1	1	2	0	0	0	0	0
Tom Davis (Wis.-Platteville 1960) 1981, 82RR	2	5	2	0	0	0	0	1
Gary Williams (Maryland 1967) 1983, 85	2	3	2	0	0	0	0	0
Jim O'Brien (Boston College 1971) 1994RR, 96, 97	3	5	3	0	0	0	0	1
Al Skinner (Massachusetts 1974) 2001, 02	2	1	2	0	0	0	0	0
TOTAL	13	17	14	0	0	0	0	3
BOSTON U.								
Matt Zunic (George Washington 1942) 1959RR	1	2	1	0	0	0	0	1
Rick Pitino (Massachusetts 1974) 1983	1	0	1	0	0	0	0	0
Mike Jarvis (Northeastern 1968) 1988, 90	2	0	2	0	0	0	0	0
Dennis Wolff (Connecticut 1978) 1997, 2002	2	0	2	0	0	0	0	0
TOTAL	6	2	6	0	0	0	0	1
BOWLING GREEN								
Harold Anderson (Otterbein 1924) 1959, 62, 63	3	1	4	0	0	0	0	0
Bill Fitch (Coe 1954) 1968	1	0	1	0	0	0	0	0
TOTAL	4	1	5	0	0	0	0	0
BRADLEY								
Forrest "Forddy" Anderson (Stanford 1942) 1950-2d, 54-2d	2	6	4	0	2	0	0	0
Bob Vanatta (Central Methodist 1945) 1955RR	1	2	1	0	0	0	0	1
Dick Versace (Wisconsin 1964) 1980, 86	2	1	2	0	0	0	0	0
Stan Albeck (Bradley 1955) 1988	1	0	1	0	0	0	0	0
Jim Molinari (Ill. Wesleyan 1977) 1996	1	0	1	0	0	0	0	0
TOTAL	7	9	7	0	2	0	0	1
BRIGHAM YOUNG								
Stan Watts (Brigham Young 1938) 1950RR, 51RR, 57, 65, 69, 71, 72	7	4	10	0	0	0	0	2
Frank Arnold (Idaho St. 1956) 1979, 80, 81RR	3	3	3	0	0	0	0	1
Ladell Andersen (Utah St. 1951) 1984, 87, 88	3	2	3	0	0	0	0	0
Roger Reid (Weber St. 1967) 1990, 91, 92, 93, 95	5	2	5	0	0	0	0	0
Steve Cleveland (UC Irvine 1976) 2001	1	0	1	0	0	0	0	0
TOTAL	19	11	22	0	0	0	0	3
BROWN								
George Allen (West Virginia 1935) 1939RR	1	0	1	0	0	0	0	1
Mike Cingiser (Brown 1962) 1986	1	0	1	0	0	0	0	0
TOTAL	2	0	2	0	0	0	0	1
BUCKNELL								
Charles Woollum (William & Mary 1962) 1987, 89	2	0	2	0	0	0	0	0
TOTAL	2	0	2	0	0	0	0	0
BUTLER								
Paul "Tony" Hinkle (Chicago 1921) 1962	1	2	1	0	0	0	0	0
Barry Collier (Butler 1976) 1997, 98, 2000	3	0	3	0	0	0	0	0
Thad Matta (Butler 1990) 2001	1	1	1	0	0	0	0	0
TOTAL	5	3	5	0	0	0	0	0
CALIFORNIA*								
Clarence "Nibs" Price (California 1914) 1946-4th	1	1	2	0	0	0	1	0
Pete Newell (Loyola Marymount 1940) 1957RR, 58RR, 59-CH, 60-2d	4	10	3	1	1	0	0	2
Lou Campanelli (Montclair St. 1960) 1990	1	1	1	0	0	0	0	0

	Yrs.	Won	Lost	CH	2D	3d%	4th	RR
Todd Bozeman (Rhode Island 1986) 1993, 94, 96	3	2	3	0	0	0	0	0
Ben Braun (Wisconsin 1975) 1997, 2001, 02	3	3	3	0	0	0	0	0
TOTAL	12	17	12	1	1	0	1	2
UC SANTA BARB.								
Jerry Pimm (Southern California 1961) 1988, 90	2	1	2	0	0	0	0	0
Bob Williams (San Jose St. 1975) 2002	1	0	1	0	0	0	0	0
TOTAL	3	1	3	0	0	0	0	0
CAL ST. FULLERTON								
Bob Dye (Idaho St. 1962) 1978RR	1	2	1	0	0	0	0	1
TOTAL	1	2	1	0	0	0	0	1
CAL ST. LOS ANGELES								
Bob Miller (Occidental 1953) 1974	1	0	1	0	0	0	0	0
TOTAL	1	0	1	0	0	0	0	0
CAL ST. NORTHRIDGE								
Bobby Braswell (Cal St. Northridge 1984) 2001	1	0	1	0	0	0	0	0
TOTAL	1	0	1	0	0	0	0	0
CAMPBELL								
Billy Lee (Barton 1971) 1992	1	0	1	0	0	0	0	0
TOTAL	1	0	1	0	0	0	0	0
CANISIUS								
Joseph Curran (Canisius 1943) 1955RR, 56RR, 57	3	6	3	0	0	0	0	2
John Beilein (Wheeling Jesuit 1975) 1996	1	0	1	0	0	0	0	0
TOTAL	4	6	4	0	0	0	0	2
CATHOLIC								
John Long (Catholic 1928) 1944RR	1	0	2	0	0	0	0	1
TOTAL	1	0	2	0	0	0	0	1
CENTRAL CONN. ST.								
Howie Dickenmann (Central Conn. St. 1970) 2000, 02	2	0	2	0	0	0	0	0
TOTAL	2	0	2	0	0	0	0	0
UCF								
Kirk Speraw (Iowa 1980) 1994, 96	2	0	2	0	0	0	0	0
TOTAL	2	0	2	0	0	0	0	0
CENTRAL MICH.								
Dick Parfitt (Central Mich. 1953) 1975, 77	2	2	2	0	0	0	0	0
Charlie Coles [Miami (Ohio) 1965] 1987	1	0	1	0	0	0	0	0
TOTAL	3	2	3	0	0	0	0	0
COL. OF CHARLESTON								
John Kresse [St. John's (N.Y.) 1964] 1994, 97, 98, 99	4	1	4	0	0	0	0	0
TOTAL	4	1	4	0	0	0	0	0
CHARLESTON SO.								
Tom Conrad (Old Dominion 1979) 1997	1	0	1	0	0	0	0	0
TOTAL	1	0	1	0	0	0	0	0
CHARLOTTE								
Lee Rose (Transylvania 1958) 1977-4th	1	3	2	0	0	0	1	0
Jeff Mullins (Duke 1964) 1988, 92, 95	3	0	3	0	0	0	0	0
Melvin Watkins (Charlotte 1977) 1997, 98	2	2	2	0	0	0	0	0
Bob Lutz (Charlotte 1980) 1999, 2001, 02	3	2	3	0	0	0	0	0
TOTAL	9	7	10	0	0	0	1	0
CHATTANOOGA								
Murray Arnold (American 1960) 1981, 82, 83	3	1	3	0	0	0	0	0
Mack McCarthy (Virginia Tech 1974) 1988, 93, 94, 95, 97	5	2	5	0	0	0	0	0
TOTAL	8	3	8	0	0	0	0	0
CINCINNATI								
George Smith (Cincinnati 1935) 1958, 59-3d, 60-3d	3	7	3	0	0	2	0	0
Ed Jucker (Cincinnati 1940) 1961-CH, 62-CH, 63-2d	3	11	1	2	1	0	0	0
Tay Baker (Cincinnati 1950) 1966	1	0	2	0	0	0	0	0
Gale Catlett (West Virginia 1963) 1975, 76, 77	3	2	3	0	0	0	0	0
Bob Huggins (West Virginia 1977) 1992-T3d, 93RR, 94, 95,96RR, 97, 98, 99, 2000, 01, 02	11	18	11	0	0	1	0	2
TOTAL	21	38	20	2	1	3	0	2
CCNY								
Nat Holman (Savage School of Phys. Ed. 1917) 1947-4th, 50-CH	2	4	2	1	0	0	1	0
TOTAL	2	4	2	1	0	0	1	0

	Yrs.	Won	Lost	CH	2D	3d%	4th	RR
CLEMSON*								
Bill C. Foster (Carson-Newman 1958) 1980RR	1	3	1	0	0	0	0	1
Cliff Ellis (Florida St. 1968) 1987, 89, 90	3	3	3	0	0	0	0	0
Rick Barnes (Lenoir-Rhyne 1977) 1996, 97, 98	3	2	3	0	0	0	0	0
TOTAL	7	8	7	0	0	0	0	1
CLEVELAND ST.								
Kevin Mackey (St. Anselm 1967) 1986	1	2	1	0	0	0	0	0
TOTAL	1	2	1	0	0	0	0	0
COASTAL CARO.								
Russ Bergman (LSU 1970) 1991, 93	2	0	2	0	0	0	0	0
TOTAL	2	0	2	0	0	0	0	0
COLGATE								
Jack Bruen (Catholic 1972) 1995, 96	2	0	2	0	0	0	0	0
TOTAL	2	0	2	0	0	0	0	0
COLORADO								
Forrest "Frosty" Cox (Kansas 1930) 1940RR, 42-T3d, 46RR	3	2	4	0	0	1	0	2
Horace "Bebe" Lee (Stanford 1938) 1954, 55-3d	2	3	3	0	0	1	0	0
Russell "Sox" Walseth (Colorado 1948) 1962RR, 63RR, 69	3	3	3	0	0	0	0	2
Ricardo Patton (Belmont 1980) 1997	1	1	1	0	0	0	0	0
TOTAL	9	9	11	0	0	2	0	4
COLORADO ST.								
Bill Strannigan (Wyoming 1941) 1954	1	0	2	0	0	0	0	0
Jim Williams (Utah St. 1947) 1963, 65, 66, 69RR	4	2	4	0	0	0	0	1
Boyd Grant (Colorado St. 1957) 1989, 90	2	1	2	0	0	0	0	0
TOTAL	7	3	8	0	0	0	0	1
COLUMBIA								
Gordon Ridings (Oregon 1929) 1948RR	1	0	2	0	0	0	0	1
Lou Rossini (Columbia 1948) 1951	1	0	1	0	0	0	0	0
John "Jack" Rohan (Columbia 1953) 1968	1	2	1	0	0	0	0	0
TOTAL	3	2	4	0	0	0	0	1
CONNECTICUT*								
Hugh Greer (Connecticut 1926) 1951, 54, 56, 57, 58, 59, 60	7	1	8	0	0	0	0	0
George Wigton (Ohio St. 1956) 1963	1	0	1	0	0	0	0	0
Fred Shabel (Duke 1954) 1964RR, 65, 67	3	2	3	0	0	0	0	1
Donald "Dee" Rowe (Middlebury 1952) 1976	1	1	1	0	0	0	0	0
Dom Perno (Connecticut 1964) 1979	1	0	1	0	0	0	0	0
Jim Calhoun (American Int'l 1968) 1990RR, 91, 92, 94,95RR, 96, 98RR, 99-CH, 2000, 02RR	10	26	9	1	0	0	0	4
TOTAL	23	30	23	1	0	0	0	5
COPPIN ST.								
Ron Mitchell (Edison 1984) 1990, 93, 97	3	1	3	0	0	0	0	0
TOTAL	3	1	3	0	0	0	0	0
CORNELL								
Royner Greene (Illinois 1929) 1954	1	0	2	0	0	0	0	0
Mike Dement (East Caro. 1976) 1988	1	0	1	0	0	0	0	0
TOTAL	2	0	3	0	0	0	0	0
CREIGHTON								
Eddie Hickey (Creighton 1927) 1941RR	1	1	1	0	0	0	0	1
John "Red" McManus (St. Ambrose 1949) 1962, 64	2	3	3	0	0	0	0	0
Eddie Sutton (Oklahoma St. 1958) 1974	1	2	1	0	0	0	0	0
Tom Apke (Creighton 1965) 1975, 78, 81	3	0	3	0	0	0	0	0
Tony Barone (Duke 1968) 1989, 91	2	1	2	0	0	0	0	0
Dana Altman (Eastern N.M. 1980) 1999, 2000, 01, 02	4	2	4	0	0	0	0	0
TOTAL	13	9	14	0	0	0	0	1
DARTMOUTH								
Osborne "Ozzie" Cowles (Carleton 1922) 1941RR, 42-2d, 43RR	3	4	3	0	1	0	0	2
Earl Brown (Notre Dame 1939) 1944-2d	1	2	1	0	1	0	0	0
Alvin "Doggie" Julian (Bucknell 1923) 1956, 58RR, 59	3	4	3	0	0	0	0	1
TOTAL	7	10	7	0	2	0	0	3
DAVIDSON								
Charles "Lefty" Driesell (Duke 1954) 1966, 68RR, 69RR	3	5	4	0	0	0	0	2
Terry Holland (Davidson 1964) 1970	1	0	1	0	0	0	0	0
Bobby Hussey (Appalachian St. 1962) 1986	1	0	1	0	0	0	0	0
Bob McKillop (Hofstra 1972) 1998, 2002	2	0	2	0	0	0	0	0
TOTAL	7	5	8	0	0	0	0	2

158 DIVISION I CHAMPIONSHIP—ALL-TIME TOURNAMENT RECORDS

DAYTON

	Yrs.	Won	Lost	CH	2D	3d%	4th	RR
Tom Blackburn [Wilmington (Ohio) 1931] 1952	1	1	1	0	0	0	0	0
Don Donoher (Dayton 1954) 1965, 66, 67-2d, 69, 70, 74, 84RR, 85	8	11	10	0	1	0	0	1
Jim O'Brien (St. Joseph's 1974) 1990	1	1	1	0	0	0	0	0
Oliver Purnell (Old Dominion 1975) 2000	1	0	1	0	0	0	0	0
TOTAL	11	13	13	0	1	0	0	1

DELAWARE

	Yrs.	Won	Lost	CH	2D	3d%	4th	RR
Steve Steinwedel (Mississippi St. 1975) 1992, 93	2	0	2	0	0	0	0	0
Mike Brey (George Washington 1982) 1998, 99	2	0	2	0	0	0	0	0
TOTAL	4	0	4	0	0	0	0	0

DePAUL*

	Yrs.	Won	Lost	CH	2D	3d%	4th	RR
Ray Meyer (Notre Dame 1938) 1943-T3d, 53, 56, 59, 60, 65, 76, 78RR, 79-3d, 80, 81, 82, 84	13	14	16	0	0	2	0	1
Joey Meyer (DePaul 1971) 1985, 86, 87, 88, 89, 91, 92	7	6	7	0	0	0	0	0
Pat Kennedy [King's (Pa.) 1976] 2000	1	0	1	0	0	0	0	0
TOTAL	21	20	24	0	0	2	0	1

DETROIT

	Yrs.	Won	Lost	CH	2D	3d%	4th	RR
Robert Calihan (Detroit 1940) 1962	1	0	1	0	0	0	0	0
Dick Vitale (Seton Hall 1962) 1977	1	1	1	0	0	0	0	0
Dave "Smokey" Gaines (LeMoyne-Owen 1963) 1979	1	0	1	0	0	0	0	0
Perry Watson (Eastern Mich. 1972) 1998, 99	2	2	2	0	0	0	0	0
TOTAL	5	3	5	0	0	0	0	0

DRAKE

	Yrs.	Won	Lost	CH	2D	3d%	4th	RR
Maurice John (Central Mo. St. 1941) 1969-3d, 70RR, 71RR	3	5	3	0	0	1	0	2
TOTAL	3	5	3	0	0	1	0	2

DREXEL

	Yrs.	Won	Lost	CH	2D	3d%	4th	RR
Eddie Burke (La Salle 1967) 1986	1	0	1	0	0	0	0	0
Bill Herrion (Merrimack 1981) 1994, 95, 96	3	1	3	0	0	0	0	0
TOTAL	4	1	4	0	0	0	0	0

DUKE

	Yrs.	Won	Lost	CH	2D	3d%	4th	RR
Harold Bradley (Hartwick 1934) 1955	1	0	1	0	0	0	0	0
Vic Bubas (North Carolina St. 1951) 1960RR, 63-3d, 64-2d, 66-3d	4	11	4	0	1	2	0	1
W.E. "Bill" Foster (Elizabethtown 1954) 1978-2d, 79, 80RR	3	6	3	0	1	0	0	1
Mike Krzyzewski (Army 1969) 1984, 85, 86-2d, 87, 88-T3d, 89-T3d, 90-2d, 91-CH, 92-CH, 93, 94-2d, 96, 97, 98RR, 99-2d, 2000, 01-CH, 02	18	58	15	3	4	2	0	1
TOTAL	26	75	23	3	6	4	0	3

DUQUESNE

	Yrs.	Won	Lost	CH	2D	3d%	4th	RR
Charles "Chick" Davies (Duquesne 1934) 1940-T3d	1	1	1	0	0	1	0	0
Donald "Dudey" Moore (Duquesne 1934) 1952RR	1	1	1	0	0	0	0	1
John "Red" Manning (Duquesne 1951) 1969, 71	2	2	2	0	0	0	0	0
John Cinicola (Duquesne 1955) 1977	1	0	1	0	0	0	0	0
TOTAL	5	4	5	0	0	1	0	1

EAST CARO.

	Yrs.	Won	Lost	CH	2D	3d%	4th	RR
Tom Quinn (Marshall 1954) 1972	1	0	1	0	0	0	0	0
Eddie Payne (Wake Forest 1973) 1993	1	0	1	0	0	0	0	0
TOTAL	2	0	2	0	0	0	0	0

EAST TENN. ST.

	Yrs.	Won	Lost	CH	2D	3d%	4th	RR
J. Madison Brooks (Louisiana Tech 1937) 1968	1	1	2	0	0	0	0	0
Les Robinson (North Carolina St. 1964) 1989, 90	2	0	2	0	0	0	0	0
Alan LeForce (Cumberland 1957) 1991, 92	2	1	2	0	0	0	0	0
TOTAL	5	2	6	0	0	0	0	0

EASTERN ILL.

	Yrs.	Won	Lost	CH	2D	3d%	4th	RR
Rick Samuels (Chadron St. 1971) 1992, 2001	2	0	2	0	0	0	0	0
TOTAL	2	0	2	0	0	0	0	0

EASTERN KY.

	Yrs.	Won	Lost	CH	2D	3d%	4th	RR
Paul McBrayer (Kentucky 1930) 1953, 59	2	0	2	0	0	0	0	0
Jim Baechtold (Eastern Ky. 1952) 1965	1	0	1	0	0	0	0	0
Guy Strong (Eastern Ky. 1955) 1972	1	0	1	0	0	0	0	0
Ed Byhre [Augustana (S.D.) 1966] 1979	1	0	1	0	0	0	0	0
TOTAL	5	0	5	0	0	0	0	0

EASTERN MICH.

	Yrs.	Won	Lost	CH	2D	3d%	4th	RR
Ben Braun (Wisconsin 1975) 1988, 91, 96	3	3	3	0	0	0	0	0
Milton Barnes (Albion 1979) 1998	1	0	1	0	0	0	0	0
TOTAL	4	3	4	0	0	0	0	0

EVANSVILLE

	Yrs.	Won	Lost	CH	2D	3d%	4th	RR
Dick Walters (Illinois St. 1969) 1982	1	0	1	0	0	0	0	0
Jim Crews (Indiana 1976) 1989, 92, 93, 99	4	1	4	0	0	0	0	0
TOTAL	5	1	5	0	0	0	0	0

FAIRFIELD

	Yrs.	Won	Lost	CH	2D	3d%	4th	RR
Mitch Buonaguro (Boston College 1975) 1986, 87	2	0	2	0	0	0	0	0
Paul Cormier (New Hampshire 1973) 1997	1	0	1	0	0	0	0	0
TOTAL	3	0	3	0	0	0	0	0

FDU-TEANECK

	Yrs.	Won	Lost	CH	2D	3d%	4th	RR
Tom Green (Syracuse 1971) 1985, 88, 98	3	0	3	0	0	0	0	0
TOTAL	3	0	3	0	0	0	0	0

FLORIDA*

	Yrs.	Won	Lost	CH	2D	3d%	4th	RR
Norm Sloan (North Carolina St. 1951) 1987, 88, 89	3	3	3	0	0	0	0	0
Lon Kruger (Kansas St. 1974) 1994-T3d, 95	2	4	2	0	0	1	0	0
Billy Donovan (Providence 1987) 1999, 2000-2d, 01, 02	4	8	4	0	1	0	0	0
TOTAL	9	15	9	0	1	1	0	0

FLORIDA A&M

	Yrs.	Won	Lost	CH	2D	3d%	4th	RR
Mickey Clayton (Florida A&M 1975) 1999	1	0	1	0	0	0	0	0
TOTAL	1	0	1	0	0	0	0	0

FLORIDA ATLANTIC

	Yrs.	Won	Lost	CH	2D	3d%	4th	RR
Sydney Green (UNLV 1983), 2002	1	0	1	0	0	0	0	0
TOTAL	1	0	1	0	0	0	0	0

FLORIDA INT'L

	Yrs.	Won	Lost	CH	2D	3d%	4th	RR
Bob Weltlich (Ohio St. 1967) 1995	1	0	1	0	0	0	0	0
TOTAL	1	0	1	0	0	0	0	0

FLORIDA ST.

	Yrs.	Won	Lost	CH	2D	3d%	4th	RR
Hugh Durham (Florida St. 1959) 1968, 72-2d, 78	3	4	3	0	1	0	0	0
Joe Williams (Southern Methodist 1956) 1980	1	1	1	0	0	0	0	0
Pat Kennedy [King's (Pa.) 1976] 1988, 89, 91, 92, 93RR	5	6	5	0	0	0	0	1
Steve Robinson (Radford 1981) 1998	1	1	1	0	0	0	0	0
TOTAL	10	12	10	0	1	0	0	1

FORDHAM

	Yrs.	Won	Lost	CH	2D	3d%	4th	RR
John Bach (Fordham 1948) 1953, 54	2	0	2	0	0	0	0	0
Richard "Digger" Phelps (Rider 1963) 1971	1	2	1	0	0	0	0	0
Nick Macarchuk (Fairfield 1963) 1992	1	0	1	0	0	0	0	0
TOTAL	4	2	4	0	0	0	0	0

FRESNO ST.

	Yrs.	Won	Lost	CH	2D	3d%	4th	RR
Boyd Grant (Colorado St. 1961) 1981, 82, 84	3	1	3	0	0	0	0	0
Jerry Tarkanian (Fresno St. 1956) 2000, 01	2	1	2	0	0	0	0	0
TOTAL	5	2	5	0	0	0	0	0

FURMAN

	Yrs.	Won	Lost	CH	2D	3d%	4th	RR
Joe Williams (Southern Methodist 1956) 1971, 73, 74, 75, 78	5	1	6	0	0	0	0	0
Eddie Holbrook (Lenoir-Rhyne 1962) 1980	1	0	1	0	0	0	0	0
TOTAL	6	1	7	0	0	0	0	0

GEORGE MASON

	Yrs.	Won	Lost	CH	2D	3d%	4th	RR
Ernie Nestor (Alderson-Broaddus 1968) 1989	1	0	1	0	0	0	0	0
Jim Larranaga (Providence 1971) 1999, 2001	2	0	2	0	0	0	0	0
TOTAL	3	0	3	0	0	0	0	0

GEORGE WASHINGTON

	Yrs.	Won	Lost	CH	2D	3d%	4th	RR
Bill Reinhart (Oregon 1923) 1954, 61	2	0	2	0	0	0	0	0
Mike Jarvis (Northeastern 1968) 1993, 94, 96, 98	4	3	4	0	0	0	0	0
Tom Penders (Connecticut 1967) 1999	1	0	1	0	0	0	0	0
TOTAL	7	3	7	0	0	0	0	0

GEORGETOWN

	Yrs.	Won	Lost	CH	2D	3d%	4th	RR
Elmer Ripley (No college) 1943-2d	1	2	1	0	1	0	0	0
John Thompson (Providence 1964) 1975, 76, 79, 80RR, 81, 82-2d, 83, 84-CH, 85-2d, 86, 87RR, 88, 89RR, 90, 91, 92, 94, 95, 96RR, 97	20	34	19	1	2	0	0	4
Craig Esherick (Georgetown 1978) 2001	1	2	1	0	0	0	0	0
TOTAL	22	38	21	1	3	0	0	4

	Yrs.	Won	Lost	CH	2D	3d%	4th	RR
GEORGIA*								
Hugh Durham (Florida St. 1959) 1983-T3d, 85, 87, 90, 91	5	4	5	0	0	1	0	0
Tubby Smith (High Point 1973) 1996, 97	2	2	2	0	0	0	0	0
Jim Harrick [Charleston (W.Va.) 1960] 2001, 02	2	1	2	0	0	0	0	0
TOTAL	9	7	9	0	0	1	0	0
GA. SOUTHERN								
Frank Kerns (Alabama 1957) 1983, 87, 92	3	0	3	0	0	0	0	0
TOTAL	3	0	3	0	0	0	0	0
GEORGIA ST.								
Bob Reinhart (Indiana 1961) 1991	1	0	1	0	0	0	0	0
Charles "Lefty" Driesell (Duke 1954) 2001	1	1	1	0	0	0	0	0
TOTAL	2	1	2	0	0	0	0	0
GEORGIA TECH								
John "Whack" Hyder (Georgia Tech 1937) 1960RR	1	1	1	0	0	0	0	1
Bobby Cremins (South Carolina 1970) 1985RR, 86, 87, 88, 89, 90-T3d, 91, 92, 93, 96	10	15	10	0	0	1	0	1
Paul Hewitt (St. John Fisher 1985) 2001	1	0	1	0	0	0	0	0
TOTAL	12	16	12	0	0	1	0	2
GONZAGA								
Dan Fitzgerald (Cal St. Los Angeles 1965) 1995	1	0	1	0	0	0	0	0
Dan Monson (Idaho 1985) 1999RR	1	3	1	0	0	0	0	1
Mark Few (Oregon 1987) 2000, 01, 02	3	4	3	0	0	0	0	0
TOTAL	5	7	5	0	0	0	0	1
HAMPTON								
Steve Merfeld (Wis.-La Crosse 1984) 2001, 02	2	1	2	0	0	0	0	0
TOTAL	2	1	2	0	0	0	0	0
HARDIN-SIMMONS								
Bill Scott (Hardin-Simmons 1947) 1953, 57	2	0	2	0	0	0	0	0
TOTAL	2	0	2	0	0	0	0	0
HARVARD								
Floyd Stahl (Illinois 1926) 1946RR	1	0	2	0	0	0	0	1
TOTAL	1	0	2	0	0	0	0	1
HAWAII								
Ephraim "Red" Rocha (Oregon St. 1950) 1972	1	0	1	0	0	0	0	0
Riley Wallace [Centenary (La.) 1964] 1994, 2001, 02	3	0	3	0	0	0	0	0
TOTAL	4	0	4	0	0	0	0	0
HOFSTRA								
Roger Gaeckler (Gettysburg 1965) 1976, 77	2	0	2	0	0	0	0	0
Jay Wright (Bucknell 1983) 2000, 01	2	0	2	0	0	0	0	0
TOTAL	4	0	4	0	0	0	0	0
HOLY CROSS								
Alvin "Doggie" Julian (Bucknell 1923) 1947-CH, 48-3d	2	5	1	1	0	1	0	0
Lester "Buster" Sheary (Catholic 1933) 1950RR, 53RR	2	2	3	0	0	0	0	2
Roy Leenig [Trinity (Conn.) 1942] 1956	1	0	1	0	0	0	0	0
George Blaney (Holy Cross 1961) 1977, 80, 93	3	0	3	0	0	0	0	0
Ralph Willard (Holy Cross 1967) 2001, 02	2	0	2	0	0	0	0	0
TOTAL	10	7	10	1	0	1	0	2
HOUSTON								
Alden Pasche (Rice 1932) 1956	1	0	2	0	0	0	0	0
Guy Lewis (Houston 1947) 1961, 65, 66, 67-3d, 68-4th, 70, 71, 72, 73, 78, 81, 82-T3d, 83-2d, 84-2d	14	26	18	0	2	2	1	0
Pat Foster (Arkansas 1961) 1987, 90, 92	3	0	3	0	0	0	0	0
TOTAL	18	26	23	0	2	2	1	0
HOUSTON BAPTIST								
Gene Iba (Tulsa 1963) 1984	1	0	1	0	0	0	0	0
TOTAL	1	0	1	0	0	0	0	0
HOWARD								
A.B. Williamson (N.C. A&T 1968) 19811	0	1	0	0	0	0	0	
Alfred "Butch" Beard (Louisville 1972) 1992	1	0	1	0	0	0	0	0
TOTAL	2	0	2	0	0	0	0	0
IDAHO								
Don Monson (Idaho 1955) 1981, 82	2	1	2	0	0	0	0	0
Kermit Davis Jr. (Mississippi St. 1982) 1989, 90	2	0	2	0	0	0	0	0
TOTAL	4	1	4	0	0	0	0	0
IDAHO ST.								
Steve Belko (Idaho 1939) 1953, 54, 55, 56	4	2	4	0	0	0	0	0
John Grayson (Oklahoma 1938) 1957, 58, 59	3	4	5	0	0	0	0	0
John Evans (Idaho 1948) 1960	1	0	1	0	0	0	0	0
Jim Killingsworth (Northeastern Okla. St. 1948) 1974, 77RR	2	2	2	0	0	0	0	1
Jim Boutin (Lewis & Clark 1964) 1987	1	0	1	0	0	0	0	0
TOTAL	11	8	13	0	0	0	0	1
ILLINOIS								
Doug Mills (Illinois 1930) 1942RR	1	0	2	0	0	0	0	1
Harry Combes (Illinois 1937) 1949-3d, 51-3d, 52-3d, 63RR	4	9	4	0	0	3	0	1
Lou Henson (New Mexico St. 1955) 1981, 83, 84RR, 85, 86, 87, 88, 89-T3d, 90, 93, 94, 95	12	12	12	0	0	1	0	1
Lon Kruger (Kansas St. 1974) 1997, 98 2000	3	3	3	0	0	0	0	0
Bill Self (Oklahoma St. 1985) 2001RR, 02	2	5	2	0	0	0	0	1
TOTAL	22	29	23	0	0	4	0	4
ILLINOIS ST.								
Bob Donewald (Hanover 1964) 1983, 84, 85	3	2	3	0	0	0	0	0
Bob Bender (Duke 1980) 1990	1	0	1	0	0	0	0	0
Kevin Stallings (Purdue 1982) 1997, 98	2	1	2	0	0	0	0	0
TOTAL	6	3	6	0	0	0	0	0
ILL.-CHICAGO								
Jimmy Collins (New Mexico St. 1970) 1998, 2002	2	0	2	0	0	0	0	0
TOTAL	2	0	2	0	0	0	0	0
INDIANA								
Branch McCracken (Indiana 1930) 1940-CH, 53-CH, 54, 58	4	9	2	2	0	0	0	0
Lou Watson (Indiana 1950) 1967	1	1	1	0	0	0	0	0
Bob Knight (Ohio St. 1962) 1973-3d, 75RR, 76-CH, 78, 80, 81-CH, 82, 83, 84RR, 86, 87-CH, 88, 89, 90, 91, 92-T3d, 93RR, 94, 95, 96, 97, 98, 99, 2000	24	42	21	3	0	2	0	3
Mike Davis (Alabama 1983) 2001, 02-2d	2	5	2	0	1	0	0	0
TOTAL	31	57	26	5	1	2	0	3
INDIANA ST.								
Bill Hodges (Marian 1970) 1979-2d	1	4	1	0	1	0	0	0
Royce Waltman (Slippery Rock 1964) 2000, 01	2	1	2	0	0	0	0	0
TOTAL	3	5	3	0	1	0	0	0
IONA*								
Jim Valvano (Rutgers 1967) 1979, 80	2	1	2	0	0	0	0	0
Pat Kennedy [King's (Pa.) 1976] 1984, 85	2	0	2	0	0	0	0	0
Tim Welsh (Potsdam St. 1984) 1998	1	0	1	0	0	0	0	0
Jeff Ruland (Iona 1991) 2000, 01	2	0	2	0	0	0	0	0
TOTAL	7	1	7	0	0	0	0	0
IOWA								
Frank "Bucky" O'Connor (Drake 1938) 1955-4th, 56-2d	2	5	3	0	1	0	1	0
Ralph Miller (Kansas 1942) 1970	1	1	1	0	0	0	0	0
Luther "Lute" Olson (Augsburg 1957) 1979, 80-4th, 81, 82, 83	5	7	6	0	0	0	1	0
George Raveling (Villanova 1960) 1985, 86	2	0	2	0	0	0	0	0
Tom Davis (Wis.-Platteville 1960) 1987RR, 88, 89, 91, 92, 93, 96, 97, 99	9	13	9	0	0	0	0	1
Steve Alford (Indiana 1987) 2001	1	1	1	0	0	0	0	0
TOTAL	20	27	22	0	1	0	2	1
IOWA ST.								
Louis Menze (Central Mo. St. 1928) 1944-T3d	1	1	1	0	0	1	0	0
Johnny Orr (Beloit 1949) 1985, 86, 88, 89, 92, 93	6	3	6	0	0	0	0	0
Tim Floyd (Louisiana Tech 1977) 1995, 96, 97	3	4	3	0	0	0	0	0
Larry Eustachy (Long Beach St. 1979) 2000RR, 01	2	3	2	0	0	0	0	1
TOTAL	12	11	12	0	0	1	0	1
JACKSON ST.								
Andy Stoglin (UTEP 1965) 1997, 2000	2	0	2	0	0	0	0	0
TOTAL	2	0	2	0	0	0	0	0
JACKSONVILLE								
Joe Williams (Southern Methodist 1956) 1970-2d	1	4	1	0	1	0	0	0
Tom Wasdin (Florida 1957) 1971, 73	2	0	2	0	0	0	0	0

	Yrs.	Won	Lost	CH	2D	3d%	4th	RR
Tates Locke (Ohio Wesleyan 1959) 1979	1	0	1	0	0		0	0	0
Bob Wenzel (Rutgers 1971) 1986	1	0	1	0	0		0	0	0
TOTAL	5	4	5	0	1		0	0	0
JAMES MADISON								
Lou Campanelli (Montclair St. 1960) 1981, 82, 83	3	3	3	0	0		0	0	0
Charles "Lefty" Driesell (Duke 1954) 1994	1	0	1	0	0		0	0	0
TOTAL	4	3	4	0	0		0	0	0
KANSAS								
Forrest C. "Phog" Allen (Kansas 1906) 1940-2d, 42RR, 52-CH, 53-2d	4	10	3	1	2		0	0	1
Dick Harp (Kansas 1940) 1957-2d, 60RR	2	4	2	0	1		0	0	1
Ted Owens (Oklahoma 1951) 1966RR, 67, 71-4th, 74-4th, 75, 78, 81	7	8	9	0	0		0	2	1
Larry Brown (North Carolina 1963) 1984, 85, 86-T3d, 87, 88-CH	5	14	4	1	0		1	0	0
Roy Williams (North Carolina 1972) 1990, 91-2d, 92, 93-T3d, 94, 95, 96RR, 97, 98, 99, 2000, 01, 02-T3d.	13	29	13	0	1		2	0	1
TOTAL	31	65	31	2	4		3	2	4
KANSAS ST.								
Jack Gardner (Southern California 1932) 1948-4th, 51-2d	2	4	3	0	1		0	1	0
Fred "Tex" Winter (Southern California 1947) 1956, 58-4th, 59RR, 61RR, 64-4th, 68	6	7	9	0	0		0	2	2
Lowell "Cotton" Fitzsimmons (Midwestern St. 1955) 1970	1	1	1	0	0		0	0	0
Jack Hartman (Oklahoma St. 1949) 1972RR, 73RR, 75RR, 77, 80, 81RR, 82	7	11	7	0	0		0	0	4
Lon Kruger (Kansas St. 1974) 1987, 88RR, 89, 90	4	4	4	0	0		0	0	1
Dana Altman (Eastern N.M. 1980) 1993	1	0	1	0	0		0	0	0
Tom Asbury (Wyoming 1967) 1996	1	0	1	0	0		0	0	0
TOTAL	22	27	26	0	1		0	3	7
KENT ST.								
Gary Waters (Ferris St. 1975) 1999, 2001	2	1	2	0	0		0	0	0
Stan Heath (Eastern Mich. 1988) 2002RR	1	3	1	0	0		0	0	1
TOTAL	3	4	3	0	0		0	0	1
KENTUCKY*								
Adolph Rupp (Kansas 1923) 1942-T3d, 45RR, 48-CH,49-CH, 51-CH, 52RR, 55, 56RR, 57RR, 58-CH, 59,61RR, 62RR, 64, 66-2d, 68RR, 69, 70RR, 71, 72RR	20	30	18	4	1		1	0	9
Joe B. Hall (Sewanee 1951) 1973RR, 75-2d, 77RR, 78-CH, 80, 81, 82, 83RR, 84-T3d, 85	10	20	9	1	1		1	0	3
Eddie Sutton (Oklahoma St. 1958) 1986RR, 87, 88	3	5	3	0	0		0	0	1
Rick Pitino (Massachusetts 1974) 1992RR, 93-T3d, 94, 95RR 96-CH, 97-2d	6	22	5	1	1		1	0	2
Tubby Smith (High Point 1973) 1998-CH, 99RR, 2000, 01, 02	5	14	4	1	0		0	0	1
TOTAL	44	91	39	7	3		3	0	16
LA SALLE								
Ken Loeffler (Penn St. 1924) 1954-CH, 55-2d	2	9	1	1	1		0	0	0
Jim Harding (Iowa 1949) 1968	1	0	1	0	0		0	0	0
Paul Westhead (St. Joseph's 1961) 1975, 78	2	0	2	0	0		0	0	0
Dave "Lefty" Ervin (La Salle 1968) 1980, 83	2	1	2	0	0		0	0	0
Bill "Speedy" Morris (St. Joseph's 1973) 1988, 89, 90, 92	4	1	4	0	0		0	0	0
TOTAL	11	11	10	1	1		0	0	0
LAFAYETTE								
George Davidson (Lafayette 1951) 1957	1	0	2	0	0		0	0	0
Fran O'Hanlon (Villanova 1970) 1999, 2000	2	0	2	0	0		0	0	0
TOTAL	3	0	4	0	0		0	0	0
LAMAR								
Billy Tubbs (Lamar 1958) 1979, 80	2	3	2	0	0		0	0	0
Pat Foster (Arkansas 1961) 1981, 83	2	2	2	0	0		0	0	0
Mike Deane (Potsdam St. 1974) 2000	1	0	1	0	0		0	0	0
TOTAL	5	5	5	0	0		0	0	0
LEBANON VALLEY								
George "Rinso" Marquette (Lebanon Valley 1948) 1953	1	1	2	0	0		0	0	0
TOTAL	1	1	2	0	0		0	0	0
LEHIGH								
Tom Schneider (Bucknell 1969) 1985	1	0	1	0	0		0	0	0

	Yrs.	Won	Lost	CH	2D	3d%	4th	RR
Fran McCaffery (Pennsylvania 1982) 1988	1	0	1	0	0		0	0	0
TOTAL	2	0	2	0	0		0	0	0
LIBERTY								
Jeff Meyer (Taylor 1976) 1994	1	0	1	0	0		0	0	0
TOTAL	1	0	1	0	0		0	0	0
LONG BEACH ST.*								
Jerry Tarkanian (Fresno St. 1956) 1970, 71RR, 72RR, 73	4	7	5	0	0		0	0	2
Dwight Jones (Pepperdine 1965) 1977	1	0	1	0	0		0	0	0
Seth Greenberg (FDU-Teaneck 1978) 1993, 95	2	0	2	0	0		0	0	0
TOTAL	7	7	8	0	0		0	0	2
LONG ISLAND								
Paul Lizzo (Northwest Mo. St. 1963) 1981, 84	2	0	2	0	0		0	0	0
Ray Haskins (Shaw 1972) 1997	1	0	1	0	0		0	0	0
TOTAL	3	0	3	0	0		0	0	0
LSU								
Harry Rabenhorst (Wake Forest 1921) 1953-4th, 54	2	2	4	0	0		0	1	0
Dale Brown (Minot St. 1957) 1979, 80RR, 81-4th, 84, 85, 86-T3d, 87RR, 88, 89, 90, 91, 92, 93	13	15	14	0	0		1	1	2
John Brady (Belhaven 1976) 2000	1	2	1	0	0		0	0	0
TOTAL	16	19	19	0	0		1	2	2
LOUISIANA TECH								
Andy Russo (Lake Forest 1970) 1984, 85	2	3	2	0	0		0	0	0
Tommy Joe Eagles (Louisiana Tech 1971) 1987, 89	2	1	2	0	0		0	0	0
Jerry Loyd (LeTourneau 1976) 1991	1	0	1	0	0		0	0	0
TOTAL	5	4	5	0	0		0	0	0
LA.-LAFAYETTE*								
Beryl Shipley (Delta St. 1951) 1972, 73	2	3	3	0	0		0	0	0
Bobby Paschal (Stetson 1964) 1982, 83	2	0	2	0	0		0	0	0
Marty Fletcher (Maryland 1973) 1992, 94	2	1	2	0	0		0	0	0
Jessie Evans (Eastern Mich. 1972) 2000	1	0	1	0	0		0	0	0
TOTAL	7	4	8	0	0		0	0	0
LA.-MONROE								
Mike Vining (La.-Monroe 1967) 1982, 86, 90, 91, 92, 93, 96	7	0	7	0	0		0	0	0
TOTAL	7	0	7	0	0		0	0	0
LOUISVILLE								
Bernard "Peck" Hickman (Western Ky. 1935) 1951, 59-4th, 61, 64, 67	5	5	7	0	0		0	1	0
John Dromo (John Carroll 1939) 1968	1	1	1	0	0		0	0	0
Denny Crum (UCLA 1959) 1972-4th, 74, 75-3d, 77, 78, 79, 80-CH, 81, 82-T3d, 83-T3d, 84, 86-CH, 88, 89, 90, 92, 93, 94, 95, 96, 97RR, 99, 2000	23	42	23	2	0		3	1	1
TOTAL	29	48	31	2	0		3	2	1
LOYOLA MARYMOUNT*								
William Donovan (Loyola Marymount 1950) 1961	1	1	1	0	0		0	0	0
Ron Jacobs (Southern California 1964) 1980	1	0	1	0	0		0	0	0
Paul Westhead (St. Joseph's 1961) 1988, 89, 90RR	3	4	3	0	0		0	0	1
TOTAL	5	5	5	0	0		0	0	1
LOYOLA (ILL.)								
George Ireland (Notre Dame 1936) 1963-CH, 64, 66, 68	4	7	3	1	0		0	0	0
Gene Sullivan (Notre Dame 1953) 1985	1	2	1	0	0		0	0	0
TOTAL	5	9	4	1	0		0	0	0
LOYOLA (LA.)								
Jim McCafferty [Loyola (La.) 1942] 1954, 57	2	0	2	0	0		0	0	0
Jim Harding (Iowa 1949) 1958	1	0	1	0	0		0	0	0
TOTAL	3	0	3	0	0		0	0	0
LOYOLA (MD.)								
Skip Prosser (Merchant Marine 1972) 1994	1	0	1	0	0		0	0	0
TOTAL	1	0	1	0	0		0	0	0
MANHATTAN								
Ken Norton (Long Island 1939) 1956, 58	2	1	3	0	0		0	0	0
Fran Fraschilla (Brooklyn 1980) 1993, 95	2	1	2	0	0		0	0	0
TOTAL	4	2	5	0	0		0	0	0
MARIST								
Matt Furjanic (Point Park 1973) 1986	1	0	1	0	0		0	0	0

	Yrs.	Won	Lost	CH	2D	3d%	4th	RR
Dave Magarity [St. Francis (Pa.) 1974] 1987	1	0	1	0	0	0	0	0
TOTAL	2	0	2	0	0	0	0	0
MARQUETTE								
Jack Nagle (Marquette 1940) 1955RR	1	2	1	0	0	0	0	1
Eddie Hickey (Creighton 1927) 1959, 61	2	1	3	0	0	0	0	0
Al McGuire [St. John's (N.Y.) 1951] 1968, 69RR, 71, 72, 73, 74-2d, 75, 76RR, 77-CH	9	20	9	1	1	0	0	2
Hank Raymonds (St. Louis 1948) 1978, 79, 80, 82, 83	5	2	5	0	0	0	0	0
Kevin O'Neill (McGill 1979) 1993, 94	2	2	2	0	0	0	0	0
Mike Deane (Potsdam St. 1974) 1996, 97	2	1	2	0	0	0	0	0
Tom Crean (Central Mich. 1989) 2002	1	0	1	0	0	0	0	0
TOTAL	22	28	23	1	1	0	0	3
MARSHALL*								
Jule Rivlin (Marshall 1940) 1956	1	0	1	0	0	0	0	0
Carl Tacy (Davis & Elkins 1956) 1972	1	0	1	0	0	0	0	0
Rick Huckabay (Louisiana Tech 1967) 1984, 85, 87	3	0	3	0	0	0	0	0
TOTAL	5	0	5	0	0	0	0	0
MARYLAND*								
H.A. "Bud" Millikan (Oklahoma St. 1942) 1958	1	2	1	0	0	0	0	0
Charles "Lefty" Driesell (Duke 1954) 1973RR, 75RR, 80, 81, 83, 84, 85, 86	8	10	8	0	0	0	0	2
Bob Wade (Morgan St. 1967) 1988	1	1	1	0	0	0	0	0
Gary Williams (Maryland 1967) 1994, 95, 96, 97, 98, 99, 2000, 01-T3d, 02-CH	9	19	8	1	0	1	0	0
TOTAL	19	32	18	1	0	1	0	2
MASSACHUSETTS*								
Matt Zunic (George Washington 1942) 1962	1	0	1	0	0	0	0	0
John Calipari (Clarion 1982) 1992, 93, 94, 95RR, 96-T3d	5	11	5	0	0	1	0	1
James Flint (St. Joseph's 1987) 1997, 98	2	0	2	0	0	0	0	0
TOTAL	8	11	8	0	0	1	0	1
McNEESE ST.								
Steve Welch (Southeastern La. 1971) 1989	1	0	1	0	0	0	0	0
Tic Price (Virginia Tech 1979) 2002	1	0	1	0	0	0	0	0
TOTAL	2	0	2	0	0	0	0	0
MEMPHIS*								
Eugene Lambert (Arkansas 1929) 1955, 56	2	0	2	0	0	0	0	0
Bob Vanatta (Central Methodist 1945) 1962	1	0	1	0	0	0	0	0
Gene Bartow (Truman 1953) 1973-2d	1	3	1	0	1	0	0	0
Wayne Yates (Memphis 1961) 1976	1	0	1	0	0	0	0	0
Dana Kirk (Marshall 1960) 1982, 83, 84, 85-T3d, 86	5	9	5	0	0	1	0	0
Larry Finch (Memphis 1973) 1988, 89, 92RR, 93, 95, 96	6	6	6	0	0	0	0	1
TOTAL	16	18	16	0	1	1	0	1
MERCER								
Bill Bibb (Ky. Wesleyan 1957) 1981, 85	2	0	2	0	0	0	0	0
TOTAL	2	0	2	0	0	0	0	0
MIAMI (FLA.)								
Bruce Hale (Santa Clara 1941) 1960	1	0	1	0	0	0	0	0
Leonard Hamilton (Tenn.-Martin 1971) 1998, 99, 2000, 02	4	3	4	0	0	0	0	0
TOTAL	5	3	5	0	0	0	0	0
MIAMI (OHIO)								
Bill Rohr (Ohio Wesleyan 1940) 1953, 55, 57	3	0	3	0	0	0	0	0
Dick Shrider (Ohio 1948) 1958, 66	2	1	3	0	0	0	0	0
Tates Locke (Ohio Wesleyan 1959) 1969	1	1	2	0	0	0	0	0
Darrell Hedric [Miami (Ohio) 1955] 1971, 73, 78, 84	4	1	4	0	0	0	0	0
Jerry Peirson [Miami (Ohio) 1966] 1985, 86	2	0	2	0	0	0	0	0
Joby Wright (Indiana 1972) 1992	1	0	1	0	0	0	0	0
Herb Sendek (Carnegie Mellon 1985) 1995	1	1	1	0	0	0	0	0
Charlie Coles [Miami (Ohio) 1965] 1997, 99	2	2	2	0	0	0	0	0
TOTAL	16	6	18	0	0	0	0	0
MICHIGAN#								
Osborne "Ozzie" Cowles (Carleton 1922) 1948RR	1	1	1	0	0	0	0	1
Dave Strack (Michigan 1946) 1964-3d, 65-2d, 66RR	3	7	3	0	1	1	0	1
Johnny Orr (Beloit 1949) 1974RR, 75, 76-2d, 77RR	4	7	4	0	1	0	0	2

	Yrs.	Won	Lost	CH	2D	3d%	4th	RR
Bill Frieder (Michigan 1964) 1985, 86, 87, 88	4	5	4	0	0	0	0	0
Steve Fisher (Illinois St. 1967) 1989-CH, 90, 92-2d, 93-2d, 94RR, 95, 96	7	20	6	1	2	0	0	1
Brian Ellerbe (Rutgers 1985) 1998	1	1	1	0	0	0	0	0
TOTAL	20	41	19	1	4	1	0	5
MICHIGAN ST.								
Forrest "Forddy" Anderson (Stanford 1942) 1957-4th, 59RR	2	3	3	0	0	0	1	1
George "Jud" Heathcote (Washington St. 1950) 1978RR, 79-CH, 85, 86, 90, 91, 92, 94, 95	9	14	8	1	0	0	0	1
Tom Izzo (Northern Mich. 1977) 1998, 99-T3d, 2000-CH, 01-T3d, 02	5	16	4	1	0	2	0	0
TOTAL	16	33	15	2	0	2	1	2
MIDDLE TENN.								
Jimmy Earle (Middle Tenn. 1959) 1975, 77	2	0	2	0	0	0	0	0
Stan Simpson (Ga. Southern 1961) 1982	1	1	1	0	0	0	0	0
Bruce Stewart (Jacksonville St. 1975) 1985, 87, 89	3	1	3	0	0	0	0	0
TOTAL	6	2	6	0	0	0	0	0
MINNESOTA*								
Bill Musselman (Wittenberg 1961) 1972	1	1	1	0	0	0	0	0
Jim Dutcher (Michigan 1955) 1982	1	1	1	0	0	0	0	0
Clem Haskins (Western Ky. 1967) 1989, 90RR, 94, 95, 97-T3d, 99	6	10	6	0	0	1	0	1
TOTAL	8	12	8	0	0	1	0	1
MISSISSIPPI								
Bob Weltlich (Ohio St. 1967) 1981	1	0	1	0	0	0	0	0
Rob Evans (New Mexico St. 1968) 1997, 98	2	0	2	0	0	0	0	0
Rod Barnes (Mississippi 1988) 1999, 2001, 02	3	3	3	0	0	0	0	0
TOTAL	6	3	6	0	0	0	0	0
MISSISSIPPI ST.								
James "Babe" McCarthy (Mississippi St. 1949) 1963	1	1	1	0	0	0	0	0
Richard Williams (Mississippi St. 1967) 1991, 95, 96-T3d	3	6	3	0	0	1	0	0
Rick Stansbury (Campbellsville 1982) 2002	1	1	1	0	0	0	0	0
TOTAL	5	8	5	0	0	1	0	0
MISSISSIPPI VAL.								
Lafayette Stribling (Miss. Industrial 1957) 1986, 92, 96	3	0	3	0	0	0	0	0
TOTAL	3	0	3	0	0	0	0	0
MISSOURI#								
George Edwards (Missouri 1913) 1944RR	1	1	1	0	0	0	0	1
Norm Stewart (Missouri 1956) 1976RR, 78, 80, 81, 82 83, 86, 87, 88, 89, 90, 92, 93, 94RR, 95, 99	16	12	16	0	0	0	0	2
Quin Snyder (Duke 1989) 2000, 01, 02RR	3	4	3	0	0	0	0	1
TOTAL	20	17	20	0	0	0	0	4
MONMOUTH								
Wayne Szoke (Maryland 1963) 1996	1	0	1	0	0	0	0	0
Dave Calloway [Monmouth 1991] 2001	1	0	1	0	0	0	0	0
TOTAL	2	0	2	0	0	0	0	0
MONTANA								
George "Jud" Heathcote (Washington St. 1950) 1975	1	1	2	0	0	0	0	0
Stew Morrill (Gonzaga 1974) 1991	1	0	1	0	0	0	0	0
Blaine Taylor (Montana 1982) 1992, 97	2	0	2	0	0	0	0	0
Don Holst (Northern Mont. 1975) 2002	1	0	1	0	0	0	0	0
TOTAL	5	1	6	0	0	0	0	0
MONTANA ST.								
John Breeden (Montana St. 1929) 1951	1	0	1	0	0	0	0	0
Stu Starner (Minn.-Morris 1965) 1986	1	0	1	0	0	0	0	0
Mike Durham (Montana St. 1979) 1996	1	0	1	0	0	0	0	0
TOTAL	3	0	3	0	0	0	0	0
MOREHEAD ST.								
Robert Laughlin (Morehead St. 1937) 1956, 57, 61	3	3	4	0	0	0	0	0
Wayne Martin (Morehead St. 1968) 1983, 84	2	1	2	0	0	0	0	0
TOTAL	5	4	6	0	0	0	0	0
MT. ST. MARY'S								
James Phelan (La Salle 1951) 1995, 99	2	0	2	0	0	0	0	0
TOTAL	2	0	2	0	0	0	0	0
MURRAY ST.								
Cal Luther (Valparaiso 1951) 1964, 69	2	0	2	0	0	0	0	0
Steve Newton (Indiana St. 1963) 1988, 90, 91	3	1	3	0	0	0	0	0

CHAMPIONSHIPS

	Yrs.	Won	Lost	CH	2D	3d%	4th	RR
Scott Edgar (Pitt.-Johnstown 1978) 1992, 95	2	0	2	0	0	0	0	0
Mark Gottfried (Alabama 1987) 1997, 98	2	0	2	0	0	0	0	0
Tevester Anderson (Ark.-Pine Bluff 1962) 1999, 2002	2	0	2	0	0	0	0	0
TOTAL	11	1	11	0	0	0	0	0
NAVY								
Ben Carnevale (New York U. 1938) 1947RR, 53, 54RR, 59, 60	5	4	6	0	0	0	0	2
Paul Evans (Ithaca 1967) 1985, 86RR	2	4	2	0	0	0	0	1
Pete Herrmann (Geneseo St. 1970) 1987	1	0	1	0	0	0	0	0
Don DeVoe (Ohio St. 1964) 1994, 97, 98	3	0	3	0	0	0	0	0
TOTAL	11	8	12	0	0	0	0	3
NEBRASKA								
Moe Iba (Oklahoma St. 1962) 1986	1	0	1	0	0	0	0	0
Danny Nee (St. Marys of the Plains 1971) 1991, 92, 93, 94, 98	5	0	5	0	0	0	0	0
TOTAL	6	0	6	0	0	0	0	0
UNLV								
Jerry Tarkanian (Fresno St. 1956) 1975, 76, 77-3d, 83, 84, 85, 86, 87-T3d, 88, 89RR, 90-CH, 91-T3d	12	30	11	1	0	3	0	1
Bill Bayno (Sacred Heart 1985) 1998, 2000	2	0	2	0	0	0	0	0
TOTAL	14	30	13	1	0	3	0	1
NEVADA								
Sonny Allen (Marshall 1959) 1984, 85	2	0	2	0	0	0	0	0
TOTAL	2	0	2	0	0	0	0	0
NEW MEXICO								
Bob King (Iowa 1947) 1968	1	0	2	0	0	0	0	0
Norm Ellenberger (Butler 1955) 1974, 78	2	2	2	0	0	0	0	0
Dave Bliss (Cornell 1965) 1991, 93, 94, 96, 97, 98, 99	7	4	7	0	0	0	0	0
TOTAL	10	6	11	0	0	0	0	0
NEW MEXICO ST.*								
George McCarty (New Mexico St. 1950) 1952	1	0	2	0	0	0	0	0
Presley Askew (Southeastern Okla. 1930) 1959, 60	2	0	2	0	0	0	0	0
Ken Hayes (Northeastern St. 1956) 1979	1	0	1	0	0	0	0	0
Neil McCarthy (Sacramento St. 1965) 1990, 91, 92, 93, 94	5	3	5	0	0	0	0	0
Lou Henson (New Mexico St. 1955) 1967, 68, 69, 70-3d, 71, 75, 99	7	7	8	0	0	1	0	0
TOTAL	16	10	18	0	0	1	0	0
NEW ORLEANS								
Benny Dees (Wyoming 1958) 1987	1	1	1	0	0	0	0	0
Tim Floyd (Louisiana Tech 1977) 1991, 93	2	0	2	0	0	0	0	0
Tic Price (Virginia Tech 1979) 1996	1	0	1	0	0	0	0	0
TOTAL	4	1	4	0	0	0	0	0
NEW YORK U.								
Howard Cann (New York U. 1920) 1943RR, 45-2d, 46RR	3	3	4	0	1	0	0	2
Lou Rossini (Columbia 1948) 1960-4th, 62, 63	3	6	5	0	0	0	1	0
TOTAL	6	9	9	0	1	0	1	2
NIAGARA								
Frank Layden (Niagara 1955) 1970	1	1	2	0	0	0	0	0
TOTAL	1	1	2	0	0	0	0	0
NICHOLLS ST.								
Rickey Broussard (La.-Lafayette 1970) 1995, 98	2	0	2	0	0	0	0	0
TOTAL	2	0	2	0	0	0	0	0
NORTH CAROLINA								
Bill Lange (Wittenberg 1921) 1941RR	1	0	2	0	0	0	0	1
Ben Carnevale (New York U. 1938) 1946-2d	1	2	1	0	1	0	0	0
Frank McGuire [St. John's (N.Y.) 1936] 1957-CH, 59	2	5	1	1	0	0	0	0
Dean Smith (Kansas 1953) 1967-4th, 68-2d, 69-4th, 72-3d, 75 76, 77-2d, 78, 79, 80, 81-2d, 82-CH, 83RR, 84, 85RR 86, 87RR, 88RR, 89, 90, 91-T3d, 92, 93-CH, 94, 95-T3d, 96, 97-T3d	27	65	27	2	3	4	2	4
Bill Guthridge (Kansas St. 1963) 1998-T3d, 99, 2000-T3d	3	8	3	0	0	2	0	0
Matt Doherty (North Carolina 1984) 2001	1	1	1	0	0	0	0	0
TOTAL	35	81	35	3	4	6	2	5
N.C. A&T								
Don Corbett [Lincoln (Mo.) 1965] 1982, 83, 84, 85, 86, 87, 88	7	0	7	0	0	0	0	0
Jeff Capel (Fayetteville St. 1977) 1994	1	0	1	0	0	0	0	0
Roy Thomas (Baylor 1974) 1995	1	0	1	0	0	0	0	0
TOTAL	9	0	9	0	0	0	0	0
UNC GREENSBORO								
Randy Peele (Va. Wesleyan 1980) 1996	1	0	1	0	0	0	0	0
Fran McCaffery (Pennsylvania 1982) 2001	1	0	1	0	0	0	0	0
TOTAL	2	0	2	0	0	0	0	0
UNC WILMINGTON								
Jerry Wainwright (Colorado Col. 1968) 2000, 02	2	1	2	0	0	0	0	0
TOTAL	2	1	2	0	0	0	0	0
NORTH CAROLINA ST.*								
Everett Case (Wisconsin 1923) 1950-3d, 51RR, 52, 54, 56	5	6	6	0	0	1	0	1
Press Maravich (Davis & Elkins 1941) 1965	1	1	1	0	0	0	0	0
Norm Sloan (North Carolina St. 1951) 1970, 74-CH, 80	3	5	2	1	0	0	0	0
Jim Valvano (Rutgers 1967) 1982, 83-CH, 85RR, 86RR 87, 88, 89	7	14	6	1	0	0	0	2
Les Robinson (North Carolina St. 1964) 1991	1	1	1	0	0	0	0	0
Herb Sendek (Carnegie Mellon 1985) 2002	1	1	1	0	0	0	0	0
TOTAL	18	28	17	2	0	1	0	3
NORTH TEXAS								
Jimmy Gales (Alcorn St. 1963) 1988	1	0	1	0	0	0	0	0
TOTAL	1	0	1	0	0	0	0	0
NORTHEASTERN								
Jim Calhoun (American Int'l 1966) 1981, 82, 84, 85, 86	5	3	5	0	0	0	0	0
Karl Fogel (Colby 1968) 1987, 91	2	0	2	0	0	0	0	0
TOTAL	7	3	7	0	0	0	0	0
NORTHERN ARIZ.								
Ben Howland (Weber St. 1980) 1998	1	0	1	0	0	0	0	0
Mike Adras (UC Santa Barb. 1983) 2000	1	0	1	0	0	0	0	0
TOTAL	2	0	2	0	0	0	0	0
NORTHERN ILL.								
John McDougal (Evansville 1950) 1982	1	0	1	0	0	0	0	0
Jim Molinari (Ill. Wesleyan 1977) 1991	1	0	1	0	0	0	0	0
Brian Hammel (Bentley 1975) 1996	1	0	1	0	0	0	0	0
TOTAL	3	0	3	0	0	0	0	0
NORTHERN IOWA								
Eldon Miller (Wittenberg 1961) 1990	1	1	1	0	0	0	0	0
TOTAL	1	1	1	0	0	0	0	0
NORTHWESTERN ST.								
Mike McConathy (Louisiana Tech 1977) 2001	1	1	1	0	0	0	0	0
TOTAL	1	1	1	0	0	0	0	0
NOTRE DAME								
John Jordan (Notre Dame 1935) 1953RR, 54RR, 57, 58RR, 60, 63	6	8	6	0	0	0	0	3
Johnny Dee (Notre Dame 1946) 1965, 69, 70, 71	4	2	6	0	0	0	0	0
Richard "Digger" Phelps (Rider 1963) 1974,75, 76, 77, 78-4th, 79RR, 80, 81, 85, 86, 87, 88, 89, 90	14	15	16	0	0	0	1	1
Mike Brey (George Washington 1982) 2001, 02	2	2	2	0	0	0	0	0
TOTAL	26	27	30	0	0	0	1	4
OHIO								
James Snyder (Ohio 1941) 1960, 61, 64RR, 65, 70, 72, 74	7	3	8	0	0	0	0	1
Danny Nee (St. Mary of the Plains 1971) 1983, 85	2	1	2	0	0	0	0	0
Larry Hunter (Ohio 1971) 1994	1	0	1	0	0	0	0	0
TOTAL	10	4	11	0	0	0	0	1
OHIO ST.								
Harold Olsen (Wisconsin 1917) 1939-2d, 44-T3d, 45-T3d, 46-3d	4	6	4	0	1	3	0	0
William "Tippy" Dye (Ohio St. 1937) 1950RR	1	1	1	0	0	0	0	1
Fred Taylor (Ohio St. 1950) 1960-CH, 61-2d, 62-2d, 68-3d, 71RR	5	14	4	1	2	1	0	1
Eldon Miller (Wittenberg 1961) 1980, 82, 83, 85	4	3	4	0	0	0	0	0
Gary Williams (Maryland 1967) 1987	1	1	1	0	0	0	0	0
Randy Ayers [Miami (Ohio) 1978] 1990, 91, 92RR	3	6	3	0	0	0	0	1
Jim O'Brien (Boston College 1971) 1999-T3d, 2000, 01, 02	4	6	4	0	0	1	0	0
TOTAL	22	37	21	1	3	5	0	3

	Yrs.	Won	Lost	CH	2D	3d%	4th	RR
OKLAHOMA								
Bruce Drake (Oklahoma 1929) 1939-T3d, 43RR, 47-2d	3	4	3	0	1	1	0	1
Dave Bliss (Cornell 1965) 1979	1	1	1	0	0	0	0	0
Billy Tubbs (Lamar 1958) 1983, 84, 85RR, 86, 87, 88-2d, 89, 90, 92	9	15	9	0	1	0	0	1
Kelvin Sampson (UNC Pembroke 1978) 1995, 96, 97, 98, 99, 2000, 01, 02-T3d	8	7	8	0	0	1	0	0
TOTAL	21	27	21	0	2	2	0	2
OKLAHOMA CITY								
Doyle Parrack (Oklahoma St. 1945) 1952, 53, 54, 55	4	1	5	0	0	0	0	0
A.E. "Abe" Lemons (Oklahoma City 1949) 1956RR, 57RR, 63, 64, 65, 66, 73	7	7	8	0	0	0	0	2
TOTAL	11	8	13	0	0	0	0	2
OKLAHOMA ST.								
Henry Iba [Westminster (Mo.) 1928] 1945-CH, 46-CH, 49-2d, 51-4th, 53-RR, 54-RR, 58RR, 65RR	8	15	7	2	1	0	1	4
Paul Hansen (Oklahoma City 1950) 1983	1	0	1	0	0	0	0	0
Eddie Sutton (Oklahoma St. 1958) 1991, 92, 93, 94, 95-T3d, 98, 99, 2000RR, 01, 02	10	15	10	0	0	1	0	1
TOTAL	19	30	18	2	1	1	1	5
OLD DOMINION								
Paul Webb (William & Mary 1951) 1980, 82, 85	3	0	3	0	0	0	0	0
Tom Young (Maryland 1958) 1986	1	1	1	0	0	0	0	0
Oliver Purnell (Old Dominion 1975) 1992	1	0	1	0	0	0	0	0
Jeff Capel (Fayetteville St. 1977) 1995, 97	2	1	2	0	0	0	0	0
TOTAL	7	2	7	0	0	0	0	0
ORAL ROBERTS								
Ken Trickey (Middle Tenn. 1954) 1974RR	1	2	1	0	0	0	0	1
Dick Acres (UC Santa Barb.) 1984	1	0	1	0	0	0	0	0
TOTAL	2	2	2	0	0	0	0	1
OREGON								
Howard Hobson (Oregon 1926) 1939-CH	1	3	0	1	0	0	0	0
John Warren (Oregon 1928) 1945RR	1	1	1	0	0	0	0	1
Steve Belko (Idaho 1939) 1960RR, 61	2	2	2	0	0	0	0	1
Jerry Green (Appalachian St. 1968) 1995	1	0	1	0	0	0	0	0
Ernie Kent (Oregon 1977) 2000, 02RR	2	3	2	0	0	0	0	1
TOTAL	7	9	6	1	0	0	0	3
OREGON ST.*								
Amory "Slats" Gill (Oregon St. 1925) 1947RR, 49-4th,55RR, 62RR, 63-4th, 64	6	8	8	0	0	0	2	3
Paul Valenti (Oregon St. 1942) 1966RR	1	1	1	0	0	0	0	1
Ralph Miller (Kansas 1942) 1975, 80, 81, 82RR, 84, 85, 88, 89	8	3	9	0	0	0	0	1
Jim Anderson (Oregon St. 1959) 1990	1	0	1	0	0	0	0	0
TOTAL	16	12	19	0	0	0	2	5
PACIFIC (CAL.)								
Dick Edwards (Culver-Stockton 1952) 1966, 67RR, 71	3	2	4	0	0	0	0	1
Stan Morrison (California 1962) 1979	1	0	1	0	0	0	0	0
Bob Thomason [Pacific (Cal.) 1971] 1997	1	0	1	0	0	0	0	0
TOTAL	5	2	6	0	0	0	0	1
PENN ST.								
John Lawther [Westminster (Pa.) 1919] 1942RR	1	1	1	0	0	0	0	1
Elmer Gross (Penn St. 1942) 1952, 54-3d	2	4	3	0	0	1	0	0
John Egli (Penn St. 1947) 1955, 65	2	1	3	0	0	0	0	0
Bruce Parkhill (Lock Haven 1971) 1991	1	1	1	0	0	0	0	0
Jerry Dunn (George Mason 1980) 1996, 2001	2	2	2	0	0	0	0	0
TOTAL	9	9	11	0	0	1	0	1
PENNSYLVANIA								
Howard "Howie" Dallmar (Stanford 1948) 1953	1	1	1	0	0	0	0	0
Dick Harter (Pennsylvania 1953) 1970, 71RR	2	2	2	0	0	0	0	1
Chuck Daly (Bloomsburg 1953) 1972RR, 73, 74, 75	4	3	5	0	0	0	0	1
Bob Weinhauer (Cortland St. 1961) 1978, 79-4th, 80, 82	4	6	5	0	0	0	1	0
Craig Littlepage (Pennsylvania 1973) 1985	1	0	1	0	0	0	0	0
Tom Schneider (Bucknell 1969) 1987	1	0	1	0	0	0	0	0

	Yrs.	Won	Lost	CH	2D	3d%	4th	RR
Fran Dunphy (La Salle 1970) 1993, 94, 95, 99, 2000, 02	6	1	6	0	0	0	0	0
TOTAL	19	13	21	0	0	0	1	2
PEPPERDINE								
Al Duer (Emporia St. 1929) 1944RR	1	0	2	0	0	0	0	1
R.L. "Duck" Dowell (Northwest Mo. St. 1933) 1962	1	1	1	0	0	0	0	0
Gary Colson (David Lipscomb 1956) 1976, 79	2	2	2	0	0	0	0	0
Jim Harrick [Charleston (W.Va.) 1960] 1982, 83, 85, 86	4	1	4	0	0	0	0	0
Tom Asbury (Wyoming 1967) 1991, 92, 94	3	0	3	0	0	0	0	0
Jan van Breda Kolff (Vanderbilt 1974) 2000	1	1	1	0	0	0	0	0
Paul Westphal (Southern California 1972) 2002	1	0	1	0	0	0	0	0
TOTAL	13	5	14	0	0	0	0	1
PITTSBURGH								
Henry Carlson (Pittsburgh 1917) 1941-T3d	1	1	1	0	0	1	0	0
Bob Timmons (Pittsburgh 1933) 1957, 58, 63	3	1	4	0	0	0	0	0
Charles "Buzz" Ridl [Westminster (Pa.) 1942] 1974RR	1	2	1	0	0	0	0	1
Roy Chipman (Maine 1961) 1981, 82, 85	3	1	3	0	0	0	0	0
Paul Evans (Ithaca 1967) 1987, 88, 89, 91, 93	5	3	5	0	0	0	0	0
Ben Howland (Weber St. 1980) 2002	1	2	1	0	0	0	0	0
TOTAL	14	10	15	0	0	1	0	1
PORTLAND								
Al Negratti (Seton Hall 1943) 1959	1	0	1	0	0	0	0	0
Rob Chavez (Mesa St. 1980) 1996	1	0	1	0	0	0	0	0
TOTAL	2	0	2	0	0	0	0	0
PRAIRIE VIEW								
Elwood Plummer (Jackson St. 1966) 1998	1	0	1	0	0	0	0	0
TOTAL	1	0	1	0	0	0	0	0
PRINCETON#								
Franklin Cappon (Michigan 1924) 1952, 55, 60	3	0	5	0	0	0	0	0
J.L. "Jake" McCandless (Princeton 1951) 1961	1	1	2	0	0	0	0	0
Butch van Breda Kolff (Princeton 1947) 1963, 64, 65-3d, 67	4	7	5	0	0	1	0	0
Pete Carril (Lafayette 1952) 1969, 76, 77, 81, 83, 84, 89, 90, 91, 92, 96	11	4	11	0	0	0	0	0
Bill Carmody [Union (N.Y.) 1975] 1997, 98	2	1	2	0	0	0	0	0
John Thompson III (Princeton 1989) 2001	1	0	1	0	0	0	0	0
TOTAL	22	13	26	0	0	1	0	0
PROVIDENCE								
Joe Mullaney (Holy Cross 1949) 1964, 65RR, 66	3	2	3	0	0	0	0	1
Dave Gavitt (Dartmouth 1959) 1972, 73-4th, 74, 77, 78	5	5	6	0	0	0	1	0
Rick Pitino (Massachusetts 1974) 1987 tie-3d	1	4	1	0	0	1	0	0
Rick Barnes (Lenior-Rhyne 1977) 1989, 90, 94	3	0	3	0	0	0	0	0
Pete Gillen (Fairfield 1968) 1997RR	1	3	1	0	0	0	0	1
Tim Welsh (Potsdam St. 1984) 2001	1	0	1	0	0	0	0	0
TOTAL	14	14	15	0	0	1	1	2
PURDUE								
George King [Charleston (W.Va.) 1950] 1969-2d	1	3	1	0	1	0	0	0
Fred Schaus (West Virginia 1949) 1977	1	0	1	0	0	0	0	0
Lee Rose (Transylvania 1958) 1980-3d	1	5	1	0	0	1	0	0
Gene Keady (Kansas St. 1958) 1983, 84, 85, 86, 87, 88, 90, 91, 93, 94RR, 95, 96, 97, 98, 99, 2000RR	16	18	16	0	0	0	0	2
TOTAL	19	26	19	0	1	1	0	2
RADFORD								
Ron Bradley (Eastern Nazarene 1973) 1998	1	0	1	0	0	0	0	0
TOTAL	1	0	1	0	0	0	0	0
RHODE ISLAND								
Ernie Calverley (Rhode Island 1946) 1961, 66	2	0	2	0	0	0	0	0
Jack Kraft (St. Joseph's 1942) 1978	1	0	1	0	0	0	0	0
Tom Penders (Connecticut 1967) 1988	1	2	1	0	0	0	0	0
Al Skinner (Massachusetts 1974) 1993, 97	2	1	2	0	0	0	0	0
Jim Harrick [Charleston (W.Va.) 1960] 1998, 99	2	3	2	0	0	0	0	1
TOTAL	8	6	8	0	0	0	0	1

RICE

	Yrs.	Won	Lost	CH	2D	3d%	4th	RR
Byron "Buster" Brannon (TCU 1933) 1940RR, 42RR	2	1	3	0	0	0	0	2
Don Suman (Rice 1944) 1954	1	1	1	0	0	0	0	0
Don Knodel [Miami (Ohio) 1953] 1970	1	0	1	0	0	0	0	0
TOTAL	4	2	5	0	0	0	0	2

RICHMOND

	Yrs.	Won	Lost	CH	2D	3d%	4th	RR
Dick Tarrant (Fordham 1951) 1984, 86, 88, 90, 91	5	5	5	0	0	0	0	0
John Beilein (Wheeling Jesuit 1975) 1998	1	1	1	0	0	0	0	0
TOTAL	6	6	6	0	0	0	0	0

RIDER

	Yrs.	Won	Lost	CH	2D	3d%	4th	RR
John Carpenter (Penn St. 1958) 1984	1	0	1	0	0	0	0	0
Kevin Bannon (St. Peter's 1979) 1993, 94	2	0	2	0	0	0	0	0
TOTAL	3	0	3	0	0	0	0	0

ROBERT MORRIS

	Yrs.	Won	Lost	CH	2D	3d%	4th	RR
Matt Furjanic (Point Park 1973) 1982, 83	2	1	2	0	0	0	0	0
Jarrett Durham (Duquesne 1971) 1989, 90, 92	3	0	3	0	0	0	0	0
TOTAL	5	1	5	0	0	0	0	0

RUTGERS

	Yrs.	Won	Lost	CH	2D	3d%	4th	RR
Tom Young (Maryland 1958) 1975, 76-4th, 79, 83	4	5	5	0	0	0	1	0
Bob Wenzel (Rutgers 1971) 1989, 91	2	0	2	0	0	0	0	0
TOTAL	6	5	7	0	0	0	1	0

ST. BONAVENTURE

	Yrs.	Won	Lost	CH	2D	3d%	4th	RR
Eddie Donovan (St. Bonaventure 1950) 1961	1	2	1	0	0	0	0	0
Larry Weise (St. Bonaventure 1958) 1968, 70-4th	2	4	4	0	0	0	1	0
Jim Satalin (St. Bonaventure 1969) 1978	1	0	1	0	0	0	0	0
Jim Baron (St. Bonaventure 1977) 2000	1	0	1	0	0	0	0	0
TOTAL	5	6	7	0	0	0	1	0

ST. FRANCIS (PA.)

	Yrs.	Won	Lost	CH	2D	3d%	4th	RR
Jim Baron (St. Bonaventure 1977) 1991	1	0	1	0	0	0	0	0
TOTAL	1	0	1	0	0	0	0	0

ST. JOHN'S (N.Y.)

	Yrs.	Won	Lost	CH	2D	3d%	4th	RR
Frank McGuire [St. John's (N.Y.) 1936] 1951RR, 52-2d	2	5	2	0	1	0	0	1
Joe Lapchick (No college) 1961	1	0	1	0	0	0	0	0
Frank Mulzoff [St. John's (N.Y.) 1951] 1973	1	0	1	0	0	0	0	0
Lou Carnesecca [St. John's (N.Y.) 1946] 1967, 68, 69, 76, 77, 78, 79RR, 80, 82, 83, 84, 85-T3d, 86, 87, 88, 90, 91RR, 92	18	17	20	0	0	1	0	2
Brian Mahoney (Manhattan 1971) 1993	1	1	1	0	0	0	0	0
Fran Fraschilla (Brooklyn 1980) 1998	1	0	1	0	0	0	0	0
Mike Jarvis (Northeastern 1968) 1999RR, 2000, 02	3	4	3	0	0	0	0	1
TOTAL	27	27	29	0	1	1	0	4

ST. JOSEPH'S*

	Yrs.	Won	Lost	CH	2D	3d%	4th	RR
John "Jack" Ramsay (St. Joseph's 1949) 1959, 60, 61-3d, 62, 63RR, 65, 66	7	8	11	0	0	1	0	1
John "Jack" McKinney (St. Joseph's 1957) 1969, 71, 73, 74	4	0	4	0	0	0	0	0
Jim Lynam (St. Joseph's 1964) 1981RR	1	3	1	0	0	0	0	1
Jim Boyle (St. Joseph's 1964) 1982, 86	2	1	2	0	0	0	0	0
Phil Martelli (Widener 1976) 1997, 2001	2	3	2	0	0	0	0	0
TOTAL	16	15	20	0	0	1	0	2

ST. LOUIS

	Yrs.	Won	Lost	CH	2D	3d%	4th	RR
Eddie Hickey (Creighton 1927) 1952RR, 57	2	1	3	0	0	0	0	1
Charlie Spoonhour (School of Ozarks 1961) 1994, 95, 98	3	2	3	0	0	0	0	0
Lorenzo Romar (Washington 1980) 2000	1	0	1	0	0	0	0	0
TOTAL	6	3	7	0	0	0	0	1

ST. MARY'S (CAL.)

	Yrs.	Won	Lost	CH	2D	3d%	4th	RR
James Weaver (DePaul 1947) 1959RR	1	1	1	0	0	0	0	1
Lynn Nance (Washington 1965) 1989	1	0	1	0	0	0	0	0
Ernie Kent (Oregon 1977) 1997	1	0	1	0	0	0	0	0
TOTAL	3	1	3	0	0	0	0	1

ST. PETER'S

	Yrs.	Won	Lost	CH	2D	3d%	4th	RR
Ted Fiore (Seton Hall 1962) 1991, 95	2	0	2	0	0	0	0	0
TOTAL	2	0	2	0	0	0	0	0

SAMFORD

	Yrs.	Won	Lost	CH	2D	3d%	4th	RR
Jimmy Tillette (Our Lady of Holy Cross 1975) 1999, 2000	2	0	2	0	0	0	0	0
TOTAL	2	0	2	0	0	0	0	0

SAN DIEGO

	Yrs.	Won	Lost	CH	2D	3d%	4th	RR
Jim Brovelli (San Francisco 1964) 1984	1	0	1	0	0	0	0	0
Hank Egan (Navy 1960) 1987	1	0	1	0	0	0	0	0
TOTAL	2	0	2	0	0	0	0	0

SAN DIEGO ST.

	Yrs.	Won	Lost	CH	2D	3d%	4th	RR
Tim Vezie (Denver 1967) 1975, 76	2	0	2	0	0	0	0	0
Dave "Smokey" Gaines (LeMoyne-Owen 1963) 1985	1	0	1	0	0	0	0	0
Steve Fisher (Illinois St. 1967) 2002	1	0	1	0	0	0	0	0
TOTAL	4	0	4	0	0	0	0	0

SAN FRANCISCO

	Yrs.	Won	Lost	CH	2D	3d%	4th	RR
Phil Woolpert (Loyola Marymount 1940) 1955-CH, 56-CH, 57-3d, 58	4	13	2	2	0	1	0	0
Peter Peletta (Sacramento St. 1950) 1963, 64RR, 65RR	3	3	3	0	0	0	0	2
Bob Gaillard (San Francisco 1962) 1972, 73RR, 74RR, 77, 78	5	4	5	0	0	0	0	2
Dan Belluomini (San Francisco 1964) 1979	1	1	1	0	0	0	0	0
Peter Barry (San Francisco 1970) 1981, 82	2	0	2	0	0	0	0	0
Phil Mathews (UC Irvine 1972) 1998	1	0	1	0	0	0	0	0
TOTAL	16	21	14	2	0	1	0	4

SAN JOSE ST.

	Yrs.	Won	Lost	CH	2D	3d%	4th	RR
Walter McPherson (San Jose St. 1940) 1951	1	0	1	0	0	0	0	0
Bill Berry (Michigan St. 1965) 1980	1	0	1	0	0	0	0	0
Stan Morrison (California 1962) 1996	1	0	1	0	0	0	0	0
TOTAL	3	0	3	0	0	0	0	0

SANTA CLARA

	Yrs.	Won	Lost	CH	2D	3d%	4th	RR
Bob Feerick (Santa Clara 1941) 1952-4th, 53RR, 54RR, 60	4	6	6	0	0	0	1	2
Dick Garibaldi (Santa Clara 1957) 1968RR, 69RR, 70	3	3	3	0	0	0	0	2
Carroll Williams (San Jose St. 1955) 1987	1	0	1	0	0	0	0	0
Dick Davey [Pacific (Cal.) 1964] 1993, 95, 96	3	2	3	0	0	0	0	0
TOTAL	11	11	13	0	0	0	1	4

SEATTLE#

	Yrs.	Won	Lost	CH	2D	3d%	4th	RR
Al Brightman [Charleston (W.Va.)] 1953, 54, 55, 56	4	4	6	0	0	0	0	0
John Castellani (Notre Dame 1952) 1958-2d	1	4	1	0	1	0	0	0
Vince Cazzetta (Arnold 1950) 1961, 62	2	0	2	0	0	0	0	0
Clair Markey (Seattle 1963) 1963	1	0	1	0	0	0	0	0
Bob Boyd (Southern California 1953) 1964	1	2	1	0	0	0	0	0
Lionel Purcell (UC Santa Barb. 1952) 1967	1	0	1	0	0	0	0	0
Morris Buckwalter (Utah 1956) 1969	1	0	1	0	0	0	0	0
TOTAL	11	10	13	0	1	0	0	0

SETON HALL

	Yrs.	Won	Lost	CH	2D	3d%	4th	RR
P. J. Carlesimo (Fordham 1971) 1988, 89-2d, 91RR, 92, 93, 94	6	12	6	0	1	0	0	1
Tommy Amaker (Duke 1987) 2000	1	2	1	0	0	0	0	0
TOTAL	7	14	7	0	1	0	0	1

SIENA

	Yrs.	Won	Lost	CH	2D	3d%	4th	RR
Mike Deane (Potsdam St. 1974) 1989	1	1	1	0	0	0	0	0
Paul Hewitt (St. John Fisher 1985) 1999	1	0	1	0	0	0	0	0
Rob Lanier (St. Bonaventure 1990) 2002	1	1	1	0	0	0	0	0
TOTAL	3	2	3	0	0	0	0	0

SOUTH ALA.

	Yrs.	Won	Lost	CH	2D	3d%	4th	RR
Cliff Ellis (Florida St. 1968) 1979, 80	2	0	2	0	0	0	0	0
Ronnie Arrow (Southwest Tex. St. 1969) 1989, 91	2	1	2	0	0	0	0	0
Bill Musselman (Wittenberg 1962) 1997	1	0	1	0	0	0	0	0
Bob Weltlich (Ohio St. 1967) 1998	1	0	1	0	0	0	0	0
TOTAL	6	1	6	0	0	0	0	0

SOUTH CAROLINA

	Yrs.	Won	Lost	CH	2D	3d%	4th	RR
Frank McGuire [St. John's (N.Y.) 1936] 1971, 72, 73, 74	4	4	5	0	0	0	0	0
George Felton (South Carolina 1975) 1989	1	0	1	0	0	0	0	0
Eddie Fogler (North Carolina 1970) 1997, 98	2	0	2	0	0	0	0	0
TOTAL	7	4	8	0	0	0	0	0

SOUTH CAROLINA ST.

	Yrs.	Won	Lost	CH	2D	3d%	4th	RR
Cy Alexander (Catawba 1975) 1989, 96, 98, 2000	4	0	4	0	0	0	0	0
TOTAL	4	0	4	0	0	0	0	0

SOUTH FLA.

	Yrs.	Won	Lost	CH	2D	3d%	4th	RR
Bobby Paschal (Stetson 1964) 1990, 92	2	0	2	0	0	0	0	0
TOTAL	2	0	2	0	0	0	0	0

SOUTHEAST MO. ST.

	Yrs.	Won	Lost	CH	2D	3d%	4th	RR
Gary Garner (Missouri 1965) 2000	1	0	1	0	0	0	0	0
TOTAL	1	0	1	0	0	0	0	0

SOUTHERN U.

	Yrs.	Won	Lost	CH	2D	3d%	4th	RR
Carl Stewart (Grambling 1954) 1981	1	0	1	0	0	0	0	0

	Yrs.	Won	Lost	CH	2D	3d%	4th	RR
Robert Hopkins (Grambling 1956) 1985	1	0	1	0	0		0	0	0
Ben Jobe (Fisk 1956) 1987, 88, 89, 93	4	1	4	0	0		0	0	0
TOTAL	6	1	6	0	0		0	0	0

SOUTHERN CALIFORNIA

	Yrs.	Won	Lost	CH	2D	3d%	4th	RR
Justin "Sam" Barry (Lawrence 13) 1940-T3d	1	1	1	0	0	1	0	0
Forrest Twogood (Iowa 1929) 1954-4th, 60, 61	3	3	5	0	0	0	1	0
Bob Boyd (Southern California 1953) 1979	1	1	1	0	0	0	0	0
Stan Morrison (California 1962) 1982, 85	2	0	2	0	0	0	0	0
George Raveling (Villanova 1960) 1991, 92	2	1	2	0	0	0	0	0
Henry Bibby (UCLA 1972) 1997, 2001RR, 02	3	3	3	0	0	0	0	1
TOTAL	12	9	14	0	0	1	1	1

SOUTHERN ILL.

	Yrs.	Won	Lost	CH	2D	3d%	4th	RR
Paul Lambert (William Jewell 1956) 1977	1	1	1	0	0	0	0	0
Rich Herrin (McKendree 1956) 1993, 94, 95	3	0	3	0	0	0	0	0
Bruce Webber (Wis.-Milwaukee 1978) 2002	1	2	1	0	0	0	0	0
TOTAL	5	3	5	0	0	0	0	0

SOUTHERN METHODIST

	Yrs.	Won	Lost	CH	2D	3d%	4th	RR
E.O. "Doc" Hayes (North Texas 1927) 1955, 56-4th, 57, 65, 66, 67RR	6	7	8	0	0	0	1	1
Dave Bliss (Cornell 1965) 1984, 85, 88	3	3	3	0	0	0	0	0
John Shumate (Notre Dame 1974) 1993	1	0	1	0	0	0	0	0
TOTAL	10	10	12	0	0	0	1	1

SOUTHERN MISS.

	Yrs.	Won	Lost	CH	2D	3d%	4th	RR
M.K. Turk (Livingston 1964) 1990, 91	2	0	2	0	0	0	0	0
TOTAL	2	0	2	0	0	0	0	0

SOUTHERN UTAH

	Yrs.	Won	Lost	CH	2D	3d%	4th	RR
Bill Evans (Southern Utah 1972) 2001	1	0	1	0	0	0	0	0
TOTAL	1	0	1	0	0	0	0	0

SOUTHWEST MO. ST.

	Yrs.	Won	Lost	CH	2D	3d%	4th	RR
Charlie Spoonhour (School of Ozarks 1961) 1987, 88, 89, 90, 92	5	1	5	0	0	0	0	0
Steve Alford (Indiana 1987) 1999	1	2	1	0	0	0	0	0
TOTAL	6	3	6	0	0	0	0	0

SOUTHWEST TEX. ST.

	Yrs.	Won	Lost	CH	2D	3d%	4th	RR
Jim Wooldridge (Louisiana Tech 1977) 1994	1	0	1	0	0	0	0	0
Mike Miller (Tex. A&M-Commerce 1987) 1997	1	0	1	0	0	0	0	0
TOTAL	2	0	2	0	0	0	0	0

SPRINGFIELD

	Yrs.	Won	Lost	CH	2D	3d%	4th	RR
Ed Hickox (Ohio Wesleyan 1905) 1940RR	1	0	1	0	0	0	0	1
TOTAL	1	0	1	0	0	0	0	1

STANFORD

	Yrs.	Won	Lost	CH	2D	3d%	4th	RR
Everett Dean (Indiana 1921) 1942-CH	1	3	0	1	0	0	0	0
Mike Montgomery (Long Beach St. 1968) 1989, 92, 95, 96, 97, 98-T3d, 99, 2000, 01RR, 02	10	14	10	0	0	1	0	1
TOTAL	11	17	10	1	0	1	0	1

SYRACUSE

	Yrs.	Won	Lost	CH	2D	3d%	4th	RR
Marc Guley (Syracuse 1936) 1957RR	1	2	1	0	0	0	0	1
Fred Lewis (Eastern Ky. 1946) 1966RR	1	1	1	0	0	0	0	1
Roy Danforth (Southern Miss. 1962) 1973, 74, 75-4th, 76	4	5	5	0	0	0	1	0
Jim Boeheim (Syracuse 1966) 1977, 78, 79, 80, 83, 84, 85, 86, 87-2d, 88, 89RR, 90, 91, 92, 94, 95, 96-2d, 98, 99, 2000, 01	21	32	21	0	2	0	0	1
TOTAL	27	40	28	0	2	0	1	3

TEMPLE

	Yrs.	Won	Lost	CH	2D	3d%	4th	RR
Josh Cody (Vanderbilt 1920) 1944RR	1	1	1	0	0	0	0	1
Harry Litwack (Temple 1930) 1956-3d, 58-3d, 64, 67, 70, 72	6	7	6	0	0	2	0	0
Don Casey (Temple 1970) 1979	1	0	1	0	0	0	0	0
John Chaney (Bethune-Cookman 1955) 1984, 85, 86, 87, 88RR, 90, 91RR, 92, 93RR, 94, 95, 96, 97, 98, 99RR, 2000, 01RR	17	23	17	0	0	0	0	5
TOTAL	25	31	25	0	0	2	0	6

TENNESSEE

	Yrs.	Won	Lost	CH	2D	3d%	4th	RR
Ramon "Ray" Mears [Miami (Ohio) 1949] 1967, 76, 77	3	0	4	0	0	0	0	0
Don DeVoe (Ohio St. 1964) 1979, 80, 81, 82, 83, 89	6	5	6	0	0	0	0	0
Jerry Green (Appalachian St. 1968) 1998, 99, 2000, 01	4	3	4	0	0	0	0	0
TOTAL	13	8	14	0	0	0	0	0

TENNESSEE ST.

	Yrs.	Won	Lost	CH	2D	3d%	4th	RR
Frankie Allen (Roanoke 1971) 1993, 94	2	0	2	0	0	0	0	0
TOTAL	2	0	2	0	0	0	0	0

TENNESSEE TECH

	Yrs.	Won	Lost	CH	2D	3d%	4th	RR
Johnny Oldham (Western Ky. 1948) 1958, 63	2	0	2	0	0	0	0	0
TOTAL	2	0	2	0	0	0	0	0

TEXAS

	Yrs.	Won	Lost	CH	2D	3d%	4th	RR
H.C. "Bully" Gilstrap (Texas 1922) 1943-T3d	1	1	1	0	0	1	0	0
Jack Gray (Texas 1935) 1939RR, 47-3d	2	2	3	0	0	1	0	1
Harold Bradley (Hartwick 1934) 1960, 63	2	2	3	0	0	0	0	0
Leon Black (Texas 1953) 1972, 74	2	1	3	0	0	0	0	0
A.E. "Abe" Lemons (Oklahoma City 1949) 1979	1	0	1	0	0	0	0	0
Tom Penders (Connecticut 1967) 1989, 90RR, 91, 92, 94, 95, 96, 97	8	10	8	0	0	0	0	1
Rick Barnes (Lenior-Rhyne 1977) 1999, 2000, 01, 02	4	3	4	0	0	0	0	0
TOTAL	20	19	23	0	0	2	0	2

TEXAS A&M

	Yrs.	Won	Lost	CH	2D	3d%	4th	RR
John Floyd (Oklahoma St. 1941) 1951	1	0	1	0	0	0	0	0
Shelby Metcalf (Tex. A&M-Commerce 1953) 1964, 69, 75, 80, 87	5	3	6	0	0	0	0	0
TOTAL	6	3	7	0	0	0	0	0

TCU

	Yrs.	Won	Lost	CH	2D	3d%	4th	RR
Byron "Buster" Brannon (TCU 1933) 1952, 53, 59	3	3	3	0	0	0	0	0
Johnny Swaim (TCU 1953) 1968RR, 71	2	1	2	0	0	0	0	1
Jim Killingsworth (Northeastern Okla. St. 1948) 1987	1	1	1	0	0	0	0	0
Billy Tubbs (Lamar 1958) 1998	1	0	1	0	0	0	0	0
TOTAL	7	5	7	0	0	0	0	1

TEXAS-SAN ANTONIO

	Yrs.	Won	Lost	CH	2D	3d%	4th	RR
Ken Burmeister [St. Mary's (Tex.) 1971] 1988	1	0	1	0	0	0	0	0
Tim Carter (Kansas 1979) 1999	1	0	1	0	0	0	0	0
TOTAL	2	0	2	0	0	0	0	0

TEXAS SOUTHERN

	Yrs.	Won	Lost	CH	2D	3d%	4th	RR
Robert Moreland (Tougaloo 1962) 1990, 94, 95	3	0	3	0	0	0	0	0
TOTAL	3	0	3	0	0	0	0	0

TEXAS TECH

	Yrs.	Won	Lost	CH	2D	3d%	4th	RR
Polk Robison (Texas Tech 1935) 1954, 56, 61	3	1	3	0	0	0	0	0
Gene Gibson (Texas Tech 1950) 1962	1	1	2	0	0	0	0	0
Gerald Myers (Texas Tech 1959) 1973, 76, 85, 86	4	1	4	0	0	0	0	0
James Dickey (Central Ark. 1976) 1993, 96	2	2	2	0	0	0	0	0
Bob Knight (Ohio St. 1962) 2002	1	0	1	0	0	0	0	0
TOTAL	11	5	12	0	0	0	0	0

TOLEDO

	Yrs.	Won	Lost	CH	2D	3d%	4th	RR
Jerry Bush [St. John's (N.Y.) 1938] 1954	1	0	1	0	0	0	0	0
Bob Nichols (Toledo 1953) 1967, 79, 80	3	1	3	0	0	0	0	0
TOTAL	4	1	4	0	0	0	0	0

TOWSON

	Yrs.	Won	Lost	CH	2D	3d%	4th	RR
Terry Truax (Maryland 1968) 1990, 91	2	0	2	0	0	0	0	0
TOTAL	2	0	2	0	0	0	0	0

TRINITY (TEX.)

	Yrs.	Won	Lost	CH	2D	3d%	4th	RR
Bob Polk (Evansville 1939) 1969	1	0	1	0	0	0	0	0
TOTAL	1	0	1	0	0	0	0	0

TUFTS

	Yrs.	Won	Lost	CH	2D	3d%	4th	RR
Richard Cochran (Tufts 1934) 1945RR	1	0	2	0	0	0	0	1
TOTAL	1	0	2	0	0	0	0	1

TULANE

	Yrs.	Won	Lost	CH	2D	3d%	4th	RR
Perry Clark (Gettysburg 1974) 1992, 93, 95	3	3	3	0	0	0	0	0
TOTAL	3	3	3	0	0	0	0	0

TULSA

	Yrs.	Won	Lost	CH	2D	3d%	4th	RR
Clarence Iba (Panhandle St. 1936) 1955	1	1	1	0	0	0	0	0
Nolan Richardson (UTEP 1965) 1982, 84, 85	3	0	3	0	0	0	0	0
J.D. Barnett (Winona St. 1966) 1986, 87	2	0	2	0	0	0	0	0
Tubby Smith (High Point 1973) 1994, 95	2	4	2	0	0	0	0	0
Steve Robinson (Radford 1981) 1996, 97	2	1	2	0	0	0	0	0
Bill Self (Oklahoma St. 1985) 1999, 2000RR	2	4	2	0	0	0	0	1
John Phillips (Oklahoma St. 1973) 2002	1	1	1	0	0	0	0	0
TOTAL	13	11	13	0	0	0	0	1

UCLA*

	Yrs.	Won	Lost	CH	2D	3d%	4th	RR
John Wooden (Purdue 1932) 1950RR, 52, 56, 62-4th, 63, 64-CH, 65-CH, 67-CH, 68-CH, 69-CH, 70-CH, 71-CH, 72-CH, 73-CH, 74-3d, 75-CH	16	47	10	10	0	1	1	1

	Yrs.	Won	Lost	CH	2D	3d%	4th	RR
Gene Bartow (Truman 1953) 1976-3d, 77	2	5	2	0	0	1	0	0
Gary Cunningham (UCLA 1962) 1978, 79RR	2	3	2	0	0	0	0	1
Larry Brown (North Carolina 1963) 1980-2d, 81	2	5	2	0	1	0	0	0
Larry Farmer (UCLA 1973) 1983	1	0	1	0	0	0	0	0
Walt Hazzard (UCLA 1964) 1987	1	1	1	0	0	0	0	0
Jim Harrick [Charleston (W.Va.) 1960] 1989, 90, 91, 92RR, 93, 94, 95-CH, 96	8	13	7	1	0	0	0	0
Steve Lavin (Chapman 1988) 1997RR, 98, 99, 2000, 01, 02	6	11	6	0	0	0	0	1
TOTAL	**38**	**85**	**31**	**11**	**1**	**2**	**1**	**4**

UTAH

	Yrs.	Won	Lost	CH	2D	3d%	4th	RR
Vadal Petersen (Utah 1920) 1944-CH, 45RR	2	3	2	1	0	0	0	1
Jack Gardner (Southern California 1932) 1955, 56RR, 59, 60, 61-4th, 66-4th	6	8	9	0	0	0	2	1
Jerry Pimm (Southern California 1960) 1977, 78, 79, 81, 83	5	5	5	0	0	0	0	0
Lynn Archibald (Fresno St. 1968) 1986	1	0	1	0	0	0	0	0
Rick Majerus (Marquette 1970) 1991, 93, 95, 96, 97RR, 98-2d, 99, 2000, 02	9	16	9	0	1	0	0	1
TOTAL	**23**	**32**	**26**	**1**	**1**	**0**	**2**	**3**

UTAH ST.

	Yrs.	Won	Lost	CH	2D	3d%	4th	RR
E.L. "Dick" Romney (Utah 1917) 1939RR	1	1	1	0	0	0	0	1
Ladell Andersen (Utah St. 1951) 1962, 63, 64, 70RR, 71	5	4	7	0	0	0	0	1
Gordon "Dutch" Belnap (Utah St. 1958) 1975, 79	2	0	2	0	0	0	0	0
Rod Tueller (Utah St. 1959) 1980, 83, 88	3	0	3	0	0	0	0	0
Larry Eustachy (Long Beach St. 1979) 1998	1	0	1	0	0	0	0	0
Steve Morrill (Gonzaga 1974) 2000, 01	2	1	2	0	0	0	0	0
TOTAL	**14**	**6**	**16**	**0**	**0**	**0**	**0**	**2**

UTEP

	Yrs.	Won	Lost	CH	2D	3d%	4th	RR
Don Haskins (Oklahoma St. 1953) 1963, 64, 66-CH, 67, 70, 75, 84, 85, 86, 87, 88, 89, 90, 92	14	14	13	1	0	0	0	0
TOTAL	**14**	**14**	**13**	**1**	**0**	**0**	**0**	**0**

VALPARAISO

	Yrs.	Won	Lost	CH	2D	3d%	4th	RR
Homer Drew (William Jewell 1966) 1996, 97, 98, 99, 2000, 02	6	2	6	0	0	0	0	0
TOTAL	**6**	**2**	**6**	**0**	**0**	**0**	**0**	**0**

VANDERBILT

	Yrs.	Won	Lost	CH	2D	3d%	4th	RR
Roy Skinner (Presbyterian 1952) 1965RR, 74	2	1	3	0	0	0	0	1
C.M. Newton (Kentucky 1952) 1988, 89	2	2	2	0	0	0	0	0
Eddie Fogler (North Carolina 1970) 1991, 93	2	2	2	0	0	0	0	0
Jan van Breda Kolff (Vanderbilt 1974) 1997	1	0	1	0	0	0	0	0
TOTAL	**7**	**5**	**8**	**0**	**0**	**0**	**0**	**1**

VILLANOVA*

	Yrs.	Won	Lost	CH	2D	3d%	4th	RR
Alex Severance (Villanova 1929) 1939-T3d, 49RR, 51, 55	4	4	4	0	0	1	0	1
Jack Kraft (St. Joseph's 1942) 1962RR, 64, 69, 70RR, 71-2d, 72	6	11	7	0	1	0	0	2
Rollie Massimino (Vermont 1956) 1978RR, 80, 81, 82RR, 83RR, 84, 85-CH, 86, 88RR, 90, 91	11	20	10	1	0	0	0	4
Steve Lappas (CCNY 1977) 1995, 96, 97, 99	4	2	4	0	0	0	0	0
TOTAL	**25**	**37**	**25**	**1**	**1**	**1**	**0**	**7**

VIRGINIA

	Yrs.	Won	Lost	CH	2D	3d%	4th	RR
Terry Holland (Davidson 1964) 1976, 81-3d, 82, 83RR, 84-T3d, 86, 87, 89RR, 90	9	15	9	0	0	2	0	2
Jeff Jones (Virginia 1982) 1991, 93, 94, 95RR, 97	5	6	5	0	0	0	0	1
Pete Gillen (Fairfield 1968) 2001	1	0	1	0	0	0	0	0
TOTAL	**15**	**21**	**15**	**0**	**0**	**2**	**0**	**3**

VA. COMMONWEALTH

	Yrs.	Won	Lost	CH	2D	3d%	4th	RR
J.D. Barnett (Winona St. 1966) 1980, 81, 83, 84, 85	5	4	5	0	0	0	0	0
Sonny Smith (Milligan 1958) 1996	1	0	1	0	0	0	0	0
TOTAL	**6**	**4**	**6**	**0**	**0**	**0**	**0**	**0**

VMI

	Yrs.	Won	Lost	CH	2D	3d%	4th	RR
Louis "Weenie" Miller (Richmond 1947) 1964	1	0	1	0	0	0	0	0
Bill Blair (VMI 1964) 1976RR	1	2	1	0	0	0	0	1
Charlie Schmaus (VMI 1966) 1977	1	1	1	0	0	0	0	0
TOTAL	**3**	**3**	**3**	**0**	**0**	**0**	**0**	**1**

VIRGINIA TECH

	Yrs.	Won	Lost	CH	2D	3d%	4th	RR
Howard Shannon (Kansas St. 1948) 1967RR	1	2	1	0	0	0	0	1
Don DeVoe (Ohio St. 1964) 1976	1	0	1	0	0	0	0	0
Charles Moir (Appalachian St. 1952) 1979, 80, 85, 86	4	2	4	0	0	0	0	0
Bill C. Foster (Carson-Newman 1958) 1996	1	1	1	0	0	0	0	0
TOTAL	**7**	**5**	**7**	**0**	**0**	**0**	**0**	**1**

WAKE FOREST

	Yrs.	Won	Lost	CH	2D	3d%	4th	RR
Murray Greason (Wake Forest 1926) 1939RR, 53	2	1	2	0	0	0	0	0
Horace "Bones" McKinney (North Carolina 1946) 1961RR, 62-3d	2	6	2	0	0	1	0	1
Carl Tacy (Davis & Elkins 1956) 1977RR, 81, 82, 84RR	4	5	4	0	0	0	0	2
Dave Odom (Guilford 1965) 1991, 92, 93, 94, 95, 96RR, 97, 2001	8	10	8	0	0	0	0	2
Skip Prosser (Merchant Marine 1972) 2002	1	1	1	0	0	0	0	0
TOTAL	**17**	**23**	**17**	**0**	**0**	**1**	**0**	**5**

WASHINGTON

	Yrs.	Won	Lost	CH	2D	3d%	4th	RR
Clarence "Hec" Edmundson (Idaho 1909) 1943RR	1	0	2	0	0	0	0	1
Art McLarney (Washington St. 1932) 1948RR	1	1	2	0	0	0	0	1
William "Tippy" Dye (Ohio St. 1937) 1951RR, 53-3d	2	5	2	0	0	1	0	1
Marv Harshman (Pacific Lutheran 1942) 1976, 84, 85	3	2	3	0	0	0	0	0
Andy Russo (Lake Forest 1970) 1986	1	0	1	0	0	0	0	0
Bob Bender (Duke 1980) 1998, 99	2	2	2	0	0	0	0	0
TOTAL	**10**	**10**	**11**	**0**	**0**	**1**	**0**	**3**

WASHINGTON ST.

	Yrs.	Won	Lost	CH	2D	3d%	4th	RR
Jack Friel (Washington St. 1923) 1941-2d	1	2	1	0	1	0	0	0
George Raveling (Villanova 1960) 1980, 83	2	1	2	0	0	0	0	0
Kelvin Sampson (UNC Pembroke 1978) 1994	1	0	1	0	0	0	0	0
TOTAL	**4**	**3**	**4**	**0**	**1**	**0**	**0**	**0**

WAYNE ST. (MICH.)

	Yrs.	Won	Lost	CH	2D	3d%	4th	RR
Joel Mason (Western Mich. 1936) 1956	1	1	2	0	0	0	0	0
TOTAL	**1**	**1**	**2**	**0**	**0**	**0**	**0**	**0**

WEBER ST.

	Yrs.	Won	Lost	CH	2D	3d%	4th	RR
Dick Motta (Utah St. 1953) 1968	1	0	1	0	0	0	0	0
Phil Johnson (Utah St. 1953) 1969, 70, 71	3	2	3	0	0	0	0	0
Gene Visscher (Weber St. 1966) 1972, 73	2	1	2	0	0	0	0	0
Neil McCarthy (Sacramento St. 1965) 1978, 79, 80, 83	4	1	4	0	0	0	0	0
Ron Abegglen (Brigham Young 1962) 1995, 99	2	2	2	0	0	0	0	0
TOTAL	**12**	**6**	**13**	**0**	**0**	**0**	**0**	**0**

WEST TEXAS A&M

	Yrs.	Won	Lost	CH	2D	3d%	4th	RR
W.A. "Gus" Miller (West Texas A&M 1927) 1955	1	0	1	0	0	0	0	0
TOTAL	**1**	**0**	**1**	**0**	**0**	**0**	**0**	**0**

WEST VIRGINIA

	Yrs.	Won	Lost	CH	2D	3d%	4th	RR
Fred Schaus (West Virginia 1949) 1955, 56, 57, 58, 59-2d, 60	6	6	6	0	1	0	0	0
George King [Charleston (W.Va.) 1950] 1962, 63, 65	3	2	3	0	0	0	0	0
Raymond "Bucky" Waters (North Carolina St. 1957) 1967	1	0	1	0	0	0	0	0
Gale Catlett (West Virginia 1963) 1982, 83, 84, 86, 87, 89, 92, 98	8	5	8	0	0	0	0	0
TOTAL	**18**	**13**	**18**	**0**	**1**	**0**	**0**	**0**

WESTERN CARO.

	Yrs.	Won	Lost	CH	2D	3d%	4th	RR
Phil Hopkins (Gardner-Webb 1972) 1996	1	0	1	0	0	0	0	0
TOTAL	**1**	**0**	**1**	**0**	**0**	**0**	**0**	**0**

WESTERN KY.*

	Yrs.	Won	Lost	CH	2D	3d%	4th	RR
Ed Diddle (Centre 1921) 1940RR, 60, 62	3	3	4	0	0	0	0	1
Johnny Oldham (Western Ky. 1948) 1966, 67, 70, 71-3d	4	6	4	0	0	1	0	0
Jim Richards (Western Ky. 1959) 1976, 78	2	1	2	0	0	0	0	0
Gene Keady (Kansas St. 1958) 1980	1	0	1	0	0	0	0	0
Clem Haskins (Western Ky. 1967) 1981, 86	2	1	2	0	0	0	0	0
Murray Arnold (American 1960) 1987	1	1	1	0	0	0	0	0
Ralph Willard (Holy Cross 1967) 1993, 94	2	2	2	0	0	0	0	0
Matt Kilcullen (Lehman 1976) 1995	1	1	1	0	0	0	0	0
Dennis Felton (Howard 1985) 2001, 02	2	0	2	0	0	0	0	0
TOTAL	**18**	**15**	**19**	**0**	**0**	**1**	**0**	**1**

	Yrs.	Won	Lost	CH	2D	3d%	4th	RR
WESTERN MICH.								
Eldon Miller (Wittenberg 1961) 1976	1	1	1	0	0	0	0	0
Bob Donewald (Hanover 1964) 1998	1	1	1	0	0	0	0	0
TOTAL	2	2	2	0	0	0	0	0
WICHITA ST.								
Ralph Miller (Kansas 1942) 1964RR.....	1	1	1	0	0	0	0	1
Gary Thompson (Wichita St. 1954) 1965-4th...........................	1	2	2	0	0	0	1	0
Harry Miller (Eastern N.M. 1951) 1976	1	0	1	0	0	0	0	0
Gene Smithson (North Central 1961) 1981RR, 85....................	2	3	2	0	0	0	0	1
Eddie Fogler (North Carolina 1970) 1987, 88...............................	2	0	2	0	0	0	0	0
TOTAL	7	6	8	0	0	0	1	2
WILLIAMS								
Alex Shaw (Michigan 1932) 1955.........	1	0	1	0	0	0	0	0
TOTAL	1	0	1	0	0	0	0	0
WINTHROP								
Gregg Marshall (Randolph-Macon 1985) 1999, 2000, 01, 02......................	4	0	4	0	0	0	0	0
TOTAL	4	0	4	0	0	0	0	0
WISCONSIN								
Harold "Bud" Foster (Wisconsin 1930) 1941-CH, 47RR	2	4	1	1	0	0	0	1
Stu Jackson (Seattle 1978) 1994..........	1	1	1	0	0	0	0	0
Dick Bennett (Ripon 1965) 1997, 99, 2000-T-3d............................	3	4	3	0	0	1	0	0
Brad Soderberg (Wis.-Stevens Point 1985) 2001	1	0	1	0	0	0	0	0
Bo Ryan (Wilkes 1969) 2002	1	1	1	0	0	0	0	0
TOTAL	8	10	7	1	0	1	0	1
WIS.-GREEN BAY								
Dick Bennett (Ripon 1965) 1991, 94, 95	3	1	3	0	0	0	0	0
Mike Heideman (Wis.-La Crosse 1971) 1996	1	0	1	0	0	0	0	0
TOTAL	4	1	4	0	0	0	0	0
WRIGHT ST.								
Ralph Underhill (Tennessee Tech 1964) 1993	1	0	1	0	0	0	0	0
TOTAL	1	0	1	0	0	0	0	0

	Yrs.	Won	Lost	CH	2D	3d%	4th	RR
WYOMING								
Everett Shelton (Phillips 1923) 1941RR, 43-CH, 47RR, 48RR, 49RR, 52RR, 53, 58	8	4	12	1	0	0	0	5
Bill Strannigan (Wyoming 1941) 1967...	1	0	2	0	0	0	0	0
Jim Brandenburg (Colorado St. 1958) 1981, 82, 87	3	4	3	0	0	0	0	0
Benny Dees (Wyoming 1958) 1988.......	1	0	1	0	0	0	0	0
Steve McClain (Chadron St. 1984) 2002	1	1	1	0	0	0	0	0
TOTAL	14	9	19	1	0	0	0	5
XAVIER								
Jim McCafferty [Loyola (La.) 1942] 1961	1	0	1	0	0	0	0	0
Bob Staak (Connecticut 1971) 1983	1	0	1	0	0	0	0	0
Pete Gillen (Fairfield 1968) 1986, 87, 88, 89, 90, 91, 93....................	7	5	7	0	0	0	0	0
Skip Prosser (Merchant Marine 1972) 1995, 97, 98, 2001	4	1	4	0	0	0	0	0
Thad Matta (Butler 1990) 2002	1	1	1	0	0	0	0	0
TOTAL	14	7	14	0	0	0	0	0
YALE								
Howard Hobson (Oregon 1926) 1949RR	1	0	2	0	0	0	0	1
Joe Vancisin (Dartmouth 1944) 1957, 62	2	0	2	0	0	0	0	0
TOTAL	3	0	4	0	0	0	0	1

%National 3d-place games did not start until 1946 and ended with 1981; in other years, two teams tied for third and both listed this column. RR Regional runner-up, or one victory from Final Four, thus in the top eight.

 # NOTES ON TEAMS AND COACHES:
MICHIGAN: Steve Fisher coached Michigan in the 1989 tournament; Bill Freider was the coach during the regular season.
MISSOURI: Rich Daly coached Missouri in the 1989 tournament due to Norm Stewart's illness; Missouri credits the entire 1989 season to Stewart.
PRINCETON: J.L. McCandless coached Princeton in the 1961 tournament; Franklin Cappon suffered a heart attack 11 games into the season; Princeton credits the1961 regular season to Cappon and the postseason to McCandless.
SEATTLE: Clair Markey coached Seattle in the 1963 tournament due to Vince Cazetta's resignation.

* TEAMS VACATING NCAA TOURNAMENT ACTION

Teams	Years	Record	Placing	Conference
Alabama	1987	2-1		Southeastern
Arizona	1999	0-1		Pacific 10
Arizona St.	1995	2-1		Pacific 10
Austin Peay.............	1973	1-2		Ohio Valley
California	1996	0-1		Pacific 10
Clemson	1990	2-1		Atlantic Coast
Connecticut.............	1996	2-1		Big East
DePaul	1986-89	6-4		Independent
Florida	1987-88	3-2		Southeastern
Georgia	1985	1-1		Southeastern
Iona	1980	1-1		Independent
Kentucky.................	1988	2-1		Southeastern
Long Beach St.	1971-73	6-3	2 RR	Pacific Coast
La.-Lafayette	1972-73	3-3		Southland
Loyola Marymount....	1980	0-1		West Coast
Marshall	1987	0-1		Southern
Maryland	1988	1-1		Atlantic Coast
Massachusetts	1996	4-1	3d	Atlantic 10
Memphis	1982-86	9-5	3d	Metro
Minnesota	1972, 94-95, 97	6-4	3d	Big Ten
Missouri	1994	3-1	RR	Big Eight
New Mexico St.	1992-94	3-3		Big West
North Carolina St.....	1987-88	0-2		Atlantic Coast
Oregon St.	1980-82	2-3	RR	Pacific 10
Purdue	1996	1-1		Big Ten
St. Joseph's	1961	3-1	3d	Middle Atlantic
Texas Tech	1996	2-1		Southwest
UCLA	1980, 99	5-2	2d	Pacific 10
Villanova	1971	4-1	2d	Independent
Western Ky.	1971	4-1	3d	Ohio Valley
30 schools	50 years	78-52	2 2d, 5 3d, 4 RR	

Official NCAA Records	Yrs	Won	Lost	CH	2d	3d	4th	RR
Alabama	13	13	13	0	0	0	0	0
Arizona	19	32	18	1	1	2	0	2
Arizona St.	10	9	11	0	0	0	0	3
Austin Peay	3	1	3	0	0	0	0	0
California.....................	10	16	10	1	1	0	1	2
Clemson	6	6	6	0	0	0	0	1
Connecticut...................	21	25	21	1	0	0	0	4
DePaul	17	14	20	0	0	2	0	1
Florida	6	12	6	0	0	1	0	0
Georgia	7	5	7	0	0	1	0	0
Iona	6	0	6	0	0	0	0	0
Kentucky	42	87	37	7	3	3	0	16
Long Beach St.	4	1	5	0	0	0	0	0
La.-Lafayette	5	1	5	0	0	0	0	0
Loyola Marymount	4	5	4	0	0	0	0	1
Marshall	4	0	4	0	0	0	0	0
Maryland	17	25	17	0	0	1	0	2
Massachusetts	7	7	7	0	0	0	0	1
Memphis	11	9	11	0	1	0	0	1
Minnesota	4	6	4	0	0	1	0	1
Missouri	17	10	17	0	0	0	0	2
New Mexico St.	13	7	15	0	0	1	0	0
North Carolina St.	15	27	14	2	0	1	0	3
Oregon St.	13	10	16	0	0	0	2	4
Purdue	18	25	18	0	1	1	0	2
St. Joseph's	15	12	19	0	0	0	0	2
Texas Tech	9	3	10	0	0	0	0	0
UCLA	35	78	28	11	0	2	1	4
Villanova	24	33	24	1	0	1	0	7
Western Ky.	16	11	17	0	0	0	0	1

CHAMPIONSHIPS

Final Four All-Tournament Teams

(First player listed on each team was the outstanding player in the Final Four)

1939— Not chosen.

1940— Marvin Huffman, Indiana
Howard Engleman, Kansas
Bob Allen, Kansas
Jay McCreary, Indiana
William Menke, Indiana

1941-51— Not chosen.

1952— Clyde Lovellette, Kansas
Bob Zawoluk, St. John's (N.Y.)
John Kerr, Illinois
Ron MacGilvray, St. John's (N.Y.)
Dean Kelley, Kansas

1953— B.H. Born, Kansas
Bob Houbregs, Washington
Bob Leonard, Indiana
Dean Kelley, Kansas
Don Schlundt, Indiana

1954— Tom Gola, La Salle
Chuck Singley, La Salle
Jesse Arnelle, Penn St.
Roy Irvin, Southern California
Bob Carney, Bradley

1955— Bill Russell, San Francisco
Tom Gola, La Salle
K.C. Jones, San Francisco
Jim Ranglos, Colorado
Carl Cain, Iowa

1956— Hal Lear, Temple
Bill Russell, San Francisco
Carl Cain, Iowa
Hal Perry, San Francisco
Bill Logan, Iowa

1957— Wilt Chamberlain, Kansas
Len Rosenbluth, North Carolina
John Green, Michigan St.
Gene Brown, San Francisco
Pete Brennan, North Carolina

1958— Elgin Baylor, Seattle
John Cox, Kentucky
Guy Rodgers, Temple
Charley Brown, Seattle
Vern Hatton, Kentucky

1959— Jerry West, West Virginia
Oscar Robertson, Cincinnati
Darrall Imhoff, California
Don Goldstein, Louisville
Denny Fitzpatrick, California

1960— Jerry Lucas, Ohio St.
Oscar Robertson, Cincinnati
Mel Nowell, Ohio St.
Darrall Imhoff, California
Tom Sanders, New York U.

1961— Jerry Lucas, Ohio St.
Bob Wiesenhahn, Cincinnati
Larry Siegfried, Ohio St.
Carl Bouldin, Cincinnati
Vacated†

1962— Paul Hogue, Cincinnati
Jerry Lucas, Ohio St.
Tom Thacker, Cincinnati
John Havlicek, Ohio St.
Len Chappell, Wake Forest

1963— Art Heyman, Duke
Tom Thacker, Cincinnati
Les Hunter, Loyola (Ill.)
George Wilson, Cincinnati
Ron Bonham, Cincinnati

1964— Walt Hazzard, UCLA
Jeff Mullins, Duke
Bill Buntin, Michigan
Willie Murrell, Kansas St.
Gail Goodrich, UCLA

1965— Bill Bradley, Princeton
Gail Goodrich, UCLA
Cazzie Russell, Michigan
Edgar Lacey, UCLA
Kenny Washington, UCLA

1966— Jerry Chambers, Utah
Pat Riley, Kentucky

Jack Marin, Duke
Louie Dampier, Kentucky
Bobby Joe Hill, UTEP

1967— Lew Alcindor, UCLA
Don May, Dayton
Mike Warren, UCLA
Elvin Hayes, Houston
Lucius Allen, UCLA

1968— Lew Alcindor, UCLA
Lynn Shackelford, UCLA
Mike Warren, UCLA
Lucius Allen, UCLA
Larry Miller, North Carolina

1969— Lew Alcindor, UCLA
Rick Mount, Purdue
Charlie Scott, North Carolina
Willie McCarter, Drake
John Vallely, UCLA

1970— Sidney Wicks, UCLA
Jimmy Collins, New Mexico St.
John Vallely, UCLA
Artis Gilmore, Jacksonville
Curtis Rowe, UCLA

1971— Vacated†
Vacated†
Vacated†
Steve Patterson, UCLA
Sidney Wicks, UCLA

1972— Bill Walton, UCLA
Keith Wilkes, UCLA
Bob McAdoo, North Carolina
Jim Price, Louisville
Ron King, Florida St.

1973— Bill Walton, UCLA
Steve Downing, Indiana
Ernie DiGregorio, Providence
Larry Finch, Memphis
Larry Kenon, Memphis

1974— David Thompson, North Carolina St.
Bill Walton, UCLA
Tom Burleson, North Carolina St.
Monte Towe, North Carolina St.
Maurice Lucas, Marquette

1975— Richard Washington, UCLA
Kevin Grevey, Kentucky
Dave Myers, UCLA
Allen Murphy, Louisville
Jim Lee, Syracuse

1976— Kent Benson, Indiana
Scott May, Indiana
Rickey Green, Michigan
Marques Johnson, UCLA
Tom Abernethy, Indiana

1977— Butch Lee, Marquette
Mike O'Koren, North Carolina
Cedric Maxwell, Charlotte
Bo Ellis, Marquette
Walter Davis, North Carolina
Jerome Whitehead, Marquette

1978— Jack Givens, Kentucky
Ron Brewer, Arkansas
Mike Gminski, Duke
Rick Robey, Kentucky
Jim Spanarkel, Duke

1979— Earvin Johnson, Michigan St.
Greg Kelser, Michigan St.
Larry Bird, Indiana St.
Mark Aguirre, DePaul
Gary Garland, DePaul

1980— Darrell Griffith, Louisville
Vacated†
Joe Barry Carroll, Purdue
Vacated†
Rodney McCray, Louisville

1981— Isiah Thomas, Indiana
Jeff Lamp, Virginia
Jim Thomas, Indiana
Landon Turner, Indiana
Al Wood, North Carolina

1982— James Worthy, North Carolina
Patrick Ewing, Georgetown
Eric Floyd, Georgetown
Michael Jordan, North Carolina
Sam Perkins, North Carolina

1983— Akeem Olajuwon, Houston
Thurl Bailey, North Carolina St.
Sidney Lowe, North Carolina St.

Milt Wagner, Louisville
Dereck Whittenburg, North Carolina St.

1984— Patrick Ewing, Georgetown
Michael Graham, Georgetown
Akeem Olajuwon, Houston
Michael Young, Houston
Alvin Franklin, Houston

1985— Patrick Ewing, Georgetown
Ed Pinckney, Villanova
Dwayne McClain, Villanova
Harold Jensen, Villanova
Gary McLain, Villanova

1986— Pervis Ellison, Louisville
Billy Thompson, Louisville
Johnny Dawkins, Duke
Mark Alarie, Duke
Tommy Amaker, Duke

1987— Keith Smart, Indiana
Sherman Douglas, Syracuse
Derrick Coleman, Syracuse
Armon Gilliam, UNLV
Steve Alford, Indiana

1988— Danny Manning, Kansas
Milt Newton, Kansas
Stacey King, Oklahoma
Dave Sieger, Oklahoma
Sean Elliott, Arizona

1989— Glen Rice, Michigan
Rumeal Robinson, Michigan
Danny Ferry, Duke
Gerald Greene, Seton Hall
John Morton, Seton Hall

1990— Anderson Hunt, UNLV
Stacey Augmon, UNLV
Larry Johnson, UNLV
Phil Henderson, Duke
Dennis Scott, Georgia Tech

1991— Christian Laettner, Duke
Bobby Hurley, Duke
Bill McCaffrey, Duke
Mark Randall, Kansas
Anderson Hunt, UNLV

1992— Bobby Hurley, Duke
Grant Hill, Duke
Christian Laettner, Duke
Jalen Rose, Michigan
Chris Webber, Michigan

1993— Donald Williams, North Carolina
Eric Montross, North Carolina
George Lynch, North Carolina
Chris Webber, Michigan
Jamal Mashburn, Kentucky

1994— Corliss Williamson, Arkansas
Corey Beck, Arkansas
Scotty Thurman, Arkansas
Grant Hill, Duke
Antonio Lang, Duke

1995— Ed O'Bannon, UCLA
Toby Bailey, UCLA
Corliss Williamson, Arkansas
Clint McDaniel, Arkansas
Bryant Reeves, Oklahoma St.

1996— Tony Delk, Kentucky
Ron Mercer, Kentucky
Marcus Camby, Massachusetts
Todd Burgan, Syracuse
John Wallace, Syracuse

1997— Miles Simon, Arizona
Mike Bibby, Arizona
Ron Mercer, Kentucky
Scott Padgett, Kentucky
Bobby Jackson, Minnesota

1998— Jeff Sheppard, Kentucky
Scott Padgett, Kentucky
Arthur Lee, Stanford
Michael Doleac, Utah
Andre Miller, Utah

1999— Richard Hamilton, Connecticut
Khalid El-Amin, Connecticut
Ricky Moore, Connecticut
Elton Brand, Duke
Trajan Langdon, Duke

2000— Mateen Cleaves, Michigan St.
Udonis Haslem, Florida
Charlie Bell, Michigan St.
A.J. Granger, Michigan St.
Morris Peterson, Michigan St.

2001— Shane Battier, Duke
Mike Dunleavy, Duke
Richard Jefferson, Arizona
Jason Williams, Duke
Loren Woods, Arizona

2002— Juan Dixon, Maryland
Lonny Baxter, Maryland
Chris Wilcox, Maryland
Dane Fife, Indiana
Kyle Hornsby, Indiana

†These student-athletes and the teams they represented were declared ineligible after the tournament. Under NCAA rules, the teams' and student-athletes' records were deleted and the teams' places in the final standings were vacated: 1961—John Egan, St. Joseph's; 1971—Howard Porter, Villanova; Hank Siemiontkowski, Villanova; Jim McDaniels, Western Kentucky; 1980—Kiki Vandeweghe, UCLA; Rod Foster, UCLA.

National Invitation Tournament Year-by-Year Results

Season	Champion	Score	Runner-Up	Third Place	Fourth Place
1938	Temple	60-36	Colorado	Oklahoma St.	New York U.
1939	Long Island	44-32	Loyola (Ill.)	Bradley	St. John's (N.Y.)
1940	Colorado	51-40	Duquesne	Oklahoma St.	DePaul
1941	Long Island	56-42	Ohio	CCNY	Seton Hall
1942	West Virginia	47-45	Western Ky.	Creighton	Toledo
1943	St. John's (N.Y.)	48-27	Toledo	Wash. & Jeff.	Fordham
1944	St. John's (N.Y.)	47-39	DePaul	Kentucky	Oklahoma St.
1945	DePaul	71-54	Bowling Green	St. John's (N.Y.)	Rhode Island
1946	Kentucky	46-45	Rhode Island	West Virginia	Muhlenberg
1947	Utah	49-45	Kentucky	North Carolina St.	West Virginia
1948	St. Louis	65-52	New York U.	Western Ky.	DePaul
1949	San Francisco	48-47	Loyola (Ill.)	Bowling Green	Bradley
1950	CCNY	69-61	Bradley	St. John's (N.Y.)	Duquesne
1951	Brigham Young	62-43	Dayton	St. John's (N.Y.)	Seton Hall
1952	La Salle	75-64	Dayton	St. Bonaventure	Duquesne
1953	Seton Hall	58-46	St. John's (N.Y.)	Duquesne	Manhattan
1954	Holy Cross	71-62	Duquesne	Niagara	Western Ky.
1955	Duquesne	70-58	Dayton	Cincinnati	St. Francis (Pa.)
1956	Louisville	93-80	Dayton	St. Joseph's	St. Francis (N.Y.)
1957	Bradley	84-83	Memphis	Tampa	St. Bonaventure
1958	Xavier	78-74(ot)	Dayton	St. Bonaventure	St. John's (N.Y.)
1959	St. John's (N.Y.)	76-71(ot)	Bradley	New York U.	Providence
1960	Bradley	88-72	Providence	Utah St.	St. Bonaventure
1961	Providence	62-59	St. Louis	Holy Cross	Dayton
1962	Dayton	73-67	St. John's (N.Y.)	Loyola (Ill.)	Duquesne
1963	Providence	81-66	Canisius	Marquette	Villanova
1964	Bradley	86-54	New Mexico	Army	New York U.
1965	St. John's (N.Y.)	55-51	Villanova	Army	New York U.
1966	Brigham Young	97-84	New York U.	Villanova	Army
1967	Southern Ill.	71-56	Marquette	Rutgers	Marshall
1968	Dayton	61-48	Kansas	Notre Dame	St. Peter's
1969	Temple	89-76	Boston College	Tennessee	Army
1970	Marquette	65-53	St. John's (N.Y.)	Army	LSU
1971	North Carolina	84-66	Georgia Tech	St. Bonaventure	Duke
1972	Maryland	100-69	Niagara	Jacksonville	St. John's (N.Y.)
1973	Virginia Tech	92-91(ot)	Notre Dame	North Carolina	Alabama
1974	Purdue	87-81	Utah	Boston College	Jacksonville
1975	Princeton	80-69	Providence	Oregon	St. John's (N.Y.)
1976	Kentucky	81-76	Charlotte	North Carolina St.	Providence
1977	St. Bonaventure	94-91	Houston	Villanova	Alabama
1978	Texas	101-93	North Carolina St.	Rutgers	Georgetown
1979	Indiana	53-52	Purdue	Alabama	Ohio St.
1980	Virginia	58-55	Minnesota	Illinois	UNLV
1981	Tulsa	86-84(ot)	Syracuse	Purdue	West Virginia
1982	Bradley	67-58	Purdue	+ Georgia	+Oklahoma
1983	Fresno St.	69-60	DePaul	+ Nebraska	+Wake Forest
1984	Michigan	83-63	Notre Dame	Virginia Tech	La.-Lafayette
1985	UCLA	65-62	Indiana	Tennessee	Louisville
1986	Ohio St.	73-63	Wyoming	Louisiana Tech	Florida
1987	Southern Miss.	84-80	La Salle	Nebraska	Ark.-Little Rock
1988	Connecticut	72-67	Ohio St.	Colorado St.	Boston College
1989	St. John's (N.Y.)	73-65	St. Louis	UAB	Michigan St.
1990	Vanderbilt	74-72	St. Louis	Penn St.	New Mexico
1991	Stanford	78-72	Oklahoma	Colorado	Massachusetts
1992	Virginia	81-76	Notre Dame	Utah	Florida
1993	Minnesota	92-61	Georgetown	UAB	Providence
1994	Villanova	80-73	Vanderbilt	Siena	Kansas St.
1995	Virginia Tech	65-64(ot)	Marquette	Penn St.	Canisius
1996	Nebraska	60-56	St. Joseph's	Tulane	Alabama
1997	Michigan	82-73	Florida St.	Connecticut	Arkansas

Season	Champion	Score	Runner-Up	Third Place	Fourth Place
1998	Minnesota	79-72	Penn St.	Georgia	Fresno St.
1999	California	61-60	Clemson	Xavier	Oregon
2000	Wake Forest	71-61	Notre Dame	Penn St.	North Carolina St.
2001	Tulsa	79-60	Alabama	Memphis	Detroit
2002	Memphis	72-62	South Carolina	Syracuse	Temple

+tied for third place

POSTSEASON CHARITY GAME

During World War II, the American Red Cross sponsored a basketball game to raise money for the war effort. The game featured that year's NCAA champion versus the NIT champion.

Season	Winner	Score	Loser	Site
1943	Wyoming (NCAA champion)	52-47(ot)	St. John's (N.Y.) (NIT champion)	New York
1944	Utah (NCAA champion)	43-36	St. John's (N.Y.) (NIT champion)	New York
1945	Oklahoma St. (NCAA champion)	52-44	DePaul (NIT champion)	New York

NABC All-Star Game Results

Season	Winner	Score	MVP	Winning Coach	Losing Coach	Attendance
1963	East	77-70	Art Heyman, Duke	Harold Anderson	Cliff Wells	9,000
1964	West	79-78	Willie Murrell, Kansas St.	Slats Gill	Jack Gardner	9,700
1965	West	87-74	Gail Goodrich, UCLA	Doggie Julian	Joe Lapchick	7,000
1966	East	126-99	Cazzie Russell, Michigan	Taps Gallagher	Forrest Twogood	8,000
1967	East	102-93	Sonny Dove, St. John's (N.Y.)	Ben Carnevale	Everest Shelton	7,300
1968	West	95-88	Pete Maravich, LSU	Phog Allen & Tex Winter	Art Schabinger & John Bach	14,500
1969	East	104-80	Neal Walk, Florida	Tony Hinkle	Branch McCracken	6,100
1970	East	116-102	Charlie Scott, North Carolina	Nat Holman	Bud Foster	14,756
1971	East	106-104 (ot)	Jim McDaniels, Western Ky.	Dutch Lonborg	Vadal Peterson	13,178
1972	East	96-91 (ot)	Billy Shepard, Butler	Howard Hobson	Henry Iba	7,856
1973	West	98-94	Jim Brewer, Minnesota	Stan Watts	Adolph Rupp	8,609
1974	East	105-85	Marvin Barnes, Providence	Harry Litwack	John Hyder	8,396
1975	West	110-89	Gus Williams, Southern California	Bruce Drake	Eddie Hickey	NA
1976	West	101-98	Chuckie Williams, Kansas St.	Marv Harshman	Dean Smith	5,951
1977	East	114-93	Ernie Grunfeld, Tennessee	Bob Knight	Johnny Orr	6,537
1978	East	93-87	Butch Lee, Marquette	Frank McGuire	Al McGuire	4,275
1979	East	114-109	Greg Deane, Utah	Joe B. Hall	Bill Foster	7,472
1980	East	88-79	Mike O'Koren, North Carolina	Bill Hodges	Jud Heathcote	7,600
1981	West	99-97	Danny Ainge, Brigham Young	Larry Brown	Denny Crum	3,116
1982	West	102-68	Ricky Frazier, Missouri	Dale Brown	Bob Knight	3,965
1983	West	99-94	Darrell Walker, Arkansas	John Thompson	Dean Smith	4,178
1984	West	111-77	Fred Reynolds, UTEP	Marv Harshman	Jim Valvano	4,126
1985	West	97-90	Lorenzo Charles, North Carolina St.	Guy Lewis	Joe B. Hall	10,464
1986	West	94-92	David Wingate, Georgetown	Rollie Massimino	Lou Carnesecca	7,009
1987	West	92-91	David Robinson, Navy	Denny Crum	Mike Krzyzewski	8,041
1988	East	97-91	David Rivers, Notre Dame	Jim Boeheim	Jerry Tarkanian	8,528
1989	West	150-111	Tim Hardaway, UTEP	Lute Olson	Billy Tubbs	7,541
1990	East	127-126	Travis Mays, Texas	P.J. Carlesimo	Steve Fisher	7,161
1991	West	122-113	Jimmy Oliver, Purdue	Nolan Richardson	Bobby Cremins	8,000
1992	West	117-93	Doug Christie, Pepperdine	Roy Williams	Clem Haskins	10,344
1993	West	104-95	Ervin Johnson, New Orleans	Bob Huggins	Mike Krzyzewski	6,604
1994	East	77-73	Charlie Ward, Florida St.	Clarence "Bighouse" Gaines	Guy Lewis	6,500
1995	West	117-88	Fred Hoiberg, Iowa St.	Lute Olson	Lon Kruger	7,900
1996	East	99-92	Danetri Hill, Florida	Eddie Sutton	Jim Harrick	5,500
1997	East	105-94	James Collins, Florida St.	Jim Boeheim	Norm Stewart	6,019
1998	East	102-89	Felipe Lopez, St. John's (N.Y.)	Clem Haskins	Steve Lavin	8,998
1999	West	93-86	Doug Swenson, Creighton	Rick Majerus	Tubby Smith	6,753

Year	Score NABC-Opp.	NABC MVP	NABC Coach	Opponent	Attendance
2000	80-82	Kenyon Jones, San Francisco	Jim Calhoun	Harlem Globetrotters	8,000
2001	63-75	Kyle Hill, Eastern Mich.	Gene Keady	Harlem Globetrotters	15,253
2002	86-76	Tony Akins, Georgia Tech	Tom Izzo	Harlem Globetrotters	8,758

Game Sites: 1963-67—Lexington, Kentucky; 1968-70—Indianapolis, Indiana; 1971-74—Dayton, Ohio; 1975-77—Tulsa, Ok.; 1978-present—same city as the NCAA Final Four.

Division II Championship

2002 Results

FIRST ROUND
Charleston (W.Va.) 96, Alderson-Broaddus 93 (ot)
Belmont Abbey 76, W. Va. Wesleyan 59
Rockhurst 75, Mo. Western St. 68
Incarnate Word 72, Tarleton St. 59
Cal St. Bakersfield 84, Montana St.-Billings 81
Seattle Pacific 82, BYU-Hawaii 57
Neb.-Omaha 88, Fort Lewis 58
Metro St. 66, Minnesota-Duluth 61
Johnson Smith 73, Augusta St. 70
Winston-Salem 90, Wingate 75
West Ga. 76, Delta St. 71
Valdosta St. 62, Paine 57
Mass.-Lowell 72, Bentley 70
Pace 92, Queens (N.Y.) 88
Findlay 70, Gannon 53
Lewis 67, Hillsdale 53

SECOND ROUND
Indiana (Pa.) 91, Charleston (W.Va.) 81
Salem Int'l 75, Belmont Abbey 69
Rockhurst 75, Northeastern St. 70 (2 ot)
Northwest Mo. St. 61, Incarnate Word 56
Cal St. San B'dino 66, Cal St. Bakersfield 62
Humboldt St. 89, Seattle Pacific 82
South Dakota St. 96, Neb.-Omaha 76
Metro St. 59, Neb.-Kearney 51
Carson-Newman 77, Johnson Smith 66
Shaw 62, Winston-Salem 61
West Ga. 77, Tampa 69
Valdosta St. 80, Henderson St. 54
Adelphi 72, Mass.-Lowell 57
Assumption 91, Pace 73
Ky. Wesleyan 94, Findlay 89
Lewis 62, Michigan Tech 51

REGIONAL FINALS
Indiana (Pa.) 85, Salem Int'l 81
Northwest Mo. St. 79, Rockhurst 73
Cal St. San B'dino 80, Humboldt St. 65
Metro St. 87, South Dakota St. 86
Shaw 69, Carson-Newman 68
West Ga. 81, Valdosta St. 69
Adelphi 77, Assumption 56
Ky. Wesleyan 80, Lewis 75

QUARTERFINALS
Shaw 102, West Ga. 84
Indiana (Pa.) 78, Northwest Mo. St. 72
Metro St. 65, Cal St. San B'dino 48
Ky. Wesleyan 71, Adelphi 46

SEMIFINALS
Metro St. 82, Indiana (Pa.) 52
Ky. Wesleyan 101, Shaw 92

CHAMPIONSHIP
Metro St. 80, Ky. Wesleyan 72

Box Scores

SEMIFINALS
MARCH 21
AT EVANSVILLE, INDIANA
Metro St. 82, Indiana (Pa.) 52

Metro St.	FG-FGA	FT-FTA	RB	PF	TP
Patrick Mutombo	6-10	5-5	1	4	17
Lester Strong	4-6	1-2	5	4	9
Lee Bethea	6-13	0-0	5	0	15
Luke Kendall	4-11	2-3	3	2	12
Clayton Smith	4-5	0-2	4	0	8
Joe Kelly	1-3	0-0	0	2	3
O.J. Thomas	0-0	0-0	1	0	0
Mark Worthington	0-1	0-2	0	3	0
Mike Buggs	4-5	8-10	3	1	16
Chris Ford	1-1	0-0	0	0	2
Ryon Nickle	0-0	0-0	0	0	0
Ben Ortner	0-1	0-0	4	1	0
Team			7		
TOTALS	30-56	16-24	33	19	82

Indiana (Pa.)	FG-FGA	FT-FTA	RB	PF	TP
Leon Piper	3-6	3-5	7	1	9
Fannar Olafsson	2-3	0-0	1	3	4
Dennis Mims	4-6	3-6	9	3	11
Wes Layton	2-4	0-0	3	3	6
Aaron Faulkner	1-12	2-2	2	3	4
Sean Whalen	0-3	0-0	0	2	0
Eric Castorina	1-2	3-4	0	2	5
Chad Curran	0-0	0-0	1	0	0
Mike Mangel	1-2	0-0	0	1	3
Keenan Holmes	3-6	1-4	3	1	8
Felix Davila	1-3	0-0	1	3	2
Team			5		
TOTALS	18-47	12-21	32	52	

Halftime: Metro St. 39, Indiana (Pa.) 15. Three-point field goals: Metro St. 6-16 (Mutombo 0-1, Bethea 3-7, Kendall 2-3, Kelly 1-3, Worthington 0-1, Buggs 0-1); Indiana (Pa.) 4-19 (Layton 2-4, Faulkner 0-7, Whalen 0-3, Castorina 0-1, Mangel 1-2, Holmes 1-2). Officials: Jerry Hill, Bobby Vetkoetter, Haywood Bostic. Attendance: 3,894.

Ky. Wesleyan 101, Shaw 92

Ky. Wesleyan	FG-FGA	FT-FTA	RB	PF	TP
Tyrus Boswell	5-10	2-5	5	3	12
Ronald Evans	6-18	6-6	6	2	21
DeWayne Floyd	1-2	1-2	4	1	3
Chris Landry	6-11	5-6	8	1	19
Beau Green	3-4	0-0	0	1	6
Gene Evans	0-0	0-0	0	0	0
Dewayne Rogers	0-0	0-0	1	0	0
Matt Enos	0-0	0-0	0	0	0
Trey Ferguson	0-1	2-2	1	1	2
Bobby Zuerner	5-9	8-10	2	0	22
Nathan Fortener	0-0	0-0	0	1	0
J.T. Riddle	0-0	0-0	0	0	0
Jeff McGowan	0-0	0-0	0	0	0
Marshall Sanders	4-7	8-10	11	4	16
Team			5		
TOTALS	30-62	32-41	43	14	101

Shaw	FG-FGA	FT-FTA	RB	PF	TP
Ronald Murray	10-21	2-4	9	5	23
Kenyon Booker	5-10	2-2	7	4	12
Steve Bynes	4-5	0-0	0	4	8
Gerald Raymond	2-11	2-2	2	2	6
Cedric Lusk	2-2	0-0	4	1	6
Willie Donaldson	0-0	0-0	0	1	0
Leroy Mosley	0-1	0-0	1	2	0
Van Williams	3-8	0-0	0	2	8
Harrell Butler	2-3	1-2	2	1	5
Jarett Kearse	8-12	2-3	2	4	24
Clarence Taylor	0-0	0-0	0	0	0
Team			5		
Totals	36-73	9-13	32	26	92

Halftime: Ky. Wesleyan 41, Shaw 40. Three-point field goals: Ky. Wesleyan 9-22 (Boswell 0-1, Evans 3-8, Landry 2-4, Green 0-1, Ferguson 0-1, Zuerner 4-7); Shaw 11-29 (Murray 1-4, Raymond 0-7, Lusk 2-2, Williams 2-7, Kearse 6-9). Disqualifications: Murray. Technical fouls: Shaw bench. Officials: Doug Votava, James Bruno, Paul Vargo. Attendance: 3,894.

CHAMPIONSHIP
MARCH 23
AT EVANSVILLE, INDIANA
Metro St. 80, Ky. Wesleyan 72

Ky. Wesleyan	FG-FGA	FT-FTA	RB	PF	TP
Tyrus Boswell	3-4	0-0	6	3	6
Ronald Evans	5-14	1-2	6	4	12
DeWayne Floyd	1-4	0-0	2	3	3
Chris Landry	7-15	1-3	6	2	17
Beau Green	2-4	4-4	1	4	9
Gene Evans	0-0	0-0	0	0	0
Dewayne Rogers	1-3	0-0	2	0	2
Trey Ferguson	0-1	0-0	0	0	0
Bobby Zuerner	2-8	4-4	1	3	10
Marshall Sanders	4-7	5-7	12	2	13
Team			3		
TOTALS	25-60	15-20	39	21	72

Metro St.	FG-FGA	FT-FTA	RB	PF	TP
Luke Kendall	4-12	0-0	1	3	8
Patrick Mutombo	12-21	5-6	6	3	29
Lester Strong	5-8	1-2	11	4	11
Lee Bethea	7-13	4-4	4	2	19
Clayton Smith	3-3	3-6	1	3	9
Joe Kelly	0-1	0-0	0	0	0
O.J. Thomas	0-0	0-0	0	0	0
Mark Worthington	0-2	0-0	1	1	0
Mike Buggs	1-2	2-2	1	0	4
Ben Ortner	0-0	0-1	2	1	0
Team			5		
TOTALS:	32-62	15-21	30	19	80

Halftime: Ky. Wesleyan 32, Metro St. 28. Three-point field goals: Ky. Wesleyan 7-24 (Evans 1-5, Floyd 1-2, Landry 2-4, Green 1-3, Rogers 0-1, Ferguson 0-1, Zuerner 2-8); Metro St. 1-14 (Kendall 0-6, Bethea 1-5, Kelly 0-1, Worthington 0-2). Officials: Doug Votava, Jerry Hill, James Bruno. Attendance: 5,119.

Year-by-Year Results

Season	Champion	Score	Runner-Up	Third Place	Fourth Place
1957	Wheaton (Ill.)	89-65	Ky. Wesleyan	Mt. St. Mary's	Cal St. Los Angeles
1958	South Dakota	75-53	St. Michael's	Evansville	Wheaton (Ill.)
1959	Evansville	83-67	Southwest Mo. St.	N.C. A&T	Cal St. Los Angeles
1960	Evansville	90-69	Chapman	Ky. Wesleyan	Cornell College
1961	Wittenberg	42-38	Southeast Mo. St.	South Dakota St.	Mt. St. Mary's
1962	Mt. St. Mary's	58-57(ot)	Sacramento St.	Southern Ill.	Neb. Wesleyan
1963	South Dakota St.	44-42	Wittenberg	Oglethorpe	Southern Ill.
1964	Evansville	72-59	Akron	N.C. A&T	Northern Iowa
1965	Evansville	85-82(ot)	Southern Ill.	North Dakota	St. Michael's
1966	Ky. Wesleyan	54-51	Southern Ill.	Akron	North Dakota
1967	Winston-Salem	77-74	Southwest Mo. St.	Ky. Wesleyan	Illinois St.
1968	Ky. Wesleyan	63-52	Indiana St.	Trinity (Tex.)	Ashland
1969	Ky. Wesleyan	75-71	Southwest Mo. St.	**American Int'l	Ashland
1970	Philadelphia U.	76-65	Tennessee St.	UC Riverside	Buffalo St.
1971	Evansville	97-82	Old Dominion	**La.-Lafayette	Ky. Wesleyan

CHAMPIONSHIPS

Photo by Chris Hall/NCAA Photos

Metro State point guard Clayton Smith lived up to the Roadrunners' nickname.

Season	Champion	Score	Runner-Up	Third Place	Fourth Place
1972	Roanoke	84-72	Akron	Tennessee St.	Eastern Mich.
1973	Ky. Wesleyan	78-76(ot)	Tennessee St.	Assumption	Brockport St.
1974	Morgan St.	67-52	Southwest Mo. St.	Assumption	New Orleans
1975	Old Dominion	76-74	New Orleans	Assumption	Chattanooga
1976	Puget Sound	83-74	Chattanooga	Eastern Ill.	Old Dominion
1977	Chattanooga	71-62	Randolph-Macon	North Ala.	Sacred Heart
1978	Cheyney	47-40	Wis.-Green Bay	Eastern Ill.	UCF
1979	North Ala.	64-50	Wis.-Green Bay	Cheyney	Bridgeport
1980	Virginia Union	80-74	New York Tech	Fla. Southern	North Ala.
1981	Fla. Southern	73-68	Mt. St. Mary's	Cal Poly	Wis.-Green Bay
1982	Dist. Columbia	73-63	Fla. Southern	Ky. Wesleyan	Cal St. Bakersfield
1983	Wright St.	92-73	Dist. Columbia	* Cal St. Bakersfield	* Morningside
1984	Central Mo. St.	81-77	St. Augustine's	* Ky. Wesleyan	* North Ala.
1985	Jacksonville St.	74-73	South Dakota St.	* Ky. Wesleyan	* Mt. St. Mary's
1986	Sacred Heart	93-87	Southeast Mo. St.	* Cheyney	* Fla. Southern
1987	Ky. Wesleyan	92-74	Gannon	* Delta St.	* Mont. St.-Billings
1988	Mass.-Lowell	75-72	Alas. Anchorage	Fla. Southern	Troy St.
1989	N.C. Central	73-46	Southeast Mo. St.	UC Riverside	Jacksonville St.
1990	Ky. Wesleyan	93-79	Cal St. Bakersfield	North Dakota	Morehouse
1991	North Ala.	79-72	Bridgeport	* Cal St. Bakersfield	* Virginia Union
1992	Virginia Union	100-75	Bridgeport	* Cal St. Bakersfield	* Calif. (Pa.)
1993	Cal St. Bakersfield	85-72	Troy St.	* Wayne St. (Mich.)	* New Hamp. Col.
1994	Cal St. Bakersfield	92-86	Southern Ind.	* Washburn	* New Hamp. Col.
1995	Southern Ind.	71-63	UC Riverside	* Norfolk St.	* Indiana (Pa.)
1996	Fort Hays St.	70-63	Northern Ky.	* Virginia Union	* Calif. (Pa.)
1997	Cal St. Bakersfield	57-56	Northern Ky.	* Salem Int'l	* Lynn
1998	UC Davis	83-77	Ky. Wesleyan	* Virginia Union	* St. Rose
1999	Ky. Wesleyan	75-60	Metro St.	* Truman	* Fla. Southern
2000	Metro St.	97-99	Ky. Wesleyan	* Mo. Southern St.	* Seattle Pacific
2001	Ky. Wesleyan	72-63	Washburn	Western Wash.	Tampa
2002	Metro St.	80-72	Ky. Wesleyan	Shaw	Indiana (Pa.)

*Indicates tied for third. **Student-athletes representing American International in 1969 and La.-Lafayette in 1971 were declared ineligible after the tournament. Under NCAA rules, the teams' and ineligible student-athletes' records were deleted, and the teams' places in the final standings were vacated.*

Photo by Chris Hall/NCAA Photos

Metro State's Lee Bethea scores two of his 19 points in the title game.

Season	Site of Finals	Coach of Champion	Outstanding Player Award
1957	Evansville, Ind.	Lee Pfund, Wheaton (Ill.)	Mel Peterson, Wheaton (Ill.)
1958	Evansville, Ind.	Duane Clodfelter, South Dakota	Ed Smallwood, Evansville
1959	Evansville, Ind.	Arad McCutchan, Evansville	Hugh Ahlering, Evansville
1960	Evansville, Ind.	Arad McCutchan, Evansville	Ed Smallwood, Evansville
1961	Evansville, Ind.	Ray Mears, Wittenberg	Don Jacobsen, South Dakota St.
1962	Evansville, Ind.	James Phelan, Mt. St. Mary's	Ron Rohrer, Sacramento St.
1963	Evansville, Ind.	Jim Iverson, South Dakota St.	Wayne Rasmussen, South Dakota St.
1964	Evansville, Ind.	Arad McCutchan, Evansville	Jerry Sloan, Evansville
1965	Evansville, Ind.	Arad McCutchan, Evansville	Jerry Sloan, Evansville
1966	Evansville, Ind.	Guy Strong, Ky. Wesleyan	Sam Smith, Ky. Wesleyan
1967	Evansville, Ind.	C.E. Gaines, Winston-Salem	Earl Monroe, Winston-Salem
1968	Evansville, Ind.	Bob Daniels, Ky. Wesleyan	Jerry Newsom, Indiana St.
1969	Evansville, Ind.	Bob Daniels, Ky. Wesleyan	George Tinsley, Ky. Wesleyan
1970	Evansville, Ind.	Herb Magee, Philadelphia U.	Ted McClain, Tennessee St.
1971	Evansville, Ind.	Arad McCutchan, Evansville	Don Buse, Evansville
1972	Evansville, Ind.	Charles Moir, Roanoke	Hal Johnston, Roanoke
1973	Evansville, Ind.	Bob Jones, Ky. Wesleyan	Mike Williams, Ky. Wesleyan
1974	Evansville, Ind.	Nathaniel Frazier, Morgan St.	Marvin Webster, Morgan St.
1975	Evansville, Ind.	Sonny Allen, Old Dominion	Wilson Washington, Old Dominion
1976	Evansville, Ind.	Don Zech, Puget Sound	Curt Peterson, Puget Sound
1977	Springfield, Mass.	Ron Shumate, Chattanooga	Wayne Golden, Chattanooga
1978	Springfield, Mo.	John Chaney, Cheyney	Andrew Fields, Cheyney
1979	Springfield, Mo.	Bill Jones, North Ala.	Perry Oden, North Ala.
1980	Springfield, Mass.	Dave Robbins, Virginia Union	Keith Valentine, Virginia Union
1981	Springfield, Mass.	Hal Wissel, Fla. Southern	John Ebeling, Fla. Southern
1982	Springfield, Mass.	Wil Jones, Dist. Columbia	Michael Britt, Dist. Columbia
1983	Springfield, Mass.	Ralph Underhill, Wright St.	Gary Monroe, Wright St.
1984	Springfield, Mass.	Lynn Nance, Central Mo. St.	Ron Nunnelly, Central Mo. St.
1985	Springfield, Mass.	Bill Jones, Jacksonville St.	Mark Tetzlaff, South Dakota St.
1986	Springfield, Mass.	Dave Bike, Sacred Heart	Roger Younger, Sacred Heart
1987	Springfield, Mass.	Wayne Chapman, Ky. Wesleyan	Sam Smith, Ky. Wesleyan
1988	Springfield, Mass.	Don Doucette, Mass.-Lowell	Leo Parent, Mass.-Lowell
1989	Springfield, Mass.	Michael Bernard, N.C. Central	Miles Clarke, N.C. Central
1990	Springfield, Mass.	Wayne Chapman, Ky. Wesleyan	Wade Green, Cal St. Bakersfield
1991	Springfield, Mass.	Gary Elliott, North Ala.	Lambert Shell, Bridgeport
1992	Springfield, Mass.	Dave Robbins, Virginia Union	Derrick Johnson, Virginia Union
1993	Springfield, Mass.	Pat Douglass, Cal St. Bakersfield	Tyrone Davis, Cal St. Bakersfield
1994	Springfield, Mass.	Pat Douglass, Cal St. Bakersfield	Stan Gouard, Southern Ind.
1995	Louisville, Ky.	Bruce Pearl, Southern Ind.	William Wilson, UC Riverside
1996	Louisville, Ky.	Gary Garner, Fort Hays St.	Sherick Simpson, Fort Hays St.
1997	Louisville, Ky.	Pat Douglass, Cal St. Bakersfield	Kebu Stewart, Cal St. Bakersfield
1998	Louisville, Ky.	Bob Williams, Ky. Wesleyan	Antonio Garcia, Ky. Wesleyan
1999	Louisville, Ky.	Bob Williams, Ky. Wesleyan	Antonio Garcia, Ky. Wesleyan
2000	Louisville, Ky.	Mike Dunlap, Metro St.	DeMarcos Anzures, Metro St.
2001	Bakersfield, Calif.	Ray Harper, Ky. Wesleyan	Lorico Duncan, Ky. Wesleyan
2002	Evansville, Ind.	Mike Dunlap, Metro St.	Patrick Mutombo, Metro St.

Individual Records

(Three-game minimum for series records and percentages)

POINTS, GAME
54—Willie Jones, American (91) vs. Evansville (101), 1960; Bill Fennelly, Central Mo. St. (112) vs. Jacksonville St. (91), 1980.

POINTS, TOURNAMENT
185—Jack Sullivan, Mt. St. Mary's, 1957 (36 vs. CCNY, 48 vs. N.C. Central, 39 vs. Rider, 19 vs. Ky. Wesleyan, 43 vs. Cal. St. Los Angeles).

FIELD GOALS, GAME
22—Phil Jackson, North Dakota (107) vs. Parsons (56), 1967.

FIELD GOALS, TOURNAMENT
71—Jack Sullivan, Mt. St. Mary's, 1957 (14 vs. CCNY, 19 vs. N.C. Central, 16 vs. Rider, 8 vs. Ky. Wesleyan, 14 vs. Cal. St. Los Angeles).

THREE-POINT FIELD GOALS, GAME
11—Kenny Warren, Cal St. Bakersfield (98) vs. Grand Canyon (68), 1993.

THREE-POINT FIELD GOALS, TOURNAMENT
22—Kenny Warren, Cal St. Bakersfield, 1993 (11 vs. Grand Canyon, 3 vs. Alas. Anchorage, 5 vs. N.C. Central, 1 vs. Wayne St. [Mich.], 2 vs. Troy St.).

FREE THROWS, GAME
24—Dave Twardzik, Old Dominion (102) vs. Norfolk St. (97), 1971.

FREE THROWS, TOURNAMENT
55—Don Jacobsen, South Dakota St., 1961 (9 vs. Cornell College, 22 vs. Prairie View, 9 vs. UC Santa Barb., 11 vs. Southeast Mo. St., 4 vs. Mt. St. Mary's).

HIGHEST FREE-THROW PERCENTAGE, GAME
(Minimum 18 Made)
100.0%—Ralph Talley, Norfolk St. (70) vs. Virginia Union (60), 1986 (18-18).

ASSISTS, GAME
20—Steve Ray, Bridgeport (132) vs. Stonehill (127) (ot), 1989.

ASSISTS, TOURNAMENT
49—Tyrone Tate, Southern Ind., 1994 (8 vs. Ky. Wesleyan, 3 vs. Wayne St. [Mich.], 16 vs. South Dakota, 16 vs. New Hamp. Col., 6 vs. Cal St. Bakersfield).

REBOUNDS, TOURNAMENT (SINCE 1968)
99—Marvin Webster, Morgan St., 1974 (5 games).

Team Records

(Three-game minimum for tournament records and percentages)

POINTS, GAME
132—Bridgeport vs. Stonehill (127) (ot), 1989; Central Okla. vs. Washburn (114), 1992.

POINTS, TOURNAMENT
567—Southern Ind., 1995 (95 vs. Hillsdale, 102 vs. Ky. Wesleyan, 102 vs. Northern Ky., 108 vs. New Hamp. Col., 89 vs. Norfolk St., 71 vs. UC Riverside).

FIELD GOALS, GAME
54—Bentley (129) vs. Stonehill (118), 1989.

FIELD GOALS, TOURNAMENT
198—Southern Ind., 1995 (37 vs. Hillsdale, 37 vs. Ky. Wesleyan, 34 vs. Northern Ky., 40 vs. New Hamp. Col., 26 vs. Norfolk St., 24 vs. UC Riverside).

THREE-POINT FIELD GOALS, GAME
23—Troy St. (126) vs. New Hamp. Col (123), 1993.

THREE-POINT FIELD GOALS, TOURNAMENT
57—Troy St., 1993 (9 vs. Fla. Southern, 14 vs. Delta St., 6 vs. Washburn, 23 vs. New Hamp. Col., 5 vs. Cal St. Bakersfield).

FREE THROWS, GAME
46—Evansville (110) vs. N.C. A&T (92), 1959.

FREE THROWS, TOURNAMENT
142—Mt. St. Mary's, 1957.

ASSISTS, GAME
36—Troy St. (126) vs. New Hamp. Col. (123), 1993.

ASSISTS, TOURNAMENT
120—North Dakota, 1990.

All-Tournament Teams

Most Outstanding Player.
#Participation voided by action of the NCAA Council.

1957
*Mel Peterson, Wheaton (Ill.)
Jack Sullivan, Mt. St. Mary's
Mason Cope, Ky. Wesleyan
Bob Whitehead, Wheaton (Ill.)
Jim Daniels, South Dakota

1958
*Ed Smallwood, Evansville
Jim Browne, St. Michael's
Jim Daniels, South Dakota
Mel Peterson, Wheaton (Ill.)
Dick Zeitler, St. Michael's

1959
*Hugh Ahlering, Evansville
Joe Cotton, N.C. A&T
Jack Israel, Southwest Mo. St.
Paul Benes, Hope
Leo Hill, Cal St. Los Angeles

1960
*Ed Smallwood, Evansville
Dale Wise, Evansville
Tom Cooke, Chapman
Gary Auten, Ky. Wesleyan
William Jones, American

1961
*Don Jacobsen, South Dakota St.
John O'Reilly, Mt. St. Mary's
George Fisher, Wittenberg
Vivan Reed, Southeast Mo. St.
Carl Ritter, Southeast Mo. St.

1962
*Ron Rohrer, Sacramento St.
Jim Mumford, Neb. Wesleyan
Ed Spila, Southern Ill.
John O'Reilly, Mt. St. Mary's
Ed Pfeiffer, Mt. St. Mary's

1963
*Wayne Rasmussen, South Dakota St.
Tom Black, South Dakota St.
Bob Cherry, Wittenberg
Bill Fisher, Wittenberg
Al Thrasher, Wittenberg

1964
*Jerry Sloan, Evansville
Maurice McHartley, N.C. A&T
Larry Humes, Evansville
Bill Stevens, Akron
Buster Briley, Evansville

1965
*Jerry Sloan, Evansville
Richard Tarrant, St. Michael's
Walt Frazier, Southern Ill.
George McNeil, Southern Ill.
Larry Humes, Evansville

1966
*Sam Smith, Ky. Wesleyan
Clarence Smith, Southern Ill.
George McNeil, Southern Ill.
David Lee, Southern Ill.
Phil Jackson, North Dakota

1967
*Earl Monroe, Winston-Salem
Lou Shepherd, Southwest Mo. St.
Sam Smith, Ky. Wesleyan
Danny Bolden, Southwest Mo. St.
Dallas Thornton, Ky. Wesleyan

1968
*Jerry Newsom, Indiana St.
Larry Jeffries, Trinity (Tex.)
George Tinsley, Ky. Wesleyan
Fred Hardman, Indiana St.
Dallas Thornton, Ky. Wesleyan

1969
*George Tinsley, Ky. Wesleyan
Curtis Perry, Southwest Mo. St.
Tommy Hobgood, Ky. Wesleyan
Mert Bancroft, Southwest Mo. St.
Bob Rutherford, American Int'l

1970
*Ted McClain, Tennessee St.
Randy Smith, Buffalo St.
Carl Poole, Philadelphia U.
Howard Lee, UC Riverside
John Pierantozzi, Philadelphia U.

1971
*Don Buse, Evansville
#Dwight Lamar, La.-Lafayette
Rick Coffey, Evansville
John Duncan, Ky. Wesleyan
Skip Noble, Old Dominion

1972
*Hal Johnston, Roanoke
Leonard Robinson, Tennessee St.
Lloyd Neal, Tennessee St.
Jay Piccola, Roanoke
Len Paul, Akron

1973
*Mike Williams, Ky. Wesleyan
Ron Gilliam, Brockport St.
Mike Boylan, Assumption
Leonard Robinson, Tennessee St.
Roger Zornes, Ky. Wesleyan

1974
*Marvin Webster, Morgan St.
John Grochowalski, Assumption
Randy Magers, Southwest Mo. St.
William Doolittle, Southwest Mo. St.
Alvin O'Neal, Morgan St.

1975
*Wilson Washington, Old Dominion
Wilbur Holland, New Orleans
John Grochowalski, Assumption
Joey Caruthers, Old Dominion
Paul Brennan, Assumption

1976
*Curt Peterson, Puget Sound
Wayne Golden, Chattanooga
Jeff Fuhrmann, Old Dominion
Jeff Furry, Eastern Ill.
Brant Gibler, Puget Sound

1977
*Wayne Golden, Chattanooga
Joe Allen, Randolph-Macon
Otis Boddie, North Ala.
William Gordon, Chattanooga
Hector Olivencia, Sacred Heart

1978
*Andrew Fields, Cheyney
Kenneth Hynson, Cheyney
Tom Anderson, Wis.-Green Bay
Charlie Thomas, Eastern Ill.
Jerry Prather, UCF

1979
*Perry Oden, North Ala.
Carlton Hurdle, Bridgeport
Ron Ripley, Wis.-Green Bay

Ron Darby, North Ala.
Rory Lindgren, Wis.-Green Bay

1980
*Keith Valentine, Virginia Union
Larry Holmes, Virginia Union
Bobby Jones, New York Tech
John Ebeling, Fla. Southern
Johnny Buckmon, North Ala.

1981
*John Ebeling, Fla. Southern
Mike Hayes, Fla. Southern
Durelle Lewis, Mt. St. Mary's
Jim Rowe, Mt. St. Mary's
Jay Bruchak, Mt. St. Mary's

1982
*Michael Britt, Dist. Columbia
John Ebeling, Fla. Southern
Dwight Higgs, Ky. Wesleyan
Earl Jones, Dist. Columbia
Wayne McDaniel, Cal St. Bakersfield

1983
*Gary Monroe, Wright St.
Anthony Bias, Wright St.
Fred Moore, Wright St.
Earl Jones, Dist. Columbia
Michael Britt, Dist. Columbia

1984
*Ron Nunnelly, Central Mo. St.
Brian Pesko, Central Mo. St.
Kenneth Bannister, St. Augustine's
Rod Drake, Ky. Wesleyan
Robert Harris, North Ala.

1985
*Mark Tetzlaff, South Dakota St.
Dave Bennett, Ky. Wesleyan
Melvin Allen, Jacksonville St.
Robert Spurgeon, Jacksonville St.
Darryle Edwards, Mt. St. Mary's

1986
*Roger Younger, Sacred Heart
Kevin Stevens, Sacred Heart
Keith Johnson, Sacred Heart
Riley Ellis, Southeast Mo. St.
Ronny Rankin, Southeast Mo. St.

1987
*Sam Smith, Ky. Wesleyan
Andra Whitlow, Ky. Wesleyan
John Worth, Ky. Wesleyan

Mike Runski, Gannon
Jerome Johnson, Mont. St.-Billings

1988
*Leo Parent, Mass.-Lowell
Bobby Licare, Mass.-Lowell
Averian Parrish, Alas. Anchorage
Jerry Johnson, Fla. Southern
Darryl Thomas, Troy St.

1989
*Miles Clarke, N.C. Central
Dominique Stephens, N.C. Central
Antoine Sifford, N.C. Central
Earnest Taylor, Southeast Mo. St.
Maurice Pullum, UC Riverside

1990
*Wade Green, Cal St. Bakersfield
LeRoy Ellis, Ky. Wesleyan
Corey Crowder, Ky. Wesleyan
Dave Vonesh, North Dakota
Vincent Mitchell, Ky. Wesleyan

1991
*Lambert Shell, Bridgeport
Pat Morris, Bridgeport
Fred Stafford, North Ala.
Allen Williams, North Ala.
Carl Wilmer, North Ala.

1992
*Derrick Johnson, Virginia Union
Reggie Jones, Virginia Union
Winston Jones, Bridgeport
Steve Wills, Bridgeport
Kenney Toomer, Calif. (Pa.)

1993
*Tyrone Davis, Cal St. Bakersfield
Roheen Oats, Cal St. Bakersfield
Terry McCord, Troy St.
Wayne Robertson, New Hamp. Col.
Danny Lewis, Wayne St. (Mich.)

1994
*Stan Gouard, Southern Ind.
Kenny Warren, Cal St. Bakersfield
Reggie Phillips, Cal St. Bakersfield
Roheen Oats, Cal St. Bakersfield
Tyrone Tate, Southern Ind.

1995
*William Wilson, UC Riverside
Brian Huebner, Southern Ind.
Chad Gilbert, Southern Ind.

Boo Purdom, UC Riverside
Corey Williams, Norfolk St.

1996
*Sherick Simpson, Fort Hays St.
Paul Cluxton, Northern Ky.
LaRon Moore, Northern Ky.
Alonzo Goldston, Fort Hays St.
Kebu Stewart, Cal St. Bakersfield

1997
*Kebu Stewart, Cal St. Bakersfield
Cliff Clinton, Northern Ky.
Paul Cluxton, Northern Ky.
Shannon Minor, Northern Ky.
Terrance Springer, Salem Int'l

1998
*Antonio Garcia, Ky. Wesleyan
Dana Williams, Ky. Wesleyan
Jason Cox, Ky. Wesleyan
Dante Ross, Ky. Wesleyan
William Davis, Virginia Union

1999
*Antonio Garcia, Ky. Wesleyan
Dana Williams, Ky. Wesleyan
Lee Barlow, Metro St.
DeMarcos Anzures, Metro St.
Innocent Kere, Fla. Southern

2000
*DeMarcos Anzures, Metro St.
Kane Oakley, Metro St.
John Bynum, Metro St.
Lee Barlow, Metro St.
Lorico Duncan, Ky. Wesleyan

2001
*Lorico Duncan, Ky. Wesleyan
Marshall Sanders, Ky. Wesleyan
Ewan Auguste, Washburn
Ryan Murphy, Washburn
Sylvere Bryan, Washburn

2002
*Patrick Mutombo, Metro St.
Clayton Smith, Metro St.
Chris Landry, Ky. Wesleyan
Ronald Evans, Ky. Wesleyan
Ronald Murray, Shaw

#The participation of Dwight Lamar (Louisiana-Lafayette) in the 1971 tournament was voided by action of the NCAA Council.

Division III Championship

2002 Results

FIRST ROUND
Wis.-Oshkosh 71, Ripon 56
Lewis & Clark 81, Claremont-M-S 59
Hope 54, St. Norbert 53
Gust. Adolphus 74, Edgewood 65
Maryville (Tenn.) 70, Webster 45
Wittenberg 75, Franklin 44
Lycoming 78, Gettysburg 59
Bethany (W.Va.) 110, Pitt.-Bradford 98
Williams 121, Cazenovia 49
Union (N.Y.) 75, Lasell 73
Western Conn. St. 92, Salem St. 89
Trinity (Conn.) 75, Colby-Sawyer 47
Alvernia 76, Ithaca 67
Cabrini 85, Merchant Marine 73
Clark (Mass.) 84, Suffolk 77

SECOND ROUND
Wis.-Oshkosh 88, St. Thomas (Minn.) 85 (ot)
Lewis & Clark 70, Mississippi Col. 57
Carthage 63, Hope 57
Gust. Adolphus 88, Buena Vista 60
Washington (Mo.) 71, Maryville (Tenn.) 57
DePauw 89, Wittenberg 76
Randolph-Macon 79, Lycoming 62
Otterbein 121, Bethany (W.Va.) 98
Rochester 66, Williams 51
Babson 63, Union (N.Y.) 50
Amherst 82, Western Conn. St. 77
Brockport St. 80, Trinity (Conn.) 61
Elizabethtown 95, Alvernia 84
Cabrini 47, Wm. Paterson 43
Clark (Mass.) 101, Staten Island 72
Catholic 74, Hampden-Sydney 66

SECTIONAL SEMIFINALS
Lewis & Clark 79, Wis.-Oshkosh 71
Carthage 71, Gust. Adolphus 65
DePauw 90, Washington (Mo.) 87
Otterbein 85, Randolph-Macon 72
Rochester 71, Babson 60
Brockport St. 69, Amherst 64
Elizabethtown 87, Cabrini 85
Clark (Mass.) 75, Catholic 72

SECTIONAL CHAMPIONSHIPS
Carthage 85, Lewis & Clark 70
Otterbein 87, DePauw 79
Rochester 71, Brockport St. 62
Elizabethtown 94, Clark (Mass.) 90

SEMIFINALS
Otterbein 70, Carthage 66
Elizabethtown 93, Rochester 83 (ot)

THIRD PLACE
Carthage 72, Rochester 51

CHAMPIONSHIP
Otterbein 102, Elizabethtown 83

Box Scores

SEMIFINALS
MARCH 15
AT SALEM, VIRGINIA

Elizabethtown 93, Rochester 83 (ot)

Rochester	FG-FGA	FT-FTA	RB	PF	TP
Tim Sweeney	1-7	2-2	5	5	5
Jeff Joss	2-7	1-2	0	4	7
Seth Hauben	16-25	7-11	18	4	39
Gabe Perez	1-6	0-0	0	1	2
Ryan Kadlubowski	2-4	0-0	4	1	4
Justin Hughes	1-3	0-0	0	1	2
Matt Conacher	4-6	1-2	5	2	9
Andy Larkin	0-0	0-0	0	0	0
Brian Jones	4-7	0-0	11	5	8
Makedo Wisseh	3-10	1-4	3	3	7
Team			4		
TOTALS	34-75	12-21	50	26	83

Elizabethtown	FG-FGA	FT-FTA	RB	PF	TP
Rocky Parise	1-2	4-6	1	0	7
Chad Heller	6-12	5-5	4	3	18
Brian Loftus	4-6	6-8	3	2	14
Bob Porambo	7-9	2-3	2	4	21
Jon English	9-14	1-3	4	2	19
Ian Daecher	2-5	4-4	2	3	8
Jim Barron	0-0	0-0	1	3	0
Brian Marquette	2-4	1-2	0	2	6
Darryl Brown	0-0	0-0	1	0	0
Justin Edwards	0-0	0-0	0	1	0
Team			5		
TOTALS	31-52	23-31	23	20	93

Halftime: Elizabethtown 36, Rochester 31. End of regulation: Tied at 75. Three-point field goals: Rochester 3-13 (Sweeney 1-5, Joss 2-6, Wisseh 0-2); Elizabethtown 8-15 (Parise 1-1, Heller 1-4, Loftus 0-1, Porambo 5-6, Marquette 1-3). Disqualifications: Sweeney, Jones. Officials: Pete Duglenski, Richard Collins, Mike Stephens. Attendance: 2,705.

Otterbein 70, Carthage 66

Carthage	FG-FGA	FT-FTA	RB	PF	TP
Jim Oboikowitch	0-0	0-0	1	3	0
Jason Wiertel	3-8	4-4	4	2	10
Antoine McDaniel	8-19	0-0	5	1	19
Rob Garnes	5-15	6-8	14	3	16
Bart Fabian	4-12	0-0	2	4	12
Tim Shorts	1-2	0-0	1	1	3
Carthage	FG-FGA	FT-FTA	RB	PF	TP

Johnny Meier	0-1	0-0	0	0	0
Scott Steger	0-0	0-0	0	0	0
Ryan Hargesheimer	2-2	0-0	2	0	4
Theo Powell	1-3	0-0	2	1	2
Team			2		
TOTALS:	24-62	10-12	33	15	66

Otterbein	FG-FGA	FT-FTA	RB	PF	TP
Robert Mock	1-2	0-0	8	1	2
Scott Hadley	0-3	0-0	0	3	0
Jeff Gibbs	13-25	4-6	15	3	30
Tony Borghese	1-5	2-2	0	1	5
Kevin Shay	7-13	0-0	6	2	17
Kyle Walton	2-4	2-2	2	0	7
Phil Susi	0-1	0-0	2	0	0
Mo Ross	3-9	2-2	6	0	9
Team			4		
TOTALS	27-62	10-12	43	10	70

Halftime: Carthage 40, Otterbein 36. Three-point field goals: Carthage 8-25 (Wiertel 0-1, McDaniel 3-8, Garnes 0-1, Fabian 4-12, Shorts 1-2, Meier 0-1); Otterbein 6-15 (Hadley 0-3, Gibbs 0-1, Borghese 1-2, Shay 3-5, Walton 1-1, Ross 1-3). Officials: Carl Gartittos, Tim Ebersole, Rod Strobl. Attendance: 2,681.

THIRD PLACE
MARCH 16
AT SALEM, VIRGINIA
Carthage 72, Rochester 51

Carthage	FG-FGA	FT-FTA	RB	PF	TP
Jim Oboikowitch	1-2	2-2	6	0	4
Jason Wiertel	13-27	7-7	7	3	33
Antoine McDaniel	3-10	2-2	4	1	10
Rob Garnes	3-7	3-3	5	4	9
Bart Fabian	2-6	0-0	9	2	5
Tim Shorts	1-2	0-0	1	0	2
Johnny Meier	0-0	0-0	0	0	0
Pat Kalamatas	0-1	2-2	2	0	2
Bernard Middleton	0-0	0-0	0	0	0
Orlando Wilson	0-0	0-0	0	0	0
Trevor Cockayne	0-2	0-0	0	0	0
Paul Reiff	0-3	0-0	2	1	0
Scott Steger	0-2	0-0	0	0	0
Ryan Hargesheimer	0-0	0-0	2	2	0
Theo Powell	3-3	1-2	1	3	7
Team			4		
TOTALS	26-65	17-18	43	16	72

Rochester	FG-FGA	FT-FTA	RB	PF	TP
Seth Hauben	4-10	1-4	10	1	9
Ryan Kadlubowski	2-4	0-0	2	2	4
Tim Sweeney	3-6	0-1	0	3	8
Jeff Joss	1-6	0-0	4	4	3
Gabe Perez	0-5	0-0	1	0	0
Justin Hughes	1-2	0-0	0	0	2
Matt Lyons,	0-0	0-0	0	0	0
Macky Berbman-Clark	0-0	0-2	0	0	0

Rochester	FG-FGA	FT-FTA	RB	PF	TP
Brendan McAllister	0-0	0-0	0	0	0
Ryan Mee	1-4	0-0	1	0	3
Matt Conacher	2-6	2-2	5	1	6
Brian Jones	5-6	2-4	4	2	12
Ross Briggs	2-3	0-0	0	1	4
Makedo Wisseh	0-2	0-1	3	1	0
Team			6		
TOTALS	21-54	5-14	36	15	51

Halftime: Carthage 39, Rochester 25. Three-point field goals: Carthage 3-15 (Wiertel 0-2, McDaniel 2-5, Fabian 1-5, Cockayne 0-1, Reiff 0-1, Steger 0-1); Rochester 4-12 (Tim Sweeney 2-3, Joss 1-3, Perez 0-1, Hughes 0-1, Mee 1-4). Officials: Jeff Bryant, Carl Blair, Tim Comer. Attendance: 2,852.

CHAMPIONSHIP
MARCH 16
AT SALEM, VIRGINIA
Otterbein 102, Elizabethtown 83

Otterbein	FG-FGA	FT-FTA	RB	PF	TP
Tony Borghese	4-11	11-14	3	1	21
Kevin Shay	10-20	5-6	5	3	29
Robert Mock	1-2	0-0	2	4	2
Jeff Gibbs	9-18	7-10	25	3	25
Scott Hadley	3-5	0-0	8	3	6
Joey Starling	0-0	0-0	0	0	0
Micheaux Robinson	0-0	0-0	0	0	0
Kyle Walton	2-2	2-2	2	2	7
Phil Susi	0-0	0-0	0	1	0
Mike Fry	0-0	0-0	0	0	0
Mo Ross	4-8	0-0	3	0	12
Matt Carpenter	0-0	0-0	0	0	0
Neil Hohman	0-0	0-0	0	0	0
Team			1		
TOTALS:	33-66	25-32	49	17	102

Elizabethtown	FG-FGA	FT-FTA	RB	PF	TP
Jim Barron	1-3	2-2	0	1	4
Chad Heller	2-9	4-4	5	4	9
Brian Loftus	7-15	1-1	6	4	17
Bob Porambo	7-15	1-2	7	3	17
Jon English	6-11	2-3	4	2	14
Ian Daecher	3-4	4-6	2	2	10
Rocky Parise	4-11	0-0	0	4	9
Brian Marquette	1-5	0-0	3	2	3
Darryl Brown	0-0	0-0	1	0	0
Justin Edwards	0-2	0-0	1	0	0
Team			7		
TOTALS	31-75	14-18	35	23	83

Halftime: Elizabethtown 54, Otterbein 48. Three-point field goals: Otterbein 11-24 (Borghese 2-6, Shay 4-9, Hadley 0-2, Walton 1-1, Ross 4-6); Elizabethtown 7-26 (Barron 1-4, Heller 1-2, Porambo 2-5, Parise 1-6, Marquette 1-3, Edwards 0-1). Officials: Mike Spanier, John Yorkovich, Carl Britt. Attendance: 2,852.

Year-by-Year Results

Season	Champion	Score	Runner-Up	Third Place	Fourth Place
1975	LeMoyne-Owen	57-54	Rowan	Augustana (Ill.)	Brockport St.
1976	Scranton	60-57	Wittenberg	Augustana (Ill.)	Plattsburgh St.
1977	Wittenberg	79-66	Oneonta St.	Scranton	Hamline
1978	North Park	69-57	Widener	Albion	Stony Brook
1979	North Park	66-62	Potsdam St.	Frank. & Marsh.	Centre
1980	North Park	83-76	Upsala	Wittenberg	Longwood
1981	Potsdam St.	67-65(ot)	Augustana (Ill.)	Ursinus	Otterbein
1982	Wabash	83-62	Potsdam St.	Brooklyn	Cal St. Stanislaus
1983	Scranton	64-63	Wittenberg	Roanoke	Wis.-Whitewater
1984	Wis.-Whitewater	103-86	Clark (Mass.)	DePauw	Upsala
1985	North Park	72-71	Potsdam St.	Neb. Wesleyan	Widener
1986	Potsdam St.	76-73	LeMoyne-Owen	Neb. Wesleyan	New Jersey City
1987	North Park	106-100	Clark (Mass.)	Wittenberg	Richard Stockton
1988	Ohio Wesleyan	92-70	Scranton	Neb. Wesleyan	Hartwick
1989	Wis.-Whitewater	94-86	Col. of New Jersey	Southern Me.	Centre
1990	Rochester	43-42	DePauw	Washington (Md.)	Calvin
1991	Wis.-Platteville	81-74	Frank. & Marsh.	Otterbein	Ramapo
1992	Calvin	62-49	Rochester	Wis.-Platteville	New Jersey City
1993	Ohio Northern	71-68	Augustana (Ill.)	Rowan	Mass.-Dartmouth
1994	Lebanon Valley	66-59†	New York U.	Wittenberg	St. Thomas (Minn.)
1995	Wis.-Platteville	69-55	Manchester	Rowan	Trinity (Conn.)
1996	Rowan	100-93	Hope	Ill. Wesleyan	Frank. & Marsh.
1997	Ill. Wesleyan	89-86	Neb. Wesleyan	Williams	Alvernia
1998	Wis.-Platteville	69-56	Hope	Williams	Wilkes

Photo by Andres Alonso/NCAA Photos

Rebounding machine Jeff Gibbs of Otterbein had 25 boards in the championship game.

Season	Champion	Score	Runner-Up	Third Place	Fourth Place
1999	Wis.-Platteville	76-75(ot)	Hampden-Sydney	Connecticut Col.	Wm. Paterson
2000	Calvin	79-75	Wis-Eau Claire	Salem St.	Frank. & Marsh.
2001	Catholic	76-62	Wm. Paterson	Ill. Wesleyan	Ohio Northern
2002	Otterbein	102-83	Elizabethtown	Carthage	Rochester

Season	Site of Finals	Coach of Champion	Outstanding Player Award
1975	Reading, Pa.	Jerry Johnson, LeMoyne-Owen	Bob Newman, LeMoyne-Owen
1976	Reading, Pa.	Bob Bessoir, Scranton	Jack Maher, Scranton
1977	Rock Island, Ill.	Larry Hunter, Wittenberg	Rick White, Wittenberg
1978	Rock Island, Ill.	Dan McCarrell, North Park	Michael Harper, North Park
1979	Rock Island, Ill.	Dan McCarrell, North Park	Michael Harper, North Park
1980	Rock Island, Ill.	Dan McCarrell, North Park	Michael Thomas, North Park
1981	Rock Island, Ill.	Jerry Welsh, Potsdam St.	Maxwell Artis, Augustana (Ill.)
1982	Grand Rapids, Mich.	Mac Petty, Wabash	Pete Metzelaars, Wabash
1983	Grand Rapids, Mich.	Bob Bessoir, Scranton	Bill Bessoir, Scranton
1984	Grand Rapids, Mich.	Dave Vander Meulen, Wis.-Whitewater	Andre McKoy, Wis.-Whitewater
1985	Grand Rapids, Mich.	Bosco Djurickovic, North Park	Earnest Hubbard, North Park
1986	Grand Rapids, Mich.	Jerry Welsh, Potsdam St.	Roosevelt Bullock, Potsdam St.
1987	Grand Rapids, Mich.	Bosco Djurickovic, North Park	Michael Starks, North Park
1988	Grand Rapids, Mich.	Gene Mehaffey, Ohio Wesleyan	Scott Tedder, Ohio Wesleyan
1989	Springfield, Ohio	Dave Vander Meulen, Wis.-Whitewater	Greg Grant, Col. of New Jersey
1990	Springfield, Ohio	Mike Neer, Rochester	Chris Fite, Rochester
1991	Springfield, Ohio	Bo Ryan, Wis.-Platteville	Shawn Frison, Wis.-Platteville
1992	Springfield, Ohio	Ed Douma, Calvin	Steve Honderd, Calvin
1993	Buffalo, N.Y.	Joe Campoli, Ohio Northern	Kirk Anderson, Augustana (Ill.)
1994	Buffalo, N.Y.	Pat Flannery, Lebanon Valley	Mike Rhoades, Lebanon Valley / Adam Crawford, New York U.
1995	Buffalo, N.Y.	Bo Ryan, Wis.-Platteville	Ernie Peavy, Wis.-Platteville
1996	Salem, Va.	John Giannini, Rowan	Terrence Stewart, Rowan
1997	Salem, Va.	Dennie Bridges, Ill. Wesleyan	Bryan Crabtree, Ill. Wesleyan
1998	Salem, Va.	Bo Ryan, Wis.-Platteville	Ben Hoffmann, Wis.-Platteville
1999	Salem, Va.	Bo Ryan, Wis.-Platteville	Merrill Brunson, Wis.-Platteville
2000	Salem, Va.	Kevin Vande Streek, Calvin	Sherm Carstensen, Calvin
2001	Salem, Va.	Mike Lonergan, Catholic	Pat Maloney, Catholic
2002	Salem, Va.	Dick Reynolds, Otterbein	Jeff Gibbs, Otterbein

Individual Records

(Minimum three games for series records.)

POINTS, GAME
49—Gerald Reece, William Penn (85) vs. North Park (81), 1981.

POINTS, TOURNAMENT
177—Michael Nogelo, Williams, 1998 (31 vs. Trinity [Conn.], 30 vs. Springfield, 25 vs. Hamilton, 35 vs. St. Lawrence, 18 vs. Wis.-Platteville, 38 vs. Wilkes).

SCORING AVERAGE, TOURNAMENT
36.3—Greg Grant, Col. of New Jersey, 1988 (40 vs. Bridgewater [Va.], 45 vs. Emory & Henry, 24 vs. Hartwick).

FIELD GOALS, GAME
21—Gerald Reece, William Penn (85) vs. North Park (81), 1981.

FIELD GOALS, TOURNAMENT
68—Greg Grant, Col. of New Jersey, 1989 (11 vs. Shenandoah, 11 vs. New Jersey City, 16 vs. Potsdam St., 16 vs. Southern Me., 14 vs. Wis.-Whitewater).

THREE-POINT FIELD GOALS, GAME
12—Kirk Anderson, Augustana (Ill.) (100) vs. Wis.-Platteville (86), 1993.

THREE-POINT FIELD GOALS, TOURNAMENT
35—Kirk Anderson, Augustana (Ill.), 1993 (4 vs. DePauw, 5 vs. Beloit, 4 vs. La Verne, 12 vs. Wis.-Platteville, 6 vs. Rowan, 4 vs. Ohio Northern).

FREE THROWS, GAME
21—Tom Montsma, Calvin (88) vs. Wabash (76), 1980.

FREE THROWS, TOURNAMENT
52—Daimen Hunter, Alvernia, 1997 (6 vs. Lebanon Valley, 14 vs. Goucher, 5 vs. Rochester Inst., 11 vs. Salisbury St., 0 vs. Ill. Wesleyan, 16 vs. Williams).

ASSISTS, GAME
20—Matt Nadelhoffer, Wheaton (Ill.) (131) vs. Grinnell (117), 1996.

ASSISTS, TOURNAMENT
62—Ricky Spicer, Wis.-Whitewater, 1989.

REBOUNDS, TOURNAMENT
83—Jeff Gibbs, Otterbein, 2002.

REBOUNDING AVERAGE, TOURNAMENT
16.6—Jeff Gibbs, Otterbein, 2002 (13 vs. Bethany (W.Va.), 6 vs. Randolph Macon, 24 vs. DePauw; 15 vs. Carthage; 25 vs. Elizabethtown).

Team Records

(Minimum three games for tournament records.)

POINTS, GAME
132—Ill. Wesleyan vs. Grinnell (91), 2001.

POINTS, TOURNAMENT
594—Rowan, 1996 (130 vs. York [N.Y.], 102 vs. New Jersey City, 85 vs. Williams, 98 vs. Richard Stockton, 79 vs. Ill. Wesleyan, 100 vs. Hope).

FIELD GOALS, GAME
52—Wheaton (Ill.) (131) vs. Grinnell (117), 1996.

FIELD GOALS, TOURNAMENT
206—Rowan, 1996 (45 vs. York [N.Y.], 31 vs. New Jersey City, 29 vs. Williams, 35 vs. Richard Stockton, 32 vs. Ill. Wesleyan, 34 vs. Hope).

THREE-POINT FIELD GOALS, GAME
22—Grinnell (117) vs. Wheaton (Ill.) (131), 1996.

THREE-POINT FIELD GOALS, TOURNAMENT
59—Augustana (Ill.), 1993 (6 vs. DePauw, 11 vs. Beloit, 11 vs. La Verne, 14 vs. Wis.-Platteville, 9 vs. Rowan, 8 vs. Ohio Northern).

FREE THROWS, GAME
43—Capital (103) vs. Va. Wesleyan (93), 1982; Potsdam St. (91) vs. New Jersey City (89), 1986.

FREE THROWS, TOURNAMENT
137—Catholic, 2001 (18 vs. CCNY; 11 vs. Widener; 18 vs. Brockport St.; 25 vs. Clark (Mass.); 33 vs. Ohio Northern; 32 vs. Wm. Paterson).

ASSISTS, GAME
34—Hampden-Sydney (105) vs. Greensboro (79), 1995.

ASSISTS, TOURNAMENT
136—Neb. Wesleyan, 1997 (25 vs. Buena Vista, 17 vs. Gust. Adolphus, 22 vs. Hope, 23 vs. Wis.-Stevens Point, 26 vs. Williams, 23 vs. Ill. Wesleyan).

All-Tournament Teams

Most Outstanding Player.

1975
*Robert Newman, LeMoyne-Owen
Clint Jackson, LeMoyne-Owen
Dan Panaggio, Brockport St.
Bruce Hamming, Augustana (Ill.)
Greg Ackles, Rowan

1976
*Jack Maher, Scranton
Tom Dunn, Wittenberg
Bob Heubner, Wittenberg
Ronnie Wright, Plattsburgh St.
Terry Lawrence, Augustana (Ill.)

1977
*Rick White, Wittenberg
Phil Smyczek, Hamline
Paul Miernicki, Scranton
Clyde Eberhardt, Wittenberg
Ralph Christian, Oneonta St.

1978
*Michael Harper, North Park
Dennis James, Widener
John Nibert, Albion
Earl Keith, Stony Brook
Tom Florentine, North Park

1979
*Michael Harper, North Park
Don Marsh, Frank. & Marsh.
Derrick Rowland, Potsdam St.

Michael Thomas, North Park
Modzel Greer, North Park

1980
*Michael Thomas, North Park
Ellonya Green, Upsala
Steve Keenan, Upsala
Tyronne Curtis, Wittenberg
Keith French, North Park

1981
*Max Artis, Augustana (Ill.)
Bill Rapier, Augustana (Ill.)
Ed Jachim, Potsdam St.
Derrick Rowland, Potsdam St.
Ron Stewart, Otterbein

1982
*Pete Metzelaars, Wabash
Doug Cornfoot, Cal St. Stanislaus
Rick Davis, Brooklyn
Merlin Nice, Wabash
Leroy Witherspoon, Potsdam St.
Maurice Woods, Potsdam St.

1983
*Bill Bessoir, Scranton
Mickey Banas, Scranton
Jay Ferguson, Wittenberg
Mark Linde, Wis.-Whitewater
Gerald Holmes, Roanoke

1984
*Andre McKoy, Wis.-Whitewater
Mark Linde, Wis.-Whitewater
James Gist, Upsala
Dan Trant, Clark (Mass.)
David Hathaway, DePauw

1985
*Earnest Hubbard, North Park
Justyne Monegain, North Park
Dana Janssen, Neb. Wesleyan
Brendan Mitchell, Potsdam St.
Lou Stevens, Widener

1986
*Roosevelt Bullock, Potsdam St.
Barry Stanton, Potsdam St.
Johnny Mayers, New Jersey City
Michael Neal, LeMoyne-Owen
Dana Janssen, Neb. Wesleyan

1987
*Michael Starks, North Park
Mike Barach, North Park
Steve Iannarino, Wittenberg
Kermit Sharp, Clark (Mass.)
Donald Ellison, Richard Stockton

1988
*Scott Tedder, Ohio Wesleyan
Lee Rowlinson, Ohio Wesleyan
J.P. Andrejko, Scranton
Charlie Burt, Neb. Wesleyan
Tim McGraw, Hartwick

1989
*Greg Grant, Col. of New Jersey
Danny Johnson, Centre
Jeff Bowers, Southern Me.
Ricky Spicer, Wis.-Whitewater
Elbert Gordon, Wis.-Whitewater
Jeff Seifriz, Wis.-Whitewater

1990
*Chris Fite, Rochester
Brett Crist, DePauw
Chris Brandt, Washington (Md.)
Brett Hecko, DePauw
Steve Honderd, Calvin

1991
*Shawn Frison, Wis.-Platteville
James Bradley, Otterbein
Robby Jeter, Wis.-Platteville
Will Lasky, Frank. & Marsh.
David Wilding, Frank. & Marsh.

1992
*Steve Honderd, Calvin
Matt Harrison, Calvin
Mike LeFebre, Calvin
Chris Fite, Rochester
Kyle Meeker, Rochester

1993
*Kirk Anderson, Augustana (Ill.)
Mark Gooden, Ohio Northern
Aaron Madry, Ohio Northern
Steven Haynes, Mass.-Dartmouth
Keith Wood, Rowan

1994
*Mike Rhoades, Lebanon Valley
*Adam Crawford, New York U.
Jonathan Gabriel, New York U.
John Harper, Lebanon Valley
Matt Croci, Wittenberg

1995
*Ernie Peavy, Wis.-Platteville
Brad Knoy, Manchester
Kyle Hupfer, Manchester
Aaron Lancaster, Wis.-Platteville
Charles Grasty, Rowan

1996
*Terrence Stewart, Rowan
Antwan Dasher, Rowan
Joel Holstege, Hope
Duane Bosma, Hope
Chris Simich, Ill. Wesleyan

1997
*Bryan Crabtree, Ill. Wesleyan
Korey Coon, Ill. Wesleyan
Mitch Mosser, Neb. Wesleyan
Damien Hunter, Alvernia
Michael Nogelo, Williams

1998
*Ben Hoffmann, Wis.-Platteville
Andre Dalton, Wis.-Platteville
Joel Holstege, Hope
Michael Nogelo, Williams
Dave Jannuzzi, Wilkes

1999
*Merrill Brunson, Wis.-Platteville
Mike Jones, Wis.-Platteville
T.J. Grimes, Hampden-Sydney
Jeremy Harris, Hampden-Sydney
Horace Jenkins, Wm. Paterson

2000
*Sherm Carstensen, Wis.-Eau Claire
Jeremy Veenstra, Calvin
Aaron Winkle, Calvin
Tishaun Jenkins, Salem St.
Alex Kraft, Frank. & Marsh.

2001
*Pat Maloney, Catholic
Matt Hilleary, Catholic
Horace Jenkins, Wm. Paterson
Chad Bostleman, Ohio Northern
Luke Kasten, Ill. Wesleyan

2002
*Jeff Gibbs, Otterbein
Kevin Shay, Otterbein
Bob Porambo, Elizabethtown
Seth Hauben Carthage
Jason Wiertel, Carthage

CHAMPIONSHIPS

Statistical Leaders

2002 Division I Individual Leaders

Points Per Game

Name, Team	CL	Ht	Pos	G	FGM	3FG	FT	PTS	PPG
1. Jason Conley, VMI	Fr.	6-5	F	28	285	79	171	820	29.3
2. Henry Domercant, Eastern Ill.	Jr.	6-4	G	31	262	104	189	817	26.4
3. Mire Chatman, Tex.-Pan American	Sr.	6-2	G	29	265	65	165	760	26.2
4. Ernest Bremer, St. Bonaventure	Sr.	6-2	G	30	231	88	188	738	24.6
5. Melvin Ely, Fresno St.	Sr.	6-10	C	28	246	0	161	653	23.3
6. Lynn Greer, Temple	Sr.	6-2	G	31	226	95	172	719	23.2
7. Nick Stapleton, Austin Peay	Sr.	6-1	G	32	270	72	130	742	23.2
8. Keith McLeod, Bowling Green	Sr.	6-2	G	33	224	89	218	755	22.9
9. Chris Davis, North Texas	Jr.	6-5	G	29	217	46	173	653	22.5
10. Ricky Minard, Morehead St.	So.	6-4	F	29	227	65	127	646	22.3
11. Kevin Martin, Western Caro.	Fr.	6-6	G	28	196	73	154	619	22.1
12. Steve Logan, Cincinnati	Sr.	6-0	G	35	246	86	192	770	22.0
Damon Hancock, Southern Methodist	Sr.	6-4	G	26	183	48	158	572	22.0
14. #Casey Jacobsen, Stanford	Jr.	6-6	G	30	205	64	184	658	21.9
15. Michael Watson, UMKC	So.	6-0	G	29	221	92	101	635	21.9
16. David Bailey, Loyola (Ill.)	Jr.	5-8	G	30	224	54	149	651	21.7
17. Troy Bell, Boston College	Jr.	6-1	G	32	207	65	212	691	21.6
18. Richard Toussaint, Bethune-Cookman	Jr.	6-3	G	29	197	2	229	625	21.6
19. #Jason Williams, Duke	Jr.	6-2	G	35	249	108	140	746	21.3
20. Leon Rodgers, Northern Ill.	Sr.	6-6	F	28	195	33	173	596	21.3
21. #Dajuan Wagner, Memphis	Fr.	6-3	G	36	265	66	166	762	21.2
22. Antawn Dobie, Long Island	Sr.	6-0	G	26	188	48	126	550	21.2
23. Chris Monroe, George Washington	Jr.	6-3	G	28	167	55	203	592	21.1
24. Jermaine Hall, Wagner	Jr.	6-5	F	29	240	4	126	610	21.0
25. Reece Gaines, Louisville	Jr.	6-6	G	32	209	91	164	673	21.0
26. Dan Dickau, Gonzaga	Sr.	6-0	G	32	195	117	165	672	21.0
27. Rasual Butler, La Salle	Sr.	6-7	F	32	233	57	147	670	20.9
28. Desmond Cambridge, Alabama A&M	Sr.	6-0	G	2 9	175	80	170	600	20.7
29. Preston Shumpert, Syracuse	Sr.	6-6	F	36	256	88	144	744	20.7
30. Thomas Terrell, Georgia St.	Sr.	6-7	F	31	214	94	113	635	20.5
31. Juan Dixon, Maryland	Sr.	6-3	G	36	251	92	141	735	20.4
32. Justin Burdine, Murray St.	Sr.	6-1	G	32	239	99	75	652	20.4
33. Jason Gardner, Arizona	Jr.	5-10	G	34	197	106	192	692	20.4
34. Jerry Green, UC Irvine	Jr.	6-3	G	32	212	47	180	651	20.3
35. #Caron Butler, Connecticut	So.	6-7	F	34	253	30	155	691	20.3
36. Predrag Savovic, Hawaii	Sr.	6-6	G	25	163	75	106	507	20.3
37. Paul Haynes, Grambling	Sr.	6-8	F	28	195	41	135	566	20.2
38. Hector Romero, New Orleans	Jr.	6-7	F	28	188	11	178	565	20.2
39. Lamayn Wilson, Troy St.	Sr.	6-8	F	28	215	59	75	564	20.1
40. Marcus Hatten, St. John's (N.Y.)	Jr.	6-1	G	3 2	212	57	163	644	20.1
41. Mario Porter, Rider	Sr.	6-6	F	28	216	22	108	562	20.1
42. Dwayne Archbold, Siena	Sr.	6-6	G	36	231	99	154	715	19.9
43. #Drew Gooden, Kansas	Jr.	6-10	F	37	285	10	154	734	19.8
44. #Kareem Rush, Missouri	Jr.	6-6	F	36	249	111	103	712	19.8
45. Tommy Adams, Hampton	Sr.	6-3	G	33	213	106	120	652	19.8
46. Earl Hunt, Brown	Jr.	6-4	G	27	173	49	138	533	19.7
47. Theron Smith, Ball St.	Jr.	6-8	F	35	233	45	176	687	19.6
48. Andrew Wisniewski, Centenary (La.)	So.	6-3	G	27	165	53	146	529	19.6
49. Doug Wrenn, Washington	So.	6-0	G	28	207	18	114	546	19.5
50. Junior Blount, TCU	Jr.	6-0	G	31	203	83	114	603	19.5
51. Luis Flores, Manhattan	So.	6-2	G	29	180	39	164	563	19.4
52. Ricky Cottrill, Eastern Mich.	So.	6-0	G	30	186	78	132	582	19.4
53. Altron Jackson, South Fla.	Sr.	6-6	F	32	218	58	122	616	19.3
54. Casey Frandsen, Portland	So.	6-3	G	30	183	98	113	577	19.2
55. Rahsaan Johnson, Monmouth	Sr.	6-0	G	29	197	62	100	556	19.2
56. Sam Clancy, Southern California	Sr.	6-7	F	32	218	1	138	611	19.1
57. Mike Sweetney, Georgetown	So.	6-8	F	29	185	0	182	552	19.0
58. Ryan Humphrey, Notre Dame	Sr.	6-8	F	31	231	3	122	587	18.9
59. Maurice Bailey, Sacred Heart	So.	6-0	G	22	138	17	123	416	18.9
60. Tamar Slay, Marshall	Sr.	6-9	G	30	196	80	95	567	18.9
61. Elvin Mims, Southern Miss.	Jr.	6-5	F	25	186	41	71	472	18.9
62. Darrell Tucker, San Francisco	Jr.	6-9	F	28	191	28	118	528	18.9
63. T.J. Sorrentine, Vermont	So.	5-11	G	29	179	90	98	546	18.8
64. Mceverett Powers, Texas-San Antonio	Sr.	6-7	F	29	163	0	218	544	18.8
65. Kyle Williams, Howard	Jr.	6-6	F	31	211	64	95	581	18.7
66. Andre Emmett, Texas Tech	So.	6-5	G	32	242	9	106	599	18.7
67. Tyray Pearson, Iowa St.	Sr.	6-7	F	31	209	0	162	580	18.7
68. Steven Barber, Texas-Arlington	Sr.	5-10	G	27	163	57	119	502	18.6
69. Frederick Jones, Oregon	Sr.	6-4	G	35	215	51	169	650	18.6
70. Abe Jackson, Boise St.	Sr.	6-7	F	30	185	92	95	557	18.6

#entered NBA draft

Field-Goal Percentage

(Min. five FG made per game)

Name, Team	CL	Ht	Pos	G	FGM	FGA	FG%
1. Adam Mark, Belmont	So.	6-8	F	26	150	212	70.8
2. #Carlos Boozer, Duke	Jr.	6-9	C	35	230	346	66.5
3. David Harrison, Colorado	Fr.	7-0	C	27	139	218	63.8
4. Rolan Roberts, Southern Ill.	Sr.	6-6	C	36	209	346	60.4
5. Jermaine Hall, Wagner	Jr.	6-5	F	29	240	400	60.0
6. Chris Sockwell, St. Francis (N.Y.)	Jr.	6-8	C	29	155	260	59.6
7. Len Matela, Bowling Green	Sr.	6-9	C	33	192	323	59.4
8. Justin Rowe, Maine	Jr.	7-0	C	30	158	266	59.4
9. James Moore, New Mexico St.	So.	6-8	F	32	184	310	59.4
10. Nick Collison, Kansas	Jr.	6-9	F	37	245	414	59.2
11. Damien Kinloch, Tennessee Tech	Jr.	6-8	C	34	186	316	58.9
12. Henry Williams, South Ala.	Jr.	6-6	F	28	141	241	58.5
13. Travis Reed, Long Beach St.	Sr.	6-8	C	30	177	303	58.4
14. Patrick Doctor, American	Sr.	6-0	G	30	166	286	58.0
15. Omar Barlett, Jacksonville St.	Jr.	6-8	C	29	155	269	57.6
16. Chris Hester, Eastern Wash.	Jr.	6-3	G	30	163	283	57.6
17. #Curtis Borchardt, Stanford	Jr.	7-0	C	29	171	297	57.6
18. Louis Truscott, Houston	Jr.	6-7	F	32	162	282	57.4
19. Kevin Johnson, Tulsa	Jr.	6-7	F	34	192	335	57.3
20. Michael Harris, Rice	Fr.	6-6	F	29	154	269	57.2
21. Reggie Borges, Oral Roberts	Jr.	6-8	F	30	150	263	57.0
22. Mike Sweetney, Georgetown	So.	6-8	F	29	185	326	56.7
23. Jason Jennings, Arkansas St.	Jr.	7-0	C	30	170	300	56.7
24. Marcus Smallwood, Northern Ill.	So.	6-6	G	28	141	250	56.4
25. Melvin Ely, Fresno St.	Sr.	6-10	C	28	246	437	56.3
26. Udonis Haslem, Florida	Sr.	6-9	C	31	159	283	56.2
27. Ryan Gomes, Providence	Fr.	6-7	F	24	132	236	55.9
28. Mario Austin, Mississippi St.	So.	6-9	C	35	209	375	55.7
29. Trevor Gaines, Vermont	Sr.	6-7	C	29	191	343	55.7
30. Erwin Dudley, Alabama	Jr.	6-8	F	35	207	372	55.6

#entered NBA draft

Three-Point Field-Goal Percentage

(Min. 1.5 FGM)

Name, Team	CL	Ht	Pos	G	3FG	3FGA	3FG%
1. Dante Swanson, Tulsa	Jr.	5-10	G	33	73	149	49.0
2. Cain Doliboa, Wright St.	Sr.	6-7	G	28	104	217	47.9
3. Jake Sullivan, Iowa St.	So.	6-1	G	28	60	127	47.2
4. Jeff Boschee, Kansas	Sr.	6-1	G	37	110	237	46.4
5. Ray Abellard, UCF	Jr.	5-10	G	29	80	173	46.2
6. Cameron Crisp, Tennessee Tech	So.	6-3	G	34	72	156	46.2
7. John Hamilton, Weber St.	So.	6-3	G	29	76	165	46.1
8. Eric Channing, New Mexico St.	Sr.	6-4	G	31	81	176	46.0
9. Jordan Kardos, Ill.-Chicago	Sr.	6-2	G	34	69	150	46.0
10. Dan Dickau, Gonzaga	Sr.	6-0	G	32	117	256	45.7
11. Mike Ames, Delaware	So.	6-3	G	30	73	160	45.6
12. Peter Anderer, Davidson	Jr.	6-1	G	31	84	185	45.4
13. Salim Stoudamire, Arizona	Fr.	6-1	G	34	73	161	45.3
14. Jason Kapono, UCLA	Jr.	6-8	F	33	87	192	45.3
Nick Moore, Toledo	Jr.	6-1	G	29	87	192	45.3
16. Josh Copperwood, Tennessee St.	Jr.	6-3	G	27	56	124	45.2
17. Anthony Thomas, Furman	Sr.	6-4	G	31	88	195	45.1
18. Douglas Ruben, New Mexico	Jr.	6-5	G	30	66	147	44.9
19. Brady Richeson, Southwest Tex. St.	Jr.	5-11	G	28	57	127	44.9
20. Chris Hill, Michigan St.	Fr.	6-3	G	31	66	148	44.6
21. David Falknor, Akron	Sr.	6-7	F	28	76	171	44.4
Steve Esterkamp, Ohio	Jr.	6-6	F	28	56	126	44.4
23. Nick Jacobson, Utah	So.	6-4	G	30	71	160	44.4
24. Brendan Plavich, Vanderbilt	So.	6-2	G	32	86	195	44.1
25. Luke Ridnour, Oregon	So.	6-2	G	35	93	211	44.1
26. Craig Dawson, Wake Forest	Sr.	6-5	G	34	100	227	44.1
27. Mike Mclaren, Dartmouth	Fr.	6-3	G	27	58	133	43.6
28. Tony Brown, Utah St.	Jr.	6-3	G	31	75	172	43.6
29. Brian Conklin, Nebraska	So.	6-11	F	28	65	150	43.3
Ronnie Jones, Wis.-Milwaukee	Jr.	5-9	G	29	65	150	43.3

Three-Point Field Goals Per Game

Name, Team	CL	Ht	Pos	G	3FG	3PG
1. Cain Doliboa, Wright St.	Sr.	6-7	G	28	104	3.7
2. Jobey Thomas, Charlotte	Sr.	6-4	G	30	110	3.7
3. Dan Dickau, Gonzaga	Sr.	6-0	G	32	117	3.7
4. Wes Burtner, Belmont	Sr.	6-5	F	28	100	3.6
Jason Morgan, St. Francis (N.Y.)	Sr.	6-4	G	28	100	3.6
6. Sharif Chambliss, Penn St.	So.	6-0	G	28	99	3.5

Name, Team	CL	Ht	Pos	G	3FG	3PG
7. Travis Cantrell, Citadel	Sr.	6-2	G	29	102	3.5
8. Bryan Buchanan, IUPUI	Jr.	6-1	G	25	84	3.4
9. Henry Domercant, Eastern Ill.	Jr.	6-4	G	31	104	3.4
10. Nick Zachery, Ark.-Little Rock	So.	6-3	G	28	93	3.3
11. Clarence Gilbert, Missouri	Sr.	6-2	G	36	118	3.3
12. Jannero Pargo, Arkansas	Sr.	6-2	G	29	95	3.3
13. Casey Frandsen, Portland	So.	6-3	G	30	98	3.3
14. Tommy Adams, Hampton	Sr.	6-3	G	33	106	3.2
15. Jerome Coleman, Rutgers	Jr.	6-2	G	31	99	3.2
16. Clay Click, Southwest Tex. St.	Sr.	6-3	G	26	83	3.2
17. Cary Cochran, Nebraska	Sr.	6-1	G	28	89	3.2
18. Michael Watson, UMKC	So.	6-0	G	29	92	3.2
19. Jamel Bradley, South Carolina	Sr.	6-2	G	37	117	3.2
20. Tony Akins, Georgia Tech	Sr.	5-11	G	31	98	3.2
David Bell, Montana	Jr.	6-1	G	31	98	3.2
Brett Nelson, Florida	Jr.	6-4	G	31	98	3.2
23. Gary Buchanan, Villanova	Jr.	6-3	G	32	101	3.2
24. Luke Mcdonald, Drake	So.	6-6	G	29	91	3.1
25. Jason Gardner, Arizona	Jr.	5-10	G	34	106	3.1
26. T.J. Sorrentine, Vermont	So.	5-11	G	29	90	3.1
27. Justin Burdine, Murray St.	Sr.	6-1	G	32	99	3.1
28. #Jason Williams, Duke	Jr.	6-2	G	35	108	3.1
29. #Kareem Rush, Missouri	Jr.	6-6	F	36	111	3.1
30. Abe Jackson, Boise St.	Sr.	6-7	F	30	92	3.1

#entered NBA draft

Free-Throw Percentage

Name, Team	CL	Ht	Pos	G	FT	FTA	FT%
1. Cary Cochran, Nebraska	Sr.	6-1	G	28	71	77	92.2
2. Gary Buchanan, Villanova	Jr.	6-3	G	32	112	123	91.1
3. Cain Doliboa, Wright St.	Sr.	6-7	G	28	80	88	90.9
4. Salim Stoudamire, Arizona	Fr.	6-1	G	34	103	114	90.4
5. Jake Sullivan, Iowa St.	So.	6-1	G	28	117	130	90.0
6. Jobey Thomas, Charlotte	Sr.	6-4	G	30	98	109	89.9
7. Juan Dixon, Maryland	Sr.	6-3	G	36	141	157	89.8
8. Chris Spatola, Army	Sr.	6-1	G	28	113	126	89.7
9. Eric Channing, New Mexico St.	Sr.	6-4	G	31	93	104	89.4
10. Travis Cantrell, Citadel	Sr.	6-2	G	29	92	103	89.3
11. Henry Domercant, Eastern Ill.	Jr.	6-4	G	31	189	212	89.2
12. Kyle Korver, Creighton	Jr.	6-7	F	29	97	109	89.0
13. Donta Richardson, Wyoming	Jr.	6-2	G	31	113	127	89.0
14. Chris Thomas, Notre Dame	Fr.	6-1	G	33	120	135	88.9
15. Greg Lakey, Loyola Marymount	Sr.	6-9	F	29	79	89	88.8
16. Curtis Allen, Washington	So.	6-0	G	29	101	114	88.6
17. Luke Recker, Iowa	Sr.	6-6	G	35	108	122	88.5
18. James Gillingham, Bradley	So.	6-4	G	29	123	139	88.5
19. Clay Click, Southwest Tex. St.	Sr.	6-3	G	26	69	78	88.5
20. Troy Bell, Boston College	Jr.	6-1	G	32	212	240	88.3
21. Jonathan Hargett, West Virginia	Fr.	5-11	G	26	89	101	88.1
22. #Roger Mason, Jr., Virginia	Jr.	6-5	G	29	133	151	88.1
23. Glenn Stokes, American	Sr.	6-0	G	30	81	92	88.0
24. Marquis Sykes, Morehead St.	Jr.	6-0	G	29	73	83	88.0
25. Lynn Greer, Temple	Sr.	6-2	G	31	172	197	87.3
26. Steve Logan, Cincinnati	Sr.	6-0	G	35	192	220	87.3
Brian Cook, Illinois	Jr.	6-10	F	35	96	110	87.3
28. Luis Flores, Manhattan	So.	6-2	G	29	164	188	87.2
29. Frederick Jones, Oregon	Sr.	6-4	G	35	169	194	87.1
30. D.J. Munir, Stony Brook	So.	6-3	G	28	106	122	86.9

#entered NBA draft

Rebounds Per Game

Name, Team	CL	Ht	Pos	G	REB	RPG
1. Jeremy Bishop, Quinnipiac	Jr.	6-6	F	29	347	12.0
2. Bruce Jenkins, N.C. A&T	Sr.	6-6	F	28	329	11.8
3. #Curtis Borchardt, Stanford	Jr.	7-0	C	29	332	11.4
4. #Drew Gooden, Kansas	Jr.	6-10	F	37	423	11.4
5. Corey Jackson, Nevada	Sr.	6-7	F	29	323	11.1
6. Reggie Evans, Iowa	Sr.	6-8	F	34	378	11.1
7. Trevor Gaines, Vermont	Sr.	6-7	C	29	320	11.0
8. Theron Smith, Ball St.	Jr.	6-8	F	35	381	10.9
9. Ryan Humphrey, Notre Dame	Sr.	6-8	F	31	337	10.9
10. Stephane Pelle, Colorado	Jr.	6-9	F	29	314	10.8
11. Hector Romero, New Orleans	Jr.	6-7	F	28	302	10.8
12. J.R. Vanhoose, Marshall	Sr.	6-10	C	30	319	10.6
13. Kelly Wise, Memphis	Sr.	6-10	C	32	330	10.3
14. Donald Cole, Sam Houston St.	Jr.	6-8	C	28	287	10.3
15. Rashod Kent, Rutgers	Sr.	6-6	F	31	317	10.2
16. Darrell Tucker, San Francisco	Jr.	6-9	F	28	284	10.1
17. Ryan Blankson, Loyola (Ill.)	Sr.	6-6	F	30	304	10.1

Name, Team	CL	Ht	Pos	G	REB	RPG
18. Greg Lewis, Winthrop	Sr.	6-6	F	31	313	10.1
19. Chris Brown, New Hampshire	Sr.	6-4	F	28	282	10.1
20. James Singleton, Murray St.	Jr.	6-8	F	31	312	10.1
21. Amien Hicks, Morris Brown	Jr.	6-8	F	28	281	10.0
22. Mike Sweetney, Georgetown	So.	6-8	F	29	290	10.0
23. Andy Savtchenko, Radford	Sr.	7-0	C	31	309	10.0
24. Dexter Hall, South Carolina St.	Sr.	6-8	F	31	305	9.8
25. Mike Wallace, Southwest Mo. St.	Sr.	6-5	C	32	314	9.8
26. David West, Xavier	Jr.	6-9	F	32	313	9.8
27. Travis Watson, Virginia	Jr.	6-8	F	28	272	9.7
28. Tyrone Levett, Alabama St.	Sr.	6-5	F	32	308	9.6
29. Jorge Rochin, Portland	Sr.	6-7	C	30	287	9.6
30. Sam Clancy, Southern California	Sr.	6-7	F	32	302	9.4

#entered NBA draft

Assists Per Game

Name, Team	CL	Ht	Pos	G	AST	APG
1. T.J. Ford, Texas	Fr.	5-10	G	33	273	8.3
2. Steve Blake, Maryland	Jr.	6-3	G	36	286	7.9
3. Edward Scott, Clemson	Jr.	6-0	G	30	238	7.9
4. Sean Kennedy, Marist	Sr.	6-2	G	28	222	7.9
5. Chris Thomas, Notre Dame	Fr.	6-1	G	33	252	7.6
6. Matt Montague, Brigham Young	Sr.	6-0	G	30	217	7.2
7. Brandin Knight, Pittsburgh	Jr.	6-0	G	35	251	7.2
8. Mychal Covington, Oakland	Sr.	6-4	G	28	198	7.1
9. Reggie Kohn, South Fla.	Jr.	6-1	G	32	220	6.9
10. Aaron Miles, Kansas	Fr.	6-1	G	37	252	6.8
11. Guilherme Da Luz, Furman	Jr.	6-3	G	31	206	6.6
12. Sean Peterson, Ga. Southern	Sr.	6-1	G	28	186	6.6
13. Marquis Sykes, Morehead St.	Jr.	6-0	G	29	189	6.5
14. Brandon Pardon, Bowling Green	Sr.	6-1	G	33	209	6.3
15. Delvon Arrington, Florida St.	Sr.	5-11	G	29	182	6.3
16. Jameer Nelson, St. Joseph's	So.	6-0	G	30	188	6.3
17. Luke Walton, Arizona	Jr.	6-8	G	31	194	6.3
18. John Salmons, Miami (Fla.)	Jr.	6-7	G	32	195	6.1
19. Courtney Eldridge, UNC Greensboro	Sr.	5-9	G	30	182	6.1
20. Derrick Zimmerman, Mississippi St.	Jr.	6-2	G	35	210	6.0
David Morris, Dayton	Sr.	5-10	G	32	192	6.0
Ashley Robinson, Mississippi Val.	Sr.	5-8	G	29	174	6.0
23. Marques Green, St. Bonaventure	So.	5-7	G	30	179	6.0
24. Chris Duhon, Duke	So.	6-1	G	35	208	5.9
25. Victor Tarver, Southern U.	Jr.	5-7	G	26	154	5.9
26. Corey Santee, TCU	Fr.	6-2	G	31	180	5.8
27. Kevin Braswell, Georgetown	Sr.	6-2	G	30	173	5.8
28. Brandon Granville, Southern California	Sr.	5-9	G	32	184	5.8
29. Andrew Wisniewski, Centenary (La.)	So.	6-3	G	27	155	5.7
30. Desmond Cambridge, Alabama A&M	Sr.	6-0	G	29	166	5.7

Blocked Shots Per Game

Name, Team	CL	Ht	Pos	G	BLKS	BKPG
1. Wojciech Myrda, La.-Monroe	Sr.	7-2	C	32	172	5.4
2. D'or Fischer, Northwestern St.	So.	6-11	C	30	133	4.4
3. Emeka Okafor, Connecticut	Fr.	6-9	C	34	138	4.1
4. Justin Rowe, Maine	Jr.	7-0	C	30	121	4.0
5. Deng Gai, Fairfield	Fr.	6-9	F	29	115	4.0
6. Nick Billings, Binghamton	Fr.	7-0	C	21	80	3.8
7. Moussa Badiane, East Caro.	Fr.	6-10	C	24	87	3.6
8. Jason Jennings, Arkansas St.	Sr.	7-0	C	30	101	3.4
9. Kendrick Moore, Oral Roberts	Jr.	6-8	C	31	103	3.3
10. Robert Battle, Drexel	Jr.	6-8	C	28	91	3.3
11. Kyle Davis, Auburn	So.	6-10	C	24	77	3.2
12. Vili Morton, UC Riverside	So.	6-8	F	26	83	3.2
13. Melvin Ely, Fresno St.	Sr.	6-10	C	28	88	3.1
14. Michael Southall, La.-Lafayette	Fr.	6-11	C	31	97	3.1
15. Cedric Suitt, Pepperdine	Sr.	6-11	C	31	96	3.1
16. Neil Ashby, Chattanooga	Sr.	6-8	F	29	89	3.1
17. #Curtis Borchardt, Stanford	Jr.	7-0	C	29	83	2.9
18. Ryan Humphrey, Notre Dame	Sr.	6-8	F	31	87	2.8
19. Hondre Brewer, San Francisco	Sr.	7-0	C	28	78	2.8
20. Jeremy Sargent, Tenn.-Martin	Sr.	6-8	C	28	74	2.6
21. Lonnie Jones, Ball St.	Sr.	7-0	C	34	89	2.6
22. David West, Xavier	Jr.	6-9	F	32	80	2.5
23. Chris Wiedemann, Columbia	Jr.	6-10	C	27	67	2.5
24. L.F. Likcholitov, Va. Commonwealth	Sr.	6-11	C	32	79	2.5
25. James Jones, Miami (Fla.)	Jr.	6-8	F	32	78	2.4
26. Rolan Roberts, Southern Ill.	Sr.	6-6	C	36	87	2.4
27. Raynell Brewer, McNeese St.	Sr.	7-1	C	29	70	2.4
Danny Granger, Bradley	Fr.	6-8	F	29	70	2.4

STATISTICAL LEADERS

Name, Team	CL	Ht	Pos	G	BLKS	BKPG
29. William McDonald, Grambling	Jr.	6-9	F	27	65	2.4
30. Nosa Obasuyi, Radford	Sr.	6-10	C	31	74	2.4

#entered NBA draft

Steals Per Game

Name, Team	CL	Ht	Pos	G	ST	STPG
1. Desmond Cambridge, Alabama A&M	Sr.	6-0	G	29	160	5.5
2. John Linehan, Providence	Sr.	5-9	G	31	139	4.5
3. Mire Chatman, Tex.-Pan American	Sr.	6-2	G	29	105	3.6
4. Marques Green, St. Bonaventure	So.	5-7	G	30	102	3.4
5. Marcus Hatten, St. John's (N.Y.)	Jr.	6-1	G	32	105	3.3
6. Carlos Morban, Florida Int'l	Fr.	6-2	G	29	87	3.0
7. Jason Conley, VMI	Fr.	6-5	F	28	82	2.9
8. James Thues, Syracuse	So.	5-10	G	36	101	2.8
9. Markus Carr, Cal St. Northridge	Sr.	6-1	G	28	78	2.8
10. Kevin Braswell, Georgetown	Sr.	6-2	G	30	81	2.7
11. Alexis McMillan, Stetson	Jr.	6-4	G	26	69	2.7

Name, Team	CL	Ht	Pos	G	ST	STPG
12. Von Damien Green, Manhattan	Sr.	5-10	G	29	76	2.6
13. Courtney Eldridge, UNC Greensboro	Sr.	5-9	G	30	78	2.6
14. Jay Heard, Jacksonville St.	Jr.	6-3	G	29	75	2.6
15. Juan Dixon, Maryland	Sr.	6-3	G	36	92	2.6
16. Ricky Minard, Morehead St.	So.	6-4	F	29	73	2.5
17. Garrett Richardson, Tennessee St.	So.	6-3	G	28	70	2.5
18. Dwyane Wade, Marquette	Fr.	6-4	G	32	79	2.5
19. Chuck Eidson, South Carolina	Sr.	6-7	F	37	91	2.5
20. Andrew Gellert, Harvard	Sr.	6-1	G	26	63	2.4
21. Travarus Bennett, Minnesota	Sr.	6-7	F	31	75	2.4
22. Chris Caldwell, Liberty	Sr.	6-0	G	30	72	2.4
Robby Collum, Western Mich.	Jr.	6-1	G	30	72	2.4
24. Brian Allen, Towson	Jr.	6-0	G	28	67	2.4
Demarcus Wilkins, Florida A&M	So.	6-0	G	28	67	2.4
26. David Sykes, Southwest Tex. St.	Jr.	6-5	G	26	62	2.4
27. Darius Lane, Seton Hall	Sr.	6-4	G	29	69	2.4
28. Brandin Knight, Pittsburgh	Jr.	6-0	G	35	82	2.3
29. Chris Duhon, Duke	So.	6-1	G	35	81	2.3
30. Thomas Jackson, Butler	Sr.	5-9	G	32	74	2.3

2002 Division I Game Highs

Individual Highs

ASSISTS

Name, Team	CL	Ht	Pos	Opponent	Date	AST
1. Brad Boyd, La.-Lafayette	So.	6-5	F	North Texas	01/24/02	17
Sean Peterson, Ga. Southern	Sr.	6-1	G	Western Caro.	01/21/02	17
Imari Sawyer, DePaul	So.	6-2	G	Youngstown St.	11/25/01	17
4. Kevin Braswell, Georgetown	Sr.	6-2	G	Rutgers	03/02/02	16
Steve Logan, Cincinnati	Sr.	6-0	G	Coppin St.	12/08/01	16
6. Aaron Miles, Kansas	Fr.	6-1	G	Texas Tech	03/09/02	15
Matt Montague, Brigham Young	Sr.	6-0	G	Wyoming	02/02/02	15
Curtis Allen, Washington	So.	6-0	G	Arizona St.	01/10/02	15
Matt Montague, Brigham Young	Sr.	6-0	G	Idaho	12/15/01	15
10. Brandin Knight, Pittsburgh	Jr.	6-0	G	Miami (Fla.)	03/08/02	14
Brandin Knight, Pittsburgh	Jr.	6-0	G	West Virginia	03/02/02	14
Mychal Covington, Oakland	Sr.	6-4	G	Valparaiso	02/21/02	14
D.J. Munir, Stony Brook	So.	6-3	G	Northeastern	02/17/02	14
Antawn Dobie, Long Island	Sr.	6-0	G	UMBC	02/15/02	14
Steve Blake, Maryland	Jr.	6-3	G	North Carolina	01/09/02	14
Brandon Pardon, Bowling Green	Sr.	6-1	G	Northern Ill.	01/08/02	14
J.P. Spatola, Army	So.	6-1	G	New Hampshire	01/07/02	14
Reggie Kohn, South Fla.	Jr.	6-1	G	TCU	01/05/02	14
Edward Scott, Clemson	Jr.	6-0	G	Charleston So.	12/22/01	14
T.J. Ford, Texas	Fr.	5-10	G	Arizona	11/17/01	14

BLOCKED SHOTS

Name, Team	CL	Ht	Pos	Opponent	Date	BLKS
1. Wojciech Myrda, La.-Monroe	Sr.	7-2	C	Texas-San Antonio	01/17/02	13
2. D'or Fischer, Northwestern St.	So.	6-11	C	Siena	11/21/01	12
3. Wojciech Myrda, La.-Monroe	Sr.	7-2	C	Nicholls St.	02/16/02	11
4. Cedric Suitt, Pepperdine	Sr.	6-11	C	San Diego	01/26/02	10
Wojciech Myrda, La.-Monroe	Sr.	7-2	C	Sam Houston St.	01/24/02	10
Wojciech Myrda, La.-Monroe	Sr.	7-2	C	Texas-Arlington	01/07/02	10
Wojciech Myrda, La.-Monroe	Sr.	7-2	C	Stephen F. Austin	01/05/02	10
Wojciech Myrda, La.-Monroe	Sr.	7-2	C	Holy Cross	12/29/01	10
Deng Gai, Fairfield	Fr.	6-9	F	St. Francis (N.Y.)	12/11/01	10
10. Wojciech Myrda, La.-Monroe	Sr.	7-2	C	Texas-San Antonio	03/06/02	9
Kendrick Moore, Oral Roberts	Jr.	6-8	F	IUPUI	03/04/02	9
Emeka Okafor, Connecticut	Fr.	6-9	C	Boston College	02/16/02	9
L.F. Likcholitov, Va. Commonwealth	Sr.	6-11	C	Drexel	02/02/02	9
Emeka Okafor, Connecticut	Fr.	6-9	C	Rutgers	01/30/02	9
Nick Billings, Binghamton	Fr.	7-0	C	Colgate	01/28/02	9
Emeka Okafor, Connecticut	Fr.	6-9	C	Arizona	01/26/02	9
D'or Fischer, Northwestern St.	So.	6-11	C	Texas-San Antonio	01/19/02	9
Justin Rowe, Maine	Jr.	7-0	C	Stony Brook	01/06/02	9
Melvin Ely, Fresno St.	Sr.	6-10	C	Tulsa	01/05/02	9
Robert Battle, Drexel	Jr.	6-8	C	Northeastern	12/18/01	9
Ryan Lewis, Jacksonville	Jr.	6-9	C	Savannah St.	12/08/01	9
Kyle Davis, Auburn	So.	6-10	C	Louisiana Tech	12/04/01	9

FIELD-GOAL PERCENTAGE
(Minimum 10 FGM)

Name, Team	CL	Opponent	Date	FG%	FGM	FGA
1. Justin Rowe, Maine	Jr.	Binghamton	01/31/02	100.0	11	11
Patrick Doctor, American	Sr.	Lafayette	02/09/02	100.0	10	10
Omar Barlett, Jacksonville St.	Jr.	Belmont	02/04/02	100.0	10	10
Ben Hunt, Stephen F. Austin	Jr.	La.-Monroe	01/05/02	100.0	10	10
5. Damien Kinloch, Tennessee Tech	Jr.	Austin Peay	01/17/02	92.3	12	13
6. Dusty Rychart, Minnesota	Sr.	Penn St.	03/07/02	91.7	11	12
Reece Gaines, Louisville	Jr.	Charlotte	03/02/02	91.7	11	12
Robert Archibald, Illinois	Sr.	Penn St.	02/20/02	91.7	11	12
Dan Champagne, Oakland	Sr.	Chicago St.	02/02/02	91.7	11	12
Charlie Davis, Tulsa	Jr.	Southern Methodist	01/19/02	91.7	11	12
Sam Spann, Fairfield	Sr.	Iona	01/18/02	91.7	11	12
T.J. Cummings, UCLA	So.	South Carolina	11/21/01	91.7	11	12
13. Kason Mims, Quinnipiac	So.	Sacred Heart	02/14/02	90.9	10	11
Jarrad Odle, Indiana	Sr.	Louisville	02/09/02	90.9	10	11
Andre Brown, DePaul	So.	East Caro.	01/23/02	90.9	10	11
Jermaine Boyette, Weber St.	Jr.	Sacramento St.	01/12/02	90.9	10	11
Curtis Borchardt, Stanford	Jr.	Long Beach St.	12/15/01	90.9	10	11
Michael Southall, La.-Lafayette	Fr.	Loyola (La.)	12/13/01	90.9	10	11
Tom Bellairs, Air Force	Sr.	Arkansas St.	12/05/01	90.9	10	11
John Allison, Purdue	Sr.	Oakland	12/02/01	90.9	10	11
David West, Xavier	Jr.	Miami (Ohio)	11/28/01	90.9	10	11
David Przybyszewski, Vanderbilt	Fr.	Hampton	11/23/01	90.9	10	11

FREE-THROW PERCENTAGE
(Minimum 12 FTM)

Name, Team	CL	Opponent	Date	FT%	FT	FTA
1. Lynn Greer, Temple	Sr.	St. Joseph's	02/02/02	100.0	18	18
Henry Domercant, Eastern Ill.	Jr.	Loyola (Ill.)	12/15/01	100.0	17	17
Troy Bell, Boston College	Jr.	Iowa St.	12/11/01	100.0	17	17
Damany Hendrix, Lamar	Jr.	Texas-Arlington	02/16/02	100.0	16	16
Marcus Moore, Washington St.	So.	Arizona St.	01/12/02	100.0	16	16
Rashon Brown, Akron	Sr.	Northern Ill.	02/20/02	100.0	15	15
Douglas Ruben, New Mexico	Jr.	UNLV	02/05/02	100.0	15	15
Dimeco Childress, East Tenn. St.	Sr.	Davidson	02/09/02	100.0	14	14
Luis Flores, Manhattan	So.	St. Peter's	01/30/02	100.0	14	14
Frederick Jones, Oregon	Sr.	Arizona St.	12/20/01	100.0	14	14
Uka Agbai, Boston College	Jr.	Pittsburgh	03/07/02	100.0	13	13
Rasual Butler, La Salle	Sr.	Rhode Island	02/23/02	100.0	13	13
Wayne Smith, Duquesne	Sr.	George Washington	02/16/02	100.0	13	13
Chris Williams, Ball St.	Jr.	Northern Ill.	02/05/02	100.0	13	13
Guilherme Da Luz, Furman	Jr.	Citadel	01/28/02	100.0	13	13
Willie Taylor, Va. Commonwealth	Jr.	UAB	12/15/01	100.0	13	13
Kyle Barker, Navy	Jr.	Davidson	12/01/01	100.0	13	13
Darius Songaila, Wake Forest	Sr.	Minnesota	11/27/01	100.0	13	13
Jake Sullivan, Iowa St.	Jr.	St. Louis	11/23/01	100.0	13	13
Jason Gardner, Arizona	Jr.	Arizona St.	03/07/02	100.0	12	12
Mike Manciel, Central Mich.	Jr.	Toledo	03/07/02	100.0	12	12
Laurie Bridges, La.-Lafayette	So.	Arkansas St.	03/04/02	100.0	12	12
Jermaine Hall, Wagner	Jr.	St. Francis (N.Y.)	02/20/02	100.0	12	12

Name, Team	CL	Opponent	Date	FT%	FT	FTA
Luke Mcdonald, Drake	So.	Bradley	02/16/02	100.0	12	12
Nate Williams, Western Ky.	Jr.	Florida Int'l	01/31/02	100.0	12	12
Bronski Dockery, St. Francis (N.Y.)	Jr.	Robert Morris	01/26/02	100.0	12	12
Brandon Miller, Butler	Jr.	Ill.-Chicago	01/26/02	100.0	12	12
Curtis Allen, Washington	So.	Oregon	01/24/02	100.0	12	12
Chris Brown, New Hampshire	Sr.	Hartford	01/24/02	100.0	12	12
David Schuck, UNC Greensboro	Sr.	East Tenn. St.	01/14/02	100.0	12	12

POINTS

Name, Team	CL	Ht	Pos	Opponent	Date	PTS
1. Desmond Cambridge, Alabama A&M	Sr.	6-0	G	Texas Southern	02/25/02	50
2. Casey Jacobsen, Stanford	Jr.	6-6	G	Arizona St.	01/31/02	49
3. Lynn Greer, Temple	Sr.	6-2	G	Wisconsin	12/03/01	47
4. Mire Chatman, Tex.-Pan American	Sr.	6-2	G	Tex. A&M-Corp. Chris	02/09/02	46
5. T.J. Sorrentine, Vermont	So.	5-11	G	Northeastern	01/17/02	45
Mike Helms, Oakland	So.	6-0	G	Western Mich.	12/29/01	45
Errick Greene, Maine	Sr.	6-3	G	Norfolk St.	12/11/01	45
8. Ronald Blackshear, Marshall	Sr.	6-5	G	Akron	03/01/02	44
Rasual Butler, La Salle	Sr.	6-7	F	Rhode Island	02/23/02	44
Mire Chatman, Tex.-Pan American	Sr.	6-2	G	New Mexico St.	02/11/02	44
David Webber, Central Mich.	Sr.	6-2	G	Miami (Ohio)	01/05/02	44
12. Brian Burke, Lafayette	Sr.	6-5	G	Lehigh	02/20/02	43
Lynn Greer, Temple	Sr.	6-2	G	Fordham	01/30/02	43
Steven Barber, Texas-Arlington	Sr.	5-10	G	Texas-San Antonio	01/24/02	43
Lamayn Wilson, Troy St.	Sr.	6-8	F	Fla. Atlantic	01/12/02	43
16. Junior Blount, TCU	Jr.	6-0	G	Tulane	02/26/02	42
Dimeco Childress, East Tenn. St.	Sr.	6-3	G	Western Caro.	02/16/02	42
Jason Conley, VMI	Fr.	6-5	F	Western Caro.	02/09/02	42
Keith McLeod, Bowling Green	Sr.	6-2	G	Buffalo	01/12/02	42
Troy Bell, Boston College	Jr.	6-1	G	Iowa St.	12/11/01	42
David Bailey, Loyola (Ill.)	Jr.	5-8	G	Tex. A&M-Corp. Chris	11/29/01	42
22. Tayshaun Prince, Kentucky	Sr.	6-9	G	Tulsa	03/16/02	41
James Felton, Fairleigh Dickinson	Sr.	6-10	C	Long Island	02/23/02	41
Christian Sonier, Prairie View	So.	5-10	G	Ark.-Pine Bluff	02/16/02	41
Steve Logan, Cincinnati	Sr.	6-0	G	Southern Miss.	02/15/02	41
Casey Jacobsen, Stanford	Jr.	6-6	G	Oregon	02/07/02	41
Eric Channing, New Mexico St.	Sr.	6-4	G	North Texas	01/26/02	41
Jerry Green, UC Irvine	Sr.	6-3	G	Pepperdine	11/20/01	41
29. Chris Williams, Ball St.	Jr.	6-3	G	South Fla.	03/12/02	40
J Locklier, Washington St.	Sr.	6-9	C	Centenary (La.)	03/02/02	40

REBOUNDS

Name, Team	CL	Ht	Pos	Opponent	Date	REB
1. Andre Brown, DePaul	So.	6-9	F	TCU	02/06/02	27
Amien Hicks, Morris Brown	Jr.	6-6	F	Clark Atlanta	01/14/02	27
3. Jamal Brown, TCU	Jr.	6-7	F	North Texas	12/23/01	26
4. Nicholas Egland, Southern U.	Fr.	6-6	G	Ark.-Pine Bluff	01/12/02	25
5. Ellis Myles, Louisville	So.	6-7	F	Tennessee St.	12/01/01	23
6. Brandon Hunter, Ohio	Jr.	6-7	F	Marshall	02/16/02	22
7. Drew Gooden, Kansas	Jr.	6-10	F	Texas Tech	03/09/02	21
Curtis Borchardt, Stanford	Jr.	7-0	C	Arizona	02/02/02	21
Adam Sonn, Belmont	Jr.	6-8	C	UCF	01/17/02	21
Ryan Blankson, Loyola (Ill.)	Sr.	6-6	F	Cleveland St.	01/03/02	21
Drew Gooden, Kansas	Jr.	6-10	F	South Carolina St.	12/15/01	21
Theron Smith, Ball St.	Jr.	6-8	F	IPFW	12/06/01	21
13. Louis Truscott, Houston	Jr.	6-7	F	Tulane	02/19/02	20
Chris Brown, New Hampshire	Sr.	6-4	F	Boston U.	02/10/02	20
Mike Sweetney, Georgetown	So.	6-8	F	Notre Dame	02/09/02	20
Vili Morton, UC Riverside	So.	6-8	F	Long Beach St.	02/02/02	20
Paul Reed, UCF	Sr.	6-8	F	Marist	12/22/01	20
Cory Violette, Gonzaga	So.	6-8	C	Fresno St.	12/06/01	20
Amien Hicks, Morris Brown	Jr.	6-6	F	Boston College	12/04/01	20
Curtis Borchardt, Stanford	Jr.	7-0	C	Purdue	11/24/01	20
Andy Savtchenko, Radford	Sr.	7-0	C	Purdue	11/21/01	20
Rasual Butler, La Salle	Sr.	6-7	F	Morris Brown	11/18/01	20

STEALS

Name, Team	CL	Ht	Pos	Opponent	Date	ST
1. Jehiel Lewis, Navy	Sr.	6-3	G	Bucknell	01/12/02	12
2. Travis Demanby, Fresno St.	Jr.	6-4	G	Oklahoma St.	02/10/02	11
John Linehan, Providence	Sr.	5-9	G	Rutgers	01/22/02	11
Drew Schifino, West Virginia	Fr.	6-3	G	Ark. Monticello	12/01/01	11
Chris Thomas, Notre Dame	Fr.	6-1	G	New Hampshire	11/16/01	11
6. Desmond Cambridge, Alabama A&M	Sr.	6-0	G	Morris Brown	01/30/02	10
Altron Jackson, South Fla.	Sr.	6-6	F	Florida St.	01/02/02	10
8. Deshaun Williams, Syracuse	Jr.	6-3	G	Boston College	03/03/02	9
Steve Esterkamp, Ohio	Jr.	6-6	F	Marshall	02/02/02	9
John Linehan, Providence	Sr.	5-9	G	Boston College	02/02/02	9
Desmond Cambridge, Alabama A&M	Sr.	6-0	G	Prairie View	01/26/02	9

Jason Conley of VMI led the country in scoring average as a freshman last year.

Name, Team	CL	Ht	Pos	Opponent	Date	ST
James Thues, Syracuse	So.	5-10	G	Rutgers	01/02/02	9
13. Juan Dixon, Maryland	Sr.	6-3	G	Florida St.	02/26/02	8
D.J. Munir, Stony Brook	So.	6-3	G	Northeastern	02/17/02	8
Jeremy Sargent, Tenn.-Martin	Sr.	6-8	C	Eastern Ill.	02/16/02	8
Mire Chatman, Tex.-Pan American	Sr.	6-2	G	New Mexico St.	02/11/02	8
Carlos Morban, Florida Int'l	Fr.	6-2	G	La.-Lafayette	02/09/02	8
Pierre Wooten, Winthrop	Jr.	6-3	G	Radford	02/09/02	8
Carlos Morban, Florida Int'l	Fr.	6-2	G	South Ala.	01/23/02	8
Juan Dixon, Maryland	Sr.	6-3	G	North Carolina	01/09/02	8
John Linehan, Providence	Sr.	5-9	G	Texas	01/07/02	8
Von Damien Green, Manhattan	Sr.	5-10	G	Fordham	12/27/01	8
John Linehan, Providence	Sr.	5-9	G	Sacred Heart	12/19/01	8
Chauncey Bryant, McNeese St.	Sr.	5-9	G	La.-Monroe	12/01/01	8
Marcus Hatten, St. John's (N.Y.)	Jr.	6-1	G	Fordham	12/01/01	8
Marcus Hatten, St. John's (N.Y.)	Jr.	6-1	G	Tennessee	11/24/01	8
Mire Chatman, Tex.-Pan American	Sr.	6-2	G	Sul Ross St.	11/17/01	8

THREE-POINT FIELD GOAL PERCENTAGE
(Min. seven 3FGM)

Name, Team	CL	Opponent	Date	3FG%	3FG	3FGA
1. Nick Moore, Toledo	Jr.	Akron	02/13/02	100.0	7	7
Bronski Dockery, St. Francis (N.Y.)	Jr.	Central Conn. St.	12/03/01	100.0	7	7
Lionel Armstead, West Virginia	Sr.	Ark. Monticello	12/01/01	100.0	7	7
4. Marcus Bullock, New Hampshire	So.	Army	01/07/02	88.9	8	9
5. Adam Fellers, Campbell	Sr.	Fla. Atlantic	02/07/02	87.5	7	8
Robby Collum, Western Mich.	Jr.	Ohio	01/26/02	87.5	7	8
Jannero Pargo, Arkansas	Jr.	Florida	01/26/02	87.5	7	8
David Falknor, Akron	Sr.	Bowling Green	01/23/02	87.5	7	8
Jacques Vigneault, Cornell	Jr.	Yale	01/12/02	87.5	7	8
Anthony Thomas, Furman	Sr.	Methodist	11/28/01	87.5	7	8
Darius Lane, Seton Hall	Sr.	San Francisco	11/16/01	87.5	7	8
12. Cory Ryan, Bowling Green	Jr.	Defiance	11/24/01	85.7	6	7
13. Ronnie Jones, Wis.-Milwaukee	Jr.	Youngstown St.	01/02/02	83.3	10	12
14. Quentin Mitchell, Western Ill.	Sr.	Southern Utah	02/07/02	81.8	9	11
15. Marcus Bullock, New Hampshire	So.	Maine	02/14/02	80.0	8	10
Luke Spencer-Gardner, Oral Roberts	So.	Southern Utah	01/24/02	80.0	8	10
17. Chris Thomas, Notre Dame	Fr.	Rutgers	02/06/02	77.8	7	9
Josh Copperwood, Tennessee St.	Jr.	Morehead St.	01/28/02	77.8	7	9
Casey Frandsen, Portland	So.	Idaho St.	01/02/02	77.8	7	9
20. Markius Barnes, Oral Roberts	Sr.	UMKC	02/02/02	75.0	9	12

STATISTICAL LEADERS

Name, Team	CL	Opponent	Date	3FG%	3FG	3FGA
Dan Dickau, Gonzaga	Sr.	Loyola Marymount	01/19/02	75.0	9	12
Joe Shipp, California	Jr.	Fresno St.	12/11/01	75.0	9	12

THREE-POINT FIELD GOALS

Name, Team	CL	Ht	Pos	vs. Opponent	Date	3FG
1. Ronald Blackshear, Marshall	So.	6-5	G	Akron	03/01/02	14
2. Clarence Gilbert, Missouri	Sr.	6-2	G	Colorado	02/23/02	12
3. T.J. Sorrentine, Vermont	So.	5-11	G	Northeastern	01/17/02	11
4. Wes Burtner, Belmont	Sr.	6-5	F	Troy St.	02/09/02	10
Ronnie Jones, Wis.-Milwaukee ..	Jr.	5-9	G	Youngstown St.	01/02/02	10
Earnest Porter, Nicholls St.	Jr.	6-4	G	Troy St.	12/17/01	10
7. Quentin Mitchell, Western Ill. ...	Sr.	6-4	G	Southern Utah	02/07/02	9
Markius Barnes, Oral Roberts....	Sr.	6-3	G	UMKC	02/02/02	9
Eric Channing, New Mexico St.	Sr.	6-4	G	North Texas	01/26/02	9
Dan Dickau, Gonzaga	Sr.	6-0	G	Loyola Marymount	01/19/02	9
Travis Cantrell, Citadel	Sr.	6-2	G	Western Caro.	01/12/02	9
Joe Shipp, California	Jr.	6-5	F	Fresno St.	12/11/01	9
Douglas Ruben, New Mexico....	Jr.	6-5	G	Pacific (Cal.)	11/23/01	9

Name, Team	CL	Ht	Pos	vs. Opponent	Date	3FG
14. Clarence Gilbert, Missouri	Sr.	6-2	G	Iowa St.	03/07/02	8
John Humphrey, Middle Tenn. ..	Jr.	6-2	G	Western Ky.	02/23/02	8
Jerome Coleman, Rutgers..........	Jr.	6-2	G	Miami (Fla.)	02/17/02	8
Reggie Kohn, South Fla.	Jr.	6-1	G	TCU	02/16/02	8
Thomas Terrell, Georgia St.	Sr.	6-7	F	Troy St.	02/16/02	8
Steve Logan, Cincinnati	Sr.	6-0	G	Southern Miss.	02/15/02	8
Marcus Bullock, New Hampshire	So.	6-0	G	Maine	02/14/02	8
T.J. Sorrentine, Vermont	So.	5-11	G	Binghamton	02/13/02	8
Thomas Terrell, Georgia St.	Sr.	6-7	F	Fla. Atlantic	02/08/02	8
Dan Dickau, Gonzaga	Sr.	6-0	G	Portland	02/02/02	8
Luke Spencer-Gardner, Oral Roberts	So.	6-1	G	Southern Utah	01/24/02	8
Clarence Gilbert, Missouri	Sr.	6-2	G	Oklahoma	01/21/02	8
Steve Reynolds, Western Mich. .	Sr.	6-7	F	Kent St.	01/19/02	8
Abe Jackson, Boise St.	Sr.	6-7	F	Fresno St.	01/17/02	8
Matt Broermann, Indiana St.	Jr.	6-5	G	Wichita St.	01/16/02	8
David Bell, Montana	Jr.	6-1	G	Portland St.	01/12/02	8
Marcus Bullock, New Hampshire	So.	6-0	G	Army	01/07/02	8

Team Highs

FIELD-GOAL PERCENTAGE

Rank Team	Opponent	Date	FG%	FGM	FGA
1. UCLA	South Carolina	11/21/01	72.9	35	48
2. Air Force	Montana St.	11/30/01	71.4	25	35
3. Colorado St.	Denver	12/15/01	71.1	27	38
4. Houston	Tennessee	12/30/01	70.0	35	50
5. Brigham Young	Fort Lewis	12/12/01	69.6	39	56
6. Minnesota	Michigan	01/09/02	69.4	34	49
7. Samford	Stetson	01/05/02	69.0	29	42
8. Davidson	Oglethorpe	11/23/01	69.0	49	71
9. Wright St.	Wis.-Green Bay	01/19/02	68.8	33	48
10. Villanova	VMI	12/22/01	68.5	37	54

THREE-POINT FIELD-GOAL PERCENTAGE
(Minimum 10 3FGM)

Rank Team	Opponent	Date	3FG%	3FG	3FGA
1. Kent St.	Buffalo	01/22/02	76.5	13	17
2. Bowling Green	Defiance	11/24/01	75.0	12	16
3. New Hampshire	Maine	02/14/02	73.9	17	23
4. Centenary (La.	Tex.-Pan American	02/25/02	73.3	11	15
5. Houston	Memphis	03/07/02	71.4	10	14
Evansville	Northern Iowa	02/05/02	71.4	10	14
Holy Cross	Navy	02/02/02	71.4	10	14
Villanova	Virginia Tech	01/30/02	71.4	10	14
Utah	Pepperdine	12/01/01	71.4	10	14
10. Campbell	Mercer	01/02/02	70.6	12	17

THREE-POINT FIELD GOALS MADE

Rank Team	Opponent	Date	3FG
1. Missouri	Colorado	02/23/02	20
Nicholls St.	Troy St.	12/17/01	20
3. Louisville	South Fla.	02/01/02	19
St. Bonaventure	Temple	01/16/02	19
5. Richmond	Duquesne	03/02/02	18
Nebraska	Kansas	02/24/02	18
Temple	Fordham	01/30/02	18
Lafayette	Howard	12/30/01	18
Cincinnati	La.-Monroe	12/20/01	18
10. St. Bonaventure	Richmond	03/07/02	17

FREE-THROW PERCENTAGE
(Minimum 15 Made)

Rank Team	Opponent	Date	FT%	FT	FTA
1. Southern California	Oregon	03/08/02	100.0	22	22
Western Caro.	Davidson	01/02/02	100.0	21	21
Maine	Vermont	01/11/02	100.0	18	18
Central Conn. St.	Robert Morris	02/04/02	100.0	16	16
La Salle	George Washington	01/13/02	100.0	16	16
Tulsa	Buffalo	12/20/01	100.0	16	16
7. Richmond	La Salle	01/05/02	96.7	29	30
8. Temple	St. Joseph`s	02/02/02	96.3	26	27
9. Miami (Fla.)	Boston College	01/29/02	96.2	25	26
10. Oregon St.	Washington St.	02/23/02	95.5	21	22

HOME-COURT STREAKS THAT ENDED IN 2002

Rank When Lost Team	Lost To	Date Lost	Score	Streak
1. Michigan St.	Wisconsin	01/12/02	63-64	53
1. Detroit	Wis.-Green Bay	02/11/02	61-65	39
2. Iowa St.	San Jose St.	12/01/01	62-64	39
3. Utah St.	UC Irvine	01/10/02	66-67	31
3. Illinois	Michigan St.	02/03/02	61-67	28
5. Boston College	Pittsburgh	01/05/02	74-77	25
4. Fresno St.	Louisiana Tech	01/26/02	64-71	25
6. Georgia St.	Jacksonville	01/12/02	72-84	25
5. Col. of Charleston	Belmont Abbey	12/08/01	67-70	24
4. Southern Utah	UC Riverside	12/08/01	64-66	24

POINTS

Rank	Team	Opponent	Date	PTS
1.	Sacred Heart	Fairleigh Dickinson	12/01/01	133
	Western Caro.	Toccoa Falls Inst.	11/26/01	133
3.	Fairleigh Dickinson	Sacred Heart	12/01/01	130
4.	Long Island	Fairleigh Dickinson	02/23/02	122
5.	UNLV	New Mexico	03/07/02	120
6.	Kentucky	Kentucky St.	12/15/01	118
7.	New Mexico	UNLV	03/07/02	117
	South Fla.	TCU	01/05/02	117
	Missouri	Southern U.	12/06/01	117
10.	Kent St.	Marshall	02/19/02	116

WINNING STREAKS THAT ENDED IN 2002

Rank When Lost	Team	Lost To	Date Lost	Score	Streak
1.	Duke	at Florida St.	01/06/02	76-77	22
1.	Kent St.	Indiana	03/23/02	69-81	21
1.	Cincinnati	at Marquette	02/02/02	60-74	20
1.	Central Conn. St.	Pittsburgh	03/15/02	54-71	19
2.	Western Ky.	Stanford	03/14/02	68-84	18

2002 Division I Team Leaders

Scoring Offense

Team	GM	W-L	PTS	PPG
1. Kansas	37	33-4	3365	90.9
2. Duke	35	31-4	3112	88.9
3. Oregon	35	26-9	2994	85.5
4. TCU	31	16-15	2645	85.3
5. Maryland	36	32-4	3060	85.0
6. Arizona	34	24-10	2793	82.1
7. Wake Forest	34	21-13	2789	82.0
8. East Tenn. St.	28	18-10	2281	81.5
9. Wagner	29	19-10	2362	81.4
10. Pepperdine	31	22-9	2519	81.3
11. Gonzaga	33	0-0	2677	81.1
12. Georgetown	30	19-11	2433	81.1
13. Stanford	30	20-10	2420	80.7
14. St. Bonaventure	30	17-13	2416	80.5
15. Florida	31	22-9	2495	80.5
16. St. Francis (N.Y.)	29	18-11	2327	80.2
17. Tulsa	34	27-7	2726	80.2
18. Memphis	36	27-9	2879	80.0
19. Alabama A&M	29	19-10	2318	79.9
20. Missouri	36	24-12	2877	79.9
21. Alcorn St.	31	21-10	2473	79.8
22. Colorado	29	15-14	2312	79.7
23. Ga. Southern	28	16-12	2230	79.6
24. Tex.-Pan American	30	20-10	2389	79.6
25. Virginia	29	17-12	2308	79.6
26. Hampton	33	26-7	2623	79.5
27. Texas Tech	32	23-9	2532	79.1
28. Quinnipiac	30	14-16	2370	79.0
29. Notre Dame	33	22-11	2601	78.8
30. Tennessee Tech	34	27-7	2675	78.7

Scoring Margin

Team	GM	W-L	PTS
1. Duke	35	31-4	3112
2. Cincinnati	35	31-4	2738
3. Kansas	37	33-4	3365
4. Gonzaga	33	0-0	2677
5. Maryland	36	32-4	3060
6. Florida	31	22-9	2495
7. Oklahoma	36	31-5	2807
8. Western Ky.	32	28-4	2491
9. Oregon	35	26-9	2994
10. Butler	32	26-6	2251
11. Marquette	33	26-7	2413
12. Kent St.	36	30-6	2732
13. Valparaiso	33	25-8	2564
14. Pittsburgh	35	29-6	2530
15. Memphis	36	27-9	2879
16. Tennessee Tech	34	27-7	2675
17. Georgetown	30	19-11	2433
18. Tulsa	34	27-7	2726
19. Notre Dame	33	22-11	2601
20. Xavier	32	26-6	2317
21. Illinois	35	26-9	2708
22. Pennsylvania	32	25-7	2342
23. Dayton	32	21-11	2339
24. Alabama	35	27-8	2658
25. Utah St.	31	23-8	2076
26. Ohio St.	32	24-8	2362
27. Hawaii	33	27-6	2367
28. Kentucky	32	22-10	2460
29. East Tenn. St.	28	18-10	2281
30. Col. of Charleston	30	21-9	2082

Rebound Margin

Team	GM	W-L
1. Gonzaga	33	0-0
2. Louisiana Tech	32	22-10
3. Kansas	37	33-4
4. Stanford	30	20-10
5. Dayton	32	21-11

Team	GM	W-L
6. Michigan St.	31	19-12
7. Wyoming	31	22-9
8. Tennessee Tech	34	27-7
9. Central Conn. St.	32	27-5
10. Virginia Tech	28	10-18
11. Memphis	36	27-9
12. Utah St.	31	23-8
13. Mississippi St.	35	27-8
14. Colorado	29	15-14
15. Western Ky.	32	28-4
16. Oklahoma St.	32	23-9
17. Pittsburgh	35	29-6
18. Cincinnati	35	31-4
19. Oklahoma	36	31-5
20. Vermont	29	21-8
21. Murray St.	32	19-13
22. Ga. Southern	28	16-12
23. Holy Cross	33	18-15
24. Kentucky	32	22-10
Villanova	32	19-13
26. Jacksonville	30	18-12
27. Iowa	35	19-16
28. Clemson	30	13-17
29. Southwest Mo. St.	32	17-15
30. Weber St.	29	18-11

Blocked Shots Per Game

Team	GM	W-L	BLKS	BKPG
1. Connecticut	34	27-7	236	6.9
2. Rutgers	31	18-13	215	6.9
3. Fairfield	29	12-17	199	6.9
4. La.-Monroe	32	20-12	217	6.8
5. Georgetown	30	19-11	191	6.4
6. Maine	30	12-18	182	6.1
7. Maryland	36	32-4	216	6.0
8. Miami (Fla.)	32	24-8	190	5.9
9. Chattanooga	30	16-14	175	5.8
10. Kansas	37	33-4	210	5.7
11. Northwestern St.	31	13-18	175	5.6
12. Syracuse	36	23-13	201	5.6
13. Fresno St.	34	19-15	187	5.5
Va. Commonwealth	32	21-11	176	5.5
15. Auburn	28	12-16	151	5.4
16. Arkansas St.	31	15-16	166	5.4
17. Indiana	37	25-12	192	5.2
18. Radford	31	15-16	160	5.2
19. La.-Lafayette	31	20-11	159	5.1
Pepperdine	31	22-9	159	5.1
21. Iona	30	13-17	153	5.1
McNeese St.	30	21-9	153	5.1
23. Jacksonville	30	18-12	152	5.1
24. Oral Roberts	31	17-14	156	5.0
25. Virginia Tech	28	10-18	139	5.0
26. Notre Dame	33	22-11	163	4.9
27. Murray St.	32	19-13	158	4.9
28. Col. of Charleston	30	21-9	146	4.9
29. Grambling	28	9-19	136	4.9
Sam Houston St.	28	14-14	136	4.9

Assists Per Game

Team	GM	W-L	AST	APG
1. Kansas	37	33-4	767	20.7
2. Maryland	36	32-4	714	19.8
3. Notre Dame	33	22-11	629	19.1
4. Texas Tech	32	23-9	588	18.4
5. Belmont	28	11-17	506	18.1
6. Duke	35	31-4	625	17.9
7. Quinnipiac	30	14-16	530	17.7
8. Pennsylvania	32	25-7	561	17.5
9. Colorado	29	15-14	508	17.5
10. South Fla.	32	19-13	555	17.3
11. Valparaiso	33	25-8	570	17.3
12. Tulsa	34	27-7	586	17.2
13. Wagner	29	19-10	498	17.2
14. Baylor	30	14-16	514	17.1
15. Dayton	32	21-11	546	17.1
16. Sam Houston St.	28	14-14	477	17.0
17. North Carolina	28	8-20	476	17.0
18. Illinois	35	26-9	590	16.9
Pittsburgh	35	29-6	590	16.9
20. Jackson St.	28	9-19	471	16.8
21. Florida	31	22-9	519	16.7
22. Tennessee Tech	34	27-7	569	16.7
23. Portland St.	28	12-16	468	16.7
24. TCU	31	16-15	517	16.7
25. Brown	27	17-10	448	16.6
26. Oregon	35	26-9	580	16.6
27. Hawaii	33	27-6	546	16.5
28. DePaul	28	9-19	463	16.5
29. Morehead St.	29	18-11	476	16.4
Wis.-Milwaukee	29	16-13	476	16.4

Steals Per Game

Team	GM	W-L	ST	STPG
1. Alabama A&M	29	19-10	395	13.6
2. Ark.-Pine Bluff	28	2-26	311	11.1
3. Providence	31	15-16	342	11.0
4. Syracuse	36	23-13	394	10.9
5. Tenn.-Martin	29	15-14	310	10.7
6. Arkansas	29	14-15	306	10.6
7. Rutgers	31	18-13	324	10.5
8. Cal St. Northridge	28	12-16	289	10.3
9. VMI	28	10-18	287	10.3
10. Tennessee St.	28	11-17	286	10.2
11. Valparaiso	33	25-8	334	10.1
12. Georgetown	30	19-11	303	10.1
13. St. John's (N.Y.)	32	20-12	323	10.1
14. Duke	35	31-4	351	10.0
15. Stetson	26	10-16	259	10.0
16. Florida	31	22-9	307	9.9
17. Manhattan	29	20-9	286	9.9
18. UNLV	32	21-11	315	9.8
19. Northeastern	28	7-21	272	9.7
20. St. Bonaventure	30	17-13	291	9.7
21. Kansas	37	33-4	357	9.6
22. South Carolina	37	22-15	356	9.6
23. St. Francis (N.Y.)	29	18-11	278	9.6
24. Oakland	30	17-13	287	9.6
25. Florida Int'l	30	10-20	286	9.5
26. Fla. Atlantic	31	19-12	294	9.5
27. Tex.-Pan American	30	20-10	284	9.5
28. Troy St.	28	18-10	265	9.5
29. Ark.-Little Rock	29	18-11	271	9.3
30. Southern Utah	27	11-16	252	9.3

Scoring Defense

Team	GM	W-L	OPP PTS	OPP PPG
1. Columbia	28	11-17	1596	57.0
2. Princeton	28	16-12	1606	57.4
3. Butler	32	26-6	1849	57.8
4. Utah St.	31	23-8	1800	58.1
5. Northwestern	29	16-13	1715	59.1
6. Holy Cross	33	18-15	1968	59.6
7. Samford	29	15-14	1748	60.3
8. Cincinnati	35	31-4	2115	60.4
9. Marquette	33	26-7	2004	60.7
10. Col. of Charleston	30	21-9	1824	60.8
11. UC Santa Barb.	31	20-11	1889	60.9
12. Pittsburgh	35	29-6	2133	60.9
13. Utah	30	21-9	1839	61.3
14. Richmond	36	22-14	2213	61.5
15. Air Force	28	9-19	1722	61.5
16. South Carolina	37	22-15	2279	61.6
17. UNC Wilmington	33	23-10	2034	61.6
18. UMKC	29	18-11	1796	61.9
19. St. Louis	31	15-16	1939	62.5
20. Xavier	32	26-6	2003	62.6

Team	GM	W-L	OPP PTS	OPP PPG
21. Indiana	37	25-12	2316	62.6
22. Southeastern La.	27	7-20	1697	62.9
23. Idaho	28	9-19	1764	63.0
24. Hawaii	33	27-6	2081	63.1
25. Central Conn. St.	32	27-5	2018	63.1
26. McNeese St.	30	21-9	1909	63.6
27. Delaware St.	29	16-13	1846	63.7
28. Pennsylvania	32	25-7	2039	63.7
29. Dayton	32	21-11	2040	63.8
30. Michigan St.	31	19-12	1978	63.8

Field-Goal Percentage Defense

Team	GM	W-L	OPP FG	OPP FGA	OPP FG%
1. Va. Commonwealth	32	21-11	767	2052	37.4
2. Cincinnati	35	31-4	761	2035	37.4
3. Col. of Charleston	30	21-9	663	1762	37.6
4. Davidson	31	21-10	692	1822	38.0
5. Connecticut	34	27-7	830	2182	38.0
6. UC Santa Barb.	31	20-11	623	1625	38.3
7. Gonzaga	33	0-0	773	2006	38.5
8. Boston U.	32	22-10	687	1760	39.0
9. Villanova	32	19-13	739	1883	39.2
10. La.-Lafayette	31	20-11	709	1803	39.3
11. Utah St.	31	23-8	655	1665	39.3
12. Siena	36	17-19	817	2076	39.4
13. Memphis	36	27-9	864	2190	39.5
14. Pittsburgh	35	29-6	765	1937	39.5
15. Rutgers	31	18-13	713	1805	39.5
16. Georgetown	30	19-11	759	1920	39.5
17. Michigan St.	31	19-12	684	1730	39.5
18. Notre Dame	33	22-11	835	2102	39.7
19. Detroit	31	18-13	676	1701	39.7
20. Syracuse	36	23-13	809	2028	39.9
21. Maryland	36	32-4	920	2304	39.9
22. Dayton	32	21-11	717	1793	40.0
23. Xavier	32	26-6	753	1883	40.0
24. Miami (Fla.)	32	24-8	754	1885	40.0
25. Fresno St.	34	19-15	871	2174	40.1
26. Marquette	33	26-7	706	1758	40.2
27. Kansas	37	33-4	991	2467	40.2
28. Hofstra	32	12-20	771	1918	40.2
29. Auburn	28	12-16	653	1624	40.2
30. Columbia	28	11-17	553	1374	40.2

Field-Goal Percentage

Team	GM	W-L	FGM	FGA	FG%
1. Kansas	37	33-4	1259	2487	50.6
2. Duke	35	31-4	1093	2209	49.5
3. Bowling Green	33	24-9	834	1709	48.8
4. Oregon	35	26-9	1014	2082	48.7
5. Ohio St.	32	24-8	825	1702	48.5
6. Ohio	28	17-11	741	1531	48.4
7. Morehead St.	29	18-11	796	1647	48.3
8. Connecticut	34	27-7	972	2012	48.3
9. Maryland	36	32-4	1083	2248	48.2
10. Hampton	33	26-7	933	1940	48.1
11. Tennessee Tech	34	27-7	915	1906	48.0
12. Mississippi St.	35	27-8	943	1965	48.0
13. Wright St.	28	17-11	698	1455	48.0
14. Pennsylvania	32	25-7	815	1701	47.9
15. Wake Forest	34	21-13	1001	2094	47.8
16. Portland St.	28	12-16	723	1513	47.8
17. Samford	29	15-14	614	1285	47.8
18. Wis.-Green Bay	30	9-21	684	1434	47.7
19. Tex.-Pan American	30	20-10	847	1776	47.7
20. Colorado St.	30	12-18	731	1533	47.7
21. Tulsa	34	27-7	961	2016	47.7
22. San Diego St.	33	21-12	906	1902	47.6
23. UC Irvine	32	21-11	783	1652	47.4
24. Houston	33	18-15	828	1749	47.3
25. Marquette	33	26-7	871	1841	47.3
26. Eastern Wash.	30	17-13	706	1496	47.2
27. UCLA	33	21-12	902	1912	47.2
28. Marshall	30	15-15	824	1751	47.1
29. Utah St.	31	23-8	751	1596	47.1
30. Belmont	28	11-17	698	1484	47.0

Free-Throw Percentage

Team	GM	W-L	FT	FTA	FT%
1. Morehead St.	29	18-11	485	619	78.4
2. Loyola Marymount	29	9-20	466	600	77.7
3. Illinois St.	31	17-14	427	551	77.5
4. Miami (Fla.)	32	24-8	523	678	77.1
5. Michigan St.	31	19-12	442	573	77.1
6. Oregon	35	26-9	662	861	76.9
7. Oklahoma	36	31-5	549	716	76.7
8. Southeast Mo. St.	28	6-22	428	560	76.4
9. Brigham Young	30	18-12	523	688	76.0
10. UMKC	29	18-11	361	475	76.0
11. St. Bonaventure	30	17-13	514	677	75.9
12. Akron	31	10-21	554	731	75.8
13. UC Santa Barb.	31	20-11	479	634	75.6
14. North Carolina St.	34	23-11	561	743	75.5
15. Belmont	28	11-17	360	477	75.5
16. Michigan	29	11-18	384	509	75.4
17. Ball St.	35	23-12	567	752	75.4
18. Brown	27	17-10	494	656	75.3
19. Tulsa	34	27-7	545	724	75.3
20. Southwest Mo. St.	32	17-15	490	651	75.3
21. Bowling Green	33	24-9	593	791	75.0
22. Iowa St.	31	15-14	458	613	74.7
23. Lafayette	29	15-14	458	613	74.7
24. UNC Greensboro	31	20-11	524	702	74.6
25. Marist	28	19-9	468	627	74.6
26. Siena	36	17-19	561	754	74.4
27. Pacific (Cal.)	30	20-10	464	624	74.4
28. Portland St.	28	12-16	361	486	74.3
29. Miami (Ohio)	31	13-18	418	563	74.2
30. Villanova	32	19-13	509	686	74.2

Three-Point Field Goals Made Per Game

Team	GM	W-L	3FG	3PG
1. St. Bonaventure	30	17-13	314	10.5
2. Dartmouth	27	9-18	263	9.7
3. Nebraska	28	13-15	267	9.5
4. Belmont	28	11-17	264	9.4
5. Troy St.	28	18-10	258	9.2
6. Baylor	30	14-16	273	9.1
7. Missouri	36	24-12	326	9.1
8. Mississippi Val.	29	12-17	258	8.9
9. Wis.-Milwaukee	29	16-13	257	8.9
10. Ball St.	35	23-12	310	8.9
11. Vanderbilt	32	17-15	282	8.8
12. Temple	34	19-15	298	8.8
13. Butler	32	26-6	280	8.8
14. Western Ky.	32	28-4	279	8.7
15. Oregon	35	26-9	304	8.7
16. Duke	35	31-4	301	8.6
17. Samford	29	15-14	249	8.6
18. Southern U.	27	7-20	230	8.5
19. Georgia Tech	31	15-16	261	8.4
20. Marshall	30	15-15	252	8.4
21. Valparaiso	33	25-8	275	8.3
22. Portland	28	12-16	233	8.3
23. Pennsylvania	32	25-7	266	8.3
24. Charlotte	30	18-12	247	8.2
Seton Hall	30	12-18	247	8.2
26. North Carolina St.	34	23-11	278	8.2
27. Louisville	32	19-13	261	8.2
28. Portland	30	6-24	242	8.1
29. Davidson	31	21-10	249	8.0
30. Western Mich.	30	17-13	240	8.0

Three-Point Field-Goal Percentage

Team	GM	W-L	3FG	3FGA	3FG%
1. Marshall	30	15-15	252	595	42.4
2. Oregon	35	26-9	304	721	42.2
3. Kansas	37	33-4	224	536	41.8
4. Indiana	37	25-12	270	659	41.0
5. Portland St.	28	12-16	233	570	40.9
6. UCF	29	17-12	200	492	40.7
7. Southwest Mo. St.	32	17-15	201	495	40.6
8. Utah	30	21-9	236	582	40.5
9. Ill.-Chicago	34	20-14	251	619	40.5
10. Tulsa	34	27-7	259	639	40.5
11. Wright St.	28	17-11	222	548	40.5
12. UC Santa Barb.	31	20-11	201	499	40.3
13. Pennsylvania	32	25-7	266	668	39.8
14. Southwest Tex. St.	28	12-16	215	541	39.7
15. Brigham Young	30	18-12	170	428	39.7
16. Wis.-Green Bay	30	9-21	189	477	39.6
17. Connecticut	34	27-7	154	391	39.4
18. Southern Utah	27	11-16	195	496	39.3
19. Michigan St.	31	19-12	180	458	39.3
20. Weber St.	29	18-11	191	486	39.3
21. Villanova	32	19-13	187	477	39.2
22. Dartmouth	27	9-18	263	671	39.2
23. Gonzaga	33	0-0	237	606	39.1
24. Missouri	36	24-12	326	834	39.1
25. Bowling Green	33	24-9	203	520	39.0
26. Drake	29	14-15	232	595	39.0
27. UCLA	33	21-12	223	572	39.0
28. Oral Roberts	31	17-14	218	560	38.9
29. Centenary (La.)	27	14-13	169	438	38.6
30. Eastern Wash.	30	17-13	177	460	38.5

Turnovers Per Game

Team	GM	W-L	TO	TOPG
1. Butler	32	26-6	322	10.1
2. Richmond	36	22-14	370	10.3
3. Temple	34	19-15	356	10.5
4. UMKC	29	18-11	314	10.8
5. Kent St.	36	30-6	391	10.9
6. Nebraska	28	13-15	317	11.3
7. St. Bonaventure	30	17-13	347	11.6
8. Detroit	31	18-13	364	11.7
9. Marist	28	19-9	329	11.8
10. Oklahoma	36	31-5	427	11.9
11. Cincinnati	35	31-4	416	11.9
12. Southern California	32	22-10	389	12.2
13. Miami (Ohio)	31	13-18	377	12.2
14. UNC Wilmington	33	23-10	403	12.2
15. St. Joseph's	31	19-12	381	12.3
16. Hawaii	33	27-6	407	12.3
17. Texas Tech	32	23-9	397	12.4
18. Denver	28	8-20	349	12.5
19. Northern Iowa	29	14-15	364	12.6
20. Ball St.	35	23-12	443	12.7
21. Dartmouth	27	9-18	344	12.8
22. Wofford	29	11-18	371	12.8
23. Ill.-Chicago	34	20-14	435	12.8
24. Tulsa	34	27-7	436	12.8
25. Delaware St.	29	16-13	372	12.8
26. Canisius	30	10-20	387	12.9
27. Idaho	28	9-19	362	12.9
28. Wisconsin	32	19-13	414	12.9
29. Drexel	28	14-14	363	13.0
30. Boston U.	32	22-10	415	13.0

Won-Lost Percentage

Team	W	L	Pct
1. Kansas	33	4	89.2
2. Maryland	32	4	88.9
3. Cincinnati	31	4	88.6
Duke	31	4	88.6
5. Western Ky.	28	4	87.5
6. Oklahoma	31	5	86.1
7. Central Conn. St.	27	5	84.4
8. Kent St.	30	6	83.3
9. Pittsburgh	29	6	82.9
10. Hawaii	27	6	81.8
11. Butler	26	6	81.3
Xavier	26	6	81.3
13. Connecticut	27	7	79.4
Tennessee Tech	27	7	79.4
Tulsa	27	7	79.4
16. Hampton	26	7	78.8
Marquette	26	7	78.8
18. Pennsylvania	25	7	78.1
19. Southern Ill.	28	8	77.8
20. Alabama	27	8	77.1

Team	W	L	Pct
Mississippi St.	27	8	77.1
22. Valparaiso	25	8	75.8
23. Memphis	27	9	75.0
Miami (Fla.)	24	8	75.0

Team	W	L	Pct
Ohio St.	24	8	75.0
26. Illinois	26	9	74.3
Oregon	26	9	74.3

Team	W	L	Pct
28. Utah St.	23	8	74.2
29. Bowling Green	24	9	72.7
30. Vermont	21	8	72.4

2003 Division I Top Returnees

Career Totals

MOST POINTS

Seniors	Ht.	Yrs.	G	FG	3FG	FT	Pts.	Avg.
1. Troy Bell, Boston College	6-1	3	91	537	194	583	1,851	20.3
2. Henry Domercant, Eastern Ill.	6-3	3	91	609	201	373	1,792	19.7
3. Chris Davis, North Texas	6-5	3	84	598	161	387	1,744	20.8
4. Chris Monroe, George Washington	6-3	3	89	491	144	535	1,661	18.7
5. Jason Kapono, UCLA	6-8	3	98	528	253	299	1,608	16.4
6. Jermaine Hall, Wagner	6-5	3	85	641	9	301	1,592	18.7
7. Theron Smith, Ball St.	6-8	3	96	543	116	351	1,553	16.2
8. Earl Hunt, Brown	6-4	3	81	521	112	372	1,526	18.8
9. Jason Gardner, Arizona	5-10	3	104	429	252	402	1,512	14.5
10. Brett Blizzard, UNC Wilmington	6-4	3	94	490	262	247	1,489	15.8

Juniors	Ht.	Yrs.	G	FG	3FG	FT	Pts.	Avg.
1. Ricky Minard, Morehead St.	6-4	2	56	381	127	208	1,097	19.6
2. Michael Watson, UMKC	6-0	2	59	378	177	135	1,068	18.1
3. Jarvis Hayes, Georgia	6-6	2	57	390	103	134	1,017	17.8
4. Mike Sweetney, Georgetown	6-8	2	62	344	0	286	974	15.7
4. T.J. Sorrentine, Vermont	5-11	2	58	318	160	178	974	16.8
6. Luke McDonald, Drake	6-5	2	57	305	177	143	930	16.3
7. Paul Haynes, Grambling	6-8	2	54	317	78	215	927	17.2
8. Mike Helms, Oakland	6-0	2	58	292	59	224	867	14.9
9. Mark Bigelow, Brigham Young	6-6	2	58	270	109	217	866	14.9
10. Jameer Nelson, St. Joseph's	6-0	2	63	275	92	202	844	13.4
10. Todd Billet, Virginia	6-0	2	58	271	158	144	844	14.6

SCORING AVERAGE

Seniors (Min. 1,200 Pts.)	Ht.	Yrs.	G	FG	3FG	FT	Pts.	Avg.
1. Chris Davis, North Texas	6-5	3	84	598	161	387	1,744	20.8
2. Troy Bell, Boston College	6-1	3	91	537	194	583	1,851	20.3
3. Henry Domercant, Eastern Ill.	6-3	3	91	609	201	373	1,792	19.7
4. Earl Hunt, Brown	6-4	3	81	521	112	372	1,526	18.8
5. Jermaine Hall, Wagner	6-5	3	85	641	9	301	1,592	18.7
6. Chris Monroe, George Washington	6-3	3	89	491	144	535	1,661	18.7
7. Jason Kapono, UCLA	6-8	3	98	528	253	299	1,608	16.4
8. Karim Souchu, Furman	6-7	3	86	549	113	199	1,410	16.4
9. Darrell Tucker, San Francisco	6-9	3	85	491	73	325	1,380	16.2
10. Theron Smith, Ball St.	6-8	3	96	543	116	351	1,553	16.2

Juniors (Min. 800 Pts.)	Ht.	Yrs.	G	FG	3FG	FT	Pts.	Avg.
1. Ricky Minard, Morehead St.	6-4	2	56	381	127	208	1,097	19.6
2. Michael Watson, UMKC	6-0	2	59	378	177	135	1,068	18.1
3. Jarvis Hayes, Georgia	6-6	2	57	390	103	134	1,017	17.8
4. Paul Haynes, Grambling	6-8	2	54	317	78	215	927	17.2
5. T.J. Sorrentine, Vermont	5-11	2	58	318	160	178	974	16.8
6. Luke McDonald, Drake	6-5	2	57	305	177	143	930	16.3
7. Mike Sweetney, Georgetown	6-8	2	62	344	0	286	974	15.7
8. Mike Helms, Oakland	6-0	2	58	292	59	224	867	14.9
9. Mark Bigelow, Brigham Young	6-6	2	58	270	109	217	866	14.9
10. Todd Billet, Virginia	6-0	2	58	271	158	144	844	14.6

HIGHEST FIELD-GOAL PERCENTAGE

Seniors (Min. 300 FGM)	Ht.	Yrs.	G	FG	FGA	Pct.
1. Jermaine Hall, Wagner	6-5	3	85	641	1,108	57.9
2. Nick Collison, Kansas	6-9	3	104	577	1,019	56.6
3. Kevin Johnson, Tulsa	6-7	3	99	411	726	56.6
4. Alai Nuualiitia, Brown	6-7	3	81	359	663	54.1
5. David West, Xavier	6-9	3	94	513	951	53.9
6. Erwin Dudley, Alabama	6-8	3	100	526	988	53.2
7. Travis Watson, Virginia	6-8	3	88	435	840	51.8
8. Mike Manciel, Central Mich.	6-5	3	72	306	598	51.2

	Ht.	Yrs.	G	FG	FGA	Pct.
9. Alvin Pettway, Alabama St.	6-9	3	88	359	705	50.9
10. Kirk Hinrich, Kansas	6-3	3	104	383	759	50.5

Juniors (Min. 240 FGM)	Ht.	Yrs.	G	FG	FGA	Pct.
1. Henry Williams, South Ala.	6-6	2	61	248	431	57.5
2. James Moore, New Mexico St.	6-8	2	60	304	535	56.8
3. Mike Sweetney, Georgetown	6-8	2	62	344	634	54.3
4. Mario Austin, Mississippi St.	6-9	2	66	308	582	52.9
5. Ricky Minard, Morehead St.	6-4	2	56	381	770	49.5
6. Andre Emmett, Texas Tech	6-5	2	60	325	676	48.1
7. Justin Reed, Mississippi	6-8	2	66	327	683	47.9
8. Luke McDonald, Drake	6-5	2	57	305	646	47.2
9. Jack Sullivan, Iowa St.	6-1	2	59	255	552	46.2
10. Jameer Nelson, St. Joseph's	6-0	2	63	275	613	44.9

MOST THREE-POINT FIELD GOALS MADE PER GAME

Seniors (Min. 120 3FGM)	Ht.	Yrs.	G	3FG	Avg.
1. Brett Blizzard, UNC Wilmington	6-4	3	94	262	2.79
2. Gary Buchanan, Villanova	6-3	3	96	249	2.59
3. Brian Chase, Virginia Tech	5-10	3	75	194	2.59
4. Jason Kapono, UCLA	6-8	3	98	253	2.58
5. Clay Tucker, Wis.-Milwaukee	6-4	3	82	210	2.56
6. Jason Gardner, Arizona	5-10	3	104	252	2.42
7. Brett Nelson, Florida	6-3	3	99	228	2.30
8. Henry Domercant, Eastern Ill.	6-3	3	91	201	2.21
9. Troy Bell, Boston College	6-1	3	91	194	2.13
10. Jason Coleman, McNeese St.	6-3	3	87	180	2.07

Juniors (Min. 80 3FGM)	Ht.	Yrs.	G	3FG	Avg.
1. E.J. Gallup, Albany (N.Y.)	6-4	2	37	123	3.32
2. Luke McDonald, Drake	6-5	2	57	177	3.11
3. Michael Watson, UMKC	6-0	2	59	177	3.00
4. Nick Zachery, Ark.-Little Rock	6-3	2	46	134	2.91
5. T.J. Sorrentine, Vermont	5-11	2	58	160	2.76
6. Todd Billet, Virginia	6-0	2	58	158	2.72
7. Casey Frandsen, Portland	6-3	2	40	98	2.45
8. Ricky Cottrill, Eastern Mich.	6-0	2	41	99	2.41
9. Ricky Minard, Morehead St.	6-4	2	56	127	2.27
10. Brendan Plavich, Vanderbilt	6-2	2	62	134	2.16

HIGHEST THREE-POINT FIELD-GOAL PERCENTAGE

Seniors (Min. 120 3FGM)	Ht.	Yrs.	G	3FG	3FGA	Pct.
1. Jason Kapono, UCLA	6-8	3	98	253	549	46.1
2. Kirk Hinrich, Kansas	6-3	3	104	146	327	44.6
3. Nick Moore, Toledo	6-1	3	93	187	419	44.6
4. Dante Swanson, Tulsa	5-10	3	107	161	367	43.9
5. Peter Anderer, Davidson	6-1	3	73	133	312	42.6
6. Brian Chase, Virginia Tech	5-10	3	75	194	463	41.9
7. Brett Blizzard, UNC Wilmington	6-4	3	94	262	629	41.7
8. Douglas Ruben, New Mexico	6-5	2	85	153	377	40.6
9. Henry Domercant, Eastern Ill.	6-3	3	91	201	506	39.7
10. Gary Buchanan, Villanova	6-3	3	96	249	632	39.4

Juniors (Min. 80 3FGM)	Ht.	Yrs.	G	3FG	3FGA	Pct.
1. Jack Sullivan, Iowa St.	6-1	2	59	121	263	46.0
2. Mike Ames, Delaware	6-3	2	57	92	207	44.4
3. Luke McDonald, Drake	6-5	2	57	177	401	44.1
4. Cameron Crisp, Tennessee Tech	6-3	2	63	85	194	43.8
5. Brian Conklin, Nebraska	6-11	2	58	88	204	43.1
6. John Hamilton, Weber St.	6-3	2	58	107	250	42.8
7. Nick Jacobson, Utah	6-4	2	61	108	257	42.0
8. Marquess Green, St. Bonaventure	5-7	2	58	89	215	41.4
9. Steve Drabyn, Belmont	6-0	2	53	107	259	41.3
10. Mark Bigelow, Brigham Young	6-6	2	58	109	267	40.8

HIGHEST FREE-THROW PERCENTAGE

Seniors (Min. 175 FTM)	Ht.	Yrs.	G	FG	FGA	Pct.
1. Gary Buchanan, Villanova	6-3	3	96	278	300	92.7
2. Brent Jolly, Tennessee Tech	6-5	3	91	226	248	91.1
3. Troy Bell, Boston College	6-1	3	91	583	665	87.7
4. Henry Domercant, Eastern Ill.	6-3	3	91	373	434	85.9
5. Jason Kapono, UCLA	6-8	3	98	299	366	81.7
6. LaVell Blanchard, Michigan	6-7	3	85	274	337	81.3
7. Kirk Hinrich, Kansas	6-3	3	104	200	246	81.3
8. Ravii Givens, Stetson	5-9	3	80	228	281	81.1
9. Earl Hunt, Brown	6-4	3	81	372	463	80.3
10. Douglas Ruben, New Mexico	6-5	2	85	266	338	78.7
Juniors (Min. 110 FTM)						
1. Jack Sullivan, Iowa St.	6-1	2	59	168	188	89.4
2. James Gillingham, Bradley	6-4	2	60	212	245	86.5
3. Luke McDonald, Drake	6-5	2	57	143	166	86.1
4. Curtis Allen, Washington	6-0	2	59	134	157	85.4
5. Ricky Cottrill, Eastern Mich.	6-0	2	41	164	193	85.0
6. D.J. Munir, Stony Brook	6-3	2	56	172	203	84.7
7. Luis Flores, Manhattan	6-2	2	58	199	236	84.3
8. Marquess Green, St. Bonaventure	5-7	2	58	154	183	84.2
9. Luke Ridnour, Oregon	6-2	2	63	172	205	83.9
10. Maris Laksa, Providence	6-9	2	49	114	137	83.2

MOST REBOUNDS

Seniors	Ht.	Yrs.	G	Reb.	Avg.
1. David West, Xavier	6-9	3	94	930	9.9
2. Erwin Dudley, Alabama	6-8	3	100	908	9.1
3. Theron Smith, Ball St.	6-8	3	96	862	9.0
4. Travis Watson, Virginia	6-8	3	88	794	9.0
5. Nick Collison, Kansas	6-9	3	104	763	7.3
6. Stephane Pelle, Colorado	6-9	3	91	756	8.3
7. Brandon Hunter, Ohio	6-7	3	89	725	8.1
8. Lewis Arline, Lamar	6-8	3	87	680	7.8
9. Darrell Tucker, San Francisco	6-9	3	85	678	8.0
10. LaVell Blanchard, Michigan	6-7	3	85	640	7.5
Juniors					
1. Mike Sweetney, Georgetown	6-8	2	62	535	8.6
2. Ron Robinson, Central Conn. St.	6-7	2	60	510	8.5
3. Ellis Myles, Louisville	6-7	2	63	468	7.4
4. Justin Reed, Mississippi	6-8	2	66	410	6.2
5. Paul Haynes, Grambling	6-8	2	54	386	7.1
6. Louis Truscott, Houston	6-7	2	64	386	6.0
7. Damien Wilkins, Georgia	6-6	2	60	348	5.8
8. Ricky Minard, Morehead St.	6-4	2	56	331	5.9
9. Andre Emmett, Texas Tech	6-5	2	60	314	5.2
10. Rans Brempong, Western Caro.	6-8	2	59	310	5.3

MOST REBOUNDS PER GAME

Seniors (Min. 500 Rebs.)	Ht.	Yrs.	G	Reb.	Avg.
1. David West, Xavier	6-9	3	94	930	9.9
2. Erwin Dudley, Alabama	6-8	3	100	908	9.1
3. Travis Watson, Virginia	6-8	3	88	794	9.0
4. Theron Smith, Ball St.	6-8	3	96	862	9.0
5. Stephane Pelle, Colorado	6-9	3	91	756	8.3
6. Brandon Hunter, Ohio	6-7	3	89	725	8.1
7. Darrell Tucker, San Francisco	6-9	3	85	678	8.0
8. Lewis Arline, Lamar	6-8	3	87	680	7.8
9. LaVell Blanchard, Michigan	6-7	3	85	640	7.5
10. Nick Collison, Kansas	6-9	3	104	763	7.3
Juniors (Min. 280 Rebs.)					
1. Mike Sweetney, Georgetown	6-8	2	62	535	8.6
2. Ron Robinson, Central Conn. St.	6-7	2	60	510	8.5
3. Ellis Myles, Louisville	6-7	2	63	468	7.4
4. Paul Haynes, Grambling	6-8	2	54	386	7.1
5. Justin Reed, Mississippi	6-8	2	66	410	6.2
6. Louis Truscott, Houston	6-7	2	64	386	6.0
7. Ricky Minard, Morehead St.	6-4	2	56	331	5.9
8. Damien Wilkins, Georgia	6-6	2	60	348	5.8
9. Kyle Davis, Auburn	6-10	2	54	300	5.6
10. Jarvis Hayes, Georgia	6-6	2	57	303	5.3

MOST ASSISTS PER GAME

Seniors (Min. 280 Asts.)	Ht.	Yrs.	G	Ast.	Avg.
1. Steven Blake, Maryland	6-3	3	107	751	7.0
2. Elliott Prasse-Freeman, Harvard	6-3	3	79	498	6.3
3. Brandin Knight, Pittsburgh	6-0	3	94	576	6.1
4. Guilherme Da Luz, Furman	6-3	3	89	519	5.8
5. Marquis Sykes, Morehead St.	6-0	3	84	442	5.3
6. Kirk Hinrich, Kansas	6-3	3	104	538	5.2
7. Edward Scott, Clemson	6-0	3	84	434	5.2
8. David Bailey, Loyola (Ill.)	5-8	3	86	422	4.9
9. Reggie Kohn, South Fla.	6-1	3	94	452	4.8
10. Ravii Givens, Stetson	5-9	3	80	381	4.8
Juniors (Min. 150 Asts.)					
1. Jameer Nelson, St. Joseph's	6-0	2	63	401	6.4
2. Imari Sawyer, DePaul	6-2	2	47	270	5.7
3. Andre Barrett, Seton Hall	5-8	2	61	320	5.2
4. Marquess Green, St. Bonaventure	5-7	2	58	301	5.2
5. Chris Duhon, Duke	6-1	2	74	382	5.2
6. T.J. Sorrentine, Vermont	5-11	2	58	275	4.7
7. Luke Ridnour, Oregon	6-2	2	63	282	4.5
8. Todd Billet, Virginia	6-0	2	58	246	4.2
9. Andrew Wisniewski, Centenary (La.)	6-3	2	45	175	3.9
10. Garrett Richardson, Tennessee St.	6-3	2	57	217	3.8

MOST BLOCKED SHOTS PER GAME

Seniors (Min. 90 Blks.)	Ht.	Yrs.	G	Blk.	Avg.
1. William McDonald, Grambling	6-9	2	52	127	2.4
2. David West, Xavier	6-9	3	94	176	1.9
3. Chris Wiedemann, Columbia	6-10	3	81	148	1.8
4. Kevin Johnson, Tulsa	6-7	3	99	175	1.8
5. Robert Battle, Drexel	6-8	3	78	130	1.7
6. Nick Collison, Kansas	6-9	3	104	169	1.6
7. Wesley Wilson, Georgetown	6-11	2	63	98	1.6
8. James Jones, Miami (Fla.)	6-8	3	94	142	1.5
9. Jermaine Hall, Wagner	6-5	3	85	99	1.2
10. Travis Watson, Virginia	6-8	3	88	90	1.0
Juniors (Min. 70 Blks.)					
1. D'or Fischer, Northwestern St.	6-11	2	62	202	3.3
2. Kyle Davis, Auburn	6-10	2	54	161	3.0
3. Rans Brempong, Western Caro.	6-8	2	59	159	2.7
4. Eddy Fobbs, Sam Houston St.	6-11	2	57	120	2.1
5. Mike Sweetney, Georgetown	6-8	2	62	71	1.1

MOST STEALS PER GAME

Seniors (Min. 120 Stls.)	Ht.	Yrs.	G	Stl.	Avg.
1. Chuck Eidson, South Carolina	6-7	3	84	212	2.5
2. Brandin Knight, Pittsburgh	6-0	3	94	228	2.4
3. Troy Bell, Boston College	6-1	3	91	202	2.2
4. Dedrick Dye, Wagner	6-0	3	85	171	2.0
5. Brett Blizzard, UNC Wilmington	6-4	3	94	180	1.9
6. Brian Allen, Towson	5-11	3	82	151	1.8
7. Steven Blake, Maryland	6-3	3	107	184	1.7
8. Guilherme Da Luz, Furman	6-3	3	89	153	1.7
9. Karim Souchu, Furman	6-7	3	86	147	1.7
10. Marquis Daniels, Auburn	6-6	3	77	130	1.7
Juniors (Min. 70 Stls.)					
1. Marquess Green, St. Bonaventure	5-7	2	58	147	2.5
2. Garrett Richardson, Tennessee St.	6-3	2	57	133	2.3
3. Demarcus Wilkins, Florida A&M	6-0	2	48	112	2.3
4. Ricky Minard, Morehead St.	6-4	2	56	122	2.2
5. Chris Duhon, Duke	6-1	2	74	158	2.1
6. James Thues, Syracuse	5-10	2	60	113	1.9
7. T.J. Sorrentine, Vermont	5-11	2	58	96	1.7
8. Kyle Williams, Howard	6-6	2	47	73	1.6
9. Michael Watson, UMKC	6-0	2	59	90	1.5
10. Jameer Nelson, St. Joseph's	6-0	2	63	95	1.5

2002 Division II Individual Leaders

Points Per Game

Name, Team	CL	Ht	Pos	G	FGM	3FG	FT	PTS	PPG
1. Angel Figueroa, Dowling	So.	6-5	F	25	216	79	143	654	26.2
2. Clint Keown, S.C.-Aiken	Sr.	6-2	G	28	222	84	163	691	24.7
3. John Flynn, Grand Valley St.	Sr.	6-0	G	28	237	34	165	673	24.0
4. Ronald Murray, Shaw	Sr.	6-0	G	33	256	45	220	777	23.5
5. Leon Smith, Bluefield St.	Fr.	6-1	G	25	190	88	108	576	23.0
6. Curtis Small, Southampton	Sr.	6-0	G	29	231	97	109	668	23.0
7. Lavar Griffin, Virginia St.	Sr.	-	-	26	222	78	71	593	22.8
8. Malik Moore, American Int'l	Sr.	6-4	G	29	223	74	141	661	22.8
9. Justin Leith, Merrimack	So.	6-6	F	25	247	14	61	569	22.8
10. Austin Nichols, Humboldt St.	So.	6-5	G	29	194	37	216	641	22.1
11. Antoine Sims, Johnson Smith	Sr.	5-10	G	31	231	110	108	680	21.9
12. Jerome Beasley, North Dakota	Jr.	6-10	F	29	251	14	114	630	21.7
13. Craig Zeigler, Lincoln Memorial	Sr.	6-3	G	27	201	83	101	586	21.7
14. Lamont Turner, Mo. Western St.	Sr.	6-3	F	30	267	31	83	648	21.6
15. Todd Manuel, St. Anselm	Sr.	6-2	G	30	193	82	174	642	21.4
16. Robert Day, Western Ore.	So.	6-5	G	27	184	62	138	568	21.0
Ronald Johnson, Cal St. Los Angeles	Jr.	6-3	F	27	182	25	179	568	21.0
18. Jason Lewis, Southampton	Sr.	6-5	F	27	239	7	80	565	20.9
19. Mars Mellish, N.J. Inst. of Tech.	Sr.	6-0	G	27	191	82	100	564	20.9
20. Marcus Wallace, Ferris St.	So.	6-3	G	26	190	66	93	539	20.7
21. Michael Jebbia, West Liberty St.	Sr.	6-2	G	28	236	49	58	579	20.7
22. Gerald Redding, Millersville	Jr.	6-4	G	27	187	66	110	550	20.4
23. Dantrail Coleman, Central Okla.	Sr.	6-0	G	26	158	73	140	529	20.3
24. Alexus Foyle, BYU-Hawaii	Sr.	6-0	G	29	250	2	87	589	20.3
25. Craig Sanders, Northern Ky.	Jr.	6-3	G	27	180	82	106	548	20.3
26. Matt Miller, Drury	Sr.	6-1	G	25	166	78	97	507	20.3
27. Kevyn McBride, Alderson-Broaddus	Sr.	6-4	F	30	211	67	119	608	20.3
28. Demond Tapscott, Shepherd	Sr.	6-0	G	21	144	76	59	423	20.1
29. Brian Atkins, Concord	So.	6-0	G	27	194	51	101	540	20.0
30. Justin Thompson, Central Wash.	Sr.	6-5	F	25	186	28	98	498	19.9
31. Cedric Brooks, Pittsburg St.	Jr.	6-0	G	27	188	66	95	537	19.9
32. Jeff Davenport, Cal St. Stanislaus	Jr.	6-5	G	27	180	57	117	534	19.8
33. David Grenade, Southern Conn. St.	Sr.	6-5	F	27	166	52	148	532	19.7
Ramzee Stanton, West Chester	Jr.	-	-	27	204	0	124	532	19.7
35. Mike Taylor, West Virginia St.	So.	6-1	G	27	160	83	128	531	19.7
36. Phil Sellers, St. Rose	Sr.	6-6	F	30	217	0	153	587	19.6
37. Gary Boodnikoff, Augusta St.	Sr.	6-7	G	30	183	89	130	585	19.5
Adrian Penland, Lander	Jr.	6-1	G	28	192	91	71	546	19.5
39. Jacob Poole, Cal St. Dom. Hills	Sr.	5-9	G	22	158	36	76	428	19.5
40. Tim Washington, Bowie St.	Sr.	6-8	C	26	177	1	150	505	19.4
41. Kevin Fletcher, UC-Colo. Spgs	Sr.	6-10	C	25	178	12	117	485	19.4
42. Ron Evans, Ky. Wesleyan	Sr.	6-5	F	34	227	78	127	659	19.4
43. Larry Boykin, LeMoyne-Owen	Jr.	6-3	G	27	188	40	106	522	19.3
44. Marques Cunningham, Longwood	Sr.	6-0	G	23	156	35	97	444	19.3
45. Ben Dewar, Lake Superior St.	Jr.	6-5	G	27	165	61	130	521	19.3
46. Al Elliott, Pace	Sr.	6-2	G	28	163	65	147	538	19.2
47. Kenny Dye, Lincoln (Mo.)	Sr.	6-3	G	26	187	33	89	496	19.1
Denver Tenbroek, North Dakota St.	Jr.	6-4	F	26	162	75	97	496	19.1
49. Damien Jackson, West Va. Wesleyan	Sr.	6-2	F	29	198	35	122	553	19.1
50. Gerrit Eades, St. Martin's	Sr.	-	-	26	182	38	89	491	18.9
51. Koran Godwin, North Fla.	Sr.	6-4	G	27	163	44	138	508	18.8
52. Jermaine Brown, Minn. St.-Mankato	Jr.	6-5	F	26	198	0	93	489	18.8
53. Rodney Keener, GC&SU	Jr.	6-0	G	27	191	63	61	506	18.7
54. Wykeen Kelly, Salem Int'l	Jr.	6-0	G	31	208	58	106	580	18.7
55. Kenny Tate, Edinboro	Sr.	6-3	G	27	199	4	101	503	18.6
56. Fred Hooks, Humboldt St.	So.	6-5	F	29	210	1	118	539	18.6
57. Niki Arinze, Henderson St.	Sr.	6-6	F	28	190	5	133	518	18.5
Milan Pepper, Southwestern Okla.	Sr.	6-1	G	28	188	28	114	518	18.5
Tyrone Smith, Elizabeth City St.	So.	5-11	G	28	159	44	156	518	18.5
60. Curtis Tonge, Barry	Sr.	6-6	G	26	179	44	78	480	18.5
61. Isaac Kincaid, Ashland	Jr.	6-3	G	27	164	51	118	497	18.4
62. Tyrone Palmer, Tex. A&M-Commerce	Sr.	6-9	F	29	180	58	115	533	18.4
63. Patrick Pope, St. Augustine's	Jr.	6-0	G	25	153	71	82	459	18.4
64. Dameion Baker, Mount Olive	Jr.	6-4	G	26	170	15	122	477	18.3
65. Manny Clifton, Washburn	Jr.	6-5	F	28	184	19	124	511	18.3
66. Byron Johnson, Belmont Abbey	Sr.	6-6	F	30	201	1	144	547	18.2
67. Shawn Alexander, Winston-Salem	Sr.	6-2	G	28	174	50	110	508	18.1
68. Gabe Maldonado, N.M. Highlands	Sr.	5-7	G	26	138	90	104	470	18.1
69. Peter Bullock, Alas. Anchorage	So.	6-6	F	27	191	4	101	487	18.0
70. Brian Westre, Mo.-Rolla	So.	6-9	C	28	198	0	109	505	18.0

Field-Goal Percentage

(Minimum five FGM)

Name, Team	CL	Ht	Pos	G	FGM	FGA	FG%
1. Brett Barnard, Le Moyne	So.	6-8	C	27	141	211	66.8
2. Steve Bynes, Shaw	Sr.	6-9	C	33	197	296	66.6
3. Raymond Strachan, Columbia Union	Jr.	6-6	G	26	164	248	66.1
4. Kantonio Davis, Montevallo	Jr.	6-6	F	27	140	213	65.7
5. Matt Jones, South Dakota St.	Fr.	6-6	F	30	161	247	65.2
6. Jon Sheppard, Northeastern St.	Jr.	-	-	30	174	268	64.9
7. Chris Ellis, Mesa St.	Sr.	6-5	F	27	142	225	63.1
8. David Siebrands, UNC Pembroke	Jr.	6-6	C	27	164	264	62.1
9. Byron Johnson, Belmont Abbey	Sr.	6-6	F	30	201	327	61.5
10. Ramzee Stanton, West Chester	Jr.	-	-	27	204	333	61.3
11. Brad Hansen, Northern St.	Sr.	6-8	C	28	171	280	61.1
12. Matt Rowan, Northwest Mo. St.	Sr.	6-7	C	32	164	269	61.0
13. Melroy McKelvey, Fort Hays St.	Jr.	6-7	F	27	148	244	60.7
14. Jamar Brown, Southern Colo.	Sr.	6-9	C	26	164	271	60.5
15. Bobby Miehlke, Lake Superior St.	Sr.	6-7	F	28	160	267	59.9
16. Tyrus Boswell, Ky. Wesleyan	Sr.	6-7	C	34	242	404	59.9
17. Cochise Valentine, Southwestern Okla.	Jr.	6-5	F	28	185	309	59.9
18. Mark Debaun, Central Mo. St.	Jr.	6-5	F	27	144	241	59.8
19. J.T. Luginski, Michigan Tech	Jr.	6-7	C	30	170	285	59.6
20. Ed Williams, Adelphi	Sr.	6-6	F	31	171	288	59.4
21. Dennis Mims, Indiana (Pa.)	Sr.	6-9	F	31	196	331	59.2
22. Damian Matacz, Northern Mich.	Sr.	6-9	C	26	149	252	59.1
23. Jason Pritchett, Central Okla.	Jr.	6-7	F	26	143	242	59.1
24. Jason Lewis, Southampton	Sr.	6-5	F	27	239	405	59.0
25. Vincent Bridgewater, Tarleton St.	Jr.	6-8	F	33	230	393	58.5
26. Dominique Liverpool, Glenville St.	So.	6-8	C	28	148	253	58.5
27. Jason Schneeweis, Minn.-Duluth	Jr.	6-9	C	30	168	288	58.3
28. Jeff Weirsma, Erskine	Jr.	6-7	F	27	180	310	58.1
29. R'Cell Harris, Emporia St.	Sr.	6-8	F	26	162	280	57.9
30. Charles Ward, St. Augustine's	Sr.	-	-	25	144	250	57.6
31. Davin Winkley, Rockhurst	Sr.	6-5	F	30	201	350	57.4
32. Jason Dunham, Salem Int'l	Sr.	6-7	F	29	148	259	57.1
33. Corey Seegers, St. Joseph's (Ind.)	So.	6-8	C	21	119	209	56.9
34. Danny Jones, Tarleton St.	Jr.	6-7	F	33	191	337	56.7
35. Wayne Taylor, Virginia Union	Jr.	-	-	26	132	233	56.7

Three-Point Field-Goal Percentage

(Min. 2.0 3FGM/G)

Name, Team	CL	Ht	Pos	G	3FG	3FGA	3FG%
1. Jared Ramirez, Northern Colo.	Sr.	6-1	G	27	60	115	52.2
2. Stephen Dye, Alderson-Broaddus	Fr.	6-2	G	30	111	223	49.8
3. Bobby Zuerner, Ky. Wesleyan	So.	6-1	G	31	70	145	48.3
4. Forrest Witt, St. Cloud St.	Jr.	6-2	G	28	74	156	47.4
5. Sundance Wicks, Northern St.	Jr.	6-5	G	28	70	148	47.3
6. Paul Marshall, South Dakota	Sr.	6-1	G	27	75	162	46.3
7. Kyle Gribble, Carson-Newman	Jr.	6-4	G	31	66	144	45.8
8. Aaron Farley, Harding	Jr.	5-9	G	27	63	139	45.3
9. Scott Majkrzak, North Dakota St.	Sr.	6-2	G	26	57	126	45.2
10. Ryan Stefanski, Calif. (Pa.)	Jr.	6-3	G	29	118	262	45.0
11. Rodney Keener, GC&SU	Jr.	6-0	G	27	63	141	44.7
12. Robert Day, Western Ore.	So.	6-5	G	27	62	139	44.6
13. Jamal Shivers, Bowie St.	Sr.	6-3	G	27	60	136	44.1
14. Adam Tesch, Southwest St.	Sr.	6-0	G	29	105	239	43.9
15. Kevyn Mcbride, Alderson-Broaddus	Sr.	6-4	F	30	67	153	43.8
16. Ramel Curry, Cal St. Bakersfield	Sr.	6-2	G	29	69	158	43.7
17. Jason Marcotte, Michigan Tech	Fr.	5-10	G	30	75	172	43.6
18. Paul Cordasco, Molloy	So.	0-6	G	27	61	140	43.6
19. Aaron Austin, Northern Colo.	Fr.	6-3	G	27	67	154	43.5
20. Jess Mcelree, UC Davis	Jr.	6-6	C	27	54	125	43.2
21. Gerald Raymond, Shaw	Jr.	6-2	G	32	117	271	43.2
22. Wes Layton, Indiana (Pa.)	Sr.	5-11	G	33	66	153	43.1
23. Jay Carlington, Pace	Sr.	6-0	G	29	94	218	43.1
Kevin Hatch, Fort Lewis	Jr.	6-4	F	30	94	218	43.1
25. Gary Boodnikoff, Augusta St.	Sr.	6-7	G	30	89	207	43.0
26. Jason Williams, Arkansas Tech	Jr.	6-2	G	26	55	128	43.0
27. Kyle Bixler, Charleston (W.Va.)	Sr.	6-0	G	32	98	229	42.8
28. Stephen Moss-Kelley, Bowie St.	Jr.	6-6	F	28	74	173	42.8

STATISTICAL LEADERS

Name, Team	CL	Ht	Pos	G	3FG	3FGA	3FG%
29. Derrick Brown, Coker	Sr.	6-2	G	26	99	232	42.7
30. Matt Miller, Drury	Sr.	6-1	G	25	78	183	42.6
31. Derek Rodgerson, Franklin Pierce	So.	6-0	G	26	60	141	42.6
32. Ron Evans, Ky. Wesleyan	Sr.	6-5	F	34	78	184	42.4
33. Matt Chambless, Colo. Christian	Sr.	6-5	G	27	61	144	42.4
34. Brady Webb, Emporia St.	Fr.	6-8	F	26	57	135	42.2
35. Jiri Mikl, Truman	Jr.	6-7	F	24	65	154	42.2

Three-Point Field Goals Per Game

Name, Team	CL	Ht	Pos	G	3FG	3PG
1. Danny Phillips, Mont. St.-Billings	Sr.	-	-	28	120	4.3
2. Ryan Stefanski, Calif. (Pa.)	Jr.	6-3	G	29	118	4.1
3. Derrick Brown, Coker	Sr.	6-2	G	26	99	3.8
4. Tarvoris Uzoigwe, Henderson St.	Fr.	5-9	G	28	106	3.8
5. Michael Gordon, Columbia Union	Jr.	6-0	G	23	87	3.8
6. Stephen Dye, Alderson-Broaddus	Fr.	6-2	G	30	111	3.7
7. Gerald Raymond, Shaw	Jr.	6-2	G	32	117	3.7
8. Adam Tesch, Southwest St.	Sr.	6-0	G	29	105	3.6
9. Demond Tapscott, Shepherd	Sr.	6-0	G	21	76	3.6
10. Antoine Sims, Johnson Smith	Sr.	5-10	G	31	110	3.5
11. Mark Huppe, Truman	Fr.	6-1	G	26	92	3.5
12. Leon Smith, Bluefield St.	Fr.	6-1	G	25	88	3.5
13. Gabe Maldonado, N.M. Highlands	Sr.	5-7	G	26	90	3.5
14. Tony Crawford, Belmont Abbey	Sr.	5-10	G	31	106	3.4
15. Ronald Donaldson, West Virginia St.	Jr.	5-8	G	27	91	3.4
16. Curtis Small, Southampton	Sr.	6-0	G	29	97	3.3
17. Tim Lee, Southern N.H.	Jr.	6-2	G	28	93	3.3
18. Adrian Penland, Lander	Jr.	6-1	G	28	91	3.3
19. Jay Carlington, Pace	Sr.	6-0	G	29	94	3.2
20. Chris Benson, Queens (N.C.)	Jr.	6-3	G	26	84	3.2
21. John Davis, Albany St. (Ga.)	Jr.	6-2	G	28	89	3.2
22. Jamie Shannon, Lincoln Memorial	Jr.	5-9	G	23	73	3.2
23. Angel Figueroa, Dowling	So.	6-5	F	25	79	3.2
24. Scott Land, Cal St. Chico	Fr.	6-4	G	26	82	3.2
25. Kevin Hatch, Fort Lewis	Jr.	6-4	F	30	94	3.1
26. Matt Miller, Drury	Sr.	6-1	G	25	78	3.1
27. Mike Taylor, West Virginia St.	So.	6-1	G	27	83	3.1
Craig Zeigler, Lincoln Memorial	Sr.	6-3	G	27	83	3.1
29. Kyle Bixler, Charleston (W.Va.)	Sr.	6-0	G	32	98	3.1
30. Mars Mellish, N.J. Inst. of Tech.	Sr.	6-0	G	27	82	3.0
Craig Sanders, Northern Ky.	Sr.	6-3	G	27	82	3.0
32. Clint Keown, S.C.-Aiken	Sr.	6-2	G	28	84	3.0
Lavar Griffin, Virginia St.	Sr.	-	-	26	78	3.0
34. Gary Boodnikoff, Augusta St.	Sr.	6-7	G	30	89	3.0
35. Jay Deshields, Bloomsburg	Sr.	6-4	G	28	82	2.9

Free-Throw Percentage

(Min. 2.5 FTM/G)

Name, Team	CL	Ht	Pos	G	FT	FTA	FT%
1. Curtis Small, Southampton	Sr.	6-0	G	29	109	116	94.0
2. Steve Serwatka, Clarion	Sr.	-	-	26	66	72	91.7
3. Sean Nolen, Northern Colo.	So.	6-0	G	27	85	93	91.4
4. Reggie Moore, Wheeling Jesuit	Jr.	6-0	G	28	118	130	90.8
5. Todd Manuel, St. Anselm	Sr.	6-2	G	30	174	193	90.2
6. Ryan Bucci, C.W. Post	Sr.	6-0	G	28	114	127	89.8
7. Eddin Santiago, Mo. Southern St.	Sr.	6-1	G	28	141	158	89.2
8. Nick Johnson, Seattle Pacific	Sr.	6-3	G	29	90	101	89.1
9. Matt Miller, Drury	Sr.	6-1	G	25	97	109	89.0
10. Mike Palm, Western Wash.	Jr.	6-10	C	27	121	136	89.0
11. Drew Carlson, Minn. St.-Mankato	Jr.	6-2	G	25	85	96	88.5
12. Cris Brunson, Southern Ind.	Fr.	6-1	G	30	91	103	88.3
13. Kashif Reyes, Chaminade	Jr.	5-10	G	25	66	75	88.0
14. Kelvin Parker, Northwest Mo. St.	So.	5-11	G	32	109	124	87.9
15. Mike Taylor, West Virginia St.	So.	6-1	G	27	128	146	87.7
16. Todd Jones, Cal St. Bakersfield	Sr.	6-5	G	28	71	81	87.7
17. Darren McCrillis, Harding	So.	5-9	G	27	98	112	87.5
18. Joe Bakhoum, Okla. Panhandle	Sr.	6-0	G	20	96	110	87.3
19. Clint Keown, S.C.-Aiken	Sr.	6-2	G	28	163	187	87.2
20. Derrick Schantz, South Dakota St.	Jr.	6-6	F	30	76	88	86.4
21. Royce Bryan, Bemidji St.	Jr.	6-0	G	28	80	93	86.0
22. Bj Brant, St. Cloud St.	Jr.	6-7	C	28	71	83	85.5
Adrian Penland, Lander	Jr.	6-1	G	28	71	83	85.5
24. Aaron Farley, Harding	Jr.	5-9	G	27	123	144	85.4
25. Marty Perry, SIU-Edwardsville	Sr.	6-0	G	25	70	82	85.4
26. Igor Majoras, Southwest Baptist	Sr.	6-7	F	26	92	108	85.2
27. Ronald Donaldson, West Virginia St.	Jr.	5-8	G	27	72	85	84.7
Darren Herrington, Tex. A&M-Kingsville	Jr.	6-2	G	26	72	85	84.7
29. Elad Inbar, Mass.-Lowell	So.	6-6	G	29	94	111	84.7
30. Damar Lopez, Mansfield	Sr.	5-11	G	22	105	124	84.7

Name, Team	CL	Ht	Pos	G	FT	FTA	FT%
31. Robbie Seabrook, Anderson (S.C.)	Jr.	6-3	G	28	103	122	84.4
32. Austin Nichols, Humboldt St.	So.	6-5	G	29	216	256	84.4
Tyrone Johnson, Pace	Sr.	6-2	G	29	81	96	84.4
34. Brian Larrabee, Southern N.H.	Jr.	6-5	F	28	182	216	84.3
Greg Moody, Mount Olive	Sr.	5-8	G	26	91	108	84.3

Rebounds Per Game

Name, Team	CL	Ht	Pos	G	REB	RPG
1. Danny Jones, Tarleton St.	Jr.	6-7	F	33	416	12.6
2. Dominique Liverpool, Glenville St.	So.	6-8	C	28	346	12.4
3. Fred Hooks, Humboldt St.	So.	6-5	F	29	342	11.8
4. Jamar Thompkins, West Va. Wesleyan	Sr.	6-8	F	29	333	11.5
5. John Laramore, Texas Lutheran	Sr.	6-8	F	25	287	11.5
6. Dennis Mims, Indiana (Pa.)	Sr.	6-9	F	31	349	11.3
7. Ramzee Stanton, West Chester	Jr.	-	-	27	297	11.0
8. Dwight Windom, Lincoln Memorial	Jr.	6-6	F	27	291	10.8
9. Jim Reeves, Philadelphia U.	Sr.	6-6	F	28	299	10.7
10. Craig Griffin, Merrimack	Jr.	6-4	F	26	277	10.7
11. Niki Arinze, Henderson St.	Sr.	6-6	F	28	296	10.6
12. Kenny Tate, Edinboro	Sr.	6-3	G	27	283	10.5
13. Dominic Callori, UC Davis	Jr.	6-6	F	27	282	10.4
14. Michael Beaton, Mercy	Jr.	6-5	F	26	271	10.4
15. Brian Atkins, Concord	So.	6-0	F	27	278	10.3
16. Scott Salisbury, BYU-Hawaii	Jr.	-	-	29	297	10.2
17. Jason Lewis, Southampton	Sr.	6-5	F	27	275	10.2
18. Jason Pritchett, Central Okla.	Jr.	6-7	F	26	261	10.0
19. Kevin Fletcher, UC-Colo. Spgs.	Sr.	6-10	C	25	250	10.0
20. Jeff Weirsma, Erskine	Jr.	6-7	F	27	268	9.9
21. Jason Schneeweis, Minn.-Duluth	Jr.	6-9	C	30	293	9.8
22. Sylvere Bryan, Tampa	Sr.	6-11	C	29	279	9.6
23. Jason Bauer, Grand Valley St.	Jr.	6-0	C	27	259	9.6
24. Brian Westre, Mo.-Rolla	So.	6-9	C	28	268	9.6
25. Matt Mlynarchek, Hillsdale	Jr.	6-10	C	27	257	9.5
26. Emory Ogletree, Charleston (W.Va.)	Sr.	6-5	F	32	299	9.3
27. Mark Roush, Morningside	So.	6-6	F	26	241	9.3
28. John Harden, Albany St. (Ga.)	Sr.	6-7	C	26	240	9.2
29. Cochise Valentine, Southwestern Okla.	Jr.	6-5	F	28	257	9.2
30. Tyrus Boswell, Ky. Wesleyan	Sr.	6-7	C	34	310	9.1
31. Scott Kassel, Mo.-St. Louis	Sr.	6-0	G	26	237	9.1
32. Mike Campbell, Ashland	Fr.	6-4	C	27	240	8.9
33. Tim Washington, Bowie St.	Jr.	6-8	C	26	231	8.9
34. Dock Ellis, Cal St. Bakersfield	Sr.	6-8	C	29	257	8.9
35. Derick Singleton, St. Paul's	Sr.	-	-	26	230	8.8

Assists Per Game

Name, Team	CL	Ht	Pos	G	AST	APG
1. Pat Delany, St. Anselm	Sr.	6-2	G	30	234	7.8
2. Eddin Santiago, Mo. Southern St.	Sr.	6-1	G	28	214	7.6
3. Ross Hodge, Tex. A&M-Commerce	Jr.	6-0	G	29	213	7.3
4. Ryan Stock, Southwest Baptist	Jr.	6-3	G	27	188	7.0
5. Josh Mueller, South Dakota	Fr.	5-11	G	27	180	6.7
6. Yuta Tabuse, BYU-Hawaii	Jr.	6-0	G	29	187	6.4
7. Lorinza Harrington, Wingate	Sr.	6-4	G	32	204	6.4
8. Mark White, Humboldt St.	So.	6-2	G	29	181	6.2
9. Ronald Murray, Shaw	Sr.	6-0	G	33	205	6.2
10. Matt Fryer, St. Rose	Sr.	5-8	G	30	186	6.2
11. Dashi Leon, Pitt.-Johnstown	Jr.	5-8	G	27	164	6.1
12. Jay Gibbons, Clayton St.	Jr.	6-3	G	28	168	6.0
13. Sotirios Karapostolou, Southern N.H.	Jr.	6-4	G	28	167	6.0
14. David Carse, Mont. St.-Billings	So.	6-0	G	28	166	5.9
15. Ky O'Dell, St. Mary's (Tex.)	So.	6-0	G	26	150	5.8
Dustin Smith, Arkansas Tech	Jr.	6-3	G	26	150	5.8
17. Cedric Powell, Fla. Southern	Sr.	6-0	G	28	161	5.8
18. Shahar Golan, Assumption	So.	6-2	G	30	172	5.7
19. Devonaire Deas, Winston-Salem	Sr.	6-6	G	25	143	5.7
20. Keyode Rogers, Concord	Jr.	6-0	G	26	147	5.7
21. Rob Thorpe, Le Moyne	So.	5-11	G	27	152	5.6
22. Jamie Holden, St. Joseph's (Ind.)	So.	5-9	G	26	145	5.6
23. Tyrone Smith, Elizabeth City St.	So.	5-11	G	28	156	5.6
24. Sullivan Phillips, Columbia Union	Sr.	6-4	F	27	150	5.6
25. Greg Moody, Mount Olive	Sr.	5-8	G	26	139	5.3
26. Jason Boucher, Grand Valley St.	Jr.	6-0	G	28	149	5.3
27. Jeremy Brooks, Valdosta St.	Jr.	5-11	G	32	170	5.3
28. Mario Porter, North Dakota	Sr.	6-4	G	29	154	5.3
29. Ryan Luckman, Bloomsburg	Jr.	6-4	G	26	137	5.3
30. Desmond Merriweather, Lane	So.	5-10	G	25	130	5.2
31. Jacob Poole, Cal St. Dom. Hills	Sr.	5-9	G	22	114	5.2
32. Royce Bryan, Bemidji St.	Jr.	6-0	G	28	145	5.2
33. Terry Duncan, Southern Ark.	Sr.	6-0	G	26	134	5.2

Name, Team	CL	Ht	Pos	G	AST	APG
34. Shane Burnison, Augustana (S.D.)	Sr.	6-5	F	27	139	5.1
35. John Redding, Dowling	Sr.	6-0	G	27	138	5.1

Blocked Shots Per Game

Name, Team	CL	Ht	Pos	G	BLKS	BKPG
1. George Bailey, Lock Haven	Jr.	6-8	F	20	79	4.0
2. Bilal Salaam, Kutztown	Fr.	6-7	F	25	97	3.9
3. Rich Edwards, Adelphi	Sr.	6-7	C	31	103	3.3
4. Sylvere Bryan, Tampa	Sr.	6-11	C	29	95	3.3
5. Marco Spears, Johnson Smith	Jr.	6-5	F	31	93	3.0
6. Jeff Weirsma, Erskine	Jr.	6-7	F	27	80	3.0
7. Aaron Davis, Southern Conn. St.	Jr.	6-6	C	25	74	3.0
8. Charles Boyd, Fort Valley St.	Sr.	6-7	F	27	79	2.9
9. Dennis Mims, Indiana (Pa.)	Sr.	6-9	F	31	90	2.9
10. Ryan Pitts, Lenoir-Rhyne	So.	6-9	C	27	76	2.8
11. Adam Wetzel, Neb.-Omaha	So.	-	-	33	90	2.7
12. Niki Arinze, Henderson St.	Sr.	6-6	F	28	73	2.6
Keith Branch, Albany St. (Ga.)	Sr.	6-8	G	28	73	2.6
14. Byron Johnson, Belmont Abbey	Sr.	6-6	F	30	75	2.5
Wayne Taylor, Virginia Union	Jr.	-	-	26	65	2.5
16. Christophe Humbert, Fla. Southern	Jr.	6-8	C	29	72	2.5
17. Nick Gibbs, St. Martin's	Jr.	-	-	26	64	2.5
18. Vincent Bridgewater, Tarleton St.	Jr.	6-8	F	33	81	2.5
19. Todd Williams, S.C.-Aiken	So.	6-8	F	25	61	2.4
20. Alex Luyk, Catawba	So.	6-9	C	27	61	2.3
21. Fred Hooks, Humboldt St.	So.	6-5	F	29	65	2.2
22. Jamaal Thomas, Angelo St.	Sr.	6-8	C	29	63	2.2
23. Desmond Peoples, St. Augustine's	So.	6-7	F	25	52	2.1
24. Brad Hansen, Northern St.	Sr.	6-8	C	28	58	2.1
Willard Winn, Armstrong Atlantic	Sr.	6-7	F	28	58	2.1
26. Chris Northcross, Hillsdale	So.	6-7	C	25	51	2.0
27. Kamar Zachery, Columbus St.	So.	6-5	F	28	55	2.0
28. Carl Mitchell, Northern Ky.	Sr.	6-9	F	27	53	2.0
29. Joshua Allen, Alderson-Broaddus	So.	6-6	F	30	57	1.9
30. Derrick Brown, Davis & Elkins	Sr.	-	-	27	51	1.9
Jai Pradia, Pittsburg St.	Sr.	6-7	C	27	51	1.9
32. Charles Paul, Concordia (N.Y.)	Jr.	6-9	C	22	41	1.9
33. Demarcus Bolton, East Central	Sr.	6-6	G	27	49	1.8
34. Burgess Williams, West Virginia St.	Sr.	6-0	G	21	38	1.8
35. Mike Phenizee, Clayton St.	Jr.	6-9	C	28	50	1.8

Steals Per Game

Name, Team	CL	Ht	Pos	G	ST	STPG
1. Shahar Golan, Assumption	So.	6-2	G	30	106	3.5
2. Eddin Santiago, Mo. Southern St.	Sr.	6-1	G	28	97	3.5
3. Tyrone Smith, Elizabeth City St.	So.	5-11	G	28	92	3.3
4. Lorinza Harrington, Wingate	Sr.	6-4	G	32	105	3.3
5. Marcus Best, Winston-Salem	Sr.	6-2	G	29	90	3.1
6. Marlin Murphy, St. Joseph's (Ind.)	Sr.	5-7	G	26	80	3.1
7. Cedric Powell, Fla. Southern	Sr.	6-0	G	28	86	3.1
8. Mars Mellish, N.J. Inst. of Tech.	Sr.	6-0	G	27	79	2.9
9. Jamie Holden, St. Joseph's (Ind.)	So.	5-9	G	26	75	2.9
10. Lucas LeCour, Cal Poly Pomona	Sr.	6-3	G	27	77	2.9
11. Sotirios Karapostolou, Southern N.H.	Jr.	6-4	G	28	79	2.8
Clint Keown, S.C.-Aiken	Sr.	6-2	G	28	79	2.8
13. Larry Taylor, Mo. Western St.	Jr.	6-4	G	30	84	2.8
14. Angel Figueroa, Dowling	So.	6-5	F	25	69	2.8
15. Malik Moore, American Int'l	Sr.	6-4	G	29	80	2.8
16. Christon Simmons, Fayetteville St.	Sr.	6-2	G	25	68	2.7
17. Carl Vault, Harding	Sr.	6-2	G	23	62	2.7
18. Kurt Patik, Fort Lewis	Jr.	6-4	F	30	80	2.7
19. Desmond Merriweather, Lane	So.	5-10	G	25	66	2.6
20. Antoine Sims, Johnson Smith	Sr.	5-10	G	31	79	2.5
21. Devonaire Deas, Winston-Salem	Sr.	6-6	G	25	63	2.5
22. Matt Fryer, St. Rose	Sr.	5-8	G	30	75	2.5
Andrew Harding, Glenville St.	So.	5-9	G	28	70	2.5
Jarel Cherry, St. Martin's	So.	-	-	26	65	2.5
25. Krik Maher, Mercy	Jr.	6-4	G	23	57	2.5
26. Kyle Hunt, Findlay	Sr.	6-7	F	30	74	2.5
27. Scott Fleming, Northwest Mo. St.	Jr.	6-3	G	32	78	2.4
28. Jason Boucher, Grand Valley St.	So.	6-0	G	28	68	2.4
29. Carlton Epps, Ferris St.	Fr.	6-2	G	24	58	2.4
30. Lee Bethea, Metro St.	Sr.	6-3	G	35	84	2.4
Leon Smith, Bluefield St.	Fr.	6-1	G	25	60	2.4
32. Luke Kendall, Metro St.	So.	6-4	G	35	83	2.4
33. Gerald Redding, Millersville	Sr.	6-4	G	27	63	2.3
Ryan Stock, Southwest Baptist	Jr.	6-3	G	27	63	2.3
Edderick Womack, Kennesaw St.	Sr.	5-11	G	27	63	2.3

2002 Division II Game Highs

Individual Highs

ASSISTS

Name, Team	CL	Ht	Pos	Opponent	Date	AST
1. Kelly West, West Liberty St.	So.	5-3	G	Fairmont St.	01/26/02	16
1. Pat Delany, St. Anselm	Sr.	6-2	G	Southern Conn. St.	02/18/02	17
2. Josh Mueller, South Dakota	Fr.	5-11	G	Northern Colo.	02/02/02	16
Bryson Vaughan, Alas. Anchorage	Jr.	6-1	G	Western Ore.	01/10/02	16
4. Pat Delany, St. Anselm	Sr.	6-2	G	Bentley	03/02/02	15
Sullivan Phillips, Columbia Union	Sr.	6-4	F	Strayer	02/12/02	15
6. Ira Taylor, Cal St. Stanislaus	Jr.	6-0	G	UC Davis	02/22/02	14
Yuta Tabuse, BYU-Hawaii	Jr.	6-0	G	Mont. St.-Billings	02/18/02	14
Anthony Reid, Virginia St.	Jr.	6-0	G	Bowie St.	02/12/02	14
Matt Fryer, St. Rose	Sr.	5-8	G	Stonehill	02/02/02	14
Abdul Smith, Bridgeport	So.	-	-	Queens (N.Y.)	01/30/02	14
Darren McCrillis, Harding	So.	5-9	G	Ark. Baptist	01/17/02	14
Kevin Petty, Catawba	Jr.	5-8	G	Wingate	01/16/02	14
Ryan Stock, Southwest Baptist	Jr.	6-3	G	Okla. Panhandle	12/07/01	14
14. Eddin Santiago, Mo. Southern St.	Sr.	6-1	G	Mo. Western St.	02/20/02	13
Rob Thorpe, Le Moyne	So.	5-11	G	Roberts Wesleyan	12/29/01	13

BLOCKED SHOTS

Name, Team	CL	Ht	Pos	Opponent	Date	BLKS
1. Jeff Weirsma, Erskine	Jr.	6-7	F	Limestone	02/25/02	11
2. Bilal Salaam, Kutztown	Fr.	6-7	F	Edinboro	12/02/01	10
3. Desmond Peoples, St. Augustine's	So.	6-7	F	Elizabeth City St.	01/15/02	9
Aaron Davis, Southern Conn. St.	Jr.	6-6	C	Saint Rose	01/10/02	9
Jamar Thompkins, West Va. Wesleyan	Sr.	6-8	F	Rio Grande	11/27/01	9
6. Matt Smith, Lander	Jr.	7-0	C	Augusta St.	03/01/02	8
Burgess Williams, West Virginia St.	Sr.	6-0	G	West Va. Tech	01/12/02	8
Christophe Humbert, Fla. Southern	Jr.	6-8	C	Rochester	01/02/02	8
Fred Hooks, Humboldt St.	So.	6-5	F	Barry	11/16/01	8

FIELD GOAL PERCENTAGE
(Minimum 10 FGM)

Name, Team	CL	Opponent	Date	FG%	FGM	FGA
1. Chris Mortellaro, Drury	So.	Lincoln (Mo.)	02/20/02	100.0	12	12
Mike Zieja, St. Anselm	Jr.	Southern Conn. St.	02/18/02	100.0	12	12

STATISTICAL LEADERS

Name, Team	CL	Opponent	Date	FG%	FGM	FGA
Chris Turner, Dist. Columbia	Jr.	Millersville	12/08/01	100.0	12	12
Yuri Whyms, Western Ore.	Jr.	St. Martin`s	01/17/02	100.0	11	11
Ernest Scott, Valdosta St.	So.	P.R.-Cayey	11/16/01	100.0	11	11
Ryan Pitts, Lenoir-Rhyne	So.	Mars Hill	02/23/02	100.0	10	10
Tim Black, Arkansas Tech	So.	Ala.-Huntsville	11/27/01	100.0	10	10
8. Ryan Boles, Calif. (Pa.)	Sr.	Kutztown	12/22/01	92.3	12	13
John Hopf, Winona St.	Fr.	Viterbo	12/18/01	92.3	12	13
10. Carl Edwards, Charleston (W.Va.)	So.	Fairmont St.	02/07/02	91.7	11	

FREE-THROW PERCENTAGE
(Minimum 10 FTM)

Name, Team	CL	Opponent	Date	FT%	FT	FTA
1. Todd Manuel, St. Anselm	Sr.	Central Wash.	12/28/01	100.0	14	14
Willie Bryant, Lynn....................	Sr.	Grand Valley St.	11/17/01	100.0	14	14
Sean Hilgenberg, Augustana (S.D.)	Sr.	Neb.-Omaha	02/15/02	100.0	13	13
Eddin Santiago, Mo. Southern St.	Sr.	Northwest Mo. St.	02/09/02	100.0	13	13
Andy Collins, Davis & Elkins	Jr.	West Va. Tech	01/24/02	100.0	13	13
Austin Hansen, South Dakota St.	Jr.	North Dakota	03/02/02	100.0	12	12
Brad Napier, West Virginia St....	Sr.	West Va. Tech	02/23/02	100.0	12	12
Ronald Murray, Shaw	Sr.	Johnson Smith	02/16/02	100.0	12	12
Kelvin Parker, Northwest Mo. St.	So.	Southwest Baptist	02/16/02	100.0	12	12
Brad Ring, West Liberty St.	Sr.	West Virginia St.	02/11/02	100.0	12	12
Brett Godette, Merrimack	So.	Mass.-Lowell	02/09/02	100.0	12	12
Corey Tabron, N.C. Central	Jr.	Bowie St.	01/08/02	100.0	12	12
Matt Britton, Morningside	So.	Northern Colo.	01/05/02	100.0	12	12
Cris Brunson, Southern Ind........	Fr.	Brescia	12/29/01	100.0	12	12
Chris Turner, Dist. Columbia	Jr.	Millersville	12/08/01	100.0	12	12
Kris Sivertsen, Midwestern St.	Jr.	Angelo St.	12/01/01	100.0	12	12
Damon Bailey, Mo. Western St.	Jr.	Lincoln (Mo.)	11/24/01	100.0	12	12

POINTS

Name, Team	CL	Ht	Pos	vs. Opponent	Date	PTS
1. Todd Manuel, St. Anselm	Sr.	6-2	G	Bentley	01/03/02	52
2. Curtis Small, Southampton	Sr.	6-0	G	Concordia (N.Y.)	01/15/02	49
3. Kevyn Mcbride, Alderson-Broaddus	Sr.	6-4	F	Charleston (W.Va.)	03/07/02	48
Angel Figueroa, Dowling	So.	6-5	F	Concordia (N.Y.)	02/20/02	48
5. Angel Figueroa, Dowling	So.	6-5	F	New York Tech	02/13/02	47
Jason Lewis, Southampton	Sr.	6-5	F	C.W. Post	12/12/01	47
7. Gerrit Eades, St. Martin's	Sr.	-	-	Alas. Anchorage	02/09/02	46
8. Jason Pryor, Longwood	Sr.	6-2	G	Charleston (W.Va.)	12/12/01	44
9. Leon Smith, Bluefield St.	Fr.	6-1	G	Davis & Elkins	02/16/02	43
10. Clint Keown, S.C.-Aiken	Sr.	6-2	G	North Fla.	02/27/02	42

REBOUNDS

Name, Team	CL	Ht	Pos	Opponent	Date	REB
1. Dominic Callori, UC Davis	Jr.	6-6	F	Sonoma St.	12/16/01	24
2. Jason Lewis, Southampton	Sr.	6-5	F	Molloy	12/15/01	23
David Covington, N.C. Central	Jr.	6-7	F	Wingate	12/05/01	23
4. Brendon Boyce, Bridgeport......	Sr.	-	-	Southampton	02/07/02	22
Steve Anderson, South Dakota	So.	6-7	F	Mo. Western St.	11/20/01	22
6. John Laramore, Texas Lutheran	Sr.	6-8	F	Schreiner	02/19/02	21
Anthony Walton, Southeastern Okla.	Sr.	6-7	F	Cameron	02/09/02	21
Eric Collier, West Fla.	Sr.	7-6	F	Southern Ark.	12/08/01	21
Scott Salisbury, BYU-Hawaii	Jr.	-	-	UC Davis	11/16/01	21
10. Fred Hooks, Humboldt St.	So.	6-5	F	Central Wash.	02/23/02	20

STEALS

Name, Team	CL	Ht	Pos	Opponent	Date	ST
1. David Plum, Davis & Elkins	Sr.	6-0	G	West Va. Tech	01/24/02	9
Matt Fryer, St. Rose	Sr.	5-8	G	Bentley	12/30/01	9
Eyal Leib, Mass.-Lowell	Sr.	6-3	G	Southern Conn. St.	12/11/01	9
Patrick Pope, St. Augustine's	Jr.	6-0	G	St. Paul`s	12/04/01	9
Shahar Golan, Assumption	So.	6-2	G	Southern Conn. St.	12/01/01	9
Yusef Aziz, Seattle Pacific........	Jr.	6-4	F	Northwest (Wash.)	11/27/01	9
7. Eric Faber, Rollins	Fr.	6-0	G	Fla. Southern	02/20/02	8
Norton Edmonds, Central Okla.	Jr.	5-10	G	Cameron	01/24/02	8
Lorinza Harrington, Wingate	Sr.	6-4	G	Lenoir-Rhyne	01/23/02	8
Jon Wagner, Augustana (S.D.) ..	So.	6-0	G	Morningside	12/30/01	8

THREE-POINT FIELD GOAL PERCENTAGE
(Minimum eight 3FGM)

Name, Team	Opponent	Date	3FG%	3FG	3FGA
1. G.J. Macon, Alas. Anchorage ..	Northwest Nazarene	02/28/02	80.0	8	10
Paul Marshall, South Dakota......	Western St. (Colo.)	12/01/01	80.0	8	10
3. Ron Hood, GC&SU	Francis Marion	01/26/02	78.6	11	14
4. Mark Drake, Alas. Anchorage ..	Western Ore.	01/10/02	75.0	9	12
5. Andy Young, West Ga.	Shorter	12/04/01	69.2	9	13

THREE-POINT FIELD GOALS MADE

Team	Opponent	Date	3FG
1. Ron Hood, GC&SU	Francis Marion	01/26/02	11
Ryan Stefanski, Calif. (Pa.)	Cheyney	12/01/01	11
3. Clint Keown, S.C.-Aiken	North Fla.	02/27/02	10
Bryan Biley, Southern Ark.	Ark. Monticello	02/23/02	10
Isaac Gildea, Humboldt St.	St. Martin`s	02/21/02	10
Jamie Carrier, Winona St.	Minn.-Morris	01/26/02	10
Brent Welton, Philadelphia U.	Mercy	01/14/02	10
8. Tim Lee, Southern N.H.	New Haven	02/20/02	9
Mark Drake, Alas. Anchorage	Western Ore.	02/16/02	9
Joey Ramirez, Western N.M.	BYU-Hawaii	02/16/02	9

Team Highs

FIELD-GOAL PERCENTAGE

Team	Opponent	Date	FG%	FGM	FGA
1. Midwestern St.	Cameron	02/09/02	71.1	32	45
2. Drury	Lincoln (Mo.)	02/20/02	71.0	44	62
3. West Virginia St.	Bluefield St.	02/21/02	69.5	41	59
4. Calif. (Pa.)	Ohio St.-Newark	12/17/01	69.1	47	68
5. Northern Ky.	Central St. (Ohio)	12/17/01	68.5	37	54
6. S.C.-Spartanburg	Presbyterian	12/04/01	68.4	26	38
7. Neb.-Omaha	St. Cloud St.	01/12/02	66.7	38	57
West Va. Tech	Bluefield St.	01/31/02	66.7	34	51
Virginia Union	Virginia St.	02/09/02	66.7	28	42

THREE-POINT FIELD-GOAL PERCENTAGE
(Minimum 10 3FGM)

Team	Opponent	Date	3FG%	3FG	3FGA
1. Northwest Mo. St.	Pittsburg St.	02/02/02	80.0	12	15
2. Minn.-Mankato	Viterbo	12/12/01	73.7	14	19
3. West Tex. A&M	Okla. Panhandle	12/15/01	73.3	11	15
Johnson Smith	Eckerd	11/30/01	73.3	11	15
5. St. Cloud St.	Minn.-Morris	11/24/01	72.2	13	18
6. St. Mary's (Tex.)	National Christian	02/20/02	71.4	15	21
7. Mo. Southern St.	Emporia St.	01/19/02	70.6	12	17
8. Neb.-Omaha	St. Cloud St.	01/12/02	68.8	11	16
9. St. Leo	Rollins	02/13/02	66.7	14	21
Drury	Oakland City	01/07/02	66.7	14	21

THREE-POINT FIELD-GOALS MADE

Team	Opponent	Date	3FG
1. Mont. St.-Billings	P.R.-Bayamon	12/07/01	22
2. Ark.-Monticello	Ark. Baptist	02/14/02	21
GC&SU	Francis Marion	01/26/02	21
4. Charleston (W.Va.)	Bluefield St.	02/23/02	20
Tampa	Monmouth (Ill.)	01/02/02	20
6. Shaw	Virginia Union	02/12/02	19
Southwest St.	Minn.-Morris	02/02/02	19
8. Tex. A&M-Kingsville	Abilene Christian	02/14/02	18
Northern St.	Minn.-Morris	01/19/02	18
Lincoln Memorial	Ashland	12/03/01	18

FREE-THROW PERCENTAGE

Rank Team	Opponent	Date	FT%	FT	FTA
1. Winona St.	Minn.-Crookston	02/16/02	100.0	15	15
West Fla.	Southern Ark.	12/08/01	100.0	15	15
3. Drury	Okla. Panhandle	01/05/02	96.7	29	30
4. Millersville	Calif. (Pa.)	01/12/02	96.2	25	26
5. Augustana (S.D.)	St. Cloud St.	01/05/02	95.7	22	23
Wheeling Jesuit	Bluefield St.	12/30/01	95.7	22	23

Rank Team	Opponent	Date	FT%	FT	FTA
7. Armstrong Atlantic	S.C.-Spartanburg	01/19/02	95.5	21	22
8. West Liberty St.	Fairmont St.	02/21/02	95.2	20	21
9. Franklin Pierce	Bentley	02/05/02	95.0	19	20
Alderson-Broaddus	Davis & Elkins	02/02/02	95.0	19	20

POINTS
(Minimum 114 Points)

Team	Opponent	Date	PTS	OPP PTS
1. Ark.-Monticello	Rhema	12/11/01	147	0
2. Findlay	Mich.-Dearborn	12/06/01	137	0
3. Clarion	Practical Bible	11/16/01	133	75

Team	Opponent	Date	PTS	OPP PTS
4. Charleston (W.Va.)	Bluefield St.	02/23/02	130	74
5. Drury	Lincoln (Mo.)	02/20/02	129	89
6. South Dakota St.	Minn.-Morris	12/15/01	127	60
7. St. Joseph's (Ind.)	Purdue-Calumet	12/20/01	126	65
Mont. St.-Billings	Great Falls	12/15/01	126	0
Lincoln (Mo.)	Mo. Western St.	11/24/01	126	112
10. Mo. Southern St.	Emporia St.	01/19/02	125	82

2002 Division II Team Leaders

Scoring Offense

Team	GM	W-L	PTS	PPG
1. Mont. St.-Billings	28	21-7	2559	91.4
2. Ky. Wesleyan	34	31-3	3104	91.3
3. Southern Ind.	30	22-8	2708	90.3
4. South Dakota St.	30	24-6	2706	90.2
5. Humboldt St.	29	25-4	2588	89.2
6. Charleston (W.Va.)	32	25-7	2812	87.9
7. Shaw	33	28-5	2871	87.0
8. Salem Int'l	31	26-5	2688	86.7
9. Findlay	30	23-7	2592	86.4
10. Bowie St.	28	20-8	2416	86.3
11. Western Wash.	27	21-6	2325	86.1
12. Pfeiffer	28	16-12	2406	85.9
13. Lincoln (Mo.)	26	14-12	2217	85.3
14. Dowling	27	14-13	2273	84.2
15. Northern Colo.	27	14-13	2272	84.1
16. South Dakota	27	19-8	2268	84.0
17. Central Okla.	26	10-16	2181	83.9
18. Wingate	33	26-7	2766	83.8
19. Harding	27	16-11	2263	83.8
20. Mo. Western St.	30	23-7	2498	83.3
21. Wheeling Jesuit	28	16-12	2330	83.2
22. St. Cloud St.	28	21-7	2327	83.1
23. Mo. Southern St.	28	20-8	2324	83.0
24. Southampton	29	17-12	2406	83.0
25. Central Wash.	26	16-10	2153	82.8
26. Neb.-Kearney	30	24-6	2481	82.7
27. Angelo St.	29	18-11	2398	82.7
28. Grand Valley St.	28	15-13	2315	82.7
29. St. Anselm	30	19-11	2465	82.2
30. West Va. Wesleyan	29	21-8	2378	82.0
31. Fort Lewis	30	21-9	2459	82.0
32. Northern St.	28	20-8	2294	81.9
33. Seattle Pacific	29	24-5	2370	81.7
34. Johnson Smith	31	23-8	2533	81.7
35. Alderson-Broaddus	30	22-8	2450	81.7

Scoring Margin

Team	GM	W-L	PTS
1. Ky. Wesleyan	34	31-3	3104
2. Salem Int'l	31	26-5	2688
3. Northern St.	28	20-8	2294
4. Northwest Mo. St.	32	29-3	2522
5. Tampa	29	26-3	2238
6. Adelphi	31	28-3	2448
7. South Dakota St.	30	24-6	2706
8. Metro St.	35	29-6	2762
9 Tarleton St.	33	25-8	2461

Team	GM	W-L	PTS
10. Seattle Pacific	29	24-5	2370
11. Belmont Abbey	31	25-6	2477
12. Findlay	30	23-7	2592
13. Carson-Newman	31	26-5	2506
14. South Dakota	27	19-8	2268
15. Cal St. San B'dino	30	28-2	2151
16. Michigan Tech	30	27-3	2384
17. Shaw	33	28-5	2871
18. Valdosta St.	32	24-8	2345
19. Northeastern St.	30	28-2	2122
20. Incarnate Word	29	25-4	2158
21. Humboldt St.	29	25-4	2588
22. Western Wash.	27	21-6	2325
23. Calif. (Pa.)	29	23-6	2326
24. Neb.-Kearney	30	24-6	2481
25. Southern Ind.	30	22-8	2708
26. Indiana (Pa.)	33	28-5	2634
27. Mo. Southern St.	28	20-8	2324
28. Gannon	28	21-7	2135
29. Mont. St.-Billings	28	21-7	2559
30. Charleston (W.Va.)	32	25-7	2812
31. St. Cloud St.	28	21-7	2327
32. Neb.-Omaha	33	24-9	2688
33. Southwest St.	29	21-8	2211
34. Fla. Southern	29	20-9	2279
35. Mo. Western St.	30	23-7	2498

Rebound Margin

Team	GM	W-L	REB
1. Tarleton St.	33	25-8	1420
2. Salem Int'l	31	26-5	1340
3. Ky. Wesleyan	34	31-3	1507
4. South Dakota St.	30	24-6	1350
5. Charleston (W.Va.)	32	25-7	1424
6. Indiana (Pa.)	33	28-5	1432
7. Western Wash.	27	21-6	1095
8. Henderson St.	28	21-7	1134
9. Minn.-Duluth	30	19-11	1196
10. Tampa	29	26-3	1175
11. Cal St. Bakersfield	29	24-5	1120
12. Southern Ind.	30	22-8	1248
13. Lake Superior St.	28	17-11	1109
14. North Fla.	27	13-14	1092
15. Incarnate Word	29	25-4	1106
16. Delta St.	29	22-7	1142
17. Eckerd	28	21-7	1130
18. Queens (N.Y.)	30	19-11	1178
19. Lynn	26	15-11	1021
20. Fayetteville St.	27	18-9	1080

Team	GM	W-L	REB
21. Calif. (Pa.)	29	23-6	1113
22. Southwest Baptist	27	12-15	1068
23. Longwood	26	13-13	1061
24. Adelphi	31	28-3	1328
25. Washburn	28	20-8	1074
26. Rockhurst	30	24-6	1175
27. Virginia Union	26	12-14	1045
28. Cal St. San B'dino	30	28-2	1134
29. Glenville St.	28	15-13	1215
30. Pfeiffer	28	16-12	1246
31. Eastern N.M.	27	15-12	1044
32. Michigan Tech	30	27-3	1099
33. Chaminade	27	16-11	1013
34. Mass.-Lowell	29	20-9	1019
35. Wayne St. (Mich.)	27	15-12	996

Scoring Defense

Team	GM	W-L	OPP PTS	OPP PPG
1. Tusculum	28	15-13	1600	57.1
2. Northeastern St.	30	28-2	1755	58.5
3. Cal St. San B'dino	30	28-2	1763	58.8
4. Tarleton St.	33	25-8	1994	60.4
5. Valdosta St.	32	24-8	1947	60.8
6. Incarnate Word	29	25-4	1806	62.3
7. Tampa	29	26-3	1810	62.4
8. Cal St. Bakersfield	29	24-5	1813	62.5
9. Henderson St.	28	21-7	1759	62.8
10. Mass.-Lowell	29	20-9	1826	63.0
11. Northwest Mo. St.	32	29-3	2042	63.8
12. S.C.-Spartanburg	27	11-16	1726	63.9
13. Minn.-Duluth	30	19-11	1923	64.1
14. Adelphi	31	28-3	1991	64.2
15. Cal Poly Pomona	27	18-9	1742	64.5
16. Metro St.	35	29-6	2263	64.7
17. Gannon	28	21-7	1819	65.0
18. Lewis	32	25-7	2079	65.0
19. St. Mary's (Tex.)	26	11-15	1701	65.4
20. Minn. St. Moorhead	27	17-10	1768	65.5
21. Ala.-Huntsville	26	17-9	1707	65.7
22. Barry	26	14-12	1708	65.7
23. Wayne St. (Mich.)	27	15-12	1775	65.7
24. Eckerd	28	21-7	1841	65.8
25. Lynn	26	15-11	1721	66.2
26. Southwest St.	29	21-8	1921	66.2
27. Northern St.	28	20-8	1855	66.3
28. West Chester	27	18-9	1792	66.4
29. Belmont Abbey	31	25-6	2063	66.5
30. Philadelphia U.	28	19-9	1866	66.6

Team	GM	W-L	OPP PTS	OPP PPG
31. Michigan Tech	30	27-3	2003	66.8
32. Fayetteville St.	27	18-9	1805	66.9
33. Delta St.	29	22-7	1940	66.9
34. Hillsdale	28	20-8	1879	67.1
35. American Int'l	29	16-13	1947	67.1

Field-Goal Percentage Defense

Team	FG	FGA	Pct.
1. Southern Ind.	1,014	1,937	52.3
2. Grand Valley St.	898	1,737	51.7
3. Mesa St.	711	1,384	51.4
4. Salem Int'l	953	1,886	50.5
5. West Tex. A&M	823	1,632	50.4
6. Hawaii-Hilo	807	1,616	49.9
7. Calif. (Pa.)	772	1,546	49.9
8. Washburn	991	1,988	49.8
9. Western Wash.	927	1,861	49.8
10. Shaw	713	1,438	49.6
11. Armstrong Atlantic	846	1,708	49.5
12. Neb.-Kearney	914	1,856	49.2
13. Westminster (Pa.)	778	1,584	49.1
14. Longwood	908	1,851	49.1
15. Northeastern St.	765	1,563	48.9
16. Lincoln (Mo.)	849	1,736	48.9
17. Seattle Pacific	774	1,584	48.9
18. Southern Colo.	737	1,509	48.8
19. St. Michael's	967	1,981	48.8
20. Michigan Tech	703	1,441	48.8
21. Winona St.	867	1,778	48.8
22. South Dakota	739	1,516	48.7
23. S.C.-Spartanburg	627	1,287	48.7
24. Drury	747	1,535	48.7
25. Delta St.	782	1,611	48.5
26. Northern St.	797	1,643	48.5
27. Alas. Anchorage	887	1,830	48.5
28. Harding	675	1,395	48.4
29. Cheyney	741	1,532	48.4
30. Wingate	941	1,946	48.4
31. Miles	762	1,579	48.3
32. Hawaii Pacific	805	1,670	48.2
33. Northern Ky.	989	2,054	48.1
34. Lake Superior St.	770	1,600	48.1
35. Mo. Western St.	813	1,694	48.0

Field-Goal Percentage Defense

Team	GM	W-L	OPP FG	OPP FGA	OPP FG%
1. Tarleton St.	33	25-8	657	1837	35.8
2. Tusculum	28	15-13	563	1504	37.4
3. Indiana (Pa.)	33	28-5	781	2068	37.8
4. Adelphi	31	28-3	761	2002	38.0
5. Tampa	29	26-3	617	1612	38.3
6. Valdosta St.	32	24-8	676	1764	38.3
7. Fla. Southern	29	20-9	653	1687	38.7
8. Cheyney	27	17-10	671	1730	38.8
9. South Dakota St.	30	24-6	796	2050	38.8
10. Mass.-Lowell	29	20-9	573	1472	38.9
11. Henderson St.	28	21-7	651	1668	39.0
12. Gannon	28	21-7	630	1596	39.5
Belmont Abbey	31	25-6	750	1900	39.5
14. Cal St. San B'dino	28	28-2	627	1585	39.6
15. Eckerd	28	21-7	688	1727	39.8
16. LeMoyne-Owen	27	13-14	703	1762	39.9
17. Cal St. Bakersfield	29	24-5	610	1526	40.0
18. Fayetteville St.	27	18-9	602	1494	40.2
19. Virginia Union	26	12-14	650	1616	40.2
20. Northern St.	28	20-8	665	1648	40.4
21. Columbus St.	28	19-9	739	1831	40.4
22. Salem Int'l	31	26-5	749	1849	40.5
23. Minn.-Duluth	30	19-11	702	1730	40.6
24. Michigan Tech	30	27-3	723	1781	40.6
25. Rockhurst	30	24-6	696	1712	40.7
26. Northeastern St.	30	28-2	633	1555	40.7
27. South Dakota	27	19-8	675	1657	40.7
28. Wayne St. (Mich.)	27	15-12	571	1401	40.8
29. Minn. St. Moorhead	27	17-10	612	1501	40.8

Team	GM	W-L	OPP FG	OPP FGA	OPP FG%
30. Delta St.	29	22-7	664	1623	40.9
31. Calif. (Pa.)	29	23-6	714	1743	41.0
32. Clayton St.	28	19-9	649	1583	41.0
33. GC&SU	27	15-12	679	1653	41.1
34. Lewis	32	25-7	747	1814	41.2
35. Fairmont St.	28	17-11	677	1643	41.2

Field-Goal Percentage

Team	GM	W-L	FGM	FGA	FG%
1. Neb.-Kearney	30	24-6	899	1762	51.0
2. Mesa St.	27	16-11	704	1393	50.5
3. Michigan Tech	30	27-3	847	1680	50.4
4. Southern Colo.	26	11-15	695	1379	50.4
5. Southern Ind.	30	22-8	988	1962	50.4
6. Metro St.	35	29-6	1075	2146	50.1
7. Shaw	33	28-5	1021	2042	50.0
8. South Dakota St.	30	24-6	924	1853	49.9
9. Fort Hays St.	28	21-7	758	1531	49.5
10. Salem Int'l	31	26-5	985	1990	49.5
11. Northern St.	28	20-8	819	1661	49.3
12. Seattle Pacific	29	24-5	830	1688	49.2
13. Lincoln (Mo.)	26	14-12	822	1672	49.2
14. Calif. (Pa.)	29	23-6	819	1666	49.2
15. Ky. Wesleyan	34	31-3	1100	2251	48.9
16. Carson-Newman	31	26-5	881	1803	48.9
17. Northeastern St.	30	28-2	746	1527	48.9
18. St. Augustine's	25	12-13	731	1508	48.5
19. Mo. Western St.	30	23-7	927	1913	48.5
20. Findlay	30	23-7	938	1938	48.4
21. BYU-Hawaii	29	19-10	837	1734	48.3
22. Pittsburg St.	27	17-10	734	1523	48.2
23. Western Wash.	27	21-6	814	1692	48.1
24. Johnson Smith	31	23-8	898	1875	47.9
25. Harding	27	16-11	781	1631	47.9
26. Valdosta St.	32	24-8	906	1893	47.9
27. Assumption	30	24-6	870	1819	47.8
28. Northern Colo.	27	14-13	758	1587	47.8
29. Indiana (Pa.)	33	28-5	932	1952	47.7
30. Charleston (W.Va.)	32	25-7	1036	2174	47.7
31. Queens (N.C.)	29	19-10	846	1776	47.6
32. Northwest Mo. St.	32	29-3	866	1818	47.6
33. Chadron St.	27	15-12	723	1518	47.6
34. Montevallo	27	10-17	761	1599	47.6
35. Eckerd	28	21-7	768	1614	47.6

Free-Throw Percentage

Team	GM	W-L	FT	FTA	FT%
1. St. Cloud St.	28	21-7	461	587	78.5
2. St. Anselm	30	19-11	482	616	78.2
3. Neb.-Kearney	30	24-6	504	649	77.7
4. Seattle Pacific	29	24-5	517	669	77.3
5. Michigan Tech	30	27-3	474	614	77.2
6. Northern Colo.	27	14-13	529	687	77.0
7. Minn. St.-Mankato	26	9-17	333	434	76.7
8. Drury	27	12-15	487	638	76.3
9. Humboldt St.	29	25-4	693	908	76.3
10. Mont. St.-Billings	28	21-7	654	859	76.1
11. West Virginia St.	27	9-18	468	620	75.5
12. Bloomsburg	28	14-14	443	587	75.5
13. Western Wash.	27	21-6	534	708	75.4
14. Presbyterian	28	12-16	492	656	75.0
Indianapolis	27	15-12	285	380	75.0
16. Wheeling Jesuit	28	16-12	523	698	74.9
17. South Dakota	27	19-8	468	625	74.9
18. Gannon	28	21-7	473	633	74.7
19. Pfeiffer	28	16-12	519	696	74.6
20. Metro St.	35	29-6	413	554	74.5
21. Colo. Christian	27	10-17	414	556	74.5
22. Incarnate Word	29	25-4	518	696	74.4
23. Harding	27	16-11	515	693	74.3
24. Augustana (S.D.)	27	14-13	434	585	74.2
25. North Dakota	29	19-10	435	587	74.1
26. Rollins	28	18-10	458	622	73.6
27. Adams St.	27	7-20	440	598	73.6
28. Cal St. Los Angeles	27	11-16	451	613	73.6
29. Northern Ky.	27	19-8	430	585	73.5
30. Grand Valley St.	28	15-13	509	693	73.4

Team	GM	W-L	FT	FTA	FT%
31. South Dakota St.	30	24-6	656	894	73.4
32. Abilene Christian	26	7-19	358	488	73.4
33. Northwest Mo. St.	32	29-3	567	773	73.4
34. Anderson (S.C.)	28	18-10	393	536	73.3
35. Minn. St. Moorhead	27	17-10	328	448	73.2

Three-Point Field Goals Per Game

Team	GM	W-L	3FG	3PG
1. St. Anselm	30	19-11	301	10.0
2. Fort Lewis	30	21-9	300	10.0
3. Alderson-Broaddus	30	22-8	299	10.0
4. Bowie St.	28	20-8	273	9.8
5. UNC Pembroke	27	12-15	260	9.6
6. Mont. St.-Billings	28	21-7	267	9.5
7. Truman	26	3-23	246	9.5
8. North Dakota St.	26	11-15	245	9.4
9. Lincoln Memorial	27	14-13	249	9.2
10. Coker	28	11-17	258	9.2
11. Northern Ky.	27	19-8	244	9.0
12. Northeastern St.	30	28-2	271	9.0
13. Southwest St.	29	21-8	261	9.0
14. Bentley	30	20-10	267	8.9
15. Augustana (S.D.)	27	14-13	240	8.9
16. Columbus St.	28	19-9	247	8.8
17. Indianapolis	27	15-12	238	8.8
18. Bemidji St.	28	17-11	245	8.8
19. South Dakota	27	19-8	234	8.7
20. Anderson (S.C.)	28	18-10	242	8.6
21. Ala.-Huntsville	26	17-9	224	8.6
22. UC San Diego	29	8-21	249	8.6
23. Adelphi	31	28-3	266	8.6
24. Arkansas Tech	26	12-14	222	8.5
Bluefield St.	26	3-22	222	8.5
Southern Colo.	26	11-15	222	8.5
27. Calif. (Pa.)	29	23-6	247	8.5
28. Ark.-Monticello	26	9-17	219	8.4
29. Northern Colo.	27	14-13	227	8.4
30. Lees-McRae	28	8-20	235	8.4
31. Pace	29	21-8	243	8.4
32. Southampton	29	17-12	242	8.3
33. Northern St.	28	20-8	233	8.3
34. Winona St.	27	14-13	223	8.3
35. Belmont Abbey	31	25-6	254	8.2

Three-Point Field-Goal Percentage

Team	GM	W-L	3FG	3FGA	3FG%
1. Michigan Tech	30	27-3	216	499	43.3
2. UC Davis	27	15-12	199	466	42.7
3. Southern Colo.	26	11-15	222	523	42.4
4. Alderson-Broaddus	30	22-8	299	705	42.4
5. Calif. (Pa.)	29	23-6	247	591	41.8
6. Northern Colo.	27	14-13	227	547	41.5
7. Fort Hays St.	28	21-7	210	509	41.3
8. Southwest St.	29	21-8	261	633	41.2
9. Quincy	26	7-19	176	431	40.8
10. Carson-Newman	31	26-5	253	620	40.8
11. Ky. Wesleyan	34	31-3	275	675	40.7
12. Southern Ind.	30	22-8	200	492	40.7
13. Northeastern St.	30	28-2	271	675	40.1
14. Colo. Christian	27	10-17	164	410	40.0
15. Pitt.-Johnstown	27	12-15	197	494	39.9
16. South Dakota	27	19-8	234	590	39.7
17. Arkansas Tech	26	12-14	222	562	39.5
18. North Dakota	29	19-10	220	558	39.4
19. St. Anselm	30	19-11	301	764	39.4
20. Minn. St. Moorhead	27	17-10	218	554	39.4
21. North Dakota St.	26	11-15	245	623	39.3
22. St. Edward's	27	4-23	179	456	39.3
23. Johnson Smith	31	23-8	225	575	39.1
24. Drury	27	12-15	188	482	39.0
25. Mesa St.	27	16-11	174	449	38.8
26. St. Cloud St.	28	21-7	226	584	38.7
27. Charleston (W.Va.)	32	25-7	219	568	38.6
28. Western Ore.	27	10-17	179	467	38.3
29. Belmont Abbey	31	25-6	254	663	38.3
30. Barton	28	19-9	207	541	38.3

Team	GM	W-L	3FG	3FGA	3FG%
31. Grand Valley St.	28	15-13	198	518	38.2
32. Cal St. Bakersfield	29	24-5	176	464	37.9
33. N.M. Highlands	26	8-18	198	523	37.9
34. Neb.-Kearney	30	24-6	179	474	37.8
35. Ala.-Huntsville	26	17-9	224	594	37.7

Won-Lost Percentage

Team	W	L	Pct
1. Cal St. San B'dino	28	2	93.3
Northeastern St.	28	2	93.3
3. Ky. Wesleyan	31	3	91.2
4. Northwest Mo. St.	29	3	90.6
5. Adelphi	28	3	90.3

Team	W	L	Pct
6. Michigan Tech	27	3	90.0
7. Tampa	26	3	89.7
8. Humboldt St.	25	4	86.2
Incarnate Word	25	4	86.2
10. Indiana (Pa.)	28	5	84.8
Shaw	28	5	84.8
12. Carson-Newman	26	5	83.9
Salem Int'l	26	5	83.9
14. Metro St.	29	5	82.9
15. Cal St. Bakersfield	24	5	82.8
Seattle Pacific	24	5	82.8
17. Belmont Abbey	25	6	80.6
18. Assumption	24	6	80.0
Neb.-Kearney	24	6	80.0
Rockhurst	24	6	80.0

Team	W	L	Pct
South Dakota St.	24	6	80.0
22. Calif. (Pa.)	23	6	79.3
23. Wingate	26	7	78.8
24. Charleston (W.Va.)	25	7	78.1
Lewis	25	7	78.1
26. Western Wash.	21	6	77.8
27. Findlay	23	7	76.7
Mo. Western St.	23	7	76.7
29. Delta St.	22	7	75.9
Winston-Salem	22	7	75.9
31. Tarleton St.	25	8	75.8
32. Valdosta St.	24	8	75.0
Eckerd	21	7	75.0
Fort Hays St.	21	7	75.0
Gannon	21	7	75.0

2002 Division III Individual Leaders

Scoring

	Name, Team	CL	Ht	Pos	G	FGM	3FG	FT	PTS	PPG
1.	Patrick Glover, Johnson St.	Jr.	6-4	F	24	237	28	147	649	27.0
2.	Steve Wood, Grinnell	So.	6-1	G	24	222	52	150	646	26.9
3.	Keith Schubert, Bethany (W.Va.)	Sr.	6-4	F	29	260	55	184	759	26.2
4.	Colin Tabb, Trinity (Conn.)	Sr.	6-4	F	25	191	66	171	619	24.8
5.	K.B. Debord, Concordia-Austin	Sr.	-	-	24	222	37	110	591	24.6
6.	Willie Chandler, Misericordia	Jr.	6-5	G	29	234	65	168	701	24.2
7.	Kyle Williford, Bridgewater (Va.)	Sr.	6-7	F	26	231	46	119	627	24.1
8.	Brandon Jones, St. Mary's (Md.)	Sr.	6-1	G	26	224	63	101	612	23.5
9.	Jeff Gibbs, Otterbein	Sr.	6-3	C	32	281	0	190	752	23.5
10.	Tim Dworak, Wis.-Oshkosh	Jr.	6-7	F	30	247	16	194	704	23.5
11.	Matt Beacon, Pitt.-Bradford	Jr.	6-4	C	28	262	0	126	650	23.2
12.	Jesse DuPerow, Marietta	Sr.	6-6	F	26	218	64	103	603	23.2
13.	Nolan Larry, Wash. & Jeff.	Jr.	6-2	G	25	189	61	137	576	23.0
14.	Damien Strahorn, Colby	Sr.	-	-	24	196	82	76	550	22.9
15.	Robert Hennigan, Emerson	So.	6-5	F	25	164	71	173	572	22.9
16.	Aaron Galletta, Union (N.Y.)	Sr.	6-7	G	29	228	92	115	663	22.9
17.	Victor Garcia, Knox	Jr.	5-11	G	23	166	43	147	522	22.7
18.	Derek Reich, Chicago	Jr.	-	-	25	204	33	125	566	22.6
19.	Andy O'Brien, York (Pa.)	Jr.	6-3	G	27	224	49	114	611	22.6
20.	Matt Glynn, Puget Sound	So.	6-3	G	25	185	58	126	554	22.2
21.	Zareh Avedian, Cal Lutheran	So.	6-6	F	24	198	32	102	530	22.1
22.	Brian Turner, Rutgers-Camden	Sr.	6-4	G	25	185	72	106	548	21.9
	Rashad Williams, Brandeis	Sr.	6-4	F	25	211	27	99	548	21.9
24.	Chad Plotke, Kenyon	Sr.	6-4	F	24	173	51	129	526	21.9
25.	Robert Moore, Mary Hardin-Baylor	Sr.	6-5	F	25	229	11	77	546	21.8
26.	Seth Harms, Neb. Wesleyan	Sr.	6-6	F	24	200	1	119	520	21.7
27.	Thomas Drakeford, McMurry	Sr.	6-4	G	26	200	55	107	562	21.6
28.	Rich Melzer, Wis.-River Falls	So.	6-8	F	26	232	1	96	561	21.6
29.	Frank Jackson, Gallaudet	So.	6-4	G	24	199	18	94	510	21.3
30.	Drew Carstens, Augustana (Ill.)	So.	6-2	G	24	128	42	208	506	21.1
31.	Pierre Bowery, Frostburg St.	Jr.	6-5	F	28	214	12	150	590	21.1
32.	Terron Buchanon, Albright	So.	-	-	24	178	36	113	505	21.0
33.	Dave Stantial, Keene St.	Sr.	6-4	F	27	179	120	90	568	21.0
34.	Leo Jones, Wesleyan (Conn.)	Sr.	6-2	G	23	185	33	80	483	21.0
35.	Jason Larson, Wis.-Eau Claire	Jr.	6-1	G	20	140	34	104	418	20.9
36.	Michael O'Steen, Oswego St.	Jr.	6-1	G	30	219	70	113	621	20.7
37.	Josh Iserloth, Wis.-Stevens Point	Jr.	6-8	F	27	193	58	113	557	20.6
38.	Jake Royal, Lincoln (Pa.)	Jr.	6-3	G	24	170	97	56	493	20.5
39.	Chuck Cassidy, Cazenovia	Jr.	6-4	G	25	165	60	115	505	20.2
40.	Aubrey Shelton, Puget Sound	Fr.	6-6	F	24	173	12	126	484	20.2
41.	Ricky Sirois, New England	Sr.	-	-	24	160	38	125	483	20.1
42.	Dave Street, Centenary (N.J.)	So.	6-3	G	20	136	54	75	401	20.1
43.	Robert Anderson, Ramapo	Sr.	6-2	G	29	202	61	113	578	19.9
44.	Ray Robinson, Waynesburg	Jr.	6-0	G	27	212	66	48	538	19.9
45.	Brendan Twomey, Mt. St. Mary (N.Y.)	So.	6-2	G	25	160	102	71	493	19.7

	Name, Team	CL	Ht	Pos	G	FGM	3FG	FT	PTS	PPG
	Steve Vega, Clarkson	Sr.	5-7	G	25	138	81	136	493	19.7
47.	Jimmie Greeno, Daniel Webster	Sr.	5-11	G	26	187	15	122	511	19.7
48.	Jimmy Evans, Nazareth	Jr.	6-5	F	27	181	87	80	529	19.6
49.	Mike Moler, Muskingum	Sr.	5-8	G	26	171	74	90	506	19.5
50.	O.J. Gulley, Linfield	So.	6-0	G	25	180	22	104	486	19.4
51.	Kevin Matthews, Western Conn. St.	Sr.	5-10	G	24	187	12	80	466	19.4
52.	Rod Overmyer, Bluffton	Sr.	6-4	F	26	157	71	119	504	19.4
53.	Adam Jones, Buena Vista	Sr.	-	-	29	186	80	108	560	19.3
	Royce Malkowski, Edgewood	Sr.	6-5	F	29	205	34	116	560	19.3
55.	David Paul, Staten Island	Sr.	6-6	F	29	215	10	118	558	19.2
56.	Harry Grabert, Bridgewater St.	Sr.	6-3	F	27	180	5	154	519	19.2
57.	Jermaine Woods, Chris. Newport	Jr.	6-3	G	28	200	97	39	536	19.1
58.	Bob Donlan, Claremont-M-S	Sr.	6-2	F	24	153	64	88	458	19.1
59.	Brandon Zaleski, Moravian	Fr.	6-6	F	25	191	3	92	477	19.1
60.	Asmar Fortney, Rutgers-Newark	Sr.	6-4	F	25	168	47	93	476	19.0
	Mark Lesko, Muhlenberg	Sr.	6-8	F	25	178	5	115	476	19.0
62.	Jason Wiertel, Carthage	Sr.	6-8	F	30	227	5	112	571	19.0
63.	Jay Harris, Clarke	Jr.	6-5	F	25	173	33	95	474	19.0
64.	Andy Gilbert, Bethel (Minn.)	Jr.	6-6	F	27	181	49	98	509	18.9
65.	Joe Finley, Hamilton	Jr.	6-5	F	25	181	0	109	471	18.8
	Will Mensah, Utica/Rome	Sr.	6-2	G	25	162	62	85	471	18.8
67.	Aubrey Lewis-Beyers, Wis.-Whitewater	Jr.	6-3	G	28	179	0	169	527	18.8
68.	Ronald Merriwether, Shenandoah	Sr.	6-1	G	27	185	64	74	508	18.8
69.	Bennie West, Howard Payne	So.	6-2	G	25	182	11	95	470	18.8
70.	Mike Tyszka, Hilbert	Sr.	6-7	F	24	157	9	128	451	18.8

Field-Goal Percentage

(Minimum five FGM/G)

	Name, Team	CL	Ht	Pos	G	FGM	FGA	FG%
1.	Omar Warthen, Neumann	Jr.	6-5	C	27	135	202	66.8
2.	Jeff Gibbs, Otterbein	Sr.	6-3	C	32	281	421	66.7
3.	John Thomas, Fontbonne	Jr.	6-8	G	24	158	237	66.7
4.	Pat Fitzsimons, Amherst	Jr.	6-8	F	29	160	241	66.4
5.	Tim Dworak, Wis.-Oshkosh	Jr.	6-7	F	30	247	381	64.8
6.	Kevin Matthews, Western Conn. St.	Sr.	5-10	G	24	187	289	64.7
7.	Jonathon Jarrett, Sewanee	Jr.	-	-	23	133	206	64.6
8.	Kanem Johnson, Wesleyan (Conn.)	So.	6-5	G	25	185	287	64.5
9.	Edmund Johnson, Wis.-River Falls	Sr.	6-5	F	25	126	198	63.6
10.	Darryl Munroe, Hunter	Sr.	6-5	C	26	177	279	63.4
11.	Andre Peterson, Potsdam St.	Sr.	6-3	F	27	183	289	63.3
12.	Giles Westie, Babson	Sr.	6-6	C	29	160	255	62.7
13.	Kim Maina, McMurry	Sr.	6-9	G	26	133	213	62.4
14.	Bryan Depew, Whitworth	So.	6-5	F	27	176	286	61.5
15.	Henry Grant, Beloit	Jr.	6-4	F	23	168	274	61.3
16.	Matt Beacon, Pitt.-Bradford	Jr.	6-4	C	28	262	428	61.2

STATISTICAL LEADERS

Name, Team	CL	Ht	Pos	G	FGM	FGA	FG%
17. Dallas Crawley, Marymount (Va.)	Sr.	6-6	C	26	162	265	61.1
18. Joe Ringger, DePauw	Jr.	6-7	C	28	195	324	60.2
19. Bennie West, Howard Payne	So.	6-2	G	25	182	303	60.1
20. Brandon Zaleski, Moravian	Fr.	6-6	F	25	191	319	59.9
21. Eric McDonald, Lake Forest	Fr.	6-4	F	23	143	239	59.8
22. David Paul, Staten Island	Sr.	6-6	F	29	215	360	59.7
23. Joe DesJean, Wabash	Jr.	6-6	F	26	170	285	59.6
24. Eric Robertson, Bethel (Minn.)	So.	-	-	26	143	240	59.6
25. Jeremy Miklovic, Defiance	Fr.	6-9	C	27	141	237	59.5
26. Bryan Nelson, Wooster	Jr.	6-4	F	26	176	296	59.5
27. Steve Adams, Johns Hopkins	Jr.	6-6	F	24	120	202	59.4
28. K.B. Debord, Concordia-Austin	Sr.	-	-	24	222	374	59.4
29. Aron Mcmillian, Guilford	Sr.	6-9	C	25	132	223	59.2
30. Mark Lesko, Muhlenberg	Sr.	6-8	F	25	178	301	59.1
31. Jared Hite, Rensselaer	So.	6-5	F	23	122	207	58.9
32. Steve Krueger, Wis.-Stout	Sr.	6-9	C	25	156	265	58.9
Josh Quattrocchi, Franklin	Sr.	6-6	F	29	156	265	58.9
34. Brian Cagle, Mass.-Dartmouth	Jr.	6-5	G	28	188	320	58.8
35. Greg Sutton, St. Lawrence	Sr.	6-6	F	28	146	250	58.4

Three-Point Field-Goal Percentage

(Min. 2.0 3FGM/G)

Name, Team	CL	Ht	Pos	G	3FG	3FGA	3FG%
1. Doug Schneider, Pitt.-Bradford	Jr.	6-3	F	28	78	143	54.5
2. Eddie Hebert, Wis.-La Crosse	Sr.	6-3	G	26	54	105	51.4
3. Kyle Vogt, Lakeland	Sr.	5-11	G	26	66	134	49.3
4. Finn Rebassoo, Occidental	Jr.	6-4	F	25	59	120	49.2
5. John Ely, York (Pa.)	Sr.	5-10	G	27	110	226	48.7
6. Josh Iserloth, Wis.-Stevens Point	Jr.	6-8	F	27	58	120	48.3
7. Mike McGlynn, Tufts	Jr.	6-2	G	25	102	212	48.1
8. Brett Repasky, Bethel (Minn.)	Sr.	6-2	G	27	57	119	47.9
9. .Nate Collord, Wheaton (Ill.)	Jr.	5-10	G	21	50	105	47.6
10. Kevin Wise, Catholic	Jr.	6-4	G	29	98	209	46.9
11. Scott Beebe, Gordon	Jr.	5-11	G	27	112	241	46.5
12. Champ Albano, Staten Island	Sr.	6-0	G	28	66	143	46.2
13. Bob Donlan, Claremont-M-S	Sr.	6-2	F	24	64	139	46.0
14. Nevada Smith, Bethany (W.Va.)	Sr.	6-0	G	29	109	237	46.0
15. Rusty Fordham, Sewanee	Sr.	-	-	25	50	110	45.5
16. Brendan Finn, St. Thomas (Minn.)	Jr.	5-11	G	28	81	179	45.3
17. Chuck Cassidy, Cazenovia	Jr.	6-4	G	25	60	133	45.1
18. Marcus Harvey, Chapman	Jr.	6-3	G	25	73	162	45.1
19. Ryan Sinclair, N.C. Wesleyan	So.	6-1	G	28	59	131	45.0
20. Ethan Slavin, Westfield St.	Jr.	5-10	G	25	53	118	44.9
21. Bryan Bertola, Loras	Sr.	6-2	G	23	50	112	44.6
22. Nick Scherer, Wis.-Oshkosh	Jr.	6-2	G	30	86	193	44.6
23. Matt Mooney, Centre	Sr.	6-0	G	25	95	214	44.4
24. Landon Lewis, Chapman	Fr.	6-3	G	25	71	160	44.4
25. Lorcan Precious, Hunter	So.	6-0	G	26	55	124	44.4
26. Joe Nixon, DePauw	Sr.	6-5	F	28	88	199	44.2
27. Antoine McDaniel, Carthage	Jr.	6-2	G	30	61	138	44.2
28. Rod Emmons, Wittenberg	So.	6-0	G	30	60	136	44.1
29. Noah Brocious, Cal Lutheran	Jr.	6-2	G	25	78	177	44.1
30. Ben Earle, Gordon	So.	6-5	F	26	74	168	44.0
31. Matt Uthoff, Loras	So.	6-2	G	27	55	125	44.0
32. Brendan Twomey, Mt. St. Mary (N.Y.)	So.	6-2	G	25	102	232	44.0
33. Ian Findlay, Emerson	Sr.	6-2	G	24	75	172	43.6
34. Stacey Keyes, Mississippi Col.	Sr.	6-0	G	24	68	157	43.3
35. Adam Jones, Buena Vista	Sr.	-	-	29	80	185	43.2

Three-Point Field Goals Per Game

Name, Team	CL	Ht	Pos	G	3FG	3PG
1. Steve Nordlund, Grinnell	So.	6-4	F	24	137	5.7
2. Dave Stantial, Keene St.	Sr.	6-4	F	27	120	4.4
3. Scott Beebe, Gordon	Jr.	5-11	G	27	112	4.1
4. Mike McGlynn, Tufts	Jr.	6-2	G	25	102	4.1
Brendan Twomey, Mt. St. Mary (N.Y.)	So.	6-2	G	25	102	4.1
6. John Ely, York (Pa.)	Sr.	5-10	G	27	110	4.1
7. Jake Royal, Lincoln (Pa.)	Jr.	6-3	G	24	97	4.0
8. Kazy Payne, Utica/Rome	Jr.	5-8	G	25	101	4.0
9. Matt Mooney, Centre	Sr.	6-0	G	25	95	3.8
10. Nevada Smith, Bethany (W.Va.)	Sr.	6-0	G	29	109	3.8
11. Nick Malinowski, Grinnell	So.	6-5	F	24	88	3.7
12. Jermaine Woods, Chris. Newport	Jr.	6-3	G	28	97	3.5
13. Damien Strahorn, Colby	Jr.	-	-	24	82	3.4
14. Tommy Wesner, Lycoming	Jr.	5-11	G	28	95	3.4
15. Kevin Wise, Catholic	Jr.	6-4	G	29	98	3.4
16. John Gleason, Springfield	Sr.	6-1	G	27	91	3.4
17. Tom Nadeau, Me.-Farmington	Sr.	5-10	G	20	67	3.4
18. Aaron Fries, Ohio Northern	Jr.	6-0	G	25	83	3.3
19. Andy Connell, Muskingum	Jr.	6-1	G	26	86	3.3

Name, Team	CL	Ht	Pos	G	3FG	3PG
20. Trevor Walker, Clark (Mass.)	So.	6-4	F	29	94	3.2
21. Steve Vega, Clarkson	Sr.	5-7	G	25	81	3.2
22. Jimmy Evans, Nazareth	Jr.	6-5	F	27	87	3.2
23. Derek James, MacMurray	Jr.	6-0	G	25	80	3.2
24. Aaron Galletta, Union (N.Y.)	Sr.	6-7	G	29	92	3.2
25. Joe Nixon, DePauw	Sr.	6-5	F	28	88	3.1
26. Ian Findlay, Emerson	Jr.	6-2	G	24	75	3.1
27. Noah Brocious, Cal Lutheran	Jr.	6-2	G	25	78	3.1
28. Doug Billet, Marywood	Jr.	6-1	G	23	71	3.1
29. Ralph Lora, Kean	Sr.	6-2	G	25	77	3.1
30. James Wallace, Va. Wesleyan	Sr.	5-11	G	26	79	3.0
31. Dom Ionadi, Carnegie Mellon	Sr.	6-0	G	23	69	3.0
32. Zach Carlson, Grinnell	Jr.	6-1	G	24	71	3.0
33. Marcus Harvey, Chapman	Jr.	6-3	G	25	73	2.9
34. Brendan Finn, St. Thomas (Minn.)	Jr.	5-11	G	28	81	2.9
35. Brian Turner, Rutgers-Camden	Sr.	6-4	G	25	72	2.9

Free-Throw Percentage

(Min. 2.5 FTM/G)

Name, Team	CL	Ht	Pos	G	FT	FTA	FT%
1. Jason Luisi, Suffolk	Sr.	-	-	28	87	94	92.6
2. Shawn Mccormick, Baldwin-Wallace	Sr.	6-4	G	26	74	80	92.5
3. Kyle Vogt, Lakeland	Sr.	5-11	G	26	71	78	91.0
4. Kevin Broene, Calvin	So.	6-3	G	27	81	89	91.0
5. Mike Moler, Muskingum	Sr.	5-8	G	26	90	99	90.9
6. Steve Kohl, Ripon	Sr.	6-0	G	26	102	113	90.3
7. Robby Pridgen, Roanoke	Jr.	6-2	G	27	125	139	89.9
8. .Scott Beebe, Gordon	Jr.	5-11	G	27	71	79	89.9
9. Joe Witherspoon, Gordon	Jr.	6-3	F	27	106	118	89.8
10. Steve Vega, Clarkson	Sr.	5-7	G	25	136	152	89.5
11. Derrick Rogers, Averett	Sr.	6-2	F	26	80	90	88.9
12. Jim Conrad, Ohio Northern	So.	6-0	G	25	79	89	88.8
13. Brendan Carney, Colby-Sawyer	Sr.	5-8	G	28	70	79	88.6
14. Coffey Anderson, Howard Payne	Sr.	6-6	G	25	72	82	87.8
Joe Nixon, DePauw	Sr.	6-5	F	28	72	82	87.8
16. Dirk Rhinehart, Kalamazoo	Jr.	6-2	G	27	121	138	87.7
17. Kevin Shay, Otterbein	Sr.	6-2	G	33	113	129	87.6
18. Josh Stanek, Coe	Sr.	6-0	G	26	84	96	87.5
19. Bryan Depew, Whitworth	So.	6-5	F	27	102	117	87.2
20. Bob Donlan, Claremont-M-S	Sr.	6-2	F	24	88	101	87.1
21. Steve Glasgow, Monmouth (Ill.)	Sr.	6-1	G	22	67	77	87.0
22. Tennyson Whitted, Ramapo	Jr.	5-9	G	29	106	122	86.9
23. Isaac Brooks, Goucher	So.	5-10	G	26	79	91	86.8
24. Colin Tabb, Trinity (Conn.)	Sr.	6-4	F	25	171	197	86.8
25. Tony Borghese, Otterbein	Fr.	5-10	G	33	120	139	86.3
26. Chris Zimmerman, Susquehanna	So.	5-8	G	26	87	101	86.1
27. Alex Wilson, Bates	Sr.	6-6	F	24	99	115	86.1
28. Dan Archambault, Wis.-Eau Claire	Fr.	6-2	G	24	68	79	86.1
29. John Gleason, Springfield	Sr.	6-1	G	27	80	93	86.0
30. Victor Garcia, Knox	Jr.	5-11	G	23	147	171	86.0
31. Clint Ferguson, Rose-Hulman	Sr.	6-3	G	25	67	78	85.9
32. Drew Logan, Blackburn	Sr.	-	-	25	108	126	85.7
Steve King, Fontbonne	Jr.	6-1	G	24	78	91	85.7
34. David Mayle, Hiram	Jr.	6-4	F	24	100	117	85.5
35. Derek Ricketts, Anderson (Ind.)	Jr.	6-3	G	26	73	86	84.9

Rebounds Per Game

Name, Team	CL	Ht	Pos	G	REB	RPG
1. Jeff Gibbs, Otterbein	Sr.	6-3	C	32	523	16.3
2. Pat Reardon, Mass. Liberal Arts	Jr.	6-10	C	23	302	13.1
3. Jed Johnson, Maine Maritime	Jr.	6-7	F	23	285	12.4
4. Joe Corbett, Hobart	Jr.	6-6	F	24	293	12.2
5. Jared Hite, Rensselaer	So.	6-5	F	23	276	12.0
6. Darren Pugh, Lebanon Valley	Jr.	6-8	C	27	315	11.7
7. Dan Luciano, Ursinus	Jr.	6-9	F	24	261	10.9
8. Jonathan Bird, Caltech	Jr.	-	-	22	230	10.5
9. Eddie Washetas, Maranatha Baptist	So.	-	-	27	282	10.4
10. Luis Melo, Mt. St. Mary (N.Y.)	Sr.	6-4	G	27	278	10.3
11. Michael Atkins, Shenandoah	Jr.	6-9	C	27	277	10.3
12. Michael Parker, Springfield	Sr.	6-3	F	26	266	10.2
13. Robert Moore, Mary Hardin-Baylor	Sr.	6-5	F	25	255	10.2
Derek Reich, Chicago	Jr.	-	-	25	255	10.2
15. Kyle McNamar, Curry	Sr.	6-6	F	25	254	10.2
16. John Mietus, Lewis & Clark	Jr.	6-7	F	30	304	10.1
17. Ryan Kelly, Roger Williams	Sr.	6-4	F	27	270	10.0
Billy Rea, Eastern Conn. St.	Sr.	6-7	C	26	260	10.0
19. Tillman Sims, Alvernia	Jr.	6-6	F	28	279	10.0
20. Jesse Lisiecka, Nazareth	Sr.	6-5	C	26	256	9.8

Name, Team	CL	Ht	Pos	G	REB	RPG
21. Jamal Lyons, Eastern Nazarene	So.	6-6	F	26	255	9.8
22. Joe DesJean, Wabash	Jr.	6-6	F	26	254	9.8
Jesse DuPerow, Marietta	Sr.	6-6	F	26	254	9.8
24. Mark Lesko, Muhlenberg	Sr.	6-8	F	25	244	9.8
25. Drew Demuth, Williams	Jr.	6-5	F	28	273	9.8
Patrick Glover, Johnson St.	Jr.	6-4	F	24	234	9.8
27. C.J. Rodgers, Union (N.Y.)	Sr.	6-4	F	23	224	9.7
28. Billy Allen, Mass.-Boston	Fr.	6-6	G	25	243	9.7
29. Royce Malkowski, Edgewood	Sr.	6-5	F	29	279	9.6
30. Craig Negangard, Eureka	So.	6-4	F	25	237	9.5
31. Steve Erfle, Ursinus	Jr.	6-8	F	24	226	9.4
32. Russ Churchwell, Oglethorpe	So.	6-5	F	25	234	9.4
33. Omar Warthen, Neumann	Jr.	6-5	C	27	251	9.3
34. Seth Harms, Neb. Wesleyan	Sr.	6-6	F	24	223	9.3
35. Davidek Herron, Hobart	Jr.	6-6	F	25	232	9.3

Assists Per Game

Name, Team	CL	Ht	Pos	G	AST	APG
1. Tennyson Whitted, Ramapo	Jr.	5-9	G	29	319	11.0
2. Trevelle Boyd, East Tex. Baptist	Jr.	5-11	G	24	169	7.0
3. .Rocky Parise, Elizabethtown	Sr.	5-10	G	32	217	6.8
4. .Danny Kanamori, MIT	Fr.	5-10	G	25	169	6.8
5. Tim Gaspar, Mass.-Dartmouth	Jr.	-	-	29	196	6.8
6. Steve Kohl, Ripon	Sr.	6-0	G	26	175	6.7
7. Ryan Keating, St. John's (Minn.)	Sr.	6-0	G	21	137	6.5
8. Richard Jackson, Mount Union	Sr.	6-1	G	27	176	6.5
9. Michael Crotty, Williams	So.	6-0	G	28	180	6.4
Mike Howland, DePauw	Sr.	5-11	G	28	180	6.4
11. Scott Johnson, Bethany (W.Va.)	Sr.	5-10	G	29	186	6.4
12. Tom Drumm, Cazenovia	Sr.	6-3	G	27	170	6.3
13. Lorcan Precious, Hunter	So.	6-0	G	26	156	6.0
14. Diego Reino, Drew	Sr.	5-10	G	25	149	6.0
15. Greg Leone, Hamilton	So.	6-1	G	25	148	5.9
16. Keith Darden, Concordia-Austin	So.	-	-	25	147	5.9
17. Rafi Hargrove, New Jersey City	Sr.	5-7	G	29	168	5.8
18. Steve King, Fontbonne	Jr.	6-1	G	24	138	5.8
19. Greg Vecchione, Chapman	Sr.	5-11	G	22	126	5.7
20. Curtis Miller, Albertus Magnus	So.	5-7	G	25	143	5.7
21. Bobby Henning, Catholic	Fr.	5-8	G	27	154	5.7
22. Aaron Kiffer, Pitt.-Bradford	Fr.	6-0	G	28	159	5.7
23. Sean Brown, Frostburg St.	Sr.	5-9	G	28	158	5.6
24. Evan Fowler, Mary Washington	So.	6-0	G	26	146	5.6
25. Jeff Weld, Castleton St.	Jr.	5-10	G	25	140	5.6
26. Rashad Clark, Oneonta St.	Jr.	6-1	G	26	145	5.6
Chris Zimmerman, Susquehanna	So.	5-8	G	26	145	5.6
28. Brandon Hansen, Neb. Wesleyan	So.	6-1	G	22	122	5.5
29. Albert Haskins, Chris. Newport	Sr.	6-1	G	28	155	5.5
30. Michael Irwin, New York U.	Jr.	5-3	G	25	138	5.5
31. Tyson Thompson, Shenandoah	Jr.	5-9	G	27	149	5.5
32. Fareed Burton, Lincoln (Pa.)	So.	5-11	G	24	132	5.5
33. Mike Sullivan, Salisbury	Sr.	5-11	G	25	135	5.4
34. Adam Fischer, Fontbonne	Jr.	6-1	G	23	124	5.4
35. Bobby Jenkins, N.C. Wesleyan	So.	5-10	G	28	150	5.4

Blocked Shots Per Game

Name, Team	CL	Ht	Pos	G	BLKS	BKPG
1. Kyle McNamar, Curry	Sr.	6-6	F	25	107	4.3
2. Antonio Ramos, Clarke	Sr.	7-3	C	25	98	3.9
3. Arthur Hatch, Methodist	So.	6-0	G	26	98	3.8
4. Rob Smith, N.C. Wesleyan	Jr.	6-9	C	26	96	3.7
5. Jawara Stephenson, Wesley	Fr.	6-10	C	24	84	3.5
6. John Thomas, Fontbonne	Jr.	6-8	C	24	79	3.3
7. Patrick Stirk, New Paltz St.	Sr.	6-7	C	22	70	3.2
8. Terry Gray, Chris. Newport	Jr.	6-6	C	28	89	3.2
9. Charles Simmons, Aurora	So.	6-5	G	24	76	3.2
10. John Mcbride, Gordon	Sr.	6-10	C	25	77	3.1

Name, Team	CL	Ht	Pos	G	BLKS	BKPG
11. Jamal Lyons, Eastern Nazarene	So.	6-6	F	26	79	3.0
12. Don Overbeek, Hope	Jr.	6-10	C	30	91	3.0
13. Mamadou Gueye, Johnson & Wales	Sr.	6-7	C	25	73	2.9
14. Jarriot Rook, Washington (Mo.)	Jr.	6-8	C	27	78	2.9
15. Adam Rue, Augustana (Ill.)	Jr.	6-10	C	23	62	2.7
16. Pat Fitzsimons, Amherst	Jr.	6-8	F	29	76	2.6
Matt Hilleary, Catholic	Jr.	6-6	C	29	76	2.6
18. Jayson Douthwright, Albertus Magnus	Jr.	6-4	C	26	66	2.5
19. Omar Boothe, Montclair St.	Sr.	6-3	G	27	68	2.5
20. Jesse DuPerow, Marietta	Sr.	6-6	F	26	65	2.5
Ryan Niemic, Heidelberg	Sr.	6-9	C	26	65	2.5
22. Garrett Ingram, Illinois Col.	Jr.	6-10	C	24	59	2.5
23. Jeff Gibbs, Otterbein	Sr.	6-3	C	32	78	2.4
24. Rockland Owens, Sul Ross St.	Fr.	6-5	F	25	60	2.4
25. Joe DesJean, Wabash	Jr.	6-6	F	26	61	2.3
26. Joel Leichtnam, Castleton St.	So.	6-8	F	25	58	2.3
27. Ron McIntyre, Wilkes	Sr.	6-6	F	26	60	2.3
28. Craig Coupe, Tufts	Fr.	6-7	C	25	55	2.2
Mark Lesko, Muhlenberg	Sr.	6-8	F	25	55	2.2
30. Luke Hennings, Blackburn	Jr.	-	-	25	54	2.2
31. Cam Scribner, Haverford	Jr.	6-9	C	20	43	2.2
32. Pat Adams, Buffalo St.	Jr.	6-3	C	23	49	2.1
33. Rich Melzer, Wis.-River Falls	So.	6-8	F	26	55	2.1
34. Michael Atkins, Shenandoah	Jr.	6-9	C	27	56	2.1
35. Corey Days, Trinity (Conn.)	Jr.	6-5	F	20	41	2.1

Steals Per Game

Name, Team	CL	Ht	Pos	G	ST	STPG
1. Tennyson Whitted, Ramapo	Jr.	5-9	G	29	138	4.8
2. Ken Heiser, Grinnell	So.	6-0	G	24	84	3.5
3. Ricky Hollis, Brockport St.	Sr.	5-10	G	31	108	3.5
4. Tim Gaspar, Mass.-Dartmouth	Jr.	-	-	29	97	3.3
5. Keith Darden, Concordia-Austin	So.	-	-	25	81	3.2
6. Chaz Williamson, Widener	Sr.	5-8	G	27	87	3.2
7. .Bennie West, Howard Payne	So.	6-2	G	25	78	3.1
8. .Irv Jenkins, New Jersey City	Sr.	6-1	G	28	86	3.1
9. Tom Roeder, St. Joseph's (N.Y.)	Sr.	6-1	G	26	79	3.0
10. Conrad Burnside, Richard Stockton	Sr.	6-2	F	26	78	3.0
Demajo Clemens, Greenville	Jr.	6-1	G	24	72	3.0
12. Jason Fulford, Brooklyn	Fr.	5-9	G	25	74	3.0
Brendan Twomey, Mt. St. Mary (N.Y.)	So.	6-2	G	25	74	3.0
14. Daniel Waguespack, Millsaps	Sr.	6-5	F	25	73	2.9
15. Jeff Hines, Babson	So.	6-1	G	30	87	2.9
16. Mark Buri, St. Thomas (Minn.)	Sr.	6-0	G	28	80	2.9
17. Jeffrey Allen, Concordia-Austin	So.	6-1	G	25	71	2.8
18. Joe Howell, Fitchburg St.	Jr.	6-3	F	25	70	2.8
Will Mensah, Utica/Rome	Sr.	6-2	G	25	70	2.8
20. Jaimar Mansel, Roanoke	Sr.	6-0	G	27	74	2.7
21. Steve Vega, Clarkson	Sr.	5-7	G	25	68	2.7
22. Matt Tabash, Washington (Mo.)	Jr.	5-10	G	27	73	2.7
23. Lerick Charles, Mass. Liberal Arts	Jr.	6-0	G	20	54	2.7
24. Brian Turner, Rutgers-Camden	Sr.	6-4	G	25	67	2.7
25. Bryan Dlugolenski, Salve Regina	Jr.	5-11	G	29	77	2.7
26. Rafael Cardoso, Salve Regina	Jr.	5-8	G	28	74	2.6
27. John Alesi, Baruch	Jr.	6-2	G	22	58	2.6
28. Devon Downing, Alfred	Sr.	6-2	G	25	64	2.6
O.J. Gulley, Linfield	So.	6-0	G	25	64	2.6
30. Adam Harper, Amherst	So.	6-2	G	22	56	2.5
Kenny Spranger, Monmouth (Ill.)	Sr.	6-5	F	22	56	2.5
32. Steve Wood, Grinnell	So.	6-1	G	24	61	2.5
33. Kevin Christensen, Wis. Lutheran	Fr.	6-2	G	25	63	2.5
34. Justin Bryant, Johnson & Wales	Jr.	6-1	G	29	73	2.5
35. Tillman Sims, Alvernia	Jr.	6-6	F	28	70	2.5

STATISTICAL LEADERS

2002 Division III Game Highs

Individual Highs

ASSISTS

	Name, Team	CL	Ht	Pos	Opponent	Date	AST
1.	Troy DeCook, Rockford	Jr.	6-2	F	Grinnell	12/14/01	19
2.	Tennyson Whitted, Ramapo	Jr.	5-9	G	Rowan	02/06/02	15
	Mike Howland, DePauw	Sr.	5-11	G	Rhodes	01/27/02	15
	Diego Reino, Drew	Sr.	5-10	G	Wilkes	01/12/02	15
5.	Tennyson Whitted, Ramapo	Jr.	5-9	G	New Jersey City	03/03/02	14
	Tennyson Whitted, Ramapo	Jr.	5-9	G	Col. of New Jersey	01/26/02	14
7.	Trevelle Boyd, East Tex. Baptist	Jr.	5-11	G	Louisiana Col.	02/07/02	13
	Ricky Davis, Lakeland	So.	6-0	G	Wis. Lutheran	01/26/02	13
	Barrett Karvis, Oglethorpe	Jr.	5-8	G	La Grange	01/16/02	13
	Victor Garcia, Knox	Jr.	5-11	G	Grinnell	01/15/02	13
	Danny Kanamori, MIT	Fr.	5-10	G	Polytechnic (N.Y.)	12/08/01	13
	Marcus Bixler, Bluffton	Jr.	6-1	F	Concordia (Ind.)	11/17/01	13

BLOCKED SHOTS

	Name, Team	CL	Ht	Pos	Opponent	Date	BLKS
1.	Antonio Ramos, Clarke	Sr.	7-3	C	Mt. Mercy	12/04/01	12
2.	Kyle McNamar, Curry	Sr.	6-6	F	New England	01/26/02	11
3.	Kyle McNamar, Curry	Sr.	6-6	F	Mount Ida	01/19/02	10
4.	Kyle McNamar, Curry	Sr.	6-6	F	Lasell	01/17/02	9
5.	Terry Gray, Chris. Newport	Jr.	6-6	C	Greensboro	02/17/02	8
	Dietrich Maertens, Centenary (N.J.)	Sr.	6-9	C	Farmingdale	02/16/02	8
	Jesse Foote, Rochester Inst.	Fr.	6-10	C	Ithaca	02/08/02	8
	Michael Atkins, Shenandoah	Jr.	6-9	C	Averett	02/02/02	8
	Jesse DuPerow, Marietta	Sr.	6-6	F	John Carroll	12/08/01	8
	Arthur Hatch, Methodist	So.	6-0	G	Fayetteville St.	12/04/01	8

FIELD-GOAL PERCENTAGE
(Minimum 10 FGM)

	Name, Team	CL	Opponent	Date	FG%	FGM	FGA
1.	Joe Howell, Fitchburg St.	Jr.	Framingham St.	01/22/02	100	11	11
	Scott Chodor, Wash. & Jeff.	So.	Pitt.-Greensburg	11/26/01	100	11	11
	Marcus Ross, Savannah A&D	Sr.	Huntingdon	02/12/02	100	10	10
	Luke Feddersen, Cornell College	Jr.	Dubuque	01/08/02	100	10	10

FREE-THROW PERCENTAGE
(Minimum 10 made)

	Name, Team	CL	Opponent	Date	FT%	FT	FTA
1.	Scott Study, Franklin	Jr.	Hanover	02/22/02	100	17	17
	Michael O'Steen, Oswego St.	Jr.	Buffalo St.	02/16/02	100	14	14
	Kyle Williford, Bridgewater (Va.)	Sr.	Roanoke	01/16/02	100	14	14
	Richard Sommers, Emory	So.	Washington (Mo.)	01/11/02	100	14	14
	Victor Garcia, Knox	Jr.	Illinois Col.	01/29/02	100	13	13
	Kari Hannula, St. Norbert	Jr.	Lake Forest	01/26/02	100	13	13
	Aubrey Lewis-Beyers, Wis.-Whitewater	Jr.	Purdue-Calumet	11/24/01	100	13	13
	Todd Richards, Mount Union	Sr.	Marietta	02/20/02	100	12	12
	Mark Buri, St. Thomas (Minn.)	Sr.	Macalester	02/11/02	100	12	12
	Kalonji Kadima, Wis.-Stevens Point	Sr.	Wis.-Eau Claire	02/06/02	100.0	12	12

POINTS

	Name, Team	CL	Ht	Pos	Opponent	Date	PTS
1.	Kyle Williford, Bridgewater (Va.)	Sr.	6-7	F	Roanoke	01/16/02	56
2.	Eric McDonald, Lake Forest	Fr.	6-4	F	Grinnell	12/08/01	50
3.	Robert Hennigan, Emerson	So.	6-5	F	Suffolk	02/07/02	47
4.	Ben Earle, Gordon	So.	6-5	F	Bates	01/10/02	45
	Terron Buchanon, Albright	So.	-	-	Endicott	01/03/02	45
	Aaron Galletta, Union (N.Y.)	Sr.	6-7	G	Cazenovia	12/19/01	45
7.	Lydale Waller, Southern Vt.	Jr.	5-9	G	Suffolk	02/09/02	44
	Brandon Henderson, Lake Erie	Jr.	6-1	G	Pitt.-Greensburg	02/02/02	44
	Steve Wood, Grinnell	So.	6-1	G	Beloit	01/26/02	44
	Victor Garcia, Knox	Jr.	5-11	G	Beloit	01/25/02	44

REBOUNDS

	Name, Team	CL	Ht	Pos	Opponent	Date	REB
1.	Kyle Williford, Bridgewater (Va.)	Sr.	6-7	F	Emory & Henry	01/12/02	24
2.	Jeff Gibbs, Otterbein	Sr.	6-3	C	Concordia-Austin	11/27/01	23
3.	Kyle McNamar, Curry	Sr.	6-6	F	New England Col.	01/22/02	22
	Eddie Washetas, Maranatha Baptist	So.	-	-	Wis. Lutheran	01/19/02	22
	Jesse DuPerow, Marietta	Sr.	6-6	F	Susquehanna	12/19/01	22
	Pat Adams, Buffalo St.	Sr.	6-6	C	Utica/Rome	12/08/01	22
7.	Jed Johnson, Maine Maritime	Jr.	6-7	F	Mount Ida	01/27/02	21
	Kyle McNamar, Curry	Sr.	6-6	F	New England	01/26/02	21
	Chris Bowman, Lehman	Jr.	6-3	F	Brooklyn	01/19/02	21
	Jeff Gibbs, Otterbein	Sr.	6-3	C	Heidelberg	01/19/02	21

STEALS

	Name, Team	CL	Ht	Pos	Opponent	Date	ST
1.	Daniel Waguespack, Millsaps	Sr.	6-5	F	Hendrix	02/17/02	11
2.	Tim Dworak, Wis.-Oshkosh	Jr.	6-7	F	Wis.-Superior	02/19/02	9
	Ted Bezel, Gwynedd-Mercy	So.	5-11	G	Goucher	02/05/02	9
	Drew Demerath, St. Norbert	So.	6-1	G	Carroll (Wis.)	12/08/01	9
	Steve Wood, Grinnell	So.	6-1	G	Faith Bapt. Bible	11/20/01	9
6.	Irv Jenkins, New Jersey City	Sr.	6-1	G	Montclair St.	02/13/02	8
	Irv Jenkins, New Jersey City	Sr.	6-1	G	Rutgers-Camden	02/09/02	8
	Chris Palm, Macalester	Sr.	6-1	G	Bethel (Minn.)	01/23/02	8
	Mario Mungia, McMurry	So.	5-10	G	Mary Hardin-Baylor	01/19/02	8
	Brett Johnson, St. Mary's (Minn.)	Sr.	5-11	G	Macalester	01/14/02	8

THREE-POINT FIELD-GOAL PERCENTAGE
(Minimum seven 3FGM)

	Name, Team	CL	Opponent	Date	3FG%	3FG	3FGA
1.	Josh Iserloth, Wis.-Stevens Point	Jr.	Wis.-River Falls	01/09/02	100.0	8	8
2.	Nathanael Haynie, Me.-Farmington	So.	Thomas	01/30/02	90.9	10	11
3.	Tim Folan, Williams	Jr.	Union (N.Y.)	11/20/01	90.0	9	10
4.	Ryan Rogan, Scranton	Fr.	Springfield	11/17/01	88.9	8	9
5.	Matt Kukla, Wis.-River Falls	So.	Wis.-Stout	01/02/02	87.5	7	8
	Corey Rich, Albright	Jr.	Moravian	12/05/01	87.5	7	8
	Jim Zinn, DeSales	So.	Centenary (N.J.)	11/29/01	87.5	7	8
8.	Greg Kloepping, Monmouth (Ill.)		Tampa	01/02/02	84.6	11	13
9.	Ben Earle, Gordon	So.	Bates	01/10/02	83.3	10	12
10.	Jay Kreider, Johns Hopkins	Jr.	Ursinus	01/26/02	80.0	8	10

THREE-POINT FIELD GOALS MADE

	Name, Team	CL	Ht	Pos	Opponent	Date	3FG
1.	Matt Mooney, Centre	Sr.	6-0	G	Rhodes	02/01/02	11
	Steve Nordlund, Grinnell	So.	6-4	F	Carroll (Wis.)	01/11/02	11
	Jake Royal, Lincoln (Pa.)	Jr.	6-3	G	Gallaudet	01/07/02	11
	Greg Kloepping, Monmouth (Ill.)	Sr.	6-2	G	Tampa	01/02/02	11
5.	John Gleason, Springfield	Sr.	6-1	G	Coast Guard	02/09/02	10
	Adam Jones, Buena Vista	Sr.	-	-	Dubuque	02/09/02	10
	Nathanael Haynie, Me.-Farmington	So.	6-0	G	Thomas	01/30/02	10
	Ben Earle, Gordon	So.	6-5	F	Bates	01/10/02	10
	Travis Brett, Earlham	Sr.	6-0	G	DePauw	01/08/02	10
10.	Kerry Betz, Richard Stockton	Sr.	6-2	G	Ramapo	03/02/02	9

Team Highs

FIELD-GOAL PERCENTAGE

	Name, Team	Opponent	Date	FG%	FGM	FGA
1.	Rockford	Grinnell	12/14/01	82.2	60	73
2.	Lawrence	Grinnell	02/01/02	79.7	47	59
3.	Monmouth (Ill.)	Grinnell	01/08/02	76.6	49	64
4.	Wis.-La Crosse	Grinnell	11/25/01	73.8	48	65
5.	Roger Williams	Elms	12/11/01	72.5	37	51
6.	Martin Luther	Grinnell	11/17/01	71.4	55	77
7.	Lake Forest	Grinnell	12/08/01	71.1	54	76
8.	Mississippi Col.	Ozarks (Ark.)	02/02/02	70.8	34	48
9.	Wis.-La Crosse	Grinnell	12/09/01	70.0	49	70
10.	Knox	Grinnell	01/15/02	69.0	40	58

THREE-POINT FIELD-GOAL PERCENTAGE
(Minimum 10 3FGM)

	Team	Opponent	Date	3FG%	3FG	3FGA
1.	Mt. St. Mary (N.Y.)	CCNY	12/04/01	85.7	12	14
2.	Waynesburg	Ohio-Eastern	01/09/02	77.8	14	18
3.	Carroll (Wis.)	Ripon	02/09/02	75.0	12	16
4.	Buena Vista	Loras	02/22/02	73.3	11	15
5.	Occidental	Pomona-Pitzer	01/16/02	72.2	13	18
6.	Widener	Moravian	01/16/02	71.4	10	14
	Neb. Wesleyan	Doane	01/02/02	71.4	10	14
	Rochester	Nazareth	11/20/01	71.4	10	14
9.	Augustana (Ill.)	Beloit	11/28/01	70.6	12	17
	Waynesburg	Pitt.-Greensburg	11/28/01	70.6	12	17

THREE-POINT FIELD GOALS MADE

	Team	Opponent	Date	3FG
1.	Grinnell	Carroll (Wis.)	01/11/02	31
2.	Grinnell	Carroll (Wis.)	02/02/02	30
3.	Grinnell	Ripon	01/25/02	28
4.	Grinnell	Wis.-La Crosse	12/09/01	25
5.	Grinnell	Martin Luther	11/17/01	22
6.	Chapman	Life Bible	02/05/02	21
	Southern Me.	Thomas	01/24/02	21
8.	Wittenberg	Hiram	02/09/02	20
9.	New England Col.	Notre Dame (N.H.)	12/11/01	19
10.	Muskingum	John Carroll	02/06/02	18

FREE-THROW PERCENTAGE
(Minimum 15 FTM)

	Team	Opponent	Date	FT%	FT	FTA
1.	Utica	Ithaca	01/22/02	100.0	20	20
	Marietta	Ohio Northern	02/09/02	100.0	19	19
	Concordia-M'head	Augsburg	12/05/01	100.0	16	16
	Wis.-River Falls	Wis.-Platteville	01/16/02	100.0	15	15

	Team	Opponent	Date	FT%	FT	FTA
5.	Baldwin-Wallace	Otterbein	12/05/01	95.8	23	24
	Lakeland	Milwaukee Engr.	12/04/01	95.8	23	24
7.	Earlham	Wooster	01/19/02	95.7	22	23
	Otterbein	Capital	12/01/01	95.7	22	23
	Heidelberg	Simpson	11/17/01	95.7	22	23
10.	Heidelberg	Wilmington (Ohio)	01/12/02	95.2	20	21

POINTS

	Team	Opponent	Date	PTS	OPP PTS
1.	Wis.-La Crosse	Grinnell	12/09/01	146	0
2.	Grinnell	Carroll (Wis.)	01/11/02	143	85
3.	Lake Forest	Grinnell	12/08/01	140	0
	Grinnell	Colorado Col.	12/02/01	140	0
5.	Grinnell	Beloit	01/26/02	139	126
6.	Rockford	Grinnell	12/14/01	138	0
7.	Grinnell	Wis.-La Crosse	12/09/01	136	146
8.	Grinnell	Ripon	01/25/02	135	123
	Grinnell	Lake Forest	12/08/01	135	140
10.	Martin Luther	Grinnell	11/17/01	134	131

2002 Division III Team Leaders

Scoring Offense

	Team	G	W-L	PTS	PPG
1.	Grinnell	24	12-12	2997	124.9
2.	Defiance	28	18-10	2554	91.2
3.	Elizabethtown	32	29-3	2903	90.7
4.	Keene St.	28	23-5	2528	90.3
5.	Linfield	25	14-11	2222	88.9
6.	Clark (Mass.)	29	23-6	2536	87.4
7.	Bethany (W.Va.)	29	21-8	2505	86.4
8.	Puget Sound	25	11-14	2157	86.3
9.	Greenville	25	9-16	2146	85.8
10.	York (Pa.)	27	21-6	2312	85.6
11.	McMurry	26	20-6	2223	85.5
12.	Lasell	28	21-7	2387	85.3
13.	Lewis & Clark	30	24-6	2547	84.9
14.	Brockport St.	31	28-3	2621	84.5
15.	Otterbein	33	30-3	2787	84.5
16.	Fontbonne	24	18-6	2019	84.1
17.	Pitt.-Bradford	28	23-5	2353	84.0
18.	Emory & Henry	27	14-13	2258	83.6
19.	Frostburg St.	28	16-12	2326	83.1
20.	Howard Payne	25	13-12	2069	82.8
21.	DePauw	28	24-4	2315	82.7
22.	Lincoln (Pa.)	24	11-13	1982	82.6
23.	Hampden-Sydney	29	23-6	2394	82.6
24.	Anderson (Ind.)	26	15-11	2137	82.2
25.	Washington (Mo.)	27	25-2	2212	81.9
26.	Catholic	29	26-3	2375	81.9
	Franklin	29	20-9	2375	81.9
28.	Widener	27	19-8	2209	81.8
29.	Mass.-Dartmouth	29	21-8	2371	81.8
	Wesleyan (Conn.)	25	15-10	2041	81.6
31.	Suffolk	28	17-11	2283	81.5
32.	Concordia-Austin	25	15-10	2035	81.4
33.	Western Conn. St.	28	21-7	2279	81.4
34.	St. Joseph's (Me.)	28	18-10	2271	81.1
35.	Plymouth St.	29	18-11	2352	81.1

Scoring Margin

	Team	GM	W-L	PTS	PPG
1.	Brockport St.	31	28-3	2621	84.5
2.	Washington (Mo.)	27	25-2	2212	81.9
3.	Elizabethtown	32	29-3	2903	90.7
4.	Wittenberg	30	26-4	2409	80.3
5.	Gust. Adolphus	29	24-5	2275	78.4
6.	Waynesburg	27	18-9	2174	80.5
7.	Occidental	25	18-7	1889	75.6
8.	Babson	30	25-5	2151	71.7
9.	Catholic	29	26-3	2375	81.9
10.	Maryville (Tenn.)	29	24-5	2263	78.0
11.	Keene St.	28	23-5	2528	90.3
12.	Hampden-Sydney	29	23-6	2394	82.6
13.	Williams	28	22-6	2186	78.1
14.	Chapman	25	18-7	1946	77.8
15.	Cal Lutheran	25	20-5	1978	79.1
16.	Carthage	30	28-2	2269	75.6
17.	Clark (Mass.)	29	23-6	2536	87.4
18.	Colby-Sawyer	28	22-6	2234	79.8
19.	Chris. Newport	28	23-5	2233	79.8
20.	Bethel (Minn.)	27	21-6	2081	77.1
21.	Lasell	28	21-7	2387	85.3
22.	Randolph-Macon	30	24-6	2177	72.6
23.	Wooster	28	21-7	2195	78.4
24.	DePauw	28	24-4	2315	82.7
25.	Mississippi Col.	24	21-3	1782	74.3
26.	Otterbein	33	30-3	2787	84.5
27.	Wis.-Stevens Point	27	21-6	2114	78.3
28.	St. Thomas (Minn.)	28	24-4	2082	74.4
29.	Hanover	26	21-5	1964	75.5
30.	Buena Vista	29	23-6	2321	80.0
31.	Whitworth	27	20-7	2100	77.8
32.	Rochester	30	24-6	2106	70.2
33.	Mass.-Dartmouth	29	21-8	2371	81.8
34.	Claremont-M-S	26	21-5	1905	73.3
35.	Lewis & Clark	30	24-6	2547	84.9

Rebound Margin

	Team	GM	W-L	REB
1.	Wittenberg	30	26-4	1276
2.	Grove City	27	17-10	1114
3.	Otterbein	33	30-3	1368
4.	Williams	28	22-6	1115
5.	DeSales	26	16-10	1133
6.	King's (Pa.)	29	22-7	1217
	Staten Island	29	22-7	1155
8.	Rochester	30	24-6	1125
9.	Ursinus	24	8-16	1016
10.	Waynesburg	27	18-9	1123
11.	Keene St.	28	23-5	1341
12.	Rowan	25	15-10	1033
13.	Chapman	25	18-7	948
14.	Colby-Sawyer	28	22-6	1227
15.	Shenandoah	27	15-12	1196
16.	Buena Vista	29	23-6	1133
17.	Wooster	28	21-7	1056
18.	Beloit	23	13-10	911
19.	St. Lawrence	30	21-9	1206
20.	Ramapo	29	21-8	1202
21.	Cortland St.	27	11-16	1010
22.	Maryville (Mo.)	24	10-14	1026
23.	Johns Hopkins	24	15-9	946
24.	Catholic	29	26-3	1233
25.	Penn St.-Behrend	27	18-9	933
26.	Neumann	28	21-7	1150
27.	Elizabethtown	32	29-3	1271
28.	Capital	28	23-5	992
29.	Hampden-Sydney	29	23-6	1169
30.	Washington (Mo.)	27	25-2	1114
31.	St. Thomas (Minn.)	28	24-4	1051
32.	Cornell College	27	12-15	1056
33.	Manchester	27	16-11	1025
34.	Wm. Paterson	29	19-10	1025
35.	Neb. Wesleyan	25	13-12	871

STATISTICAL LEADERS

Scoring Defense

Team	GM	W-L	OPP PTS	OPP PPG
1. Babson	30	25-5	1693	56.4
2. Trinity (Tex.)	25	18-7	1474	59.0
3. Frank. & Marsh.	29	24-5	1712	59.0
4. Edgewood	29	18-11	1715	59.1
5. Rochester	30	24-6	1790	59.7
6. Randolph-Macon	30	24-6	1807	60.2
7. Occidental	25	18-7	1506	60.2
8. Penn St.-Behrend	27	18-9	1630	60.4
9. Rowan	25	15-10	1521	60.8
10. New York U.	25	14-11	1530	61.2
11. Wm. Paterson	29	19-10	1777	61.3
12. Albion	26	17-9	1607	61.8
13. Richard Stockton	29	20-9	1795	61.9
14. Carthage	30	28-2	1862	62.1
15. Mississippi Col.	24	21-3	1493	62.2
16. Wittenberg	30	26-4	1868	62.3
17. Pomona-Pitzer	24	14-10	1495	62.3
18. Rose-Hulman	25	14-11	1561	62.4
19. Gust. Adolphus	29	24-5	1816	62.6
20. St. Thomas (Minn.)	28	24-4	1759	62.8
21. Washington (Mo.)	27	25-2	1697	62.9
22. Maryville (Tenn.)	29	24-5	1823	62.9
23. Claremont-M-S	26	21-5	1641	63.1
24. St. John's (Minn.)	26	15-11	1642	63.2
25. Cortland St.	27	11-16	1706	63.2
26. Williams	28	22-6	1775	63.4
27. Buffalo St.	23	15-8	1461	63.5
28. Chapman	25	18-7	1592	63.7
29. St. Norbert	26	21-5	1657	63.7
30. Alvernia	28	22-6	1788	63.9
31. MIT	25	15-10	1598	63.9
32. Hanover	26	21-5	1667	64.1
33. Gettysburg	27	20-7	1736	64.3
34. Bethel (Minn.)	27	21-6	1746	64.7
35. Lakeland	26	16-10	1683	64.7

Field-Goal Percentage

Team	GM	W-L	FGM
1. Wis.-Oshkosh	30	24-6	784
2. DePauw	28	24-4	838
3. Wis.-Stevens Point	27	21-6	750
4. Elizabethtown	32	29-3	1073
5. Claremont-M-S	26	21-5	690
6. Pitt.-Bradford	28	23-5	842
7. Otterbein	33	30-3	999
8. Whitworth	27	20-7	744
9. Brockport St.	31	28-3	944
10. Buena Vista	29	23-6	801
11. Wis.-River Falls	26	17-9	704
12. Gust. Adolphus	29	24-5	831
13. Wooster	28	21-7	824
14. Lewis & Clark	30	24-6	916
15. Franklin	29	20-9	771
16. Grove City	27	17-10	690
17. Wis.-Whitewater	28	21-7	800
18. Cal Lutheran	25	20-5	684
19. Wilkes	26	15-11	788
20. Bridgewater (Va.)	26	17-9	704
21. Rockford	25	18-7	737
22. Widener	27	19-8	806
23. Wesleyan (Conn.)	25	15-10	754
24. St. Norbert	26	21-5	674
25. Greenville	25	9-16	789
26. Fontbonne	24	18-6	721
27. Capital	28	23-5	713
28. Defiance	28	18-10	924
29. Wis.-Stout	25	12-13	654
30. Carthage	30	28-2	808
31. Lakeland	26	16-10	660
32. St. John's (Minn.)	26	15-11	659
33. Beloit	23	13-10	653
34. St. Thomas (Minn.)	28	24-4	745
35. Pacific (Ore.)	24	11-13	661

Three-Point Field Goals Per Game

Team	GM	W-L	3FG
1. Grinnell	24	12-12	490
2. Muskingum	26	10-16	296
3. Southern Me.	26	10-16	271
4. New England Col.	24	4-20	246
5. Bethany (W.Va.)	29	21-8	285
6. Gordon	27	16-11	262
7. Clark (Mass.)	29	23-6	279
8. Bowdoin	25	16-9	240
9. Lewis & Clark	30	24-6	287
10. Chapman	25	18-7	237
11. Keene St.	28	23-5	257
12. Lake Forest	23	9-14	210
13. Bethel (Minn.)	27	21-6	246
14. Puget Sound	25	11-14	225
15. Pitt.-Bradford	28	23-5	250
16. Benedictine (Ill.)	25	13-12	222
17. Wittenberg	30	26-4	265
Fontbonne	24	18-6	212
19. Alfred	25	11-14	220
20. Wis.-La Crosse	26	17-9	228
21. York (Pa.)	27	21-6	235
22. Greenville	25	9-16	214
23. Colorado Col.	24	9-15	205
24. Centre	25	16-9	211
25. Me.-Farmington	25	11-14	210
26. N.C. Wesleyan	28	20-8	235
27. Pacific (Ore.)	24	11-13	201
28. Chicago	25	15-10	208
29. Marywood	23	1-22	191
30. MacMurray	25	15-10	206
31. Coast Guard	24	10-14	197
New England	24	8-16	197
33. Millikin	25	8-17	205
34. Defiance	28	18-10	229
35. Va. Wesleyan	26	16-10	212

Field-Goal Percentage Defense

Team	GM	W-L	OPP FG
1. Rowan	25	15-10	503
2. Washington (Mo.)	27	25-2	600
3. MIT	25	15-10	542
4. Grove City	27	17-10	607
5. Endicott	27	16-11	575
6. Johns Hopkins	24	15-9	520
7. Trinity (Tex.)	25	18-7	489
8. Gordon	27	16-11	631
9. Frank. & Marsh.	29	24-5	628
10. Maine Maritime	23	14-9	563
11. Catholic	29	26-3	711
12. Roger Williams	27	16-11	685
13. Albion	26	17-9	542
14. Brockport St.	31	28-3	691
15. Williams	28	22-6	612
16. Lincoln (Pa.)	24	11-13	688
17. Colby-Sawyer	28	22-6	658
18. Bowdoin	25	16-9	576
19. Babson	30	25-5	587
20. Wittenberg	30	26-4	644
21. Chris. Newport	28	23-5	690
22. Concordia (Wis.)	28	16-12	636
23. Buffalo St.	23	15-8	50
24. New York U.	25	14-11	555
25. Maryville (Tenn.)	29	24-5	624
26. Kalamazoo	27	17-10	550
27. Trinity (Conn.)	25	19-6	607
28. Occidental	25	18-7	543
29. Buena Vista	29	23-6	711
30. Lehman	27	17-10	641
31. N.C. Wesleyan	28	20-8	706
32. Alvernia	28	22-6	617
33. St. Thomas (Minn.)	28	24-4	641
34. Pomona-Pitzer	24	14-10	517
35. Wooster	28	21-7	608

Free-Throw Percentage

Team	GM	W-L	FT
1. Moravian	25	14-11	407
2. Muskingum	26	10-16	291
3. Baldwin-Wallace	26	7-19	375
4. Blackburn	25	14-11	383
5. Catholic	29	26-3	556
6. Roanoke	27	17-10	423
7. Bluffton	26	10-16	433
8. Wis.-Oshkosh	30	24-6	484
9. Otterbein	33	30-3	591
10. Whitworth	27	20-7	428
11. Hanover	26	21-5	412
12. Lakeland	26	16-10	328
13. Wartburg	28	20-8	463
14. Franklin	29	20-9	675
15. Wis.-River Falls	26	17-9	367
16. Calvin	27	20-7	439
17. Puget Sound	25	11-14	488
18. Coe	26	13-13	354
19. Mount Union	27	18-9	405
20. Ripon	26	19-7	447
21. Bridgewater (Va.)	26	17-9	378
22. Cal Lutheran	25	20-5	432
23. Chapman	25	18-7	395
24. Clarkson	29	19-10	412
25. Heidelberg	27	10-17	367
26. Bates	24	13-11	381
27. Occidental	25	18-7	296
28. Centre	25	16-9	423
29. Bethany (W.Va.)	29	21-8	514
30. Manchester	27	16-11	428
31. Wooster	28	21-7	352
32. Hendrix	24	5-19	329
33. Wis.-Stevens Point	27	21-6	395
34. Chicago	25	15-10	350
35. Wis.-Eau Claire	25	11-14	374

Three-Point Field-Goal Percentage

Team	GM	W-L	3FG	3FGA
1. Gordon	27	16-11	262	590
2. Pitt.-Bradford	28	23-5	250	580
3. Wis.-Stevens Point	27	21-6	219	514
4. Lakeland	26	16-10	147	346
5. Wittenberg	30	26-4	265	632
6. Wis.-Oshkosh	30	24-6	223	534
7. Chapman	25	18-7	237	568
8. Maryville (Tenn.)	29	24-5	209	502
9. Claremont-M-S	26	21-5	190	457
10. Franklin	29	20-9	158	385
11. York (Pa.)	27	21-6	235	580
12. N.C. Wesleyan	28	20-8	235	583
13. Bethel (Minn.)	27	21-6	246	612
14. Capital	28	23-5	134	334
15. Cal Lutheran	25	20-5	178	445
16. Kalamazoo	27	17-10	212	534
17. Wheaton (Ill.)	25	16-9	163	411
18. Mississippi Col.	24	21-3	159	402
19. Occidental	25	18-7	201	509
20. Augustana (Ill.)	25	17-8	158	401
21. Bethany (W.Va.)	29	21-8	285	725
22. Buena Vista	29	23-6	189	481
23. Baldwin-Wallace	26	7-19	174	443
24. Emerson	25	12-13	187	480
25. Wis.-La Crosse	26	17-9	228	587
26. Kenyon	24	6-18	195	503
27. Clark (Mass.)	29	23-6	279	721
28. St. Thomas (Minn.)	28	24-4	208	538
29. Whitworth	27	20-7	184	476
30. Wooster	28	21-7	195	505
31. Lewis & Clark	30	24-6	287	746
32. Suffolk	28	17-11	147	383
33. Wartburg	28	20-8	203	529
34. Mt. St. Mary (N.Y.)	27	16-11	198	517
35. Keene St.	28	23-5	257	673

Won-Lost Percentage

Team	W	L	Pct
1. Carthage	28	2	93.3
2. Washington (Mo.)	25	2	92.6
3. Otterbein	30	3	90.9
4. Elizabethtown	29	3	90.6
5. Brockport St.	28	3	90.3
6. Catholic	26	3	89.7
7. Mississippi Col.	21	3	87.5
8. Wittenberg	26	4	86.7
9. DePauw	24	4	85.7
St. Thomas (Minn.)	24	4	85.7

Team	W	L	Pct
11. Babson	25	5	83.3
12. Frank. & Marsh.	24	5	82.8
Gust. Adolphus	24	5	82.8
Maryville (Tenn.)	24	5	82.8
Merchant Marine	24	5	82.8
16. Capital	23	5	82.1
Chris. Newport	23	5	82.1
Keene St.	23	5	82.1
Pitt.-Bradford	23	5	82.1
20. Claremont-M-S	21	5	80.8
Hanover	21	5	80.8
St. Norbert	21	5	80.8
23. Lewis & Clark	24	6	80.0

Team	W	L	Pct
Randolph-Macon	24	6	80.0
Rochester	24	6	80.0
Wis.-Oshkosh	24	6	80.0
Cal Lutheran	20	5	80.0
28. Buena Vista	23	6	79.3
Clark (Mass.)	23	6	79.3
Hampden-Sydney	23	6	79.3
31. Alvernia	22	6	78.6
Colby-Sawyer	22	6	78.6
Williams	22	6	78.6
34. Bethel (Minn.)	21	6	77.8
Wis.-Stevens Point	21	6	77.8

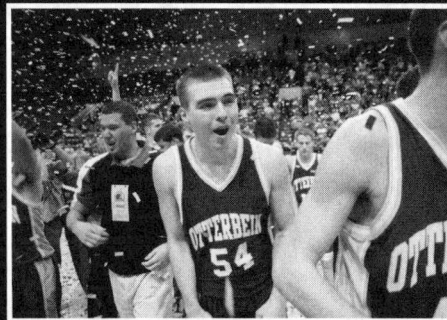

Conferences

2002 Division I Conference Standings

AMERICA EAST CONFERENCE

Team	Conference W	L	Pct.	Full Season W	L	Pct.
Boston U. #	13	3	.813	22	10	.688
Vermont	13	3	.813	21	8	.724
Hartford	10	6	.625	14	18	.438
New Hampshire	8	8	.500	11	17	.393
Maine	7	9	.438	12	18	.400
Binghamton	6	10	.375	9	19	.321
Albany (N.Y.)	5	11	.313	8	20	.286
Northeastern	5	11	.313	7	21	.250
Stony Brook	5	11	.313	6	22	.214

ATLANTIC COAST CONFERENCE

Team	Conference W	L	Pct.	Full Season W	L	Pct.
Maryland	15	1	.938	32	4	.889
Duke #	13	3	.813	31	4	.886
North Carolina St.	9	7	.563	23	11	.676
Wake Forest	9	7	.563	21	13	.618
Georgia Tech	7	9	.438	15	16	.484
Virginia	7	9	.438	17	12	.586
Clemson	4	12	.250	13	17	.433
Florida St.	4	12	.250	12	17	.414
North Carolina	4	12	.250	8	20	.286

ATLANTIC SUN CONFERENCE

Team	Conference W	L	Pct.	Full Season W	L	Pct.
Georgia St.	14	6	.700	20	11	.645
Troy St.	14	6	.700	18	10	.643
Fla. Atlantic #	13	7	.650	19	12	.613
Jacksonville	12	8	.600	18	12	.600
Samford	12	8	.600	15	14	.517
UCF	12	8	.600	17	12	.586
Belmont	8	12	.400	11	17	.393
Jacksonville St.	8	12	.400	13	16	.448
Stetson	7	13	.350	10	16	.385
Campbell	6	14	.300	8	19	.296
Mercer	4	16	.200	6	23	.207

ATLANTIC 10 CONFERENCE

East Division	Conference W	L	Pct.	Full Season W	L	Pct.
St. Joseph's	12	4	.750	19	12	.613
Temple	12	4	.750	19	15	.559
St. Bonaventure	8	8	.500	17	13	.567
Massachusetts	6	10	.375	13	16	.448
Fordham	4	12	.250	8	20	.286
Rhode Island	4	12	.250	8	20	.286

West Division	Conference W	L	Pct.	Full Season W	L	Pct.
Xavier #	14	2	.875	26	6	.813
Richmond	11	5	.688	22	14	.611
Dayton	10	6	.625	21	11	.656
La Salle	6	10	.375	15	17	.469
George Washington	5	11	.313	12	16	.429
Duquesne	4	12	.250	9	19	.321

BIG EAST CONFERENCE

East Division	Conference W	L	Pct.	Full Season W	L	Pct.
Connecticut #	13	3	.813	27	7	.794
Miami (Fla.)	10	6	.625	24	8	.750
St. John's (N.Y.)	9	7	.563	20	12	.625
Boston College	8	8	.500	20	12	.625
Villanova	7	9	.438	19	13	.594
Providence	6	10	.375	15	16	.484
Virginia Tech	4	12	.250	10	18	.357

West Division	Conference W	L	Pct.	Full Season W	L	Pct.
Pittsburgh	13	3	.813	29	6	.829
Notre Dame	10	6	.625	22	11	.667
Syracuse	9	7	.563	23	13	.639
Georgetown	9	7	.563	19	11	.633
Rutgers	8	8	.500	18	13	.581
Seton Hall	5	11	.313	12	18	.400
West Virginia	1	15	.063	8	20	.286

BIG SKY CONFERENCE

Team	Conference W	L	Pct.	Full Season W	L	Pct.
Montana St.	12	2	.857	20	10	.667
Eastern Wash.	10	4	.714	17	13	.567
Weber St.	8	6	.571	18	11	.621
Montana #	7	7	.500	16	15	.516
Northern Ariz.	7	7	.500	14	14	.500
Portland St.	6	8	.429	12	16	.429
Idaho St.	3	11	.214	10	17	.370
Sacramento St.	3	11	.214	9	19	.321

BIG SOUTH CONFERENCE

Team	Conference W	L	Pct.	Full Season W	L	Pct.
UNC Asheville	10	4	.714	13	15	.464
Winthrop #	10	4	.714	19	12	.613
Radford	9	5	.643	15	16	.484
Charleston So.	8	6	.571	12	17	.414
Elon	7	7	.500	13	16	.448
Coastal Caro.	5	9	.357	8	20	.286
High Point	5	9	.357	11	19	.367
Liberty	2	12	.143	5	25	.167

BIG TEN CONFERENCE

Team	Conference W	L	Pct.	Full Season W	L	Pct.
Illinois	11	5	.688	26	9	.743
Indiana	11	5	.688	25	12	.676
Ohio St. #	11	5	.688	24	8	.750
Wisconsin	11	5	.688	19	13	.594
Michigan St.	10	6	.625	19	12	.613
Minnesota	9	7	.563	18	13	.581
Northwestern	7	9	.438	16	13	.552
Iowa	5	11	.313	19	16	.543
Michigan	5	11	.313	11	18	.379
Purdue	5	11	.313	13	18	.419
Penn St.	3	13	.188	7	21	.250

BIG 12 CONFERENCE

Team	Conference W	L	Pct.	Full Season W	L	Pct.
Kansas #	16	0	1.000	33	4	.892
Oklahoma #	13	3	.813	31	5	.861
Oklahoma St.	10	6	.625	23	9	.719
Texas	10	6	.625	22	12	.647
Texas Tech	10	6	.625	23	9	.719
Missouri	9	7	.563	24	12	.667
Kansas St.	6	10	.375	13	16	.448
Nebraska	6	10	.375	13	15	.464
Colorado	5	11	.313	15	14	.517
Baylor	4	12	.250	14	16	.467
Iowa St.	4	12	.250	12	19	.387
Texas A&M	3	13	.188	9	22	.290

BIG WEST CONFERENCE

Team	Conference W	L	Pct.	Full Season W	L	Pct.
UC Irvine	13	5	.722	21	11	.656
Utah St.	13	5	.722	23	8	.742
Cal St. Northridge	11	7	.611	12	16	.429
Pacific (Cal.)	11	7	.611	20	10	.667
UC Santa Barb. #	11	7	.611	20	11	.645
Cal Poly	9	9	.500	15	12	.556
Long Beach St.	9	9	.500	13	17	.433
Idaho	6	12	.333	9	19	.321
UC Riverside	5	13	.278	8	18	.308
Cal St. Fullerton	2	16	.111	5	22	.185

COLONIAL ATHLETIC ASSOCIATION

Team	Conference W	L	Pct.	Full Season W	L	Pct.
UNC Wilmington #	14	4	.778	23	10	.697
George Mason	13	5	.722	19	10	.655
Drexel	11	7	.611	14	14	.500
Va. Commonwealth	11	7	.611	21	11	.656
Delaware	9	9	.500	14	16	.467
Old Dominion	7	11	.389	13	16	.448
Towson	7	11	.389	11	18	.379
William & Mary	7	11	.389	10	19	.345

Team	Conference W	L	Pct.	Full Season W	L	Pct.
James Madison	6	12	.333	14	15	.483
Hofstra	5	13	.278	12	20	.375

CONFERENCE USA

American Division	Conference W	L	Pct.	Full Season W	L	Pct.
Cincinnati #	14	2	.875	31	4	.886
Marquette	13	3	.813	26	7	.788
Charlotte	11	5	.688	18	12	.600
St. Louis	9	7	.563	15	16	.484
Louisville	8	8	.500	19	13	.594
East Caro.	5	11	.313	12	18	.400
DePaul	2	14	.125	9	19	.321

National Division	Conference W	L	Pct.	Full Season W	L	Pct.
Memphis	12	4	.750	27	9	.750
Houston	9	7	.563	18	15	.545
South Fla.	8	8	.500	19	13	.594
TCU	6	10	.375	16	15	.516
UAB	6	10	.375	13	17	.433
Tulane	5	11	.313	14	15	.483
Southern Miss.	4	12	.250	10	17	.370

HORIZON LEAGUE

Team	Conference W	L	Pct.	Full Season W	L	Pct.
Butler	12	4	.750	26	6	.813
Detroit	11	5	.688	18	13	.581
Wis.-Milwaukee	11	5	.688	16	13	.552
Loyola (Ill.)	9	7	.563	17	13	.567
Wright St.	9	7	.563	17	11	.607
Ill.-Chicago #	8	8	.500	20	14	.588
Cleveland St.	6	10	.375	12	16	.429
Wis.-Green Bay	4	12	.250	9	21	.300
Youngtown St.	2	14	.125	5	23	.179

IVY GROUP

Team	Conference W	L	Pct.	Full Season W	L	Pct.
Pennsylvania	11	3	.786	25	7	.781
Princeton	11	3	.786	16	12	.571
Yale	11	3	.786	21	11	.656
Brown	8	6	.571	17	10	.630
Harvard	7	7	.500	14	12	.538
Columbia	4	10	.286	11	17	.393
Cornell	2	12	.143	5	22	.185
Dartmouth	2	12	.143	9	18	.333

METRO ATLANTIC ATHLETIC CONFERENCE

Team	Conference W	L	Pct.	Full Season W	L	Pct.
Marist	13	5	.722	19	9	.679
Rider	13	5	.722	17	11	.607
Manhattan	12	6	.667	20	9	.690
Niagara	12	6	.667	18	14	.563
Iona	10	8	.556	13	17	.433
Fairfield	9	9	.500	12	17	.414
Siena #	9	9	.500	17	19	.472
Canisius	5	13	.278	10	20	.333
Loyola (Md.)	4	14	.222	5	23	.179
St. Peter's	3	15	.167	4	24	.143

MID-AMERICAN CONFERENCE

East Division	Conference W	L	Pct.	Full Season W	L	Pct.
Kent St. #	17	1	.944	30	6	.833
Bowling Green	12	6	.667	24	9	.727
Ohio	11	7	.611	17	11	.607
Miami (Ohio)	9	9	.500	13	18	.419
Marshall	8	10	.444	15	15	.500
Buffalo	7	11	.389	12	18	.400
Akron	5	13	.278	10	21	.323

West Division	Conference W	L	Pct.	Full Season W	L	Pct.
Ball St.	12	6	.667	23	12	.657
Toledo	11	7	.611	16	14	.533
Western Mich.	10	8	.556	17	13	.567

#won conference tournament

CONFERENCES

West Division	Conference			Full Season		
	W	L	Pct.	W	L	Pct.
Northern Ill.	8	10	.444	12	16	.429
Central Mich.	5	13	.278	9	19	.321
Eastern Mich.	2	16	.111	6	24	.200

MID-CONTINENT CONFERENCE

Team	Conference			Full Season		
	W	L	Pct.	W	L	Pct.
Valparaiso #	12	2	.857	25	8	.758
Oakland	10	4	.714	17	13	.567
Oral Roberts	10	4	.714	17	14	.548
Southern Utah	8	6	.571	11	16	.407
UMKC	7	7	.500	18	11	.621
IUPUI	6	8	.429	15	15	.500
Western Ill.	3	11	.214	12	16	.429
Chicago St.	0	14	.000	2	26	.071

MID-EASTERN ATHLETIC CONFERENCE

Team	Conference			Full Season		
	W	L	Pct.	W	L	Pct.
Hampton #	16	1	.941	26	7	.788
Delaware St.	11	6	.647	16	13	.552
Howard	11	6	.647	18	13	.581
N.C. A&T	10	7	.588	11	17	.393
South Carolina St.	10	7	.588	15	16	.484
Florida A&M	9	8	.529	9	19	.321
Norfolk St.	9	8	.529	10	19	.345
Bethune-Cookman	7	10	.412	12	17	.414
Md.-East. Shore	7	11	.389	11	18	.379
Coppin St.	3	15	.167	6	25	.194
Morgan St.	2	16	.111	3	25	.107

MISSOURI VALLEY CONFERENCE

Team	Conference			Full Season		
	W	L	Pct.	W	L	Pct.
Creighton #	14	4	.778	23	9	.719
Southern Ill.	14	4	.778	28	8	.778
Illinois St.	12	6	.667	17	14	.548
Southwest Mo. St.	11	7	.611	17	15	.531
Drake	9	9	.500	14	15	.483
Wichita St.	9	9	.500	15	15	.500
Northern Iowa	8	10	.444	14	15	.483
Bradley	5	13	.278	9	20	.310
Evansville	4	14	.222	7	21	.250
Indiana St.	4	14	.222	6	22	.214

MOUNTAIN WEST CONFERENCE

Team	Conference			Full Season		
	W	L	Pct.	W	L	Pct.
Wyoming	11	3	.786	22	9	.710
Utah	10	4	.714	21	9	.700
UNLV	9	5	.643	21	11	.656
Brigham Young	7	7	.500	18	12	.600
San Diego St. #	7	7	.500	21	12	.636
New Mexico	6	8	.429	16	14	.533
Air Force	3	11	.214	9	19	.321
Colorado St.	3	11	.214	12	18	.400

NORTHEAST CONFERENCE

Team	Conference			Full Season		
	W	L	Pct.	W	L	Pct.
Central Conn. St. #	19	1	.950	27	5	.844
UMBC	15	5	.750	20	9	.690
Wagner	15	5	.750	19	10	.655
Monmouth	14	6	.700	18	12	.600
St. Francis (N.Y.)	13	7	.650	18	11	.621
Robert Morris	11	9	.550	12	18	.400
Quinnipiac	10	10	.500	14	16	.467
Sacred Heart	7	13	.350	8	20	.286
Long Island	5	15	.250	5	22	.185
St. Francis (Pa.)	5	15	.250	6	21	.222
Fairleigh Dickinson	4	16	.200	4	25	.138
Mt. St. Mary's	2	18	.100	3	24	.111

OHIO VALLEY CONFERENCE

Team	Conference			Full Season		
	W	L	Pct.	W	L	Pct.
Tennessee Tech	15	1	.938	27	7	.794
Morehead St.	11	5	.688	18	11	.621
Murray St. #	10	6	.625	19	13	.594
Austin Peay	8	8	.500	14	18	.438
Eastern Ill.	7	9	.438	15	16	.484
Tenn.-Martin	7	9	.438	15	14	.517
Tennessee St.	7	9	.438	11	17	.393
Southeast Mo. St.	4	12	.250	6	22	.214
Eastern Ky.	3	13	.188	7	20	.259

PACIFIC-10 CONFERENCE

Team	Conference			Full Season		
	W	L	Pct.	W	L	Pct.
Oregon	14	4	.778	26	9	.743
Arizona #	12	6	.667	24	10	.706
California	12	6	.667	23	9	.719
Southern California	12	6	.667	22	10	.688
Stanford	12	6	.667	20	10	.667
UCLA	11	7	.611	21	12	.636
Arizona St.	7	11	.389	14	15	.483
Washington	5	13	.278	11	18	.379
Oregon St.	4	14	.222	12	17	.414
Washington St.	1	17	.056	6	21	.222

PATRIOT LEAGUE

Team	Conference			Full Season		
	W	L	Pct.	W	L	Pct.
American	10	4	.714	18	12	.600
Holy Cross #	9	5	.643	18	15	.545
Bucknell	8	6	.571	13	16	.448
Colgate	8	6	.571	17	11	.607
Lafayette	8	6	.571	15	14	.517
Army	6	8	.429	12	16	.429
Navy	5	9	.357	10	20	.333
Lehigh	2	12	.143	5	23	.179

SOUTHEASTERN CONFERENCE

Eastern Division	Conference			Full Season		
	W	L	Pct.	W	L	Pct.
Florida	10	6	.625	22	9	.710
Georgia	10	6	.625	22	10	.688
Kentucky	10	6	.625	22	10	.688
Tennessee	7	9	.438	15	16	.484
South Carolina	6	10	.375	22	15	.595
Vanderbilt	6	10	.375	17	15	.531

Western Division	Conference			Full Season		
	W	L	Pct.	W	L	Pct.
Alabama	12	4	.750	27	8	.771
Mississippi St. #	10	6	.625	27	8	.771
Mississippi	9	7	.563	20	11	.645
LSU	6	10	.375	19	15	.559
Arkansas	6	10	.375	14	15	.483
Auburn	4	12	.250	12	16	.429

SOUTHERN CONFERENCE

North Division	Conference			Full Season		
	W	L	Pct.	W	L	Pct.
Davidson #	11	5	.688	21	10	.677
UNC Greensboro	11	5	.688	20	11	.645
East Tenn. St.	11	5	.688	18	10	.643
Western Caro.	6	10	.375	12	16	.429
Appalachian St.	5	11	.313	10	18	.357
VMI	5	11	.313	10	18	.357

South Division	Conference			Full Season		
	W	L	Pct.	W	L	Pct.
Col. of Charleston	9	7	.563	21	9	.700
Ga. Southern	9	7	.563	16	12	.571
Chattanooga	9	7	.563	16	14	.533
Citadel	8	8	.500	17	12	.586
Furman	7	9	.438	17	14	.548
Wofford	5	11	.313	11	18	.379

SOUTHLAND CONFERENCE

Team	Conference			Full Season		
	W	L	Pct.	W	L	Pct.
McNeese St. #	17	3	.850	21	9	.700
La.-Monroe	15	5	.750	20	12	.625
Texas-San Antonio	13	7	.650	19	10	.655
Lamar	11	9	.550	15	14	.517
Southwest Tex. St.	10	10	.500	12	16	.429
Stephen F. Austin	10	10	.500	13	15	.464
Northwestern St.	9	11	.450	13	18	.419
Sam Houston St.	9	11	.450	14	14	.500
Texas-Arlington	9	11	.450	12	15	.444
Southeastern La.	6	14	.300	7	20	.259
Nicholls St.	1	19	.050	2	25	.074

SOUTHWESTERN ATHLETIC CONFERENCE

Team	Conference			Full Season		
	W	L	Pct.	W	L	Pct.
Alcorn St. #	16	2	.889	21	10	.677
Alabama A&M	12	6	.667	19	10	.655
Alabama St.	12	6	.667	19	13	.594
Texas Southern	10	8	.556	11	17	.393
Mississippi Val.	9	9	.500	12	17	.414
Jackson St.	8	10	.444	9	19	.321
Prairie View	8	10	.444	10	20	.333
Grambling	7	11	.389	9	19	.321
Southern U.	6	12	.333	7	20	.259
Ark.-Pine Bluff	2	16	.111	2	26	.071

SUN BELT CONFERENCE

East Division	Conference			Full Season		
	W	L	Pct.	W	L	Pct.
Western Ky. #	13	1	.929	28	4	.875
Ark.-Little Rock	8	6	.571	18	11	.621
Middle Tenn.	6	8	.429	14	15	.483
Arkansas St.	5	9	.357	15	16	.484
Florida Int'l	4	10	.286	10	20	.333

West Division	Conference			Full Season		
	W	L	Pct.	W	L	Pct.
La.-Lafayette	11	4	.733	20	11	.645
New Mexico St.	11	4	.733	20	12	.625
New Orleans	9	6	.600	15	14	.517
North Texas	8	7	.533	15	14	.517
Denver	3	12	.200	8	20	.286
South Ala.	2	13	.133	7	21	.250

WEST COAST CONFERENCE

Team	Conference			Full Season		
	W	L	Pct.	W	L	Pct.
Gonzaga #	13	1	.929	29	4	.879
Pepperdine	13	1	.929	22	9	.710
San Francisco	8	6	.571	13	15	.464
Santa Clara	8	6	.571	13	15	.464
San Diego	7	7	.500	16	13	.552
St. Mary's (Cal.)	3	11	.214	9	20	.310
Loyola Marymount	2	12	.143	9	20	.310
Portland	2	12	.143	6	24	.200

WESTERN ATHLETIC CONFERENCE

Team	Conference			Full Season		
	W	L	Pct.	W	L	Pct.
Hawaii #	15	3	.833	27	6	.818
Tulsa	15	3	.833	27	7	.794
Louisiana Tech	14	4	.778	22	10	.688
Southern Methodist	10	8	.556	15	14	.517
Fresno St.	9	9	.500	19	15	.559
Nevada	9	9	.500	17	13	.567
Boise St.	6	12	.333	13	17	.433
Rice	5	13	.278	10	19	.345
San Jose St.	4	14	.222	10	22	.313
UTEP	3	15	.167	10	22	.313

INDEPENDENTS

	W	L	Pct.
Tex.-Pan American	20	10	.667
Centenary (La.)	14	13	.519
Morris Brown	4	25	.138

#won conference tournament

Division I Conference Champions Season By Season

Regular-season and conference tournament champions; No. refers to the number of teams in the conference or tournament.

AMERICA EAST CONFERENCE

Season	No.	Regular Season
1980	10	Boston U./Northeastern
1981	9	Northeastern
1982	9	Northeastern
1983	9	Boston U./New Hampshire
1984	8	Northeastern
1985	9	Northeastern/Canisius
1986	10	Northeastern
1987	10	Northeastern
1988	10	Siena
1989	10	Siena
1990	7	Northeastern
1991	6	Northeastern
1992	8	Delaware
1993	8	Drexel/Northeastern
1994	8	Drexel
1995	9	Drexel
1996	10	Drexel
1997	10	Boston U.
1998	10	Delaware/Boston U.
1999	10	Delaware/Drexel
2000	10	Hofstra
2001	10	Hofstra
2002	9	Boston U./Vermont

Season	No.	Conference Tournament
1980	8	Holy Cross
1981	6	Northeastern
1982	6	Northeastern
1983	9	Boston U.
1984	8	Northeastern
1985	9	Northeastern
1986	10	Northeastern
1987	10	Northeastern
1988	10	Boston U.
1989	10	Siena
1990	7	Boston U.
1991	6	Northeastern
1992	8	Delaware
1993	8	Delaware
1994	8	Drexel
1995	9	Drexel
1996	10	Drexel
1997	10	Boston U.
1998	10	Delaware
1999	10	Delaware
2000	10	Hofstra
2001	10	Hofstra
2002	8	Boston U.

AMERICAN SOUTH CONFERENCE

Season	No.	Regular Season
1988	6	Louisiana Tech/New Orleans
1989	6	New Orleans
1990	6	Louisiana Tech/New Orleans
1991	7	New Orleans/Arkansas St.

Season	No.	Conference Tournament
1988	6	Louisiana Tech
1989	6	Louisiana Tech
1990	6	New Orleans
1991	7	Louisiana Tech

AMERICAN WEST CONFERENCE

Season	No.	Regular Season
1995	4	Southern Utah
1996	4	Cal Poly

Season	No.	Conference Tournament
1995	4	Southern Utah
1996	4	Southern Utah

ATLANTIC COAST CONFERENCE

Season	No.	Regular Season
1954	8	Duke
1955	8	North Carolina St.
1956	8	North Carolina St./North Carolina
1957	8	North Carolina
1958	8	Duke
1959	8	North Carolina St./North Carolina
1960	8	North Carolina
1961	8	North Carolina
1962	8	Wake Forest
1963	8	Duke
1964	8	Duke
1965	8	Duke
1966	8	Duke
1967	8	North Carolina
1968	8	North Carolina
1969	8	North Carolina
1970	8	South Carolina
1971	8	North Carolina
1972	7	North Carolina
1973	7	North Carolina St.
1974	7	North Carolina St.
1975	7	Maryland
1976	7	North Carolina
1977	7	North Carolina
1978	7	North Carolina
1979	7	Duke/North Carolina
1980	8	Maryland
1981	8	Virginia
1982	8	North Carolina/Virginia
1983	8	North Carolina/Virginia
1984	8	North Carolina
1985	8	Georgia Tech/North Carolina/North Carolina St.
1986	8	Duke
1987	8	North Carolina
1988	8	North Carolina
1989	8	North Carolina St.
1990	8	Clemson
1991	8	Duke
1992	9	Duke
1993	9	North Carolina
1994	9	Duke
1995	9	Maryland/North Carolina/Virginia/Wake Forest
1996	9	Georgia Tech
1997	9	Duke
1998	9	Duke
1999	9	Duke
2000	9	Duke
2001	9	Duke/North Carolina
2002	9	Maryland

Season	No.	Conference Tournament
1954	8	North Carolina St.
1955	8	North Carolina St.
1956	8	North Carolina St.
1957	8	North Carolina
1958	8	Maryland
1959	8	North Carolina St.
1960	8	Duke
1961	7	Wake Forest
1962	8	Wake Forest
1963	8	Duke
1964	8	Duke
1965	8	North Carolina St.
1966	8	Duke
1967	8	North Carolina
1968	8	North Carolina
1969	8	North Carolina
1970	8	North Carolina St.
1971	8	South Carolina
1972	7	North Carolina
1973	7	North Carolina St.
1974	7	North Carolina St.
1975	7	North Carolina
1976	7	Virginia
1977	7	North Carolina
1978	7	Duke
1979	7	North Carolina
1980	8	Duke
1981	8	North Carolina
1982	8	North Carolina
1983	8	North Carolina St.
1984	8	Maryland
1985	8	Georgia Tech
1986	8	Duke
1987	8	North Carolina St.
1988	8	Duke
1989	8	North Carolina
1990	8	Georgia Tech
1991	7	North Carolina
1992	9	Duke
1993	9	Georgia Tech
1994	9	North Carolina
1995	9	Wake Forest
1996	9	Wake Forest
1997	9	North Carolina
1998	9	North Carolina
1999	9	Duke
2000	9	Duke
2001	9	Duke
2002	9	Duke

ATLANTIC SUN CONFERENCE

Season	No.	Regular Season
1979	8	La.-Monroe
1980	7	La.-Monroe
1981	9	Houston Baptist
1982	9	Ark.-Little Rock
1983	8	Ark.-Little Rock
1984	8	Houston Baptist
1985	8	Ga. Southern
1986	8	Ark.-Little Rock
1987	10	Ark.-Little Rock
1988	10	Ark.-Little Rock/Ga. Southern
1989	10	Ga. Southern
1990	9	Centenary (La.)
1991	8	Texas-San Antonio
1992	8	Ga. Southern
1993	7	Florida Int'l
1994	10	Col. of Charleston
1995	11	Col. of Charleston
1996	12	Col. of Charleston (East)/Samford (West)/Southeastern La. (West)
1997	12	Col. of Charleston (East)/Samford (West)
1998	12	Col. of Charleston (East)/Georgia St. (West)
1999	11	Samford
2000	10	Georgia St./Troy St.
2001	10	Georgia St.
2002	11	Georgia St./Troy St.

Season	No.	Conference Tournament
1979	6	La.-Monroe
1980	7	Centenary (La.)
1981	9	Mercer
1982	7	La.-Monroe
1983	8	Ga. Southern
1984	8	Houston Baptist
1985	8	Mercer
1986	8	Ark.-Little Rock
1987	8	Ga. Southern
1988	8	Texas-San Antonio
1989	8	Ark.-Little Rock
1990	8	Ark.-Little Rock
1991	8	Georgia St.
1992	8	Ga. Southern
1993		DNP
1994	8	UCF
1995	8	Florida Int'l
1996	8	UCF
1997	8	Col. of Charleston
1998	8	Col. of Charleston
1999	8	Samford
2000	10	Samford
2001	10	Georgia St.
2002	8	Fla. Atlantic

ATLANTIC 10 CONFERENCE

Season	No.	Regular Season
1977	8	Rutgers (Eastern)/West Virginia (Western)/Penn St. (Western)
1978	8	Rutgers/Villanova
1979	8	Villanova
1980	8	Villanova/Duquesne/Rutgers
1981	8	Rhode Island/Duquesne
1982	8	West Virginia
1983	10	Rutgers (Eastern)/St. Bonaventure (Western)/West Virginia (Western)
1984	10	Temple
1985	10	West Virginia
1986	10	St. Joseph's
1987	10	Temple
1988	10	Temple
1989	10	West Virginia
1990	10	Temple
1991	10	Rutgers
1992	9	Massachusetts
1993	8	Massachusetts
1994	9	Massachusetts

Season	No.	Regular Season
1995	9	Massachusetts
1996	12	Massachusetts (East)/ George Washington (West)/ Virginia Tech (West)
1997	12	St. Joseph's (East)/Xavier (West)
1998	12	Temple (East)/Xavier (West)/ George Washington (West)/ Dayton (West)
1999	12	Temple (East)/George Washington (West)
2000	12	Temple (East)/Dayton (West)
2001	11	St. Joseph's
2002	12	Temple (East)/St. Joseph's (East)/Xavier (West)

Season	No.	Conference Tournament
1977	8	Duquesne
1978	8	Villanova
1979	8	Rutgers
1980	8	Villanova
1981	8	Pittsburgh
1982	8	Pittsburgh
1983	10	West Virginia
1984	10	West Virginia
1985	10	Temple
1986	10	St. Joseph's
1987	10	Temple
1988	10	Temple
1989	10	Rutgers
1990	10	Temple
1991	10	Penn St.
1992	9	Massachusetts
1993	8	Massachusetts
1994	9	Massachusetts
1995	9	Massachusetts
1996	12	Massachusetts
1997	12	St. Joseph's
1998	12	Xavier
1999	12	Rhode Island
2000	12	Temple
2001	11	Temple
2002	12	Xavier

BIG EAST CONFERENCE

Season	No.	Regular Season
1980	7	Syracuse/Georgetown/ St. John's (N.Y.)
1981	8	Boston College
1982	8	Villanova
1983	9	Boston College/Villanova/ St. John's (N.Y.)
1984	9	Georgetown
1985	9	St. John's (N.Y.)
1986	9	St. John's (N.Y.)/Syracuse
1987	9	Syracuse/Georgetown/Pittsburgh
1988	9	Pittsburgh
1989	9	Georgetown
1990	9	Connecticut/Syracuse
1991	9	Syracuse
1992	10	Seton Hall/Georgetown/ St. John's (N.Y.)
1993	10	Seton Hall
1994	10	Connecticut
1995	10	Connecticut
1996	13	Georgetown (Big East 7)/ Connecticut (Big East 6)
1997	13	Georgetown (Big East 7)/ Villanova (Big East 6)/ Boston College (Big East 6)
1998	13	Syracuse (Big East 7)/ Connecticut (Big East 6)
1999	13	Connecticut
2000	13	Syracuse/Miami (Fla.)
2001	14	Boston College (East)/ Notre Dame (West)
2002	14	Connecticut (East)/Pittsburgh (West)

Season	No.	Conference Tournament
1980	7	Georgetown
1981	8	Syracuse
1982	8	Georgetown
1983	9	St. John's (N.Y.)
1984	9	Georgetown
1985	9	Georgetown
1986	9	St. John's (N.Y.)
1987	9	Georgetown
1988	9	Syracuse
1989	9	Georgetown
1990	9	Connecticut
1991	9	Seton Hall
1992	10	Syracuse

Season	No.	Conference Tournament
1993	10	Seton Hall
1994	10	Providence
1995	10	Villanova
1996	13	Connecticut
1997	13	Boston College
1998	13	Connecticut
1999	13	Connecticut
2000	13	St. John's (N.Y.)
2001	12	Boston College
2002	12	Connecticut

BIG EIGHT CONFERENCE

(Note: The Big Eight and Missouri Valley conferences share the same history from 1908-28.)

Season	No.	Regular Season
1908	6	Kansas
1909	6	Kansas
1910	6	Kansas
1911	5	Kansas
1912	6	Nebraska/Kansas
1913	6	Nebraska
1914	7	Kansas/Nebraska
1915	7	Kansas
1916	7	Nebraska
1917	7	Kansas St.
1918	7	Missouri
1919	8	Kansas St.
1920	8	Missouri
1921	9	Missouri
1922	9	Missouri/Kansas
1923	9	Kansas
1924	9	Kansas
1925	9	Kansas
1926	10	Kansas
1927	10	Kansas
1928	10	Oklahoma
1929	6	Oklahoma
1930	6	Missouri
1931	6	Kansas
1932	6	Kansas
1933	6	Kansas
1934	6	Kansas
1935	6	Iowa St.
1936	6	Kansas
1937	6	Kansas/Nebraska
1938	6	Kansas
1939	6	Missouri/Oklahoma
1940	6	Kansas/Missouri/Oklahoma
1941	6	Iowa St./Kansas
1942	6	Kansas/Oklahoma
1943	6	Kansas
1944	6	Iowa St./Oklahoma
1945	6	Iowa St.
1946	6	Kansas
1947	6	Oklahoma
1948	7	Kansas St.
1949	7	Nebraska/Oklahoma
1950	7	Kansas/Kansas St./Nebraska
1951	7	Kansas St.
1952	7	Kansas
1953	7	Kansas
1954	7	Kansas/Colorado
1955	7	Colorado
1956	7	Kansas St.
1957	7	Kansas
1958	7	Kansas St.
1959	8	Kansas St.
1960	8	Kansas/Kansas St.
1961	8	Kansas St.
1962	8	Colorado
1963	8	Colorado/Kansas St.
1964	8	Kansas St.
1965	8	Oklahoma St.
1966	8	Kansas
1967	8	Kansas
1968	8	Kansas St.
1969	8	Colorado
1970	8	Kansas St.
1971	8	Kansas
1972	8	Kansas St.
1973	8	Kansas St.
1974	8	Kansas
1975	8	Kansas
1976	8	Missouri
1977	8	Kansas St.
1978	8	Kansas
1979	8	Oklahoma
1980	8	Missouri
1981	8	Missouri
1982	8	Missouri

Season	No.	Regular Season
1983	8	Missouri
1984	8	Oklahoma
1985	8	Oklahoma
1986	8	Kansas
1987	8	Missouri
1988	8	Oklahoma
1989	8	Oklahoma
1990	8	Missouri
1991	8	Oklahoma St./Kansas
1992	8	Kansas
1993	8	Kansas
1994	8	Missouri
1995	8	Kansas
1996	8	Kansas

Season	No.	Conference Tournament
1977	8	Kansas St.
1978	8	Missouri
1979	8	Oklahoma
1980	8	Kansas St.
1981	8	Kansas
1982	8	Missouri
1983	8	Oklahoma St.
1984	8	Kansas
1985	8	Oklahoma
1986	8	Kansas
1987	8	Missouri
1988	8	Oklahoma
1989	8	Missouri
1990	8	Oklahoma
1991	8	Missouri
1992	8	Kansas
1993	8	Missouri
1994	8	Nebraska
1995	8	Oklahoma St.
1996	8	Iowa St.

BIG SKY CONFERENCE

Season	No.	Regular Season
1964	6	Montana St.
1965	6	Weber St.
1966	6	Weber St./Gonzaga
1967	6	Gonzaga/Montana St.
1968	6	Weber St.
1969	6	Weber St.
1970	6	Weber St.
1971	6	Weber St.
1972	6	Weber St.
1973	8	Weber St.
1974	8	Idaho St./Montana
1975	8	Montana
1976	8	Boise St./Weber St./Idaho St.
1977	8	Idaho St.
1978	8	Montana
1979	8	Weber St.
1980	8	Weber St.
1981	8	Idaho
1982	8	Idaho
1983	8	Weber St./Nevada
1984	8	Weber St.
1985	8	Nevada
1986	8	Northern Ariz./Montana
1987	8	Montana St.
1988	9	Boise St.
1989	9	Boise St./Idaho
1990	9	Idaho
1991	9	Montana
1992	9	Montana
1993	8	Idaho
1994	8	Weber St./Idaho St.
1995	8	Montana/Weber St.
1996	8	Montana St.
1997	9	Northern Ariz.
1998	9	Northern Ariz.
1999	9	Weber St.
2000	9	Montana/Eastern Wash.
2001	9	Cal St. Northridge
2002	8	Montana St.

Season	No.	Conference Tournament
1976	8	Boise St.
1977	8	Idaho St.
1978	8	Weber St.
1979	8	Weber St.
1980	8	Weber St.
1981	8	Idaho
1982	8	Idaho
1983	8	Weber St.
1984	8	Nevada
1985	8	Nevada
1986	7	Montana St.

Season	No.	Conference Tournament
1987	8	Idaho St.
1988	9	Boise St.
1989	9	Idaho
1990	9	Idaho
1991	9	Montana
1992	6	Montana
1993	6	Boise St.
1994	6	Boise St.
1995	6	Weber St.
1996	6	Montana St.
1997	6	Montana
1998	6	Northern Ariz.
1999	6	Weber St.
2000	6	Northern Ariz.
2001	6	Cal St. Northridge
2002	6	Montana

BIG SOUTH CONFERENCE

Season	No.	Regular Season
1986	8	Charleston So.
1987	8	Charleston So.
1988	7	Coastal Caro.
1989	7	Coastal Caro.
1990	7	Coastal Caro.
1991	8	Coastal Caro.
1992	8	Radford
1993	9	Towson
1994	10	Towson
1995	9	UNC Greensboro
1996	9	UNC Greensboro
1997	8	Liberty/UNC Asheville
1998	7	UNC Asheville
1999	6	Winthrop
2000	8	Radford
2001	8	Radford
2002	8	Winthrop/UNC Asheville

Season	No.	Conference Tournament
1986	8	Charleston So.
1987	8	Charleston So.
1988	7	Winthrop
1989	7	UNC Asheville
1990	7	Coastal Caro.
1991	8	Coastal Caro.
1992	8	Campbell
1993	9	Coastal Caro.
1994	8	Liberty
1995	8	Charleston So.
1996	8	UNC Greensboro
1997	8	Charleston So.
1998	7	Radford
1999	6	Winthrop
2000	6	Winthrop
2001	6	Winthrop
2002	8	Winthrop

BIG TEN CONFERENCE

Season	No.	Regular Season
1906	6	Minnesota
1907	5	Chicago/Minnesota/Wisconsin
1908	5	Chicago/Wisconsin
1909	8	Chicago
1910	8	Chicago
1911	8	Purdue/Minnesota
1912	8	Purdue/Wisconsin
1913	9	Wisconsin
1914	9	Wisconsin
1915	9	Illinois
1916	9	Wisconsin
1917	9	Minnesota/Illinois
1918	10	Wisconsin
1919	10	Minnesota
1920	10	Chicago
1921	10	Michigan/Wisconsin/Purdue
1922	10	Purdue
1923	10	Iowa/Wisconsin
1924	10	Wisconsin/Illinois/Chicago
1925	10	Ohio St.
1926	10	Purdue/Indiana/Michigan/Iowa
1927	10	Michigan
1928	10	Indiana/Purdue
1929	10	Wisconsin/Michigan
1930	10	Purdue
1931	10	Northwestern
1932	10	Purdue
1933	10	Northwestern/Ohio St.
1934	10	Purdue
1935	10	Purdue/Illinois/Wisconsin
1936	10	Indiana/Purdue
1937	10	Minnesota/Illinois

Season	No.	Regular Season
1938	10	Purdue
1939	10	Ohio St.
1940	10	Purdue
1941	10	Wisconsin
1942	10	Illinois
1943	10	Illinois
1944	10	Ohio St.
1945	10	Iowa
1946	10	Ohio St.
1947	9	Wisconsin
1948	9	Michigan
1949	9	Illinois
1950	9	Ohio St.
1951	10	Illinois
1952	10	Illinois
1953	10	Indiana
1954	10	Indiana
1955	10	Iowa
1956	10	Iowa
1957	10	Indiana/Michigan St.
1958	10	Indiana
1959	10	Michigan St.
1960	10	Ohio St.
1961	10	Ohio St.
1962	10	Ohio St.
1963	10	Ohio St./Illinois
1964	10	Michigan/Ohio St.
1965	10	Michigan
1966	10	Michigan
1967	10	Indiana/Michigan St.
1968	10	Ohio St./Iowa
1969	10	Purdue
1970	10	Iowa
1971	10	Ohio St.
1972	10	Minnesota
1973	10	Indiana
1974	10	Indiana/Michigan
1975	10	Indiana
1976	10	Indiana
1977	10	Michigan
1978	10	Michigan St.
1979	10	Michigan St./Purdue/Iowa
1980	10	Indiana
1981	10	Indiana
1982	10	Minnesota
1983	10	Indiana
1984	10	Illinois/Purdue
1985	10	Michigan
1986	10	Michigan
1987	10	Indiana/Purdue
1988	10	Purdue
1989	10	Indiana
1990	10	Michigan St.
1991	10	Ohio St./Indiana
1992	10	Ohio St.
1993	11	Indiana
1994	11	Purdue
1995	11	Purdue
1996	11	Purdue
1997	11	Minnesota
1998	11	Michigan St./Illinois
1999	11	Michigan St.
2000	11	Michigan St./Ohio St.
2001	11	Michigan St./Illinois
2002	11	Illinois/Ohio St./Indiana/Wisconsin

Season	No.	Conference Tournament
1998	11	Michigan
1999	11	Michigan St.
2000	11	Michigan St.
2001	11	Iowa
2002	11	Ohio St.

BIG 12 CONFERENCE

Season	No.	Regular Season
1997	12	Kansas
1998	12	Kansas
1999	12	Texas
2000	12	Iowa St.
2001	12	Iowa St.
2002	12	Kansas

Season	No.	Conference Tournament
1997	12	Kansas
1998	12	Kansas
1999	12	Kansas
2000	12	Iowa St.
2001	12	Oklahoma
2002	12	Oklahoma

BIG WEST CONFERENCE

Season	No.	Regular Season
1970	6	Long Beach St.
1971	6	Long Beach St.
1972	7	Long Beach St.
1973	7	Long Beach St.
1974	7	Long Beach St.
1975	6	Long Beach St.
1976	6	Long Beach St./Cal St. Fullerton
1977	7	Long Beach St./San Diego St.
1978	8	Fresno St./San Diego St.
1979	8	Pacific (Cal.)
1980	8	Utah St.
1981	8	Fresno St.
1982	8	Fresno St.
1983	9	UNLV
1984	10	UNLV
1985	10	UNLV
1986	10	UNLV
1987	10	UNLV

Season	No.	Conference Tournament
1988	10	UNLV
1989	10	UNLV
1990	10	UNLV
1991	10	UNLV
1992	10	UNLV
1993	10	New Mexico St.
1994	10	New Mexico St.
1995	10	Utah St.
1996	10	Long Beach St.
1997	12	Nevada (Eastern)/New Mexico St. (Eastern)/Utah St. (Eastern)/Pacific (Cal.) (Western)
1998	1	Utah St. (Eastern)/Pacific (Cal.) (Western)
1999	12	Boise St. (Eastern)/New Mexico St. (Eastern)/UC Santa Barb. (Western)
2000	12	Utah St. (Eastern)/Long Beach St. (Western)
2001	9	UC Irvine
2002	10	Utah St./UC Irvine

Season	No.	Conference Tournament
1976	4	San Diego St.
1977	7	Long Beach St.
1978	7	Cal St. Fullerton
1979	8	Pacific (Cal.)
1980	7	San Jose St.
1981	7	Fresno St.
1982	7	Fresno St.
1983	8	UNLV
1984	8	Fresno St.
1985	8	UNLV
1986	8	UNLV
1987	8	UNLV
1988	10	Utah St.
1989	10	UNLV
1990	10	UNLV
1991	8	UNLV
1992	8	New Mexico St.
1993	8	Long Beach St.
1994	10	New Mexico St.
1995	10	Long Beach St.
1996	6	San Jose St.
1997	8	Pacific (Cal.)
1998	8	Utah St.
1999	8	New Mexico St.
2000	8	Utah St.
2001	8	Utah St.
2002	8	UC Santa Barb.

BORDER CONFERENCE

Season	No.	Regular Season
1932	5	Arizona
1933	6	Texas Tech
1934	6	Texas Tech
1935	6	Texas Tech
1936	7	Arizona
1937	7	New Mexico St.
1938	7	New Mexico St.
1939	7	New Mexico St.
1940	7	New Mexico St.
1941		DNP
1942	9	West Tex. A&M
1943	8	West Tex. A&M
1944	4	Northern Ariz.
1945	9	New Mexico
1946	9	Arizona
1947	9	Arizona
1948	9	Arizona

Season	No.	Regular Season
1949	9	Arizona
1950	9	Arizona
1951	9	Arizona
1952	8	New Mexico St./West Tex. A&M
1953	8	Arizona/Hardin-Simmons
1954	7	Texas Tech
1955	7	Texas Tech/West Tex. A&M
1956	7	Texas Tech
1957	6	UTEP
1958	6	Arizona St.

Season	No.	Conference Tournament
1959	6	Arizona St./New Mexico St./UTEP
1960	6	New Mexico St.
1961	6	Arizona St./New Mexico St.
1962	5	Arizona St.

COLONIAL ATHLETIC ASSOCIATION

Season	No.	Regular Season
1983	6	William & Mary
1984	6	Richmond
1985	8	Navy/Richmond
1986	8	Navy
1987	8	Navy
1988	8	Richmond
1989	8	Richmond
1990	8	James Madison
1991	8	James Madison
1992	8	Richmond/James Madison
1993	8	James Madison/Old Dominion
1994	8	James Madison/Old Dominion
1995	8	Old Dominion
1996	9	Va. Commonwealth
1997	9	Old Dominion/UNC Wilmington
1998	9	William & Mary/UNC Wilmington
1999	9	George Mason
2000	9	James Madison/George Mason
2001	9	Richmond
2002	10	UNC Wilmington

Season	No.	Conference Tournament
1983	6	James Madison
1984	6	Richmond
1985	8	Navy
1986	8	Navy
1987	8	Navy
1988	8	Richmond
1989	8	George Mason
1990	8	Richmond
1991	8	Richmond
1992	8	Old Dominion
1993	8	East Caro.
1994	8	James Madison
1995	8	Old Dominion
1996	9	Va. Commonwealth
1997	9	Old Dominion
1998	9	Richmond
1999	9	George Mason
2000	9	UNC Wilmington
2001	6	George Mason
2002	10	UNC Wilmington

CONFERENCE USA

Season	No.	Regular Season
1996	11	Tulane (Red)/Memphis (White)/Cincinnati (Blue)
1997	12	Tulane (Red)/Memphis (White)/Charlotte (White)/Cincinnati (Blue)
1998	12	Cincinnati (American)/Memphis (National)
1999	12	Cincinnati (American)/UAB (National)
2000	12	Cincinnati (American)/Tulane (National)/South Fla. (National)
2001	12	Cincinnati (American)/Southern Miss. (National)
2002	14	Cincinnati (American)/Memphis (National)

Season	No.	Conference Tournament
1996	11	Cincinnati
1997	12	Marquette
1998	12	Cincinnati
1999	12	Charlotte
2000	12	St. Louis
2001	12	Charlotte
2002	12	Cincinnati

EAST COAST CONFERENCE

Season	No.	Regular Season
1959	10	St. Joseph's
1960	10	St. Joseph's
1961	10	St. Joseph's
1962	10	St. Joseph's
1963	9	St. Joseph's
1964	8	Temple
1965	8	St. Joseph's
1966	10	St. Joseph's
1967	12	Temple
1968	11	La Salle
1969	12	Temple
1970	12	St. Joseph's (East)/Rider (West)/Lehigh (West)/Lafayette (West)
1971	13	St. Joseph's (East)/Lafayette (West)
1972	13	Temple (East)/Rider (West)
1973	13	St. Joseph's (East)/Lafayette (West)
1974	13	St. Joseph's (East)/La Salle (East)/Rider (West)
1975	12	American (East)/La Salle (East)/Lafayette (West)
1976	12	St. Joseph's (East)/Lafayette (West)
1977	12	Temple (East)/Hofstra (East)/Lafayette (West)
1978	12	La Salle (East)/Lafayette (West)
1979	12	Temple (East)/Bucknell (West)
1980	12	St. Joseph's (East)/Lafayette (West)
1981	12	American (East)/Lafayette (West)/Rider (West)
1982	12	Temple (East)/West Chester (West)
1983	10	American (East)/La Salle (East)/Hofstra (East)/Rider (West)
1984	9	Bucknell
1985	8	Bucknell
1986	8	Drexel
1987	8	Bucknell
1988	8	Lafayette
1989	8	Bucknell
1990	8	Towson/Hofstra/Lehigh
1991	7	Towson
1992	7	Hofstra
1993		DNP
1994	6	Troy St.

Season	No.	Conference Tournament
1975	12	La Salle
1976	12	Hofstra
1977	12	Hofstra
1978	12	La Salle
1979	12	Temple
1980	12	La Salle
1981	12	St. Joseph's
1982	12	St. Joseph's
1983	10	La Salle
1984	9	Rider
1985	8	Lehigh
1986	8	Drexel
1987	8	Bucknell
1988	8	Lehigh
1989	8	Bucknell
1990	8	Towson
1991	7	Towson
1992	7	Towson
1993		DNP
1994	6	Hofstra

GREAT MIDWEST CONFERENCE

Season	No.	Regular Season
1992	6	DePaul/Cincinnati
1993	6	Cincinnati
1994	7	Marquette
1995	7	Memphis

Season	No.	Conference Tournament
1992	6	Cincinnati
1993	6	Cincinnati
1994	7	Cincinnati
1995	7	Cincinnati

GULF STAR CONFERENCE

Season	No.	Regular Season
1985	6	Southeast La.
1986	6	Sam Houston St.
1987	6	Stephen F. Austin

HORIZON LEAGUE CONFERENCE

Season	No.	Regular Season
1980	6	Loyola (Ill.)
1981	7	Xavier
1982	7	Evansville
1983	8	Loyola (Ill.)
1984	8	Oral Roberts
1985	8	Loyola (Ill.)
1986	8	Xavier
1987	7	Evansville/Loyola (Ill.)
1988	6	Xavier
1989	7	Evansville
1990	8	Xavier
1991	8	Xavier
1992	6	Evansville
1993	8	Evansville/Xavier
1994	8	Xavier
1995	11	Xavier
1996	9	Wis.-Green Bay
1997	9	Butler
1998	8	Detroit/Ill.-Chicago
1999	8	Detroit
2000	8	Butler
2001	8	Butler
2002	9	Butler

Season	No.	Conference Tournament
1980	6	Oral Roberts
1981	7	Oklahoma City
1982	7	Evansville
1983	8	Xavier
1984	8	Oral Roberts
1985	8	Loyola (Ill.)
1986	7	Xavier
1987	7	Xavier
1988	6	Xavier
1989	7	Evansville
1990	8	Dayton
1991	8	Xavier
1992	8	Evansville
1993	8	Evansville
1994	6	Detroit
1995	10	Wis.-Green Bay
1996	8	Northern Ill.
1997	9	Butler
1998	8	Butler
1999	8	Detroit
2000	8	Butler
2001	8	Butler
2002	9	Ill.-Chicago

IVY GROUP

Season	No.	Regular Season
1902	5	Yale
1903	5	Yale
1904	6	Columbia
1905	5	Columbia
1906	5	Pennsylvania
1907	6	Yale
1908	5	Pennsylvania
1909-10		DNP
1911	5	Columbia
1912	6	Columbia
1913	5	Cornell
1914	6	Cornell/Columbia
1915	6	Yale
1916	6	Pennsylvania
1917	6	Yale
1918	6	Pennsylvania
1919	5	Pennsylvania
1920	6	Pennsylvania
1921	6	Pennsylvania
1922	6	Princeton
1923	6	Yale
1924	6	Cornell
1925	6	Princeton
1926	6	Columbia
1927	6	Dartmouth
1928	6	Pennsylvania
1929	6	Pennsylvania
1930	6	Columbia
1931	6	Columbia
1932	6	Princeton
1933	6	Yale
1934	7	Pennsylvania
1935	7	Pennsylvania
1936	7	Columbia
1937	7	Pennsylvania
1938	7	Dartmouth
1939	7	Dartmouth

Season	No.	Regular Season
1940	7	Dartmouth
1941	7	Dartmouth
1942	7	Dartmouth
1943	7	Dartmouth
1944	5	Dartmouth
1945	4	Pennsylvania
1946	5	Dartmouth
1947	7	Columbia
1948	7	Columbia
1949	7	Yale
1950	7	Princeton
1951	7	Columbia
1952	7	Princeton
1953	7	Pennsylvania
1954	8	Cornell
1955	8	Princeton
1956	8	Dartmouth
1957	8	Yale
1958	8	Dartmouth
1959	8	Dartmouth
1960	8	Princeton
1961	8	Princeton
1962	8	Yale
1963	8	Princeton
1964	8	Princeton
1965	8	Princeton
1966	8	Pennsylvania
1967	8	Princeton
1968	8	Columbia
1969	8	Princeton
1970	8	Pennsylvania
1971	8	Pennsylvania
1972	8	Pennsylvania
1973	8	Pennsylvania
1974	8	Pennsylvania
1975	8	Pennsylvania
1976	8	Princeton
1977	8	Princeton
1978	8	Pennsylvania
1979	8	Pennsylvania
1980	8	Pennsylvania
1981	8	Princeton
1982	8	Pennsylvania
1983	8	Princeton
1984	8	Princeton
1985	8	Pennsylvania
1986	8	Brown
1987	8	Pennsylvania
1988	8	Cornell
1989	8	Princeton
1990	8	Princeton
1991	8	Princeton
1992	8	Princeton
1993	8	Pennsylvania
1994	8	Pennsylvania
1995	8	Pennsylvania
1996	8	Princeton
1997	8	Princeton
1998	8	Princeton
1999	8	Pennsylvania
2000	8	Pennsylvania
2001	8	Princeton
2002	8	Pennsylvania/Yale/Princeton

METRO ATLANTIC ATHLETIC CONFERENCE

Season	No.	Regular Season
1982	6	St. Peter's
1983	6	Iona
1984	8	La Salle/St. Peter's/Iona
1985	8	Iona
1986	8	Fairfield
1987	8	St. Peter's
1988	8	La Salle
1989	8	La Salle
1990	12	Holy Cross (North)/ La Salle (South)
1991	9	Siena
1992	9	Manhattan
1993	8	Manhattan
1994	8	Canisius
1995	8	Manhattan
1996	8	Fairfield/Iona
1997	8	Iona
1998	10	Iona
1999	10	Niagara/Siena
2000	10	Siena
2001	10	Iona/Siena/Niagara
2002	10	Marist/Rider

Season	No.	Conference Tournament
1982	6	Fordham
1983	6	Fordham
1984	8	Iona
1985	8	Iona
1986	8	Fairfield
1987	8	Fairfield
1988	8	La Salle
1989	8	La Salle
1990	12	La Salle
1991	9	St. Peter's
1992	9	La Salle
1993	8	Manhattan
1994	8	Loyola (Md.)
1995	8	St. Peter's
1996	8	Canisius
1997	8	Fairfield
1998	10	Iona
1999	10	Siena
2000	10	Iona
2001	10	Iona
2002	10	Siena

METROPOLITAN COLLEGIATE ATHLETIC CONFERENCE

Season	No.	Regular Season
1976	6	Tulane
1977	7	Louisville
1978	7	Florida St.
1979	7	Louisville
1980	7	Louisville
1981	7	Louisville
1982	7	Memphis
1983	7	Louisville
1984	8	Memphis/Louisville
1985	8	Memphis
1986	7	Louisville
1987	7	Louisville
1988	7	Louisville
1989	7	Florida St.
1990	8	Louisville
1991	8	Southern Miss.
1992	7	Tulane
1993	7	Louisville
1994	7	Louisville
1995	7	Charlotte

Season	No.	Conference Tournament
1976	6	Cincinnati
1977	7	Cincinnati
1978	7	Louisville
1979	7	Virginia Tech
1980	7	Louisville
1981	7	Louisville
1982	7	Memphis
1983	7	Louisville
1984	8	Memphis
1985	8	Memphis
1986	7	Louisville
1987	7	Memphis
1988	7	Louisville
1989	5	Louisville
1990	8	Louisville
1991	8	Florida St.
1992	7	Charlotte
1993	7	Louisville
1994	7	Louisville
1995	7	Louisville

METROPOLITAN NEW YORK CONFERENCE

Season	No.	Regular Season
1943	8	St. John's (N.Y.)
1944-45		DNP
1946	7	New York U./St. John's (N.Y.)
1947	7	St. John's (N.Y.)
1948	7	New York U.
1949	7	Manhattan/St. John's (N.Y.)
1950	7	CCNY
1951	7	St. John's (N.Y.)
1952	7	St. John's (N.Y.)
1953	7	Manhattan
1954	7	St. Francis (N.Y.)
1955	7	Manhattan
1956	7	St. Francis (N.Y.)
1957	7	New York U.
1958	7	St. John's (N.Y.)
1959	7	Manhattan
1960	7	New York U.
1961	7	St. John's (N.Y.)
1962	7	St. John's (N.Y.)
1963	7	Fordham

MID-AMERICAN ATHLETIC CONFERENCE

Season	No.	Regular Season
1947	5	Butler/Cincinnati
1948	6	Cincinnati
1949	6	Cincinnati
1950	6	Cincinnati
1951	5	Cincinnati
1952	7	Miami (Ohio)/Western Mich.
1953	7	Miami (Ohio)
1954	8	Toledo
1955	8	Miami (Ohio)
1956	7	Marshall
1957	7	Miami (Ohio)
1958	7	Miami (Ohio)
1959	7	Bowling Green
1960	7	Ohio
1961	7	Ohio
1962	7	Bowling Green
1963	7	Bowling Green
1964	7	Ohio
1965	7	Ohio
1966	7	Miami (Ohio)
1967	7	Toledo
1968	7	Bowling Green
1969	7	Miami (Ohio)
1970	6	Ohio
1971	6	Miami (Ohio)
1972	6	Ohio
1973	7	Miami (Ohio)
1974	7	Ohio
1975	8	Central Mich.
1976	10	Western Mich.
1977	10	Central Mich.
1978	10	Miami (Ohio)
1979	10	Toledo
1980	10	Toledo
1981	10	Ball St./Northern Ill./Toledo/ Western Mich./Bowling Green
1982	10	Ball St.
1983	10	Bowling Green
1984	10	Miami (Ohio)
1985	10	Ohio
1986	10	Miami (Ohio)
1987	9	Central Mich.
1988	9	Eastern Mich.
1989	9	Ball St.
1990	9	Ball St.
1991	9	Eastern Mich.
1992	8	Miami (Ohio)
1993	10	Ball St./Miami (Ohio)
1994	10	Ohio
1995	10	Miami (Ohio)
1996	10	Eastern Mich.
1997	10	Bowling Green/Miami (Ohio)
1998	12	Akron (East)/Ball St. (West)/
1999	13	Miami (Ohio)(East)/Toledo (West)
2000	13	Bowling Green (East)/ Ball St. (West)/Toledo (West)
2001	13	Kent St. (East)/ Central Mich. (West)
2002	13	Kent St. (East)/Ball St. (West)

Season	No.	Conference Tournament
1980	7	Toledo
1981	7	Ball St.
1982	7	Northern Ill.
1983	7	Ohio
1984	7	Miami (Ohio)
1985	7	Ohio
1986	7	Ball St.
1987	7	Central Mich.
1988	7	Eastern Mich.
1989	8	Ball St.
1990	8	Ball St.
1991	8	Eastern Mich.
1992	8	Miami (Ohio)
1993	10	Ball St.
1994	8	Ohio
1995	8	Ball St.
1996	8	Eastern Mich.
1997	8	Miami (Ohio)
1998	8	Eastern Mich.
1999	8	Kent St.
2000	13	Ball St.
2001	13	Kent St.
2002	13	Kent St.

MID-CONTINENT CONFERENCE

Season	No.	Regular Season
1983	8	Western Ill.
1984	8	Ill.-Chicago
1985	8	Cleveland St.
1986	8	Cleveland St.
1987	8	Southwest Mo. St.
1988	8	Southwest Mo. St.
1989	8	Southwest Mo. St.
1990	7	Southwest Mo. St.
1991	9	Northern Ill.
1992	9	Wis.-Green Bay
1993	9	Cleveland St.
1994	10	Wis.-Green Bay
1995	10	Valparaiso
1996	10	Valparaiso
1997	8	Valparaiso
1998	9	Valparaiso
1999	8	Valparaiso
2000	9	Oakland
2001	9	Southern Utah/Valparaiso
2002	8	Valparaiso

Season	No.	Conference Tournament
1984	8	Western Ill.
1985	8	Eastern Ill.
1986	8	Cleveland St.
1987	8	Southwest Mo. St.
1988		DNP
1989	7	Southwest Mo. St.
1990	7	Northern Iowa
1991	8	Wis.-Green Bay
1992	8	Eastern Ill.
1993	8	Wright St.
1994	8	Wis.-Green Bay
1995	6	Valparaiso
1996	8	Valparaiso
1997	8	Valparaiso
1998	7	Valpairaso
1999	7	Valparaiso
2000	7	Valparaiso
2001	8	Southern Utah
2002	8	Valparaiso

MID-EASTERN ATHLETIC CONFERENCE

Season	No.	Regular Season
1972	7	N.C. A&T
1973	7	Md.-East. Shore
1974	7	Md.-East. Shore/Morgan St.
1975	7	N.C. A&T
1976	7	N.C. A&T/Morgan St.
1977	7	South Carolina St.
1978	7	N.C. A&T
1979	7	N.C. A&T
1980	7	Howard
1981	6	N.C. A&T
1982	7	N.C. A&T
1983	7	Howard
1984	6	N.C. A&T
1985	7	N.C. A&T
1986	8	N.C. A&T
1987	8	Howard
1988	9	N.C. A&T
1989	9	South Carolina St.
1990	9	Coppin St.
1991	9	Coppin St.
1992	9	N.C. A&T/Howard
1993	9	Coppin St.
1994	9	Coppin St.
1995	9	Coppin St.
1996	10	Coppin St./South Carolina St.
1997	10	Coppin St.
1998	11	Coppin St.
1999	11	Coppin St./South Carolina St.
2000	11	South Carolina St.
2001	11	Hampton/South Carolina St.
2002	11	Hampton

Season	No.	Conference Tournament
1972	7	N.C. A&T
1973	7	N.C. A&T
1974	7	Md.-East. Shore
1975	7	N.C. A&T
1976	7	N.C. A&T
1977	7	Morgan St.
1978	7	N.C. A&T
1979	7	N.C. A&T
1980	7	Howard
1981	6	Howard
1982	7	N.C. A&T
1983	7	N.C. A&T
1984	6	N.C. A&T
1985	6	N.C. A&T
1986	6	N.C. A&T
1987	7	N.C. A&T
1988	7	N.C. A&T
1989	8	South Carolina St.
1990	8	Coppin St.
1991	9	Florida A&M
1992	9	Howard
1993	9	Coppin St.
1994	9	N.C. A&T
1995	9	N.C. A&T
1996	8	South Carolina St.
1997	9	Coppin St.
1998	9	South Carolina St.
1999	10	Florida A&M
2000	11	South Carolina St.
2001	11	Hampton
2002	11	Hampton

MISSOURI VALLEY CONFERENCE

(Note: The Big Eight and Missouri Valley conferences share the same history from 1908-28.)

Season	No.	Regular Season
1908	6	Kansas
1909	6	Kansas
1910	6	Kansas
1911	5	Kansas
1912	6	Nebraska/Kansas
1913	6	Nebraska
1914	7	Kansas/Nebraska
1915	7	Kansas
1916	7	Nebraska
1917	7	Kansas St.
1918	7	Missouri
1919	8	Kansas St.
1920	8	Missouri
1921	8	Missouri
1922	9	Missouri/Kansas
1923	9	Kansas
1924	9	Kansas
1925	9	Kansas
1926	10	Kansas
1927	10	Kansas
1928	10	Oklahoma
1929	5	Washington (Mo.)
1930	5	Creighton/Washington (Mo.)
1931	5	Creighton/Oklahoma St.
1932	5	Creighton
1933	6	Butler
1934	6	Butler
1935	7	Creighton/Drake
1936	7	Creighton/Oklahoma St./Drake
1937	7	Oklahoma St.
1938	7	Oklahoma St.
1939	8	Oklahoma St./Drake
1940	7	Oklahoma St.
1941	7	Creighton
1942	6	Oklahoma St./Creighton
1943	6	Creighton
1944	4	Oklahoma St.
1945	5	Oklahoma St.
1946	6	Oklahoma St.
1947	7	St. Louis
1948	6	Oklahoma St.
1949	6	Oklahoma St.
1950	7	Bradley
1951	8	Oklahoma St.
1952	6	St. Louis
1953	6	Oklahoma St.
1954	6	Oklahoma St.
1955	6	Tulsa/St. Louis
1956	7	Houston
1957	7	St. Louis
1958	8	Cincinnati
1959	8	Cincinnati
1960	7	Cincinnati
1961	7	Cincinnati
1962	7	Bradley/Cincinnati
1963	7	Cincinnati
1964	7	Drake/Wichita St.
1965	8	Wichita St.
1966	8	Cincinnati
1967	8	Louisville
1968	9	Louisville
1969	9	Drake/Louisville
1970	9	Drake
1971	8	Drake/Louisville/St. Louis
1972	8	Memphis/Louisville
1973	10	Memphis
1974	9	Louisville
1975	8	Louisville
1976	7	Wichita St.
1977	7	Southern Ill./New Mexico St.
1978	9	Creighton
1979	9	Indiana St.
1980	9	Bradley
1981	9	Wichita St.
1982	10	Bradley
1983	10	Wichita St.
1984	9	Tulsa/Illinois St.
1985	9	Tulsa
1986	9	Bradley
1987	8	Tulsa
1988	8	Bradley
1989	8	Creighton
1990	8	Southern Ill.
1991	9	Creighton
1992	10	Southern Ill./Illinois St.
1993	10	Illinois St.
1994	10	Southern Ill./Tulsa
1995	11	Tulsa
1996	11	Bradley
1997	10	Illinois St.
1998	10	Illinois St.
1999	10	Evansville
2000	10	Indiana St.
2001	10	Creighton
2002	10	Southern Ill./Creighton

Season	No.	Conference Tournament
1977	8	Southern Ill.
1978	9	Creighton
1979	8	Indiana St.
1980	8	Bradley
1981	8	Creighton
1982	8	Tulsa
1983	8	Illinois St.
1984	8	Tulsa
1985	8	Wichita St.
1986	8	Tulsa
1987	7	Wichita St.
1988	8	Bradley
1989	8	Creighton
1990	8	Illinois St.
1991	9	Creighton
1992	8	Southwest Mo. St.
1993	8	Southern Ill.
1994	8	Southern Ill.
1995	8	Southern Ill.
1996	8	Tulsa
1997	10	Illinois St.
1998	10	Illinois St.
1999	10	Creighton
2000	10	Creighton
2001	10	Indiana St.
2002	10	Creighton

MOUNTAIN STATES CONFERENCE

Season	No.	Regular Season
1938	7	Colorado/Utah
1939	7	Colorado
1940	7	Colorado
1941	7	Wyoming
1942	7	Colorado
1943	5	Wyoming
1944	7	Utah
1945	7	Utah
1946	7	Wyoming
1947	7	Wyoming
1948	6	Brigham Young
1949	6	Wyoming
1950	6	Brigham Young
1951	6	Brigham Young
1952	8	Wyoming
1953	8	Wyoming
1954	8	Colorado
1955	8	Utah
1956	8	Utah
1957	8	Brigham Young
1958	8	Wyoming
1959	8	Utah
1960	8	Utah
1961	8	Colorado St./Utah
1962	8	Utah

MOUNTAIN WEST

Season	No.	Regular Season
2000	8	UNLV/Utah

Season	No.	Regular Season
2001	8	Brigham Young/Wyoming/Utah
2002	8	Wyoming

Season	No.	Conference Tournament
2000	8	UNLV
2001	7	Brigham Young
2002	8	San Diego St.

NEW ENGLAND CONFERENCE

Season	No.	Regular Season
1938	5	Rhode Island
1939	5	Rhode Island
1940	5	Rhode Island
1941	5	Rhode Island
1942	5	Rhode Island
1943	5	Rhode Island
1944	4	Rhode Island
1945		DNP
1946	5	Rhode Island

NEW JERSEY-NEW YORK 7 CONFERENCE

Season	No.	Regular Season
1977	7	Columbia/Seton Hall
1978	7	Rutgers/St. John's (N.Y.)
1979	7	Rutgers

NORTHEAST CONFERENCE

Season	No.	Regular Season
1982	11	Fairleigh Dickinson (North)/Robert Morris (South)
1983	10	Long Island (North)/Robert Morris (South)
1984	9	Long Island/Robert Morris
1985	8	Marist
1986	9	Fairleigh Dickinson
1987	9	Marist
1988	9	Fairleigh Dickinson/Marist
1989	9	Robert Morris
1990	9	Robert Morris
1991	9	St. Francis (Pa.)/Fairleigh Dickinson
1992	9	Robert Morris
1993	10	Rider
1994	10	Rider
1995	10	Rider
1996	10	Mt. St. Mary's
1997	10	Long Island
1998	9	Long Island
1999	11	UMBC
2000	12	Central Conn. St.
2001	12	St. Francis (N.Y.)
2002	12	Central Conn. St.

Season	No.	Conference Tournament
1982	8	Robert Morris
1983	8	Robert Morris
1984	8	Long Island
1985	8	Fairleigh Dickinson
1986	8	Marist
1987	6	Marist
1988	6	Fairleigh Dickinson
1989	6	Robert Morris
1990	6	Robert Morris
1991	7	St. Francis (Pa.)
1992	9	Robert Morris
1993	10	Rider
1994	10	Rider
1995	10	Mt. St. Mary's
1996	10	Monmouth
1997	8	Long Island
1998	8	Fairleigh Dickinson
1999	8	Mt. St. Mary's
2000	8	Central Conn. St.
2001	7	Monmouth
2002	8	Central Conn. St.

OHIO VALLEY CONFERENCE

Season	No.	Regular Season
1949	8	Western Ky.
1950	7	Western Ky.
1951	7	Murray St.
1952	7	Morehead St.
1953	6	Eastern Ky.
1954	6	Western Ky.
1955	6	Western Ky.
1956	6	Morehead St./Tennessee Tech/Western Ky.
1957	6	Morehead St./Western Ky.
1958	7	Tennessee Tech
1959	7	Eastern Ky.
1960	7	Western Ky.
1961	7	Morehead St./Western Ky./Eastern Ky.
1962	6	Western Ky.
1963	7	Tennessee Tech/Morehead St.
1964	8	Murray St.
1965	8	Eastern Ky.
1966	8	Western Ky.
1967	8	Western Ky.
1968	8	East Tenn. St./Murray St.
1969	8	Murray St./Morehead St.
1970	8	Western Ky.
1971	8	Western Ky.
1972	8	Eastern Ky./Morehead St./Western Ky.
1973	8	Austin Peay
1974	8	Austin Peay/Morehead St.
1975	8	Middle Tenn.
1976	8	Western Ky.
1977	8	Austin Peay
1978	8	Middle Tenn./Eastern Ky.
1979	7	Eastern Ky.
1980	7	Western Ky./Murray St.
1981	8	Western Ky.
1982	8	Murray St./Western Ky.
1983	8	Murray St.
1984	8	Morehead St.
1985	8	Tennessee Tech
1986	8	Akron/Middle Tenn.
1987	8	Middle Tenn.
1988	8	Murray St.
1989	7	Middle Tenn./Murray St.
1990	7	Murray St.
1991	7	Murray St.
1992	8	Murray St.
1993	9	Tennessee St.
1994	9	Murray St.
1995	9	Murray St./Tennessee St.
1996	9	Murray St.
1997	10	Austin Peay/Murray St.
1998	10	Murray St.
1999	10	Murray St.
2000	10	Southeast Mo. St./ Murray St.
2001	9	Tennessee Tech
2002	9	Tennessee Tech

Season	No.	Conference Tournament
1949	8	Western Ky.
1950	7	Eastern Ky.
1951	7	Murray St.
1952	7	Western Ky.
1953	6	Western Ky.
1954	6	Western Ky.
1955	6	Eastern Ky.
1956-63		DNP
1964	8	Murray St.
1965	8	Western Ky.
1966	8	Western Ky.
1967	8	Tennessee Tech
1968-74		DNP
1975	4	Middle Tenn.
1976	8	Western Ky.
1977	4	Middle Tenn.
1978	4	Western Ky.
1979	4	Eastern Ky.
1980	4	Western Ky.
1981	4	Western Ky.
1982	4	Middle Tenn.
1983	4	Morehead St.
1984	4	Morehead St.
1985	7	Middle Tenn.
1986	7	Akron
1987	7	Austin Peay
1988	7	Murray St.
1989	7	Middle Tenn.
1990	7	Murray St.
1991	7	Murray St.
1992	7	Murray St.
1993	6	Tennessee St.
1994	7	Tennessee St.
1995	7	Murray St.
1996	7	Austin Peay
1997	8	Murray St.
1998	8	Murray St.
1999	8	Murray St.
2000	8	Southeast Mo. St.
2001	8	Eastern Ill.
2002	8	Murray St.

PACIFIC-10 CONFERENCE

Season	No.	Regular Season
1916	3	California/Oregon St.
1917	6	Washington St.
1918		DNP
1919	6	Oregon
1920	6	Stanford
1921	6	Stanford
1922	8	Idaho
1923	8	Idaho
1924	9	California
1925	8	California
1926	9	California
1927	9	California
1928	10	Southern California
1929	10	California
1930	9	Southern California
1931	9	Washington
1932	9	California
1933	9	Oregon St.
1934	9	Washington
1935	9	Southern California
1936	9	Stanford
1937	9	Stanford
1938	10	Stanford
1939	9	Oregon
1940	9	Southern California
1941	9	Washington St.
1942	9	Stanford
1943	9	Washington
1944	8	Washington (North)/California (South)
1945	8	Oregon (North)/UCLA (South)
1946	9	California
1947	9	Oregon St.
1948	9	Washington
1949	9	Oregon St.
1950	9	UCLA
1951	9	Washington
1952	9	UCLA
1953	9	Washington
1954	9	Southern California
1955	9	Oregon St.
1956	9	UCLA
1957	9	California
1958	9	Oregon St./California
1959	9	California
1960	5	California
1961	5	Southern California
1962	5	UCLA
1963	5	UCLA/Stanford
1964	6	UCLA
1965	8	UCLA
1966	8	Oregon St.
1967	8	UCLA
1968	8	UCLA
1969	8	UCLA
1970	8	UCLA
1971	8	UCLA
1972	8	UCLA
1973	8	UCLA
1974	8	UCLA
1975	8	UCLA
1976	8	UCLA
1977	8	UCLA
1978	8	UCLA
1979	10	UCLA
1980	10	Oregon St.
1981	10	Oregon St.
1982	10	Oregon St.
1983	10	UCLA
1984	10	Washington/Oregon St.
1985	10	Washington/Southern California
1986	10	Arizona
1987	10	UCLA
1988	10	Arizona
1989	10	Arizona
1990	10	Oregon St./Arizona
1991	10	Arizona
1992	10	UCLA
1993	10	Arizona
1994	10	Arizona
1995	10	UCLA
1996	10	UCLA
1997	10	UCLA
1998	10	Arizona
1999	10	Stanford
2000	10	Arizona/Stanford
2001	10	Stanford
2002	10	Oregon

Season	No.	Conference Tournament
1987	10	UCLA
1988	10	Arizona
1989	10	Arizona
1990	10	Arizona
1991-2001		DNP
2002	8	Arizona

PATRIOT LEAGUE

Season	No.	Regular Season
1991	7	Fordham
1992	8	Bucknell/Fordham
1993	8	Bucknell
1994	8	Navy/Fordham/Colgate/Holy Cross
1995	8	Bucknell/Colgate
1996	7	Colgate/Navy
1997	7	Navy
1998	7	Lafayette/Navy
1999	7	Lafayette
2000	7	Lafayette/Navy
2001	7	Holy Cross
2002	8	American

Season	No.	Conference Tournament
1991	7	Fordham
1992	8	Fordham
1993	8	Holy Cross
1994	8	Navy
1995	8	Colgate
1996	7	Colgate
1997	7	Navy
1998	7	Navy
1999	7	Lafayette
2000	7	Lafayette
2001	7	Holy Cross
2002	8	Holy Cross

ROCKY MOUNTAIN CONFERENCE

Season	No.	Regular Season
1922	6	Colorado Col.
1923	5	Colorado Col.
1924	6	Colorado Col.
1925	12	Colorado Col. (East)/Brigham Young (West)
1926	12	Colorado St. (East)/Utah (West)
1927	12	Colorado Col. (East)/Montana St. (West)
1928	12	Wyoming (East)/Montana St. (West)
1929	12	Colorado (East)/Montana St. (West)
1929	12	Colorado (East)/Montana St. (West)
1930	12	Colorado (East)/Montana St. (West)/Utah St. (West)
1931	12	Wyoming (East)/Utah (West)
1932	12	Wyoming (East)/Brigham Young (West)/Utah (West)
1933	12	Wyoming (East)/Colorado St. (East)/Brigham Young (West)/Utah (West)
1934	12	Wyoming (East)/Brigham Young (West)
1935	12	Northern Colo. (East)/Utah St. (West)
1936	12	Wyoming (East)/Utah (West)
1937	12	Denver (East)/Colorado (East)/Montana St. (West)/Utah (West)
1938	5	Montana St.
1939	5	Northern Colo.
1940	5	Northern Colo.
1941	5	Northern Colo.
1942	5	Northern Colo.
1943	3	Northern Colo.
1944	3	Colorado Col.
1945	3	Colorado Col.
1946	5	Colorado St.
1947	5	Montana St.
1948	4	Colorado St.
1949	5	Colorado St.
1950	6	Montana St.
1951	6	Montana St.
1952	6	Colorado St./Montana St.
1953	6	Idaho St.
1954	6	Idaho St.
1955	6	Idaho St.
1956	6	Idaho St.
1957	6	Idaho St.
1958	6	Idaho St.

Season	No.	Regular Season
1959	6	Idaho St.
1960	6	Idaho St.

SOUTHEASTERN CONFERENCE

Season	No.	Regular Season
1933	13	Kentucky
1934	13	Alabama
1935	13	LSU/Kentucky
1936	13	Tennessee
1937	13	Kentucky
1938	13	Georgia Tech
1939	13	Kentucky
1940	13	Kentucky
1941	12	Tennessee
1942	12	Kentucky
1943	12	Tennessee
1944	6	Kentucky
1945	12	Kentucky
1946	12	Kentucky
1947	12	Kentucky
1948	12	Kentucky
1949	12	Kentucky
1950	12	Kentucky
1951	12	Kentucky
1952	12	Kentucky
1953	11	LSU
1954	12	Kentucky/LSU
1955	12	Kentucky
1956	12	Alabama
1957	12	Kentucky
1958	12	Kentucky
1959	12	Mississippi St.
1960	12	Auburn
1961	12	Mississippi St.
1962	12	Mississippi St./Kentucky
1963	12	Mississippi St.
1964	12	Kentucky
1965	11	Vanderbilt
1966	11	Kentucky
1967	10	Tennessee
1968	10	Kentucky
1969	10	Kentucky
1970	10	Kentucky
1971	10	Kentucky
1972	10	Tennessee/Kentucky
1973	10	Kentucky
1974	10	Vanderbilt/Alabama
1975	10	Kentucky/Alabama
1976	10	Alabama
1977	10	Kentucky/Tennessee
1978	10	Kentucky
1979	10	LSU
1980	10	Kentucky
1981	10	LSU
1982	10	Kentucky/Tennessee
1983	10	Kentucky
1984	10	Kentucky
1985	10	LSU
1986	10	Kentucky
1987	10	Alabama
1988	10	Kentucky*
1989	10	Florida
1990	10	Georgia
1991	10	Mississippi St./LSU
1992	12	Kentucky (Eastern)/Arkansas (Western)
1993	12	Vanderbilt (Eastern)/Arkansas (Western)
1994	12	Florida (Eastern)/Kentucky (Eastern)/Arkansas (Western)
1995	12	Kentucky (Eastern)/Arkansas (Western)/Mississippi St. (Western)
1996	12	Kentucky (Eastern)/Mississippi St. (Western)
1997	12	South Carolina (Eastern)/Mississippi (Western)
1998	12	Kentucky (Eastern)/Mississippi (Western)
1999	12	Tennessee (Eastern)/Auburn (Western)
2000	12	Tennessee (Eastern)/Florida (Eastern)/Kentucky (Eastern)/LSU (Western)
2001	12	Florida (Eastern)/Kentucky (Eastern)/Mississippi (Western)
2002	12	Georgia (Eastern)/Kentucky (Eastern)/Florida (Eastern)/Alabama (Western)

Season	No.	Conference Tournament
1933	13	Kentucky
1934	10	Alabama
1935		DNP
1936	9	Tennessee
1937	8	Kentucky
1938	11	Georgia Tech
1939	12	Kentucky
1940	12	Kentucky
1941	12	Tennessee
1942	12	Kentucky
1943	11	Tennessee
1944	6	Kentucky
1945	11	Kentucky
1946	12	Kentucky
1947	12	Kentucky
1948	12	Kentucky
1949	12	Kentucky
1950	12	Kentucky
1951	12	Vanderbilt
1952	12	Kentucky
1953-78		DNP
1979	10	Tennessee
1980	10	LSU
1981	10	Mississippi
1982	10	Alabama
1983	10	Georgia
1984	10	Kentucky
1985	10	Auburn
1986	10	Alabama
1987	10	Alabama
1988	10	Kentucky*
1989	10	Alabama
1990	9	Alabama
1991	9	Alabama
1992	11	Kentucky
1993	12	Kentucky
1994	12	Kentucky
1995	12	Kentucky
1996	12	Mississippi St.
1997	12	Kentucky
1998	12	Kentucky
1999	12	Kentucky
2000	12	Arkansas
2001	12	Kentucky
2002	12	Mississippi St.

*later vacated

SOUTHERN CONFERENCE

Season	No.	Regular Season
1922	13	Virginia
1923	19	North Carolina
1924	21	Tulane
1925	21	North Carolina
1926	22	Kentucky
1927	22	South Carolina
1928	22	Auburn
1929	23	Wash. & Lee
1930	23	Alabama
1931	22	Georgia
1932	23	Kentucky/Maryland
1933	10	South Carolina
1934	10	South Carolina
1935	10	North Carolina
1936	16	Wash. & Lee
1937	16	Wash. & Lee
1938	15	North Carolina
1939	15	Wake Forest
1940	15	Duke
1941	15	North Carolina
1942	16	Duke
1943	15	Duke
1944	12	North Carolina
1945	14	South Carolina
1946	16	North Carolina
1947	16	North Carolina St.
1948	16	North Carolina St.
1949	16	North Carolina St.
1950	16	North Carolina St.
1951	17	North Carolina St.
1952	17	West Virginia
1953	17	North Carolina St.
1954	10	George Washington
1955	10	West Virginia
1956	10	George Washington/West Virginia
1957	10	West Virginia
1958	10	West Virginia
1959	9	West Virginia
1960	9	Virginia Tech
1961	9	West Virginia

Season	No.	Regular Season
1962	9	West Virginia
1963	9	West Virginia
1964	9	Davidson
1965	10	Davidson
1966	9	Davidson
1967	9	West Virginia
1968	9	Davidson
1969	8	Davidson
1970	8	Davidson
1971	7	Davidson
1972	8	Davidson
1973	8	Davidson
1974	8	Furman
1975	8	Furman
1976	8	VMI
1977	10	Furman/VMI
1978	8	Appalachian St.
1979	9	Appalachian St.
1980	9	Furman
1981	9	Appalachian St./Davidson/Chattanooga
1982	9	Chattanooga
1983	9	Chattanooga
1984	9	Marshall
1985	9	Chattanooga
1986	9	Chattanooga
1987	9	Marshall
1988	9	Marshall
1989	8	Chattanooga
1990	8	East Tenn. St.
1991	8	East Tenn. St./Furman/Chattanooga
1992	8	East Tenn. St./Chattanooga
1993	10	Chattanooga
1994	10	Chattanooga
1995	10	Marshall (Northern)/Chattanooga (Southern)
1996	10	Davidson (Northern)/Western Caro. (Southern)
1997	10	Davidson (Northern)/Marshall (Northern)/Chattanooga (Southern)
1998	11	Appalachian St. (North)/Davidson (North)/Chattanooga (South)
1999	12	Appalachian St.(North)/Col. of Charleston (South)
2000	12	Appalachian St. (North)/Col. of Charleston (South)
2001	12	East Tenn. St. (North)/Col. of Charleston (South)
2002	12	Davidson (North)/UNC Greensboro (North)/East Tenn. St. (North)/Col. of Charleston (South)/Ga. Southern(Southern)/Chattanooga (Southern)

Season	No.	Conference Tournament
1921		Kentucky
1922	23	North Carolina
1923	22	Mississippi St.
1924	16	North Carolina
1925	17	North Carolina
1926	16	North Carolina
1927	14	Vanderbilt
1928	16	Mississippi
1929	16	North Carolina St.
1930	16	Alabama
1931	16	Maryland
1932	16	Georgia
1933	8	South Carolina
1934	8	Wash.& Lee
1935	8	North Carolina
1936	8	North Carolina
1937	8	Wash.& Lee
1938	8	Duke
1939	11	Clemson
1940	8	North Carolina
1941	8	Duke
1942	8	Duke
1943	8	George Washington
1944	8	Duke
1945	8	North Carolina
1946	8	Duke
1947	8	North Carolina St.
1948	10	North Carolina St.
1949	8	North Carolina St.
1950	8	North Carolina St.
1951	8	North Carolina St.
1952	8	North Carolina St.
1953	8	Wake Forest
1954	8	George Washington
1955	8	West Virginia
1956	8	West Virginia
1957	8	West Virginia
1958	8	West Virginia
1959	8	West Virginia
1960	8	West Virginia
1961	8	George Washington
1962	8	West Virginia
1963	8	West Virginia
1964	8	VMI
1965	8	West Virginia
1966	8	Davidson
1967	8	West Virginia
1968	8	Davidson
1969	8	Davidson
1970	8	Davidson
1971	7	Furman
1972	8	East Caro.
1973	8	Furman
1974	8	Furman
1975	8	Furman
1976	8	VMI
1977	7	VMI
1978	8	Furman
1979	8	Appalachian St.
1980	8	Furman
1981	8	Chattanooga
1982	8	Chattanooga
1983	8	Chattanooga
1984	8	Marshall
1985	8	Marshall
1986	8	Davidson
1987	8	Marshall
1988	8	Chattanooga
1989	8	East Tenn. St.
1990	8	East Tenn. St.
1991	8	East Tenn. St.
1992	8	East Tenn. St.
1993	10	Chattanooga
1994	10	Chattanooga
1995	10	Chattanooga
1996	9	Western Caro.
1997	10	Chattanooga
1998	10	Davidson
1999	12	Col. of Charleston
2000	12	Appalachian St.
2001	12	UNC Greensboro
2002	12	Davidson

SOUTHLAND CONFERENCE

Season	No.	Regular Season
1964	5	Lamar
1965	5	Abilene Christian/Arkansas St.
1966	5	Abilene Christian
1967	5	Arkansas St.
1968	5	Abilene Christian
1969	5	Trinity (Tex.)
1970	5	Lamar
1971	5	Arkansas St.
1972	7	Louisiana Tech
1973	7	Louisiana Tech
1974	3	Arkansas St.
1975	5	McNeese St.
1976	6	Louisiana Tech
1977	6	Lafayette
1978	6	McNeese St./Lamar
1979	6	Lamar
1980	6	Lamar
1981	6	Lamar
1982	6	Lafayette
1983	7	Lamar
1984	7	Lamar
1985	7	Louisiana Tech
1986	7	La.-Monroe
1987	6	Louisiana Tech
1988	8	North Texas
1989	8	North Texas
1990	8	La.-Monroe
1991	8	La.-Monroe
1992	10	Texas-San Antonio
1993	10	La.-Monroe
1994	10	La.-Monroe
1995	10	Nicholls St.
1996	10	La.-Monroe
1997	10	McNeese St./La.-Monroe/Southwest Tex. St.
1998	10	Nicholls St.
1999	10	Southwest Tex. St.
2000	11	Sam Houston St.
2001	11	McNeese St.
2002	11	McNeese St.

Season	No.	Conference Tournament
1981	6	Lamar
1982	5	Lafayette
1983	7	Lamar
1984	7	Louisiana Tech
1985	7	Louisiana Tech
1986	7	La.-Monroe
1987	6	Louisiana Tech
1988	6	North Texas
1989	6	McNeese St.
1990	7	La.-Monroe
1991	4	La.-Monroe
1992	6	La.-Monroe
1993	6	La.-Monroe
1994	8	Southwest Tex. St.
1995	8	Nicholls St.
1996	6	La.-Monroe
1997	6	Southwest Tex. St.
1998	6	Nicholls St.
1999	6	Texas-San Antonio
2000	8	Lamar
2001	8	Northwestern St.
2002	6	McNeese St.

SOUTHWEST CONFERENCE

Season	No.	Regular Season
1915	5	Texas
1916	5	Texas
1917	3	Texas
1918	5	Rice
1919	5	Texas
1920	6	Texas A&M
1921	5	Texas A&M
1922	6	Texas A&M
1923	6	Texas A&M
1924	8	Texas
1925	8	Oklahoma St.
1926	7	Arkansas
1927	7	Arkansas
1928	7	Arkansas
1929	7	Arkansas
1930	7	Arkansas
1931	7	TCU
1932	7	Baylor
1933	7	Texas
1934	7	TCU
1935	7	Arkansas/Rice/Southern Methodist
1936	7	Arkansas
1937	7	Southern Methodist
1938	7	Arkansas
1939	7	Texas
1940	7	Rice
1941	7	Arkansas
1942	7	Rice/Arkansas
1943	7	Texas/Rice
1944	7	Arkansas/Rice
1945	7	Rice
1946	7	Baylor
1947	7	Texas
1948	7	Baylor
1949	7	Arkansas/Baylor/Rice
1950	7	Baylor/Arkansas
1951	7	Texas A&M/TCU/Texas
1952	7	TCU
1953	7	TCU
1954	7	Rice/Texas
1955	7	Southern Methodist
1956	7	Southern Methodist
1957	7	Southern Methodist
1958	8	Arkansas/Southern Methodist
1959	8	TCU
1960	8	Texas
1961	8	Texas Tech
1962	8	Southern Methodist/Texas Tech
1963	8	Texas
1964	8	Texas A&M
1965	8	Southern Methodist/Texas
1966	8	Southern Methodist
1967	8	Southern Methodist
1968	8	TCU
1969	8	Texas A&M
1970	8	Rice
1971	8	TCU
1972	8	Texas/Southern Methodist
1973	8	Texas Tech
1974	8	Texas
1975	8	Texas A&M
1976	9	Texas A&M
1977	9	Arkansas

Season	No.	Regular Season
1978	9	Texas/Arkansas
1979	9	Texas/Arkansas
1980	9	Texas A&M
1981	9	Arkansas
1982	9	Arkansas
1983	9	Houston
1984	9	Houston
1985	9	Texas Tech
1986	9	TCU/Texas/Texas A&M
1987	9	TCU
1988	9	Southern Methodist
1989	9	Arkansas
1990	9	Arkansas
1991	9	Arkansas
1992	8	Houston/Texas
1993	8	Southern Methodist
1994	8	Texas
1995	8	Texas/Texas Tech
1996	8	Texas Tech

Season	No.	Conference Tournament
1976	9	Texas Tech
1977	9	Arkansas
1978	9	Houston
1979	9	Arkansas
1980	9	Texas A&M
1981	9	Houston
1982	9	Arkansas
1983	9	Houston
1984	9	Houston
1985	8	Texas Tech
1986	8	Texas Tech
1987	8	Texas A&M
1988	8	Southern Methodist
1989	8	Arkansas
1990	8	Arkansas
1991	9	Arkansas
1992	8	Houston
1993	8	Texas Tech
1994	8	Texas
1995	7	Texas
1996	8	Texas Tech

SOUTHWESTERN ATHLETIC CONFERENCE

Season	No.	Regular Season
1957	6	Texas Southern
1958	6	Texas Southern
1959	8	Grambling
1960	8	Grambling
1961	8	Prairie View
1962	7	Prairie View
1963	8	Grambling
1964	8	Grambling/Jackson St.
1965	8	Southern U.
1966	8	Alcorn St./Grambling
1967	8	Alcorn St./Ark.-Pine Bluff/Grambling
1968	8	Alcorn St./Jackson St.
1969	8	Alcorn St.
1970	8	Jackson St.
1971	7	Grambling
1972	7	Grambling
1973	7	Alcorn St.
1974	7	Jackson St.
1975	7	Jackson St.
1976	7	Alcorn St.
1977	7	Texas Southern
1978	7	Jackson St./Southern U.
1979	7	Alcorn St.
1980	7	Alcorn St.
1981	7	Alcorn St./Southern U.
1982	7	Alcorn St./Jackson St.
1983	8	Texas Southern
1984	8	Alcorn St.
1985	8	Alcorn St.
1986	8	Alcorn St./Southern U.
1987	8	Grambling
1988	8	Southern U.
1989	8	Grambling/Southern U./Texas Southern
1990	8	Southern U.
1991	8	Jackson St.
1992	8	Mississippi Val./Texas Southern
1993	8	Jackson St.
1994	8	Texas Southern
1995	8	Texas Southern
1996	8	Jackson St./Mississippi Val.
1997	8	Mississippi Val.

Season	No.	Regular Season
1998	9	Texas Southern
1999	9	Alcorn St.
2000	10	Alcorn St.
2001	10	Alabama St.
2002	10	Alcorn St.

Season	No.	Conference Tournament
1980	7	Alcorn St.
1981	7	Southern U.
1982	7	Alcorn St.
1983	7	Alcorn St.
1984	8	Alcorn St.
1985	4	Southern U.
1986	8	Mississippi Val.
1987	8	Southern U.
1988	8	Southern U.
1989	8	Southern U.
1990	8	Texas Southern
1991	8	Jackson St.
1992	8	Mississippi Val.
1993	8	Southern U.
1994	8	Texas Southern
1995	6	Texas Southern
1996	6	Mississippi Val.
1997	8	Jackson St.
1998	8	Prairie View
1999	8	Alcorn St.
2000	8	Jackson St.
2001	8	Alabama St.
2002	8	Alcorn St.

SUN BELT CONFERENCE

Season	No.	Regular Season
1977	6	Charlotte
1978	6	Charlotte
1979	6	South Ala.
1980	8	South Ala.
1981	7	Va. Commonwealth/South Ala./UAB
1982	6	UAB
1983	8	Va. Commonwealth/Old Dominion
1984	8	Va. Commonwealth
1985	8	Va. Commonwealth
1986	8	Old Dominion
1987	8	Western Ky.
1988	8	Charlotte
1989	8	South Ala.
1990	8	UAB
1991	8	South Ala.
1992	11	Louisiana Tech/Lafayette
1993	10	New Orleans
1994	10	Western Ky.
1995	10	Western Ky.
1996	10	Ark.-Little Rock/New Orleans
1997	10	New Orleans/South Ala.
1998	10	South Ala./Arkansas St.
1999	8	Louisiana Tech
2000	9	Lafayette/South Ala.
2001	12	Western Ky. (East)/South Ala. (West)
2002	11	Western Ky. (East)/La.-Lafayette (South)/New Mexico St. (South)

Season	No.	Conference Tournament
1977	6	Charlotte
1978	6	New Orleans
1979	6	Jacksonville
1980	8	Va. Commonwealth
1981	7	Va. Commonwealth
1982	6	UAB
1983	8	UAB
1984	8	UAB
1985	8	Va. Commonwealth
1986	8	Jacksonville
1987	8	UAB
1988	8	Charlotte
1989	8	South Ala.
1990	8	South Fla.
1991	8	South Ala.
1992	11	Lafayette
1993	9	Western Ky.
1994	10	Lafayette
1995	10	Western Ky.
1996	10	New Orleans
1997	10	South Ala.
1998	10	South Ala.
1999	8	Arkansas St.
2000	9	Lafayette
2001	11	Western Ky.
2002	11	Western Ky.

WEST COAST CONFERENCE

Season	No.	Regular Season
1953	5	Santa Clara
1954	5	Santa Clara
1955	5	San Francisco
1956	8	San Francisco
1957	8	San Francisco
1958	7	San Francisco
1959	7	St. Mary's (Cal.)
1960	7	Santa Clara
1961	7	Loyola Marymount
1962	7	Pepperdine
1963	7	San Francisco
1964	7	San Francisco
1965	8	San Francisco
1966	8	Pacific (Cal.)
1967	8	Pacific (Cal.)
1968	8	Santa Clara
1969	8	Santa Clara
1970	8	Santa Clara
1971	8	Pacific (Cal.)
1972	8	San Francisco
1973	8	San Francisco
1974	8	San Francisco
1975	8	UNLV
1976	7	Pepperdine
1977	8	San Francisco
1978	8	San Francisco
1979	8	San Francisco
1980	9	San Francisco/St. Mary's (Cal.)
1981	8	San Francisco/Pepperdine
1982	8	Pepperdine
1983	7	Pepperdine
1984	7	San Diego
1985	7	Pepperdine
1986	8	Pepperdine
1987	8	San Diego
1988	8	Loyola Marymount
1989	8	St. Mary's (Cal.)
1990	8	Loyola Marymount
1991	8	Pepperdine
1992	8	Pepperdine
1993	8	Pepperdine
1994	8	Gonzaga
1995	8	Santa Clara
1996	8	Gonzaga/Santa Clara
1997	8	St. Mary's (Cal.)/Santa Clara
1998	8	Gonzaga
1999	8	Gonzaga
2000	8	Pepperdine
2001	8	Gonzaga
2002	8	Gonzaga/Pepperdine

Season	No.	Conference Tournament
1987	8	Santa Clara
1988	8	Loyola Marymount
1989	8	Loyola Marymount
1990		DNP
1991	8	Pepperdine
1992	8	Pepperdine
1993	8	Santa Clara
1994	8	Pepperdine
1995	8	Gonzaga
1996	8	Portland
1997	8	St. Mary's (Cal.)
1998	8	San Francisco
1999	8	Gonzaga
2000	8	Gonzaga
2001	8	Gonzaga
2002	8	Gonzaga

WESTERN ATHLETIC CONFERENCE

Season	No.	Regular Season
1963	6	Arizona St.
1964	6	New Mexico/Arizona St.
1965	6	Brigham Young
1966	6	Utah
1967	6	Wyoming/Brigham Young
1968	6	New Mexico
1969	6	Brigham Young/Wyoming
1970	8	UTEP
1971	8	Brigham Young
1972	8	Brigham Young
1973	8	Arizona St.
1974	8	New Mexico
1975	8	Arizona St.
1976	8	Arizona
1977	8	Utah
1978	8	New Mexico
1979	7	Brigham Young
1980	8	Brigham Young

Season	No.	Regular Season
1981	9	Utah/Wyoming
1982	9	Wyoming
1983	9	UTEP/Utah
1984	9	UTEP
1985	9	UTEP
1986	9	Wyoming/UTEP/Utah
1987	9	UTEP
1988	9	Brigham Young
1989	9	Colorado St.
1990	9	Colorado St./Brigham Young
1991	9	Utah
1992	9	UTEP/Brigham Young
1993	10	Brigham Young/Utah
1994	10	New Mexico
1995	10	Utah
1996	10	Utah
1997	16	Fresno St. (Pacific)/Hawaii (Pacific)/Utah (Mountain)
1998	16	TCU (Pacific)/Utah (Mountain)
1999	16	UNLV (Mountain)/Tulsa (Mountain)/Utah (Pacific)
2000	8	Tulsa
2001	9	Fresno St.
2002	10	Hawaii/Tulsa

Season	No.	Conference Tournament
1984	9	UTEP
1985	9	San Diego St.
1986	9	UTEP
1987	9	Wyoming
1988	9	Wyoming
1989	9	UTEP
1990	9	UTEP
1991	9	Brigham Young
1992	8	Brigham Young
1993	10	New Mexico
1994	10	Hawaii
1995	10	Utah
1996	10	New Mexico
1997	12	Utah
1998	12	UNLV
1999	12	Utah
2000	8	Fresno St.
2001	9	Hawaii
2002	10	Hawaii

WESTERN NEW YORK LITTLE THREE CONFERENCE

Season	No.	Regular Season
1947	3	Canisius
1948	3	Niagara
1949	3	Niagara
1950	3	Canisius/Niagara/St. Bonaventure
1951	3	St. Bonaventure
1952		DNP
1953	3	Niagara
1954	3	Niagara
1955	3	Niagara
1956	3	Canisius
1957	3	Canisius/St. Bonaventure
1958	3	St. Bonaventure

YANKEE CONFERENCE

Season	No.	Regular Season
1947	6	Vermont
1948	6	Connecticut
1949	6	Connecticut
1950	6	Rhode Island
1951	6	Connecticut
1952	6	Connecticut
1953	6	Connecticut
1954	6	Connecticut
1955	6	Connecticut
1956	6	Connecticut
1957	6	Connecticut
1958	6	Connecticut
1959	6	Connecticut
1960	6	Connecticut
1961	6	Rhode Island
1962	6	Massachusetts
1963	6	Massachusetts
1964	6	Connecticut/Rhode Island
1965	6	Connecticut
1966	6	Connecticut/Rhode Island
1967	6	Connecticut
1968	6	Massachusetts/Rhode Island
1969	6	Massachusetts
1970	6	Connecticut/Massachusetts
1971	6	Massachusetts
1972	6	Rhode Island
1973	7	Massachusetts
1974	7	Massachusetts
1975	7	Massachusetts

INDEPENDENTS
(Best Record)

Season	No.	Regular Season
1946	30	Yale
1947	32	Duquesne
1948	40	Bradley
1949	34	Villanova
1950	36	Toledo
1951	37	Dayton
1952	42	Seton Hall
1953	42	Seattle
1954	39	Holy Cross/Seattle
1955	41	Marquette
1956	35	Temple
1957	32	Seattle
1958	29	Temple
1959	32	St. Bonaventure
1960	34	Providence
1961	35	Memphis
1962	34	Loyola (Ill.)
1963	47	Loyola (Ill.)
1964	51	UTEP
1965	45	Providence
1966	44	UTEP
1967	47	Boston College
1968	47	Houston
1969	47	Boston College
1970	52	Jacksonville
1971	55	Marquette
1972	59	Oral Roberts
1973	68	Providence
1974	73	Notre Dame
1975	79	Tex.-Pan American
1976	79	Rutgers
1977	73	UNLV
1978	70	DePaul
1979	68	Syracuse
1980	55	DePaul
1981	54	DePaul
1982	52	DePaul
1983	19	New Orleans
1984	19	DePaul
1985	22	Notre Dame
1986	17	Notre Dame
1987	18	DePaul
1988	18	Akron
1989	22	Akron
1990	19	Wright St.
1991	17	DePaul
1992	12	Penn St.
1993	14	Wis.-Milwaukee
1994	6	Southern Utah
1995	2	Notre Dame
1996	2	Oral Roberts
1997	3	Oral Roberts
1998	0	
1999	2	Denver
2000	5	Tex.-Pan American
2001	5	Stony Brook
2002	3	Tex.-Pan American

CONSECUTIVE REGULAR-SEASON WINNER

No.	Team	Conference	Seasons
13	UCLA	Pacific-10	1967-79
10	Connecticut	Yankee	1951-60
10	UNLV	Big West	1983-92
9	Kentucky	Southeastern	1944-52
8	Idaho St.	Rocky Mountain	1953-60
8	Long Beach St.	Big West	1970-77
7	Cincinnati	Conference USA	1996-2002
7	Coppin St.	Mid-Eastern	1993-99
7	Dartmouth	Ivy	1938-44
7	Murray St.	Ohio Valley	1994-2000
7	Rhode Island	New England	1938-44
6	Arizona	Border	1946-51
6	Cincinnati	Missouri Valley	1958-63
6	Davidson	Southern	1968-73
6	Kansas	Missouri Valley	1922-27
6	Kentucky	Southeastern	1968-73
6	Pennsylvania	Ivy	1970-75
6	Weber St.	Big Sky	1968-73

CONSECUTIVE CONFERENCE TOURNAMENT WINNER

No.	Team	Conference	Seasons
7	Kentucky	Southeastern	1944-50
7	N.C. A&T	Mid-Eastern	1982-88
6	North Carolina St.	Southern	1947-52
6	Valparaiso	Mid-Continent	1995-2000
6	West Virginia	Southern	1955-60
5	Massachusetts	Atlantic 10	1992-96
4	Arizona	Pacific-10	1988-90, 2002
4	Cincinnati	Great Midwest	1992-95
4	Duke	Atlantic Coast	1999-2002
4	East Tenn. St.	Southern	1989-92
4	Gonzaga	West Coast	1999-2002
4	Kentucky	Southeastern	1992-95
4	La.-Monroe	Southland	1990-93
4	Northeastern	America East	1984-87
4	Winthrop	Big South	1999-2002
3	23 tied		

Division I Conference Alignment History

CHANGES FOR 2002-03

Team	Old Conference	New Conference
Gardner-Webb	new to Division I	Atlantic Sun
IPFW	new to Division I	Independent
Savannah St.	new to Division I	Independent
Tex. A&M-Corp. Chris.	new to Division I	Independent

AMERICA EAST CONFERENCE
(1980-present)
ECAC North (1980-82)
ECAC North Atlantic (1983-89)
North Atlantic (1990-96)
America East (1997-present)

Albany (N.Y.)	2002-present
Binghamton	2002-present
Boston U.	1980-present
Canisius	1980-89
Colgate	1980-90
Delaware	1992-2001
Drexel	1992-2001
Hartford	1986-present
Hofstra	1995-2001
Holy Cross	1980-83
Maine	1980-present

New Hampshire	1980-present
Niagara	1980-89
Northeastern	1980-present
Rhode Island	1980
Siena	1985-89
Stony Brook	2002-present
Towson	1996-2001
Vermont	1980-present

AMERICAN SOUTH CONFERENCE (1988-91)

Arkansas St.	1988-91
UCF	1991
Lamar	1988-91
Louisiana Tech	1988-91
New Orleans	1988-91
Lafayette	1988-91
Tex.-Pan American	1988-91

AMERICAN WEST CONFERENCE (1995-96)

Cal Poly	1995-96
Cal St. Northridge	1995-96
Sacramento St.	1995-96
Southern Utah	1995-96

ATLANTIC COAST CONFERENCE (1954-present)

Clemson	1954-present
Duke	1954-present
Florida St.	1992-present
Georgia Tech	1980-present
Maryland	1954-present
North Carolina	1954-present
North Carolina St.	1954-present
South Carolina	1954-71
Virginia	1954-present
Wake Forest	1954-present

ATLANTIC SUN CONFERENCE (1979-present)
Trans America Athletic (1979-2001)

Ark.-Little Rock	1981-91
Belmont	2002-present
Campbell	1995-present
Centenary (La.)	1979-99
UCF	1993-present
Col. of Charleston	1993-98
Fla. Atlantic	1994-present
Florida Int'l	1992-98
Gardner-Webb	2003-present
Georgia Southern	1981-92
Georgia St.	1985-present
Hardin-Simmons	1979-89
Jacksonville	1999-present
Houston Baptist	1979-89
Jacksonville St.	1996-present
Mercer	1979-present
Nicholls St.	1983-84
La.-Monroe	1979-82
Northwestern St.	1981-84
Oklahoma City	1979
Samford	1979-present
Southeastern La.	1992-97
Stetson	1987-present
Tex.-Pan American	1979-80
Troy St.	1998-present

ATLANTIC 10 CONFERENCE (1977-present)
Eastern Collegiate Basketball League (1977-78)
Eastern AA (1979-82)
Eastern 8
Atlantic 10 (1983-present)

Dayton	1996-present
Duquesne	1977-92, 94-present
Fordham	1996-present
George Washington	1977-present
La Salle	1996-present
Massachusetts	1977-present
Penn St.	1977-79, 83-91
Pittsburgh	1977-82
Rhode Island	1981-present
Richmond	2002-present
Rutgers	1977-95
St. Bonaventure	1980-present
St. Joseph's	1983-present

Temple	1983-present
Villanova	1977-80
Virginia Tech	1996-2000
West Virginia	1977-95
Xavier	1996-present

BIG EAST CONFERENCE (1980-present)

Boston College	1980-present
Connecticut	1980-present
Georgetown	1980-present
Miami (Fla.)	1992-present
Notre Dame	1996-present
Pittsburgh	1983-present
Providence	1980-present
Rutgers	1996-present
St. John's (N.Y.)	1980-present
Seton Hall	1980-present
Syracuse	1980-present
Villanova	1981-present
Virginia Tech	2001-present
West Virginia	1996-present

BIG EIGHT CONFERENCE (1908-96)
Missouri Valley (1908-28)
Big Six (1929-47)
Big Seven (1948-58)
Big Eight (1959-96)

Colorado	1948-96
Drake	1908-28
Grinnell	1919-28
Iowa St.	1908-96
Kansas	1908-96
Kansas St.	1914-96
Missouri	1908-96
Nebraska	1908-19, 21-96
Oklahoma	1920-96
Oklahoma St.	1926-28, 59-96
Washington (Mo.)	1908-10, 12-28

BIG SKY CONFERENCE (1964-present)

Boise St.	1971-96
Cal St. Northridge	1997-2001
Eastern Wash.	1988-present
Gonzaga	1964-79
Idaho	1964-96
Idaho St.	1964-present
Montana	1964-present
Montana St.	1964-present
Nevada	1980-92
Northern Ariz.	1971-present
Portland St.	1999-present
Sacramento St.	1997-present
Weber St.	1964-present

BIG SOUTH CONFERENCE (1986-present)

Armstrong Atlantic	1986-87
Augusta St.	1986-91
Campbell	1986-94
Charleston So.	1986-present
Coastal Caro.	1986-present
Davidson	1991-92
Elon	2000-present
High Point	2000-present
Liberty	1992-present
UMBC	1993-98
UNC Asheville	1986-present
UNC Greensboro	1993-97
Radford	1986-present
Towson	1993-95
Winthrop	1986-present

BIG TEN CONFERENCE (1895-present)
Intercollegiate Conference of Faculty Representatives
Western Intercollegiate
Big Nine (1947-48)
Big Ten (1912-46, 49-present)

Chicago	1895-46
Illinois	1895-present
Indiana	1899-present
Iowa	1899-present
Michigan	1895-present

Michigan St.	1949-present
Minnesota	1895-present
Northwestern	1895-present
Ohio St.	1912-present
Penn St.	1993-present
Purdue	1895-present
Wisconsin	1895-present

BIG 12 CONFERENCE (1997-present)

Baylor	1997-present
Colorado	1997-present
Iowa St.	1997-present
Kansas	1997-present
Kansas St.	1997-present
Missouri	1997-present
Nebraska	1997-present
Oklahoma	1997-present
Oklahoma St.	1997-present
Texas	1997-present
Texas A&M	1997-present
Texas Tech	1997-present

BIG WEST CONFERENCE (1970-present)
Pacific Coast (1970-88)
Big West (1989-present)

Boise St.	1997-2001
UC Irvine	1978-present
UC Riverside	2002-present
UC Santa Barb.	1970-74, 77-present
Cal Poly	1997-present
Cal St. Fullerton	1975-present
Cal St. Los Angeles	1970-74
Cal St. Northridge	2002-present
Fresno St.	1970-92
Idaho	1997-present
Long Beach St.	1970-present
Nevada	1993-2000
UNLV	1983-96
New Mexico St.	1984-2000
North Texas	1997-2000
Pacific (Cal.)	1972-present
San Diego St.	1970-78
San Jose St.	1970-96
Utah St.	1979-present

BORDER CONFERENCE (1932-40, 42-62)

Arizona	1932-40, 42-61
Arizona St.	1932-40, 42-43, 44-62
Hardin-Simmons	1942-43, 45-62
New Mexico	1932-40, 42, 45-51
New Mexico St.	1932-40, 42-62
Northern Ariz.	1932-40, 42-53
Texas Tech	1933-40, 42-56
UTEP	1936-40, 42-43, 44-62
West Tex. A&M	1942-43, 45-62

COLONIAL ATHLETIC ASSOCIATION (1983-present)

American	1985-2001
Delaware	2002-present
Drexel	2002-present
East Caro.	1983-2001
George Mason	1983-present
Hofstra	2002-present
James Madison	1983-present
Navy	1983-91
UNC Wilmington	1985-present
Old Dominion	1992-present
Richmond	1983-2001
Towson	2002-present
Va. Commonwealth	1996-present
William & Mary	1983-present

CONFERENCE USA (1996-present)

UAB	1996-present
Charlotte	1996-present
Cincinnati	1996-present
DePaul	1996-present
East Caro.	2002-present
Houston	1997-present
Louisville	1996-present
Marquette	1996-present
Memphis	1996-present
St. Louis	1996-present

South Fla.	1996-present
Southern Miss.	1996-present
TCU	2002-present
Tulane	1996-present

EAST COAST CONFERENCE (1959-92, 94)

Middle Atlantic (1959-74)
East Coast (1975-92, 94)

American	1967-84
Brooklyn	1992
Bucknell	1959-90
Buffalo	1992, 94
Central Conn. St.	1991-92, 94
Chicago St.	1994
Delaware	1959-91
Drexel	1959-91
Gettysburg	1959-74
Hofstra	1966-92, 94
Lafayette	1959-90
La Salle	1959-83
Lehigh	1959-90
UMBC	1991-92
Muhlenberg	1959-64
Northeastern Ill.	1994
Rider	1967-92
Rutgers	1959-62
St. Joseph's	1959-82
Temple	1959-82
Towson	1983-92
Troy St.	1994
West Chester	1966-67, 69-74

GREAT MIDWEST CONFERENCE (1992-95)

UAB	1992-95
Cincinnati	1992-95
Dayton	1994-95
DePaul	1992-95
Marquette	1992-95
Memphis	1992-95
St. Louis	1992-95

GULF STAR CONFERENCE (1985-87)

Nicholls St.	1985-87
Northwestern St.	1985-87
Sam Houston St.	1985-87
Southeastern La.	1985-87
Southwest Tex. St.	1985-87
Stephen F. Austin	1985-87

HORIZON LEAGUE (1980-present)
Midwestern Collegiate (1980-2001)

Butler	1980-present
Cleveland St.	1995-present
Dayton	1989-93
Detroit	1981-present
Duquesne	1993
Evansville	1980-94
Ill.-Chicago	1995-present
La Salle	1993-95
Loyola (Ill.)	1980-present
Marquette	1990-91
Northern Ill.	1995-97
Oklahoma City	1980-85
Oral Roberts	1980-87
St. Louis	1983-91
Wis.-Green Bay	1995-present
Wis.-Milwaukee	1995-present
Wright St.	1995-present
Xavier	1980-95
Youngstown St.	2002-present

IVY GROUP (1902-08, 11-18, 20-present)
Eastern Intercollegiate League

Brown	1954-present
Columbia	1902-08, 11-18, 20-present
Cornell	1902-08, 11-18, 20-present
Dartmouth	1912-18, 20-present
Harvard	1902-04, 06-07, 34-43, 47-present
Pennsylvania	1904-08, 11-18, 20-present
Princeton	1902-08, 11-18, 20-44, 46-present
Yale	1902-08, 11-18, 20-43, 47-present

METRO ATLANTIC ATHLETIC CONFERENCE (1982-present)

Army	1982-90
Canisius	1990-present
Fairfield	1982-present
Fordham	1982-90
Holy Cross	1984-90
Iona	1982-present
La Salle	1984-92
Loyola (Md.)	1990-present
Manhattan	1982-present
Marist	1998-present
Niagara	1990-present
Rider	1998-present
St. Peter's	1982-present
Siena	1990-present

METROPOLITAN COLLEGIATE ATHLETIC CONFERENCE (1976-95)

Charlotte	1992-95
Cincinnati	1976-91
Florida St.	1977-91
Georgia Tech	1976-78
Louisville	1976-95
Memphis	1976-91
St. Louis	1976-82
South Carolina	1984-91
South Fla.	1992-95
Southern Miss.	1983-95
Tulane	1976-85, 90-95
Va. Commonwealth	1992-95
Virginia Tech	1979-95

METROPOLITAN COLLEGIATE CONFERENCE (1966-69)

Fairleigh Dickinson	1966-69
Hofstra	1966-69
Iona	1966-69
Long Island	1966-69
Manhattan	1966-69
New York U.	1966-67
St. Peter's	1966-69
St. Francis (N.Y.)	1966-68
Seton Hall	1966-69
Wagner	1966-69

METROPOLITAN NEW YORK CONFERENCE (1943, 46-63)

CCNY	1943, 46-63
Brooklyn	1943, 46-63
Fordham	1943, 46-63
Hofstra	1943
Manhattan	1943, 46-63
New York U.	1943, 46-63
St. Francis (N.Y.)	1943, 46-63
St. John's (N.Y.)	1943, 46-63

MID-AMERICAN ATHLETIC CONFERENCE (1947-present)

Akron	1993-present
Ball St.	1976-present
Bowling Green	1954-present
Buffalo	1999-present
Butler	1947-50
Central Mich.	1973-present
Cincinnati	1947-53
Eastern Mich.	1975-present
Kent St.	1952-present
Marshall	1954-69, 98-present
Miami (Ohio)	1948-present
Northern Ill.	1976-86, 98-present
Ohio	1947-present
Toledo	1952-present
Wayne St. (Mich.)	1947
Western Mich.	1948-present
Case Reserve	1947-55

MID-CONTINENT CONFERENCE (1983-present)

Akron	1991-92
Buffalo	1995-98
Central Conn. St.	1995-97
Chicago St.	1995-present
Cleveland St.	1983-94
Eastern Ill.	1983-96
Ill.-Chicago	1983-94
IUPUI	1999-present
UMKC	1995-present
Northeastern Ill.	1995-98
Northern Ill.	1991-94
Northern Iowa	1983-91
Oakland	2000-present
Oral Roberts	1998-present
Southern Utah	1998-present
Southwest Mo. St.	1983-90
Troy St.	1995-97
Valparaiso	1983-present
Western Ill.	1983-present
Wis.-Green Bay	1983-94
Wis.-Milwaukee	1994
Wright St.	1992-94
Youngstown St.	1993-2001

MID-EASTERN ATHLETIC CONFERENCE (1972-present)

Bethune-Cookman	1981-present
Coppin St.	1986-present
Delaware St.	1972-87, 89-present
Florida A&M	1981-83, 88-present
Hampton	1996-present
Howard	1972-present
Md.-East. Shore	1972-79, 83-present
Morgan St.	1972-80, 85-present
Norfolk St.	1998-present
N.C. A&T	1972-present
N.C. Central	1972-80
South Carolina St.	1972-present

MISSOURI VALLEY CONFERENCE (1908-present)

Bradley	1949-51, 56-present
Butler	1933-34
Cincinnati	1958-70
Creighton	1928-43, 46-48, 78-present
Detroit	1950-57
Drake	1908-51, 57-present
Evansville	1995-present
Grinnell	1919-39
Houston	1951-60
Illinois St.	1982-present
Indiana St.	1978-present
Iowa St.	1908-28
Kansas	1908-28
Kansas St.	1914-28
Louisville	1965-75
Memphis	1968-73
Missouri	1908-28
Nebraska	1908-19, 21-28
New Mexico St.	1973-83
Northern Iowa	1992-present
North Texas	1958-75
Oklahoma	1920-28
Oklahoma St.	1926-57
St. Louis	1938-43, 45-74
Southern Ill.	1976-present
Southwest Mo. St.	1991-present
Tulsa	1935-96
Washburn	1935-41
Washington (Mo.)	1908-10, 12-47
West Tex. A&M	1973-86
Wichita St.	1946-present

MOUNTAIN STATES CONFERENCE (1911-43, 46-62)

Rocky Mountain (1911-37)
Big Seven (1938-43, 46-47)
Skyline Six (1948-51)
Skyline Eight (1952-62)
Mountain States (1938-43, 46-62)

Brigham Young	1924-42, 46-62
Colorado	1911-42, 46-47
Colorado Col.	1911-37
Colorado Mines	1911-37

Colorado St.	1911-22, 24-42, 46-62
Denver	1911-42, 46-62
Montana	1952-62
Montana St.	1925-37
New Mexico	1952-62
Northern Colo.	1925-37
Utah	1924-42, 46-62
Utah St.	1924-42, 46-62
Western St.	1925-37
Wyoming	1923-43, 46-62

MOUNTAIN WEST CONFERENCE (2000-present)

Air Force	2000-present
Brigham Young	2000-present
Colorado St.	2000-present
UNLV	2000-present
New Mexico	2000-present
San Diego St.	2000-present
Utah	2000-present
Wyoming	2000-present

NEW JERSEY-NEW YORK 7 CONFERENCE (1977-79)

Columbia	1977-79
Fordham	1977-79
Manhattan	1977-79
Princeton	1977-79
Rutgers	1977-79
St. John's (N.Y.)	1977-79
Seton Hall	1977-79

NORTHEAST CONFERENCE (1982-present)
ECAC Metro (1982-88)
Northeast (1989-present)

Baltimore	1982-83
Central Conn. St.	1998-present
Fairleigh Dickinson	1982-present
Long Island	1982-present
Loyola (Md.)	1982-89
Marist	1982-97
UMBC	1999-present
Monmouth	1986-present
Mt. St. Mary's	1990-present
Quinnipiac	1999-present
Rider	1993-97
Robert Morris	1982-present
Sacred Heart	2000-present
St. Francis (N.Y.)	1982-present
St. Francis (Pa.)	1982-present
Siena	1982-84
Towson	1982
Wagner	1982-present

OHIO VALLEY CONFERENCE (1949-present)

Akron	1981-87
Austin Peay	1964-present
Eastern Ill.	1997-present
Eastern Ky.	1949-present
East Tenn. St.	1958-78
Evansville	1949-52
Louisville	1949
Marshall	1949-52
Middle Tenn.	1953-2000
Morehead St.	1949-present
Murray St.	1949-present
Southeast Mo. St.	1992-present
Tenn.-Martin	1993-present
Tennessee St.	1988-present
Tennessee Tech	1949-present
Western Ky.	1949-82
Youngstown St.	1982-88

PACIFIC-10 CONFERENCE (1916-17, 19-present)
Pacific Coast (1916-59)
Big Five (1960-62)
Big Six (1963)
Athletic Association of Western Universities— AAWU (1963-68)
Pacific 8 (1969-78)
Pacific-10 (1979-present)

Arizona	1979-present
Arizona St.	1979-present

California	1916-17, 19-present
Idaho	1922-59
Montana	1924-29
Oregon	1917, 19-59, 65-present
Oregon St.	1916-17, 19-59, 65-present
Southern California	1922-24, 26-present
Stanford	1917, 19-43, 46-present
UCLA	1928-present
Washington	1916-17, 19-present
Washington St.	1917, 19-59, 64-present

PATRIOT LEAGUE (1991-present)

American	2002-present
Army	1991-present
Bucknell	1991-present
Colgate	1991-present
Fordham	1991-95
Holy Cross	1991-present
Lafayette	1991-present
Lehigh	1991-present
Navy	1992-present

SOUTHEASTERN CONFERENCE (1933-present)

Alabama	1933-43, 45-present
Arkansas	1992-present
Auburn	1933-43, 45-present
Florida	1933-43, 45-present
Georgia	1933-present
Georgia Tech	1933-64
Kentucky	1933-52, 54-present
LSU	1933-present
Mississippi	1933-43, 45-present
Mississippi St.	1933-43, 45-present
Sewanee	1933-40
South Carolina	1992-present
Tennessee	1933-43, 45-present
Tulane	1933-66
Vanderbilt	1933-present

SOUTHERN CONFERENCE (1922-present)
Southern Intercollegiate Athletic Association— SIAA (1895-1921)

Appalachian St.	1973-present
Alabama	1922-32
Auburn	1922-32
Col. of Charleston	1999-present
Chattanooga	1977-present
Citadel	1937-present
Clemson	1922-53
Davidson	1937-88, 93-present
Duke	1929-53
East Caro.	1966-77
East Tenn. St.	1979-present
Florida	1923-32
Furman	1937-42, 45-present
George Washington	1942-43, 46-70
Georgia	1922-32
Ga. Southern	1993-present
Ga. Tech	1922-32
Kentucky	1922-32
LSU	1923-32
Marshall	1977-97
Maryland	1924-53
Mississippi	1923-32
Mississippi St.	1922-30, 32
North Carolina	1922-53
UNC Greensboro	1998-present
North Carolina St.	1922-53
Richmond	1937-76
South Carolina	1923-53
Sewanee	1924-32
Tennessee	1922-32
Tulane	1923-32
Vanderbilt	1923-32
Virginia	1922-37
VMI	1926-present
Virginia Tech	1922-65
Wake Forest	1937-43, 45-53
Wash. & Lee	1922-43, 46-58
West Virginia	1951-68
Western Caro.	1977-present
William & Mary	1937-77
Wofford	1998-present

SOUTHLAND CONFERENCE (1964-present)

Abilene Christian	1964-73
Arkansas St.	1964-87
Lamar	1964-87, 99-present
Louisiana Tech	1972-87
Lafayette	1972-82
La.-Monroe	1983-present
McNeese St.	1973-present
Nicholls St.	1992-present
North Texas	1983-96
Northwestern St.	1988-present
Sam Houston St.	1988-present
Southeastern La.	1998-present
Southwest Tex. St.	1988-present
Stephen F. Austin	1988-present
Texas-Arlington	1964-86, 88-present
Texas-San Antonio	1992-present
Trinity (Tex.)	1964-72

SOUTHWEST CONFERENCE (1915-96)

Arkansas	1924-91
Baylor	1915-96
Houston	1976-96
Oklahoma St.	1918, 22-25
Phillips	1920
Rice	1915-16, 18-96
Southern Methodist	1919-96
Southwestern (Tex.)	1915-16
Texas	1915-96
Texas A&M	1915-96
TCU	1924-96
Texas Tech	1958-96

SOUTHWESTERN ATHLETIC CONFERENCE (1978-present)

Alabama A&M	2000-present
Alabama St.	1983-present
Alcorn St.	1978-present
Ark.-Pine Bluff	1999-present
Grambling	1978-present
Jackson St.	1978-present
Mississippi Val.	1978-present
Prairie View	1978-present
Southern U.	1978-present
Texas Southern	1978-present

SUN BELT CONFERENCE (1977-present)

UAB	1980-91
Ark.-Little Rock	1992-present
Arkansas St.	1992-present
UCF	1992
Charlotte	1977-91
Denver	2000-present
Florida Int'l	1999-present
Georgia St.	1977-81
Jacksonville	1977-98
Lamar	1992-98
Lafayette	1992-present
Louisiana Tech	1992-2001
Middle Tenn.	2001-present
New Mexico St.	2001-present
New Orleans	1977-80, 92-present
North Texas	2001-present
Old Dominion	1983-91
South Ala.	1977-present
South Fla.	1977-91
Tex.-Pan American	1992-98
Va. Commonwealth	1980-91
Western Ky.	1983-present

WEST COAST CONFERENCE (1953-present)

UC Santa Barb.	1965-69
Fresno St.	1956-57
Gonzaga	1980-present
Loyola Marymount	1956-present
Nevada	1970-79
UNLV	1970-75
Pacific (Cal.)	1953-71
Pepperdine	1956-present
Portland	1977-present
St. Mary's (Cal.)	1953-present

San Diego	1980-present
San Francisco	1953-82, 86-present
San Jose St.	1953-69
Santa Clara	1953-present
Seattle	1972-80

WESTERN ATHLETIC CONFERENCE (1963-present)

Air Force	1981-99
Arizona	1963-78
Arizona St.	1963-78
Boise St.	2002-present
Brigham Young	1963-99
Colorado St.	1970-99
Fresno St.	1993-present
Hawaii	1980-99
Louisiana Tech	2002-present
Nevada	2001-present

UNLV	1997-99
New Mexico	1963-present
Rice	1997-99
San Diego St.	1979-present
San Jose St.	1997-present
Southern Methodist	1997-present
TCU	1997-2001
Tulsa	1997-present
UTEP	1970-present
Utah	1963-99
Wyoming	1963-99

WESTERN NEW YORK LITTLE THREE CONFERENCE (1947-51, 53-58)

Canisius	1947-51, 53-58
Niagara	1947-51, 53-58
St. Bonaventure	1947-51, 53-58

YANKEE CONFERENCE (1938-43, 46-76)

Boston U.	1973-76
Connecticut	1938-43, 46-76
Maine	1938-43, 46-76
Massachusetts	1947-76
New Hampshire	1938-43, 46-76
Northeastern	1938-43, 46
Rhode Island	1938-43, 46-76
Vermont	1947-76

Division I Alignment History

Abilene Christian	1971-73
Air Force	1958-present
Akron	1948-50, 1981-present
Alabama	1948-present
Alabama A&M	2000-present
Alabama St.	1983-present
UAB	1980-present
Albany (N.Y.)	2000-present
Alcorn St.	1978-present
American	1967-present
Appalachian St.	1974-present
Arizona	1948, 1951-present
Arizona St.	1951-present
Arkansas	1948-present
Ark.-Little Rock	1979-present
Ark.-Pine Bluff	1999-present
Arkansas St.	1971-present
Armstrong St.	1987
Army	1948-present
Auburn	1948-present
Augusta	1985-91
Austin Peay	1964-present
Baldwin-Wallace	1948-53
Ball St.	1972-present
Baltimore	1979-83
Baylor	1948-present
Belmont	2000-present
Bethune-Cookman	1981-present
Binghamton	2002-present
Boise St.	1972-present
Boston College	1948-present
Boston U.	1948-49, 1958-present
Bowling Green	1948-present
Bradley	1948-present
Brigham Young	1948-present
Brooklyn	1948-49, 1983-92
Brown	1948-present
Bucknell	1948-present
Buffalo	1974-77, 1992-present
Butler	1948-present
California	1948-present
UC Irvine	1978-present
UC Riverside	2002-present
UC Santa Barb.	1964-present
Cal Poly	1995-present
Cal St. Fullerton	1975-present
Cal St.-Los Angeles	1971-75
Cal St. Northridge	1991-present
Campbell	1978-present
Canisius	1948-present
Case Reserve	1948-55
Catholic	1977-81
Centenary (La.)	1960-present
Central Conn. St.	1987-present
UCF	1985-present

Central Mich.	1974-present
Col. of Charleston	1992-present
Charleston So.	1975-present
Charlotte	1973-present
Chattanooga	1978-present
Chicago St.	1985-present
Cincinnati	1948-present
Citadel	1948-present
CCNY	1948-53
Clemson	1948-present
Cleveland St.	1973-present
Coastal Caro.	1987-present
Colgate	1948-present
Colorado	1948-present
Colorado St.	1948-present
Columbia	1948-present
Connecticut	1948, 1952-present
Coppin St.	1986-present
Cornell	1948-present
Creighton	1948-56, 1960-present
Dartmouth	1948-present
Davidson	1948-present
Dayton	1948-present
Delaware	1958-present
Delaware St.	1974-present
Denver	1948-80, 1999-present
DePaul	1948-present
Detroit	1948-present
Drake	1948-present
Drexel	1974-present
Duke	1948-present
Duquesne	1948-present
East Caro.	1965-present
East Tenn. St.	1959-present
Eastern Ill.	1982-present
Eastern Ky.	1948, 1952-present
Eastern Mich.	1974-present
Eastern Wash.	1984-present
Elon	2000-present
Evansville	1978-present
Fairfield	1965-present
Fairleigh Dickinson	1968-present
Florida	1948-present
Florida A&M	1979-present
Fla. Atlantic	1994-present
Florida Int'l	1988-present
Florida St.	1957-present
Fordham	1948-present
Fresno St.	1956-58, 1971-present
Furman	1948-present
Gardner-Webb	2003-present
George Mason	1979-present
George Washington	1948-present
Georgetown	1948-present
Georgia	1948-present

Gettysburg	1948-51, 1959-73
Ga. Southern	1974-present
Georgia St.	1974-present
Georgia Tech	1948-present
Gonzaga	1953-present
Grambling	1978-present
Hamline	1948
Hampton	1996-present
Hardin-Simmons	1951-63, 1965-90
Hartford	1985-present
Harvard	1948-present
Hawaii	1971-present
High Point	2000-present
Hofstra	1967-present
Holy Cross	1948-present
Houston	1951-present
Houston Baptist	1974-89
Howard	1974-present
Idaho	1948-present
Idaho St.	1959-present
Illinois	1948-present
Ill.-Chicago	1982-present
Illinois St.	1972-present
Indiana	1948-present
Indiana St.	1948, 1972-present
IPFW	2003-present
IUPUI	1999-present
Iona	1954-present
Iowa	1948-present
Iowa St.	1948-present
Jackson St.	1978-present
Jacksonville	1967-present
Jacksonville St.	1996-present
James Madison	1977-present
John Carroll	1948-55
Kansas	1948-present
Kansas St.	1948-present
Kent St.	1948, 1952-present
Kentucky	1948-52, 1954-present
Ky. Wesleyan	1957-58
La Salle	1948-present
Lafayette	1948-present
Lamar	1970-present
Lawrence Tech	1948
Lehigh	1948-present
Liberty	1989-present
Long Beach St.	1970-present
Long Island	1948-51, 1969-present
Lafayette	1972-73, 1976-present
La.-Monroe	1974-present
LSU	1948-present
Louisiana Tech	1974-present
Louisville	1948-present
Loyola Marymount	1950-present
Loyola (La.)	1952-53, 1955-72

School	Years
Loyola (Ill.)	1948-present
Loyola (Md.)	1948-50, 1982-present
Maine	1962-present
Manhattan	1948-present
Marist	1982-present
Marquette	1948-present
Marshall	1948, 1954-present
Maryland	1948-present
UMBC	1987-present
Md.-East. Shore	1974-75, 1982-present
Massachusetts	1962-present
McNeese St.	1974-present
Memphis St.	1956-present
Mercer	1974-present
Miami (Fla.)	1949-53, 1955-71, 1986-present
Miami (Ohio)	1948-present
Michigan	1948-present
Michigan St.	1948-present
Middle Tenn.	1959-present
Minnesota	1948-present
Mississippi	1948-present
Mississippi St.	1948-present
Mississippi Val.	1980-present
Missouri	1948-present
UMKC	1990-present
Monmouth	1984-present
Montana	1948, 1952-present
Montana St.	1948, 1958-present
Morehead St.	1956-present
Morgan St.	1985-present
Morris Brown	2002-present
Mt. St. Mary's	1989-present
Muhlenberg	1948-63
Murray St.	1954-present
Navy	1948-present
Nebraska	1948-present
UNLV	1970-present
Nevada	1948, 1970-present
New Hampshire	1962-present
New Mexico	1951-present
New Mexico St.	1951-present
New Orleans	1976-present
New York U.	1948-71; 84
Niagara	1948-present
Nicholls St.	1981-present
Norfolk St.	1998-present
North Carolina	1948-present
UNC Asheville	1987-present
UNC Greensboro	1992-present
UNC Wilmington	1977-present
N.C. A&T	1974-present
North Carolina St.	1948-present
North Texas	1958-present
Northeastern	1973-present
Northeastern Ill.	1991-98
Northern Ariz.	1951-53, 1972-present
Northern Colo.	1974-78
Northern Ill.	1968-present
Northern Iowa	1981-present
Northwestern	1948-present
Northwestern La.	1977-present
Notre Dame	1948-present
Oakland	2000-present
Ohio	1948-present
Ohio St.	1948-present
Oklahoma	1948-present
Oklahoma City	1951-85
Oklahoma St.	1948-present
Old Dominion	1977-present
Oral Roberts	1972-89, 1994-present
Oregon	1948-present
Oregon St.	1948-present
Pacific (Cal.)	1954-present
Penn St.	1948-present
Pennsylvania	1948-present
Pepperdine	1956-present
Pittsburgh	1948-present
Portland	1954-present
Portland St.	1973-81, 1999-present
Prairie View	1981-present
Princeton	1948-present
Providence	1949, 1958-present
Purdue	1948-present
Quinnipiac	1999-present
Radford	1985-present
Regis	1962-64
Rhode Island	1948-present
Rice	1948-present
Richmond	1948-present
Rider	1968-present
Robert Morris	1977-present
Rutgers	1948-present
Sacramento St.	1992-present
Sacred Heart	2000-present
St. Bonaventure	1948-present
St. Francis (N.Y.)	1948-present
St. Francis (Pa.)	1956-present
St. John's (N.Y.)	1948-present
St. Joseph's	1948-present
St. Louis	1948-present
St. Mary's (Cal.)	1948-present
St. Peter's	1965-present
Sam Houston St.	1987-present
Samford	1973-present
San Diego	1980-present
San Diego St.	1971-present
San Francisco	1948-82, 1986-present
San Jose St.	1953-present
Santa Clara	1948-present
Savannah St.	2003-present
Scranton	1948
Seattle	1953-80
Seton Hall	1948-present
Siena	1948-49, 1951-60, 1977-present
South Ala.	1972-present
South Carolina	1948-present
South Carolina St.	1974-present
South Fla.	1974-present
Southeast Mo. St.	1992-present
Southeastern La.	1981-89, 1991-present
Southern U.	1978-present
Southern California	1948-present
Southern Ill.	1968-present
Southern Methodist	1948-present
Southern Miss.	1969, 1973-present
Southern Utah St.	1989-present
Southwest Mo. St.	1983-present
Southwest Tex. St.	1985-present
Stanford	1948-present
Stephen F. Austin	1987-present
Stetson	1972-present
Stony Brook	2000-present
Syracuse	1948-present
Temple	1948-present
Tennessee	1948-present
Tenn.-Martin	1993-present
Tennessee St.	1978-present
Tennessee Tech	1956-present
Texas	1948-present
Texas-Arlington	1969-present
Texas A&M	1948-present
Tex. A&M-Corp. Chris.	1973, 2003-present
TCU	1948-present
Tex.-Pan American	1969-present
UTEP	1951-present
Texas-San Antonio	1982-present
Texas Southern	1978-present
Texas Tech	1951-present
Texas Wesleyan	1948
Toledo	1948-present
Towson	1980-present
Trinity (Texas)	1971-73
Troy St.	1994-present
Tulane	1948-85, 1990-present
Tulsa	1948-present
UCLA	1948-present
U.S. Int'l	1982-91
Utah	1948-present
Utah St.	1948-present
Utica	1982-87
Valparaiso	1948-58, 1977-present
Vanderbilt	1948-present
Vermont	1962-present
Villanova	1948-present
Virginia	1948-present
Va. Commonwealth	1974-present
VMI	1948-present
Virginia Tech	1948-present
Wagner	1977-present
Wake Forest	1948-present
Washington	1948-present
Washington (Mo.)	1948-50, 1954-60
Wash. & Lee	1948-59
Washington St.	1948-present
Wayne St. (Neb.)	1948-50
Weber St.	1964-present
West Chester	1974-82
West Texas	1951-86
West Virginia	1948-present
Western Caro.	1977-present
Western Ill.	1982-present
Western Ky.	1948-present
Western Mich.	1948-present
Wichita St.	1948-present
William & Mary	1948-present
Winthrop	1987-present
Wisconsin	1948-present
Wis.-Green Bay	1982-present
Wis.-Milwaukee	1974-80, 1991-present
Wofford	1996-present
Wright St.	1988-present
Wyoming	1948-present
Xavier	1948-present
Yale	1948-present
Youngstown St.	1948, 1982-present

2002 Division II Conference Standings

CALIFORNIA COLLEGIATE ATHLETIC ASSOCIATION

	Conference			Full Season		
Team	W	L	Pct.	W	L	Pct.
Cal St. San B'dino #.	21	1	.955	28	2	.933
Cal St. Bakersfield....	18	4	.818	24	5	.828
Cal Poly Pomona......	15	7	.682	18	9	.667
San Fran. St.	13	9	.591	15	13	.536
UC Davis.................	12	10	.545	15	12	.556
Cal St. Dom. Hills.....	11	11	.500	12	15	.444
Cal St. Los Angeles ..	9	13	.409	11	16	.407
Sonoma St.	9	13	.409	11	16	.407
Grand Canyon.........	8	14	.364	10	17	.370
Cal St. Stanislaus	7	15	.318	10	17	.370
UC San Diego	5	17	.227	8	21	.276
Cal St. Chico	4	18	.182	6	21	.222

CAROLINAS INTERCOLLEGIATE ATHLETIC CONFERENCE

	Conference			Full Season		
Team	W	L	Pct.	W	L	Pct.
Belmont Abbey #	16	4	.800	25	6	.806
Anderson (S.C.)	16	4	.800	18	10	.643
Queens (N.C.)	15	5	.750	19	10	.655
Barton.....................	14	6	.700	19	9	.679
Pfeiffer	12	8	.600	16	12	.571
Longwood	10	10	.500	13	13	.500
Erskine....................	9	11	.450	11	16	.407
Mount Olive	8	12	.400	12	14	.462
Coker	8	12	.400	11	17	.393
Limestone	7	13	.350	12	16	.429
Lees-McRae.............	4	16	.200	8	20	.286
St. Andrews.............	1	19	.050	2	25	.074

 # Won conference tournament or playoff.

CENTRAL INTERCOLLEGIATE ATHLETIC ASSOCIATION

	Conference			Full Season		
Eastern Division	W	L	Pct.	W	L	Pct.
Shaw #..................	9	1	.900	28	5	.848
Bowie St.	9	1	.900	20	8	.714
Elizabeth City St.	5	5	.500	13	15	.464
Virginia Union	3	7	.300	12	14	.462
Virginia St.	2	8	.200	6	20	.231
St. Paul's................	2	8	.200	4	22	.154
Western Division						
Johnson Smith..........	9	1	.900	23	8	.742
Winston-Salem	7	3	.700	22	7	.759
Fayetteville St..........	5	5	.500	18	9	.667
N.C. Central...........	5	5	.500	9	18	.333
St. Augustine's	2	8	.200	12	13	.480
Livingstone..............	2	8	.200	5	21	.192

 # Won conference tournament or playoff.

GREAT LAKES INTERCOLLEGIATE ATHLETIC CONFERENCE

	Conference			Full Season		
North Division	W	L	Pct.	W	L	Pct.
Michigan Tech #......	16	2	.889	27	3	.900
Northwood..............	10	8	.556	18	11	.621
Lake Superior St.......	8	10	.444	17	11	.607
Grand Valley St.	8	10	.444	15	13	.536
Northern Mich.	7	11	.389	14	12	.538
Saginaw Valley	2	16	.111	5	21	.192
Ferris St..................	1	17	.056	4	22	.154

	Conference			Full Season		
South Division	W	L	Pct.	W	L	Pct.
Findlay...................	12	5	.706	23	7	.767
Gannon	12	5	.706	21	7	.750
Hillsdale.................	11	6	.647	20	8	.714
Ashland	11	6	.647	18	9	.667
Wayne St. (Mich.)....	10	7	.588	15	12	.556
Mercyhurst..............	6	11	.353	13	13	.500

 # Won conference tournament or playoff.

GREAT LAKES VALLEY CONFERENCE

	Conference			Full Season		
Team	W	L	Pct.	W	L	Pct.
Ky. Wesleyan	19	1	.950	31	3	.912
Lewis #	15	5	.750	25	7	.781
Northern Ky.............	15	5	.750	19	8	.704
Southern Ind.	14	6	.700	22	8	.733
Indianapolis.............	11	9	.550	15	12	.556
Wis.-Parkside...........	9	11	.450	14	14	.500
Bellarmine	9	11	.450	12	15	.444
Mo.-St. Louis	6	14	.300	10	17	.370
St. Joseph's (Ind.)	5	15	.250	8	18	.308
Quincy....................	4	16	.200	7	19	.269
SIU-Edwardsville.......	3	17	.150	7	19	.269

*#won conference tournament; *ineligible for conference championship*

 # Won conference tournament or playoff.

GREAT NORTHWEST ATHLETIC CONFERENCE

	Conference			Full Season		
Team	W	L	Pct.	W	L	Pct.
Humboldt St............	15	3	.833	25	4	.862
Seattle Pacific	15	3	.833	24	5	.828
Western Wash.	15	3	.833	21	6	.778
Central Wash.	9	9	.500	16	10	.615
Alas. Anchorage	9	9	.500	9	18	.333
St. Martin's.............	8	10	.444	10	16	.385
Northwest Nazarene	7	11	.389	10	18	.357
Western Ore.	6	12	.333	10	17	.370
Seattle	4	14	.222	6	23	.207
Alas. Fairbanks........	2	16	.111	4	23	.148

GULF SOUTH CONFERENCE

	Conference			Full Season		
East Division	W	L	Pct.	W	L	Pct.
Valdosta St.............	10	4	.714	24	8	.750
West Ga. #............	9	5	.643	24	9	.727
West Fla.	8	6	.571	16	12	.571
Montevallo	8	6	.571	10	17	.370
Ala.-Huntsville	7	7	.500	17	9	.654
Lincoln Memorial......	5	9	.357	14	13	.519
North Ala...............	5	9	.357	10	15	.400
West Ala................	4	10	.286	11	15	.423

	Conference			Full Season		
West Division	W	L	Pct.	W	L	Pct.
Henderson St.	13	3	.813	21	7	.750
Delta St..................	12	4	.750	22	7	.759
Southern Ark...........	9	7	.563	16	10	.615
Harding	8	8	.500	16	11	.593
Arkansas Tech	8	8	.500	12	14	.462
Central Ark.............	7	9	.438	11	14	.440
Ark.-Monticello.........	6	10	.375	9	17	.346
Ouachita Baptist	5	11	.313	13	13	.500
Christian Bros.	4	12	.250	7	19	.269

 # Won conference tournament or playoff.

HEARTLAND CONFERENCE

	Conference			Full Season		
Team	W	L	Pct.	W	L	Pct.
Incarnate Word	8	2	.800	25	4	.862
Rockhurst................	8	2	.800	24	6	.800
Lincoln (Mo.)...........	7	3	.700	14	12	.538
Drury	4	6	.400	12	15	.444
St. Mary's (Tex.).......	2	8	.200	11	15	.423
St. Edward's	1	9	.100	4	23	.148

LONE STAR CONFERENCE

	Conference			Full Season		
North Division	W	L	Pct.	W	L	Pct.
Northeastern St. #....	11	1	.917	28	2	.933
Southwestern Okla. ..	10	2	.833	18	10	.643
Midwestern St.	6	6	.500	13	14	.481
East Central	6	6	.500	10	17	.370
Cameron	3	9	.250	11	15	.423
Central Okla...........	3	9	.250	10	16	.385
Southeastern Okla. ...	3	9	.250	10	16	.385

	Conference			Full Season		
South Division	W	L	Pct.	W	L	Pct.
Tarleton St.	10	2	.833	25	8	.758
Tex. A&M-Kingsville..	8	4	.667	15	13	.536
Angelo St.	6	6	.500	18	11	.621
West Tex. A&M	6	6	.500	16	10	.615
Eastern N.M.	6	6	.500	15	12	.556
Tex. A&M-Commerce	4	8	.333	10	19	.345
Abilene Christian	2	10	.167	6	20	.231

 # Won conference tournament or playoff.

MID-AMERICA INTERCOLLEGIATE ATHLETICS ASSOCIATION

	Conference			Full Season		
Team	W	L	Pct.	W	L	Pct.
Northwest Mo. St. #.	16	2	.889	29	3	.906
Mo. Western St........	16	2	.889	23	7	.767
Mo. Southern St.	12	6	.667	20	8	.714
Washburn	12	6	.667	20	8	.714
Pittsburg St.	11	7	.611	17	10	.630
Mo.-Rolla................	6	12	.333	13	15	.464
Southwest Baptist	6	12	.333	12	15	.444
Central Mo. St.	6	12	.333	12	15	.444
Emporia St.	4	14	.222	7	19	.269
Truman	1	17	.056	3	23	.115

NEW YORK COLLEGIATE ATHLETIC CONFERENCE

	Conference			Full Season		
Team	W	L	Pct.	W	L	Pct.
Adelphi..................	21	1	.955	28	3	.903
Philadelphia U.	17	5	.773	19	9	.679
Queens (N.Y.) #	15	7	.682	19	11	.633
Southampton............	14	8	.636	17	12	.586
New York Tech	13	9	.591	18	15	.545
Dowling	13	9	.591	14	13	.519
Bridgeport	11	11	.500	14	14	.500
St. Thomas Aquinas..	9	13	.409	11	16	.407
C.W. Post	8	14	.364	13	15	.464
Molloy	6	16	.273	8	19	.296
Concordia (N.Y.)	4	18	.182	4	22	.154
Mercy	1	21	.045	2	24	.077

NORTH CENTRAL CONFERENCE

	Conference			Full Season		
Team	W	L	Pct.	W	L	Pct.
South Dakota St. # ...	15	3	.833	24	6	.800
Neb.-Omaha	13	5	.722	24	9	.727
St. Cloud St.	12	6	.667	21	7	.750
North Dakota..........	12	6	.667	19	10	.655
South Dakota	11	7	.611	19	8	.704
Northern Colo.	9	9	.500	14	13	.519
Augustana (S.D.)......	7	11	.389	14	13	.519
Minn. St.-Mankato....	5	13	.278	9	17	.346
North Dakota St.	5	13	.278	11	15	.423
Morningside	1	17	.056	4	22	.154

 # Won conference tournament or playoff.

NORTHEAST-10 CONFERENCE

	Conference			Full Season		
Team	W	L	Pct.	W	L	Pct.
Assumption..............	18	4	.818	24	6	.800
Pace	17	5	.773	21	8	.724
Mass.-Lowell	16	6	.727	20	9	.690
Bentley #................	16	6	.727	20	10	.667
St. Anselm	13	9	.591	19	11	.633
Southern N.H.	13	9	.591	17	11	.607
St. Rose..................	12	10	.545	17	13	.567
American Int'l	12	10	.545	16	13	.552
Franklin Pierce	12	10	.545	15	12	.556
Southern Conn. St. ..	11	11	.500	14	13	.519
St. Michael's	7	15	.318	11	16	.407
Le Moyne	7	15	.318	11	16	.407
Merrimack..............	5	17	.227	6	20	.231
Bryant....................	4	18	.182	7	19	.269
Stonehill	2	20	.091	4	22	.154

NORTHERN SUN INTERCOLLEGIATE CONFERENCE

	Conference			Full Season		
Team	W	L	Pct.	W	L	Pct.
Northern St.............	14	4	.778	20	8	.714
Minn.-Duluth #	14	4	.778	19	11	.633
Southwest St.	13	5	.722	21	8	.724
Bemidji St...............	13	5	.722	17	11	.607
Minn. St.-Moorhead..	11	7	.611	17	10	.630
Winona St...............	10	8	.556	14	13	.519
Concordia-St.Paul.....	5	13	.278	9	18	.333
Minn.-Crookston	5	13	.278	7	19	.269
Wayne St. (Neb.).....	4	14	.222	8	19	.296
Minn.-Morris	1	17	.056	3	24	.111

PACIFIC WEST CONFERENCE

Pacific Division	Conference W	L	Pct.	Full Season W	L	Pct.
Mont. St.-Billings # ...	10	5	.667	21	7	.750
BYU-Hawaii	10	5	.667	19	10	.655
Hawaii Pacific	9	6	.600	17	9	.654
Hawaii-Hilo	8	7	.533	18	9	.667
Chaminade	8	7	.533	16	11	.593
Western N.M.	0	15	.000	1	23	.042

PEACH BELT ATHLETIC CONFERENCE

North Division	Conference W	L	Pct.	Full Season W	L	Pct.
Augusta St. #	14	5	.737	22	8	.733
UNC Pembroke	8	11	.421	12	15	.444
S.C.-Spartanburg	8	11	.421	11	16	.407
S.C.-Aiken	7	12	.368	12	16	.429
Lander	6	13	.316	11	17	.393
Francis Marion	2	17	.105	4	23	.148

South Division	Conference W	L	Pct.	Full Season W	L	Pct.
Clayton St.	15	4	.789	19	9	.679
Kennesaw St.	13	6	.684	20	10	.667
Columbus St.	13	6	.684	19	9	.679
GC&SU	10	9	.526	15	12	.556
North Fla.	10	9	.526	13	14	.481
Armstrong Atlantic	8	11	.421	13	15	.464

 # Won conference tournament or playoff.

PENNSYLVANIA STATE ATHLETIC CONFERENCE

Eastern Division	Conference W	L	Pct.	Full Season W	L	Pct.
West Chester	10	2	.833	18	9	.667
Millersville	10	2	.833	17	10	.630
Cheyney	8	4	.667	17	10	.630
Bloomsburg	6	6	.500	14	14	.500
Mansfield	4	8	.333	9	16	.360
Kutztown	3	9	.250	6	19	.240
East Stroudsburg	1	11	.083	4	20	.167

Western Division	Conference W	L	Pct.	Full Season W	L	Pct.
Indiana (Pa.) #	9	3	.750	28	5	.848
Calif. (Pa.)	9	3	.750	23	6	.793
Edinboro	9	3	.750	18	9	.667
Clarion	7	5	.583	15	11	.577
Lock Haven	4	8	.333	8	18	.308
Shippensburg	3	9	.250	9	17	.346
Slippery Rock	1	11	.083	7	19	.269

ROCKY MOUNTAIN ATHLETIC CONFERENCE

East Division	Conference W	L	Pct.	Full Season W	L	Pct.
Neb.-Kearney	18	1	.947	24	6	.800
Metro St.	16	3	.842	29	6	.829
Fort Hays St.	14	5	.737	21	7	.750
Chadron St.	9	10	.474	15	12	.556
Regis (Colo.)	9	10	.474	12	15	.444
Colo.-Christian	7	12	.368	10	17	.370
Colorado Mines	3	16	.158	5	21	.192

West Division	Conference W	L	Pct.	Full Season W	L	Pct.
Fort Lewis #	14	5	.737	21	9	.700
Mesa St.	12	7	.632	16	11	.593
Southern Colo.	7	12	.368	11	15	.423
UC-Colo. Spgs.	7	12	.368	9	17	.346
N.M. Highlands	7	12	.368	8	18	.308
Adams St.	5	14	7.000	7	20	.259
Western St.	5	14	.263	6	20	.231

 # Won conference tournament or playoff.

SOUTH ATLANTIC CONFERENCE

Team	Conference W	L	Pct.	Full Season W	L	Pct.
Carson-Newman #	13	1	.929	26	5	.839
Wingate	11	3	.786	26	7	.788
Catawba	9	5	.643	19	8	.704
Tusculum	8	6	.571	15	13	.536
Lenoir-Rhyne	8	6	.571	10	17	.370
Presbyterian	4	10	.286	12	16	.429
Mars Hill	2	12	.143	4	21	.160
Newberry	1	13	.071	3	23	.115

SOUTHERN INTERCOLLEGIATE ATHLETIC CONFERENCE

Team	Conference W	L	Pct.	Full Season W	L	Pct.
Clark Atlanta	12	6	.667	16	9	.640
Morehouse	11	7	.611	19	10	.655
Miles	11	7	.611	16	11	.593
Paine #	11	7	.611	16	13	.552
Kentucky St.	11	7	.611	14	14	.500
LeMoyne-Owen	10	8	.556	13	14	.481
Fort Valley St.	8	10	.444	11	16	.407
Albany St. (Ga.)	7	11	.389	9	19	.321
Tuskegee	5	13	.278	7	20	.259
Lane	4	14	.222	8	18	.308

 # Won conference tournament or playoff.

SUNSHINE STATE CONFERENCE

Team	Conference W	L	Pct.	Full Season W	L	Pct.
Tampa #	13	1	.929	26	3	.897
Eckerd	10	4	.714	21	7	.750
Fla. Southern	9	5	.643	20	9	.690
Rollins	9	5	.643	18	10	.643
Barry	7	7	.500	14	12	.538
Lynn	6	8	.429	15	11	.577
St. Leo	1	13	.071	7	20	.259
Florida Tech	1	13	.071	6	20	.231

 # Won conference tournament or playoff.

WEST VIRGINIA INTERCOLLEGIATE ATHLETIC CONFERENCE

Team	Conference W	L	Pct.	Full Season W	L	Pct.
Salem Int'l	15	3	.833	26	5	.839
Alderson-Broaddus #	15	3	.833	22	8	.733
West Va. Wesleyan	15	3	.833	21	8	.724
Charleston (W.Va.)	14	4	.778	25	7	.781
Glenville St.	12	6	.667	15	13	.536
Fairmont St.	10	8	.556	17	11	.607
West Liberty St.	10	8	.556	14	14	.500
Wheeling Jesuit	9	9	.500	16	12	.571
Concord	10	8	.556	13	14	.481
Shepherd	7	11	.389	10	17	.370
West Va. St.	7	11	.389	9	18	.333
Davis & Elkins	4	14	.222	7	20	.259
West Va. Tech	4	14	.222	7	20	.259
Bluefield St.	2	16	.111	3	22	.120
Ohio Valley*	1	17	.056	3	23	.115

 # Won conference tournament or playoff.

* Not eligible for conference title.

DIVISION II INDEPENDENTS

Team	Full Season W	L	Pct.
Okla. Panhandle	5	22	.185
Pitt.-Johnstown	12	15	.444
Dist. Columbia	18	9	.667
Columbia Union	10	17	.370
New Haven	14	13	.519
Oakland City	10	16	.385

2002 Division III Conference Standings

ALLEGHENY MOUNTAIN COLLEGIATE CONFERENCE

Team	Conference W	L	Pct.	Full Season W	L	Pct.
Pitt.-Bradford #	11	1	.917	23	5	.821
Penn St.-Behrend	9	3	.750	18	9	.667
Frostburg St.	9	3	.750	16	12	.571
Pitt.-Greensburg	5	7	.417	8	17	.320
La Roche	3	9	.250	9	18	.333
Penn St.-Altoona	3	9	.250	4	22	.154
Lake Erie	2	10	.167	8	18	.308

 # Won conference tournament or playoff.

AMERICAN SOUTHWEST CONFERENCE

East Division	Conference W	L	Pct.	Full Season W	L	Pct.
Mississippi Col. #	11	1	.917	21	3	.875
Ozarks (Ark.)	7	5	.583	14	12	.538
Austin	7	5	.583	11	14	.440
Texas-Dallas	5	7	.417	13	12	.520
East Tex. Baptist	5	7	.417	12	12	.500
LeTourneau *	4	8	.333	8	17	.320
Louisiana Col. *	3	9	.250	6	18	.250

Western Division	Conference W	L	Pct.	Full Season W	L	Pct.
McMurry	10	3	.769	20	6	.769
Mary Hardin-Baylor	10	4	.714	15	11	.577
Texas Lutheran	9	5	.643	13	12	.520
Concordia-Austin	8	6	.571	15	10	.600
Howard Payne	8	6	.571	13	12	.520
Sul Ross St.	7	6	.538	12	13	.480
Schreiner	2	12	.143	4	20	.167
Hardin-Simmons	1	13	.071	2	22	.083

 # Won conference tournament or playoff.

* Not eligible for conference title.

CAPITAL ATHLETIC CONFERENCE

Team	Conference W	L	Pct.	Full Season W	L	Pct.
Catholic #	13	1	.929	26	3	.897
York (Pa.)	12	2	.857	21	6	.778
Marymount (Va.)	10	4	.714	19	9	.679
Goucher	6	8	.429	13	13	.500
Mary Washington	6	8	.429	10	16	.385
Salisbury	4	10	.286	8	17	.320
Gallaudet	3	11	.214	7	19	.269
St. Mary's (Md.)	2	12	.143	5	21	.192

 # Won conference tournament or playoff.

CENTENNIAL CONFERENCE

East Division	Conference W	L	Pct.	Full Season W	L	Pct.
Muhlenberg	10	3	.769	19	6	.760
Ursinus	7	6	.538	8	16	.333
Washington (Md.)	5	8	.385	10	14	.417
Swarthmore	2	11	.154	6	19	.240
Haverford	2	11	.154	3	21	.125

West Division	Conference W	L	Pct.	Full Season W	L	Pct.
Frank. & Marsh.	11	2	.846	24	5	.828
Gettysburg #	10	3	.769	20	7	.741
Johns Hopkins	9	4	.692	15	9	.625
Dickinson	7	6	.538	13	12	.520
Western Md.	2	11	.154	6	19	.240

 # Won conference tournament or playoff.

CITY UNIVERSITY OF NEW YORK ATHLETIC CONFERENCE

North Division	Conference W	L	Pct.	Full Season W	L	Pct.
Lehman	8	5	.615	17	10	.630
John Jay	8	5	.615	17	7	.708
Baruch	8	5	.615	16	8	.667
Hunter	5	8	9.000	10	16	.385
CCNY	5	8	.385	11	16	.407

South Division	W	L	Pct.	W	L	Pct.
Staten Island #	10	3	.769	22	7	.759
Medgar Evers	9	4	.692	20	9	.690
York (N.Y.)	7	6	.538	13	14	.481
New York City Tech *	4	9	.308	5	18	.217
Brooklyn *	1	12	.077	5	20	.200

Won conference tournament or playoff.

* Not eligible for conference title.

COLLEGE CONFERENCE OF ILLINOIS AND WISCONSIN

	Conference			Full Season		
Team	W	L	Pct.	W	L	Pct.
Carthage	13	1	.929	28	2	.933
Augustana (Ill.)	9	5	.643	17	8	.680
Elmhurst	9	5	.643	16	9	.640
Wheaton (Ill.)	6	8	.429	16	9	.640
Ill. Wesleyan	6	8	.429	12	13	.480
North Park	6	8	.429	11	14	.440
North Central	4	10	.286	8	17	.320
Millikin	3	11	.214	8	17	.320

COMMONWEALTH COAST CONFERENCE

	Conference			Full Season		
Team	W	L	Pct.	W	L	Pct.
Colby-Sawyer #	10	1	.909	22	6	.786
Salve Regina	9	2	.818	20	9	.690
Curry	8	3	.727	13	12	.520
Roger Williams	8	3	.727	16	11	.593
Gordon	6	5	.545	16	11	.593
Endicott	6	5	.545	16	11	.593
Eastern Nazarene	5	6	.455	10	16	.385
Anna Maria	4	7	.364	10	16	.385
Nichols	4	7	.364	10	14	.417
New England	4	7	.364	8	16	.333
Wentworth Inst.	2	9	.182	5	20	.200
New England Col.	0	11	.000	4	20	.167

Won conference tournament or playoff.

DIXIE INTERCOLLEGIATE ATHLETIC CONFERENCE

	Conference			Full Season		
Team	W	L	Pct.	W	L	Pct.
Chris. Newport	11	3	.786	23	5	.821
N.C. Wesleyan #	10	4	.714	20	8	.714
Methodist	10	4	.714	16	11	.593
Shenandoah	9	5	.643	15	12	.556
Greensboro	6	8	.429	11	15	.423
Ferrum	5	9	.357	10	16	.385
Chowan	3	11	.214	7	19	.269
Averett	2	12	.143	4	22	.154

Won conference tournament or playoff.

EMPIRE ATHLETIC ASSOCIATION

	Conference			Full Season		
Team	W	L	Pct.	W	L	Pct.
Ithaca #	11	3	.786	16	10	.615
Nazareth	10	4	.714	17	10	.630
St. John Fisher	8	6	.571	13	13	.500
Elmira	7	7	.500	10	15	.400
Rochester Inst.	7	7	.500	14	12	.538
Alfred	6	8	.429	11	14	.440
Utica	6	8	.429	9	15	.375
Hartwick	1	13	.071	4	21	.160

Won conference tournament or playoff.

GREAT NORTHEAST ATHLETIC CONFERENCE

	Conference			Full Season		
	W	L	Pct.	W	L	Pct.
North Division						
Western New Eng.	9	4	.692	16	10	.615
Rivier	7	6	.538	10	14	.417
Southern Vt.	7	6	.538	15	12	.556
Norwich	2	11	.154	6	18	.250
South Division	W	L	Pct.	W	L	Pct.
Suffolk #	10	3	.769	17	11	.607
Emerson	9	4	.692	12	13	.480
Johnson & Wales	9	4	.692	16	13	.552
Daniel Webster	2	11	.154	4	22	.154
Albertus Magnus	8	5	.615	11	15	.423
Emmanuel	2	11	.154	5	19	.208

Won conference tournament or playoff.

HEARTLAND COLLEGIATE ATHLETIC CONFERENCE

	Conference			Full Season		
Team	W	L	Pct.	W	L	Pct.
Hanover	11	3	.786	21	5	.808
Defiance	10	4	.714	18	10	.643
Manchester	9	5	.643	16	11	.593
Franklin #	8	6	.571	20	9	.690
Anderson (Ind.)	7	7	.500	15	11	.577
Mt. St. Joseph	5	9	.357	9	17	.346
Bluffton	3	11	.214	10	16	.385
Transylvania	3	11	.214	4	20	.167

Won conference tournament or playoff.

IOWA INTERCOLLEGIATE ATHLETIC CONFERENCE

	Conference			Full Season		
Team	W	L	Pct.	W	L	Pct.
Buena Vista #	16	2	.889	23	6	.793
Wartburg	14	4	.778	20	8	.714
Simpson	12	6	.667	14	12	.538
Loras	11	7	.611	15	12	.556
Coe	11	7	.611	13	13	.500
Cornell College	9	9	.500	12	15	.444
Upper Iowa	7	11	.389	12	15	.444
Central (Iowa)	4	14	.222	5	21	.192
Dubuque	3	15	.167	6	19	.240
Luther	3	15	.167	3	22	.120

Won conference tournament or playoff.

LAKE MICHIGAN CONFERENCE

	Conference			Full Season		
Team	W	L	Pct.	W	L	Pct.
Wis. Lutheran	9	3	.750	14	11	.560
Lakeland	9	3	.750	16	10	.615
Edgewood #	8	4	.667	18	11	.621
Concordia (Wis.)	6	6	.500	16	12	.571
Marian (Wis.)	6	6	.500	14	11	.560
Maranatha Baptist	3	9	.250	12	15	.444
Milwaukee Engr.	1	11	.083	7	20	.259

Won conference tournament or playoff.

LITTLE EAST CONFERENCE

	Conference			Full Season		
Team	W	L	Pct.	W	L	Pct.
Keene St.	12	2	.857	23	5	.821
Western Conn. St. #	10	4	.714	21	7	.750
Mass.-Dartmouth	10	4	.714	21	8	.724
Plymouth St.	8	6	.571	18	11	.621
Eastern Conn. St.	8	6	.571	13	13	.500
Southern Me.	4	10	.286	10	16	.385
Mass.-Boston	4	10	.286	9	16	.360
Rhode Island Col.	0	14	.000	1	24	.040

Won conference tournament or playoff.

MASSACHUSETTS STATE COLLEGE ATHLETIC CONFERENCE

	Conference			Full Season		
Team	W	L	Pct.	W	L	Pct.
Salem St. #	11	1	.917	21	7	.750
Fitchburg St.	7	5	.583	16	11	.593
Westfield St.	6	6	.500	11	14	.440
Worcester St.	6	6	.500	8	18	.308
Bridgewater St.	5	7	.417	11	16	.407
Framingham St.	4	8	.333	13	14	.481
Mass. Liberal Arts	3	9	.250	5	18	.217

Won conference tournament or playoff.

MICHIGAN INTERCOLLEGIATE ATHLETIC ASSOCIATION

	Conference			Full Season		
Team	W	L	Pct.	W	L	Pct.
Calvin	9	3	.750	20	7	.741
Hope #	8	4	.667	21	9	.700
Kalamazoo	8	4	.667	17	10	.630
Albion	7	5	.583	17	9	.654
Adrian	6	6	.500	14	12	.538
Olivet	4	8	.333	10	16	.385
Alma	0	12	.000	3	22	.120

Won conference tournament or playoff.

MIDDLE ATLANTIC CONFERENCE

Commonwealth League	Conference			Full Season		
	W	L	Pct.	W	L	Pct.
Elizabethtown #	13	1	.929	29	3	.906
Widener	11	3	.786	19	8	.704
Lebanon Valley	10	4	.714	18	9	.667
Susquehanna	7	7	.500	14	12	.538
Moravian	6	8	.429	14	11	.560
Messiah	4	10	.286	9	16	.360
Juniata	3	11	.214	10	14	.417
Albright	2	12	.143	4	21	.160
Freedom League						
King's (Pa.)	10	4	.714	22	7	.759
Lycoming #	10	4	.714	20	8	.714
Scranton	9	5	.643	12	13	.480
DeSales	7	7	.500	16	10	.615
Wilkes	7	7	.500	15	11	.577
Drew	6	8	.429	12	13	.480
FDU-Madison	6	8	.429	10	14	.417
Delaware Valley	1	13	.071	6	19	.240

Won conference tournament or playoff.

MIDWEST CONFERENCE

	Conference			Full Season		
Team	W	L	Pct.	W	L	Pct.
St. Norbert	16	0	1.000	21	5	.808
Ripon #	11	5	.688	19	7	.731
Illinois Col.	9	7	.563	13	11	.542
Grinnell	9	7	.563	12	12	.500
Beloit	8	8	.500	13	10	.565
Monmouth (Ill.)	8	8	.500	9	13	.409
Lawrence	7	9	.438	9	14	.391
Lake Forest	6	10	.375	9	14	.391
Knox	4	12	.250	5	18	.217
Caroll (Wis.)	2	14	.125	2	21	.087

Won conference tournament or playoff.

MINNESOTA INTERCOLLEGIATE ATHLETIC CONFERENCE

	Conference			Full Season		
Team	W	L	Pct.	W	L	Pct.
St. Thomas (Minn.)	18	2	.900	24	4	.857
Gust. Adolphus	17	3	.850	24	5	.828
Bethel (Minn.) #	15	5	.750	21	6	.778
Macalester	13	7	.650	16	11	.593
St. John's (Minn.)	13	7	.650	15	11	.577
Carleton	9	11	.450	10	16	.385
Concordia-M'head	7	13	.350	8	17	.320
Augsburg	6	14	.300	10	15	.400
St. Mary's (Minn.)	5	15	.250	5	19	.208
St. Olaf	5	15	.250	9	16	.360
Hamline	2	18	.100	3	22	.120

Won conference tournament or playoff.

NEW ENGLAND SMALL COLLEGE ATHLETIC CONFERENCE

	Conference			Full Season		
Team	W	L	Pct.	W	L	Pct.
Trinity (Conn.)	8	1	.889	19	6	.760
Williams	7	2	.778	22	6	.786
Connecticut Col.	6	3	.667	16	9	.640
Amherst #	5	4	.556	22	7	.759
Bowdoin	5	4	.556	16	9	.640
Wesleyan (Conn.)	4	5	.444	15	10	.600
Tufts	3	6	.333	12	13	.480
Colby	3	6	.333	10	15	.400
Middlebury	3	6	.333	11	13	.458
Bates	1	8	.111	13	11	.542

Won conference tournament or playoff.

NEW ENGLAND WOMEN'S & MEN'S ATHLETIC CONFERENCE

	Conference			Full Season		
Team	W	L	Pct.	W	L	Pct.
Clark (Mass.)	11	1	.917	23	6	.793
Babson #	10	2	.833	25	5	.833
Springfield	7	5	.583	18	9	.667
MIT	5	7	.417	15	10	.600
Wheaton (Mass.)	4	8	.333	13	14	.481
Coast Guard	4	8	.333	10	14	.417
Worcester Tech	1	11	.083	5	20	.200

Won conference tournament or playoff.

NEW JERSEY ATHLETIC CONFERENCE

Team	Conference			Full Season		
	W	L	Pct.	W	L	Pct.
Montclair St.	12	6	.667	19	9	.679
Richard Stockton	12	6	.667	20	9	.690
Ramapo	12	6	.667	21	8	.724
Wm. Paterson #	11	7	.611	19	10	.655
New Jersey City	11	7	.611	18	11	.621
Rowan	10	8	.556	15	10	.600
Rutgers-Camden	8	10	.444	14	11	.560
Col. of New Jersey	6	12	.333	11	14	.440
Kean	5	13	.278	10	15	.400
Rutgers-Newark	3	15	.167	7	18	.280

Won conference tournament or playoff.

NORTH COAST ATHLETIC CONFERENCE

Team	Conference			Full Season		
	W	L	Pct.	W	L	Pct.
Wittenberg #	15	1	.938	26	4	.867
Wooster	13	3	.813	21	7	.750
Wabash	12	4	.750	15	11	.577
Allegheny	8	8	.500	11	14	.440
Ohio Wesleyan	8	8	.500	12	15	.444
Earlham	7	9	.438	11	15	.423
Denison	7	9	.438	6	20	.231
Hiram	6	10	.375	9	16	.360
Kenyon	4	12	.250	6	18	.250
Oberlin	0	16	.000	0	25	.000

Won conference tournament or playoff.

NORTHEASTERN ATHLETIC CONFERENCE

Team	Conference			Full Season		
	W	L	Pct.	W	L	Pct.
Cazenovia	6	2	.750	16	11	.593
Keuka	5	3	.625	7	18	.280
D'Youville	4	4	.500	14	12	.538
Hilbert	4	4	.500	9	17	.346
Medaille	1	7	.125	3	22	.120

NORTHERN ILLINOIS-IOWA INTERCOLLEGIATE CONFERENCE

Team	Conference			Full Season		
	W	L	Pct.	W	L	Pct.
Rockford	10	2	.833	18	7	.720
Aurora	9	3	.750	18	7	.720
Benedictine (Ill.)	8	4	.667	13	12	.520
Clarke	6	6	.500	11	14	.440
Concordia (Ill.)	4	8	.333	7	18	.280
Dominican	3	9	.250	6	19	.240
Eureka	2	10	.167	5	20	.200

NORTHWEST CONFERENCE OF INDEPENDENT COLLEGES

Team	Conference			Full Season		
	W	L	Pct.	W	L	Pct.
Lewis & Clark #	13	3	.813	24	6	.800
Whitworth	12	4	.750	20	7	.741
Willamette	12	4	.750	18	8	.692
Linfield	9	7	.563	14	11	.560
Pacific Lutheran	7	9	.438	14	11	.560
Puget Sound	7	9	.438	11	14	.440
Pacific (Ore.)	6	10	.375	11	13	.458
Whitman	6	10	.375	10	15	.400
George Fox	0	16	.000	3	22	.120

Won conference tournament or playoff.

OHIO ATHLETIC CONFERENCE

Team	Conference			Full Season		
	W	L	Pct.	W	L	Pct.
Otterbein #	15	3	.833	30	3	.909
Capital	14	4	.778	23	5	.821
Mount Union	12	6	.667	18	9	.667
Ohio Northern	12	6	.667	18	8	.692
John Carroll	10	8	.556	12	13	.480
Marietta	8	10	.444	13	13	.500
Muskingum	5	13	.278	10	16	.385
Heidelberg	5	13	.278	10	17	.370
Wilmington (Ohio)	5	13	.278	6	19	.240
Baldwin-Wallace	4	14	.222	7	19	.269

Won conference tournament or playoff.

OLD DOMINION ATHLETIC CONFERENCE

Team	Conference			Full Season		
	W	L	Pct.	W	L	Pct.
Randolph-Macon	16	2	.889	24	6	.800
Va. Wesleyan	14	4	.778	16	10	.615
Hampden-Sydney #	13	5	.722	23	6	.793
Roanoke	11	7	.611	17	10	.630
Bridgewater (Va.)	11	7	.611	17	9	.654
Guilford	10	8	.556	15	11	.577
Emory & Henry	7	11	.389	14	13	.519
Wash. & Lee	4	14	.222	7	18	.280
East. Mennonite	3	15	.167	5	20	.200
Lynchburg	1	17	.056	2	23	.080

Won conference tournament or playoff.

PENNSYLVANIA ATHLETIC CONFERENCE

Team	Conference			Full Season		
	W	L	Pct.	W	L	Pct.
Alvernia	14	2	.875	22	6	.786
Misericordia	12	4	.750	19	10	.655
Neumann	12	4	.750	21	7	.750
Cabrini #	10	6	.625	19	12	.613
Gwynedd-Mercy	9	7	.563	13	12	.520
Eastern	6	10	.375	10	16	.385
Arcadia	5	11	.313	6	20	.231
Wesley	4	12	.250	10	16	.385
Marywood	0	16	.000	1	22	.043

Won conference tournament or playoff.

PRESIDENTS' ATHLETIC CONFERENCE

Team	Conference			Full Season		
	W	L	Pct.	W	L	Pct.
Bethany (W.Va.) #	9	1	.900	21	8	.724
Thiel	5	4	.556	11	15	.423
Grove City	5	5	.500	17	10	.630
Waynesburg	3	6	.333	18	9	.667
Wash. & Jeff.	1	7	.125	6	19	.240
Westminster (Pa.)*	0	0	.000	10	15	.400

Won conference tournament or playoff.

* Not eligible for conference title.

ST. LOUIS INTERCOLLEGIATE ATHLETIC CONFERENCE

Team	Conference			Full Season		
	W	L	Pct.	W	L	Pct.
Webster	11	3	.786	13	13	.500
Fontbonne	10	4	.714	18	6	.750
MacMurray	9	5	.643	15	10	.600
Blackburn	7	7	14.000	14	11	.560
Westminster (Mo.)	6	8	.429	13	12	.520
Maryville (Mo.)	6	8	.429	10	14	.417
Greenville	4	10	.286	9	16	.360
Principia	3	11	.214	8	14	.364

SKYLINE CONFERENCE

Team	Conference			Full Season		
	W	L	Pct.	W	L	Pct.
Merchant Marine #	18	1	.947	24	5	.828
Manhattanville	15	4	.789	20	9	.690
Mt. St. Mary (N.Y.)	11	7	.611	14	12	.538
Old Westbury	10	8	.556	16	11	.593
Yeshiva	8	9	.471	14	12	.538
Stevens Tech	7	10	.412	8	17	.320
St. Joseph's (N.Y.)	5	12	.294	8	17	.320
Maritime (N.Y.)	4	14	.222	6	21	.222
Mt. St. Vincent	2	15	.118	7	19	.269

Won conference tournament or playoff.

SOUTHERN CALIFORNIA INTER-COLLEGIATE ATHLETIC CONFERENCE

Team	Conference			Full Season		
	W	L	Pct.	W	L	Pct.
Claremont-M-S	13	1	.929	21	5	.808
Cal Lutheran	12	2	.857	20	5	.800
Occidental	9	5	.643	18	7	.720
Pomona-Pitzer	9	5	.643	14	10	.583
La Verne	6	8	.429	10	14	.417
Whittier	4	10	.286	9	16	.360
Redlands	3	11	.214	9	16	.360
Caltech	0	14	.000	2	20	.091

SOUTHERN COLLEGIATE ATHLETIC CONFERENCE

Team	Conference			Full Season		
	W	L	Pct.	W	L	Pct.
DePauw	16	2	.889	24	4	.857
Trinity (Tex.)	14	4	.778	18	7	.720
Millsaps	12	6	.667	18	7	.720
Rose-Hulman	12	6	.667	14	11	.560
Centre	10	8	.556	16	9	.640
Southwestern (Tex.)	8	10	.444	10	15	.400
Rhodes	7	11	.389	10	15	.400
Sewanee	6	12	.333	11	14	.440
Hendrix	3	15	.167	5	19	.208
Oglethorpe	2	16	.111	4	21	.160

STATE UNIVERSITY OF NEW YORK ATHLETIC CONFERENCE

Team	Conference			Full Season		
	W	L	Pct.	W	L	Pct.
Brockport St. #	14	2	.875	28	3	.903
Buffalo St.	11	5	.688	15	8	.652
Plattsburgh St.	11	5	.688	16	11	.593
Potsdam St.	10	6	.625	14	13	.519
Geneseo St.	10	6	.625	16	11	.593
Oswego St.	9	7	.563	18	12	.600
Cortland St.	6	10	.375	11	16	.407
Oneonta St.	6	10	.375	10	16	.385
Fredonia St.	5	11	.313	14	13	.538
Utica/Rome	4	12	.250	10	15	.400
New Paltz St.	2	14	.125	3	22	.120

UNIVERSITY ATHLETIC ASSOCIATION

Team	Conference			Full Season		
	W	L	Pct.	W	L	Pct.
Washington (Mo.) #	14	0	1.000	25	2	.926
Rochester	12	2	.857	24	6	.800
Chicago	10	4	.714	15	10	.600
New York U.	7	7	.500	14	11	.560
Emory	4	10	.286	9	16	.360
Brandeis	3	11	.214	8	17	.320
Carnegie Mellon	3	11	.214	9	16	.360
Case Reserve	3	11	.214	7	17	.292

Won conference tournament or playoff.

UPSTATE COLLEGIATE ATHLETIC ASSOCIATION

Team	Conference			Full Season		
	W	L	Pct.	W	L	Pct.
Union (N.Y.)	11	3	.786	21	8	.724
St. Lawrence #	10	4	.714	21	9	.700
Clarkson	9	5	.643	19	10	.655
Hamilton	8	6	.571	16	9	.640
Hobart	7	7	.500	12	13	.480
Rensselaer	7	7	.500	11	12	.478
Vassar	3	11	.214	9	15	.375
Skidmore	1	13	.071	6	19	.240

Won conference tournament or playoff.

WISCONSIN INTERCOLLEGIATE ATHLETIC CONFERENCE

Team	Conference			Full Season		
	W	L	Pct.	W	L	Pct.
Wis.-Oshkosh	11	5	.688	24	6	.800
Wis.-Stevens Point	11	5	.688	21	6	.778
Wis.-Whitewater	11	5	.688	21	7	.750
Wis.-La Crosse	10	6	.625	17	9	.654
Wis.-River Falls	9	7	.563	17	9	.654
Wis.-Platteville	7	9	.438	14	12	.538
Wis.-Stout	7	9	.438	12	13	.480
Wis.-Eau Claire	3	13	.188	11	14	.440
Wis.-Superior	3	13	.188	11	15	.423

DIVISION III INDEPENDENTS

Team	Full Season		
	W	L	Pct.
Maryville (Tenn.)	24	5	.828
Lasell	21	7	.750
Chapman	18	7	.720
St. Joseph's (Me.)	18	10	.643
Menlo	16	10	.615
Maine Maritime	14	9	.609
Cal St. Hayward	16	12	.571

Team	Full Season W	L	Pct.	Team	Full Season W	L	Pct.	Team	Full Season W	L	Pct.
Johnson St.	14	11	.560	Stillman	11	14	.440	Castleton St.	7	18	.280
Neb. Wesleyan	13	12	.520	Colorado Col.	9	15	.375	Elms	6	20	.231
Savannah A&D	13	12	.520	St. Scholastica	8	16	.333	Thomas More	5	20	.200
Lincoln (Pa.)	11	13	.458	Villa Julie	8	16	.333	Centenary (N.J.)	4	19	.174
Martin Luther	10	12	.455	Millikin	8	17	.320				
Me.-Farmington	11	14	.440	Bard	6	15	.286				

Attendance Records

Attendance

2002 Attendance Summary

(For All NCAA Varsity Teams)

	Total Teams	Games or Sessions	2002 Attendance	Avg.	Change in Total	Change in Avg.
Home Attendance, NCAA Div. I	*321	*4,357	*22,016,723	5,053	109,916	-4
NCAA Championship Tournament		*35	720,433	20,584	124,358	3,553
Other Div. I Neutral-Site Attendance		*242	*1,762,455	7,283	164,782	-2,060
NCAA DIVISION I TOTALS	*321	*4,634	*24,499,611	5,287	399,056	-24
Home Attendance, NCAA Division II	258	3,369	2,990,641	888	38,672	11
Home Attendance, NCAA Division III	357	*4,251	1,804,209	424	-41,834	-20
Neutral-Site Attendance for Divisions II & III		*108	*62,508	579	–	–
NCAA Division II Tournament Neutral Sites		16	24,409	1,526	–	–
NCAA Division III Tournament Neutral Sites		7	13,862	1,980	–	–
NATIONAL TOTALS FOR 2002	936	*12,385	*29,395,240	2,373	446,147	-19

* Record high. NOTES: The neutral-site attendance for Division II and III does not include any tournaments. The total attendance figures for the Division II Tournament were 60,258 for a 2,152 average over 28 sessions and the Division III Tournament figures were 74,437 for a 1,618 average over 46 sessions.

Division I Championship Tournament

Round	Site	Att.	Site	Att.	Site	Att.	Site	Att.
Opening Round	Dayton	8,611						
1st Round	Albuquerque	13,606	Dallas	19,072	Pittsburgh	16,717	St. Louis	22,370
	Albuquerque	15,612	Dallas	19,111	Pittsburgh	16,717	St. Louis	22,739
	Chicago	20,822	Greenville	13,641	Sacramento	15,826	Washington	19,348
	Chicago	20,898	Greenville	13,925	Sacramento	16,087	Washington	19,309
2nd Round	Albuquerque	15,857	Dallas	19,267	Pittsburgh	16,717	St. Louis	28,665
	Chicago	21,515	Greenville	13,962	Sacramento	16,126	Washington	19,327
Regional Semifinal	Lexington	22,016	Madison	15,999	San Jose	18,040	Syracuse	28,742
Regional Final	Lexington	22,016	Madison	15,999	San Jose	18,040	Syracuse	28,440

Final Four

	Site	Att.
National Semifinal	Atlanta	52,647
National Final	Atlanta	52,647
Final Four Total		105,294

Total Tournament Attendance 720,433
Average Per Session 20,584

All Division I Conferences

	Total Teams	Games or Sessions	Entire Season 2002 Attendance	Average	Change In Avg.	Conference Tournament Total Sessions	Total Attendance	Average
1. Big Ten	11	169	2,258,255	13,362	-21	5	94,402	18,880
2. Southeastern	12	192	2,094,195	10,907	-75	6	107,715	17,953
3. Atlantic Coast	9	148	1,582,300	10,691	-1,069	5	111,913	22,383
4. Big 12	12	194	*1,948,759	*10,045	637	6	104,740	17,457
5. Mountain West	8	126	1,163,056	*9,231	86	4	53,682	13,421
6. Big East	14	229	1,987,417	8,679	-188	6	114,558	19,093
7. Conference USA #	14	226	*1,920,276	8,497	-496	6	70,089	11,682
8. Pacific 10	10	151	1,212,828	8,032	321	4	67,819	16,955
9. Missouri Valley	10	141	880,460	6,244	-129	5	43,633	8,727
10. Atlantic 10 #	12	162	930,640	5,745	-250	6	49,555	8,259
11. Western Athletic #	10	139	737,664	5,307	-679	5	32,119	6,424
12. Mid-American	13	176	697,421	3,963	84	9	55,020	6,113
13. Horizon #	9	124	438,676	3,538	-53	5	19,308	3,862
14. Sun Belt #	11	153	535,706	3,501	600	5	20,201	4,040
15. Colonial #	10	131	454,407	3,469	-208	5	22,444	4,489
16. Ohio Valley	9	125	365,332	2,923	-473	6	9,798	1,633
17. Big West #	10	137	375,053	2,738	-770	4	11,906	2,977
18. Big Sky #	8	103	278,426	2,703	180	3	12,244	4,081
19. Mid-Continent #	8	107	281,444	2,630	202	4	6,320	1,580
20. West Coast	8	111	275,692	2,484	157	4	18,506	4,627
21. Ivy	8	99	243,790	*2,463	315	–	–	–
22. Metro Atlantic	10	125	298,785	2,390	136	6	33,429	5,572
23. Southern	12	167	380,949	2,281	60	6	28,354	4,726
24. Mid-Eastern	11	122	245,448	2,012	132	9	40,694	4,522
25. Southwestern	10	121	217,786	1,800	-213	6	19,379	3,230
26. Southland	11	132	229,623	1,740	228	5	19,650	3,930
27. Patriot #	8	104	176,447	1,697	119	3	9,459	3,153
28. America East #	9	105	143,842	1,370	-563	4	8,286	2,072
29. Atlantic Sun #	11	138	179,675	1,302	-97	4	4,170	1,043
30. Northeast	12	158	186,609	1,181	49	4	8,857	2,214
31. Big South	8	105	113,690	1,083	-299	4	5,270	1,318
Independent #	3	36	93,376	2,594	1,172	–	–	–

* Record high for that conference.   ** All-time high for any conference.   # Different lineups in 2001.

NOTE: Entire season total attendance includes the conference tournaments.

Leading Division II Conferences

Rank	Division II	Total Teams	Games or Sessions	2002 Attendance	Average	Change In Avg.
1.	North Central	10	145	369,858	2,551	433
2.	Mid-America	10	136	215,794	1,587	-62
3.	CIAA	12	139	206,813	1,488	-38
4.	Great Lakes Valley	11	154	191,849	1,246	36
5.	Great Northwest	8	115	135,743	1,180	–
6.	SIAC	10	107	125,303	1,171	-191
7.	Northern Sun	8	109	127,367	1,169	127
8.	Lone Star	14	181	182,748	1,010	48
9.	California	12	164	157,822	962	22
10.	Pacific West	6	92	78,423	852	-141

Leading Division III Conferences

Rank	Division III	Total Teams	Games or Sessions	2002 Attendance	Average	Change In Avg.
1.	Michigan	7	79	98,263	1,244	81
2.	Illinois & Wisconsin	8	98	96,049	980	-151
3.	Wisconsin State	9	115	93,268	811	-51
4.	Ohio	10	126	96,205	764	28
5.	Northwest	9	99	61,000	616	31
6.	Minnesota	11	133	80,693	607	81
7.	Iowa	11	125	74,374	595	-56
8.	Heartland Collegiate	7	87	51,656	594	124
9.	North Coast	10	123	72,374	588	-35
10.	Dixie	8	96	52,610	548	-94

Leading Teams

DIVISION I

Rank	School	G	Attendance	Average
1.	Kentucky	15	315,203	21,014
2.	Louisville	19	359,655	18,929
3.	Indiana	11	189,013	17,183
4.	Syracuse	19	323,438	17,023
5.	Ohio St.	17	282,250	16,603
6.	Wisconsin	13	214,860	16,528
7.	New Mexico	19	312,090	16,426
8.	North Carolina	16	261,109	16,319
9.	Kansas	13	211,700	16,285
10.	Memphis	21	340,723	16,225
11.	Illinois	14	226,480	16,177
12.	Iowa	17	258,511	15,207
13.	Arkansas	16	241,033	15,065
14.	Michigan St.	17	250,903	14,759
15.	Arizona	13	189,072	14,544
16.	Tennessee	14	199,221	14,230
17.	Maryland	15	212,495	14,166
18.	Texas Tech	17	233,626	13,743
19.	Connecticut	15	205,640	13,709
20.	North Carolina St.	18	242,419	13,468
21.	Marquette	16	202,882	12,680
22.	Minnesota	18	219,498	12,194
23.	Dayton	17	206,213	12,130
24.	Iowa St.	17	205,869	12,110
25.	Cincinnati	15	180,865	12,058
26.	Missouri	16	192,650	12,041
27.	Utah	16	190,246	11,890
28.	Oklahoma St.	15	178,240	11,883
29.	Purdue	15	178,027	11,868
30.	St. Louis	16	185,565	11,598

2002 DIVISION I TEAM-BY-TEAM ATTENDANCE

Team	G	Attendance	Avg.
Air Force	11	22,359	2,033
Akron	12	28,780	2,398
Alabama	17	167,180	9,834
Alabama A&M	14	27,947	1,996
Alabama St.	14	27,358	1,954
UAB	14	50,731	3,624
Albany (N.Y.)	12	19,787	1,649
Alcorn St.	12	29,622	2,469
American	14	22,816	1,630
Appalachian St.	13	31,878	2,452
Arizona	13	189,072	14,544
Arizona St.	17	118,730	6,984
Ark.-Little Rock	13	59,371	4,567
Ark.-Pine Bluff	9	7,243	805
Arkansas	16	241,033	15,065
Arkansas St.	13	66,115	5,086
Army	14	17,860	1,276
Auburn	16	151,200	9,450
Austin Peay	13	32,985	2,537
Ball St.	14	93,917	6,708
Baylor	16	109,494	6,843
Belmont	12	9,543	795
Bethune-Cookman	13	23,573	1,813
Binghamton	12	17,907	1,492
Boise St.	15	74,924	4,995
Boston College	16	105,631	6,602
Boston U.	13	12,822	986
Bowling Green	14	49,630	3,545
Bradley	13	117,935	9,072

Team	G	Attendance	Avg.
Brigham Young	16	138,073	8,630
Brown	13	20,959	1,612
Bucknell	10	13,743	1,374
Buffalo	12	28,642	2,387
Butler	13	80,705	6,208
California	18	181,683	10,094
UC Irvine	12	38,013	3,168
UC Riverside	11	15,388	1,399
UC Santa Barb.	13	36,795	2,830
Cal Poly	13	35,602	2,739
Cal St. Fullerton	13	12,667	974
Cal St. Northridge	13	16,959	1,305
Campbell	13	9,674	744
Canisius	12	18,443	1,537
Centenary (La.)	13	21,316	1,640
Central Conn. St.	15	38,708	2,581
UCF	16	17,350	1,084
Central Mich.	13	31,658	2,435
Col. of Charleston	17	64,900	3,818
Charleston So.	11	5,146	468
Charlotte	14	104,770	7,484
Chattanooga	14	45,603	3,257
Chicago St.	12	5,860	488
Cincinnati	15	180,865	12,058
Citadel	14	28,828	2,059
Clemson	16	130,500	8,156
Cleveland St.	16	48,968	3,061
Coastal Caro.	12	8,736	728
Colgate	13	9,938	764
Colorado	16	80,093	5,006
Colorado St.	14	45,610	3,258
Columbia	11	17,072	1,552
Connecticut	15	205,640	13,709
Coppin St.	9	6,767	752
Cornell	12	15,098	1,258
Creighton	15	99,199	6,613
Dartmouth	13	14,996	1,154
Davidson	13	31,314	2,409
Dayton	17	206,213	12,130
Delaware	12	59,378	4,948
Delaware St.	10	19,833	1,983
Denver	13	12,247	942
DePaul	15	73,069	4,871
Detroit	12	37,236	3,103
Drake	13	51,109	3,931
Drexel	12	20,907	1,742
Duke	13	121,082	9,314
Duquesne	13	45,340	3,488
East Caro.	15	69,043	4,603
East Tenn. St.	13	35,148	2,704
Eastern Ill.	13	37,569	2,890
Eastern Ky.	13	36,250	2,788
Eastern Mich.	15	28,207	1,880
Eastern Wash.	12	25,789	2,149
Elon	12	10,511	876
Evansville	14	81,503	5,822
Fairfield	12	35,387	2,949
Fairleigh Dickinson	12	8,003	667
Florida	15	162,069	10,805
Florida A&M	9	15,868	1,763
Fla. Atlantic	13	16,471	1,267
Florida Int'l	14	8,428	602
Florida St.	16	82,853	5,178
Fordham	10	28,960	2,896
Fresno St.	17	165,250	9,721
Furman	15	20,780	1,385

ATTENDANCE RECORDS

Team	G	Attendance	Avg.
George Mason	14	44,481	3,177
George Washington	12	31,381	2,615
Georgetown	17	139,304	8,194
Georgia	13	117,834	9,064
Ga. Southern	14	22,536	1,610
Georgia St.	12	20,956	1,746
Georgia Tech	16	112,040	7,003
Gonzaga	13	51,967	3,997
Grambling	12	10,223	852
Hampton	10	35,136	3,514
Hartford	10	11,809	1,181
Harvard	12	14,635	1,220
Hawaii	17	126,274	7,428
High Point	16	15,583	974
Hofstra	11	28,104	2,555
Holy Cross	12	23,885	1,990
Houston	14	56,263	4,019
Howard	12	18,247	1,521
Idaho	14	19,876	1,420
Idaho St.	11	25,424	2,311
Illinois	14	226,480	16,177
Illinois St.	13	84,120	6,471
Ill.-Chicago	13	43,373	3,336
Indiana	11	189,013	17,183
Indiana St.	14	71,851	5,132
IUPUI	13	16,966	1,305
Iona	11	19,190	1,745
Iowa	17	258,511	15,207
Iowa St.	17	205,869	12,110
Jackson St.	13	29,213	2,247
Jacksonville	13	11,833	910
Jacksonville St.	11	22,859	2,078
James Madison	12	53,589	4,466
Kansas	13	211,700	16,285
Kansas St.	17	100,557	5,915
Kent St.	12	59,130	4,928
Kentucky	15	315,203	21,014
La Salle	11	31,044	2,822
Lafayette	13	33,320	2,563
Lamar	13	34,707	2,670
Lehigh	12	18,122	1,510
Liberty	13	21,557	1,658
Long Beach St.	14	28,812	2,058
Long Island	13	7,390	568
LSU	17	145,078	8,534
Louisiana Tech	15	43,440	2,896
La.-Lafayette	13	49,865	3,836
La.-Monroe	12	41,095	3,425
Louisville	19	359,655	18,929
Loyola (Ill.)	13	32,868	2,528
Loyola (Md.)	11	6,376	580
Loyola Marymount	14	28,193	2,014
Maine	11	17,749	1,614
Manhattan	12	19,878	1,657
Marist	14	33,493	2,392
Marquette	16	202,882	12,680
Marshall	14	68,084	4,863
Maryland	15	212,495	14,166
UMBC	11	17,312	1,574
Md.-East. Shore	10	15,225	1,523
Massachusetts	14	75,959	5,426
McNeese St.	13	37,594	2,892
Memphis	21	340,723	16,225
Mercer	11	6,878	625
Miami (Fla.)	16	74,415	4,651
Miami (Ohio)	13	57,479	4,106
Michigan	15	167,352	11,157
Michigan St.	17	250,903	14,759
Middle Tenn.	13	31,472	2,421
Minnesota	18	219,498	12,194
Mississippi	14	94,953	6,782
Mississippi St.	14	79,642	5,689
Mississippi Val.	11	19,671	1,788
Missouri	16	192,650	12,041
UMKC	15	53,233	3,549
Monmouth	12	23,041	1,920
Montana	13	47,686	3,668
Montana St.	14	65,674	4,691
Morehead St.	14	35,892	2,564
Morgan St.	10	13,808	1,381
Morris Brown	9	29,576	3,286
Mt. St. Mary's	13	16,258	1,251
Murray St.	15	41,061	2,737
Navy	14	31,825	2,273
Nebraska	16	130,053	8,128

Team	G	Attendance	Avg.
Nevada	14	84,712	6,051
UNLV	20	210,221	10,511
New Hampshire	14	14,745	1,053
New Mexico	19	312,090	16,426
New Mexico St.	16	128,651	8,041
New Orleans	12	21,374	1,781
Niagara	12	21,042	1,754
Nicholls St.	12	6,254	521
Norfolk St.	10	17,780	1,778
North Carolina	16	261,109	16,319
N.C. A&T	10	27,563	2,756
North Carolina St.	18	242,419	13,468
UNC Asheville	12	12,150	1,013
UNC Greensboro	12	15,174	1,265
UNC Wilmington	13	71,534	5,503
North Texas	13	23,521	1,809
Northeastern	11	6,477	589
Northern Ariz.	12	20,453	1,704
Northern Ill.	12	27,154	2,263
Northern Iowa	12	41,080	3,423
Northwestern	13	62,995	4,846
Northwestern St.	10	13,501	1,350
Notre Dame	13	143,257	11,020
Oakland	11	19,308	1,755
Ohio	13	92,884	7,145
Ohio St.	17	282,250	16,603
Oklahoma	16	166,658	10,416
Oklahoma St.	15	178,240	11,883
Old Dominion	15	48,896	3,260
Oral Roberts	13	61,471	4,729
Oregon	16	129,972	8,123
Oregon St.	15	91,104	6,074
Pacific (Cal.)	14	45,741	3,267
Penn St.	14	113,964	8,140
Pennsylvania	13	63,496	4,884
Pepperdine	12	27,368	2,281
Pittsburgh	18	122,457	6,803
Portland	14	19,437	1,388
Portland St.	12	12,073	1,006
Prairie View	12	23,587	1,966
Princeton	13	67,205	5,170
Providence	17	136,095	8,006
Purdue	15	178,027	11,868
Quinnipiac	12	10,376	865
Radford	12	17,171	1,431
Rhode Island	11	25,111	2,283
Rice	15	31,587	2,106
Richmond	16	80,554	5,035
Rider	13	20,314	1,563
Robert Morris	15	15,383	1,026
Rutgers	17	98,638	5,802
Sacramento St.	14	13,676	977
Sacred Heart	13	7,378	568
St. Bonaventure	12	70,038	5,837
St. Francis (N.Y.)	14	6,144	439
St. Francis (Pa.)	13	11,818	909
St. John's (N.Y.)	15	139,484	9,299
St. Joseph's	12	43,633	3,636
St. Louis	16	185,565	11,598
St. Mary's (Cal.)	13	17,909	1,378
St. Peter's	9	5,582	620
Sam Houston St.	10	18,275	1,828
Samford	12	20,047	1,671
San Diego	17	54,870	3,228
San Diego St.	15	92,475	6,165
San Francisco	13	45,569	3,505
San Jose St.	14	21,363	1,526
Santa Clara	13	21,308	1,639
Seton Hall	13	108,438	8,341
Siena	13	85,651	6,589
South Ala.	15	28,651	1,910
South Carolina	18	162,742	9,041
South Carolina St.	10	10,954	1,095
South Fla.	15	77,959	5,197
Southeast Mo. St.	14	57,722	4,123
Southeastern La.	12	8,721	727
Southern California	13	93,177	7,167
Southern Ill.	13	83,502	6,423
Southern Methodist	14	52,904	3,779
Southern Miss.	13	41,324	3,179
Southern U.	11	10,702	973
Southern Utah	11	30,001	2,727
Southwest Mo. St.	15	88,943	5,930
Southwest Tex. St.	12	20,642	1,720

Team	G	Attendance	Avg.
Stanford	13	78,215	6,017
Stephen F. Austin	13	19,313	1,486
Stetson	12	15,606	1,301
Stony Brook	9	12,510	1,390
Syracuse	19	323,438	17,023
Temple	14	99,723	7,123
Tennessee	14	199,221	14,230
Tennessee St.	12	26,644	2,220
Tennessee Tech	15	50,834	3,389
Tenn.-Martin	14	41,047	2,932
Texas	15	150,225	10,015
Texas A&M	14	84,854	6,061
TCU	18	71,789	3,988
Texas Southern	11	19,756	1,796
Texas Tech	17	233,626	13,743
Texas-Arlington	13	9,581	737
UTEP	16	113,089	7,068
Tex.-Pan American	14	42,484	3,035
Texas-San Antonio	12	19,940	1,662
Toledo	13	61,084	4,699
Towson	12	13,430	1,119
Troy St.	11	27,294	2,481
Tulane	15	35,549	2,370
Tulsa	16	129,561	8,098
UCLA	15	150,321	10,021
Utah	16	190,246	11,890
Utah St.	16	113,294	7,081
Valparaiso	12	54,362	4,530
Vanderbilt	17	150,325	8,843
Vermont	11	25,890	2,354
Villanova	19	139,173	7,325
Virginia	17	133,612	7,860
Va. Commonwealth	14	66,031	4,717
VMI	12	25,142	2,095
Virginia Tech	15	52,511	3,501
Wagner	13	21,554	1,658
Wake Forest	16	174,277	10,892
Washington	12	78,877	6,573
Washington St.	15	33,858	2,257
Weber St.	13	62,018	4,771
West Virginia	13	84,378	6,491
Western Caro.	13	25,219	1,940
Western Ill.	16	33,923	2,120
Western Ky.	14	90,064	6,433
Western Mich.	14	35,677	2,548
Wichita St.	14	117,585	8,399
William & Mary	11	25,613	2,328
Winthrop	13	17,566	1,351
Wisconsin	13	214,860	16,528
Wis.-Green Bay	14	41,432	2,959
Wis.-Milwaukee	13	41,943	3,226
Wofford	14	25,679	1,834
Wright St.	14	66,441	4,746
Wyoming	14	140,370	10,026
Xavier	14	143,129	10,224
Yale	12	30,329	2,527
Youngstown St.	12	30,843	2,570

LARGEST DIVISION I AVERAGE ATTENDANCE INCREASE FROM PREVIOUS YEAR

Rank	School	G	2002 Avg.	2001 Avg.	Change in Avg.
1.	Texas Tech	17	13,743	9,557	4,186
2.	La.-Monroe	12	3,425	935	2,490
3.	Western Ky.	14	6,433	4,007	2,426
4.	Indiana	11	17,183	14,905	2,278
5.	Pittsburgh	18	6,803	4,832	1,971
6.	Texas A&M	14	6,061	4,119	1,942
7.	Southern Ill.	13	6,423	4,483	1,940
8.	Southern California	13	7,167	5,323	1,844
9.	Miami (Fla.)	16	4,651	2,898	1,753
10.	Ball St.	14	6,708	4,983	1,725
11.	San Diego St.	15	6,165	4,538	1,627
12.	Louisville	19	18,929	17,443	1,486
13.	Marquette	16	12,680	11,194	1,486
14.	Butler	13	6,208	4,738	1,470
15.	Baylor	16	6,843	5,378	1,465
16.	Oral Roberts	13	4,729	3,407	1,322
17.	Kent St.	12	4,928	3,621	1,307
18.	Boston College	13	6,602	5,341	1,261
19.	UCLA	15	10,021	8,765	1,256
20.	Ark.-Little Rock	13	4,567	3,328	1,239

Rank	School	G	2002 Avg.	2001 Avg.	Change in Avg.
21.	Connecticut	15	13,709	12,543	1,166
22.	Mississippi St.	14	5,689	4,568	1,121
23.	Vermont	11	2,354	1,243	1,111
24.	Mississippi	14	6,782	5,687	1,095
25.	New Mexico St.	16	8,041	6,981	1,060
26.	Georgia	13	9,064	8,026	1,038

DIVISION I ALL GAMES ATTENDANCE (HOME, ROAD, NEUTRAL)

Rk.	School	Attendance
1.	Indiana	644,641
2.	Maryland	623,898
3.	Kentucky	605,924
4.	Kansas	586,331
5.	Iowa	526,451
6.	Louisville	524,133
7.	Illinois	521,389
8.	Syracuse	504,832
9.	Oklahoma	503,296
10.	Ohio St.	500,165
11.	Connecticut	497,414
12.	North Carolina St.	478,317
13.	Missouri	467,452
14.	Memphis	465,533
15.	Arizona	458,993
16.	Michigan St.	447,081
17.	Texas Tech	437,327
18.	Duke	431,314
19.	North Carolina	424,139
20.	Alabama	418,340
21.	Wisconsin	415,906
22.	Tennessee	411,728
23.	Wake Forest	411,027
24.	Arkansas	409,793
25.	New Mexico	404,954

DIVISION II

Rank	Division II	G/S	Attendance	Avg.
1.	South Dakota St.	17	75,633	4,449
2.	North Dakota	15	57,850	3,857
3.	Ky. Wesleyan	18	69,302	3,850
4.	South Dakota	15	45,655	3,044
5.	St. Cloud St.	15	43,597	2,906
6.	Northern St.	16	46,242	2,890
7.	Washburn	15	43,005	2,867
8.	Gardner-Webb	17	48,044	2,826
9.	UC Davis	13	36,324	2,794
10.	Virginia St.	10	26,322	2,632
11.	Johnson Smith	12	31,461	2,622
12.	North Dakota St.	15	38,073	2,538
13.	Augustana (S.D.)	14	35,502	2,536
14.	Winston-Salem	10	24,211	2,421
15.	Neb.-Kearney	13	31,361	2,412
16.	Southern Ind.	15	34,550	2,303
17.	Southwest St.	14	30,344	2,167
18.	Minn. St.-Mankato	14	30,078	2,148
19.	Pittsburg St.	13	27,908	2,147
20.	Gannon	16	33,981	2,124
21.	Fayetteville St.	11	23,127	2,102
22.	Northwest Mo. St.	15	31,100	2,073
23.	Mo. Southern St.	14	27,850	1,989
24.	Alas. Anchorage	17	33,146	1,950
25.	Cal St. Bakersfield	14	26,854	1,918
26.	Harding	16	30,533	1,908
27.	Angelo St.	15	28,567	1,904
28.	Morehouse	13	22,252	1,712
29.	Neb.-Omaha	15	25,350	1,690
30.	Cal St. San B'dino	15	24,312	1,621

DIVISION III

Rank	Division III	G/S	Attendance	Avg.
1.	Calvin	13	37,613	2,893
2.	Hope	16	35,272	2,205
3.	Ill. Wesleyan	11	22,890	2,081
4.	Otterbein	17	34,843	2,050
5.	Gust. Adolphus	13	20,298	1,561
6.	Wis.-Stevens Point	14	19,332	1,381
7.	Mississippi Col.	11	14,919	1,356
8.	Carthage	15	19,900	1,327
9.	Chris. Newport	17	22,289	1,311
10.	Wooster	15	18,485	1,232
11.	Buena Vista	15	17,606	1,174
12.	Wittenberg	16	18,789	1,174

Rank	Division III	G/S	Attendance	Avg.
13.	King's (Pa.)	14	15,164	1,083
14.	Hamilton	10	10,736	1,074
15.	Elizabethtown	15	16,100	1,073
16.	Wis.-Platteville	11	11,477	1,043
17.	Wheaton (Ill.)	14	14,550	1,039
18.	Hampden-Sydney	15	15,536	1,036
19.	North Park	11	10,805	982
20.	Wis.-Stout	11	10,724	975
21.	Whitworth	11	10,701	973
22.	Keene St.	17	16,323	960
23.	Capital	14	13,388	956
24.	Defiance	14	13,280	949
25.	St. Thomas (Minn.)	15	14,154	944
26.	Wilkes	14	13,200	943
27.	Scranton	9	8,325	925
28.	Bethel (Minn.)	13	11,800	908
29.	Linfield	9	8,100	900
30.	Pacific (Ore.)	12	10,750	896

Annual NCAA Attendance

ALL DIVISIONS

Season	Teams	Attendance	Per Game Average	Change in Avg.	
1977	717	23,324,040	2,710	—	—
1978	726	23,590,952	2,678	Down	32
1979	718	24,482,516	2,757	Up	79
1980	715	24,861,722	2,765	Up	8
1981	730	25,159,358	2,737	Down	28
1982	741	25,416,017	2,727	Down	10
1983	755	26,122,785	2,706	Down	21
1984	750	26,271,613	2,728	Up	22
1985	753	26,584,426	2,712	Down	16
1986	760	26,368,815	2,654	Down	58
1987	760	26,797,644	2,698	Up	44
1988	761	27,452,948	2,777	Up	79
1989	772	28,270,260	2,814	Up	37
1990	767	28,740,819	*2,860	Up	46
1991	796	29,249,583	2,796	Down	64
1992	813	29,378,161	2,747	Down	49
1993	831	28,527,348	2,703	Down	44
1994	858	28,390,491	2,604	Down	99
1995	868	28,548,158	2,581	Down	23
1996	866	28,225,352	2,563	Down	18
1997	865	27,738,284	2,508	Down	55
1998	895	28,031,879	2,445	Down	63
1999	926	28,505,428	2,401	Down	44
2000	932	29,024,876	2,410	Up	9
2001	*937	28,949,093	2,392	Down	18
2002	936	*29,395,240	2,373	Down	19

DIVISION I

Season	Teams	Attendance	Per Game Average	Change in Avg.	
1976	235	15,059,892	4,759	—	—
1977	245	16,469,250	5,021	Up	262
1978	254	17,669,080	5,124	Up	103
1979	257	18,649,383	5,271	Up	147
1980	261	19,052,743	5,217	Down	54
1981	264	19,355,690	5,131	Down	86
1982	273	19,789,706	5,191	Up	60
1983	274	20,488,437	5,212	Up	21
1984	276	20,715,426	5,243	Up	31
1985	282	21,394,261	5,258	Up	15
1986	283	21,244,519	5,175	Down	83
1987	290	21,756,709	5,205	Up	30
1988	290	22,463,476	5,443	Up	238
1989	293	23,059,429	5,565	Up	122
1990	292	23,581,823	5,721	Up	156
1991	295	23,777,437	*5,735	Up	14
1992	298	23,893,993	5,643	Down	92
1993	298	23,321,655	5,635	Down	8
1994	301	23,275,158	5,571	Down	64
1995	302	23,560,495	5,641	Up	70
1996	305	23,542,652	5,588	Down	53
1997	305	23,190,856	5,485	Down	103
1998	306	23,282,774	5,459	Down	26
1999	310	23,587,824	5,451	Down	8
2000	318	24,281,774	5,386	Down	65
2001	318	24,100,555	5,311	Down	75
2002	*321	*24,499,611	5,287	Down	24

DIVISION II

Season	Teams	Attendance	Per Game Average	Change in Avg.	
1977	177	*3,846,907	*1,811	—	—
1978	173	3,168,419	1,515	Down	296
1979	172	3,295,149	1,535	Up	20
1980	177	3,324,670	1,479	Down	56
1981	190	3,543,766	1,486	Up	7
1982	190	3,329,518	1,391	Down	95
1983	195	3,364,184	1,324	Down	67
1984	189	3,199,307	1,306	Down	18
1985	181	2,988,083	1,255	Down	51
1986	184	2,946,020	1,204	Down	51
1987	179	2,893,392	1,220	Up	16
1988	175	2,902,400	1,242	Up	22
1989	189	3,157,464	1,273	Up	31
1990	189	3,104,462	1,223	Down	50
1991	204	3,388,232	1,221	Down	2
1992	214	3,395,684	1,188	Down	33
1993	220	3,201,765	1,145	Down	43
1994	243	3,219,979	1,036	Down	109
1995	244	3,125,974	992	Down	44
1996	242	2,918,802	938	Down	54
1997	242	2,873,311	915	Down	23
1998	252	2,976,420	904	Down	8
1999	*266	3,063,436	892	Down	15
2000	258	2,942,477	882	Down	10
2001	261	2,951,969	877	Down	5
2002	258	2,990,641	888	Up	11

DIVISION III

Season	Teams	Attendance	Per Game Average	Change in Avg.	
1977	295	*2,881,400	*912	—	—
1978	299	2,632,678	816	Down	96
1979	289	2,427,688	770	Down	46
1980	277	2,387,142	783	Up	13
1981	276	2,132,000	693	Down	90
1982	278	2,183,895	711	Up	18
1983	286	2,148,736	685	Down	26
1984	286	2,233,340	701	Up	16
1985	290	2,081,452	629	Down	72
1986	293	2,053,693	615	Down	14
1987	291	2,021,459	606	Down	9
1988	296	1,970,823	583	Down	23
1989	290	1,935,058	573	Down	10
1990	286	1,939,795	581	Up	8
1991	297	1,967,087	564	Down	17
1992	301	1,962,598	553	Down	11
1993	313	1,883,283	531	Down	22
1994	314	1,741,867	493	Down	38
1995	322	1,802,301	487	Down	6
1996	319	1,730,357	472	Down	15
1997	318	1,626,240	444	Down	28
1998	337	1,736,409	447	Up	3
1999	350	1,824,391	446	Down	1
2000	*356	1,750,621	426	Down	20
2001	*358	1,846,043	444	Up	18
2002	357	1,804,209	424	Down	20

*record

Annual Conference Attendance Champions

DIVISION I

Season	Conference	Teams	Attendance	P/G Avg.
1976	Atlantic Coast	7	863,082	9,590
1977	Big Ten	10	1,346,889	9,977
1978	Big Ten	10	1,539,589	11,238
1979	Big Ten	10	1,713,380	12,238
1980	Big Ten	10	1,877,048	12,189
1981	Big Ten	10	1,779,892	12,026
1982	Big Ten	10	1,688,834	11,810
1983	Big Ten	10	1,747,910	11,499
1984	Big Ten	10	1,774,140	12,069
1985	Big Ten	10	1,911,325	12,097
1986	Big Ten	10	1,908,629	11,929
1987	Big Ten	10	1,805,263	11,877
1988	Big Ten	10	1,925,617	12,423
1989	Big Ten	10	1,971,110	12,635
1990	Big Ten	10	2,017,407	*13,449
1991	Big Ten	10	2,042,836	13,095
1992	Big Ten	10	1,994,144	12,865
1993	Big Ten	11	2,163,693	12,728

Season	Conference	Teams	Attendance	P/G Avg.
1994	Big Ten	11	2,107,600	12,696
1995	Big Ten	11	2,058,763	12,708
1996	Big Ten	11	2,106,810	12,769
1997	Big Ten	11	2,004,893	12,376
1998	Big Ten	11	2,166,264	12,450
1999	Big Ten	11	2,204,556	13,361
2000	Big Ten	11	*2,255,913	13,428
2001	Big Ten	11	*2,342,022	13,383
2002	Big Ten	11	2,258,255	13,362

DIVISION II

Season	Conference	Teams	Attendance	P/G Avg.
1979	Central Intercollegiate	12	375,370	2,760
1980	Mid-Continent	5	189,193	2,782
1981	North Central Intercollegiate	8	312,410	2,840
1982	North Central Intercollegiate	8	290,995	2,622
1983	North Central Intercollegiate	8	356,777	2,567
1984	North Central Intercollegiate	10	392,154	2,801
1985	North Central Intercollegiate	10	380,087	2,639
1986	North Central Intercollegiate	10	379,701	2,601
1987	North Central Intercollegiate	10	393,940	2,626
1988	North Central Intercollegiate	10	413,956	2,797
1989	North Central Intercollegiate	10	438,403	2,923
1990	North Central Intercollegiate	10	436,292	2,889
1991	North Central Intercollegiate	10	438,746	2,868
1992	North Central Intercollegiate	10	*482,213	*3,014
1993	North Central Intercollegiate	10	408,624	2,919
1994	North Central Intercollegiate	10	362,572	2,627
1995	North Central Intercollegiate	10	382,042	2,497
1996	North Central Intercollegiate	10	341,119	2,336
1997	North Central Intercollegiate	10	319,703	2,160
1998	North Central Intercollegiate	10	315,918	2,225
1999	North Central Intercollegiate	10	299,228	2,050
2000	North Central Intercollegiate	10	300,257	2,114
2001	North Central Intercollegiate	10	300,822	2,118
2002	North Central Intercollegiate	10	369,858	2,551

DIVISION III

Season	Conference	Teams	Attendance	P/G Avg.
1990	Wisconsin State University	9	*170,276	*1,362
1991	Wisconsin State University	7	84,615	1,128
1992	Michigan Intercollegiate	7	89,549	1,163
1993	Michigan Intercollegiate	7	97,624	1,236
1994	Michigan Intercollegiate	7	97,418	1,203
1995	Michigan Intercollegiate	7	86,353	1,183
1996	Michigan Intercollegiate	7	80,376	1,058
1997	Michigan Intercollegiate	7	81,370	1,085
1998	Michigan Intercollegiate	8	91,267	941
1999	Michigan Intercollegiate	8	87,055	957
2000	Michigan Intercollegiate	8	111,310	1,091
2001	Michigan Intercollegiate	7	95,378	1,163
2002	Michigan Intercollegiate	7	98,263	1,244

*record

Annual Team Attendance Champions

DIVISION I

Season	Champion	Games	Attendance	Avg.
1970	Illinois	11	157,206	14,291
1971	Illinois	11	177,408	16,128
1972	Brigham Young	12	261,815	21,818
1973	Brigham Young	14	260,102	18,579
1974	Brigham Young	10	162,510	16,251
1975	Minnesota	13	219,047	16,850
1976	Indiana	12	202,700	16,892
1977	Kentucky	14	312,527	22,323
1978	Kentucky	16	373,367	23,335
1979	Kentucky	15	351,042	23,403
1980	Kentucky	15	352,511	23,501
1981	Kentucky	15	354,996	23,666
1982	Kentucky	16	371,093	23,193
1983	Kentucky	15	356,776	23,785
1984	Kentucky	16	380,453	23,778
1985	Syracuse	15	388,049	25,870
1986	Syracuse	19	498,850	26,255
1987	Syracuse	19	474,214	24,959
1988	Syracuse	16	461,223	28,826
1989	Syracuse	19	*537,949	28,313
1990	Syracuse	16	478,686	*29,918
1991	Syracuse	17	497,179	29,246
1992	Syracuse	17	460,752	27,103

Season	Champion	Games	Attendance	Avg.
1993	Syracuse	16	405,620	25,351
1994	Syracuse	17	419,039	24,649
1995	Syracuse	16	387,925	24,245
1996	Kentucky	13	310,633	23,895
1997	Kentucky	13	309,457	23,804
1998	Kentucky	12	287,354	23,946
1999	Kentucky	13	303,771	23,367
2000	Kentucky	14	314,267	22,448
2001	Kentucky	12	261,435	21,786
2002	Kentucky	15	315,203	21,014

DIVISION II

Season	Champion	Avg.
1977	Evansville	4,576
1978	Norfolk St.	4,226
1979	Norfolk St.	4,984
1980	Norfolk St.	4,917
1981	North Dakota St.	5,300
1982	North Dakota St.	4,385
1983	North Dakota St.	6,057
1984	Norfolk St.	*6,663
1985	Norfolk St.	6,116
1986	St. Cloud St.	4,539
1987	North Dakota St.	4,820
1988	Southeast Mo. St.	5,227
1989	Southeast Mo. St.	5,052
1990	Southeast Mo. St.	5,287
1991	Southeast Mo. St.	5,370
1992	North Dakota	4,943
1993	Alabama A&M	4,748
1994	South Dakota	4,852
1995	Alabama A&M	5,141
1996	South Dakota St.	4,945
1997	South Dakota St.	4,423
1998	South Dakota St.	5,350
1999	Ky. Wesleyan	4,247
2000	South Dakota St.	4,077
2001	Morehouse	4,404
2002	South Dakota St.	4,449

*record

DIVISION III

Season	Champion	Avg.
1977	Scranton	2,707
1978	Calvin	3,630
1979	Savannah St.	2,870
1980	Savannah St.	2,917
1981	Potsdam St.	2,873
1982	Wis.-Stevens Point	2,929
1983	Augustana (Ill.)	3,033
1984	Hope	2,144
1985	Wis.-Stevens Point	2,313
1986	Calvin	2,570
1987	Concordia-M'head	2,869
1988	Calvin	2,627
1989	Calvin	2,544
1990	Calvin	2,622
1991	Hope	2,480
1992	Calvin	2,757
1993	Calvin	*4,018
1994	Calvin	2,734
1995	Calvin	2,792
1996	Hope	2,409
1997	Calvin	2,821
1998	Ill. Wesleyan	2,615
1999	Hope	2,440
2000	Calvin	3,496
2001	Calvin	3,369
2002	Calvin	2,893

*record

Annual NCAA Tournament Attendance

DIVISION I

Season	Sess.	Attend.	P/G Avg.
1939	5	15,025	3,005
1940	5	36,880	7,376
1941	5	48,055	9,611
1942	5	24,372	4,874
1943	5	56,876	11,375
1944	5	59,369	11,874
1945	5	67,780	13,556
1946	5	73,116	14,623
1947	5	72,959	14,592
1948	5	72,523	14,505
1949	5	66,077	13,215
1950	5	75,464	15,093
1951	9	110,645	12,294
1952	10	115,712	11,571
1953	14	127,149	9,082
1954	15	115,391	7,693
1955	15	116,983	7,799
1956	15	132,513	8,834
1957	14	108,891	7,778
1958	14	176,878	12,634
1959	14	161,809	11,558
1960	16	155,491	9,718
1961	14	169,520	12,109
1962	14	177,469	12,676
1963	14	153,065	10,933
1964	14	140,790	10,056
1965	13	140,673	10,821
1966	13	140,925	10,840
1967	14	159,570	11,398
1968	14	160,888	11,492
1969	15	165,712	11,047
1970	16	146,794	9,175
1971	16	207,200	12,950
1972	16	147,304	9,207
1973	16	163,160	10,198

ATTENDANCE RECORDS

Season	Sess.	Attend.	P/G Avg.
1974	16	154,112	9,632
1975	18	183,857	10,214
1976	18	202,502	11,250
1977	18	241,610	13,423
1978	18	227,149	12,619
1979	22	262,101	11,914
1980	26	321,260	12,356
1981	26	347,414	13,362
1982	26	427,251	16,433
1983	28	364,356	13,013
1984	28	397,481	14,196
1985	34	422,519	12,427
1986	34	499,704	14,697
1987	34	654,744	19,257
1988	34	558,998	16,441
1989	34	613,242	18,037
1990	34	537,138	15,798
1991	34	665,707	19,580
1992	34	580,462	17,072
1993	34	707,719	20,815
1994	34	578,007	17,000
1995	34	539,440	15,866
1996	34	643,290	18,920
1997	34	634,584	18,664
1998	34	682,530	20,074
1999	34	*720,685	*21,197
2000	34	638,577	18,782
2001	35	596,075	17,031
2002	35	720,433	20,584

DIVISION II

Season	Sess.	Attend.	P/G Avg.
1977	22	*87,602	*3,982
1978	22	83,058	3,775
1979	22	66,446	3,020
1980	22	50,649	2,302
1981	22	69,470	3,158
1982	22	67,925	3,088
1983	22	70,335	3,197
1984	22	81,388	3,699
1985	22	81,476	3,703
1986	22	71,083	3,231
1987	22	77,934	3,542
1988	22	72,462	3,294
1989	20	69,008	3,450
1990	20	64,212	3,211
1991	20	59,839	2,992

Season	Sess.	Attend.	P/G Avg.
1992	20	60,629	3,031
1993	20	56,125	2,806
1994	20	60,511	3,026
1995	36	86,767	2,410
1996	28	65,882	2,353
1997	28	66,626	2,380
1998	28	59,946	2,141
1999	28	49,144	1,755
2000	28	50,130	1,790
2001	28	60,418	2,158
2002	28	60,258	2,152

*record

DIVISION III

Season	Sess.	Attend.	P/G Avg.
1977	21	38,881	1,851
1978	21	37,717	1,796
1979	22	43,850	1,993
1980	22	46,518	2,114
1981	22	58,432	*2,656
1982	22	44,973	2,044
1983	22	51,093	2,322
1984	22	42,152	1,916
1985	22	39,154	1,780
1986	22	53,500	2,432
1987	22	48,150	2,189
1988	22	43,787	1,990
1989	28	49,301	1,761
1990	26	50,527	1,943
1991	34	56,942	1,675
1992	34	65,257	1,919
1993	34	49,675	1,461
1994	34	54,848	1,613
1995	59	*88,684	1,503
1996	58	87,437	1,508
1997	58	70,647	1,218
1998	42	63,330	1,508
1999	42	53,928	1,284
2000	42	62,527	1,489
2001	42	77,110	1,836
2002	46	74,437	1,618

*record

Division I Attendance Records

SINGLE GAME (PAID)
68,112—LSU (87) vs. Notre Dame (64), Jan. 20, 1990, at Louisiana Superdome, New Orleans (regular-season game)

SINGLE GAME (TURNSTILE)
58,903—North Carolina (78) vs. Kansas (68) and Michigan (81) vs. Kentucky (78) (ot), Apr. 3, 1993 (NCAA semifinals), at Louisiana Superdome, New Orleans

HOME COURT, SINGLE GAME
33,048—Syracuse (62) vs. Georgetown (58), Mar. 3, 1991, at Carrier Dome, Syracuse, N.Y.

HOME-COURT AVERAGE, SEASON
29,918—Syracuse, 1990 (478,686 in 16 games at Carrier Dome)

HOME-COURT TOTAL, SEASON
537,949—Syracuse, 1989 (19 games)

FULL-SEASON AVERAGE, ALL GAMES
(home, road, neutral, tournaments)
22,501—Syracuse, 1989 (855,053 in 38 games)

FULL-SEASON TOTAL, ALL GAMES
(home, road, neutral, tournaments)
855,053—Syracuse, 1989 (38 games)

TOP 10 ATTENDANCE GAMES (PAID)*
68,112—LSU (87) vs. Notre Dame (64), Jan. 20, 1990, at Louisiana Superdome, New Orleans

66,144—LSU (82) vs. Georgetown (80), Jan. 28, 1989, at Louisiana Superdome, New Orleans

64,959—Indiana (74) vs. Syracuse (73), Mar. 30, 1987 (NCAA final); Indiana (97) vs. UNLV (93) and Syracuse (77) vs. Providence (63), Mar. 28, 1987 (NCAA semifinals), at Louisiana Superdome, New Orleans

64,151—North Carolina (77) vs. Michigan (71), Apr. 5, 1993 (NCAA final); North Carolina (78) vs. Kansas (68) and Michigan (81) vs. Kentucky (78) (ot), Apr. 3, 1993 (NCAA semifinals), at Louisiana Superdome, New Orleans

61,612—North Carolina (63) vs. Georgetown (62), Mar. 29, 1982 (NCAA final); North Carolina (68) vs. Houston (63) and Georgetown (50) vs. Louisville (46), Mar. 27, 1982 (NCAA semifinals), at Louisiana Superdome, New Orleans

61,304—LSU (84) vs. Texas (83), Jan. 3, 1992, at Louisiana Superdome, New Orleans

52,693—Houston (71) vs. UCLA (69), Jan. 20, 1968, at The Astrodome, Houston

52,647—Maryland (64) vs. Indiana (52), Apr. 1, 2002 (NCAA final); Maryland (97) vs. Kansas (88) and Indiana (73) vs. Oklahoma

(64), Mar. 30, 2002 (NCAA semifinals), at Georgia Dome, Atlanta

50,379—Duke (71) vs. Michigan (51), Apr. 6, 1992 (NCAA final); Duke (81) vs. Indiana (78) and Michigan (76) vs. Cincinnati (72), Apr. 4, 1992 (NCAA semifinals), at Hubert H. Humphrey Metrodome, Minneapolis

47,100—Duke (72) vs. Kansas (65), Apr. 1, 1991 (NCAA final); Kansas (79) vs. North Carolina (73) and Duke (79) vs. UNLV (77), Mar. 30, 1991 (NCAA semifinals), at RCA Dome, Indianapolis

*Note: Figures for games at the Final Four include the media.

TOP FIVE ATTENDANCE GAMES (TURNSTILE)
58,903—North Carolina (78) vs. Kansas (68) and Michigan (81) vs. Kentucky (78) (ot), Apr. 3, 1993 (NCAA semifinals), at Louisiana Superdome, New Orleans

56,707—Indiana (74) vs. Syracuse (73), Mar. 30, 1987 (NCAA final), at Louisiana Superdome, New Orleans

56,264—North Carolina (77) vs. Michigan (71), Apr. 5, 1993 (NCAA final), at Louisiana Superdome, New Orleans

55,841—Indiana (97) vs. UNLV (93) and Syracuse (77) vs. Providence (63), Mar. 28, 1987 (NCAA semifinals), at Louisiana Superdome, New Orleans

54,321—LSU (82) vs. Georgetown (80), Jan. 28, 1989, at Louisiana Superdome, New Orleans

TOP 10 REGULAR-SEASON GAMES (PAID)

68,112 —LSU (87) vs. Notre Dame (64), Jan. 20, 1990, at Louisiana Superdome, New Orleans

66,144—LSU (82) vs. Georgetown (80), Jan. 28, 1989, at Louisiana Superdome, New Orleans

61,304—LSU (84) vs. Texas (83), Jan. 3, 1992, at Louisiana Superdome, New Orleans

52,693—Houston (71) vs. UCLA (69), Jan. 20, 1968, at The Astrodome, Houston

45,214—Louisville (101) vs. Indiana (79) and Notre Dame (81) vs. Kentucky (65), Dec. 3, 1988, at RCA Dome, Indianapolis

43,601—Notre Dame (69) vs. Louisville (54) and Kentucky (82) vs. Indiana (76), Dec. 5, 1987, at RCA Dome, Indianapolis

41,071—Kentucky (89) vs. Indiana (82), Dec. 2, 1995, at RCA Dome, Indianapolis

40,128—Louisville (84) vs. Notre Dame (73) and Indiana (71) vs. Kentucky (69), Dec. 2, 1989, at RCA Dome, Indianapolis

38,504—Kentucky (75) vs. Indiana (72), Dec. 6, 1997, at RCA Dome, Indianapolis

38,194 —Indiana (96) vs. Kentucky (84), Dec. 4, 1993, at RCA Dome, Indianapolis

ON-CAMPUS REGULAR-SEASON, SINGLE GAME

33,048—Syracuse (62) vs. Georgetown (58), Mar. 3, 1991, at Carrier Dome, Syracuse, N.Y.

33,015—Syracuse (89) vs. Georgetown (87), Mar. 4, 1990 (ot), at Carrier Dome, Syracuse, N.Y.

32,996—Syracuse (68) vs. Georgetown (72), Feb. 23, 1992, at Carrier Dome, Syracuse, N.Y.

32,820—Syracuse (90) vs. Connecticut (86), Feb. 10, 1990, at Carrier Dome, Syracuse, N.Y.

32,763—Syracuse (89) vs. Pittsburgh (68), Feb. 24, 1991, at Carrier Dome, Syracuse, N.Y.

32,747—Syracuse (65) vs. Notre Dame (66), Feb. 17, 1990, at Carrier Dome, Syracuse, N.Y.

32,683—Syracuse (82) vs. Georgetown (76) (ot), Mar. 5, 1989, at Carrier Dome, Syracuse, N.Y.

32,633—Syracuse (78) vs. Seton Hall (64), Jan. 19, 1991, at Carrier Dome, Syracuse, N.Y.

32,602—Syracuse (71) vs. Georgetown (72), Feb. 22, 1987, at Carrier Dome, Syracuse, N.Y.

32,589—Syracuse (85) vs. Georgetown (64), Feb. 10, 1996, at Carrier Dome, Syracuse, N.Y.

2002 Division I Attendance Single-Game Highs

REGULAR-SEASON

29,379—Kentucky (66) vs. Indiana (52), Dec. 22, 2001, RCA Dome, Indianapolis

29,215—Syracuse (69) vs. Georgetown (75), Feb. 24, 2002, Carrier Dome, Syracuse, NY

24,895—Kentucky (82) vs. Louisville (62), Dec. 29, 2001, Rupp Arena, Lexington, KY

23,606—Kentucky (70) vs. Florida (67), Mar. 2, 2002, Rupp Arena, Lexington, KY

23,544—Alabama (64) vs. Kentucky (82), Jan. 26, 2002, Rupp Arena, Lexington, KY

POSTSEASON

52,647—Maryland (64) vs. Indiana (52), Apr. 1, 2002 (NCAA final); Maryland (97) vs. Kansas (88) and Indiana (73) vs. Oklahoma (64), Mar. 30, 2002 (NCAA semifinals), at Georgia Dome, Atlanta

28,742—Maryland (78) vs. Kentucky (68) and Connecticut (71) vs. Southern Ill. (59), Mar. 22, 2002 (East Region semifinals), at Carrier Dome, Syracuse, N.Y. (28,440 in final)

28,665—Kentucky (87) vs. Tulsa (82) and Kansas (86) vs. Stanford (63), Mar. 16, 2002 (NCAA second round), at Trans World Dome, St. Louis

23,895—Sessions 2, 3, 4 & 5, Mar. 8-10, 2002 (Atlantic Coast Conference Tournament), at Charlotte Coliseum, Charlotte, N.C.

22,508—Mississippi St. (64) vs. Florida (52) and South Carolina (70) vs. Kentucky (57), Mar. 8, 2002 (Session 4 of Southeastern Conference Tournament), at Georgia Dome, Atlanta

Division II Attendance Records

PAID ATTENDANCE

13,913 —Evansville (93) vs. Ky. Wesleyan (87), Feb. 13, 1960, at Roberts Stadium, Evansville, Indiana

13,240—La.-Lafayette (105) vs. Ky. Wesleyan (83), March 19, 1971, at Roberts Stadium, Evansville, Indiana (NCAA third place)

13,124—Evansville (97) vs. Old Dominion (82), March 20, 1971, at Roberts Stadium, Evansville, Indiana (NCAA final)

Division III Attendance Records

PAID ATTENDANCE

11,442—Hope (70) vs. Calvin (56), Jan. 29, 1997, at Van Andel Arena, Grand Rapids, Michigan

ATTENDANCE RECORDS

Playing-Rules History

Dr. James Naismith's 13 Original Rules of Basketball

Photo from NCAA archives

1. The ball may be thrown in any direction with one or both hands.
2. The ball may be batted in any direction with one or both hands (never with the fist).
3. A player cannot run with the ball. The player must throw it from the spot on which he catches it, allowance to be made for a man who catches the ball when running at a good speed if he tries to stop.
4. The ball must be held in or between the hands; the arms or body must not be used for holding it.
5. No shouldering, holding, pushing, tripping, or striking in any way the person of an opponent shall be allowed; the first infringement of this rule by any player shall count as a foul, the second shall disqualify him until the next goal is made, or, if there was evident intent to injure the person, for the whole of the game, no substitute allowed.
6. A foul is striking at the ball with the fist, violation of Rules 3, 4, and such as described in Rule 5.
7. If either side makes three consecutive fouls, it shall count a goal for the opponents (consecutive means without the opponents in the mean time making a foul).
8. A goal shall be made when the ball is thrown or batted from the grounds into the basket and stays there, providing those defending the goal do not touch or disturb the goal. If the ball rests on the edges, and the opponent moves the basket, it shall count as a goal.
9. When the ball goes out of bounds, it shall be thrown into the field of play by the person first touching it. In case of a dispute, the umpire shall throw it straight into the field. The thrower-in is allowed five seconds; if he holds it longer, it shall go to the opponent. If any side persists in delaying the game, the umpire shall call a foul on that side.
10. The umpire shall be judge of the men and shall note the fouls and notify the referee when three consecutive fouls have been made. He shall have power to disqualify men according to Rule 5.
11. The referee shall be judge of the ball and shall decide when the ball is in play, in bounds, to which side it belongs, and shall keep the time. He shall decide when a goal has been made, and keep account of the goals with any other duties that are usually performed by a referee.
12. The time shall be two 15-minute halves, with five minutes' rest between.
13. The side making the most goals in that time shall be declared the winner. In case of a draw, the game may, by agreement of the captains, be continued until another goal is made.

Note: These original rules were published in January 1892 in the Springfield College school newspaper, The Triangle.

Important Rules Changes by Year

1891-92
• The 13 original rules of basketball are written by Dr. James Naismith in December 1891 in Springfield, Massachusetts.

1894-95
• The free-throw line is moved from 20 to 15 feet.

1895-96
• A field goal changes from three to two points, and free throws from three points to one point.

1896-97
• Backboards are installed.

1900-01
• A dribbler may not shoot for a field goal and may dribble only once, and then with two hands.

1908-09
• A dribbler is permitted to shoot. The dribble is defined as the "continuous passage of the ball," making the double dribble illegal.
• A second official is added for games in an effort to curb the rough play.

1910-11
• Players are disqualified upon committing their fourth personal foul.
• No coaching is allowed during the progress of the game by anybody connected with either team. A warning is given for the first violation and a free throw is awarded after that.

1913-14
• The bottom of the net is left open.

1914-15
• College, YMCA and AAU rules are made the same.

1920-21
• A player can re-enter the game once. Before this rule, if a player left the game, he could not re-enter for the rest of the game.
• The backboards are moved 2 feet from the wall of the court. Before this rule, players would "climb" the padded wall to sink baskets.

1921-22
• Running with the ball changes from a foul to a violation.

1923-24
• The player fouled must shoot his own free throws. Before this rule, one person usually shot all his team's free throws.

1928-29
• The charging foul by the dribbler is introduced.

1930-31
• A held ball may be called when a closely guarded player is withholding the ball from play for five seconds. The result will be a jump ball.
• The maximum circumference of the ball is reduced from 32 to 31 inches, and the maximum weight from 23 to 22 ounces.

1932-33
• The 10-second center (division) line is introduced to reduce stalling.
• No player can stand in the free-throw lane with the ball for more than three seconds.

1933-34
• A player may re-enter the game twice.

1934-35
• The circumference of the ball again is reduced to between 29½ and 30¼ inches.

1935-36
- No offensive player can remain in the free-throw lane, with or without the ball, for more than three seconds.
- After a made free throw, the team scored upon shall put the ball in play at the end of the court where the goal had been scored.

1937-38
- The center jump after every goal scored is eliminated.

1938-39
- The ball will be thrown in from out of bounds at mid-court by the team shooting a free throw after a technical foul. Before, the ball was put into play with a center jump after a technical-foul free throw.
- The circumference of the ball is established as 30 inches.

1939-40
- Teams have the choice of whether to take a free throw or take the ball out of bounds at mid-court. If two or more free throws are awarded, this option applies to the last throw.
- The backboards are moved from 2 to 4 feet from the end line to permit freer movement under the basket.

1940-41
- Fan-shaped backboards are made legal.

1942-43
- Any player who is eligible to start an overtime period will be allowed an extra personal foul, increasing the total so disqualification is on the fifth foul.

1944-45
- Defensive goaltending is banned.
- Five personal fouls disqualify a player. An extra foul is not permitted in overtime games.
- Unlimited substitution is introduced.
- It becomes a violation for an offensive player to remain in the free-throw lane for more than three seconds.

1946-47
- Transparent backboards are authorized.

1947-48
- The clock is stopped on every dead ball the last three minutes of the second half and of every overtime period. This includes every time a goal is scored because the ball is considered dead until put into play again. (This rule was abolished in 1951.)

1948-49
- Coaches are allowed to speak to players during a timeout.

1951-52
- Games are to be played in four 10-minute quarters. Before this, games were played in two 20-minute halves.

1952-53
- Teams can no longer waive free throws in favor of taking the ball out of bounds.
- The one-and-one free-throw rule is introduced, although the bonus is used only if the first shot is missed. The rule will be in effect the entire game except the last three minutes, when every foul results in two free throws.

1954-55
- The one-and-one free throw is changed so that the bonus shot is given only if the first shot is made.
- Games are changed back to being played in two 20-minute halves.

1955-56
- The two-shot penalty in the last three minutes of the game is eliminated. The one-and-one is now in effect the entire game.

1956-57
- The free-throw lane is increased from 6 feet to 12 feet. On the lineup for a free throw, the two spaces adjacent to the end line must be occupied by opponents of the free-thrower. In the past, one space was marked "H" for a home team player to occupy, and across the lane the first space was marked "V" for a visiting team player to stand in.
- Grasping the basket is now classified as a technical foul under unsportsmanlike tactics.

1957-58
- Offensive goaltending is now banned, as an addition to the original 1945 rule.
- One free throw for each common foul is taken for the first six personal fouls by one team in each half, and the one-and-one is used thereafter.

- On uniforms, the use of the single digit numbers one and two and any digit greater than five is prohibited.
- A ball that passes over the backboard—either front to back or back to front—is considered out of bounds.

1964-65
- Coaches must remain seated on the bench except while the clock is stopped or to direct or encourage players on the court. This rule is to help keep coaches from inciting undesirable crowd reactions toward the officials.

1967-68
- The dunk is made illegal during the game and pregame warm-up.

1970-71
- During a jump ball, a nonjumper may not change his position from the time the official is ready to make the toss until after the ball has been touched.

1972-73
- The free throw on the first six common fouls each half by a team is eliminated.
- Players cannot attempt to create the false impression that they have been fouled in charging/guarding situations or while screening when the contact was only incidental. An official can charge the "actor" with a technical foul for unsportsmanlike conduct if, in the official's opinion, the actor is making a travesty of the game.
- Freshmen are eligible to play varsity basketball. This was the result of a change in the NCAA bylaws, not the basketball playing rules.

1973-74
- Officials may now penalize players for fouls occurring away from the ball, such as grabbing, holding and setting illegal screens.

1974-75
- During a jump ball, a non-jumper on the restraining circle may move around the circle after the ball has left the official's hands.
- A player charged with a foul is no longer required to raise his hand. (In 1978, however, it was strongly recommended that a player start raising his hand again.)

1976-77
- The dunk is made legal again.

1981-82
- The jump ball is used only at the beginning of the game and the start of each overtime. An alternating arrow will indicate possession in jump-ball situations during the game.
- All fouls charged to bench personnel shall be assessed to the head coach.

1982-83
- When the closely guarded five-second count is reached, it is no longer a jump-ball situation. It is a violation, and the ball is awarded to the defensive team out of bounds.

1983-84
- Two free throws are taken for each common foul committed within the last two minutes of the second half and the entire overtime period, if the bonus rule is in effect. (This rule was rescinded one month into the season.)

1984-85
- The coaching box is introduced, whereby a coach and all bench personnel must remain in the 28-foot-long coaching box unless seeking information from the scorers' table.

1985-86
- The 45-second clock is introduced. The team in control of the ball must now shoot for a goal within 45 seconds after it attains team control.
- If a shooter is fouled intentionally and the shot is missed, the penalty will be two shots and possession of the ball out of bounds to the team that was fouled.
- The head coach may stand throughout the game, while all other bench personnel must remain seated.

1986-87
- The three-point field goal is introduced and set at 19 feet 9 inches from the center of the basket.
- A coach may leave the confines of the bench at any time without penalty to correct a scorer's or timer's mistake. A technical foul is assessed if there is no mistake. (This was changed the next year to a timeout.) Also, a television replay may be used to prevent or rectify a scorer's or timer's mistake or a malfunction of the clock.

1987-88
- Each intentional personal foul carries a two-shot penalty plus possession of the ball.

1988-89

• Any squad member who participates in a fight will be ejected from the game and will be placed on probation. If that player participates in a second fight during the season, he will be suspended for one game. A third fight involving the same person results in suspension for the rest of the season including championship competition.

1990-91

• Beginning with the team's 10th personal foul in a half, two free throws are awarded for each common foul, except player-control fouls.
• Three free throws are awarded when a shooter is fouled during an unsuccessful three-point try.
• The fighting rule is amended. The first time any squad member or bench personnel participates in a fight he will be suspended for the team's next game. If that same person participates in a second fight, he will be suspended for the rest of the season, including championship competition.

1991-92

• Contact technical fouls count toward the five fouls for player disqualification and toward the team fouls in reaching bonus free-throw situations.
• The shot clock is reset when the ball strikes the basket ring, not when a shot leaves the shooter's hands as it had been ever since the rule was introduced in 1986.

1992-93

• Unsporting technical fouls, in addition to contact technical fouls, count toward the five fouls for player disqualification and toward the team fouls in reaching bonus free-throw situations.

1993-94

• The shot clock is reduced to 35 seconds from 45. The team in control of the ball must shoot for a goal within 35 seconds after it gains team control.
• A foul shall be ruled intentional if, while playing the ball, a player causes excessive contact with an opponent.
• The game clock will be stopped after successful field goals in the last minute of the game and the last minute of any overtime period with no substitution allowed.
• The five-second dribbling violation when closely guarded is eliminated.
• The rule concerning the use of profanity is expanded to include abusive and obscene language in an effort to curtail verbal misconduct by players and coaches.

1994-95

• The inner circle at mid-court is eliminated.
• Scoring is restricted to a tap-in when (3/10) (.3) of a second or less remain on the game clock or shot clock.
• The fighting and suspension rules are expanded to include coaches and team personnel.

1995-96

• All unsporting technical fouls charged to anyone on the bench count toward the team foul total.

• Teams are allowed one 20-second timeout per half. This was an experimental rule in the 1994-95 season.

1996-97

• Teams shall warm up and shoot at the end of the court farthest from their own bench for the first half. Previously, teams had the choice of baskets in the first half.
• In games not involving commercial electronic media, teams are entitled to four full-length timeouts and two 20-second timeouts per game. In games involving commercial electronic media, teams are entitled to two full-length timeouts and three 20-second timeouts per game.

1997-98

• The five-second dribbling violation when closely guarded is reinstated.
• Timeout requests can be made by a player on the court or by the head coach.

1998-99

• In a held-ball situation initiated by the defense, the ball shall be awarded to the defensive team. Previously, possession was awarded by the direction of the possession arrow.

1999-00

• Held-ball change from previous season rescinded.
• Twenty-second timeouts increased to 30 seconds in length. New electronic-media timeout format adopted.
• Uniform numbers one and two are permitted.
• Officials must consult courtside television monitors, when available, to judge whether a game-deciding last-second shot in the second half or any extra period counts. (This was passed during the season.)

2000-01

• Technical fouls divided into direct (two-shot penalty) and indirect (one-shot penalty) with ball returned to point of interruption.

2001-02

• Both direct and indirect technical fouls penalized by two shots and returned to point of interruption.
• Officials can check an official courtside monitor to determine if a try is a three- or two-point attempt, regardless of whether the try is successful.

2002-03

• Composite ball can be used without mutual consent of coaches.
• Two free-throw lane spaces closest to the free-thrower shall remain unoccupied.
• No free throws to offended team in bonus for personal fouls committed by team while in team control or in possession of the ball during a throw-in (team-control foul).

Important Rules Changes by Subject

Ball: 1930-31, The maximum circumference of the ball is reduced from 32 to 31 inches, and the maximum weight from 23 to 22 ounces. 1934-35, The circumference of the ball again is reduced to between 29 1/2 and 30 1/4 inches. 1938-39, The circumference of the ball is established as 30 inches. 2002-03, Mutual consent no longer needed for composite ball to be legal.

Basket Equipment: 1896-97, Backboards are installed. 1913-14, The bottom of the net is left open. 1920-21, The backboards are moved 2 feet from the wall of the court. Before this rule, players would "climb" the padded wall to sink baskets. 1939-40, The backboards are moved from 2 to 4 feet from the end line to permit freer movement under the basket. 1940-41, Fan-shaped backboards are made legal. 1946-47, Transparent backboards are authorized. 1957-58, A ball that passes over the backboard—either front to back or back to front—is considered out of bounds. 1996-97, Teams shall warm up and shoot at the end of the court farthest from their own bench for the first half. Previously, teams had the choice of baskets in the first half. 2002-03, For Division I, shot clocks had to be mounted and recessed on backboard, red warning light had to be added and game clock had to show 10th-of-a-second display.

Block/Charge: 1928-29, The charging foul by the dribbler is introduced. 1972-73, Players cannot attempt to create the false impression that they have been fouled in charging/guarding situations or while screening when the contact was only

incidental. An official can charge the "actor" with a technical foul for unsportsman-like conduct if, in the official's opinion, the actor is making a travesty of the game.

Clock Stoppage: 1947-48, The clock is stopped on every dead ball the last three minutes of the second half and of every extra period. This includes every time a goal is scored because the ball is considered dead until put into play again. (This rule was abolished in 1951.)

Closely Guarded: 1982-83, When the closely guarded five-second count is reached, it is no longer a jump-ball situation. It is a violation, and the ball is awarded to the defensive team out of bounds. 1993-94, The five-second dribbling violation when closely guarded is eliminated. 1997-98, The five-second dribbling violation when closely guarded is reinstated.

Coaching: 1910-11, No coaching is allowed during the progress of the game by anybody connected with either team. A warning is given for the first violation and a free throw is awarded after that. 1948-49, Coaches are allowed to speak to players during a timeout. 1964-65, Coaches must remain seated on the bench except while the clock is stopped or to direct or encourage players on the court. This rule is to help keep coaches from inciting undesirable crowd reactions toward the officials. 1984-85, The coaching box is introduced, whereby a coach and all bench personnel must remain in the 28-foot-long coaching box unless seeking information from the scorers' table. 1985-86, The head coach may stand throughout the game, while all

other bench personnel must remain seated. 1986-87, A coach may leave the confines of the bench at any time without penalty to correct a scorer's or timer's mistake. A technical foul is assessed if there is no mistake. (This penalty was changed the next year to a timeout.) Also, a television replay may be used to prevent or rectify a scorer's or timer's mistake or a malfunction of the clock. 1994-95, The fighting and suspension rules are expanded to include coaches and team personnel. 1995-96, All unsporting technical fouls charged to anyone on the bench count toward the team foul total.

Dunk: 1967-68, The dunk is made illegal during the game and pregame warm-up. 1976-77, The dunk is made legal again but remains illegal during warm-up.

Field Goals: 1895-96, A field goal changes from three to two points, and free throws from three points to one point.

Fighting: 1988-89, Any squad member who participates in a fight will be ejected from the game and will be placed on probation. If that individual participates in a second fight during the season, he will be suspended for one game. A third fight involving the same person results in suspension for the rest of the season including championship competition. 1990-91, The fighting rule is amended. The first time any squad member or bench personnel participates in a fight he will be suspended for the team's next game. If that same person participates in a second fight, he will be suspended for the rest of the season, including championship competition. 1994-95, The fighting and suspension rules are expanded to include coaches and team personnel.

Fouling Out: 1910-11, Players are disqualified upon committing their fourth personal foul. 1942-43, Any player who is eligible to start an extra period will be allowed an extra personal foul, increasing the total so disqualification is on the fifth foul. 1944-45, Five personal fouls disqualify a player. An extra foul is not permitted in overtime games. 1991-92, Contact technical fouls count toward the five fouls for player disqualification and toward the team fouls in reaching bonus free-throw situations.

Free Throws: 1894-95, The free-throw line is moved from 20 to 15 feet. 1923-24, The player fouled must shoot his own free throws. Before this rule, one person usually shot all his team's free throws. 1935-36, After a made free throw, the team scored upon shall put the ball in play at the end of the court where the goal had been scored. 1939-40, Teams have the choice of whether to take a free throw or take the ball out of bounds at mid-court. If two or more free throws are awarded, this option applies to the last throw. 1952-53, Teams can no longer waive free throws in favor of taking the ball out of bounds. 1952-53, The one-and-one free-throw rule is introduced, although the bonus is used only if the first shot is missed. The rule will be in effect the entire game except the last three minutes, when every foul is two shots. 1954-55, The one-and-one free throw is changed so that the bonus shot is given only if the first shot is made. 1955-56, The two-shot penalty in the last three minutes of the game is eliminated. The one-and-one is now in effect the entire game. 1956-57, The free-throw lane is increased from 6 feet to 12 feet. On the lineup for a free throw, the two spaces adjacent to the end line must be occupied by opponents of the free thrower. In the past, one space was marked "H" for a home team player to occupy, and across the lane the first space was marked "V" for a visiting team player to stand in. 1957-58, One free throw for each common foul is taken for the first six personal fouls by one team in each half, and the one-and-one is used thereafter. 1972-73, The free throw on the first six common fouls each half by a team is eliminated. 1974-75, A player charged with a foul is no longer required to raise his hand. (In 1978, however, it was strongly recommended that a player start raising his hand again.) 1983-84, Two free throws are taken for each common foul committed within the last two minutes of the second half and the entire overtime period, if the bonus rule is in effect. (This rule was rescinded one month into the season.) 1985-86, If a shooter is fouled intentionally and the shot is missed, the penalty will be two shots and possession of the ball out of bounds to the team that was fouled. 1987-88, Each intentional personal foul carries a two-shot penalty plus possession of the ball. 1990-91, Beginning with the team's 10th personal foul in a half, two free throws are awarded for each common foul, except player-control fouls. 1990-91, Three free throws are awarded when a shooter is fouled during an unsuccessful three-point try. 1991-92, Contact technical fouls count toward the five fouls for player disqualification and toward the team fouls in reaching bonus free-throw situations. 1992-93, Unsporting technical fouls, in addition to contact technical fouls, count toward the five fouls for player disqualification and toward the team fouls in reaching bonus free-throw situations. 1995-96, All unsporting technical fouls charged to anyone on the bench count toward the team foul total. 2000-01, Number of players permitted on free-throw lane reduced from eight to six. 2002-03, Lane spaces closest to the free-thrower shall remain unoccupied.

Freshmen: 1972-73, Freshmen are eligible to play varsity basketball. This was the result of a change in the NCAA bylaws, not the basketball playing rules.

Goaltending/Basket Interference: 1944-45, Defensive goaltending is banned. 1957-58, Offensive goaltending is now banned, as an addition to the original 1945 rule.

Held Ball: 1930-31, A held ball may be called when a closely guarded player is withholding the ball from play for five seconds. The result will be a jump ball. 1998-99, In a held-ball situation initiated by the defense, the ball shall be awarded to the defensive team. Previously, possession was awarded by the direction of the possession arrow. This was rescinded the next season.

Intentional Foul: 1985-86, If a shooter is fouled intentionally and the shot is missed, the penalty will be two shots and possession of the ball out of bounds to the team that was fouled. 1987-88, Each intentional personal foul carries a two-shot penalty plus possession of the ball. 1993-94, A foul shall be ruled intentional if, while playing the ball, a player causes excessive contact with an opponent.

Jump Ball/Alternate Possession: 1930-31, A held ball may be called when a closely guarded player is withholding the ball from play for five seconds. The result will be a jump ball. 1937-38, The center jump after every goal scored is eliminated. 1970-71, During a jump ball, a non-jumper may not change his position from the time the official is ready to make the toss until after the ball has been touched. 1974-75, During a jump ball, a non-jumper on the restraining circle may move around it after the ball has left the official's hands. 1981-82, The jump ball is used only at the beginning of the game and the start of each extra period. An alternating arrow will indicate possession in held-ball situations during the game. 1994-95, The inner circle at mid-court is eliminated.

Lines: 1894-95, The free-throw line is moved from 20 to 15 feet. 1932-33, The 10-second center (division) line is introduced to reduce stalling. 1956-57, The free-throw lane is increased from 6 feet to 12 feet. On the lineup for a free throw, the two spaces adjacent to the end line must be occupied by opponents of the free-thrower. In the past, one space was marked "H" for a home team player to occupy, and across the lane the first space was marked "V" for a visiting team player to stand in. 1984-85, The coaching box is introduced, whereby a coach and all bench personnel must remain in the 28-foot-long coaching box unless seeking information from the scorers' table. 1986-87, The three-point field goal is introduced and set at 19 feet 9 inches from the center of the basket. 1994-95, The inner circle at mid-court is eliminated.

Officials: 1908-09, A second official is added for games in an effort to curb the rough play. 1977-78, The option of a third official is allowed.

Out of Bounds: 1957-58, A ball that passes over the backboard—either front to back or back to front—is considered out of bounds.

Overtime: 1942-43, Any player who is eligible to start an extra period will be allowed an extra personal foul, increasing the total so disqualification is on the fifth foul. 1944-45, An extra foul is not permitted in overtime games. 1993-94, The game clock will be stopped after successful field goals in the last minute of the game and the last minute of any extra period with no substitution allowed.

Periods: 1951-52, Games are to be played in four 10-minute quarters. Before this, games were played in two 20-minute halves. 1954-55, Games are changed back to being played in two 20-minute halves. 1996-97, Teams shall warm up and shoot at the end of the court farthest from their own bench for the first half. Previously, teams had the choice of baskets in the first half.

Rough Play: 1908-09, A second official is added for games in an effort to curb the rough play. 1939-40, Teams have the choice of whether to take a free throw or take the ball out of bounds at mid-court. If two or more free throws are awarded, this option applies to the last throw. 1952-53, Teams can no longer waive free throws in favor of taking the ball out of bounds. 1957-58, One free throw for each common foul is taken for the first six personal fouls by one team in each half, and the one-and-one is used thereafter. 1972-73, The free throw on the first six common fouls each half by a team is eliminated. 1973-74, Officials may now penalize players for fouls occurring away from the ball, such as grabbing, holding and setting illegal screens. 1974-75, A player charged with a foul is no longer required to raise his hand. (In 1978, however, it was strongly recommended that a player start raising his hand again.) 1983-84, Two free throws are taken for each common foul committed within the last two minutes of the second half and the entire overtime period, if the bonus rule is in effect. (This rule was rescinded one month into the season.) 1987-88, Each intentional personal foul carries a two-shot penalty plus possession of the ball. 1990-91, Beginning with the team's 10th personal foul in a half, two free throws are awarded for each common foul, except player-control fouls. 1991-92, Contact technical fouls count toward the five fouls for player disqualification and toward the team fouls in reaching bonus free-throw situations. 1992-93, Unsporting technical fouls, in addition to contact technical fouls, count toward the five fouls for player disqualification and toward the team fouls in reaching bonus free-throw situations. 1993-94, A foul shall be ruled intentional if, while playing the ball, a player causes excessive contact with an opponent. 2000-01, Number of players permitted on free-throw lane reduced from eight to six.

Shot Clock/Stalling: 1932-33, The 10-second center (division) line is introduced to reduce stalling. 1985-86, The 45-second clock is introduced. The team in control of the ball must now shoot for a goal within 45 seconds after it attains team control. 1991-92, The shot clock is reset when the ball strikes the basket ring, not when a shot leaves the shooter's hands as it had been ever since the rule was introduced in 1986. 1993-94, The shot clock is reduced to 35 seconds from 45. The team in control of the ball must shoot for a goal within 35 seconds after it gains team control. 1993-94, The game clock will be stopped after successful field goals in the last minute of the game and the last minute of any overtime period with no substitution allowed.

Shot in Closing Seconds: 1994-95, Scoring is restricted to a tap-in when 3/10 (.3) of a second or less remain on the game clock or shot clock. 1999-00, During the season, rules committee made rule that requires official to look at courtside monitor to decipher if a potential game-determining shot in the last second of the game or overtime should count.

Substitution: 1920-21, A player can re-enter the game once. Before this rule, if a player left the game, he could not re-enter for the rest of the game. 1933-34, A player may re-enter the game twice. 1944-45, Unlimited substitution is introduced. 1993-94, The game clock will be stopped after successful field goals in the last minute of the game and the last minute of any extra period with no substitution allowed.

Technical Fouls: 1938-39, The ball will be thrown in from out of bounds at mid-court by the team shooting a free throw after a technical foul. Before, the ball was put into play with a center jump after a technical-foul free throw. 1956-57, Grasping the basket is now classified as a technical foul under unsportsmanlike tactics. 1981-

82, All fouls charged to bench personnel shall be assessed to the head coach. 1988-89, Any squad member who participates in a fight will be ejected from the game and will be placed on probation. If that player participates in a second fight during the season, he will be suspended for one game. A third fight involving the same person results in suspension for the rest of the season including championship competition. 1990-91, The fighting rule is amended. The first time any squad member or bench personnel participates in a fight he will be suspended for the team's next game. If that same person participates in a second fight, he will be suspended for the rest of the season, including championship competition. 1991-92, Contact technical fouls count toward the five fouls for player disqualification and toward the team fouls in reaching bonus free-throw situations. 1992-93, Unsporting technical fouls, in addition to contact technical fouls, count toward the five fouls for player disqualification and toward the team fouls in reaching bonus free-throw situations. 1993-94, The rule concerning the use of profanity is expanded to include abusive and obscene language in an effort to curtail verbal misconduct by players and coaches. 1994-95, The fighting and suspension rules are expanded to include coaches and team personnel. 2000-01, technical fouls divided into direct (two-shot penalty) and indirect (one-shot penalty) with ball returned to point of interruption. 2001-02, Both direct and indirect technical fouls penalized by two shots and return to point of interruption.

Television Replay: 1986-87, A coach may leave the confines of the bench at any time without penalty to correct a scorer's or timer's mistake. A technical foul is assessed if there is no mistake. (This was changed the next year to a timeout.) Also, a television replay may be used to prevent or rectify a scorer's or timer's mistake or a malfunction of the clock. 1999-00, Officials must consult courtside television monitors, when available, to judge whether a game-deciding last-second shot in the second half or any extra period counts. (This was passed during season.) 2001-02, Officials can check an official courtside monitor to determine if a try is a three- or two-point attempt, regardless of whether the try is successful.

Three Seconds: 1932-33, No player can stand in the free-throw lane with the ball more than three seconds. 1935-36, No offensive player can remain in the free-throw lane, with or without the ball, for more than three seconds. 1944-45, It becomes a violation for an offensive player to remain in the free-throw lane more than three seconds.

Three-Point Shot: 1986-87, The three-point field goal is introduced and set at 19 feet 9 inches from the center of the basket. 1990-91, Three free throws are awarded when a shooter is fouled during an unsuccessful three-point try.

Timeouts: 1948-49, Coaches are allowed to speak to players during a timeout. 1995-96, Teams are allowed one 20-second timeout per half. This was an experimental rule in the 1994-95 season. 1996-97, In games not involving commercial electronic media, teams are entitled to four full-length timeouts and two 20-second timeouts per game. In games involving commercial electronic media, teams are entitled to two full-length timeouts and three 20-second timeouts per game. 1997-98, Timeout requests can be made by a player on the court or by the head coach. 1999-00, Twenty-second timeouts increased to 30 seconds in length. New electronic-media timeout format adopted.

Traveling: 1900-01, A dribbler may not shoot for a field goal and may dribble only once, and then with two hands. 1908-09, A dribbler is permitted to shoot. The dribble is defined as the "continuous passage of the ball," making the double dribble illegal. 1921-22, Running with the ball changes from a foul to a violation.

Uniforms: 1957-58, On uniforms, the use of the single digit numbers one and two and any digit greater than five is prohibited. 1999-00, Uniform numbers one and two are permitted.

Division I Basketball Firsts

The First Time...

Playing rules were published:
January 1892 in the Springfield College school newspaper, The Triangle.

A game was played:
January 20, 1892, at the Training School of the International YMCA College, now known as Springfield College in Massachusetts.

A game was played in public:
March 11, 1892, at Springfield College. A crowd of 200 saw the students defeat the teachers, 5-1.

A full schedule of games was played by a college:
1894 when the University of Chicago compiled a 6-1 season record.

A game between two colleges was played:
February 9, 1895, when the Minnesota School of Agriculture defeated Hamline, 9-3. Nine players were allowed on the court at the same time for both teams.

A game between two colleges was played with five players on each team:
January 16, 1896, when Chicago defeated Iowa, 15-12, in Iowa City. Iowa's starting lineup was composed of a YMCA team that just happened to be university students.

A game between two true college teams with five players on a team was played:
1897 when Yale defeated Pennsylvania, 32-10.

A conference season was played:
1901-02 by the East League, known today as the Ivy Group.

A conference tournament was played:
1921 by the Southern Conference. Kentucky was the winner.

A consensus all-America team was selected:
1929. Members were Charley Hyatt, Pittsburgh; Joe Schaaf, Pennsylvania; Charles Murphy, Purdue; Vern Corbin, California; Thomas Churchill, Oklahoma; and John Thompson, Montana State.

The National Invitation Tournament was played:
1938 when Temple was the winner.

A college game was televised:
February 28, 1940, when Pittsburgh defeated Fordham, 50-37, at Madison Square Garden in New York City. In the second game, New York University defeated Georgetown, 50-27.

The three-point shot was used experimentally in a game:
February 7, 1945, Columbia defeated Fordham, 73-58. The three-point line was set at 21 feet from the basket and Columbia scored 11 "long goals" to Fordham's nine. Also, free-throwers had an option to take their shots from the regular 15-foot distance for one point or from 21 feet for two points. Eight "long fouls" were made during the game.

The 12-foot free-throw lane was used experimentally in a game:
February 7, 1945, Columbia defeated Fordham, 73-58 in the same game as mentioned above. The free-throw lane was widened from 6 feet to 12 for this game and the rule was adopted 11 years later.

An Associated Press poll was published:
1949, when St. Louis was ranked No. 1. By the end of the season, Kentucky had taken over the top spot.

NCAA Tournament Firsts

The first game:
March 17, 1939, when Villanova defeated Brown, 42-30, in Philadelphia.

The first championship game:
March 27, 1939, when Oregon defeated Ohio State, 46-33, in Evanston, Illinois.

The first time two teams from the same conference played in the NCAA tournament:
1944 when Iowa State and Missouri, both of the Big Six, played in the Western regional.

The first time four teams advanced to the final site:
1946 (North Carolina, Ohio State, Oklahoma State and California).

The first championship game televised:
1946 locally in New York City by WCBS-TV. Oklahoma State defeated North Carolina, 43-40. An estimated 500,000 watched the game on television.

The first repeat champion:
Oklahoma State followed its 1945 championship with a title in 1946.

First NCAA championship team to have an integrated roster of white and black players:
CCNY's 1950 squad is believed to be the first integrated championship team.

The first time conference champions qualified automatically:
1951.

The first time a conference champion qualified automatically for the NCAA tournament instead of the regular-season champion:
1952, North Carolina State finished second in the Southern Conference but won the conference postseason tournament.

The first time there were four regional sites:
1952.

The first time games were televised regionally:
1952.

The first time a Final Four was played on Friday and Saturday:
1954.

The first tournament championship game televised nationally:
1954 for a broadcast rights fee of $7,500.

The first time an undefeated team won the NCAA championship:
1956 when San Francisco went 29-0.

The first time two teams from the same state played in the NCAA title game:

1961 when Cincinnati defeated Ohio State, 70-65, in overtime.

The first championship team to start five African-Americans:
UTEP in 1966—Harry Flournoy, David Lattin, Bobby Joe Hill, Orsten Artis, Willie Cager.

The first time the Final Four was played on Thursday and Saturday:
1969.

The first time the Final Four was played on Saturday and Monday:
1973.

The first NCAA title game televised during prime time:
UCLA's win over Memphis in 1973 was televised by NBC.

The first time television rights totaled more than $1 million:
1973.

The first public draw for Final Four tickets:
1973 for the 1974 championship.

The first time teams other than the conference champion could be chosen at large from the same conference:
1975.

The first reference to the term "Final Four":
1975 Official Collegiate Basketball Guide, page 5 in national preview-review section written by Ed Chay of the Cleveland Plain Dealer. Chay wrote, "Outspoken Al McGuire of Marquette, whose team was one of the final four in Greensboro, was among several coaches who said it was good for college basketball that UCLA was finally beaten."

The first time two teams from the same conference played in the Final Four title game:
1976 when Indiana defeated Michigan, 86-68. Both teams were Big Ten members.

The first time the seeding process was used to align teams in the bracket:
1978.

The first reference to term "Final Four" is capitalized:
1978 Official Collegiate Basketball Guide (page 7, first line).

The first time all teams were seeded in the bracket:
1979.

The first public lottery for Final Four tickets:
1979.

The first time more than two teams from the same conference were allowed in the NCAA tournament:
1980.

The first time none of the No. 1 seeds in the NCAA tournament advanced to the Final Four:
1980.

The first time the Rating Percentage Index (RPI), a computer ranking system, was used as an aid in evaluating teams for at-large selections and seeding:
1981.

The first time two No. 1 seeds in the NCAA tournament advanced to the Final Four:
1981.

The first time a Final Four logo was produced that was specific to the site of the championship game:
1981, when the final game was played in Philadelphia and the logo included the Liberty Bell.

The first live television broadcast of the selection show announcing the NCAA tournament bracket:
1982.

The first time CBS was awarded the television rights for the NCAA tournament:
1982.

The first time a men's and women's team from the same school advanced to the Final Four in the same year:
1983, when both Georgia teams lost in the national semifinals.

The first time awards were presented to all participating teams in the NCAA championship tournament:
1984.

The first time 64 teams participated in the NCAA tournament:
1985.

The first time three teams from the same conference advanced to the Final Four:
1985, when Georgetown, St. John's (New York) and Villanova represented the Big East.

The first time all 64 NCAA tournament teams were subject to drug testing:
1987.

The first time neutral courts were used in all rounds of the NCAA tournament:
1989.

The first time all the Nos. 1 and 2 seeds in the NCAA tournament advanced to the Sweet Sixteen:
1989.

The first time a bearded coach advanced to the Final Four:
P.J. Carlesimo of Seton Hall in 1989.

The first time a minimum facility seating capacity of 12,000 for first and second rounds and regionals was established:
1993.

The first time three No. 1 seeds in the NCAA tournament advanced to the Final Four:
1993.

The first time two former Final Four most outstanding players returned to the Final Four:
1995, when North Carolina's Donald Williams (1993) and Arkansas' Corliss Williamson (1994) returned to the Final Four.

The first NCAA tournament MOP:
Marv Huffman of Indiana in 1940.

The first freshman named NCAA tournament MOP:
Arnie Ferrin of Utah in 1944.

The first two-time NCAA tournament MOP:
Bob Kurland of Oklahoma State in 1945 and 1946.

The first NCAA tournament MOP not to play on the national championship team:
B.H. Born of Kansas in 1953.

The first football Heisman Trophy winner to play in the Final Four:
Terry Baker of Oregon State in 1963.

The first three-time NCAA tournament MOP:
Lew Alcindor of UCLA in 1967, 1968 and 1969.

The first player to play for two teams in the Final Four championship game:
Bob Bender with Indiana 1976 and Duke 1978.

The first coach to win the NCAA title in his first year as a head coach:
Steve Fisher of Michigan in 1989.

The First Team(s)...

To win 30 games in a season:
Wyoming went 31-2 in 1943.

To win a football bowl game and the NCAA tournament title in the same academic year:
Oklahoma State won the Cotton Bowl and the NCAA championship in 1944-45.

To be ranked No. 1 in the final regular-season poll and go on to win the NCAA championship:

Kentucky ended the 1949 regular season ranked No. 1 and proceeded to win its second NCAA title.

To win the NCAA tournament and the NIT in the same year:
CCNY won both tournaments in 1950.

To play for the national championship in both football and basketball in the same academic year:
Oklahoma lost in both the Orange Bowl and the Final Four title game in 1987-88.

Representing the same school to be ranked No. 1 in the men's and women's polls:
Connecticut's men's and women's basketball programs were ranked No. 1 in their respective top 25 polls February 13, 1995.

The First Coach...

Who also happened to be the inventor of the game:
Dr. James Naismith invented the game in December 1891 at Springfield College in Massachusetts.

To lead his team to a finish among the final four teams in the nation in his first season as a head coach:
Ray Meyer of DePaul in 1943.

To be recognized as coach of the year:
Phil Woolpert of San Francisco was named the 1955 coach of the year by United Press International.

To take two different schools to the NCAA championship game:
Frank McGuire in 1957 with North Carolina after St. John's (New York) in 1952.

To win the NCAA championship after playing for an NCAA championship team:
Bob Knight coached Indiana to the championship in 1976 after playing for the 1960 Ohio State champions.

To take two different teams to the Final Four:
Forddy Anderson and Frank McGuire. Anderson—Bradley in 1950 (first year) and Michigan State in 1957; McGuire—St. John's (New York) (first year) in 1952 and North Carolina in 1957.

Steve Fisher's 1989 Michigan team won the national title in his first year as head coach. Fisher now coaches at San Diego State.

To take two different teams to the NCAA tournament:

Ben Carnevale—North Carolina in 1946 (first year) and Navy in 1947.

To take three different teams to the NCAA tournament:

Eddie Hickey—Creighton in 1941 (first year), Saint Louis in 1952 and Marquette in 1959.

To take four different teams to the NCAA tournament:

Eddie Sutton—Creighton in 1974 (first year), Arkansas in 1977, Kentucky in 1986 and Oklahoma State in 1991.

The First Player...

To be named consensus all-American three times:

John Wooden of Purdue from 1930-32.

To score 1,000 points in his career:

Christian Steinmetz of Wisconsin from 1903-05.

To score 50 points in one game:

Hank Luisetti of Stanford, who scored 50 in a win over Duquesne, January 1, 1938.

To popularize the jump shot:

Hank Luisetti of Stanford in 1936-38.

African-American to be named to the consensus all-America team:

Don Barksdale of UCLA in 1947.

To score 2,000 points in his career:

Jim Lacy of Loyola (Md.) scored 2,154 points in 1946-49.

To lead the nation in scoring during the regular season and play for the NCAA championship team in the same year:

Clyde Lovellette of Kansas in 1952.

To achieve 2,000 points and 2,000 rebounds in his career:

Tom Gola of La Salle scored 2,462 points and pulled down 2,201 rebounds in 1952-55.

To grab 50 rebounds in one game:

Bill Chambers of William and Mary brought down 51 boards against Virginia on February 14, 1953.

To grab 700 rebounds in a season:

Walt Dukes of Seton Hall brought down 734 boards during the 1953 season.

To score 100 points in a game:

Frank Selvy of Furman scored 100 points in a 149-95 victory over Newberry on February 13, 1954, in Greenville, South Carolina.

To score 1,000 points in a single season:

Frank Selvy of Furman scored 1,209 during the 1954 season.

To average 40 points a game for a season:

Frank Selvy of Furman averaged 41.7 points a game during the 1954 season.

To average 30 points a game for a career:

Frank Selvy of Furman averaged 32.5 points a game from 1952-54.

To average more than 20 points and 20 rebounds per game during his career:

Bill Russell of San Francisco from 1954-56. He averaged 20.7 points and 20.3 rebounds.

Recognized as the player of the year:

Tom Gola of La Salle was named the 1955 player of the year by United Press International.

To score 3,000 points in his career:

Pete Maravich of LSU scored 3,667 points from 1968-70.

To average 40 points a game for a career:

Pete Maravich of LSU averaged 44.2 points a game from 1968-70.

To lead the nation in scoring and rebounding in the same season:

Xavier McDaniel of Wichita State in 1985.

To make 400 three-point field goals in his career:

Doug Day of Radford hit 401 three-pointers from 1990-93.

2002 Results, All Divisions

2001-2002 Results—All Divisions

Following is an alphabetical listing of the 2001-02 season's game-by-game scores for the men's teams of the member colleges and universities of the National Collegiate Athletic Association.

Below each team's name and location appear the name of its 2001-02 head coach and his alma mater. All other information is from the 2001-02 season. Divisional designation for each team is indicated in the upper right-hand corner of each listing.

Squares (■) indicate home games and daggers (†) indicate neutral-site games.

All records are restricted to varsity games between four-year college institutions.

The 2002-03 schedules and updated information can be found on the World Wide Web at www.ncaa.org.

ABILENE CHRISTIAN
Abilene, TX 79699 II

Coach: Mike Martin, Southeastern Okla. 1965

2001-02 RESULTS (6-20)
92	Okla. Panhandle ■	80
59	St. Edward's ■	78
53	Okla. Panhandle	71
58	St. Edward's	75
87	Texas Col. ■	71
89	Central Okla. ■	91
52	Northeastern St. ■	82
69	Southern Ind.	103
76	Ky. Wesleyan	109
68	Southeastern Okla. ■	65
55	East Central	76
73	Cameron ■	71
77	Southwestern Okla. ■	82
58	Midwestern St.	75
76	Tex. A&M-Commerce ■	74
41	Tex. A&M-Kingsville ■	59
61	Eastern N.M.	82
58	West Tex. A&M	80
114	Angelo St. ■	105
59	Tarleton St. ■	61
56	Angelo St.	85
50	Tarleton St.	97
59	Tex. A&M-Kingsville	103
75	Tex. A&M-Commerce	85
70	West Tex. A&M ■	82
70	Eastern N.M. ■	71

Nickname: Wildcats
Colors: Purple & White
Arena: Moody Coliseum
  Capacity: 4,600; Year Built: 1968
AD: Shanon Hays
SID: Lance Fleming

ADAMS ST.
Alamosa, CO 81102 II

Coach: Larry Mortensen, Adams St. 1988

2001-02 RESULTS (7-20)
91	Southwestern Okla. ■	83
49	St. Mary's (Tex.) ■	53
67	St. Mary's (Tex.)	73
74	Salem Int'l †	84
57	Southern Utah	67
65	Westminster (Utah) †	84
73	Western N.M. ■	69
72	Regis (Colo.)	76
77	Colo. Christian	80
74	Chadron St. ■	65
84	Colorado Mines ■	75
86	Northern Colo. ■	101
71	Metro St.	97
61	Neb.-Kearney	86
65	Fort Hays St. ■	75

80	Fort Lewis	87
99	N.M. Highlands	106
68	Mesa St. ■	76
75	Western St. ■	70
73	UC-Colo. Spgs.	66
59	Southern Colo.	85
80	N.M. Highlands ■	102
82	Fort Lewis ■	94
66	Western St.	80
62	Mesa St.	87
78	Southern Colo.	65
71	UC-Colo. Spgs. ■	82

Nickname: Grizzlies
Colors: Green & White
Arena: Plachy Hall
  Capacity: 3,200; Year Built: 1960
AD: Jeff Geiser
SID: Chris Day

ADELPHI
Garden City, NY 11530 II

Coach: Jim Ferry, Keene St. 1990

2001-02 RESULTS (28-3)
72	Bentley	70
90	Merrimack	67
93	Dowling	80
60	Philadelphia U.	66
73	St. Thomas Aquinas ■	52
67	Mass.-Lowell	54
101	Concordia (N.Y.) ■	71
84	NYIT	69
74	Queens (N.Y.) ■	57
69	New Haven	56
74	Molloy	60
75	C.W. Post ■	65
78	Bridgeport	59
81	Southampton ■	67
91	Mercy	72
94	Philadelphia U. ■	73
59	St. Thomas Aquinas	48
93	Dowling ■	76
112	Concordia (N.Y.)	66
71	NYIT ■	54
81	Queens (N.Y.)	64
67	Molloy	57
96	C.W. Post	81
80	Bridgeport ■	63
80	Southampton	65
87	Mercy ■	59
85	Molloy ■	68
66	NYIT †	68
72	Mass.-Lowell †	57
77	Assumption †	56
46	Ky. Wesleyan †	71

Nickname: Panthers
Colors: Black & Gold
Arena: Woodruff Hall
  Capacity: 800; Year Built: 1929
AD: Robert E. Hartwell
SID: Suzette Thweatt

ADRIAN
Adrian, MI 49221.................III

Coach: Buck Riley, Southwest Okla. 1967

2001-02 RESULTS (14-12)
82	Trinity (Conn.) †	75
77	Rutgers-Newark	67
74	Ohio Wesleyan	93
90	Rochester College ■	66
84	Heidelberg	96
82	Goshen ■	67
77	Bluffton	67
94	Earlham	78
98	Spring Arbor	113
60	Wm. Paterson †	70
100	Penn St.-Altoona †	97
73	Alma ■	61
62	Hope ■	80
57	Albion ■	70
76	Calvin	95
62	Kalamazoo	71
80	Rochester College	73
67	Olivet ■	62
93	Alma	78
58	Hope	65
59	Albion	41
68	Calvin ■	72
78	Kalamazoo ■	66
85	Siena Heights ■	92
101	Olivet	76
57	Albion	76

Nickname: Bulldogs
Colors: Gold & Black
Arena: Merillat Center
  Capacity: 1,350; Year Built: 1990
AD: C. Henry Mensing
SID: Darcy Gifford

AIR FORCE
USAF Academy, CO 80840-5001 I

Coach: Joe Scott, Princeton 1987

2001-02 RESULTS (9-19)
68	Yale †	62
58	Missouri	86
52	Denver ■	44
53	Navy	71
70	Montana St. †	65
52	Fresno St.	68
67	Arkansas St. ■	63
53	Oakland ■	57
53	Denver	63
66	Liberty	54
44	Tennessee Tech ■	64
57	Northern Ariz.	56
54	UNLV ■	66
52	Tex.-Pan American	58
47	New Mexico	50
57	Utah	63
74	Brigham Young ■	64
57	Colorado St.	60
76	Wyoming	83
67	San Diego St. ■	54
47	New Mexico ■	44
51	Utah	59
51	Brigham Young	67
48	Wyoming ■	51
51	Colorado St. ■	59
66	UNLV	73
47	San Diego St.	49
67	Wyoming †	69

Nickname: Falcons
Colors: Blue & Silver
Arena: Clune Arena
  Capacity: 6,002; Year Built: 1968
AD: Col. Randall Spetman
SID: Jerry Cross

AKRON
Akron, OH 44325....................I

Coach: Dan Hipsher, Bowling Green 1977

2001-02 RESULTS (10-21)
67	Iona	64
61	Monmouth †	64
59	Hampton †	67
90	Liberty †	56
64	Oakland †	71
62	William & Mary †	74
68	Western Ky. ■	78
60	Buffalo	79
66	Cleveland St. ■	79
76	Mount Union ■	70
57	Cincinnati †	73
80	Niagara ■	79
57	Ohio ■	68
60	Eastern Mich. ■	61
48	Miami (Ohio)	50
54	Kent St. ■	78
66	Ball St.	78
87	Bowling Green ■	86
83	Central Mich. ■	73
74	Ohio	73
89	Buffalo ■	81
63	Marshall	78
89	Western Mich. ■	94
72	Toledo	77
76	Eastern Mich.	83
88	Northern Ill. ■	80
46	Bowling Green	76
57	Kent St.	67
87	Marshall ■	104
90	Western Mich.	83
58	Bowling Green †	60

Nickname: Zips
Colors: Blue & Gold
Arena: James A. Rhodes Arena
  Capacity: 5,942; Year Built: 1983
AD: Michael J. Thomas
SID: Gregg Bach

ALABAMA
Tuscaloosa, AL 35487...............I

Coach: Mark Gottfried, Alabama 1987

2001-02 RESULTS (27-8)
107	Mississippi Val. ■	67
83	Samford ■	51
68	Missouri †	75
81	Memphis †	70
76	Utah ■	61
90	McNeese St. ■	61
74	Chattanooga ■	68
57	UCLA †	79
99	Jacksonville St. ■	57
70	Temple †	67
90	Alabama A&M ■	54
79	Notre Dame †	76
76	Florida A&M ■	52
93	Bethune-Cookman ■	46
76	LSU ■	74
92	Vanderbilt ■	79
56	Auburn	59
72	Georgia	72
85	Mississippi St. ■	73
64	Kentucky	61
109	Arkansas ■	94
57	LSU	48
79	Mississippi ■	59
62	Mississippi St.	76
52	South Carolina	51
95	Tennessee ■	82
59	Arkansas	67
65	Florida ■	64
73	Auburn ■	68
56	Mississippi	84

91	Tennessee †	72
65	South Carolina †	57
58	Mississippi St. †	61
86	Fla. Atlantic †	78
58	Kent St. †	71

Nickname: Crimson Tide
Colors: Crimson & White
Arena: Coleman Coliseum
   Capacity: 15,043; Year Built: 1968
AD: Mal Moore
SID: Becky Hopf

ALABAMA A&M
Normal, AL 35762 I

Coach: L. Vann Pettaway,
   Alabama A&M 1980
2001-02 RESULTS (19-10)

75	Tuskegee ■	59
75	Detroit	98
45	Mississippi St.	70
77	Athens St. ■	63
90	Jackson St.	80
88	Grambling	89
54	Alabama	90
89	Ark.-Pine Bluff ■	66
65	Mississippi Val. ■	81
63	Alabama St.	64
68	Savannah St.	57
82	Southern U.	68
82	Alcorn St.	91
92	Prairie View ■	72
73	Texas Southern ■	56
79	Morris Brown	71
92	Ark.-Pine Bluff	73
84	Mississippi Val.	72
57	Alabama St. ■	51
95	Savannah St. ■	53
80	Southern U. ■	82
91	Alcorn St. ■	86
88	Morris Brown ■	63
74	Prairie View	63
99	Texas Southern	100
105	Jackson St. ■	83
81	Grambling ■	76
114	Prairie View ■	82
61	Alabama St. †	64

Nickname: Bulldogs
Colors: Maroon & White
Arena: Elmore Health Science Building
   Capacity: 6,000; Year Built: 1973
AD: James A. Martin Sr.
SID: Ashley Balch

ALABAMA ST.
Montgomery, AL 36101-0271 I

Coach: Rob Spivery, Ashland 1972
2001-02 RESULTS (19-13)

52	Oregon	92
55	Long Beach St. †	74
43	Western Mich. †	63
61	Mobile ■	65
71	Florida A&M ■	58
64	Iowa	73
55	La Salle †	42
80	Montevallo ■	70
80	Morris Brown	67
62	Grambling	55
71	Jackson St.	63
77	Morris Brown ■	46
61	Birmingham-So.	65
57	Mississippi Val. ■	52
96	Ark.-Pine Bluff ■	73
64	Alabama A&M ■	63
61	Alcorn St.	75
67	Southern U.	57
71	Texas Southern ■	76
78	Prairie View ■	73
75	Mississippi Val.	72
68	Ark.-Pine Bluff	70
51	Alabama A&M	57

73	Alcorn St. ■	59
61	Southern U. ■	57
49	Texas Southern	64
58	Prairie View	65
82	Grambling ■	74
61	Jackson St. ■	60
60	Jackson St. ■	56
64	Alabama A&M †	61
67	Alcorn St. †	70

Nickname: Hornets
Colors: Black & Gold
Arena: Joe L. Reed Academe
   Capacity: 8,000; Year Built: 1992
AD: Robert Spivery
SID: Ronnie Johnson

UAB
Birmingham, AL 35294-0110 I

Coach: Murry Bartow, UAB 1985
2001-02 RESULTS (13-17)

79	Eastern Mich. †	66
79	Miami (Fla.) †	81
58	La Salle †	63
59	Richmond ■	60
82	Bradley ■	50
69	Murray St.	74
102	Alcorn St. ■	61
74	UNLV ■	68
76	Va. Commonwealth	82
81	Louisiana Tech ■	63
53	La Salle	56
88	Jackson St. ■	68
67	Florida A&M ■	49
77	Louisville ■	88
63	East Caro. ■	54
36	Southern Miss.	50
59	Marquette	67
71	Houston ■	80
81	Memphis	102
80	Tulane ■	63
77	TCU	71
65	South Fla.	81
64	Memphis ■	46
68	TCU ■	78
72	Tulane	83
47	St. Louis	53
83	South Fla. ■	78
66	Southern Miss. ■	56
72	Houston	76
62	South Fla. †	65

Nickname: Blazers
Colors: Forest Green & Old Gold
Arena: Bartow Arena
   Capacity: 8,500; Year Built: 1987
AD: Watson Brown
SID: Aaron Jordan

ALA.-HUNTSVILLE
Huntsville, AL 35899 II

Coach: Lennie Acuff, Shorter 1988
2001-02 RESULTS (17-9)

76	GC&SU †	75
70	Fort Valley St. †	62
68	Athens St.	61
71	Carson-Newman	87
60	Arkansas Tech	50
61	Montevallo ■	63
58	West Fla.	68
75	Athens St. ■	62
68	Tenn. Temple ■	44
84	Shorter ■	49
64	Kennesaw St.	60
94	Arkansas Tech ■	76
65	North Ala.	57
72	West Ga.	71
77	Oakland City ■	82
53	Valdosta St. ■	69
84	West Ala.	73
68	Montevallo	62
62	West Fla. ■	68

69	Lincoln Memorial	63
63	North Ala. ■	66
68	West Ga. ■	65
64	Oakland City	50
64	Valdosta St.	77
60	West Ala. ■	71
89	Lincoln Memorial ■	76

Nickname: Chargers
Colors: Royal Blue & White
Arena: Spragins Hall
   Capacity: 2,000; Year Built: 1977
AD: James E. Harris
SID: Antoine Bell

ALAS. ANCHORAGE
Anchorage, AK 99508..............II

Coach: Charlie Bruns, Eastern Wash.
   1968
2001-02 RESULTS (9-18)

66	Indiana ■	101
54	Tennessee ■	74
63	Oregon St. ■	72
78	BYU-Hawaii ■	84
73	BYU-Hawaii ■	74
76	Mo.-Rolla ■	78
70	Alas. Fairbanks	62
67	Wyoming	85
64	Angelo St. ■	78
87	Angelo St. ■	93
68	St. Martin's ■	58
79	Central Wash. ■	72
87	Western Ore.	68
72	Humboldt St.	76
67	Western Wash.	87
64	Seattle Pacific	95
73	Seattle ■	53
81	Northwest Nazarene ■	71
90	Alas. Fairbanks ■	76
88	Central Wash.	93
64	St. Martin's	97
88	Humboldt St. ■	91
110	Western Ore. ■	105
86	Seattle Pacific ■	95
70	Western Wash. ■	71
82	Northwest Nazarene	79
68	Seattle	79

Nickname: Seawolves
Colors: Green & Gold
Arena: UAA Sports Center
   Capacity: 1,450; Year Built: 1977
AD: Steve Cobb
SID: Nate Sagan

ALAS. FAIRBANKS
Fairbanks, AK 99775-7500 II

Coach: Al Sokaitis, Mass. Liberal Arts
   1976
2001-02 RESULTS (4-23)

59	Western Wash.	101
74	Evergreen St. ■	85
86	Evergreen St. ■	87
70	Washington ■	82
58	Mississippi ■	75
50	Radford ■	89
71	Southern Colo.	80
68	Northern Colo. †	93
62	Alas. Anchorage ■	70
67	UC San Diego ■	50
76	UC San Diego ■	74
67	Central Wash. ■	84
51	St. Martin's ■	70
86	Humboldt St.	93
75	Western Ore.	86
56	Seattle Pacific	81
65	Northwest Nazarene ■	80
54	Seattle ■	48
76	Alas. Anchorage	90
60	St. Martin's	66
58	Central Wash.	79
66	Western Ore. ■	82

65	Humboldt St. ■	94
71	Western Wash. ■	80
62	Seattle Pacific ■	97
74	Seattle	69
73	Northwest Nazarene	97

Nickname: Nanooks
Colors: Blue & Gold
Arena: Patty Center
   Capacity: 2,000; Year Built: 1962
AD: Jake Poole
SID: Scott Roselius

ALBANY ST. (GA.)
Albany, GA 31705 II

Coach: John Davis, Albany St. (Ga.)
   1969
2001-02 RESULTS (10-18)

62	Clayton St. ■	70
59	GC&SU ■	63
80	Lane ■	84
79	Kentucky St. ■	83
67	GC&SU	79
50	Valdosta St. ■	74
58	Ga. Southern	66
73	Clayton St.	64
77	West Ga. †	82
61	Paine	77
83	Clark Atlanta	78
73	Morehouse ■	66
67	Fort Valley St. ■	56
63	Tuskegee ■	54
75	Miles	72
59	LeMoyne-Owen	80
79	Lane	65
61	Kentucky St.	62
50	Valdosta St.	54
53	Paine ■	56
78	Clark Atlanta ■	82
57	Morehouse	78
80	Fort Valley St.	73
70	Tuskegee	71
59	Miles ■	63
73	LeMoyne-Owen ■	62
83	Lane †	62
73	Paine †	78

Nickname: Golden Rams
Colors: Blue & Gold
Arena: HPER Gym Complex
   Capacity: 4,000; Year Built: 1998
AD: John I. Davis
SID: Edythe Bradley

ALBANY (N.Y.)
Albany, NY 12222 I

Coach: Will Brown, Dowling 1993
2001-02 RESULTS (8-20)

72	Lafayette ■	80
62	Ohio St.	87
65	Quinnipiac ■	79
48	Siena	60
65	Syracuse ■	91
51	Bucknell	50
61	Yale	73
60	Army ■	68
61	Robert Morris	58
43	Vermont	71
52	Maine	59
61	Binghamton ■	69
66	Maine ■	73
41	Columbia ■	40
56	Dartmouth	77
60	New Hampshire	71
49	Boston U. ■	64
51	Northeastern ■	50
74	New Hampshire ■	57
65	Stony Brook	54
56	Binghamton	75
51	Hartford	62
61	Vermont ■	45
59	Northeastern	79

56	Boston U.	68
51	Hartford ■	48
47	Stony Brook ■	48
49	Hartford †	65

Nickname: Great Danes
Colors: Purple & Gold
Arena: Recreation & Convocation Center
 Capacity: 5,000; Year Built: 1992
AD: Lee McElroy
SID: Brian DePasquale

ALBERTUS MAGNUS
New Haven, CT 06511-1189...III

Coach: Bob McMahon, Boston U. 1976

2001-02 RESULTS (11-15)

67	Wheaton (Mass.)	71
80	Mount Ida †	88
61	Western Conn. St. ■	79
80	Newbury	87
72	Nichols	84
92	Eastern Conn. St.	87
64	Wesleyan (Conn.) ■	98
65	Framingham St.	74
72	Coast Guard ■	71
63	Westfield St. ■	75
62	Gordon	80
101	Notre Dame (N.H.) ■	61
64	Norwich	48
78	Suffolk ■	83
75	Daniel Webster	70
83	Emmanuel (Mass.) ■	75
78	Johnson & Wales	87
55	Emerson ■	53
80	Southern Vt. ■	62
58	Western New Eng. ■	80
88	Emmanuel (Mass.)	67
71	Rivier ■	60
95	Emerson	91
97	Suffolk	110
66	Johnson & Wales ■	84
55	Johnson & Wales	78

Nickname: Falcons
Colors: Royal Blue & White
Arena: Cosgrove Marcus Messer Center
 Capacity: 700; Year Built: 1989
AD: Joseph A. Tonelli
SID: Jeff Mills

ALBION
Albion, MI 49224...III

Coach: Mike Turner, Arizona 1970

2001-02 RESULTS (17-9)

56	Bluffton ■	54
65	Ohio Dominican ■	62
70	Manchester	58
70	Mich.-Dearborn †	57
65	Walsh	81
87	Madonna ■	55
71	Northwood	79
82	North Park	71
90	Buffalo St. †	59
74	Elmhurst	68
72	Dominican (Ill.) ■	45
69	Wis.-Whitewater ■	73
65	Olivet	62
70	Adrian	57
72	Kalamazoo ■	75
65	Calvin ■	57
73	Alma	58
73	Hope	78
61	Olivet ■	62
41	Adrian ■	59
62	Kalamazoo	67
65	Calvin	64
64	Alma ■	41
53	Hope ■	39
76	Adrian ■	57
61	Calvin	69

Nickname: Britons
Colors: Purple & Gold

Arena: Kresge Gymnasium
 Capacity: 1,400; Year Built: 1925
AD: Peter Hart
SID: Bobby Lee

ALBRIGHT
Reading, PA 19612-5234.........III

Coach: Rick Ferry, Susquehanna 1985

2001-02 RESULTS (4-21)

80	Col. of New Jersey	79
59	Apprentice †	100
80	Alvernia	92
74	Wilkes ■	89
48	DeSales	79
68	Frank. & Marsh.	100
80	Moravian ■	83
99	Messiah	95
83	Gwynedd-Mercy ■	71
95	Marymount (Va.) †	97
82	Endicott †	85
74	Marymount (Va.) ■	82
81	Lebanon Valley ■	100
65	Susquehanna ■	77
86	Lincoln (Pa.) ■	102
92	Juniata ■	100
62	Elizabethtown	99
70	Widener ■	100
77	Messiah ■	75
74	Moravian	86
56	Susquehanna	91
79	Lebanon Valley ■	80
62	Juniata	80
61	Widener	99
53	Elizabethtown ■	89

Nickname: Lions
Colors: Red & White
Arena: Bollman Center
 Capacity: 2,500; Year Built: 1950
AD: Sally Stetler
SID: Jim Wagner

ALCORN ST.
Alcorn State, MS 39096-7500 ...I

Coach: Davey L. Whitney, Kentucky St. 1953

2001-02 RESULTS (21-10)

72	New Mexico St.	82
82	Tougaloo ■	70
60	Southern Miss.	66
55	New Mexico	87
61	UAB	102
48	Hawaii	62
79	Prairie View	77
88	Texas Southern	83
86	Jackson St. ■	75
99	Grambling ■	87
88	Mississippi Val. ■	77
73	Ark.-Pine Bluff	65
75	Alabama St. ■	61
91	Alabama A&M ■	82
64	Morris Brown	68
86	Southern U.	69
76	UTEP	80
81	Jackson St.	78
87	Grambling	85
87	Mississippi Val. ■	86
84	Ark.-Pine Bluff ■	66
59	Alabama St.	73
86	Alabama A&M	91
87	Southern U. ■	73
92	Morris Brown ■	69
93	Texas Southern ■	86
92	Prairie View ■	77
108	Grambling ■	84
87	Texas Southern †	65
70	Alabama St. †	67
77	Siena †	81

Nickname: Braves
Colors: Purple & Gold
Arena: Davey L. Whitney Complex

 Capacity: 7,000; Year Built: 1974
AD: Robert Raines
SID: Peter G. Forest

ALDERSON-BROADDUS
Philippi, WV 26416...II

Coach: Brett Vincent, Marshall 1991

2001-02 RESULTS (22-8)

79	Roberts Wesleyan †	85
75	Nyack †	62
83	Campbellsville ■	79
75	Shaw	104
74	Campbellsville	93
92	West Liberty St. ■	84
66	Salem Int'l ■	103
86	Ohio Valley ■	71
91	Wheeling Jesuit ■	76
70	Shepherd	66
70	Pitt.-Johnstown ■	74
107	Bluefield St. ■	103
83	Pitt.-Johnstown	80
81	West Virginia St. ■	79
87	Charleston (W.Va.) ■	85
69	Concord	73
93	Fairmont St. ■	89
66	Davis & Elkins ■	61
61	West Va. Wesleyan ■	74
77	Pitt.-Johnstown	60
84	Glenville St. ■	67
77	West Va. Tech	55
99	Davis & Elkins	83
102	West Va. Wesleyan ■	96
90	Shepherd ■	81
73	Glenville St.	68
82	Fairmont St. †	78
77	Salem Int'l †	71
88	Charleston (W.Va.)	86
93	Charleston (W.Va.) †	96

Nickname: Battlers
Colors: Blue, Gray & Gold
Arena: Rex Pyles Arena
 Capacity: 2,500; Year Built: 1968
AD: Jerrell D. Long
SID: Michelle Odai

ALFRED
Alfred, NY 14802...III

Coach: Jay Murphy, Brockport St. 1981

2001-02 RESULTS (11-14)

67	Bowdoin †	81
79	D'Youville †	70
65	Hilbert	70
80	Cazenovia	71
81	Geneseo St. ■	74
70	Cortland St. ■	54
64	St. Lawrence	83
55	Le Moyne	70
77	Mercy †	66
83	St. John Fisher ■	72
94	Elmira ■	82
68	Ithaca ■	71
71	Pitt.-Bradford	82
76	Rochester Inst. ■	79
75	Hartwick	68
65	Utica	62
92	St. John Fisher	93
55	Nazareth	66
64	Rochester Inst.	70
68	Allegheny	77
72	Utica ■	60
74	Hartwick ■	63
64	Nazareth ■	66
47	Ithaca	61
79	Elmira	84

Nickname: Saxons
Colors: Purple & Gold
Arena: James A. McLane Physical
 Capacity: 3,200; Year Built: 1971
AD: James M. Moretti
SID: Mark Whitehouse

ALLEGHENY
Meadville, PA 16335...III

Coach: Phil Ness, Lafayette 1978

2001-02 RESULTS (11-14)

64	Grove City	77
72	Wash. & Jeff. †	64
64	Alma ■	58
63	Muskingum ■	46
88	Thiel	86
67	Ohio Wesleyan	77
100	Hiram ■	65
66	Wittenberg ■	72
64	Gannon	105
78	Edinboro ■	83
73	Earlham	64
72	Wabash	71
80	Kenyon	61
70	Wooster	82
63	Ohio Wesleyan ■	70
92	Hiram	80
67	Denison ■	68
63	Oberlin ■	70
61	Wittenberg	86
77	Alfred ■	68
63	Wooster ■	91
73	Kenyon ■	63
65	Oberlin	79
74	Denison	88
72	Wooster	82

Nickname: Gators
Colors: Blue & Gold
Arena: Wise Center
 Capacity: 1,000; Year Built: 1997
AD: Larry Lee
SID: Jeff Schaefer

ALMA
Alma, MI 48801...III

Coach: Kevin Skaggs, Western Mich. 1980

2001-02 RESULTS (3-22)

72	Nazareth †	81
68	Oberlin †	52
58	Allegheny	64
77	Westminster (Pa.) †	84
54	Spring Arbor ■	62
69	Aquinas	83
66	Kendall †	73
79	Cornerstone ■	84
68	Anderson (Ind.)	69
67	Grace Bible (Mich.) ■	62
66	Bethel (Ind.) ■	83
61	Adrian ■	73
78	Finlandia	63
58	Kalamazoo	68
71	Olivet ■	81
70	Hope ■	86
58	Albion ■	73
67	Calvin	76
78	Adrian	93
57	Kalamazoo ■	78
60	Olivet	62
78	Hope	82
41	Albion	64
55	Calvin ■	69
73	Hope	86

Nickname: Scots
Colors: Maroon & Cream
Arena: Cappaert Gymnasium
 Capacity: 3,000; Year Built: 1967
AD: James Cole
SID: Dave Girrard

ALVERNIA
Reading, PA 19607...III

Coach: John McCloskey, Kutztown 1964

2001-02 RESULTS (22-6)

68	Hunter ■	53
61	Staten Island ■	63
92	Albright ■	80
62	Lycoming	56
59	Kutztown ■	53
75	Lebanon Valley	64
66	Marywood ■	53
68	Eastern ■	44
89	Wesley	76
69	Delaware Valley	60
67	Gettysburg	76
66	Arcadia	46
77	Gwynedd-Mercy ■	53
62	Neumann	61
85	Cabrini	71
69	Misericordia	89
78	Wesley ■	63
65	Gwynedd-Mercy ■	68
92	Arcadia ■	62
89	Marywood	58
62	Cabrini ■	61
68	Neumann ■	65
73	Eastern	55
73	Misericordia ■	65
88	Wesley ■	50
72	Cabrini ■	81
76	Ithaca ■	67
84	Elizabethtown	95

Nickname: Crusaders
Colors: Maroon & Gold
Arena: Physical Education Center
   Capacity: 1,000; Year Built: 1987
AD: John McCloskey
SID: Jon King

AMERICAN
Washington, DC 20016 I

Coach: Jeff Jones, Virginia 1982

2001-02 RESULTS (18-12)

53	Maryland	83
55	St. Francis (Pa.)	52
55	Fairleigh Dickinson ■	48
70	Col. of Charleston ■	76
51	Pennsylvania ■	61
65	Radford	76
86	N.C. A&T	72
71	Howard	80
57	Vanderbilt	85
77	Florida St.	72
58	Wagner ■	69
94	Liberty ■	73
68	Fairfield ■	67
76	Colgate	59
58	Army ■	40
52	Lafayette ■	57
69	Bucknell ■	52
65	Lehigh	59
54	Holy Cross	63
67	Navy ■	66
72	Colgate ■	58
74	Army	59
74	Lafayette	77
78	Bucknell	67
70	Lehigh ■	67
62	Navy	50
44	Holy Cross ■	68
82	Lehigh †	69
66	Lafayette †	58
54	Holy Cross ■	58

Nickname: Eagles
Colors: AU Red & Blue
Arena: Bender Arena
   Capacity: 4,500; Year Built: 1988
AD: Tom George
SID: Shaun May

AMERICAN INT'L
Springfield, MA 01109-3189 II

Coach: Arthur Luptowski,
Bloomsburg 1973

2001-02 RESULTS (16-13)

80	Wilmington (Del.) †	56
70	West Chester	74
60	Assumption	66
64	Bryant ■	50
68	Southern Conn. St.	65
49	St. Rose	50
62	Pace	70
82	Bentley	87
72	St. Rose	70
57	Dowling	77
59	Stonehill	48
82	Merrimack ■	65
66	New Haven ■	63
75	Bryant	66
59	Assumption ■	74
53	Southern Conn. St. ■	66
68	Pace ■	56
59	Mass.-Lowell	63
77	Southern N.H. ■	78
62	Franklin Pierce	60
85	St. Anselm ■	80
78	St. Michael's	77
70	Le Moyne	61
82	Stonehill ■	67
65	Merrimack	70
73	Bentley ■	80
73	Southern Conn. St. ■	51
71	Pace	68
75	St. Anselm	89

Nickname: Yellow Jackets
Colors: Gold, White & Black
Arena: Henry A. Butova Gym
   Capacity: 2,500; Year Built: 1965
AD: Robert E. Burke
SID: George Sylvester

AMHERST
Amherst, MA 01002 III

Coach: David Hixon, Amherst 1975

2001-02 RESULTS (22-7)

116	Mass. Liberal Arts ■	57
80	Rivier ■	54
79	Vassar	68
77	Clark (Mass.)	87
75	Western New Eng.	60
75	Westfield St. †	64
74	Worcester St. ■	47
86	Embry-Riddle	93
78	Berea †	62
86	Colby-Sawyer ■	62
72	Williams ■	70
85	Wesleyan (Conn.) ■	74
45	Williams	74
69	Middlebury	76
86	Lasell	75
92	Bates ■	69
86	Tufts ■	71
107	Trinity (Conn.) ■	110
75	Salve Regina	56
73	Wesleyan (Conn.)	59
66	Connecticut Col.	73
92	Brandeis	73
85	Bowdoin ■	79
86	Colby ■	73
71	Bowdoin	61
69	Williams †	62
85	Trinity (Conn.)	78
82	Western Conn. St. ■	77
64	Brockport St.	69

Nickname: Lord Jeffs
Colors: Purple & White
Arena: LeFrak Gymnasium

Capacity: 2,450; Year Built: 1986
AD: Peter J. Gooding
SID: Kevin Graber

ANDERSON (IND.)
Anderson, IN 46012-3495 III

Coach: Denny Lehnus, Anderson 1965

2001-02 RESULTS (15-11)

90	Maryville (Mo.)	75
83	Webster †	56
75	Judson (Ill.)	79
98	Wis. Lutheran ■	82
66	Aurora ■	82
98	Defiance	104
75	Mt. St. Joseph ■	61
74	Manchester ■	76
88	Thomas More	85
69	Alma	68
70	Texas-Dallas	77
60	Neb. Wesleyan †	57
84	Bluffton	77
67	Transylvania	65
89	Franklin ■	71
74	Hanover ■	73
72	Mt. St. Joseph	80
95	Defiance ■	96
104	Thomas More ■	85
90	Manchester	99
100	Bluffton ■	78
110	Ind.-Northwest ■	54
81	Franklin	84
75	Transylvania ■	61
81	Hanover	92
69	Franklin	91

Nickname: Ravens
Colors: Orange & Black
Arena: O.C. Lewis Gym
   Capacity: 3,000; Year Built: 1962
AD: A. Barrett Bates
SID: Justin Bates

ANDERSON (S.C.)
Anderson, SC 29621 II

Coach: Doug Novak, Tennessee 1990

2001-02 RESULTS (18-10)

55	Charleston So.	62
68	Presbyterian ■	70
65	Emmanuel (Ga.)	68
76	Coker	66
72	Augusta St. †	87
86	S.C.-Aiken	77
69	Mount Olive ■	67
79	Barton	80
70	Belmont Abbey	81
95	Lees-McRae ■	66
72	Longwood	85
71	St. Andrews ■	65
83	Limestone	68
73	Queens (N.C.) ■	67
91	Pfeiffer †	81
70	Erskine ■	62
72	Coker ■	60
98	Mount Olive	90
86	Barton ■	64
91	Belmont Abbey ■	78
51	Lees-McRae	54
67	Longwood ■	64
78	St. Andrews	58
80	Limestone ■	63
72	Wingate ■	83
77	Queens (N.C.)	69
58	Limestone ■	46
58	Queens (N.C.) †	83

Nickname: Trojans
Colors: Gold & Black
Arena: Abney Athletic Center
   Capacity: 1,500; Year Built: 1979

AD: Robert G. Beville
SID: Cobb Oxford

ANGELO ST.
San Angelo, TX 76909 II

Coach: Joe Esposito, Marist 1988

2001-02 RESULTS (18-11)

70	Lake Superior St. †	79
98	Minn.-Morris †	75
88	Chadron St.	86
83	Southwest Baptist ■	72
77	Huston-Tillotson ■	70
88	Midwestern St.	89
69	Northeastern ■	71
109	Central Okla.	83
97	Hillsdale Free Will ■	54
103	S'western Adventist ■	60
78	Alas. Anchorage	64
93	Alas. Anchorage	87
68	East Central	67
80	Southeastern Okla.	102
88	Southwestern Okla.	84
79	Cameron ■	61
69	Tex. A&M-Kingsville ■	54
83	Tex. A&M-Commerce ■	71
82	West Tex. A&M	80
73	Eastern N.M.	61
105	Abilene Christian	114
60	Tarleton St.	90
85	Abilene Christian ■	56
75	Tarleton St. ■	76
84	Tex. A&M-Commerce	97
74	Tex. A&M-Kingsville	100
80	Eastern N.M. ■	86
88	West Tex. A&M	62
72	Southwestern Okla.	75

Nickname: Rams
Colors: Blue & Gold
Arena: ASU PE Building
   Capacity: 4,224; Year Built: 1973
AD: Jerry Vandergriff
SID: M.L. Stark Hinkle

ANNA MARIA
Paxton, MA 01612-1198 III

Coach: David Shea, Anna Maria 1993

2001-02 RESULTS (10-16)

95	Lyndon St. †	83
52	Williams †	90
95	Johnson & Wales ■	87
61	Worcester St.	64
80	Becker ■	64
63	Johnson St.	76
69	Me.-Farmington †	91
69	WPI	74
45	Salem St.	99
92	Newbury †	76
72	Fitchburg St. ■	82
77	Newbury	69
69	Eastern Nazarene	74
101	New England Col.	93
85	Framingham St. ■	87
70	Roger Williams ■	86
77	New England	84
57	Endicott	56
60	Salve Regina ■	70
74	Nichols	67
87	Gordon ■	75
61	Wentworth Inst.	65
66	Elms	61
63	Curry	83
65	Colby-Sawyer ■	80
54	Colby-Sawyer	86

Nickname: Amcats
Colors: Royal Blue & White
Arena: Fuller Activities Center
   Capacity: 500; Year Built: 1986

AD: Leonard Smith
SID: Joseph Brady

APPALACHIAN ST.

Boone, NC 28608 I

Coach: Houston Fancher, Middle Tenn. 1988

2001-02 RESULTS (10-18)

61	Richmond	62
93	East Caro. ■	87
107	Barton ■	61
69	Charlotte	71
66	Tennessee	97
95	Liberty ■	77
66	Clemson	76
91	North Greenville ■	44
76	TCU	110
76	UNC Asheville	79
66	East Tenn. St.	75
63	UNC Greensboro	87
89	Ga. Southern ■	101
81	Chattanooga ■	67
71	Western Caro. ■	79
78	Furman	91
91	VMI ■	93
101	Gardner-Webb ■	93
78	Citadel	74
66	Western Caro.	62
72	Davidson ■	82
81	VMI	88
55	Col. of Charleston	79
85	Wofford ■	69
62	Davidson	60
68	UNC Greensboro ■	83
72	East Tenn. St. ■	79
61	Col. of Charleston	85

Nickname: Mountaineers
Colors: Black & Gold
Arena: Holmes Convocation Center
Capacity: 8,325; Year Built: 2000
AD: Roachel Laney
SID: Kelby Siler

ARCADIA

Glenside, PA 19038-3295........III

Coach: Kevin McGeehan, Gettysburg 1995

2001-02 RESULTS (6-20)

62	Elizabethtown	93
90	East. Mennonite †	79
48	Muhlenberg	76
55	Gettysburg ■	70
53	Wesley	62
61	King's (Pa.)	85
60	Misericordia	62
58	Neumann ■	60
50	Richard Stockton ■	70
45	Widener	77
58	Eastern ■	56
46	Alvernia ■	66
70	Delaware Valley	72
51	Cabrini ■	70
77	Marywood	61
54	Gwynedd-Mercy ■	71
81	Wesley ■	76
74	DeSales ■	85
58	Neumann	81
74	Misericordia ■	83
81	Cabrini	77
62	Alvernia	92
50	Eastern	68
97	Marywood ■	62
57	Gwynedd-Mercy	80
68	Misericordia	100

Nickname: Knights
Colors: Scarlet & Gray
Arena: Kuch Center
Capacity: 1,500; Year Built: 1993
AD: Shirley M. Liddle
SID: Tom Carlin

ARIZONA

Tucson, AZ 85721-0096 I

Coach: Lute Olson, Augsburg 1956

2001-02 RESULTS (24-10)

71	Maryland †	67
75	Florida †	71
88	Texas	74
97	Kansas ■	105
87	Illinois †	82
79	Purdue †	66
60	Michigan St.	74
76	Oregon St.	73
75	Oregon	105
94	Pepperdine ■	71
74	Valparaiso ■	70
80	Oregon ■	90
93	Oregon St. ■	87
92	Washington St.	85
74	Washington	69
97	Southern California ■	80
96	UCLA ■	86
72	Arizona St.	88
98	Connecticut ■	100
68	California	58
88	Stanford	82
91	Washington ■	82
85	Washington St. ■	68
76	UCLA	77
89	Southern California	94
83	Arizona St. ■	75
71	Stanford ■	76
99	California ■	53
73	Arizona St. †	56
90	California †	78
81	Southern California †	71
86	UC Santa Barb. †	81
68	Wyoming †	60
67	Oklahoma †	88

Nickname: Wildcats
Colors: Cardinal & Navy
Arena: McKale Center
Capacity: 14,545; Year Built: 1973
AD: Jim Livengood
SID: Richard Paige

ARIZONA ST.

Tempe, AZ 85287-2505 I

Coach: Rob Evans, New Mexico St. 1968

2001-02 RESULTS (14-15)

92	Stephen F. Austin ■	61
69	Portland St. ■	79
70	Brigham Young	82
73	UC Riverside ■	64
100	Prairie View ■	62
71	Utah ■	62
72	Montana St. ■	69
90	Oregon	103
57	Oregon St.	62
77	Canisius ■	54
77	Northwestern ■	60
67	Oregon St. ■	58
95	Oregon ■	88
68	Washington	81
81	Washington St.	71
79	UCLA ■	82
73	Southern California ■	81
88	Arizona ■	72
81	Stanford	90
59	California	67
96	Washington St. ■	45
86	Washington ■	74
61	Southern California	83
69	UCLA	68
75	Arizona	83
80	California ■	91
76	Stanford ■	81
56	Arizona †	73
91	UNLV	96

Nickname: Sun Devils
Colors: Maroon & Gold
Arena: Wells Fargo Arena
Capacity: 14,198; Year Built: 1974
AD: Eugene Smith
SID: Doug Tammaro

ARKANSAS

Fayetteville, AR 72701 I

Coach: Nolan Richardson, UTEP 1965

2001-02 RESULTS (14-15)

64	Maine ■	47
71	Wake Forest ■	76
71	Oral Roberts ■	57
79	Tulsa	75
54	Oklahoma ■	69
90	Southwest Tex. St. ■	68
91	Illinois †	94
89	UNC Greensboro ■	74
98	Chattanooga ■	84
76	Oklahoma St. †	85
97	Elon ■	52
90	Memphis	73
83	Auburn	77
75	Mississippi St. ■	64
69	LSU	75
60	South Carolina ■	62
64	Mississippi ■	70
67	Georgia	81
94	Florida ■	92
94	Alabama	109
62	Auburn ■	60
67	Mississippi	79
53	Tennessee	64
63	LSU ■	67
67	Alabama ■	59
58	Kentucky	71
83	Mississippi St.	89
81	Vanderbilt ■	67
61	Tennessee †	68

Nickname: Razorbacks
Colors: Cardinal & White
Arena: Bud Walton Arena
Capacity: 19,200; Year Built: 1993
AD: J. Frank Broyles
SID: Robby Edwards

ARKANSAS ST.

State University, AR 72467.........I

Coach: Dickey Nutt, Oklahoma St. 1982

2001-02 RESULTS (15-16)

107	Central Methodist ■	75
97	Briar Cliff ■	57
109	Ark.-Pine Bluff ■	66
91	Nevada ■	61
90	Jackson St.	79
77	Mississippi Val.	79
85	Southern Miss. ■	61
63	Air Force	67
83	Mississippi St.	91
94	Mississippi Val. ■	49
68	Georgia †	80
70	Boston College †	76
77	Portland †	74
60	UMKC †	58
98	Tex. A&M-Corp. Chris.	102
78	Denver ■	58
70	North Texas ■	76
58	Ark.-Little Rock ■	78
74	South Ala.	68
57	Florida Int'l	56
65	New Orleans ■	68
64	Middle Tenn.	83
42	Western Ky.	45
63	Ark.-Little Rock	65
83	Middle Tenn. ■	51
46	Western Ky. ■	50
50	La.-Lafayette	53
59	New Mexico St.	69
64	Florida Int'l ■	54
58	Denver †	53
59	La.-Lafayette †	74

Nickname: Indians
Colors: Scarlet & Black
Arena: Convocation Center
Capacity: 10,563; Year Built: 1987
AD: Dean Lee
SID: Bill Bowen

ARKANSAS TECH

Russellville, AR 72801-2222 II

Coach: Robert Thompson, Belhaven 1992

2001-02 RESULTS (12-14)

46	Ark.-Little Rock	83
75	Oakland City ■	58
87	Lane ■	65
50	Ala.-Huntsville ■	60
63	Southeastern Okla.	74
76	Southwestern Okla.	87
92	Southwestern Okla. ■	73
73	Southeastern Okla. ■	75
82	Ozarks (Ark.) ■	70
76	Ala.-Huntsville	94
83	Christian Bros. ■	77
85	Delta St.	82
74	Ouachita Baptist ■	71
77	Ark.-Monticello	81
69	Central Ark. ■	60
61	Henderson St.	65
74	Southern Ark. ■	71
68	Harding ■	72
85	Christian Bros.	87
81	Delta St. ■	88
76	Ouachita Baptist	68
57	Ark.-Monticello ■	55
72	Central Ark.	66
71	Henderson St. ■	87
74	Southern Ark.	84
76	Harding	79

Nickname: Wonder Boys
Colors: Green & Gold
Arena: Tucker Coliseum
Capacity: 3,500; Year Built: 1976
AD: Joe Foley
SID: Larry Smith

ARK.-LITTLE ROCK

Little Rock, AR 72204.................I

Coach: Porter Moser, Creighton 1990

2001-02 RESULTS (18-11)

60	Massachusetts	66
83	Arkansas Tech ■	46
81	Mississippi St.	93
76	Ark.-Pine Bluff ■	52
83	Southeast Mo. St.	74
61	St. Louis	58
92	Central Ark. ■	57
75	Austin Peay ■	61
88	Colorado St.	79
69	Austin Peay	88
83	Morgan St. ■	56
93	Grambling	69
71	Florida Int'l	57
84	North Texas ■	74
79	Denver ■	63
78	Arkansas St.	58
72	New Orleans	73
72	South Ala. ■	65
85	Western Ky.	95
65	Middle Tenn.	68
65	Arkansas St. ■	63
79	Western Ky. ■	83
71	Middle Tenn. ■	52
73	New Mexico St.	81
58	La.-Lafayette	61
53	Southern Miss. ■	60
79	Florida Int'l ■	54
71	New Orleans	67
53	La.-Lafayette †	67

Nickname: Trojans
Colors: Maroon & Silver
Arena: Alltel Arena
  Capacity: 18,000; Year Built: 1999
AD: Chris Peterson
SID: Kevin Taukersley

ARK.-MONTICELLO
Monticello, AR 71656-3596 II

Coach: Mike Newell, Sam Houston St. 1973

2001-02 RESULTS (9-17)

55	UTEP	88
57	TCU †	100
86	Northwestern St. †	107
40	Austin Peay †	74
66	Louisiana Tech	83
63	Marshall	93
73	West Virginia	105
94	Ozarks (Ark.) ■	50
147	Rhema ■	66
79	Harding	77
76	Christian Bros.	87
67	Delta St. ■	70
58	Ouachita Baptist	82
81	Arkansas Tech ■	77
73	Central Ark.	74
64	Henderson St. ■	78
75	Southern Ark.	73
85	Harding ■	82
67	Christian Bros. ■	56
60	Delta St.	75
68	Ouachita Baptist ■	61
55	Arkansas Tech	57
119	Ark. Baptist ■	79
76	Central Ark. ■	95
75	Henderson St.	83
87	Southern Ark. ■	90

Nickname: Boll Weevils
Colors: Kelly Green & White
Arena: Steelman Fieldhouse
  Capacity: 2,600; Year Built: 1959
AD: Alvy Early
SID: Tim Munn

ARK.-PINE BLUFF
Pine Bluff, AR 71601 I

Coach: Harold Blevins, Ark.-Pine Bluff 1970

2001-02 RESULTS (2-26)

81	Colorado	98
74	Wyoming	94
66	Arkansas St.	109
52	Ark.-Little Rock	76
42	Gonzaga	92
75	Washington St.	91
43	Iowa St.	66
64	Drake	93
68	Mississippi Val.	80
49	Marquette	100
53	Mississippi	95
66	Alabama A&M	89
73	Alabama St.	96
61	Southern U. ■	66
65	Alcorn St. ■	73
63	Prairie View	76
60	Texas Southern	74
72	Grambling ■	84
81	Jackson St.	79
73	Alabama A&M ■	92
70	Alabama St. ■	68
86	Southern U.	90
66	Alcorn St.	84
83	Prairie View ■	89
70	Texas Southern ■	73
77	Grambling	91
61	Jackson St.	83
58	Mississippi Val. ■	77

Nickname: Golden Lions
Colors: Black & Gold
Arena: K.L. Johnson HPER Complex
  Capacity: 4,500; Year Built: 1982
AD: H.O. Clemmons
SID: Carl Whimper

ARMSTRONG ATLANTIC
Savannah, GA 31419-1997 II

Coach: John Marhefka, Hiram 1993

2001-02 RESULTS (13-15)

57	Presbyterian	66
59	Wingate	73
78	Francis Marion	69
50	Lander ■	53
68	Savannah St. ■	52
83	Claflin ■	63
53	Savannah St.	51
69	Carson-Newman ■	85
58	Lenoir-Rhyne	57
60	S.C.-Spartanburg ■	53
94	UNC Pembroke ■	88
56	S.C.-Aiken ■	59
79	Columbus St. ■	76
76	Francis Marion ■	55
76	S.C.-Spartanburg	64
53	GC&SU ■	54
71	UNC Pembroke ■	74
55	Augusta St.	78
76	Kennesaw St.	82
59	Clayton St.	67
71	North Fla.	74
54	Clayton St. ■	70
93	North Fla.	69
76	Columbus St.	87
53	GC&SU	75
80	Kennesaw St. ■	55
68	S.C.-Spartanburg †	60
68	Columbus St.	72

Nickname: Pirates
Colors: Maroon & Gold
Arena: Alumni Arena
  Capacity: 5,000; Year Built: 1995
AD: Eddie Aenchbacher
SID: Chad Jackson

ARMY
West Point, NY 10996-2101 I

Coach: Pat Harris, Army 1979

2001-02 RESULTS (12-16)

72	Coast Guard ■	61
74	Quinnipiac ■	66
87	Maritime (N.Y.) ■	44
49	Notre Dame	86
73	Yale	83
64	Columbia ■	69
57	Binghamton ■	69
68	Albany (N.Y.)	60
71	Stony Brook ■	60
58	Marist ■	71
93	Brown	92
65	Cornell	90
73	New Hampshire	84
69	Lehigh ■	62
40	American	58
53	Bucknell	56
85	Lafayette ■	72
57	Holy Cross ■	46
61	Navy	79
72	Colgate	82
77	Lehigh	72
59	American	74
62	Bucknell ■	65
78	Lafayette	69
57	Holy Cross	77
65	Colgate ■	82
73	Navy ■	63
59	Bucknell †	70

Nickname: Black Knights/Cadets
Colors: Black, Gold & Gray
Arena: Christl Arena
  Capacity: 5,043; Year Built: 1985
SID: Mike Albright

ASHLAND
Ashland, OH 44805 II

Coach: Roger Lyons, Ashland 1974

2001-02 RESULTS (18-9)

94	Tiffin ■	82
84	Malone	80
94	West Va. Wesleyan	77
89	Lincoln Memorial ■	79
88	Saginaw Valley	73
75	Northwood	76
84	Central Wash. †	87
63	Seattle Pacific †	76
93	Tiffin	84
109	Wilberforce ■	62
103	Lincoln Memorial ■	94
72	Northern Mich. ■	56
73	Michigan Tech ■	79
112	Lake Superior St. ■	61
75	Grand Valley St.	74
83	Ferris St.	72
92	Findlay	80
58	Wayne St. (Mich.) ■	75
85	Hillsdale	79
79	Gannon	71
69	Mercyhurst	71
75	Findlay ■	76
57	Hillsdale	68
64	Wayne St. (Mich.)	60
81	Mercyhurst ■	68
60	Gannon ■	55
76	Northwood †	84

Nickname: Eagles
Colors: Purple & Gold
Arena: Charles Kates Gym
  Capacity: 3,200; Year Built: 1967
AD: Bill Goldring
SID: Al King

ASSUMPTION
Worcester, MA 01609 II

Coach: Tom Ackerman, St. Vincent 1979

2001-02 RESULTS (24-6)

66	American Int'l ■	60
91	Teikyo Post ■	49
77	Pace	83
73	Southern Conn. St. ■	62
77	St. Rose	67
81	Southern Conn. St.	74
72	Bentley ■	70
75	Bridgeport ■	69
70	West Chester ■	60
72	Bryant	55
83	Merrimack	68
69	Stonehill	54
76	Bryant ■	70
105	New Haven	96
74	American Int'l	59
70	Pace ■	58
79	St. Rose ■	77
68	Southern N.H.	77
84	Franklin Pierce ■	73
74	Mass.-Lowell	76
89	St. Michael's ■	81
69	Le Moyne	67
79	St. Anselm ■	76
88	Merrimack ■	71
70	Bentley	82
86	Stonehill ■	67
76	St. Rose ■	69
64	Bentley ■	72
91	Pace †	73
56	Adelphi †	77

Nickname: Greyhounds
Colors: Royal Blue & White
Arena: Andrew Laska Gym
  Capacity: 3,000; Year Built: 1962
AD: Rita M. Castagna
SID: Steve Morris

AUBURN
Auburn , AL 36849-5113 I

Coach: Cliff Ellis, Florida St. 1968

2001-02 RESULTS (12-16)

63	High Point ■	59
75	Jacksonville St. ■	53
56	Rutgers	57
78	McNeese St. ■	74
67	Florida Int'l ■	55
66	Louisiana Tech ■	67
72	Virginia †	77
78	Marshall †	60
73	South Ala. ■	58
83	UNC Asheville ■	38
64	Southern Miss. ■	55
77	Arkansas ■	83
65	Mississippi	69
59	Alabama ■	56
67	Vanderbilt	73
58	LSU	75
62	Kentucky ■	69
59	Tennessee	82
64	Mississippi St. ■	72
60	Arkansas	62
75	Georgia ■	72
65	Mississippi ■	62
53	Mississippi St.	89
61	Florida	89
50	South Carolina ■	46
68	Alabama	73
54	LSU ■	59
63	Florida †	81

Nickname: Tigers
Colors: Orange & Blue
Arena: Beard-Eaves Memorial
  Capacity: 10,500; Year Built: 1969
AD: David E. Housel
SID: Chuck Gallina

AUGSBURG
Minneapolis, MN 55454 III

Coach: Brian Ammann, Augsburg 1985

2001-02 RESULTS (10-15)

77	Dakota Wesleyan †	69
75	Wis.-Eau Claire	61
90	St. Scholastica ■	72
69	Crown	46
69	Carleton ■	65
72	Concordia-M'head	79
76	Hamline ■	63
49	St. Thomas (Minn.) ■	62
64	Northwestern (Minn.) ■	81
46	Macalester	80
69	St. Mary's (Minn.) ■	72
49	St. John's (Minn.)	76
65	St. Olaf ■	86
68	Bethel (Minn.)	87
78	Gust. Adolphus ■	75
53	Carleton	78
87	Concordia-M'head ■	68
74	Hamline	63
68	Macalester ■	83
59	St. Mary's (Minn.)	54
68	St. Thomas (Minn.)	92
46	St. John's (Minn.) ■	67
70	St. Olaf	78
54	Bethel (Minn.) ■	81
56	Gust. Adolphus	76

Nickname: Auggies
Colors: Maroon & Gray
Arena: Si Melby Hall

Capacity: 2,200; Year Built: 1961
AD: Paul Grauer
SID: Don Stoner

AUGUSTA ST.
Augusta, GA 30904 II

Coach: Gary Tuell, Louisville 1973

2001-02 RESULTS (22-8)
86	West Ga. ■	79
48	Wayne St. (Mich.) †	70
113	P.R.-Mayaguez †	81
72	S.C.-Aiken	68
71	North Fla. ■	66
80	West Ga.	83
87	Anderson (S.C.) †	72
82	St. Leo †	65
77	GC&SU	73
52	Columbus St. ■	61
77	Kennesaw St.	96
80	UNC Pembroke ■	60
91	Paine †	82
72	Lander ■	67
97	Francis Marion ■	57
84	Columbus St.	72
70	Clayton St.	67
78	Armstrong Atlantic ■	55
62	S.C.-Spartanburg ■	55
78	UNC Pembroke ■	82
83	Lander	79
51	S.C.-Spartanburg	57
88	Kennesaw St. ■	71
79	Francis Marion	73
70	North Fla.	56
61	S.C.-Aiken ■	65
68	Lander †	45
69	Columbus St.	65
79	Kennesaw St. †	67
70	Johnson Smith †	73

Nickname: Jaguars
Colors: Royal Blue & White
Arena: ASU Athletic Complex
   Capacity: 2,216; Year Built: 1991
AD: Clint Bryant
SID: John Bush

AUGUSTANA (ILL.)
Rock Island, IL 61201-2296 III

Coach: Grey Giovanine, Central Mo. St.
1981

2001-02 RESULTS (17-8)
74	Coe	83
103	Beloit ■	96
71	Eastern Ill.	87
84	Rockford ■	72
80	Marycrest Int'l	90
83	St. Ambrose ■	68
83	Eureka	70
87	Mount St. Clare ■	74
89	Clarke ■	52
74	Cornell College	38
76	Central (Iowa)	68
84	North Central ■	56
85	Ill. Wesleyan	77
85	Wheaton (Ill.) ■	71
76	Millikin	78
83	Elmhurst	87
63	Carthage ■	64
80	North Central	45
92	North Park ■	70
73	Wheaton (Ill.)	80
81	Elmhurst ■	61
63	North Park	61
82	Millikin ■	79
106	Ill. Wesleyan ■	92
70	Carthage	84

Nickname: Vikings
Colors: Gold & Blue
Arena: Carver PE Center
   Capacity: 3,200; Year Built: 1971

AD: Gregory D. Wallace
SID: Dave Wrath

AUGUSTANA (S.D.)
Sioux Falls, SD 57197 II

Coach: Perry Ford, Jamestown 1978

2001-02 RESULTS (14-13)
110	Hamline ■	89
73	Concordia-St. Paul ■	56
91	Florida Tech †	74
70	Eckerd	69
109	Western St. (Colo.) ■	74
71	Southwest St. ■	74
80	North Dakota St. ■	101
59	North Dakota ■	63
87	Bellevue ■	79
73	Wayne St. (Neb.)	62
73	South Dakota	90
94	Morningside	61
82	Minn. St.-Mankato ■	69
69	St. Cloud St. ■	84
83	South Dakota St.	96
80	Northern Colo.	93
80	Neb.-Omaha ■	85
84	Morningside ■	53
78	South Dakota ■	71
68	St. Cloud St.	83
66	Minn. St.-Mankato	60
76	South Dakota St. ■	94
77	Neb.-Omaha ■	87
96	Northern Colo. ■	88
60	North Dakota	88
89	North Dakota St.	81
72	Neb.-Omaha	85

Nickname: Vikings
Colors: Navy & Yellow
Arena: Elmen Center
   Capacity: 4,000; Year Built: 1988
AD: Bill Gross
SID: Karen Madsen

AURORA
Aurora, IL 60506 III

Coach: James Lancaster, Aurora 1986

2001-02 RESULTS (18-7)
90	MacMurray †	85
49	Calvin	82
71	Carleton ■	69
89	Ind.-Northwest †	57
82	Anderson (Ind.)	66
72	Trinity Int'l ■	52
72	Millikin	67
58	Ill. Wesleyan	81
78	Beloit	84
80	Webster ■	70
91	Blackburn ■	58
78	North Central	79
65	Concordia (Ill.) ■	51
74	Benedictine (Ill.) ■	63
79	Rockford	59
79	Eureka ■	64
79	Dominican (Ill.)	62
84	Judson (Ill.)	80
76	Clarke	73
71	Benedictine (Ill.)	77
82	Rockford ■	86
65	Eureka	70
74	Dominican (Ill.) ■	67
84	Concordia (Ill.)	67
77	Clarke ■	68

Nickname: Spartans
Colors: Royal Blue & White
Arena: Thornton Gymnasium
   Capacity: 2,200; Year Built: 1970
AD: Mark Walsh
SID: Lane Stahl

AUSTIN
Sherman, TX 75090-4440 III

Coach: Chris Oestreich, St. Mary's Plains
1988

2001-02 RESULTS (11-14)
76	Texas Wesleyan ■	69
55	Mary Hardin-Baylor ■	80
69	Loyola (La.) †	77
84	S'western Assemblie †	92
57	Texas Lutheran ■	60
63	Schreiner ■	58
60	Ozarks (Ark.) ■	63
56	Marian (Wis.) ■	59
78	Huntington ■	55
81	Howard Payne ■	79
70	Sul Ross St. ■	72
60	Texas Wesleyan	77
81	Texas-Dallas ■	76
75	Dallas ■	78
74	LeTourneau	97
69	East Tex. Baptist ■	70
53	Mississippi Col. ■	71
98	Louisiana Col. ■	82
53	Mississippi Col.	64
60	Louisiana Col.	58
69	Texas-Dallas	66
74	Dallas	88
89	Ozarks (Ark.)	84
88	LeTourneau ■	78
75	East Tex. Baptist ■	62

Nickname: Kangaroos
Colors: Crimson & Gold
Arena: Hughey Gym
   Capacity: 2,000; Year Built: 1949
AD: Timothy P. Millerick
SID: Chuck Sadowski

AUSTIN PEAY
Clarksville, TN 37044-4576 I

Coach: Dave Loos, Memphis 1970

2001-02 RESULTS (14-18)
75	Marian (Ind.) ■	42
58	Oklahoma St.	81
44	Siena †	62
84	Providence †	93
74	Ark.-Monticello †	40
54	Binghamton †	51
60	Ball St.	81
61	Ark.-Little Rock	75
75	Western Ky. ■	77
88	Ark.-Little Rock ■	69
61	Dayton	76
90	Webster ■	68
68	Memphis	109
82	Eastern Ky.	70
86	Eastern Ill. ■	64
73	Western Ky.	75
65	Tenn.-Martin ■	71
68	Murray St. ■	62
67	Tennessee Tech ■	74
81	Tennessee St. ■	68
70	Eastern Ill.	73
68	Southeast Mo. St. ■	67
69	Tenn.-Martin	68
70	Eastern Ky. ■	59
65	Morehead St. ■	68
68	Murray St.	78
67	Tennessee St.	78
84	Tennessee Tech	86
51	Morehead St.	66
80	Southeast Mo. St. ■	47
72	Tenn.-Martin ■	69
77	Tennessee Tech †	86

Nickname: Governors
Colors: Red & White
Arena: Winfield Dunn Center
   Capacity: 9,092; Year Built: 1975
AD: Dave Loos
SID: Brad Kirtley

AVERETT
Danville, VA 24541 III

Coach: Kirk Chandler, Elon 1981

2001-02 RESULTS (4-22)
92	Hampden-Sydney ■	97
51	Frank. & Marsh. †	81
125	Gallaudet	113
79	Lynchburg	78
102	Emory & Henry ■	112
59	Apprentice ■	64
85	Lynchburg ■	97
58	Williams ■	85
61	Savannah A&D †	69
54	Eastern Conn. St. †	87
66	Apprentice	86
70	Ferrum ■	68
80	Shenandoah ■	100
73	Chris. Newport ■	78
75	Greensboro ■	80
72	Methodist ■	85
74	Chowan ■	92
59	N.C. Wesleyan ■	71
68	Ferrum	81
45	Shenandoah ■	74
62	Chris. Newport	86
76	Greensboro	80
61	Methodist	89
70	Chowan ■	76
87	N.C. Wesleyan ■	80
71	Chris. Newport †	96

Nickname: Cougars
Colors: Navy & Gold
Arena: Grant Center
   Capacity: 2,000; Year Built: 1998
AD: Vesa Hiltunen
SID: Sam Ferguson

BABSON
Babson Park, MA 02457-0310 .III

Coach: Steve Brennan, Bates 1987

2001-02 RESULTS (25-5)
83	Johnson & Wales ■	46
82	Plymouth St. ■	73
82	Emerson	70
78	Mount Ida	70
80	Salem St. ■	70
76	Tufts ■	63
79	Suffolk ■	65
84	Flagler	87
83	Roger Williams	54
71	Bowdoin ■	41
58	MIT	45
71	Brandeis	48
78	Coast Guard ■	42
63	Clark (Mass.)	75
84	Eastern Nazarene ■	36
69	WPI ■	41
64	Springfield ■	42
83	Wheaton (Mass.) ■	70
76	MIT ■	51
58	Coast Guard	44
90	Clark (Mass.) ■	79
62	WPI	31
50	Springfield	64
82	Wheaton (Mass.) ■	63
68	Salve Regina	66
69	WPI ■	38
72	Springfield †	56
44	Wheaton (Mass.) †	42
63	Union (N.Y.) ■	50
60	Rochester †	71

Nickname: Beavers
Colors: Green & White
Arena: Staake Gymnasium
   Capacity: 1,000; Year Built: 1989
AD: Frank Millerick
SID: Chris Buck

BALDWIN-WALLACE
Berea, OH 44017 III

Coach: Steve Bankson, Graceland 1963

2001-02 RESULTS (7-19)
89	Moravian †	94
65	Phila. Bible †	51
86	Thiel ■	78
68	Bethany (W.Va.)	75
67	Marietta	73
81	Otterbein	108
87	Muskingum ■	79
85	Wilmington (Ohio)	92
81	Heidelberg ■	82
82	Marian (Ind.) †	87
74	Illinois Col. †	91
58	Ohio Northern ■	77
89	Mount Union	84
73	Capital ■	75
68	John Carroll ■	73
72	Muskingum	65
80	Otterbein ■	90
83	Wilmington (Ohio) ■	84
68	Heidelberg	73
75	Ohio Northern	84
72	Mount Union ■	75
73	Capital	85
87	John Carroll	91
72	Marietta ■	69
77	Muskingum	66
59	Capital	83

Nickname: Yellow Jackets
Colors: Brown & Gold
Arena: Ursprung Gymnasium
  Capacity: 2,800; Year Built: 1949
AD: Stephen Bankson
SID: Kevin Ruple

BALL ST.
Muncie, IN 47306 I

Coach: Tim Buckley, Bemidji St. 1986

2001-02 RESULTS (23-12)
93	Kansas †	91
91	UCLA †	73
71	Duke †	83
106	Elon ■	65
81	Austin Peay ■	60
113	IPFW ■	89
61	Indiana	74
103	IUPUI	81
66	Butler ■	75
68	Indiana St.	54
70	Oklahoma St. †	82
54	Kent St.	81
63	Eastern Mich.	45
89	Central Mich. ■	77
68	Toledo	59
92	Bowling Green ■	79
78	Akron ■	66
74	Western Mich. ■	61
77	Miami (Ohio)	80
95	Marshall	98
90	Eastern Mich. ■	56
86	Northern Ill.	81
71	Ohio	85
87	Buffalo ■	63
81	Toledo ■	63
65	Western Mich.	80
74	Miami (Ohio) ■	58
68	Northern Ill. ■	69
81	Central Mich.	77
62	Miami (Ohio) †	50
57	Bowling Green †	69
98	South Fla. ■	92
76	St. Joseph's	54
75	LSU	65
47	South Carolina	82

Nickname: Cardinals
Colors: Cardinal & White
Arena: University Arena

Capacity: 11,500; Year Built: 1992
SID: Joe Hernandez

BARD
Annandale-On-Hudson, NY 12504-5000 III

Coach: Phil Roloson, Ulster County CC

2001-02 RESULTS (6-15)
72	Webb Inst.	51
63	Sarah Lawrence	65
81	Simon's Rock	27
55	Albany Pharmacy ■	78
73	Pratt ■	84
80	Webb Inst.	47
59	Hampshire	46
69	Polytechnic (N.Y.) ■	89
75	Albany Pharmacy	103
45	Newbury	92
71	St. Joseph's (Brkln) ■	75
54	Old Westbury	112
82	Pratt	84
53	Purchase St.	104
72	Becker ■	98
55	Cooper Union ■	62
75	Hampshire ■	59
70	St. Joseph's (Brkln) †	91
70	Cooper Union	85
64	Berkeley ■	72
66	Simon's Rock ■	40

Nickname: Raptors
Colors: White & Black
Arena: Stevenson Gym
  Capacity: 850; Year Built: 1988
AD: Kristen E. Hall
SID: Phillip Roloson

BARRY
Miami Shores, FL 33161 II

Coach: Cesar Odio, Fla. Southern 1981

2001-02 RESULTS (14-12)
84	Humboldt St. †	94
73	UC Davis	85
73	P.R.-Mayaguez ■	64
99	P.R.-Cayey	54
53	Fla. Memorial	60
82	Nova Southeastern ■	64
68	Fla. Memorial ■	64
72	Mo. Western St. †	82
77	St. Edward's ■	67
88	N.J. Inst. of Tech. ■	70
78	Nova Southeastern	57
71	Fla. Southern	60
68	Tampa	74
70	Rollins ■	60
47	Eckerd	61
73	Lynn ■	74
75	St. Leo	61
58	Florida Tech	57
52	Tampa ■	63
67	Rollins	73
60	Eckerd ■	70
68	Lynn	58
60	St. Leo	47
69	Florida Tech ■	53
59	Fla. Southern ■	71
51	Rollins †	65

Nickname: Buccaneers
Colors: Red, Black & Silver
Arena: Health & Sports Center
  Capacity: 1,500; Year Built: 1990
AD: Michael L. Covone
SID: Dennis Jezek

BARTON
Wilson, NC 27893-7000 II

Coach: Ron Lievense, St. Thomas (Minn.) 1981

2001-02 RESULTS (19-9)
80	St. Paul's	76
76	Barber-Scotia †	71
77	Virginia St.	88
61	Appalachian St.	107
84	St. Paul's ■	60
92	St. Andrews	77
76	Virginia St. ■	63
86	Limestone ■	64
80	Anderson (S.C.) ■	79
101	Pfeiffer	97
91	Erskine ■	79
80	Coker	61
95	Mount Olive ■	76
74	Queens (N.C.)	94
70	Belmont Abbey ■	81
102	Lees-McRae	83
72	Longwood ■	54
65	St. Andrews ■	47
58	Limestone	62
64	Anderson (S.C.)	86
69	Pfeiffer ■	86
70	Erskine	76
61	Coker ■	60
93	Mount Olive	67
89	Queens (N.C.) ■	76
92	Belmont Abbey ■	66
90	Pfeiffer ■	85
69	Belmont Abbey †	89

Nickname: Bulldogs
Colors: Royal Blue & White
Arena: Wilson Gym
  Capacity: 2,500; Year Built: 1966
AD: Gary W. Hall
SID: John Hackney

BARUCH
New York, NY 10010-5585 III

Coach: Ray Rankis, Lehman 1976

2001-02 RESULTS (10-9)
47	New York U.	67
56	New Paltz St.	54
75	Concordia (N.Y.)	71
68	Yeshiva ■	48
71	John Jay	59
61	Lehman ■	69
67	Western Conn. St.	86
80	Hunter ■	69
77	CCNY	91
85	Brooklyn	76
84	Staten Island	92
64	York (N.Y.)	55
77	Lehman	75
63	John Jay ■	76
95	Hunter	85
71	CCNY	79
80	John Jay †	64
64	Staten Island †	66
72	Montclair St.	77

Nickname: Bearcats
Colors: Navy Blue and Columbia Blue
Arena: Baruch College ARC Arena
  Capacity: 800; Year Built: 2002
AD: William Eng
SID: Eric John Kloiber

BATES
Lewiston, ME 04240 III

Coach: Joe Reilly, Trinity (Conn.) 1991

2001-02 RESULTS (13-11)
67	Wheaton (Mass.)	55
76	Southern Me.	78
110	New England ■	63
83	Colby-Sawyer	90
104	Thomas ■	51
81	Suffolk †	91
68	Bowdoin ■	63
57	Me.-Farmington	51
88	Eastern Nazarene	67

62	Endicott	55
78	Gordon ■	76
88	Colby ■	75
84	Wentworth Inst. ■	53
110	New England Col. ■	75
104	Tufts	111
69	Amherst	92
96	Trinity (Conn.) ■	105
53	Bowdoin	71
79	Colby	91
66	Middlebury ■	101
87	Williams ■	83
74	Connecticut Col. ■	85
74	Wesleyan (Conn.) ■	77

Nickname: Bobcats
Colors: Garnet
Arena: Alumni Gymnasium
  Capacity: 750; Year Built: 1925
AD: Suzanne R. Coffey
SID: Adam Levin

BAYLOR
Waco, TX 76798-7096 I

Coach: Dave Bliss, Cornell 1965

2001-02 RESULTS (14-16)
107	Hardin-Simmons ■	48
88	Texas-Arlington ■	64
81	Sacred Heart ■	55
92	Southern Methodist ■	90
92	Cal St. Fullerton ■	56
60	Rice	75
95	North Texas ■	81
99	Centenary (La.) ■	66
97	P.R.-Mayaguez †	58
65	Florida Int'l †	61
66	Tex.-Pan American †	72
81	TCU	92
68	Colorado St. ■	53
79	Iowa St. ■	74
57	Oklahoma St. ■	68
78	Texas	102
73	Kansas St. ■	70
60	Texas A&M	63
63	Texas ■	69
88	Colorado	95
97	Texas A&M ■	45
57	Oklahoma	70
81	Missouri ■	80
65	Texas Tech	90
72	Kansas	87
54	Oklahoma ■	65
64	Oklahoma St.	77
55	Nebraska	75
89	Texas Tech ■	91
73	Kansas St. †	74

Nickname: Bears
Colors: Green & Gold
Arena: Ferrell Center
  Capacity: 10,284; Year Built: 1988
AD: Thomas I. Stanton
SID: Heath Nielsen

BECKER
Leicester, MA 01524 III

2001-02 RESULTS (1-24)
50	Vassar	77
52	Wentworth Inst. †	65
54	Stonehill	81
74	Daniel Webster ■	94
64	Anna Maria	80
47	Gordon ■	58
71	Fitchburg St. ■	82
69	St. Joseph's (Me.)	107
51	Worcester St. †	65
68	Mount Ida	96
59	Maine Maritime	97
69	Elms ■	84
69	Lasell	109
70	Johnson St.	92

78	Eastern Nazarene	88
98	Bard	72
83	Lasell ■	108
83	Westfield St.	100
79	Elms	90
68	Maine Maritime ■	90
74	Mount Ida ■	89
84	Nichols	88
57	Framingham St. ■	69
77	Newbury ■	87
84	Elms	97

Nickname: Hawks
Colors: Royal Blue/White/Scarlet
Arena: Leicester Gymnasium
  Capacity: 500; Year Built: 1972
AD: Gene Alley
SID: Herb Whitworth

BELLARMINE
Louisville, KY 40205-0671.........II

Coach: Charlie Just, Ohio Northern
1977
2001-02 RESULTS (12-15)

70	Erskine ■	53
85	Findlay ■	93
83	SIU-Edwardsville	72
68	Lewis	84
79	St. Joseph's (Ind.) ■	68
65	Indianapolis	83
103	Mid-Continent ■	75
89	Christian Bros.	87
59	Ky. Wesleyan ■	73
78	Mercyhurst †	88
65	Western Wash. †	85
71	Mo.-St. Louis ■	63
86	Quincy	83
60	Lewis ■	80
71	Wis.-Parkside ■	53
77	Indianapolis	79
72	Northern Ky.	76
62	Ky. Wesleyan	90
94	Southern Ind.	116
77	Quincy ■	86
94	SIU-Edwardsville ■	81
72	Wis.-Parkside	59
90	St. Joseph's (Ind.)	74
73	Northern Ky. ■	95
56	Southern Ind. ■	103
81	Mo.-St. Louis ■	74
50	Lewis †	51

Nickname: Knights
Colors: Scarlet & Silver
Arena: Knights Hall
  Capacity: 3,000; Year Built: 1960
AD: Rick Bagby
SID: Shannon Satterly

BELMONT
Nashville, TN 37212-3757 I

Coach: Rick Byrd, Tennessee 1976
2001-02 RESULTS (11-17)

71	Southern Ill.	82
74	Valparaiso ■	72
37	Jacksonville	58
65	Middle Tenn. ■	59
90	Campbell ■	78
68	Georgia St. ■	59
95	Stetson	106
63	Stanford	97
78	Santa Clara †	71
72	Navy	78
55	Florida	107
75	Troy St. ■	80
87	Mercer ■	65
74	Jacksonville St.	72
66	Samford ■	60
59	UCF	76
66	Fla. Atlantic	69
78	UCF ■	86
78	Fla. Atlantic ■	80

64	Samford	62
71	Jacksonville St. ■	91
68	Mercer	81
64	Troy St.	65
79	Stetson ■	82
91	Jacksonville ■	68
69	Georgia St.	71
84	Campbell	67
79	Georgia St. †	82

Nickname: Bruins
Colors: Red, White & Navy Blue
Arena: Municipal Auditorium
  Capacity: 8,354; Year Built: 1962
AD: Michael D. Strickland
SID: Matt Wilson

BELMONT ABBEY
Belmont, NC 28012-1802 II

Coach: Darren Metress, Belmont Abbey
1988
2001-02 RESULTS (25-6)

67	Benedict †	62
72	Paine	69
60	Johnson Smith	79
70	Wingate ■	69
72	Longwood	67
70	Col. of Charleston	67
94	Francis Marion ■	47
91	St. Andrews	66
82	Limestone	57
81	Anderson (S.C.) ■	70
82	Pfeiffer ■	64
60	Erskine	67
74	Coker	59
78	Mount Olive	63
81	Barton ■	70
78	Queens (N.C.) ■	83
116	Lees-McRae	73
95	Longwood ■	67
75	St. Andrews	56
92	Limestone ■	56
78	Anderson (S.C.)	91
97	Pfeiffer	84
76	Erskine ■	56
80	Coker ■	62
106	Mount Olive ■	56
66	Barton	92
72	Coker ■	48
89	Barton †	69
78	Queens (N.C.) †	60
76	West Va. Wesleyan †	59
69	Salem Int'l †	75

Nickname: Crusaders
Colors: Red & White
Arena: The Wheeler Center
  Capacity: 1,500; Year Built: 1971
AD: Eliane Kebbe
SID: Matt Kline

BELOIT
Beloit, WI 53511-5595 III

Coach: Cecil Youngblood,
Augustana (Ill.) 1976
2001-02 RESULTS (13-10)

80	Chicago	70
56	Ohio Northern †	68
96	Augustana (Ill.)	103
80	Carroll (Wis.) ■	69
58	Rockford	50
74	Lawrence	68
84	Aurora ■	78
87	Goucher †	70
73	Virgin Islands	68
74	St. Norbert ■	83
66	Ripon	74
96	Lake Forest ■	81
74	Monmouth (Ill.)	78
113	Grinnell ■	106
72	Illinois Col.	68
91	Knox	87

126	Grinnell	139
59	Carroll (Wis.)	65
69	Monmouth (Ill.) ■	68
60	Lake Forest	58
80	Ripon ■	81
79	Lawrence	89
66	St. Norbert	75

Nickname: Buccaneers
Colors: Navy Blue & Gold
Arena: Flood Arena
  Capacity: 2,250; Year Built: 1986
AD: Edward J. DeGeorge
SID: Keith Domke

BEMIDJI ST.
Bemidji, MN 56601-2699.........II

Coach: Jeff Guiot, Pittsburg St.
2001-02 RESULTS (17-11)

89	Mayville St.	80
57	St. Cloud St.	85
78	North Dakota ■	89
87	Bethel (Minn.) ■	94
89	Finlandia	83
76	Michigan Tech	90
77	Wayne St. (Neb.) ■	75
66	Southwest St. ■	63
66	Northern Mich. ■	72
71	Valley City St. ■	69
94	Minn.-Crookston	92
66	Minn. St. Moorhead	76
82	Minn.-Duluth ■	80
84	Minn.-Morris ■	54
69	Northern St. ■	93
47	Winona St.	60
80	Concordia-St. Paul	77
81	Southwest St.	84
77	Wayne St. (Neb.) ■	68
71	Minn. St. Moorhead ■	59
71	Minn.-Crookston ■	62
61	Minn.-Duluth	57
79	Northern St.	76
78	Minn.-Morris	60
91	Concordia-St. Paul ■	76
65	Winona St. ■	85
70	Winona St. ■	69
58	Minn.-Duluth †	69

Nickname: Beavers
Colors: Kelly Green & White
Arena: BSU Gymnasium
  Capacity: 2,000; Year Built: 1959
AD: Rick Goeb
SID: Andy Bartlett

BENEDICTINE (ILL.)
Lisle, IL 60532-0900 III

Coach: Keith Bunkenburg,
Benedictine (Ill.) 1989
2001-02 RESULTS (13-12)

79	St. Scholastica †	69
82	Loras	65
74	Siena Heights †	84
76	Puget Sound †	72
87	Schreiner †	81
56	Ill. Wesleyan	84
86	North Central	92
72	Trinity Int'l	55
69	Elmhurst ■	78
69	Concordia (Wis.) ■	77
57	Chicago	63
63	Aurora	74
74	Clarke ■	55
47	Eastern Ill.	77
78	Dominican (Ill.) ■	70
85	Eureka	54
58	Rockford ■	67
64	Concordia (Ill.)	62
77	Aurora ■	71
60	Clarke	74
63	Lakeland	66
60	Dominican (Ill.)	64

80	Eureka ■	71
62	Rockford	61
72	Concordia (Ill.) ■	43

Nickname: Eagles
Colors: Cardinal & White
Arena: Dan & Ada Rice Center
  Capacity: 2,000; Year Built: 1976
AD: John Ostrowski
SID: Jill Redmond

BENTLEY
Waltham, MA 02154-4705.......II

Coach: Jay Lawson, New Hampshire
1979
2001-02 RESULTS (20-10)

70	Adelphi ■	72
79	Merrimack	69
101	Stonehill	56
90	Le Moyne ■	79
82	St. Michael's	66
89	St. Anselm ■	75
87	American Int'l ■	82
70	Assumption	72
68	New Haven †	63
67	St. Rose	84
95	St. Anselm	90
89	Bryant ■	64
80	Le Moyne	77
91	St. Michael's ■	78
73	New Haven ■	77
87	Merrimack ■	70
91	Stonehill ■	71
68	St. Rose	60
79	Southern Conn. St.	67
74	Pace	83
79	Franklin Pierce ■	84
85	Southern N.H. ■	84
51	Mass.-Lowell ■	76
56	Bryant	59
82	Assumption ■	70
80	American Int'l	73
88	Southern N.H.	74
72	Assumption	64
78	St. Anselm ■	72
70	Mass.-Lowell †	72

Nickname: Falcons
Colors: Blue & Gold
Arena: Charles Dana PE Center
  Capacity: 2,600; Year Built: 1973
AD: Robert DeFelice
SID: Dick Lipe

BETHANY (W.VA.)
Bethany, WV 26032-0417 III

Coach: Rob Clune, Albany (N.Y.) 1981
2001-02 RESULTS (21-8)

92	Gwynedd-Mercy †	72
84	York (Pa.)	90
74	La Roche	71
75	Baldwin-Wallace ■	68
88	Notre Dame (Ohio) ■	59
108	Wheeling Jesuit	100
95	Ohio-Eastern †	87
80	Frostburg St. ■	89
97	Kenyon	98
103	Carroll (Wis.) †	75
76	Embry-Riddle	115
71	Colgate	102
72	Apprentice ■	87
77	Penn St.-Altoona	73
78	Westminster (Pa.)	77
90	Wash. & Jeff. ■	66
82	Waynesburg ■	71
83	Thiel	73
58	Grove City	50
85	Westminster (Pa.) ■	68
111	Pitt.-Greensburg ■	86
82	Wash. & Jeff.	78
88	Waynesburg	89
75	Thiel ■	59

96	Grove City ■	91
88	Waynesburg ■	78
89	Grove City ■	74
110	Pitt.-Bradford	98
98	Otterbein	121

Nickname: Bison
Colors: Kelly Green & White
Arena: Hummel Field House
Capacity: 1,400; Year Built: 1948
AD: Janice L. Forsty
SID: Brian Rose

BETHEL (MINN.)
St. Paul, MN 55112-6999 III

Coach: Bob Bjorklund, Minnesota 1973

2001-02 RESULTS (21-6)

109	Mt. Senario ■	33
75	Northwestern (Minn.) ■	73
94	Bemidji St.	87
71	St. Thomas (Minn.)	79
61	Macalester ■	65
84	Martin Luther	74
83	St. Mary's (Minn.) ■	71
90	St. Olaf ■	57
78	St. John's (Minn.)	63
55	Carleton	50
88	Hamline	75
66	Gust. Adolphus ■	70
87	Augsburg ■	68
75	Concordia-M'head	65
73	St. Thomas (Minn.) ■	50
59	Macalester	74
67	St. Olaf	52
75	St. John's (Minn.) ■	64
76	St. Mary's (Minn.)	72
93	Carleton ■	57
90	Hamline ■	74
66	Gust. Adolphus	68
81	Augsburg	54
86	Concordia-M'head ■	66
72	Carleton	53
66	Gust. Adolphus	59
61	St. Thomas (Minn.)	73

Nickname: Royals
Colors: Blue & Gold
Arena: Robertson PE Center
Capacity: 2,000; Year Built: 1971
AD: David Klostreich
SID: Greg Peterson

BETHUNE-COOKMAN
Daytona Beach, FL 32114-3099.I

Coach: Horace Broadnax, Georgetown 1986

2001-02 RESULTS (12-17)

81	Iona ■	74
77	Florida A&M ■	98
73	La.-Lafayette	83
61	Georgetown	91
69	Md.-East. Shore	55
55	South Ala.	68
65	Oklahoma	102
46	Alabama	93
75	South Carolina St. ■	78
75	N.C. A&T ■	67
65	Savannah St.	52
66	Delaware St.	86
66	Howard	73
60	Canisius ■	53
96	Coppin St. ■	72
64	Morgan St. ■	66
69	Hampton ■	85
58	Norfolk St.	67
76	Md.-East. Shore ■	70
61	South Carolina St.	59
60	N.C. A&T	62
56	Delaware St. ■	67
72	Howard ■	69
99	South Ala. ■	104
83	Morgan St.	72
64	Coppin St.	80

57	Florida A&M	53
82	Md.-East. Shore †	70
52	Howard †	71

Nickname: Wildcats
Colors: Maroon & Gold
Arena: Moore Gymnasium
Capacity: 3,000; Year Built: 1953
AD: Lynn Thompson
SID: Charles D. Jackson

BINGHAMTON
Binghamton, NY 13902-6000....I

Coach: Al Walker, Brockport St. 1981

2001-02 RESULTS (9-19)

49	Dartmouth ■	46
56	Syracuse	103
52	George Washington	69
53	Stony Brook †	51
54	Oral Roberts ■	70
51	Austin Peay †	54
70	Elon †	77
69	Army	57
60	North Carolina	61
60	Stony Brook	52
66	Hartford ■	68
65	Quinnipiac ■	89
69	Albany (N.Y.)	61
50	Boston U.	62
94	Northeastern	76
62	Stony Brook ■	66
60	Maine	83
81	Northeastern ■	64
53	Boston U. ■	55
58	Colgate ■	62
69	Maine	80
69	New Hampshire	79
75	Albany (N.Y.) ■	56
80	Vermont ■	83
71	Vermont	86
63	Hartford	88
67	St. Francis (N.Y.)	71
85	New Hampshire ■	67

Nickname: Bearcats
Colors: Green & Black
Arena: West Gym
Capacity: 2,275; Year Built: 1970
AD: Joel Thirer
SID: John Hartrick

BIRMINGHAM-SO.
Birmingham, AL 35254 I

2001-02 RESULTS (13-14)

62	Southeast Mo. St.	51
52	Jacksonville St. ■	63
69	Stetson ■	82
53	Winthrop	67
34	Butler	70
62	Florida St.	78
71	Texas Col. ■	59
72	La.-Lafayette	84
65	Elon ■	58
77	Sewanee ■	43
55	Idaho St. †	59
38	Centenary (La.) †	56
65	Alabama St. ■	61
83	Liberty ■	65
74	High Point ■	57
65	Fla. Atlantic ■	59
67	Coastal Caro.	74
44	Charleston So.	71
47	Savannah St.	44
62	Charleston So. ■	60
60	Elon	67
68	High Point	65
56	Winthrop ■	63
88	Coastal Caro. ■	80
61	East Caro.	73
66	Liberty	70
82	Savannah St. ■	47

Nickname: Panthers

Colors: Black & Gold
Arena: Bill Battle Coliseum
Capacity: 1,800; Year Built: 1980
AD: Joe Dean Jr.
SID: Jason Falls

BLACKBURN
Carlinville, IL 62626 III

Coach: Joe Ramsey, Southern Ill. 1965

2001-02 RESULTS (14-11)

68	Purdue-Calumet †	82
82	Ind.-Northwest †	51
75	Millikin ■	73
71	Illinois Col.	82
75	Mt. St. Joseph †	74
62	Rockford	61
68	Hannibal-La Grange	44
88	Iowa Wesleyan ■	82
76	Eureka ■	62
58	Aurora	91
55	Washington (Mo.) ■	71
90	Fontbonne ■	85
63	Westminster (Mo.)	62
81	Greenville ■	85
69	Principia ■	52
62	MacMurray ■	65
58	Webster ■	66
68	Maryville (Mo.) ■	52
69	Fontbonne	75
74	Westminster (Mo.) ■	64
82	Greenville	86
70	Principia	65
70	MacMurray ■	66
56	Webster	59
47	Maryville (Mo.)	56

Nickname: Battlin' Beavers
Colors: Scarlet & Black
Arena: Dawes Gymnasium
Capacity: 500; Year Built: 1938
AD: Joe Ramsey
SID: Matt Patterson

BLOOMSBURG
Bloomsburg, PA 17815 II

Coach: Charles Chronister, East Stroudsburg 1963

2001-02 RESULTS (14-14)

74	Calif. (Pa.) †	80
62	Daemen †	59
67	Pitt.-Johnstown ■	62
89	New Haven ■	83
78	Lock Haven	58
56	Clarion	68
60	New Haven	77
85	Dist. Columbia ■	72
83	Shippensburg ■	73
73	Indiana (Pa.) ■	95
77	Pitt.-Johnstown	85
65	Slippery Rock	43
69	Edinboro	84
74	Cheyney	72
77	Calif. (Pa.) †	82
70	Kutztown	61
65	West Chester	73
82	East Stroudsburg ■	69
90	Mansfield ■	82
77	Millersville ■	89
69	Cheyney ■	71
64	Kutztown ■	62
65	Mansfield	71
77	East Stroudsburg	63
71	Millersville	76
70	West Chester ■	81
60	West Chester	54
66	Calif. (Pa.) †	68

Nickname: Huskies
Colors: Maroon & Gold
Arena: E.H. Nelson Fieldhouse
Capacity: 3,000; Year Built: 1972
AD: Mary Gardner
SID: Tom McGuire

BLUEFIELD ST.
Bluefield, WV 24701-2198 II

Coach: Terry Brown, Bluefield St. 1975

2001-02 RESULTS (3-23)

70	Cumberland (Ky.) †	115
73	Five Towns †	74
89	Mount Olive ■	106
81	Concord ■	78
66	Gardner-Webb	101
69	Salem Int'l	98
98	Wheeling Jesuit	120
83	Fairmont St. ■	89
99	West Virginia St.	106
82	Concord ■	101
72	Charleston (W.Va.) ■	98
80	Ohio Valley	66
103	Alderson-Broaddus ■	107
63	West Va. Wesleyan ■	94
74	Shepherd	84
78	Glenville St.	89
90	West Va. Tech.	110
69	Fairmont St.	89
84	Wheeling Jesuit ■	88
96	West Liberty St. ■	105
70	Concord	74
102	Davis & Elkins ■	87
71	West Va. Tech ■	82
89	West Virginia St. ■	104
74	Charleston (W.Va.)	130
92	Salem Int'l	116

Nickname: Big Blues
Colors: Blue & Gold
Arena: Ned Shott Gymnasium
Capacity: 1,500; Year Built: 1969
AD: Terry W. Brown
SID: Terry Brown

BLUFFTON
Bluffton, OH 45817-1196 III

Coach: Guy Neal, Bowling Green 1982

2001-02 RESULTS (10-16)

54	Albion	56
84	Concordia (Mich.) †	67
64	Earlham ■	62
53	Manchester	83
51	Hanover ■	74
67	Adrian ■	77
55	Mt. St. Joseph	66
85	Denison	65
90	Hiram †	67
85	Heidelberg	83
68	Bridgewater (Va.) ■	92
85	Millikin ■	82
82	Franklin	94
77	Anderson (Ind.) ■	84
93	Thomas More ■	90
61	Transylvania ■	64
94	Defiance	100
50	Hanover	95
93	Manchester ■	99
96	Mt. St. Joseph ■	90
78	Anderson (Ind.)	100
93	Franklin ■	97
87	Transylvania	78
106	Defiance ■	103
80	Thomas More	88
90	Defiance	91

Nickname: Beavers
Colors: Royal Purple & White
Arena: Founders Hall
Capacity: 1,500; Year Built: 1952
AD: Carlin B. Carpenter
SID: Tim Stried

BOISE ST.
Boise, ID 83725-1020 I

Coach: Rod Jensen, Redlands 1975

2001-02 RESULTS (13-17)

53	Portland St. ■	60
49	Utah	64
68	Idaho ■	59
42	Eastern Wash. ■	47
70	Idaho	44
76	Lewis-Clark St. ■	64
59	San Diego	85
77	Wyoming ■	74
67	Southern Utah ■	49
55	Northern Ariz. ■	44
67	Southern Methodist	80
36	Louisiana Tech	59
61	San Jose St. ■	52
62	Hawaii ■	64
62	Rice	59
60	Tulsa	80
56	Fresno St. ■	72
64	Nevada ■	73
51	UTEP	72
56	Hawaii	67
51	San Jose St.	62
56	Tulsa ■	70
78	Rice ■	62
86	Nevada	94
61	Fresno St.	58
81	UTEP ■	72
67	Louisiana Tech ■	80
80	Southern Methodist ■	63
73	UTEP †	72
53	Tulsa	72

Nickname: Broncos
Colors: Orange & Blue
Arena: Pavilion
  Capacity: 12,200; Year Built: 1982
AD: Gene Bleymaier
SID: Brad Larrondo

BOSTON COLLEGE
Chestnut Hill, MA 02467-3861 ..I

Coach: Al Skinner, Massachusetts 1974

2001-02 RESULTS (20-12)

82	Boston U. ■	65
80	New Hampshire ■	77
88	Penn St. ■	65
96	St. Bonaventure †	82
83	Michigan	74
90	Morris Brown ■	65
80	Massachusetts ■	78
86	Iowa St.	81
75	Holy Cross ■	51
67	Miami (Ohio) †	73
76	Arkansas St. †	70
67	Holy Cross †	57
81	Seton Hall	66
74	Pittsburgh ■	77
88	Villanova	81
43	Georgetown ■	70
57	St. John's (N.Y.) ■	64
77	Virginia Tech ■	68
78	Duke ■	88
70	Miami (Fla.)	65
61	Providence	64
73	Virginia Tech	76
76	Miami (Fla.) ■	63
89	Providence ■	79
77	Connecticut	79
62	St. John's (N.Y.)	71
69	Villanova ■	67
61	Connecticut ■	75
69	Syracuse	65
60	Rutgers †	55
62	Pittsburgh †	76
57	Texas †	70

Nickname: Eagles
Colors: Maroon & Gold
Arena: Silvio O. Conte Forum
  Capacity: 8,606; Year Built: 1988
AD: Gene DeFilippo
SID: Mike Enright

BOSTON U.
Boston, MA 02215 I

Coach: Dennis Wolff, Connecticut 1978

2001-02 RESULTS (22-10)

69	New Orleans †	63
61	Iowa	90
65	Boston College	82
70	St. Peter's ■	58
76	George Washington	79
61	Holy Cross	49
51	Harvard ■	41
47	Columbia	68
79	Dartmouth ■	58
62	Providence	68
79	Wis.-Green Bay	75
71	UC Irvine †	77
70	New Hampshire	65
65	Vermont ■	74
70	Hartford	56
62	Binghamton ■	50
90	Stony Brook ■	54
95	Northeastern	88
64	Albany (N.Y.)	49
55	Binghamton	53
42	Hartford ■	44
85	Vermont	89
61	Maine	59
63	New Hampshire ■	56
63	Northeastern ■	57
68	Albany (N.Y.) ■	56
64	Stony Brook	62
72	Maine ■	61
86	Northeastern †	76
63	Hartford ■	60
66	Maine ■	40
52	Cincinnati †	90

Nickname: Terriers
Colors: Scarlet & White
Arena: Case Gym
  Capacity: 1,800; Year Built: 1971
AD: Gary Strickler
SID: Stephan Lemon

BOWDOIN
Brunswick, ME 04011 III

Coach: Tim Gilbride, Providence 1974

2001-02 RESULTS (16-9)

81	Alfred †	67
67	Rochester	85
93	New England ■	63
61	Southern Me.	59
72	Suffolk ■	60
105	Thomas ■	37
63	Bates	68
67	Norwich	52
41	Babson	71
71	Colby-Sawyer ■	77
76	Plymouth St. ■	64
80	Colby	48
79	Wesleyan (Conn.)	87
75	Connecticut Col.	74
58	Maine Maritime	48
76	Middlebury ■	71
84	Williams ■	54
86	St. Joseph's (Me.) ■	74
71	Bates ■	53
68	Colby ■	78
64	Me.-Farmington ■	57
79	Amherst	85
57	Trinity (Conn.)	82
61	Amherst	71

Nickname: Polar Bears
Colors: White
Arena: Morrell Gymnasium
  Capacity: 2,000; Year Built: 1965
AD: Jeffrey H. Ward
SID: Jac Coyne

BOWIE ST.
Bowie, MD 20715-9465 II

Coach: Luke D'Alessio, Catholic 1983

2001-02 RESULTS (20-8)

82	Dist. Columbia	85
90	Winston-Salem ■	83
84	St. Augustine's	101
87	St. Mary's (Md.)	64
125	Washington Bible ■	60
101	Livingstone ■	90
95	St. Paul's	81
98	Shepherd ■	85
82	Fairmont St. †	67
83	Wheeling Jesuit	85
88	Virginia St. ■	78
81	N.C. Central	88
64	Fayetteville St.	68
77	Shaw	86
91	Johnson Smith	89
89	Columbia Union ■	83
90	Virginia Union ■	75
96	Elizabeth City St.	90
84	Pitt.-Johnstown ■	71
78	Virginia Union	77
89	Columbia Union	83
94	Shaw ■	77
81	Virginia St.	72
94	St. Paul's ■	75
65	Cheyney	70
95	Elizabeth City St. ■	89
66	Fayetteville St. †	63
67	Johnson Smith †	84

Nickname: Bulldogs
Colors: Black & Gold
Arena: A.C. Jordan Arena
  Capacity: 4,000; Year Built: 1973
AD: Charles Davis
SID: Scott Rouch

BOWLING GREEN
Bowling Green, OH 43403........I

Coach: Dan Dakich, Indiana 1985

2001-02 RESULTS (24-9)

82	Mississippi †	78
74	Washington †	81
73	Delaware †	70
107	Defiance ■	80
65	Michigan	59
61	Marist ■	58
64	Duquesne	62
84	UNC Wilmington ■	83
84	Evansville	72
77	Detroit	60
65	Indiana St.	55
82	Central Mich.	81
91	Northern Ill. ■	61
85	Buffalo	73
79	Ball St.	92
76	Toledo ■	57
86	Akron	87
67	Kent St. ■	70
78	Western Mich.	66
64	Miami (Ohio) ■	61
64	Kent St.	76
80	Ohio ■	64
83	Marshall ■	60
82	Eastern Mich. ■	61
62	Toledo	66
65	Miami (Ohio)	50
76	Akron ■	46
73	Buffalo ■	58
78	Ohio	85
60	Akron †	58
69	Ball St. †	57
59	Kent St. †	70
69	Butler	81

Nickname: Falcons
Colors: Orange & Brown
Arena: Anderson Arena

Capacity: 5,000; Year Built: 1960
AD: Paul Krebs
SID: J.D. Campbell

BRADLEY
Peoria, IL 61625 I

Coach: Jim Molinari, Ill. Wesleyan 1977

2001-02 RESULTS (9-20)

63	La.-Lafayette ■	41
84	Western Ill.	69
50	UAB	82
50	Southern California ■	60
60	Texas-Arlington ■	61
61	Northern Iowa ■	67
42	La.-Lafayette ■	43
87	Hampton	84
46	Weber St. †	68
67	Sam Houston St. †	77
64	Wichita St.	70
68	Drake ■	65
64	Southwest Mo. St.	60
55	Evansville	60
49	Southern Ill. ■	55
63	Creighton	76
55	Illinois St. ■	58
66	Wichita St. ■	49
60	Indiana St. ■	57
67	Northern Iowa	81
51	Illinois St.	60
67	Evansville ■	62
66	Indiana St.	71
54	Drake	68
49	Southwest Mo. St. ■	51
64	Creighton ■	80
73	Southern Ill.	84
70	Indiana St. †	58
44	Southern Ill. †	66

Nickname: Braves
Colors: Red & White
Arena: Carver Arena
  Capacity: 11,300; Year Built: 1982
AD: Kenneth E. Kavanagh
SID: Bobby Parker

BRANDEIS
Waltham, MA 02454-9110 III

Coach: Chris Ford

2001-02 RESULTS (8-17)

74	Endicott ■	80
92	Nichols ■	89
94	Wheaton (Mass.) ■	56
54	Clark (Mass.)	98
76	WPI ■	58
75	Suffolk	79
81	Emerson ■	76
88	Carnegie Mellon ■	87
63	Rochester ■	73
48	Babson ■	71
55	New York U.	64
80	Tufts	92
60	Chicago	73
55	Washington (Mo.)	102
63	Middlebury ■	60
86	Case Reserve ■	65
63	Emory	64
60	Emory	77
88	Case Reserve	70
59	Rochester	67
72	Carnegie Mellon	76
73	Amherst	92
71	Washington (Mo.) ■	95
77	Chicago ■	86
64	New York U. ■	66

Nickname: Judges
Colors: Blue & White
Arena: Auerbach Arena
  Capacity: 2,500; Year Built: 1992
AD: Jeffrey W. Cohen
SID: Jack Molloy

BRIDGEPORT
Bridgeport, CT 06601 II

Coach: Mike Ruane, Alvernia 1992

2001-02 RESULTS (14-14)
64	Green Mountain ■	47
61	Southern N.H. ■	77
76	Molloy ■	61
79	NYIT	84
72	Philadelphia U. ■	70
79	Mercy ■	59
69	Assumption	75
68	St. Vincent †	64
84	Dowling ■	66
78	Southampton	86
84	Concordia (N.Y.) ■	78
59	Adelphi ■	78
60	St. Thomas Aquinas	66
64	C.W. Post	81
55	Molloy	52
53	NYIT ■	59
53	Philadelphia U.	67
64	Queens (N.Y.) ■	74
57	Mercy	50
67	Dowling	74
77	Southampton ■	61
68	Concordia (N.Y.)	60
63	Adelphi	80
67	St. Thomas Aquinas ■	53
57	Queens (N.Y.)	61
84	C.W. Post ■	75
66	Philadelphia U.	61
70	Queens (N.Y.) †	88

Nickname: Purple Knights
Colors: Purple & White
Arena: Harvey Hubbell Gym
  Capacity: 2,000; Year Built: 1963
AD: Joseph DiPuma
SID: Mike Ruane

BRIDGEWATER (VA.)
Bridgewater, VA 22812-1599 ...III

Coach: Bill Leatherman, Milligan 1966

2001-02 RESULTS (17-9)
61	Dallas †	54
66	Howard Payne †	76
87	Villa Julie	72
61	Randolph-Macon	75
74	Christendom ■	48
78	Ferrum	67
77	Wash. & Lee ■	55
92	Bluffton	68
103	Ohio Dominican †	96
78	East. Mennonite	54
62	Hampden-Sydney	65
65	Lynchburg ■	50
47	Va. Wesleyan	69
87	Emory & Henry	69
92	Guilford ■	80
99	Roanoke ■	107
84	East. Mennonite ■	63
66	Hampden-Sydney ■	62
86	Lynchburg	65
80	Roanoke	64
57	Guilford	66
91	Emory & Henry ■	81
61	Randolph-Macon ■	74
71	Va. Wesleyan ■	76
73	Wash. & Lee	53
60	Roanoke †	67

Nickname: Eagles
Colors: Cardinal & Vegas Gold
Arena: Nininger Hall
  Capacity: 1,200; Year Built: 1957
AD: Curtis L. Kendall
SID: Steve Cox

BRIDGEWATER ST.
Bridgewater, MA 02325-9998 ..III

Coach: Joe Farroba, Boston St. 1976

2001-02 RESULTS (11-16)
78	Newbury †	67
83	Eastern Nazarene ■	66
82	Mass.-Dartmouth	90
66	Wheaton (Mass.) ■	71
66	Wentworth Inst.	55
86	Emmanuel (Mass.)	80
86	Plymouth St.	93
50	Stonehill	65
57	Eastern Nazarene †	60
85	Curry ■	80
53	Westfield St.	65
71	Rhode Island Col. ■	73
63	Framingham St. ■	61
77	Mass. Liberal Arts	74
70	Mass.-Boston ■	75
57	Worcester St.	66
62	Salem St. ■	71
70	Fitchburg St. ■	52
70	Westfield St. ■	63
62	Salve Regina	71
52	Framingham St.	51
76	Mass. Liberal Arts ■	83
55	Worcester St. ■	57
73	Salem St.	92
52	Fitchburg St.	56
72	Worcester St.	69
52	Salem St.	76

Nickname: Bears
Colors: Crimson & White
Arena: Dr. Adrian Tinsley Center
  Capacity: 1,000; Year Built: 2002
AD: John C. Harper
SID: Mike Holbrook

BRIGHAM YOUNG
Provo, UT 84602 I

Coach: Steve Cleveland, UC Irvine 1976

2001-02 RESULTS (18-12)
70	San Diego	59
82	Arizona St. ■	70
58	UC Santa Barb.	68
81	Utah St.	90
65	Weber St. ■	47
61	Creighton ■	52
101	Fort Lewis ■	53
70	Idaho ■	48
81	Stanford †	76
84	Cal St. Northridge ■	70
79	Southern Utah ■	58
65	San Francisco ■	51
79	Pepperdine	82
75	San Diego St. ■	64
60	UNLV ■	47
58	New Mexico	73
64	Air Force	74
66	Utah	71
85	Wyoming ■	70
57	Colorado St. ■	52
70	UNLV	73
73	San Diego St.	77
68	New Mexico ■	62
67	Air Force ■	51
63	Utah ■	61
60	Wyoming	76
75	Colorado St.	79
51	San Diego St. †	62
78	UC Irvine ■	55
69	Memphis	80

Nickname: Cougars
Colors: Blue, White & Tan
Arena: Marriott Center
  Capacity: 22,700; Year Built: 1971
AD: Q. Val Hale
SID: Brett Pyne

BYU-HAWAII
Laie, HI 96762-1294 II

Coach: Ken Wagner, Brigham Young 1979

2001-02 RESULTS (19-10)
90	UC Davis	86
84	Humboldt St. †	119
87	Cal St. Chico	80
63	Cal St. San B'dino ■	75
85	Metro St.	70
84	Alas. Anchorage	78
89	Mo.-Rolla †	79
74	Alas. Anchorage	73
97	Montana St.-Northern ■	86
104	Lincoln (Mo.) ■	105
70	Columbia ■	65
94	New Mexico St. ■	84
67	Tulsa ■	88
74	Hawaii-Hilo ■	81
83	Hawaii-Hilo ■	78
78	Mont. St.-Billings	89
80	Mont. St.-Billings	120
76	Western N.M.	74
82	Chaminade	80
82	Hawaii Pacific ■	65
51	Hawaii Pacific	70
94	Western N.M. ■	62
80	Western N.M. ■	69
94	Mont. St.-Billings ■	76
68	Hawaii-Hilo	75
78	Hawaii Pacific ■	64
91	Chaminade	78
86	Chaminade	82
57	Seattle Pacific †	82

Nickname: Seasiders
Colors: Crimson, Gray & Gold
Arena: Cannon Activities Center
  Capacity: 4,338; Year Built: 1981
AD: Randy Day
SID: Scott Lowe

BROCKPORT ST.
Brockport, NY 14420-2989 III

Coach: Nelson Whitmore, St. John Fisher 1992

2001-02 RESULTS (28-3)
102	Brooklyn Tech †	43
96	New York U.	85
102	St. John Fisher ■	70
85	Medaille †	61
97	Nazareth	66
72	Cortland St.	49
89	Plattsburgh St. ■	64
98	Oswego St. ■	70
78	Wm. Paterson	69
91	New Paltz St.	62
91	Utica/Rome ■	78
101	Oneonta St. ■	73
95	Keuka †	53
73	Geneseo St. †	60
78	Rochester Inst. †	58
55	Buffalo St.	74
74	Cortland St. ■	48
59	Geneseo St.	52
70	Oswego St.	61
81	Utica/Rome ■	55
79	Buffalo St. ■	72
99	Potsdam St.	87
76	Plattsburgh St.	88
89	Fredonia St. ■	55
106	New Paltz St. ■	50
100	Oneonta St. †	71
82	Potsdam St. †	64
92	Oswego St. †	78
80	Trinity (Conn.) ■	61
69	Amherst	64
62	Rochester ■	71

Nickname: Golden Eagles
Colors: Green & Gold
Arena: Tuttle North Gym
  Capacity: 3,000; Year Built: 1973
AD: Linda J. Case
SID: Eric McDowell

BROOKLYN
Brooklyn, NY 11210-2889 III

Coach: Steve Podias, Fordham 1978

2001-02 RESULTS (5-20)
101	Berkeley ■	34
71	Gwynedd-Mercy	99
79	Maritime (N.Y.)	78
101	St. Joseph's (Brkln) ■	80
65	New York U. ■	68
62	Rutgers-Newark ■	85
65	York (N.Y.)	67
71	Purchase St. ■	81
58	Staten Island	72
101	St. Joseph's (Brkln)	83
79	NYCCT ■	97
67	Medgar Evers	82
77	Purchase St.	88
76	Baruch ■	85
69	Lehman	94
53	John Jay ■	89
60	Hunter	88
74	CCNY ■	88
59	Yeshiva ■	77
66	York (N.Y.) ■	78
49	Staten Island ■	73
83	NYCCT	63
80	Medgar Evers ■	91
61	St. Joseph's (L.I.) ■	63
58	CCNY	75

Nickname: Bridges
Colors: Maroon & Gold
Arena: Roosevelt Gymnasium
  Capacity: 800; Year Built: 1935
AD: Bruce Filosa
SID: Adam Engerow

BROWN
Providence, RI 02912 I

Coach: Glen Miller, Connecticut 1986

2001-02 RESULTS (17-10)
82	Vermont †	58
60	Central Conn. St.	66
90	Northeastern	88
103	Wagner ■	100
67	Providence	60
81	High Point	69
63	Holy Cross	76
87	Stony Brook ■	60
91	Rhode Island ■	76
76	Maine	89
92	Army ■	93
95	Navy ■	83
99	Coast Guard ■	67
72	Cornell ■	59
63	Columbia ■	50
87	Yale	82
77	Yale ■	80
81	Harvard	89
74	Dartmouth	71
56	Princeton ■	70
74	Pennsylvania ■	84
52	Columbia	41
81	Cornell	78
63	Pennsylvania	82
47	Princeton	73
85	Dartmouth ■	70
92	Harvard ■	83

Nickname: Bears
Colors: Brown, Red & White
Arena: Pizzitola Sports Center
  Capacity: 3,100; Year Built: 1989
AD: David T. Roach
SID: Chris Humm

BRYANT
Smithfield, RI 02917-1284 II

Coach: Max Good, Eastern Ky. 1969

2001-02 RESULTS (7-19)

76	Dominican (N.Y.)	61
83	Holy Family †	99
50	American Int'l	64
67	St. Rose	70
62	New Haven ■	56
66	Southern Conn. St.	75
80	Stonehill ■	53
56	Pace ■	77
64	Pace	74
85	St. Joseph's (Me.) ■	76
55	Assumption ■	72
64	Bentley	89
59	Merrimack	73
70	Assumption	76
66	American Int'l ■	75
71	St. Rose ■	77
71	Southern Conn. St. ■	73
59	Franklin Pierce	69
76	Mass.-Lowell ■	84
78	Southern N.H.	86
73	Le Moyne ■	59
72	St. Anselm ■	93
61	St. Michael's ■	73
59	Bentley ■	56
58	Stonehill	46
66	Merrimack ■	78

Nickname: Bulldogs
Colors: Black & Gold
Arena: Bryant Athletic Center
  Capacity: 2,400; Year Built: 1971
AD: Dan Gavitt
SID: Chuck Sullivan

BUCKNELL
Lewisburg, PA 17837 I

Coach: Pat Flannery, Bucknell 1980

2001-02 RESULTS (13-16)

55	Central Conn. St.	68
60	Vermont †	77
62	Rider	75
44	St. Francis (Pa.)	59
71	Cornell ■	62
45	Villanova	69
50	Albany (N.Y.) ■	51
70	UMBC ■	67
57	Penn St.	78
56	South Fla.	59
68	Hofstra †	60
58	Mt. St. Mary's	46
49	Canisius	66
65	Lafayette ■	64
49	Navy	64
56	Army ■	53
52	American	69
80	Colgate	75
69	Lehigh ■	50
65	Holy Cross ■	73
68	Lafayette	74
76	Navy ■	56
65	Army	62
67	American ■	78
68	Colgate ■	57
75	Holy Cross	73
64	Lehigh	75
70	Army †	59
57	Holy Cross †	64

Nickname: Bison
Colors: Orange & Blue
Arena: Davis Gymnasium
  Capacity: 2,300; Year Built: 1938
AD: John P. Hardt
SID: Jon Terry

BUENA VISTA
Storm Lake, IA 50588-9990 III

Coach: Brian VanHaaften,
Northwestern (Iowa)

2001-02 RESULTS (23-6)

96	Clarke ■	77
78	Sioux Falls	85
64	Gust. Adolphus †	78
88	Neb. Wesleyan	85
74	Wartburg	65
68	Northwestern (Iowa) ■	82
63	Central (Iowa)	58
80	Simpson	68
77	Cal Lutheran	66
63	Gettysburg †	61
77	Coe ■	55
96	Cornell College ■	56
69	Dubuque	57
94	Loras	70
66	Luther ■	59
98	Upper Iowa ■	80
88	Simpson ■	83
71	Central (Iowa) ■	53
70	Cornell College	76
83	Coe	67
86	Wartburg ■	76
69	Loras ■	66
112	Dubuque ■	51
68	Upper Iowa	83
73	Luther	38
110	Central (Iowa) ■	82
95	Loras ■	70
85	Wartburg ■	73
60	Gust. Adolphus ■	88

Nickname: Beavers
Colors: Blue & Gold
Arena: Siebens Center
  Capacity: 4,000; Year Built: 1969
AD: Jan Travis
SID: Paul Misner

BUFFALO
Buffalo, NY 14260 I

Coach: Reggie Witherspoon, Empire St. 1995

2001-02 RESULTS (12-18)

62	Niagara	63
100	Chicago St.	92
58	Canisius ■	56
55	Rhode Island	57
73	New Hampshire ■	72
65	Cornell	54
79	Akron ■	60
75	Tulsa †	80
63	Navy †	54
80	Valparaiso †	87
62	Syracuse	83
70	Eastern Mich.	51
70	Northern Ill.	72
66	Kent St. ■	65
73	Bowling Green ■	85
61	Ohio ■	62
82	Marshall	78
53	Kent St.	91
57	Northwestern ■	63
75	Northern Ill. ■	65
81	Akron	89
52	Miami (Ohio) ■	66
59	Western Mich. ■	60
63	Ball St.	87
69	Central Mich. ■	57
42	Toledo	54
87	Marshall ■	62
68	Miami (Ohio)	78
58	Bowling Green	73
60	Miami (Ohio)	71

Nickname: Bulls
Colors: Royal Blue & White
Arena: Alumni Arena
  Capacity: 8,500; Year Built: 1982
AD: Robert J. Arkeilpane
SID: Jon Fuller

BUFFALO ST.
Buffalo, NY 14222-1095 III

Coach: Richard Bihr, Buffalo St. 1969

2001-02 RESULTS (15-8)

59	Oberlin ■	50
59	Nazareth ■	67
59	Oswego St.	64
95	Oneonta St. ■	76
69	Utica/Rome ■	58
59	Albion †	90
73	Wartburg †	65
84	D'Youville ■	68
75	Hilbert ■	54
76	Geneseo St. ■	52
68	Potsdam St.	47
78	New Paltz St.	49
61	Oneonta St.	60
74	Brockport St. ■	55
63	Potsdam St. ■	76
93	Plattsburgh St. ■	77
70	Fredonia St.	46
72	Brockport St.	79
91	Utica/Rome	88
53	Geneseo St.	59
78	Cortland St. ■	52
73	Oswego St. ■	80
48	Cortland St. †	49

Nickname: Bengals
Colors: Orange & Black
Arena: Sports Arena
  Capacity: 3,500; Year Built: 1991
AD: Jerry S. Boyes
SID: Jeff Ventura

BUTLER
Indianapolis, IN 46208-3485.....I

Coach: Todd Lickliter, Butler 1979

2001-02 RESULTS (26-6)

73	Radford †	56
76	Delaware †	59
67	Washington †	64
69	Indiana St. ■	49
74	Purdue	68
70	Birmingham-So.	34
76	Lipscomb	56
101	Evansville ■	65
77	Northern Iowa	65
66	Mt. St. Mary's	46
75	Ball St.	66
45	Samford †	37
66	Indiana †	64
87	Wright St. ■	90
62	Cleveland St.	45
54	Detroit	63
68	Youngstown St.	50
64	Wis.-Green Bay ■	41
72	Wis.-Milwaukee ■	73
78	Loyola (Ill.) ■	48
82	Ill.-Chicago	73
59	Wis.-Milwaukee	58
72	Wright St.	57
61	Detroit ■	48
70	Cleveland St. ■	45
77	Wis.-Green Bay	74
75	Youngstown St.	50
56	Loyola (Ill.)	60
85	Ill.-Chicago ■	61
48	Wis.-Green Bay †	49
81	Bowling Green ■	69
65	Syracuse	66

Nickname: Bulldogs
Colors: Blue & White
Arena: Hinkle Fieldhouse
  Capacity: 11,043; Year Built: 1928
AD: John C. Parry
SID: Jim McGrath

C.W. POST
Brookville, NY 11548 II

Coach: Tom Galeazzi, Cortland St. 1961

2001-02 RESULTS (13-15)

83	Holy Family †	79
64	Dominican (N.Y.)	60
69	St. Thomas Aquinas	70
87	Dowling ■	92
71	Concordia (N.Y.)	82
87	Southampton	101
69	Queens (N.Y.) ■	71
83	Merrimack	65
71	P.R.-Cayey	53
76	P.R.-Arecibo	64
70	P.R.-Rio Piedras	76
70	Mercy	56
61	Philadelphia U. ■	68
65	Adelphi	75
67	Molloy ■	70
75	NYIT	66
81	Bridgeport ■	64
63	St. Thomas Aquinas ■	59
68	Dowling	87
71	Concordia (N.Y.) ■	57
77	Southampton ■	91
55	Queens (N.Y.)	62
102	Mercy ■	69
67	Philadelphia U.	76
81	Adelphi ■	96
88	Molloy	70
71	NYIT ■	59
75	Bridgeport	84

Nickname: Pioneers
Colors: Green & Gold
Arena: Conolly Gym
  Capacity: 600; Year Built: 1960
AD: Vincent Salamone
SID: Brad Sullivan

CABRINI
Radnor, PA 19087-3698 III

Coach: John Dzik, West Chester 1972

2001-02 RESULTS (19-12)

63	St. Norbert †	60
86	Siena Heights †	95
73	Loras	83
95	Widener ■	92
63	Marywood	37
79	Wesley ■	57
63	Cheyney	69
77	Hartwick †	60
59	Mt. St. Joseph †	62
78	Pacific Lutheran †	79
74	Shenandoah ■	64
75	Neumann ■	79
95	Eastern	75
70	Arcadia	51
63	Gwynedd-Mercy	51
71	Alvernia ■	85
62	Misericordia ■	52
68	Neumann	64
69	Wesley	63
70	Marywood ■	40
77	Arcadia ■	81
81	Eastern ■	63
61	Alvernia	62
65	Gwynedd-Mercy ■	70
59	Misericordia	57
92	Gwynedd-Mercy ■	57
81	Alvernia	72
71	Neumann	67
85	Merchant Marine	73
47	Wm. Paterson	43
85	Elizabethtown †	87

Nickname: Cavaliers
Colors: Royal Blue & White
Arena: Sacred Heart Gymnasium

Capacity: 750; Year Built: 1958
AD: John L. Dzik
SID: Rich Schepis

CALIFORNIA

Berkeley, CA 94720 I

Coach: Ben Braun, Wisconsin 1975

2001-02 RESULTS (23-9)

70	Princeton ■	58
56	Eastern Wash. ■	27
67	Santa Clara ■	60
71	New Mexico ■	62
59	South Fla.	79
88	St. Louis ■	63
97	Fresno St. ■	75
78	Mt. St. Mary's ■	50
69	Harvard ■	54
76	Penn St. ■	73
62	Stanford	82
68	Stanford ■	54
72	Oregon	76
61	Oregon St.	53
62	Washington ■	50
90	Washington St. ■	57
92	Southern California	91
57	UCLA	64
58	Arizona ■	68
67	Arizona St. ■	59
73	Oregon St. ■	58
107	Oregon ■	103
77	Washington St.	56
60	Washington	75
69	UCLA ■	51
83	Southern California ■	64
91	Arizona St.	80
53	Arizona	99
67	UCLA †	61
78	Arizona †	90
82	Pennsylvania †	75
50	Pittsburgh	63

Nickname: Golden Bears
Colors: Blue & Gold
Arena: Haas Pavilion
Capacity: 11,813; Year Built: 1999
AD: Stephen Gladstone
SID: Herb Benenson

UC DAVIS

Davis, CA 95616-8674 II

Coach: Brian Fogel, Sonoma St. 1989

2001-02 RESULTS (15-12)

86	BYU-Hawaii ■	90
85	Barry ■	73
88	Cal St. Hayward	53
69	UC Irvine	74
81	Cal St. Los Angeles ■	75
67	Cal St. Dom. Hills ■	63
70	San Fran. St.	69
70	Sonoma St.	73
85	Western Ore.	78
82	Cal Poly Pomona ■	74
60	Cal St. San B'dino ■	68
66	Cal St. Bakersfield	70
82	Cal St. Stanislaus	73
81	Grand Canyon ■	70
86	UC San Diego ■	79
87	Cal St. Chico ■	103
68	Cal St. Chico	72
70	Cal St. Dom. Hills	76
73	Cal St. Los Angeles	72
77	Sonoma St. ■	51
71	San Fran. St. ■	57
55	Cal St. San B'dino	72
85	Cal Poly Pomona	71
67	Cal St. Stanislaus ■	75
62	Cal St. Bakersfield ■	72
91	UC San Diego	78
93	Grand Canyon	99

Nickname: Aggies
Colors: Yale Blue & Gold

Arena: Recreation Hall
Capacity: 7,600; Year Built: 1977
AD: Greg Warzecka
SID: Mike Robles

UC IRVINE

Irvine, CA 92697-4125 I

Coach: Pat Douglass, Pacific (Cal.) 1972

2001-02 RESULTS (21-11)

71	St. Mary's (Cal.) ■	64
96	Pepperdine ■	93
52	Illinois St. †	58
68	Oakland †	61
64	Kent St. †	75
71	Loyola Marymount	59
74	UC Davis ■	69
52	San Diego	63
74	UCLA	75
75	Long Beach St. ■	69
79	Lipscomb †	62
77	Boston U. †	71
68	Cal St. Fullerton ■	58
72	UC Riverside ■	53
67	Utah St.	66
92	Idaho	54
62	Pacific (Cal.) ■	58
72	Cal St. Northridge ■	73
81	UC Santa Barb.	70
47	Cal Poly	50
72	UC Riverside	64
72	Cal St. Fullerton	46
52	Idaho ■	38
61	Utah St. ■	62
82	Cal St. Northridge	80
61	Pacific (Cal.)	73
77	Cal Poly ■	63
71	UC Santa Barb. ■	67
70	Long Beach St.	86
72	Long Beach St. †	65
61	UC Santa Barb. †	66
55	Brigham Young	78

Nickname: Anteaters
Colors: Blue & Gold
Arena: Bren Events Center
Capacity: 5,000; Year Built: 1987
SID: Bob Olson

UC RIVERSIDE

Riverside, CA 92521 I

Coach: John Masi, UC Riverside 1970

2001-02 RESULTS (8-18)

67	Portland	75
64	Arizona St.	73
58	Fresno St.	75
72	Montana St. †	82
50	UCLA	65
66	Southern Utah	64
71	UC Santa Cruz ■	64
56	UC Santa Barb. ■	68
81	Cal Poly ■	77
100	Sacramento St. ■	66
73	Long Beach St.	67
53	UC Irvine	72
68	Cal St. Fullerton ■	60
42	Utah St. ■	68
58	Idaho ■	60
59	Pacific (Cal.)	71
69	Cal St. Northridge	84
64	UC Irvine ■	72
66	Long Beach St. ■	69
70	Cal St. Fullerton	58
67	Idaho	56
42	Utah St.	59
64	Cal St. Northridge ■	73
75	Pacific (Cal.) ■	87
65	Cal Poly	90
58	UC Santa Barb.	80

Nickname: Highlanders
Colors: Blue & Gold
Arena: UCR Student Rec Center

Capacity: 3,168; Year Built: 1994
AD: Stanley M. Morrison
SID: Ross French

UC SAN DIEGO

La Jolla, CA 92093-0531..........II

Coach: Greg Lanthier, Point Loma 1987

2001-02 RESULTS (8-21)

104	Redlands ■	44
62	San Diego	89
53	San Diego St.	98
62	Holy Names †	53
76	UC Santa Cruz	54
65	Sonoma St. ■	74
62	San Fran. St. ■	71
62	Cal St. Bakersfield ■	85
71	Cal St. Stanislaus ■	57
50	Alas. Fairbanks	67
74	Alas. Fairbanks	76
50	Cal St. Los Angeles	77
81	Cal St. Dom. Hills	87
70	Cal Poly Pomona ■	64
54	Cal St. San B'dino ■	74
88	Cal St. Chico	87
79	UC Davis	86
73	Grand Canyon ■	78
76	Grand Canyon	72
65	San Fran. St.	82
69	Sonoma St.	76
63	Cal St. Stanislaus	67
82	Cal St. Bakersfield	89
83	Cal St. Dom. Hills ■	93
72	Cal St. Los Angeles ■	82
55	Cal St. San B'dino	71
66	Cal Poly Pomona	88
78	UC Davis ■	91
101	Cal St. Chico ■	91

Nickname: Tritons
Colors: Blue & Gold
Arena: RIMAC Arena
Capacity: 5,000; Year Built: 1995
AD: Earl W. Edwards
SID: Bill Gannon

UC SANTA BARB.

Santa Barbara, CA 93106.........I

Coach: Bob Williams, San Jose St. 1976

2001-02 RESULTS (20-11)

51	Westmont ■	42
69	San Francisco	49
62	Southern California	73
68	Brigham Young ■	58
62	St. Mary's (Cal.) ■	51
70	Loyola Marymount	77
68	Pepperdine ■	51
68	UC Riverside	56
64	Cal St. Fullerton	62
86	Detroit †	59
59	Santa Clara	61
76	Idaho ■	53
56	Utah St. ■	60
57	Cal St. Northridge	54
70	Pacific (Cal.)	73
74	Cal Poly	67
70	UC Irvine ■	81
82	Long Beach St. ■	50
64	Utah St.	72
37	Idaho	40
70	Pacific (Cal.) ■	57
58	Cal St. Northridge ■	51
69	Cal Poly ■	66
74	Long Beach St.	77
67	UC Irvine	71
54	Cal St. Fullerton ■	52
80	UC Riverside ■	58
74	Cal Poly †	65
66	UC Irvine †	61
60	Utah St. †	56
81	Arizona †	86

Nickname: Gauchos
Colors: Blue & Gold
Arena: The Thunderdome
Capacity: 6,000; Year Built: 1979
AD: Gary A. Cunningham
SID: Bill Mahoney

UC SANTA CRUZ

Santa Cruz, CA 95064 III

2001-02 RESULTS (7-17)

113	Goldey-Beacom ■	37
69	Southern Ore.	75
58	Oregon Tech †	101
59	Willamette ■	66
54	UC San Diego ■	76
39	St. Mary's (Cal.)	95
64	UC Riverside	71
98	Cal Christian ■	83
61	Warner Southern	78
82	Wis. Lutheran †	74
86	Bethany (Cal.)	90
75	Cal St. Monterey Bay ■	87
61	Notre Dame de Namur ■	64
67	Menlo ■	75
33	Holy Names ■	62
58	Dominican (Cal.)	72
80	Cal St. Hayward	92
59	Cal Maritime ■	66
90	Simpson (Cal.) ■	78
84	Pacific Union	69
66	Notre Dame de Namur	86
77	Menlo	73
80	Bethany (Cal.) ■	71
67	Cal St. Monterey Bay	87

Nickname: Banana Slugs
Colors: Blue & Gold
Arena: West Field House
Capacity: 300
AD: Greg Harshaw
SID: Dorth Raphaely

CALIF. (PA.)

California, PA 15419................II

Coach: Bill Brown, Ohio 1974

2001-02 RESULTS (23-6)

80	Bloomsburg †	74
73	St. Vincent	64
100	Pitt.-Greensburg ■	52
85	Cheyney ■	60
87	West Chester ■	96
68	Virginia Union	55
117	Ohio St.-Newark ■	48
77	East Stroudsburg	73
84	Kutztown	64
86	Ohio Valley ■	72
74	Franklin Pierce ■	69
85	Mansfield	72
73	Edinboro	88
73	Millersville ■	78
85	Slippery Rock ■	70
70	Lock Haven	65
82	Bloomsburg †	77
91	Shippensburg ■	68
71	Indiana (Pa.) ■	70
101	Edinboro ■	72
59	Clarion	61
67	Slippery Rock	56
76	Shippensburg	56
84	Lock Haven ■	60
85	Clarion ■	78
75	Indiana (Pa.)	83
82	Edinboro ■	70
68	Bloomsburg †	66
68	Indiana (Pa.) †	71

Nickname: Vulcans
Colors: Red & Black
Arena: Hamer Hall
Capacity: 2,500; Year Built: 1962
AD: Thomas G. Pucci
SID: David Smith

CAL LUTHERAN
Thousand Oaks, CA 91360-2787 III

Coach: Rich Rider, Truman 1968

2001-02 RESULTS (20-5)
90	La Sierra	92
86	Cal St. Los Angeles ■	74
100	LIFE Bible ■	52
118	Cal Christian	81
82	Vanguard ■	71
63	Holy Names ■	57
70	Chapman	58
66	Buena Vista ■	77
76	Cal St. Hayward ■	71
71	Ill. Wesleyan ■	97
90	Cal Christian ■	57
59	Claremont-M-S ■	58
91	Occidental	80
78	Caltech	33
82	Whittier ■	63
81	La Verne ■	53
89	Redlands	72
66	Pomona-Pitzer	42
60	Claremont-M-S	64
69	Occidental ■	65
86	Caltech ■	35
72	Whittier	61
84	La Verne	79
88	Redlands ■	81
61	Pomona-Pitzer	62

Nickname: Kingsmen
Colors: Purple & Gold
Arena: CLU Gymnasium
  Capacity: 500; Year Built: 1962
AD: Bruce Bryde
SID: John Czimbal

CAL POLY
San Luis Obispo, CA 93407 I

Coach: Kevin Bromley, Colorado St. 1983

2001-02 RESULTS (15-12)
57	Northern Ariz.	75
70	St. Mary's (Cal.) ■	50
100	Portland St. ■	79
64	Vanderbilt	69
75	Lipscomb	51
75	Eastern Wash.	70
72	Oregon St.	68
61	Cal St. Fullerton	60
77	UC Riverside	81
82	Cal St. Stanislaus ■	74
61	Utah St. ■	58
72	Idaho ■	57
54	Pacific (Cal.)	70
62	Cal St. Northridge	72
67	UC Santa Barb. ■	74
75	Long Beach St. ■	63
50	UC Irvine ■	47
56	Idaho	54
53	Utah St.	85
77	Cal St. Northridge ■	65
84	Pacific (Cal.) ■	79
66	UC Santa Barb.	69
63	UC Irvine	77
80	Long Beach St.	83
90	UC Riverside ■	65
62	Cal St. Fullerton ■	64
65	UC Santa Barb. †	74

Nickname: Mustangs
Colors: Green & Gold
Arena: Robert A. Mott Gymnasium
  Capacity: 3,032; Year Built: 1960
AD: John F. Mc Cutcheon
SID: Brian Thurmond

CAL POLY POMONA
Pomona, CA 91768 II

Coach: Greg Kamansky, UC San Diego 1988

2001-02 RESULTS (18-9)
65	Vanguard	52
50	Azusa Pacific	64
97	La Verne ■	63
70	Cal St. Stanislaus	65
67	Cal St. Bakersfield	47
54	Cal St. Los Angeles ■	50
71	Cal St. Dom. Hills ■	62
80	Mont. St.-Billings	105
75	Dominican (Cal.) ■	59
74	UC Davis	82
81	Cal St. Chico	71
64	UC San Diego	70
93	Grand Canyon	66
69	San Fran. St. ■	44
59	Sonoma St. ■	54
63	Cal St. San B'dino ■	66
56	Cal St. San B'dino	67
86	Cal St. Stanislaus ■	57
70	Cal St. Bakersfield ■	65
59	Cal St. Dom. Hills	69
73	Cal St. Los Angeles	58
76	Cal St. Chico ■	57
71	UC Davis ■	85
86	Grand Canyon ■	69
88	UC San Diego ■	66
67	Sonoma St.	62
63	San Fran. St.	67

Nickname: Broncos
Colors: Green & Gold
Arena: Kellogg Gym
  Capacity: 5,000; Year Built: 1966
AD: Dan Bridges
SID: Steve Quintero

CAL ST. BAKERSFIELD
Bakersfield, CA 93311-1099 II

Coach: Henry Clark, Mont. St. Billings 1980

2001-02 RESULTS (24-5)
84	Cal St. Hayward ■	59
70	Seattle †	51
76	Western Ore.	55
58	Cal St. San B'dino ■	65
47	Cal Poly Pomona	67
85	UC San Diego	62
81	Grand Canyon	57
75	Cal St. Stanislaus ■	60
60	UC-Colo. Spgs.	51
60	Whitworth	45
59	San Fran. St.	54
75	Sonoma St.	68
70	UC Davis ■	66
79	Cal St. Chico ■	59
65	Cal St. Los Angeles ■	44
70	Cal St. Dom. Hills ■	64
89	Cal St. Stanislaus	68
62	Cal St. San B'dino	60
65	Cal Poly Pomona	70
77	Grand Canyon ■	65
89	UC San Diego ■	82
72	Sonoma St. ■	53
70	San Fran. St. ■	58
79	Cal St. Chico	78
72	UC Davis	62
80	Cal St. Dom. Hills ■	66
64	Cal St. Los Angeles	77
84	Mont. St.-Billings †	81
62	Cal St. San B'dino	66

Nickname: Roadrunners
Colors: Blue & Gold
Arena: Centennial Garden
  Capacity: 10,800; Year Built: 1998
AD: Rudy Carvajal
SID: Kevin Gilmore

CAL ST. CHICO
Chico, CA 95929 II

Coach: Prescott Smith, Southwestern Okla. 1965

2001-02 RESULTS (6-21)
95	Oregon Tech	93
80	BYU-Hawaii	87
93	Dominican (Cal.) ■	72
76	Central Wash. ■	96
85	Cal St. Dom. Hills ■	67
63	Cal St. Los Angeles ■	76
68	San Fran. St.	71
60	Sonoma St.	90
67	Santa Clara	92
68	Cal St. San B'dino ■	74
71	Cal Poly Pomona ■	81
69	Cal St. Stanislaus	84
59	Cal St. Bakersfield	79
87	UC San Diego ■	88
77	Grand Canyon ■	85
103	UC Davis	87
72	UC Davis ■	68
59	Cal St. Los Angeles	76
86	Cal St. Dom. Hills	89
71	San Fran. St. ■	79
89	Sonoma St. ■	102
57	Cal Poly Pomona	76
45	Cal St. San B'dino	71
78	Cal St. Bakersfield ■	79
78	Cal St. Stanislaus ■	77
105	Grand Canyon	108
91	UC San Diego	101

Nickname: Wildcats
Colors: Cardinal & White
Arena: Art Acker Gym
  Capacity: 1,997; Year Built: 1962
AD: Anita S. Barker
SID: Teresa Clements

CAL ST. DOM. HILLS
Carson, CA 90747 II

Coach: Larry Hauser, Chicago St. 1971

2001-02 RESULTS (12-15)
70	Cal Baptist ■	72
59	Pomona-Pitzer ■	53
67	Cal St. Chico	85
63	UC Davis	67
50	Cal St. San B'dino	66
62	Cal Poly Pomona ■	71
54	Hawaii Pacific	78
68	Hawaii-Hilo	90
76	Concordia (Cal.)	89
66	Grand Canyon ■	72
87	UC San Diego ■	81
64	Sonoma St. ■	57
71	San Fran. St. ■	73
78	Cal St. Stanislaus	83
64	Cal St. Bakersfield	70
77	Cal St. Los Angeles	74
72	Cal St. Los Angeles ■	67
76	UC Davis ■	70
89	Cal St. Chico ■	86
69	Cal Poly Pomona ■	59
57	Cal St. San B'dino ■	65
93	UC San Diego	83
85	Grand Canyon	77
61	San Fran. St.	64
72	Sonoma St.	62
66	Cal St. Bakersfield ■	80
82	Cal St. Stanislaus ■	63

Nickname: Toros
Colors: Cardinal Red & Gold
Arena: Torodome
  Capacity: 4,200; Year Built: 1978
AD: Ron Prettyman
SID: Patrick Guillen

CAL ST. FULLERTON
Fullerton, CA 92834-6810 I

Coach: Donny Daniels, Cal St. Fullerton 1977

2001-02 RESULTS (5-22)
58	Pepperdine	75
43	San Francisco ■	70
84	Loyola Marymount ■	70
56	Baylor	92
71	Wyoming	86
79	Sacramento St.	85
86	Pt. Loma Nazarene ■	50
106	Sacramento St. ■	97
60	Cal Poly ■	61
62	UC Santa Barb. ■	64
68	Northern Ariz.	80
58	UC Irvine ■	68
60	Long Beach St. ■	68
60	UC Riverside.	68
65	Utah St. ■	51
59	Idaho ■	63
68	Cal St. Northridge	92
48	Pacific (Cal.)	82
60	Long Beach St. ■	77
46	UC Irvine	72
58	UC Riverside ■	70
45	Utah St.	60
53	Idaho	65
61	Pacific (Cal.) ■	67
59	Cal St. Northridge ■	73
52	UC Santa Barb.	54
64	Cal Poly	62

Nickname: Titans
Colors: Navy, Orange & White
Arena: Titan Gym
  Capacity: 3,500; Year Built: 1964
AD: Brian Quinn
SID: Mel Franks

CAL ST. HAYWARD
Hayward, CA 94542 III

Coach: [missing]

2001-02 RESULTS (16-12)
59	Cal St. Bakersfield	84
53	UC Davis ■	88
66	Lewis-Clark St. †	83
67	Oregon Tech †	80
80	Notre Dame de Namur †	73
59	San Francisco	94
86	La Verne ■	78
85	Redlands	73
77	Gettysburg †	89
71	Cal Lutheran ■	76
102	Simpson (Cal.) ■	62
75	Holy Names ■	66
71	Dominican (Cal.) ■	68
83	Cal Maritime	101
93	Bethany (Cal.) ■	67
87	Pacific Union	70
68	Cal St. Monterey Bay ■	73
92	UC Santa Cruz ■	80
91	Notre Dame de Namur	76
82	Menlo	71
85	Cal Maritime ■	68
83	Simpson (Cal.)	78
88	Pacific Union ■	49
62	Holy Names	81
65	Dominican (Cal.)	84
57	Cal St. Monterey Bay †	55
78	Notre Dame de Namur †	63
40	Holy Names †	70

Nickname: Pioneers
Colors: Red & White
Arena: Pioneer Gym
  Capacity: 5,000; Year Built: 1967
AD: Debby DeAngelis
SID: Marty Valdez

CAL ST. LOS ANGELES
Los Angeles, CA 90032-8240 ...II

Coach: Dave Yanai,
Long Beach St. 1966

2001-02 RESULTS (11-16)

86	Christian Heritage ■	.79
74	Cal Lutheran	.86
70	Vanguard ■	.65
75	UC Davis	.81
76	Cal St. Chico	.63
50	Cal Poly Pomona ■	.54
69	Cal St. San B'dino	.76
58	Cal Baptist ■	.64
62	Azusa Pacific ■	.68
77	UC San Diego ■	.50
63	Grand Canyon ■	.57
64	San Fran. St. ■	.73
70	Sonoma St. ■	.52
44	Cal St. Bakersfield	.65
75	Cal St. Stanislaus	.76
74	Cal St. Dom. Hills ■	.77
67	Cal St. Dom. Hills	.72
76	Cal St. Chico ■	.59
72	UC Davis ■	.73
54	Cal St. San B'dino ■	.55
58	Cal Poly Pomona ■	.73
76	Grand Canyon	.74
82	UC San Diego	.72
69	Sonoma St.	.72
55	San Fran. St.	.66
75	Cal St. Stanislaus ■	.73
77	Cal St. Bakersfield ■	.64

Nickname: Golden Eagles
Colors: Black & Gold
Arena: Eagles Nest
  Capacity: 5,000; Year Built: 1947
AD: Carol M. Dunn
SID: Chris Hughes

CAL ST. NORTHRIDGE
Northridge, CA 91330 I

Coach: Bobby Braswell,
Cal St. Northridge 1984

2001-02 RESULTS (12-16)

75	Nevada ■	.85
101	Dominican (Cal.) ■	.47
65	Howard	.99
70	San Diego St.	.80
64	Wyoming	.86
65	Nevada	.74
60	Southern Ill. ■	.74
56	Utah St.	.73
57	Idaho	.56
70	Brigham Young	.84
66	San Diego ■	.82
70	Pacific (Cal.) ■	.59
54	UC Santa Barb. ■	.57
72	Cal Poly	.62
66	Long Beach St. ■	.54
73	UC Irvine	.72
92	Cal St. Fullerton ■	.68
84	UC Riverside ■	.69
58	Pacific (Cal.)	.74
65	Cal Poly	.77
51	UC Santa Barb.	.58
80	UC Irvine ■	.82
60	Long Beach St. ■	.73
73	UC Riverside	.64
73	Cal St. Fullerton	.59
63	Idaho ■	.46
62	Utah St. ■	.54
66	Pacific (Cal.) †	.78

Nickname: Matadors
Colors: Red, White & Black
Arena: The Matadome
  Capacity: 1,600; Year Built: 1962
AD: Richard Dull
SID: Ryan Finney

CAL ST. SAN B'DINO
San Bernardino, CA 92407-2397
....II

Coach: Larry Reynolds,
UC Riverside 1976

2001-02 RESULTS (28-2)

75	BYU-Hawaii	.63
70	Metro St. †	.62
64	Christian Heritage ■	.54
81	Cal St. Stanislaus	.51
65	Cal St. Bakersfield	.58
66	Cal St. Dom. Hills	.50
76	Cal St. Los Angeles ■	.69
81	Pt. Loma Nazarene ■	.64
111	Mont. St.-Billings ■	.65
74	Cal St. Chico	.68
68	UC Davis	.60
68	Grand Canyon	.65
74	UC San Diego	.54
67	Sonoma St. ■	.52
68	San Fran. St. ■	.47
66	Cal Poly Pomona	.63
67	Cal Poly Pomona ■	.56
60	Cal St. Bakersfield ■	.62
76	Cal St. Stanislaus ■	.52
55	Cal St. Los Angeles	.54
65	Cal St. Dom. Hills	.57
72	UC Davis ■	.55
71	Cal St. Chico ■	.45
71	UC San Diego ■	.55
97	Grand Canyon ■	.73
80	San Fran. St. ■	.61
69	Sonoma St. ■	.55
66	Cal St. Bakersfield ■	.62
80	Humboldt St. ■	.65
48	Metro St. †	.65

Nickname: Coyotes
Colors: Columbia Blue & Black
Arena: Coussoulis Arena
  Capacity: 5,000; Year Built: 1995
AD: Nancy P. Simpson
SID: Mike Murphy

CAL ST. STANISLAUS
Turlock, CA 95382-0299 II

Coach: Mike Terpstra, Northwest
Nazarene

2001-02 RESULTS (10-17)

99	Bethany (Cal.) ■	.68
80	Cal St. Monterey Bay ■	.61
72	Albertson	.87
98	Northwest Nazarene	.95
51	Cal St. San B'dino ■	.81
65	Cal Poly Pomona ■	.70
64	Grand Canyon	.63
57	UC San Diego	.71
60	Cal St. Bakersfield	.75
74	Cal Poly	.82
53	Sonoma St.	.71
68	San Fran. St.	.63
84	Cal St. Chico ■	.69
73	UC Davis ■	.82
83	Cal St. Dom. Hills ■	.78
76	Cal St. Los Angeles ■	.75
68	Cal St. Bakersfield ■	.89
57	Cal Poly Pomona	.86
52	Cal St. San B'dino	.76
67	UC San Diego ■	.63
81	Grand Canyon ■	.82
71	San Fran. St. ■	.82
65	Sonoma St. ■	.70
75	UC Davis	.67
77	Cal St. Chico	.78
73	Cal St. Los Angeles	.75
63	Cal St. Dom. Hills	.82

Nickname: Warriors
Colors: Red & Gold
Arena: Warrior Gym

Capacity: 2,000; Year Built: 1978
AD: Milton E. Richards
SID: Will Keener

CALTECH
Pasadena, CA 91125 III

Coach: Gene Victor,
Cal St. Los Angeles 1959

2001-02 RESULTS (2-20)

61	Cooper Union †	.60
41	S'western (Ariz.) †	.71
46	LIFE Bible ■	.54
9	San Jose Christian ■	.33
49	MIT	.82
47	LIFE Bible ■	.40
33	Chapman	.75
48	Amer. Indian Bib. ■	.61
30	Pomona-Pitzer	.80
34	Claremont-M-S ■	.67
33	Cal Lutheran ■	.78
36	Occidental ■	.81
42	Redlands	.71
41	Whittier ■	.83
32	La Verne ■	.100
33	Pomona-Pitzer ■	.85
35	Claremont-M-S	.74
35	Cal Lutheran	.86
38	Occidental ■	.66
48	Redlands ■	.79
44	Whittier	.73
46	La Verne ■	.77

Nickname: Beavers
Colors: Orange, Black, & White
Arena: Braun Athletic Center
  Capacity: 300; Year Built: 1992
AD: Timothy D. Downes
SID: Brent Reger

CALVIN
Grand Rapids, MI 49546-4388 III

Coach: Kevin Vande Streek, Dordt 1981

2001-02 RESULTS (20-7)

73	Orchard Lake ■	.58
82	Aurora ■	.49
104	Aquinas ■	.76
79	Aquinas †	.75
84	Cornerstone †	.90
63	Wheaton (Ill.)	.69
95	Ferris St. ■	.76
79	Cornerstone	.82
100	Spring Arbor ■	.63
77	Defiance	.73
73	Milwaukee Engr. †	.61
93	Hannibal-La Grange †	.59
66	Olivet ■	.58
42	Kalamazoo	.65
95	Adrian ■	.76
57	Albion	.65
70	Hope	.68
76	Alma ■	.67
91	Olivet	.60
71	Kalamazoo ■	.65
80	Orchard Lake	.63
72	Adrian	.68
64	Albion ■	.65
78	Hope ■	.64
69	Alma	.55
69	Albion ■	.61
63	Hope ■	.70

Nickname: Knights
Colors: Maroon & Gold
Arena: Calvin Fieldhouse
  Capacity: 4,500; Year Built: 1965
AD: Marvin A. Zuidema
SID: Jeff Febus

CAMERON
Lawton, OK 73505-6377 II

Coach: Garrette Mantle,
Southeastern Okla. 1988

2001-02 RESULTS (11-15)

75	Oral Roberts	.71
81	National Christian ■	.52
88	Rhema ■	.63
68	Eastern N.M. ■	.64
63	West Tex. A&M ■	.59
63	Washburn †	.74
60	Central Mo. St. †	.83
53	Tarleton St.	.76
70	Tex. A&M-Kingsville ■	.60
63	Tex. A&M-Commerce ■	.58
71	Abilene Christian	.73
61	Angelo St.	.79
60	Southwestern Okla. ■	.85
77	Okla. Panhandle ■	.70
49	Midwestern St.	.58
72	Central Okla.	.90
65	Northeastern St. ■	.67
57	East Central	.60
62	Southeastern Okla. ■	.55
66	Okla. Panhandle	.75
66	Midwestern St. ■	.84
50	Southwestern Okla.	.58
84	Central Okla. ■	.78
58	Northeastern St.	.70
58	East Central ■	.55
70	Southeastern Okla.	.73

Nickname: Aggies
Colors: Gold & Black
Arena: Aggie Gymnasium
  Capacity: 1,800; Year Built: 1958
AD: Sam Carroll
SID: Steve Doughty

CAMPBELL
Buies Creek, NC 27506 I

Coach: Billy Lee, Atlanta Christian 1971

2001-02 RESULTS (8-19)

60	Fla. Atlantic	.77
59	LSU	.83
93	UNC Pembroke ■	.77
77	UNC Asheville ■	.72
75	Furman ■	.78
78	Belmont	.90
53	Furman	.83
71	Georgia St.	.85
81	Troy St. ■	.88
56	Coastal Caro.	.67
47	Florida St.	.93
77	Mercer ■	.76
86	UCF	.99
53	Jacksonville ■	.67
91	Stetson ■	.82
55	Samford	.69
84	Jacksonville St. ■	.79
64	Georgia St. ■	.81
56	Samford ■	.53
66	Jacksonville St. †	.78
69	Stetson	.72
57	Jacksonville	.85
92	Fla. Atlantic ■	.87
86	UCF ■	.84
71	Troy St.	.81
85	Mercer	.88
67	Belmont ■	.84

Nickname: Fighting Camels
Colors: Orange & Black
Arena: Carter Gymnasium
  Capacity: 945; Year Built: 1953
AD: Stan Williamson
SID: Stan Cole

CANISIUS
Buffalo, NY 14208-1098 I

Coach: Mike MacDonald,
St. Bonaventure 1988

2001-02 RESULTS (10-20)

65	Cornell ■	48
56	Buffalo	58
76	St. Joseph's	82
65	Iona	75
46	Rider ■	63
73	Notre Dame ■	84
54	Arizona St.	77
70	La.-Lafayette †	73
69	Fairfield ■	77
66	Bucknell ■	49
81	Marist ■	80
74	Morgan St.	68
62	Rider	65
53	Bethune-Cookman	60
76	Siena ■	68
62	St. Peter's †	71
74	Loyola (Md.) ■	65
43	Siena	63
60	Iona ■	61
51	Loyola (Md.)	54
71	St. Peter's ■	73
62	Manhattan ■	61
69	Marist	63
53	Manhattan	73
65	Niagara ■	80
54	Fairfield	72
82	Niagara	86
88	Loyola (Md.) †	62
85	Rider †	84
60	Niagara †	70

Nickname: Golden Griffins
Colors: Blue & Gold
Arena: Koessler Athletic Center
  Capacity: 1,800; Year Built: 1969
AD: Timothy J. Dillon
SID: Marc Gignac

CAPITAL
Columbus, OH 43209-2394 III

Coach: Damon Goodwin, Dayton 1986

2001-02 RESULTS (23-5)

77	St. Olaf ■	61
95	Texas Lutheran ■	71
73	Ohio Dominican ■	69
76	Marietta	74
62	Wooster	55
87	Otterbein	90
58	Mount Union ■	59
76	Ohio Northern ■	84
79	Muskingum ■	69
89	Denison	63
74	Mt. St. Joseph ■	67
77	Ohio Wesleyan	68
65	John Carroll	54
63	Wilmington (Ohio)	47
75	Baldwin-Wallace	73
76	Heidelberg ■	73
53	Ohio Northern	50
62	Mount Union ■	57
78	Muskingum	64
71	Marietta ■	65
103	John Carroll	84
67	Wilmington (Ohio) ■	61
85	Baldwin-Wallace ■	73
77	Heidelberg	67
67	Otterbein ■	70
83	Baldwin-Wallace ■	59
80	Mount Union †	63
67	Otterbein	69

Nickname: Crusaders
Colors: Purple & White
Arena: The Capital Center
  Capacity: 2,100; Year Built: 2001
AD: Roger Welsh
SID: Leonard Reich

CARLETON
Northfield, MN 55057 III

Coach: Guy Kalland,
Concordia-M'head 1974

2001-02 RESULTS (10-16)

69	Aurora	71
82	Chicago	87
81	Pillsbury ■	52
81	Puget Sound †	98
70	Pacific Lutheran	82
65	Augsburg	69
71	Gust. Adolphus ■	85
63	Macalester	70
78	St. John's (Minn.)	73
88	Hamline	80
58	Concordia-M'head ■	52
50	Bethel (Minn.) ■	55
73	St. Mary's (Minn.) ■	60
70	St. Thomas (Minn.)	86
66	St. Olaf	60
78	Augsburg ■	53
78	Gust. Adolphus	86
53	Macalester ■	45
82	Hamline	64
60	Concordia-M'head	62
53	St. John's (Minn.) ■	55
57	Bethel (Minn.)	93
68	St. Mary's (Minn.)	60
57	St. Thomas (Minn.) ■	59
75	St. Olaf	79
53	Bethel (Minn.)	72

Nickname: Knights
Colors: Maize & Blue
Arena: West Gymnasium
  Capacity: 1,850; Year Built: 1964
AD: Leon Lunder
SID: Eric Sieger

CARNEGIE MELLON
Pittsburgh, PA 15213-3890 III

Coach: Tony Wingen, Springfield 1982

2001-02 RESULTS (9-16)

83	Wash. & Jeff. †	80
67	Grove City ■	78
59	Notre Dame (Ohio) ■	56
43	Juniata	64
73	Rochester	86
75	Penn St.-Behrend	82
69	Thiel	71
61	Johns Hopkins	74
69	Hiram	65
87	Brandeis	88
49	New York U.	65
85	Penn St.-Altoona	53
94	Wash. & Jeff.	66
77	La Roche ■	74
72	Case Reserve ■	76
88	Emory ■	78
59	Chicago	86
72	Washington (Mo.)	76
66	Washington (Mo.) ■	71
73	Chicago ■	87
60	New York U. ■	68
76	Brandeis ■	72
85	Emory	97
88	Case Reserve	77
44	Rochester ■	51

Nickname: Tartans
Colors: Cardinal, White & Grey
Arena: Skibo Gymnasium
  Capacity: 1,500; Year Built: 1924
AD: John H. Harvey
SID: Jon Surmacz

CARROLL (WIS.)
Waukesha, WI 53186-5593 III

Coach: Sean McDonough,
Marquette 1991

2001-02 RESULTS (2-21)

61	Lakeland ■	77
71	Milwaukee Engr. ■	77
62	Wis.-Stevens Point	83
69	Beloit	80
65	Carthage	79
59	St. Norbert ■	77
66	Wis.-Whitewater	95
75	Bethany (W.Va.) †	103
67	Hobart †	74
45	Ripon	67
85	Grinnell ■	143
74	Knox	86
91	Lawrence ■	96
73	Illinois Col. ■	77
82	Monmouth (Ill.) ■	93
59	Lake Forest	74
73	Illinois Col.	80
65	Beloit ■	59
81	Knox ■	80
122	Grinnell ■	143
58	St. Norbert	76
82	Ripon ■	95
68	Lawrence	81

Nickname: Pioneers
Colors: Orange & White
Arena: Van Male Fieldhouse
  Capacity: 2,000; Year Built: 1965
AD: Kris Jacobsen
SID: Rick Mobley

CARSON-NEWMAN
Jefferson City, TN 37760 II

Coach: Dale Clayton, Milligan 1973

2001-02 RESULTS (26-5)

66	Findlay †	81
54	Erskine †	62
67	Lincoln Memorial	75
87	Ala.-Huntsville ■	71
87	S.C.-Aiken ■	70
91	Lincoln Memorial ■	61
67	S.C.-Aiken	61
85	Armstrong Atlantic	69
96	UNC Pembroke †	90
79	West Va. Tech	61
74	Wingate	76
104	Mars Hill ■	60
69	Presbyterian	59
79	Maryville (Tenn.) ■	76
78	Lenoir-Rhyne ■	54
64	Tusculum	50
94	Newberry	82
72	Maryville (Tenn.)	61
95	Catawba	77
87	Wingate ■	75
91	Mars Hill	64
97	Presbyterian ■	83
75	Lenoir-Rhyne	70
62	Tusculum ■	52
101	Newberry ■	70
71	Catawba ■	67
105	Newberry ■	74
88	Tusculum †	51
76	Wingate †	62
77	Johnson Smith	66
68	Shaw ■	69

Nickname: Eagles
Colors: Orange & Blue
Arena: Holt Fieldhouse
  Capacity: 2,000; Year Built: 1961
AD: David W. Barger
SID: Marlin Curnutt

CARTHAGE
Kenosha, WI 53140 III

Coach: Bosko Djurickovic,
North Park 1973

2001-02 RESULTS (28-2)

72	Mt. St. Joseph †	50
74	Illinois Col.	69

CASE RESERVE
Cleveland, OH 44106 III

Coach: Adam Hutchinson, Amherst
1993

2001-02 RESULTS (7-17)

66	Chicago	49
101	Dominican (Ill.) ■	62
66	Savannah A&D ■	50
79	Carroll (Wis.)	65
69	Olivet Nazarene ■	56
84	Palm Beach Atl.	61
75	Malone †	63
76	Marycrest Int'l	68
75	St. Xavier ■	71
75	Elmhurst ■	76
84	Millikin ■	68
71	Wheaton (Ill.)	61
72	Ill. Wesleyan ■	49
64	Augustana (Ill.)	63
80	North Park	62
70	Elmhurst	63
76	Ill. Wesleyan	56
85	North Central ■	52
83	North Central	73
74	North Park ■	59
74	Millikin	61
83	Wheaton (Ill.) ■	72
84	Augustana (Ill.) ■	70
63	Hope	57
71	Gust. Adolphus †	65
85	Lewis & Clark ■	70
66	Otterbein †	70
72	Rochester †	51

Nickname: Redmen
Colors: Red, White & Black
Arena: PE Center
  Capacity: 2,500; Year Built: 1964
AD: Robert R. Bonn
SID: Steve Marovich

Coach: Adam Hutchinson, Amherst
1993

2001-02 RESULTS (7-17)

69	Washington (Md.) †	76
67	Johns Hopkins	93
45	Wittenberg	85
84	Hiram ■	63
76	Lake Erie	62
83	Notre Dame (Md.)	67
55	Grove City ■	74
43	Wooster	94
65	Ohio Northern †	80
84	Oberlin ■	54
85	Emory	78
68	Chicago ■	77
92	Washington (Mo.) ■	97
76	Carnegie Mellon	72
53	Rochester	98
65	Brandeis	86
62	New York U.	78
71	New York U. ■	63
70	Brandeis ■	88
49	Washington (Mo.) ■	82
64	Chicago	80
43	Rochester ■	76
77	Carnegie Mellon ■	88
78	Emory ■	94

Nickname: Spartans
Colors: Blue, Gray & White
Arena: Emerson PE Center
  Capacity: 1,220; Year Built: 1958
AD: David M. Hutter
SID: Creg Jantz

CASTLETON ST.
Castleton, VT 05735 III

Coach: Ted Shipley, Lyndon St. 1987

2001-02 RESULTS (7-18)

48	Plattsburgh St.	77
68	Norwich ■	88
77	Oneonta St. ■	92
75	Southern Vt.	104
87	Curry †	86

50	Norwich	74
62	Dartmouth	89
74	Curry ■	78
79	Green Mountain	73
68	Norwich ■	61
81	Emmanuel (Mass.)	78
95	New England Col. ■	85
51	Middlebury	70
82	Notre Dame (N.H.)	94
68	Johnson St.	79
82	Lyndon St.	77
72	Plymouth St.	90
80	Utica/Rome ■	90
68	Green Mountain ■	79
70	Johnson St. ■	77
78	St. Joseph (Vt.) ■	85
54	Gordon ■	73
88	Lyndon St.	76
96	Notre Dame (N.H.) ■	102
59	St. Joseph (Vt.)	70

Nickname: Spartans
Colors: Green & White
Arena: Glenbrook
  Capacity: 1,000; Year Built: 1959
AD: Deanna Tyson
SID: Tim Barrett

CATAWBA
Salisbury, NC 28144-2488 II

Coach: Jim Baker, Catawba 1978
2001-02 RESULTS (19-8)

98	Pfeiffer	90
103	Claflin ■	66
87	Livingstone	77
87	Reinhardt ■	66
87	St. Andrews ■	78
84	Winston-Salem ■	89
90	N.C. Central ■	77
89	Allen ■	62
79	Johnson Smith ■	85
76	N.C. Central	75
75	Livingstone ■	68
87	Lenoir-Rhyne ■	78
71	Tusculum	61
96	Mars Hill	70
102	Wingate ■	97
84	Newberry	70
71	Presbyterian ■	64
80	Apprentice ■	71
77	Carson-Newman ■	95
69	Lenoir-Rhyne	76
53	Tusculum ■	46
58	Mars Hill ■	59
76	Wingate	91
78	Newberry ■	77
73	Presbyterian	68
67	Carson-Newman	71
74	Presbyterian ■	83

Nickname: Indians
Colors: Blue & White
Arena: Goodman Gym
  Capacity: 3,500; Year Built: 1970
AD: Dennis Davidson
SID: Jim Lewis

CATHOLIC
Washington, DC 20064 III

Coach: Mike Lonergan, Catholic 1988
2001-02 RESULTS (26-3)

68	Wm. Paterson	71
90	Scranton ■	83
72	York (Pa.)	69
86	Goucher ■	67
80	Villa Julie	60
77	Haverford	50
90	McDaniel	55
76	Lebanon Valley ■	59
87	Lycoming ■	70
88	Swarthmore ■	53
62	Edgewood ■	59
90	Salisbury	79

104	Gallaudet ■	63
84	Johns Hopkins	79
81	Mary Washington	63
86	Marymount (Va.) ■	67
88	St. Mary's (Md.) ■	62
92	Goucher	85
94	York (Pa.) ■	78
91	Gallaudet	71
75	Salisbury ■	64
70	Marymount (Va.)	79
70	Mary Washington ■	47
102	St. Mary's (Md.)	76
85	St. Mary's (Md.) ■	65
77	Goucher ■	61
64	Marymount (Va.)	56
74	Hampden-Sydney ■	68
72	Clark (Mass.) ■	75

Nickname: Cardinals
Colors: Cardinal Red & Black
Arena: DuFour Center
  Capacity: 2,000; Year Built: 1985
AD: Robert J. Talbot
SID: Chris Panter

CAZENOVIA
Cazenovia, NY 13035 III

Coach: Todd Widrick, Le Moyne 1985
2001-02 RESULTS (16-11)

81	Keuka †	77
71	St. John Fisher	83
71	Alfred	80
72	Clarkson	68
66	Potsdam St.	76
72	Hobart ■	65
105	Baptist Bible (Pa.) ■	98
80	Marietta †	81
75	Union (N.Y.) †	81
86	Tufts †	81
64	Union (N.Y.)	62
87	Ithaca ■	86
92	Medaille ■	78
87	Utica	83
73	Hilbert	67
73	D'Youville ■	78
82	Le Moyne	88
85	Medaille	66
54	Rochester Inst.	84
70	D'Youville	62
87	Cortland St.	76
75	Hilbert ■	73
76	Keuka	78
104	Keuka ■	90
76	Elmira	75
78	Hilbert †	86
49	Williams	121

Nickname: Wildcats
Colors: Navy Blue & Gold
Arena: Schneweiss Athletic Center
  Capacity: 800; Year Built: 1988
AD: Marvin Christopher
SID: Todd Widrick

CENTENARY (LA.)
Shreveport, LA 71134-1188 I

Coach: Kevin Johnson, Tex.-Pan American 88
2001-02 RESULTS (14-13)

87	East Tex. Baptist ■	67
76	Tulane	92
89	LeTourneau ■	62
99	Southern U.	69
62	Stephen F. Austin ■	51
75	Vanderbilt	77
48	Louisiana Tech	68
66	Baylor	99
57	Rice	66
59	Utah St.	74
56	Birmingham-So. †	38
73	Texas A&M	63
72	Northwestern St.	89
74	Gardner-Webb ■	58

80	Tex. A&M-Corp. Chris. ■	81
82	Texas Col. ■	59
52	Lipscomb	51
67	Gardner-Webb	78
84	Louisiana Tech ■	71
61	Tex.-Pan American ■	58
64	Lipscomb	54
62	La.-Lafayette	77
107	Ark. Baptist ■	59
57	Northwestern St.	65
73	Tex. A&M-Corp. Chris. ■	77
85	Tex.-Pan American ■	67
80	Washington St.	102

Nickname: Gentlemen
Colors: Maroon & White
Arena: Gold Dome
  Capacity: 3,000; Year Built: 1971
AD: David Bedard
SID: Jason Behenna

CENTENARY (N.J.)
Hackettstown, NJ 07840 III

Coach: Abe Kasbo, Seton Hall
2001-02 RESULTS (4-19)

78	Maritime (N.Y.) †	90
85	New Paltz St. †	77
61	Manhattanville ■	94
72	Farmingdale St.	85
48	DeSales	110
71	Delaware Valley ■	66
48	Wm. Paterson	83
55	Misericordia	83
64	CCNY	72
65	King's (Pa.) ■	100
55	Skidmore	65
74	Rutgers-Camden	89
76	Widener	96
65	Lehman ■	84
85	Col. of New Jersey ■	100
74	Mt. St. Vincent ■	62
58	FDU-Madison	78
66	Phila. Bible ■	72
44	Indiana (Pa.)	92
73	Medgar Evers ■	91
80	Baptist Bible (Pa.)	78
75	Hunter ■	102
62	Farmingdale St. ■	93

Nickname: Cyclones
Colors: Blue & White
Arena: Reeves Center
  Capacity: 250; Year Built: 1954
AD: Diane Finnan
SID: Josh Huber

CENTRAL (IOWA)
Pella, IA 50219 III

Coach: Dan Mason, North Park 1983
2001-02 RESULTS (5-21)

85	Northwestern (Iowa) †	91
87	Trinity Christian †	93
86	Iowa Wesleyan ■	84
68	Luther	57
50	St. Cloud St.	88
58	Buena Vista ■	63
85	Wartburg ■	98
57	Dordt ■	76
64	Mt. Mercy	69
68	Augustana (Ill.) ■	76
75	Simpson ■	82
53	Upper Iowa	67
67	Coe	68
60	Cornell College	81
69	Dubuque ■	60
53	Loras ■	56
88	Upper Iowa ■	67
63	Wartburg	68
53	Buena Vista	71
67	Simpson	79
62	Luther	65
62	Cornell College ■	71
58	Coe	75

76	Loras	87
70	Dubuque	59
82	Buena Vista	110

Nickname: Dutch
Colors: Red & White
Arena: Kuyper Gymnasium
  Capacity: 3,000; Year Built: 1970
AD: Al Dorenkamp
SID: Larry Happel

CENTRAL ARK.
Conway, AR 72035-0001 II

Coach: Charles Hervey
2001-02 RESULTS (11-14)

86	Lambuth	85
80	Central Okla.	94
90	St. Xavier †	85
72	Grand Canyon	74
65	Incarnate Word †	82
70	St. Edward's	75
57	Ark.-Little Rock	92
84	Okla. Panhandle ■	78
70	Southern Ark.	86
67	Harding	84
81	Christian Bros. ■	65
53	Delta St.	72
67	Ouachita Baptist ■	62
60	Arkansas Tech	69
74	Ark.-Monticello	73
78	Ark. Baptist ■	74
67	Henderson St.	64
67	Southern Ark. ■	67
64	Harding	80
75	Christian Bros.	67
66	Delta St. ■	68
67	Ouachita Baptist	73
66	Arkansas Tech ■	72
95	Ark.-Monticello ■	76
72	Henderson St. ■	70

Nickname: Bears
Colors: Purple & Gray
Arena: Jeff Farris Center
  Capacity: 6,500; Year Built: 1973
AD: William Lide
SID: Steve East

CENTRAL CONN. ST.
New Britain, CT 06050-4010 I

Coach: Howie Dickenman, Central Conn. St. 1970
2001-02 RESULTS (27-5)

44	Oklahoma	66
68	Bucknell ■	55
66	Brown ■	60
73	Hartford †	59
60	Niagara †	55
69	St. Francis (N.Y.) ■	82
80	Mt. St. Mary's	69
66	UMBC	62
107	Long Island	76
49	Massachusetts ■	64
67	Loyola (Md.) ■	50
63	Providence	94
77	Wagner ■	71
76	Sacred Heart ■	47
84	Quinnipiac	74
76	UMBC ■	58
50	Monmouth ■	42
78	Sacred Heart	69
76	Quinnipiac ■	66
66	St. Francis (Pa.)	49
64	Robert Morris	55
90	Fairleigh Dickinson ■	62
63	Monmouth	62
83	Wagner	69
100	Long Island ■	65
83	Fairleigh Dickinson	65
80	St. Francis (Pa.) ■	59
70	Robert Morris ■	62
65	Sacred Heart †	54
58	St. Francis (N.Y.) †	54

78 Quinnipiac ■ 71
54 Pittsburgh 71

Nickname: Blue Devils
Colors: Blue & White
Arena: Detrick Gymnasium
    Capacity: 4,500; Year Built: 1965
AD: Charles Jones Jr.
SID: Gene Gumbs

UCF
Orlando, FL 32816-3555 I

Coach: Kirk Speraw, Iowa 1980
2001-02 RESULTS (17-12)
92 P.R.-Mayaguez ■ 58
72 Hampton 73
82 East Caro. 72
73 Jacksonville ■ 72
66 Fla. Atlantic 78
101 Florida A&M ■ 76
100 Chicago St. 67
69 Jacksonville St. 72
58 Samford 59
63 Marist 78
75 Stetson 69
99 Campbell ■ 86
84 Georgia St. ■ 92
74 Troy St. 85
81 Mercer 71
76 Belmont ■ 59
62 Fla. Atlantic ■ 56
86 Belmont 78
79 South Fla. ■ 84
86 Mercer ■ 53
58 Troy St. ■ 64
83 Georgia St. 73
84 Campbell 86
72 Samford ■ 56
68 Jacksonville St. ■ 50
78 Stetson 65
80 Jacksonville 82
84 Samford ■ 74
64 Georgia St. ■ 82

Nickname: Golden Knights
Colors: Black & Gold
Arena: UCF Arena
    Capacity: 5,100; Year Built: 1991
AD: Steve Orsini
SID: Chris Showiak

CENTRAL MICH.
Mount Pleasant, MI 48859-0001 I

Coach: Jay Smith, Saginaw Valley 1984
2001-02 RESULTS (9-19)
75 Tri-State ■ 53
65 Dayton 81
76 Georgia St. ■ 52
64 Oklahoma 81
79 Loyola (Ill.) ■ 72
54 George Mason 65
63 Illinois St. 72
68 Detroit ■ 77
81 Bowling Green ■ 82
94 Miami (Ohio) ■ 100
77 Ball St. 89
67 Western Mich. 81
88 Marshall ■ 84
86 Eastern Mich. 73
75 Toledo 61
73 Akron 83
91 Northern Ill. ■ 93
70 Western Mich. ■ 67
42 Toledo 58
66 Kent St. ■ 96
50 Ohio 64
57 Buffalo 69
76 Eastern Mich. ■ 57
70 Northern Ill. 80
57 Marshall 82
77 Ball St. ■ 81

65 Ohio..................................56
54 Toledo † 62

Nickname: Chippewas
Colors: Maroon & Gold
Arena: Rose Arena
    Capacity: 5,200; Year Built: 1973
AD: Herbert W. Deromedi
SID: Don Helinski

CENTRAL MO. ST.
Warrensburg, MO 64093 II

Coach: Don Doucette, Boston St. 1976
2001-02 RESULTS (12-15)
56 Evangel ■ 76
72 Lincoln (Mo.) † 78
88 St. Mary (Kan.) † 71
76 York (Neb.) ■ 66
94 William Penn ■ 60
64 Okla. Panhandle ■ 53
98 St. Mary's (Tex.) † 85
83 Cameron † 60
61 Pittsburg St. 72
64 Mo. Western St. ■ 74
73 Truman ■ 61
62 Mo. Southern St. 70
89 Southwest Baptist ■ 88
61 Mo.-Rolla 60
61 Washburn ■ 85
54 Northwest Mo. St. 78
90 Emporia St. ■ 83
52 Pittsburg St. ■ 61
55 Mo. Western St. 71
54 Truman 58
78 Mo. Southern St. ■ 65
63 Southwest Baptist 77
32 Mo.-Rolla ■ 53
65 Washburn 83
54 Northwest Mo. St. ■ 72
97 Emporia St. ■ 92
51 Northwest Mo. St................100

Nickname: Mules
Colors: Cardinal & Black
Arena: CMSU Multipurpose Building
    Capacity: 8,500; Year Built: 1976
AD: Jerry M. Hughes
SID: Bill Turnage

CENTRAL OKLA.
Edmond, OK 73034 II

Coach: Jim Seward, Hiram Scott 1969
2001-02 RESULTS (10-16)
106 Ark. Baptist ■ 72
94 Central Ark. ■ 80
87 Harding 93
86 Tex. A&M-Kingsville ■ 106
102 Tex. A&M-Commerce ■ 71
91 Abilene Christian 89
83 Angelo St. 109
94 Drury † 78
77 Washburn † 91
56 Metro St. † 81
93 Lock Haven † 84
85 Eastern N.M. 88
85 West Tex. A&M ■ 68
54 Tarleton St. 90
101 East Central ■ 97
69 Southeastern Okla. 73
90 Cameron 72
90 Southwestern Okla. 96
57 Northeastern St. 83
65 Midwestern St. ■ 69
81 East Central 98
95 Southeastern Okla. ■ 59
78 Cameron 84
104 Southwestern Okla. ■ 108
78 Northeastern St. 93
80 Midwestern St. 91

Nickname: Bronchos
Colors: Bronze & Blue

Arena: Hamilton Field House
    Capacity: 3,000; Year Built: 1965
AD: John E. Wagnon
SID: Mike Kirk

CENTRAL WASH.
Ellensburg, WA 98926.............II

Coach: Greg Sparling, Central Wash.
    1993
2001-02 RESULTS (16-10)
104 Northwest (Wash.) ■ 73
87 Sonoma St. † 76
96 Cal St. Chico 76
91 Warner Pacific ■ 79
100 Seattle Pacific ■ 101
81 Western Wash. ■ 84
87 Ashland † 84
81 Drury † 68
90 St. Anselm † 92
67 Coker † 65
84 Alas. Fairbanks ■ 67
72 Alas. Anchorage 79
77 Northwest Nazarene 82
73 Seattle 83
88 Humboldt St. ■ 74
79 Western Ore. ■ 70
70 St. Martin's ■ 75
85 Western Wash. 88
59 Seattle Pacific 84
93 Alas. Anchorage ■ 88
79 Alas. Fairbanks ■ 58
61 Seattle 50
92 Northwest Nazarene ■ 80
97 Western Ore. 77
72 Humboldt St. 85
88 St. Martin's 62

Nickname: Wildcats
Colors: Crimson & Black
Arena: Nicholson Pavilion
    Capacity: 3,500; Year Built: 1959
AD: Jack Bishop
SID: Jonathan Gordon

CENTRE
Danville, KY 40422-1394.........III

Coach: Greg Mason, Centre 1994
2001-02 RESULTS (16-9)
74 Maryville (Tenn.) ■ 72
66 Hanover 74
82 Berea † 72
68 DePauw 83
56 Rose-Hulman 62
67 Sewanee ■ 45
83 Concordia (Ill.) ■ 64
71 Berea ■ 68
70 Rhodes ■ 60
72 Hendrix ■ 53
70 Millsaps 71
71 Oglethorpe 56
97 Thomas More ■ 88
80 Trinity (Tex.) ■ 86
72 Southwestern (Tex.) ■ 61
84 Transylvania 44
69 Sewanee 52
102 Rhodes 104
80 Hendrix 48
78 Millsaps ■ 81
75 Oglethorpe ■ 63
48 Trinity (Tex.) 55
78 Southwestern (Tex.) 75
79 DePauw ■ 88
80 Rose-Hulman ■ 60

Nickname: Colonels
Colors: Gold & White
Arena: Alumni Memorial Gym
    Capacity: 1,800; Year Built: 1950
AD: Brian Chafin
SID: Ed Rall

CHADRON ST.
Chadron, NE 69337-2690........II

Coach: Dan Beebe, Chadron St. 1992
2001-02 RESULTS (15-12)
79 Huron 55
73 Huron 70
86 Angelo St. 88
100 St. Edward's † 93
88 Great Falls ■ 69
87 Mont. St.-Billings 98
80 Mesa St. ■ 76
95 Western St. (Colo.) ■ 68
65 Adams St. 74
70 UC-Colo. Spgs. ■ 62
88 Southern Colo. ■ 75
86 N.M. Highlands ■ 71
77 Fort Lewis 81
78 Colorado Col. ■ 58
85 Colorado Mines ■ 72
64 Metro St. ■ 83
88 Colo. Christian ■ 64
78 Regis (Colo.) ■ 71
67 Fort Hays St. 74
78 Neb.-Kearney ■ 115
67 Metro St. 77
85 Colorado Mines 64
89 Colo. Christian 86
68 Regis (Colo.) 73
70 Fort Hays St. ■ 85
78 Neb.-Kearney ■ 90
54 Metro St. 76

Nickname: Eagles
Colors: Cardinal & White
Arena: Armstrong
    Capacity: 3,200; Year Built: 1965
AD: Bradley Roy Smith
SID: Con Marshall

CHAMINADE
Honolulu, HI 96816-1578 II

Coach: Aaron Griess, Colorado Col.
    1993
2001-02 RESULTS (16-11)
61 South Carolina † 74
62 Seton Hall ■ 74
73 Houston † 76
88 North Park ■ 73
64 San Fran. St. ■ 51
86 Hastings ■ 72
89 Western St. (Colo.) 75
70 Northern Colo. 89
78 Colo. Christian 72
59 Presbyterian ■ 49
88 Coe ■ 73
81 Mont. St.-Billings ■ 75
76 Mont. St.-Billings ■ 77
72 Western N.M. ■ 57
81 Hawaii Pacific 78
69 Hawaii Pacific 70
59 Hawaii-Hilo 62
80 BYU-Hawaii 82
83 Western N.M. 81
92 Western N.M. 89
79 Mont. St.-Billings ■ 108
78 Great Falls 76
74 Hawaii-Hilo ■ 62
69 Hawaii-Hilo ■ 67
76 Hawaii Pacific ■ 63
78 BYU-Hawaii ■ 91
82 BYU-Hawaii ■ 86

Nickname: Silverswords
Colors: Royal Blue & White
Arena: McCabe Gym
    Capacity: 2,500
AD: Aaron Griess
SID: John Hemenway

CHAPMAN
Orange, CA 92866 III

Coach: Mike Bokosky, Fort Lewis 1978
2001-02 RESULTS (18-7)
97	LIFE Bible ■	.38
78	Cooper Union ■	.42
62	Whittier	.80
82	Redlands	.88
76	Newport News †	.69
84	Redlands	.64
63	Lewis & Clark †	.95
81	La Verne	.76
59	Claremont-M-S ■	.73
75	Caltech ■	.33
58	Cal Lutheran ■	.70
52	Occidental	.68
75	Pacific Union †	.45
84	West Coast Chrst. †	.43
64	Richard Stockton †	.69
74	Whittier ■	.52
73	La Sierra	.65
79	San Jose Christian	.63
79	Cal Christian	.67
96	S'western (Ariz.) ■	.62
91	S'western (Ariz.)	.81
90	LIFE Bible ■	.63
108	Cal Christian ■	.66
84	San Jose Christian ■	.58
82	La Sierra ■	.62

Nickname: Panthers
Colors: Cardinal & Gray
Arena: Hutton Sports Center
    Capacity: 2,400; Year Built: 1978
AD: David Currey
SID: Doug Aiken

COL. OF CHARLESTON
Charleston, SC 29424 I

Coach: John Kresse, St. John's (N.Y.) 1964
2001-02 RESULTS (21-9)
76	Furman	.72
76	Charleston So. ■	.48
74	Stetson ■	.58
81	Francis Marion ■	.45
76	American	.70
64	Coastal Caro. †	.47
67	Belmont Abbey ■	.70
60	UNC Wilmington	.58
66	North Carolina	.60
70	Georgia St. †	.63
86	La.-Monroe ■	.60
68	Radford ■	.61
64	Wofford ■	.66
67	Chattanooga	.69
71	East Tenn. St. ■	.64
73	Wofford	.61
63	VMI	.55
77	Citadel ■	.65
57	Ga. Southern ■	.60
52	UNC Greensboro	.63
62	Furman	.45
58	Citadel	.60
79	Appalachian St. ■	.55
81	Western Caro.	.64
86	Chattanooga ■	.62
70	Davidson ■	.73
54	Ga. Southern	.70
85	Appalachian St. ■	.61
76	East Tenn. St.	.75
43	Furman ■	.44

Nickname: Cougars
Colors: Maroon & White
Arena: F. Mitchell Johnson Center
    Capacity: 3,500; Year Built: 1983
AD: Jerry I. Baker
SID: Tony Ciuffo

CHARLESTON (W.VA.)
Charleston, WV 25304 II

Coach: Jayson Gee, Charleston (W.Va.) 1988
2001-02 RESULTS (25-7)
82	Lenoir-Rhyne †	.70
79	Pfeiffer	.81
96	Oakland City ■	.72
91	Virginia St.	.72
88	Longwood ■	.80
80	Rio Grande †	.63
95	Concord	.86
95	Virginia St.	.78
82	Oakland City	.81
82	West Va. Tech ■	.81
89	West Virginia St.	.80
98	Bluefield St.	.72
76	Salem Int'l	.73
99	Davis & Elkins ■	.65
79	Shepherd ■	.66
85	Glenville St.	.86
85	Alderson-Broaddus	.87
79	West Va. Wesleyan ■	.100
74	Concord ■	.72
87	West Liberty St.	.65
87	Fairmont St. ■	.90
94	Ohio Valley ■	.59
95	Wheeling Jesuit	.86
114	West Virginia St. ■	.72
85	West Va. Tech	.72
130	Bluefield St. ■	.74
77	West Va. Tech ■	.69
80	Glenville St. ■	.76
66	West Va. Wesleyan ■	.64
86	Alderson-Broaddus ■	.88
96	Alderson-Broaddus †	.93
81	Indiana (Pa.)	.91

Nickname: Golden Eagles
Colors: Maroon & Gold
Arena: Eddie King Gym
    Capacity: 2,500; Year Built: 1888
AD: Tom Nozica
SID: Drew Meighen

CHARLESTON SO.
Charleston, SC 29423-8087 I

Coach: Jim Platt, Concordia (Ill.) 1973
2001-02 RESULTS (12-17)
48	Col. of Charleston	.76
62	Anderson (S.C.) ■	.55
60	William & Mary ■	.71
56	Georgia St.	.67
70	Citadel †	.66
69	VMI	.90
64	North Greenville ■	.55
54	Virginia	.74
50	North Carolina St.	.70
45	Clemson	.82
41	South Carolina	.86
63	UNC Asheville	.87
69	Elon	.75
71	High Point	.77
89	Liberty ■	.64
74	Radford ■	.63
71	Birmingham-So. ■	.44
66	Winthrop	.63
73	Coastal Caro. ■	.77
60	Birmingham-So.	.62
52	Radford	.70
66	Liberty	.53
60	High Point ■	.55
61	Elon ■	.52
55	Fairfield	.70
55	Winthrop ■	.57
77	UNC Asheville ■	.68
78	Coastal Caro.	.69
64	Elon †	.83

Nickname: Buccaneers
Colors: Blue & Gold
Arena: CSU Fieldhouse
    Capacity: 1,500; Year Built: 1965

AD: Hank Small
SID: To be named

CHARLOTTE
Charlotte, NC 28223 I

Coach: Bobby Lutz, Charlotte 1980
2001-02 RESULTS (18-12)
65	Davidson ■	.51
61	Indiana	.65
100	Long Beach St.	.81
71	Appalachian St. ■	.69
64	Temple	.72
63	Valparaiso ■	.70
62	Richmond ■	.42
52	Florida †	.73
86	UTEP ■	.58
56	Miami (Fla.)	.64
97	George Washington	.87
76	Marquette	.68
58	Cincinnati	.71
84	East Caro.	.75
77	St. Louis ■	.49
81	South Fla.	.78
77	Louisville ■	.71
87	East Caro. ■	.52
97	DePaul	.83
83	Houston	.68
66	Cincinnati ■	.85
54	St. Louis	.73
75	Memphis ■	.63
81	DePaul ■	.57
52	Marquette	.66
96	Tulane ■	.54
88	Louisville	.90
78	Tulane †	.69
55	Cincinnati †	.71
63	Notre Dame †	.82

Nickname: 49ers
Colors: Green & White
Arena: Dale F. Halton Arena
    Capacity: 9,105; Year Built: 1996
AD: Judith W. Rose
SID: Thomas E. Whitestone

CHATTANOOGA
Chattanooga, TN 37403-2598 ..I

Coach: Henry Dickerson, Charleston (W. Va.) 1973
2001-02 RESULTS (16-14)
89	Tenn. Wesleyan ■	.59
82	Liberty †	.57
84	Notre Dame †	.97
57	Vanderbilt †	.69
63	Murray St.	.72
56	Kent St.	.75
68	Alabama	.74
70	Illinois St. ■	.59
83	Bluefield Col. ■	.51
84	Arkansas	.98
71	Murray St. ■	.58
76	Sam Houston St. ■	.59
71	Weber St. ■	.63
77	UNC Greensboro ■	.74
69	Col. of Charleston ■	.67
61	Davidson	.63
67	Appalachian St.	.81
79	Wofford ■	.77
64	Citadel	.72
65	Furman ■	.76
66	East Tenn. St.	.61
103	Ga. Southern ■	.91
84	Citadel ■	.77
70	Wofford	.45
67	Furman	.68
91	VMI ■	.64
62	Col. of Charleston	.86
68	Ga. Southern ■	.84
91	Western Caro. ■	.71
57	UNC Greensboro †	.67

Nickname: Mocs
Colors: Navy Blue & Gold

Arena: The McKenzie Arena
    Capacity: 11,218; Year Built: 1982
AD: Steve Sloan
SID: Jeff Romero

CHEYNEY
Cheyney, PA 19319-0200 II

Coach: Robert Marshall, Cheyney 1980
2001-02 RESULTS (17-10)
62	Columbia Union	.78
79	Lincoln (Pa.) †	.73
72	Caldwell ■	.76
60	Calif. (Pa.)	.85
44	Indiana (Pa.)	.84
69	Cabrini ■	.63
87	Clarion ■	.78
83	Lock Haven ■	.68
63	Edinboro	.66
63	Slippery Rock	.47
74	East Stroudsburg ■	.65
82	Shippensburg ■	.65
72	Bloomsburg ■	.74
80	Mansfield ■	.74
72	West Chester ■	.74
80	Kutztown ■	.73
67	Millersville	.76
50	East Stroudsburg	.48
71	Bloomsburg	.69
63	West Chester ■	.48
91	Millersville ■	.89
77	Mansfield	.74
70	Bowie St. ■	.65
95	Columbia Union ■	.85
60	Kutztown	.69
77	Millersville ■	.75
81	Indiana (Pa.) ■	.86

Nickname: Wolves
Colors: Blue & White
Arena: Cope Hall
    Capacity: 1,500; Year Built: 1961
AD: Eve Atkinson
SID: Lenn Margolis

CHICAGO
Chicago, IL 60637 III

Coach: Mike McGrath, DePauw 1992
2001-02 RESULTS (15-10)
70	Beloit ■	.80
77	Ohio Wesleyan ■	.70
63	Wheaton (Ill.)	.67
87	Carleton ■	.82
49	Carthage ■	.66
60	Ill. Wesleyan ■	.65
79	Kalamazoo ■	.72
79	Lake Forest	.68
52	DePauw	.72
52	Rhodes	.54
63	Benedictine (Ill.) ■	.57
62	Washington (Mo.)	.65
77	Case Reserve	.68
86	Emory	.65
73	Brandeis ■	.60
71	New York U. ■	.49
86	Carnegie Mellon ■	.59
51	Rochester	.54
52	Rochester	.55
87	Carnegie Mellon	.73
103	Emory ■	.78
80	Case Reserve ■	.64
59	New York U.	.57
86	Brandeis	.77
62	Washington (Mo.) ■	.64

Nickname: Maroons
Colors: Maroon & White
Arena: Henry Crown Field House
    Capacity: 1,500; Year Built: 1931
AD: Thomas Weingartner
SID: Dave Hilbert

CHICAGO ST.
Chicago, IL 60628-1598 I

Coach: Bo Ellis, Marquette 1977
2001-02 RESULTS (2-26)

49	Marquette	102
92	Buffalo ■	100
42	Northwestern	80
62	Wis.-Green Bay	78
81	Youngstown St. ■	72
47	Wis.-Milwaukee	84
67	UCF	100
63	DePaul	79
87	Lakeland ■	58
73	Loyola (Ill.)	85
56	Wichita St. ■	78
77	Oakland	88
54	IUPUI	61
62	IPFW	79
77	Western Ill.	82
66	Valparaiso ■	78
49	Southern Utah	69
53	UMKC	67
62	Oral Roberts	91
59	IUPUI ■	92
73	Oakland ■	78
63	Valparaiso	100
69	Western Ill.	93
35	Southern Utah ■	57
86	IPFW ■	88
64	Oral Roberts ■	94
48	UMKC ■	61
50	Valparaiso †	81

Nickname: Cougars
Colors: Green & White
Arena: Jacoby Dickens Center
  Capacity: 2,500; Year Built: 1971
AD: Al Avant
SID: Mark Johnson

CHOWAN
Murfreesboro, NC 27855.........III

Coach: Bob Burke, Campbell 1969
2001-02 RESULTS (7-19)

99	Elmira †	95
67	Lycoming	89
92	Me.-Presque Isle †	58
74	Frostburg St. ■	72
94	Villa Julie	99
66	Apprentice	76
53	Apprentice ■	63
79	Lycoming ■	87
74	Wesley ■	75
65	John Jay †	67
70	Delaware Valley †	62
58	N.C. Wesleyan	72
60	Methodist	65
58	Greensboro ■	62
67	Chris. Newport	80
72	Shenandoah	81
92	Averett ■	74
61	Ferrum	87
60	N.C. Wesleyan ■	66
57	Methodist ■	66
57	Greensboro	70
48	Chris. Newport ■	82
67	Shenandoah ■	82
76	Averett	70
81	Ferrum	67
75	Methodist	84

Nickname: Braves
Colors: Columbia Blue & White
Arena: Helms Center
  Capacity: 3,000; Year Built: 1979
AD: Debra P. Warren
SID: Meredith Davies Long

CHRISTIAN BROS.
Memphis, TN 38104 II

Coach: Mike Nienaber, Mississippi Col. 1976

2001-02 RESULTS (7-19)

74	Central St. (Ohio) †	81
87	Ferris St. †	79
87	LeMoyne-Owen ■	90
54	Memphis	86
78	West Ala.	67
87	Bellarmine ■	89
77	Mo.-Rolla	85
78	LeMoyne-Owen	94
81	Mo.-Rolla ■	71
87	Arkansas Tech	83
87	Ark.-Monticello	76
65	Central Ark.	81
66	Henderson St. ■	72
72	Southern Ark.	98
75	Harding	85
68	West Ala.	70
66	Delta St. ■	63
87	Ouachita Baptist	84
87	Arkansas Tech	85
56	Ark.-Monticello	67
67	Central Ark.	75
59	Henderson St.	61
64	Southern Ark. ■	65
63	Harding ■	96
64	Delta St.	70
84	Ouachita Baptist ■	73

Nickname: Buccaneers
Colors: Scarlet & Gray
Arena: De La Salle Gymnasium
  Capacity: 2,000; Year Built: 1951
AD: Michael Daush
SID: Keith Smith

CHRIS. NEWPORT
Newport News, VA 23606-2998 III

Coach: C.J. Woollum, Ky. Wesleyan 1971

2001-02 RESULTS (23-5)

64	Greensboro	59
72	Marymount (Va.) ■	67
75	Va. Wesleyan ■	51
103	Temple Baptist ■	66
111	St. Mary's (Md.) ■	83
83	St. Lawrence ■	70
83	Salisbury	69
60	Randolph-Macon ■	78
68	Savannah A&D ■	55
80	Frostburg St. ■	71
88	Haverford ■	56
78	New Jersey City †	74
62	Shenandoah ■	57
97	Ferrum	78
78	Averett	73
80	Chowan ■	67
67	N.C. Wesleyan ■	74
80	Methodist	64
58	Shenandoah	73
71	Ferrum ■	55
86	Averett ■	62
82	Chowan	48
89	N.C. Wesleyan ■	91
81	Methodist ■	63
76	Greensboro ■	55
96	Averett †	71
90	Shenandoah †	68
75	N.C. Wesleyan †	77

Nickname: Captains
Colors: Blue & Silver
Arena: Freeman Center
  Capacity: 2,300; Year Built: 2000
AD: C.J. Woollum
SID: Francis Tommasino

CINCINNATI
Cincinnati, OH 45221-0021 I

Coach: Bob Huggins, West Virginia 1977

2001-02 RESULTS (31-4)

62	Oklahoma St.	69
83	Wright St. ■	54
74	UNLV ■	61
77	Dayton ■	55
74	Duquesne ■	41
90	Coppin St. ■	39
68	Toledo ■	55
75	Xavier	55
77	Richmond ■	46
102	La.-Monroe †	66
90	Mississippi St. †	56
79	Purdue †	62
73	Akron †	57
72	East Caro.	62
71	Charlotte ■	58
83	Houston	62
89	DePaul ■	72
77	Louisville ■	50
54	St. Louis	50
78	South Fla.	68
75	East Caro. ■	48
60	Marquette	74
85	Charlotte	66
103	Wake Forest	94
67	St. Louis ■	53
89	Southern Miss. ■	37
79	DePaul	62
63	Marquette ■	62
71	Louisville	74
80	Memphis ■	75
79	South Fla. †	57
71	Charlotte †	55
77	Marquette †	63
90	Boston U. †	52
101	UCLA †	105

Nickname: Bearcats
Colors: Red & Black
Arena: Myrl Shoemaker Center
  Capacity: 13,176; Year Built: 1989
AD: Robert G. Goin
SID: Tom Hathaway

CITADEL
Charleston, SC 29409-6150 I

Coach: Pat Dennis, Wash. & Lee 1978
2001-02 RESULTS (17-12)

69	Flagler	62
53	North Carolina St.	63
67	William & Mary ■	62
83	Navy ■	47
66	Charleston So. †	70
97	Emmanuel (Ga.) ■	59
69	Davidson	50
65	Philander Smith	51
72	Greensboro ■	40
57	South Carolina	73
74	Coastal Caro.	62
89	South Carolina St.	81
74	East Tenn. St. ■	61
64	Wofford	73
105	Western Caro.	97
85	Ga. Southern ■ †	80
72	Chattanooga ■	64
65	Col. of Charleston	77
74	Appalachian St. ■	78
75	Furman	83
77	Chattanooga	84
60	Col. of Charleston ■	58
68	UNC Greensboro	81
64	Furman ■	70
86	Ga. Southern	95
75	VMI	55
72	Wofford ■	63
80	VMI †	70
58	Davidson †	71

Nickname: Bulldogs
Colors: Blue & White
Arena: McAlister Field House
  Capacity: 6,000; Year Built: 1939
AD: Les Robinson
SID: Andy Solomon

CCNY
New York, NY 10031 III

Coach: Andre Stampfel, Baruch 1996
2001-02 RESULTS (11-16)

67	Ramapo	89
61	Roger Williams †	75
72	Purchase St.	83
62	Lehman	64
78	Skidmore	74
56	St. John Fisher †	72
61	Mt. St. Mary (N.Y.) ■	68
74	Hunter	92
72	Centenary (N.J.) ■	64
85	Mt. St. Vincent	87
69	Yeshiva	61
81	St. Joseph's (Brkln)	49
64	St. Joseph's (L.I.)	58
63	Merchant Marine ■	86
68	John Jay	71
91	Baruch	77
63	Medgar Evers ■	82
75	NYCCT ■	78
74	Staten Island	75
75	York (N.Y.) ■	52
88	Brooklyn	74
73	Lehman ■	78
76	Hunter ■	58
76	John Jay ■	86
79	Baruch ■	71
75	Brooklyn ■	58
61	Staten Island †	75

Nickname: Beavers
Colors: Lavender & Black
Arena: Nat Holman Gymnasium
  Capacity: 3,500; Year Built: 1972
AD: Robert Coleman
SID: Derrick Harrison

CLAREMONT-M-S
Claremont, CA 91711-6400 III

Coach: Ken Scalmanini, Cal Poly Pomona 1993
2001-02 RESULTS (21-5)

98	Puget Sound	85
84	Pacific Lutheran ■	93
72	Southwestern (Tex.) †	62
64	Savannah A&D ■	66
81	Hope Int'l ■	55
73	Chapman	59
63	Holy Names ■	59
90	Concordia (Cal.)	85
75	Culver-Stockton ■	82
76	Pacific (Ore.) ■	53
92	La Sierra †	63
58	Cal Lutheran	59
67	Caltech	34
82	Redlands ■	70
85	La Verne	68
79	Pomona-Pitzer ■	71
77	Occidental ■	67
64	Whittier	63
64	Cal Lutheran ■	60
74	Caltech ■	35
71	Redlands	63
73	La Verne ■	60
51	Pomona-Pitzer	49
49	Occidental	47
84	Whittier ■	52
59	Lewis & Clark	81

Nickname: Stags
Colors: Maroon, Gold & White

Arena: Ducey Gymnasium
 Capacity: 1,200; Year Built: 1959
AD: Michael Sutton
SID: Kelly Beck

CLARION
Clarion, PA 16214................II

Coach: Ron Righter, St. Joseph's 1975
2001-02 RESULTS (15-11)
72	Shippensburg ■	42
133	Practical Bible ■	75
73	Franklin Pierce ■	86
85	Felician	80
82	Mansfield ■	86
68	Bloomsburg ■	56
78	Cheyney	87
70	West Chester	54
55	Millersville	64
91	East Stroudsburg ■	61
77	Kutztown ■	56
62	Edinboro	76
67	Indiana (Pa.)	72
75	New Haven	87
70	Lock Haven ■	46
77	Slippery Rock	55
74	Shippensburg	79
61	Calif. (Pa.) ■	59
78	Edinboro ■	74
59	Lock Haven	61
68	Pitt.-Johnstown	57
74	Slippery Rock ■	60
82	Indiana (Pa.) ■	71
78	Calif. (Pa.)	85
74	New Haven ■	67
55	Indiana (Pa.)	62

Nickname: Golden Eagles
Colors: Blue & Gold
Arena: W.S. Tippin Gymnasium
 Capacity: 4,000; Year Built: 1968
AD: Robert Carlson
SID: Rich Herman

CLARK ATLANTA
Atlanta, GA 30314................II

Coach: Anthony Witherspoon,
 Clark Atlanta 1977
2001-02 RESULTS (10-15)
89	N.C. Central †	73
65	Paine	66
75	St. Augustine's ■	83
61	Shaw ■	85
81	Morehouse ■	91
85	Tuskegee ■	99
71	Fort Valley St. ■	77
78	Albany St. (Ga.) ■	83
57	Morris Brown	63
72	Miles ■	64
88	LeMoyne-Owen ■	83
90	Lane	85
92	Kentucky St.	99
77	Morehouse	87
80	Fort Valley St.	75
82	Albany St. (Ga.)	78
86	Morris Brown †	84
70	Miles	81
71	LeMoyne-Owen	75
98	Lane	84
91	Kentucky St. ■	80
105	Tuskegee ■	93
83	Morehouse †	88

Nickname: Panthers
Colors: Red, Black & Grey
Arena: L.S. Epps Gym
 Capacity: 1,800
AD: Brenda Edmond
SID: Charles Ward

CLARK (MASS.)
Worcester, MA 01610-1477.....III

Coach: Paul Phillips, Assumption 1976
2001-02 RESULTS (23-6)
82	Va. Wesleyan †	76
84	Wilkes	72
80	Wesleyan (Conn.)	83
98	Brandeis ■	54
111	Lasell †	101
78	Williams	80
87	Amherst ■	77
83	Mass.-Boston ■	75
90	Worcester St.	59
113	Frostburg St. †	71
63	Frank. & Marsh. †	73
87	Wheaton (Mass.)	70
75	Babson	63
85	MIT ■	83
78	WPI	57
100	Springfield ■	76
92	Coast Guard	74
108	Trinity (Conn.)	75
76	Wheaton (Mass.) ■	69
79	Babson	90
90	MIT	82
87	WPI ■	55
77	Springfield	66
91	Coast Guard ■	64
92	Wheaton (Mass.) ■	100
84	Suffolk ■	77
101	Staten Island	72
75	Catholic	72
90	Elizabethtown †	94

Nickname: Cougars
Colors: Scarlet & White
Arena: Kneller Athletic Center
 Capacity: 2,000; Year Built: 1977
AD: Linda S. Moulton
SID: Joe Brady

CLARKE
Dubuque, IA 52001................III

Coach: Jon Davison, Dubuque 1961
2001-02 RESULTS (11-14)
77	Buena Vista	96
83	Wis. Lutheran ■	80
89	Cornell College ■	79
67	Wis.-Platteville ■	83
69	Knox	57
68	Mt. Mercy	74
89	Kendall ■	86
52	Augustana (Ill.)	89
62	Viterbo ■	69
61	Dubuque ■	75
67	William Penn ■	79
50	Concordia (Ill.) ■	46
55	Benedictine (Ill.) ■	74
70	Dominican (Ill.)	67
76	Faith Bapt. Bible ■	44
63	Rockford ■	71
75	Eureka	71
73	Aurora ■	76
67	Concordia (Ill.)	69
74	Benedictine (Ill.) ■	60
62	Dominican (Ill.) ■	56
69	Upper Iowa ■	72
49	Rockford	72
66	Eureka ■	59
68	Aurora	77

Nickname: Crusaders
Colors: Navy & Gold
Arena: Kehl Center
 Capacity: 900; Year Built: 1994
AD: Curt Long
SID: Jerry Hanson

CLARKSON
Potsdam, NY 13699-5830.......III

Coach: Tobin Anderson, Wesley 1995
2001-02 RESULTS (19-10)
81	Potsdam St. †	80
78	St. Lawrence †	80
77	Plattsburgh St. ■	64
105	Oneonta St. ■	66
68	Cazenovia ■	72
97	Keuka ■	56
91	St. Lawrence	84
82	George Fox †	70
90	Gallaudet †	63
68	Utica	60
61	Union (N.Y.) ■	55
90	Skidmore ■	67
78	Rensselaer ■	95
80	Vassar	52
64	Hamilton	83
64	Hobart	69
55	Williams	69
68	Vassar ■	58
58	Rensselaer	37
88	Potsdam St. ■	76
65	Skidmore	55
59	Union (N.Y.)	70
66	St. Lawrence	72
72	Hobart ■	61
70	Hamilton ■	62
58	St. Lawrence †	61
78	Rochester Inst. ■	64
64	Oswego St. †	60
61	St. Lawrence	71

Nickname: Golden Knights
Colors: Green & Gold
Arena: Alumni Gymnasium
 Capacity: 2,000; Year Built: 1952
AD: Sean Frazier
SID: Tommy Szarka

CLAYTON ST.
Morrow, GA 30260................II

Coach: Gordon Gibbons, Springfield
 1968
2001-02 RESULTS (19-9)
70	Albany St. (Ga.)	62
83	West Ga.	99
87	Mobile ■	76
83	UNC Pembroke ■	73
76	Kennesaw St.	56
91	Edward Waters ■	80
64	Albany St. (Ga.) ■	73
61	Morehouse ■	63
72	S.C.-Aiken	70
64	S.C.-Spartanburg	59
89	GC&SU ■	99
72	North Fla.	66
64	Columbus St.	60
73	UNC Pembroke	57
76	Kennesaw St. ■	55
67	Augusta St.	70
62	West Ga. ■	78
65	Columbus St. ■	84
76	Francis Marion	69
67	Armstrong Atlantic ■	59
65	GC&SU	62
70	Armstrong Atlantic	54
71	S.C.-Spartanburg ■	66
86	North Fla. ■	82
66	Lander	68
83	Francis Marion ■	79
77	S.C.-Aiken †	61
69	Kennesaw St. †	72

Nickname: Lakers
Colors: Blue & Orange
Arena: Athletics Center
 Capacity: 2,000; Year Built: 1983
AD: Mason Barfield
SID: Gid Rowell

CLEMSON
Clemson, SC 29634................I

Coach: Larry Shyatt, Wooster 1973
2001-02 RESULTS (13-17)
55	Wake Forest	96
70	Morris Brown †	57
81	La Salle †	69
65	Miami (Fla.) †	67
85	Wofford ■	82
79	Penn St.	66
83	Coastal Caro. ■	54
80	Duke	96
76	Appalachian St. ■	66
59	South Carolina	81
88	Elon ■	78
61	Winthrop ■	66
82	Charleston So. ■	45
78	Hartford †	48
65	Yale ■	68
83	Georgia Tech	76
68	Virginia ■	52
79	North Carolina St.	80
90	Maryland	99
63	Florida St.	68
69	North Carolina	87
88	Duke ■	98
50	Georgia Tech ■	74
71	Virginia	85
118	Wake Forest ■	115
54	North Carolina St.	83
68	Maryland ■	84
87	Florida St. ■	78
78	North Carolina	96
84	Florida St. †	91

Nickname: Tigers
Colors: Orange & Purple
Arena: Littlejohn Coliseum
 Capacity: 11,020; Year Built: 1968
AD: Terry Don Phillips
SID: Tim Bourret

CLEVELAND ST.
Cleveland, OH 44115-2440......I

Coach: Rollie Massimino, Vermont 1956
2001-02 RESULTS (12-16)
65	IUPUI	82
64	St. Bonaventure ■	79
72	Vermont	69
83	Siena ■	66
56	Stony Brook	64
79	Akron ■	66
63	Florida St.	76
90	Prairie View ■	53
82	Duquesne ■	64
62	Kent St. ■	66
79	Norfolk St. ■	69
63	Loyola (Ill.)	87
83	Ill.-Chicago	69
45	Butler ■	62
71	Youngstown St. ■	58
64	Wright St. ■	68
50	Detroit	53
69	Wis.-Milwaukee	78
50	Wis.-Green Bay	61
81	Loyola (Ill.) ■	60
76	Ill.-Chicago ■	70
72	Wright St.	87
45	Butler	70
58	Youngstown St.	48
62	Detroit	72
69	Wis.-Milwaukee ■	67
66	Wis.-Green Bay ■	74
63	Detroit	67

Nickname: Vikings
Colors: Forest Green & White
Arena: Henry J. Goodman Arena
 Capacity: 13,610; Year Built: 1991
AD: Lee Reed
SID: Paulette Welch

SCHEDULES/RESULTS

COAST GUARD
New London, CT 06320-4195..III

Coach: Peter Barry, San Francisco 1970
2001-02 RESULTS (10-14)
61	Army	.72
94	Johnson & Wales	.73
74	Wentworth Inst. ■	.43
55	Trinity (Conn.) ■	.65
90	Rhode Island Col.	.61
101	Nichols ■	.78
85	Merchant Marine ■	.77
71	Albertus Magnus	.72
67	Brown	.99
64	Wheaton (Mass.)	.68
42	Babson	.78
51	MIT ■	.64
59	Springfield	.60
67	Connecticut Col.	.75
58	WPI ■	.46
74	Clark (Mass.) ■	.92
67	Wheaton (Mass.) ■	.64
44	Babson	.58
68	MIT	.50
52	Springfield ■	.65
80	Roger Williams	.63
72	WPI	.59
64	Clark (Mass.)	.91
48	Springfield	.59

Nickname: Bears
Colors: Blue & White
Arena: John Merriman Gymnasium
  Capacity: 2,400; Year Built: 1964
AD: Raymond Cieplik
SID: Jason Southard

COASTAL CARO.
Conway, SC 29528-6054..........I

Coach: Pete Strickland, Pittsburgh 1979
2001-02 RESULTS (8-20)
41	Xavier	.72
51	Georgetown	.76
79	Western Caro. ■	.73
54	Clemson	.83
47	Col. of Charleston †	.64
71	East Tenn. St. ■	.85
81	South Carolina St. ■	.89
67	Old Dominion	.81
67	Campbell ■	.56
62	Citadel	.74
71	Navy	.90
71	High Point	.87
80	Elon	.91
71	Radford ■	.82
80	Liberty ■	.86
74	Birmingham-So. ■	.67
88	UNC Asheville ■	.78
77	Charleston So.	.73
49	Winthrop ■	.68
58	Liberty	.54
60	Radford	.76
80	Elon ■	.75
98	High Point ■	.76
80	Birmingham-So.	.88
81	UNC Asheville	.92
74	Winthrop	.100
69	Charleston So. ■	.78
66	Radford †	.81

Nickname: Chanticleers
Colors: Coastal Green, Bronze & Black
Arena: Kimbel Arena
  Capacity: 1,037; Year Built: 1974
AD: Warren Koegel
SID: Wayne White

COE
Cedar Rapids, IA 52402-5092 .III

Coach: Brent Brase,
Cornell College 1990
2001-02 RESULTS (13-13)
71	Wis.-Platteville	.79
62	Wis.-Stevens Point ■	.81
68	Mt. Mercy	.73
83	Augustana (Ill.) ■	.74
85	Dubuque	.66
80	Washington (Mo.)	.100
73	Luther ■	.58
73	Upper Iowa ■	.71
79	Mt. Mercy ■	.73
73	Chaminade	.88
55	Buena Vista	.77
68	Wartburg	.69
76	Loras	.74
68	Central (Iowa) ■	.67
71	Simpson ■	.78
69	Cornell College ■	.72
72	Loras ■	.82
78	Upper Iowa	.54
87	Luther	.81
80	Wartburg ■	.59
62	Buena Vista ■	.83
88	Dubuque ■	.65
70	Simpson	.89
75	Central (Iowa)	.58
74	Cornell College	.61
65	Loras	.87

Nickname: Kohawks
Colors: Crimson & Gold
Arena: Moray L. Eby Fieldhous
  Capacity: 2,600; Year Built: 1931
AD: John Chandler
SID: To be named

COKER
Hartsville, SC 29550................II

Coach: Dan Schmotzer,
St. Edwards 1974
2001-02 RESULTS (11-17)
75	Morris ■	.56
66	Francis Marion	.55
52	Pfeiffer	.65
66	Anderson (S.C.) ■	.76
48	Wingate	.53
64	Rollins	.73
65	Central Wash. †	.67
79	Erskine ■	.68
58	Queens (N.C.)	.75
76	Mount Olive	.71
61	Barton	.80
59	Belmont Abbey ■	.74
93	Lees-McRae ■	.75
80	Longwood	.76
63	St. Andrews ■	.57
46	Limestone	.59
60	Anderson (S.C.)	.72
64	Pfeiffer ■	.72
54	Erskine	.50
55	Queens (N.C.) ■	.80
64	Mount Olive ■	.62
60	Barton	.61
62	Belmont Abbey	.80
93	Lees-McRae	.77
65	Longwood ■	.81
73	Mount Olive	.71
48	Belmont Abbey	.72

Nickname: Cobras
Colors: Navy Blue & Gold
Arena: Timberlake-Lawnon Gym
  Capacity: 750; Year Built: 1963
AD: C. Timothy Griggs
SID: Cale Bigbee

COLBY
Waterville, ME 04901-8849.....III

Coach: Dick Whitmore, Bowdoin 1965
2001-02 RESULTS (10-14)
79	St. Joseph's (Me.) †	.71
74	Husson †	.76
105	Thomas ■	.61
100	Mount Ida †	.73
59	Framingham St. †	.48
78	Maine Maritime ■	.56
71	Colby-Sawyer ■	.73
71	Southern Me.	.80
88	New Paltz St. †	.81
62	Hamilton	.89
75	St. Joseph's (Me.) ■	.83
75	Bates	.88
48	Bowdoin ■	.80
62	Connecticut Col.	.74
84	Wesleyan (Conn.)	.89
65	Williams ■	.81
82	Middlebury ■	.74
88	New England	.63
60	Tufts ■	.75
91	Bates ■	.79
71	Me.-Farmington ■	.74
78	Bowdoin	.68
60	Trinity (Conn.)	.81
73	Amherst	.86

Nickname: White Mules
Colors: Blue & Gray
Arena: Wadsworth Gymnasium
  Capacity: 2,500; Year Built: 1966
AD: Marcella K. Zalot
SID: To be named

COLBY-SAWYER
New London, NH 03257 III

Coach: Bill Foti, New Hampshire 1986
2001-02 RESULTS (22-6)
79	Connecticut Col. †	.66
86	Mass.-Dartmouth	.89
90	Bates ■	.83
91	Wesleyan (Conn.) †	.83
73	Colby	.71
71	Keene St. †	.87
83	Norwich ■	.49
81	Eastern Nazarene ■	.61
71	St. Joseph (Vt.) ■	.46
77	Bowdoin	.71
62	Amherst	.86
85	Wentworth Inst.	.54
96	New England	.69
101	Nichols ■	.55
72	Gordon ■	.69
99	New England Col.	.66
67	Salve Regina	.74
77	Middlebury	.84
84	Roger Williams ■	.66
100	Curry ■	.60
80	Notre Dame (N.H.)	.64
64	Endicott	.47
94	Rivier	.75
80	Anna Maria	.65
86	Anna Maria ■	.54
69	Roger Williams ■	.52
69	Salve Regina ■	.54
47	Trinity (Conn.)	.75

Nickname: Chargers
Colors: Royal Blue and White
Arena: David L. Coffin Fieldhouse
  Capacity: 650; Year Built: 1991
AD: Deborah McGrath
SID: Adam Kamras

COLGATE
Hamilton, NY 13346-1304 I

Coach: Emmett Davis, St. Lawrence
1981
2001-02 RESULTS (17-11)
46	Holy Cross	.42
99	Long Island	.87
77	Northern Ariz. ■	.78
80	Oral Roberts ■	.68
51	Syracuse	.70
68	Cornell	.55
87	Yale ■	.75
76	Harvard	.64
85	Hobart ■	.48
73	Dartmouth ■	.65
61	Notre Dame ■	.92
102	Bethany (W.Va.) ■	.71
55	New Hampshire	.69
59	American ■	.76
74	Lehigh	.95
93	Navy ■	.95
75	Bucknell ■	.80
71	Lafayette	.67
62	Binghamton	.58
82	Army ■	.72
58	American	.72
84	Lehigh ■	.52
58	Holy Cross ■	.55
66	Navy	.65
57	Bucknell	.68
82	Army	.65
85	Lafayette ■	.73
71	Lafayette †	.74

Nickname: Raiders
Colors: Maroon, Gray & White
Arena: Cotterell Court
  Capacity: 3,091; Year Built: 1966
AD: Mark H. Murphy
SID: Bob Cornell

COLORADO
Boulder, CO 80309..................I

Coach: Ricardo Patton, Belmont 1980
2001-02 RESULTS (15-14)
98	Ark.-Pine Bluff ■	.81
77	Regis (Colo.) ■	.56
108	Rice	.80
75	St. Joseph's ■	.81
73	Georgia	.81
75	Colorado St.	.70
84	Montana	.71
106	Southern U. ■	.74
93	Wis.-Milwaukee ■	.87
68	St. Mary's (Cal.) ■	.51
85	Kansas	.97
84	Morris Brown	.44
67	Nebraska	.75
63	Iowa St. ■	.61
77	Missouri	.92
85	Kansas St. ■	.71
55	Oklahoma St. ■	.64
95	Baylor	.88
73	Kansas	.100
84	Nebraska ■	.61
95	Texas	.104
63	Iowa St.	.89
79	Texas Tech ■	.97
64	Kansas St.	.66
83	Missouri ■	.96
92	Texas A&M	.77
71	Oklahoma	.82
67	Nebraska †	.60
73	Kansas †	.102

Nickname: Buffaloes
Colors: Silver, Gold & Black
Arena: Coors Events/Conference Center
  Capacity: 11,064; Year Built: 1979
AD: Richard A. Tharp
SID: David Plati

COLO. CHRISTIAN
Lakewood, CO 80226 II

Coach: Brannon Hays, Cal Lutheran
1993
2001-02 RESULTS (10-17)
96	Langston ■	.88
74	Rockhurst	.77
71	Mo.-Rolla †	.73
78	Rockhurst ■	.80
97	North Central ■	.71
80	Adams St. ■	.77
65	UC-Colo. Spgs.	.69
94	Southern Colo.	.93
99	Great Falls ■	.76

72	Chaminade ■	78
85	N.M. Highlands ■	83
87	Fort Lewis ■	79
61	Western St. (Colo.)	83
72	Mesa St.	88
86	Fort Hays St. ■	84
84	Neb.-Kearney ■	93
64	Chadron St.	88
79	Colorado Mines	74
65	Regis (Colo.) ■	80
58	Metro St. ■	64
58	Fort Hays St.	78
73	Neb.-Kearney	94
86	Chadron St. ■	89
80	Colorado Mines ■	70
68	Regis (Colo.)	75
64	Metro St.	74
68	Neb.-Kearney	84

Nickname: Cougars
Colors: Blue & Gold
Arena: CCU Gymnasium
  Capacity: 1,800; Year Built: 1990
AD: Lisa Parker
SID: Matt Cingoranelli

COLORADO COL.
Colorado Springs, CO 80903 ..III

Coach: Mike McCubbin, Grinnell 1988
2001-02 RESULTS (9-15)

62	Whittier ■	53
70	McMurry ■	73
65	Schreiner ■	75
77	Puget Sound ■	94
66	UC-Colo. Spgs.	75
75	Cornell College	85
117	Grinnell	140
65	Bellevue ■	79
66	Westminster (Utah) ■	86
82	Neb. Wesleyan ■	59
102	Dallas	76
74	Mississippi Col. †	82
58	Thomas More †	60
73	Hartwick †	72
86	Southwestern (Kan.) ■	52
76	Hardin-Simmons	69
58	Chadron St.	78
52	Fort Lewis	85
74	Hastings	68
65	Colorado Mines ■	57
72	UC-Colo. Spgs. ■	52
69	Hastings	81
64	Neb.-Kearney	80
59	Neb. Wesleyan	69

Nickname: Tigers
Colors: Black & Gold
Arena: J. Juan Reid Gymnasium
  Capacity: 1,000; Year Built: 1970
AD: Joel Nielsen
SID: Dave Moross

COLORADO MINES
Golden, CO 80401 II

Coach: Pryor Orser, Eastern Mont. 1990
2001-02 RESULTS (5-21)

51	Azusa Pacific ■	72
57	Queens (N.Y.) ■	79
62	Northern Colo. ■	60
88	Rocky Mountain ■	81
70	Western St. (Colo.) ■	67
54	Mesa St. ■	76
75	Adams St.	84
63	St. Martin's	69
44	Western Wash.	72
70	Southern Colo.	80
70	UC-Colo. Spgs. ■	74
56	Fort Lewis	67
71	N.M. Highlands	70
48	Metro St. ■	86
72	Chadron St.	85
65	Regis (Colo.) ■	69

74	Colo. Christian ■	79
57	Colorado Col.	65
63	Neb.-Kearney ■	81
75	Fort Hays St.	62
54	Metro St.	79
64	Chadron St. ■	85
58	Regis (Colo.)	64
70	Colo. Christian	80
54	Neb.-Kearney ■	63
61	Fort Hays St. ■	66

Nickname: Orediggers
Colors: Silver & Blue
Arena: Volk Gymnasium
  Capacity: 1,000; Year Built: 1959
AD: Marvin L. Kay
SID: Kacey Kingry

COLORADO ST.
Fort Collins, CO 80523-6011 I

Coach: Dale Layer, Eckerd 1979
2001-02 RESULTS (12-18)

80	Montana Tech ■	50
79	Washington St.	75
66	South Carolina St. †	48
61	Hawaii †	59
69	Weber St. †	72
54	Gardner-Webb	56
58	South Carolina	66
70	Colorado ■	75
79	Ark.-Little Rock ■	88
74	Denver	61
80	Southern Ill. ■	62
92	IPFW ■	71
53	Baylor	68
83	Morris Brown ■	46
72	Wyoming	95
69	San Diego St.	81
68	UNLV	75
60	Air Force ■	57
64	New Mexico ■	70
62	Utah	67
52	Brigham Young ■	57
69	Wyoming ■	72
70	Michigan ■	66
63	San Diego St. ■	75
91	UNLV ■	96
60	New Mexico	72
59	Air Force	51
62	Utah ■	72
79	Brigham Young ■	75
66	Utah †	69

Nickname: Rams
Colors: Green & Gold
Arena: Moby Arena
  Capacity: 8,745; Year Built: 1966
AD: Jeffrey A. Hathaway
SID: Gary Ozzello

UC-COLO. SPGS.
Colorado Springs, CO 80933-7150 II

Coach: Ed Pipes, Okla. Christian 1978
2001-02 RESULTS (9-17)

74	Minn.-Duluth †	66
53	Caldwell †	59
44	Murray St.	109
75	Colorado Col. ■	66
63	Neb.-Kearney	84
48	Fort Hays St.	71
69	Colo. Christian ■	65
69	Regis (Colo.) ■	64
51	Cal St. Bakersfield	60
46	Spring Hill †	64
62	Chadron St.	70
74	Colorado Mines	70
52	Metro St. ■	81
67	Western St. (Colo.)	61
65	Mesa St.	80
73	Fort Lewis ■	84
79	N.M. Highlands ■	84

54	Southern Colo. ■	73
66	Adams St. ■	73
52	Colorado Col.	72
76	Western St. (Colo.) ■	74
65	Mesa St.	57
69	Fort Lewis	104
74	N.M. Highlands ■	80
60	Southern Colo.	78
82	Adams St.	71

Nickname: Mountain Lions
Colors: Black & Gold
Arena: Lions Den
  Capacity: 500; Year Built: 1988
AD: Ruben A. Cubero
SID: Doug Fitzgerald

COLUMBIA
New York, NY 10027................I

Coach: Armond Hill, Princeton 1985
2001-02 RESULTS (11-17)

66	Northeastern †	54
59	Marist	69
52	Haverford ■	37
54	Providence	68
53	Lehigh ■	47
52	Lafayette ■	48
69	Army	64
68	Boston U. ■	47
65	BYU-Hawaii	70
55	Valparaiso †	71
74	Navy †	72
55	UCLA	64
59	San Diego St.	75
54	Yale	65
50	Brown	63
40	Albany (N.Y.) ■	41
56	Cornell ■	40
54	Cornell	42
41	Princeton	49
54	Pennsylvania	53
52	Harvard ■	55
51	Dartmouth ■	57
41	Brown ■	52
56	Yale ■	76
62	Dartmouth	58
56	Harvard	59
47	Pennsylvania ■	51
48	Princeton ■	49

Nickname: Lions
Colors: Columbia Blue & White
Arena: Levien Gym
  Capacity: 3,408; Year Built: 1974
AD: John Reeves
SID: Casey Taylor

COLUMBIA UNION
Takoma Park, MD 20912 II

Coach: Sandy Smith, Winston-Salem
2001-02 RESULTS (10-17)

62	Elizabeth City St. ■	60
78	Cheyney ■	62
63	Kutztown ■	67
43	Winston-Salem ■	69
76	St. Paul's	67
63	Winston-Salem	67
52	Shepherd	65
64	Fairmont St.	74
53	Mercyhurst	77
68	Edinboro	76
78	Pace ■	87
56	Fla. Southern	94
61	Eckerd	74
57	Kutztown	49
83	Bowie St.	89
72	Elizabeth City St.	74
56	Dist. Columbia ■	72
89	Strayer ■	87
75	Lincoln (Pa.)	98
84	Pfeiffer	83
78	West Va. Tech ■	67

83	Bowie St. ■	89
96	Lincoln (Pa.) ■	87
87	Strayer ■	72
75	Shepherd ■	60
85	Cheyney	95
79	Dist. Columbia	87

Nickname: Pioneers
Colors: Blue & Gold
Arena: The Pit
  Capacity: 350; Year Built: 1954
AD: Brad Durby
SID: Josh McClure

COLUMBUS ST.
Columbus, GA 31907-5645......II

Coach: Herbert Greene, Auburn 1967
2001-02 RESULTS (19-9)

113	Tuskegee ■	90
66	Morehouse	80
82	Tuskegee	77
79	West Ga. ■	78
83	S.C.-Spartanburg	79
94	GC&SU ■	70
98	West Ga.	101
87	Tuskegee ■	78
83	Johnson Smith ■	79
61	Augusta St.	52
74	North Fla. ■	62
76	Armstrong Atlantic	79
60	Clayton St. ■	64
78	S.C.-Aiken	65
72	Augusta St. ■	84
64	North Fla.	87
84	Clayton St.	65
72	S.C.-Aiken ■	70
83	Kennesaw St. ■	82
95	UNC Pembroke	87
94	Francis Marion	71
62	GC&SU	68
87	Armstrong Atlantic ■	76
72	Lander	70
77	Kennesaw St.	80
89	Lander ■	62
72	Armstrong Atlantic ■	68
65	Augusta St.	69

Nickname: Cougars
Colors: Red, White & Blue
Arena: Lumpkin Center
  Capacity: 4,500; Year Built: 2000
AD: Herbert Greene
SID: Mike Peacock

CONCORD
Athens, WV 24712 II

Coach: Steve Cox, Salem Int'l 1974
2001-02 RESULTS (13-14)

45	Tusculum	50
74	West Virginia St. †	87
78	Bluefield St.	81
75	West Va. Tech ■	70
62	Tusculum ■	58
80	West Virginia St. ■	77
78	Davis & Elkins	91
86	Charleston (W.Va.) ■	95
68	Winston-Salem	87
88	Glenville St. †	70
101	Bluefield St.	82
61	Fairmont St.	87
73	Glenville St. ■	86
93	Davis & Elkins ■	48
99	Ohio Southern ■	76
74	West Va. Wesleyan ■	90
64	Shepherd	74
73	Alderson-Broaddus ■	69
72	Charleston (W.Va.)	74
57	Salem Int'l	84
83	West Liberty St. ■	71
87	Wheeling Jesuit ■	84
74	Bluefield St. ■	70
74	West Virginia St.	70

64	West Va. Tech	68
89	Ohio Valley	67
66	Wheeling Jesuit ■	87

Nickname: Mountain Lions
Colors: Maroon & Gray
Arena: Carter Center
  Capacity: 2,000; Year Built: 1972
AD: Steven Lee
SID: Ronald Macosko

CONCORDIA (ILL.)
River Forest, IL 60305-1499......III

Coach: Brian Miller, Wis.-Milwaukee
1987

2001-02 RESULTS (7-18)

65	Maranatha Baptist ■	61
68	Upper Iowa ■	88
61	Doane ■	93
78	Lake Forest ■	85
69	Wheaton (Ill.) ■	81
76	Milwaukee Engr. †	73
57	Edgewood ■	71
81	Webster ■	69
71	Wis. Lutheran	85
64	Centre	83
78	Westminster (Pa.) †	92
51	Aurora	65
46	Clarke	50
64	Dominican (Ill.) ■	70
68	Eureka ■	59
62	Rockford	81
53	Concordia (Mich.) †	66
61	Concordia (Wis.)	69
62	Benedictine (Ill.) ■	64
69	Clarke ■	67
77	Dominican (Ill.)	72
71	Eureka	67
53	Rockford ■	73
67	Aurora ■	84
43	Benedictine (Ill.)	72

Nickname: Cougars
Colors: Maroon & Gold
Arena: Geisman Gymnasium
  Capacity: 2,200; Year Built: 1964
AD: Janet L. Fisher
SID: Jim Egan

CONCORDIA (N.Y.)
Bronxville, NY 10708 II

Coach: John Dwinell, Springfield 1981

2001-02 RESULTS (4-22)

70	Pace	97
71	Baruch ■	75
82	Mercy ■	81
82	C.W. Post ■	71
71	Adelphi	101
71	Philadelphia U. ■	84
66	West Fla. †	102
61	North Fla.	84
59	Queens (N.Y.)	82
64	NYIT ■	86
78	Bridgeport	84
96	Southampton ■	105
57	Molloy	80
58	Dowling	102
66	Queens (N.Y.) ■	84
84	Mercy	91
57	C.W. Post	71
66	Adelphi ■	112
65	Philadelphia U.	88
66	St. Thomas Aquinas ■	63
74	NYIT	85
60	Bridgeport ■	68
96	Southampton	107
87	Molloy ■	77
57	St. Thomas Aquinas	72
86	Dowling ■	105

Nickname: Clippers
Colors: Blue & Gold
Arena: Meyer Athletic Center

Capacity: 1,000; Year Built: 1963
AD: Ivan Marquez
SID: Kris Zeiter

CONCORDIA (WIS.)
Mequon, WI 53097-2402........III

Coach: Pete Gnan, Minn. St.-Mankato
1985

2001-02 RESULTS (16-12)

67	Ripon	87
74	Ill. Wesleyan †	72
56	Lake Forest	65
87	Eureka †	49
82	Rockford	86
70	Martin Luther ■	45
74	Maranatha Baptist ■	59
88	Logan Chiropractic †	52
113	Concordia (Mo.)	93
59	Lakeland	65
77	Benedictine (Ill.)	69
52	Edgewood	53
65	Milwaukee Engr. ■	58
61	Marian (Wis.)	55
67	Wis. Lutheran ■	84
75	Lincoln Chrst.	61
67	Maranatha Baptist	77
65	Concordia (Neb.) ■	67
69	Concordia (Ill.) ■	61
66	Lakeland ■	63
59	Edgewood ■	53
59	Marian (Wis.) ■	79
85	Milwaukee Engr. ■	54
76	Wis. Lutheran	77
67	Wis.-Whitewater ■	87
52	Marian (Wis.) ■	48
72	Wis. Lutheran ■	48
63	Edgewood	69

Nickname: Falcons
Colors: Royal Blue & White
Arena: Fieldhouse
  Capacity: 2,000; Year Built: 1989
AD: Robert, M Barnhill
SID: Mike Bartholomew

CONCORDIA-AUSTIN
Austin, TX 78705-2799 III

Coach: Jim Jost

2001-02 RESULTS (15-10)

105	Houston Baptist ■	88
89	St. Edward's ■	88
98	East Tex. Baptist	94
71	Otterbein ■	98
66	Texas-Dallas	75
88	Dallas	79
68	Mary Hardin-Baylor ■	73
83	Savannah A&D ■	78
93	Texas Wesleyan ■	83
68	Lawrence ■	71
69	Mississippi Col. ■	66
72	Louisiana Col. ■	73
86	Texas Lutheran ■	74
108	Schreiner ■	93
91	McMurry ■	75
74	Hardin-Simmons ■	64
86	Howard Payne ■	82
79	Sul Ross St. ■	64
55	Mary Hardin-Baylor	78
71	Howard Payne	83
61	Sul Ross St.	75
81	Texas Lutheran ■	89
102	Schreiner ■	65
84	McMurry	98
87	Hardin-Simmons	72

Nickname: Tornados
Colors: Purple & White
Arena: Woltman Center
  Capacity: 1,600; Year Built: 1982
AD: Linda Lowery
SID: Jim Jost

CONCORDIA-M'HEAD
Moorhead, MN 56562-3597 ...III

Coach: Duane Siverson, Yankton 1978

2001-02 RESULTS (8-17)

54	Minn. St. Moorhead ■	70
59	Black Hills St.	75
80	Mayville St. ■	69
87	Hamline	84
79	Augsburg ■	72
68	St. Olaf	66
58	St. Mary's (Minn.)	59
63	Gust. Adolphus ■	71
71	Wis.-Superior	72
72	Briar Cliff ■	84
52	Carleton	58
53	St. Thomas (Minn.)	75
45	Macalester ■	54
69	St. Mary's (Minn.)	49
54	St. John's (Minn.)	56
65	Bethel (Minn.) ■	75
81	Hamline ■	58
68	Augsburg	87
78	St. Olaf ■	73
62	Carleton ■	60
53	Gust. Adolphus	90
60	St. Thomas (Minn.) ■	68
70	Macalester	72
67	St. John's (Minn.)	69
66	Bethel (Minn.)	86

Nickname: Cobbers
Colors: Maroon & Gold
Arena: Memorial Auditorium
  Capacity: 3,500; Year Built: 1951
AD: Armin Pipho
SID: Jim Cella

CONCORDIA-ST. PAUL
St. Paul, MN 55104 II

2001-02 RESULTS (9-18)

76	Trinity Bible (N.D.)	50
63	Wis.-Milwaukee	77
56	Augustana (S.D.)	73
75	South Dakota St. ■	83
35	Northern St.	84
84	Minn.-Morris	75
73	St. Cloud St. ■	99
74	Hamline ■	53
100	Mt. Senario	59
59	Minn. St.-Mankato	76
80	North Cent. (Minn.)	67
55	Winona St.	75
53	Southwest St. ■	73
67	Wayne St. (Neb.) ■	65
54	Minn. St. Moorhead	90
87	Minn.-Crookston	73
46	Minn.-Duluth ■	68
77	Bemidji St. ■	80
69	Minn.-Morris ■	61
77	Northern St. ■	80
67	Winona St.	83
48	Wayne St. (Neb.)	71
51	Southwest St.	91
96	Minn.-Crookston ■	94
61	Minn. St. Moorhead ■	74
76	Bemidji St.	91
60	Minn.-Duluth	78

Nickname: Golden Bears
Colors: Navy & Vegas Gold
AD: David Herbster
SID: To be named

CONNECTICUT
Storrs, CT 06269 I

Coach: Jim Calhoun,
American Int'l 1968

2001-02 RESULTS (27-7)

84	Vanderbilt ■	71
110	New Hampshire ■	58

84	George Washington †	76
65	Maryland †	77
80	Northeastern ■	44
69	Massachusetts	59
95	Quinnipiac ■	79
70	St. Bonaventure ■	88
86	Virginia Tech ■	74
76	Miami (Fla.) ■	75
67	Oklahoma ■	69
95	Virginia Tech ■	60
70	Villanova ■	65
69	Providence	62
86	North Carolina ■	54
75	St. John's (N.Y.) ■	70
100	Arizona	98
53	Rutgers	61
66	Miami (Fla.)	68
67	Providence ■	56
83	St. John's (N.Y.)	85
46	Villanova ■	40
79	Boston College ■	77
75	Georgetown	74
95	West Virginia ■	73
75	Boston College	61
90	Seton Hall ■	78
72	Villanova †	70
82	Notre Dame †	77
74	Pittsburgh †	65
78	Hampton †	67
77	North Carolina St. †	74
71	Southern Ill. †	59
82	Maryland †	90

Nickname: Huskies
Colors: Navy & White
Arena: Harry A.Gampel Pavilion
  Capacity: 10,027; Year Built: 1990
AD: Lew Perkins
SID: Kyle Muncy

CONNECTICUT COL.
New London, CT 06320-4196..III

Coach: Lynn Ramage, West Liberty St.
1992

2001-02 RESULTS (16-9)

66	Colby-Sawyer †	79
93	Johnson St. †	80
77	Scranton ■	82
74	Roger Williams	62
82	Johnson & Wales ■	86
89	Mass. Liberal Arts	74
90	Lasell ■	87
89	Elms	77
69	Eastern Conn. St. ■	70
54	MIT	57
69	Salve Regina	54
92	Hunter ■	68
74	Colby	62
74	Bowdoin ■	75
75	Coast Guard	67
80	Wesleyan (Conn.) ■	65
64	Middlebury	63
62	Williams	72
80	Elms ■	73
68	Trinity (Conn.)	71
73	Amherst ■	66
101	Mass. Liberal Arts ■	95
85	Bates	74
89	Tufts	84
61	Wesleyan (Conn.) ■	75

Nickname: Camels
Colors: Royal Blue & White
Arena: Luce Fieldhouse/Gymnasium
  Capacity: 800; Year Built: 1984
AD: Stanton Ching
SID: Mike Salerno

COPPIN ST.
Baltimore, MD 21216-3698 I

Coach: Ron Mitchell, Edison St. 1984

2001-02 RESULTS (6-25)

51	Towson †	53
76	Loyola (Md.)	68
68	Morgan St.	66
44	George Mason	80
59	Norfolk St. ■	63
69	Hampton ■	81
39	Cincinnati	90
49	Louisville	75
59	Florida Int'l †	63
57	P.R.-Mayaguez	56
50	Niagara †	78
49	Penn St. †	66
51	Harvard †	55
47	Missouri	74
46	Delaware St.	57
67	Howard	84
59	Md.-East. Shore ■	64
72	Bethune-Cookman	96
61	Florida A&M	75
50	South Carolina St. ■	54
55	N.C. A&T	66
51	Norfolk St.	69
51	Hampton	78
65	Delaware St. ■	67
72	Howard ■	88
64	Md.-East. Shore	68
64	Florida A&M ■	67
80	Bethune-Cookman ■	64
72	Morgan St. ■	65
61	Norfolk St. †	46
45	Delaware St. †	54

Nickname: Eagles
Colors: Royal Blue & Gold
Arena: Coppin Center
　Capacity: 1,720; Year Built: 1987
AD: Ronald Mitchell
SID: David Popham

CORNELL
Ithaca, NY 14853 I

Coach: Steve Donahue, Ursinus 1984

2001-02 RESULTS (5-22)

48	Canisius	65
48	Notre Dame	78
62	Bucknell	71
58	Syracuse	76
55	Colgate ■	68
77	Ithaca ■	45
54	Buffalo ■	65
44	Lafayette	73
69	Lehigh ■	61
40	James Madison †	56
41	Richmond	52
68	Georgia Tech	86
90	Army ■	65
59	Brown	72
74	Yale	79
40	Columbia	56
42	Columbia ■	54
63	Pennsylvania	75
38	Princeton	60
56	Dartmouth ■	62
63	Harvard ■	62
65	Yale ■	80
78	Brown ■	81
46	Harvard	55
70	Dartmouth	61
57	Princeton ■	61
53	Pennsylvania ■	78

Nickname: Big Red
Colors: Carnelian & White
Arena: Newman Arena
　Capacity: 4,473; Year Built: 1989
AD: J. Andrew Noel
SID: Jeremy Hartigan

CORNELL COLLEGE
Mt. Vernon, IA 52314-1098 III

Coach: Ed Timm, Central (Iowa) 1985

2001-02 RESULTS (12-15)

72	Hannibal-La Grange †	59
56	Culver-Stockton	63
54	Mt. Mercy	81
79	Clarke	89
61	Loras	65
85	Colorado Col. ■	75
71	Upper Iowa ■	77
67	Luther ■	55
76	Iowa Wesleyan ■	82
38	Augustana (Ill.) ■	74
65	Wartburg	77
56	Buena Vista	96
84	Dubuque	85
76	Simpson	74
81	Central (Iowa) ■	60
72	Coe	69
72	Dubuque ■	53
77	Luther	74
79	Upper Iowa	72
76	Buena Vista ■	70
56	Wartburg ■	77
41	Loras ■	68
71	Central (Iowa)	62
60	Simpson	78
61	Coe ■	74
79	Simpson	76
56	Wartburg	61

Nickname: Rams
Colors: Purple & White
Arena: Cornell Fieldhouse
　Capacity: 2,500; Year Built: 1953
AD: Tina Hill
SID: Darren Miller

CORTLAND ST.
Cortland, NY 13045 III

Coach: Tom Spanbauer, Cortland St. 1983

2001-02 RESULTS (11-16)

63	FDU-Madison †	58
57	Medgar Evers †	60
50	Elmira ■	44
54	Alfred	70
49	Brockport St. ■	72
51	Fredonia St.	41
57	Ithaca	63
54	Misericordia †	66
57	Southern Vt. †	44
51	Plattsburgh St.	71
71	Oswego St.	75
64	Hartwick ■	58
69	Plattsburgh St. ■	58
52	Potsdam St. ■	64
52	New Paltz St. ■	69
48	Brockport St.	74
58	Utica/Rome ■	74
51	Geneseo St.	61
59	Fredonia St. ■	53
72	Oneonta St. ■	66
76	Cazenovia ■	87
67	New Paltz St.	52
78	Utica/Rome ■	60
52	Buffalo St.	78
56	Geneseo St.	57
49	Buffalo St. †	48
75	Oswego St. †	83

Nickname: Red Dragons
Colors: Red & White
Arena: Corey Gymnasium
　Capacity: 3,500; Year Built: 1973
AD: Robert McBee
SID: Fran Elia

CREIGHTON
Omaha, NE 68178-0001 I

Coach: Dana Altman, Eastern N.M. 1980

2001-02 RESULTS (23-9)

72	N.C. A&T ■	51
94	Western Ky. ■	91

(continued)

102	Grambling ■	64
77	TCU	82
52	Brigham Young	61
76	Nebraska ■	70
70	Indiana St. ■	46
61	Western Ky.	95
65	Xavier	72
90	Mississippi Val. ■	65
76	Illinois St.	62
79	Northern Iowa	85
88	Evansville ■	74
76	Southwest Mo. St.	72
63	Illinois St. ■	56
76	Bradley ■	63
67	Wichita St.	55
57	Evansville	41
80	Southwest Mo. St. ■	74
77	Southern Ill. ■	79
64	Indiana St.	63
83	Northern Iowa ■	56
95	Drake	91
69	Wichita St. ■	67
62	Southern Ill.	65
80	Bradley	64
73	Drake ■	75
80	Northern Iowa †	65
90	Illinois St. †	63
84	Southern Ill. †	76
83	Florida †	82
60	Illinois †	72

Nickname: Bluejays
Colors: Blue & White
Arena: Omaha Civic Auditorium
　Capacity: 9,377; Year Built: 1954
AD: Bruce D. Rasmussen
SID: Michael Molde

CURRY
Milton, MA 02186 III

Coach: Sean Casey, Keene St. 1993

2001-02 RESULTS (13-12)

75	WPI	82
95	Daniel Webster	86
60	Springfield ■	61
86	Castleton St. †	87
85	Lyndon St. †	102
91	Hampshire ■	68
76	Gordon	70
78	Castleton St.	74
80	Bridgewater St.	85
78	Tufts	99
64	Endicott ■	73
74	Salve Regina	84
77	Lasell ■	91
81	Mount Ida ■	68
93	New England Col. ■	87
99	Eastern Nazarene ■	91
85	New England ■	70
90	Notre Dame (N.H.) ■	77
78	Nichols	60
60	Colby-Sawyer	100
83	Wentworth Inst.	78
83	St. Joseph's (Me.) ■	92
83	Anna Maria ■	63
81	Roger Williams ■	67
69	Endicott ■	70

Nickname: Colonels
Colors: Purple & White
Arena: Miller Gymnasium
　Capacity: 300; Year Built: 1952
AD: Steve Nelson
SID: Ken Golner

DALLAS
Irving, TX 75062 III

Coach: Brian Stanfield, Drury 1990

2001-02 RESULTS (15-13)

54	Bridgewater (Va.) †	61
72	Southwestern (Tex.)	62
56	Texas-Dallas	61
53	Mary Hardin-Baylor ■	59

(continued)

79	Concordia-Austin ■	88
56	Southwestern (Tex.) ■	62
47	Trinity (Tex.) ■	63
65	Neb. Wesleyan †	69
76	Colorado Col.	102
61	Huntington	52
55	Neb. Wesleyan ■	74
68	Schreiner	75
77	Texas Lutheran	71
85	Ozarks (Ark.)	73
78	Austin	75
88	Louisiana Col.	66
65	East Tex. Baptist	74
84	LeTourneau	75
84	Texas-Dallas	75
70	East Tex. Baptist ■	87
68	LeTourneau ■	74
92	Ozarks (Ark.) ■	78
88	Austin ■	74
91	Dallas Christian ■	63
93	Louisiana Col.	80
88	Philander Smith †	81
88	Texas Wesleyan †	82
72	Rochester College †	68

Nickname: Crusaders
Colors: Navy & White
Arena: Maher Athletic Center
　Capacity: 1,000; Year Built: 1965
AD: Richard L. Strockbine
SID: Patty Danko

DANIEL WEBSTER
Nashua, NH 03063-1300........III

Coach: John Griffith, Southern Me. 1979

2001-02 RESULTS (4-22)

64	Gordon ■	93
86	Curry	95
53	WPI	69
94	Becker ■	74
99	New England Col.	107
82	Elms ■	76
73	Framingham St. ■	77
51	Southern Vt.	81
59	Fitchburg St.	75
80	Nichols	104
87	New England ■	90
50	River ■	54
70	Albertus Magnus ■	75
74	Fisher ■	84
57	Western New Eng.	84
68	Suffolk ■	95
50	Norwich ■	62
87	Emmanuel (Mass.)	92
54	Emerson ■	86
69	Newbury	74
68	Western New Eng. ■	97
71	Johnson & Wales	83
76	Norwich	74
67	Southern Vt. ■	62
72	River	89
62	Western New Eng.	75

Nickname: Eagles
Colors: Navy & White, Red
Arena: Vagge Gymnasium
　Capacity: 600; Year Built: 1977
AD: John Griffith
SID: Greg Andruskevich

DARTMOUTH
Hanover, NH 03755 I

Coach: Dave Faucher, New Hampshire 1972

2001-02 RESULTS (9-18)

46	Binghamton	49
54	Vermont	73
72	New Hampshire	70
58	Holy Cross ■	47
72	Lehigh ■	67
89	Castleton St. ■	62
58	Boston U.	79
53	Harvard	70

70	Quinnipiac	68
65	Colgate	73
62	Southeastern La. †	59
60	New Mexico	77
57	Harvard ■	88
71	Pennsylvania ■	87
46	Princeton ■	57
77	Albany (N.Y.) ■	56
65	Hartford ■	67
55	Yale ■	73
71	Brown ■	74
62	Cornell	56
57	Columbia	51
68	Princeton	79
62	Pennsylvania	100
58	Columbia ■	62
61	Cornell ■	70
70	Brown	85
59	Yale	88

Nickname: Big Green
Colors: Green & White
Arena: Leede Arena
 Capacity: 2,100; Year Built: 1986
AD: Jo Ann Harper
SID: Kathy Slattery

DAVIDSON
Davidson, NC 28036 I

Coach: Bob McKillop, Hofstra 1972
2001-02 RESULTS (21-10)

51	Charlotte	65
58	North Carolina	54
114	Oglethorpe ■	45
81	Navy ■	79
66	Elon ■	59
50	Citadel	69
70	St. Bonaventure	79
91	Wash. & Jeff. ■	47
69	Georgia Tech †	83
75	Pennsylvania	71
85	Hamilton ■	49
71	Duke †	106
74	Western Caro.	71
63	Chattanooga ■	61
73	Furman ■	70
79	VMI ■	68
73	East Tenn. St. ■	66
58	UNC Greensboro	57
67	Western Caro. ■	70
72	Wofford ■	61
82	Appalachian St.	72
53	UNC Greensboro ■	48
78	East Tenn. St.	85
64	Ga. Southern ■	56
60	Appalachian St. ■	62
73	Col. of Charleston	70
77	VMI	81
71	Citadel †	58
68	UNC Greensboro †	58
62	Furman †	57
64	Ohio St. †	69

Nickname: Wildcats
Colors: Red & Black
Arena: Belk Arena
 Capacity: 5,700; Year Built: 1989
AD: James Murphy
SID: Rick Bender

DAVIS & ELKINS
Elkins, WV 26241-3996 II

Coach: Amrit Rayfield,
Davis & Elkins 1997
2001-02 RESULTS (7-20)

62	West Va. Wesleyan †	81
74	Southern Va. †	71
71	Wheeling Jesuit	98
71	Shepherd	82
91	Concord ■	78
59	Fairmont St.	74
59	Salem Int'l	98

74	Waynesburg	99
75	West Liberty St. ■	69
99	Ohio Valley ■	86
114	West Va. Wesleyan ■	109
65	Charleston (W.Va.)	99
48	Concord	93
98	Ohio Valley	83
74	West Va. Tech ■	72
58	West Virginia St. ■	85
71	Southern Va.	90
65	Salem Int'l ■	86
61	Alderson-Broaddus	66
77	Glenville St.	88
67	Shepherd ■	80
55	Dist. Columbia	87
83	Alderson-Broaddus ■	99
87	Bluefield St.	102
83	Glenville St. ■	92
63	West Va. Wesleyan	82
62	Glenville St.	78

Nickname: Senators
Colors: Scarlet & White
Arena: Memorial Gymnasium
 Capacity: 1,875; Year Built: 1950
SID: To be named

DAYTON
Dayton, OH 45469 I

Coach: Oliver Purnell,
Old Dominion 1975
2001-02 RESULTS (21-11)

69	Toledo ■	50
81	Central Mich. ■	65
57	Villanova	59
55	Cincinnati	77
85	Morehead St. ■	41
51	Marquette	73
82	Eastern Ky. ■	70
83	Purdue †	72
76	Austin Peay ■	61
69	St. Louis ■	63
60	Miami (Ohio) ■	23
59	Xavier ■	66
83	George Washington ■	59
88	Duquesne	44
68	Richmond ■	52
71	La Salle	69
59	Xavier	75
83	Massachusetts ■	68
75	St. Bonaventure ■	81
92	Fordham ■	78
54	Richmond	63
82	Duquesne ■	50
66	Rhode Island ■	57
89	George Washington	59
68	St. Joseph's	70
70	Temple ■	75
95	La Salle ■	72
90	Rhode Island †	71
81	St. Joseph's †	74
59	Xavier †	66
80	Detroit ■	69
59	Tennessee Tech ■	68

Nickname: Flyers
Colors: Red & Blue
Arena: University of Dayton Arena
 Capacity: 13,511; Year Built: 1969
AD: Ted Kissell
SID: Doug Hauschild

DEPAUL
Chicago, IL 60614 I

Coach: Pat Kennedy, King's 1975
2001-02 RESULTS (9-19)

70	Fordham ■	61
60	Syracuse	74
107	Youngstown St. ■	69
55	Notre Dame †	82
75	Ohio	77
94	Fairfield †	90

65	Murray St. ■	69
95	Long Island ■	69
79	Chicago St. ■	63
60	Temple	58
63	Missouri ■	62
63	Tulane ■	73
74	St. Louis	92
63	South Fla. ■	70
72	Cincinnati	89
68	Marquette ■	87
80	East Caro.	58
67	Louisville	97
83	Charlotte	97
75	UNLV	90
83	TCU ■	92
62	East Caro. ■	51
72	Louisville ■	76
57	Charlotte	81
62	Cincinnati ■	79
61	Memphis	88
63	St. Louis ■	72
53	Marquette	72

Nickname: Blue Demons
Colors: Scarlet & Blue
Arena: Allstate Arena
 Capacity: 17,500; Year Built: 1980
AD: Jean Lenti Ponsetto
SID: Scott Reed

DEPAUW
Greencastle, IN 46135............III

Coach: Bill Fenlon, Northwestern 1979
2001-02 RESULTS (24-4)

94	Savannah A&D †	76
88	Transylvania †	84
90	Oberlin ■	78
78	Wabash	66
83	Centre ■	68
80	Sewanee ■	61
72	Chicago ■	52
81	Hendrix	68
78	Rhodes	74
75	Millsaps ■	60
97	Oglethorpe ■	62
101	Earlham ■	106
85	Southwestern (Tex.)	77
56	Trinity (Tex.)	66
71	Rose-Hulman ■	67
102	Hendrix ■	63
78	Rhodes ■	67
66	Millsaps	71
99	Oglethorpe	71
94	Judson (Ill.) ■	80
81	Southwestern (Tex.) ■	54
68	Trinity (Tex.) ■	66
65	Rose-Hulman	57
88	Centre	79
87	Sewanee	70
89	Wittenberg ■	76
90	Washington (Mo.) †	87
79	Otterbein	87

Nickname: Tigers
Colors: Old Gold & Black
Arena: Neal Fieldhouse
 Capacity: 2,800; Year Built: 1982
AD: Page Cotton Jr.
SID: Bill Wagner

DEFIANCE
Defiance, OH 43512 III

Coach: Tom Palombo,
Va. Wesleyan 1989
2001-02 RESULTS (18-10)

105	Ind.-East ■	69
103	Shawnee St. ■	91
84	Heidelberg ■	78
80	Bowling Green	107
104	Anderson (Ind.) ■	98
92	Franklin	89
99	Urbana ■	87

74	Hanover	87
78	Ohio Northern	92
73	Calvin ■	77
82	Muhlenberg †	89
90	Muskingum	102
72	Manchester ■	76
91	Transylvania	77
105	Urbana	83
92	Mt. St. Joseph	96
100	Bluffton ■	94
105	Franklin ■	93
96	Anderson (Ind.)	95
84	Hanover ■	81
107	Thomas More ■	72
106	Transylvania ■	69
86	Manchester	77
80	Mt. St. Joseph ■	65
103	Bluffton	106
91	Bluffton ■	90
85	Manchester †	81
87	Franklin †	92

Nickname: Yellow Jackets
Colors: Purple & Gold
Arena: Weaner Community Center
 Capacity: 1,800; Year Built: 1964
AD: Dick Kaiser
SID: Mike Partee

DELAWARE
Newark, DD 19716 I

Coach: David Henderson, Duke 1986
2001-02 RESULTS (14-16)

62	Wichita St. †	47
59	Butler †	76
70	Bowling Green †	73
84	La Salle ■	78
57	St. Joseph's	84
78	High Point ■	63
50	UNC Greensboro	65
78	Rider	94
83	George Mason	56
75	Loyola (Md.) ■	55
51	James Madison ■	50
53	William & Mary	59
58	Old Dominion	60
65	UNC Wilmington	60
57	Va. Commonwealth	68
44	Pennsylvania	50
78	Drexel ■	73
53	Towson	59
67	Hofstra	74
75	Va. Commonwealth ■	70
75	Old Dominion ■	70
57	George Mason ■	69
89	Drexel	97
57	Towson	61
66	UNC Wilmington ■	69
82	William & Mary ■	72
75	Hofstra ■	63
65	James Madison	64
85	Drexel †	59
54	UNC Wilmington †	69

Nickname: Fightin' Blue Hens
Colors: Blue & Gold
Arena: Bob Carpenter Center
 Capacity: 5,000; Year Built: 1992
AD: Edgar N. Johnson
SID: Mike Hirschman

DELAWARE ST.
Dover, DE 19901 I

Coach: Greg Jackson, St. Paul's 1982
2001-02 RESULTS (16-13)

69	Hartford ■	57
60	Maine	52
53	Maryland	77
61	Old Dominion	72
78	South Carolina St.	63
63	N.C. A&T	76
62	Eastern Mich.	75

70	Fordham	80
79	Fairleigh Dickinson	73
44	Villanova	67
57	Towson	64
57	Coppin St. ■	46
77	Morgan St. ■	67
86	Bethune-Cookman ■	66
65	Florida A&M ■	50
55	Hampton	58
82	Norfolk St.	62
77	Md.-East. Shore ■	67
55	South Carolina St. ■	61
75	N.C. A&T ■	61
67	Coppin St.	65
54	Morgan St.	52
67	Bethune-Cookman	56
62	Florida A&M	69
58	Hampton	63
66	Norfolk St. ■	73
71	Howard	64
54	Coppin St. †	45
56	Howard †	65

Nickname: Hornets
Colors: Red & Columbia Blue
Arena: Memorial Hall
 Capacity: 3,000; Year Built: 1982
AD: Hallie Gregory
SID: Dennis Jones

DELAWARE VALLEY
Doylestown, PA 18901-2699 III

Coach: Bob Simmons, Wilkes 1993
2001-02 RESULTS (6-19)
67	East. Mennonite †	66
75	Elizabethtown	102
74	Phila. Bible ■	68
111	Valley Forge Chrst. ■	64
84	Lincoln (Pa.)	81
66	Centenary (N.J.)	71
55	Scranton ■	72
73	Lycoming ■	88
60	Alvernia ■	69
60	Lebanon Valley	71
62	Chowan †	70
72	Arcadia ■	70
69	King's (Pa.)	100
51	DeSales	68
58	Moravian ■	64
53	Wilkes ■	66
52	Drew	62
62	FDU-Madison ■	67
64	Lycoming	84
58	Scranton	76
71	DeSales ■	61
74	King's (Pa.) ■	90
69	Wilkes	74
66	FDU-Madison	77
64	Drew ■	69

Nickname: Aggies
Colors: Green & Gold
Arena: James Work Gymnasium
 Capacity: 1,800; Year Built: 1969
AD: Frank Wolfgang
SID: Matthew Levy

DELTA ST.
Cleveland, MS 38733 II

Coach: Steve Rives,
Mississippi Col 1972
2001-02 RESULTS (22-7)
75	North Ala.	66
68	SIU-Edwardsville	65
84	Miles ■	65
87	LeMoyne-Owen ■	76
89	Tougaloo ■	48
70	Mississippi Val.	75
76	Tougaloo	65
80	Ouachita Baptist	72
82	Arkansas Tech ■	85
70	Ark.-Monticello	67

72	Central Ark. ■	53
62	Henderson St.	76
77	Southern Ark. ■	64
74	Harding ■	73
72	Mississippi Val. ■	59
63	Christian Bros.	66
68	Ouachita Baptist ■	49
88	Arkansas Tech	81
75	Ark.-Monticello ■	60
68	Central Ark.	66
64	Henderson St. ■	59
78	Southern Ark.	73
77	Harding	81
70	Christian Bros. ■	64
110	Ark. Baptist ■	60
77	Montevallo †	73
50	Valdosta St. †	66
71	West Ga. †	76
100	Selma †	57

Nickname: Statesmen
Colors: Green & White
Arena: Walter Sillers Coliseum
 Capacity: 4,000; Year Built: 1961
AD: James H. Jordan
SID: Fred Sington

DENISON
Granville, OH 43023 III

Coach: Bill Lee, Cornerstone 1988
2001-02 RESULTS (6-20)
76	Emory & Henry	92
76	N.C. Wesleyan †	83
69	Mt. Vernon Naz.	86
57	Grove City	66
60	Wittenberg ■	96
73	Oberlin ■	68
62	Wabash	75
65	Bluffton ■	85
63	Capital	89
58	Otterbein	99
58	Hanover †	85
60	La Roche ■	64
71	Wooster ■	83
51	Ohio Wesleyan ■	75
72	Earlham ■	71
73	Hiram	71
69	Wittenberg	100
66	Oberlin ■	70
68	Allegheny ■	67
80	Kenyon ■	72
68	Wabash ■	79
77	Hiram ■	87
77	Earlham	83
70	Kenyon	88
88	Allegheny ■	74
53	Wabash	89

Nickname: Big Red
Colors: Red & White
Arena: Livingston Gymnasium
 Capacity: 3,500; Year Built: 1949
AD: Larry Scheiderer
SID: Jack Hire

DENVER
Denver, CO 80208 I

Coach: Terry Carroll,
Northern Iowa 1978
2001-02 RESULTS (8-20)
83	Montana Tech ■	65
44	Air Force	52
68	Wyoming ■	71
57	Manhattan	81
92	Morris Brown	76
49	St. Louis	63
63	Air Force ■	53
61	Colorado St. ■	74
79	Tex. A&M-Corp. Chris.	81
82	New Mexico St. ■	86
68	Drake	72
58	Arkansas St.	78

63	Ark.-Little Rock	79
78	Morris Brown ■	50
72	Florida Int'l ■	69
70	North Texas ■	78
59	Western Ky. ■	86
62	New Mexico St.	68
58	La.-Lafayette	70
57	North Texas	83
78	Tex. A&M-Corp. Chris. ■	68
76	South Ala. ■	58
73	New Orleans	74
64	South Ala.	60
47	Middle Tenn.	62
60	La.-Lafayette ■	74
46	New Orleans	69
53	Arkansas St. †	58

Nickname: Pioneers
Colors: Crimson & Gold
Arena: Magness Arena
 Capacity: 7,200; Year Built: 1999
AD: M. Dianne Murphy
SID: Daniel Lust

DESALES
Center Valley, PA 18034-9568..III

Coach: Scott Coval,
William & Mary 1986
2001-02 RESULTS (16-10)
85	Stevens Tech ■	69
70	Moravian ■	55
50	Misericordia	57
110	Centenary (N.J.) ■	48
79	Albright ■	48
61	FDU-Madison	68
70	King's (Pa.) ■	61
82	Villa Julie	57
82	Marywood ■	58
88	Waynesburg ■	78
62	Wilkes	87
68	Delaware Valley ■	51
71	Scranton	72
83	Lycoming ■	76
85	Arcadia	74
79	Drew ■	73
69	King's (Pa.)	71
58	Muhlenberg	72
73	FDU-Madison ■	58
61	Delaware Valley	71
88	Lancaster Bible ■	49
80	Wilkes ■	86
91	Scranton ■	78
68	Drew	50
59	Lycoming	73
80	Misericordia	86

Nickname: Bulldogs
Colors: Navy Blue & Scarlet
Arena: Billera Hall
 Capacity: 1,000; Year Built: 1964
AD: Scott Coval
SID: B.J. Spigelmyer

DETROIT
Detroit, MI 48219-0900 I

Coach: Perry Watson,
Eastern Mich. 1972
2001-02 RESULTS (18-13)
70	Michigan St.	80
98	Alabama A&M ■	75
73	Wyoming ■	57
67	Western Mich. ■	62
95	Eastern Mich.	69
67	Oakland	93
54	Maryland	79
63	Toledo	40
77	Central Mich.	68
60	Bowling Green	77
59	UC Santa Barb. †	86
47	UMBC †	50
61	Ill.-Chicago	62
49	Loyola (Ill.)	55

63	Butler ■	54
75	Wright St. ■	74
66	Youngstown St.	51
53	Cleveland St. ■	50
52	Wis.-Green Bay	40
48	Wis.-Milwaukee	66
74	Ill.-Chicago	67
48	Butler	61
69	Wright St.	64
61	Wis.-Green Bay ■	65
55	Loyola (Ill.) ■	53
72	Cleveland St.	62
63	Youngstown St. ■	52
94	Wis.-Milwaukee ■	61
67	Cleveland St. ■	63
68	Ill.-Chicago †	79
69	Dayton	80

Nickname: Titans
Colors: Red, White & Blue
Arena: Calihan Hall
 Capacity: 8,837; Year Built: 1952
AD: Bradford E. Kinsman
SID: Mark Engel

DICKINSON
Carlisle, PA 17013 III

Coach: David Frohman, Indiana 1972
2001-02 RESULTS (13-12)
89	Lynchburg ■	63
56	Muskingum ■	64
70	Lebanon Valley ■	71
72	Susquehanna	81
60	Ursinus	69
72	Shippensburg	80
64	York (Pa.)	70
66	Muhlenberg	71
75	Messiah	64
73	Moravian	65
77	FDU-Madison †	66
73	Swarthmore ■	59
85	McDaniel ■	66
55	Elizabethtown ■	82
90	Johns Hopkins ■	81
55	Frank. & Marsh.	63
88	Eastern ■	78
56	Gettysburg	64
52	Haverford	45
79	Juniata	66
79	Washington (Md.) ■	70
69	McDaniel	47
52	Johns Hopkins	69
61	Frank. & Marsh. ■	63
75	Gettysburg ■	66

Nickname: Red Devils
Colors: Red & White
Arena: Kline Center
 Capacity: 2,000; Year Built: 1980
AD: Les J. Poolman
SID: Charlie McGuire

DIST. COLUMBIA
Washington, DC 20008 II

Coach: Mike McLeese,
Elizabeth City St. 1974
2001-02 RESULTS (18-9)
85	Bowie St. ■	82
83	Shepherd ■	48
70	West Chester	68
45	Millersville	60
79	Longwood	95
54	Indiana (Pa.) ■	58
85	Millersville ■	67
79	Mansfield ■	63
72	Bloomsburg	85
54	Franklin Pierce †	57
80	Ohio Valley †	72
72	Indiana (Pa.)	79
72	Virginia Union	71
72	Southern Va.	71
95	Pitt.-Johnstown ■	71

77	Mansfield	81
72	Columbia Union	56
65	Kutztown	62
81	West Chester ■	55
90	Southern Va. ■	63
81	Shepherd	85
87	Davis & Elkins ■	55
78	Virginia Union	73
77	Kutztown ■	60
91	St. Augustine's ■	83
64	Pitt.-Johnstown	69
87	Columbia Union ■	79

Nickname: Firebirds
Colors: Red & Yellow
Arena: Physical Activities Center
   Capacity: 3,000; Year Built: 1976
AD: Mike McLeese
SID: Bernard S. Payton

DOMINICAN (ILL.)
River Forest, IL 60305 III

2001-02 RESULTS (5-20)
66	North Park	76
52	Lewis	89
57	Elmhurst	91
55	Humboldt St. †	102
62	Carthage	101
58	Lakeland †	56
52	Edgewood	81
85	Milwaukee Engr. †	71
63	North Park ■	94
77	Humboldt St. ■	83
45	Albion	72
62	Ohio Wesleyan †	70
54	Marian (Wis.)	76
72	Eureka ■	55
70	Concordia (Ill.)	64
67	Clarke ■	70
70	Benedictine (Ill.)	78
62	Aurora ■	79
66	Rockford	76
71	Eureka	76
72	Concordia (Ill.) ■	77
56	Clarke	62
64	Benedictine (Ill.) ■	60
67	Aurora	74
75	Rockford ■	85

Nickname: Stars
Colors: Royal Blue & Black
AD: Barb Bolich
SID: To be named

DOWLING
Oakdale, NY 11769 II

Coach: Mike Voyack, St. John's (N.Y.)
   1995

2001-02 RESULTS (14-13)
80	Adelphi ■	93
80	Molloy	79
113	Mercy ■	70
92	C.W. Post	87
79	Merrimack	94
83	St. Thomas Aquinas	92
75	Mass.-Lowell †	78
77	American Int'l ■	57
70	St. Michael's	85
66	Bridgeport	84
68	Queens (N.Y.) ■	70
102	Southampton	98
79	NYIT ■	86
61	Philadelphia U.	75
102	Concordia (N.Y.) ■	58
94	Mercy	64
87	C.W. Post ■	68
76	Adelphi	93
88	Molloy ■	85
87	St. Thomas Aquinas ■	79
74	Bridgeport ■	67
91	Queens (N.Y.)	96

99	Southampton ■	104
94	NYIT	80
78	Philadelphia U. ■	67
105	Concordia (N.Y.)	86
73	Queens (N.Y.)	78

Nickname: Golden Lions
Colors: Blue & Gold
Arena: Lasalle Center
   Capacity: 1,500
AD: Robert Dranoff
SID: Mark Sosna

DRAKE
Des Moines, IA 50311-4505......I

Coach: Kurt Kanaskie, La Salle 1980

2001-02 RESULTS (14-15)
74	Sam Houston St. †	65
63	Hawaii	74
73	Oral Roberts	68
74	Western Ill.	80
93	Ark.-Pine Bluff ■	64
85	Indiana St. ■	71
59	Iowa	101
72	Iowa St. ■	58
57	Northern Ill. ■	79
71	Fla. Atlantic ■	79
72	Denver ■	68
56	Northern Iowa	71
65	Bradley ■	68
83	Illinois St. ■	73
65	Wichita St.	81
63	Evansville	61
71	Northern Iowa ■	77
64	Southern Ill. ■	79
54	Illinois St.	68
80	Wichita St. ■	64
78	Evansville ■	67
51	Southwest Mo. St.	65
57	Southern Ill.	66
91	Creighton ■	95
68	Bradley ■	54
62	Indiana St.	60
68	Southwest Mo. St. ■	61
75	Creighton	73
63	Illinois St. †	64

Nickname: Bulldogs
Colors: Blue & White
Arena: Drake Knapp Center
   Capacity: 7,002; Year Built: 1992
AD: Dave Blank
SID: Mike Mahon

DREW
Madison, NJ 07940................III

Coach: Mark Coleman, St. Lawrence
   1983

2001-02 RESULTS (12-13)
86	New Paltz St. ■	55
70	Maritime (N.Y.) ■	47
53	Hawaii-Hilo †	92
43	Whitworth †	82
60	Menlo †	69
70	Moravian ■	78
64	Messiah ■	58
65	King's (Pa.)	76
50	Scranton	81
80	Lycoming ■	74
76	Wilkes ■	72
69	Ursinus	71
68	FDU-Madison	77
62	Delaware Valley ■	52
79	Phila. Bible	64
73	DeSales	79
60	Scranton ■	61
60	Swarthmore	57
62	King's (Pa.) ■	58
63	Wilkes	75
97	Farmingdale St. ■	77
63	Lycoming	91

68	FDU-Madison ■	64
50	DeSales ■	68
69	Delaware Valley ■	64

Nickname: Rangers
Colors: Green & Blue
Arena: Baldwin Gym
   Capacity: 800; Year Built: 1958
AD: Connee Zotos
SID: Jennifer Brauner

DREXEL
Philadelphia, PA 19104 I

Coach: Bruiser Flint, St. Joseph's 1987

2001-02 RESULTS (14-14)
67	Marist	75
87	Northeastern †	76
55	Rider	68
80	Pennsylvania †	89
71	James Madison	58
84	Lafayette ■	88
70	La Salle †	80
64	St. Joseph's	85
83	Northeastern ■	72
70	Hofstra ■	58
87	Niagara ■	82
84	Va. Commonwealth ■	73
66	Old Dominion	74
58	William & Mary	56
62	Towson	68
69	James Madison ■	59
73	Delaware	78
84	Hofstra	74
100	George Mason ■	69
78	William & Mary ■	61
65	Va. Commonwealth	77
50	UNC Wilmington	63
97	Delaware ■	89
80	Old Dominion ■	70
64	George Mason	79
68	UNC Wilmington ■	65
65	Towson ■	81
59	Delaware †	85

Nickname: Dragons
Colors: Navy Blue & Gold
Arena: Daskalakis Athletic Center
   Capacity: 2,300; Year Built: 1975
AD: Eric A. Zillmer
SID: Mike Tuberosa

DRURY
Springfield, MO 65802 II

Coach: Gary Stanfield, John Brown
   1969

2001-02 RESULTS (12-15)
80	Midwestern St.	86
66	Oakland City	77
80	Langston ■	73
91	North Ala. ■	85
75	Truman	80
68	Southwest Baptist ■	75
81	Pittsburg St. ■	101
78	Central Okla. †	94
68	Central Wash. ■	81
86	Trevecca Nazarene †	81
59	Master's †	83
77	Lee †	90
76	Lock Haven ■	61
102	Harris-Stowe ■	57
91	Okla. Panhandle	81
107	Oakland City ■	82
88	St. Edward's ■	80
56	Incarnate Word	71
76	St. Mary's (Tex.)	83
74	Rockhurst ■	87
93	Lincoln (Mo.)	100
91	Okla. Panhandle ■	84
85	St. Edward's	82
82	St. Mary's (Tex.) ■	76
78	Incarnate Word ■	80

129	Lincoln (Mo.) ■	89
68	Rockhurst	78

Nickname: Panthers
Colors: Scarlet & Gray
Arena: Weiser Gymnasium
   Capacity: 2,250; Year Built: 1948
AD: Bruce Harger
SID: Dan Cashel

DUBUQUE
Dubuque, IA 52001 III

Coach: Mike Elbe, Quincy 1986

2001-02 RESULTS (6-19)
46	Wis.-Platteville ■	70
66	Coe ■	85
77	Iowa Wesleyan ■	92
66	Loras	68
82	Knox ■	74
75	Cardinal Stritch †	98
75	Clarke	61
67	Tri-State †	53
68	Luther	96
67	Upper Iowa	80
85	Cornell College ■	84
57	Buena Vista ■	69
61	Wartburg ■	82
71	Mt. Mercy ■	89
60	Central (Iowa)	69
57	Simpson	73
53	Cornell College	72
62	Loras ■	75
87	Upper Iowa ■	81
60	Luther ■	57
65	Coe	88
68	Wartburg	88
51	Buena Vista	112
35	Simpson ■	71
59	Central (Iowa) ■	70

Nickname: Spartans
Colors: Blue & White
Arena: McCormick Gym
   Capacity: 1,500; Year Built: 1916
SID: Jason Hughes

DUKE
Durham, NC 27708-0555 I

Coach: Mike Krzyzewski, Army 1969

2001-02 RESULTS (31-4)
80	Seton Hall †	79
81	South Carolina †	56
83	Ball St. †	71
104	Portland ■	62
80	Iowa †	62
96	Clemson	80
82	Temple ■	57
104	Michigan	83
93	N.C. A&T ■	51
95	Kentucky †	92
92	San Diego St. ■	79
106	Davidson †	71
76	Florida St.	77
104	Georgia Tech ■	79
76	North Carolina St.	57
99	Maryland ■	78
103	Wake Forest ■	80
88	Boston College	78
94	Virginia ■	81
87	North Carolina	58
98	Clemson ■	88
80	Florida St. ■	49
95	Georgia Tech	63
108	North Carolina St. ■	71
73	Maryland	87
90	Wake Forest	61
97	St. John's (N.Y.) ■	55
84	Virginia	87
93	North Carolina ■	68
60	North Carolina †	48
79	Wake Forest †	64
91	North Carolina St. †	61

84	Winthrop †	37
84	Notre Dame †	77
73	Indiana †	74

Nickname: Blue Devils
Colors: Royal Blue & White
Arena: Cameron Indoor Stadium
  Capacity: 9,314; Year Built: 1939
AD: Joe Alleva
SID: Jon Jackson

DUQUESNE
Pittsburgh, PA 15282 I

Coach: Danny Nee, St. Mary's Plains 1971
2001-02 RESULTS (9-19)

76	Md.-East. Shore ■	52
82	Vermont ■	77
60	Ohio	73
41	Cincinnati	74
62	Bowling Green ■	64
52	UNC Wilmington	64
68	West Virginia	61
63	Pittsburgh †	78
64	Cleveland St.	82
84	Liberty ■	66
64	George Mason ■	48
50	George Washington	74
48	Temple ■	85
44	Dayton ■	88
54	La Salle ■	62
89	St. Bonaventure ■	96
47	St. Joseph's ■	63
51	Richmond ■	55
65	Xavier	79
95	Fordham ■	66
78	Massachusetts ■	69
72	Rhode Island	69
50	Dayton	82
79	George Washington ■	69
65	La Salle	80
66	Xavier ■	80
57	Richmond ■	83
66	St. Bonaventure †	81

Nickname: Dukes
Colors: Red & Blue
Arena: A.J. Palumbo Center
  Capacity: 6,200; Year Built: 1988
AD: Brian Colleary
SID: Dave Saba

EARLHAM
Richmond, IN 47374 III

Coach: Jeff Justus, Rose-Hulman 1978
2001-02 RESULTS (11-15)

55	Transylvania	70
64	Savannah A&D †	67
79	Rose-Hulman ■	71
62	Bluffton	64
77	Wilmington (Ohio) ■	52
79	Wooster ■	88
79	Kenyon	80
78	Oberlin	69
78	Adrian ■	94
72	Mt. St. Joseph ■	69
71	Franklin ■	67
64	Allegheny ■	73
81	Hiram ■	67
106	DePauw	101
71	Denison	72
63	Wabash ■	72
70	Wooster	86
70	Kenyon ■	56
57	Ohio Wesleyan	83
38	Wittenberg ■	70
59	Oberlin	69
68	Wabash	63
83	Denison ■	77
60	Wittenberg	81
60	Ohio Wesleyan ■	57
51	Wittenberg	78

Nickname: Quakers
Colors: Maroon & White
Arena: Schuckman Court
  Capacity: 1,800; Year Built: 1999
AD: Frank Carr
SID: Jon Mires

EAST CARO.
Greenville, NC 27858-4353 I

Coach: Bill Herrion, Merrimack 1981
2001-02 RESULTS (12-18)

79	Rutgers †	74
71	Northwestern †	68
47	North Carolina St.	71
87	Appalachian St.	93
72	UCF ■	82
62	Virginia Tech	90
54	UNC Greensboro	56
52	Old Dominion ■	53
64	S.C.-Spartanburg ■	52
81	Middle Tenn. ■	71
90	Radford	86
85	Lees-McRae ■	44
62	Cincinnati ■	72
54	UAB	63
75	Charlotte ■	84
87	Louisville ■	77
72	St. Louis	85
58	DePaul ■	80
52	Charlotte	87
48	Cincinnati	75
69	St. Louis ■	63
58	Marquette	70
51	DePaul	62
61	Southern Miss. ■	58
73	Birmingham-So. ■	61
42	Louisville	75
63	Houston ■	46
51	Marquette ■	46
63	TCU	66
49	Houston †	58

Nickname: Pirates
Colors: Purple & Gold
Arena: Williams Arena at Minges
  Capacity: 8,000; Year Built: 1967
AD: Mike Hamrick
SID: Jody Jones

EAST CENTRAL
Ada, OK 74820 II

Coach: Wayne Cobb, Southeastern Okla. 1965
2001-02 RESULTS (10-17)

54	Harding	61
78	Sterling (Kan.) ■	82
89	Rhema †	72
89	National Christian †	51
69	Ouachita Baptist	75
58	Tarleton St. ■	68
65	Tex. A&M-Commerce	72
65	Tex. A&M-Kingsville	69
76	Harding	75
63	Ouachita Baptist ■	67
67	Angelo St. ■	68
76	Abilene Christian ■	55
66	West Tex. A&M	81
63	Eastern N.M.	67
97	Central Okla.	101
75	Northeastern St. ■	64
61	Southeastern Okla. ■	49
69	Midwestern St.	75
60	Cameron	57
57	Southwestern Okla. ■	84
98	Central Okla. ■	81
54	Northeastern St.	68
67	Southeastern Okla.	58
87	Midwestern St. ■	58
55	Cameron	58
58	Southwestern Okla.	65
68	Tex. A&M-Kingsville	71

Nickname: Tigers
Colors: Orange & Black
Arena: Kerr Activities Center
  Capacity: 2,771; Year Built: 1973
AD: Tim Green
SID: Zac Underwood

EAST STROUDSBURG
East Stroudsburg, PA 18301 II

Coach: Mike Power, Lehigh
2001-02 RESULTS (4-20)

75	N.J. Inst. of Tech.	70
55	Shippensburg ■	64
67	Edinboro ■	74
61	Slippery Rock ■	48
54	Bloomfield ■	55
63	N.J. Inst. of Tech. ■	49
42	Felician ■	65
73	Calif. (Pa.) ■	77
67	Indiana (Pa.) ■	81
51	Shippensburg	83
65	Cheyney ■	74
61	Clarion	91
51	Lock Haven	62
75	Mansfield	89
35	Millersville ■	53
69	Bloomsburg	82
54	Kutztown	48
48	Cheyney	50
62	West Chester ■	70
46	Mansfield ■	65
65	Millersville	66
55	Kutztown ■	68
63	Bloomsburg ■	77
56	West Chester	66

Nickname: Warriors
Colors: Red & Black
Arena: Koehler Fieldhouse
  Capacity: 2,650; Year Built: 1967
AD: Joy M. Richman
SID: Peter Nevins

EAST TENN. ST.
Johnson City, TN 37614 I

Coach: Ed DeChellis, Penn St. 1982
2001-02 RESULTS (18-10)

90	Guilford ■	61
62	Virginia	85
71	Va. Commonwealth	79
66	South Carolina	83
77	UNC Asheville ■	71
85	Coastal Caro. ■	71
79	Radford ■	54
84	James Madison ■	57
110	Shenandoah ■	60
109	Virginia-Wise ■	66
77	Vanderbilt	86
75	Appalachian St. ■	66
61	Citadel	74
64	Col. of Charleston	71
101	VMI ■	90
92	UNC Greensboro	104
66	Davidson	73
71	Wofford ■	58
61	Chattanooga ■	66
96	VMI	77
100	Ga. Southern ■	65
86	Western Caro.	76
85	Davidson ■	78
90	UNC Greensboro ■	76
91	Western Caro. ■	77
78	Furman	67
79	Appalachian St.	72
75	Col. of Charleston	76

Nickname: Buccaneers
Colors: Blue & Gold
Arena: Memorial Center
  Capacity: 13,000; Year Built: 1977
AD: Todd Stansbury
SID: Phil Hess

EAST TEX. BAPTIST
Marshall, TX 75670-1498 III

Coach: Leland Hand, East Tex. Baptist
2001-02 RESULTS (12-12)

67	Centenary (La.)	87
94	Concordia-Austin ■	98
79	Jarvis Christian ■	81
86	Sul Ross St. ■	77
79	Howard Payne ■	100
70	Wiley	69
99	Jarvis Christian	79
75	LeTourneau	69
81	Wiley ■	68
87	Hardin-Simmons	82
75	McMurry	95
92	Louisiana Col.	81
63	Mississippi Col.	75
85	Ozarks (Ark.) ■	92
70	Austin	69
74	Dallas ■	65
70	Texas-Dallas ■	57
82	LeTourneau ■	78
87	Dallas	70
65	Texas-Dallas	86
84	Louisiana Col. ■	89
62	Mississippi Col. ■	91
87	Ozarks (Ark.)	90
62	Austin	75

Nickname: Tigers
Colors: Blue & Gold
AD: Kent Reeves
SID: To be named

EASTERN
St. Davids, PA 19087-3696 III

Coach: Mike Schauer, Wheaton (Ill.) 1993
2001-02 RESULTS (10-16)

78	Messiah	68
63	Gordon	70
53	Elizabethtown ■	81
65	Baptist Bible (Pa.)	45
44	Alvernia	68
52	Misericordia ■	62
56	Arcadia	58
58	King's (Pa.) †	74
67	Oswego St. †	75
93	Valley Forge Chrst. ■	53
75	Cabrini	95
86	Wesley	78
73	Neumann ■	92
78	Pa. Col. of Bible ■	47
83	Marywood ■	55
78	Dickinson	88
69	Gwynedd-Mercy ■	64
72	Misericordia	77
52	Neumann	77
71	Wesley ■	67
63	Cabrini	81
68	Arcadia ■	50
84	Marywood	45
55	Alvernia ■	73
56	Gwynedd-Mercy	67
71	Neumann	83

Nickname: Eagles
Colors: Maroon & White
Arena: Eastern College Gym
  Capacity: 600
AD: Harry Gutelius
SID: Mark Birtwistle

EASTERN CONN. ST.
Willimantic, CT 06226 III

Coach: Barry Davis, St. Lawrence 1980
2001-02 RESULTS (13-13)

78	Salve Regina ■	89
78	Westfield St. ■	55
75	Trinity (Conn.) ■	87
87	Wesleyan (Conn.)	102

82	Rhode Island Col.	74
73	Worcester St. ■	51
87	Albertus Magnus ■	92
72	Plymouth St. ■	94
70	Connecticut Col.	69
66	Roanoke	75
87	Averett †	54
85	Mass.-Boston ■	77
75	Mass.-Dartmouth ■	72
99	Southern Me.	88
78	Keene St.	98
87	Wheaton (Mass.)	94
78	Rhode Island Col. ■	59
76	Western Conn. St.	72
67	Plymouth St.	79
69	Endicott	60
63	Mass.-Boston	75
65	Keene St. ■	76
85	Mass.-Dartmouth	75
68	Western Conn. St. ■	82
70	Southern Me. ■	60
83	Plymouth St.	84

Nickname: Warriors
Colors: Blue & White
Arena: Geissler Gymnasium
  Capacity: 3,000; Year Built: 1974
AD: Joyce Wong
SID: Bob Molta

EASTERN ILL.
Charleston, IL 61920-3099 I

Coach: Rick Samuels, Chadron St. 1971
2001-02 RESULTS (15-16)

98	St. Joseph's (Ind.) ■	58
53	Illinois	93
65	Georgia Tech †	70
60	Pennsylvania †	77
73	Hartford †	57
52	Indiana St.	50
87	Augustana (Ill.) ■	71
86	Evansville	76
81	Western Ill.	72
94	Loyola (Ill.) ■	78
50	Oklahoma	109
59	Ohio St.	72
73	Northern Ill.	86
64	Austin Peay	86
84	Southeast Mo. St. ■	74
72	Morehead St. ■	71
86	Eastern Ky. ■	59
77	Benedictine (Ill.) ■	47
88	Murray St.	86
79	Tenn.-Martin	81
73	Austin Peay ■	70
92	Tennessee Tech	97
76	Tennessee St.	94
70	Eastern Ky.	76
76	Morehead St.	68
76	Murray St. ■	77
62	Tenn.-Martin ■	68
87	Southeast Mo. St.	102
88	Tennessee St. ■	84
68	Tennessee Tech ■	85
56	Murray St.	103

Nickname: Panthers
Colors: Blue & Gray
Arena: Lantz Arena
  Capacity: 5,300; Year Built: 1966
AD: Richard A. McDuffie
SID: Dave Kidwell

EASTERN KY.
Richmond, KY 40475-3101 I

Coach: Travis Ford, Kentucky 1994
2001-02 RESULTS (7-20)

91	Wilmington (Ohio) ■	56
62	Western Ill. ■	71
78	Wyoming	98
90	Marietta ■	71
74	Memphis	111

60	High Point	70
70	Dayton	82
57	Western Ill.	70
77	Louisville	94
70	Austin Peay ■	82
61	Tennessee Tech ■	90
68	Tennessee St. ■	69
75	Southeast Mo. St.	95
59	Eastern Ill.	86
100	IPFW ■	96
71	Morehead St.	84
108	Tenn.-Martin ■	100
92	Murray St. ■	81
59	Austin Peay	70
48	Tennessee Tech	71
76	Eastern Ill. ■	70
74	Southeast Mo. St. ■	81
63	Tennessee St.	66
60	Morehead St. ■	76
74	Murray St.	85
77	Tenn.-Martin	82

Nickname: Colonels
Colors: Maroon & White
Arena: McBrayer Arena
  Capacity: 6,500; Year Built: 1963
SID: Karl Park

EAST. MENNONITE
Harrisonburg, VA 22802 III

Coach: Tom Baker, East. Mennonite
1981
2001-02 RESULTS (5-20)

66	Delaware Valley †	67
79	Arcadia †	90
73	Shenandoah	68
55	Va. Wesleyan ■	70
51	Ferrum †	60
83	Christendom †	52
38	Randolph-Macon ■	66
51	VMI	77
54	Bridgewater (Va.) ■	78
68	Lynchburg	56
66	Hampden-Sydney ■	81
73	Wash. & Lee ■	76
48	Guilford ■	70
94	Emory & Henry ■	95
63	Bridgewater (Va.)	84
66	Southern Va. ■	77
75	Roanoke	87
69	Lynchburg ■	59
68	Hampden-Sydney	106
66	Randolph-Macon	77
73	Emory & Henry	81
55	Guilford	71
45	Va. Wesleyan	69
86	Wash. & Lee ■	68
62	Roanoke ■	82

Nickname: Royals
Colors: Royal Blue & White
Arena: University Gym
  Capacity: 1,800; Year Built: 1999
AD: Larry Martin
SID: Seth McGuffin

EASTERN MICH.
Ypsilanti, MI 48197 I

Coach: Jim Boone, West Va. St. 1981
2001-02 RESULTS (6-24)

66	UAB †	79
56	Miami (Fla.) †	93
67	Morris Brown †	55
61	Md.-East. Shore ■	65
79	Tennessee Tech ■	86
69	Detroit ■	95
75	Delaware St. ■	62
76	Wis.-Green Bay ■	106
85	Concordia (Mich.) ■	54
58	Michigan	88
72	Western Caro. ■	59
51	Buffalo ■	70

45	Ball St. ■	63
61	Akron ■	60
60	Toledo ■	85
75	Marshall	97
56	Miami (Ohio)	72
73	Central Mich. ■	86
66	Ohio	80
72	Northern Ill.	84
62	Kent St. ■	82
56	Ball St.	90
94	Western Mich.	101
85	Northern Ill. ■	90
61	Bowling Green	82
83	Akron ■	76
57	Central Mich.	76
52	Western Mich. ■	71
68	Toledo	74
53	Toledo	89

Nickname: Eagles
Colors: Green & White
Arena: Convocation Center
  Capacity: 8,824; Year Built: 1998
AD: David L. Diles
SID: Jim Streeter

EASTERN NAZARENE
Quincy, MA 02170-2999 III

Coach: Tim Swanson,
Northwest Nazarene 1991
2001-02 RESULTS (10-16)

75	Elms ■	60
66	Bridgewater St. ■	83
75	Fisher ■	78
69	Rhode Island Col. ■	59
53	Worcester St.	51
67	MIT	73
61	Colby-Sawyer	81
76	Emerson ■	89
70	Mount Ida ■	79
56	NYIT †	77
60	Bridgewater St. †	57
67	Bates ■	88
67	Salem St.	75
74	Anna Maria ■	69
90	Nichols ■	67
36	Babson	84
75	New England Col. ■	69
67	Roger Williams	75
91	Curry	99
88	Becker ■	78
80	New England	77
72	Endicott ■	73
59	Salve Regina ■	71
59	Gordon ■	82
74	Wentworth Inst.	63
51	Salve Regina	69

Nickname: Crusaders
Colors: Red & White
Arena: Lahue Center
  Capacity: 1,600; Year Built: 1973
AD: Dr. Nancy B. Detwiler
SID: Carolyn Morse

EASTERN N.M.
Portales, NM 88130 II

Coach: Shawn Scanlan, Kansas 1978
2001-02 RESULTS (15-12)

75	Western N.M. †	61
101	N.M. Highlands	91
80	N.M. Highlands ■	61
64	Cameron	68
71	Southwestern Okla.	73
74	Midwestern St. ■	66
73	Lubbock Chrst.	74
89	Okla. Panhandle ■	69
88	Central Okla.	85
51	Northeastern St.	70
75	Southeastern Okla.	58
67	East Central ■	63
82	New Mexico St.	98

48	Tarleton St.	65
81	Okla. Panhandle ■	77
82	Abilene Christian ■	61
61	Angelo St. ■	73
82	West Tex. A&M	73
70	Tex. A&M-Commerce ■	75
77	Tex. A&M-Kingsville †	73
70	Tex. A&M-Kingsville	79
70	Tex. A&M-Commerce	71
80	Tarleton St.	87
81	West Tex. A&M	77
86	Angelo St.	80
71	Abilene Christian	70
59	Northeastern St.	71

Nickname: Greyhounds
Colors: Green & Silver
Arena: Greyhound Arena
  Capacity: 4,800; Year Built: 1967
AD: Michael Maguire
SID: Robert McKinney

EASTERN ORE.
La Grande, OR 97850-2899 III

Coach: Art Furman, Minn. St.-Mankato
1978
2001-02 RESULTS (6-19)

69	Walla Walla ■	65
70	Whitman	68
51	Carroll (Mont.)	65
73	Trinity Baptist	69
43	Whitworth	97
85	Walla Walla	89
52	Western Baptist	77
71	Concordia (Ore.) ■	67
45	Gonzaga	105
72	Evergreen St.	105
53	Northwest (Wash.)	82
64	Cascade ■	75
72	Warner Pacific ■	93
70	Southern Ore.	83
66	Oregon Tech	83
62	Concordia (Ore.)	80
71	Western Baptist	101
67	Albertson	71
66	Northwest (Wash.) ■	65
90	Evergreen St. ■	93
63	Warner Pacific	72
90	Cascade	69
65	Oregon Tech ■	71
73	Southern Ore. ■	79
80	Albertson	90

Nickname: Mountaineers
Colors: Navy Blue & Vegas Gold
Arena: Quinn Coliseum
  Capacity: 2,500
AD: Rob Cashell
SID: Sam Ghrist

EASTERN WASH.
Cheney, WA 99004 I

Coach: Ray Giacoletti, Minot St. 1984
2001-02 RESULTS (17-13)

68	St. Joseph's †	67
27	California	56
103	Northwest (Wash.) ■	71
68	Minnesota	86
47	Boise St. ■	42
75	St. Martin's ■	59
74	Gonzaga	84
59	Idaho	48
70	Cal Poly ■	75
61	Portland	68
58	San Diego St.	86
67	St. Mary's (Cal.)	73
60	Indiana †	73
59	Samford †	48
79	Montana ■	46
81	Montana St. ■	90
88	Portland St. ■	79
78	Weber St.	89

76	Idaho St.	.71
63	Northern Ariz. ■	.70
87	Sacramento St. ■	.67
66	Montana St.	.62
80	Montana	.78
78	Portland St.	.62
70	Idaho St. ■	.60
68	Weber St. ■	.66
81	Sacramento St.	.71
75	Northern Ariz. ■	.80
62	Weber St. †	.57
66	Montana ■	.70

Nickname: Eagles
Colors: Red & White
Arena: Reese Court
  Capacity: 5,000; Year Built: 1975
AD: Scott Barnes
SID: Dave Cook

ECKERD
St. Petersburg, FL 33711 II

Coach: Tom Ryan, Eckerd 1987
2001-02 RESULTS (21-7)

96	P.R.-Cayey ■	.70
61	Franklin ■	.56
102	P.R.-Bayamon ■	.69
69	Augustana (S.D.) ■	.70
61	Five Towns †	.46
75	Johnson Smith †	.76
86	Queens (N.C.) ■	.76
76	Nova Southeastern ■	.69
63	Nova Southeastern	.61
74	Columbia Union ■	.61
87	Monmouth (Ill.) ■	.48
80	Fla. Memorial ■	.50
90	Lynn	.83
81	Florida Tech ■	.65
66	St. Leo	.51
61	Barry ■	.47
78	Fla. Southern	.86
66	Rollins	.80
48	Tampa ■	.68
101	Florida Tech	.70
80	St. Leo ■	.55
70	Barry	.60
83	Fla. Southern ■	.77
71	Rollins ■	.68
54	Tampa	.66
72	Lynn ■	.60
84	St. Leo †	.76
71	Fla. Southern †	.77

Nickname: Tritons
Colors: Red, White & Black
Arena: McArthur Center
  Capacity: 1,300; Year Built: 1970
AD: George Meese
SID: Sara Weber

EDGEWOOD
Madison, WI 53711-1998 III

Coach: Steven Larson, Wis.-Oshkosh 1974
2001-02 RESULTS (18-11)

48	Loras	.51
64	St. Scholastica †	.54
64	St. Norbert †	.69
47	Wis.-Stevens Point †	.62
50	Wis.-Oshkosh	.54
78	Northland ■	.49
76	Ripon ■	.69
58	Wis. Lutheran	.67
81	Dominican (Ill.) ■	.52
71	Concordia (Ill.) ■	.57
65	Maranatha Baptist ■	.56
60	Wis.-Parkside	.54
53	Concordia (Wis.) ■	.52
74	N.C. Wesleyan †	.64
59	Catholic	.62
51	Lakeland	.64

68	Wis.-Platteville	.73
50	Marian (Wis.) ■	.39
66	Milwaukee Engr. ■	.55
70	Wis. Lutheran ■	.75
68	Maranatha Baptist	.57
53	Concordia (Wis.)	.59
69	Lakeland ■	.58
70	Marian (Wis.)	.60
64	Milwaukee Engr.	.63
73	Maranatha Baptist ■	.54
61	Milwaukee Engr. ■	.49
69	Concordia (Wis.) ■	.63
65	Gust. Adolphus	.74

Nickname: Eagles
Colors: Black, Red & White
Arena: Todd Wehr Edgedome
  Capacity: 1,000; Year Built: 1961
AD: Steven Larson
SID: Josh Larson

EDINBORO
Edinboro, PA 16444-0001 II

Coach: Greg Walcavich, Rutgers 1973
2001-02 RESULTS (18-9)

69	Gannon	.72
57	Wooster	.74
69	Mercyhurst	.74
74	East Stroudsburg	.67
80	Kutztown	.77
76	Columbia Union ■	.68
69	Millersville	.79
83	Allegheny	.78
92	Lake Erie ■	.83
66	Cheyney ■	.63
57	West Chester ■	.71
88	Calif. (Pa.) ■	.73
77	Mansfield ■	.72
84	Bloomsburg ■	.69
76	Clarion ■	.62
74	Shippensburg	.66
83	Mercyhurst ■	.70
82	Lock Haven ■	.72
63	Indiana (Pa.)	.81
72	Calif. (Pa.)	.101
80	Slippery Rock ■	.66
74	Clarion	.78
77	Indiana (Pa.) ■	.75
83	Shippensburg ■	.75
75	Slippery Rock ■	.64
81	Lock Haven ■	.70
70	Calif. (Pa.)	.82

Nickname: Fighting Scots
Colors: Red & White
Arena: McComb Fieldhouse
  Capacity: 4,000; Year Built: 1970
AD: Bruce R. Baumgartner
SID: Bob Shreve

ELIZABETH CITY ST.
Elizabeth City, NC 27909 II

Coach: Barry Hamler, Clinch Valley 1957
2001-02 RESULTS (13-15)

60	Columbia Union	.62
73	Pitt.-Johnstown †	.66
69	Queens (N.Y.) †	.62
76	Johnson Smith ■	.81
90	Winston-Salem	.106
74	Montevallo	.77
70	Wingate	.91
74	North Fla. ■	.68
76	Fort Valley St. ■	.63
65	Shaw ■	.90
81	Virginia St. †	.77
71	St. Augustine's	.88
75	Fayetteville St. ■	.77
74	Columbia Union ■	.72
93	St. Paul's	.80
70	Virginia Union	.77

90	Bowie St. ■	.96
70	Shaw	.85
81	Livingstone	.71
80	St. Paul's ■	.54
95	N.C. Central ■	.96
94	Virginia St. ■	.85
89	Bowie St.	.95
69	Virginia Union ■	.65
86	Livingstone †	.78
64	Winston-Salem †	.84

Nickname: Vikings
Colors: Royal Blue & White
Arena: R.L. Vaughan Center
  Capacity: 5,000; Year Built: 1976
AD: Edward McLean
SID: April Emory

ELIZABETHTOWN
Elizabethtown, PA 17022-2298 III

Coach: Robert Schlosser, East Stoudsburg 1977
2001-02 RESULTS (29-3)

93	Arcadia ■	.62
102	Delaware Valley ■	.75
80	Frank. & Marsh.	.83
81	Eastern	.53
89	Johns Hopkins ■	.64
88	Scranton ■	.73
95	Widener	.83
107	Susquehanna ■	.79
96	Gettysburg	.57
99	Shenandoah ■	.83
85	King's (Pa.)	.65
85	Me.-Farmington †	.53
106	Moravian ■	.82
92	Juniata	.83
82	Dickinson	.55
83	Lebanon Valley ■	.67
99	Albright †	.62
84	Messiah	.67
95	Susquehanna	.71
77	Widener ■	.79
96	Juniata †	.49
87	Moravian	.73
95	Lebanon Valley	.66
101	Messiah ■	.74
89	Albright	.53
80	Susquehanna ■	.77
85	Widener	.73
95	Alvernia ■	.84
87	Cabrini †	.85
94	Clark (Mass.) †	.90
93	Rochester †	.83
83	Otterbein †	.102

Nickname: Blue Jays
Colors: Blue & Grey
Arena: Thompson Gymnasium
  Capacity: 2,400; Year Built: 1969
AD: Nancy J. Latimore
SID: Ian Showalter

ELMHURST
Elmhurst, IL 60126-3296...........III

Coach: Mark Scherer, Eureka 1983
2001-02 RESULTS (16-9)

50	Wis.-Whitewater	.59
79	Milwaukee Engr.	.71
91	Dominican (Ill.) ■	.57
56	Olivet Nazarene ■	.76
81	Maryville (Mo.) †	.74
81	Fontbonne	.65
53	St. Norbert ■	.59
79	Manchester	.59
78	Benedictine (Ill.) ■	.69
83	Wartburg	.58
68	Albion ■	.74
70	Ill. Wesleyan	.80
76	Carthage	.75
87	North Central ■	.71

87	Augustana (Ill.) ■	.83
77	Wheaton (Ill.) ■	.80
78	Millikin	.76
63	Carthage ■	.70
61	Augustana (Ill.)	.81
71	Ill. Wesleyan ■	.61
80	Wheaton (Ill.)	.87
83	North Park ■	.79
75	North Central	.62
94	Millikin ■	.65
92	North Park	.89

Nickname: Bluejays
Colors: Blue & White
Arena: R.A. Faganel Hall
  Capacity: 1,800; Year Built: 1983
AD: Christopher Ragsdale
SID: Hope Wagner

ELMIRA
Elmira, NY 14901 III

Coach: Pat Donnelly, Mansfield 1992
2001-02 RESULTS (10-15)

95	Chowan †	.99
77	Gallaudet †	.80
56	Le Moyne	.72
67	Pitt.-Bradford ■	.69
44	Cortland St.	.50
77	Keuka	.66
57	New York U.	.69
71	Lycoming ■	.77
82	Alfred	.94
73	St. John Fisher	.81
84	Ithaca ■	.61
72	Houghton	.59
58	Hartwick	.56
65	Rochester Inst. ■	.60
71	Nazareth ■	.77
85	Houghton ■	.74
56	Utica ■	.63
70	Hartwick ■	.63
67	Ithaca	.86
68	Nazareth	.80
60	Rochester Inst.	.71
67	Utica	.58
75	St. John Fisher ■	.61
84	Alfred ■	.79
75	Cazenovia ■	.76

Nickname: Soaring Eagles
Colors: Purple & Gold
Arena: Speidel Gymnasium
  Capacity: 1,000; Year Built: 1995
AD: Patricia A. Thompson
SID: Pat Donnelly

ELMS
Chicopee, MA 01013-2839 III

Coach: Aaron Patterson, Springfield
2001-02 RESULTS (6-20)

60	Eastern Nazarene	.75
79	Newbury †	.92
77	Westfield St.	.89
81	Southern Vt.	.91
69	Gordon ■	.79
76	Daniel Webster	.82
44	Trinity (Conn.)	.72
77	Connecticut Col. ■	.89
100	Roger Williams ■	.113
60	Western New Eng. ■	.77
50	Maine Maritime ■	.57
54	Endicott	.64
84	Becker	.69
82	Emerson	.78
61	Maine Maritime	.72
75	Nichols	.77
74	Lasell ■	.77
73	Connecticut Col.	.80
90	Becker ■	.79
61	Anna Maria	.66
56	Lasell	.93

90	Newbury	88
97	Becker ■	84
50	Lasell	71

Nickname: Blazers
Colors: Green & Gold
Arena: Picknelly Arena
    Capacity: 481; Year Built: 1994
AD: Louise McCleary
SID: Kathleen Bantley

ELON
Elon, NC 27244-2010 I

Coach: Mark Simons, Aquinas 1972

2001-02 RESULTS (13-16)

94	N.C. A&T ■	82
67	Wake Forest	87
93	Lynchburg ■	51
59	Florida St.	89
55	UNC Greensboro ■	70
65	Ball St.	106
77	Binghamton †	70
59	Davidson	66
97	Bluefield Col. ■	80
78	Clemson	88
58	Birmingham-So.	65
52	Arkansas	97
61	Radford ■	58
75	Charleston So. ■	69
91	Coastal Caro. ■	80
64	Winthrop ■	76
64	UNC Asheville ■	76
75	Liberty ■	53
63	High Point ■	73
63	Liberty	56
67	Birmingham-So. ■	60
71	Winthrop ■	64
75	Coastal Caro. ■	80
52	Charleston So.	61
58	UNC Asheville ■	72
60	Radford	81
74	High Point ■	66
83	Charleston So. †	64
66	Winthrop †	77

Nickname: Phoenix
Colors: Maroon & Gold
Arena: Koury Center/Alumni Gym
    Capacity: 1,768; Year Built: 1949
AD: Alan J. White
SID: Matt Eviston

EMERSON
Boston, MA 02116 III

Coach: Hank Smith, Franklin Pierce

2001-02 RESULTS (12-13)

80	MIT ■	90
70	Babson ■	82
78	Mass.-Boston	82
71	Wheaton (Mass.) ■	106
82	Wentworth Inst.	70
76	Brandeis	81
64	Salem St.	82
89	Eastern Nazarene	76
65	WPI	54
66	Roger Williams ■	88
69	Western New Eng.	79
72	Johnson & Wales	59
110	Emmanuel (Mass.) ■	79
65	Rivier ■	53
83	Suffolk	71
78	Elms ■	82
89	Southern Vt. ■	85
53	Albertus Magnus	55
90	Endicott ■	93
86	Daniel Webster	54
92	Emmanuel (Mass.) ■	75
80	Suffolk ■	76
75	Norwich	67
91	Albertus Magnus ■	95
75	Johnson & Wales ■	93

Nickname: Lions
Colors: Purple & Black
Arena: Wang YMCA
    Capacity: 1,200
AD: Hank Smith
SID: Michael Burns

EMMANUEL (MASS.)
Boston, MA 02115 III

Coach: Lance Tucker, Boston U. 1975

2001-02 RESULTS (5-20)

105	Thomas ■	56
81	Lasell ■	101
100	Notre Dame (N.H.) ■	94
85	Newbury	83
87	Mount Ida	90
80	Bridgewater St. ■	86
69	Baruch	92
63	Lehman	74
78	Castleton St. ■	81
88	Johnson St. ■	92
73	Suffolk ■	91
79	Emerson	110
73	Southern Vt.	91
83	Johnson & Wales ■	96
75	Albertus Magnus	83
55	Norwich	73
72	Wesleyan (Conn.) ■ ■	105
92	Daniel Webster ■	87
102	Rivier	97
75	Emerson ■	92
67	Albertus Magnus ■	88
74	Western New Eng.	94
80	Johnson & Wales	90
74	Suffolk	94
61	Suffolk	89

Nickname: Saints
Colors: Navy Blue & Gold
Arena: Marian Hall Gymnasium
    Capacity: 450; Year Built: 1956
AD: Andy Yosinoff
SID: Alexis Mastronardi

EMORY
Atlanta, GA 30322 III

Coach: Brett Zuver, Lake Superior St. 1991

2001-02 RESULTS (9-16)

84	La Grange	76
92	Flagler †	104
70	Sewanee	87
103	N.C. Wesleyan ■	91
89	Oglethorpe	94
82	Rust ■	83
78	Maryville (Tenn.)	107
54	Furman	87
88	Sewanee ■	76
78	Case Reserve ■	85
65	Rochester	77
91	Washington (Mo.) ■	96
65	Chicago ■	86
78	Carnegie Mellon	88
64	New York U.	81
64	Brandeis	63
101	Piedmont ■	79
77	Brandeis ■	60
73	New York U. ■	83
78	Chicago	103
47	Washington (Mo.)	93
97	Carnegie Mellon ■	85
59	Rochester ■	96
83	Oglethorpe ■	70
94	Case Reserve	78

Nickname: Eagles
Colors: Blue & Gold
Arena: Woodruff PE Center
    Capacity: 2,000; Year Built: 1983
AD: Charles J. Gordon
SID: John Arenberg

EMORY & HENRY
Emory, VA 24327-0947 III

Coach: Bob Johnson, Dickinson 1968

2001-02 RESULTS (14-13)

92	Denison	76
66	Maryville (Tenn.) ■	85
70	Virginia Intermont	66
94	Mary Washington	90
86	Roanoke	99
72	Hampden-Sydney	97
112	Averett	102
101	Guilford ■	85
97	Lynchburg ■	63
76	Va. Wesleyan ■	93
70	Randolph-Macon ■	89
103	Warren Wilson ■	72
69	Bridgewater (Va.)	87
95	East. Mennonite	94
81	Warren Wilson	73
82	Hampden-Sydney ■	88
76	Wash. & Lee ■	75
91	Randolph-Macon	85
81	Va. Wesleyan	91
60	Wash. & Lee	62
81	East. Mennonite ■	73
81	Bridgewater (Va.) ■	91
93	Roanoke ■	96
88	Lynchburg	76
67	Guilford	78
79	Va. Wesleyan †	77
95	Hampden-Sydney †	105

Nickname: Wasps
Colors: Blue & Gold
Arena: King Health & Physical Ed
    Capacity: 1,300; Year Built: 1970
AD: Fred Selfe
SID: Nathan Graybeal

EMPORIA ST.
Emporia, KS 66801-5087 II

Coach: David Moe, Texas Lutheran 1986

2001-02 RESULTS (7-19)

65	Rockhurst	80
61	Salem Int'l †	76
69	St. Mary's (Tex.)	62
108	Okla. Panhandle ■	67
77	Fort Hays St.	92
86	Newman	90
74	Rockhurst ■	90
93	Okla. Panhandle	81
57	Northwest Mo. St. ■	75
80	Mo.-Rolla ■	71
77	Pittsburg St.	94
81	Mo. Western St. ■	97
79	Truman	75
83	Southwest Baptist ■	76
82	Mo. Southern St.	125
64	Washburn	80
83	Central Mo. St. ■	90
79	Northwest Mo. St.	91
66	Mo.-Rolla	82
77	Pittsburg St. ■	90
59	Mo. Western St.	85
71	Truman	61
69	Southwest Baptist	79
85	Mo. Southern St. ■	98
75	Washburn ■	80
92	Central Mo. St.	97

Nickname: Hornets
Colors: Old Gold & Black
Arena: White Auditorium
    Capacity: 5,000; Year Built: 1940
AD: Kent Weiser
SID: Don Weast

ENDICOTT
Beverly, MA 01915 III

Coach: James Cosgrove, St. Anselm 1987

2001-02 RESULTS (16-11)

80	Brandeis	74
53	Kean †	89
56	Keene St.	82
63	Wheaton (Mass.) ■	62
64	Johnson & Wales ■	49
56	Framingham St.	54
69	Rivier ■	58
69	Roger Williams ■	58
60	Springfield	66
85	Albright †	82
55	Bates ■	62
73	Curry	64
67	Gordon ■	68
64	Elms ■	54
72	Nichols	56
61	Wentworth Inst. ■	49
56	Anna Maria	57
60	Eastern Conn. St. ■	69
93	Emerson	90
57	WPI ■	51
73	Eastern Nazarene	72
83	New England Col. ■	73
47	Colby-Sawyer ■	64
49	Salve Regina	51
78	New England	80
70	Curry	69
50	Salve Regina	62

Nickname: Gulls
Colors: Blue, Kelly Green & White
Arena: Post Center Arena
    Capacity: 1,400; Year Built: 1999
AD: Larry R. Hiser
SID: To be named

ERSKINE
Due West, SC 29639 II

Coach: Mark Peeler, Sewanee 1984

2001-02 RESULTS (11-16)

53	Bellarmine	70
62	Carson-Newman †	54
91	Emmanuel (Ga.)	94
56	Presbyterian ■	64
69	Pfeiffer ■	66
89	Newberry	79
50	Tusculum ■	56
75	Queens (N.C.)	77
68	Coker	79
78	Mount Olive ■	80
79	Barton	91
67	Belmont Abbey ■ ■	60
88	Lees-McRae	64
67	Longwood	60
88	St. Andrews ■	77
80	Limestone ■	71
62	Anderson (S.C.)	70
64	Pfeiffer	82
76	Queens (N.C.) ■	85
50	Coker ■	54
71	Mount Olive	74
76	Barton ■	70
56	Belmont Abbey	76
55	Lees-McRae ■	63
79	Longwood ■	77
74	St. Andrews	67
59	Limestone	60

Nickname: The Flying Fleet
Colors: Maroon & Gold
Arena: Galloway PE Center
    Capacity: 2,000; Year Built: 1980
AD: Joseph H. Sherer
SID: Thomas Holland

EUREKA
Eureka, IL 61530-1500.............III

Coach: Mike DeGeorge, Monmouth (Ill.) 1992

2001-02 RESULTS (5-20)

64	Millikin ■	97
89	Knox ■	76
53	Webster †	63
49	Concordia (Wis.) †	87
73	Greenville	77
65	Ripon †	107
67	Northland †	52
87	Lincoln Chrst. ■	85
73	Fontbonne	94
66	Marycrest Int'l ■	71
62	Blackburn	76
70	Augustana (Ill.) ■	83
68	Westminster (Mo.) ■	81
55	Dominican (Ill.)	72
45	Rockford	92
59	Concordia (Ill.)	68
64	Aurora	79
54	Benedictine (Ill.) ■	85
71	Clarke ■	75
76	Dominican (Ill.) ■	71
67	Rockford	83
67	Concordia (Ill.) ■	71
70	Aurora ■	65
71	Benedictine (Ill.)	80
59	Clarke	66

Nickname: Red Devils
Colors: Maroon & Gold
Arena: Reagan Gym
  Capacity: 2,200; Year Built: 1970
AD: Joe Barth
SID: Shelly Lindsey

EVANSVILLE
Evansville, IN 47722 I

Coach: Jim Crews, Indiana 1976

2001-02 RESULTS (7-21)

87	Youngstown St. ■	64
64	Western Ky.	90
78	Tennessee St.	101
61	Ill.-Chicago	64
67	Miami (Ohio) ■	63
76	Eastern Ill. ■	86
65	Butler	101
72	Bowling Green ■	84
77	Wis.-Green Bay ■	69
82	Southwest Mo. St. ■	93
72	Southern Ill.	82
40	Indiana St.	45
74	Creighton	88
60	Bradley ■	55
61	Drake ■	63
63	Wichita St.	81
55	Southwest Mo. St.	76
41	Creighton ■	57
62	Southern Ill.	101
67	Drake	78
83	Northern Iowa ■	77
62	Bradley	67
55	Illinois St. ■	73
71	Indiana St. ■	82
67	Northern Iowa	65
83	Wichita St. ■	81
73	Illinois St.	82
75	Northern Iowa †	78

Nickname: Purple Aces
Colors: Purple, White & Orange
Arena: Roberts Stadium
  Capacity: 12,144; Year Built: 1956
AD: Bill McGillis
SID: Bob Boxell

FAIRFIELD
Fairfield, CT 06430-5195 I

Coach: Tim O'Toole, Fairfield 1986

2001-02 RESULTS (12-17)

62	Harvard	68
59	Michigan	88
57	Rhode Island ■	59
78	Iona ■	82
90	DePaul †	94
75	St. Francis (N.Y.) ■	71
57	UNC Wilmington	82
77	Canisius	69
67	American	68
95	St. Peter's ■	75
72	Manhattan	88
77	Niagara	79
69	Rider ■	57
79	Iona	90
64	Loyola (Md.) ■	53
72	Loyola (Md.) ■	48
84	Marist	93
77	Niagara ■	80
70	Manhattan ■	73
56	St. John's (N.Y.) ■	95
59	Rider	73
79	Siena ■	72
70	Charleston So.	55
64	Marist ■	76
60	Siena	57
72	Canisius ■	54
93	St. Peter's	61
81	Manhattan †	74
63	Siena †	83

Nickname: Stags
Colors: Red & White
Arena: Arena at Harbor Yard
  Capacity: 9,500; Year Built: 2001
SID: Jack Jones

FAIRLEIGH DICKINSON
Teaneck, NJ 07666 I

Coach: Tom Green, Syracuse 1971

2001-02 RESULTS (4-25)

57	San Jose St. †	65
66	Prairie View †	77
66	Rutgers †	70
48	American	55
63	Loyola (Md.) ■	74
69	Wagner ■	78
130	Sacred Heart ■	133
56	Hartford	73
73	Seton Hall	95
73	Delaware St. ■	79
45	Kansas St.	88
66	St. Francis (N.Y.)	75
109	Long Island	86
72	UMBC ■	87
81	Mt. St. Mary's ■	61
63	Sacred Heart	75
57	Robert Morris ■	86
79	Quinnipiac	84
69	Mt. St. Mary's	64
70	UMBC	81
76	St. Francis (N.Y.) ■	86
62	Monmouth	83
62	Central Conn. St.	90
89	Quinnipiac ■	82
61	Robert Morris	65
68	St. Francis (Pa.)	72
65	Central Conn. St. ■	83
115	Long Island	122
63	Monmouth	73

Nickname: Knights
Colors: Blue & Red
Arena: Rothman Center
  Capacity: 5,000; Year Built: 1987
SID: Drew Brown

FDU-MADISON
Madison, NJ 07940................III

Coach: Roger Kindel, Seton Hall 1972

2001-02 RESULTS (10-14)

58	Cortland St. †	63
50	Montclair St.	66
67	Stevens Tech	64
80	Hunter	92
85	John Jay	87
54	Wilkes	76
68	DeSales ■	61
79	NYCCT ■	59
74	Staten Island ■	77
65	Salisbury †	59
66	Dickinson †	77
66	Scranton ■	61
71	Lycoming	80
77	Drew	68
52	King's (Pa.)	64
67	Delaware Valley	62
87	Wilkes ■	69
78	Centenary (N.J.) ■	58
58	DeSales	73
72	Lycoming ■	76
65	Scranton	79
64	Drew	68
77	Delaware Valley ■	66
70	King's (Pa.) ■	75

Nickname: Devils
Colors: Cardinal and Navy
Arena: Ferguson Recreation Center
  Capacity: 3,000; Year Built: 1995
AD: William T. Klika
SID: Scott Giglio

FAIRMONT ST.
Fairmont, WV 26554................II

Coach: Butch Haswell, Fairmont St. 1973

2001-02 RESULTS (17-11)

76	Ohio St. Lima ■	28
69	New Haven ■	68
66	Lock Haven	71
67	Daemen ■	55
74	Columbia Union	64
74	Davis & Elkins ■	59
94	Ohio-Eastern ■	64
67	Bowie St. †	82
89	Bluefield St. †	83
71	Glenville St. ■	73
68	West Va. Wesleyan	84
59	Shepherd	61
87	Concord ■	61
70	Ohio Valley	57
69	Wheeling Jesuit	83
75	West Liberty St.	80
83	Salem Int'l	84
89	Alderson-Broaddus	93
89	Bluefield St. ■	69
90	Charleston (W.Va.)	87
67	West Virginia St.	66
64	West Va. Tech ■	58
84	Ohio Valley ■	66
88	Wheeling Jesuit ■	71
76	West Liberty St. ■	74
65	Salem Int'l	79
78	Shepherd ■	62
78	Alderson-Broaddus †	82

Nickname: Falcons
Colors: Maroon & White
Arena: Joe Retton Arena
  Capacity: 4,000; Year Built: 1978
AD: David W. Cooper
SID: Jim Brinkman

FARMINGDALE ST.
Farmingdale, NY 11735-1021 .III

2001-02 RESULTS (3-14)

84	St. Joseph's (L.I.)	93
74	Staten Island ■	83
76	Molloy	95
68	Southern Conn. St. †	89
85	Centenary (N.J.) ■	72
71	Oneonta St.	92
70	Montclair St. ■	81
69	New Jersey City	89
85	Ramapo ■	91
75	Lasell †	102
69	Old Westbury	70
87	Ramapo	105
70	New Paltz St.	62
77	Drew	97
67	John Jay ■	69
86	Lincoln (Pa.) ■	102
93	Centenary (N.J.)	62

Nickname: Rams
Colors: Green & White
AD: Michael Harrington
SID: To be named

FAYETTEVILLE ST.
Fayetteville, NC 28301-4298 II

Coach: Mike Bernard, Kentucky St. 1970

2001-02 RESULTS (18-9)

81	Morehouse	83
80	Lane †	63
78	Mount Olive	73
69	Newberry †	57
79	Queens (N.C.)	67
55	Johnson Smith †	51
66	Methodist	70
65	St. Andrews ■	66
66	Virginia Union ■	59
68	Bowie St. ■	64
85	Johnson Smith ■	87
87	St. Augustine's ■	72
77	Elizabeth City St.	75
63	Livingstone	56
92	Shaw ■	90
73	St. Paul's ■	61
51	Winston-Salem	72
70	N.C. Central ■	54
61	St. Augustine's	81
67	N.C. Central	65
62	Benedict ■	49
74	Winston-Salem ■	80
73	Johnson Smith	74
61	Virginia St.	58
76	Livingstone ■	67
50	St. Paul's †	45
63	Bowie St. †	66

Nickname: Broncos
Colors: Royal Blue & Lilly White
Arena: Capel Arena
  Capacity: 4,000; Year Built: 1995
AD: William Carver
SID: Marion Crowe

FERRIS ST.
Big Rapids, MI 49307-2295 II

Coach: Edgar Wilson, Michigan St. 1978

2001-02 RESULTS (4-22)

71	Northern Ky.	79
79	Christian Bros. †	87
79	Olivet ■	59
71	Aquinas ■	72
72	Findlay	91
76	Calvin	95

67	Gannon ■	73
55	Mercyhurst	67
75	St. Joseph's (Ind.) ■	103
71	Grand Canyon	69
57	Mesa St. †	54
57	Hillsdale	94
79	Wayne St. (Mich.)	92
72	Ashland ■	83
66	Northwood	71
85	Grand Valley St. ■	86
65	Saginaw Valley ■	77
65	Lake Superior St. ■	71
53	Michigan Tech	77
63	Northern Mich.	80
68	Lake Superior St.	91
66	Northwood ■	75
75	Grand Valley St.	78
81	Saginaw Valley	80
65	Northern Mich. ■	72
61	Michigan Tech ■	91

Nickname: Bulldogs
Colors: Crimson & Gold
Arena: Jim Wink Arena
  Capacity: 2,400; Year Built: 1999
AD: Tom Kirinovic
SID: Rob Bentley

FERRUM
Ferrum, VA 24088 III

Coach: Ed Wills, North Carolina 1994
2001-02 RESULTS (10-16)

67	Wesley †	80
62	York (N.Y.) †	54
71	Lynchburg ■	62
60	East. Mennonite †	51
67	Bridgewater (Va.)	78
73	Lynchburg	67
60	Randolph-Macon ■	68
70	Webber	78
89	Fla. Christian †	78
68	Averett	70
78	Chris. Newport ■	97
69	Shenandoah	74
74	Methodist ■	76
66	Greensboro	58
81	N.C. Wesleyan	83
87	Chowan	61
81	Averett ■	68
73	Apprentice	83
55	Chris. Newport ■	71
75	Shenandoah ■	68
62	Methodist	60
61	Greensboro	67
66	Apprentice ■	69
72	N.C. Wesleyan ■	88
67	Chowan ■	81
71	N.C. Wesleyan †	102

Nickname: Panthers
Colors: Black & Gold
Arena: Swartz Gymnasium
  Capacity: 1,200; Year Built: 1960
AD: T. Michael Kinder
SID: Gary Holden

FINDLAY
Findlay, OH 45840.................II

Coach: Ron Niekamp, Miami (Ohio) 1972
2001-02 RESULTS (23-7)

81	Carson-Newman †	66
93	Bellarmine	85
87	Tiffin	66
91	Ferris St. ■	72
100	Grand Valley St. ■	82
137	Mich.-Dearborn ■	90
120	St. Mary's (Mich.) ■	70
102	Tiffin ■	54
82	North Ala.	67
103	Shawnee St. ■	78
102	Huntington ■	72

88	Northwood ■	72
88	Saginaw Valley ■	66
80	Northern Mich.	59
79	Lake Superior St.	92
91	Michigan Tech	80
80	Ashland ■	92
66	Hillsdale ■	69
88	Wayne St. (Mich.) ■	84
74	Mercyhurst	76
77	Gannon	87
76	Ashland	75
71	Wayne St. (Mich.)	68
60	Hillsdale	59
71	Gannon ■	57
106	Mercyhurst ■	64
68	Hillsdale †	67
72	Northwood †	77
70	Gannon †	53
89	Ky. Wesleyan	94

Nickname: Oilers
Colors: Orange & Black
Arena: Croy Gym
  Capacity: 2,200; Year Built: 1969
AD: Steven Rackley
SID: Dave Leisering

FITCHBURG ST.
Fitchburg, MA 01420-2697......III

Coach: Jack Scott, Clark (Mass.) 1994
2001-02 RESULTS (16-11)

90	New England Col. †	64
55	Keene St.	77
59	Mass.-Boston	74
50	Gordon	69
84	Western New Eng. ■	78
90	Mount Ida	85
82	Becker	71
75	Daniel Webster ■	59
59	Wheaton (Mass.) ■	53
82	Anna Maria	72
67	Worcester St. ■	65
58	Salem St.	71
67	Lasell	88
76	Nichols	63
71	Westfield St. ■	69
80	Framingham St.	76
78	Mass. Liberal Arts ■■	77
52	Bridgewater St.	70
66	Worcester St.	52
55	Salem St. ■	82
61	Westfield St.	90
62	Framingham St. ■	61
73	Mass. Liberal Arts	85
56	Bridgewater St. ■	52
85	Mass. Liberal Arts ■	68
59	Framingham St. †	61
90	Keene St.	106

Nickname: Falcons
Colors: Green, Gold & White
Arena: Recreation Center
  Capacity: 1,000; Year Built: 2000
AD: Sue E. Lauder
SID: Rusty Eggen

FLORIDA
Gainesville, FL 32611 I

Coach: Billy Donovan, Providence 1987
2001-02 RESULTS (22-9)

104	Tennessee	100
72	Temple †	64
71	Arizona †	75
68	Florida St.	47
108	New Hampshire	56
81	Tulane ■	65
74	Michigan St.	70
92	South Fla.	73
73	Charlotte †	52
103	High Point ■	49
76	New Orleans ■	60
94	Stetson ■	66

107	Belmont ■	55
69	South Carolina ■	60
95	Vanderbilt	85
102	LSU ■	70
79	Georgia ■	84
92	Arkansas	94
68	Kentucky ■	70
76	Mississippi St. ■	48
72	South Carolina	63
80	Vanderbilt ■	54
85	Georgia	70
51	Mississippi	68
89	Auburn ■	61
64	Alabama	65
68	Tennessee ■	62
67	Kentucky	70
81	Auburn †	63
52	Mississippi St. †	62
82	Creighton †	83

Nickname: Gators
Colors: Orange & Blue
Arena: Stephen C. O'Connell Center
  Capacity: 12,000; Year Built: 1980
AD: Jeremy Foley
SID: Steve McClain

FLORIDA A&M
Tallahassee, FL 32307................I

Coach: Mike Gillespie, DePaul 1974
2001-02 RESULTS (9-19)

62	Georgia Tech	97
55	Mississippi St.	92
98	Bethune-Cookman	77
72	Wofford	77
58	Alabama St.	71
54	Md.-East. Shore	85
76	UCF	101
55	Northwestern	58
62	Miami (Fla.)	90
52	Alabama	76
49	UAB	67
70	N.C. A&T ■	66
69	South Carolina St. ■	72
76	Howard	82
50	Delaware St.	65
72	Morgan St. ■	66
75	Coppin St. ■	61
73	Norfolk St. ■	61
65	Hampton	97
73	Md.-East. Shore ■	61
73	N.C. A&T	81
72	South Carolina St.	73
55	Howard	58
69	Delaware St. ■	62
67	Coppin St.	64
67	Morgan St.	50
53	Bethune-Cookman ■	57
91	Morgan St. †	94

Nickname: Rattlers
Colors: Orange & Green
Arena: Gaither Athletic Center
  Capacity: 3,365; Year Built: 1963
AD: Kenneth Riley
SID: Alvin Hollins

FLA. ATLANTIC
Boca Raton, FL 33431-0991 I

Coach: Sidney Green, UNLV 1983
2001-02 RESULTS (19-12)

58	Jacksonville ■	73
90	Georgia St. ■	77
77	Campbell ■	60
65	Hofstra	67
107	St. Mary's (Md.) ■	73
76	Jacksonville	72
48	Miami (Fla.)	74
82	Stetson	71
78	UCF ■	66
91	Liberty	80
84	Va. Commonwealth ■	88

66	Samford	68
74	Jacksonville St.	71
79	Drake ■	71
94	Mercer	73
100	Troy St.	107
59	Birmingham-So.	65
69	Belmont ■	66
56	UCF	62
80	Belmont	78
67	Troy St. ■	66
72	Mercer ■	71
87	Campbell	92
71	Georgia St.	76
78	Jacksonville St. ■■	68
50	Samford ■	68
77	Stetson	74
59	Jacksonville †	50
55	Jacksonville St. †	47
76	Georgia St. †	75
78	Alabama †	86

Nickname: Owls
Colors: Blue, Red & Grey
Arena: FAU Gymnasium
  Capacity: 5,000; Year Built: 1984
AD: Thomas Cargill
SID: Katrina McCormack

FLORIDA INT'L
Miami, FL 33199......................I

Coach: Donnie Marsh, Frank. & Marsh. 1979
2001-02 RESULTS (10-20)

70	St. Peter's ■	59
65	Texas-San Antonio ■	71
85	Florida Tech ■	68
49	Princeton	44
82	IPFW ■	80
55	Auburn	67
59	Miami (Fla.)	77
61	West Virginia	74
63	Coppin St. †	59
61	Baylor †	65
55	Oral Roberts †	66
64	Vermont ■	69
54	Long Island ■	50
57	Ark.-Little Rock ■	71
54	Western Ky. ■	65
67	Middle Tenn. ■	60
49	Pennsylvania	75
79	North Texas	78
69	Denver	72
56	Arkansas St. ■	57
66	South Ala.	56
69	New Orleans ■	55
64	Western Ky.	66
69	Middle Tenn.	71
70	New Mexico St.	77
60	La.-Lafayette ■	65
77	UNLV	83
54	Arkansas St.	64
54	Ark.-Little Rock	79
71	North Texas †	84

Nickname: Golden Panthers
Colors: Blue & Gold
Arena: Golden Panther Arena
  Capacity: 5,000; Year Built: 1986
AD: Rick Mello
SID: Rich Kelch

FLA. SOUTHERN
Lakeland, FL 33801-5698 II

Coach: Tony Longa, UCF 1987
2001-02 RESULTS (20-9)

76	Nova Southeastern ■	59
81	P.R.-Mayaguez ■	71
108	North Fla.	104
76	Embry-Riddle ■	89
78	Northern Colo. †	89
71	Southern Colo.	62

102	Webber ■	61
83	Warner Southern ■	74
94	Columbia Union ■	56
98	Molloy ■	56
94	Rochester College ■	49
75	Morehouse	85
60	Barry ■	71
93	St. Leo ■	45
75	Florida Tech	59
68	Lynn	63
86	Eckerd ■	78
79	Tampa	81
59	Rollins ■	55
90	St. Leo	62
80	Florida Tech ■	60
64	Lynn	73
77	Eckerd	83
84	Tampa ■	76
72	Rollins	76
71	Barry	59
63	Lynn †	62
77	Eckerd †	71
45	Tampa †	62

Nickname: Moccasins
Colors: Scarlet & White
Arena: Jenkins Field House
  Capacity: 2,500; Year Built: 1966
AD: Lois Webb
SID: Tim Carpenter

FLORIDA ST.
Tallahassee, FL 32306...............I

Coach: Steve Robinson, Radford 1981
2001-02 RESULTS (12-17)

47	Florida	68
93	Savannah St. ■	41
89	Elon ■	59
50	Northwestern ■	57
78	Birmingham-So. ■	62
69	Western Caro. ■	79
72	Wake Forest	93
76	Cleveland St. ■	63
72	American ■	77
78	Virginia Tech ■	49
93	Campbell ■	47
78	South Fla.	74
77	Duke ■	76
62	North Carolina St.	77
81	North Carolina ■	71
74	Virginia	91
68	Clemson ■	63
63	Maryland	84
46	Georgia Tech	77
80	Wake Forest ■	89
49	Duke	80
67	North Carolina St. ■	76
85	North Carolina	95
66	Virginia ■	59
78	Clemson	87
63	Maryland ■	96
78	Georgia Tech ■	86
91	Clemson †	84
59	Maryland †	85

Nickname: Seminoles
Colors: Garnet & Gold
Arena: Leon County Civic Center
  Capacity: 12,200; Year Built: 1981
AD: David R. Hart Jr.
SID: Chuck Walsh

FLORIDA TECH
Melbourne, FL 32901...............II

Coach: Kris Olson, Iowa St. 1994
2001-02 RESULTS (6-20)

67	Jacksonville	77
84	P.R.-Rio Piedras ■	68
68	Florida Int'l	85
74	Augustana (S.D.) †	91
97	P.R.-Bayamon †	96
72	Nova Southeastern	65

67	Fort Valley St.	85
61	Valdosta St.	76
82	Nova Southeastern ■	71
59	Valdosta St. ■	75
83	Wilmington (Del.) ■	69
78	St. Leo	62
65	Eckerd	81
59	Fla. Southern ■	75
62	Rollins	86
58	Tampa ■	82
58	Lynn	81
57	Barry ■	58
70	Eckerd ■	101
60	Fla. Southern	80
73	Rollins ■	83
67	Tampa	88
71	Lynn ■	83
53	Barry	69
69	St. Leo ■	73
61	Tampa †	75

Nickname: Panthers
Colors: Crimson & Gray
Arena: Percy Hedgecock Gymnasium
  Capacity: 1,400; Year Built: 1964
AD: William K. Jurgens
SID: Dean Watson

FONTBONNE
St Louis, MO 63105-3098.......III

Coach: Lee McKinney, Southeast Mo St 1960
2001-02 RESULTS (18-6)

95	Purdue-North Cent. †	89
85	Moody Bible	65
79	Illinois Tech	58
101	St. Louis Christian ■	70
65	Elmhurst ■	81
94	Eureka ■	73
70	Rose-Hulman	65
96	St. Louis Christian ■	75
77	Savannah A&D ■	57
67	P.R.-Bayamon	74
85	Blackburn	90
93	Principia ■	78
87	MacMurray ■	73
69	Webster	72
95	Maryville (Mo.) ■	89
114	Greenville ■	109
95	Westminster (Mo.) ■	85
75	Blackburn ■	69
84	Principia	71
94	MacMurray ■	72
85	Webster ■	77
73	Maryville (Mo.)	75
78	Greenville	72
61	Westminster (Mo.) ■	65

Nickname: Griffins
Colors: Purple & Gold
Arena: Dunham Student Activities
  Capacity: 1,800; Year Built: 1993
AD: Lee McKinney
SID: Lance Thorohsu

FORDHAM
Bronx, NY 10458-5155.............I

Coach: Bob Hill, Bowling Green 1971
2001-02 RESULTS (8-20)

61	DePaul	70
84	South Fla.	104
78	Siena ■	69
78	Iona	74
67	St. John's (N.Y.)	76
55	Marquette	79
80	Delaware St. ■	70
63	Northwestern †	60
72	Manhattan †	82
57	Seton Hall †	66
75	Holy Cross	95
75	Temple ■	86
58	Xavier	88

95	Massachusetts ■	86
72	St. Joseph's	83
71	Rhode Island ■	58
87	St. Bonaventure ■	81
74	La Salle ■	63
74	Temple	91
66	Duquesne	95
78	Dayton	92
77	St. Joseph's ■	84
64	Rhode Island ■	70
84	St. Bonaventure	90
54	Massachusetts	67
50	Richmond	67
68	George Washington ■	70
63	La Salle †	83

Nickname: Rams
Colors: Maroon & White
Arena: Rose Hill Gym
  Capacity: 3,470; Year Built: 1926
AD: Francis X. McLaughlin
SID: Joe DiBari

FORT HAYS ST.
Hays, KS 67601...............II

Coach: Mark Johnson, Pittsburg St. 1993
2001-02 RESULTS (21-7)

90	Bethany (Kan.) ■	56
82	Tabor	48
64	Rockhurst	73
86	Central Christian ■	67
92	Emporia St. ■	77
90	Southern Colo.	74
71	UC-Colo. Spgs. ■	48
96	Newman ■	93
82	N.M. Highlands ■	68
64	Fort Lewis	86
68	Mesa St. ■	55
81	Western St. (Colo.) ■	41
75	Adams St.	65
88	Rockhurst ■	87
84	Colo. Christian	92
61	Regis (Colo.)	53
65	Neb.-Kearney ■	69
82	Metro St.	81
74	Chadron St.	67
62	Colorado Mines ■	75
78	Colo. Christian ■	58
70	Regis (Colo.) ■	49
69	Neb.-Kearney	71
76	Metro St.	72
85	Chadron St.	70
66	Colorado Mines	61
76	Mesa St. ■	62
86	Neb.-Kearney †	94

Nickname: Tigers
Colors: Black & Gold
Arena: Gross Memorial Coliseum
  Capacity: 6,814; Year Built: 1973
AD: Thomas E. Spicer
SID: Steve Webster

FORT LEWIS
Durango, CO 81301-3999.......II

Coach: Bob Hofman, Colorado 1974
2001-02 RESULTS (21-9)

69	Southern Utah	86
65	Grand Canyon	75
97	St. Xavier	94
103	Western N.M. ■	88
90	Westminster (Utah) ■	80
82	Metro St.	88
53	Brigham Young	101
84	Neb.-Kearney ■	97
86	Fort Hays St. ■	64
71	Regis (Colo.)	79
79	Colo. Christian	87
67	Colorado Mines ■	56
81	Chadron St. ■	77
94	N.M. Highlands ■	74
87	Adams St. ■	80

85	Colorado Col. ■	52
84	UC-Colo. Spgs. ■	73
71	Southern Colo.	53
100	Western St. (Colo.) ■	71
71	Mesa St. ■	85
91	N.M. Highlands	88
94	Adams St.	82
104	UC-Colo. Spgs. ■	69
85	Southern Colo. ■	71
97	Western St. (Colo.)	85
72	Mesa St.	65
72	Regis (Colo.) ■	71
95	Metro St. †	86
72	Neb.-Kearney †	71
58	Neb.-Omaha †	88

Nickname: Skyhawks
Colors: Navy Blue & Gold
Arena: FLC Fieldhouse
  Capacity: 2,750
AD: David L. Preszler
SID: To be named

FORT VALLEY ST.
Fort Valley, GA 31030.............II

Coach: Michael Moore, Albany St. (Ga) 1984
2001-02 RESULTS (12-15)

85	Montevallo	73
62	Ala.-Huntsville †	70
64	West Fla. ■	66
93	Kentucky St. ■	75
94	Lane	87
58	West Fla.	75
78	Montevallo †	76
85	Florida Tech ■	67
52	Mercer	61
63	Elizabeth City St.	76
77	Clark Atlanta	71
64	Paine ■	60
55	Tuskegee	52
56	Albany St. (Ga.)	67
62	Morehouse ■	64
81	LeMoyne-Owen	77
70	Miles	71
55	Kentucky St.	89
90	Lane	79
75	Clark Atlanta ■	80
82	Tuskegee ■	74
69	Paine	72
73	Albany St. (Ga.) ■	80
58	Morehouse	68
76	LeMoyne-Owen ■	67
54	Miles ■	59
59	Kentucky St. †	85

Nickname: Wildcats
Colors: Old Gold & Blue
Arena: George Woodward Gymnasium
  Capacity: 1,345; Year Built: 1959
AD: Gwendolyn Reeves
SID: Russell Boone

FRAMINGHAM ST.
Framingham, MA 01701-9101.III

Coach: Don Spellam
2001-02 RESULTS (13-14)

69	WPI ■	48
59	Lasell	76
78	Mass.-Boston	75
48	Colby †	59
46	MIT	77
54	Endicott ■	56
77	Daniel Webster	73
63	Newbury ■	51
74	Albertus Magnus	65
67	Mass. Liberal Arts ■	66
61	Bridgewater St.	63
76	Worcester St. ■	71
87	Anna Maria	85
68	Salem St.	85

76 Fitchburg St. ■ 80
54 Westfield St. ■ 42
62 Nichols 74
81 Mass. Liberal Arts 71
51 Bridgewater St. ■ 52
63 Worcester St. 66
56 Salem St. ■ 76
61 Fitchburg St. 62
54 Westfield St. 74
69 Becker 57
76 Westfield St. ■ 71
61 Fitchburg St. † 59
60 Salem St. 83

Nickname: Rams
Colors: Black & Gold
Arena: Dwight Gymnasium
 Capacity: 450
AD: Thomas M. Kelley
SID: Carey Williams

FRANCIS MARION
Florence, SC 29501-0547 II

Coach: John Schweitz, Richmond 1988

2001-02 RESULTS (4-23)
59 Mars Hill † 79
77 Emmanuel (Ga.) † 72
55 Coker ■ 66
45 Col. of Charleston 81
69 Armstrong Atlantic ■ 78
63 GC&SU 64
56 Allen 52
47 Belmont Abbey ■ 94
64 Millersville ■ 89
72 S.C.-Aiken ■ 75
68 UNC Pembroke ■ 69
69 Lander 82
55 Armstrong Atlantic 76
57 Augusta St. 97
88 North Fla. ■ 99
49 S.C.-Spartanburg 82
74 GC&SU ■ 96
75 UNC Pembroke 95
69 Clayton St. ■ 76
83 S.C.-Spartanburg 82
78 Kennesaw St. 90
71 Columbus St. ■ 94
49 Lander ■ 67
73 Augusta St. ■ 79
86 S.C.-Aiken 72
79 Clayton St. 83
83 Kennesaw St. † 96

Nickname: Patriots
Colors: Red, White & Blue
Arena: Smith University Center
 Capacity: 3,027; Year Built: 1974
AD: Murray Hartzler
SID: Michael Hawkins

FRANKLIN
Franklin, IN 46131 III

Coach: Kerry Prather, Indiana 1977

2001-02 RESULTS (20-9)
92 Webber 80
56 Eckerd 61
99 Millikin ■ 87
62 Mt. St. Joseph 58
89 Defiance ■ 92
86 Hanover 84
90 Goshen ■ 82
81 Marian (Ind.) ■ 79
84 Wabash 76
69 Rose-Hulman 53
67 Earlham 71
94 Bluffton ■ 82
93 Thomas More ■ 85
78 Manchester 84
71 Anderson (Ind.) 89
76 Transylvania ■ 79
93 Defiance 105
83 Mt. St. Joseph ■ 72

104 Ind.-Northwest ■ 56
72 Hanover ■ 76
94 Thomas More 82
97 Bluffton 93
84 Anderson (Ind.) ■ 81
75 Manchester ■ 72
76 Transylvania 63
91 Anderson (Ind.) ■ 69
83 Hanover 79
92 Defiance † 87
44 Wittenberg 75

Nickname: Grizzlies
Colors: Navy Blue & Old Gold
Arena: Spurlock Center
 Capacity: 1,500; Year Built: 1975
AD: Kerry N. Prather
SID: Kevin Elixman

FRANK. & MARSH.
Lancaster, PA 17604-3003 III

Coach: Glenn Robinson, West Chester 1967

2001-02 RESULTS (24-5)
85 Springfield ■ 61
77 Salem St. ■ 67
83 Elizabethtown ■ 80
81 Averett † 51
67 Phila. Sciences † 57
84 Wesley ■ 61
66 Muhlenberg 63
100 Albright ■ 68
75 McDaniel ■ 47
66 Salisbury ■ 47
67 Lincoln (Pa.) ■ 59
73 Clark (Mass.) † 63
52 Goucher 61
52 Ursinus 46
69 Gettysburg 79
56 Lebanon Valley ■ 62
63 Dickinson ■ 55
61 Johns Hopkins 68
80 Washington (Md.) ■ 71
78 McDaniel 57
62 Swarthmore 48
59 Gettysburg ■ 44
54 Haverford 52
63 Dickinson 61
61 Johns Hopkins ■ 54
70 Ursinus ■ 56
47 Gettysburg ■ 50
71 Lebanon Valley ■ 59
82 King's (Pa.) ■ 65

Nickname: Diplomats
Colors: Blue & White
Arena: Mayser Center
 Capacity: 3,000; Year Built: 1960
AD: Robert D. Bunnell
SID: Edward Haas

FRANKLIN PIERCE
Rindge, NH 03461 II

Coach: David Chadbourne, St. Joseph's (Me.) 1987

2001-02 RESULTS (15-12)
86 Longwood † 77
86 Clarion 73
85 St. Rose 87
76 Southern Conn. St. ■ 69
65 Southern N.H. ■ 86
51 Mass.-Lowell 74
75 St. Rose ■ 69
66 St. Anselm 84
57 Dist. Columbia † 54
69 Calif. (Pa.) 74
70 Pace ■ 72
82 Le Moyne ■ 76
78 St. Michael's ■ 67
82 Southern Conn. St. 50
79 Pace 71
66 Le Moyne 75

79 St. Michael's ■ 89
71 St. Anselm ■ 64
69 Bryant ■ 59
73 Assumption 84
60 American Int'l ■ 62
84 Bentley 79
69 Stonehill ■ 61
80 Merrimack 77
72 Southern N.H. 75
79 Mass.-Lowell ■ 73
78 St. Rose 79

Nickname: Ravens
Colors: Crimson, Gray & Black
Arena: FPC Fieldhouse
 Capacity: 2,000; Year Built: 1967
AD: Bruce Kirsh
SID: Doug Monson

FREDONIA ST.
Fredonia, NY 14063 III

Coach: Kevin Moore, Brockport St. 1983

2001-02 RESULTS (8-16)
68 Hobart † 81
57 Goucher † 71
86 Medaille ■ 66
45 Penn St.-Behrend ■ 61
69 St. John Fisher 56
41 Cortland St. 51
76 Oneonta St. ■ 74
75 Hilbert 68
72 Oswego St. 70
60 Potsdam St. 80
55 Plattsburgh St. 75
56 Penn St.-Behrend 83
65 New Paltz St. 73
33 Gannon 64
86 Plattsburgh St. ■ 80
42 Potsdam St. ■ 56
46 Buffalo St. ■ 70
64 Utica/Rome 78
53 Cortland St. 59
63 Geneseo St. ■ 71
58 Oneonta St. 63
55 Brockport St. 89
83 Oswego St. ■ 69
83 New Paltz St. ■ 52

Nickname: Blue Devils
Colors: Blue & White
Arena: Steele Hall
 Capacity: 3,500; Year Built: 1983
AD: Gregory Prechtl
SID: Donna Valone

FRESNO ST.
Fresno, CA 93740-0048 I

Coach: Jerry Tarkanian, Fresno St. 1955

2001-02 RESULTS (19-15)
92 Montana 70
65 Southern California ■ 58
61 Wake Forest † 62
63 Michigan St. † 58
73 Pacific (Cal.) 65
75 UC Riverside ■ 58
68 Air Force ■ 52
75 San Francisco ■ 65
77 Gonzaga † 87
78 San Diego St. 93
75 California 97
91 Savannah St. ■ 52
73 Hawaii 83
80 San Jose St. 68
87 Rice ■ 61
86 Tulsa ■ 85
85 Nevada 88
72 Boise St. 56
80 UTEP 77
78 Southern Methodist ■ 70
64 Louisiana Tech ■ 71
63 Tulsa 78
63 Rice 76

57 Nevada ■ 66
58 Oklahoma St. ■ 52
72 UTEP ■ 64
58 Boise St. ■ 61
63 Louisiana Tech 66
86 Southern Methodist 78
72 San Jose St. ■ 60
79 Hawaii ■ 82
72 Louisiana Tech † 69
65 Tulsa 81
75 Temple ■ 81

Nickname: Bulldogs
Colors: Bulldog Red & Blue
Arena: Selland Arena
 Capacity: 10,132; Year Built: 1966
AD: Scott Johnson
SID: Steve Weakland

FROSTBURG ST.
Frostburg, MD 21532-1099 III

Coach: Webb Hatch, VMI 1969

2001-02 RESULTS (16-12)
89 Marietta ■ 77
71 Widener ■ 81
72 Chowan 74
90 Wash. & Jeff. 80
81 Shenandoah 92
89 Bethany (W.Va.) 80
87 Lake Erie ■ 76
74 Mt. Aloysius 57
71 Chris. Newport 80
71 Clark (Mass.) † 113
66 Lincoln (Pa.) † 71
71 Pitt.-Greensburg ■ 67
57 Penn St.-Behrend 66
101 Penn St.-Altoona 66
80 Pitt.-Bradford ■ 92
85 Gallaudet 91
85 La Roche ■ 70
88 Lake Erie 76
93 Villa Julie 76
80 Penn St.-Behrend ■ 50
87 Waynesburg 89
92 Pitt.-Greensburg 85
79 Pitt.-Bradford 96
100 Penn St.-Altoona ■ 51
86 La Roche 78
99 Penn St.-Altoona ■ 63
83 Penn St.-Behrend † 74
99 Pitt.-Bradford 102

Nickname: Bobcats
Colors: Red, White & Black
Arena: Bobcat Arena
 Capacity: 3,600; Year Built: 1977
AD: Ralph Brewer
SID: Chris Starke

FURMAN
Greenville, SC 29613 I

Coach: Larry Davis, Asbury 1978

2001-02 RESULTS (17-14)
72 Col. of Charleston ■ 76
62 Georgia 75
82 Asbury ■ 41
78 Campbell 75
87 Methodist ■ 65
83 Campbell ■ 53
69 UNC Asheville ■ 58
87 Emory ■ 54
60 Wisconsin 68
59 St. Louis 73
81 Macalester ■ 54
65 Gardner-Webb ■ 81
65 Ga. Southern ■ 59
49 Wofford 59
67 Western Caro. 77
70 Davidson ■ 73
91 Appalachian St. ■ 78
76 Chattanooga 65
68 VMI 76

83	Citadel ■	75
45	Col. of Charleston	62
78	Ga. Southern	86
68	Chattanooga ■	67
70	Citadel	64
55	Wofford ■	48
67	East Tenn. St. ■	78
67	UNC Greensboro	70
65	Western Caro. †	61
73	Ga. Southern †	70
44	Col. of Charleston	43
57	Davidson †	62

Nickname: Paladins
Colors: Purple & White
Arena: Timmons Arena
 Capacity: 5,500; Year Built: 1997
AD: Gary Clark
SID: Hunter Reid

GALLAUDET
Washington, DC 20002-3695 ..III

Coach: James DeStefano, Gallaudet 1985

2001-02 RESULTS (7-19)

55	Lycoming	78
80	Elmira †	77
76	Villa Julie	82
80	Phila. Sciences ■	81
113	Averett †	125
94	St. Mary's (Md.) ■	81
66	Marymount (Va.) ■	82
87	Washington (Md.) ■	92
66	Utica/Rome †	59
63	Clarkson †	90
87	Lincoln (Pa.)	90
58	York (Pa.)	92
63	Catholic	104
71	Salisbury ■	69
77	Goucher ■	84
91	Frostburg St. ■	85
52	Mary Washington ■	99
73	Marymount (Va.)	76
69	St. Mary's (Md.)	72
71	Catholic ■	91
70	McDaniel ■	68
96	York (Pa.) ■	99
56	Goucher	72
59	Salisbury	54
65	Mary Washington	82
78	York (Pa.)	91

Nickname: Bison
Colors: Buff & Blue
Arena: Field House
 Capacity: 1,892; Year Built: 1984
AD: James DeStefano
SID: Richard Coco

GANNON
Erie, PA 16541-0001 II

Coach: Jerry Slocum, King's (N.Y.) 1975

2001-02 RESULTS (21-7)

72	Edinboro ■	69
84	Nyack ■	49
92	Indiana (Pa.)	65
97	Roberts Wesleyan ■	63
73	Ferris St.	67
92	Grand Valley St.	67
105	Allegheny ■	64
66	Pitt.-Johnstown	55
119	Tiffin ■	76
98	Pace ■	61
64	Michigan Tech ■	60
77	Lake Superior St. ■	64
67	Northern Mich. ■	56
80	Saginaw Valley	68
78	Northwood	83
84	Wayne St. (Mich.)	78
61	Hillsdale	59
64	Fredonia St. ■	33
71	Mercyhurst ■	69

71	Ashland ■	79
87	Findlay ■	77
70	Hillsdale ■	52
56	Wayne St. (Mich.) ■	70
66	Mercyhurst	48
57	Findlay	71
55	Ashland	60
76	Lake Superior St. †	86
53	Findlay †	70

Nickname: Golden Knights
Colors: Maroon & Gold
Arena: Hammermill Center
 Capacity: 2,800; Year Built: 1949
AD: Mike Corbett
SID: Dan Teliski

GARDNER-WEBB
Boiling Springs, NC 28017 II

2001-02 RESULTS (23-9)

130	St. Mary's (Md.) ■ ■	81
77	Ga. Southern	88
85	Asbury ■	60
67	James Madison	85
56	Colorado St. ■	54
57	Kansas St.	75
106	Ga. Southern ■	99
101	Bluefield St. ■	66
68	Limestone ■	51
68	Va. Commonwealth ■	75
71	South Ala.	66
79	Yale †	69
81	Furman ■	65
80	Murray St.	66
58	Centenary (La.)	74
78	Tex. A&M-Corp. Chris.	86
84	Tex.-Pan American	94
93	Appalachian St.	101
78	Centenary (La.) ■	67
81	Brevard ■	68
86	Tex. A&M-Corp. Chris. ■	76
75	Savannah St.	67
95	Lipscomb	89
79	Southern Wesleyan ■	61
86	Tex.-Pan American ■	79
79	Savannah St. ■	50
77	Lipscomb	76
95	Emmanuel (Ga.)	82
75	Tenn. Temple ■	62
97	Trinity Christian ■	59
75	Cedarville ■	65
94	Mt. Vernon Naz. ■	103

Nickname: Runnin' Bulldogs
Colors: Scarlet, White & Black
Arena: Paul Porter Arena
 Capacity: 5,000; Year Built: 1982
AD: Chuck Burch
SID: Thomas Goodwin

GENESEO ST.
Geneseo, NY 14454...............III

Coach: Steve Minton, Heidelberg 1986

2001-02 RESULTS (16-11)

93	Medaille †	58
61	Penn St.-Behrend	54
72	D'Youville ■	68
81	Ithaca ■	68
74	Alfred	81
87	Utica/Rome ■	66
82	Oswego St.	80
74	Plattsburgh St. ■	75
57	Ithaca	64
52	Buffalo St. ■	76
91	Oneonta St. ■	81
86	New Paltz St. ■	77
93	Roberts Wesleyan ■	88
60	Brockport St. †	73
70	St. John Fisher †	54
74	Utica/Rome ■	71
61	Oneonta St.	87
84	New Paltz St.	78

52	Brockport St. ■	59
61	Cortland St.	51
71	Fredonia St.	63
54	Plattsburgh St.	64
52	Potsdam St.	63
59	Buffalo St. ■	53
57	Cortland St.	56
61	Potsdam St. †	67
69	Oswego St.	78

Nickname: Blue Knights
Colors: Navy Blue & White
Arena: Alumni Fieldhouse
 Capacity: 3,000; Year Built: 1973
AD: Marilyn Moore
SID: George Gagnier

GEORGE FOX
Newberg, OR 97132-2697 III

Coach: Mark Vernon, George Fox 1977

2001-02 RESULTS (3-22)

63	Cascade	64
78	Northwest (Wash.) ■	93
73	Cascade ■	82
61	Pacific (Ore.)	66
79	Northwest (Wash.)	65
69	Willamette	89
70	Clarkson †	82
50	Utica/Rome †	48
70	Holy Names	76
86	Pacific Lutheran	91
97	Puget Sound ■	106
77	Lewis & Clark	102
96	Linfield ■	115
81	Northwest Chrst. ■	72
73	Whitworth	83
67	Whitman	88
87	Linfield	100
78	Lewis & Clark ■	95
69	Pacific (Ore.) ■	73
75	Pacific Lutheran ■	84
85	Northwest Chrst.	89
75	Puget Sound	83
44	Willamette ■	56
60	Whitman ■	82
98	Whitworth ■	100

Nickname: Bruins
Colors: Navy & Gold
AD: Craig Taylor
SID: To be named

GEORGE MASON
Fairfax, VA 22030....................I

Coach: Jim Larranaga, Providence 1971

2001-02 RESULTS (19-10)

86	Niagara ■	71
65	Miami (Ohio)	70
67	Toledo ■	64
80	Coppin St. ■	44
71	Mississippi	70
65	Central Mich. ■	54
66	Southern Ill. ■	73
56	Delaware ■	83
86	Winthrop †	66
48	Duquesne	64
80	William & Mary ■	71
71	Towson ■	42
51	UNC Wilmington ■	68
76	Old Dominion ■	67
82	Hofstra ■	68
64	Towson	52
59	Va. Commonwealth	75
69	Drexel	100
80	James Madison ■	68
69	Delaware	57
62	Hofstra	61
59	UNC Wilmington	56
79	Drexel ■	64
51	William & Mary	54
83	Va. Commonwealth ■	80
81	James Madison	74

78	Old Dominion	63
76	Hofstra †	82
64	St. Joseph's ■	73

Nickname: Patriots
Colors: Green & Gold
Arena: Patriot Center
 Capacity: 10,000; Year Built: 1985
AD: Thomas J. O'Connor
SID: Carlton D. White

GEORGE WASHINGTON
Washington, DC 20052.............I

Coach: Karl Hobbs, Connecticut 1985

2001-02 RESULTS (12-16)

69	Marshall †	64
48	Western Ky. †	73
63	Texas A&M	87
69	Binghamton ■	52
116	Yale ■	102
79	Boston U. ■	76
76	Connecticut †	84
60	Princeton †	57
68	Old Dominion	64
83	Providence	77
87	Charlotte ■	97
92	St. Bonaventure ■	86
74	Duquesne ■	50
59	Dayton	83
75	La Salle ■	72
63	Xavier ■	71
74	St. Joseph's	92
60	Massachusetts	73
62	Rhode Island ■	75
53	Richmond ■	61
70	La Salle	83
58	Temple ■	80
75	Xavier	89
69	Duquesne	79
59	Dayton ■	89
53	Richmond ■	49
70	Fordham	68
62	Massachusetts †	73

Nickname: Colonials
Colors: Buff & Blue
Arena: Charles E. Smith Center
 Capacity: 5,000; Year Built: 1975
AD: Jack E. Kvancz
SID: Brad Bower

GEORGETOWN
Washington, DC 20057-1121 I

Coach: Craig Esherick, Georgetown 1978

2001-02 RESULTS (19-11)

108	Marymount (Va.) ■	47
59	Georgia †	73
76	Coastal Caro. ■	51
91	Towson ■	40
103	Grambling	69
91	Bethune-Cookman ■	61
70	South Carolina	68
91	Morgan St. ■	65
87	Norfolk St. ■	68
99	Howard ■	80
55	Virginia ■	61
91	UCLA	98
71	Miami (Fla.) ■	79
87	Rutgers	89
70	Boston College	43
84	Seton Hall ■	58
67	Pittsburgh ■	58
83	Notre Dame ■	73
56	Pittsburgh	67
75	Syracuse ■	60
84	West Virginia ■	77
111	Notre Dame ■	116
84	Seton Hall	77
72	Villanova	83
74	Connecticut ■	75
75	Syracuse	69

87 West Virginia............77
88 Rutgers ■............69
68 Providence †............67
76 Miami (Fla.) †............84

Nickname: Hoyas
Colors: Blue & Gray
Arena: MCI Center
   Capacity: 20,600; Year Built: 1997
AD: Joseph C. Lang
SID: Bill Shapland

GEORGIA
Athens, GA 30602-1661 I

Coach: Jim Harrick,
Charleston (W.Va.) 1960
2001-02 RESULTS (22-10)
75 Furman ■............62
73 Georgetown †............59
94 Ga. Southern †............73
61 Samford ■............55
81 Colorado............73
78 Georgia St. †............83
77 Minnesota ■............55
95 Georgia Tech ■............82
79 South Ala.............70
91 Pepperdine ■............74
80 Arkansas St. †............68
64 Miami (Ohio) †............59
44 Hawaii............54
82 Vanderbilt ■............69
88 Kentucky............84
73 Tennessee ■............70
72 Alabama............77
84 Florida............79
81 Arkansas ■............67
84 Vanderbilt............86
67 South Carolina............80
79 Mississippi............72
86 Mississippi St.............68
72 Auburn............75
70 Florida ■............85
78 Kentucky ■............69
55 LSU............54
82 South Carolina ■............75
63 Tennessee............71
76 LSU †............78
85 Murray St. †............68
75 Southern Ill. †............77

Nickname: Bulldogs
Colors: Red & Black
Arena: Stegeman Coliseum
   Capacity: 10,523; Year Built: 1963
AD: Vincent J. Dooley
SID: Tim Hix

GC&SU
Milledgeville, GA 31061............II

Coach: Terry Sellers,
Aub.-Montgomery 1976
2001-02 RESULTS (15-12)
75 Ala.-Huntsville †............76
95 Montevallo............85
88 Paine ■............72
63 Albany St. (Ga.)............59
64 Francis Marion ■............63
70 Columbus St.............94
79 Albany St. (Ga.) ■............67
61 Johnson Smith †............67
76 Tuskegee †............73
85 UNC Pembroke............70
73 Augusta St. ■............77
74 North Fla.............88
99 Clayton St.............89
77 Kennesaw St. ■............90
86 North Fla.............74
88 Lander............81
54 Armstrong Atlantic............53
96 Francis Marion............74
74 S.C.-Spartanburg............75
93 UNC Pembroke ■............81

62 Clayton St. ■............65
61 S.C.-Aiken............62
68 Columbus St. ■............62
68 Kennesaw St.............70
75 Armstrong Atlantic ■............53
49 S.C.-Spartanburg ■............58
66 Lander †............71

Nickname: Bobcats
Colors: Navy Blue & Hunter Green
Arena: Centennial Center
   Capacity: 4,071; Year Built: 1989
AD: Stan Aldridge
SID: Brad Muller

GA. SOUTHERN
Statesboro, GA 30460-8086......I

Coach: Jeff Price, Pikeville 1981
2001-02 RESULTS (16-12)
85 North Ga. ■............51
88 Gardner-Webb ■............77
73 Georgia †............94
77 Wichita St.............97
87 Illinois St. ■............76
64 UNLV............79
99 Gardner-Webb............106
86 Savannah St.............63
92 Mercer ■............69
66 Albany St. (Ga.) ■............58
59 Furman............65
100 VMI ■............60
101 Appalachian St.............89
67 UNC Greensboro ■............79
80 Citadel............85
86 Wofford ■............73
96 Western Caro. ■............67
60 Col. of Charleston............57
91 Chattanooga ■............103
80 Savannah St. ■............41
65 East Tenn. St.............100
86 Furman ■............78
67 Wofford............76
56 Davidson............64
95 Citadel ■............86
84 Chattanooga............68
70 Col. of Charleston ■............54
70 Furman †............73

Nickname: Eagles
Colors: Blue & White
Arena: Hanner Fieldhouse
   Capacity: 4,378; Year Built: 1969
AD: Samuel Q. Baker
SID: Joey Warren

GEORGIA ST.
Atlanta, GA 30303-3083 I

Coach: Lefty Driesell, Duke 1954
2001-02 RESULTS (20-11)
77 Fla. Atlantic............90
72 Jacksonville ■............84
82 Valdosta St. ■............71
52 Central Mich.............76
67 Charleston So. ■............56
59 Belmont............68
83 Georgia †............78
90 Mercer ■............79
85 Campbell ■............71
63 Mississippi St. †............72
95 St. Joseph's †............90
63 Col. of Charleston †............70
84 Troy St. ■............67
92 UCF............84
89 Stetson ■............73
75 Jacksonville St.............81
59 Samford............63
81 Campbell............64
80 Jacksonville St. ■............61
60 Samford ■............48
81 Jacksonville............75
94 Stetson............79
73 UCF ■............83

76 Fla. Atlantic ■............71
82 Mercer............74
102 Troy St.............88
71 Belmont ■............69
82 Belmont †............79
82 UCF............64
75 Fla. Atlantic †............76
62 Tennessee Tech............64

Nickname: Panthers
Colors: Blue, White & Red
Arena: GSU Sports Arena
   Capacity: 5,000; Year Built: 1972
AD: Greg Manning
SID: Charlie Taylor

GEORGIA TECH
Atlanta, GA 30332-0455 I

Coach: Paul Hewitt, St. John Fisher 1985
2001-02 RESULTS (15-16)
97 Florida A&M ■............62
74 Pennsylvania............79
70 Eastern Ill. †............65
66 Illinois †............105
54 St. Louis †............67
62 Wisconsin ■............61
77 North Carolina ■............83
82 Georgia............95
96 Syracuse †............80
83 Davidson †............69
79 Wofford ■............70
69 Tulane ■............79
92 IUPUI ■............98
86 Cornell ■............68
76 Clemson ■............83
79 Duke............104
87 Maryland ■............92
71 North Carolina St.............84
65 Virginia............69
74 Wake Forest ■............87
77 Florida St. ■............46
86 North Carolina............74
74 Clemson............50
63 Duke ■............95
65 Maryland............85
60 St. Louis............40
65 North Carolina St. ■............59
82 Virginia............80
90 Wake Forest ■............77
86 Florida St.............78
83 Wake Forest †............92

Nickname: Yellow Jackets
Colors: Old Gold & White
Arena: Alexander Memorial Coliseum
   Capacity: 9,191; Year Built: 1956
AD: David T. Braine
SID: Mike Stamus

GETTYSBURG
Gettysburg, PA 17325-1668 III

Coach: George Petrie, Lebanon Valley
1972
2001-02 RESULTS (20-7)
64 John Carroll ■............60
75 Lebanon Valley ■............63
92 Messiah ■............79
70 Arcadia............55
80 Marymount (Va.) ■............58
73 Washington (Md.)............57
65 Johns Hopkins............57
67 York (Pa.)............57
57 Elizabethtown ■............96
60 Navy............78
89 Cal St. Hayward †............77
61 Buena Vista †............63
76 Alvernia ■............67
62 Muhlenberg............70
79 Frank. & Marsh. ■............69
86 McDaniel............64
64 Dickinson ■............56
69 Swarthmore............51

68 Johns Hopkins............65
85 Haverford ■............45
44 Frank. & Marsh.............59
84 McDaniel ■............65
67 Ursinus ■............66
66 Dickinson............75
68 Muhlenberg............59
50 Frank. & Marsh.............47
59 Lycoming............78

Nickname: Bullets
Colors: Orange & Blue
Arena: Bream Gymnasium
   Capacity: 3,000; Year Built: 1962
AD: David Wright
SID: Matt Daskivich

GLENVILLE ST.
Glenville, WV 26351................II

Coach: Robert Williams, Ithaca 1988
2001-02 RESULTS (15-13)
95 Southern Va. ■............70
81 West Va. Wesleyan ■............94
60 Pitt.-Johnstown............63
85 Ohio Valley............69
71 Slippery Rock............81
105 Ohio Southern ■............59
76 Ky. Wesleyan............105
55 Lincoln (Mo.) †............93
70 Concord †............88
73 Fairmont St.............71
86 Wheeling Jesuit ■............84
78 Salem Int'l ■............83
86 Concord............73
76 West Virginia St.............69
86 Charleston (W.Va.) ■............85
89 Bluefield St. ■............78
87 West Va. Tech............68
95 West Liberty St. ■............97
71 Shepherd............63
88 Davis & Elkins ■............77
82 West Va. Wesleyan ■............92
67 Alderson-Broaddus............84
77 Shepherd ■............75
74 West Va. Wesleyan............75
92 Davis & Elkins............83
68 Alderson-Broaddus ■............73
78 Davis & Elkins ■............62
76 Charleston (W.Va.)............80

Nickname: Pioneers
Colors: Royal Blue & White
Arena: Jesse Lilly Gym
   Capacity: 1,600; Year Built: 1950
AD: Greg Bamberger
SID: Jodi Devereux

GONZAGA
Spokane, WA 99258-0066 I

Coach: Mark Few, Oregon 1987
2001-02 RESULTS (29-4)
58 Illinois............76
83 Montana ■............63
65 St. John's (N.Y.) †............58
67 Texas †............64
63 Marquette †............72
92 Ark.-Pine Bluff ■............42
93 Portland St. ■............58
84 Eastern Wash. ■............74
87 Fresno St. †............77
67 Washington............47
67 Washington St. ■............44
105 Eastern Ore. ■............45
79 Monmouth............54
83 St. Joseph's............80
95 New Mexico............90
83 Santa Clara ■............81
75 San Diego ■............62
75 Pepperdine............88
94 Loyola Marymount............60
93 San Francisco ■............73
70 St. Mary's (Cal.) ■............52

102	Portland ■	67
94	Portland	80
84	Santa Clara	69
77	San Diego	76
72	Loyola Marymount ■	51
91	Pepperdine ■	78
70	San Francisco	54
74	St. Mary's (Cal.)	55
82	Loyola Marymount †	64
87	San Diego	79
96	Pepperdine †	90
66	Wyoming †	74

Nickname: Bulldogs, Zags
Colors: Blue, White & Red
Arena: The Kennel
  Capacity: 4,000; Year Built: 1960
AD: Michael L. Roth
SID: Oliver Pierce

GORDON
Wenham, MA 01984-1899 III

Coach: Troy Justice, Neb. Christian 1988
2001-02 RESULTS (16-11)

93	Daniel Webster	64
70	Eastern ■	63
69	Fitchburg St. ■	50
79	Elms	69
58	Becker	47
80	Salem St.	72
70	Curry ■	76
72	Mass. Liberal Arts	77
66	Northwestern (Minn.) †	93
78	Houston Baptist	92
80	Albertus Magnus ■	62
76	Bates	78
54	Nichols	66
68	Endicott	67
66	Salve Regina ■	59
69	Colby-Sawyer	72
70	Johnson St. ■	58
50	Roger Williams	69
78	Newbury	47
77	Wentworth Inst. ■	59
73	Castleton St.	54
75	Anna Maria	87
82	Eastern Nazarene ■	59
85	New England ■	74
84	New England Col. ■	58
69	Roger Williams	72
74	Mass.-Dartmouth	89

Nickname: Fighting Scots
Colors: Blue & White
Arena: Bennett Center
  Capacity: 2,300; Year Built: 1996
AD: Joe Hakes
SID: Steve Leonard

GOUCHER
Towson, MD 21204-2794 III

Coach: Leonard Trevino, Texas Tech 1987
2001-02 RESULTS (13-13)

68	Merchant Marine	85
71	Fredonia St. †	57
74	Johns Hopkins ■	66
64	Mary Washington	56
67	Catholic	86
65	Villa Julie	62
74	Roanoke ■	92
67	Montclair St.	74
70	Beloit †	87
89	Virgin Islands	76
74	Gwynedd-Mercy ■	64
61	Frank. & Marsh. ■	52
90	St. Mary's (Md.) ■	72
81	Marymount (Va.) ■	74
72	York (Pa.)	94
84	Gallaudet	77
78	Salisbury	90
85	Catholic ■	92
84	Mary Washington ■	75
77	Marymount (Va.)	83
60	St. Mary's (Md.)	72
72	Gallaudet ■	56
78	York (Pa.) ■	85
56	Salisbury ■	58
66	Mary Washington ■	65
61	Catholic	77

Nickname: Gophers
Colors: Blue & Gold
Arena: Sports/Recreation Center
  Capacity: 1,200; Year Built: 1991
AD: Geoffrey Miller
SID: Mike Sanders

GRAMBLING
Grambling, LA 71245.............I

Coach: Larry Wright
2001-02 RESULTS (9-19)

81	Wiley ■	54
61	Tulsa	104
68	Villanova	82
69	Georgetown	103
64	Creighton	102
76	Missouri	100
91	Northwestern St. ■	88
55	Alabama St. ■	62
89	Alabama A&M ■	88
69	Ark.-Little Rock	93
67	Virginia	112
87	Southern U.	106
87	Alcorn St.	99
79	Prairie View	61
66	Texas Southern ■	55
91	Jackson St.	96
84	Ark.-Pine Bluff	72
87	Mississippi Val.	91
81	Southern U. ■	80
85	Alcorn St. ■	87
73	Prairie View	75
68	Texas Southern	87
98	Jackson St. ■	83
91	Ark.-Pine Bluff ■	77
87	Mississippi Val. ■	99
74	Alabama St.	82
76	Alabama A&M	81
84	Alcorn St.	108

Nickname: Tigers
Colors: Black & Gold
Arena: Tiger Memorial Gym
  Capacity: 4,500; Year Built: 1954
AD: Albert Dennis
SID: T. Scott Boatright

GRAND CANYON
Phoenix, AZ 85017 II

Coach: Leighton McCrary, Philander Smith 1974
2001-02 RESULTS (10-17)

75	Fort Lewis ■	65
74	Central Ark. ■	72
84	Sonoma St. ■	92
85	San Fran. St. ■	80
63	Cal St. Stanislaus ■	64
57	Cal St. Bakersfield ■	81
69	Ferris St. ■	71
75	Mesa St. ■	82
78	Walsh ■	89
72	Cal St. Dom. Hills ■	66
57	Cal St. Los Angeles ■	63
65	Cal St. San B'dino ■	68
66	Cal Poly Pomona ■	93
70	UC Davis ■	81
85	Cal St. Chico	77
78	UC San Diego ■	73
72	UC San Diego	76
76	Sonoma St.	72
73	San Fran. St.	80
65	Cal St. Bakersfield	77
82	Cal St. Stanislaus ■	81
74	Cal St. Los Angeles ■	76
77	Cal St. Dom. Hills ■	85
69	Cal Poly Pomona ■	86
73	Cal St. San B'dino	97
108	Cal St. Chico	105
99	UC Davis ■	93

Nickname: Antelopes
Colors: Purple & White
Arena: Antelope Gym
  Capacity: 2,000; Year Built: 1994
AD: John Pierson
SID: Rebecca Brutlag

GRAND VALLEY ST.
Allendale, MI 49401 II

Coach: Terry Smith, Michigan St. 1984
2001-02 RESULTS (15-13)

86	Neb.-Omaha †	84
78	Lynn †	90
86	Southern Ind. †	112
108	Cornerstone †	117
101	Aquinas †	69
81	Northwood	84
82	Findlay	100
98	Grace Bible (Mich.) ■	67
79	Mercyhurst ■	66
67	Gannon ■	92
104	Finlandia ■	60
92	Rochester College ■	62
69	Wayne St. (Mich.) ■	59
62	Wayne St. (Mich.)	77
70	Hillsdale	74
74	Ashland ■	75
86	Mich.-Dearborn	63
86	Ferris St.	85
81	Lake Superior St. ■	62
97	Saginaw Valley ■	75
69	Northern Mich.	76
63	Michigan Tech	80
94	Northwood ■	81
64	Lake Superior St.	70
78	Ferris St. ■	75
99	Saginaw Valley	96
79	Michigan Tech ■	85
82	Northern Mich. ■	80

Nickname: Lakers
Colors: Blue, Black & White
Arena: Grand Valley Field House
  Capacity: 4,010; Year Built: 1982
AD: Tim W. Selgo
SID: Tim Nott

GREENSBORO
Greensboro, NC 27401-1875 ..III

Coach: Eddie Payne, Wake Forest 1973
2001-02 RESULTS (11-15)

59	Chris. Newport ■	64
66	Johns Hopkins	61
68	Washington (Md.) †	47
53	Wash. & Lee	56
71	Milligan	69
53	Maryville (Tenn.) ■	68
54	Guilford †	61
91	Warren Wilson ■	56
40	Citadel	72
68	Maryville (Tenn.)	81
45	Milligan ■	56
52	Methodist	68
75	N.C. Wesleyan ■	72
62	Chowan	58
80	Averett ■	75
58	Ferrum	66
63	Shenandoah ■	72
62	Methodist ■	66
76	N.C. Wesleyan	79
70	Chowan	57
77	Piedmont ■	56
80	Averett ■	75
67	Ferrum ■	61
73	Shenandoah	75
55	Chris. Newport	76
62	Shenandoah	63

Nickname: The Pride
Colors: Green, White & Silver
Arena: Hanes Gymnasium
  Capacity: 850; Year Built: 1964
AD: Kim A. Strable
SID: Bob Lowe

GREENVILLE
Greenville, IL 62246..............III

Coach: George Barber, Asbury 1986
2001-02 RESULTS (9-16)

88	Wis. Lutheran	95
76	Rockford †	88
119	St. Louis Pharmacy ■	86
77	Eureka ■	73
78	McKendree	111
100	St. Louis Christian ■	50
92	Judson (Ill.) ■	97
90	Knox ■	88
72	Wheaton (Ill.)	88
112	Sanford Brown	67
81	Lincoln Chrst.	86
77	Westminster (Mo.) ■	79
75	Webster	76
85	Blackburn	81
97	Maryville (Mo.) ■	75
76	Principia	59
109	Fontbonne	114
68	MacMurray ■	86
90	Westminster (Mo.)	104
81	Webster ■	86
86	Blackburn ■	82
84	Maryville (Mo.)	105
77	Principia ■	88
72	Fontbonne ■	78
84	MacMurray	91

Nickname: Panthers
Colors: Orange & Black
Arena: H.J. Long Gymnasium
  Capacity: 2,000; Year Built: 1960
AD: Doug Faulkner
SID: B.J. Schneck

GRINNELL
Grinnell, IA 50112.................III

Coach: David Arseneault, Colby 1976
2001-02 RESULTS (12-12)

131	Martin Luther	134
123	Faith Bapt. Bible ■	100
124	Wis.-La Crosse	127
126	Mt. Mercy ■	116
140	Colorado Col. ■	117
135	Lake Forest ■	140
136	Wis.-La Crosse	146
129	Rockford ■	138
124	Illinois Col. ■	130
124	Monmouth (Ill.)	131
143	Carroll (Wis.) ■	85
128	Lawrence ■	89
110	Knox	108
106	Beloit	113
94	St. Norbert ■	117
135	Ripon ■	123
139	Beloit ■	126
110	Lawrence	128
143	Carroll (Wis.)	122
135	Monmouth (Ill.) ■	121
107	Illinois Col.	113
130	Knox ■	91
111	Lake Forest	93
114	St. Norbert	125

Nickname: Pioneers
Colors: Scarlet & Black
Arena: Darby Gym
  Capacity: 1,250; Year Built: 1942
AD: Diane (Dee) Fairchild
SID: Andy Holmes

GROVE CITY
Grove City, PA 16127-2104 III

Coach: Steve Lamie, Grove City 1985

2001-02 RESULTS (17-10)
77	Allegheny ■	64
78	Carnegie Mellon	67
53	Penn St.-Behrend	56
66	Denison ■	57
77	Juniata ■	58
55	Geneva ■	64
74	Case Reserve	55
53	Hilbert	57
76	La Roche	61
75	Penn St.-Altoona ■	64
60	Wm. Paterson ■	53
63	Merchant Marine †	65
78	Wash. & Jeff. †	59
95	Medaille ■	65
73	Penn St.-Altoona	61
78	Waynesburg ■	60
67	Thiel ■	79
74	Wash. & Jeff.	59
111	Westminster (Pa.)	101
50	Bethany (W.Va.) ■	58
75	Waynesburg	64
63	Thiel	64
80	Wash. & Jeff. ■	58
69	Westminster (Pa.) ■	76
91	Bethany (W.Va.)	96
77	Thiel	62
74	Bethany (W.Va.)	89

Nickname: Wolverines
Colors: Crimson & White
Arena: College Arena
   Capacity: 1,800; Year Built: 1953
AD: Christopher Smith
SID: Joe Klimchak

GUILFORD
Greensboro, NC 27410-4173 ..III

Coach: Butch Estes, North Carolina 1971

2001-02 RESULTS (15-11)
61	East Tenn. St.	90
100	Atlanta Christian	71
77	Southeastern Fla.	68
77	Lynchburg	47
61	Greensboro †	54
85	Emory & Henry	101
71	Hampden-Sydney ■	74
73	Western Caro.	77
64	Wash. & Lee	55
44	Randolph-Macon ■	80
58	Va. Wesleyan	55
95	Roanoke ■	81
70	East. Mennonite	48
80	Bridgewater (Va.)	92
65	Wash. & Lee ■	51
86	Lynchburg ■	59
108	Roanoke Bible ■	32
79	Hampden-Sydney	88
68	Va. Wesleyan	71
56	Randolph-Macon	72
112	Roanoke Bible	49
66	Bridgewater (Va.) ■	57
71	East. Mennonite ■	55
63	Roanoke	75
78	Emory & Henry ■	67
55	Hampden-Sydney	57

Nickname: Quakers
Colors: Crimson & Gray
Arena: Ragan-Brown
   Capacity: 2,500; Year Built: 1980
AD: Marion Kirby
SID: Dave Walters

GUST. ADOLPHUS
St. Peter, MN 56082-1498 III

Coach: Mark Hanson, Gust. Adolphus 1983

2001-02 RESULTS (24-5)
97	Martin Luther ■	52
95	Luther ■	47
78	Buena Vista †	64
87	Simpson †	73
75	Northwestern (Minn.)	59
81	St. Olaf ■	60
85	Carleton ■	71
87	St. Mary's (Minn.) ■	65
71	Concordia-M'head	63
61	St. John's (Minn.) ■	58
72	St. Thomas (Minn.)	75
86	Macalester ■	77
70	Bethel (Minn.)	66
95	Hamline ■	69
75	Augsburg	78
84	St. Olaf	58
86	Carleton	78
59	St. Mary's (Minn.) ■	31
68	St. John's (Minn.)	53
58	St. Thomas (Minn.) ■	61
90	Concordia-M'head ■	53
64	Macalester	62
68	Bethel (Minn.) ■	66
121	Hamline	59
76	Augsburg ■	56
59	Bethel (Minn.) ■	66
74	Edgewood ■	65
88	Buena Vista	60
65	Carthage	71

Nickname: Golden Gusties
Colors: Black & Gold
Arena: Gus Young Court
   Capacity: 3,000; Year Built: 1984
AD: Alan Molde
SID: Tim Kennedy

GWYNEDD-MERCY
Gwynedd Valley, PA 19437-0901
....III

Coach: Kevin Newsome, Sonoma St. 1982

2001-02 RESULTS (14-12)
72	Bethany (W.Va.) †	92
88	Hiram †	84
66	Swarthmore ■	56
99	Brooklyn ■	71
71	Ursinus ■	65
72	Misericordia ■	65
80	Neumann	90
97	Marywood ■	68
75	Widener	94
71	Albright	83
64	Rowan ■	62
64	Goucher	74
53	Alvernia	77
51	Cabrini ■	63
71	Arcadia	54
69	Wesley ■	77
52	Misericordia	64
64	Eastern	69
87	Marywood	62
68	Alvernia ■	65
62	Neumann ■	66
83	Wesley	64
70	Cabrini	65
80	Arcadia ■	57
67	Eastern ■	56
57	Cabrini	92

Nickname: Griffins
Colors: Cardinal & Gold
Arena: Griffin Complex

Capacity: 1,200; Year Built: 1991
AD: Keith Mondillo
SID: Rich Schepis

HAMILTON
Clinton, NY 13323 III

Coach: Tom Murphy, Springfield 1960

2001-02 RESULTS (16-9)
80	Hartwick	52
92	Middlebury	83
69	Utica	57
61	Hilbert	54
84	Wartburg †	73
84	Wis.-Oshkosh †	93
49	Davidson	85
112	Notre Dame (N.H.) ■	64
89	Colby ■	62
85	Rensselaer ■	75
56	Vassar ■	67
79	Williams ■	76
79	Union (N.Y.) ■	83
95	Skidmore ■	82
81	Hobart	57
83	Clarkson ■	64
86	St. Lawrence ■	90
83	Hobart ■	52
80	Skidmore ■	67
80	Union (N.Y.) ■	84
86	Vassar	59
81	Rensselaer	67
79	St. Lawrence	83
62	Clarkson	70
66	Union (N.Y.)	80

Nickname: Continentals
Colors: Buff & Blue
Arena: Margaret Bundy Scott Fieldhouse
   Capacity: 2,500; Year Built: 1978
AD: Thomas Murphy/David Thompson
SID: Stephen Jaynes

HAMLINE
St. Paul, MN 55104.................III

Coach: Tom Gilles, Iowa 1986

2001-02 RESULTS (3-22)
70	Crown ■	53
89	Augustana (S.D.)	110
56	Martin Luther ■	91
47	Northwestern (Minn.)	68
84	Concordia-M'head ■	87
52	St. Thomas (Minn.)	84
63	Augsburg	76
56	St. Olaf ■	58
53	Concordia-St. Paul	74
80	Carleton	88
50	St. Mary's (Minn.) ■	60
75	Bethel (Minn.) ■	88
69	St. John's (Minn.) ■	81
69	Gust. Adolphus	95
63	Macalester ■	79
58	Concordia-M'head	81
60	St. Thomas (Minn.) ■	86
63	Augsburg ■	74
64	Carleton ■	82
73	St. Olaf	72
70	St. Mary's (Minn.) ■	57
74	Bethel (Minn.)	90
62	St. John's (Minn.)	82
59	Gust. Adolphus ■	121
88	Macalester	92

Nickname: Pipers
Colors: Red & Grey
Arena: Hutton Fieldhouse
   Capacity: 2,000
AD: Dan O'Brien
SID: Tom Gilles

HAMPDEN-SYDNEY
Hampden-Sydney, VA 23943 III

Coach: Tony Shaver, North Carolina 1976

2001-02 RESULTS (23-6)
79	Hilbert ■	36
105	Wabash ■	65
97	Averett	92
108	Apprentice ■	75
97	Emory & Henry ■	72
100	Lynchburg	58
74	Guilford	71
98	La Grange ■	77
98	John Carroll †	76
65	Bridgewater (Va.) ■	62
81	East. Mennonite	66
63	Randolph-Macon	67
81	Roanoke	66
78	Wash. & Lee	51
57	Va. Wesleyan ■	60
88	Emory & Henry	82
88	Guilford ■	79
62	Bridgewater (Va.)	66
106	East. Mennonite ■	68
80	Wash. & Lee ■	63
87	Roanoke ■	69
104	Lynchburg ■	57
51	Randolph-Macon ■	60
70	Va. Wesleyan	78
57	Guilford ■	55
105	Emory & Henry †	95
55	Randolph-Macon †	48
92	N.C. Wesleyan	79
68	Catholic	74

Nickname: Tigers
Colors: Garnet & Gray
Arena: S. Douglas Fleet Gym
   Capacity: 2,500; Year Built: 1979
AD: Joseph E. Bush
SID: Dan McCormick

HAMPTON
Hampton, VA 23668 I

Coach: Steve Merfeld, Wis.-La Crosse 1984

2001-02 RESULTS (26-7)
77	North Carolina	69
73	UCF ■	72
85	Vanderbilt †	100
67	Akron †	59
83	Hawaii Pacific	76
78	Morgan St.	70
81	Coppin St.	69
85	Norfolk St. ■	67
84	Old Dominion	77
84	Bradley	87
74	Western Ill.	77
66	Montana St.	80
91	Troy St. †	100
86	Md.-East. Shore ■	71
81	South Carolina St.	75
82	N.C. A&T	68
58	Delaware St. ■	55
79	Howard ■	58
85	Bethune-Cookman	69
97	Florida A&M ■	65
89	Morgan St.	74
78	Coppin St. ■	51
64	William & Mary	59
81	Md.-East. Shore	63
87	South Carolina St. ■	73
72	N.C. A&T ■	61
63	Delaware St.	58
81	Howard	82
92	Norfolk St.	89
93	Morgan St. †	70

80	South Carolina St. †	70
80	Howard †	62
67	Connecticut †	78

Nickname: Pirates
Colors: Royal Blue & White
Arena: Convocation Center
  Capacity: 7,200; Year Built: 1993
AD: Malcolm Avery
SID: Patricia Harvey

HANOVER
Hanover, IN 47243-0108.........III

Coach: Mike Beitzel, Wooster 1968
2001-02 RESULTS (21-5)
58	Webster †	53
93	Maryville (Mo.) ■	59
84	Wabash	75
74	Centre ■	66
63	Washington (Mo.) ■	55
66	Ind.-Southeast	64
74	Bluffton	51
84	Franklin ■	86
87	Defiance ■	74
78	Rose-Hulman ■	71
53	St. Norbert †	56
85	Denison †	58
77	Transylvania	70
63	Manchester	61
60	Mt. St. Joseph ■	59
63	Thomas More	55
73	Anderson (Ind.)	74
95	Bluffton ■	50
81	Defiance	84
76	Franklin	72
71	Manchester ■	53
75	Transylvania ■	50
82	Thomas More ■	52
78	Mt. St. Joseph	55
92	Anderson (Ind.)	81
79	Franklin	83

Nickname: Panthers
Colors: Red & Blue
Arena: John Collier Arena
  Capacity: 2,000; Year Built: 1995
AD: Lynn Hall
SID: To be named

HARDIN-SIMMONS
Abilene, TX 79698.................III

Coach: Dylan Howard, UAB 1989
2001-02 RESULTS (2-22)
48	Baylor	107
47	Ill. Wesleyan	88
44	Washington (Mo.)	98
45	Mississippi Col.	69
58	McMurry	90
72	Texas Wesleyan	79
45	Texas-Arlington	103
82	East Tex. Baptist ■	87
75	LeTourneau ■	73
69	Colorado Col.	76
95	Sul Ross St. ■	88
64	Howard Payne ■	72
88	Texas Wesleyan ■	97
51	Mary Hardin-Baylor	88
64	Concordia-Austin	74
90	Schreiner	105
53	Texas Lutheran	74
87	McMurry ■	93
91	Schreiner ■	108
75	Texas Lutheran ■	86
71	Sul Ross St.	92
71	Howard Payne	88
57	Mary Hardin-Baylor ■	85
72	Concordia-Austin	87

Nickname: Cowboys
Colors: Purple & Gold
Arena: Mabee Complex
  Capacity: 3,003; Year Built: 1979

AD: John Neese
SID: Chad Grubbs

HARDING
Searcy, AR 72149-0001 II

Coach: Jeff Morgan, West Tex. A&M 1989
2001-02 RESULTS (16-11)
108	Jarvis Christian ■	78
61	East Central ■	54
86	Louisiana Tech	102
93	Central Okla. ■	87
77	Southwest Baptist ■	75
118	Wiley ■	79
74	Southeastern Okla. ■	58
100	Central Baptist ■	79
75	East Central	76
77	Ark.-Monticello ■	79
84	Central Ark.	67
83	Henderson St. ■	88
79	Southern Ark.	83
113	Ark. Baptist ■	56
85	Christian Bros. ■	75
73	Delta St. ■	74
93	Ouachita Baptist ■	76
72	Arkansas Tech ■	68
82	Ark.-Monticello	85
80	Central Ark. ■	64
64	Henderson St.	72
78	Southern Ark. ■	92
96	Christian Bros.	63
81	Delta St. ■	77
79	Ouachita Baptist	82
79	Arkansas Tech	76
73	Valdosta St. †	95

Nickname: Bisons
Colors: Black & Gold
Arena: Rhodes Fieldhouse
  Capacity: 3,000; Year Built: 1949
AD: Greg Harnden
SID: Scott Goode

HARTFORD
West Hartford, CT 06117-1599..I

Coach: Larry Harrison, Pittsburgh 1978
2001-02 RESULTS (14-18)
57	Delaware St.	69
54	Iowa St.	83
52	St. Louis †	85
46	Southern Ill. †	78
57	Eastern Ill. †	73
59	Central Conn. St. †	73
58	Winthrop †	55
38	Manhattan	76
73	Fairleigh Dickinson ■	56
52	Siena	68
53	Rutgers	63
48	Clemson †	78
68	Binghamton	66
64	Northeastern ■	61
56	Boston U. ■	70
78	New Hampshire ■	80
50	Maine	47
78	Vermont ■	65
67	Dartmouth	65
70	New Hampshire	74
76	Stony Brook ■	70
44	Boston U.	42
66	Northeastern	67
59	Maine ■	47
62	Albany (N.Y.) ■	51
57	Md.-East. Shore ■	61
80	Stony Brook	73
88	Binghamton ■	63
48	Albany (N.Y.)	51
66	Vermont	75
65	Albany (N.Y.) †	49
60	Boston U.	63

Nickname: Hawks
Colors: Scarlet & White

Arena: The Chase Family Arena
  Capacity: 4,475; Year Built: 1990
AD: Pat Meiser-McKnett
SID: Thomas Pincince

HARTWICK
Oneonta, NY 13820-4020.......III

Coach: Tim McGraw, Hartwick 1988
2001-02 RESULTS (4-21)
89	Oneonta St. ■	93
76	Rhode Island Col. ■	71
85	St. Joseph's (L.I.)	64
52	Hamilton ■	80
58	Union (N.Y.)	62
77	Baptist Bible (Mo.)	79
74	Skidmore ■	69
64	Cabrini †	77
57	Linfield †	78
72	Colorado Col. †	73
67	Nazareth	77
58	Rochester Inst.	74
58	Cortland St.	64
71	Utica	67
56	Elmira ■	58
68	Alfred ■	75
59	St. John Fisher ■	62
52	Ithaca	62
63	Elmira	70
69	Utica ■	71
59	St. John Fisher	67
63	Alfred	74
46	Ithaca ■	66
54	Rochester Inst. ■	60
71	Nazareth ■	74

Nickname: Hawks
Colors: Royal Blue & White
Arena: Binder PE Center
  Capacity: 1,800; Year Built: 1968
AD: Kenneth Kutler
SID: Bill Sodoma

HARVARD
Boston, MA 02163-1012...........I

Coach: Frank Sullivan, Westfield St. 1973
2001-02 RESULTS (14-12)
68	Fairfield ■	62
57	Holy Cross	65
64	Lehigh	62
68	Northeastern ■	61
64	Stony Brook ■	59
41	Boston U.	51
64	Colgate ■	76
70	New Hampshire	65
70	Dartmouth ■	53
54	Vermont	74
81	Sacred Heart ■	69
54	California	69
55	Coppin St. †	51
88	Dartmouth	57
48	Princeton ■	50
78	Pennsylvania ■	75
89	Brown ■	81
57	Yale ■	66
55	Columbia	52
62	Cornell	63
51	Pennsylvania	78
59	Princeton	70
55	Cornell ■	46
59	Columbia ■	56
72	Yale	77
83	Brown	92

Nickname: Crimson
Colors: Crimson, Black & White
Arena: Lavietes Pavilion
  Capacity: 2,195; Year Built: 1926
AD: Robert L. Scalise
SID: John Veneziano

HAVERFORD
Haverford, PA 19041-1392 III

Coach: Michael Mucci, Villanova 1977
2001-02 RESULTS (3-21)
43	Wash. & Lee †	71
53	Tufts ■	75
37	Columbia	52
67	Union (N.Y.)	77
43	Rensselaer	78
57	Lebanon Valley ■	71
58	Johns Hopkins ■	73
55	Ursinus	67
50	Catholic	77
53	Col. of New Jersey ■	54
56	Chris. Newport	88
79	Southern Me. †	83
56	McDaniel	81
68	Muhlenberg ■	86
72	Washington (Md.) ■	75
70	Swarthmore ■	60
45	Dickinson ■	52
65	Phila. Sciences ■	63
84	Ursinus ■	78
45	Gettysburg	85
59	Muhlenberg	83
52	Frank. & Marsh. ■	54
69	Washington (Md.) ■	76
53	Swarthmore	59

Nickname: Fords
Colors: Scarlet & Black
Arena: Alumni Field House
  Capacity: 1,200; Year Built: 1957
AD: Gregory Kannerstein
SID: John Douglas

HAWAII
Honolulu, HI 96822-2370..........I

Coach: Riley Wallace, Centenary (La.) 1964
2001-02 RESULTS (27-6)
76	Norfolk St. ■	52
74	Drake	63
89	Mercer †	72
59	Colorado St. †	61
60	Wisconsin †	57
60	Northwestern St. ■	58
62	Alcorn St. ■	48
58	San Diego St. ■	61
75	Portland ■	68
67	Iona ■	56
54	Georgia	44
83	Fresno St. ■	73
58	Nevada ■	40
70	UTEP	68
64	Boise St.	62
81	Louisiana Tech ■	61
83	Southern Methodist ■	74
53	San Jose St.	57
88	Rice	79
90	Tulsa	82
67	Boise St. ■	56
75	UTEP ■	60
85	Southern Methodist	76
57	Louisiana Tech	61
71	San Jose St. ■	46
86	Tulsa ■	85
79	Rice ■	50
69	Nevada	79
82	Fresno St.	79
71	San Jose St. †	56
90	Nevada †	68
73	Tulsa	59
58	Xavier †	70

Nickname: Rainbow Warriors
Colors: Green, Black, Silver & White
Arena: Stan Sheriff Center
  Capacity: 10,300; Year Built: 1994
AD: Herman Frazier
SID: Derek Inouchi

SCHEDULES/RESULTS

HAWAII PACIFIC
Honolulu, HI 96813 II

Coach: Anthony Sellitto, Colorado Col. 1961

2001-02 RESULTS (18-9)

70	Neb.-Kearney ■	60
58	Notre Dame ■	98
81	Liberty ■	46
76	Hampton ■	83
65	St. Martin's ■	61
56	Seattle Pacific	86
87	Montana St.-Northern ■	76
86	Lincoln (Mo.) ■	74
94	Cal St. Monterey Bay ■	70
78	Cal St. Dom. Hills ■	54
69	Presbyterian ■	58
80	Olivet Nazarene ■	68
78	Chaminade ■	81
70	Chaminade ■	69
68	Western N.M. ■	60
73	Western N.M. ■	67
56	Mont. St.-Billings ■	67
69	Hawaii-Hilo ■	66
65	BYU-Hawaii ■	82
70	BYU-Hawaii ■	51
84	Mont. St.-Billings ■	81
73	Mont. St.-Billings ■	51
78	Western N.M. ■	71
63	Chaminade	76
64	BYU-Hawaii ■	78
72	Hawaii-Hilo	78
97	Hawaii-Hilo	69

Nickname: Sea Warriors
Colors: Columbia Blue & Kelly Green
Arena: Neal Blaisdell Center
Capacity: 7,500
AD: Russell Dung
SID: Trey Garman

HAWAII-HILO
Hilo, HI 96720-4091 II

Coach: Jeff Law, Plattsburgh St. 1985

2001-02 RESULTS (18-9)

91	Neb.-Kearney ■	84
84	Cal St. Monterey Bay ■	62
92	Drew †	53
62	Wisconsin ■	78
62	LSU	64
87	South Carolina St. ■	69
63	San Fran. St. ■	61
90	Lincoln (Mo.) ■	89
83	Potsdam St. ■	59
90	Cal St. Dom. Hills ■	68
92	Concordia (Cal.) ■	82
71	Asbury ■	64
92	Western N.M. ■	56
70	Western N.M. ■	52
92	Mont. St.-Billings ■	81
81	BYU-Hawaii	74
78	BYU-Hawaii	83
62	Chaminade ■	59
66	Hawaii Pacific	69
74	Mont. St.-Billings	83
79	Mont. St.-Billings	95
90	Western N.M.	64
62	Chaminade	74
67	Chaminade	69
75	BYU-Hawaii ■	68
78	Hawaii Pacific ■	72
69	Hawaii Pacific ■	97

Nickname: Vulcans
Colors: Red, White & Blue
Arena: Afook-Chinen Civic Center
Capacity: 3,000; Year Built: 1955
AD: Kathleen McNally
SID: Kelly Leong

HEIDELBERG
Tiffin, OH 44883-2462 III

Coach: John Hill, Heidelberg 1970

2001-02 RESULTS (10-17)

81	North Central	60
62	Simpson †	57
78	Defiance	84
69	Urbana	70
96	Adrian	84
61	Muskingum	66
79	John Carroll	81
72	Otterbein ■	88
61	Marietta ■	84
82	Baldwin-Wallace ■	81
71	Lake Erie ■	64
83	Bluffton ■	85
44	Mount Union ■	66
70	Ohio Northern ■	84
73	Wilmington (Ohio) ■	60
73	Capital	76
68	Otterbein	85
56	John Carroll ■	79
80	Marietta ■	74
73	Baldwin-Wallace ■	68
63	Mount Union	70
66	Ohio Northern	77
76	Wilmington (Ohio)	74
67	Capital ■	77
71	Muskingum ■	87
73	Wilmington (Ohio) ■	59
69	Otterbein	78

Nickname: Berg
Colors: Red, Orange & Black
Arena: Seiberling Gymnasium
Capacity: 1,900; Year Built: 1952
AD: Jerry McDonald
SID: Toby Boyce

HENDERSON ST.
Arkadelphia, AR 71999-0001 ...II

Coach: Rand Chappell, Southwest Mo. St. 1985

2001-02 RESULTS (21-7)

75	Jarvis Christian ■	50
80	Lane †	56
61	Oakland City †	47
83	Wiley ■	53
73	West Fla. †	48
67	North Ala.	55
96	Ark. Baptist ■	63
63	Seattle Pacific †	68
52	Northeastern St. †	59
71	Quincy	69
76	Southern Ark. ■	56
88	Harding	83
72	Christian Bros.	66
76	Delta St. ■	62
76	Ouachita Baptist	59
65	Arkansas Tech ■	61
78	Ark.-Monticello	64
64	Central Ark. ■	67
63	Southern Ark.	60
72	Harding ■	64
61	Christian Bros. ■	59
59	Delta St.	64
82	Ouachita Baptist ■	68
87	Arkansas Tech	71
83	Ark.-Monticello ■	75
70	Central Ark.	72
56	West Fla. †	60
54	Valdosta St. †	80

Nickname: Reddies
Colors: Red & Gray
Arena: Wells Center
Capacity: 2,100; Year Built: 1971
AD: Sam Goodwin
SID: To be named

HENDRIX
Conway, AR 72032-3080 III

Coach: Cliff Garrison, Central Ark. 1962

2001-02 RESULTS (5-19)

99	Central Baptist ■	90
65	Rust ■	78
66	Ohio Wesleyan †	88
83	Maryville (Mo.) †	92
62	Trinity (Tex.)	78
53	Southwestern (Tex.)	61
56	Rust	65
68	DePauw ■	81
57	Rose-Hulman ■	86
47	Sewanee	74
53	Centre	72
67	Rhodes	58
49	Oglethorpe ■	76
56	Millsaps ■	74
63	DePauw	102
58	Rose-Hulman	81
67	Sewanee ■	58
48	Centre ■	80
78	Central Baptist ■	71
83	Rhodes ■	67
65	Oglethorpe	84
54	Millsaps	83
47	Trinity (Tex.) ■	51
52	Southwestern (Tex.) ■	85

Nickname: Warriors
Colors: Orange & Black
Arena: Ivan H. Grove
Capacity: 1,200; Year Built: 1961
AD: Danny Powell
SID: Jason Rhodes

HIGH POINT
High Point, NC 27262-3598 I

Coach: Jerry Steele, Wake Forest 1961

2001-02 RESULTS (11-19)

59	Auburn	63
63	William & Mary ■	57
66	UNC Wilmington ■	74
91	Warren Wilson ■	42
69	Brown	81
70	Eastern Ky. ■	60
63	Delaware ■	78
55	Wright St. ■	77
63	Oklahoma	107
49	Florida	103
93	Covenant ■	60
87	Coastal Caro. ■	71
77	Charleston So. ■	71
57	Birmingham-So.	74
72	UNC Asheville	83
77	Radford	78
75	Winthrop ■	83
73	Liberty	58
73	Elon ■	63
71	Winthrop	81
61	UNC Asheville ■	67
65	Birmingham-So. ■	68
55	Charleston So.	60
76	Coastal Caro.	98
60	Radford ■	78
99	Liberty ■	98
66	Elon	74
72	UNC Asheville †	71
72	Radford †	70
48	Winthrop †	70

Nickname: Panthers
Colors: Purple & White
Arena: Millis Center
Capacity: 2,565; Year Built: 1992
AD: Woody Gibson
SID: Lee Owen

HILBERT
Hamburg, NY 14075-1597 III

Coach: Richard Walsh, Canisius 1980

2001-02 RESULTS (9-17)

36	Hampden-Sydney	79
44	Walsh †	61
70	Alfred ■	65
61	Nazareth	68
47	Rochester Inst.	72
64	Oswego St.	69
54	Hamilton ■	61
57	Grove City	53
68	Fredonia St. ■	75
64	Medaille †	52
54	Buffalo St.	75
57	Hobart ■	69
51	Thiel	81
74	D'Youville	78
67	Cazenovia ■	73
54	La Roche	64
75	Medaille ■	62
73	Keuka ■	63
59	Pitt.-Bradford ■	77
73	Cazenovia	75
66	Medaille	63
55	Keuka	72
86	D'Youville ■	64
71	Medaille ■	65
86	Cazenovia †	78
50	Keuka †	56

Nickname: Hawks
Colors: Royal Blue & White
Arena: Brad Hafner Recreation Center
Capacity: 1,200; Year Built: 1973
AD: Richard Walsh
SID: Matt Palisin

HILLSDALE
Hillsdale, MI 49242-1298 II

Coach: Ed Douma, Calvin 1966

2001-02 RESULTS (20-8)

74	Saginaw Valley	56
71	Northwood †	66
91	Tiffin ■	71
86	Olivet ■	56
78	Northwood ■	72
95	Saginaw Valley ■	78
64	Lewis	63
91	Kalamazoo ■	78
78	St. Francis (Ill.) ■	72
83	Shippensburg ■	72
86	West Va. Wesleyan ■	71
94	Ferris St.	70
74	Grand Valley St. ■	70
53	Michigan Tech	72
82	Northern Mich.	61
83	Lake Superior St.	71
76	Mercyhurst	72
59	Gannon ■	61
69	Findlay	66
79	Ashland	85
65	Wayne St. (Mich.) ■	68
52	Gannon	70
65	Mercyhurst	57
68	Ashland ■	57
59	Findlay ■	60
69	Wayne St. (Mich.)	62
67	Findlay †	68
53	Lewis †	67

Nickname: Chargers
Colors: Royal Blue & White
Arena: Jesse Philips Arena
Capacity: 2,500; Year Built: 1989
AD: Michael J. Kovalchik
SID: Homer Hendricks

HIRAM
Hiram, OH 44234-0067 III

Coach: Sean McDonnell, Boston College 1996

2001-02 RESULTS (6-19)
69	York (Pa.)	94
84	Gwynedd-Mercy †	88
63	Case Reserve	84
95	Notre Dame (Ohio)	73
81	Oberlin	83
65	Allegheny	100
57	Ohio Wesleyan	78
65	Carnegie Mellon ■	69
96	Pitt.-Greensburg ■	78
67	Bluffton †	90
67	Lake Erie †	93
58	Wabash	92
67	Earlham	81
70	Thiel	97
51	Wittenberg ■	91
71	Denison ■	73
86	Kenyon	80
80	Allegheny ■	92
59	Oberlin	69
69	Wooster	88
54	Ohio Wesleyan ■	51
87	Denison	77
60	Wittenberg	103
60	Wooster ■	93
99	Kenyon ■	87

Nickname: Terriers
Colors: Red & Blue
Arena: Price Gymnasium
  Capacity: 2,000; Year Built: 1959
AD: Thomas E. Mulligan
SID: Jason Tirotta

HOBART
Geneva, NY 14456 III

Coach: Richard Roche, Hobart 1987

2001-02 RESULTS (12-13)
81	Fredonia St. †	68
72	Merchant Marine	81
51	Rochester	70
87	Ithaca ■	74
76	Rochester Inst. ■	90
65	Cazenovia	72
71	Utica	66
48	Colgate	85
69	Ripon †	81
74	Carroll (Wis.) †	67
69	Hilbert	57
79	Vassar ■	50
69	Rensselaer ■	78
86	Skidmore	57
71	Union (N.Y.)	77
57	Hamilton ■	81
57	St. Lawrence ■	55
69	Clarkson ■	64
52	Hamilton	83
69	Union (N.Y.) ■	70
96	Skidmore ■	65
71	Rensselaer	65
73	Vassar	61
61	Clarkson	72
45	St. Lawrence	68

Nickname: Statesmen
Colors: Royal Purple and Orange
Arena: Bristol Gym
  Capacity: 1,500; Year Built: 1965
AD: Michael J. Hanna
SID: Ken DeBolt

HOFSTRA
Hempstead, NY 11549.............I

Coach: Tom Pecora, Adelphi 1983

2001-02 RESULTS (12-20)
67	Fla. Atlantic ■	65
67	Kent St. †	64
60	South Fla. †	79
82	Illinois St. †	80
67	Iona †	54
65	Syracuse	91
76	Stony Brook ■	67
75	St. John's (N.Y.)	89
67	Manhattan	74
58	Drexel	70
71	Ill.-Chicago †	79
60	Bucknell †	68
67	Old Dominion ■	66
58	UNC Wilmington ■	69
77	Va. Commonwealth ■	62
49	James Madison ■	68
68	George Mason	82
68	William & Mary ■	59
74	Drexel ■	84
74	Delaware ■	67
62	Towson	60
54	UNC Wilmington	78
67	Va. Commonwealth	69
61	George Mason ■	62
71	James Madison ■	80
57	William & Mary	61
53	Old Dominion	69
63	Delaware	75
60	Towson ■	61
72	Towson †	52
82	George Mason †	76
54	Va. Commonwealth †	70

Nickname: Pride
Colors: Gold, White and Blue
Arena: Hofstra Arena
  Capacity: 5,124; Year Built: 1999
AD: Harry H. Royle
SID: Jeremy Kniffin

HOLY CROSS
Worcester, MA 01610-2395 I

Coach: Ralph Willard, Holy Cross 1967

2001-02 RESULTS (18-15)
42	Colgate ■	46
85	Quinnipiac ■	57
65	Harvard ■	57
62	Manhattan	75
47	Dartmouth	58
49	Boston U. ■	61
67	Massachusetts	56
76	Brown ■	63
51	Boston College	75
59	Iona †	71
60	Portland †	43
57	Boston College †	67
49	Radford †	66
57	La.-Monroe †	63
95	Fordham ■	75
50	Princeton	52
70	Navy ■	57
58	Lafayette	64
72	Lehigh	66
46	Army	57
63	American ■	54
73	Bucknell	65
62	Navy	54
76	Lafayette ■	70
55	Colgate	58
79	Lehigh ■	40
77	Army ■	57
73	Bucknell ■	75
68	American	44
59	Navy †	41
64	Bucknell †	57
58	American	54
59	Kansas †	70

Nickname: Crusaders
Colors: Royal Purple
Arena: Hart Recreation Center
  Capacity: 3,600; Year Built: 1975

AD: Richard M. Regan Jr.
SID: Frank Mastrandrea

HOPE
Holland, MI 49422-9000 III

Coach: Glenn Van Wieren, Hope 1964

2001-02 RESULTS (21-9)
88	Trinity Christian ■	64
78	Northwestern (Iowa) ■	81
71	Spring Arbor	72
80	Manchester ■	46
61	Cornerstone	75
80	Trinity Christian	76
78	Aquinas	73
80	Huntington ■	91
79	North Central	69
83	Grace Bible (Mich.) ■	51
80	Madonna ■	67
69	Mount Union ■	43
87	Kalamazoo ■	60
80	Adrian	62
81	Olivet	82
86	Alma	70
68	Calvin ■	70
78	Albion ■	73
75	Kalamazoo	68
65	Adrian ■	58
93	Olivet ■	72
86	Orchard Lake ■	73
82	Alma	78
64	Calvin	78
39	Albion	53
86	Alma ■	73
68	Kalamazoo †	67
70	Calvin	63
54	St. Norbert	53
57	Carthage	63

Nickname: Flying Dutchmen
Colors: Blue & Orange
Arena: Holland Civic Center
  Capacity: 2,550; Year Built: 1954
AD: Raymond E. Smith
SID: Tom Renner

HOUSTON
Houston, TX 77204...................I

Coach: Ray McCallum, Ball St. 1983

2001-02 RESULTS (18-15)
60	UCLA †	71
78	Kansas †	95
76	Chaminade †	73
62	Rice ■	61
75	North Texas ■	69
82	Texas Southern	79
64	Texas Tech ■	71
89	Southwest Tex. St. ■	62
69	LSU	73
66	North Carolina St.	67
91	Tennessee St. ■	60
64	St. Louis	67
69	Tulane	66
62	Cincinnati	83
82	TCU ■	71
99	Prairie View	85
80	UAB	71
74	Southern Miss. ■	66
66	Memphis ■	84
66	San Diego St.	78
68	Charlotte	83
68	Southern Miss.	60
69	TCU	87
91	South Fla. ■	75
76	Memphis	73
85	Tulane ■	81
46	East Caro.	63
57	South Fla.	88
76	UAB ■	72
58	East Caro. †	49
80	Memphis †	74

Nickname: Cougars
Colors: Scarlet & White
Arena: Hofheinz Pavilion
  Capacity: 8,479; Year Built: 1969
AD: Dave Maggard
SID: Chris Burkhalter

HOWARD
Washington, DC 20059............I

Coach: Frankie Allen, Roanoke 1971

2001-02 RESULTS (18-13)
76	Mercer †	68
66	Virginia	115
72	St. Francis (N.Y.) ■	85
99	Cal St. Northridge ■	65
71	Miami (Fla.)	87
71	N.C. A&T	64
58	South Carolina St.	63
80	American ■	71
88	St. Francis (Pa.) ■	67
80	Georgetown	99
77	Towson †	57
84	Lafayette	93
93	Morgan St. ■	76
84	Coppin St. ■	67
82	Florida A&M ■	76
73	Bethune-Cookman ■	66
84	Norfolk St.	87
58	Hampton	79
75	Md.-East. Shore ■	65
75	N.C. A&T ■	77
81	South Carolina St. ■	72
64	Morgan St.	66
88	Coppin St.	72
58	Florida A&M ■	55
69	Bethune-Cookman	72
73	Norfolk St. ■	63
82	Hampton ■	81
64	Delaware St. ■	71
71	Bethune-Cookman †	52
65	Delaware St. †	56
62	Hampton †	80

Nickname: Bison
Colors: Blue, White & Red
Arena: Burr Gymnasium
  Capacity: 2,700; Year Built: 1963
AD: Sondra Norrell-Thomas
SID: Edward Hill Jr.

HOWARD PAYNE
Brownwood, TX 76801 III

Coach: Charles Pattillo, Howard Payne 1965

2001-02 RESULTS (13-12)
81	Southwestern (Tex.)	66
76	Bridgewater (Va.) †	66
74	Texas Wesleyan	84
70	Wayland Baptist ■	84
98	LeTourneau	84
100	East Tex. Baptist	79
88	Texas-Dallas	85
83	Sul Ross St. ■	72
63	Incarnate Word	81
79	Austin ■	81
98	Ozarks (Ark.) ■	108
78	McMurry	84
72	Hardin-Simmons	64
86	Texas Lutheran ■	66
96	Schreiner	81
82	Concordia-Austin	86
67	Mary Hardin-Baylor	79
61	Sul Ross St.	95
83	Concordia-Austin ■	71
90	Mary Hardin-Baylor ■	85
85	McMurry ■	99
88	Hardin-Simmons ■	71

| 73 | Marquette † | 85 |
| 50 | Vanderbilt | 59 |

81	Texas Wesleyan ■	84
91	Texas Lutheran	98
99	Schreiner	93

Nickname: Yellow Jackets
Colors: Gold & Blue
Arena: Brownwood Coliseum
    Capacity: 5,000; Year Built: 1968
AD: Vance Gibson
SID: Nadir Dalleh

HUMBOLDT ST.
Arcata, CA 95521-8299 II

Coach: Tom Wood, UC Davis 1971

2001-02 RESULTS (25-4)

94	Barry †	84
119	BYU-Hawaii †	84
103	San Fran. St. ■	83
85	Southern Ore. ■	74
102	Dominican (Ill.) †	55
98	Sonoma St.	91
114	Northwest Nazarene	105
74	Seattle	71
83	Dominican (Ill.)	77
76	Sonoma St. ■	64
104	Western Ore. ■	78
93	Alas. Fairbanks ■	86
76	Alas. Anchorage ■	72
74	Central Wash.	88
84	St. Martin's	70
84	Seattle Pacific ■	78
100	Western Wash. ■	86
82	Seattle ■	67
101	Northwest Nazarene ■	77
80	Western Ore.	68
91	Alas. Anchorage	88
94	Alas. Fairbanks	65
102	St. Martin's ■	73
85	Central Wash. ■	72
66	Western Wash. ■	76
78	Seattle Pacific	81
89	Seattle Pacific †	82
65	Cal St. San B'dino	80

Nickname: Lumberjacks
Colors: Green & Gold
Arena: HSU East Gym
    Capacity: 1,400; Year Built: 1956
AD: Dan Collen
SID: Dan Pambianco

HUNTER
New York, NY 10021 III

Coach: Bill Healy, St. Joseph's 1983

2001-02 RESULTS (10-16)

53	Alvernia	68
74	New Jersey City †	79
92	FDU-Madison ■	80
74	John Jay	83
92	CCNY ■	74
67	Western Conn. St.	77
57	New York U.	54
78	Rutgers-Newark ■	68
66	St. Lawrence †	97
70	Scranton	84
76	Lehman	72
69	Baruch	80
68	Connecticut Col.	92
78	NYCCT	63
70	Staten Island ■	73
87	Ursinus ■	85
81	York (N.Y.) ■	85
88	Brooklyn ■	60
71	Medgar Evers ■	75
86	John Jay ■	84
58	CCNY	76
59	Lehman ■	77
85	Baruch ■	95
67	Manhattanville	76
102	Centenary (N.J.)	75
87	Medgar Evers ■	88

Nickname: Hawks
Colors: Purple, White & Gold
Arena: Hunter College Sportsplex
    Capacity: 1,500; Year Built: 1985
AD: Terry Ann Wansart
SID: Damion Jones

IDAHO
Moscow, ID 83843-2302 I

Coach: Leonard Perry, Idaho 1995

2001-02 RESULTS (9-19)

86	Western Mont. ■	72
59	Boise St.	68
66	Portland ■	71
44	Boise St. ■	70
55	Washington St.	81
48	Eastern Wash. ■	59
48	Montana ■	47
48	Pacific (Cal.) ■	52
48	Brigham Young	70
56	Cal St. Northridge ■	57
75	Sacramento St.	63
53	UC Santa Barb.	76
57	Cal Poly	72
69	Long Beach St. ■	67
54	UC Irvine ■	92
60	UC Riverside	58
63	Cal St. Fullerton	59
46	Utah St.	57
54	Cal Poly ■	56
40	UC Santa Barb. ■	37
38	UC Irvine	52
64	Long Beach St.	62
56	UC Riverside ■	67
65	Cal St. Fullerton ■	53
56	Utah St.	65
46	Cal St. Northridge	63
49	Pacific (Cal.)	57
41	Utah St. †	61

Nickname: Vandals
Colors: Silver & Gold
Arena: Cowan Spectrum
    Capacity: 7,000; Year Built: 1975
AD: Mike R. Bohn
SID: Becky Paull

IDAHO ST.
Pocatello, ID 83209 I

Coach: Doug Oliver, San Jose St. 1973

2001-02 RESULTS (10-17)

56	Loyola Marymount	67
96	Portland	90
73	Southern Utah ■	71
59	Utah St.	64
96	Montana Tech ■	72
72	Texas-San Antonio †	81
76	Southern U. †	71
51	Southern Utah	68
73	Western Mont. ■	69
58	Utah	75
59	Birmingham-So. †	55
56	Utah St.	74
83	Portland ■	79
87	Sacramento St. ■	79
77	Northern Ariz. ■	64
47	Montana St.	78
65	Montana	74
77	Portland St. ■	87
71	Eastern Wash. ■	76
46	Weber St. ■	65
76	Northern Ariz.	77
80	Sacramento St.	90
79	Montana ■	64
59	Montana St. ■	63
60	Eastern Wash.	70
78	Portland St.	91
82	Weber St.	88

Nickname: Bengals
Colors: Orange & Black
Arena: Reed Gymnasium
    Capacity: 3,241; Year Built: 1951

AD: Howard L. Gauthier
SID: Frank Mercogliano

ILLINOIS
Champaign, IL 61820 I

Coach: Bill Self, Oklahoma St. 1985

2001-02 RESULTS (26-9)

76	Gonzaga ■	58
93	Eastern Ill. ■	53
78	Pennsylvania †	71
105	Georgia Tech †	66
75	Southern Ill. †	72
63	Maryland	76
80	Tex. A&M-Corp. Chris. ■	56
82	Arizona †	87
94	Arkansas †	91
98	Western Ill. ■	62
87	Illinois St. ■	73
72	Missouri †	61
87	Loyola (Ill.) ■	72
76	Minnesota ■	53
66	Wisconsin	72
75	Purdue	84
94	Michigan ■	70
77	Iowa ■	66
80	Wisconsin ■	48
57	Indiana	88
67	Ohio St.	78
61	Michigan St. ■	67
68	Michigan	60
69	Purdue ■	67
63	Michigan St.	61
75	Seton Hall	65
83	Penn St. ■	56
56	Northwestern	41
70	Indiana ■	62
67	Minnesota	66
92	Minnesota †	76
88	Ohio St. †	94
93	San Diego St. †	64
72	Creighton †	60
69	Kansas †	73

Nickname: Fighting Illini
Colors: Orange & Blue
Arena: Assembly Hall
    Capacity: 16,450; Year Built: 1963
AD: Ronald E. Guenther
SID: Kent Brown

ILLINOIS COL.
Jacksonville, IL 62650-2299 III

Coach: Mike Worrell, Urbana 1986

2001-02 RESULTS (13-11)

89	Sanford Brown	44
82	Blackburn ■	71
69	Carthage ■	74
79	Knox ■	58
70	MacMurray ■	85
79	Millikin ■	64
58	Wittenberg ■	81
91	Baldwin-Wallace †	74
130	Grinnell	124
67	Lake Forest	71
72	Ripon ■	77
55	St. Norbert ■	68
79	Monmouth (Ill.) ■	69
77	Carroll (Wis.) ■	73
68	Beloit	72
83	Lawrence ■	60
80	Carroll (Wis.) ■	73
105	Knox	79
44	St. Norbert	66
69	Ripon	82
77	Lake Forest ■	46
113	Grinnell ■	107
69	Monmouth (Ill.)	90
47	Ripon †	87

Nickname: Blueboys
Colors: Blue & White
Arena: Memorial Gymnasium
    Capacity: 2,000; Year Built: 1951

AD: Gale F. Vaughn
SID: Jim Murphy

ILLINOIS ST.
Normal, IL 61790-2660 I

Coach: Tom Richardson, St. Xavier 1977

2001-02 RESULTS (17-14)

74	Weber St. ■	70
58	UC Irvine †	52
46	Pittsburgh †	65
80	Hofstra †	82
76	Ga. Southern	87
82	Texas-San Antonio	88
65	Samford ■	54
72	Central Mich. ■	63
59	Chattanooga	70
73	Illinois	87
48	Kent St. ■	61
62	Creighton ■	76
58	Southern Ill.	79
81	Wichita St. ■	71
73	Drake	83
68	Indiana St. ■	56
56	Creighton	63
61	Southwest Mo. St. ■	60
58	Bradley	55
68	Drake ■	54
70	Northern Iowa ■	55
63	Southwest Mo. St.	68
60	Bradley ■	51
67	Indiana St.	61
73	Evansville	55
84	Southern Ill. ■	70
66	Wichita St.	77
71	Northern Iowa	66
82	Evansville ■	73
64	Drake †	63
63	Creighton †	90

Nickname: Redbirds
Colors: Red & White
Arena: Redbird Arena
    Capacity: 10,600; Year Built: 1989
AD: Perk Weisenburger
SID: Todd Kober

ILL. WESLEYAN
Bloomington, IL 61702-2900 III

Coach: Scott Trost, Minn.-Morris 1985

2001-02 RESULTS (12-12)

72	Concordia (Wis.) †	74
51	Ripon	73
88	Hardin-Simmons ■	47
84	Benedictine (Ill.) ■	56
65	Chicago ■	60
81	Aurora ■	58
58	Washington (Mo.)	81
81	Olivet Nazarene	88
73	St. Xavier †	67
97	Cal Lutheran	71
80	Elmhurst ■	70
77	Augustana (Ill.) ■	85
102	North Park ■	68
49	Carthage	72
63	Millikin	61
60	Wheaton (Ill.)	55
76	North Central ■	79
56	Carthage ■	76
61	Elmhurst	71
55	North Park	68
85	Wheaton (Ill.) ■	74
92	Augustana (Ill.)	106
74	North Central	77
82	Millikin	79

Nickname: Titans
Colors: Green & White
Arena: Shirk Center
    Capacity: 2,680; Year Built: 1994
AD: Dennis Bridges
SID: Stew Salowitz

ILL.-CHICAGO
Chicago, IL 60608 I

Coach: Jimmy Collins, New Mexico St. 1970

2001-02 RESULTS (20-14)

70	Indiana St. ■	54
96	St. Joseph's (Ind.) ■	53
64	Evansville ■	61
68	Southern Ill.	76
65	Old Dominion	71
93	North Central ■	53
86	Northern Ill. ■	69
73	Purdue	80
86	Texas A&M †	82
86	Southwest Mo. St. †	80
74	Mississippi St. †	77
79	Hofstra †	71
78	South Fla.	82
62	Detroit ■	61
69	Cleveland St. ■	83
75	Wis.-Green Bay	66
49	Wis.-Milwaukee	75
65	Loyola (Ill.)	76
99	IPFW	80
85	Youngstown St. ■	69
73	Butler ■	82
68	Wright St. ■	66
67	Detroit	74
70	Cleveland St.	76
63	Youngstown St.	57
73	Wis.-Milwaukee ■	71
75	Wis.-Green Bay ■	67
76	Loyola (Ill.) ■	63
62	Wright St.	63
61	Butler	85
75	Wis.-Milwaukee †	63
79	Detroit †	68
76	Loyola (Ill.) †	75
63	Oklahoma †	71

Nickname: Flames
Colors: Navy Blue & Fire Engine Red
Arena: UIC Pavilion
    Capacity: 9,200; Year Built: 1982
AD: James W. Schmidt
SID: Anne Schoenherr

INCARNATE WORD
San Antonio, TX 78209............II

Coach: Al Grushkin, Ogelthorpe 1975

2001-02 RESULTS (25-4)

67	Midwestern St.	65
81	Southwestern Okla. ■	70
78	Tex. A&M-Commerce ■	58
85	Midwestern St. ■	88
82	Central Ark. †	65
59	Loyola (La.) †	42
77	Texas Lutheran	63
81	Howard Payne ■	63
66	Tex. A&M-Kingsville ■	59
73	SIU-Edwardsville ■	72
76	Southeastern Okla. †	47
86	National Christian †	54
69	Lawrence ■	57
86	Rollins ■	65
68	Lincoln (Mo.)	76
55	Rockhurst	59
71	Drury ■	56
70	St. Edward's	65
74	Okla. Panhandle	61
72	St. Mary's (Tex.)	63
82	Lincoln (Mo.) ■	75
65	Rockhurst ■	50
84	Okla. Panhandle ■	72
80	Drury	78
87	National Christian ■	43
87	St. Edward's ■	75
66	St. Mary's (Tex.) ■	50
72	Tarleton St. †	59
56	Northwest Mo. St. †	61

Nickname: Crusaders
Colors: Red, Black & White
Arena: McDermott Center
    Capacity: 2,000; Year Built: 1990
AD: Mark Papich
SID: Wayne Witt

INDIANA
Bloomington, IN 47408-1590 I

Coach: Mike Davis, Thomas Edison 1995

2001-02 RESULTS (25-12)

65	Charlotte	61
101	Alas. Anchorage	66
49	Marquette †	50
77	Texas †	71
79	North Carolina	66
60	Southern Ill.	72
76	Notre Dame ■	75
74	Ball St. ■	61
53	Miami (Fla.)	58
52	Kentucky †	66
87	Eastern Wash. †	60
64	Butler †	66
59	Northwestern	44
61	Penn St. ■	54
83	Michigan St. ■	65
77	Iowa	66
67	Ohio St.	73
85	Penn St.	51
88	Illinois ■	57
66	Purdue ■	52
74	Minnesota	88
79	Iowa ■	51
77	Louisville	62
63	Wisconsin ■	64
75	Michigan	55
63	Ohio St. ■	57
54	Michigan St.	57
62	Illinois	70
79	Northwestern ■	67
67	Michigan St. †	56
60	Iowa †	62
75	Utah †	56
76	UNC Wilmington †	67
74	Duke †	73
81	Kent St. †	69
73	Oklahoma †	64
52	Maryland †	64

Nickname: Hoosiers
Colors: Cream & Crimson
Arena: Assembly Hall
    Capacity: 17,357; Year Built: 1971
AD: Michael McNeely
SID: Jeff Fanter

INDIANA (PA.)
Indiana, PA 15705-1077 II

Coach: Gary Edwards, Va. Wesleyan 1979

2001-02 RESULTS (28-5)

83	Taylor (Ind.) †	67
65	Gannon	92
84	West Chester ■	71
84	Cheyney	44
58	Dist. Columbia	54
86	Southern Va. ■	60
80	Kutztown	74
81	East Stroudsburg	67
111	Husson ■	83
95	Bloomsburg	73
103	Mansfield	87
79	Dist. Columbia ■	72
86	Millersville ■	49
92	Shippensburg	57
72	Clarion ■	67
75	Slippery Rock	60
70	Calif. (Pa.)	71
81	Edinboro ■	63
92	Centenary (N.J.) ■	44

95	Lock Haven ■	64
63	Shippensburg ■	56
67	Slippery Rock ■	50
75	Edinboro	77
71	Clarion	82
78	Lock Haven	77
83	Calif. (Pa.) ■	75
62	Clarion	55
86	Cheyney	81
71	Calif. (Pa.) †	68
91	Charleston (W.Va.) ■	81
85	Salem Int'l ■	81
78	Northwest Mo. St. †	72
52	Metro St. †	82

Nickname: Indians
Colors: Crimson & Gray
Arena: Memorial Field House
    Capacity: 2,365; Year Built: 1966
AD: Frank J. Condino
SID: Michael Hoffman

INDIANA ST.
Terre Haute, IN 47809...............I

Coach: Royce Waltman, Slippery Rock 1964

2001-02 RESULTS (6-22)

54	Ill.-Chicago	70
54	Valparaiso ■	71
49	Butler ■	69
50	Eastern Ill.	52
66	IUPUI ■	56
74	Murray St. ■	66
71	Drake	85
46	Creighton	70
58	Wyoming ■	72
54	Ball St.	68
55	Bowling Green ■	65
45	Evansville ■	40
70	Northern Iowa ■	71
56	Illinois St.	68
63	Wichita St.	64
73	Southern Ill.	91
71	Northern Iowa	65
53	Southwest Mo. St. ■	59
57	Bradley	60
84	Wichita St.	87
63	Creighton ■	64
61	Illinois St. ■	67
71	Bradley ■	66
82	Evansville	71
60	Drake ■	62
74	Southern Ill. ■	84
58	Southwest Mo. St.	70
58	Bradley †	70

Nickname: Sycamores
Colors: Blue & White
Arena: Hulman Center
    Capacity: 10,200; Year Built: 1972
AD: Andrea Myers
SID: Kent Johnson

IPFW
Fort Wayne, IN 46805-1499 II

Coach: Doug Noll, Malone 1979

2001-02 RESULTS (7-21)

73	Morehead St. ■	82
60	Toledo	69
62	Wright St.	75
80	Florida Int'l	82
68	Michigan St.	81
65	Maine †	73
62	Michigan	91
89	Ball St.	113
111	Indiana Tech ■	100
65	Tri-State	62
71	Colorado St.	92
59	Montana St.	63
59	Oregon St.	84
70	Long Beach St.	105

72	San Diego St.	90
79	Chicago St.	62
96	Eastern Ky.	100
80	Ill.-Chicago	99
77	Oakland ■	71
80	Middle Tenn.	90
81	Lipscomb ■	85
81	Concordia (Mich.) ■	60
66	Loyola (Ill.)	77
60	IUPUI	82
94	Grace (Ind.) ■	77
88	Chicago St.	86
71	Youngstown St.	78
66	UMKC	81

Nickname: Mastodons
Colors: Blue & White
Arena: Gates Sports Center
    Capacity: 2,700; Year Built: 1981
AD: Mark A. Pope
SID: Michael Jewell

IUPUI
Indianapolis, IN 46202.............I

Coach: Ron Hunter, Miami (Ohio) 1986

2001-02 RESULTS (15-15)

82	Cleveland St. ■	65
72	Middle Tenn.	76
96	Olivet Nazarene ■	71
109	Indiana Tech ■	82
56	Indiana St. ■	66
70	Ohio St.	83
81	Ball St. ■	103
90	Morehead St. ■	81
70	Mississippi †	77
86	Mississippi Val. †	74
98	Georgia Tech	92
80	Southern Utah ■	67
61	Chicago St. ■	54
76	Oral Roberts	85
64	UMKC	63
61	Western Mich.	62
69	Oakland	83
73	Valparaiso ■	74
59	Western Ill. ■	58
92	Chicago St.	59
53	Southern Utah	61
54	UMKC ■	55
71	Oral Roberts ■	88
82	IPFW †	60
92	Oakland ■	94
81	Western Ill.	77
75	Valparaiso	95
90	Oakland †	84
58	Oral Roberts †	53
55	Valparaiso †	88

Nickname: Jaguars
Colors: Red & Gold
Arena: IUPUI Gymnasium
    Capacity: 2,000; Year Built: 1982
AD: Michael R. Moore
SID: Kevin Buerge

INDIANAPOLIS
Indianapolis, IN 46227-3697 II

Coach: Todd Sturgeon, DePauw 1988

2001-02 RESULTS (15-12)

68	Seattle Pacific	67
65	Northwest Nazarene †	58
73	Wis.-Parkside	76
77	St. Joseph's (Ind.) ■	45
53	Northern Ky.	76
83	Bellarmine	65
90	Southern Ind. ■	91
82	Mo.-St. Louis ■	73
70	Michigan Tech	79
47	Marian (Ind.) ■	62
72	Oakland City ■	67
74	SIU-Edwardsville	71
64	Lewis	74

89	St. Joseph's (Ind.) ■	.79
63	Brescia ■	.52
79	Bellarmine ■	.77
100	Ky. Wesleyan ■	106
64	Mo.-St. Louis	.63
87	Quincy	.70
69	Lewis ■	.74
67	Wis.-Parkside ■	.54
61	Northern Ky. ■	.80
88	Ky. Wesleyan ■	.94
68	Southern Ind.	.86
82	Quincy	.76
93	SIU-Edwardsville ■	.68
79	Southern Ind. †	.82

Nickname: Greyhounds
Colors: Crimson & Grey
Arena: Nicoson Hall
  Capacity: 4,000; Year Built: 1960
AD: David J. Huffman
SID: Joe Gentry

IONA
New Rochelle, NY 10801 I

Coach: Jeff Ruland, Iona 1991
2001-02 RESULTS (13-17)

64	Akron ■	.67
74	Bethune-Cookman	.81
61	Rhode Island	.66
74	Fordham ■	.78
54	Hofstra †	.67
73	Wagner	.88
82	Fairfield	.78
75	Canisius ■	.65
71	Holy Cross †	.59
56	Hawaii	.67
57	Miami (Ohio) †	.51
73	Seton Hall ■	.99
58	Manhattan †	.69
70	Siena ■	.79
85	St. Peter's	.53
79	Rider ■	.82
68	Loyola (Md.) ■	.63
80	Marist	.96
90	Fairfield ■	.79
71	Siena	.84
75	Manhattan ■	.70
61	Canisius ■	.60
74	Niagara	.84
81	St. Peter's ■	.83
71	Marist ■	.79
64	Loyola (Md.) ■	.50
65	Rider ■	.63
77	Niagara ■	.76
66	Manhattan	.81
83	Niagara †	.89

Nickname: Gaels
Colors: Maroon & Gold
Arena: Mulcahy Center
  Capacity: 2,611; Year Built: 1974
AD: Shawn Brennan
SID: Mike Laprey

IOWA
Iowa City, IA 52242 I

Coach: Steve Alford, Indiana 1987
2001-02 RESULTS (19-16)

89	Md.-East. Shore ■	.59
90	Boston U. ■	.61
75	Louisiana Tech ■	.67
75	Memphis †	.71
77	Missouri †	.78
62	Duke †	.80
73	Alabama St. ■	.64
86	Southern Methodist ■	.69
76	Northern Iowa	.78
78	Iowa St.	.53
101	Drake ■	.59
83	Missouri	.65
89	Kansas St. ■	.70

77	Mercer ■	.43
69	Wisconsin ■	.57
62	Ohio St.	.72
70	Northwestern ■	.60
66	Indiana ■	.77
66	Illinois	.77
50	Northwestern	.63
75	Michigan St. ■	.71
68	Purdue ■	.73
81	Penn St. ■	.64
51	Indiana	.79
78	Minnesota ■	.86
65	Penn St.	.71
66	Ohio St. ■	.72
56	Wisconsin	.64
76	Michigan	.56
79	Michigan St. ■	.93
87	Purdue †	.72
58	Wisconsin †	.56
62	Indiana †	.60
64	Ohio St. †	.81
61	LSU ■	.63

Nickname: Hawkeyes
Colors: Old Gold & Black
Arena: Carver-Hawkeye Arena
  Capacity: 15,500; Year Built: 1983
AD: Robert A. Bowlsby
SID: Steve Roe

IOWA ST.
Ames, IA 50011 I

Coach: Larry Eustachy,
Long Beach St. 1979
2001-02 RESULTS (12-19)

83	Hartford ■	.54
57	Southern Ill. †	.66
77	St. Louis †	.72
77	Pennsylvania †	.84
64	Savannah St. ■	.39
71	Wis.-Milwaukee ■	.62
62	San Jose St. ■	.64
66	Ark.-Pine Bluff ■	.43
53	Iowa ■	.78
81	Boston College	.86
58	Drake	.72
77	Md.-East. Shore ■	.54
88	Northern Iowa ■	.69
69	Morris Brown ■	.45
74	Baylor	.79
71	Missouri ■	.67
66	Oklahoma St. ■	.69
61	Colorado	.63
52	Kansas St.	.63
81	Kansas ■	.88
84	Nebraska	.86
50	Texas A&M ■	.52
43	Texas Tech	.69
73	Missouri	.76
89	Colorado ■	.63
85	Nebraska ■	.79
66	Kansas	102
73	Kansas St. ■	.71
75	Oklahoma	.89
76	Texas ■	.79
59	Missouri †	.79

Nickname: Cyclones
Colors: Cardinal & Gold
Arena: James H. Hilton Coliseum
  Capacity: 14,092; Year Built: 1971
AD: Bruce Van De Velde
SID: Mike Green

ITHACA
Ithaca, NY 14850 III

Coach: Jim Mullins, Connecticut 1980
2001-02 RESULTS (16-10)

84	Westfield St. †	.76
63	Salve Regina †	.55
68	Geneseo St. ■	.81

74	Hobart	.87
45	Cornell	.77
69	St. Lawrence ■	.72
63	Cortland St. ■	.57
76	Pitt.-Bradford	.89
64	Geneseo St.	.57
86	Cazenovia	.87
62	St. John Fisher	.53
71	Alfred	.68
61	Elmira	.84
68	Utica	.75
86	Nazareth ■	.67
71	Rochester Inst. ■	.68
86	Oneonta St. ■	.72
62	Hartwick ■	.52
71	Utica ■	.72
86	Elmira ■	.67
56	Rochester Inst.	.39
64	Nazareth	.47
66	Hartwick	.46
61	Alfred ■	.47
65	St. John Fisher ■	.62
67	Alvernia	.76

Nickname: Bombers
Colors: Blue & Gold
Arena: Ben Light Gymnasium
  Capacity: 2,500; Year Built: 1964
AD: Kristen Ford
SID: Mike Warwick

JACKSON ST.
Jackson, MS 39217 I

Coach: Andy Stoglin, UTEP 1965
2001-02 RESULTS (9-19)

87	Prairie View ■	.61
58	Southern Miss.	.83
68	Stephen F. Austin ■	.59
79	Arkansas St. ■	.90
68	Missouri	106
96	Louisiana Tech ■	.99
63	McNeese St. ■	.70
41	Oklahoma St.	.90
80	Alabama A&M ■	.90
63	Alabama St. ■	.71
59	Louisiana Tech	.74
68	UAB	.88
75	Alcorn St.	.86
68	Southern U.	.60
66	Texas Southern ■	.57
96	Grambling ■	.91
78	Mississippi Val.	.85
79	Ark.-Pine Bluff	.81
78	Alcorn St. ■	.81
81	Southern U. ■	.91
74	Texas Southern	.71
68	Prairie View	.55
83	Grambling	.98
89	Mississippi Val. ■	.75
83	Ark.-Pine Bluff ■	.61
83	Alabama A&M	105
60	Alabama St.	.61
56	Alabama St.	.60

Nickname: Tigers
Colors: Blue & White
Arena: Williams Athletics Center
  Capacity: 8,000; Year Built: 1981
AD: Roy E. Culberson
SID: Sam Jefferson

JACKSONVILLE
Jacksonville, FL 32211-3394 I

Coach: Hugh Durham, Florida St. 1959
2001-02 RESULTS (18-12)

73	Fla. Atlantic	.58
84	Georgia St.	.72
77	Florida Tech	.67
73	New Orleans ■	.58
72	Fla. Atlantic	.76
58	Belmont ■	.37

72	UCF	.73
67	Stetson ■	.57
91	Savannah St. ■	.49
90	Texas	.96
67	Wichita St.	.65
64	Oral Roberts †	.73
52	Niagara †	.64
85	P.R.-Mayaguez †	.43
58	Savannah St.	.55
69	Jacksonville St. ■	.67
58	Samford ■	.65
67	Campbell	.53
75	Mercer ■	.62
74	Troy St. ■	.71
58	Stetson	.68
74	Mercer	.58
61	Troy St.	.76
75	Georgia St. ■	.81
85	Campbell ■	.57
51	Samford	.52
100	Jacksonville St.	.98
68	Belmont ■	.91
82	UCF ■	.80
50	Fla. Atlantic †	.59

Nickname: Dolphins
Colors: Green & White
Arena: Swisher Gymnasium
  Capacity: 1,500; Year Built: 1953
AD: Hugh Durham
SID: Jamie Zeitz

JACKSONVILLE ST.
Jacksonville, AL 36265-1602 I

Coach: Mike LaPlante, Maine 1989
2001-02 RESULTS (13-16)

53	Auburn	.75
63	Birmingham-So.	.52
52	Troy St.	.70
53	Mercer	.71
57	Alabama	.99
72	UCF ■	.69
71	Fla. Atlantic ■	.74
59	Samford	.57
67	Jacksonville	.69
83	Stetson	.89
72	Belmont ■	.74
81	Georgia St. ■	.75
79	Campbell ■	.84
59	Samford ■	.56
64	Savannah St.	.55
61	Georgia St.	.80
78	Campbell	.66
83	Savannah St. ■	.63
91	Belmont	.71
90	Stetson ■	.78
98	Jacksonville ■	100
72	Morris Brown	.77
68	Fla. Atlantic	.78
50	UCF	.68
90	Morris Brown ■	.59
95	Mercer ■	.68
60	Troy St. †	.79
69	Troy St. †	.62
47	Fla. Atlantic †	.55

Nickname: Gamecocks
Colors: Red & White
Arena: Pete Mathews Coliseum
  Capacity: 5,500; Year Built: 1974
AD: Tom Seitz
SID: Greg Seitz

JAMES MADISON
Harrisonburg, VA 22807 I

Coach: Sherman Dillard, James Madison
1978
2001-02 RESULTS (14-15)

58	North Carolina St.	.75
85	Gardner-Webb ■	.67
58	Drexel ■	.71

91	West Virginia ■	75
77	Liberty	67
57	East Tenn. St.	84
85	Penn St.	69
84	Morgan St. ■	66
56	Cornell †	40
94	VMI †	84
50	Delaware	51
75	Va. Commonwealth	82
68	Hofstra ■	49
59	Drexel	69
59	UNC Wilmington	63
59	William & Mary	77
86	Towson ■	75
67	Old Dominion ■	61
68	George Mason	80
58	William & Mary ■	63
67	Va. Commonwealth ■	65
61	UNC Wilmington ■	69
80	Hofstra	71
68	Old Dominion	73
83	Towson	71
74	George Mason ■	81
64	Delaware	65
78	William & Mary †	67
62	UNC Wilmington †	78

Nickname: Dukes
Colors: Purple & Gold
Arena: JMU Convocation Center
Capacity: 7,156; Year Built: 1982
AD: Jeffrey T. Bourne
SID: Gary Michael

JOHN CARROLL
University Hgts., OH 44118-4581 ...III

Coach: Mike Moran, Xavier 1973
2001-02 RESULTS (12-13)

66	Lebanon Valley †	76
60	Gettysburg	64
81	Trevecca Nazarene †	91
81	Berry †	67
68	Wilmington (Ohio) ■	56
81	Heidelberg ■	79
65	Marietta	78
84	Ohio Northern	99
61	Mount Union ■	81
91	St. Lawrence †	88
76	Hampden-Sydney †	98
54	Capital	65
84	Muskingum ■	78
63	Otterbein	82
73	Baldwin-Wallace	68
74	Marietta ■	81
79	Heidelberg	56
86	Ohio Northern ■	70
81	Mount Union	80
84	Capital ■	103
96	Muskingum	86
84	Otterbein ■	89
91	Baldwin-Wallace ■	87
81	Wilmington (Ohio)	72
73	Ohio Northern	85

Nickname: Blue Streaks
Colors: Blue & Gold
Arena: Don Shula Sports Center
Capacity: 2,400; Year Built: 1957
AD: Anthony J. DeCarlo
SID: Chris Wenzler

JOHN JAY
New York, NY 10019 ...III

Coach: Guy Rancourt, Western Conn. St. 1997
2001-02 RESULTS (18-8)

56	Rutgers-Camden ■	60
79	New Paltz St. ■	68
87	FDU-Madison ■	85
83	Hunter ■	74
69	Vassar	67

59	Baruch ■	71
63	Col. of New Jersey ■	58
65	Maritime (N.Y.)	55
67	Chowan †	65
67	Lebanon Valley	71
69	New York U. ■	48
73	Stevens Tech ■	69
71	CCNY ■	68
66	Lehman	72
71	Staten Island	79
67	York (N.Y.) ■	71
89	Brooklyn	53
88	Polytechnic (N.Y.) ■	38
62	NYCCT	59
84	Hunter	86
76	Baruch	63
86	CCNY	76
68	Lehman ■	64
69	Medgar Evers ■	57
69	Farmingdale St.	67
64	Baruch †	80

Nickname: Bloodhounds
Colors: Blue & Gold
Arena: College Gym
Capacity: 700; Year Built: 1989
AD: Susan Larkin
SID: Terry Small

JOHNS HOPKINS
Baltimore, MD 21218-2684 ...III

Coach: Bill Nelson, Brockport St. 1965
2001-02 RESULTS (15-9)

61	Greensboro ■	66
93	Case Reserve ■	67
66	Goucher	74
69	Otterbein †	81
92	Roanoke †	86
64	Elizabethtown	89
73	Haverford	58
57	Gettysburg	65
74	Carnegie Mellon ■	61
72	Oneonta St. †	58
93	Bethany (Cal.) †	60
84	Washington (Md.)	76
87	Villa Julie ■	59
79	Catholic ■	84
81	Dickinson	90
74	McDaniel ■	44
68	Frank. & Marsh. ■	61
95	Ursinus ■	63
65	Gettysburg ■	68
62	Muhlenberg	52
69	Swarthmore ■	56
69	Dickinson ■	52
67	McDaniel	36
54	Frank. & Marsh.	61

Nickname: Blue Jays
Colors: Columbia Blue & Black
Arena: White Athletic Center
Capacity: 1,200; Year Built: 1965
AD: Thomas P. Calder
SID: Ernie Larossa

JOHNSON & WALES
Providence, RI 02903 ...III

Coach: Todd Finn,
2001-02 RESULTS (16-13)

46	Babson	83
70	Worcester St. †	65
87	Anna Maria	95
73	Coast Guard ■	94
49	Endicott	64
86	Connecticut Col.	82
57	Roger Williams	58
66	Salve Regina	75
66	Mount Ida	65
60	Rhode Island Col. ■	60
47	Mass.-Dartmouth	88
71	Plymouth St. ■	65
73	Southern Vt. ■	70

59	Emerson ■	72
66	Western New Eng. ■	75
96	Emmanuel (Mass.)	83
80	Suffolk ■	94
87	Albertus Magnus ■	78
82	Rivier	79
72	Norwich	64
81	Suffolk	97
83	Daniel Webster ■	71
90	Emmanuel (Mass.) ■	80
93	Emerson	75
84	Albertus Magnus	66
78	Albertus Magnus ■	55
83	Western New Eng.	69
71	Suffolk †	76
76	Salve Regina	83

Nickname: Wildcats
Colors: Red, Gold & Royal Blue
Arena: Harborside Student Center
Capacity: 1,500; Year Built: 1998
AD: John Parente
SID: John Parente

JOHNSON SMITH
Charlotte, NC 28216 ...II

Coach: Steve Joyner, Johnson Smith 1973
2001-02 RESULTS (23-8)

110	Robert Morris (Ill.) ■	59
70	Virginia Union	56
79	Belmont Abbey ■	60
57	Virginia Union †	64
63	Lenoir-Rhyne †	58
76	Eckerd †	75
51	Fayetteville St. †	55
81	Elizabeth City St.	76
85	LeMoyne-Owen ■	65
85	Catawba	79
67	GC&SU †	61
79	Columbus St.	83
102	St. Paul's ■	74
87	Fayetteville St.	85
89	Bowie St.	91
86	Winston-Salem ■	71
93	St. Augustine's	80
84	Winston-Salem	71
89	N.C. Central	86
79	Livingstone	70
89	Virginia St. ■	75
88	Livingstone	74
96	St. Augustine's	82
99	Shaw	102
74	Fayetteville St. ■	73
103	N.C. Central	105
81	St. Augustine's †	59
84	Bowie St. †	67
68	Shaw †	82
73	Augusta St. †	70
66	Carson-Newman	77

Nickname: Golden Bulls
Colors: Blue & Gold
Arena: Brayboy Gymnasium
Capacity: 2,500; Year Built: 1961
AD: Henry White
SID: Patricia Harvey

JOHNSON ST.
Johnson, VT 05656-9464 ...III

Coach: Charles Mason, Concordia-Mont. 1991
2001-02 RESULTS (14-11)

63	Mass.-Dartmouth	102
80	Connecticut Col. †	93
84	Plymouth St. ■	88
75	Norwich	77
76	Anna Maria	63
60	Middlebury	87
79	Thomas	58
98	Lyndon St.	57
90	New England Col.	78

92	Emmanuel (Mass.)	88
75	St. Joseph (Vt.)	51
83	Green Mountain ■	69
79	Castleton St.	68
75	Plattsburgh St.	88
58	Gordon	70
92	Becker	70
77	Castleton St.	70
82	Hampshire	58
81	Notre Dame (N.H.) ■	93
73	Green Mountain	80
93	Lyndon St. ■	81
61	St. Joseph (Vt.) ■	68
86	Notre Dame (N.H.)	71
63	St. Joseph (Vt.)	71

Nickname: Badgers
Colors: Green, Blue & White
Arena: Carter Gymnasium
Capacity: 700; Year Built: 1965
AD: Barbara Lougee Fountain
SID: Gregory Dixon

JUNIATA
Huntingdon, PA 16652 ...III

Coach: Greg Curley, Allegheny 1995
2001-02 RESULTS (10-14)

87	Villa Julie ■	74
74	Methodist ■	58
73	Norwich †	49
64	Carnegie Mellon	43
88	Penn St.-Altoona ■	42
58	Grove City	77
80	Messiah	69
46	Widener ■	64
87	York (Pa.) ■	88
63	Pitt.-Greensburg	51
68	Susquehanna	74
80	Villa Julie	61
83	Elizabethtown	92
100	Albright	92
72	Moravian	86
58	Lebanon Valley ■	67
54	Widener	64
66	Dickinson	79
51	Messiah ■	75
49	Elizabethtown	96
72	Susquehanna ■	80
80	Albright ■	62
56	Lebanon Valley	67
60	Moravian ■	64

Nickname: Eagles
Colors: Yale Blue & Old Gold
Arena: Kennedy Sports & Recreation Center
Capacity: 1,500; Year Built: 1982
AD: Lawrence R. Bock
SID: Bub Parker

KALAMAZOO
Kalamazoo, MI 49006-3295 ...III

Coach: Joe Haklin, Wabash 1973
2001-02 RESULTS (17-10)

68	Lake Forest ■	49
81	Madonna	73
74	Concordia (Mich.) ■	36
64	Goshen ■	48
57	Marian (Ind.) †	73
87	Mich.-Dearborn †	46
72	Chicago	79
82	Cornerstone †	94
89	St. Joseph (Vt.) †	66
78	Hillsdale	91
61	Purdue-Calumet	57
60	Marietta	61
91	Kenyon †	64
60	Hope	87
65	Calvin ■	42
68	Alma ■	58
75	Albion	72
71	Adrian ■	62

70	Olivet	.66
68	Hope ■	.75
65	Calvin	.71
78	Alma	.57
67	Albion ■	.62
66	Adrian	.78
86	Olivet ■	.67
75	Olivet ■	.67
67	Hope †	.68

Nickname: Hornets
Colors: Orange & Black
Arena: Anderson Athletic Center
    Capacity: 2,000; Year Built: 1980
AD: Robert L. Kent
SID: Steve Wideen

KANSAS
Lawrence, KS 66045-8881 I

Coach: Roy Williams,
North Carolina 1972

2001-02 RESULTS (33-4)

91	Ball St. †	.93
95	Houston †	.78
80	Seton Hall †	.62
105	Pittsburg St. ■	.62
105	Arizona	.97
83	Wake Forest ■	.76
79	UMKC ■	.68
78	Princeton	.62
106	South Carolina St. ■	.73
108	North Dakota	.77
93	Tulsa †	.85
81	Valparaiso	.73
97	Colorado	.85
96	Nebraska ■	.57
77	UCLA	.87
79	Oklahoma St.	.61
74	Oklahoma	.67
88	Iowa St.	.81
86	Texas A&M	.74
105	Missouri ■	.73
100	Colorado ■	.73
98	Kansas St.	.71
108	Texas Tech ■	.81
110	Texas	.103
87	Baylor	.72
102	Iowa St. ■	.66
88	Nebraska	.87
103	Kansas St. ■	.68
95	Missouri	.92
102	Colorado †	.73
90	Texas Tech †	.50
55	Oklahoma †	.64
70	Holy Cross †	.59
86	Stanford †	.63
73	Illinois †	.69
104	Oregon †	.86
88	Maryland †	.97

Nickname: Jayhawks
Colors: Crimson & Blue
Arena: Allen Fieldhouse
    Capacity: 16,300; Year Built: 1955
AD: Allen Bohl
SID: Mitch Germann

KANSAS ST.
Manhattan, KS 66502-3355 I

Coach: Jim Wooldridge,
Louisiana Tech 1977

2001-02 RESULTS (13-16)

64	Troy St. ■	.60
68	Wis.-Green Bay ■	.55
65	Mississippi ■	.67
79	Tennessee St. ■	.73
75	Gardner-Webb ■	.57
56	Wichita St.	.65
56	Northwestern	.79
84	North Texas ■	.70
64	Western Caro. ■	.66
70	Iowa	.89

88	Fairleigh Dickinson ■	.45
49	Texas Tech	.74
66	Missouri ■	.81
70	Baylor	.73
63	Iowa St. ■	.52
71	Colorado	.85
74	Missouri	.86
71	Texas	.70
70	Oklahoma St. ■	.61
71	Kansas ■	.98
82	Nebraska	.99
69	Texas A&M ■	.38
62	Oklahoma	.73
66	Colorado	.64
71	Iowa St.	.73
68	Kansas	.103
67	Nebraska ■	.58
74	Baylor †	.73
52	Oklahoma †	.63

Nickname: Wildcats
Colors: Purple & White
Arena: Bramlage Coliseum
    Capacity: 13,500; Year Built: 1988
AD: Tim Weiser
SID: Garry Bowman

KEAN
Union, NJ 07083 III

Coach: Bruce Hamburger, Kean 1981

2001-02 RESULTS (10-15)

83	Nichols †	.54
89	Endicott †	.53
84	New Jersey City ■	.82
51	Rowan	.66
63	Rutgers-Newark ■	.53
71	Col. of New Jersey	.72
74	Staten Island	.77
85	Montclair St.	.92
72	Ramapo	.84
73	Scranton ■	.57
69	NYCCT	.55
64	Maritime (N.Y.) †	.48
75	Villa Julie	.84
51	Richard Stockton	.61
70	Rutgers-Camden	.71
75	Wm. Paterson ■	.78
84	Col. of New Jersey ■	.58
53	Rutgers-Newark	.41
53	Rowan ■	.56
69	New Jersey City	.73
65	Ramapo ■	.70
58	Montclair St. ■	.61
43	Richard Stockton ■	.62
52	Wm. Paterson	.62
82	Rutgers-Camden ■	.72

Nickname: Cougars
Colors: Blue & Silver
Arena: D'angola Gymnasium
    Capacity: 700; Year Built: 1958
AD: Glenn Hedden
SID: Jack McKiernan

KEENE ST.
Keene, NH 03435-0000 III

Coach: Rob Colbert, Marist 1992

2001-02 RESULTS (23-5)

108	Notre Dame (N.H.) ■	.63
77	Fitchburg St. ■	.55
82	Endicott ■	.56
88	Springfield	.92
99	Mass.-Boston ■	.77
87	Colby-Sawyer †	.71
93	Rivier	.66
104	Southern Me. ■	.75
87	Western Conn. St. ■	.78
88	Middlebury ■	.73
89	Mass.-Dartmouth ■	.85
98	Eastern Conn. St. ■	.78
87	Rhode Island Col.	.39
104	Mass.-Boston	.98

90	Plymouth St.	.77
111	Southern Vt. ■	.73
88	Southern Me.	.86
88	Tufts	.85
91	Rhode Island Col. ■	.61
76	Eastern Conn. St.	.65
88	Lasell	.81
83	Western Conn. St.	.90
83	Plymouth St. ■	.64
91	Mass.-Dartmouth	.95
67	Plymouth St. ■	.62
83	Western Conn. St. ■	.86
106	Fitchburg St.	.90
92	Plymouth St. †	.94

Nickname: Owls
Colors: Red & White
Arena: Spaulding Gym
    Capacity: 2,100; Year Built: 1968
AD: John C. Ratliff
SID: Stuart Kaufman

KENNESAW ST.
Kennesaw, GA 30144-5591 II

Coach: Tony Ingle, Huntington 1976

2001-02 RESULTS (20-10)

77	Shaw	.86
86	North Ga. ■	.73
70	West Ga. ■	.81
85	Montevallo	.73
67	North Fla.	.70
56	Clayton St. ■	.76
60	Ala.-Huntsville ■	.64
82	Montevallo ■	.65
69	UNC Pembroke ■	.65
91	Lander ■	.72
96	Augusta St. ■	.77
90	GC&SU	.77
71	S.C.-Aiken ■	.59
90	North Fla. ■	.78
55	Clayton St.	.76
69	S.C.-Spartanburg ■	.67
80	Lander	.70
82	Armstrong Atlantic ■	.76
82	Columbus St.	.83
90	Francis Marion	.78
87	Paine ■	.57
71	Augusta St.	.88
70	GC&SU ■	.68
64	S.C.-Aiken	.61
80	Columbus St. ■	.77
55	Armstrong Atlantic	.80
96	Francis Marion †	.83
86	UNC Pembroke †	.77
72	Clayton St. †	.69
67	Augusta St. †	.79

Nickname: Fighting Owls
Colors: Black & Gold
Arena: Spec Landrum Centre
    Capacity: 1,008; Year Built: 1963
AD: Dave Waples
SID: Steve Ruthsatz

KENT ST.
Kent, OH 44242-0001 I

Coach: Stan Heath, Eastern Mich. 1988

2001-02 RESULTS (30-6)

90	Mercyhurst ■	.68
64	Hofstra ■	.67
83	Robert Morris	.55
75	UC Irvine †	.64
68	Kentucky †	.82
75	Chattanooga ■	.56
70	Youngstown St.	.75
56	Xavier	.62
61	Illinois St.	.48
66	Cleveland St.	.62
93	St. Bonaventure ■	.82
81	Ball St. ■	.54
73	Marshall	.70
65	Buffalo	.66

71	Ohio ■	.56
78	Akron	.54
75	Western Mich. ■	.72
91	Buffalo ■	.53
70	Bowling Green	.67
82	Eastern Mich. ■	.62
79	Toledo ■	.52
76	Bowling Green	.64
96	Central Mich. ■	.66
73	Northern Ill.	.61
73	Miami (Ohio) ■	.57
116	Marshall ■	.76
70	Ohio	.67
67	Akron ■	.57
70	Miami (Ohio)	.67
82	Marshall †	.70
86	Toledo †	.61
70	Bowling Green †	.59
69	Oklahoma St. †	.61
71	Alabama †	.58
78	Pittsburgh †	.73
69	Indiana †	.81

Nickname: Golden Flashes
Colors: Navy Blue & Gold
Arena: Memorial Athletic & Convocation
Center
    Capacity: 6,327; Year Built: 1950
AD: Laing E. Kennedy
SID: Will Roleson

KENTUCKY
Lexington, KY 40506-0033 I

Coach: Tubby Smith, High Point 1973

2001-02 RESULTS (22-10)

52	Western Ky. ■	.64
90	Marshall ■	.73
94	Morehead St. ■	.75
82	Kent St. †	.68
99	VMI ■	.57
79	North Carolina ■	.59
118	Kentucky St. ■	.63
92	Duke †	.95
66	Indiana †	.52
82	Louisville ■	.62
101	Tulane †	.67
69	Mississippi St.	.74
84	Georgia ■	.88
51	South Carolina	.50
87	Mississippi ■	.64
72	Notre Dame	.65
69	Auburn	.62
61	Alabama ■	.64
70	Florida	.68
91	South Carolina ■	.74
74	Tennessee	.76
68	LSU	.56
67	Vanderbilt ■	.59
69	Georgia	.78
64	Tennessee ■	.61
71	Arkansas ■	.58
73	Vanderbilt	.86
70	Florida ■	.67
57	South Carolina †	.70
83	Valparaiso †	.68
87	Tulsa †	.82
68	Maryland †	.78

Nickname: Wildcats
Colors: Blue & White
Arena: Rupp Arena
    Capacity: 23,000; Year Built: 1976
AD: Terry Mobley
SID: Brooks Downing

KENTUCKY ST.
Frankfort, KY 40601 II

Coach: Winston Bennett, Kentucky 1987

2001-02 RESULTS (14-14)

80	N.C. Central	.88
75	Fort Valley St.	.93
83	Albany St. (Ga.)	.79

83	Shawnee St. ■	89
79	Oakland City	76
63	Kentucky	118
61	Ky. Wesleyan	105
95	Miles ■	88
87	LeMoyne-Owen ■	92
77	Lane ■	75
75	Morehouse	72
78	Tuskegee	64
88	Central St. (Ohio) ■	84
100	Paine ■	102
99	Clark Atlanta ■	92
89	Fort Valley St. ■	75
62	Albany St. (Ga.) ■	61
55	Miles	78
77	LeMoyne-Owen	88
94	Lane	95
88	Morehouse ■	85
82	Tuskegee ■	79
66	Central St. (Ohio)	86
63	Western Ky.	100
82	Paine	75
80	Clark Atlanta	91
85	Fort Valley St. †	59
77	Paine †	81

Nickname: Thorobreds
Colors: Green & Gold
Arena: William Exum HPER Center
Capacity: 2,750; Year Built: 1994
AD: Derrick Ramsey
SID: Ron Braden

KY. WESLEYAN
Owensboro, KY 42302-1039 II

Coach: Ray Harper, Ky. Wesleyan 1985

2001-02 RESULTS (31-3)

109	Central St. (Ohio) ■	93
106	Quincy	100
82	SIU-Edwardsville	53
82	Wis.-Parkside ■	69
88	St. Joseph's (Ind.) ■	67
64	Northern Ky.	62
73	Bellarmine	59
105	Glenville St. ■	76
105	Kentucky St.	61
109	Abilene Christian ■	76
92	Oakland City ■	59
88	Southern Ind.	94
86	Mo.-St. Louis	57
109	SIU-Edwardsville ■	65
92	Lewis ■	63
94	St. Joseph's (Ind.)	68
106	Indianapolis	100
90	Bellarmine ■	62
120	Lincoln (Mo.)	81
80	Mo.-St. Louis ■	64
113	Quincy ■	63
80	Lewis	73
90	Wis.-Parkside	79
94	Indianapolis ■	88
99	Northern Ky. ■	76
96	Southern Ind. ■	68
89	Mo.-St. Louis †	59
80	Southern Ind. †	77
65	Lewis †	77
94	Findlay ■	89
80	Lewis ■	75
71	Adelphi †	46
101	Shaw †	92
72	Metro St. †	80

Nickname: Panthers
Colors: Purple & White
Arena: Owensboro Sportscenter
Capacity: 5,002; Year Built: 1949
AD: Larry E. Moore
SID: Roy Pickerill

KENYON
Gambier, OH 43022-9223 III

Coach: Dave Kunka, Ill. Wesleyan 1993

2001-02 RESULTS (6-18)

71	Sewanee	91
70	Piedmont †	64
120	Wash. & Jeff.	121
77	Mt. Vernon Naz. ■	97
84	Lake Erie ■	87
65	Wabash	91
80	Earlham ■	79
59	Wooster	92
98	Bethany (W.Va.) ■	97
64	Kalamazoo †	91
63	Marietta	106
53	Ohio Wesleyan ■	73
53	Wittenberg	86
61	Allegheny ■	80
85	Oberlin ■	78
80	Hiram ■	86
56	Earlham	70
63	Wabash ■	65
72	Denison	80
59	Wooster ■	96
83	Oberlin	67
63	Allegheny	73
88	Denison ■	70
87	Hiram	99

Nickname: Lords
Colors: Purple & White
Arena: Tomsich Arena
Capacity: 2,000; Year Built: 1981
AD: Peter Smith
SID: Mart Fuller

KEUKA
Keuka Park, NY 14478-0098 ...III

Coach: George Winder, Rochester 1986

2001-02 RESULTS (7-18)

77	Cazenovia †	81
73	Southern Vt. †	78
63	York (Pa.) †	88
66	Medaille †	90
73	Potsdam St.	77
56	Clarkson	97
66	Elmira ■	77
67	Nazareth ■	76
75	D'Youville †	100
53	Brockport St. †	95
62	Roberts Wesleyan †	99
58	Nazareth †	68
80	Oneonta St.	82
74	NYCCT	76
63	Hilbert	73
70	D'Youville ■	58
63	Medaille	52
57	Pitt.-Bradford ■	85
78	Cazenovia ■	76
90	Cazenovia	104
72	Hilbert ■	55
64	Medaille ■	51
52	Utica	90
58	D'Youville †	53
56	Hilbert †	50

Nickname: Storm
Colors: Green & Gold
Arena: Weed Physical Arts Center
Capacity: 1,800; Year Built: 1973
AD: David M. Sweet
SID: Doug Lippincott

KING'S (PA.)
Wilkes-Barre, PA 18711-0801 ..III

Coach: J.P. Andrejko, Scranton 1988

2001-02 RESULTS (22-7)

95	Lincoln (Pa.) †	76
66	Susquehanna	64
107	Baptist Bible (Pa.) ■	67
65	Marywood	58
81	Misericordia ■	79
85	Arcadia ■	61
76	Drew ■	65
61	DeSales	70

74	Eastern †	58
71	Wis.-Platteville †	65
100	Centenary (N.J.)	65
65	Elizabethtown ■	85
74	Me.-Farmington ■	47
100	Delaware Valley ■	69
62	Scranton	68
94	Lycoming	96
64	FDU-Madison ■	52
70	Wilkes	59
71	DeSales ■	69
58	Drew	62
79	Scranton	68
90	Delaware Valley	74
84	Lycoming ■	73
92	Wilkes ■	73
75	FDU-Madison	70
89	Wilkes	84
64	Lycoming ■	72
76	Misericordia †	73
65	Frank. & Marsh.	82

Nickname: Monarchs
Colors: Red & Gold
Arena: Scandlon Gym
Capacity: 3,200; Year Built: 1968
AD: Tom Baker
SID: Bob Ziadie

KNOX
Galesburg, IL 61401-4999 III

Coach: Tim Heimann, Knox 1970

2001-02 RESULTS (5-18)

76	Eureka	89
67	Rockford ■	70
77	Principia ■	58
57	Clarke ■	69
58	Illinois Col.	79
66	MacMurray	82
83	Monmouth (Ill.)	79
88	Greenville	90
74	Dubuque	82
80	Lake Forest ■	96
64	St. Norbert ■	71
86	Carroll (Wis.) ■	74
108	Grinnell ■	110
60	Lawrence	78
74	Ripon	97
87	Beloit ■	91
64	Lawrence ■	58
79	Illinois Col. ■	105
80	Carroll (Wis.)	81
55	St. Norbert	81
103	Lake Forest	92
91	Grinnell	130
56	Monmouth (Ill.) ■	66

Nickname: Prairie Fire
Colors: Purple & Gold
Arena: Memorial Gym
Capacity: 3,000; Year Built: 1951
AD: Dan Calandro
SID: Kevin Vest

KUTZTOWN
Kutztown, PA 19530-0721 II

Coach: Bernie Driscoll, Dickinson 1977

2001-02 RESULTS (6-19)

67	Columbia Union	63
53	Neumann	58
53	Alvernia	59
73	Slippery Rock ■	75
77	Edinboro ■	80
74	Mansfield	85
74	Indiana (Pa.) ■	80
64	Calif. (Pa.) ■	84
49	Columbia Union ■	57
64	Shippensburg	62
62	Millersville ■	67
74	Lock Haven	57
56	Clarion	77
54	West Chester	63

61	Bloomsburg ■	70
73	Cheyney	80
62	Dist. Columbia	65
48	East Stroudsburg ■	54
64	Millersville	73
49	West Chester ■	63
62	Bloomsburg	64
68	East Stroudsburg ■	55
60	Dist. Columbia	77
73	Mansfield ■	64
69	Cheyney ■	60

Nickname: Golden Bears
Colors: Maroon & Gold
Arena: Keystone Hall
Capacity: 4,000; Year Built: 1971
AD: Clark Yeager
SID: Josh Leiboff

LA ROCHE
Pittsburgh, PA 15237...............III

Coach: Scott Lang, Clarion 1993

2001-02 RESULTS (9-18)

71	Bethany (W.Va.) ■	74
71	Muskingum	82
68	Waynesburg ■	74
71	Lake Erie	78
95	Thiel ■	81
70	Mt. Aloysius	63
61	Grove City	76
68	Slippery Rock ■	69
56	Geneva ■	85
64	Denison	60
75	Penn St.-Altoona ■	63
63	Pitt.-Bradford	81
74	Carnegie Mellon	77
76	Pitt.-Greensburg	66
65	Penn St.-Behrend ■	69
70	Frostburg St.	85
64	Hilbert ■	54
73	Wash. & Jeff.	83
83	Lake Erie ■	94
72	Pitt.-Bradford ■	69
59	Penn St.-Altoona	63
53	Penn St.-Behrend	65
80	Wash. & Jeff. ■	64
65	Pitt.-Greensburg	70
78	Frostburg St. ■	86
95	Pitt.-Greensburg †	69
70	Pitt.-Bradford †	90

Nickname: Redhawks
Colors: Red & White
Arena: Kerr Fitness & Sports Center
Capacity: 1,200; Year Built: 1993
AD: Jim Tinkey
SID: Scott Lang

LA SALLE
Philadelphia, PA 19141-1199 I

Coach: Billy Hahn, Maryland 1975

2001-02 RESULTS (15-17)

63	Morris Brown †	49
69	Clemson †	81
63	UAB †	58
78	Delaware	84
61	Villanova	58
63	Southern Methodist †	72
42	Alabama St. †	55
56	Rutgers ■	81
80	Drexel †	70
71	Seton Hall	68
56	UAB ■	53
70	Marist	64
57	Richmond	77
62	St. Bonaventure ■	68
72	George Washington	75
62	Duquesne	54
67	Xavier ■	71
69	Dayton ■	71
63	Fordham	74
76	Pennsylvania ■	81

83	George Washington ■	70
71	St. Joseph's †	80
47	Massachusetts	62
71	Temple ■	67
59	Richmond ■	56
80	Duquesne ■	65
77	Rhode Island ■	64
53	Xavier	68
72	Dayton	95
83	Fordham †	63
72	Temple †	66
60	Richmond †	68

Nickname: Explorers
Colors: Blue & Gold
Arena: Tom Gola Arena
  Capacity: 4,000; Year Built: 1972
AD: Thomas Brennan
SID: Kevin Currie

LA VERNE
La Verne, CA 91750-4443 III

Coach: Dan Mulville, UC San Diego 1990

2001-02 RESULTS (10-14)

69	Linfield ■	82
86	La Sierra ■	63
63	Cal Poly Pomona	97
73	Albertson †	67
81	Menlo	71
66	Menlo ■	77
76	Chapman ■	81
74	Vanguard	94
78	Cal St. Hayward ■	86
82	Hope Int'l	65
74	Occidental	95
65	Redlands	73
84	Whittier ■	59
68	Claremont-M-S ■	85
53	Cal Lutheran	81
59	Pomona-Pitzer	67
100	Caltech ■	32
61	Occidental ■	73
84	Redlands ■	77
85	Whittier	78
60	Claremont-M-S	73
79	Cal Lutheran ■	84
71	Pomona-Pitzer ■	64
77	Caltech	46

Nickname: Leopards, Leos
Colors: Orange & Green
Arena: Student Center Gym
  Capacity: 900; Year Built: 1973
AD: Jimmy M. Paschal
SID: Will Darity

LAFAYETTE
Easton, PA 18042......................I

Coach: Fran O'Hanlon, Villanova 1970

2001-02 RESULTS (15-14)

80	Albany (N.Y.) ■	72
66	Penn St.	75
69	Miami (Fla.)	79
69	St. Peter's ■	66
80	Marist ■	86
48	Columbia	52
88	Drexel	84
73	Cornell ■	44
90	Scranton ■	47
61	Princeton	67
93	Howard ■	84
66	Rider ■	86
64	Bucknell	65
64	Holy Cross ■	58
57	American	52
72	Army	85
66	Pennsylvania	73
92	Navy	79
67	Colgate ■	71
68	Lehigh	63
74	Bucknell ■	68
70	Holy Cross	76

77	American ■	74
69	Army ■	78
80	Navy ■	72
98	Lehigh ■	93
73	Colgate	85
74	Colgate †	71
58	American †	66

Nickname: Leopards
Colors: Maroon & White
Arena: Kirby Sports Center
  Capacity: 3,500; Year Built: 1973
AD: Jeff Cohen/Bruce McCutcheon
SID: Phil LaBella

LAKE ERIE
Painesville, OH 44077 III

2001-02 RESULTS (8-18)

57	Geneva †	71
70	Notre Dame (Ohio) †	74
100	Marygrove †	87
71	St. Mary's (Mich.)	78
87	Kenyon	84
62	Case Reserve ■	76
78	La Roche ■	71
76	Frostburg St.	87
87	Notre Dame (Ohio)	68
82	D'Youville ■	93
64	Heidelberg	71
93	Hiram †	67
83	Edinboro	92
82	Thiel	81
56	Penn St.-Behrend	70
78	Pitt.-Greensburg	86
71	Pitt.-Bradford	76
81	Penn St.-Altoona ■	82
88	Medaille ■	71
76	Frostburg St. ■	88
94	La Roche	83
80	Pitt.-Greensburg ■	84
54	Penn St.-Behrend ■	74
76	Penn St.-Altoona	78
79	Pitt.-Bradford ■	86
57	Penn St.-Behrend	65

Nickname: Storm
Colors: Green & White
Arena: Lincoln Gym
  Capacity: 1,000; Year Built: 1978
AD: James Schweickert
SID: To be named

LAKE FOREST
Lake Forest, IL 60045 III

Coach: Chris Conger, Wisconsin 1995

2001-02 RESULTS (9-14)

49	Kalamazoo	68
59	Wis.-River Falls ■	72
65	Concordia (Wis.) ■	56
70	Webster ■	63
85	Concordia (Ill.)	78
67	Milwaukee Engr.	72
75	Monmouth (Ill.) ■	65
140	Grinnell	135
68	Chicago ■	79
96	Knox	80
71	Illinois Col. ■	67
81	Beloit	96
73	Ripon ■	78
55	St. Norbert ■	63
63	Lawrence	73
74	Carroll (Wis.) ■	59
74	St. Norbert	83
85	Monmouth (Ill.)	75
69	Ripon	77
58	Beloit ■	60
46	Illinois Col.	77
92	Knox ■	103
93	Grinnell ■	111

Nickname: Foresters
Colors: Red & Black
Arena: Sports Center

Capacity: 1,200; Year Built: 1968
AD: Jackie A. Slaats
SID: Scott Rucker

LAKE SUPERIOR ST.
Sault Ste. Marie, MI 49783 II

Coach: Marty McDermott, North Dakota 1993

2001-02 RESULTS (17-11)

79	Angelo St. †	70
86	North Dakota St.	76
72	Grace Bible (Mich.) ■	39
70	Northern Mich.	86
75	Northland Bapt. ■	47
67	Michigan Tech	68
100	St. Mary's (Mich.)	72
80	Ohio Valley ■	51
104	Ohio Valley ■	47
60	Mercyhurst	76
64	Gannon	77
61	Ashland	112
63	Wayne St. (Mich.) ■	73
92	Findlay	79
71	Hillsdale ■	83
97	Northwood ■	84
62	Grand Valley St.	81
71	Ferris St.	65
96	Finlandia	43
99	Saginaw Valley	84
77	Northwood	78
91	Ferris St. ■	68
70	Grand Valley St. ■	64
86	Michigan Tech	100
70	Northern Mich. ■	59
81	Saginaw Valley ■	70
86	Gannon †	76
71	Michigan Tech †	88

Nickname: Lakers
Colors: Royal Blue & Gold
Arena: James Norris Center
  Capacity: 2,500; Year Built: 1976
AD: Bill Crawford
SID: Jill Rheaume

LAKELAND
Sheboygan, WI 53082-0359 ...III

Coach: Paul Combs, Ripon 1993

2001-02 RESULTS (16-10)

77	Carroll (Wis.) ■	61
68	Lawrence †	64
64	Finlandia	68
72	Northland	48
64	Maranatha Baptist	49
61	Savannah A&D †	71
56	Dominican (Ill.) †	58
83	Milwaukee Engr. ■	72
76	Wis. Lutheran	91
63	Wis.-Parkside ■	73
65	Concordia (Wis.) ■	59
58	Chicago St.	87
68	Rensselaer †	58
68	Randolph-Macon	73
80	Rockford ■	72
64	Edgewood ■	51
81	Northland Bapt. ■	52
57	Marian (Wis.)	50
86	Milwaukee Engr.	71
92	Wis. Lutheran ■	68
63	Concordia (Wis.)	66
69	Maranatha Baptist ■	57
58	Edgewood	69
66	Benedictine (Ill.) ■	63
64	Marian (Wis.)	57
72	Milwaukee Engr. ■	75

Nickname: Muskies
Colors: Navy & Gold
Arena: Todd Wehr Center
  Capacity: 1,500; Year Built: 1985
AD: Jane Bouche
SID: John Weber

LAMAR
Beaumont, TX 77710 I

Coach: Mike Deane, Potsdam St. 1974

2001-02 RESULTS (15-14)

57	Stephen F. Austin	56
62	Rice	91
74	Texas A&M ■	77
87	Texas Southern ■	58
79	Maine †	65
71	Michigan St.	80
58	Tex.-Pan American	69
69	Tex. A&M-Corp. Chris.	67
67	Texas-San Antonio	74
78	Southwest Tex. St.	77
82	Northwestern St. ■	65
65	McNeese St. ■	73
89	Sam Houston St. ■	87
61	Texas-Arlington	80
82	Nicholls St. ■	64
59	Southeastern La. ■	63
81	Northwestern St.	77
66	La.-Monroe	92
72	Texas-San Antonio ■	78
84	Southwest Tex. St. ■	91
82	Nicholls St.	74
55	Southeastern La.	51
65	Stephen F. Austin ■	62
94	Texas-Arlington ■	85
46	McNeese St.	74
73	La.-Monroe ■	76
64	Sam Houston St.	58
53	Stephen F. Austin ■	36
57	McNeese St.	71

Nickname: Cardinals
Colors: Red & White
Arena: Montagne Center
  Capacity: 10,080; Year Built: 1984
AD: Billy Tubbs
SID: Daucy Crizer

LANDER
Greenwood, SC 29649-2099 ...II

Coach: Roger Bagwell, Lander 1973

2001-02 RESULTS (11-17)

58	Winthrop	60
83	Allen ■	71
60	Presbyterian †	67
60	Newberry †	52
75	Virginia St. ■	69
53	Armstrong Atlantic	50
64	S.C.-Spartanburg ■	57
80	Presbyterian ■	67
69	North Fla. ■	78
72	Kennesaw St.	91
65	S.C.-Spartanburg	68
82	Francis Marion ■	69
67	Augusta St.	72
81	GC&SU	88
75	UNC Pembroke ■	66
67	S.C.-Aiken ■	71
70	Kennesaw St. ■	80
85	North Fla.	86
72	North Greenville ■	77
62	S.C.-Aiken	64
79	Augusta St. ■	83
67	Francis Marion	49
58	UNC Pembroke	65
70	Columbus St. ■	72
68	Clayton St. ■	66
62	Columbus St.	89
71	GC&SU †	66
45	Augusta St. †	68

Nickname: Senators
Colors: Blue & Gold
Arena: Finis Horne Arena
  Capacity: 2,500; Year Built: 1993
AD: Jefferson J. May
SID: Bob Stoner

RESULTS

LANE
Jackson, TN 38301-4598.........II

Coach: J.L. Perry, Lane 1971
2001-02 RESULTS (8-18)

63	Fayetteville St. †	80
66	Rust ■	63
56	Henderson St. †	80
65	Arkansas Tech	87
84	Albany St. (Ga.)	80
87	Fort Valley St.	94
80	West Ala. ■	71
69	Rust	68
71	LeMoyne-Owen ■	93
71	Miles ■	75
75	Kentucky St.	77
58	Tuskegee	74
68	Morehouse	87
85	Clark Atlanta ■	90
101	Paine ■	112
88	West Ala.	69
65	Albany St. (Ga.) ■	79
79	Fort Valley St. ■	90
69	LeMoyne-Owen	86
61	Miles	80
95	Kentucky St. ■	94
109	Tuskegee ■	92
89	Morehouse ■	85
84	Clark Atlanta	98
58	Paine	63
62	Albany St. (Ga.) †	83

Nickname: Dragons
Colors: Cardinal Red & Royal Blue
Arena: J.F. Lane Center
Capacity: 2,500; Year Built: 1974
AD: J.L. Perry
SID: William Head

LASELL
Newton, MA 02466 III

Coach: Chris Harvey, Worcester St.
2001-02 RESULTS (21-7)

83	Yeshiva †	75
101	Emmanuel (Mass.)	81
76	Framingham St. ■	59
79	St. Joseph's (Me.) ■	70
73	Mount Ida ■	65
101	Clark (Mass.) †	111
104	St. Joseph (Vt.) ■	56
94	Nichols	79
87	Connecticut Col.	90
89	Maine Maritime	66
61	Westfield St. ■	73
88	Fitchburg St. ■	67
91	Curry	77
102	Farmingdale St. †	75
83	Manhattanville	75
75	Amherst ■	86
109	Becker ■	69
60	Western Conn. St.	89
81	Mount Ida ■	79
77	Elms	74
108	Becker	83
81	Keene St.	88
97	Newbury	50
93	Elms ■	56
81	Maine Maritime ■	57
71	Elms ■	50
69	Maine Maritime ■	65
73	Union (N.Y.)	75

Nickname: Lasers
Colors: Columbia & Navy
Arena: Lasell Gymnasium
Capacity: 300; Year Built: 1997
AD: Kristy Walter
SID: Jessica Cormier

LAWRENCE
Appleton, WI 54912-0599.......III

Coach: John Tharp, Beloit 1991

2001-02 RESULTS (9-14)

94	Milwaukee Engr. †	64
64	Lakeland †	68
69	Wis.-Oshkosh	79
71	Marian (Wis.) ■	72
69	Ripon ■	54
68	Beloit ■	74
63	Mary Hardin-Baylor	79
71	Concordia-Austin	68
57	Incarnate Word	69
52	St. Norbert ■	62
56	Monmouth (Ill.)	66
89	Grinnell	128
96	Carroll (Wis.)	91
78	Knox ■	60
73	Lake Forest ■	63
60	Illinois Col.	83
58	Knox	64
56	St. Norbert ■	71
128	Grinnell ■	110
56	Monmouth (Ill.) ■	60
89	Beloit	79
81	Carroll (Wis.) ■	68
66	Ripon	84

Nickname: Vikings
Colors: Navy & White
Arena: Alexander Gym
Capacity: 1,000; Year Built: 1929
AD: Kimberly N. Tatro
SID: Joe VandenAcker

LE MOYNE
Syracuse, NY 13214-1399 II

Coach: Steve Evans, Union (N.Y.) 1994
2001-02 RESULTS (11-16)

72	Elmira ■	56
70	St. Anselm ■	77
79	Bentley	90
90	Merrimack ■	87
92	Stonehill	89
82	St. Michael's	65
52	St. Rose ■	62
70	Alfred ■	55
86	Roberts Wesleyan ■	78
55	Mass.-Lowell ■	65
76	Franklin Pierce	82
81	Southern N.H. ■	89
59	Mass.-Lowell	82
77	Bentley ■	80
77	Merrimack	62
74	Stonehill ■	70
75	Franklin Pierce ■	66
58	Southern N.H.	78
88	Cazenovia ■	82
73	St. Anselm	100
79	St. Michael's ■	62
59	Bryant	73
67	Assumption ■	69
61	American Int'l	70
55	Pace ■	67
81	Southern Conn. St.	93
63	St. Anselm	81

Nickname: Dolphins
Colors: Green & Gold
Arena: Ted Grant Court
Capacity: 2,000; Year Built: 1954
AD: Richard Rockwell
SID: Mike Donlin

LEBANON VALLEY
Annville, PA 17003-1400 III

Coach: Brad McAlester, Southampton 1953
2001-02 RESULTS (18-9)

76	John Carroll †	66
63	Gettysburg	75
71	Dickinson	70
68	Ursinus	66
71	Haverford	57
64	Alvernia	75
67	Susquehanna	62
67	Moravian	66
59	Catholic	76
71	Delaware Valley ■	60
71	John Jay	67
100	Albright ■	81
73	Widener ■	80
62	Frank. & Marsh. ■	56
67	Elizabethtown	83
71	Messiah ■	63
64	Juniata	58
64	Moravian ■	71
73	Susquehanna ■	62
78	Widener	73
80	Albright	79
66	Elizabethtown ■	95
67	Juniata	56
73	Messiah	57
61	Widener	77
67	Penn St.-Behrend ■	61
59	Frank. & Marsh.	71

Nickname: Flying Dutchmen
Colors: Blue, White & Red
Arena: Lynch Memorial Gymnasium
Capacity: 1,400; Year Built: 1950
AD: Kathleen Tierney
SID: Gregg Matalas

LEES-McRAE
Banner Elk, NC 28604-0128 II

Coach: Randy Unger, Taylor 1976
2001-02 RESULTS (8-20)

87	Bacone	79
93	Central Baptist	81
77	Okla. Sci. & Arts	104
71	Salem Int'l	103
108	Free Will Baptist	63
94	Queens (N.C.)	108
44	East Caro.	85
68	Longwood ■	71
71	St. Andrews	81
66	Limestone ■	81
66	Anderson (S.C.)	95
94	Pfeiffer ■	93
64	Erskine ■	88
75	Coker	93
67	Mount Olive	86
83	Barton ■	102
73	Belmont Abbey ■	116
65	Queens (N.C.)	95
67	Longwood	88
84	St. Andrews ■	58
82	Limestone	96
54	Anderson (S.C.) ■	51
97	Pfeiffer	106
63	Erskine	55
77	Coker ■	93
73	Mount Olive ■	87
55	Longwood	51
78	Queens (N.C.)	110

Nickname: Bobcats
Colors: Forest Green & Gold
Arena: Williams Gym
Capacity: 1,200; Year Built: 1975
AD: Ried Estus
SID: Barbara Russo

LEHIGH
Bethlehem, PA 18015-3089 I

Coach: Sal Mentesana, Providence 1969
2001-02 RESULTS (5-23)

91	St. Francis (N.Y.)	100
73	Wagner ■	80
62	Harvard ■	64
47	Columbia	53
67	Dartmouth	64
75	Vermont	83
48	Penn St.	61
72	New Hampshire ■	49
72	Swarthmore ■	40
61	Cornell	69
76	Portland	73
55	Oregon St.	78
58	Pennsylvania ■	74
62	Army ■	69
79	Colgate ■	74
85	Navy	92
66	Holy Cross ■	72
59	American ■	65
50	Bucknell	69
63	Lafayette ■	68
72	Army ■	77
52	Colgate	84
61	Navy ■	66
40	Holy Cross	79
67	American	70
93	Lafayette	98
75	Bucknell ■	64
69	American †	82

Nickname: Mountain Hawks
Colors: Brown & White
Arena: Stabler Arena
Capacity: 5,600; Year Built: 1979
AD: Joseph D. Sterrett
SID: Michael Garland Jr.

LEHMAN
Bronx, NY 10468-1589 III

Coach: Steve Schluman, Syracuse 1989
2001-02 RESULTS (17-10)

101	Utica †	100
59	Utica/Rome	80
64	CCNY	62
67	Purchase St.	61
88	Berkeley ■	32
75	NYCCT	71
69	St. Joseph's (L.I.) ■	68
69	Baruch	61
55	Wm. Paterson ■	64
67	Col. of New Jersey	78
84	St. Joseph's (Brkln)	60
74	Emmanuel (Mass.) ■	63
72	Hunter ■	76
84	Centenary (N.J.)	65
72	John Jay ■	66
54	York (N.Y.)	60
94	Brooklyn ■	69
92	Medgar Evers ■	96
85	Old Westbury ■	80
62	Staten Island ■	59
78	CCNY	73
75	Baruch ■	77
77	Hunter	59
64	John Jay	68
86	Polytechnic (N.Y.)	32
55	York (N.Y.) †	71
70	Richard Stockton	72

Nickname: Lightning
Colors: Blue, Green & White
Arena: Lehman College APEX
Capacity: 1,000; Year Built: 1994
AD: Dr. Martin L. Zwiren
SID: Eric Harrison

LEMOYNE-OWEN
Memphis, TN 38126 II

Coach: Jerry Johnson, Fayetteville St. 1951
2001-02 RESULTS (13-14)

70	Southern Ark. ■	83
60	Southern Ark. †	69
76	Delta St.	87
90	Christian Bros. ■	87
83	Morehouse ■	74
80	Tuskegee ■	67
65	Johnson Smith	85
94	Christian Bros. ■	78
93	Lane	71
92	Kentucky St.	87
71	Rust ■	48
79	Miles	76
61	Paine	69

83	Clark Atlanta	88
77	Fort Valley St. ■	81
80	Albany St. (Ga.) ■	59
67	Morehouse	74
61	Tuskegee	74
86	Lane ■	69
88	Kentucky St. ■	77
74	Rust	95
64	Miles ■	67
76	Paine	68
75	Clark Atlanta ■	71
67	Fort Valley St.	76
62	Albany St. (Ga.)	73
61	Miles †	62

Nickname: Magicians
Colors: Purple & Old Gold
Arena: Bruce Hall
  Capacity: 1,000; Year Built: 1954
AD: E. D. Wilkens
SID: Willie Patterson

LENOIR-RHYNE
Hickory, NC 28603 II

Coach: John Lentz, Lenoir-Rhyne 1974
2001-02 RESULTS (10-17)
65	Paine	80
61	Benedict	71
70	Charleston (W.Va.) †	82
82	Brevard †	64
58	Johnson Smith †	63
52	Five Towns †	57
49	Newberry †	65
69	Brevard ■	72
55	TCU	93
79	Paine ■	61
58	UNC Pembroke †	60
57	Armstrong Atlantic	58
78	Catawba	87
70	Newberry	69
66	Tusculum ■	54
54	Carson-Newman	78
73	Presbyterian	67
72	Wingate ■	92
63	Mars Hill	61
76	Catawba ■	69
72	Newberry ■	56
64	Tusculum	74
70	Carson-Newman ■	75
65	Presbyterian	62
47	Wingate	67
61	Mars Hill ■	55
44	Tusculum	46

Nickname: Bears
Colors: Red & Black
Arena: Shuford Memorial Gym
  Capacity: 3,200; Year Built: 1957
AD: Neill McGeachy
SID: Michael MacEachern

LETOURNEAU
Longview, TX 75607-7001 III

2001-02 RESULTS (3-13)
62	Centenary (La.)	89
84	Howard Payne ■	98
110	Sul Ross St. ■	81
69	East Tex. Baptist ■	75
56	Tex.-Pan American	101
74	McMurry	95
73	Hardin-Simmons	75
61	Mississippi Col.	72
97	Austin	74
73	Ozarks (Ark.) ■	86
75	Dallas ■	84
78	East Tex. Baptist	82
74	Dallas	68
55	Mississippi Col. ■	60
78	Austin ■	88
67	Ozarks (Ark.)	78

Nickname: YellowJackets
Colors: Blue & Gold
Arena: Solheim Arena
  Capacity: 1,200; Year Built: 1996
AD: Bernie Balikian
SID: John E. Inman

LEWIS
Romeoville, IL 60446 II

Coach: Jim Whitesell, Luther 1982
2001-02 RESULTS (25-7)
89	Dominican (Ill.) ■	52
75	St. Francis (Ill.) ■	50
73	Northern Ky. ■	88
84	Bellarmine ■	68
75	Southern Ind.	82
66	Mo.-St. Louis	58
84	SIU-Edwardsville ■	60
63	Hillsdale ■	64
84	Winona St. ■	58
61	St. Mary's (Tex.)	60
72	Northwood ■	60
76	St. Joseph's (Ind.)	72
74	Indianapolis ■	64
80	Bellarmine	60
63	Ky. Wesleyan	92
67	Mo.-St. Louis ■	64
79	Quincy ■	77
75	Wis.-Parkside ■	68
74	Indianapolis	69
67	Northern Ky.	72
73	Ky. Wesleyan ■	80
81	Southern Ind. ■	68
78	Quincy	56
70	SIU-Edwardsville	57
65	Wis.-Parkside	57
69	St. Joseph's (Ind.)	66
51	Bellarmine †	50
70	Wis.-Parkside †	58
77	Ky. Wesleyan †	65
67	Hillsdale †	53
62	Michigan Tech †	51
75	Ky. Wesleyan	80

Nickname: Flyers
Colors: Red & White
Arena: Neil Carey Arena
  Capacity: 855; Year Built: 1961
AD: Paul Ruddy
SID: Mickey Smith

LEWIS & CLARK
Portland, OR 97219-7899 III

Coach: Bob Gaillard, San Francisco 1962
2001-02 RESULTS (24-6)
87	Cascade ■	72
73	Westminster (Utah) †	76
111	Lewis-Clark St.	105
94	Bethany (Cal.) †	62
114	Whittier †	98
95	Chapman †	63
79	Cascade	71
91	Warner Pacific ■	94
69	Holy Names †	62
72	Whitworth ■	86
78	Whitman ■	64
60	Pacific (Ore.)	78
102	George Fox ■	77
69	Willamette	54
104	Linfield	65
84	Pacific Lutheran ■	77
92	Puget Sound	83
95	George Fox	78
77	Whitman	64
74	Whitworth	79
74	Pacific (Ore.) ■	72
78	Puget Sound ■	68
78	Willamette ■	67
94	Pacific Lutheran	86
102	Linfield ■	84
101	Whitworth ■	86

81	Claremont-M-S ■	59
70	Mississippi Col.	57
79	Wis.-Oshkosh †	71
70	Carthage	85

Nickname: Pioneers
Colors: Orange & Black
Arena: Pamplin Sports Center
  Capacity: 2,300; Year Built: 1969
AD: Steve Wallo
SID: Tom Galbraith

LIBERTY
Lynchburg, VA 24502-2269 I

Coach: Mel Hankinson, Indiana (Pa.) 1965
2001-02 RESULTS (5-25)
61	Vanderbilt	96
88	Shenandoah ■	71
57	Chattanooga †	82
46	Hawaii Pacific	81
56	Akron †	90
77	Appalachian St.	95
80	Fla. Atlantic ■	91
67	James Madison ■	77
46	Tusculum	45
49	Northwestern	66
54	Air Force ■	66
66	Duquesne	84
73	American	94
65	Birmingham-So.	83
54	UNC Asheville ■	68
64	Charleston So.	89
86	Coastal Caro.	80
48	Winthrop ■	81
53	Elon	75
58	High Point ■	73
60	Radford	79
56	Elon ■	63
54	Coastal Caro. ■	58
53	Charleston So. ■	66
69	UNC Asheville	85
62	Winthrop	69
98	High Point	99
70	Birmingham-So. ■	66
78	Radford ■	69
59	Winthrop †	66

Nickname: Flames
Colors: Red, White & Blue
Arena: Vines Center
  Capacity: 9,000; Year Built: 1990
AD: Kim Graham
SID: Todd Wetmore

LIMESTONE
Gaffney, SC 29340-3799 II

Coach: Larry Epperly, Emory & Henry 1975
2001-02 RESULTS (12-15)
91	Newberry †	82
66	S.C.-Spartanburg	53
72	Mars Hill ■	56
61	Mount Olive	70
63	Mars Hill	49
51	Gardner-Webb	68
64	Barton	86
57	Belmont Abbey ■	82
81	Lees-McRae	66
76	Longwood	80
65	St. Andrews	59
69	Queens (N.C.) ■	73
68	Anderson (S.C.) ■	83
73	Pfeiffer	89
71	Erskine	80
59	Coker ■	46
65	Mount Olive ■	80
62	Barton	58
56	Belmont Abbey	92
96	Lees-McRae ■	82
63	Longwood	73
74	St. Andrews ■	69

65	Queens (N.C.)	77
63	Anderson (S.C.)	80
88	Pfeiffer	77
60	Erskine	84
46	Anderson (S.C.)	58

Nickname: Saints
Colors: Blue, White & Gold
Arena: Timken Center
  Capacity: 1,500; Year Built: 1972
AD: Larry Epperly
SID: Larry Epperly

LINCOLN (MO.)
Jefferson City, MO 65102-0029 II

Coach: Bill Pope, Kansas 1988
2001-02 RESULTS (14-12)
87	Morningside †	61
61	Northwest Mo. St.	72
78	Central Mo. St. †	72
126	Mo. Western St.	112
72	Columbia (Mo.)	77
101	Mo. Western St.	109
95	Mo.-Rolla	99
84	Truman	60
89	Hawaii-Hilo	90
105	BYU-Hawaii	104
74	Hawaii Pacific	86
68	Southeast Mo. St.	77
93	Glenville St. †	55
87	Winston-Salem	82
76	Incarnate Word ■	68
66	St. Mary's (Tex.) ■	65
85	St. Edward's	82
100	Oakland City ■	104
81	Ky. Wesleyan	120
100	Drury ■	93
78	Rockhurst	88
75	Incarnate Word	82
75	St. Mary's (Tex.)	71
88	St. Edward's ■	68
89	Drury	129
84	Rockhurst	77

Nickname: Blue Tigers
Colors: Navy Blue & White
Arena: Jason Gym
  Capacity: 2,500; Year Built: 1958
AD: Patric Simon
SID: David Klopfer

LINCOLN (PA.)
Lincoln Univ., PA 19352 III

Coach: Robert Byars, Cheyney 1978
2001-02 RESULTS (11-13)
76	King's (Pa.) †	95
105	Ursinus †	97
73	Cheyney †	79
75	Messiah ■	76
81	Delaware Valley	84
79	Widener †	83
77	Salisbury	88
63	Neumann †	76
49	Newport News †	63
59	Frank. & Marsh.	67
76	Frostburg St. †	85
90	Gallaudet ■	87
93	Messiah	81
102	Albright	86
91	Pitt.-Greensburg ■	85
96	Mt. Aloysius	72
86	Wilmington (Del.)	64
80	Widener	92
89	Wilkes ■	91
98	Columbia Union ■	75
75	Wilkes	96
87	Columbia Union	96
102	Farmingdale St.	85
80	Mt. Aloysius	71

Nickname: Lions
Colors: Orange & Blue
Arena: Manuel Rivero Hall

Capacity: 3,000; Year Built: 1973
AD: Cyrus D. Jones
SID: To be named

LINCOLN MEMORIAL
Harrogate, TN 37752-1901 II

Coach: Jeff Tungate, Oakland 1993

2001-02 RESULTS (14-13)

123	Ohio St.-Newark ■	48
93	Union (Ky.) ■	82
75	Carson-Newman ■	67
67	Union (Ky.)	68
78	Tusculum ■	62
79	Ashland	89
61	Carson-Newman	91
72	West Ala. ■	59
81	P.R.-Cayey	70
86	P.R.-Rio Piedras †	81
89	P.R.-Bayamon	84
93	West Liberty St. †	86
94	Ashland	103
70	Tusculum	65
70	West Ga.	96
88	North Ala. ■	96
72	Montevallo	96
75	Valdosta St. ■	76
85	West Fla.	97
71	North Ala.	85
82	West Ala.	73
63	Ala.-Huntsville ■	69
96	West Ga. ■	76
92	Montevallo ■	87
52	Valdosta St.	73
91	West Fla.	90
76	Ala.-Huntsville	89

Nickname: Railsplitters
Colors: Blue & Gray
Arena: B. Frank Turner Arena
Capacity: 5,009; Year Built: 1990
AD: R. Jack Bondurant
SID: Michael Peace

LINFIELD
Mc Minnville, OR 97128-6894 .III

Coach: Larry Doty, Linfield 1978

2001-02 RESULTS (14-11)

71	Pomona-Pitzer	61
82	La Verne	69
94	Warner Pacific	108
95	Concordia (Ore.)	100
89	Whitworth ■	87
107	Western Baptist	110
95	Whitman ■	84
81	Western Baptist ■	76
82	Mt. St. Joseph †	86
78	Hartwick †	57
121	Thomas More †	90
101	Pacific Lutheran	88
86	Pacific (Ore.)	84
77	Willamette ■	72
115	George Fox	96
65	Lewis & Clark ■	104
100	Puget Sound ■	102
100	George Fox ■	87
80	Willamette	85
94	Pacific (Ore.) ■	76
79	Pacific Lutheran ■	73
84	Whitworth	90
77	Whitman	91
83	Puget Sound	94
84	Lewis & Clark	102

Nickname: Wildcats
Colors: Purple & Red
Arena: Ted Wilson Gymnasium
Capacity: 1,924; Year Built: 1989
AD: Scott Carnahan
SID: Kelly Bird

LIPSCOMB
Nashville, TN 37204-3951 I

2001-02 RESULTS (6-21)

79	Tenn.-Martin	86
70	Morris Brown	71
75	North Texas ■	74
51	Cal Poly ■	75
56	Butler ■	76
52	Northern Ariz. ■	67
87	Reinhardt ■	73
76	Sacramento St.	86
81	North Texas	102
64	Tulane	77
62	UC Irvine †	79
44	Wis.-Green Bay	77
49	Mississippi	75
60	Savannah St.	71
104	Rochester College ■	64
80	Northern Ill. ■	85
82	Tennessee St.	97
70	Tex.-Pan American	96
76	Savannah St. ■	68
51	Centenary (La.) ■	52
81	Tex. A&M-Corp. Chris. ■	79
85	IPFW	81
54	Centenary (La.)	64
89	Gardner-Webb	95
62	Tex.-Pan American ■	79
61	Tex. A&M-Corp. Chris.	75
76	Gardner-Webb	77

Nickname: Bisons
Colors: Purple & Gold
AD: Steve Potts
SID: To be named

LIVINGSTONE
Salisbury, NC 28144 II

Coach: Edward Joyner, Fla. Memorial 1974

2001-02 RESULTS (6-21)

66	Virginia Union ■	69
83	Morris ■	72
65	Xavier (La.)	80
50	West Ala. †	69
77	Catawba	87
65	Virginia Union	80
77	St. Paul's	68
77	Virginia St.	88
90	Bowie St.	101
74	Virginia Union ■	86
68	Catawba ■	75
81	Mars Hill ■	75
65	Winston-Salem ■	81
74	N.C. Central ■	70
56	Fayetteville St. ■	63
59	St. Augustine's	99
62	Shaw	82
71	Mars Hill	87
88	St. Paul's ■	75
70	Johnson Smith ■	79
71	Elizabeth City St. ■	81
74	Johnson Smith	88
67	N.C. Central	75
64	Winston-Salem	85
79	St. Augustine's ■	73
67	Fayetteville St.	76
78	Elizabeth City St. †	86

Nickname: Blue Bears
Colors: Columbia Blue & Black
Arena: Trent Gymnasium
AD: Clifton Huff
SID: Dionne Redding

LOCK HAVEN
Lock Haven, PA 17745..............II

Coach: John Wilson, Washburn 1980

2001-02 RESULTS (8-18)

67	Northwest Nazarene †	87
59	Seattle Pacific	87
71	Fairmont St. ■	66
84	Mansfield	79
58	Bloomsburg ■	78
74	Mansfield ■	63
67	West Chester	76
68	Cheyney	83
57	Washburn	76
84	Central Okla. †	93
61	Drury	76
69	Millersville	76
61	Slippery Rock	49
57	Kutztown ■	74
62	East Stroudsburg ■	51
65	Calif. (Pa.) ■	70
46	Clarion	70
72	Edinboro ■	82
56	Shippensburg ■	46
64	Slippery Rock ■	48
64	Indiana (Pa.)	95
61	Clarion ■	59
83	Shippensburg	91
60	Calif. (Pa.)	84
77	Indiana (Pa.) ■	78
70	Edinboro	81

Nickname: Bald Eagles
Colors: Crimson & White
Arena: Thomas Field House
Capacity: 2,000; Year Built: 1928
AD: Sharon E. Taylor
SID: Danielle Barney

LONG BEACH ST.
Long Beach, CA 90840-0118 I

Coach: Wayne Morgan, St. Lawrence 1973

2001-02 RESULTS (13-17)

71	Western Mich. †	64
74	Alabama St. †	55
67	Oregon	97
81	Charlotte ■	100
81	Cal St. Monterey Bay ■	46
56	Texas A&M	71
83	Pepperdine	93
68	Southern California ■	86
77	Stanford	94
68	Loyola Marymount ■	76
69	UC Irvine	75
105	IPFW ■	70
67	UC Riverside	73
68	Cal St. Fullerton ■	60
67	Idaho	69
66	Utah St.	70
54	Cal St. Northridge ■	66
78	Pacific (Cal.) ■	74
63	Cal Poly	75
50	UC Santa Barb.	82
77	Cal St. Fullerton	60
69	UC Riverside ■	66
53	Utah St. ■	60
62	Idaho ■	64
77	Pacific (Cal.)	63
73	Cal St. Northridge	60
77	UC Santa Barb. ■	74
83	Cal Poly ■	80
86	UC Irvine ■	70
65	UC Irvine †	72

Nickname: Forty Niners
Colors: Black & Gold
Arena: The Pyramid
Capacity: 5,000; Year Built: 1994
AD: Bill Shumard
SID: Steve Janisch

LONG ISLAND
Brooklyn, NY 11201 I

Coach: Ron Brown, John Jay 1976

2001-02 RESULTS (5-22)

87	Colgate ■	99
84	Manhattan ■	111
64	Quinnipiac	94
54	Yale	90
57	Xavier	108
76	Central Conn. St. ■	107
69	DePaul	95
57	Ohio †	110
50	Florida Int'l	54
57	Monmouth ■	73
86	Fairleigh Dickinson ■	109
64	St. Francis (Pa.)	77
66	Robert Morris	85
70	UMBC	91
57	Mt. St. Mary's ■	60
84	St. Francis (N.Y.)	92
80	St. Francis (Pa.) ■	64
75	Robert Morris ■	73
74	Monmouth	84
87	Wagner ■	97
88	Sacred Heart ■	80
81	Wagner	92
108	UMBC ■	111
65	Central Conn. St.	100
99	Sacred Heart	94
122	Fairleigh Dickinson	115
94	St. Francis (N.Y.) ■	108

Nickname: Blackbirds
Colors: Black, Silver & Royal Blue
Arena: Schwartz Athletic Center
Capacity: 1,000; Year Built: 1963
AD: John Suarez
SID: Greg Fox

LONGWOOD
Farmville, VA 23909-1899 II

Coach: Michael Leeder, Florida St. 1992

2001-02 RESULTS (13-13)

77	Franklin Pierce †	86
125	Practical Bible †	44
99	N.C. Central ■	72
95	Dist. Columbia ■	79
67	Belmont Abbey ■	72
80	Charleston (W.Va.)	88
71	Lees-McRae	68
80	Queens (N.C.) ■	83
99	St. Andrews ■	64
80	Limestone	76
85	Anderson (S.C.) ■	72
60	Erskine ■	67
76	Coker	80
95	Mount Olive ■	92
54	Barton	72
67	Belmont Abbey	95
88	Lees-McRae ■	67
66	Queens (N.C.)	67
73	St. Andrews	65
73	Limestone ■	63
64	Anderson (S.C.)	67
86	Pfeiffer ■	72
77	Erskine	79
65	Pfeiffer	110
81	Coker ■	65
51	Lees-McRae ■	55

Nickname: Lancers
Colors: Blue & White
Arena: Lancer Hall
Capacity: 2,522; Year Built: 1980
AD: Rick Mazzuto
SID: Greg Prouty

LORAS
Dubuque, IA 52004-0178 III

Coach: Chad Walthall, Concordia-M'head 1991

2001-02 RESULTS (15-12)

51	Edgewood ■	48
65	Benedictine (Ill.) ■	82

83	Cabrini ■	73
65	Cornell College ■	61
68	Dubuque ■	66
61	St. Thomas (Minn.)	73
60	Wis.-River Falls	71
53	St. John's (Minn.) †	77
81	Upper Iowa	73
72	Luther	57
74	Coe ■	76
65	Wartburg ■	69
70	Buena Vista ■	94
66	Mount St. Clare ■	64
54	Simpson	75
56	Central (Iowa)	53
82	Coe	72
75	Dubuque	62
56	Luther ■	60
66	Upper Iowa ■	77
68	Cornell College	41
66	Buena Vista	69
76	Wartburg	64
87	Central (Iowa) †	76
97	Simpson ■	69
87	Coe ■	65
70	Buena Vista	95

Nickname: Duhawks
Colors: Purple & Gold
Arena: Loras Fieldhouse
 Capacity: 1,200; Year Built: 1923
AD: Greg Capell
SID: Dave Beyer

LA.-LAFAYETTE
Lafayette, LA 70506.................I

Coach: Jessie Evans, Eastern Mich. 1972

2001-02 RESULTS (20-11)

76	McNeese St. ■	69
41	Bradley	63
71	Mississippi St. ■	79
83	Bethune-Cookman	73
65	LSU	83
84	Birmingham-So. ■	72
43	Bradley	42
81	Loyola (La.) ■	61
72	Texas Tech	89
51	Northwestern †	52
73	Canisius †	70
75	South Ala. ■	54
102	New Orleans ■	78
62	Western Ky.	63
64	Middle Tenn.	69
71	New Mexico St.	66
96	North Texas ■	78
70	Denver ■	58
73	South Ala.	68
61	New Orleans	63
77	Centenary (La.) ■	62
65	Florida Int'l	60
59	North Texas	78
53	Arkansas St.	50
61	Ark.-Little Rock ■	58
74	Denver	60
69	New Mexico St. ■	67
74	Arkansas St. †	59
67	Ark.-Little Rock †	53
70	Western Ky. †	76
63	Louisiana Tech	83

Nickname: Ragin' Cajuns
Colors: Vermilion & White
Arena: Cajundome
 Capacity: 12,800; Year Built: 1985
AD: Nelson Schexnayder Jr.
SID: Jeff Conrad

LA.-MONROE
Monroe, LA 71209-3000...........I

Coach: Mike Vining, La.-Monroe 1967

2001-02 RESULTS (20-12)

53	Samford	62
100	Tougaloo ■	62

94	TCU	90
79	McNeese St. ■	73
43	Mississippi	78
73	Sam Houston St.	81
67	Mississippi St. †	104
66	Cincinnati †	102
58	Richmond †	80
76	Texas A&M †	61
60	Col. of Charleston	86
63	Holy Cross †	57
85	Stephen F. Austin ■	72
87	Texas-Arlington ■	79
64	Southeastern La.	54
66	Nicholls St.	61
55	McNeese St.	66
72	Texas-San Antonio ■	70
70	Southwest Tex. St. ■	57
87	Sam Houston St.	67
92	Lamar ■	66
72	Northwestern St. †	64
74	Texas-San Antonio	81
51	Southwest Tex. St.	60
66	Southeastern La. ■	57
90	Nicholls St. ■	73
81	Texas-Arlington	70
51	Stephen F. Austin	52
76	Lamar	73
96	Northwestern St.	83
64	Texas-San Antonio	62
43	McNeese St.	65

Nickname: Indians
Colors: Maroon & Gold
Arena: Fant-Ewing Coliseum
 Capacity: 8,000; Year Built: 1971
AD: Bruce Hanks
SID: Hank Largin

LSU
Baton Rouge, LA 70803.............I

Coach: John Brady, Belhaven 1976

2001-02 RESULTS (19-15)

83	Campbell ■	59
97	Southern U. ■	69
74	Weber St. †	75
64	Hawaii-Hilo	62
84	Mercer †	54
83	Towson	46
91	Northwestern St. ■	54
83	La.-Lafayette ■	65
80	McNeese St. ■	57
59	New Orleans	60
73	Houston	69
61	Miami (Fla.) †	68
71	Nicholls St.	35
74	Alabama	76
75	Arkansas ■	69
70	Florida	102
75	Auburn ■	58
55	Mississippi	70
61	Mississippi St.	84
58	Tennessee ■	61
48	Alabama ■	57
63	Vanderbilt	68
56	Kentucky ■	68
68	Mississippi St. ■	65
67	Arkansas	63
53	South Carolina	66
54	Georgia	55
59	Mississippi	56
59	Auburn	54
69	Vanderbilt †	62
78	Georgia †	76
51	Mississippi St. †	57
63	Iowa	61
65	Ball St. ■	75

Nickname: Fighting Tigers
Colors: Purple & Gold
Arena: Maravich Assembly Center
 Capacity: 14,164; Year Built: 1972
AD: Skip Bertman
SID: Michael Bonnette

LOUISIANA TECH
Ruston, LA 71272.....................I

Coach: Keith Richard, La.-Monroe 1982

2001-02 RESULTS (22-10)

57	Rice ■	43
67	Iowa	75
102	Harding ■	86
83	Ark.-Monticello ■	66
99	Jackson St.	96
67	Auburn	66
67	Oklahoma	71
68	Centenary (La.) ■	48
63	UAB	81
74	Jackson St. ■	59
77	UTEP ■	63
59	Boise St.	36
71	Southern Methodist ■	74
61	Hawaii	81
78	San Jose St.	61
68	Tulsa ■	71
77	Nevada	69
71	Fresno St.	64
71	Centenary (La.)	84
70	Southern Methodist	66
77	San Jose St. ■	53
61	Hawaii ■	57
72	Rice	61
63	Tulsa	72
66	Fresno St.	63
86	Nevada ■	83
80	Boise St.	67
86	UTEP	68
69	Fresno St. †	72
83	La.-Lafayette ■	63
83	Vanderbilt ■	68
64	Villanova	67

Nickname: Bulldogs
Colors: Red & Blue
Arena: Thomas Assembly Center
 Capacity: 8,000; Year Built: 1982
AD: Jim M. Oakes
SID: Chris Weego

LOUISVILLE
Louisville, KY 40292 I

Coach: Rick Pitino, Massachusetts 1974

2001-02 RESULTS (19-13)

92	South Ala. ■	38
63	Oregon †	90
81	Tennessee St. ■	63
90	Wis.-Milwaukee ■	75
84	Murray St. ■	69
75	Coppin St. ■	49
66	Ohio St.	61
70	Tennessee Tech ■	66
73	Tennessee	72
94	Eastern Ky. ■	77
62	Kentucky	82
88	UAB	77
71	Marquette ■	75
93	TCU ■	85
77	East Caro.	87
50	Cincinnati	77
71	Charlotte	77
97	DePaul ■	67
70	Memphis	80
96	South Fla. ■	77
64	St. Louis	67
63	Indiana	77
76	DePaul	72
63	Marquette	75
75	East Caro. ■	42
50	St. Louis	56
74	Cincinnati ■	71
90	Charlotte ■	88
110	TCU †	86
76	Marquette †	84
66	Princeton ■	65
62	Temple ■	65

Nickname: Cardinals
Colors: Red, Black & White
Arena: Freedom Hall
 Capacity: 18,865; Year Built: 1956
AD: Thomas M. Jurich
SID: Kenny Klein

LOYOLA (ILL.)
Chicago, IL 60611 I

Coach: Larry Farmer, UCLA 1973

2001-02 RESULTS (17-13)

70	Marquette	80
75	Northern Ill. ■	63
76	Tennessee Tech	87
86	Tex. A&M-Corp. Chris. ■	66
72	Central Mich.	79
79	Md.-East. Shore ■	54
78	Eastern Ill.	94
72	St. Mary's (Cal.)	70
85	Chicago St. ■	73
72	Illinois	87
87	Cleveland St. ■	63
55	Detroit ■	49
91	Wis.-Milwaukee	87
72	Wis.-Green Bay	68
76	Ill.-Chicago	65
72	Youngstown St.	63
48	Butler	78
60	Wright St.	65
60	Cleveland St.	81
75	Youngstown St.	55
70	Wis.-Milwaukee ■	80
84	Wis.-Green Bay ■	74
77	IPFW	66
53	Detroit	55
63	Ill.-Chicago	76
60	Butler	56
74	Wright St.	80
90	Wright St. †	64
63	Wis.-Green Bay †	57
75	Ill.-Chicago †	76

Nickname: Ramblers
Colors: Maroon & Gold
Arena: Joseph J. Gentile Center
 Capacity: 5,200; Year Built: 1996
AD: John Planek
SID: Bill Behrns

LOYOLA (MD.)
Baltimore, MD 21210 I

Coach: Scott Hicks, Le Moyne 1988

2001-02 RESULTS (5-23)

50	Marist ■	85
66	UMBC ■	76
68	Coppin St. ■	76
74	Fairleigh Dickinson	63
59	Rutgers	71
63	Northeastern ■	74
51	Niagara	71
60	St. Peter's †	59
46	Mt. St. Mary's	55
50	Central Conn. St.	67
55	Delaware	75
56	Manhattan ■	61
50	Santa Clara	68
76	Siena ■	82
63	Iona ■	68
56	Rider	83
53	Fairfield ■	64
48	Fairfield	72
65	Canisius	74
53	Marist	67
54	Canisius ■	51
58	Siena	68
50	Iona	64
42	Niagara ■	65
88	St. Peter's	78
56	Manhattan †	67
77	Rider ■	65
62	Canisius †	88

Nickname: Greyhounds
Colors: Green & Grey
Arena: Reitz Arena
  Capacity: 3,000; Year Built: 1984
AD: Joseph Boylan
SID: David Rosenfeld

LOYOLA MARYMOUNT
Los Angeles, CA 90045-8235 I

Coach: Steve Aggers, Chadron St. 1971
2001-02 RESULTS (9-20)
60	Samford †	72
74	Mississippi Val. †	65
67	Idaho St. ■	56
70	Cal St. Fullerton	84
59	UC Irvine ■	71
80	Texas A&M	78
77	UC Santa Barb. ■	70
95	Sacramento St. ■	77
68	UNLV ■	70
76	Long Beach St.	68
67	Southern California ■	81
67	Montana	82
81	Occidental ■	55
78	Portland St.	90
66	San Francisco ■	75
75	St. Mary's (Cal.)	64
85	Portland ■	77
60	Gonzaga ■	94
60	San Diego	73
64	Santa Clara	74
59	Pepperdine	84
79	Pepperdine ■	89
44	St. Mary's (Cal.) ■	62
67	San Francisco ■	80
51	Gonzaga	72
79	Portland	83
59	Santa Clara ■	67
71	San Diego ■	87
64	Gonzaga †	82

Nickname: Lions
Colors: Crimson & Navy Blue
Arena: Albert Gersten Pavilion
  Capacity: 4,156; Year Built: 1982
AD: William S. Husak
SID: John Shaffer

LUTHER
Decorah, IA 52101-1045 III

Coach: Jeff Olinger, Luther 1985
2001-02 RESULTS (3-22)
47	Gust. Adolphus	95
64	St. Olaf ■	86
63	Wis.-La Crosse ■	65
74	Mt. Mercy ■	77
57	Central (Iowa) ■	68
58	Northwestern (Minn.)	82
58	Coe	73
55	Cornell College	67
39	St. John's (Minn.) †	60
36	Wis.-River Falls	60
96	Dubuque ■	68
57	Loras ■	72
58	Simpson ■	60
66	Upper Iowa ■	77
59	Buena Vista	66
57	Wartburg	71
40	Simpson	64
74	Cornell College ■	77
81	Coe ■	87
60	Loras	56
57	Dubuque	60
65	Central (Iowa)	62
51	Upper Iowa	65
63	Wartburg ■	64
38	Buena Vista ■	73

Nickname: Norse
Colors: Blue & White
Arena: Luther Field House

Capacity: 3,500; Year Built: 1964
AD: Joe Thompson
SID: Dave Blanchard

LYCOMING
Williamsport, PA 17701-5192 ..III

Coach: Terry Conrad, Bloomsburg 1983
2001-02 RESULTS (20-8)
78	Gallaudet ■	55
89	Chowan ■	67
82	Misericordia ■	77
56	Alvernia ■	62
78	Susquehanna ■	59
65	Wilkes ■	48
88	Delaware Valley	73
87	Chowan	79
85	Va. Wesleyan ■	82
70	Catholic	87
61	Marymount (Va.)	76
77	Elmira	71
74	Drew	80
80	FDU-Madison ■	71
96	King's (Pa.) ■	94
76	DeSales	83
58	Scranton	59
84	Delaware Valley ■	64
95	Wilkes	93
76	FDU-Madison	72
91	Drew ■	63
73	King's (Pa.)	84
77	Scranton ■	74
73	DeSales ■	59
70	Scranton ■	67
72	King's (Pa.)	64
78	Gettysburg	59
62	Randolph-Macon	79

Nickname: Warriors
Colors: Blue & Gold
Arena: Lamade Gymnasium
  Capacity: 2,300; Year Built: 1979
AD: Frank L. Girardi
SID: Robb Dietrich

LYNCHBURG
Lynchburg, VA 24501-3199......III

Coach: Ron Carr, Wofford 1982
2001-02 RESULTS (2-23)
63	Dickinson	89
63	Western Conn. St. †	68
51	Elon	93
62	Ferrum	71
78	Averett ■	79
47	Guilford ■	77
67	Ferrum ■	73
58	Hampden-Sydney ■	100
63	Emory & Henry	97
97	Averett	85
64	Va. Wesleyan ■	80
56	East. Mennonite ■	68
50	Bridgewater (Va.)	65
75	Wash. & Lee	71
72	Roanoke ■	80
59	Guilford	86
52	Randolph-Macon ■	76
59	East. Mennonite	69
65	Bridgewater (Va.) ■	86
69	Va. Wesleyan ■	90
46	Roanoke	100
59	Wash. & Lee ■	66
57	Hampden-Sydney	104
76	Emory & Henry ■	88
50	Randolph-Macon	81

Nickname: Hornets
Colors: Grey & Crimson
Arena: Turner Gym
  Capacity: 2,400; Year Built: 1970
AD: Jack M. Toms
SID: Mike Carpenter

LYNN
Boca Raton, FL 33431..............II

Coach: Andy Russo, Lake Forest 1970
2001-02 RESULTS (15-11)
76	NYIT †	64
90	Grand Valley St. †	78
90	Wingate †	82
72	P.R.-Mayaguez ■	66
63	Wayne St. (Mich.)	60
80	Voorhees ■	66
63	Nova Southeastern	55
71	Fla. Memorial	73
59	Mo. Western St. †	65
83	St. Edward's ■	67
75	Fla. Memorial ■	54
83	Eckerd ■	90
60	Rollins	63
51	Tampa ■	56
63	Fla. Southern ■	68
74	Barry	73
81	Florida Tech ■	58
74	St. Leo ■	61
65	Rollins ■	67
57	Tampa	60
73	Fla. Southern	64
58	Barry ■	68
83	Florida Tech	71
87	St. Leo ■	57
60	Eckerd	72
62	Fla. Southern †	63

Nickname: Fighting Knights
Colors: Royal Blue & White
Arena: De Hoernle Center
  Capacity: 1,500; Year Built: 1993
AD: John McCarthy
SID: Jeff Schaly

MACALESTER
St. Paul, MN 55105.................III

Coach: Curt Kietzer, St. Thomas (Minn.) 1988
2001-02 RESULTS (16-11)
65	Flagler †	73
85	Embry-Riddle	80
62	St. John's (Minn.) ■	60
65	Bethel (Minn.)	61
70	Carleton ■	63
69	Northwestern (Minn.)	77
54	Furman	81
90	Yale †	82
80	Augsburg ■	46
76	St. Olaf	74
77	Gust. Adolphus	86
54	Concordia-M'head	45
56	St. Thomas (Minn.) ■	79
64	St. Mary's (Minn.)	48
79	Hamline	63
48	St. John's (Minn.)	69
74	Bethel (Minn.) ■	59
45	Carleton	53
83	Augsburg	68
93	St. Olaf ■	84
62	Gust. Adolphus ■	64
72	Concordia-M'head ■	70
80	St. Thomas (Minn.)	86
69	St. Mary's (Minn.) ■	74
92	Hamline ■	88
83	St. John's (Minn.) ■	82
77	St. Thomas (Minn.)	86

Nickname: Scots
Colors: Orange & Blue
Arena: Macalester Gymnasium
  Capacity: 600; Year Built: 1933
AD: Irvin Cross
SID: Andy Johnson

MACMURRAY
Jacksonville, IL 62650-2590......III

Coach: Bob Gay, MacMurray 1967
2001-02 RESULTS (15-10)
85	Aurora †	90
91	Orchard Lake †	79
93	Lincoln Chrst.	92
73	Monmouth (Ill.)	67
82	Knox	66
85	Illinois Col.	70
57	Millikin	102
88	Hannibal-La Grange ■	69
55	Washington (Mo.) ■	78
61	Wis.-Superior †	65
65	Wabash	86
91	Webster	75
93	Maryville (Mo.) ■	76
73	Fontbonne	87
69	Westminster (Mo.)	68
65	Blackburn ■	62
72	Principia	82
86	Greenville	68
72	Webster ■	75
75	Maryville (Mo.)	64
72	Fontbonne	94
73	Westminster (Mo.) ■	55
66	Blackburn	70
84	Principia ■	71
91	Greenville ■	84

Nickname: Highlanders
Colors: Scarlet & Navy
Arena: Bill Wall Gymnasium
  Capacity: 1,500; Year Built: 1975
AD: Bob Gay
SID: Andy Danner

MAINE
Orono, ME 04469-5747 I

Coach: John Giannini, North Central 1984
2001-02 RESULTS (12-18)
47	Arkansas	64
56	Texas-San Antonio †	73
70	St. Peter's †	79
52	Delaware St. ■	60
71	Troy St. ■	73
65	Lamar †	79
73	IPFW †	65
67	Sacred Heart	61
81	Norfolk St.	84
60	Massachusetts	78
89	Brown	76
59	Albany (N.Y.) ■	52
65	Stony Brook	68
65	Vermont	79
73	Albany (N.Y.)	66
47	Hartford ■	50
83	Binghamton	60
72	New Hampshire	61
80	Binghamton ■	69
74	Northeastern	73
47	Hartford	59
59	Boston U. ■	61
53	Stony Brook ■	57
69	New Hampshire ■	87
52	Vermont ■	49
63	Northeastern ■	70
61	Boston U.	72
54	New Hampshire †	48
61	Vermont †	59
40	Boston U.	66

Nickname: Black Bears
Colors: Blue & White
Arena: Alfond Arena
  Capacity: 5,712; Year Built: 1977
AD: Paul Bubb
SID: Pete Lefresne

MAINE MARITIME
Castine, ME 04421 III

Coach: Chris Murphy, Maine 1973
2001-02 RESULTS (14-9)
70	Me.-Farmington	62
54	Wesleyan (Conn.) †	83
73	Unity	44
56	Colby	78
76	Wesleyan (Conn.) †	88
77	Me.-Machias ■	89
66	Lasell ■	89
78	Thomas	55
74	Me.-Presque Isle	72
57	Elms	50
68	Me.-Farmington ■	52
97	Becker ■	59
48	Bowdoin ■	58
72	Elms ■	61
66	Mount Ida ■	58
67	Me.-Machias	48
79	Thomas ■	55
58	Husson	66
90	Becker	68
57	Lasell	81
92	Mount Ida	61
71	Mount Ida †	65
65	Lasell	69

Nickname: Mariners
Colors: Royal Blue & Gold
Arena: Margaret Chase Smith Gym
 Capacity: 1,000; Year Built: 1965
AD: William J. Mottola
SID: William J. Mottola

ME.-FARMINGTON
Farmington, ME 04938 III

Coach: Dick Meader, Me.-Farmington 1968
2001-02 RESULTS (11-14)
62	Maine Maritime ■	70
106	New England ■	77
51	St. Joseph's (Me.)	63
102	Thomas ■	56
91	Notre Dame (N.H.) †	93
91	Anna Maria †	69
70	Husson ■	76
51	Bates ■	57
76	New England	79
53	Elizabethtown †	85
47	King's (Pa.)	74
77	Me.-Machias ■	75
52	Maine Maritime	68
73	St. Joseph's (Me.) ■	66
71	Husson	84
80	Lyndon St. ■	76
89	Thomas	45
73	Me.-Presque Isle ■	58
77	Me.-Fort Kent ■	75
74	Colby	71
74	Me.-Machias	78
57	Bowdoin	64
62	Me.-Fort Kent	76
69	Me.-Presque Isle	52
65	Me.-Machias	68

Nickname: Beavers
Colors: Maroon, White & Gold
Arena: Dearborn Gymnasium
 Capacity: 600; Year Built: 1963
AD: Julie Davis

MANCHESTER
North Manchester, IN 46962....III

Coach: Jamie Matthews, Ball St. 1993
2001-02 RESULTS (16-11)
65	Simpson †	70
64	North Central	63
58	Albion ■	70
46	Hope	80
83	Bluffton ■	53
70	Thomas More	67
76	Anderson (Ind.)	74
73	Transylvania	52
59	Elmhurst ■	79
81	Muskingum	70
71	Muhlenberg †	76
70	Oberlin	60
76	Defiance	72
61	Hanover ■	63
84	Franklin ■	78
82	Ind.-Northwest ■	52
65	Mt. St. Joseph	72
85	Thomas More ■	78
99	Bluffton	93
76	Transylvania ■	71
99	Anderson (Ind.) ■	90
53	Hanover	71
77	Defiance ■	86
72	Franklin	75
74	Mt. St. Joseph ■	62
70	Mt. St. Joseph ■	64
81	Defiance †	85

Nickname: Spartans
Colors: Black & Gold
Arena: Stauffer Wolfe Arena
 Capacity: 1,700; Year Built: 1983
AD: Tom Jarman
SID: Doug Shoemaker

MANHATTAN
Riverdale, NY 10471 I

Coach: Bobby Gonzalez, Buffalo St. 1986
2001-02 RESULTS (20-9)
58	Syracuse	78
75	Holy Cross ■	62
111	Long Island	84
81	Denver ■	57
76	Hartford ■	38
74	St. Peter's	57
85	St. John's (N.Y.) †	68
74	Hofstra ■	67
82	Fordham †	72
69	Iona †	58
61	Loyola (Md.)	56
98	Niagara ■	56
88	Fairfield ■	72
56	Marist	58
69	Siena	64
68	Rider ■	72
67	Marist ■	62
70	Iona	75
96	St. Peter's ■	87
73	Fairfield	70
75	Siena ■	70
61	Canisius	62
83	Niagara	94
73	Canisius ■	53
62	Rider	64
67	Loyola (Md.) †	56
81	Iona ■	66
74	Fairfield †	81
69	Villanova	84

Nickname: Jaspers
Colors: Kelly Green & White
Arena: Draddy Gymnasium
 Capacity: 3,000; Year Built: 1979
AD: Robert J. Byrnes
SID: Adrienne J. Mullikin

MANHATTANVILLE
Purchase, NY 10577 III

Coach: Brian Curtin, St. Michael's 1987
2001-02 RESULTS (20-9)
52	Rowan ■	56
94	Centenary (N.J.)	61
67	Staten Island	57
72	Yeshiva	67

MANSFIELD
Mansfield, PA 16933 II

Coach: Vince Alexander, Okla. Baptist 1989
2001-02 RESULTS (9-16)
104	Daemen	91
93	Daemen ■	64
79	Lock Haven ■	84
86	Clarion	82
63	Lock Haven	74
102	Roberts Wesleyan ■	109
85	Kutztown ■	74
63	Dist. Columbia	79
74	Shippensburg ■	67
72	Calif. (Pa.) ■	85
87	Indiana (Pa.) ■	103
55	West Chester ■	67
72	Edinboro	77
67	Slippery Rock	73
89	East Stroudsburg ■	75
74	Cheyney	80
81	Dist. Columbia ■	77
48	Millersville	75
82	Bloomsburg	90
78	West Chester	89
65	East Stroudsburg	46
71	Bloomsburg ■	65
74	Cheyney ■	77
64	Kutztown	73
80	Millersville ■	82

Nickname: Mountaineers
Colors: Red & Black
Arena: Decker Gymnasium
 Capacity: 2,500; Year Built: 1970
AD: Roger N. Maisner
SID: Steve McCloskey

MARANATHA BAPTIST
Watertown, WI 53094-0000....III

Coach: Jerry Terrill
2001-02 RESULTS (12-15)
61	Concordia (Ill.)	65
91	Purdue-Calumet †	87
67	Emmaus	53
49	Lakeland ■	64
89	Great Lake Christian ■	60
62	Cincinnati Bible	57
64	Grace Bible (Mich.) ■	49
59	Old Westbury ■	50
69	St. Joseph's (L.I.)	60
93	Mt. St. Vincent	77
59	Vassar ■	63
73	Merchant Marine	79
71	Skidmore	75
82	Purchase St. ■	49
87	Old Westbury	67
68	Stevens Tech	66
76	Mt. St. Mary (N.Y.)	69
84	Newbury ■	71
75	Lasell ■	83
73	Merchant Marine ■	72
60	Maritime (N.Y.)	49
74	St. Joseph's (L.I.) ■	64
70	Yeshiva	95
68	Mt. St. Mary (N.Y.) ■	59
60	Stevens Tech	61
76	Hunter ■	67
78	Mt. St. Vincent ■	72
81	Maritime (N.Y.)	62
74	St. Joseph's (L.I.) †	51
61	Yeshiva ■	54
72	Merchant Marine ■	73
74	New Jersey City ■	76

Nickname: Valiants
Colors: Red & White
Arena: Kennedy Gymnasium
 Capacity: 700; Year Built: 2001
AD: Gail A. Lozado
SID: Yakik Rumley

(MARANATHA BAPTIST listing continued)
59	Concordia (Wis.)	74
46	Ohio Dominican †	103
68	Trinity Int'l †	79
56	Edgewood	65
68	Northland Bapt. ■	53
45	Marian (Wis.)	87
61	Wis.-Whitewater	87
60	Wis. Lutheran	65
77	Concordia (Wis.) ■	67
67	Milwaukee Engr.	82
74	Lincoln Chrst.	55
57	Edgewood ■	68
69	Moody Bible ■	43
57	Lakeland	69
42	Marian (Wis.) ■	54
78	Milwaukee Engr. ■	70
73	Wis. Lutheran ■	67
54	Edgewood	73
70	Moody Bible †	58
55	Grace Bible (Mich.) ■	58

Nickname: Crusaders
Colors: Navy Blue & Gold
Arena: Willis Denny Gym
 Capacity: 1,000
AD: Terry Price
SID: Greg Wright

MARIAN (WIS.)
Fond Du Lac, WI 54935-4699..III

Coach: Mark Boyle, Wis.-Eau Claire 1978
2001-02 RESULTS (14-11)
88	Rockford	95
50	Wis.-Oshkosh	92
54	Wis.-Stevens Point †	67
87	Barat	107
79	Martin Luther ■	60
72	Lawrence	71
83	Cardinal Stritch ■	78
59	Illinois Tech	49
66	Wis. Lutheran	62
59	Austin	56
70	Texas-Dallas	69
70	Milwaukee Engr.	68
76	Dominican (Ill.) ■	54
55	Concordia (Wis.) ■	61
70	Maranatha Baptist ■	45
39	Edgewood	50
50	Lakeland ■	57
73	Northland Bapt.	62
73	Milwaukee Engr. ■	65
68	Wis. Lutheran ■	70
79	Concordia (Wis.)	59
54	Maranatha Baptist	42
60	Edgewood ■	70
57	Lakeland	64
48	Concordia (Wis.)	52

Nickname: Sabres
Colors: Blue, White & Scarlet
Arena: Sadoff Gym
 Capacity: 1,000; Year Built: 1982
AD: Doug Hammonds
SID: Chris Zills

MARIETTA
Marietta, OH 45750 III

Coach: Doug Foote, Morehead St. 1983
2001-02 RESULTS (13-13)
77	Frostburg St.	89
76	Waynesburg †	74
74	Capital ■	76
71	Eastern Ky.	90
73	Baldwin-Wallace ■	67
69	Muskingum	65
78	John Carroll ■	65
84	Heidelberg	61
81	Cazenovia †	80
73	Susquehanna †	67
61	Kalamazoo ■	60
106	Kenyon	63

84	Wilmington (Ohio)	70
75	Otterbein	90
62	Ohio Northern ■	58
74	Mount Union	85
81	John Carroll	74
76	Muskingum ■	82
74	Heidelberg ■	80
65	Capital	71
76	Wilmington (Ohio) ■	63
61	Otterbein ■	78
64	Ohio Northern	74
56	Mount Union	59
69	Baldwin-Wallace	72
72	Mount Union	84

Nickname: Pioneers
Colors: Navy Blue & White
Arena: Ban Johnson Fieldhouse
Capacity: 3,000; Year Built: 1929
AD: Debora Lazorik
SID: Nicole Peloquin

MARIST
Poughkeepsie, NY 12601-1387 .I

Coach: Dave Magarity, St. Francis (Pa.)
1974

2001-02 RESULTS (19-9)

85	Loyola (Md.)	50
75	Drexel ■	67
69	Columbia ■	59
80	South Ala. ■	70
59	Massachusetts	66
86	Lafayette	80
58	Bowling Green ■	61
77	Siena ■	69
80	Rider	69
78	UCF ■	63
64	La Salle ■	70
71	Army	58
71	St. Peter's	49
66	Niagara ■	70
80	Canisius	81
58	Manhattan ■	56
96	Iona ■	80
84	Niagara	78
62	Manhattan	67
93	Fairfield ■	84
67	Loyola (Md.) ■	53
79	Iona	71
63	Canisius ■	69
76	Fairfield	64
77	Rider ■	84
89	St. Peter's ■	61
60	Siena	57
76	Siena †	82

Nickname: Red Foxes
Colors: Red & White
Arena: McCann Recreation Center
Capacity: 3,944; Year Built: 1977
AD: Timothy S. Murray
SID: Jill Skotarczak

MARITIME (N.Y.)
Bronx, NY 10465 III

Coach: Howard Frajberg,
St. John's (N.Y.) 1980

2001-02 RESULTS (4-18)

47	Drew	70
90	Centenary (N.J.) †	78
44	Army	87
78	Brooklyn ■	79
62	Old Westbury ■	81
53	Yeshiva	61
50	Stevens Tech	49
55	John Jay ■	65
48	Kean †	64
54	Washington (Md.) †	68
82	St. Joseph's (L.I.) ■	71
64	Merchant Marine ■	66
52	Stevens Tech ■	65
49	Manhattanville	60

45	Merchant Marine	69
92	Old Westbury ■	67
58	St. Joseph's (L.I.)	65
76	Mt. St. Mary (N.Y.) ■	77
53	Yeshiva ■	54
57	Mt. St. Mary (N.Y.)	80
62	Manhattanville ■	81
58	Merchant Marine	79

Nickname: Privateers
Colors: Cardinal, Navy & White
Arena: Riesenberg Hall
Capacity: 800; Year Built: 1964
AD: James Migli
SID: James Migli

MARQUETTE
Milwaukee, WI 53201-1881......I

Coach: Tom Crean, Central Mich. 1989

2001-02 RESULTS (26-7)

80	Loyola (Ill.) ■	70
102	Chicago St. ■	49
85	Tennessee †	74
50	Indiana †	49
72	Gonzaga †	63
76	Texas Southern ■	40
77	Sam Houston St. ■	58
73	Dayton ■	51
79	Fordham ■	55
100	Ark.-Pine Bluff ■	49
73	Wisconsin	86
59	Wake Forest	64
85	Morris Brown ■	38
68	Charlotte	76
75	Louisville	71
61	St. Louis ■	53
67	UAB ■	59
87	DePaul ■	68
83	TCU ■	72
55	St. Louis	38
68	Tulane	66
74	Cincinnati ■	60
70	East Caro. ■	58
72	Southern Miss.	58
75	Louisville ■	63
66	Charlotte ■	52
62	Cincinnati	63
46	East Caro.	51
72	DePaul ■	53
84	Louisville ■	76
85	Houston †	73
63	Cincinnati †	77
69	Tulsa †	71

Nickname: Golden Eagles
Colors: Blue & Gold
Arena: Bradley Center
Capacity: 19,150; Year Built: 1988
AD: William L. Cords
SID: John Farina

MARS HILL
Mars Hill, NC 28754................II

Coach: Steve Roberts, Lander 1984

2001-02 RESULTS (4-21)

79	Francis Marion †	59
71	Mount Olive	83
65	Virginia-Wise ■	76
56	Limestone	72
76	North Greenville ■	85
55	Virginia-Wise	95
49	Limestone ■	63
78	Newberry ■	64
75	Livingstone	81
60	Carson-Newman	104
70	Catawba ■	96
52	Presbyterian	70
84	Wingate	105
61	North Greenville	62
51	Tusculum ■	64
61	Lenoir-Rhyne ■	63
87	Livingstone ■	71

68	Newberry	72
64	Carson-Newman ■	91
59	Catawba	58
53	Presbyterian ■	57
62	Wingate ■	77
54	Tusculum	67
55	Lenoir-Rhyne	61
72	Wingate	80

Nickname: Mountain Lions
Colors: Royal Blue & Gold
Arena: Stanford Arena
Capacity: 2,300; Year Built: 1969
AD: David Riggins
SID: Rick Baker

MARSHALL
Huntington, WV 25755 I

Coach: Greg White, Marshall 1982

2001-02 RESULTS (15-15)

64	George Washington †	69
73	Kentucky	90
72	Troy St. ■	77
96	Shepherd ■	46
93	Ark.-Monticello ■	63
71	Winthrop	65
67	Radford	63
79	Northern Ill. ■	76
60	Auburn †	78
77	Western Mich.	73
81	Massachusetts ■	66
70	Kent St. ■	73
65	Miami (Ohio)	80
97	Eastern Mich. ■	75
84	Central Mich.	88
78	Buffalo ■	82
81	West Virginia †	79
67	Toledo	77
98	Ball St. ■	95
78	Ohio	94
78	Akron ■	63
60	Bowling Green	83
82	Miami (Ohio) ■	74
66	Ohio ■	71
76	Kent St.	116
62	Buffalo	87
82	Central Mich. ■	57
104	Akron	87
97	Northern Ill. ■	93
70	Kent St. †	82

Nickname: Thundering Herd
Colors: Green & White
Arena: Henderson Center
Capacity: 9,043; Year Built: 1981
AD: Bob Marcum
SID: Randy Burnside

MARTIN LUTHER
New Ulm, MN 56073-3965.....III

Coach: James Unke, Martin Luther 1983

2001-02 RESULTS (10-12)

52	Gust. Adolphus ■	97
134	Grinnell ■	131
91	Hamline	56
45	Concordia (Wis.)	70
60	Marian (Wis.)	79
82	Viterbo	75
74	Bethel (Minn.) ■	84
99	Minn.-Morris	100
97	North Cent. (Minn.)	85
77	North Cent. (Minn.) ■	81
63	Crown	61
56	St. Scholastica ■	65
87	Northland ■	53
60	Northwestern (Minn.)	69
53	Crown	58
88	Presentation ■	77
77	St. Scholastica	71
85	Northland	70
66	Northwestern (Minn.) ■	79
82	Presentation	89

66	Crown	57
45	Northwestern (Minn.)	64

Nickname: Knights
Colors: Black, Red & White
Arena: Luther Student Center
Capacity: 1,500; Year Built: 1967
AD: James M. Unke
SID: Jeremy Belter

MARY HARDIN-BAYLOR
Belton, TX 76513 III

Coach: Ken DeWeese, Louisiana Col.
1969

2001-02 RESULTS (15-11)

73	Texas Wesleyan †	81
80	Austin	55
65	West Tex. A&M †	80
50	Tarleton St.	58
59	Dallas	53
59	Texas-Dallas	61
73	Concordia-Austin	68
58	Savannah A&D ■	67
98	S'western Assemblie ■	69
79	Lawrence ■	63
70	Mississippi Col. ■	71
110	Louisiana Col.	87
95	Schreiner	78
63	Texas Lutheran	68
88	Hardin-Simmons ■	51
85	McMurry ■	91
80	Sul Ross St. ■	71
79	Howard Payne ■	67
78	Concordia-Austin ■	55
70	Sul Ross St.	75
85	Howard Payne	90
106	Schreiner ■	59
87	Texas Lutheran ■	76
85	Hardin-Simmons	57
91	McMurry	82
55	Mississippi Col. †	65

Nickname: Crusaders
Colors: Purple, Gold & White
Arena: Mabee Gym
Capacity: 1,000; Year Built: 1957
AD: Ben Shipp
SID: Jon Wallin

MARY WASHINGTON
Fredericksburg, VA 22401-5358 III

Coach: Rod Wood, Randolph-Macon
1985

2001-02 RESULTS (10-16)

51	VMI	76
80	Christendom ■	64
90	Emory & Henry ■	94
79	Washington (Md.) ■	63
56	Goucher ■	64
67	Methodist ■	72
65	Salisbury ■	53
59	Apprentice	72
63	McDaniel	70
58	Marymount (Va.)	63
63	York (Pa.) ■	73
63	Catholic ■	81
80	St. Mary's (Md.)	75
103	Villa Julie ■	80
99	Gallaudet	52
77	Salisbury	72
75	Goucher	84
69	Apprentice ■	85
71	York (Pa.)	95
61	Marymount (Va.) ■	73
53	Wash. & Lee	61
82	St. Mary's (Md.) ■	73
70	Villa Julie	62
47	Catholic	70
82	Gallaudet ■	65
65	Goucher	66

Nickname: Eagles
Colors: Navy, Gray & White
Arena: Goolrick Gymnasium
  Capacity: 800; Year Built: 1967
AD: Edward H. Hegmann
SID: Clint Often

MARYLAND
College Park, MD 20742 I

Coach: Gary Williams, Maryland 1968
2001-02 RESULTS (32-4)

67	Arizona †	71
82	Temple †	74
83	American ■	53
77	Delaware St. ■	53
76	Illinois ■	63
61	Princeton †	53
77	Connecticut †	65
79	Detroit ■	54
91	Monmouth ■	55
56	Oklahoma	72
103	William & Mary ■	75
72	North Carolina St.	65
92	Norfolk St. ■	69
112	North Carolina ■	79
92	Georgia Tech	87
78	Duke	99
99	Clemson ■	90
85	Wake Forest	63
84	Florida St. ■	63
91	Virginia	87
89	North Carolina St. ■	73
92	North Carolina	77
85	Georgia Tech ■	65
87	Duke ■	73
84	Clemson	68
90	Wake Forest ■	89
96	Florida St.	63
112	Virginia ■	92
85	Florida St. †	59
82	North Carolina St. †	86
85	Siena †	70
87	Wisconsin †	57
78	Kentucky †	68
90	Connecticut †	82
97	Kansas †	88
64	Indiana †	52

Nickname: Terps
Colors: Red, White, Black & Gold
Arena: Cole Field House
  Capacity: 14,500; Year Built: 1955
AD: Deborah A. Yow
SID: Kevin Messenger

UMBC
Baltimore, MD 21250-0000 I

Coach: Tom Sullivan, Fordham 1972
2001-02 RESULTS (20-9)

76	Loyola (Md.)	66
73	Towson †	54
77	St. Francis (Pa.)	75
65	Robert Morris	80
78	Quinnipiac ■	71
62	Central Conn. St. ■	66
67	Bucknell	70
51	Rutgers	67
77	Towson ■	67
58	Santa Clara	59
50	Detroit †	47
87	Fairleigh Dickinson	72
75	Monmouth	72
91	Long Island ■	70
58	Central Conn. St.	76
72	Mt. St. Mary's	63
73	Monmouth ■	78
81	Fairleigh Dickinson ■	70
67	Sacred Heart	52
78	St. Francis (N.Y.)	67
75	St. Francis (Pa.)	72
84	Robert Morris ■	70
111	Long Island	108

69	Wagner	86
66	Mt. St. Mary's ■	61
81	Wagner	69
81	Sacred Heart ■	78
85	Robert Morris †	76
72	Quinnipiac †	75

Nickname: Retrievers
Colors: Black, Gold & Red
Arena: RAC Arena
  Capacity: 4,024; Year Built: 1974
SID: Steve Levy

MD.-EAST. SHORE
Princess Anne, MD 21853-1299 I

Coach: Thomas C. Trotter, Wis.-Parkside 1985
2001-02 RESULTS (11-18)

59	Iowa	89
48	New Orleans †	46
52	Duquesne	76
55	UMKC	58
65	Eastern Mich.	61
55	Bethune-Cookman ■	69
85	Florida A&M ■	54
54	Loyola (Ill.)	79
93	Towson ■	78
48	Minnesota	95
54	Iowa St.	77
71	Hampton	86
95	Norfolk St.	88
60	Morgan St.	59
64	Coppin St.	59
70	South Carolina St. ■	67
67	N.C. A&T ■	79
67	Delaware St.	77
65	Howard ■	75
70	Bethune-Cookman	76
61	Florida A&M	73
63	Hampton ■	81
68	Norfolk St. ■	70
61	Hartford	57
81	Morgan St. ■	67
68	Coppin St. ■	64
72	N.C. A&T	85
69	South Carolina St.	72
70	Bethune-Cookman †	82

Nickname: Fighting Hawks
Colors: Maroon & Gray
Arena: Hytche Athletic Center
  Capacity: 5,500; Year Built: 1998
AD: Vivian L. Fuller
SID: G. Stan Bradley

MARYMOUNT (VA.)
Arlington, VA 22207-4299 III

Coach: Chuck Driesell, Maryland 1985
2001-02 RESULTS (19-9)

47	Georgetown	108
67	Chris. Newport	72
84	Penn St.-Altoona	74
70	Salisbury ■	58
58	Gettysburg	80
82	Gallaudet	66
78	Penn St.-Altoona ■	57
71	Washington (Md.)	67
90	Villa Julie	85
76	Lycoming ■	61
97	Albright †	95
67	Springfield	71
82	Albright	74
63	Mary Washington ■	58
74	Goucher	81
104	St. Mary's (Md.) ■	85
67	Catholic	86
77	York (Pa.)	82
76	Gallaudet ■	73
74	Salisbury	71
83	Goucher ■	77
73	Mary Washington	61
79	Catholic ■	70
99	St. Mary's (Md.)	77

82	York (Pa.) ■	98
83	Salisbury ■	78
103	York (Pa.)	100
56	Catholic	64

Nickname: Saints
Colors: Royal Blue & White
Arena: Verizon Sports Arena
  Capacity: 1,000; Year Built: 1999
AD: William Finney
SID: Judy Finney

MARYVILLE (MO.)
St. Louis, MO 63141-7299 III

Coach: Dennis Kruse, Quincy 1966
2001-02 RESULTS (10-14)

75	Anderson (Ind.) ■	90
59	Hanover ■	93
65	Mo.-Rolla	88
83	Rhodes	80
92	Hendrix †	83
74	Elmhurst †	81
84	St. Louis Christian †	61
105	St. Louis Pharmacy ■	85
89	Savannah A&D ■	92
65	Mo. Baptist	89
97	Principia ■	84
76	MacMurray	93
77	Webster ■	80
75	Greenville	97
89	Fontbonne	95
76	Westminster (Mo.) ■	72
52	Blackburn	68
76	Principia	62
64	MacMurray ■	75
51	Webster	52
105	Greenville ■	84
75	Fontbonne ■	73
67	Westminster (Mo.)	76
56	Blackburn ■	47

Nickname: Saints
Colors: Red & White
Arena: Moloney Arena
  Capacity: 3,000; Year Built: 1980
AD: David R. Pierce
SID: To be named

MARYVILLE (TENN.)
Maryville, TN 37804-5907 III

Coach: Randy Lambert, Maryville (Tenn.) 1976
2001-02 RESULTS (24-5)

75	N.C. Wesleyan †	66
85	Emory & Henry	66
72	Centre	74
78	Rust ■	77
90	Covenant ■	56
68	Greensboro	53
107	Emory ■	78
75	King (Tenn.)	66
81	Thomas More	55
81	Greensboro ■	68
96	Covenant	75
100	Stillman ■	77
76	Carson-Newman	79
82	Fisk ■	45
70	Rust	57
74	Piedmont ■	59
66	Sewanee	67
102	La Grange	70
61	Carson-Newman ■	72
73	Stillman	56
72	Fisk	67
62	Huntingdon ■	48
71	Piedmont	56
79	La Grange ■	50
86	Savannah A&D ■	54
77	Piedmont	45
76	La Grange ■	71
70	Webster ■	45
57	Washington (Mo.)	71

Nickname: Scots
Colors: Orange & Garnet
Arena: Boydson Baird Gymnasium
  Capacity: 2,000; Year Built: 1971
AD: Randy Lambert
SID: Eric S. Etchison

MARYWOOD
Scranton, PA 18509-1598 III

Coach: Eric Grundman, Empire St. 1992
2001-02 RESULTS (1-22)

46	Richard Stockton †	69
87	Baptist Bible (Pa.) †	92
103	Practical Bible	80
58	King's (Pa.) ■	65
37	Cabrini ■	63
53	Alvernia	66
68	Gwynedd-Mercy	97
58	DeSales	82
74	Rutgers-Camden †	86
66	Misericordia	86
61	Arcadia	77
65	Wesley ■	72
55	Eastern	83
45	Neumann	81
79	Villa Julie	92
62	Gwynedd-Mercy ■	87
40	Cabrini	70
65	Misericordia ■	101
81	Wesley	89
58	Alvernia ■	89
45	Eastern ■	84
62	Arcadia	97
71	Neumann ■	90

Nickname: Pacers
Colors: Green & White
Arena: Health & Physical Education Center
  Capacity: 1,000
AD: Mary Jo Gunning
SID: Will Donohoe

MASSACHUSETTS
Amherst, MA 01003 I

Coach: Steve Lappas, CCNY 1977
2001-02 RESULTS (13-16)

66	Ark.-Little Rock ■	60
66	Marist	59
62	Oregon †	58
69	North Carolina St.	62
56	Holy Cross ■	67
78	Boston College	80
59	Connecticut ■	69
64	Central Conn. St.	49
78	Maine ■	60
66	Marshall	81
38	St. Joseph's ■	63
62	Ohio St. ■	70
86	Fordham	95
54	Richmond	63
63	Temple ■	53
73	George Washington ■	60
67	St. Bonaventure	65
68	Dayton ■	83
59	Rhode Island	70
69	Duquesne ■	78
62	La Salle ■	47
56	St. Bonaventure ■	60
47	Temple	64
67	St. Joseph's	72
67	Fordham ■	54
79	Rhode Island ■	69
52	Xavier	72
73	George Washington †	62
59	Xavier †	65

Nickname: Minutemen
Colors: Maroon & White
Arena: Mullins Center
  Capacity: 9,493; Year Built: 1993
AD: Ian McCaw
SID: Nick Joos

MASS.-DARTMOUTH
North Dartmouth, MA 02747-2300 III

Coach: Brian Baptiste, American Int'l 1976

2001-02 RESULTS (21-8)

102	Johnson St. ■	63
89	Colby-Sawyer ■	86
69	Worcester St.	42
90	Bridgewater St. ■	82
54	Salve Regina	59
95	Plymouth St.	76
104	Western Conn. St. ■	91
88	Johnson & Wales ■	47
71	Wis.-Platteville †	75
83	Ripon †	89
88	Southern Me. ■	79
72	Eastern Conn. St.	75
85	Keene St.	89
83	Mass.-Boston	63
95	Tufts	75
85	Plymouth St. ■	62
90	Rhode Island Col. ■	52
72	Western Conn. St.	78
64	Salem St. ■	58
77	Southern Me.	58
76	Mass.-Boston ■	68
75	Eastern Conn. St. ■	85
79	Rhode Island Col.	75
95	Keene St. ■	91
78	Southern Me. ■	67
64	Western Conn. St. †	84
89	Gordon ■	74
88	Salve Regina	68
67	Plymouth St. ■	63

Nickname: Corsairs
Colors: Blue, White & Gold
Arena: Tripp Athletic Center
Capacity: 3,000; Year Built: 1972
AD: Robert W. Mullen
SID: William Gathright

MIT
Cambridge, MA 02139-7404...III

Coach: Larry Anderson, Rust 1987

2001-02 RESULTS (15-10)

90	Emerson	80
78	Newbury	55
66	Suffolk ■	65
77	Framingham St. ■	46
68	Rensselaer ■	62
82	Caltech	49
73	Eastern Nazarene ■	67
77	Tufts	84
103	Polytechnic (N.Y.) ■	46
52	Salem St. ■	72
57	Connecticut Col. ■	54
45	Babson ■	58
66	Wentworth Inst.	37
66	Springfield ■	56
64	Coast Guard ■	51
83	Clark (Mass.)	85
73	Wheaton (Mass.)	75
51	WPI ■	49
51	Babson	76
64	Springfield	74
50	Coast Guard ■	68
82	Clark (Mass.) ■	90
78	Wheaton (Mass.) ■	73
63	WPI	59
66	Wheaton (Mass.) ■	67

Nickname: Engineers
Colors: Cardinal & Gray
Arena: Rockwell Cage
Capacity: 600
AD: Candace L. Royer
SID: Roger Crosley

MASS. LIBERAL ARTS
North Adams, MA 01247-4100III

Coach: Robert Hamilton, Middlebury 1981

2001-02 RESULTS (5-18)

74	Wentworth Inst. †	71
63	Vassar	69
57	Amherst	116
67	Middlebury ■	95
74	Connecticut Col. ■	89
72	Western New Eng.	80
63	Williams	82
77	Gordon ■	72
66	Framingham St.	67
92	Southern Vt.	94
74	Bridgewater St. ■	77
53	Worcester St. ■	79
64	Salem St.	82
77	Fitchburg St.	78
82	Westfield St.	77
71	Framingham St. ■	81
83	Bridgewater St.	76
74	Worcester St.	77
80	Salem St. ■	84
95	Connecticut Col.	101
85	Fitchburg St. ■	73
78	Westfield St. ■	108
68	Fitchburg St.	85

Nickname: Mohawks
Colors: Blue & Gold
Arena: Amsler Campus Center Gym
Capacity: 2,500; Year Built: 1975
AD: Scott F. Nichols
SID: Robert Hamilton

MASS.-BOSTON
Boston, MA 02125 III

Coach: Charlie Titus, St. Michael's 1972

2001-02 RESULTS (9-16)

74	Fitchburg St. ■	59
75	Framingham St. ■	78
72	Mount Ida ■	76
82	Emerson ■	78
65	Suffolk	77
77	Keene St.	99
75	Clark (Mass.)	83
83	Rhode Island Col. ■	79
110	Newbury †	68
70	Salem St.	87
77	Eastern Conn. St.	85
61	Plymouth St. ■	76
58	Tufts ■	78
59	Western Conn. St.	67
63	Mass.-Dartmouth ■	83
75	Bridgewater St.	70
98	Keene St. ■	104
66	Southern Me.	70
89	Rhode Island Col.	67
61	Wentworth Inst.	59
75	Eastern Conn. St. ■	63
68	Mass.-Dartmouth	76
68	Plymouth St.	89
85	Southern Me. ■	72
73	Western Conn. St. ■	95

Nickname: Beacons
Colors: Blue & White
Arena: Clark Athletic Center
Capacity: 3,500; Year Built: 1981
AD: Charlie Titus
SID: Alan Wickstrom

MASS.-LOWELL
Lowell, MA 01854 II

Coach: Ken Barer, George Washington 1988

2001-02 RESULTS (20-9)

51	Pace	56
86	St. Rose ■	73
71	Southern N.H.	54
65	NYIT ■	50
74	Franklin Pierce ■	51
54	Adelphi	67
69	Southern Conn. St. ■	36
78	Dowling †	75
64	Felician †	56
65	Le Moyne	55
44	St. Michael's	50
77	St. Anselm ■	80
82	Le Moyne ■	59
68	St. Rose	53
53	Pace	61
71	Southern Conn. St.	68
88	St. Michael's ■	78
78	St. Anselm	71
63	American Int'l ■	59
84	Bryant	76
76	Assumption ■	74
71	Stonehill ■	57
64	Merrimack	72
76	Bentley ■	51
75	Southern N.H. ■	58
73	Franklin Pierce	79
62	St. Anselm ■	65
72	Bentley †	70
57	Adelphi †	72

Nickname: River Hawks
Colors: Red, White & Royal Blue
Arena: Costello Gymnasium
Capacity: 2,100; Year Built: 1960
AD: Dana K. Skinner
SID: Chris O'Donnell

MCMURRY
Abilene, TX 79697 III

Coach: Ron Holmes, McMurry 1977

2001-02 RESULTS (20-6)

67	Neb. Wesleyan †	65
73	Colorado Col.	70
65	Wayland Baptist †	93
43	Lubbock Chrst.	73
95	Louisiana Col.	91
90	Hardin-Simmons ■	58
98	Texas Wesleyan ■	87
100	Texas Wesleyan	86
79	Lubbock Chrst. ■	68
95	LeTourneau ■	74
95	East Tex. Baptist ■	75
84	Howard Payne ■	78
99	Sul Ross St. ■	84
75	Concordia-Austin	91
91	Mary Hardin-Baylor	85
67	Texas Lutheran ■	80
104	Schreiner	94
93	Hardin-Simmons	87
83	Texas Lutheran ■	68
100	Schreiner ■	66
99	Howard Payne	85
80	Sul Ross St.	64
98	Concordia-Austin ■	84
82	Mary Hardin-Baylor ■	91
93	Ozarks (Ark.) ■	87
75	Mississippi Col. ■	88

Nickname: Indians
Colors: Maroon & White
Arena: Kimbrell Arena
Capacity: 2,250; Year Built: 1973
AD: Steve Keenum
SID: Chris Myers

MCNEESE ST.
Lake Charles, LA 70609 I

Coach: Tic Price, Virginia Tech 1979

2001-02 RESULTS (21-9)

69	La.-Lafayette	76
88	Loyola (La.) ■	46
74	Auburn	78
61	Alabama	90
73	La.-Monroe	79
67	Nicholls St. ■	60
70	Jackson St.	63
76	Southwest Tex. St. ■	66
57	LSU	80
76	Texas	80
68	Southeastern La. ■	63
71	Texas-San Antonio ■	55
75	Sam Houston St.	76
73	Lamar	65
73	Texas-San Antonio	81
76	Southwest Tex. St.	71
66	La.-Monroe ■	55
67	Texas-Arlington ■	61
60	Southeastern La.	58
74	Nicholls St.	46
67	Northwestern St.	63
65	Stephen F. Austin	49
81	Texas-Arlington	74
74	Lamar ■	46
79	Sam Houston St. ■	68
75	Northwestern St. ■	53
62	Stephen F. Austin	37
71	Lamar ■	57
65	La.-Monroe ■	43
58	Mississippi St. †	70

Nickname: Cowboys
Colors: Blue & Gold
Arena: Burton Coliseum
Capacity: 8,000; Year Built: 1986
AD: Sonny Watkins
SID: Louis Bonnette

MEDAILLE
Buffalo, NY 14214-2695..........III

Coach: Robert Hamilton

2001-02 RESULTS (1-19)

58	Geneseo St. †	93
46	Rochester	82
90	Keuka †	66
66	Fredonia St.	86
61	Brockport St. †	85
60	Utica/Rome ■	75
46	Westminster (Pa.)	77
52	Hilbert †	64
81	Waynesburg ■	86
65	Grove City	95
78	Cazenovia	92
71	Lake Erie	88
66	Cazenovia	85
62	Hilbert	75
52	Keuka	63
61	Oswego St. ■	90
63	Hilbert ■	64
39	Penn St.-Behrend ■	69
51	Keuka	64
65	Hilbert	71

Nickname: Mavericks
Colors: Scarlet/Navy/White
AD: Peter Jerebko
SID: To be named

MEDGAR EVERS
Brooklyn, NY 11225-2298 III

Coach: Robert Holford

2001-02 RESULTS (14-7)

76	Montclair St.	68
60	Cortland St. †	57
77	York (N.Y.) ■	58
58	Westfield St. †	54
70	Mt. St. Mary (N.Y.)	71
68	New Jersey City	74
89	Western Conn. St.	95
74	Staten Island ■	79
82	Brooklyn ■	67
82	CCNY	63
96	Lehman	92
75	Hunter	71
54	York (N.Y.)	52
91	Centenary (N.J.)	71
73	Staten Island	71
91	Brooklyn	80

57 John Jay ... 69
88 Hunter ... 87
68 York (N.Y.) † ... 65
57 Staten Island † ... 59
96 Ramapo ■ ... 97

Nickname: Cougars
Colors: Gold & Black
Arena: Medgar Evers College Gym
  Capacity: 300; Year Built: 1971
AD: Roy Anderson
SID: To be named

MEMPHIS
Memphis, TN 38152-3370 I

Coach: John Calipari, Clarion 1982
2001-02 RESULTS (27-9)
88 Wofford ■ ... 61
91 Old Dominion ■ ... 66
97 Northwestern St. ■ ... 69
71 Iowa † ... 75
70 Alabama † ... 81
65 Southeastern La. ■ ... 46
86 Christian Bros. ■ ... 54
111 Eastern Ky. ■ ... 74
67 Mississippi ... 71
71 Tennessee ■ ... 69
64 Temple ... 54
109 Austin Peay ■ ... 68
88 Tenn.-Martin ■ ... 58
73 Arkansas ■ ... 90
75 Southern Miss. ■ ... 53
98 TCU ... 93
78 Tulane ... 70
81 South Fla. ■ ... 62
73 Southern Miss. ... 64
102 UAB ... 81
84 Houston ... 66
80 Louisville ■ ... 70
98 TCU ■ ... 72
78 Tulane ■ ... 72
46 UAB ... 64
63 Charlotte ... 75
73 Houston ■ ... 76
71 South Fla. ... 59
88 DePaul ■ ... 61
75 Cincinnati ... 80
74 Houston † ... 80
82 UNC Greensboro ■ ... 62
80 Brigham Young ■ ... 69
79 Tennessee Tech ■ ... 73
78 Temple † ... 77
72 South Carolina † ... 62

Nickname: Tigers
Colors: Blue & Gray
Arena: The Pyramid
  Capacity: 20,004; Year Built: 1991
AD: R.C. Johnson
SID: Ron Mears

MENLO
Atherton, CA 94027-4185 III

Coach: Keith Larsen, San Fran. St.
2001-02 RESULTS (16-10)
65 Sacramento St. ... 81
77 North Park † ... 85
69 Drew † ... 60
77 Southern Ore. ■ ... 74
71 La Verne ■ ... 81
77 La Verne ... 66
63 Pomona-Pitzer ... 61
70 Cal St. Monterey Bay ... 69
83 San Jose Christian ■ ... 62
76 Cal Baptist ■ ... 90
74 Fresno Pacific ... 87
82 Bethany (Cal.) ... 72
75 UC Santa Cruz ... 67
77 Dominican (Cal.) ... 84
90 Simpson (Cal.) ... 78
59 Holy Names ■ ... 62

77 Pacific Union ■ ... 67
71 Cal St. Hayward ■ ... 82
77 Cal Maritime ... 75
86 Bethany (Cal.) ■ ... 77
73 UC Santa Cruz ■ ... 77
74 Cal St. Monterey Bay ■ ... 71
56 Holy Names † ... 55
66 Robert Morris (Ill.) † ... 80

Nickname: Oaks
Colors: Navy Blue & White
Arena: Haynes-Prim Pavilion
  Capacity: 700; Year Built: 1981
AD: Keith Larsen
SID: Nicholas Enriquez

MERCER
Macon, GA 31207 I

Coach: Mark Slonaker, Georgia 1980
2001-02 RESULTS (6-23)
68 Howard † ... 76
59 Minnesota ... 80
72 Hawaii † ... 89
72 South Carolina St. † ... 61
54 LSU † ... 84
60 Samford ■ ... 69
71 Jacksonville St. ■ ... 53
79 Georgia St. ... 90
69 Ga. Southern ... 92
61 Fort Valley St. ■ ... 52
43 Iowa ... 77
52 South Carolina ... 88
76 Campbell ... 77
65 Belmont ... 87
73 Fla. Atlantic ■ ... 94
71 UCF ■ ... 81
62 Jacksonville ... 75
71 Stetson ... 76
65 Troy St. ... 71
58 Jacksonville ■ ... 74
55 Stetson ■ ... 58
53 UCF ... 86
71 Fla. Atlantic ... 72
81 Belmont ■ ... 68
72 Troy St. ■ ... 71
74 Georgia St. ■ ... 82
88 Campbell ■ ... 85
68 Jacksonville St. ... 95
49 Samford ... 69

Nickname: Bears
Colors: Orange & Black
Arena: Porter Gym
  Capacity: 500; Year Built: 1925
AD: Bobby A. Pope
SID: Kevin Coulombe

MERCHANT MARINE
Kings Point, NY 11024-1699 III

Coach: Chris Carideo, Widener 1996
2001-02 RESULTS (24-5)
85 Goucher ■ ... 68
81 Hobart ■ ... 72
107 Mt. St. Vincent ... 79
73 New York U. ■ ... 67
79 Stevens Tech ■ ... 49
77 Coast Guard ... 85
79 Manhattanville ■ ... 73
91 Old Westbury ... 64
67 Yeshiva ■ ... 53
65 Grove City † ... 63
80 York (Pa.) ... 93
86 CCNY ... 63
66 Maritime (N.Y.) ... 64
89 Mt. St. Vincent ■ ... 72
60 Stevens Tech ... 52
94 St. Joseph's (L.I.) ... 70
72 Manhattanville ... 73
80 Mt. St. Mary (N.Y.) ■ ... 77
69 Maritime (N.Y.) ■ ... 45
56 Rowan † ... 74
78 Yeshiva ... 69

89 Old Westbury ■ ... 70
123 Polytechnic (N.Y.) ■ ... 42
90 St. Joseph's (L.I.) ■ ... 56
78 Mt. St. Mary (N.Y.) ... 69
79 Maritime (N.Y.) ■ ... 58
84 Mt. St. Mary (N.Y.) ■ ... 77
73 Manhattanville ■ ... 72
73 Cabrini ■ ... 85

Nickname: Mariners
Colors: Blue & Gray
Arena: O'Hara Hall
  Capacity: 1,200; Year Built: 1943
AD: Susan Petersen-Lubow
SID: Kim McNulty

MERCY
Dobbs Ferry, NY 10522 II

Coach: Steve Kelly, Fordham 1969
2001-02 RESULTS (2-24)
82 Geneva † ... 85
95 Practical Bible † ... 59
70 Dowling ... 113
81 Concordia (N.Y.) ... 82
87 Southampton ■ ... 92
78 NYIT ■ ... 85
59 Bridgeport ... 79
75 Roberts Wesleyan † ... 92
66 Alfred † ... 77
56 C.W. Post ... 70
52 St. Thomas Aquinas ■ ... 65
65 Molloy ... 75
72 Philadelphia U. ■ ... 107
76 Queens (N.Y.) ... 95
72 Adelphi ... 91
64 Dowling ■ ... 94
91 Concordia (N.Y.) ■ ... 84
82 Southampton ... 92
83 NYIT ... 90
50 Bridgeport ■ ... 57
69 C.W. Post ... 102
87 Molloy ■ ... 88
72 Philadelphia U. ... 78
68 Queens (N.Y.) ■ ... 98
59 Adelphi ... 87
75 St. Thomas Aquinas ... 88

Nickname: Flyers
Colors: Blue & White
Arena: Westchester Community College
  Capacity: 2,000
AD: Neil D. Judge
SID: Steve Balsan

MERCYHURST
Erie, PA 16546 II

Coach: Karl Fogel, Colby 1968
2001-02 RESULTS (13-13)
77 West Virginia St. ■ ... 72
77 Point Park ■ ... 52
68 Kent St. ... 90
74 Edinboro ■ ... 69
77 Columbia Union ■ ... 53
66 Grand Valley St. ... 79
67 Ferris St. ... 55
88 Bellarmine † ... 78
61 St. Mary's (Tex.) † ... 53
100 Roberts Wesleyan ■ ... 64
76 Lake Superior St. ... 60
56 Northern Mich. ■ ... 43
61 Michigan Tech ■ ... 75
61 Northwood ... 65
64 Saginaw Valley ... 76
72 Hillsdale ... 76
77 Wayne St. (Mich.) ... 90
70 Edinboro ... 83
69 Gannon ... 71
76 Findlay ■ ... 74
71 Ashland ■ ... 69
66 Wayne St. (Mich.) ■ ... 60
57 Hillsdale ... 65

48 Gannon ■ ... 66
68 Ashland ... 81
64 Findlay ... 106

Nickname: Lakers
Colors: Blue & Green
Arena: Mercyhurst Athletic Center
  Capacity: 1,800; Year Built: 1978
AD: Peter J. Russo
SID: John Leisering

MERRIMACK
North Andover, MA 01845 II

Coach: Bert Hammel, Bentley 1973
2001-02 RESULTS (6-20)
67 Adelphi ■ ... 90
69 Bentley ■ ... 79
63 St. Michael's ... 70
68 St. Anselm ■ ... 75
87 Le Moyne ... 90
59 St. Michael's ■ ... 86
94 Dowling ■ ... 79
65 C.W. Post ■ ... 83
51 Stonehill ... 57
68 Assumption ■ ... 83
65 American Int'l ... 82
73 Bryant ■ ... 59
77 St. Anselm ... 93
62 Le Moyne ■ ... 77
79 Stonehill ... 52
70 Bentley ... 87
68 New Haven ■ ... 70
73 Pace ... 78
69 St. Rose ■ ... 80
61 Southern Conn. St. ... 80
80 Southern N.H. ... 96
72 Mass.-Lowell ■ ... 64
77 Franklin Pierce ■ ... 80
71 Assumption ... 88
70 American Int'l ■ ... 65
78 Bryant ... 66

Nickname: Warriors
Colors: Navy Blue & Gold
Arena: Volpe Complex
  Capacity: 1,600; Year Built: 1972
AD: Robert M. DeGregorio Jr.
SID: Devin Bigoness

MESA ST.
Grand Junction, CO 81501 II

Coach: Jim Heaps, Mesa St. 1982
2001-02 RESULTS (16-11)
79 Great Falls ... 68
65 Mont. St.-Billings ... 77
91 Mont. St.-Billings ... 98
107 Wilberforce ... 84
93 Western Mont. ■ ... 76
76 Chadron St. ... 80
76 Colorado Mines ... 54
85 Metro St. ■ ... 87
82 Grand Canyon ... 75
54 Ferris St. † ... 57
55 Fort Hays St. ... 68
75 Neb.-Kearney ... 90
87 Regis (Colo.) ■ ... 70
88 Colo. Christian ■ ... 72
82 Southern Colo. ... 64
80 UC-Colo. Spgs. ... 65
94 Western St. (Colo.) ■ ... 82
76 Adams St. ... 68
76 N.M. Highlands ... 83
85 Fort Lewis ... 71
76 Southern Colo. ... 73
57 UC-Colo. Spgs. ... 65
87 Western St. (Colo.) ... 69
87 Adams St. ■ ... 62
102 N.M. Highlands ■ ... 82
65 Fort Lewis ... 72
62 Fort Hays St. ... 76

Nickname: Mavericks
Colors: Maroon, Gold & White
Arena: Brownson Arena
  Capacity: 2,500; Year Built: 1969
AD: Clarence Ross
SID: Tish Elliott

MESSIAH
Grantham, PA 17027 III

Coach: Dave Manzer,
Mt. Vernon Nazarene

2001-02 RESULTS (9-16)
68	Eastern ■	78
79	Gettysburg	92
76	Lincoln (Pa.)	75
58	Drew ■	64
81	Goldey-Beacom ■	71
69	Juniata ■	80
95	Albright ■	99
64	Dickinson ■	75
66	Baptist Bible (Pa.)	57
62	Methodist	78
74	Phila. Bible ■	56
71	Widener	79
81	Lincoln (Pa.) ■	93
72	Moravian	76
64	Susquehanna ■	74
63	Lebanon Valley	71
67	Elizabethtown ■	84
75	Albright	77
75	Juniata	51
79	Moravian ■	72
83	Widener ■	80
73	Villa Julie ■	72
74	Susquehanna	65
74	Elizabethtown	101
57	Lebanon Valley ■	73

Nickname: Falcons
Colors: Navy & White
Arena: Brubaker Auditorium
  Capacity: 1,800; Year Built: 1972
AD: Jerry Chaplin
SID: Scott Frey

METHODIST
Fayetteville, NC 28311-1420 ...III

Coach: David Smith, Methodist 1981

2001-02 RESULTS (16-11)
85	Penn St.-Altoona †	48
58	Juniata	74
73	Savannah A&D	84
67	La Grange	73
65	Furman	87
72	Mary Washington	67
70	Fayetteville St. ■	66
78	Messiah ■	62
64	Savannah A&D ■	56
68	Greensboro ■	52
65	Chowan ■	60
71	Apprentice ■	77
69	N.C. Wesleyan ■	68
76	Ferrum ■	74
85	Averett ■	72
74	Shenandoah ■	67
64	Chris. Newport ■	80
66	Greensboro	62
66	Chowan	57
61	Apprentice	82
61	N.C. Wesleyan ■	60
60	Ferrum	62
89	Averett ■	61
63	Chris. Newport ■	81
66	Shenandoah	88
84	Chowan ■	75
70	N.C. Wesleyan ■	77

Nickname: Monarchs
Colors: Green & Gold
Arena: March F. Riddle Center
  Capacity: 1,200; Year Built: 1990
AD: Bob McEvoy
SID: Lee Glenn

METRO ST.
Denver, CO 80217-3362 II

Coach: Mike Dunlap, Loyola Marymount
1980

2001-02 RESULTS (29-6)
86	Queens (N.Y.) †	36
80	Azusa Pacific †	70
70	BYU-Hawaii	85
62	Cal St. San B'dino †	70
95	Rocky Mountain ■	44
97	N.M. Highlands ■	60
88	Fort Lewis ■	82
77	Western St. (Colo.)	49
87	Mesa St.	85
90	Great Falls ■	61
81	Central Okla. †	56
74	Washburn	73
97	Adams St. ■	71
85	Southern Colo.	76
81	UC-Colo. Spgs.	52
86	Colorado Mines	48
83	Chadron St.	64
81	Fort Hays St. ■	82
73	Neb.-Kearney ■	83
64	Colo. Christian	58
74	Regis (Colo.)	62
79	Colorado Mines ■	54
77	Chadron St. ■	67
71	Neb.-Kearney	67
72	Fort Hays St.	76
77	Regis (Colo.) ■	49
74	Colo. Christian ■	64
76	Chadron St. ■	54
86	Fort Lewis †	95
66	Minn.-Duluth †	61
59	Neb.-Kearney †	51
87	South Dakota St.	86
65	Cal St. San B'dino †	48
82	Indiana (Pa.) †	52
80	Ky. Wesleyan †	72

Nickname: Roadrunners
Colors: Navy Blue & Burgundy
Arena: Auraria Events Center
  Capacity: 3,000; Year Built: 1970
AD: Joan M. McDermott
SID: Nick Garner

MIAMI (FLA.)
Coral Gables, FL 33146 I

Coach: Perry Clark, Gettysburg 1974

2001-02 RESULTS (24-8)
93	Eastern Mich. †	56
81	UAB †	79
67	Clemson †	65
79	Lafayette ■	69
74	Fla. Atlantic ■	48
87	Howard ■	71
77	Florida Int'l ■	59
64	Texas A&M	55
58	Indiana ■	53
90	Florida A&M ■	62
64	Charlotte ■	56
68	LSU †	61
71	St. Francis (Pa.) ■	48
79	Georgetown	71
75	Connecticut	76
60	St. John's (N.Y.)	71
77	Virginia Tech	68
76	Pittsburgh ■	69
102	Providence ■	96
76	Villanova ■	58
67	Boston College ■	70
68	Connecticut ■	66
65	Villanova	56
63	Boston College	76
79	St. John's (N.Y.) ■	56
61	Rutgers	64
77	Notre Dame ■	90
81	Providence	65
83	Virginia Tech ■	77
84	Georgetown †	76
71	Pittsburgh †	76
80	Missouri †	93

Nickname: Hurricanes
Colors: Orange, Green & White
Arena: Miami Arena
  Capacity: 15,388; Year Built: 1988
AD: Paul Dee
SID: Sam Henderson

MIAMI (OHIO)
Oxford, OH 45056 I

Coach: Charlie Coles, Miami (Ohio)
1965

2001-02 RESULTS (13-18)
42	UNC Wilmington	50
70	George Mason ■	65
58	Xavier ■	87
67	Wright St. ■	61
63	Evansville	67
69	Notre Dame ■	70
55	Southern California	59
73	Boston College †	67
59	Georgia †	64
51	Iona †	57
23	Dayton	60
63	Western Mich.	69
100	Central Mich.	94
80	Marshall ■	65
50	Akron ■	48
72	Eastern Mich. ■	56
61	Ohio	85
70	Northern Ill. ■	78
80	Ball St. ■	77
61	Bowling Green	64
66	Buffalo	52
64	Toledo ■	54
79	Ohio ■	55
74	Marshall	82
57	Kent St.	73
50	Bowling Green ■	65
58	Ball St.	74
78	Buffalo ■	68
67	Kent St. ■	70
71	Buffalo ■	60
50	Ball St. †	62

Nickname: RedHawks
Colors: Red & White
Arena: Millett Hall
  Capacity: 9,200; Year Built: 1968
AD: Steve Snyder
SID: Angie Renninger

MICHIGAN
Ann Arbor, MI 48109-2201 I

Coach: Tommy Amaker, Duke 1987

2001-02 RESULTS (11-18)
81	Oakland ■	73
88	Fairfield ■	59
73	Western Mich.	79
59	Bowling Green	65
74	Boston College ■	83
91	IPFW ■	62
83	Duke ■	104
88	Eastern Mich. ■	58
47	San Francisco †	55
57	Penn St.	63
79	Purdue ■	75
82	Minnesota	90
70	Illinois	94
54	Northwestern ■	58
71	Minnesota ■	69
47	Ohio St.	69
75	Vermont ■	62
44	Michigan St.	71
44	Wisconsin ■	53
60	Illinois ■	68
65	Penn St. ■	58
66	Colorado St.	70
43	Purdue	79
55	Indiana ■	75
56	Iowa	76

(record continues)

Nickname: Wolverines
Colors: Maize & Blue
Arena: Crisler Arena
  Capacity: 13,562; Year Built: 1967
AD: William C. Martin
SID: Bruce Madej

MICHIGAN ST.
East Lansing, MI 48824-1025 I

Coach: Tom Izzo, Northern Mich. 1977

2001-02 RESULTS (19-12)
80	Detroit ■	70
67	Oklahoma ■	55
58	Syracuse †	69
58	Fresno St. †	63
81	IPFW ■	68
80	Lamar ■	71
70	Florida	74
92	Nicholls St. ■	38
74	Arizona ■	60
76	UNC Asheville ■	56
78	Oakland ■	50
68	Seton Hall ■	64
64	Stanford †	75
67	Minnesota	70
65	Indiana	83
63	Wisconsin ■	64
65	Purdue ■	56
77	Penn St.	65
71	Iowa	75
71	Michigan ■	44
67	Illinois	61
49	Northwestern	61
67	Ohio St. ■	64
61	Illinois ■	63
62	Purdue	59
74	Minnesota ■	55
57	Indiana ■	54
81	Ohio St.	76
93	Iowa ■	79
56	Indiana †	67
58	North Carolina St. †	69

Nickname: Spartans
Colors: Green & White
Arena: Breslin Events Center
  Capacity: 14,659; Year Built: 1989
AD: Ronald Mason
SID: Matt Larson

MICHIGAN TECH
Houghton, MI 49931-1295 II

Coach: Kevin Luke, Northern Mich.
1982

2001-02 RESULTS (27-3)
86	Finlandia ■	60
81	Northern Mich. ■	65
89	South Dakota St. †	86
59	Montevallo †	56
90	Bemidji St. ■	76
112	St. Scholastica ■	67
68	Lake Superior St.	67
79	Indianapolis	70
77	Minn.-Duluth ■	61
60	Gannon	64
79	Ashland	73
75	Mercyhurst	61
72	Hillsdale ■	53
71	Wayne St. (Mich.) ■	70
80	Findlay ■	91
76	Saginaw Valley ■	68
78	Northern Mich.	65
74	Northwood ■	58
77	Ferris St. ■	53
80	Grand Valley St. ■	63
72	Northern Mich. ■	44
96	Saginaw Valley	79

100	Lake Superior St. ■	86
81	Northwood ■	59
85	Grand Valley St.	79
91	Ferris St.	61
78	Wayne St. (Mich.) †	70
88	Lake Superior St. †	71
79	Northwood †	65
51	Lewis †	62

Nickname: Huskies
Colors: Silver, Gold & Black
Arena: SDC Gymnasium
   Capacity: 3,200; Year Built: 1981
AD: Rick Yeo
SID: Wes Frahm

MIDDLE TENN.
Murfreesboro, TN 37132 I

Coach: Randy Wiel, North Carolina 1979

2001-02 RESULTS (14-15)

115	Bryan ■	59
76	IUPUI ■	72
74	UNC Greensboro ■	58
59	Belmont	65
53	Radford	72
65	Rice ■	52
71	Tenn.-Martin	76
88	Tennessee St. ■	79
64	Tex.-Pan American	66
71	East Caro.	81
51	South Ala.	59
69	New Orleans	64
60	Florida Int'l	67
88	New Mexico St. ■	94
69	La.-Lafayette ■	64
45	Western Ky. ■	55
63	North Texas	85
56	Tennessee	74
83	Arkansas St. ■	64
68	Ark.-Little Rock ■	65
90	IPFW	80
71	Florida Int'l ■	69
70	Tex.-Pan American ■	52
51	Arkansas St.	83
52	Ark.-Little Rock	71
62	Denver ■	47
61	Western Ky.	65
48	South Ala. †	47
48	New Mexico St. †	63

Nickname: Blue Raiders
Colors: Royal Blue & White
Arena: Murphy Athletic Center
   Capacity: 11,520; Year Built: 1972
AD: James Donnelly
SID: Ryan Simmons

MIDDLEBURY
Middlebury, VT 05753 III

Coach: Jeff Brown, Vermont 1982

2001-02 RESULTS (11-13)

68	Washington (Mo.)	99
49	Trinity (Tex.) †	90
75	St. Joseph (Vt.)	63
73	Skidmore	64
83	Hamilton ■	92
95	Mass. Liberal Arts	67
87	Johnson St. ■	60
89	Southern Vt.	96
74	Springfield ■	81
64	Norwich ■	48
73	Keene St.	88
70	Castleton St. ■	51
64	Union (N.Y.) ■	58
65	Trinity (Conn.) ■	79
76	Amherst	69
60	Brandeis	63
71	Bowdoin	76
74	Colby	82
84	Colby-Sawyer ■	77
63	Connecticut Col. ■	64

100	Wesleyan (Conn.) ■	87
101	Bates	66
88	Tufts	103
63	Williams	88

Nickname: Panthers
Colors: Blue & White
Arena: Pepin Gymnasium
   Capacity: 1,200; Year Built: 1949
AD: Russell Reilly
SID: Brad Nadeau

MIDWESTERN ST.
Wichita Falls, TX 76308-2099 ...II

Coach: Greg Giddings, Midwestern St. 1985

2001-02 RESULTS (13-14)

86	Drury ■	80
65	Incarnate Word ■	67
72	Mo. Southern St.	100
88	Incarnate Word	85
89	Angelo St. ■	88
66	Eastern N.M.	74
81	West Tex. A&M	87
66	St. Mary's (Tex.)	79
63	Tarleton St.	65
61	St. Mary's (Tex.) ■	55
64	Trinity (Tex.)	62
60	Tex. A&M-Kingsville	70
57	Tex. A&M-Commerce	54
75	Abilene Christian ■	58
68	Southwestern Okla.	89
58	Cameron ■	49
76	Southeastern Okla.	85
75	East Central ■	69
56	Northeastern St. ■	66
69	Central Okla.	65
78	Southwestern Okla. ■	83
84	Cameron	66
65	Southeastern Okla. ■	56
68	East Central	87
48	Northeastern St.	52
91	Central Okla. ■	80
60	Tarleton St.	76

Nickname: Indians
Colors: Maroon and Gold
Arena: D.L. Ligon Coliseum
   Capacity: 5,200; Year Built: 1969
AD: Jeff Ray
SID: Andy Austin

MILES
Birmingham, AL 35208 II

Coach: Roosevelt Sanders, Alabama St. 1973

2001-02 RESULTS (16-12)

66	Stillman ■	45
84	Talladega	68
65	Delta St.	84
54	Southern Ark. †	69
76	Tuskegee ■	53
61	North Ala.	76
78	West Fla. †	77
83	Talladega ■	84
76	Stillman	67
65	Morehouse ■	70
88	Kentucky St.	95
75	Lane	71
76	LeMoyne-Owen ■	79
64	Clark Atlanta	72
60	Paine	75
72	Albany St. (Ga.) ■	75
71	Fort Valley St. ■	70
60	Tuskegee	77
60	Morehouse	37
78	Kentucky St. ■	55
80	Lane ■	61
67	LeMoyne-Owen	64
81	Clark Atlanta ■	70
80	Paine ■	66
63	Albany St. (Ga.)	59

59	Fort Valley St.	54
62	LeMoyne-Owen †	61
49	Morehouse †	57

Nickname: Golden Bears
Colors: Purple & Gold
Arena: Knox-Windham Gym
   Capacity: 2,000; Year Built: 1949
AD: Augustus James
SID: LaTaiya Barnes

MILLERSVILLE
Millersville, PA 17551-0302 II

Coach: Fred Thompson, La.-Monroe 1990

2001-02 RESULTS (17-10)

67	Col. of West Va.	89
44	West Va. Wesleyan	64
61	New Haven	67
60	Dist. Columbia ■	45
77	Shippensburg	81
67	Dist. Columbia	85
79	Edinboro ■	69
70	Slippery Rock ■	48
89	Francis Marion	64
76	Lock Haven	69
64	Clarion ■	55
67	Kutztown	62
78	Calif. (Pa.) ■	73
49	Indiana (Pa.)	86
65	West Chester ■	51
53	East Stroudsburg	35
75	Mansfield ■	48
78	Col. of West Va. ■	96
76	Cheyney ■	67
73	Kutztown ■	64
89	Bloomsburg	77
66	East Stroudsburg ■	65
89	Cheyney	91
80	West Chester	91
76	Bloomsburg ■	71
82	Mansfield	80
75	Cheyney ■	77

Nickname: Marauders
Colors: Black & Gold
Arena: Pucillo Gymnasium
   Capacity: 3,000; Year Built: 1970
AD: Daniel N. Audette
SID: Greg Wright

MILLIKIN
Decatur, IL 62522-2084 III

Coach: Tim Littrell, Millikin 1977

2001-02 RESULTS (8-17)

97	Eureka	64
73	Blackburn	75
87	Franklin	99
101	Ind.-Northwest ■	57
67	Aurora	72
87	Judson (Ill.) ■	85
102	MacMurray ■	57
64	Illinois Col.	79
74	Ohio Dominican †	90
82	Bluffton	85
75	Webster	63
94	North Central	82
68	Carthage	84
82	Augustana (Ill.) ■	76
60	North Central ■	62
61	Ill. Wesleyan ■	63
76	Elmhurst	78
69	Wheaton (Ill.)	84
87	North Park ■	91
96	Wheaton (Ill.) ■	86
79	Augustana (Ill.)	82
61	Carthage ■	74
60	North Park	69
65	Elmhurst	94
79	Ill. Wesleyan	82

Nickname: Big Blue
Colors: Royal Blue & White

Arena: Griswold Gymnasium
   Capacity: 4,080; Year Built: 1970
AD: Doug Neibuhr
SID: Julie Farr

MILLSAPS
Jackson, MS 39210 III

Coach: John Stroud, Mississippi 1980

2001-02 RESULTS (18-7)

87	Loyola (La.) ■	77
74	Huntingdon ■	37
67	Huntingdon	51
88	Rust ■	71
82	Oglethorpe ■	59
63	Loyola (La.)	60
75	Rust	71
51	Southern Miss.	64
74	Southwestern (Tex.) ■	65
62	Trinity (Tex.) ■	52
60	DePauw	75
78	Rose-Hulman	74
71	Centre ■	70
72	Sewanee ■	63
61	Rhodes	66
74	Hendrix	56
72	Southwestern (Tex.)	76
60	Trinity (Tex.)	75
71	DePauw ■	66
54	Rose-Hulman ■	58
81	Centre	78
58	Sewanee	59
89	Rhodes ■	77
83	Hendrix ■	54
96	Oglethorpe	91

Nickname: Majors
Colors: Purple & White
Arena: Physical Activities Cente
   Capacity: 3,000; Year Built: 1974
AD: Ron Jurney
SID: Jeff Mitchell

MILWAUKEE ENGR.
Milwaukee, WI 53202-3109 III

Coach: Brian Good, Wisconsin 1993

2001-02 RESULTS (7-20)

64	Lawrence †	94
77	Carroll (Wis.)	71
71	Elmhurst	79
65	Illinois Tech ■	57
72	Lake Forest ■	67
72	Lakeland	83
73	Concordia (Ill.) †	76
71	Dominican (Ill.) †	85
85	Northland Bapt. ■	47
61	Wis.-Eau Claire ■	95
81	Rockford	87
81	North Park ■	76
61	Calvin †	73
75	Palm Beach Atl.	80
68	Marian (Wis.) ■	70
58	Concordia (Wis.) ■	65
72	Wis. Lutheran ■	93
55	Edgewood	66
71	Lakeland	86
82	Maranatha Baptist ■	67
65	Marian (Wis.)	73
64	Wis. Lutheran	69
54	Concordia (Wis.)	85
70	Maranatha Baptist	78
63	Edgewood ■	64
75	Lakeland	72
49	Edgewood	61

Nickname: Raiders
Colors: Red & White
Arena: US Cellular Arena
   Capacity: 12,000
AD: Daniel I. Harris
SID: Mark Ostapina

MINNESOTA
Minneapolis, MN 55455 I

Coach: Dan Monson, Idaho 1985
2001-02 RESULTS (18-13)

80	Mercer ■	59
92	UNC Asheville ■	65
86	Eastern Wash. ■	68
79	Wake Forest	85
89	Tex.-Pan American ■	72
50	UNC Wilmington ■	58
55	Georgia	77
75	Oregon ■	72
95	Md.-East. Shore ■	48
81	Nebraska ■	72
60	Texas Tech	80
53	Illinois	76
70	Michigan St. ■	67
90	Michigan ■	82
87	Purdue ■	71
64	Wisconsin	73
69	Michigan	71
89	Ohio St. ■	71
94	Penn St. ■	70
88	Indiana ■	74
86	Iowa	78
56	Northwestern	58
62	Wisconsin ■	67
55	Michigan St.	74
68	Penn St.	64
69	Northwestern ■	51
66	Illinois ■	67
84	Penn St. †	60
76	Illinois †	92
96	New Mexico ■	62
66	Richmond ■	67

Nickname: Golden Gophers
Colors: Maroon & Gold
Arena: Williams Arena
   Capacity: 14,625; Year Built: 1928
AD: Joel Maturi
SID: Bill Crumley

MINN. ST. MOORHEAD
Moorhead, MN 56563-2996 II

Coach: Mike Olson, St. Norbert 1981
2001-02 RESULTS (17-10)

70	Concordia-M'head	54
77	St. Martin's †	64
97	Western Wash.	94
69	North Dakota	72
69	North Dakota ■	79
60	Valley City St. ■	46
65	Minn.-Crookston	73
83	Valley City St.	73
77	Northland	32
75	Minn.-Duluth ■	63
76	Bemidji St. ■	66
70	Northern St.	66
91	Minn.-Morris	65
90	Concordia-St. Paul ■	54
64	Winona St.	73
69	Wayne St. (Neb.)	72
65	Southwest St.	75
74	Minn.-Crookston ■	48
59	Bemidji St.	71
45	Minn.-Duluth	71
80	Minn.-Morris ■	64
64	Northern St. ■	80
55	Winona St.	53
74	Concordia-St. Paul	61
74	Southwest St. ■	67
76	Wayne St. (Neb.) ■	48
56	Southwest St.	84

Nickname: Dragons
Colors: Scarlet & White
Arena: Alex Nemzek Hall
   Capacity: 3,400; Year Built: 1960
AD: Katy Wilson
SID: Larry Scott

MINN. ST.-MANKATO
Mankato, MN 56001 II

Coach: Dan McCarrell, North Park 1961
2001-02 RESULTS (9-17)

76	Wis.-Parkside ■	86
92	Truman ■	60
76	Sioux Falls	85
84	Southwest St. ■	88
84	Winona St.	73
78	Morningside ■	55
72	South Dakota ■	80
100	Viterbo ■	75
65	Minn.-Duluth	88
76	Concordia-St. Paul ■	59
64	St. Cloud St.	85
69	Augustana (S.D.) ■	82
66	South Dakota St.	97
77	Neb.-Omaha ■	59
81	Northern Colo. ■	79
66	North Dakota St.	65
72	North Dakota	78
78	St. Cloud St. ■	81
76	South Dakota St.	87
60	Augustana (S.D.) ■	66
88	Northern Colo.	104
61	Neb.-Omaha	73
78	North Dakota ■	87
89	North Dakota St. ■	79
53	South Dakota	94
67	Morningside	73

Nickname: Mavericks
Colors: Purple & Gold
Arena: Bresnan Arena In Taylor Center
   Capacity: 4,521; Year Built: 2000
SID: Paul Allan

MINN.-CROOKSTON
Crookston, MN 56716-5001 II

2001-02 RESULTS (7-19)

88	Valley City St. ■	65
75	Mayville St. ■	79
77	St. Cloud St. ■	86
67	Mayville St.	77
64	Morningside ■	80
67	Valley City St.	74
73	Minn. St. Moorhead ■	65
81	North Dakota St.	78
60	North Dakota	80
92	Bemidji St. ■	94
72	Minn.-Duluth	73
85	Minn.-Morris	76
74	Northern St.	84
77	Winona St.	73
73	Concordia-St. Paul ■	87
68	Southwest St.	91
74	Wayne St. (Neb.)	79
48	Minn. St. Moorhead	74
43	Minn.-Duluth	84
62	Bemidji St.	71
70	Northern St. ■	101
92	Minn.-Morris ■	69
94	Concordia-St. Paul	96
73	Winona St.	89
84	Wayne St. (Neb.) ■	71
69	Southwest St. ■	83

Nickname: Golden Eagle
Colors: Maroon & Gold
Arena: Lysaker Gym
   Capacity: 3,500; Year Built: 1970
AD: Lon Boike
SID: Nick Kornder

MINN.-DULUTH
Duluth, MN 55812-2496 II

Coach: Gary Holquist, Milton 1979
2001-02 RESULTS (19-11)

66	UC-Colo. Spgs. †	74
55	Southern Colo.	65

75	Montevallo ■	69
72	South Dakota St. ■	89
80	North Dakota St.	89
74	Southwest St. ■	54
70	Wayne St. (Neb.) ■	49
54	North Dakota	67
88	Minn. St.-Mankato	65
61	Michigan Tech ■	77
63	Minn. St. Moorhead	75
73	Minn.-Crookston	72
80	Bemidji St.	82
79	Northern St. ■	72
97	Minn.-Morris ■	53
68	Concordia-St. Paul	46
71	Winona St.	65
66	Wayne St. (Neb.)	61
65	Southwest St.	64
84	Minn.-Crookston ■	43
71	Minn. St. Moorhead	45
57	Bemidji St. ■	61
78	Minn.-Morris	55
61	Northern St.	63
77	Winona St. ■	60
78	Concordia-St. Paul ■	60
79	Wayne St. (Neb.) ■	62
69	Bemidji St. †	58
59	Southwest St. †	57
61	Metro St. †	66

Nickname: Bulldogs
Colors: Maroon & Gold
Arena: Romano Gymnasium
   Capacity: 2,759; Year Built: 1953
AD: Robert Corran
SID: Troy Andre

MINN.-MORRIS
Morris, MN 56267 II

Coach: Jim Severson, Minn.-Morris 1977
2001-02 RESULTS (3-24)

75	North Dakota St.	96
75	Angelo St. †	98
69	South Dakota	96
52	Valley City St. ■	78
72	Winona St. ■	96
75	Concordia-St. Paul ■	84
80	Crown ■	68
100	Martin Luther ■	99
60	South Dakota St.	127
90	Sioux Falls	103
59	Southwest St.	101
81	Wayne St. (Neb.)	92
76	Minn.-Crookston	85
65	Minn. St. Moorhead ■	91
54	Bemidji St.	84
53	Minn.-Duluth	97
57	Northern St.	109
61	Concordia-St. Paul	69
78	Winona St.	89
71	Wayne St. (Neb.) ■	70
56	Southwest St.	94
64	Minn. St. Moorhead	80
69	Minn.-Crookston	92
55	Minn.-Duluth ■	78
60	Bemidji St. ■	78
66	Northern St.	94
47	Northern St.	99

Nickname: Cougars
Colors: Maroon & Gold
Arena: Physical Education Center
   Capacity: 3,500; Year Built: 1971
AD: Mark Fohl
SID: Brian Curtis

MISERICORDIA
Dallas, PA 18612 III

Coach: David Martin, Wilkes 1990
2001-02 RESULTS (19-10)

87	Baptist Bible (Pa.) ■	63
63	Richard Stockton ■	66
77	Lycoming	82
57	DeSales ■	50

79	King's (Pa.)	81
65	Gwynedd-Mercy	72
62	Arcadia ■	60
83	Centenary (N.J.) ■	55
62	Eastern	52
66	Cortland St. †	54
53	Williams	76
86	Marywood ■	66
85	Wesley	68
67	Neumann ■	66
52	Cabrini	62
64	Gwynedd-Mercy ■	52
89	Alvernia ■	69
77	Eastern ■	72
83	Arcadia	74
101	Marywood	65
95	Villa Julie ■	71
68	Neumann	71
70	Wesley ■	63
63	Cabrini ■	59
65	Alvernia	73
100	Arcadia ■	68
76	Neumann ■	86
86	DeSales ■	80
73	King's (Pa.) †	76

Nickname: Cougars
Colors: Royal Blue & Gold
Arena: Anderson Sports-Health Center
   Capacity: 1,500; Year Built: 1992
AD: Michael W. Mould
SID: Scott Crispell

MISSISSIPPI
University, MS 38677 I

Coach: Rod Barnes, Mississippi 1988
2001-02 RESULTS (20-11)

78	Bowling Green †	82
75	Alas. Fairbanks	58
80	Wichita St. †	68
67	Kansas St.	65
92	Morris Brown ■	45
70	George Mason ■	71
78	La.-Monroe ■	43
71	Memphis	67
83	Tenn.-Martin †	72
77	IUPUI †	70
68	UTEP	58
95	Ark.-Pine Bluff ■	53
75	Lipscomb ■	49
76	Tennessee	82
69	Auburn ■	65
66	Mississippi St. ■	59
64	Kentucky	87
70	Arkansas	64
70	LSU ■	55
71	South Carolina ■	53
73	Vanderbilt ■	61
72	Georgia	79
59	Alabama	79
79	Arkansas ■	67
62	Auburn	65
68	Florida ■	51
59	Mississippi St.	61
56	LSU	59
84	Alabama ■	56
67	South Carolina †	69
58	UCLA †	80

Nickname: Rebels
Colors: Red & Blue
Arena: C.M. "Tad" Smith Coliseum
   Capacity: 8,700; Year Built: 1966
AD: Pete Boone
SID: Lamar Chance

MISSISSIPPI COL.
Clinton, MS 39058 III

Coach: Mike Jones, Mississippi Col. 1975
2001-02 RESULTS (21-3)

84	Wiley ■	47
76	Southwestern Aly God ■	73
68	Loyola (La.) ■	50

69	Hardin-Simmons ■	45
77	Louisiana Col. ■	53
82	Colorado Col. †	74
76	Pacific Lutheran †	64
68	Mt. St. Joseph †	65
66	Concordia-Austin	69
71	Mary Hardin-Baylor	70
72	LeTourneau ■	61
75	East Tex. Baptist ■	63
77	Louisiana Col.	74
67	Texas-Dallas	77
71	Austin	53
86	Ozarks (Ark.)	66
64	Austin ■	53
96	Ozarks (Ark.) ■	63
60	LeTourneau	55
91	East Tex. Baptist	62
76	Texas-Dallas ■	56
65	Mary Hardin-Baylor †	55
88	McMurry	75
57	Lewis & Clark ■	70

Nickname: Choctaws
Colors: Blue & Gold
Arena: A.E. Wood Coliseum
  Capacity: 3,500; Year Built: 1979
AD: Mike Jones
SID: Will Chandler

MISSISSIPPI ST.
Mississippi State, MS 39762-5509 I

Coach: Rick Stansbury, Campbellsville 1982

2001-02 RESULTS (27-8)

95	Nicholls St. ■	59
92	Florida A&M ■	55
93	Ark.-Little Rock ■	81
79	La.-Lafayette	71
70	Alabama A&M ■	45
73	South Ala. ■	66
71	Richmond	57
91	Arkansas St. ■	83
104	La.-Monroe †	67
72	Georgia St. †	63
74	Richmond †	72
56	Cincinnati †	90
77	Ill.-Chicago †	74
77	Tulane	66
74	Kentucky ■	69
64	Arkansas	75
59	Mississippi	66
92	Tennessee ■	91
73	Alabama	85
84	LSU ■	61
72	Auburn	64
48	Florida	76
68	Georgia	86
76	Alabama ■	62
65	LSU	68
89	Auburn ■	53
66	Vanderbilt	43
61	Mississippi ■	59
89	Arkansas ■	83
64	South Carolina	57
62	Florida †	52
57	LSU †	51
61	Alabama †	58
70	McNeese St. †	58
64	Texas †	68

Nickname: Bulldogs
Colors: Maroon & White
Arena: Humphrey Coliseum
  Capacity: 10,500; Year Built: 1975
AD: Larry Templeton
SID: David Rosinski

MISSISSIPPI VAL.
Itta Bena, MS 38941-1400 I

Coach: Lafayette Stribling, Miss. Industrial 1957

2001-02 RESULTS (12-17)

67	Alabama	107
65	Loyola Marymount †	74
79	Arkansas St. ■	77
75	Delta St.	70
49	Arkansas St.	94
82	Southeast Mo. St.	70
80	Ark.-Pine Bluff ■	68
82	UTEP	89
74	IUPUI †	86
65	Creighton	90
52	Alabama St.	57
81	Alabama A&M	65
77	Alcorn St. ■	88
84	Southern U. ■	77
69	Texas Southern	72
78	Prairie View	85
59	Delta St.	72
85	Jackson St. ■	78
91	Grambling ■	87
72	Alabama St. ■	75
72	Alabama A&M ■	84
86	Alcorn St.	87
73	Southern U.	88
90	Texas Southern ■	61
107	Prairie View ■	76
75	Jackson St.	89
99	Grambling	87
77	Ark.-Pine Bluff	58
61	Texas Southern	68

Nickname: Delta Devils
Colors: Forest Green & White
Arena: Harrison HPER Complex
  Capacity: 6,000; Year Built: 1970
AD: Lonza C. Hardy
SID: Marlon J. Reed

MISSOURI
Columbia, MO 65211-1050 I

Coach: Quin Snyder, Duke 1989

2001-02 RESULTS (24-12)

89	Tenn.-Martin ■	63
86	Air Force ■	58
75	Alabama †	68
78	Iowa †	77
72	Xavier †	60
106	Jackson St. ■	68
100	Grambling ■	76
69	St. Louis	67
117	Southern U. ■	67
65	Iowa ■	83
61	Illinois †	72
62	DePaul	63
74	Coppin St. ■	47
60	Nebraska ■	53
67	Iowa St.	71
81	Kansas St.	66
74	Texas A&M ■	50
92	Colorado ■	77
71	Oklahoma	84
86	Kansas St. ■	74
73	Kansas	105
81	Virginia ■	77
76	Iowa St.	73
80	Baylor	81
87	Nebraska	71
70	Texas ■	72
68	Texas Tech	91
96	Colorado	83
72	Oklahoma St. ■	69
92	Kansas ■	95
79	Iowa St. †	59
85	Texas †	89
93	Miami (Fla.) †	80
83	Ohio St. †	67
82	UCLA †	73
75	Oklahoma †	81

Nickname: Tigers
Colors: Old Gold & Black
Arena: Hearnes Center
  Capacity: 13,545; Year Built: 1972
AD: Michael F. Alden
SID: Chad Moller

UMKC
Kansas City, MO 64110 I

Coach: Rich Zvosec, Defiance 1983

2001-02 RESULTS (18-11)

48	Wis.-Green Bay ■	47
58	Md.-East. Shore ■	55
69	Southwest Mo. St. ■	63
79	Northern Iowa ■	64
70	Robert Morris ■	63
68	Kansas	79
67	Wis.-Green Bay ■	54
50	Oklahoma St. ■	62
68	Youngstown St. ■	53
58	Arkansas St. †	60
63	Wayland Baptist †	53
55	Oral Roberts	67
72	Oakland ■	63
63	IUPUI ■	64
67	Tex. A&M-Corp. Chris. ■	61
63	Western Ill.	51
60	Valparaiso	78
67	Chicago St.	53
49	Southern Utah ■	54
75	Oral Roberts ■	85
55	IUPUI	54
59	Oakland	72
63	Valparaiso ■	76
64	Western Ill. ■	52
72	Southern Utah	71
61	Chicago St. ■	48
81	IPFW ■	66
70	Southern Utah †	57
58	Valparaiso †	71

Nickname: Kangaroos
Colors: Blue & Gold
Arena: Municipal Auditorium
  Capacity: 9,827; Year Built: 1936
AD: Robert W. Thomas
SID: Pat Madden

MO.-ROLLA
Rolla, MO 65401 II

Coach: Dale Martin, Central Mo. St. 1976

2001-02 RESULTS (13-15)

88	Maryville (Mo.) ■	65
68	Regis (Colo.) †	65
73	Colo. Christian †	71
79	BYU-Hawaii †	89
78	Alas. Anchorage †	76
99	Lincoln (Mo.) ■	95
85	Christian Bros. ■	77
71	Mo.-St. Louis	67
71	Christian Bros.	81
67	Mo. Southern St. ■	75
71	Emporia St.	80
79	Southwest Baptist ■	74
78	Pittsburg St.	81
53	Washburn ■	59
60	Central Mo. St. ■	61
58	Mo. Western St.	77
68	Truman	60
73	Northwest Mo. St.	79
72	Mo. Southern St.	89
82	Emporia St. ■	66
63	Southwest Baptist	79
82	Pittsburg St. ■	72
64	Washburn	94
53	Central Mo. St.	32
67	Mo. Western St. ■	98
75	Truman ■	72
62	Northwest Mo. St.	75
54	Mo. Western St.	64

Nickname: Miners
Colors: Silver & Gold
Arena: Bullman Multi-Purpose
  Capacity: 4,550; Year Built: 1969
AD: Mark Mullin
SID: John Kean

MO.-ST. LOUIS
St. Louis, MO 63121-4499 II

Coach: Mark Bernsen, Mo.-St. Louis 1972

2001-02 RESULTS (10-17)

66	Truman	52
73	Lindenwood ■	54
69	Southern Ind. ■	53
70	SIU-Edwardsville ■	80
58	Lewis ■	66
79	Mo. Baptist ■	55
81	St. Joseph's (Ind.)	61
73	Indianapolis	82
67	Mo.-Rolla	71
80	Harris-Stowe ■	65
63	Bellarmine ■	71
57	Ky. Wesleyan ■	86
65	Quincy	67
64	Lewis	67
60	Wis.-Parkside	57
63	Indianapolis ■	64
73	Northern Ky. ■	78
64	Ky. Wesleyan	80
63	Southern Ind.	72
79	Quincy ■	67
70	SIU-Edwardsville	66
71	Mo. Baptist	81
76	Wis.-Parkside ■	58
61	St. Joseph's (Ind.) ■	63
75	Northern Ky.	88
74	Bellarmine	81
59	Ky. Wesleyan †	89

Nickname: Rivermen
Colors: Red & Gold
Arena: Mark Twain Building
  Capacity: 4,736; Year Built: 1971
AD: Patricia A. Dolan
SID: Todd Addington

MO. SOUTHERN ST.
Joplin, MO 64801-1595 II

Coach: Robert Corn, Mo. Southern St. 1978

2001-02 RESULTS (20-8)

95	St. Martin's †	72
86	Philander Smith †	60
100	Midwestern St. ■	72
63	Northeastern St.	64
77	Southeastern Okla.	71
92	Bacone ■	42
91	Okla. Panhandle ■	59
70	Rockhurst ■	59
75	Mo.-Rolla	67
86	Southwest Baptist ■	62
74	Washburn	86
70	Central Mo. St. ■	62
67	Northwest Mo. St.	90
78	Pittsburg St.	65
125	Emporia St. ■	82
73	Mo. Western St.	80
77	Truman ■	62
89	Mo.-Rolla ■	72
99	Southwest Baptist	74
83	Washburn ■	74
65	Central Mo. St.	78
94	Northwest Mo. St. ■	77
81	Pittsburg St. ■	83
98	Emporia St.	85
76	Mo. Western St. ■	91
101	Truman	62
63	Southwest Baptist ■	60
76	Northwest Mo. St.	79

Nickname: Lions
Colors: Green & Gold
Arena: Leggett & Platt A.C.
   Capacity: 3,240; Year Built: 1999
AD: Sallie Beard
SID: Joe Moore

MO. WESTERN ST.
St. Joseph, MO 64507 II

Coach: Tom Smith, Valparaiso 1967

2001-02 RESULTS (23-7)
125	William Jewell ■	99
85	South Dakota ■	98
124	St. Mary (Kan.) ■	85
112	Lincoln (Mo.) ■	126
109	Lincoln (Mo.)	101
72	Rockhurst ■	83
82	Barry †	72
65	Lynn †	59
95	Washburn	92
74	Central Mo. St.	64
70	Northwest Mo. St. ■	76
97	Emporia St. ■	81
76	Pittsburg St. ■	64
82	Truman	75
77	Mo.-Rolla	58
80	Mo. Southern St. ■	73
77	Southwest Baptist	79
73	Washburn ■	71
71	Central Mo. St. ■	55
64	Northwest Mo. St.	59
85	Emporia St. ■	59
83	Pittsburg St.	68
83	Truman ■	60
98	Mo.-Rolla	67
91	Mo. Southern St. ■	76
83	Southwest Baptist ■	52
64	Mo.-Rolla ■	54
75	Washburn	60
58	Northwest Mo. St. ■	71
68	Rockhurst †	75

Nickname: Griffons
Colors: Black & Gold
Arena: MWSC Fieldhouse
   Capacity: 3,750; Year Built: 1981
AD: Peter Chapman
SID: Brett King

MOLLOY
Rockville Centre, NY 11570-5002 II

Coach: Charles Marquardt, St. Joseph's (Me.) 1986

2001-02 RESULTS (8-19)
95	Farmingdale St. ■	76
72	Bloomfield ■	57
79	Dowling ■	80
61	Bridgeport ■	76
67	Philadelphia U. ■	61
65	St. Thomas Aquinas	67
71	Southampton ■	73
56	Fla. Southern	98
54	Tampa	79
60	Adelphi	74
75	Mercy ■	65
70	C.W. Post ■	67
80	Concordia (N.Y.) ■	57
66	Queens (N.Y.)	83
52	Bridgeport ■	55
57	Philadelphia U.	88
58	St. Thomas Aquinas ■	61
85	Dowling	88
66	Southampton	85
61	NYIT	63
57	Adelphi ■	67
88	Mercy	87
70	C.W. Post ■	88
77	Concordia (N.Y.)	87
69	Queens (N.Y.) ■	78
67	NYIT ■	53
68	Adelphi	85

Nickname: Lions
Colors: Maroon & White
Arena: Quealy Gymnasium
   Capacity: 400; Year Built: 1955
AD: Harold Herman
SID: Dan Drutz

MONMOUTH
West Long Branch, NJ 07764 I

Coach: Dave Calloway, Monmouth 1991

2001-02 RESULTS (18-12)
50	Rider ■	45
64	Akron †	61
81	Vanderbilt †	67
48	Notre Dame †	85
51	Seton Hall	72
69	Wagner ■	65
70	Princeton	76
55	Maryland	91
69	St. Peter's	61
69	Sacred Heart ■	96
54	Gonzaga ■	79
73	Long Island	57
86	St. Francis (N.Y.)	71
75	Mt. St. Mary's ■	63
72	UMBC ■	75
61	Wagner	69
57	St. Francis (Pa.) ■	55
42	Central Conn. St.	50
78	UMBC	73
84	Mt. St. Mary's	60
84	Long Island ■	74
83	Fairleigh Dickinson	62
95	Quinnipiac	88
62	Central Conn. St. ■	63
60	St. Francis (Pa.)	43
63	Robert Morris	69
88	Quinnipiac ■	71
75	St. Francis (N.Y.) ■	68
73	Fairleigh Dickinson ■	63
61	St. Francis (N.Y.) †	71

Nickname: Hawks
Colors: Royal Blue & White
Arena: Boylan Gymnasium
   Capacity: 2,500; Year Built: 1965
AD: Marilyn A. McNeil
SID: Thomas Dick

MONMOUTH (ILL.)
Monmouth, IL 61462-1998 III

Coach: Terry Glasgow, Parsons 1966

2001-02 RESULTS (9-13)
71	SIU-Edwardsville	76
83	Principia ■	77
83	Rockford ■	87
67	MacMurray ■	73
65	Lake Forest	75
79	Knox ■	83
48	Eckerd	87
81	Tampa	107
131	Grinnell ■	124
66	Lawrence ■	56
78	Beloit ■	74
69	Illinois Col.	79
64	Ripon	85
93	Carroll (Wis.)	82
62	St. Norbert ■	71
78	Ripon ■	75
75	Lake Forest ■	85
68	Beloit	69
60	Lawrence	56
121	Grinnell	135
90	Illinois Col. ■	69
66	Knox	56

Nickname: Fighting Scots
Colors: Crimson & White
Arena: Glennie Gymnasium
   Capacity: 1,600; Year Built: 1982

AD: Terry L. Glasgow
SID: Barry McNamara, Dan Nolan

MONTANA
Missoula, MT 59812-1291 I

Coach: Don Holst, Northern Mont. 1975

2001-02 RESULTS (16-15)
80	Evergreen St. ■	77
63	Gonzaga	83
67	Northern Iowa	87
72	Concordia (Cal.) ■	48
75	Washington St.	71
64	Pacific (Cal.) ■	77
75	Nevada ■	68
47	Idaho	48
71	Colorado	84
78	Navy †	61
82	Tulsa †	92
67	New Mexico St. †	79
82	Loyola Marymount ■	67
80	Weber St.	73
46	Eastern Wash.	79
99	Portland St.	88
71	Weber St. ■	90
74	Idaho St. ■	65
64	Northern Ariz.	77
88	Sacramento St.	78
56	Montana St.	76
80	Portland St. ■	66
78	Eastern Wash. ■	80
64	Idaho St.	79
86	Sacramento St. ■	53
70	Northern Ariz. ■	63
55	Montana St.	75
82	Northern Ariz. †	64
70	Montana St.	68
70	Eastern Wash.	66
62	Oregon †	81

Nickname: Grizzlies
Colors: Copper, Silver & Gold
Arena: Adams Center
   Capacity: 7,500; Year Built: 1953
AD: Wayne Hogan
SID: Dave Guffey

MONTANA ST.
Bozeman, MT 59717-3380 I

Coach: Mick Durham, Montana St. 1979

2001-02 RESULTS (20-10)
70	Fresno St.	92
51	Utah St.	66
73	Jamestown ■	58
65	Air Force †	70
82	UC Riverside †	72
55	Utah St.	60
77	Montana St.-Northern ■	69
69	Arizona St.	72
69	Wyoming †	82
63	IPFW ■	59
80	Hampton ■	66
68	San Diego ■	59
64	Weber St.	62
66	Portland	63
74	Portland St.	68
90	Eastern Wash.	81
78	Idaho St. ■	47
79	Weber St. ■	68
56	Sacramento St.	78
59	Northern Ariz.	48
76	Montana ■	56
62	Eastern Wash. ■	66
94	Portland St. ■	82
63	Idaho St.	59
62	Northern Ariz. ■	59
70	Sacramento St. ■	60
75	Montana	55
68	Montana ■	70
77	Utah St.	69
48	Richmond	63

Nickname: Bobcats
Colors: Blue & Gold
Arena: Worthington Arena
   Capacity: 7,250; Year Built: 1956
AD: Dan Davies
SID: Bill Lamberty

MONT. ST.-BILLINGS
Billings, MT 59101-0298 II

Coach: Craig Carse, Bethany (W.Va.) 1978

2001-02 RESULTS (21-7)
77	Mesa St. ■	65
98	Mesa St. ■	91
101	Minot St. ■	86
98	Chadron St. ■	87
113	P.R.-Mayaguez ■	73
121	P.R.-Mayaguez ■	79
126	Great Falls ■	101
105	Cal Poly Pomona ■	80
65	Cal St. San B'dino	111
75	Chaminade ■	81
77	Chaminade	76
81	Hawaii-Hilo	92
103	Okla. Panhandle ■	79
118	Okla. Panhandle ■	90
89	BYU-Hawaii ■	78
120	BYU-Hawaii ■	80
67	Hawaii Pacific ■	56
76	Western N.M.	74
72	Western N.M.	67
83	Hawaii-Hilo ■	74
95	Hawaii-Hilo ■	79
108	Chaminade	79
81	Hawaii Pacific	84
51	Hawaii Pacific ■	73
76	BYU-Hawaii	94
106	Western N.M. ■	83
96	Western N.M. ■	58
81	Cal St. Bakersfield †	84

Nickname: Yellowjackets
Colors: Cobalt Blue & Yellow
Arena: Alterowitz Gymnasium
   Capacity: 3,500; Year Built: 1961
AD: Gary R. Gray
SID: Travis Elam

MONTCLAIR ST.
Upper Montclair, NJ 07043 III

Coach: Ted Fiore, Seton Hall 1962

2001-02 RESULTS (19-9)
68	Medgar Evers ■	76
66	FDU-Madison ■	50
40	Rutgers-Newark ■	45
66	Richard Stockton	71
54	Wm. Paterson ■	51
53	Rowan	63
92	Kean ■	85
75	Rutgers-Camden	53
81	Farmingdale St.	70
74	Goucher ■	67
84	Worcester St. ■	74
64	Savannah A&D ■	59
77	Staten Island ■	63
87	Ramapo ■	67
56	Col. of New Jersey	53
94	New Jersey City ■	96
65	Rowan ■	63
61	Wm. Paterson	75
80	Richard Stockton ■	64
69	Rutgers-Newark	55
71	Rutgers-Camden ■	70
61	Kean	58
82	Ramapo	77
81	New Jersey City	83
76	Col. of New Jersey ■	69
42	Wm. Paterson ■	66
58	Baruch ■	72
55	New Jersey City ■	71

Nickname: Red Hawks
Colors: Scarlet & White
Arena: Panzer Gymnasium
  Capacity: 1,200; Year Built: 1954
AD: Holly P. Gera
SID: Mike Scala

MONTEVALLO
Montevallo, AL 35115-6001......II

Coach: Jeff Daniels, Montevallo 1984
2001-02 RESULTS (10-17)
73	Fort Valley St. ■	85
85	GC&SU ■	95
69	Minn.-Duluth	75
56	Michigan Tech †	59
73	Kennesaw St. ■	85
63	Ala.-Huntsville	61
70	Alabama St.	80
75	Southern Ark. †	87
76	Fort Valley St. †	78
77	Elizabeth City St. ■	74
65	Kennesaw St.	82
83	North Ala. ■	65
80	West Fla.	95
96	Lincoln Memorial ■	72
68	West Ala. ■	60
85	West Ga. ■	100
73	Valdosta St. ■	54
109	Oakland City ■	96
62	Ala.-Huntsville ■	68
91	North Ala.	89
89	West Fla. ■	81
87	Lincoln Memorial	92
69	West Ala.	75
74	West Ga. ■	70
70	Valdosta St. ■	71
78	Oakland City	90
73	Delta St. †	77

Nickname: Falcons
Colors: Purple & Gold
Arena: Myrick Hall
  Capacity: 1,500; Year Built: 1964
AD: Michael Cancilla
SID: Alfred Kojima

MORAVIAN
Bethlehem, PA 18018-6650......III

Coach: Jim Walker, Gettysburg 1965
2001-02 RESULTS (14-11)
94	Baldwin-Wallace †	89
88	Muhlenberg	75
55	DeSales	70
84	Scranton ■	87
78	Drew	70
88	Wilkes	82
74	Muhlenberg ■	68
83	Albright	80
66	Lebanon Valley ■	67
65	Dickinson ■	73
85	Salisbury ■	69
82	Elizabethtown	106
76	Messiah ■	72
64	Delaware Valley ■	58
57	Widener	80
86	Juniata ■	72
72	Swarthmore ■	56
68	Susquehanna ■	81
71	Lebanon Valley	64
86	Albright ■	74
72	Messiah	79
73	Elizabethtown ■	87
73	Widener ■	82
76	Susquehanna	79
64	Juniata	60

Nickname: Greyhounds
Colors: Blue & Grey
Arena: Johnston Hall
  Capacity: 1,200; Year Built: 1952
AD: Paul R. Moyer
SID: Mark Fleming

MOREHEAD ST.
Morehead, KY 40351-1689.......I

Coach: Kyle Macy, Kentucky 1980
2001-02 RESULTS (18-11)
82	IPFW	73
103	Shawnee St. ■	78
75	Kentucky	94
98	VMI ■	87
41	Dayton	85
80	Wright St. ■	72
77	Asbury ■	69
81	IUPUI	90
50	Samford	62
73	Vanderbilt	83
92	Tennessee St. ■	72
78	Tennessee Tech ■	81
71	Eastern Ill.	72
59	Southeast Mo. St. ■	53
86	Ohio Dominican ■	73
84	Eastern Ky. ■	71
92	Murray St. ■	83
89	Tenn.-Martin ■	88
72	Tennessee St.	91
68	Austin Peay ■	65
91	Southeast Mo. St. ■	75
68	Eastern Ill. ■	76
68	Tennessee Tech	75
76	Eastern Ky.	60
66	Austin Peay	51
84	Tenn.-Martin	72
66	Murray St.	60
91	Tennessee St. ■	82
75	Murray St. †	89

Nickname: Eagles
Colors: Blue & Gold
Arena: Ellis T. Johnson Arena
  Capacity: 6,500; Year Built: 1981
AD: Chip Smith
SID: Randy Stacy

MOREHOUSE
Atlanta, GA 30314..................II

Coach: Grady Brewer, Morehouse 1980
2001-02 RESULTS (20-9)
83	Fayetteville St. ■	81
87	N.C. Central	74
66	West Fla.	64
80	Columbus St. ■	66
74	LeMoyne-Owen	83
55	Xavier (La.) ■	60
91	Clark Atlanta ■	81
70	Miles	65
77	West Ga. †	92
63	Clayton St.	61
85	Fla. Southern ■	75
70	Paine	69
66	Albany St. (Ga.) ■	73
72	Kentucky St. ■	75
87	Lane ■	68
64	Fort Valley St. ■	62
88	Tuskegee ■	59
87	Clark Atlanta ■	77
74	LeMoyne-Owen ■	67
37	Miles ■	60
67	Paine ■	65
78	Albany St. (Ga.) ■	57
85	Kentucky St.	88
85	Lane	89
68	Fort Valley St. ■	58
76	Tuskegee ■	52
88	Clark Atlanta †	83
57	Miles †	49
49	Paine †	52

Nickname: Tigers
Colors: Maroon & White
Arena: Olympic Arena
  Capacity: 6,000; Year Built: 1996
AD: Andre' Pattillo
SID: James Nix

MORGAN ST.
Baltimore, MD 21251 I

Coach: Butch Beard, Louisville 1972
2001-02 RESULTS (3-25)
55	Pittsburgh	76
66	Coppin St. ■	68
63	Western Mich.	83
70	Hampton ■	78
66	Norfolk St. ■	79
62	Towson	67
65	Georgetown	91
56	Ark.-Little Rock	83
66	James Madison	84
47	Providence	91
76	Howard	93
67	Delaware St.	77
68	Canisius	74
59	Md.-East. Shore ■	60
66	Florida A&M	72
66	Bethune-Cookman	64
60	N.C. A&T ■	67
73	South Carolina St.	81
74	Hampton	89
69	Norfolk St.	74
66	Howard ■	64
52	Delaware St. ■	54
67	Md.-East. Shore	81
72	Bethune-Cookman ■	83
50	Florida A&M ■	67
65	Coppin St.	72
94	Florida A&M †	91
70	Hampton †	93

Nickname: Bears
Colors: Blue & Orange
Arena: Hill Field House
  Capacity: 6,500; Year Built: 1975
AD: David Y. Thomas
SID: Joseph McIver

MORNINGSIDE
Sioux City, IA 51106-1751 II

Coach: Bob Bargen, Nebraska 1973
2001-02 RESULTS (4-22)
61	Lincoln (Mo.) †	87
48	Western Ore. †	51
58	Grand View ■	77
80	Minn.-Crookston	64
69	Briar Cliff †	83
55	Minn. St.-Mankato	78
51	St. Cloud St.	87
62	Dakota Wesleyan ■	59
80	Dana ■	81
81	Mt. Marty ■	70
52	South Dakota St. ■	101
61	Augustana (S.D.) ■	94
40	Neb.-Omaha ■	87
73	Northern Colo.	101
64	North Dakota St. ■	79
67	North Dakota ■	101
75	South Dakota ■	103
53	Augustana (S.D.)	84
60	South Dakota St.	99
72	Northern Colo. ■	93
67	Neb.-Omaha	101
63	North Dakota	91
62	North Dakota St.	103
39	South Dakota	106
68	St. Cloud St. ■	98
73	Minn. St.-Mankato ■	67

Nickname: Mustangs
Colors: Maroon & White
Arena: Allee Gymnasium
  Capacity: 3,000; Year Built: 1949
AD: Jerry Schmutte
SID: Dave Rebstock

MORRIS BROWN
Atlanta, GA 30314 I

Coach: Derek Thompson
2001-02 RESULTS (5-24)
57	Clemson †	70
49	La Salle †	63
55	Eastern Mich. †	67
71	Lipscomb ■	70
41	Tulsa	88
45	Mississippi	92
65	Boston College	90
76	Denver ■	92
67	Alabama St. ■	80
47	Southern Miss.	73
46	Alabama St.	77
50	Oregon	96
45	Iowa St.	69
38	Marquette	85
46	Colorado St.	83
50	Denver	78
44	Colorado	84
48	Savannah St.	54
63	Clark Atlanta ■	57
68	Alcorn St. ■	64
74	Southern U. ■	80
71	Alabama A&M ■	79
53	Western Ky.	92
65	Savannah St.	57
77	Jacksonville St. ■	72
84	Clark Atlanta †	86
59	Jacksonville St.	90
63	Alabama A&M	88
69	Alcorn St.	92

Nickname: Wolverines
Colors: Purple & Black
Arena: John H. Lewis Gym
  Capacity: 3,000; Year Built: 1970
AD: Russell Ellington
SID: William C. Lindsey

MOUNT IDA
Newton Centre, MA 02459-3323 III

2001-02 RESULTS (9-13)
88	Albertus Magnus †	80
73	Colby †	100
76	Mass.-Boston	72
65	Lasell ■	73
70	Babson ■	78
85	Fitchburg St. ■	90
65	Johnson & Wales	66
79	Eastern Nazarene	70
90	New England	100
53	WPI	62
96	Becker ■	68
68	Curry	81
96	New England ■	86
89	Nichols ■	76
58	Maine Maritime	66
87	Roger Williams ■	74
79	Lasell	81
61	Wheaton (Mass.)	88
99	New England Col.	91
89	Becker	74
61	Maine Maritime	92
65	Maine Maritime †	71

Nickname: Mustangs
Colors: Green & White
AD: Jacqueline Palmer
SID: To be named

MOUNT OLIVE
Mount Olive, NC 28365..........II

Coach: Bill Clingan, Northeastern St.
2001-02 RESULTS (12-14)
98	Emmanuel (Ga.) ■	73
83	Mars Hill ■	71

106	Bluefield St.	89
90	West Virginia St. †	85
73	Fayetteville St. ■	78
70	Limestone ■	61
67	Anderson (S.C.)	69
103	Pfeiffer ■	107
80	Erskine	78
71	Coker ■	76
83	Queens (N.C.)	81
76	Barton	95
63	Belmont Abbey ■	78
86	Lees-McRae ■	67
92	Longwood	95
75	St. Andrews	59
80	Limestone	65
90	Anderson (S.C.) ■	98
101	Pfeiffer	109
74	Erskine ■	71
62	Coker	64
60	Queens (N.C.) ■	74
67	Barton ■	93
56	Belmont Abbey	106
87	Lees-McRae ■	73
71	Coker	73

Nickname: Trojans
Colors: Green & White
Arena: College Hall
  Capacity: 1,500; Year Built: 1987
AD: Allen M. Cassell
SID: Adam Pitterman

MT. ST. JOSEPH
Cincinnati, OH 45233-1672 III

Coach: Larry Cox, Hanover 1981
2001-02 RESULTS (9-17)

80	Otterbein ■	90
50	Carthage †	72
74	Blackburn †	75
58	Franklin ■	62
61	Anderson (Ind.)	75
71	Transylvania ■	58
66	Bluffton ■	55
69	Earlham	72
67	Capital	74
86	Linfield †	82
60	Cabrini ■	59
65	Mississippi Col. †	68
69	Thomas More ■	72
59	Hanover	60
96	Defiance ■	92
72	Manchester ■	65
80	Anderson (Ind.) ■	72
72	Franklin	83
90	Bluffton	96
68	Transylvania †	69
78	Savannah A&D ■	54
70	Thomas More ■	63
65	Defiance	80
55	Hanover ■	78
62	Manchester	74
64	Manchester ■	70

Nickname: Lions
Colors: Blue & Gold
Arena: Harrington Center
  Capacity: 2,000; Year Built: 1998
AD: Steven F. Radcliffe
SID: Dane Neumeister

MT. ST. MARY (N.Y.)
Newburgh, NY 12550 III

Coach: Duane Davis, Empire St. 1969
2001-02 RESULTS (16-11)

54	New York U.	71
88	Polytechnic (N.Y.)	46
48	Yeshiva	66
76	NYCCT ■	61
71	Medgar Evers ■	70
68	CCNY	61
61	Old Westbury	58
74	Purchase St.	69

60	Walsh †	75
69	Benedictine (Kan.) †	82
84	Stevens Tech ■	53
66	St. Joseph's (L.I.) ■	62
79	Mt. St. Vincent ■	58
69	Manhattanville ■	76
79	Vassar ■	68
70	Yeshiva ■	64
77	Merchant Marine	80
75	Stevens Tech	77
94	Mt. St. Vincent ■	76
72	St. Joseph's (L.I.) ■	55
59	Manhattanville	68
77	Maritime (N.Y.)	76
72	Old Westbury	76
80	Maritime (N.Y.) ■	57
69	Merchant Marine ■	78
59	Old Westbury ■	58
77	Merchant Marine	84

Nickname: Blue Knights
Colors: Royal Blue & Gold
Arena: Kaplan Recreation Center
  Capacity: 1,500; Year Built: 1992
AD: John J. Wright
SID: Dan Twomey

MT. ST. MARY'S
Emmitsburg, MD 21727-7799 I

Coach: Jim Phelan, La Salle 1951
2001-02 RESULTS (3-24)

59	Virginia Tech	82
57	Robert Morris	66
54	St. Francis (Pa.)	75
69	Central Conn. St. ■	80
62	Quinnipiac ■	84
55	Loyola (Md.) ■	46
46	Butler ■	66
50	California	78
72	San Jose St.	91
54	Navy	95
46	Bucknell ■	58
63	Monmouth	75
61	Fairleigh Dickinson	81
73	St. Francis (N.Y.) ■	85
60	Long Island	57
63	UMBC ■	72
64	Fairleigh Dickinson	69
60	Monmouth ■	84
70	Wagner	102
57	Sacred Heart	79
60	Robert Morris ■	65
57	St. Francis (Pa.) ■	54
60	St. Francis (N.Y.)	85
65	Quinnipiac	77
61	UMBC	66
84	Sacred Heart ■	88
58	Wagner ■	88

Nickname: Mountaineers
Colors: Blue & White
Arena: Knott Arena
  Capacity: 3,196; Year Built: 1987
AD: Harold P. Menninger
SID: Mark Vandergrift

MT. ST. VINCENT
Riverdale, NY 10471-1093 III

Coach: Chuck Mancuso,
Concordia (N.Y.) 81
2001-02 RESULTS (1-15)

79	Merchant Marine ■	107
82	Old Westbury	87
77	Manhattanville ■	93
75	Yeshiva	94
87	CCNY ■	85
66	St. Joseph's (L.I.)	68
58	Mt. St. Mary (N.Y.) ■	79
79	Stevens Tech	83
72	Merchant Marine	89
62	Centenary (N.J.)	74
76	Mt. St. Mary (N.Y.)	94

58	Stevens Tech	73
68	Old Westbury ■	84
69	St. Joseph's (L.I.) ■	88
72	Manhattanville	78
75	Yeshiva ■	81

Nickname: Dolphins
Colors: Blue, White & Gold
Arena: Cardinal Hayes Gymnasium
  Capacity: 450; Year Built: 1910
AD: Chuck Mancuso
SID: Chuck Mancuso

MOUNT UNION
Alliance, OH 44601 III

Coach: Lee Hood, Ohio Northern 1982
2001-02 RESULTS (18-9)

85	Pitt.-Greensburg ■	54
85	Rose-Hulman ■	72
68	Thiel	66
85	Westminster (Pa.) ■	52
76	Ohio Northern	58
59	Capital ■	58
63	Wilmington (Ohio)	67
106	Otterbein ■	59
81	John Carroll	61
70	Akron	76
66	Taylor (Ind.) †	56
43	Hope	69
66	Heidelberg	44
84	Baldwin-Wallace ■	89
95	Muskingum	92
85	Marietta ■	74
78	Wilmington (Ohio) ■	59
57	Capital	62
73	Otterbein	79
80	John Carroll ■	81
70	Heidelberg ■	63
75	Baldwin-Wallace ■	72
67	Muskingum ■	56
59	Marietta	56
70	Ohio Northern ■	72
84	Marietta ■	72
63	Capital †	80

Nickname: Purple Raiders
Colors: Purple & White
Arena: Timken PE Building
  Capacity: 2,300; Year Built: 1970
AD: Larry Kehres
SID: Michael DeMatteis

MUHLENBERG
Allentown, PA 18104-5586 III

Coach: Dave Madeira, Concord 1969
2001-02 RESULTS (19-6)

80	Phila. Bible ■	51
75	Moravian	88
76	Arcadia ■	48
64	Phila. Sciences	57
63	Frank. & Marsh. ■	66
68	Moravian	74
71	Dickinson	66
89	Defiance †	82
76	Manchester †	71
72	Whittier	71
67	Richard Stockton †	64
70	Gettysburg ■	62
86	Haverford ■	68
91	Widener ■	77
75	Washington (Md.) ■	58
63	Swarthmore ■	47
82	Ursinus	85
66	McDaniel	56
72	DeSales ■	58
52	Johns Hopkins ■	62
83	Haverford ■	59
82	Washington (Md.)	81
75	Swarthmore	44
80	Ursinus ■	77
59	Gettysburg	68

Nickname: Mules
Colors: Cardinal & Grey
Arena: Memorial Hall
  Capacity: 3,529; Year Built: 1954
AD: Stephen P. Erber
SID: Mike Falk

MURRAY ST.
Murray, KY 42071-3318............I

Coach: Tevester Anderson,
Arkansas AM&N 1962
2001-02 RESULTS (19-13)

100	West Fla. ■	61
109	UC-Colo. Spgs. ■	44
77	Western Ky.	101
72	Chattanooga ■	63
74	UAB ■	69
66	Indiana St.	74
69	Virginia Tech †	63
69	Louisville	84
69	DePaul	65
103	Tennessee St. ■	72
58	Chattanooga	71
63	Southern Ill. ■	67
90	Tenn.-Martin ■	76
66	Gardner-Webb ■	80
59	Tennessee Tech	78
62	Austin Peay	68
86	Eastern Ill. ■	88
85	Southeast Mo. St. ■	72
83	Morehead St.	92
81	Eastern Ky. ■	92
92	Tenn.-Martin	74
87	Tennessee St.	84
75	Tennessee Tech ■	56
78	Austin Peay ■	68
77	Eastern Ill.	76
92	Southeast Mo. St.	86
85	Eastern Ky. ■	74
60	Morehead St. ■	66
103	Eastern Ill. ■	56
89	Morehead St. †	75
70	Tennessee Tech †	69
68	Georgia †	85

Nickname: Racers
Colors: Navy & Gold
Arena: Regional Special Events Center
  Capacity: 8,600; Year Built: 1998
AD: E.W. Dennison
SID: Steve Parker

MUSKINGUM
New Concord, OH 43762 III

Coach: Jim Burson, Muskingum 1963
2001-02 RESULTS (10-16)

81	Western Conn. St. †	46
64	Dickinson	56
66	Westminster (Pa.) †	60
46	Allegheny	63
82	La Roche ■	71
66	Heidelberg ■	61
65	Marietta ■	69
79	Baldwin-Wallace ■	87
69	Capital	79
75	Wilmington (Ohio) ■	72
70	Manchester ■	81
102	Defiance ■	90
77	Otterbein ■	76
78	John Carroll	84
92	Mount Union	95
68	Ohio Northern	75
65	Baldwin-Wallace ■	72
82	Marietta	76
64	Capital ■	78
75	Wilmington (Ohio) ■	76
64	Otterbein	91
86	John Carroll ■	96
56	Mount Union	67
44	Ohio Northern ■	58
87	Heidelberg	71
66	Baldwin-Wallace ■	77

Nickname: Fighting Muskies
Colors: Black & Magenta
Arena: Muskingum Recreation Center
Capacity: 3,000; Year Built: 1986
AD: Larry Shank
SID: Bobby Lee

MCDANIEL
Westminster, MD 21157-4390 ..III

Coach: Darrell Brooks, Bowie St. 1979
2001-02 RESULTS (6-19)
77	Maryland Bible ■	68
65	Valley Forge Chrst. ■	57
57	Col. of New Jersey	89
73	Swarthmore	67
73	York (Pa.) ■	84
47	Frank. & Marsh.	75
55	Catholic	90
63	St. Mary's (Md.)	76
80	Pitt.-Greensburg ■	92
70	Mary Washington ■	63
81	Haverford ■	56
66	Dickinson	85
66	Villa Julie	85
64	Gettysburg ■	86
44	Johns Hopkins	74
69	Maryland Bible	59
56	Muhlenberg ■	66
24	Princeton	78
57	Frank. & Marsh. ■	78
59	Ursinus	73
68	Gallaudet	70
47	Dickinson ■	69
65	Gettysburg	84
36	Johns Hopkins ■	67
80	Washington (Md.) ■	88

Nickname: Green Terror
Colors: Green & Gold
Arena: Gill P.E. Learning Center
Capacity: 3,000; Year Built: 1984
AD: James M. Smith
SID: To be named

NAVY
Annapolis, MD 21402-5000 I

Coach: Don DeVoe, Ohio St. 1964
2001-02 RESULTS (10-20)
65	Wake Forest ■	87
72	Rice	75
64	Southern Methodist	81
71	Air Force ■	53
74	Ohio ■	80
47	Citadel	83
79	Davidson	81
78	Gettysburg ■	60
61	Montana †	78
54	Buffalo †	63
72	Columbia †	74
78	Belmont ■	72
95	Mt. St. Mary's ■	54
90	Coastal Caro. ■	71
83	Brown	95
57	Holy Cross	70
64	Bucknell ■	49
92	Lehigh ■	85
95	Colgate	93
79	Lafayette ■	92
79	Army ■	61
66	American	67
54	Holy Cross ■	62
56	Bucknell	76
66	Lehigh	61
65	Colgate ■	66
72	Lafayette	80
50	American ■	62
63	Army	73
41	Holy Cross †	59

Nickname: Midshipmen
Colors: Navy Blue & Gold
Arena: Alumni Hall

Capacity: 5,710; Year Built: 1991
AD: Chet Gladchuck
SID: Scott Strasemeier

NAZARETH
Rochester, NY 14618-3790 III

Coach: Mike Daley, St. Bonaventure 1966
2001-02 RESULTS (17-10)
81	Alma †	72
67	Buffalo St.	59
77	Rochester ■	78
68	Hilbert ■	61
78	D'Youville ■	72
66	Brockport St. ■	97
58	Rochester Inst. ■	47
76	Keuka	67
65	Oswego St.	71
77	Hartwick ■	67
53	Utica ■	47
66	Rochester Inst. †	74
48	Rochester	71
68	Keuka †	58
77	St. John Fisher	57
67	Ithaca	86
77	Elmira	71
66	Alfred ■	55
63	St. John Fisher ■	65
80	Elmira ■	68
47	Ithaca ■	64
66	Alfred	64
84	Utica	86
74	Hartwick	71
64	Rochester Inst. ■	63
89	Plattsburgh St. ■	81
87	St. Lawrence	99

Nickname: Golden Flyers
Colors: Purple & Gold
Arena: Robert A. Kidera Gym
Capacity: 1,200; Year Built: 1976
AD: Peter Bothner
SID: Joe Seil

NEBRASKA
Lincoln, NE 68588 I

Coach: Barry Collier, Butler 1976
2001-02 RESULTS (13-15)
69	N.C. A&T ■	57
73	Winthrop ■	65
81	Texas-San Antonio ■	63
65	Wofford ■	46
72	Western Ill. ■	53
61	Oral Roberts ■	55
70	Creighton	76
70	Sam Houston St. ■	74
72	Minnesota	81
52	Pacific (Cal.)	75
66	Savannah St. ■	47
53	Missouri	60
57	Kansas	96
75	Colorado ■	67
51	Oklahoma ■	78
66	Texas	77
63	Oklahoma St.	70
86	Iowa St. ■	84
80	Texas Tech ■	69
61	Colorado	84
99	Kansas St. ■	82
71	Missouri ■	87
79	Iowa St.	85
82	Texas A&M	72
87	Kansas ■	88
75	Baylor ■	55
58	Kansas St.	67
60	Colorado †	67

Nickname: Cornhuskers, Huskers
Colors: Scarlet & Cream
Arena: Bob Devaney Sports Center
Capacity: 13,500; Year Built: 1976

AD: C. William Byrne Jr.
SID: Jerry Trickie

NEB. WESLEYAN
Lincoln, NE 68504-2796 III

Coach: Todd Raridon, Hastings 1980
2001-02 RESULTS (13-12)
65	McMurry †	67
57	Whittier †	55
77	Simpson	70
85	Buena Vista ■	88
70	Hastings ■	73
53	Dordt	56
98	Dana ■	87
64	Mt. Marty ■	57
59	Colorado Col.	82
69	Dallas †	65
74	Dallas	55
57	Anderson (Ind.) †	60
84	Doane	70
68	Sioux Falls	71
83	Midland Lutheran	82
55	Dakota Wesleyan ■	72
66	Concordia (Neb.) ■	54
76	Northwestern (Iowa) ■	87
81	Dana	63
67	Hastings	65
57	Sioux Falls ■	63
74	Mt. Marty	88
57	Dakota Wesleyan	77
65	Midland Lutheran ■	56
69	Colorado Col. ■	59

Nickname: Prairie Wolves
Colors: Gold, Brown & Black
Arena: Snyder Arena
Capacity: 2,350; Year Built: 1995
AD: Ira Zeff
SID: Karl Skinner

NEB.-KEARNEY
Kearney, NE 68849 II

Coach: Tom Kropp, Neb.-Kearney 1976
2001-02 RESULTS (24-6)
84	Hawaii-Hilo	91
60	Hawaii Pacific	70
79	Wayne St. (Neb.)	67
73	Neb.-Omaha	81
84	UC-Colo. Spgs. ■	63
83	Southern Colo.	72
97	Fort Lewis	84
79	N.M. Highlands	66
90	Hastings	86
82	Western St. (Colo.) ■	60
90	Mesa St. ■	75
123	York (Neb.) ■	59
86	Adams St.	61
90	Regis (Colo.)	75
93	Colo. Christian	84
69	Fort Hays St.	65
83	Metro St.	73
81	Colorado Mines ■	63
115	Chadron St. ■	78
75	Regis (Colo.) ■	66
94	Colo. Christian ■	73
71	Fort Hays St. ■	69
67	Metro St. ■	71
80	Colorado Col. ■	64
63	Colorado Mines	54
90	Chadron St.	78
84	Colo. Christian	68
94	Fort Hays St. †	86
71	Fort Lewis †	72
51	Metro St. †	59

Nickname: Antelopes, Lopers
Colors: Royal Blue & Light Old Gold
Arena: Health & Sports Center
Capacity: 6,000; Year Built: 1990
AD: Jon McBride
SID: Peter Yazvac

NEB.-OMAHA
Omaha, NE 68182 II

Coach: Kevin McKenna, Creighton 1993
2001-02 RESULTS (24-9)
84	Grand Valley St. †	86
68	NYIT †	61
90	Tex. A&M-Commerce †	58
92	Dakota Wesleyan ■	59
82	Winona St. ■	65
65	San Jose St. †	59
68	Wis.-Milwaukee †	87
81	Neb.-Kearney ■	73
94	Northern Colo.	82
81	Wayne St. (Neb.) ■	70
71	Bellevue ■	55
110	Midland Lutheran ■	68
74	North Dakota St.	65
88	North Dakota	92
87	Morningside ■	40
77	South Dakota ■	70
59	Minn. St.-Mankato	77
102	St. Cloud St.	63
74	South Dakota St.	78
85	Augustana (S.D.) ■	80
85	North Dakota ■	80
77	North Dakota St. ■	65
77	South Dakota	82
101	Morningside	67
81	St. Cloud St. ■	72
73	Minn. St.-Mankato ■	61
87	Augustana (S.D.)	77
76	South Dakota St.	87
97	Northern Colo. ■	85
85	Augustana (S.D.) ■	72
53	North Dakota †	68
88	Fort Lewis †	58
76	South Dakota St.	96

Nickname: Mavericks
Colors: Black & Crimson
Arena: UNO Fieldhouse
Capacity: 3,500; Year Built: 1950
AD: Robert Danenhauer
SID: Gary Anderson

NEUMANN
Aston, PA 19014-1298 III

Coach: Brian Nugent, Temple 1993
2001-02 RESULTS (21-7)
70	Wilkes	88
73	Va. Wesleyan †	79
81	Widener	66
58	Kutztown ■	53
82	Phila. Bible	75
83	Salisbury	71
83	Widener †	74
90	Gwynedd-Mercy ■	80
60	Arcadia	58
76	Lincoln (Pa.) †	63
72	Rowan	63
79	Cabrini	75
92	Eastern	73
61	Alvernia ■	62
66	Misericordia	67
81	Marywood ■	45
80	Wesley	70
64	Cabrini ■	68
81	Arcadia ■	58
77	Eastern ■	52
66	Gwynedd-Mercy	62
71	Misericordia ■	68
65	Alvernia	68
86	Wesley ■	71
90	Marywood	71
83	Eastern ■	71
86	Misericordia	71
67	Cabrini ■	71

Nickname: Knights
Colors: Blue, Gold & White
Arena: Bruder Gym
Capacity: 350; Year Built: 1985

AD: Joseph Giunta
SID: To be named

NEVADA
Reno, NV 89557 I

Coach: Trent Johnson, Boise St. 1983

2001-02 RESULTS (17-13)

85	Cal St. Northridge	75
66	St. Mary's (Cal.)	61
61	Arkansas St.	91
84	San Francisco ■	59
78	Santa Clara ■	53
68	Montana	75
74	Cal St. Northridge ■	65
85	Southern Ore. ■	54
75	Portland St. ■	53
75	UNLV	87
91	San Jose St.	85
40	Hawaii	58
66	Tulsa ■	76
91	Rice ■	70
88	Fresno St. ■	85
64	UTEP	93
73	Boise St.	64
69	Louisiana Tech ■	77
57	Southern Methodist ■	71
64	Rice	56
68	Tulsa	73
66	Fresno St.	57
94	Boise St. ■	86
80	UTEP ■	65
74	Southern Methodist	77
83	Louisiana Tech	86
79	Hawaii ■	69
72	San Jose St. ■	76
72	Southern Methodist †	66
68	Hawaii †	90

Nickname: Wolf Pack
Colors: Silver & Blue
Arena: Lawlor Events Center
　Capacity: 11,200; Year Built: 1983
AD: Chris Ault
SID: Jason D. Houston

UNLV
Las Vegas, NV 89154 I

Coach: Charles Spoonhour,
Ozarks (Ark.) 1961

2001-02 RESULTS (21-11)

74	Wisconsin ■	69
97	Nicholls St. ■	54
61	Cincinnati	74
64	Washington	77
79	Ga. Southern ■	64
68	UAB †	74
70	Loyola Marymount	68
87	Nevada ■	75
78	Texas ■	87
101	Tennessee St. ■	83
84	Old Dominion ■	76
59	Wyoming ■	69
66	Air Force	54
63	Utah	86
47	Brigham Young	60
75	Colorado St. ■	68
80	San Diego St.	79
90	DePaul ■	75
81	New Mexico	84
73	Brigham Young ■	70
72	Utah ■	64
83	Florida Int'l ■	77
78	Wyoming	82
96	Colorado St.	91
83	San Diego St. ■	76
73	Air Force ■	66
91	New Mexico ■	82
120	New Mexico ■	117
76	Utah	79
75	San Diego St. ■	78
96	Arizona St. ■	91
65	South Carolina	75

Nickname: Rebels
Colors: Scarlet & Gray
Arena: Thomas & Mack Center
　Capacity: 18,500; Year Built: 1983
AD: John Robinson
SID: Andy Grossman

NEW ENGLAND
Biddeford, ME 04005 III

Coach: Dave Labbe, Southern Me. 1993

2001-02 RESULTS (8-16)

72	Wesleyan (Conn.) †	105
77	Me.-Farmington	106
63	Bowdoin	93
63	Bates	110
70	Southern Me. ■	108
81	Newbury ■	76
91	St. Joseph's (Me.) ■	97
86	Nichols ■	100
79	Me.-Farmington ■	76
90	Daniel Webster	87
100	Mount Ida ■	90
75	Salve Regina	91
69	Colby-Sawyer	96
93	Wentworth Inst. ■	88
86	Mount Ida	96
84	Anna Maria	77
70	Curry	85
63	Colby	88
77	Eastern Nazarene ■	80
104	New England Col. ■	85
77	Plymouth St. ■	109
66	Roger Williams	80
74	Gordon	85
80	Endicott ■	78

Nickname: Nor'easters
Colors: Royal & Grey
Arena: Campus Center
　Capacity: 1,500; Year Built: 1989
AD: Karol L'heureux
SID: Curt Smyth

NEW ENGLAND COL.
Henniker, NH 03242-3293 III

Coach: Cory McClure, Westbrook 1996

2001-02 RESULTS (3-21)

64	Fitchburg St. †	90
89	Notre Dame (Md.) ■	100
108	Lyndon St. ■	95
77	Rivier	81
107	Daniel Webster ■	99
52	Plymouth St. †	89
51	New Hampshire	96
74	Salve Regina ■	91
90	Notre Dame (Md.) ■	98
78	Johnson St.	90
85	Castleton St.	95
68	Roger Williams	85
93	Anna Maria ■	101
75	Bates ■	110
69	Eastern Nazarene ■	75
87	Curry	93
66	Colby-Sawyer ■	99
57	Wentworth Inst.	91
113	Thomas ■	82
85	New England ■	104
73	Endicott	83
91	Mount Ida ■	99
119	Nichols ■	126
58	Gordon	84

Nickname: Pilgrims
Colors: Scarlet & Royal Blue
Arena: Bridges Gym
　Capacity: 400; Year Built: 1965
AD: Lori Runksmeier
SID: Renee Hellert

NEW HAMPSHIRE
Durham, NH 03824 I

Coach: Phil Rowe, Plymouth St. 1974

2001-02 RESULTS (11-17)

53	Notre Dame	95
77	Boston College	80
70	Dartmouth ■	72
58	Connecticut	110
56	Florida ■	108
72	Buffalo	73
96	New England Col. ■	51
49	Lehigh	72
65	Harvard ■	70
72	Northeastern ■	84
65	Boston U. ■	70
69	Colgate ■	55
84	Army ■	73
80	Hartford	78
68	Vermont	81
75	Stony Brook	68
71	Albany (N.Y.) ■	60
74	Hartford ■	70
61	Maine	72
57	Albany (N.Y.)	74
79	Binghamton ■	69
82	Northeastern	81
67	Stony Brook ■	57
56	Boston U.	63
87	Maine	69
77	Vermont ■	93
67	Binghamton	85
48	Maine †	54

Nickname: Wildcats
Colors: Blue & White
Arena: Lundholm Gymnasium
　Capacity: 3,500; Year Built: 1961
AD: Marty Scarano
SID: Derek Leslie

NEW HAVEN
West Haven, CT 06516-1999 ...II

Coach: Jay Young, Marist 1986

2001-02 RESULTS (14-13)

67	Wheeling Jesuit †	54
68	Fairmont St.	69
67	Millersville ■	61
83	Bloomsburg	89
56	Bryant	62
65	Southern N.H.	81
77	Bloomsburg ■	60
66	Stonehill ■	51
77	St. Rose	95
79	Green Mountain †	56
63	Bentley †	68
55	St. Thomas Aquinas †	44
77	Pitt.-Johnstown ■	57
56	Adelphi ■	69
63	American Int'l	66
96	Assumption	105
77	Bentley	73
87	Clarion ■	75
70	Merrimack ■	68
65	Green Mountain	60
63	St. Michael's	74
72	St. Anselm	85
71	Southern Conn. St.	77
82	St. Rose ■	66
77	Teikyo Post	65
102	Southern N.H. ■	98
67	Clarion	74

Nickname: Chargers
Colors: Blue & Gold
Arena: Charger Gymnasium
　Capacity: 3,500; Year Built: 1971
AD: Deborah Chin
SID: Jason Sullivan

COL. OF NEW JERSEY
Ewing, NJ 08628-0718 III

Coach: John Castaldo,
Col. of New Jersey 1982

2001-02 RESULTS (11-14)

79	Albright ■	80
78	Palm Beach Atl. ■	68
64	Rutgers-Camden ■	61
76	Ramapo	84
89	McDaniel ■	57
59	Richard Stockton ■	62
72	Kean ■	71
91	New Jersey City	101
77	Wm. Paterson ■	59
54	Haverford	53
58	John Jay	63
78	Lehman ■	67
73	Rutgers-Newark	57
53	Montclair St. ■	56
100	Centenary (N.J.)	85
76	Rowan ■	78
58	Kean	84
82	Richard Stockton ■	75
73	Ramapo ■	78
80	Rutgers-Camden	95
44	Wm. Paterson	64
70	New Jersey City ■	86
76	Rutgers-Newark ■	67
60	Rowan	73
69	Montclair St.	76

Nickname: Lions
Colors: Blue & Gold
Arena: Packer Hall
　Capacity: 1,200; Year Built: 1962
AD: Kevin A. McHugh
SID: Ann King

NEW JERSEY CITY
Jersey City, NJ 07305-1597 III

Coach: Charles Brown, New Jersey City
1965

2001-02 RESULTS (18-11)

50	Staten Island †	69
79	Hunter †	74
82	Kean	84
74	Wm. Paterson ■	66
85	Ramapo	74
74	Rutgers-Newark	62
101	Col. of New Jersey ■	91
71	Richard Stockton	72
89	Farmingdale St. ■	69
74	Medgar Evers ■	68
81	Southern Me. †	70
74	Chris. Newport	78
67	Rutgers-Camden ■ †	63
87	Rowan ■	76
96	Montclair St.	94
86	Rutgers-Newark ■	69
77	Stevens Tech	62
64	Ramapo ■	79
70	Wm. Paterson	80
73	Kean ■	69
62	Richard Stockton ■	68
86	Col. of New Jersey	70
99	Rutgers-Camden	103
83	Montclair St. ■	81
76	Rowan	78
44	Wm. Paterson ■	60
76	Manhattanville	74
71	Montclair St.	55
83	Ramapo	101

Nickname: Gothic Knights
Colors: Green & Gold
Arena: Athletic & Fitness Center
　Capacity: 2,000; Year Built: 1994
AD: Lawrence R. Schiner
SID: Ira Thor

316 RESULTS

N.J. INST. OF TECH.
Newark, NJ 07102 II

Coach: Jim Casciano, Drexel 1974

2001-02 RESULTS (14-13)
70	East Stroudsburg ■	75
47	St. Anselm	69
79	Nyack ■	74
60	Wilmington (Del.)	71
54	Dominican (N.Y.) ■	56
62	Pitt.-Johnstown †	63
49	East Stroudsburg	63
77	Felician	74
56	Caldwell	57
65	Phila. Sciences ■	59
70	Nova Southeastern	65
70	Barry	88
71	Teikyo Post ■	73
52	Holy Family	74
61	Bloomfield	57
75	Dominican (N.Y.)	67
76	Felician ■	70
62	Nyack	51
60	Caldwell ■	63
77	Goldey-Beacom	57
74	Holy Family ■	72
81	Teikyo Post	77
84	Goldey-Beacom ■	80
76	Phila. Sciences	53
61	Bloomfield ■	64
87	Wilmington (Del.) ■	77
71	Shaw	87

Nickname: Highlanders
Colors: Scarlet & White
Arena: Entwistle Gym
    Capacity: 1,500; Year Built: 1960
AD: Leonard Kaplan
SID: Mark Mentone

NEW MEXICO
Albuquerque, NM 87131 I

Coach: Fran Fraschilla, Brooklyn 1980

2001-02 RESULTS (16-14)
66	Stanford ■	81
97	Texas Southern ■	51
85	Pacific (Cal.) ■	66
85	West Virginia ■	88
62	California	71
87	Alcorn St. ■	55
66	New Mexico St.	64
87	Tennessee Tech ■	80
70	New Mexico St. ■	49
83	UNC Greensboro ■	69
72	St. Mary's (Cal.) ■	62
77	Dartmouth ■	60
70	Northern Ariz. ■	57
90	Gonzaga ■	95
50	Air Force ■	47
73	Brigham Young ■	58
51	Utah ■	81
67	Wyoming	79
70	Colorado	64
65	San Diego St. ■	78
84	UNLV ■	81
44	Air Force	47
62	Brigham Young	68
65	Utah	66
72	Colorado St. ■	60
74	Wyoming ■	65
71	San Diego St.	84
82	UNLV	91
117	UNLV	120
62	Minnesota	96

Nickname: Lobos
Colors: Cherry & Silver
Arena: The Pit/Bob King Court
    Capacity: 18,018; Year Built: 1966
AD: Rudy Davalos
SID: Greg Remington

N.M. HIGHLANDS
Las Vegas, NM 87701 II

Coach: Ed Manzanares, New Mexico

2001-02 RESULTS (8-18)
86	Western N.M.	74
79	West Tex. A&M ■	84
91	Eastern N.M.	101
61	Eastern N.M.	80
64	Northern Ariz.	91
66	Western N.M. ■	59
60	Metro St.	97
68	Fort Hays St. ■	82
66	Neb.-Kearney ■	79
72	West Tex. A&M	77
83	Colo. Christian	85
72	Regis (Colo.)	84
71	Chadron St. ■	86
70	Colorado Mines ■	71
74	Fort Lewis	94
106	Adams St.	99
69	Southern Colo.	73
84	UC-Colo. Spgs.	79
83	Mesa St.	76
94	Western St. (Colo.) ■	91
88	Fort Lewis ■	91
102	Adams St.	80
72	Southern Colo.	83
80	UC-Colo. Spgs. ■	74
82	Mesa St.	102
88	Western St. (Colo.)	104

Nickname: Cowboys
Colors: Purple & White
Arena: Wilsom Complex
    Capacity: 5,000; Year Built: 1986
AD: Dennis Francois
SID: William Maes

NEW MEXICO ST.
Las Cruces, NM 88003 I

Coach: Lou Henson, New Mexico St. 1955

2001-02 RESULTS (20-12)
88	Texas-Arlington	71
82	Alcorn St. ■	72
94	San Diego St.	79
80	Texas Tech ■	81
73	UTEP ■	71
64	New Mexico ■	66
74	Washington ■	75
49	New Mexico	70
94	Valparaiso †	77
84	BYU-Hawaii	94
79	Montana †	67
86	Denver	82
71	North Texas	76
77	New Orleans ■	62
80	South Ala. ■	63
94	Middle Tenn.	88
67	Western Ky.	83
98	Eastern N.M. ■	82
66	La.-Lafayette ■	71
68	Denver ■	62
88	North Texas ■	71
64	New Orleans	62
78	South Ala.	74
77	Florida Int'l ■	70
98	Western N.M. ■	67
86	Tex.-Pan American	100
81	Ark.-Little Rock ■	73
69	Arkansas St. ■	59
81	UTEP	85
67	La.-Lafayette	69
63	Middle Tenn. †	48
72	Western Ky. †	73

Nickname: Aggies
Colors: Crimson & White
Arena: Pan American Center
    Capacity: 13,071; Year Built: 1968
AD: Brian Faison
SID: Sean Johnson

NEW ORLEANS
New Orleans, LA 70148 I

Coach: Monte Towe, North Carolina St.

2001-02 RESULTS (15-14)
63	Boston U. †	69
46	Md.-East. Shore †	48
71	Rollins	56
58	Jacksonville	73
80	Nicholls St.	66
61	Norfolk St. ■	54
47	Oklahoma St.	95
55	Southwest Mo. St.	71
63	Tulane	74
58	Southeastern La.	47
60	LSU ■	59
60	Florida	76
76	Western Ky. ■	90
64	Middle Tenn. ■	69
62	New Mexico St.	77
78	La.-Lafayette	102
73	Ark.-Little Rock	72
62	South Ala.	44
68	Arkansas St.	65
82	Tex. A&M-Corp. Chris.	68
55	Florida Int'l	69
62	New Mexico St. ■	64
63	La.-Lafayette ■	61
82	North Texas	75
74	Denver	73
78	South Ala. ■	67
83	North Texas ■	61
69	Denver	46
67	Ark.-Little Rock ■	71

Nickname: Privateers
Colors: Royal Blue & Silver
Arena: Kiefer Lakefront Arena
    Capacity: 10,000; Year Built: 1983
AD: Robert W. Brown
SID: Bob Boyle

NEW PALTZ ST.
New Paltz, NY 12561-2499 III

Coach: Joe Kremer, Hamilton 1990

2001-02 RESULTS (3-22)
55	Drew	86
77	Centenary (N.J.) †	85
68	John Jay	79
71	Vassar ■	55
62	York (N.Y.) ■	68
54	Baruch	56
54	Oneonta St.	61
60	Potsdam St. ■	72
81	Colby †	88
72	Notre Dame (N.H.) †	77
62	Brockport St. ■	91
69	Oswego St.	71
77	Geneseo St.	86
69	Utica/Rome ■	80
49	Buffalo St. ■	78
73	Fredonia St. ■	65
69	Cortland St.	52
79	Oswego St. ■	85
78	Geneseo St. ■	84
62	Farmingdale St. ■	70
79	Plattsburgh St.	80
52	Cortland St.	67
69	Oneonta St. ■	71
50	Brockport St.	106
52	Fredonia St.	83

Nickname: Hawks
Colors: Orange & Blue
Arena: Elting Gymnasium
    Capacity: 2,200; Year Built: 1964
AD: Tracey Ranieri/Stuart Robinson
SID: Dave Hines

NYIT
Old Westbury, NY 11568-8000 II

Coach: Sal Lagano, Hofstra 1988

2001-02 RESULTS (18-15)
64	Lynn †	76
61	Neb.-Omaha †	68
58	Tarleton St. †	73
67	Dominican (N.Y.) ■	55
77	Southampton ■	75
50	Mass.-Lowell	65
84	Bridgeport ■	79
73	Queens (N.Y.)	87
85	Mercy	78
69	Adelphi ■	84
77	Eastern Nazarene †	56
69	Stonehill	58
62	St. Thomas Aquinas ■	58
86	Concordia (N.Y.) ■	64
86	Dowling	79
66	C.W. Post ■	75
82	Southampton	62
59	Bridgeport	53
62	Queens (N.Y.) ■	59
90	Mercy ■	83
54	Adelphi	71
63	Molloy ■	61
85	Concordia (N.Y.) ■	74
50	St. Thomas Aquinas ■	64
80	Dowling	94
59	C.W. Post	71
50	Philadelphia U.	67
70	Philadelphia U. ■	50
53	Molloy	67
83	Southampton	71
68	Adelphi †	66
63	Queens (N.Y.) †	80
76	St. Rose †	81

Nickname: Bears
Colors: Navy Blue & Gold
Arena: Recreation Hall
    Capacity: 500; Year Built: 1955
AD: Clyde Doughty Jr.
SID: Ben Arcuri

NEW YORK U.
New York, NY 10012-1019 III

Coach: Joe Nesci, Brooklyn 1979

2001-02 RESULTS (14-11)
71	Mt. St. Mary (N.Y.) ■	54
85	Brockport St. ■	96
67	Baruch	47
72	St. Joseph's (L.I.) ■	46
68	Brooklyn	65
67	Merchant Marine	73
69	Elmira ■	57
54	Hunter ■	57
47	Rochester ■	50
65	Carnegie Mellon ■	49
48	John Jay	69
64	Brandeis ■	55
92	Polytechnic (N.Y.) ■	29
58	Washington (Mo.)	72
49	Chicago	71
81	Emory ■	64
78	Case Reserve ■	62
57	Stevens Tech ■	48
63	Case Reserve	71
83	Emory	73
68	Carnegie Mellon	60
48	Rochester	62
57	Chicago ■	59
43	Washington (Mo.) ■	77
66	Brandeis	64

Nickname: Violets
Colors: Purple & White
Arena: Coles Sports Center
    Capacity: 1,900; Year Built: 1981
AD: Christopher Bledsoe
SID: Jeffrey Bernstein

NEWBERRY
Newberry, SC 29108 II

Coach: Grafton Young, Warren Wilson 1979

2001-02 RESULTS (3-23)

82	Limestone †	91
76	North Greenville †	89
60	S.C.-Spartanburg ■	67
65	S.C.-Aiken	77
52	Lander †	60
57	Fayetteville St. †	69
83	Montreat †	91
65	Lenoir-Rhyne †	49
69	North Greenville	68
79	Erskine ■	89
64	Mars Hill	78
69	Lenoir-Rhyne ■	70
74	Wingate ■	96
71	North Greenville	79
50	Tusculum	72
70	Catawba ■	84
82	Carson-Newman ■	94
60	Presbyterian	77
72	Mars Hill	68
56	Lenoir-Rhyne	72
64	Wingate	95
63	Tusculum ■	68
77	Catawba	78
70	Carson-Newman	101
65	Presbyterian ■	82
74	Carson-Newman	105

Nickname: Indians
Colors: Scarlet & Gray
Arena: Eleazer Arena
  Capacity: 1,600; Year Built: 1981
AD: Andy Carter
SID: Darrell Orand

NIAGARA
Niagara Univ., NY 14109 I

Coach: Joe Mihalich, La Salle 1978

2001-02 RESULTS (18-14)

71	George Mason ■	86
63	Buffalo ■	62
75	St. Bonaventure	90
63	Winthrop †	58
55	Central Conn. St. †	60
71	Loyola (Md.) ■	51
65	Siena	77
52	St. John's (N.Y.) ■	60
85	Tex.-Pan American †	91
64	Jacksonville †	52
78	Coppin St. †	50
82	Drexel	87
79	Akron	80
70	Marist	66
56	Manhattan	98
79	Fairfield ■	77
78	Marist ■	84
72	St. Peter's	65
76	Rider ■	80
74	Siena ■	73
80	Fairfield	77
84	Iona ■	74
67	Rider	82
93	St. Peter's ■	70
94	Manhattan ■	83
65	Loyola (Md.)	42
80	Canisius ■	65
76	Iona	77
86	Canisius ■	82
89	Iona †	83
70	Canisius †	60
77	Siena †	92

Nickname: Purple Eagles
Colors: Purple and White
Arena: Gallagher Center
  Capacity: 2,400; Year Built: 1949
AD: Michael J. Hermann
SID: Mark Vandergrift

NICHOLLS ST.
Thibodaux, LA 70310 I

Coach: Rickey Broussard, La.-Lafayette 1971

2001-02 RESULTS (2-25)

59	Mississippi St.	95
54	UNLV	97
66	New Orleans ■	80
66	Loyola (La.) ■	57
60	McNeese St.	67
38	Michigan St.	92
86	Troy St.	98
59	Stephen F. Austin ■	72
59	Texas-Arlington ■	87
35	LSU	71
66	Southwest Tex. St.	87
65	Texas-San Antonio	93
66	Northwestern St. ■	73
61	La.-Monroe ■	66
64	Lamar	82
43	Sam Houston St.	84
40	Southeastern La.	56
46	McNeese St. ■	74
56	Stephen F. Austin	72
58	Texas-Arlington	81
74	Lamar ■	82
65	Sam Houston St. ■	80
72	Northwestern St.	93
73	La.-Monroe	90
51	Texas-San Antonio ■	73
59	Southwest Tex. St. ■	72
61	Southeastern La. ■	39

Nickname: Colonels
Colors: Red & Gray
Arena: David Stopher Gymnasium
  Capacity: 3,800; Year Built: 1967
AD: Robert J. Bernardi
SID: Ross Blacker

NICHOLS
Dudley, MA 01571-5000 III

Coach: Dave Sokolnicki, Nichols 1997

2001-02 RESULTS (10-14)

54	Kean †	83
89	Brandeis	92
64	Worcester St. ■	59
84	Albertus Magnus ■	72
79	Lasell ■	94
78	Coast Guard	101
100	New England	86
104	Daniel Webster ■	80
59	Union (N.Y.)	75
66	Gordon ■	54
67	Eastern Nazarene	90
63	Fitchburg St.	76
55	Colby-Sawyer	101
56	Endicott ■	72
76	Mount Ida	89
74	Framingham St. ■	62
77	Elms ■	75
60	Curry ■	78
67	Anna Maria ■	74
74	Roger Williams ■	81
72	Salve Regina	83
126	New England Col.	119
88	Becker ■	84
84	Wentworth Inst. ■	75

Nickname: Bison
Colors: Black, Green & White
Arena: Chalmers Field House
  Capacity: 500; Year Built: 2000
AD: Charlyn Robert
SID: Mike Serijan

NORFOLK ST.
Norfolk, VA 23504...................I

Coach: Wil Jones, American 1960

2001-02 RESULTS (10-19)

52	Hawaii	76
71	Sam Houston St. †	90
71	San Diego St.	78
67	Tulane	89
54	New Orleans	61
63	Coppin St.	59
79	Morgan St.	66
57	Hampton	85
84	Maine ■	81
68	Georgetown	87
69	UNC Greensboro	84
69	Cleveland St.	79
69	Maryland	92
88	Md.-East. Shore ■	95
74	N.C. A&T	73
51	South Carolina St.	75
87	Howard ■	84
62	Delaware St. ■	82
61	Florida A&M ■	73
67	Bethune-Cookman ■	58
69	Coppin St. ■	51
74	Morgan St. ■	69
70	Md.-East. Shore	68
68	N.C. A&T ■	71
82	South Carolina St. ■	86
63	Howard	73
73	Delaware St.	66
89	Hampton ■	92
46	Coppin St. †	61

Nickname: Spartans
Colors: Green & Gold
Arena: Echols Arena
  Capacity: 7,600; Year Built: 1982
AD: Orby Moss Jr.
SID: Glen Mason

NORTH ALA.
Florence, AL 35632-0001 II

Coach: Gary Elliott, Alabama 1970

2001-02 RESULTS (10-15)

66	Delta St. ■	75
78	Selma ■	63
63	Evangel †	73
85	Drury	91
76	Miles ■	61
55	Henderson St. ■	67
63	Valdosta St. ■	79
68	Southeast Mo. St.	75
83	Tuskegee	77
67	Findlay ■	82
65	Montevallo	83
57	Ala.-Huntsville ■	65
96	Lincoln Memorial	88
80	West Ala.	63
71	West Ga. ■	80
69	Athens St.	58
72	West Fla. ■	62
85	Lincoln Memorial ■	71
73	Valdosta St.	81
89	Montevallo ■	91
66	Ala.-Huntsville	63
66	West Ala. ■	73
72	West Ga.	75
82	Athens St. ■	70
76	West Fla.	83

Nickname: Lions
Colors: Purple & Gold
Arena: Flowers Hall
  Capacity: 3,500; Year Built: 1972
AD: Joel Erdmann
SID: Jeff Hodges

NORTH CAROLINA
Chapel Hill, NC 27515 I

Coach: Matt Doherty, North Carolina 1984

2001-02 RESULTS (8-20)

69	Hampton ■	77
54	Davidson ■	58
66	Indiana ■	79
83	Georgia Tech	77
59	Kentucky	79
61	Binghamton ■	60
60	Col. of Charleston ■	66
92	St. Joseph's ■	76
104	N.C. A&T ■	66
96	Texas A&M ■	62
62	Wake Forest ■	84
79	Maryland	112
67	Virginia ■	71
71	Florida St.	81
54	Connecticut	86
59	North Carolina St. ■	77
87	Clemson	69
58	Duke ■	87
74	Georgia Tech	86
66	Wake Forest	90
77	Maryland ■	92
63	Virginia	73
95	Florida St. ■	85
78	Ohio ■	86
76	North Carolina St.	98
96	Clemson ■	78
68	Duke	93
48	Duke †	60

Nickname: Tar Heels
Colors: Carolina Blue & White
Arena: Smith Center
  Capacity: 21,750; Year Built: 1986
AD: Richard Baddour
SID: Steve Kirschner

N.C. A&T
Greensboro, NC 27411 I

Coach: Curtis Hunter, North Carolina 1987

2001-02 RESULTS (11-17)

82	Elon	94
51	Creighton	72
57	Nebraska	69
53	Va. Commonwealth	66
64	Howard ■	71
76	Delaware St. ■	63
72	American ■	86
51	Duke	93
66	North Carolina	104
66	Florida A&M	70
67	Bethune-Cookman	75
73	Norfolk St. ■	74
63	N.C. Central †	57
68	Hampton ■	82
67	UNC Greensboro †	85
79	Md.-East. Shore	67
67	Morgan St.	60
66	Coppin St. ■	55
76	South Carolina St. ■	71
77	Howard	75
61	Delaware St.	75
81	Florida A&M ■	73
62	Bethune-Cookman ■	60
71	Norfolk St.	68
61	Hampton	72
85	Md.-East. Shore ■	72
58	South Carolina St.	59
61	South Carolina St. †	63

Nickname: Aggies
Colors: Blue & Gold
Arena: Ellis Corbett Sports Center
  Capacity: 6,700; Year Built: 1978
AD: Alfonso Scandrett Jr.
SID: Donal O. Ware

UNC ASHEVILLE
Asheville, NC 28804-3299 I

Coach: Eddie Biedenbach, North Carolina St. 1968

2001-02 RESULTS (13-15)

57	West Virginia	83
49	UNC Greensboro ■	75

65	Minnesota	92
72	Campbell	77
71	East Tenn. St. ■	77
72	Western Caro.	66
58	Furman	69
86	Montreat ■	91
54	North Carolina St.	92
56	Michigan St.	76
38	Auburn	83
79	Appalachian St. ■	76
87	Charleston So. ■	63
74	Radford	60
68	Liberty	54
69	Brevard ■	62
83	High Point ■	72
76	Elon ■	64
78	Coastal Caro.	88
66	Winthrop ■	73
80	Radford ■	71
67	High Point	61
85	Liberty ■	69
72	Elon	58
92	Coastal Caro. ■	81
68	Charleston So.	77
62	Winthrop	77
71	High Point †	72

Nickname: Bulldogs
Colors: Royal Blue & White
Arena: Charlie Justice Center
  Capacity: 1,100; Year Built: 1963
AD: Joni Comstock
SID: Mike Gore

N.C. CENTRAL
Durham, NC 27707 II

Coach: Phil Spence, North Carolina St.
1976

2001-02 RESULTS (9-18)

73	Clark Atlanta †	89
74	Morehouse ■	87
80	Shaw	100
88	Kentucky St. ■	80
52	Virginia St. ■	58
72	Longwood	99
83	Wingate	87
77	Catawba	90
75	West Va. Tech ■	81
75	Catawba ■	76
88	Bowie St. ■	81
94	St. Augustine's	90
70	Livingstone	74
57	N.C. A&T †	63
88	St. Augustine's ■	75
86	Johnson Smith	89
72	Winston-Salem	70
54	Fayetteville St.	70
75	Livingstone ■	67
65	Fayetteville St. ■	67
96	Elizabeth City St.	95
59	Virginia Union	79
67	Winston-Salem ■	77
60	St. Paul's ■	63
105	Johnson Smith ■	103
62	Virginia St. †	55
75	Shaw †	101

Nickname: Eagles
Colors: Maroon & Gray
Arena: McLendon-McDougald Gym
  Capacity: 3,000; Year Built: 1955
AD: Lin Dawson
SID: Kyle Serba

UNC GREENSBORO
Greensboro, NC 27402-6170 ...I

Coach: Fran McCaffery, Pennsylvania
1982

2001-02 RESULTS (20-11)

75	UNC Asheville	49
58	Middle Tenn.	74
70	Elon	55

77	St. Peter's ■	61
56	East Caro. ■	54
65	Delaware ■	50
74	Arkansas	89
84	Norfolk St. ■	69
69	New Mexico	83
54	Ohio St.	85
74	Chattanooga	77
87	Appalachian St. ■	63
80	VMI	74
79	Ga. Southern	67
104	East Tenn. St. ■	92
85	N.C. A&T †	67
77	Western Caro.	87
57	Davidson ■	58
81	Wofford	76
63	Col. of Charleston ■	52
80	Western Caro. ■	75
48	Davidson	53
81	Citadel ■	68
76	East Tenn. St.	90
74	VMI ■	71
83	Appalachian St.	68
70	Furman ■	67
70	Wofford †	41
67	Chattanooga †	57
58	Davidson †	68
62	Memphis	82

Nickname: Spartans
Colors: Gold, White & Navy
Arena: Michael B. Fleming Gym
  Capacity: 2,320; Year Built: 1989
AD: Nelson Bobb
SID: Jake Keys

UNC PEMBROKE
Pembroke, NC 28372-1510......II

Coach: John Haskins, UNC Wilmington
1980

2001-02 RESULTS (12-15)

77	Campbell	93
76	S.C.-Aiken	67
73	Clayton St.	83
87	Newport News ■	69
82	Wingate	100
79	St. Andrews ■	67
60	Lenoir-Rhyne †	58
90	Carson-Newman †	96
70	GC&SU ■	85
65	Kennesaw St.	69
88	Armstrong Atlantic ■	94
69	Francis Marion	68
60	Augusta St. ■	80
66	S.C.-Spartanburg ■	56
57	Clayton St. ■	73
66	Lander	75
74	Armstrong Atlantic	71
95	Francis Marion ■	75
81	GC&SU	93
82	Augusta St.	78
87	Columbus St. ■	95
78	S.C.-Aiken	65
65	Lander ■	58
74	S.C.-Spartanburg	81
74	North Fla.	85
77	Kennesaw St. †	86

Nickname: Braves
Colors: Black & Gold
Arena: Jones Athletic Complex
  Capacity: 3,000; Year Built: 1972
AD: Dan Kenney
SID: Pamela Mason

NORTH CAROLINA ST.
Raleigh, NC 27695-7001 I

Coach: Herb Sendek, Carnegie Mellon
1985

2001-02 RESULTS (23-11)

95	Prairie View ■	51
78	San Jose St. ■	56

71	East Caro. ■	47
75	James Madison ■	58
63	Citadel ■	53
50	Ohio St.	64
62	Massachusetts ■	69
80	Wofford ■	42
82	Syracuse	68
92	UNC Asheville ■	54
70	Charleston So.	50
67	Houston	66
65	Maryland ■	72
81	Virginia	74
77	Florida St. ■	62
57	Duke ■	76
80	Clemson	79
84	Georgia Tech ■	71
77	North Carolina	59
80	Temple ■	61
81	Wake Forest ■	82
73	Maryland	89
85	Virginia ■	68
76	Florida St.	67
71	Duke	108
83	Clemson ■	54
59	Georgia Tech	65
98	North Carolina ■	76
71	Wake Forest	83
92	Virginia †	72
86	Maryland †	82
61	Duke †	91
69	Michigan St. †	58
74	Connecticut †	77

Nickname: Wolfpack
Colors: Red & White
Arena: Raleigh Entertainment & Sports
  Center
  Capacity: 19,722; Year Built: 1999
AD: Lee G. Fowler
SID: Annabelle Vaughan

N.C. WESLEYAN
Rocky Mount, NC 27804 III

Coach: John Thompson,
UNC Greensboro 1984

2001-02 RESULTS (20-8)

66	Maryville (Tenn.) †	75
83	Denison †	76
91	Emory	103
80	Oglethorpe	60
105	Phila. Bible ■	49
102	Warren Wilson ■	50
82	Warren Wilson	52
64	Edgewood †	74
67	Swarthmore †	55
72	Chowan	58
72	Greensboro	75
86	Warren Wilson ■	57
68	Methodist ■	69
84	Shenandoah	79
74	Chris. Newport	67
83	Ferrum ■	81
71	Averett ■	59
66	Chowan	60
79	Greensboro ■	76
60	Methodist	61
69	Shenandoah ■	64
91	Chris. Newport ■	89
88	Ferrum	72
80	Averett	87
102	Ferrum †	71
77	Methodist	70
77	Chris. Newport †	75
79	Hampden-Sydney	92

Nickname: Battling Bishops
Colors: Royal Blue & Gold
Arena: Everett Gymnasium
  Capacity: 800; Year Built: 1960
AD: John M. Thompson
SID: Renny Taylor

UNC WILMINGTON
Wilmington, NC 28403-3297 I

Coach: Jerry Wainwright,
Colorado College 68

2001-02 RESULTS (23-10)

78	Wake Forest	79
50	Miami (Ohio) ■	42
74	High Point	66
72	Radford	85
54	Ohio St.	80
58	Minnesota	50
64	Duquesne ■	52
83	Bowling Green	84
58	Col. of Charleston ■	60
71	Old Dominion	67
82	Fairfield ■	57
76	Towson ■	37
69	Hofstra	58
68	George Mason ■	51
60	Delaware ■	65
58	William & Mary	56
63	James Madison ■	59
66	Old Dominion ■	56
68	Va. Commonwealth	74
56	Towson	46
78	Hofstra ■	54
63	Drexel ■	50
69	James Madison	61
56	George Mason	59
66	William & Mary ■	58
69	Delaware	66
65	Drexel	68
73	Va. Commonwealth ■	62
78	James Madison †	62
69	Delaware †	54
66	Va. Commonwealth †	51
93	Southern California †	89
67	Indiana †	76

Nickname: Seahawks
Colors: Teal, Navy & Gold
Arena: Trask Coliseum
  Capacity: 6,100; Year Built: 1977
SID: Joe Browning

NORTH CENTRAL
Naperville, IL 60566-7063 III

Coach: Benjy Taylor, Richmond 1989

2001-02 RESULTS (8-17)

60	Heidelberg ■	81
63	Manchester ■	64
91	Illinois Tech	59
78	Regis (Colo.)	95
71	Colo. Christian	97
92	Benedictine (Ill.) ■	86
53	Ill.-Chicago	93
69	Hope ■	79
79	Aurora ■	78
85	Finlandia †	60
70	Wis.-Eau Claire	79
56	Augustana (Ill.)	84
82	Millikin ■	94
71	Elmhurst	87
53	North Park ■	65
62	Millikin	60
73	North Park	77
45	Augustana (Ill.) ■	80
79	Ill. Wesleyan	76
77	Wheaton (Ill.) ■	67
52	Carthage	85
73	Carthage ■	83
62	Elmhurst ■	75
77	Ill. Wesleyan ■	74
67	Wheaton (Ill.)	76

Nickname: Cardinals
Colors: Cardinal & White
Arena: Gregory Arena
  Capacity: 3,000; Year Built: 1931
AD: Walter J. Johnson
SID: Kevin Juday

NORTH DAKOTA
Grand Forks, ND 58202 II

Coach: Rich Glas, Bemidji St. 1970

2001-02 RESULTS (19-10)
98	Jamestown ■	66
76	Minot St.	80
89	Bemidji St.	78
72	Minn. St. Moorhead ■	69
77	South Dakota St.	94
63	Augustana (S.D.)	59
67	Minn.-Duluth	54
65	Northern St.	80
80	Minn.-Crookston ■	60
77	Kansas ■	108
87	Northern Colo. ■	78
92	Neb.-Omaha ■	88
83	North Dakota St. ■	79
65	South Dakota	78
101	Morningside	67
91	St. Cloud St. ■	88
78	Minn. St.-Mankato ■	72
80	Neb.-Omaha	85
88	Northern Colo.	102
54	North Dakota St.	66
91	Morningside ■	63
87	South Dakota ■	75
87	Minn. St.-Mankato	78
73	St. Cloud St.	87
88	Augustana (S.D.) ■	60
96	South Dakota St.	78
96	Northern Colo. ■	74
68	Neb.-Omaha †	53
92	South Dakota St.	100

Nickname: Fighting Sioux
Colors: Green & White
Arena: Hyslop Sports Center
  Capacity: 4,792; Year Built: 1951
AD: Roger Thomas
SID: Joel Carlson

NORTH DAKOTA ST.
Fargo, ND 58105-5600 II

Coach: Tim Miles, Mary 1989

2001-02 RESULTS (11-15)
96	Minn.-Morris ■	75
76	Lake Superior St. ■	86
70	Northern St. ■	68
89	Minn.-Duluth ■	80
79	Minn. St. Moorhead	69
101	Augustana (S.D.)	80
82	South Dakota St.	97
78	Minn.-Crookston ■	81
92	Mayville St. ■	65
99	Minot St. ■	80
65	Neb.-Omaha ■	74
76	Northern Colo. ■	87
79	North Dakota	83
79	Morningside	64
63	South Dakota	69
65	Minn. St.-Mankato ■	66
79	St. Cloud St.	93
91	Northern Colo.	93
65	Neb.-Omaha	77
66	North Dakota ■	54
73	South Dakota ■	86
103	Morningside ■	62
68	St. Cloud St.	82
79	Minn. St.-Mankato	89
91	South Dakota St. ■	83
81	Augustana (S.D.) ■	89

Nickname: Bison
Colors: Yellow & Green
Arena: Bison Sports Arena
  Capacity: 8,000; Year Built: 1970
AD: Gene Taylor
SID: George Ellis

NORTH FLA.
Jacksonville, FL 32224-2645 II

Coach: Matt Kilcullen, Lehman 1976

2001-02 RESULTS (13-14)
60	Edward Waters ■	65
104	Fla. Southern ■	108
73	Flagler	95
70	Kennesaw St. ■	67
66	Augusta St.	71
84	Nova Southeastern ■	70
87	Green Mountain ■	55
84	Concordia (N.Y.) ■	61
68	Elizabeth City St.	74
78	Lander	69
88	GC&SU ■	74
62	Columbus St.	74
66	Clayton St. ■	72
74	GC&SU	86
78	Kennesaw St.	90
99	Francis Marion	88
80	S.C.-Aiken ■	63
87	Columbus St. ■	64
71	S.C.-Aiken	77
86	Lander ■	85
74	Armstrong Atlantic	71
67	S.C.-Spartanburg	61
69	Armstrong Atlantic ■	93
82	Clayton St.	86
56	Augusta St. ■	70
85	UNC Pembroke ■	74
91	S.C.-Aiken †	92

Nickname: Ospreys
Colors: Navy Blue & Gray
Arena: UNF Arena
  Capacity: 5,800; Year Built: 1993
AD: Richard E. Gropper
SID: B.J. Sohn

NORTH PARK
Chicago, IL 60625-4895 III

Coach: Rees Johnson, Winona St. 1965

2001-02 RESULTS (11-14)
76	Dominican (Ill.) ■	66
85	Menlo †	77
67	Whitworth †	85
73	Chaminade	88
66	Northwestern (Minn.) ■	58
82	Rockford	86
94	Dominican (Ill.)	63
71	Albion ■	82
76	Milwaukee Engr.	81
74	Judson (Ill.) ■	66
77	Wabash	80
68	Ill. Wesleyan	102
65	North Central	53
91	Wheaton (Ill.) ■	81
77	North Central ■	73
62	Carthage ■	80
70	Augustana (Ill.)	92
91	Millikin	87
61	Augustana (Ill.) ■	63
68	Ill. Wesleyan ■	55
59	Carthage	74
79	Elmhurst	83
69	Millikin ■	60
64	Wheaton (Ill.)	73
89	Elmhurst ■	92

Nickname: Vikings
Colors: Blue & Gold
Arena: North Park Gymnasium
  Capacity: 1,800; Year Built: 1958
AD: Jack Surridge
SID: Chris Nelson

NORTH TEXAS
Denton, TX 76203-6737 I

Coach: Johnny Jones, LSU 1985

2001-02 RESULTS (15-14)
79	Southwest Mo. St. ■	77
58	Oklahoma St.	77
74	Lipscomb	75
69	Houston	75
66	Southern Methodist ■	74
81	Baylor	95
70	Kansas St.	84
102	Lipscomb ■	81
89	Tennessee Tech ■	83
92	TCU	85
76	New Mexico St. ■	71
74	Ark.-Little Rock	84
76	Arkansas	70
78	Florida Int'l ■	79
100	Tex. A&M-Kingsville ■	92
78	Denver	70
85	Middle Tenn. ■	63
78	La.-Lafayette	96
71	New Mexico St.	88
98	St. Edward's ■	71
83	Denver ■	57
75	New Orleans ■	82
77	South Ala. ■	73
78	La.-Lafayette ■	59
76	Western Ky.	100
61	New Orleans	83
78	South Ala.	72
84	Florida Int'l †	71
68	Western Ky. †	82

Nickname: Mean Green
Colors: Green & White
Arena: Super Pit
  Capacity: 10,032; Year Built: 1973
AD: Rick Villarreal
SID: Jerry Scott

NORTHEASTERN
Boston, MA 02115-5096 I

Coach: Ron Everhart, Virginia Tech 1985

2001-02 RESULTS (7-21)
54	Columbia †	66
76	Drexel †	87
88	Brown ■	90
67	Northern Ariz. ■	70
61	Harvard	68
56	Virginia Tech	79
74	Loyola (Md.) ■	63
44	Connecticut	80
72	Drexel	83
80	Rider ■	68
66	Rhode Island	67
84	New Hampshire	72
61	Hartford	64
77	Vermont ■	80
91	Stony Brook ■	65
76	Binghamton ■	94
87	Vermont	102
88	Boston U. ■	95
64	Binghamton	81
50	Albany (N.Y.) ■	51
67	Hartford ■	66
73	Maine ■	74
81	New Hampshire ■	82
79	Albany (N.Y.) ■	59
57	Boston U.	63
70	Stony Brook	85
70	Maine	63
76	Boston U. †	86

Nickname: Huskies
Colors: Red & Black
Arena: Matthews Arena
  Capacity: 6,000; Year Built: 1909
SID: Jack Grinold

NORTHEASTERN ST.
Tahlequah, OK 74464-2399 II

Coach: Larry Gipson, Heidelberg 1974

2001-02 RESULTS (28-2)
76	Bacone †	34
65	Pittsburg St.	60
64	Mo. Southern St. ■	63
73	John Brown	49
72	Tex. A&M-Commerce ■	51
77	Tex. A&M-Kingsville ■	69
71	Angelo St.	69
82	Abilene Christian	52
71	Western Wash. †	70
59	Henderson St. †	52
74	West Tex. A&M ■	51
70	Eastern N.M. ■	51
85	Bacone	65
58	Tarleton St.	53
66	Southeastern Okla. ■	52
64	East Central	75
87	Southwestern Okla. ■	66
67	Cameron	65
83	Central Okla. ■	57
66	Midwestern St.	56
73	Southeastern Okla.	61
68	East Central ■	54
64	Southwestern Okla.	59
70	Cameron ■	58
93	Central Okla.	78
52	Midwestern St. ■	48
71	Eastern N.M. ■	59
65	Tex. A&M-Kingsville ■	53
66	Tarleton St. ■	50
70	Rockhurst ■	75

Nickname: Redmen
Colors: Green & White
Arena: Dobbins Fieldhouse
  Capacity: 1,200; Year Built: 1954
AD: Eddie Griffin
SID: Matt Conley

NORTHERN ARIZ.
Flagstaff, AZ 86011-5400 I

Coach: Mike Adras, UC Santa Barb. 1983

2001-02 RESULTS (14-14)
75	Cal Poly ■	57
47	Pittsburgh	58
78	Colgate	77
70	Northeastern	67
91	N.M. Highlands ■	64
67	Lipscomb	52
51	Tenn.-Martin	54
51	Oregon	86
44	Boise St.	55
64	Montana Tech ■	46
80	Cal St. Fullerton ■	68
56	Air Force ■	57
57	New Mexico	70
66	Weber St.	78
64	Idaho St.	77
63	Sacramento St.	81
77	Montana ■	64
48	Montana St. ■	59
70	Eastern Wash.	63
77	Portland St.	60
77	Idaho St. ■	76
85	Weber St. ■	79
90	Sacramento St. ■	70
59	Montana St.	62
63	Montana	70
79	Portland St. ■	88
80	Eastern Wash. ■	75
64	Montana †	82

Nickname: Lumberjacks
Colors: Blue & Gold
Arena: Walkup Skydome
  Capacity: 7,000; Year Built: 1977
AD: Steven P. Holton
SID: Steve Shaff

SCHEDULES/RESULTS

NORTHERN COLO.
Greeley, CO 80639 II

Coach: Craig Rasmuson, Ashland 1990
2001-02 RESULTS (14-13)
59	Oregon St.	64
92	Western St. (Colo.) ■	77
60	Colorado Mines	62
66	Southern Colo. ■	67
89	Fla. Southern †	78
93	Alas. Fairbanks †	68
82	Neb.-Omaha ■	94
101	Adams St.	86
89	Chaminade ■	70
78	North Dakota	87
87	North Dakota St.	76
63	South Dakota ■	67
101	Morningside ■	73
60	St. Cloud St.	85
79	Minn. St.-Mankato	81
93	Augustana (S.D.) ■	80
97	South Dakota St. ■	85
93	North Dakota St. ■	91
102	North Dakota ■	88
93	Morningside	72
87	South Dakota	98
104	Minn. St.-Mankato ■	88
86	St. Cloud St.	85
71	South Dakota St. ■	83
88	Augustana (S.D.) ■	96
85	Neb.-Omaha	97
74	North Dakota	96

Nickname: Bears
Colors: Blue & Gold
Arena: Butler Hancock Hall
　Capacity: 4,500; Year Built: 1975
AD: James E. Fallis
SID: Colin McDonough

NORTHERN ILL.
De Kalb, IL 60115-2854 I

Coach: Rob Judson, Illinois 1980
2001-02 RESULTS (12-16)
63	Loyola (Ill.)	75
50	Valparaiso ■	70
73	Sam Houston St. †	80
87	Texas Southern †	65
74	South Fla. ■	79
76	Marshall	79
69	Ill.-Chicago	86
79	Drake	57
86	Eastern Ill. ■	73
76	Ohio ■	88
72	Buffalo ■	70
61	Bowling Green	91
85	Lipscomb	80
80	Toledo	89
78	Miami (Ohio) ■	70
84	Eastern Mich. ■	72
65	Buffalo	75
95	Toledo ■	91
93	Central Mich.	91
81	Ball St. ■	86
90	Eastern Mich.	85
61	Kent St. ■	73
87	Western Mich. ■	97
80	Akron	88
80	Central Mich. ■	70
69	Ball St.	68
85	Western Mich.	86
93	Marshall	97

Nickname: Huskies
Colors: Cardinal & Black
Arena: Convocation Center
　Capacity: 9,100; Year Built: 2002
AD: Cary Groth
SID: Michael Smoose

NORTHERN IOWA
Cedar Falls, IA 50614 I

Coach: Greg McDermott, Northern Iowa
2001-02 RESULTS (14-15)
57	San Diego St. †	71
76	William & Mary †	55
87	Montana	67
83	Wis.-Green Bay	79
74	Tex.-Pan American ■	66
64	UMKC	79
78	Iowa ■	76
67	Bradley	61
65	Butler	77
69	Iowa St.	88
71	Drake ■	56
85	Creighton ■	79
71	Indiana St.	70
58	Southern Ill.	83
78	Southwest Mo. St. ■	80
77	Drake	71
65	Indiana St. ■	71
69	Southern Ill. ■	64
55	Illinois St.	70
81	Bradley ■	67
77	Evansville	83
56	Creighton	83
83	Wichita St. ■	75
62	Southwest Mo. St.	68
65	Evansville ■	67
66	Illinois St. ■	71
74	Wichita St.	86
78	Evansville †	75
65	Creighton †	80

Nickname: Panthers
Colors: Purple & Old Gold
Arena: UNI-Dome
　Capacity: 10,000; Year Built: 1976
AD: Rick Hartzell
SID: Nancy Justis

NORTHERN KY.
Highland Heights, KY 41099 II

Coach: Ken Shields, Dayton 1964
2001-02 RESULTS (19-8)
79	Ferris St. ■	71
106	Central St. (Ohio) ■	85
95	Thomas More ■	50
88	Lewis	73
54	Wis.-Parkside	67
76	Indianapolis ■	53
62	Ky. Wesleyan ■	64
83	Southern Ind. ■	82
87	Pfeiffer	97
73	Wingate	81
94	Ind.-Southeast ■	75
76	Quincy	74
70	SIU-Edwardsville	62
70	Wis.-Parkside ■	55
90	St. Joseph's (Ind.) ■	85
76	Bellarmine ■	72
90	Southern Ind.	99
78	Mo.-St. Louis	73
90	SIU-Edwardsville ■	55
72	Lewis ■	67
70	St. Joseph's (Ind.)	73
80	Indianapolis	61
95	Bellarmine	73
76	Ky. Wesleyan	99
88	Mo.-St. Louis ■	75
79	Quincy ■	75
87	Wis.-Parkside †	93

Nickname: Norse
Colors: Gold, Black & White
Arena: Regents Hall
　Capacity: 2,000; Year Built: 1972
AD: Jane Meier
SID: Don Owen

NORTHERN MICH.
Marquette, MI 49855-5391 II

Coach: Dean Ellis, Northern Mich. 1983
2001-02 RESULTS (14-12)
85	Finlandia †	66
65	Michigan Tech	81
111	Finlandia ■	63
86	Lake Superior St. ■	70
101	Mt. Senario ■	43
72	Bemidji St. ■	66
84	West Va. Wesleyan †	80
60	Shippensburg †	40
56	Ashland	72
43	Mercyhurst	56
56	Gannon	67
59	Findlay ■	80
61	Hillsdale ■	82
42	Wayne St. (Mich.) ■	75
77	Saginaw Valley ■	64
65	Michigan Tech	78
61	Northwood	60
76	Grand Valley St. ■	69
80	Ferris St.	63
44	Michigan Tech	72
94	Saginaw Valley	82
86	Northland Bapt. ■	51
55	Northwood ■	68
59	Lake Superior St.	70
72	Ferris St.	65
80	Grand Valley St.	82

Nickname: Wildcats
Colors: Old Gold & Olive Green
Arena: Berry Events Center
　Capacity: 4,000; Year Built: 1999
AD: Daniel Spielmann
SID: Jim Pinar

NORTHERN ST.
Aberdeen, SD 57401 II

Coach: Don Meyer, Northern Colo. 1967
2001-02 RESULTS (20-8)
79	Jamestown ■	55
85	Mt. Senario ■	50
113	Dakota St. ■	57
68	North Dakota St.	70
68	St. Cloud St. ■	84
81	South Dakota St.	95
84	Concordia-St. Paul ■	35
77	Winona St.	71
99	Sioux Falls ■	69
80	North Dakota ■	65
77	Wayne St. (Neb.)	67
72	Southwest St.	62
66	Minn. St. Moorhead ■	70
84	Minn.-Crookston ■	74
72	Minn.-Duluth	79
93	Bemidji St.	69
109	Minn.-Morris ■	57
75	Winona St.	55
80	Concordia-St. Paul	77
59	Southwest St. ■	65
90	Wayne St. (Neb.) ■	65
101	Minn.-Crookston	70
80	Minn. St. Moorhead	64
76	Bemidji St. ■	79
63	Minn.-Duluth ■	61
94	Minn.-Morris	66
99	Minn.-Morris ■	47
70	Southwest St. †	77

Nickname: Wolves
Colors: Maroon & Gold
Arena: Wachs Arena
　Capacity: 8,057; Year Built: 1987
AD: Robert A. Olson
SID: Bruce Bachmeier

NORTHWEST MO. ST.
Maryville, MO 64468-6001 II

Coach: Steve Tappmeyer, Southeast Mo. St. 1979
2001-02 RESULTS (29-3)
70	Western Ore. ■	55
72	Lincoln (Mo.) ■	61
85	Wis.-Stout †	48
81	Huron	66
77	Western Ore.	63
76	Seattle †	40
103	Manhattan Chrst. ■	49
89	Marycrest Int'l ■	61
75	Emporia St.	57
72	Pittsburg St.	56
76	Mo. Western St.	70
74	Truman ■	65
90	Mo. Southern St. ■	67
67	Washburn	65
82	Southwest Baptist	67
78	Central Mo. St. ■	54
79	Mo.-Rolla	73
91	Emporia St. ■	79
90	Pittsburg St.	81
59	Mo. Western St. ■	64
79	Truman	50
77	Mo. Southern St.	94
72	Washburn ■	57
99	Southwest Baptist ■	92
72	Central Mo. St.	54
75	Mo.-Rolla ■	62
100	Central Mo. St. ■	51
79	Mo. Southern St.	76
71	Mo. Western St.	58
61	Incarnate Word †	56
79	Rockhurst †	73
72	Indiana (Pa.) †	78

Nickname: Bearcats
Colors: Green & White
Arena: Bearcat Arena
　Capacity: 2,500; Year Built: 1955
AD: Bob Boerigter
SID: Andy Seeley

NORTHWEST NAZARENE
Nampa, ID 83686 II

2001-02 RESULTS (10-18)
87	Lock Haven †	67
58	Indianapolis †	65
95	Cal St. Stanislaus ■	98
86	Albertson †	99
71	Regis (Colo.)	83
105	Humboldt St. ■	114
70	Western Ore. ■	79
62	Seattle ■	57
82	Christian Heritage	84
65	Pt. Loma Nazarene	64
64	Seattle Pacific	85
76	Western Wash.	104
82	Central Wash. ■	77
76	St. Martin's ■	78
82	Seattle	73
80	Alas. Fairbanks	65
71	Alas. Anchorage	81
73	Western Ore.	70
77	Humboldt St.	101
71	Western Wash. ■	77
83	Seattle Pacific ■	86
99	Walla Walla ■	79
74	St. Martin's	78
80	Central Wash.	92
79	Belhaven †	67
66	Briar Cliff	69
79	Alas. Anchorage ■	82
97	Alas. Fairbanks ■	73

Nickname: Crusaders
Colors: Red and Black
Arena: Montgomery Fieldhouse
　Capacity: 3,500; Year Built: 1971

AD: Rich Sanders
SID: Gil Craker

NORTHWESTERN
Evanston, IL 60208 I

Coach: Bill Carmody, Union 1975
2001-02 RESULTS (16-13)

78	Va. Commonwealth †	73
68	East Caro. †	71
59	San Jose St. †	51
80	Chicago St. ■	42
57	Florida St. ■	50
79	Kansas St. ■	56
58	Florida A&M ■	55
66	Liberty ■	49
60	Fordham †	63
52	La.-Lafayette †	51
60	Arizona St.	77
44	Indiana ■	59
60	Iowa	70
48	Ohio St. ■	55
58	Michigan	54
63	Iowa ■	50
61	Purdue ■	63
63	Buffalo	57
69	Wisconsin ■	60
57	Ohio St.	58
61	Michigan St. ■	49
44	Wisconsin	73
58	Minnesota ■	56
55	Penn St.	49
61	Purdue	48
41	Illinois ■	56
51	Minnesota	69
67	Indiana	79
51	Michigan †	72

Nickname: Wildcats
Colors: Purple & White
Arena: Welsh-Ryan Arena
  Capacity: 8,117; Year Built: 1952
AD: Rick Taylor
SID: Michael Mahoney

NORTHWESTERN ST.
Natchitoches, LA 71497-0003....I

Coach: Mike McConathy, Louisiana Tech 1977
2001-02 RESULTS (13-18)

79	TCU	93
69	Memphis	97
60	UTEP †	66
107	Ark.-Monticello †	86
99	Siena †	91
58	Hawaii	60
54	LSU	91
88	Grambling	91
44	Oklahoma †	79
65	Lamar	82
66	Stephen F. Austin ■	73
79	Texas-Arlington	65
89	Centenary (La.)	72
73	Nicholls St.	66
72	Southeastern La.	63
90	Southwest Tex. St. ■	63
88	Texas-San Antonio ■	86
77	Lamar ■	81
83	Sam Houston St. ■	98
64	La.-Monroe †	72
63	McNeese St. ■	67
79	Sam Houston St.	74
69	Southwest Tex. St.	85
67	Texas-San Antonio	77
93	Nicholls St. ■	72
62	Southeastern La. ■	52
65	Centenary (La.) ■	57
58	Stephen F. Austin	66
70	Texas-Arlington ■	65
53	McNeese St.	75
83	La.-Monroe	96

Nickname: Demons
Colors: Purple, White & Orange

Arena: Prather Coliseum
  Capacity: 4,300; Year Built: 1963
AD: Gregory S. Burke
SID: Doug Ireland

NORTHWOOD
Midland, MI 48640-2398 II

Coach: Bob Taylor, Arkansas Tech 1980
2001-02 RESULTS (18-11)

82	Wayne St. (Mich.) †	74
66	Hillsdale †	71
91	Rochester College ■	71
84	Grand Valley St. ■	81
72	Hillsdale	78
62	Wayne St. (Mich.)	78
79	Albion ■	71
76	Ashland ■	75
95	St. Joseph's (Ind.) ■	72
87	Finlandia ■	61
60	Lewis	72
72	Findlay	88
65	Mercyhurst ■	61
83	Gannon ■	78
71	Ferris St. ■	66
84	Lake Superior St.	97
58	Michigan Tech ■	74
60	Northern Mich. ■	61
73	Saginaw Valley	69
78	Lake Superior St. ■	77
81	Grand Valley St.	94
75	Ferris St.	66
68	Northern Mich.	55
59	Michigan Tech	81
98	Rochester College ■	82
112	Saginaw Valley ■	85
84	Ashland †	76
77	Findlay †	72
65	Michigan Tech †	79

Nickname: Timberwolves
Colors: Columbia Blue & White
Arena: E.W. Bennett Sports Center
  Capacity: 1,260; Year Built: 1979
AD: Pat Riepma
SID: Dave Marsh

NORWICH
Northfield, VT 05663 III

Coach: Paul Booth, St. Joseph's (Vt.) 1983
2001-02 RESULTS (6-18)

64	Skidmore †	66
88	Castleton St. †	68
49	Juniata †	73
53	Notre Dame (Ohio) †	68
77	Johnson St. ■	75
82	Lyndon St. ■	70
74	Castleton St. ■	50
49	Colby-Sawyer ■	83
52	Bowdoin ■	67
61	Castleton St.	68
48	Middlebury	64
48	Albertus Magnus ■	64
56	Southern Vt. ■	60
68	Suffolk	80
68	Western New Eng. ■	71
69	Rivier ■	70
73	Emmanuel (Mass.) ■	55
62	Daniel Webster	50
64	Johnson & Wales ■	72
68	Southern Vt.	93
67	Emerson ■	75
74	Daniel Webster ■	76
76	Rivier	82
49	Western New Eng.	82

Nickname: Cadets
Colors: Maroon & Gold
Arena: Andrews Hall
  Capacity: 1,500; Year Built: 1980
AD: Anthony A. Mariano
SID: Todd Bamford

NOTRE DAME
Notre Dame, IN 46556 I

Coach: Mike Brey, George Washington 1982
2001-02 RESULTS (22-11)

95	New Hampshire ■	53
78	Cornell ■	48
98	Hawaii Pacific ■	58
97	Chattanooga †	84
85	Monmouth †	48
86	Army ■	49
82	DePaul †	55
75	Indiana	76
70	Miami (Ohio)	69
84	Canisius ■	73
76	Alabama †	79
92	Colgate ■	61
72	Villanova ■	74
67	West Virginia	64
56	Pittsburgh ■	53
51	Syracuse	56
65	Kentucky ■	72
73	Georgetown ■	83
60	Seton Hall ■	51
89	Pittsburgh ■	76
63	Seton Hall	61
89	Rutgers ■	72
116	Georgetown	111
62	Rutgers	65
65	Syracuse ■	68
89	West Virginia ■	76
90	Miami (Fla.)	77
81	St. John's (N.Y.)	84
76	Providence ■	68
83	St. John's (N.Y.) †	63
77	Connecticut †	82
82	Charlotte †	63
77	Duke †	84

Nickname: Fighting Irish
Colors: Blue & Gold
Arena: Joyce Center
  Capacity: 11,418; Year Built: 1968
AD: Kevin White
SID: Bernadette Cafarelli

OAKLAND
Rochester, MI 48309-4401.........I

Coach: Greg Kampe, Bowling Green 1978
2001-02 RESULTS (17-13)

73	Michigan	81
94	St. Mary's (Mich.) ■	73
53	Pittsburgh ■	70
61	UC Irvine †	68
77	Robert Morris	53
71	Akron †	64
71	Purdue	89
93	Detroit ■	67
57	Air Force	53
54	Wright St.	74
70	Ohio	71
50	Michigan St.	78
93	Toledo ■	68
100	Western Mich. ■	94
88	Chicago St.	77
58	Southern Utah ■	57
63	UMKC	72
61	Oral Roberts	93
83	IUPUI ■	69
93	Western Ill. ■	75
77	Valparaiso ■	86
71	IPFW	77
84	Southern Utah	60
78	Chicago St. ■	73
85	Oral Roberts ■	76
72	UMKC ■	59
94	IUPUI	92
72	Valparaiso	79
86	Western Ill.	82
84	IUPUI †	90

Nickname: Golden Grizzlies
Colors: Gold, Black & White
Arena: Athletic Center
  Capacity: 4,005; Year Built: 1998
AD: Jack G. Mehl
SID: Amy Stabley-Hirschman

OAKLAND CITY
Oakland City, IN 47660-1099 ..II

Coach: John Hayes, Oakland City 1990
2001-02 RESULTS (10-16)

75	Ohio-Chillicothe ■	83
77	Drury ■	66
58	Arkansas Tech	75
47	Henderson St. †	61
96	Mid-Continent ■	70
72	Charleston (W.Va.)	96
66	Harris-Stowe ■	68
76	Kentucky St. ■	79
108	Mid-Continent	70
52	Southern Ind.	97
67	Indianapolis ■	72
59	Ky. Wesleyan	92
81	Charleston (W.Va.) ■	82
93	Wilberforce	105
73	Brescia	81
82	Drury	107
82	Ala.-Huntsville	77
82	Hannibal-La Grange	54
96	Montevallo	109
104	Lincoln (Mo.) ■	100
102	St. Louis Christian ■	58
91	Brescia ■	97
99	Spalding	91
50	Ala.-Huntsville ■	64
89	Spalding ■	81
90	Montevallo ■	78

Nickname: Mighty Oaks
Colors: Navy & White
Arena: Johnson Center
  Capacity: 1,600; Year Built: 1987
AD: Mike Sandifar
SID: To be named

OBERLIN
Oberlin, OH 44074 III

Coach: James Sullinger, Oberlin 1978
2001-02 RESULTS (9-16)

50	Buffalo St.	59
52	Alma †	68
62	DePauw	90
56	St. Vincent ■	89
83	Hiram	81
68	Denison ■	73
69	Earlham	78
62	Wilmington (Ohio)	73
60	Manchester ■	70
54	Case Reserve	84
53	Wittenberg ■	103
76	Wash. & Jeff. ■	75
58	Wooster	78
49	Ohio Wesleyan ■	85
78	Kenyon	85
78	Wabash ■	69
70	Denison	66
69	Hiram ■	59
70	Allegheny	63
69	Earlham ■	59
67	Kenyon ■	83
62	Ohio Wesleyan	67
79	Allegheny ■	65
49	Wabash	60
56	Ohio Wesleyan	49

Nickname: Yeomen
Colors: Crimson & Gold
Arena: Philips Gymnasium
  Capacity: 1,800; Year Built: 1971
AD: George Andrews
SID: Scott Wargo

SCHEDULES/RESULTS

OCCIDENTAL

Los Angeles, CA 90041 III

Coach: Brian Newhall, Occidental 1983

2001-02 RESULTS (18-7)

74	S'western (Ariz.) †	54
76	LIFE Bible †	38
66	La Sierra ■	42
78	La Sierra	54
89	Western Baptist	69
68	Chapman ■	52
103	Western Baptist ■	46
81	Pacific Union ■	44
55	Loyola Marymount	81
113	Cal Baptist ■	58
65	Trinity (Conn.) ■	72
95	La Verne ■	74
80	Cal Lutheran ■	91
82	Pomona-Pitzer	72
81	Caltech ■	36
90	Whittier	83
67	Claremont-M-S	77
74	Redlands	63
73	La Verne	61
65	Cal Lutheran	69
52	Pomona-Pitzer ■	66
66	Caltech	38
67	Whittier ■	62
47	Claremont-M-S ■	49
82	Redlands	55

Nickname: Tigers
Colors: Orange & Black
Arena: Rush Gymnasium
    Capacity: 1,800; Year Built: 1967
AD: Dixon Farmer
SID: Jenna Panatier

OGLETHORPE

Atlanta, GA 30319-2797 III

Coach: Jim Owen, Berry 1981

2001-02 RESULTS (4-21)

55	Flagler †	71
54	La Grange	71
45	Davidson	114
60	N.C. Wesleyan ■	80
94	Emory ■	89
59	Millsaps	82
64	Trinity (Tex.) ■	85
67	Southwestern (Tex.) ■	81
59	Rose-Hulman	71
62	DePauw	97
81	Sewanee ■	87
56	Centre ■	71
97	La Grange ■	96
76	Hendrix	49
62	Rhodes	83
51	Trinity (Tex.)	67
52	Southwestern (Tex.)	72
44	Rose-Hulman ■	60
71	DePauw ■	99
56	Sewanee	80
63	Centre	75
84	Hendrix ■	65
67	Rhodes ■	77
70	Emory	83
91	Millsaps ■	96

Nickname: Stormy Petrels
Colors: Black & Gold
Arena: Dorough Fieldhouse
    Capacity: 2,000; Year Built: 1962
AD: Bob Unger
SID: Jack Berkshire

OHIO

Athens, OH 45701 I

Coach: Tim O'Shea, Boston College
1984

2001-02 RESULTS (17-11)

80	Navy	74
73	Duquesne ■	60
77	DePaul	75
71	Wisconsin ■	77
85	St. Bonaventure	97
71	Oakland ■	70
110	Long Island †	57
79	Vermont †	91
88	Northern Ill.	76
68	Akron ■	57
86	Western Mich. ■	68
56	Kent St.	71
62	Buffalo	61
85	Miami (Ohio) ■	61
80	Eastern Mich.	66
65	Western Mich.	95
73	Akron	74
94	Marshall ■	78
64	Bowling Green	80
85	Ball St. ■	71
55	Miami (Ohio)	79
64	Central Mich. ■	50
71	Marshall	66
86	North Carolina	78
67	Kent St. ■	70
68	Toledo ■	69
85	Bowling Green ■	78
56	Central Mich. ■	65

Nickname: Bobcats
Colors: Hunter Green & White
Arena: Convocation Center
    Capacity: 13,000; Year Built: 1968
AD: Thomas C. Boeh
SID: Jim Stephan

OHIO NORTHERN

Ada, OH 45810 III

Coach: Joe Campoli, Rhode Island 1964

2001-02 RESULTS (18-8)

76	Ohio Wesleyan †	58
68	Beloit †	56
82	Geneva ■	44
58	Mount Union ■	76
82	Wilmington (Ohio) ■	54
84	Capital	76
92	Defiance ■	78
99	John Carroll ■	84
57	Otterbein	79
72	Thiel †	76
80	Case Reserve †	65
77	Baldwin-Wallace	58
84	Heidelberg ■	70
58	Marietta	62
75	Muskingum ■	68
50	Capital ■	53
61	Wilmington (Ohio)	63
70	John Carroll	86
63	Otterbein ■	62
84	Baldwin-Wallace ■	75
77	Heidelberg	66
74	Marietta ■	64
58	Muskingum	44
72	Mount Union	70
85	John Carroll ■	73
59	Otterbein	91

Nickname: Polar Bears
Colors: Burnt Orange & Black
Arena: ONU Sports Center
    Capacity: 3,200; Year Built: 1975
AD: Thomas E. Simmons
SID: Tim Glon

OHIO ST.

Columbus, OH 43210 I

Coach: Jim O'Brien, Boston College
1971

2001-02 RESULTS (24-8)

78	Winthrop ■	54
87	Albany (N.Y.) ■	62
64	North Carolina St. ■	50
80	UNC Wilmington ■	54
83	IUPUI ■	70
88	Santa Clara ■	41
61	Louisville ■	66
55	Pittsburgh ■	62
72	Eastern Ill. ■	59
85	UNC Greensboro ■	54
79	Purdue	71
72	Iowa ■	62
70	Massachusetts ■	62
55	Northwestern	48
76	Penn St. ■	57
73	Indiana ■	67
69	Michigan ■	47
71	Minnesota	89
78	Illinois ■	67
58	Northwestern ■	57
92	Wisconsin	94
64	Michigan St. ■	67
72	Iowa	66
57	Indiana	63
77	Purdue ■	66
76	Michigan St. ■	81
84	Michigan	75
75	Michigan †	68
94	Illinois †	88
81	Iowa †	64
69	Davidson †	64
67	Missouri †	83

Nickname: Buckeyes
Colors: Scarlet & Gray
Arena: Value City Arena
    Capacity: 19,200; Year Built: 1998
AD: Ferdinand A. Geiger
SID: Dan Wallenberg

OHIO VALLEY

Vienna, WV 26104 II

2001-02 RESULTS (3-23)

60	Salem Int'l	101
87	Ohio Southern	72
69	Glenville St. ■	85
93	Ohio Southern ■	78
51	Lake Superior St.	80
47	Lake Superior St.	104
72	Calif. (Pa.)	86
72	Dist. Columbia †	80
57	West Va. Wesleyan ■	94
71	Alderson-Broaddus	86
86	Davis & Elkins	99
66	Bluefield St. ■	80
57	Fairmont St.	70
68	West Liberty St. ■	82
83	Davis & Elkins ■	98
56	Salem Int'l	99
84	Wheeling Jesuit ■	98
63	Shepherd	77
48	West Virginia St. ■	59
71	West Va. Tech	63
59	Charleston (W.Va.)	94
66	Fairmont St. ■	84
53	West Liberty St.	104
62	Salem Int'l ■	87
58	Wheeling Jesuit ■	78
67	Concord ■	89

Nickname: Fighting Scots
Colors: Royal Blue & Red
AD: Ron Pavan
SID: To be named

OHIO WESLEYAN

Delaware, OH 43015 III

Coach: Michael DeWitt, Ohio Wesleyan
1987

2001-02 RESULTS (12-15)

58	Ohio Northern †	76
70	Chicago	77
93	Adrian ■	74
88	Hendrix †	66

84	Rhodes	77
45	Ohio Dominican	64
77	Allegheny ■	67
63	Wooster	73
78	Hiram ■	57
68	Capital ■	77
65	Wis.-Whitewater †	74
70	Dominican (Ill.) †	62
73	Kenyon ■	53
75	Denison ■	51
85	Oberlin	49
68	Wittenberg ■	70
70	Allegheny	63
55	Wooster ■	76
83	Earlham ■	57
48	Wabash	51
51	Hiram	54
64	Wittenberg ■	67
67	Oberlin ■	62
72	Wabash ■	81
57	Earlham	60
49	Oberlin	56
69	Wittenberg	75

Nickname: Battling Bishops
Colors: Red & Black
Arena: Branch Rickey Arena
    Capacity: 2,300; Year Built: 1976
AD: John A. Martin
SID: Mark Beckenbach

OKLAHOMA

Norman, OK 73019 I

Coach: Kelvin Sampson, UNC Pembroke
1974

2001-02 RESULTS (31-5)

66	Central Conn. St. ■	44
55	Michigan St.	67
81	Central Mich. ■	64
69	Arkansas	54
80	St. Bonaventure ■	74
71	Louisiana Tech ■	67
107	High Point ■	63
102	Bethune-Cookman ■	65
109	Eastern Ill. ■	50
72	Maryland ■	56
97	Texas Southern †	55
89	Texas A&M ■	63
69	Connecticut	67
98	Texas Tech ■	72
78	Nebraska	51
67	Kansas	74
84	Missouri ■	71
79	Texas Tech	92
58	Oklahoma St. ■	53
85	Texas	84
70	Baylor ■	57
68	Texas A&M	64
72	Oklahoma St.	79
73	Kansas St. ■	62
65	Baylor	54
96	Texas ■	78
89	Iowa St. ■	75
82	Colorado	71
63	Kansas St. †	52
69	Texas †	51
64	Kansas †	55
71	Ill.-Chicago †	63
78	Xavier †	65
88	Arizona †	67
81	Missouri †	75
64	Indiana †	73

Nickname: Sooners
Colors: Crimson & Cream
Arena: Lloyd Noble Center
    Capacity: 12,000; Year Built: 1975
AD: Joseph R. Castiglione
SID: Mike Houck

OKLA. PANHANDLE

Goodwell, OK 73939 II

Coach: Charles Terry,

2001-02 RESULTS (5-22)

80	Abilene Christian	92
64	West Tex. A&M	89
71	Abilene Christian ■	53
85	Western N.M. ■	76
67	Emporia St.	108
62	Pittsburg St. †	101
59	Mo. Southern St.	91
63	Northwestern Okla. ■	76
84	Southwest Baptist	110
53	Central Mo. St.	64
60	West Tex. A&M ■	95
69	Eastern N.M. ■	89
81	Emporia St. ■	93
78	Central Ark.	84
81	Drury ■	91
61	Northwestern Okla.	91
79	Mont. St.-Billings	103
90	Mont. St.-Billings	118
70	Cameron	77
77	Eastern N.M.	81
61	Incarnate Word ■	74
81	National Christian ■	68
84	Drury	91
75	Cameron ■	66
72	Incarnate Word	84
84	National Christian	65
95	Western N.M.	101

Nickname: Aggies
Colors: Navy & Red
Arena: Carl Williams Field House
  Capacity: 2,800; Year Built: 1909
AD: Wayne Stewart
SID: Jason Cronin

OKLAHOMA ST.

Stillwater, OK 74078-5070 I

Coach: Eddie Sutton, Oklahoma St. 1958

2001-02 RESULTS (23-9)

69	Cincinnati ■	62
81	Austin Peay ■	58
83	Providence †	65
82	Siena †	64
95	TCU ■	77
77	North Texas ■	58
95	New Orleans ■	47
61	Wichita St. ■	59
90	Jackson St. ■	41
79	Northwestern St. ■	44
62	UMKC	50
85	Arkansas †	76
82	Ball St. †	70
61	Texas ■	70
68	Baylor	57
69	Iowa St.	66
61	Kansas ■	79
70	Texas Tech	94
70	Nebraska ■	63
64	Colorado ■	55
53	Oklahoma	58
61	Kansas St.	70
64	Texas Tech ■	62
52	Fresno St.	58
79	Oklahoma ■	72
71	Texas A&M ■	66
85	Texas	80
77	Baylor ■	64
69	Missouri	72
66	Texas A&M ■	51
51	Texas Tech †	73
61	Kent St. †	69

Nickname: Cowboys
Colors: Orange & Black
Arena: Gallagher-Iba Arena
  Capacity: 13,611; Year Built: 1938
AD: Harry Birdwell
SID: Mike Noteware

OLD DOMINION

Norfolk, VA 23529-0197 I

Coach: Blaine Taylor, Montana 1982

2001-02 RESULTS (13-16)

69	Sacramento St. †	52
66	Memphis	91
55	Virginia Tech ■	46
72	Delaware St. ■	61
71	Ill.-Chicago ■	65
64	George Washington ■	68
53	East Caro.	52
81	Coastal Caro. ■	67
77	Hampton	84
67	UNC Wilmington ■	71
76	UNLV	84
66	Hofstra	67
74	Drexel ■	66
60	Delaware ■	58
67	George Mason	76
66	Towson	53
77	Va. Commonwealth ■	79
56	UNC Wilmington	66
68	William & Mary ■	52
61	James Madison ■	67
70	Delaware	75
55	Towson ■	67
66	Va. Commonwealth	73
70	Drexel	80
73	James Madison ■	68
69	Hofstra ■	53
81	William & Mary	53
63	George Mason ■	78
54	Va. Commonwealth †	58

Nickname: Monarchs
Colors: Slate Blue, Sky Blue, & Silver
Arena: Ted Constant Convocation Ctr.
  Capacity: 8,600; Year Built: 2002
AD: James Jarrett
SID: Carol Hudson

OLD WESTBURY

Old Westbury, NY 11568-0210III

Coach: Bernard Tomlin, Hofstra 1976

2001-02 RESULTS (14-11)

80	Yeshiva ■	68
86	Stevens Tech ■	61
50	Manhattanville	59
81	Maritime (N.Y.) ■	62
87	Mt. St. Vincent ■	82
77	St. Joseph's (L.I.)	63
58	Mt. St. Mary (N.Y.) ■	61
64	Merchant Marine ■	91
67	Manhattanville ■	87
66	Stevens Tech	68
93	St. Joseph's (L.I.) ■	69
69	Purchase ■	48
70	Farmingdale St. ■	69
51	York (N.Y.) ■	53
80	Lehman	85
112	Bard	54
115	St. Joseph's (Brkln)	93
109	Polytechnic (N.Y.) ■	39
67	Maritime (N.Y.)	92
84	Mt. St. Vincent	68
70	Merchant Marine	89
76	Mt. St. Mary (N.Y.)	72
67	Yeshiva	75
58	Mt. St. Mary (N.Y.)	59
118	Pratt ■	66

Nickname: Panthers
Colors: Forest Green & White
Arena: Clark Center
  Capacity: 2,500; Year Built: 1891
AD: John Lonardo
SID: Matt Farrand

OLIVET

Olivet, MI 49076 III

Coach: Steve Hettinga, Olivet 1993

2001-02 RESULTS (10-16)

56	Rose-Hulman ■	58
69	Pitt.-Greensburg †	65
59	Ferris St.	79
59	Tri-State	69
79	Concordia (Mich.) ■	75
56	Hillsdale	86
75	Rochester College ■	83
79	Concordia (Mich.)	61
66	Mich.-Dearborn	70
76	Grace Bible (Mich.) ■	67
99	Madonna	85
71	Wabash	68
64	Wis.-Superior †	97
58	Calvin	66
62	Albion ■	65
82	Hope ■	81
81	Alma	71
66	Kalamazoo ■	70
62	Adrian	67
60	Calvin ■	91
62	Albion	61
72	Hope	93
62	Alma ■	60
67	Kalamazoo	86
76	Adrian ■	101
67	Kalamazoo	75

Nickname: Comets
Colors: Crimson & White
Arena: Upton Gymnasium
  Capacity: 1,500; Year Built: 1981
AD: Irv Sigler
SID: Johnny Cunningham

ONEONTA ST.

Oneonta, NY 13820-4015 III

Coach: Paul Clune, Rochester Inst. 1984

2001-02 RESULTS (10-16)

93	Hartwick	89
77	Western New Eng. †	87
92	Castleton St.	77
66	Clarkson	105
92	Farmingdale St. ■	71
61	New Paltz St. ■	54
76	Buffalo St.	95
74	Fredonia St.	76
58	Johns Hopkins †	72
71	Wesleyan (Conn.) †	94
55	Plattsburgh St. ■	71
81	Geneseo St.	91
73	Brockport St.	101
70	Oswego St. ■	66
88	Utica/Rome ■	73
60	Buffalo St. ■	61
82	Keuka ■	80
87	Geneseo St. ■	61
72	Ithaca	86
67	Potsdam St.	82
71	Plattsburgh St.	85
66	Cortland St.	72
63	Fredonia St. ■	58
71	New Paltz St.	69
70	Potsdam St. ■	72
71	Brockport St. †	100

Nickname: Red Dragons
Colors: Red & White
Arena: Dewar Arena
  Capacity: 4,000; Year Built: 1999
AD: Steve Garner
SID: Geoff Hassard

ORAL ROBERTS

Tulsa, OK 74171 I

Coach: Scott Sutton, Oklahoma St. 1994

2001-02 RESULTS (17-14)

71	Cameron ■	75
57	Arkansas ■	71
68	Drake ■	73
68	Colgate	80
70	Binghamton	54
66	Tulsa ■	73
87	Tennessee St. ■	71
55	Nebraska	61
64	Southern Methodist	82
115	Texas-Arlington ■	62
73	Jacksonville †	64
58	Tex.-Pan American †	67
66	Florida Int'l †	55
78	Stephen F. Austin ■	57
77	Texas-Arlington	83
67	UMKC	55
85	IUPUI ■	76
93	Oakland ■	61
67	Valparaiso	87
95	Western Ill.	82
70	Southern Utah ■	71
91	Chicago St. ■	62
85	UMKC ■	75
76	Oakland	85
88	IUPUI	71
84	Western Ill. ■	67
77	Valparaiso ■	74
94	Chicago St.	64
75	Southern Utah	82
86	Western Ill. †	75
53	IUPUI †	58

Nickname: Golden Eagles
Colors: Gold, Blue & White
Arena: Mabee Center
  Capacity: 10,575; Year Built: 1972
AD: R. Michael Carter
SID: Cory Rogers

OREGON

Eugene, OR 97401 I

Coach: Ernie Kent, Oregon 1977

2001-02 RESULTS (26-9)

92	Alabama St. ■	52
91	Western Mich. ■	48
97	Long Beach St. ■	67
90	Louisville †	63
58	Massachusetts †	62
78	Portland	79
72	Minnesota	75
88	Pepperdine ■	64
86	Northern Ariz. ■	51
103	Arizona St. ■	90
105	Arizona	75
96	Morris Brown ■	50
90	Arizona	80
88	Arizona St. ■	95
76	California ■	72
87	Stanford ■	79
71	Willamette	48
63	Oregon St. ■	51
92	Washington	97
94	Washington St. ■	86
91	UCLA ■	62
73	Southern California ■	69
87	Stanford	90
103	California	107
91	Oregon St. ■	62
115	Washington St. ■	77
90	Washington ■	84
67	Southern California	65
65	UCLA	62
86	Washington †	64
78	Southern California †	89
81	Montana †	62
92	Wake Forest †	87
72	Texas †	70
86	Kansas †	104

Nickname: Ducks
Colors: Green & Yellow
Arena: McArthur Court
  Capacity: 9,087; Year Built: 1927

AD: William Moos
SID: Greg Walker

OREGON ST.
Corvallis, OR 97331 I

Coach: Ritchie McKay, Seattle Pacific 1987

2001-02 RESULTS (12-17)

64	Northern Colo. ■	.59
68	Texas †	.78
63	St. John's (N.Y.) †	.66
72	Alas. Anchorage	.63
65	San Diego ■	.56
73	Southern Utah ■	.63
51	Portland St.	.46
68	Cal Poly	.72
73	Arizona ■	.76
62	Arizona St. ■	.57
84	IPFW ■	.59
78	Lehigh ■	.55
58	Arizona St.	.67
87	Arizona	.93
50	Stanford ■	.67
53	California ■	.61
51	Oregon ■	.63
74	Washington St.	.72
68	Washington	.53
51	Southern California ■	.64
48	UCLA ■	.70
58	California	.73
55	Stanford	.77
62	Oregon	.91
74	Portland	.60
63	Washington	.68
91	Washington St. ■	.55
57	UCLA	.65
45	Southern California	.79

Nickname: Beavers
Colors: Orange & Black
Arena: Gill Coliseum
  Capacity: 10,400; Year Built: 1950
AD: Mitch S. Barnhart
SID: Steve Fenk

OSWEGO ST.
Oswego, NY 13126 III

Coach: Kevin Broderick, Nazareth 1989

2001-02 RESULTS (18-12)

77	St. Lawrence ■	.83
72	Potsdam St. ■	.63
74	D'Youville	.83
69	Hilbert ■	.64
64	Buffalo St. ■	.59
80	Geneseo St.	.82
70	Brockport St.	.98
68	Embry-Riddle	.89
75	Eastern †	.67
71	Nazareth ■	.65
70	Fredonia St. ■	.72
71	New Paltz St. ■	.69
75	Cortland St. ■	.71
66	Oneonta St.	.70
64	Potsdam St.	.61
87	Utica/Rome ■	.75
74	Skidmore	.63
85	New Paltz St.	.79
70	Potsdam St. ■	.66
61	Brockport St. ■	.70
85	Plattsburgh St. ■	.58
73	Utica/Rome ■	.75
90	Medaille	.61
69	Fredonia St.	.83
80	Buffalo St. ■	.73
79	Plattsburgh St. †	.63
83	Cortland St. †	.75
78	Brockport St. †	.92
78	Geneseo St. ■	.69
60	Clarkson †	.64

Nickname: Lakers
Colors: Green, Gold & White

Arena: Max Ziel Gymnasium
  Capacity: 3,500; Year Built: 1968
AD: Sandra Moore
SID: Lyle Fulton

OTTERBEIN
Westerville, OH 43081-2006 ...III

Coach: Dick Reynolds, Otterbein 1965

2001-02 RESULTS (30-3)

90	Mt. St. Joseph	.80
81	Johns Hopkins †	.69
81	Trinity (Tex.)	.79
98	Concordia-Austin	.71
90	Capital ■	.87
108	Baldwin-Wallace ■	.81
88	Heidelberg ■	.72
59	Mount Union ■	106
79	Ohio Northern ■	.57
99	Denison ■	.58
74	St. Norbert ■	.70
73	Wittenberg ■	.64
76	Muskingum ■	.77
90	Marietta ■	.75
82	John Carroll ■	.63
93	Wilmington (Ohio)	.75
85	Heidelberg ■	.68
90	Baldwin-Wallace	.80
79	Mount Union ■	.73
62	Ohio Northern	.63
91	Muskingum ■	.64
78	Marietta	.61
89	John Carroll ■	.84
79	Wilmington (Ohio) ■	.54
70	Capital	.67
78	Heidelberg ■	.69
91	Ohio Northern ■	.59
69	Capital ■	.67
121	Bethany (W.Va.) ■	.98
85	Randolph-Macon ■	.72
87	DePauw ■	.79
70	Carthage †	.66
102	Elizabethtown †	.83

Nickname: Cardinals
Colors: Tan & Cardinal
Arena: The Rike Center
  Capacity: 3,100; Year Built: 1974
AD: Richard E. Reynolds
SID: Ed Syguda

OUACHITA BAPTIST
Arkadelphia, AR 71998-0001 ...II

Coach: Charlie Schaef, Texas Tech 1993

2001-02 RESULTS (13-13)

74	St. Edward's	.72
96	Jarvis Christian ■	.79
75	East Central ■	.69
71	William Carey ■	.82
77	Tex. A&M-Commerce ■	.57
96	Wiley ■	.81
63	St. Edward's ■	.53
79	Xavier (La.) ■	.76
67	East Central	.63
73	Tex. A&M-Commerce	.91
72	Delta St. ■	.80
71	Arkansas Tech	.74
82	Ark.-Monticello ■	.58
62	Central Ark.	.67
59	Henderson St. ■	.76
75	Southern Ark.	.79
76	Harding	.93
84	Christian Bros. ■	.68
49	Delta St.	.68
68	Arkansas Tech ■	.76
61	Ark.-Monticello	.68
73	Central Ark. ■	.67
68	Henderson St.	.82
70	Southern Ark. ■	.63
82	Harding ■	.79
73	Christian Bros.	.84

Nickname: Tigers
Colors: Purple & Gold
Arena: Vining Arena
  Capacity: 2,500
AD: David R. Sharp
SID: Chris Babb

OZARKS (ARK.)
Clarksville, AR 72830-2880......III

Coach: Matt O'Connor, Davidson 1991

2001-02 RESULTS (14-12)

87	Rust †	.61
89	Central Baptist †	.73
99	Rhema ■	.80
103	Central Baptist ■	.83
93	Schreiner ■	.79
70	Texas Lutheran ■	.76
83	Ark. Baptist ■	.88
50	Ark.-Monticello ■	.94
63	Austin ■	.60
70	Arkansas Tech ■	.82
81	Sul Ross St. ■	.75
108	Howard Payne ■	.98
73	Dallas ■	.85
65	Texas-Dallas ■ ■	.62
92	East Tex. Baptist ■	.85
86	LeTourneau ■	.73
98	Louisiana Col. ■	.91
66	Mississippi Col. ■	.86
75	Louisiana Col.	.88
63	Mississippi Col.	.96
78	Dallas	.92
69	Texas-Dallas	.75
84	Austin ■	.89
90	East Tex. Baptist ■	.87
78	LeTourneau ■	.67
87	McMurry	.93

Nickname: Eagles
Colors: Purple & Gold
Arena: Mabee Gym
  Capacity: 2,500
AD: Jack C. Jones
SID: Josh Peppas

PACE
Pleasantville, NY 10570-2799 ...II

Coach: Jim Harter, Delaware 1982

2001-02 RESULTS (21-8)

97	Concordia (N.Y.) ■ ■	.70
56	Mass.-Lowell ■	.51
79	Southern N.H.	.86
83	Assumption ■	.77
70	American Int'l ■	.62
77	Bryant	.56
87	Columbia Union	.78
74	Bryant ■	.64
90	Saginaw Valley †	.80
61	Gannon	.98
72	Franklin Pierce ■	.70
77	St. Rose	.76
99	Southern Conn. St. ■	.85
72	Southern N.H. ■	.50
61	Mass.-Lowell	.53
71	Franklin Pierce ■	.79
58	Assumption	.70
56	American Int'l	.68
78	Merrimack ■	.73
77	Stonehill	.73
83	Bentley ■	.74
98	St. Rose ■	.90
72	Southern Conn. St.	.76
67	Le Moyne	.55
71	St. Michael's	.68
88	St. Anselm ■	.81
68	American Int'l ■	.71
92	Queens (N.Y.) †	.88
73	Assumption †	.91

Nickname: Setters
Colors: Navy & Gold
Arena: Goldstein Athletics Center

Capacity: 2,400; Year Built: 2002
AD: Joseph F. O'Donnell
SID: Brian Mundy

PACIFIC (CAL.)
Stockton, CA 95211 I

Coach: Bob Thomason, Pacific (Cal.) 1971

2001-02 RESULTS (20-10)

85	Santa Clara	.83
86	Cal St. Monterey Bay ■	.65
66	New Mexico	.85
65	Southern Miss. †	.50
65	Fresno St. ■	.73
77	Montana	.64
74	San Jose St. ■	.59
52	Idaho	.48
72	San Francisco	.69
71	Utah St.	.81
75	Nebraska ■	.52
72	Concordia (Cal.) ■	.57
59	Cal St. Northridge	.70
70	Cal Poly ■	.54
73	UC Santa Barb. ■	.70
58	UC Irvine ■	.62
74	Long Beach St. ■	.78
71	UC Riverside ■	.59
82	Cal St. Fullerton ■	.48
74	Cal St. Northridge ■	.58
57	UC Santa Barb.	.70
79	Cal Poly	.84
63	Long Beach St. ■	.77
73	UC Irvine ■	.61
67	Cal St. Fullerton	.61
87	UC Riverside	.75
55	Utah St. ■	.51
57	Idaho ■	.49
78	Cal St. Northridge †	.66
65	Utah St. †	.69

Nickname: Tigers
Colors: Orange & Black
Arena: A.G. Spanos Center
  Capacity: 6,150; Year Built: 1981
AD: Lynn King
SID: Mike Millerick

PACIFIC (ORE.)
Forest Grove, OR 97116-1797 .III

Coach: Ken Schumann, George Fox 1981

2001-02 RESULTS (11-13)

72	Warner Pacific ■	.81
96	Multnomah Bible ■	.52
74	Western Baptist ■	.80
74	Northwest Chrst. ■	.61
66	George Fox	.61
116	Multnomah Bible	.55
69	Pacific Lutheran	.85
94	Redlands	.88
53	Claremont-M-S	.76
77	Puget Sound	.74
84	Linfield ■	.86
78	Lewis & Clark ■	.60
54	Willamette	.73
72	Whitman	.82
50	Whitworth	.72
80	Willamette ■	.68
73	George Fox ■	.69
76	Linfield	.94
97	Puget Sound ■	.76
52	Lewis & Clark	.74
62	Pacific Lutheran ■	.66
94	Northwest Chrst.	.86
50	Whitworth ■	.58
100	Whitman ■	.82

Nickname: Boxers
Colors: Red, Black & White
Arena: Pacific Athletic Center
  Capacity: 2,500; Year Built: 1970

AD: Judy Sherman
SID: Blake Timm

PACIFIC LUTHERAN
Tacoma, WA 98447-0003 III

Coach: Bruce Haroldson, Augustana (S.D.) 1959

2001-02 RESULTS (14-11)
97	St. Mary's (Minn.) †	91
93	Claremont-M-S †	84
76	Western Baptist ■	79
82	Carleton ■	70
61	Willamette ■	72
77	Southern Ore. ■	68
85	Pacific (Ore.) ■	69
91	Seattle ■	79
97	Thomas More †	70
64	Mississippi Col. †	76
79	Cabrini †	78
88	Linfield ■	101
91	George Fox ■	86
72	Whitman	83
60	Whitworth	94
77	Lewis & Clark	84
82	Whitworth ■	67
61	Whitman ■	72
84	George Fox	75
73	Linfield	79
96	Puget Sound ■	81
49	Willamette	81
66	Pacific (Ore.)	62
98	Puget Sound	88
86	Lewis & Clark ■	94

Nickname: Lutes
Colors: Black & Gold
Arena: Olson Auditorium
  Capacity: 3,200; Year Built: 1969
AD: Paul Hoseth
SID: Nick Dawson

PAINE
Augusta, GA 30901-3182 II

Coach: Ron Spry, Campbellsville 1975

2001-02 RESULTS (17-13)
80	Lenoir-Rhyne	65
69	Belmont Abbey ■	72
72	GC&SU	88
66	Clark Atlanta ■	65
46	Stillman	50
64	Tuskegee	63
61	Lenoir-Rhyne	79
69	Morehouse ■	70
77	Albany St. (Ga.) ■	61
60	Fort Valley St.	64
82	Augusta St. †	91
69	LeMoyne-Owen ■	61
70	Miles ■	60
102	Kentucky St.	100
112	Lane	101
77	Tuskegee ■	68
79	Clark Atlanta	73
65	Morehouse	67
56	Albany St. (Ga.)	53
80	Allen †	70
57	Kennesaw St.	87
72	Fort Valley St. ■	69
68	LeMoyne-Owen	76
66	Miles	80
75	Kentucky St. ■	82
63	Lane ■	58
78	Albany St. (Ga.) †	73
81	Kentucky St. †	77
52	Morehouse †	49
57	Valdosta St. †	62

Nickname: Lions
Colors: Purple & White
Arena: Randall Carter Gymnasium
  Capacity: 1,200; Year Built: 1952
AD: Ronnie O. Spry
SID: Andre Kent-Bright

PENNSYLVANIA
Philadelphia, PA 19104-6322 I

Coach: Fran Dunphy, La Salle 1970

2001-02 RESULTS (25-7)
79	Georgia Tech	74
71	Illinois †	78
77	Eastern Ill. †	60
84	Iowa St. †	77
89	Drexel †	80
61	American	51
75	Villanova	74
61	St. Joseph's ■	67
71	Davidson	75
68	Temple	62
74	Lehigh	58
75	Florida Int'l ■	49
87	Dartmouth	71
75	Harvard	78
50	Delaware ■	44
73	Lafayette ■	66
62	St. Joseph's	60
81	La Salle	76
75	Cornell ■	63
53	Columbia ■	54
78	Yale	83
84	Brown	74
62	Princeton	38
78	Harvard ■	51
100	Dartmouth ■	62
82	Brown ■	63
72	Yale ■	63
51	Columbia	47
78	Cornell	53
64	Princeton ■	48
77	Yale †	58
75	California †	82

Nickname: Quakers
Colors: Red & Blue
Arena: The Palestra
  Capacity: 8,722; Year Built: 1927
AD: Steve Bilsky
SID: Carla Shultzberg

PENN ST.
University Park, PA 16802..........I

Coach: Jerry Dunn, George Mason 1980

2001-02 RESULTS (7-21)
74	Yale ■	87
75	Lafayette ■	66
65	Boston College	88
66	Clemson ■	79
63	Temple	75
61	Lehigh ■	48
53	Pittsburgh	83
69	James Madison ■	85
78	Bucknell ■	57
66	Coppin St. †	49
73	California	76
63	Michigan ■	67
54	Indiana	61
51	Wisconsin ■	49
57	Ohio St.	76
65	Michigan St. ■	77
51	Indiana ■	85
63	Wisconsin	66
70	Minnesota	94
64	Iowa	81
81	Purdue ■	68
58	Michigan	65
71	Iowa ■	65
49	Northwestern ■	55
56	Illinois	83
64	Minnesota ■	68
57	Purdue	92
60	Minnesota †	84

Nickname: Nittany Lions
Colors: Blue & White
Arena: Bryce Jordan Center
  Capacity: 15,261; Year Built: 1996

AD: Timothy M. Curley
SID: Jeff Nelson

PENN ST.-ALTOONA
Altoona, PA 16601-3760 III

2001-02 RESULTS (3-20)
48	Methodist †	85
68	Villa Julie †	78
74	Marymount (Va.) ■	84
42	Juniata	88
57	Marymount (Va.)	78
45	Penn St.-Behrend	80
64	Grove City	75
97	Adrian †	100
63	La Roche	75
53	Carnegie Mellon ■	85
61	Grove City ■	73
73	Bethany (W.Va.) ■	77
66	Frostburg St. ■	101
82	Lake Erie	81
61	Waynesburg ■	76
77	Pitt.-Bradford	98
65	Penn St.-Behrend ■	68
63	La Roche ■	59
78	Lake Erie ■	76
66	Waynesburg	87
51	Frostburg St.	100
72	Pitt.-Bradford ■	102
63	Frostburg St.	99

Nickname: Lions
Colors: Navy Blue & White
AD: Fredina M. Ingold
SID: Brent Baird

PENN ST.-BEHREND
Erie, PA 16563-0101 III

Coach: Dave Niland, Le Moyne 1989

2001-02 RESULTS (18-9)
68	Mt. Aloysius ■	54
54	Geneseo St. ■	61
56	Grove City ■	53
50	Wash. & Jeff.	57
61	Fredonia St.	45
82	Carnegie Mellon ■	75
49	Pitt.-Bradford	61
80	Penn St.-Altoona ■	45
52	Thiel	58
67	Waynesburg †	68
71	Wilmington (Ohio)	66
77	Westminster (Pa.) ■	67
70	Lake Erie ■	56
66	Frostburg St. ■	57
83	Frostburg St. ■	56
69	La Roche	65
78	Pitt.-Greensburg	47
68	Penn St.-Altoona	65
69	Pitt.-Bradford ■	80
50	Frostburg St.	80
74	Lake Erie	54
65	La Roche ■	53
69	Medaille	39
76	Pitt.-Greensburg ■	62
65	Lake Erie ■	57
74	Frostburg St. †	83
61	Lebanon Valley	67

Nickname: Lions
Colors: Blue & White
Arena: Athletics & Recreation Center
  Capacity: 1,600; Year Built: 2000
AD: Brian Streeter
SID: Paul Benim

PEPPERDINE
Malibu, CA 90263 I

Coach: Paul Westphal, Southern California 1972

2001-02 RESULTS (22-9)
75	Cal St. Fullerton ■	58
93	UC Irvine	96
85	UCLA	78
74	Utah	81
93	Long Beach St. ■	83
78	Southern California †	77
51	UC Santa Barb.	68
64	Oregon	88
74	Georgia ■	91
98	Pt. Loma Nazarene ■	55
71	Arizona	94
97	West Virginia †	65
82	Brigham Young ■	79
67	St. Mary's (Cal.)	51
74	San Francisco	68
88	Gonzaga ■	79
109	Portland ■	88
74	Santa Clara	67
96	San Diego	91
84	Loyola Marymount ■	59
89	Loyola Marymount	79
79	San Francisco ■	72
68	St. Mary's (Cal.)	57
83	Portland	77
78	Gonzaga	91
90	San Diego ■	79
96	Santa Clara ■	58
77	Portland †	64
68	St. Mary's (Cal.) †	47
90	Gonzaga †	96
74	Wake Forest †	83

Nickname: Waves
Colors: Blue & Orange
Arena: Firestone Fieldhouse
  Capacity: 3,104; Year Built: 1973
AD: John G. Watson
SID: Michael Zapolski

PFEIFFER
Misenheimer, NC 28109-0960..II

Coach: Dave Davis, Warren Wilson 1983

2001-02 RESULTS (16-12)
90	Catawba	98
99	Brevard	87
81	Charleston (W.Va.) ■	79
65	Coker ■	52
74	Wingate	107
66	Erskine	69
97	Northern Ky. ■	87
107	Mount Olive	103
97	Barton ■	101
64	Belmont Abbey ■	82
93	Lees-McRae	94
74	St. Andrews	62
89	Limestone ■	73
81	Anderson (S.C.) ■	91
87	Queens (N.C.)	77
82	Erskine ■	64
72	Coker	64
83	Columbia Union	84
109	Mount Olive ■	101
86	Barton	69
84	Belmont Abbey ■	97
106	Lees-McRae ■	97
72	Longwood	86
82	St. Andrews ■	60
110	Longwood ■	65
77	Limestone	88
94	St. Andrews ■	82
85	Barton	90

Nickname: Falcons
Colors: Black & Gold
Arena: Merner Gymnasium
  Capacity: 2,500; Year Built: 1976
AD: Jeffrey H. Childress
SID: Gregg Gebhard

PHILADELPHIA U.
Philadelphia, PA 19144-5497....II

Coach: Herb Magee, Philadelphia U. 1963

2001-02 RESULTS (19-9)

63	West Liberty St. †	66
73	Felician †	79
71	West Chester ■	65
61	St. Thomas Aquinas ■	58
66	Adelphi ■	60
61	Molloy	67
70	Bridgeport	72
84	Concordia (N.Y.)	71
83	Holy Family ■	61
90	Southampton	68
68	C.W. Post	61
75	Queens (N.Y.) ■	59
107	Mercy	72
75	Dowling	61
73	Adelphi	94
88	Molloy ■	57
67	Bridgeport ■	53
66	St. Thomas Aquinas	50
88	Concordia (N.Y.) ■	65
76	C.W. Post ■	67
70	Queens (N.Y.)	69
78	Mercy ■	72
67	Dowling	78
67	NYIT ■	50
50	NYIT	70
78	Southampton ■	67
61	Bridgeport ■	66
66	Southampton ■	88

Nickname: Rams
Colors: Maroon & Grey
Arena: Bucky Harris Gym
  Capacity: 1,000; Year Built: 1960
SID: Tony Berich

PIEDMONT
Demorest, GA 30535...............III

2001-02 RESULTS (0-9)

64	Kenyon †	70
55	Sewanee	60
59	Maryville (Tenn.)	74
60	Stillman	80
79	Emory	101
55	Greensboro	77
56	Maryville (Tenn.) ■	71
89	Stillman ■	97
45	Maryville (Tenn.) ■	77

Nickname: Lions
Colors: Green & Gold
SID: To be named

PITTSBURG ST.
Pittsburg, KS 66762 II

Coach: Gene Iba, Tulsa 1963

2001-02 RESULTS (17-10)

95	Philander Smith ■	58
69	St. Martin's ■	38
60	Northeastern St. ■	65
93	Sterling (Kan.) ■	69
62	Kansas	105
101	Okla. Panhandle †	62
89	Bacone †	37
101	Drury	81
72	Central Mo. St. ■	61
56	Northwest Mo. St.	72
94	Emporia St. ■	77
81	Mo.-Rolla ■	78
64	Mo. Western St.	76
65	Mo. Southern St.	78
93	Truman ■	68
80	Southwest Baptist ■	64
75	Washburn	89
61	Central Mo. St.	52
81	Northwest Mo. St. ■	90

90	Emporia St.	77
72	Mo.-Rolla	82
68	Mo. Western St. ■	83
83	Mo. Southern St. ■	81
64	Truman	56
84	Southwest Baptist ■	61
90	Washburn ■	69
73	Washburn	80

Nickname: Gorillas
Colors: Crimson & Gold
Arena: John Lance Arena
  Capacity: 6,500; Year Built: 1971
SID: Dan Wilkes

PITTSBURGH
Pittsburgh, PA 15260 I

Coach: Ben Howland, Weber St. 1980

2001-02 RESULTS (29-6)

76	Morgan St. ■	55
58	Northern Ariz. ■	47
86	Robert Morris ■	62
70	Oakland †	53
65	Illinois St. †	46
63	South Fla. †	69
87	Savannah St. ■	35
77	St. Francis (Pa.) ■	55
83	Penn St. ■	53
58	Rhode Island ■	51
62	Ohio St.	55
78	Duquesne †	63
74	St. Francis (N.Y.) ■	61
77	St. John's (N.Y.) ■	54
77	Boston College	74
66	Rutgers	58
53	Notre Dame ■	56
69	Miami (Fla.)	76
68	Georgetown	67
72	Syracuse ■	57
67	Georgetown ■	56
76	Notre Dame	89
71	Villanova ■	59
70	Seton Hall	65
75	Syracuse	63
85	West Virginia	75
78	Rutgers ■	59
73	Seton Hall	66
92	West Virginia ■	65
76	Boston College †	62
76	Miami (Fla.) †	71
65	Connecticut †	74
71	Central Conn. St. ■	54
63	California ■	50
73	Kent St. †	78

Nickname: Panthers
Colors: Gold & Blue
Arena: Fitzgerald Field House
  Capacity: 6,798; Year Built: 1951
SID: Melissa Androutsos

PITT.-BRADFORD
Bradford, PA 16701-2898 III

2001-02 RESULTS (23-5)

86	Wooster	94
58	Randolph-Macon †	75
76	Houghton ■	77
69	Elmira	67
91	Thiel	86
61	Penn St.-Behrend ■	49
73	Pitt.-Greensburg	64
89	Ithaca ■	76
83	Scranton	81
60	St. Lawrence †	57
106	Mt. Aloysius ■	86
81	La Roche ■	63
82	Alfred ■	71
76	Lake Erie	71
52	Frostburg St.	80
98	Penn St.-Altoona ■	77
92	Pitt.-Greensburg ■	72
80	Penn St.-Behrend	69

69	La Roche	72
95	St. John Fisher ■	72
77	Hilbert	59
96	Frostburg St. ■	79
85	Keuka	57
86	Lake Erie ■	79
102	Penn St.-Altoona	72
90	La Roche †	70
102	Frostburg St.	99
98	Bethany (W.Va.) ■	110

Nickname:
Colors: Navy & Gold
SID: Fred Wallace

PITT.-JOHNSTOWN
Johnstown, PA 15904-2990.......II

Coach: Bob Rukavina, Indiana (Pa.) 1985

2001-02 RESULTS (12-15)

73	Nyack ■	60
71	Roberts Wesleyan ■	74
62	Bloomsburg	67
63	Glenville St. ■	60
66	Elizabeth City St. †	73
51	Virginia Union	69
64	West Va. Wesleyan ■	66
63	N.J. Inst. of Tech. †	62
79	Bloomfield †	63
55	Gannon ■	66
91	Husson	78
57	New Haven	77
85	Bloomsburg ■	77
74	Alderson-Broaddus	70
71	Dist. Columbia	95
80	Alderson-Broaddus ■	83
75	Mt. Aloysius ■	60
80	Virginia St. ■	91
71	Bowie St.	84
79	Roberts Wesleyan ■	89
84	Virginia St.	77
60	Alderson-Broaddus ■	77
57	Clarion	68
79	Mt. Aloysius ■	75
60	Slippery Rock ■	68
57	Shippensburg ■	54
69	Dist. Columbia ■	64

Nickname: Mountain Cats
Colors: Gold & Blue
Arena: Sports Center
  Capacity: 2,400; Year Built: 1976
AD: Michael F. Castner
SID: Chris Caputo

PLATTSBURGH ST.
Plattsburgh, NY 12901 III

Coach: Ed Jones, Brockport St. 1973

2001-02 RESULTS (16-11)

77	Castleton St. ■	48
80	Skidmore ■	70
64	Clarkson	77
62	St. Joseph (Vt.)	75
75	St. John Fisher †	84
67	Skidmore	75
80	Potsdam St. ■	67
64	Brockport St.	89
75	Geneseo St. ■	74
71	Oneonta St.	55
71	Cortland St. ■	51
75	Fredonia St. ■	55
87	St. Lawrence ■	74
58	Cortland St.	69
88	Johnson St. ■	75
80	Fredonia St.	86
77	Buffalo St. ■	93
73	St. Joseph (Vt.) ■	60
80	New Paltz St. ■	79
85	Oneonta St. ■	71
58	Oswego St.	85
64	Geneseo St. ■	54
88	Brockport St. ■	76

76	Potsdam St.	71
81	Utica/Rome ■	68
63	Oswego St. †	79
81	Nazareth	89

Nickname: Cardinals
Colors: Cardinal Red & White
Arena: Memorial Hall Gymnasium
  Capacity: 1,000; Year Built: 1961
SID: Jeremy Agor

PLYMOUTH ST.
Plymouth, NH 03264-1595 III

Coach: John Scheinman, Marist 1984

2001-02 RESULTS (18-11)

73	Worcester St. †	63
73	Babson	82
88	Johnson St.	84
85	Salem St. ■	70
76	Mass.-Dartmouth ■	95
89	New England Col. †	52
94	Eastern Conn. St.	72
93	Bridgewater St.	86
65	Johnson & Wales	71
91	Western Conn. St. ■	93
76	Mass.-Boston	61
64	Bowdoin	76
90	Rhode Island Col.	63
89	Southern Me.	79
62	Mass.-Dartmouth	85
77	Keene St. ■	90
90	Castleton St. ■	72
79	Eastern Conn. St. ■	67
76	Western Conn. St.	102
72	Southern Me. ■	71
109	New England	77
89	Mass.-Boston ■	68
64	Keene St.	83
88	Rhode Island Col. ■	64
84	Eastern Conn. St. ■	83
62	Keene St.	67
97	Roger Williams ■	70
94	Keene St.	92
63	Mass.-Dartmouth	67

Nickname: Panthers
Colors: Green & White
Arena: Foley Gymnasium
  Capacity: 2,000; Year Built: 1969
SID: Kent Cherrington

POMONA-PITZER
Claremont, CA 91711-6346.....III

Coach: Charles Katsiaficas, Tufts 1984

2001-02 RESULTS (14-10)

61	Linfield ■	71
71	Hope Int'l ■	58
63	Savannah A&D ■	79
61	Southwestern (Tex.) †	60
65	La Sierra	61
53	Cal St. Dom. Hills	59
61	Menlo	63
42	Biola	94
64	Trinity (Conn.) †	56
91	Cal Baptist †	49
80	Caltech ■	30
73	Whittier	82
72	Occidental ■	82
75	Redlands ■	70
71	Claremont-M-S	79
67	La Verne ■	59
42	Cal Lutheran ■	66
85	Caltech	33
60	Whittier ■	57
66	Occidental	62
80	Redlands	76
49	Claremont-M-S ■	51
64	La Verne	71
62	Cal Lutheran ■	61

Nickname: Sagehens
Colors: Blue, Orange & White
Arena: Voelkel Gymnasium

Capacity: 1,500; Year Built: 1989
SID: Ryan Witt

PORTLAND
Portland, OR 97203-5798 I

Coach: Michael Holton, UCLA 1983
2001-02 RESULTS (6-24)

75	UC Riverside ■	67
90	Idaho St. ■	96
62	Duke	104
71	Idaho	66
79	Oregon ■	78
80	Tex.-Pan American ■	82
75	Portland	77
68	Eastern Wash. ■	61
68	Hawaii	75
43	Holy Cross †	60
74	Arkansas St. †	77
73	Lehigh ■	76
79	Idaho St.	83
63	Montana St. ■	66
64	San Diego ■	65
73	Santa Clara ■	84
77	Loyola Marymount	85
88	Pepperdine	109
74	St. Mary's (Cal.) ■	68
69	San Francisco ■	77
67	Gonzaga	102
80	Gonzaga ■	94
80	San Diego	103
58	Santa Clara	75
77	Pepperdine ■	83
83	Loyola Marymount ■	79
60	Oregon St.	74
59	St. Mary's (Cal.)	68
81	San Francisco	97
64	Pepperdine †	77

Nickname: Pilots
Colors: Purple & White
Arena: Chiles Center
   Capacity: 5,000; Year Built: 1984
SID: Loren Wohlgemuth

PORTLAND ST.
Portland, OR 97207-0751 I

Coach: Joel Sobotka, Arizona St. 1993
2001-02 RESULTS (12-16)

60	Boise St.	53
79	Arizona St.	69
59	San Diego ■	74
79	Cal Poly	100
58	Gonzaga	93
77	Portland ■	75
46	Oregon St. ■	51
53	Nevada	75
76	Santa Clara †	63
63	Stanford	87
58	Wyoming	104
81	Concordia (Cal.) ■	65
90	Loyola Marymount ■	78
68	Montana St. ■	74
88	Montana ■	99
79	Eastern Wash.	88
87	Idaho St.	77
85	Weber St.	90
86	Sacramento St. ■	83
60	Northern Ariz. ■	77
66	Montana	80
82	Montana St.	94
62	Eastern Wash. ■	78
83	Weber St. ■	77
91	Idaho St. ■	78
88	Northern Ariz.	79
74	Sacramento St.	67
62	Weber St. †	84

Nickname: Vikings
Colors: Forest Green & White
Arena: Peter W. Stott Center
   Capacity: 1,775; Year Built: 1967
SID: Mike Lund

POTSDAM ST.
Potsdam, NY 13676-0000 III

Coach: Bill Mitchell, Michigan 1983
2001-02 RESULTS (14-13)

80	Clarkson †	81
63	Oswego St.	72
77	Keuka ■	73
76	Cazenovia ■	66
67	Plattsburgh St.	80
72	New Paltz St.	60
56	Westminster (Mo.) †	66
59	Hawaii-Hilo	83
83	Utica/Rome ■	67
80	Fredonia St. ■	60
47	Buffalo St. ■	68
84	D'Youville ■	77
61	Oswego St. ■	64
64	Cortland St.	52
69	St. Lawrence	78
76	Buffalo St.	63
56	Fredonia St.	42
66	Oswego St.	70
82	Oneonta St. ■	67
76	Clarkson	88
87	Brockport St. ■	99
63	Geneseo St. ■	52
71	Plattsburgh St. ■	76
72	Oneonta St.	70
75	Utica/Rome †	66
67	Geneseo St. †	61
64	Brockport St. †	82

Nickname: Bears
Colors: Maroon & Gray
Arena: Maxcy Hall
   Capacity: 3,600; Year Built: 1972
SID: Boyd Jones

PRAIRIE VIEW
Prairie View, TX 77446 I

Coach: Elwood Plummer, Jackson St. 1966
2001-02 RESULTS (10-20)

61	Jackson St.	87
51	North Carolina St.	95
77	Fairleigh Dickinson †	66
66	Va. Commonwealth †	82
76	Huston-Tillotson ■	77
55	Washington St.	103
63	South Fla.	86
62	Arizona St.	100
99	Paul Quinn ■	73
77	Alcorn St. ■	79
89	Southern U. ■	75
61	Wright St.	94
53	Cleveland St.	90
61	Grambling	79
85	Houston ■	99
76	Ark.-Pine Bluff ■	63
85	Mississippi Val. ■	78
72	Alabama A&M	92
73	Alabama St.	78
80	Texas Southern ■	76
90	Texas Southern	93
75	Grambling ■	73
55	Jackson St. ■	68
89	Ark.-Pine Bluff	83
76	Mississippi Val.	107
63	Alabama A&M ■	74
65	Alabama St. ■	58
98	Southern U.	95
77	Alcorn St.	92
82	Alabama A&M	114

Nickname: Panthers
Colors: Purple & Gold
Arena: William J. Nicks Building
   Capacity: 5,000; Year Built: 1968
SID: Harlan Robinson

PRESBYTERIAN
Clinton, SC 29325-2998..........II

Coach: Gregg Nibert, Marietta 1979
2001-02 RESULTS (12-16)

66	Armstrong Atlantic ■	57
81	Allen ■	66
67	Benedict ■	61
67	Lander †	60
66	S.C.-Aiken	67
70	Anderson (S.C.)	68
64	Erskine	56
59	S.C.-Spartanburg ■	62
78	Shaw ■	73
67	Lander	80
58	Hawaii Pacific	69
49	Chaminade	59
50	Tusculum	55
89	Wingate	95
59	Carson-Newman	69
70	Mars Hill ■	52
67	Lenoir-Rhyne	73
64	Catawba	71
77	Newberry ■	60
57	Tusculum ■	66
87	Wingate ■	99
83	Carson-Newman ■	97
57	Mars Hill	53
62	Lenoir-Rhyne ■	65
68	Catawba ■	73
82	Newberry	65
83	Catawba	74
75	Wingate †	76

Nickname: Blue Hose
Colors: Garnet & Blue
Arena: Ross E. Templeton Center
   Capacity: 2,500; Year Built: 1975
SID: Al Ansley

PRINCETON
Princeton, NJ 08544.................I

Coach: John Thompson III, Princeton 1989
2001-02 RESULTS (16-12)

58	California	70
63	St. Joseph's †	74
44	Florida Int'l	49
69	Rider ■	57
53	Maryland †	61
57	George Washington †	60
76	Monmouth ■	70
62	Kansas ■	78
67	Lafayette ■	61
70	Rutgers	70
52	Holy Cross ■	50
50	Harvard ■	48
57	Dartmouth	46
78	McDaniel ■	24
49	Columbia ■	41
60	Cornell ■	38
70	Brown	56
50	Yale	60
38	Pennsylvania ■	62
79	Dartmouth ■	68
70	Harvard ■	59
59	Yale ■	46
73	Brown ■	47
61	Cornell	57
49	Columbia	48
48	Pennsylvania	64
60	Yale †	76
65	Louisville	66

Nickname: Tigers
Colors: Orange & Black
Arena: Jadwin Gymnasium
   Capacity: 6,854; Year Built: 1969
SID: Jerry Price

PRINCIPIA
Elsah, IL 62028-9799 III

Coach: Garry Sprague, Principia 1986
2001-02 RESULTS (8-14)

87	St. Louis Christian ■	76
77	Monmouth (Ill.) ■	83
58	Knox	77
102	St. Louis Pharmacy ■	81
98	Sanford Brown †	41
90	Lincoln Chrst.	103
84	Maryville (Mo.)	97
78	Fontbonne	93
87	St. Louis Pharmacy ■	63
68	Westminster (Mo.) ■	56
52	Blackburn	69
59	Greenville ■	76
82	MacMurray ■	72
65	Webster	78
62	Maryville (Mo.) ■	76
71	Fontbonne ■	84
74	Westminster (Mo.)	88
106	Sanford Brown	49
65	Blackburn ■	70
88	Greenville	77
71	MacMurray	84
88	Webster ■	96

Nickname: Panthers
Colors: Gold & Blue
Arena: Hay Field House
   Capacity: 1,000; Year Built: 1967
SID: Mary Ann Sprague

PROVIDENCE
Providence, RI 02918 I

Coach: Tim Welsh, Potsdam St. 1984
2001-02 RESULTS (15-16)

79	Siena ■	54
65	Oklahoma St. †	83
93	Austin Peay †	84
69	UTEP †	60
68	Columbia ■	54
60	Brown ■	67
71	Rhode Island ■	59
48	South Carolina	67
77	George Washington ■	83
85	Sacred Heart ■	76
68	Boston U. ■	62
91	Morgan St. ■	47
94	Central Conn. St. ■	63
57	Villanova	76
66	Syracuse ■	73
48	Texas	68
78	St. John's (N.Y.) ■	57
62	Connecticut	69
96	Miami (Fla.)	102
70	Rutgers ■	55
75	St. John's (N.Y.)	70
81	West Virginia	89
64	Boston College ■	61
56	Connecticut	67
77	Virginia Tech ■	69
79	Boston College	89
72	Villanova ■	64
64	Virginia Tech	69
65	Miami (Fla.) ■	81
68	Notre Dame	76
67	Georgetown †	68

Nickname: Friars
Colors: Black & White
Arena: Dunkin' Donuts Center
   Capacity: 12,993; Year Built: 1972
SID: Arthur Parks

PUGET SOUND
Tacoma, WA 98416 III

Coach: Eric Bridgeland, Manitoba

2001-02 RESULTS (11-14)

85	Claremont-M-S ■	98
100	St. Mary's (Minn.) ■	84
72	Benedictine (Ill.) †	76
94	Colorado Col.	77
98	Carleton †	81
81	Western Baptist †	99
92	Concordia (Ore.)	78
93	Lewis-Clark St.	118
73	Western Ore.	79
74	Pacific (Ore.) ■	77
106	George Fox	97
85	Whitworth	92
85	Whitman	74
84	Willamette	100
102	Linfield	100
83	Lewis & Clark ■	92
96	Whitman ■	81
82	Whitworth ■	89
76	Pacific (Ore.)	97
81	Pacific Lutheran	96
83	George Fox ■	75
68	Lewis & Clark	78
88	Pacific Lutheran ■	98
94	Linfield ■	83
82	Willamette ■	76

Nickname: Loggers
Colors: Maroon & White
Arena: Memorial Arena
 Capacity: 4,000; Year Built: 1949
SID: Robin Hamilton

PURDUE
West Lafayette, IN 47907-1031 .I

Coach: Gene Keady, Kansas St. 1958

2001-02 RESULTS (13-18)

73	Valparaiso	69
91	Radford ■	84
62	Stanford †	78
68	Butler ■	74
75	William & Mary ■	58
89	Oakland	71
70	Xavier ■	66
66	Arizona †	79
72	Dayton †	83
80	Ill.-Chicago	73
84	Southwest Mo. St. †	83
64	Texas A&M †	71
62	Cincinnati †	79
87	Robert Morris ■	53
71	Ohio St. ■	79
75	Michigan	79
84	Illinois ■	75
71	Minnesota	87
56	Michigan St.	65
66	Wisconsin	77
63	Northwestern ■	61
73	Iowa ■	68
52	Indiana	66
68	Penn St.	81
67	Illinois	69
79	Michigan ■	43
59	Michigan St.	62
48	Northwestern	61
66	Ohio St.	77
92	Penn St. ■	57
72	Iowa †	87

Nickname: Boilermakers
Colors: Old Gold & Black
Arena: Mackey Arena
 Capacity: 14,123; Year Built: 1967
SID: Elliot Bloom

QUEENS (N.Y.)
Flushing, NY 11367 ...II

Coach: Kyrk Peponakis, St. John's (N.Y.) 1988

2001-02 RESULTS (19-11)

36	Metro St. †	86
79	Colorado Mines	57
52	Virginia Union	68
62	Elizabeth City St. †	69
82	Southampton	84
87	NYIT ■	73
71	C.W. Post ■	69
57	Adelphi	74
82	Concordia (N.Y.) ■	59
70	Dowling	68
59	Philadelphia U.	75
77	St. Thomas Aquinas	73
95	Mercy ■	76
83	Molloy	66
84	Concordia (N.Y.)	66
89	Southampton ■	92
59	NYIT	62
74	Bridgeport	64
62	C.W. Post	55
64	Adelphi ■	81
96	Dowling ■	91
69	Philadelphia U. ■	70
75	St. Thomas Aquinas ■	69
98	Mercy	68
61	Bridgeport ■	57
78	Molloy	69
78	Dowling	73
88	Bridgeport †	70
80	NYIT †	63
88	Pace †	92

Nickname: Knights
Colors: Blue & Silver
Arena: Fitzgerald Gymnasium
 Capacity: 3,000; Year Built: 1958
SID: Neal Kaufer

QUEENS (N.C.)
Charlotte, NC 28274 ...II

Coach: Bart Lundy, Winthrop 1994

2001-02 RESULTS (19-10)

68	Brevard	77
90	West Va. Tech ■	79
101	Montreat ■	96
67	Fayetteville St. ■	79
76	Eckerd	86
108	Lees-McRae	94
81	Tampa	83
77	Erskine ■	75
83	Longwood	80
75	Coker ■	58
78	St. Andrews	73
81	Mount Olive ■	83
73	Limestone	69
94	Barton ■	74
67	Anderson (S.C.)	73
83	Belmont Abbey	78
77	Pfeiffer ■	87
95	Lees-McRae ■	65
85	Erskine	76
67	Longwood ■	66
80	Coker	55
99	St. Andrews ■	80
74	Mount Olive	60
77	Limestone ■	65
76	Barton	89
69	Anderson (S.C.) ■	77
110	Lees-McRae ■	78
83	Anderson (S.C.) †	58
60	Belmont Abbey †	78

Nickname: Royals
Colors: Navy Blue and Gold
Arena: Ovens Athletic Center
 Capacity: 900; Year Built: 1989
SID: Scott Handback

QUINCY
Quincy, IL 62301-2699 ...II

Coach: Mike Foster, Missouri 1981

2001-02 RESULTS (7-19)

71	Hannibal-La Grange	61
100	Ky. Wesleyan ■	106
88	Southern Ind. ■	97
79	Truman	74
79	SIU-Edwardsville ■	81
77	Wis.-Parkside	78
89	St. Joseph's (Ind.)	79
72	Olivet Nazarene	75
69	Henderson St.	71
65	Shaw ■	69
89	Mobile ■	76
74	Northern Ky. ■	76
83	Bellarmine ■	86
80	Southern Ind.	98
67	Mo.-St. Louis	65
78	SIU-Edwardsville	82
77	Lewis	79
90	St. Joseph's (Ind.) ■	82
70	Indianapolis	87
86	Bellarmine	77
63	Ky. Wesleyan	113
67	Mo.-St. Louis	79
56	Lewis ■	78
105	Wis.-Parkside ■	110
76	Indianapolis	82
75	Northern Ky.	79

Nickname: Hawks
Colors: Brown, White & Gold
Arena: Pepsi Arena
 Capacity: 2,000; Year Built: 1950
AD: Patrick Atwell
SID: Ryan Dowd

QUINNIPIAC
Hamden, CT 06518-1940 ...I

Coach: Joe DeSantis, Fairfield 1979

2001-02 RESULTS (14-16)

57	Holy Cross	85
66	Army	74
79	Albany (N.Y.) ■	65
94	Long Island	64
71	St. Francis (N.Y.) ■	75
71	UMBC	78
84	Mt. St. Mary's	62
68	Dartmouth ■	70
79	Connecticut	95
60	St. John's (N.Y.)	97
89	Binghamton	65
86	Sacred Heart ■	78
75	Wagner	77
74	Central Conn. St. ■	84
102	St. Francis (N.Y.)	112
84	Fairleigh Dickinson ■	79
87	Wagner ■	85
66	Central Conn. St.	76
80	Robert Morris	82
79	St. Francis (Pa.)	77
88	Monmouth	95
82	Fairleigh Dickinson	89
104	Sacred Heart	87
77	Mt. St. Mary's ■	65
71	Monmouth	88
93	Robert Morris ■	73
71	St. Francis (Pa.) ■	58
87	Wagner	78
75	UMBC †	72
71	Central Conn. St.	78

Nickname: Braves
Colors: Navy & Maize
Arena: Burt Kahn Court-Athletic Center
 Capacity: 1,500; Year Built: 1969
SID: Al Carbone

RADFORD
Radford, VA 24142 ...I

Coach: Ron Bradley, Eastern Nazarene 1973

2001-02 RESULTS (15-16)

56	Butler †	73
81	Wichita St. †	82
89	Alas. Fairbanks	50
84	Purdue	91
85	UNC Wilmington ■	72
52	Richmond ■	62
72	Middle Tenn. ■	53
76	American ■	65
63	Marshall ■	67
54	East Tenn. St.	79
56	Virginia Tech	63
66	Tennessee	72
86	East Caro.	90
66	Holy Cross †	49
61	Col. of Charleston	68
58	Elon	61
60	UNC Asheville ■	74
69	Winthrop	48
82	Coastal Caro.	71
63	Charleston So.	74
78	High Point ■	77
79	Liberty ■	60
71	UNC Asheville	80
70	Charleston So. ■	52
76	Coastal Caro. ■	60
72	Winthrop	64
78	High Point	60
81	Elon ■	60
69	Liberty	78
81	Coastal Caro. †	66
70	High Point †	72

Nickname: Highlanders
Colors: Blue, Red, Green & White
Arena: Donald N. Dedmon Center
 Capacity: 5,000; Year Built: 1981
SID: Aaron Barter

RAMAPO
Mahwah, NJ 07430-1680 ...III

Coach: Chuck McBreen, Towson 1988

2001-02 RESULTS (21-8)

89	CCNY ■	67
97	Suffolk †	74
94	Wm. Paterson	65
84	Col. of New Jersey ■	76
74	New Jersey City ■	85
82	Staten Island	88
58	Rutgers-Camden	63
85	York (N.Y.) ■	63
65	Rowan ■	57
84	Kean	72
101	Yeshiva	81
67	Montclair St.	87
86	Richard Stockton ■	72
91	Farmingdale St.	85
69	Rutgers-Newark	53
69	Rutgers-Camden ■	64
79	New Jersey City	64
78	Col. of New Jersey	73
105	Farmingdale St. ■	87
70	Wm. Paterson ■	74
70	Kean	65
83	Rowan	81
77	Montclair St. ■	82
80	Rutgers-Newark ■	62
66	Richard Stockton	68
68	Richard Stockton	74
97	Medgar Evers	96
81	Richard Stockton	78
101	New Jersey City ■	83

Nickname: Roadrunners
Colors: Maroon, Black & White
Arena: Ramapo Athletic Center
 Capacity: 1,800; Year Built: 1974
SID: Rachel McCann

RANDOLPH-MACON
Ashland, VA 23005 ...III

Coach: Mike Rhoades, Lebanon Valley 1995

2001-02 RESULTS (24-6)

63	St. Thomas (Minn.) †	70
75	Pitt.-Bradford ■	58
75	Bridgewater (Va.) ■	61
82	Wash. & Lee ■	64

77	Roanoke ■	52
68	Ferrum	60
66	East. Mennonite	38
78	Chris. Newport	60
76	Staten Island ■	59
73	Lakeland ■	68
80	Guilford	44
89	Emory & Henry	70
67	Hampden-Sydney ■	63
80	Va. Wesleyan ■	67
69	Winthrop	75
69	Roanoke	66
62	Wash. & Lee	39
76	Lynchburg	52
85	Emory & Henry ■	91
72	Guilford ■	56
77	East. Mennonite ■	66
64	Va. Wesleyan	65
74	Bridgewater (Va.) ■	61
60	Hampden-Sydney ■	51
81	Lynchburg ■	50
69	Wash. & Lee †	36
71	Roanoke †	63
48	Hampden-Sydney †	55
79	Lycoming ■	62
72	Otterbein	85

Nickname: Yellow Jackets
Colors: Lemon & Black
Arena: Crenshaw Gymnasium
  Capacity: 2,500; Year Built: 1965
SID: Ann Marie Schlottman

REDLANDS
Redlands, CA 92373-0999 III

Coach: Gary Smith, Redlands 1964
2001-02 RESULTS (9-16)

44	UC San Diego	104
88	LIFE Bible ■	49
88	Chapman ■	82
88	S'western (Ariz.) ■	64
64	Chapman ■	84
70	Whittier ■	69
78	La Sierra ■	68
73	Cal St. Hayward ■	85
88	Pacific (Ore.) ■	94
81	West Coast Chrst. ■	64
73	Biola ■	100
62	Whittier	76
73	La Verne ■	65
70	Claremont-M-S	82
70	Pomona-Pitzer	75
71	Caltech ■	42
72	Cal Lutheran ■	89
63	Occidental	74
84	Whittier ■	93
77	La Verne	84
63	Claremont-M-S ■	71
76	Pomona-Pitzer ■	80
79	Caltech	48
81	Cal Lutheran ■	88
55	Occidental	82

Nickname: Bulldogs
Colors: Maroon & Gray
Arena: Currier Gym
  Capacity: 1,200; Year Built: 1929
SID: Rachel Johnson

REGIS (COLO.)
Denver, CO 80221-1099 II

Coach: Lonnie Porter, Adams St. 1968
2001-02 RESULTS (12-15)

94	Langston ■	87
56	Colorado	77
65	Mo.-Rolla †	68
50	Rockhurst	55
95	North Central ■	78
55	Rockhurst ■	69
83	Northwest Nazarene ■	71
76	Adams St. ■	72
64	UC-Colo. Spgs.	69
79	Southern Colo.	71

79	Fort Lewis ■	71
84	N.M. Highlands ■	72
70	Mesa St.	87
78	Western St. (Colo.)	88
75	Neb.-Kearney ■	90
53	Fort Hays St. ■	61
69	Colorado Mines ■	65
71	Chadron St.	78
80	Colo. Christian	65
62	Metro St.	74
66	Neb.-Kearney	75
49	Fort Hays St.	70
64	Colorado Mines ■	58
73	Chadron St. ■	68
75	Colo. Christian ■	68
49	Metro St.	77
71	Fort Lewis	72

Nickname: Rangers
Colors: Navy Blue & Gold
Arena: Regis University Fieldhouse
  Capacity: 2,500; Year Built: 1959
SID: Jeff Duggan

RENSSELAER
Troy, NY 12180-3590 III

Coach: Mike Griffin, Columbia 1965
2001-02 RESULTS (11-12)

69	Southern Vt.	72
74	Swarthmore ■	55
78	Haverford ■	43
47	Williams ■	62
62	MIT	68
95	St. Joseph (Vt.) ■	50
58	Lakeland †	68
67	Staten Island †	81
69	Stevens Tech	44
75	Hamilton	85
78	Hobart	69
70	Vassar ■	67
95	Clarkson ■	78
65	St. Lawrence ■	63
76	Union (N.Y.)	83
63	Skidmore ■	47
63	St. Lawrence	78
37	Clarkson	58
65	Hobart ■	71
67	Hamilton ■	81
69	Vassar	68
60	Skidmore ■	54
58	Union (N.Y.) ■	61

Nickname: Red Hawks
Colors: Cherry & White
Arena: Robison Gymnasium
  Capacity: 1,500; Year Built: 1920
AD: Ken Ralph
SID: Kevin Beattie

RHODE ISLAND
Kingston, RI 02881 I

Coach: Jim Baron, St. Bonaventure 1977
2001-02 RESULTS (8-20)

63	Virginia Tech	86
66	Iona ■	61
59	Fairfield	57
57	Buffalo ■	55
59	Providence	71
54	Southern California	82
43	Valparaiso	68
66	Yale	77
51	Pittsburgh	58
67	Northeastern ■	66
76	Brown	91
74	St. Bonaventure	96
71	St. Joseph's ■	87
42	Temple	60
58	Fordham ■	71
49	Xavier ■	67
75	George Washington	62
58	St. Joseph's	71
70	Massachusetts ■	59

42	Temple ■	71
69	Duquesne ■	72
70	Fordham	64
57	Dayton	66
51	Richmond ■	52
64	La Salle	77
69	Massachusetts	79
80	St. Bonaventure ■	72
71	Dayton †	90

Nickname: Rams
Colors: Light & Dark Blue & White
Arena: Keaney Gymnasium
  Capacity: 3,385; Year Built: 1953
SID: Mike Ballweg

RHODE ISLAND COL.
Providence, RI 02908 III

Coach: Mike Kelly, St. Joseph's (Me.) 1993
2001-02 RESULTS (1-24)

75	Western New Eng. †	91
71	Hartwick	76
62	Salve Regina ■	82
59	Eastern Nazarene ■	69
57	Roger Williams	59
74	Eastern Conn. St. ■	82
61	Coast Guard	90
79	Mass.-Boston	83
60	Johnson & Wales	67
60	Warner Southern	93
68	Flagler	119
87	Virginia Intermont †	96
52	Southern Me.	81
73	Bridgewater St.	71
63	Plymouth St. ■	90
51	Western Conn. St.	94
39	Keene St. ■	87
59	Eastern Conn. St.	78
52	Mass.-Dartmouth	90
67	Mass.-Boston	89
61	Keene St.	91
61	Western Conn. St. ■	84
47	Southern Me. ■	84
75	Mass.-Dartmouth ■	79
64	Plymouth St.	88

Nickname: Anchormen
Colors: Gold, White & Burgundy
Arena: Intercollegiate Athletic
  Capacity: 8,000; Year Built: 1995
SID: Scott Gibbons

RHODES
Memphis, TN 38112-1690 III

Coach: Herb Hilgeman, Miami (Ohio) 1972
2001-02 RESULTS (10-14)

80	Huntingdon	61
80	Maryville (Mo.) ■	83
77	Ohio Wesleyan ■	84
69	Southwestern (Tex.)	100
68	Trinity (Tex.)	61
61	Rust	65
54	Huntingdon	52
54	Chicago ■	52
63	Rose-Hulman ■	73
74	DePauw ■	78
60	Centre	70
59	Sewanee	61
58	Hendrix ■	67
66	Millsaps ■	61
83	Oglethorpe ■	62
51	Rose-Hulman	75
67	DePauw	78
104	Centre ■	102
65	Sewanee ■	62
67	Hendrix	83
77	Millsaps	89
77	Oglethorpe	67
71	Southwestern (Tex.) ■	61
56	Trinity (Tex.) ■	83

Nickname: Lynx
Colors: Red, Black & White
Arena: Mallory Gym
  Capacity: 2,000
SID: Laura Whiteley

RICE
Houston, TX 77251-1892 I

Coach: Willis Wilson, Rice 1982
2001-02 RESULTS (10-19)

43	Louisiana Tech	57
75	Navy ■	72
91	Lamar ■	62
80	Colorado	108
86	Stephen F. Austin	90
61	Houston	62
75	Baylor ■	60
52	Middle Tenn.	65
66	Centenary (La.) ■	57
64	Tex.-Pan American ■	81
71	Siena	60
61	Fresno St.	87
70	Nevada	91
59	Boise St. ■	62
73	UTEP ■	59
49	Southern Methodist	76
79	Hawaii ■	88
70	San Jose St. ■	58
60	Tulsa	79
56	Nevada ■	64
76	Fresno St. ■	63
75	UTEP	68
62	Boise St.	78
61	Louisiana Tech ■	72
61	Southern Methodist ■	63
62	San Jose St.	46
50	Hawaii	79
62	Tulsa ■	67
57	San Jose St. †	58

Nickname: Owls
Colors: Blue & Gray
Arena: Autry Court
  Capacity: 5,000; Year Built: 1950
SID: John Sullivan

RICHARD STOCKTON
Pomona, NJ 08240-0195 III

Coach: Gerry Mathews, Kean 1965
2001-02 RESULTS (20-9)

69	Marywood †	46
66	Misericordia	63
54	Rowan	55
71	Montclair St. ■	66
62	Col. of New Jersey ■	59
60	Wm. Paterson	56
49	Rutgers-Newark	64
72	New Jersey City ■	71
70	Arcadia	50
69	Chapman †	64
64	Muhlenberg †	67
61	Kean ■	51
72	Ramapo	86
87	Purchase St.	47
68	Rutgers-Camden	63
56	Wm. Paterson ■	58
75	Col. of New Jersey	82
64	Montclair St.	80
43	Rowan ■	40
68	New Jersey City	62
76	Stevens Tech	63
80	Rutgers-Newark ■	59
62	Kean	43
63	Rutgers-Camden ■	60
68	Ramapo ■	66
74	Ramapo ■	68
49	Wm. Paterson ■	55
72	Lehman ■	70
78	Ramapo	81

Nickname: Ospreys
Colors: Black, White & Red
Arena: Sports Center

Capacity: 3,000; Year Built: 2000
SID: Chris Rollman

RICHMOND
Richmond, VA 23173-1903........I

Coach: John Beilein, Wheeling Jesuit 1975

2001-02 RESULTS (22-14)
62	Appalachian St. ■	61
60	UAB	59
62	Radford	52
54	Va. Commonwealth ■	65
57	Mississippi St. ■	71
42	Charlotte	62
46	Cincinnati	77
72	Mississippi St. †	74
80	La.-Monroe †	58
67	Southwest Mo. St. †	60
80	VMI ■	82
52	Cornell ■	41
52	Wake Forest	67
77	La Salle ■	57
62	Xavier	72
63	Massachusetts ■	54
52	Dayton	68
75	Temple	68
55	Duquesne ■	51
61	George Washington ■	53
64	Xavier ■	67
78	St. Bonaventure	66
63	Dayton ■	54
61	St. Joseph's ■	59
56	La Salle	59
52	Rhode Island	51
49	George Washington	53
67	Fordham	50
83	Duquesne	57
78	St. Bonaventure †	69
68	La Salle †	60
60	Xavier †	73
74	Wagner ■	67
63	Montana St. ■	48
67	Minnesota	66
46	Syracuse	62

Nickname: Spiders
Colors: Red & Blue
Arena: Robins Center
    Capacity: 9,171; Year Built: 1972
SID: Stacey Brann

RIDER
Lawrenceville, NJ 08648-3099...I

Coach: Don Harnum, Susquehanna 1986

2001-02 RESULTS (17-11)
45	Monmouth	50
75	Bucknell ■	62
68	Drexel ■	55
57	Princeton	69
58	Towson	60
66	Seton Hall ■	78
69	Marist ■	80
63	Canisius	46
94	Delaware ■	78
68	Northeastern	80
86	Lafayette	66
63	Siena	64
82	Iona	79
65	Canisius ■	62
57	Fairfield	69
83	Loyola (Md.) ■	56
72	Manhattan	68
80	Niagara	76
63	St. Peter's ■	57
88	St. Peter's	52
82	Niagara ■	67
73	Fairfield ■	59
63	Iona ■	65
64	Manhattan ■	62
84	Marist	77
62	Siena ■	56

| 65 | Loyola (Md.) | 77 |
| 84 | Canisius † | 85 |

Nickname: Broncs
Colors: Cranberry & White
Arena: Alumni Gymnasium
    Capacity: 1,650; Year Built: 1959
SID: Bud Focht

RIPON
Ripon, WW 54971.................III

Coach: Bob Gillespie, Lewis 1971

2001-02 RESULTS (19-7)
87	Concordia (Wis.) ■	67
73	Ill. Wesleyan ■	51
107	Eureka †	65
69	Edgewood	76
54	Lawrence	69
89	St. Ambrose ■	77
81	Hobart †	69
89	Mass.-Dartmouth †	83
67	Carroll (Wis.) ■	45
74	Beloit ■	66
77	Illinois Col.	72
78	Lake Forest	73
66	St. Norbert	71
85	Monmouth (Ill.) ■	64
97	Knox ■	74
123	Grinnell	135
75	Monmouth (Ill.)	78
77	Lake Forest ■	69
82	Illinois Col. ■	69
81	Beloit	80
95	Carroll (Wis.)	82
53	St. Norbert ■	74
84	Lawrence ■	66
87	Illinois Col. †	47
54	St. Norbert	45
56	Wis.-Oshkosh	71

Nickname: Red Hawks
Colors: Red & White
Arena: Storzer Center
    Capacity: 1,500; Year Built: 1967
SID: Ron Ernst

RIVIER
Nashua, NH 03060-5086........III

Coach: Dave Morissette, Plymouth St. 1994

2001-02 RESULTS (8-12)
59	Williams ■	102
81	New England Col. ■	77
54	Amherst	80
70	Stevens Tech †	78
58	Endicott	69
66	Keene St. ■	93
62	Suffolk	81
82	Western New Eng. ■	78
54	Daniel Webster	50
53	Emerson	65
75	Southern Vt.	74
70	Norwich	69
54	Western New Eng.	80
79	Johnson & Wales ■	82
94	Southern Vt. ■	76
60	Albertus Magnus	71
75	Colby-Sawyer	94
82	Norwich ■	76
89	Daniel Webster ■	72
85	Southern Vt. ■	92

Nickname: Raiders
Colors: Blue & Gray
Arena: Muldoon Fitness Center
    Capacity: 300; Year Built: 1984
SID: To be named

ROANOKE
Salem, VA 24153 III

Coach: Page Moir, Virginia Tech 1984

2001-02 RESULTS (17-10)
88	York (N.Y.) ■	74
85	Wesley	63
60	Trinity (Tex.)	88
86	Johns Hopkins †	92
99	Emory & Henry ■	86
66	Va. Wesleyan	68
52	Randolph-Macon	77
92	Goucher	74
75	Eastern Conn. St. ■	66
66	Savannah A&D	54
71	Wash. & Lee ■	56
81	Guilford	95
66	Hampden-Sydney ■	81
80	Lynchburg	72
107	Bridgewater (Va.)	99
66	Randolph-Macon ■	69
74	Va. Wesleyan ■	62
87	East. Mennonite	75
76	Wash. & Lee	69
64	Bridgewater (Va.)	80
100	Lynchburg ■	46
69	Hampden-Sydney	87
96	Emory & Henry	93
75	Guilford ■	63
82	East. Mennonite	62
67	Bridgewater (Va.) †	60
63	Randolph-Macon †	71

Nickname: Maroons
Colors: Maroon & Gray
Arena: Bast Center
    Capacity: 2,000; Year Built: 1982
SID: Chris Cummings

ROBERT MORRIS
Moon Township, PA 15108-1189 I

Coach: Mark Schmidt, Boston College

2001-02 RESULTS (12-18)
62	Pittsburgh	86
55	South Fla. ■	82
55	Kent St.	83
53	Oakland ■	77
66	Mt. St. Mary's ■	57
80	UMBC ■	65
63	UMKC ■	70
86	West Virginia	102
87	Youngstown St.	80
58	Albany (N.Y.) ■	61
53	Purdue	87
69	Sacred Heart	77
63	Wagner	89
93	St. Francis (N.Y.) ■	80
85	Long Island	66
63	St. Francis (Pa.) ■	65
86	Fairleigh Dickinson	57
72	Sacred Heart ■	67
78	St. Francis (N.Y.)	91
73	Long Island ■	75
82	Quinnipiac ■	80
55	Central Conn. St. ■	64
65	Mt. St. Mary's	60
70	UMBC	84
65	Fairleigh Dickinson ■	61
69	Monmouth ■	63
58	St. Francis (Pa.)	54
73	Quinnipiac	93
63	Central Conn. St.	67
76	UMBC †	85

Nickname: Colonials
Colors: Blue & White
Arena: Charles L. Sewall Center
    Capacity: 3,056; Year Built: 1985
SID: Jim Duzyk

ROCHESTER
Rochester, NY 14627-0296 III

Coach: Mike Neer, Wash. & Lee 1970

2001-02 RESULTS (24-6)
81	D'Youville ■	72
85	Bowdoin ■	67
78	Nazareth ■	77
82	Medaille ■	46
73	York (Pa.) ■	68
70	Hobart ■	51
86	Carnegie Mellon ■	73
74	St. John Fisher ■	61
74	Rochester Inst.	37
50	New York U.	47
73	Brandeis	63
77	Emory ■	65
67	St. John Fisher	72
71	Nazareth ■	48
53	Roberts Wesleyan †	66
98	Case Reserve ■	53
48	Washington (Mo.)	65
54	Chicago	51
55	Chicago	52
63	Washington (Mo.)	65
67	Brandeis	59
62	New York U. ■	48
76	Case Reserve	43
96	Emory	59
51	Carnegie Mellon	44
66	Williams ■	51
71	Babson †	60
71	Brockport St.	62
83	Elizabethtown †	93
51	Carthage †	72

Nickname: Yellowjackets
Colors: Yellow & Blue
Arena: Louis Alexander Palestra
    Capacity: 2,250; Year Built: 1930
SID: Dennis O'Donnell

ROCHESTER INST.
Rochester, NY 14623-5603 III

Coach: Bob McVean, Brockport St. 1969

2001-02 RESULTS (14-12)
72	Hilbert ■	47
90	Hobart	76
47	Nazareth ■	58
60	D'Youville ■	69
64	York (N.Y.) ■	52
37	Rochester ■	74
66	Susquehanna †	72
75	Baptist Bible (Pa.) †	65
81	Utica ■	68
74	Hartwick ■	58
74	Nazareth †	66
92	St. John Fisher †	83
58	Brockport St. †	78
79	Alfred	76
60	Elmira	65
68	Ithaca	71
84	Cazenovia ■	54
71	St. John Fisher ■	66
70	Alfred ■	64
39	Ithaca ■	56
71	Elmira ■	60
61	St. John Fisher	72
60	Hartwick	54
72	Utica	81
63	Nazareth	64
64	Clarkson	78

Nickname: Tigers
Colors: Burnt Umber, Orange & White
Arena: Clark Memorial Gymnasium
    Capacity: 2,200; Year Built: 1968
SID: Jamie Joss

ROCKFORD
Rockford, IL 61108-2393 III

Coach: Bill Lavery, Monmouth (Ill.) 1990

2001-02 RESULTS (18-7)
66	Wis.-Superior †	76
88	Greenville †	76
95	Marian (Wis.) ■	88

70	Knox	67
87	Monmouth (Ill.)	83
86	Concordia (Wis.) ■	82
61	Blackburn ■	62
72	Augustana (Ill.)	84
50	Beloit ■	58
86	North Park ■	82
138	Grinnell	129
87	Milwaukee Engr.	81
72	Lakeland	80
92	Eureka	45
59	Aurora ■	79
81	Concordia (Ill.) ■	62
71	Clarke	63
67	Benedictine (Ill.) ■	58
76	Dominican (Ill.) ■	66
83	Eureka ■	67
86	Aurora	82
73	Concordia (Ill.)	53
72	Clarke ■	49
61	Benedictine (Ill.) ■	62
85	Dominican (Ill.)	75

Nickname: Regents
Colors: Purple, White & Black
Arena: Seaver Center
  Capacity: 1,750; Year Built: 1964
SID: John Krueger

ROCKHURST
Kansas City, MO 64110-2561 ..II

Coach: William O'Connor, St. Benedict 1972
2001-02 RESULTS (24-6)

80	Emporia St. ■	65
77	Colo. Christian ■	74
55	Regis (Colo.) ■	50
73	Fort Hays St. ■	64
80	Colo. Christian	78
69	Regis (Colo.)	55
64	Washburn ■	69
83	Mo. Western St.	72
59	Mo. Southern St.	70
75	Park ■	60
90	Emporia St.	74
68	Ottawa ■	48
71	St. Mary's (Tex.) ■	60
59	Incarnate Word ■	55
87	Fort Hays St.	88
78	St. Edward's	71
86	William Jewell	72
86	Benedictine (Kan.) ■	64
87	Drury	74
88	Lincoln (Mo.) ■	78
77	St. Mary's (Tex.)	70
50	Incarnate Word	65
79	Park	76
94	St. Edward's ■	82
81	Southwestern Okla. †	75
78	Drury ■	68
77	Lincoln (Mo.)	84
75	Mo. Western St. †	68
75	Northeastern St.	70
73	Northwest Mo. St. †	79

Nickname: Hawks
Colors: Blue & White
Arena: Mason-Halpin Field House
  Capacity: 2,000; Year Built: 1938
SID: Sid Bordman

ROGER WILLIAMS
Bristol, RI 02809 III

Coach: Tom Sienkiewicz, Villanova 1981
2001-02 RESULTS (16-11)

74	Suffolk †	79
75	CCNY †	61
62	Connecticut Col. ■	74
59	Rhode Island Col. ■	57
58	Johnson & Wales ■	57
53	Wheaton (Mass.) ■	68
58	Endicott	69
113	Elms	100

54	Babson ■	83
88	Emerson	66
72	Newbury	60
85	New England Col. ■	68
70	WPI	52
86	Anna Maria	70
75	Eastern Nazarene ■	67
69	Salve Regina	67
69	Gordon ■	50
74	Mount Ida	87
66	Colby-Sawyer	84
61	Wentworth Inst. ■	58
81	Nichols	74
80	New England ■	66
63	Coast Guard ■	80
67	Curry	81
72	Gordon ■	69
52	Colby-Sawyer	69
70	Plymouth St.	97

Nickname: Hawks
Colors: Blue & Gold
Arena: Paolino Recreation Center
  Capacity: 3,000; Year Built: 1983
SID: David Kemmy

ROLLINS
Winter Park, FL 32789 II

Coach: Tom Klusman, Rollins 1976
2001-02 RESULTS (18-10)

56	New Orleans	71
95	P.R.-Mayaguez ■	91
88	P.R.-Rio Piedras ■	74
82	P.R.-Cayey ■	62
74	Warner Southern ■	77
81	Nova Southeastern ■	66
82	St. Leo ■	78
86	Nova Southeastern ■	40
73	Coker ■	64
79	St. Anselm ■	78
53	St. Mary's (Tex.)	57
65	Incarnate Word	86
65	Tampa	75
63	Lynn ■	60
60	Barry	70
86	Florida Tech ■	62
74	St. Leo	51
80	Eckerd ■	66
55	Fla. Southern	59
67	Lynn	65
73	Barry ■	67
83	Florida Tech	73
80	St. Leo ■	79
68	Eckerd	71
76	Fla. Southern ■	72
63	Tampa ■	71
65	Barry †	51
63	Tampa †	84

Nickname: Tars
Colors: Blue & Gold
Arena: Alfond Sports Center
  Capacity: 2,500; Year Built: 2000
SID: Dean Hybl

ROSE-HULMAN
Terre Haute, IN 47803 III

Coach: Jim Shaw, Indiana 1982
2001-02 RESULTS (14-11)

58	Olivet †	56
72	Mount Union	85
71	Earlham	79
66	Sewanee ■	49
62	Centre ■	56
65	Fontbonne	70
70	Ind.-Northwest	48
53	Franklin ■	69
71	Hanover	78
73	Rhodes	63
86	Hendrix	57
71	Oglethorpe ■	59
74	Millsaps ■	78
51	Trinity (Tex.)	55

53	Southwestern (Tex.)	50
67	DePauw	71
75	Rhodes ■	51
81	Hendrix ■	58
60	Oglethorpe	44
58	Millsaps	54
34	Trinity (Tex.) ■	53
70	Southwestern (Tex.) ■	64
57	DePauw ■	65
72	Sewanee	69
60	Centre	80

Nickname: Fightin' Engineers
Colors: Old Rose & White
Arena: Hulbert Arena
  Capacity: 2,000; Year Built: 1997
SID: Kevin Lanke

ROWAN
Glassboro, NJ 08028-1701 III

Coach: Joe Cassidy, St. Joseph's 1974
2001-02 RESULTS (15-10)

56	Manhattanville	52
55	Richard Stockton ■	54
66	Kean ■	51
58	Rutgers-Camden	64
63	Montclair St. ■	53
57	Ramapo	65
54	Rutgers-Newark	51
57	Yeshiva	42
83	Newport News ■	43
63	Neumann ■	72
62	Gwynedd-Mercy	64
74	Rutgers-Newark	62
107	St. Mary's (Md.) ■	60
56	Wm. Paterson ■	57
76	New Jersey City	87
78	Col. of New Jersey ■	76
63	Montclair St.	65
72	Rutgers-Camden ■	57
56	Kean	53
40	Richard Stockton	43
74	Merchant Marine †	56
81	Ramapo ■	83
73	Wm. Paterson	75
73	Col. of New Jersey ■	60
78	New Jersey City ■	76

Nickname: Profs
Colors: Brown & Gold
Arena: Esby Gym
  Capacity: 1,500; Year Built: 1963
SID: Sheila Stevenson

RUST
Holly Springs, MS 38635 III

Coach:
2001-02 RESULTS (12-11)

61	Ozarks (Ark.) †	87
78	Hendrix	65
63	Lane	66
77	Maryville (Tenn.)	78
68	Lane ■	69
71	Millsaps	88
83	Emory	82
65	Rhodes	61
71	Millsaps ■	75
94	Crichton	71
65	Hendrix ■	56
48	LeMoyne-Owen	71
57	Maryville (Tenn.) ■	70
54	Savannah A&D	73
79	Oakwood ■	72
72	Fisk ■	66
74	Philander Smith ■	81
82	Stillman ■	76
69	Fisk	77
96	Crichton	95
95	LeMoyne-Owen ■	74
85	Savannah A&D ■	68
70	Stillman	66

Nickname: Bearcats
Colors: Blue & White

Arena: McMillan Multipurpose Center
  Capacity: 2,000; Year Built: 1971
SID: To be named

RUTGERS
Piscataway, NJ 08854-8053 I

Coach: Gary Waters, Ferris St. 1957
2001-02 RESULTS (18-13)

74	East Caro. †	79
58	Va. Commonwealth †	71
70	Fairleigh Dickinson †	66
57	Auburn ■	56
76	Stony Brook ■	37
71	Loyola (Md.) ■	59
81	La Salle	56
77	Wagner ■	61
63	Hartford ■	53
67	UMBC ■	51
68	Virginia	76
70	Princeton ■	62
66	Syracuse	87
89	Georgetown ■	87
58	Pittsburgh ■	66
54	Seton Hall	67
79	West Virginia ■	66
55	Providence	70
77	West Virginia	59
61	Connecticut ■	53
82	Syracuse ■	74
72	Notre Dame	89
80	St. Peter's ■	63
65	Notre Dame ■	62
64	Miami (Fla.) ■	61
59	Pittsburgh	78
66	Seton Hall ■	60
49	Virginia Tech	63
69	Georgetown	88
55	Boston College †	60
65	Yale ■	67

Nickname: Scarlet Knights
Colors: Scarlet
Arena: Louis Brown Athletic Center
  Capacity: 8,500; Year Built: 1978
SID: John Wooding

RUTGERS-CAMDEN
Camden, NJ 08102 III

Coach: Jim Flynn, St. Joseph's 1988
2001-02 RESULTS (14-11)

60	John Jay	56
61	Col. of New Jersey	64
59	Rutgers-Newark	58
64	Rowan ■	58
95	Valley Forge Chrst. ■	47
63	Ramapo ■	58
67	Wm. Paterson	84
53	Montclair St. ■	75
75	Waynesburg †	81
86	Marywood †	74
89	Centenary (N.J.) ■	74
63	New Jersey City	67
71	Kean ■	70
83	Lancaster Bible	60
63	Richard Stockton ■	68
64	Ramapo	69
57	Rowan	72
72	Rutgers-Newark ■	58
95	Col. of New Jersey ■	80
70	Montclair St.	71
69	Wm. Paterson ■	68
91	Phila. Bible	75
103	New Jersey City ■	99
60	Richard Stockton	63
72	Kean	82

Nickname: Scarlet Raptors
Colors: Scarlet & Silver
Arena: Rutgers Camden Gymnasium
  Capacity: 2,100; Year Built: 1973
SID: Mike Ballard

SCHEDULES/RESULTS

RUTGERS-NEWARK
Newark, NJ 07102.................III

Coach: Joe Loughran, American Int'l 1993

2001-02 RESULTS (7-18)

96	NYCCT ■	55
67	Adrian ■	77
45	Montclair St.	40
58	Rutgers-Camden ■	59
53	Kean	63
62	New Jersey City ■	74
85	Brooklyn	62
64	Richard Stockton ■	49
51	Rowan ■	54
67	Purchase St. ■	64
57	York (N.Y.) ■	63
68	Hunter	78
62	Rowan	74
57	Col. of New Jersey ■	73
67	Wm. Paterson	59
53	Ramapo	69
69	New Jersey City	86
41	Kean ■	53
58	Rutgers-Camden	72
55	Montclair St. ■	69
78	Polytechnic (N.Y.)	48
59	Richard Stockton ■	80
67	Col. of New Jersey	76
62	Ramapo ■	80
54	Wm. Paterson ■	65

Nickname: Scarlet Raiders
Colors: Scarlet
Arena: The Golden Dome
   Capacity: 2,000; Year Built: 1977
SID: John Stallings

SACRAMENTO ST.
Sacramento, CA 95819.............I

Coach: Jerome Jenkins, Regis 1990

2001-02 RESULTS (9-19)

52	Old Dominion †	69
46	Wofford †	56
81	Menlo ■	65
60	San Jose St.	62
64	St. Mary's (Cal.)	78
72	Southern Utah ■	61
85	Cal St. Fullerton ■	79
77	Loyola Marymount	95
97	Cal St. Fullerton	106
86	Lipscomb ■	76
66	UC Riverside	100
63	Idaho	75
82	Tex. A&M-Corp. Chris. ■	69
91	Dominican (Cal.) ■	73
79	Idaho St.	87
83	Weber St.	86
81	Northern Ariz. ■	63
78	Montana St. ■	56
78	Montana ■	88
83	Portland St.	86
67	Eastern Wash.	87
72	Weber St. ■	76
90	Idaho St. ■	80
70	Northern Ariz.	90
53	Montana	86
60	Montana St.	70
71	Eastern Wash. ■	81
67	Portland St. ■	74

Nickname: Hornets
Colors: Green & Gold
Arena: Hornet Gym
   Capacity: 1,300; Year Built: 1922
SID: Brian Berger

SACRED HEART
Fairfield, CT 06432-1000.........I

Coach: Dave Bike, Sacred Heart 1969

2001-02 RESULTS (8-20)

76	Stony Brook ■	71
55	Baylor	81
64	Yale	77
133	Fairleigh Dickinson	130
62	Vermont ■	85
61	Maine ■	67
96	Monmouth	69
76	Providence	85
69	Harvard	81
77	Robert Morris ■	69
67	St. Francis (Pa.) ■	70
78	Quinnipiac	86
47	Central Conn. St.	76
75	Fairleigh Dickinson ■	63
80	Wagner ■	82
67	Robert Morris	72
69	Central Conn. St. ■	78
74	Wagner	95
52	UMBC ■	67
79	Mt. St. Mary's ■	57
80	Long Island	88
76	St. Francis (N.Y.)	77
87	Quinnipiac ■	104
94	St. Francis (N.Y.) ■	86
94	Long Island ■	99
88	Mt. St. Mary's ■	84
78	UMBC	81
54	Central Conn. St. †	65

Nickname: Pioneers
Colors: Scarlet & White
Arena: William H. Pitt Center
   Capacity: 2,000; Year Built: 1997
SID: To be named

SAGINAW VALLEY
University Center, MI 48710-0001
....II

Coach: Dean Lockwood, Spring Arbor 1982

2001-02 RESULTS (5-21)

56	Hillsdale ■	74
68	Wayne St. (Mich.) ■	75
83	Spring Arbor	85
53	Mich.-Dearborn ■	80
69	Wayne St. (Mich.)	80
78	Hillsdale	95
73	Ashland ■	88
82	Rochester College ■	69
77	Concordia (Mich.) ■	59
80	Pace †	90
84	Tiffin †	77
66	Findlay	88
68	Gannon ■	80
76	Mercyhurst ■	64
68	Michigan Tech	76
64	Northern Mich.	77
77	Ferris St.	65
75	Grand Valley St.	97
69	Northwood ■	73
84	Lake Superior St. ■	99
82	Northern Mich. ■	94
79	Michigan Tech ■	96
96	Grand Valley St. ■	99
80	Ferris St. ■	81
70	Lake Superior St.	81
85	Northwood	112

Nickname: Cardinals
Colors: Red, White & Blue
Arena: James O'Neill Jr. Arena
   Capacity: 4,000; Year Built: 1989
SID: Tom Waske

ST. ANDREWS
Laurinburg, NC 28352-5598.....II

Coach: Rick Johnson, Marantha Baptist

2001-02 RESULTS (2-25)

57	S.C.-Aiken ■	78
83	Wingate ■	92
78	Catawba	87

51	Winston-Salem †	78
77	Barton ■	92
66	Fayetteville St.	65
67	UNC Pembroke	79
66	Belmont Abbey	91
81	Lees-McRae ■	71
64	Longwood	99
73	Queens (N.C.) ■	78
59	Limestone	65
65	Anderson (S.C.)	71
62	Pfeiffer ■	74
77	Erskine	88
57	Coker	63
59	Mount Olive	75
47	Barton	65
56	Belmont Abbey ■	75
58	Lees-McRae	84
65	Longwood ■	73
80	Queens (N.C.)	99
69	Limestone	74
58	Anderson (S.C.) ■	78
60	Pfeiffer	82
67	Erskine ■	74
82	Pfeiffer	94

Nickname: Knights
Colors: Royal Blue & White
Arena: Harris/Courts
   Capacity: 1,200; Year Built: 1967
SID: Marilynn Oliver

ST. ANSELM
Manchester, NH 03102-1310 ...II

Coach: Keith Dickson, New Hampshire 1979

2001-02 RESULTS (19-11)

69	N.J. Inst. of Tech. ■	47
74	St. Michael's ■	78
77	Le Moyne	70
75	Merrimack	68
75	Stonehill ■	54
75	Bentley	89
72	Southern N.H. ■	82
84	Franklin Pierce †	66
92	Central Wash. †	90
78	Rollins	79
90	Bentley ■	95
80	Mass.-Lowell	77
93	Merrimack ■	77
88	Stonehill	66
96	Southern N.H.	64
71	Mass.-Lowell ■	78
64	Franklin Pierce	71
97	St. Michael's ■	95
100	Le Moyne ■	73
85	New Haven	72
80	American Int'l	85
93	Bryant ■	72
76	Assumption	79
90	St. Rose ■	81
103	Southern Conn. St. ■	45
81	Pace	88
81	Le Moyne ■	63
65	Mass.-Lowell	62
89	American Int'l ■	75
72	Bentley	78

Nickname: Hawks
Colors: Blue & White
Arena: Stoutenburgh Gymnasium
   Capacity: 1,600; Year Built: 1961
SID: Kurt Svoboda

ST. AUGUSTINE'S
Raleigh, NC 27610.................II

Coach: Thomas Hargrove

2001-02 RESULTS (13-13)

89	Morris	71
101	Bowie St. ■	84
83	Clark Atlanta	75
57	Benedict ■	50
71	St. Paul's	64

79	Shepherd ■	54
83	St. Paul's ■	79
83	Winston-Salem	88
86	Shaw	107
90	N.C. Central	94
88	Elizabeth City St. ■	71
72	Fayetteville St.	87
80	Johnson Smith	93
99	Livingstone ■	59
75	N.C. Central	88
85	Virginia St.	63
54	Virginia Union	63
83	Winston-Salem ■	95
81	Fayetteville St. ■	61
82	Johnson Smith	96
84	Virginia St. ■	66
73	Livingstone	79
83	Dist. Columbia	91
112	Knoxville	113
83	Virginia Union †	79
59	Johnson Smith †	81

Nickname: Falcons
Colors: Blue & White
Arena: Emery Gymnasium
   Capacity: 1,000; Year Built: 1962
SID: Leon Carrington

ST. BONAVENTURE
St. Bonaventure, NY 14778 I

Coach: Jan van Breda Kolff, Vanderbilt 1974

2001-02 RESULTS (17-13)

79	Cleveland St.	64
90	Niagara ■	75
82	Boston College †	96
82	Toledo	76
74	Oklahoma	80
93	Wis.-Green Bay ■	83
97	Ohio	85
79	Davidson ■	70
78	Siena	74
88	Connecticut	70
82	Kent St.	93
86	George Washington	92
96	Rhode Island ■	74
68	La Salle	62
87	St. Joseph's	93
93	Temple ■	74
96	Duquesne ■	89
81	Fordham	87
65	Massachusetts ■	67
81	Dayton	75
66	Richmond ■	78
80	Xavier ■	79
60	Massachusetts	56
90	Fordham ■	84
71	Temple	75
84	St. Joseph's ■	91
72	Rhode Island	80
81	Duquesne †	66
69	Richmond †	78
66	Syracuse	76

Nickname: Bonnies
Colors: Brown & White
Arena: Reilly Center
   Capacity: 6,000; Year Built: 1966
SID: Steve Mest

ST. CLOUD ST.
St. Cloud, MN 56301-4498......II

Coach: Kevin Schlagel, St. Cloud St. 1976

2001-02 RESULTS (21-7)

85	Bemidji St. ■	57
86	Minn.-Crookston	77
84	Northern St.	68
88	Central (Iowa) ■	50
97	South Dakota ■	81
87	Morningside ■	51
99	Concordia-St. Paul	73

67 St. John's (Minn.) ■ 59
83 Southwest St. ■ 62
82 Wis.-La Crosse ■ 58
85 Minn. St.-Mankato ■ 64
56 South Dakota St. 79
84 Augustana (S.D.) ■ 69
85 Northern Colo. ■ 60
63 Neb.-Omaha ■ 102
88 North Dakota 91
93 North Dakota St. 79
81 Minn. St.-Mankato ■ 78
83 Augustana (S.D.) ■ 68
82 South Dakota St. ■ 90
72 Neb.-Omaha ■ 81
85 Northern Colo. 86
82 North Dakota St. ■ 68
87 North Dakota ■ 73
98 Morningside 68
73 South Dakota 60
95 South Dakota ■ 90
77 South Dakota St. 91

Nickname: Huskies
Colors: Cardinal Red & Black
Arena: Halenbeck Hall
  Capacity: 6,900; Year Built: 1965
SID: Anne Abicht

ST. EDWARD'S
Austin, TX 78704 II

Coach: Mike Jones, Angelo St.
2001-02 RESULTS (4-23)
72 Ouachita Baptist ■ 74
78 Abilene Christian 59
88 Concordia-Austin 89
79 Southwest Baptist † 85
93 Chadron St. † 100
75 Abilene Christian ■ 58
71 Loyola (La.) ■ 76
75 Central Ark. ■ 70
53 Ouachita Baptist 63
79 SIU-Edwardsville † 84
86 Tex. A&M-Kingsville † 90
51 Tarleton St. 81
67 Barry 77
67 Lynn 83
58 Tarleton St. ■ 74
80 Drury 88
71 Rockhurst ■ 78
82 Lincoln (Mo.) ■ 85
65 Incarnate Word ■ 70
64 St. Mary's (Tex.) 80
71 North Texas 98
77 Huston-Tillotson ■ 84
82 Drury ■ 85
82 Rockhurst 94
68 Lincoln (Mo.) 88
75 Incarnate Word 87
69 St. Mary's (Tex.) ■ 56

Nickname: Hilltoppers
Colors: Navy & White
Arena: Recreation & Convocation Center
  Capacity: 2,500; Year Built: 1989
SID: Kevin Jannusch

ST. FRANCIS (PA.)
Loretto, PA 15940-0600 I

Coach: Bobby Jones, Western Ky. 1984
2001-02 RESULTS (6-21)
67 Wright St. ■ 83
52 American 55
59 Bucknell ■ 44
75 UMBC ■ 77
75 Mt. St. Mary's ■ 54
55 Pittsburgh 77
67 Howard 88
60 Wake Forest 89
48 Miami (Fla.) 71
80 Wagner 81
70 Sacred Heart 67
77 Long Island ■ 64

62 St. Francis (N.Y.) ■ 64
65 Robert Morris 63
55 Monmouth 57
67 Wagner ■ 80
64 Long Island 80
66 St. Francis (N.Y.) 79
49 Central Conn. St. ■ 66
77 Quinnipiac ■ 79
72 UMBC 75
54 Mt. St. Mary's 57
43 Monmouth 60
72 Fairleigh Dickinson ■ 68
54 Robert Morris ■ 58
59 Central Conn. St. 80
58 Quinnipiac 71

Nickname: Red Flash
Colors: Red & White
Arena: Maurice Stokes Athletic Center
  Capacity: 3,500; Year Built: 1972
SID: Pat Farabaugh

ST. FRANCIS (N.Y.)
Brooklyn Heights, NY 11201-4398 I

Coach: Ron Ganulin, Long Island 1968
2001-02 RESULTS (18-11)
100 Lehigh ■ 91
90 St. Peter's ■ 83
85 Howard ■ 72
75 Quinnipiac 71
82 Central Conn. St. 69
71 Fairfield 75
82 St. John's (N.Y.) 89
61 Pittsburgh 74
75 Fairleigh Dickinson ■ 66
71 Monmouth 86
80 Robert Morris 93
64 St. Francis (Pa.) 62
85 Mt. St. Mary's 73
112 Quinnipiac ■ 102
92 Long Island ■ 84
91 Robert Morris ■ 78
79 St. Francis (Pa.) ■ 66
86 Fairleigh Dickinson 76
67 UMBC ■ 78
77 Sacred Heart ■ 76
88 Wagner 99
85 Mt. St. Mary's ■ 60
86 Sacred Heart 94
71 Wagner ■ 83
71 Binghamton ■ 67
68 Monmouth 75
108 Long Island 94
71 Monmouth † 61
54 Central Conn. St. † 58

Nickname: Terriers
Colors: Red & Blue
Arena: Pope Physical Education Center
  Capacity: 1,200; Year Built: 1971
SID: Jim Hoffman

ST. JOHN FISHER
Rochester, NY 14618 III

Coach: Rob Kornaker, Alfred
2001-02 RESULTS (13-13)
84 Southern Vt. ■ 76
83 Cazenovia 71
70 Brockport St. 102
84 Plattsburgh St. † 75
72 CCNY † 56
56 Fredonia St. 69
61 Rochester 74
72 Alfred 83
53 Ithaca ■ 62
81 Elmira 73
72 Rochester ■ 67
83 Rochester Inst. † 92
54 Geneseo St. † 70
57 Nazareth ■ 77
69 Utica 58

62 Hartwick 59
93 Alfred ■ 92
66 Rochester Inst. 71
65 Nazareth 63
72 Pitt.-Bradford 95
67 Hartwick ■ 59
60 Utica ■ 52
72 Rochester Inst. ■ 61
61 Elmira 75
62 Ithaca 65
88 St. Lawrence 97

Nickname: Cardinals
Colors: Cardinal Red & Gold
Arena: Athletic Center
  Capacity: 1,200; Year Built: 1963
SID: Norm Kieffer

ST. JOHN'S (MINN.)
Collegeville, MN 56321 III

Coach: Jim Smith, Marquette 1956
2001-02 RESULTS (15-11)
71 Wis.-Platteville ■ 79
65 Wis.-Stout ■ 72
60 Macalester 62
75 St. Thomas (Minn.) ■ 72
73 Carleton 78
59 St. Cloud St. 67
60 Luther † 39
77 Loras † 53
58 Gust. Adolphus 61
63 Bethel (Minn.) ■ 78
63 St. Olaf 56
76 Augsburg ■ 49
81 Hamline 69
56 Concordia-M'head ■ 54
61 St. Mary's (Minn.) 41
69 Macalester ■ 48
62 St. Thomas (Minn.) 68
53 Gust. Adolphus 68
64 Bethel (Minn.) 75
55 Carleton 53
90 St. Olaf ■ 76
67 Augsburg 46
82 Hamline ■ 62
69 Concordia-M'head 67
88 St. Mary's (Minn.) ■ 66
82 Macalester 83

Nickname: Johnnies
Colors: Cardinal & Blue
Arena: Sexton Arena
  Capacity: 3,500; Year Built: 1974
SID: Michael Hemmesch

ST. JOHN'S (N.Y.)
Jamaica, NY 11439 I

Coach: Mike Jarvis, Northeastern 1968
2001-02 RESULTS (20-12)
72 Stony Brook ■ 55
58 Gonzaga † 65
66 Oregon St. † 63
69 Tennessee † 55
76 Fordham ■ 67
68 Manhattan † 85
60 Niagara 52
89 Hofstra ■ 75
89 St. Francis (N.Y.) ■ 82
72 Wake Forest ■ 60
97 Quinnipiac ■ 60
54 Pittsburgh 77
72 West Virginia ■ 53
71 Miami (Fla.) ■ 60
57 Providence 78
65 Villanova ■ 63
70 Connecticut 75
70 Providence ■ 75
59 Seton Hall 63
72 Virginia Tech 63
95 Fairfield ■ 56
85 Connecticut ■ 83
56 Miami (Fla.) 79

73 Virginia Tech ■ 63
71 Boston College ■ 62
55 Duke 97
84 Notre Dame ■ 81
62 Villanova 77
64 Seton Hall † 58
63 Notre Dame † 83
70 Wisconsin † 80

Nickname: Red Storm
Colors: Red & White
Arena: Alumni Hall
  Capacity: 6,008; Year Built: 1961
SID: Dominic P. Scianna

ST. JOSEPH'S (IND.)
Rensselaer, IN 47978 II

Coach: Ken Carillo, Arizona 1984
2001-02 RESULTS (8-18)
58 Eastern Ill. 98
53 Ill.-Chicago 96
45 Indianapolis ■ 77
68 Bellarmine 79
67 Ky. Wesleyan ■ 88
61 Mo.-St. Louis ■ 81
79 Quincy ■ 89
72 Northwood 95
103 Ferris St. 75
126 East-West U. ■ 65
109 Calumet Col. ■ 62
72 Lewis 76
55 Wis.-Parkside 65
79 Indianapolis 89
85 Northern Ky. 90
68 Ky. Wesleyan ■ 94
92 Southern Ind. ■ 87
82 Quincy 90
90 SIU-Edwardsville ■ 86
66 Wis.-Parkside ■ 80
73 Northern Ky. ■ 70
74 Bellarmine ■ 90
88 Southern Ind. 102
63 Mo.-St. Louis 61
81 SIU-Edwardsville ■ 72
66 Lewis 69

Nickname: Pumas
Colors: Cardinal & Purple
Arena: Richard F. Scharf Fieldhouse
  Capacity: 2,000; Year Built: 1941
SID: Joe Danahey

ST. JOSEPH'S (L.I.)
Patchogue, NY 11772-2603 III

Coach: John Mateyko
2001-02 RESULTS (9-17)
93 Farmingdale St. ■ 84
70 York (N.Y.) 79
64 Hartwick ■ 85
46 New York U. 72
93 Pratt ■ 52
60 Manhattanville ■ 69
63 Old Westbury ■ 77
68 Lehman 69
69 Yeshiva 76
68 Mt. St. Vincent ■ 66
58 CCNY ■ 64
62 Mt. St. Mary (N.Y.) ■ 66
71 Maritime (N.Y.) 82
69 Old Westbury 93
70 Merchant Marine ■ 94
79 Purchase St. 70
73 Stevens Tech 80
69 Yeshiva ■ 56
64 Manhattanville 74
55 Mt. St. Mary (N.Y.) 72
65 Maritime (N.Y.) ■ 58
88 Mt. St. Vincent 69
63 Brooklyn 61
56 Merchant Marine 90
63 Stevens Tech ■ 50
51 Manhattanville 74

Nickname: Golden Eagles
Colors: Blue & Gold
Arena: Danzi Athletic Center
    Capacity: 1,500; Year Built: 1996
SID: Matt Aug

ST. JOSEPH'S (ME.)
Standish, ME 04084-5263 III

Coach: Rick Simonds, Southern Me.
1972
2001-02 RESULTS (18-10)
71	Colby †	79
85	Southern Me.	76
63	Me.-Farmington ■	51
70	Lasell	79
112	Lyndon St.	71
76	Me.-Fort Kent ■	81
97	New England	91
107	Becker ■	69
79	Me.-Fort Kent †	72
76	Bryant	85
83	Colby	75
87	Me.-Machias	92
89	Me.-Presque Isle	79
75	Me.-Fort Kent	59
112	Thomas	61
66	Me.-Farmington	73
63	Husson	64
81	Me.-Presque Isle ■	51
74	Bowdoin	86
88	Southern Me. ■	92
90	Thomas ■	51
92	Curry	83
65	Husson ■	61
74	Me.-Machias ■	69
98	Thomas	52
68	Me.-Fort Kent †	55
61	Husson †	54
69	Northwestern (Iowa) †	86

Nickname: Monks
Colors: Royal Blue & White
Arena: Harold Alfond Center
    Capacity: 1,500; Year Built: 1999
SID: Rob Sanicola

ST. JOSEPH'S
Philadelphia, PA 19131-1395 I

Coach: Phil Martelli, Widener 1976
2001-02 RESULTS (19-12)
67	Eastern Wash. †	68
74	Princeton †	63
81	Colorado ■	75
84	Delaware	57
82	Canisius ■	76
67	Pennsylvania	61
85	Drexel ■	64
90	Georgia St. †	95
76	North Carolina	92
80	Gonzaga ■	83
63	Massachusetts	38
87	Rhode Island	71
93	St. Bonaventure ■	87
83	Fordham ■	72
92	George Washington ■	74
63	Duquesne	47
60	Pennsylvania ■	62
73	Villanova	102
71	Rhode Island ■	58
72	Temple	82
80	La Salle †	71
84	Fordham	77
59	Richmond	61
77	Xavier	84
72	Massachusetts ■	67
70	Dayton ■	68
91	St. Bonaventure	84
84	Temple †	87
74	Dayton †	81
73	George Mason	64
54	Ball St. ■	76

Nickname: Hawks
Colors: Crimson & Gray
Arena: Alumni Memorial Fieldhouse
    Capacity: 3,200; Year Built: 1949
SID: Larry Dougherty

ST. LAWRENCE
Canton, NY 13617 III

Coach: Chris Downs, Oneonta St. 1991
2001-02 RESULTS (21-9)
83	Oswego St.	77
80	Clarkson †	78
70	Chris. Newport	83
84	Clarkson	91
72	Ithaca	69
83	Alfred	64
88	John Carroll †	91
75	La Grange †	73
97	Hunter †	66
57	Pitt.-Bradford †	60
80	Skidmore	74
83	Union (N.Y.) ■	68
74	Plattsburgh St.	87
69	Vassar	76
63	Rensselaer	65
78	Potsdam St. ■	69
55	Hobart	57
90	Hamilton	86
78	Rensselaer ■	63
69	Vassar ■	55
74	Union (N.Y.)	71
82	Skidmore	66
72	Clarkson	66
83	Hamilton ■	79
68	Hobart ■	45
61	Clarkson †	58
63	Union (N.Y.)	70
97	St. John Fisher ■	88
99	Nazareth ■	87
71	Clarkson ■	61

Nickname: Saints
Colors: Scarlet & Brown
Arena: Burkman Gymnasium
    Capacity: 1,500; Year Built: 1970
SID: Lauren Zimmerman

ST. LEO
Saint Leo, FL 33574 II

Coach: Mike Hanks, SMU 1975
2001-02 RESULTS (7-20)
73	P.R.-Mayaguez ■	56
103	P.R.-Cayey ■	50
73	P.R.-Rio Piedras ■	66
88	Nova Southeastern ■	72
71	P.R.-Bayamon ■	72
63	Webber	68
78	Rollins	82
72	Point Park ■	86
51	S.C.-Aiken	56
65	Augusta St. †	82
90	Nova Southeastern	88
62	Florida Tech ■	78
45	Fla. Southern	93
51	Eckerd ■	66
60	Tampa	78
51	Rollins ■	74
61	Barry	75
61	Lynn ■	74
62	Fla. Southern ■	90
55	Eckerd	80
49	Tampa ■	69
79	Rollins	80
47	Barry ■	60
57	Lynn	87
73	Florida Tech	69
76	Eckerd †	84

Nickname: Monarchs
Colors: Forest Green & Old Gold
Arena: Marion Bowman Center
    Capacity: 2,700; Year Built: 1970
SID: Tom O'Brien

ST. LOUIS
St. Louis, MO 63108 I

Coach: Lorenzo Romar, Washington
1980
2001-02 RESULTS (15-16)
64	Southern Ill. ■	69
85	Hartford †	52
72	Iowa St. †	77
67	Georgia Tech †	54
58	Ark.-Little Rock ■	61
67	Missouri ■	69
63	California	88
63	Denver ■	49
88	Southeast Mo. St. ■	62
73	Furman ■	59
63	Dayton	69
71	Washington ■	70
50	Southwest Mo. St.	53
67	Houston ■	64
92	DePaul ■	74
53	Marquette	61
49	Charlotte	77
85	East Caro. ■	72
50	Cincinnati ■	54
38	Marquette ■	55
46	Southern Miss.	67
63	East Caro.	69
67	Louisville	64
73	Charlotte ■	54
53	Cincinnati	67
40	Georgia Tech ■	60
53	UAB ■	47
56	Louisville ■	50
72	DePaul	63
67	Tulane	59
47	Tulane †	50

Nickname: Billikens
Colors: Blue & White
Arena: Savvis Center
    Capacity: 20,000; Year Built: 1994
SID: Doug McIlhagga

ST. MARTIN'S
Lacey, WA 98503 II

Coach: Bob Grisham, Col. of Idaho
1976
2001-02 RESULTS (10-16)
72	Mo. Southern St. †	95
38	Pittsburg St.	69
64	Minn. St. Moorhead †	77
86	Southern Colo. †	69
61	Hawaii Pacific ■	65
59	Eastern Wash.	75
53	Western Wash. ■	78
46	Seattle Pacific ■	73
92	Evergreen St. ■	106
69	Colorado Mines ■	63
58	Alas. Anchorage ■	68
70	Alas. Fairbanks	51
59	Seattle	47
78	Northwest Nazarene	76
74	Western Ore. ■	71
70	Humboldt St. ■	84
75	Central Wash.	70
59	Seattle Pacific	74
60	Western Wash.	70
66	Alas. Fairbanks ■	60
97	Alas. Anchorage ■	64
78	Northwest Nazarene ■	74
53	Seattle ■	57
73	Humboldt St.	102
81	Western Ore.	83
62	Central Wash. ■	88

Nickname: Saints
Colors: Red & White
Arena: SMC Pavillion
    Capacity: 4,300; Year Built: 1965
SID: Michael Ostlund

ST. MARY'S (CAL.)
Moraga, CA 94575 I

Coach: Randy Bennett, UC San Diego
1986
2001-02 RESULTS (9-20)
64	UC Irvine	71
61	Nevada ■	66
50	Cal Poly	70
78	Sacramento St. ■	64
51	UC Santa Barb.	62
59	San Jose St.	51
95	UC Santa Cruz ■	39
70	Loyola (Ill.) ■	72
73	Eastern Wash. ■	67
62	New Mexico	72
68	Southeastern La. †	49
51	Colorado	68
35	Utah ■	41
51	Pepperdine ■	67
64	Loyola Marymount ■	75
46	San Francisco ■	63
67	San Francisco	84
68	Portland	74
52	Gonzaga	70
60	Santa Clara ■	63
62	San Diego ■	60
62	Loyola Marymount	44
57	Pepperdine	68
72	San Diego	76
49	Santa Clara	56
68	Portland ■	59
55	Gonzaga ■	74
72	Santa Clara †	67
47	Pepperdine †	68

Nickname: Gaels
Colors: Navy Blue & Red
Arena: McKeon Pavilion
    Capacity: 3,500; Year Built: 1978
SID: Jason Santos

ST. MARY'S (MD.)
St. Mary's City, MD 20686 III

Coach: Alfred Johnson, Elizabeth City St.
1994
2001-02 RESULTS (5-21)
81	Gardner-Webb	130
73	Fla. Atlantic	107
95	Southern Va. †	81
83	Chris. Newport	111
81	Gallaudet	94
77	York (Pa.) ■	88
64	Bowie St. ■	87
72	VMI	98
76	McDaniel ■	63
59	Wilkes	86
60	Rowan	107
72	Goucher	90
75	Salisbury ■	79
85	Marymount (Va.)	104
75	Mary Washington ■	80
62	Catholic	88
65	York (Pa.)	82
59	Savannah A&D ■	71
72	Gallaudet ■	69
74	Salisbury	89
85	Villa Julie	64
72	Goucher ■	60
73	Mary Washington	82
77	Marymount (Va.) ■	99
76	Catholic	102
65	Catholic	85

Nickname: Seahawks
Colors: Navy Blue & Old Gold
Arena: Somerset Gymnasium
    Capacity: 1,420; Year Built: 1968
SID: Shawne McCoy

ST. MARY'S (MINN.)
Winona, MN 55987-1399.......III

Coach: Bob Biebel,
St. Mary's (Minn.) 1979

2001-02 RESULTS (5-19)
91	Pacific Lutheran †	97
84	Puget Sound	100
64	Winona St.	94
72	St. Olaf ■	78
65	Gust. Adolphus	87
59	Concordia-M'head ■	58
71	Bethel (Minn.)	83
52	St. Thomas (Minn.) ■	76
72	Augsburg	69
60	Hamline ■	50
60	Carleton	73
49	Concordia-M'head	69
48	Macalester ■	64
41	St. John's (Minn.) ■	61
58	Viterbo	66
87	St. Olaf	84
31	Gust. Adolphus ■	59
47	St. Thomas (Minn.) ■	64
54	Augsburg ■	59
72	Bethel (Minn.) ■	76
57	Hamline	70
60	Carleton ■	68
74	Macalester	69
66	St. John's (Minn.)	88

Nickname: Cardinals
Colors: Scarlet, Red & White
Arena: St. Mary's Fieldhouse
Capacity: 3,500; Year Built: 1965
SID: Donny Nadeau

ST. MARY'S (TEX.)
San Antonio, TX 78228-8572....II

Coach: Herman Meyer, St. Mary's (Tex.)

2001-02 RESULTS (11-15)
72	Western St. (Colo.) †	67
53	Adams St.	49
73	Adams St. ■	67
62	Emporia St. ■	69
56	Tex. A&M-Commerce	67
80	Tex. A&M-Kingsville ■	61
85	Central Mo. St. †	98
53	Mercyhurst †	61
60	Lewis ■	61
79	Midwestern St. ■	66
57	Rollins ■	53
55	Midwestern St.	61
60	Rockhurst	71
65	Lincoln (Mo.)	66
84	National Christian ■	44
83	Drury ■	76
64	Tex. A&M-Kingsville	65
80	St. Edward's ■	64
78	Huston-Tillotson ■	60
63	Incarnate Word ■	72
70	Rockhurst	77
71	Lincoln (Mo.) ■	75
76	Drury	82
94	National Christian ■	34
56	St. Edward's	69
50	Incarnate Word	66

Nickname: Rattlers
Colors: Blue & Gold
Arena: Bill Greehey Arena
Capacity: 3,500; Year Built: 2000
SID: Steve Johnson

ST. MICHAEL'S
Colchester, VT 05439...............II

Coach: Tom O'Shea, Vermont 1986

2001-02 RESULTS (11-16)
78	St. Anselm	74
70	Merrimack ■	63
64	Stonehill	66
66	Bentley ■	82
86	Merrimack	59
65	Le Moyne ■	82
86	Green Mountain	63
78	Felician ■	60
85	Dowling ■	70
50	Mass.-Lowell ■	44
67	Franklin Pierce	78
76	Southern N.H. ■	82
95	Stonehill	61
78	Bentley	91
78	Mass.-Lowell	88
89	Franklin Pierce ■	79
89	Southern N.H.	99
95	St. Anselm	97
74	New Haven ■	63
62	Le Moyne	79
81	Assumption	89
77	American Int'l ■	78
73	Bryant	61
65	Southern Conn. St. ■	72
68	Pace ■	71
79	St. Rose	93
74	Southern N.H.	104

Nickname: Purple Knights
Colors: Purple & Gold
Arena: Ross Sports Center
Capacity: 2,500; Year Built: 1974
SID: Angela Aja

ST. NORBERT
De Pere, WI 54115 III

Coach: Paul De Noble, Wis.-Oshkosh
1973

2001-02 RESULTS (21-5)
60	Cabrini †	63
77	St. Thomas Aquinas †	60
69	Edgewood †	64
66	Wis.-Oshkosh ■	81
59	Elmhurst	53
77	Carroll (Wis.)	59
56	Hanover †	53
70	Otterbein	74
83	Beloit	74
62	Lawrence ■	52
71	Knox	64
68	Illinois Col.	55
71	Ripon ■	66
63	Lake Forest ■	55
117	Grinnell ■	94
71	Monmouth (Ill.)	62
83	Lake Forest	74
71	Lawrence	56
66	Illinois Col. ■	44
81	Knox ■	55
76	Carroll (Wis.) ■	58
74	Ripon	53
75	Beloit ■	66
125	Grinnell	114
45	Ripon ■	54
53	Hope ■	54

Nickname: Green Knights
Colors: Dartmouth Green & Old Gold
Arena: Schuldes Sports Center
Capacity: 2,000; Year Built: 1979
SID: Dan Lukes

ST. OLAF
Northfield, MN 55057-1098 III

Coach: Dan Kosmoski, Minnesota 1980

2001-02 RESULTS (9-16)
61	Capital	77
93	Thiel †	76
86	Luther	64
74	Northwestern (Minn.) ■	70
60	Gust. Adolphus	81
78	St. Mary's (Minn.)	72
66	Concordia-M'head ■	68
58	Hamline	56
79	Crown	72

ST. JOHN'S / continued
57	Bethel (Minn.)	90
74	Macalester ■	76
56	St. John's (Minn.) ■	63
39	St. Thomas (Minn.) ■	64
86	Augsburg	65
60	Carleton	66
58	Gust. Adolphus ■	84
84	St. Mary's (Minn.) ■	87
73	Concordia-M'head	78
52	Bethel (Minn.) ■	67
84	Macalester	93
72	Hamline ■	73
76	St. John's (Minn.)	90
75	St. Thomas (Minn.)	91
78	Augsburg ■	70
79	Carleton ■	75

Nickname: Oles
Colors: Black & Old Gold
Arena: Skoglund Athletic Center
Capacity: 3,000; Year Built: 1968
SID: Judy Stromayer

ST. PAUL'S
Lawrenceville, VA 23868...........II

Coach: To be named,

2001-02 RESULTS (4-22)
76	Barton ■	80
69	Voorhees ■	58
60	Barton	84
67	Columbia Union ■	76
64	Wingate ■	88
51	Voorhees	66
64	St. Augustine's ■	71
68	Livingstone ■	77
81	Bowie St. ■	95
79	St. Augustine's	83
60	Barber-Scotia ■	66
74	Johnson Smith	102
41	Virginia Union †	58
82	Virginia Union ■	74
77	Winston-Salem	91
76	Shaw	96
80	Elizabeth City St. ■	93
61	Fayetteville St.	73
75	Livingstone	88
64	Virginia St.	68
76	Shaw ■	87
54	Elizabeth City St.	80
75	Bowie St.	94
63	N.C. Central	60
88	Virginia St. ■	76
45	Fayetteville St. †	50

Nickname: Tigers
Colors: Black & Orange
Arena: Taylor-Whitehead Gym
Capacity: 1,500; Year Built: 1965
SID: April Emory

ST. PETER'S
Jersey City, NJ 07306...............I

Coach: Bob Leckie, St. Peter's 1969

2001-02 RESULTS (4-24)
59	Florida Int'l	70
79	Maine †	70
83	St. Francis (N.Y.)	90
58	Boston U.	70
66	Lafayette	69
61	UNC Greensboro	77
57	Manhattan ■	74
59	Loyola (Md.) †	60
63	Seton Hall	78
61	Monmouth ■	69
49	Marist ■	71
53	Iona ■	85
75	Fairfield	95
59	Siena	73
65	Niagara ■	72
71	Canisius †	62
57	Rider	63
87	Manhattan	96
52	Rider ■	88
83	Iona	81
73	Canisius	71
70	Niagara	93
63	Rutgers	80
55	Siena	73
78	Loyola (Md.) ■	88
61	Marist	89
61	Fairfield ■	93
66	Siena †	77

Nickname: Peacocks
Colors: Blue & White
Arena: Yanitelli Center
Capacity: 3,200; Year Built: 1975
SID: Tim Camp

ST. ROSE
Albany, NY 12203 II

Coach: Brian Beaury, St. Rose 1982

2001-02 RESULTS (17-13)
87	Franklin Pierce ■	85
73	Mass.-Lowell	86
70	Bryant ■	67
50	American Int'l	49
67	Assumption	77
69	Franklin Pierce	75
70	American Int'l ■	72
62	Le Moyne	52
95	New Haven ■	77
102	Southampton ■	81
84	Bentley ■	67
85	Southern N.H.	73
76	Pace ■	77
66	Southern Conn. St.	78
53	Mass.-Lowell ■	68
77	Southern N.H. ■	67
77	Bryant	71
77	Assumption	79
70	Bentley ■	68
80	Merrimack	69
75	Stonehill ■	57
90	Pace	98
66	New Haven	82
83	Southern Conn. St. ■	80
81	St. Anselm	90
93	St. Michael's ■	79
79	Franklin Pierce ■	78
69	Assumption	76
81	NYIT †	76
101	Southampton †	113

Nickname: Golden Knights
Colors: Gold, White & Black
Arena: Activities Center
Capacity: 500; Year Built: 1977
SID: David Alexander

ST. SCHOLASTICA
Duluth, MN 55811-4199..........III

Coach: David Staniger, St. Scholastica
1992

2001-02 RESULTS (8-16)
69	Benedictine (Ill.) †	79
54	Edgewood †	64
73	St. Thomas Aquinas †	77
72	Augsburg	90
56	Wis.-Superior ■	72
56	Viterbo	79
80	Upper Iowa †	83
62	Finlandia	74
67	Michigan Tech	112
71	North Cent. (Minn.) ■	68
85	Finlandia	75
60	Wis.-Eau Claire	93
73	Finlandia †	57
70	Presentation ■	71
90	Presentation	98
78	Northland	62
65	Martin Luther	56
94	Northwestern (Minn.) ■	93
85	Crown	87

83	Northland ■	67
71	Martin Luther ■	77
54	Northwestern (Minn.)	80
87	Crown ■	67
82	Presentation †	85

Nickname: Saints
Colors: Royal Blue & Gold
Arena: Reif Center
  Capacity: 1,500; Year Built: 1975
SID: Jen Walter

ST. THOMAS (MINN.)
St. Paul, MN 55105 III

Coach: Steve Fritz, St. Thomas (Minn.) 1971

2001-02 RESULTS (24-4)

70	Randolph-Macon †	63
76	Wooster	66
76	Northwestern (Minn.) ■	46
66	Wis.-River Falls	68
79	Bethel (Minn.) ■	71
84	Hamline ■	52
72	St. John's (Minn.)	75
62	Augsburg	49
73	Loras ■	61
76	St. Mary's (Minn.)	52
75	Gust. Adolphus ■	72
75	Concordia-M'head ■	53
64	St. Olaf ■	39
79	Macalester	56
86	Carleton ■	70
50	Bethel (Minn.)	73
86	Hamline	60
68	St. John's (Minn.) ■	62
64	St. Mary's (Minn.) ■	47
61	Gust. Adolphus	58
92	Augsburg ■	68
68	Concordia-M'head	60
91	St. Olaf ■	75
86	Macalester ■	80
59	Carleton	57
86	Macalester ■	77
73	Bethel (Minn.) ■	61
85	Wis.-Oshkosh ■	88

Nickname: Tommies
Colors: Purple & Grey
Arena: Schoenecker Arena
  Capacity: 2,200; Year Built: 1982
SID: Gene McGivern

ST. THOMAS AQUINAS
Sparkill, NY 10976 II

2001-02 RESULTS (11-16)

76	Siena Heights ■	78
60	St. Norbert †	77
77	St. Scholastica †	73
58	Philadelphia U.	61
70	C.W. Post ■	69
52	Adelphi ■	73
67	Molloy ■	65
92	Dowling ■	83
56	Southampton	62
77	Green Mountain †	67
44	New Haven †	55
58	NYIT ■	62
65	Mercy	52
73	Queens (N.Y.) ■	77
66	Bridgeport ■	60
59	C.W. Post	63
48	Adelphi ■	59
61	Molloy	58
50	Philadelphia U. ■	66
79	Dowling	87
63	Concordia (N.Y.)	66
64	NYIT	50
69	Queens (N.Y.)	75
53	Bridgeport	67
72	Concordia (N.Y.) ■	57
80	Southampton	91
88	Mercy ■	75

Nickname: Spartans
Colors: Maroon & Gold
SID: To be named

SALEM INT'L
Salem, WV 26426 II

Coach: Danny Young, Grand Canyon 1990

2001-02 RESULTS (26-5)

101	Ohio Valley ■	60
99	West Va. Tech ■	75
76	Emporia St. †	61
84	Adams St. †	74
103	Lees-McRae ■	71
81	Virginia St. ■	65
98	Davis & Elkins ■	59
98	Bluefield St. ■	69
74	Bluefield Col. ■	62
85	West Va. Wesleyan ■	70
103	Alderson-Broaddus ■	66
87	Shepherd	61
83	Glenville St.	78
73	Charleston (W.Va.) ■	76
87	West Liberty St.	96
73	Wheeling Jesuit	67
99	Ohio Valley ■	56
84	Fairmont St.	83
86	Davis & Elkins	65
84	Concord	57
92	West Virginia St.	82
76	West Va. Tech	55
93	West Liberty St. ■	75
69	Wheeling Jesuit	74
87	Ohio Valley	62
79	Fairmont St. ■	65
116	Bluefield St. ■	92
91	West Liberty St. †	66
71	Alderson-Broaddus †	77
75	Belmont Abbey †	69
81	Indiana (Pa.)	85

Nickname: Tigers
Colors: Kelly Green & White
Arena: T. Edward Davis Gym
  Capacity: 1,620
SID: David Zinn

SALEM ST.
Salem, MA 01970 III

Coach: Brian Meehan, Clark (Mass.) 1986

2001-02 RESULTS (21-7)

71	Scranton †	68
67	Frank. & Marsh.	77
96	Tufts	100
70	Plymouth St.	85
70	Babson	69
72	Gordon ■	80
82	Emerson ■	64
89	Southern Me. ■	80
99	Anna Maria ■	45
87	Mass.-Boston ■	70
72	MIT	52
75	Eastern Nazarene ■	67
71	Fitchburg St.	58
71	Westfield St.	82
85	Framingham St.	68
82	Mass. Liberal Arts ■	64
71	Bridgewater St.	62
83	Worcester St. ■	80
58	Mass.-Dartmouth	64
82	Fitchburg St. ■	55
86	Westfield St. ■	76
76	Framingham St.	56
84	Mass. Liberal Arts	80
92	Bridgewater St. ■	73
70	Worcester St.	67
76	Bridgewater St. ■	52
83	Framingham St. ■	60
89	Western Conn. St.	92

Nickname: Vikings
Colors: Orange & Blue
Arena: O'Keefe Sports Center
  Capacity: 2,200; Year Built: 1976
SID: Thomas Roundy

SALISBURY
Salisbury, MD 21801-6860 III

Coach: Steve Holmes, Plattsburgh St. 1983

2001-02 RESULTS (8-17)

88	Christendom †	35
106	Shenandoah	108
86	Washington (Md.)	71
58	Marymount (Va.)	70
71	Neumann ■	83
88	Lincoln (Pa.)	77
53	Mary Washington	65
47	Frank. & Marsh.	66
69	Chris. Newport ■	83
74	Va. Wesleyan ■	71
59	FDU-Madison †	65
69	Moravian	85
79	Catholic ■	90
79	St. Mary's (Md.)	75
69	Gallaudet	71
81	York (Pa.) ■	91
90	Goucher ■	78
72	Mary Washington ■	77
71	Marymount (Va.) ■	74
89	St. Mary's (Md.) ■	74
64	Catholic	75
61	York (Pa.)	66
54	Gallaudet ■	59
58	Goucher	56
78	Marymount (Va.)	83

Nickname: Sea Gulls
Colors: Maroon & Gold
Arena: Maggs Activities Center
  Capacity: 2,000; Year Built: 1977
SID: Paul Ohanian

SALVE REGINA
Newport, RI 02840-4192 III

Coach: Michael Plansky, Fairfield 1991

2001-02 RESULTS (20-9)

89	Eastern Conn. St.	78
55	Ithaca †	63
82	Rhode Island Col.	62
68	WPI	47
59	Mass.-Dartmouth ■	54
77	Wheaton (Mass.)	83
75	Johnson & Wales ■	66
91	New England Col.	74
87	Western New Eng.	79
54	Connecticut Col.	69
91	New England	75
84	Curry ■	74
59	Gordon	66
84	Wentworth Inst.	79
67	Roger Williams ■	69
74	Colby-Sawyer ■	67
80	Suffolk	73
71	Bridgewater St. ■	62
70	Anna Maria	60
56	Amherst ■	75
71	Eastern Nazarene	59
83	Nichols ■	72
51	Endicott ■	49
66	Babson ■	68
69	Eastern Nazarene ■	51
62	Endicott ■	50
54	Colby-Sawyer	69
83	Johnson & Wales ■	76
68	Mass.-Dartmouth ■	88

Nickname: Seahawks
Colors: Blue, Green & White
Arena: Rogers Gymnasium
  Capacity: 4,000
SID: Ed Habershaw

SAM HOUSTON ST.
Huntsville, TX 77340 I

Coach: Bob Marlin, Mississippi St. 1981

2001-02 RESULTS (14-14)

70	Southeastern La. ■	71
65	Drake †	74
90	Norfolk St. †	71
69	Texas Tech	65
80	Northern Ill. †	73
58	Marquette	77
81	La.-Monroe ■	73
74	Nebraska	70
67	Southwest Tex. ■	70
74	Texas-San Antonio	90
59	Chattanooga	76
77	Bradley †	67
76	McNeese St. ■	75
87	Lamar	89
72	Texas-Arlington	75
49	Stephen F. Austin	45
84	Nicholls St. ■	43
61	La.-Monroe	87
98	Northwestern St.	83
96	Southwest Tex. St. ■	82
75	Texas-San Antonio ■	82
74	Northwestern St. ■	79
69	Southeastern La.	70
80	Nicholls St.	65
102	Texas-Arlington ■	94
71	Stephen F. Austin ■	61
68	McNeese St.	79
58	Lamar ■	64

Nickname: Bearkats
Colors: Orange & White
Arena: Johnson Coliseum
  Capacity: 6,110; Year Built: 1976
SID: Paul Ridings

SAMFORD
Birmingham, AL 35229 I

Coach: Jimmy Tillette, Lady/Holy Cross 1975

2001-02 RESULTS (15-14)

72	Loyola Marymount †	60
51	Alabama	83
62	La.-Monroe ■	53
55	Georgia	61
69	Mercer	60
68	Troy St.	65
54	Illinois St.	65
68	Fla. Atlantic ■	66
59	UCF	58
62	Morehead St. ■	50
37	Butler †	45
48	Eastern Wash. †	59
57	Jacksonville St. ■	59
89	Stetson	67
65	Jacksonville	58
60	Belmont	66
69	Campbell ■	55
63	Georgia St. ■	59
56	Jacksonville St.	59
53	Campbell	56
48	Georgia St.	60
62	Belmont ■	64
52	Jacksonville ■	51
57	Stetson ■	50
56	UCF	72
68	Fla. Atlantic	50
52	Troy St. ■	64
69	Mercer ■	49
74	UCF	84

Nickname: Bulldogs
Colors: Red & Blue
Arena: Seibert Hall
  Capacity: 4,000; Year Built: 1957
SID: Craig Threlkeld

SAN DIEGO
San Diego, CA 92110-2492......I

Coach: Brad Holland, UCLA 1979
2001-02 RESULTS (16-13)
59	Brigham Young ■	70
89	UC San Diego ■	62
74	Portland St.	59
56	Oregon St.	65
94	Washington ■	98
72	San Diego St. ■	67
85	Boise St. ■	59
63	UC Irvine ■	52
67	Southern California ■	71
81	Southern Ore. ■	47
70	Troy St. †	63
59	Montana St.	68
82	Cal St. Northridge ■	66
65	Portland	64
62	Gonzaga	75
82	Santa Clara	73
77	Santa Clara	86
73	Loyola Marymount ■	60
91	Pepperdine ■	96
71	San Francisco	87
60	St. Mary's (Cal.)	63
103	Portland ■	80
76	Gonzaga ■	77
76	St. Mary's (Cal.) ■	72
88	San Francisco ■	55
79	Pepperdine	90
87	Loyola Marymount	71
69	San Francisco ■	67
79	Gonzaga ■	87

Nickname: Toreros
Colors: Columbia Blue, Navy & White
Arena: Jenny Craig Pavilion
   Capacity: 5,100; Year Built: 2000
SID: Ted Gosen

SAN DIEGO ST.
San Diego, CA 92182...............I

Coach: Steve Fisher, Illinois St. 1967
2001-02 RESULTS (21-12)
71	Northern Iowa †	57
71	Texas Tech	81
78	Norfolk St. ■	71
79	New Mexico St.	94
98	UC San Diego ■	53
80	Cal St. Northridge ■	70
67	San Diego	72
93	Fresno St. ■	58
61	Hawaii	58
86	Eastern Wash. ■	58
79	Duke	92
75	Columbia ■	59
90	IPFW ■	72
82	Tex. A&M-Corp. Chris.	79
64	Brigham Young	75
70	Utah	76
81	Colorado St. ■	69
85	Wyoming ■	88
79	UNLV ■	80
78	Houston	66
78	New Mexico	65
54	Air Force	67
53	Utah ■	70
77	Brigham Young ■	73
75	Colorado St.	63
68	Wyoming	64
76	UNLV	83
84	New Mexico ■	71
49	Air Force ■	47
62	Brigham Young †	51
70	Wyoming †	69
78	UNLV	75
64	Illinois †	93

Nickname: Aztecs
Colors: Scarlet & Black
Arena: Cox Arena
   Capacity: 12,414; Year Built: 1997
SID: Mike May

SAN FRANCISCO
San Francisco, CA 94117-1080.I

Coach: Philip Mathews, UC Irvine 1972
2001-02 RESULTS (13-15)
79	Seton Hall ■	87
70	Cal St. Fullerton	43
49	UC Santa Barb. ■	69
59	Nevada	84
72	Xavier ■	87
65	Fresno St.	75
94	Cal St. Hayward ■	59
69	Pacific (Cal.)	72
75	Tex. A&M-Corp. Chris.	80
93	Southern U.	78
55	Michigan †	47
51	Brigham Young	65
65	Tex. A&M-Corp. Chris. ■	63
75	Loyola Marymount ■	66
68	Pepperdine ■	74
63	St. Mary's (Cal.)	46
84	St. Mary's (Cal.) ■	67
73	Gonzaga	93
77	Portland	69
87	San Diego ■	71
77	Santa Clara	59
72	Pepperdine	79
80	Loyola Marymount ■	67
67	Santa Clara	77
55	San Diego	88
54	Gonzaga ■	70
97	Portland ■	81
67	San Diego	69

Nickname: Dons
Colors: Green & Gold
Arena: War Memorial Gymnasium
   Capacity: 5,300; Year Built: 1958
SID: Peter Simon

SAN FRAN. ST.
San Francisco, CA 94132.........II

Coach: Charlie Thomas, Virginia Tech 1978
2001-02 RESULTS (15-13)
63	Dominican (Cal.)	67
64	Holy Names ■	58
83	Humboldt St.	103
61	Hawaii-Hilo	63
51	Chaminade	64
80	Grand Canyon	85
71	UC San Diego	62
71	Cal St. Chico ■	68
69	UC Davis	70
77	Sonoma St.	72
54	Cal St. Bakersfield ■	59
63	Cal St. Stanislaus	68
73	Cal St. Los Angeles	64
73	Cal St. Dom. Hills	71
44	Cal Poly Pomona	69
47	Cal St. San B'dino	68
66	Sonoma St. ■	64
82	UC San Diego ■	65
80	Grand Canyon ■	73
79	Cal St. Chico	71
57	UC Davis	71
82	Cal St. Stanislaus	71
58	Cal St. Bakersfield	70
64	Cal St. Dom. Hills ■	61
66	Cal St. Los Angeles ■	55
61	Cal St. San B'dino ■	80
67	Cal Poly Pomona ■	63

Nickname: Gators
Colors: Purple & Gold
Arena: SFSU Main Gym
   Capacity: 2,000; Year Built: 1949
SID: Jon Fuller

SAN JOSE ST.
San Jose, CA 95192 I

Coach: Steve Barnes, Azusa Pacific 1981
2001-02 RESULTS (10-22)
65	Fairleigh Dickinson †	57
56	North Carolina St.	78
51	Northwestern †	59
62	Sacramento St. ■	60
63	Santa Clara ■	65
59	Neb.-Omaha †	65
64	Iowa St.	62
51	St. Mary's (Cal.) †	59
59	Pacific (Cal.)	74
78	Notre Dame de Namur ■	65
70	Vanguard ■	72
91	Mt. St. Mary's ■	72
85	Nevada	91
68	Fresno St. ■	80
52	Boise St.	61
65	UTEP	66
66	Southern Methodist ■	68
61	Louisiana Tech	78
57	Hawaii ■	53
54	Tulsa	78
58	Rice	70
67	UTEP ■	62
62	Boise St. ■	51
53	Louisiana Tech	77
55	Southern Methodist	84
46	Hawaii	71
46	Rice ■	62
72	Tulsa ■	82
60	Fresno St.	72
76	Nevada	72
58	Rice †	57
56	Hawaii †	71

Nickname: Spartans
Colors: Gold, White & Blue
Arena: The Event Center
   Capacity: 5,000; Year Built: 1989
SID: Lawrence Fan

SANTA CLARA
Santa Clara, CA 95053..............I

Coach: Dick Davey, Pacific (Cal.) 1964
2001-02 RESULTS (13-15)
83	Pacific (Cal.) ■	85
60	California	67
49	Washington	69
65	San Jose St. ■	63
53	Nevada	78
41	Ohio St.	88
62	Wright St.	76
63	Portland St. †	76
71	Belmont †	78
92	Cal St. Chico ■	67
59	UMBC ■	58
61	UC Santa Barb. ■	59
68	Loyola (Md.) ■	50
81	Gonzaga	83
84	Portland	73
73	San Diego ■	82
86	San Diego	77
67	Pepperdine ■	74
74	Loyola Marymount ■	64
63	St. Mary's (Cal.)	60
59	San Francisco	77
69	Gonzaga ■	84
75	Portland ■	58
77	San Francisco ■	67
56	St. Mary's (Cal.) †	49
67	Loyola Marymount	59
58	Pepperdine	96
67	St. Mary's (Cal.) †	72

Nickname: Broncos
Colors: Santa Clara Red & White
Arena: Leavey Center
   Capacity: 5,000; Year Built: 1975
SID: Richard Kilwien

SAVANNAH A&D
Savannah, GA 31402-3146.....III

Coach: Cazzie Russell, Michigan 1966
2001-02 RESULTS (13-12)
76	DePauw †	94
67	Earlham †	64
84	Methodist ■	73
79	Pomona-Pitzer	63
66	Claremont-M-S	64
71	Lakeland †	61
50	Carthage	66
71	Texas Lutheran	58
67	Mary Hardin-Baylor	58
78	Concordia-Austin	83
92	Maryville (Mo.)	89
57	Fontbonne	77
55	Chris. Newport	68
72	York (N.Y.) †	65
59	Montclair St.	64
69	Averett †	61
54	Roanoke	66
56	Methodist	64
73	Rust ■	54
72	Fisk	80
71	St. Mary's (Md.)	59
54	Mt. St. Joseph	78
86	Huntingdon ■	44
68	Rust	85
54	Maryville (Tenn.)	86

Nickname: Bees
Colors: Black, White & Gold
Arena: Savannah Civic Center
   Capacity: 7,500; Year Built: 1974
SID: Michael MacEachern

SAVANNAH ST.
Savannah, GA 31404 II

2001-02 RESULTS (2-26)
54	Southern Methodist	74
41	Florida St.	93
39	Iowa St.	64
35	Pittsburgh	87
52	Armstrong Atlantic	68
63	Ga. Southern	86
49	Jacksonville	91
51	Armstrong Atlantic ■	53
56	Weber St.	87
52	Fresno St.	91
55	Jacksonville ■	58
47	Nebraska	66
71	Lipscomb ■	60
52	Bethune-Cookman ■	65
54	Morris Brown ■	48
57	Alabama A&M ■	68
68	Lipscomb	76
55	Jacksonville St. ■	64
44	Birmingham-So. ■	47
41	Ga. Southern	80
63	Jacksonville St.	83
67	Gardner-Webb ■	75
57	Morris Brown	65
53	Alabama A&M	95
62	Tex. A&M-Corp. Chris. ■	77
50	Gardner-Webb	79
47	Birmingham-So.	82
66	Tex. A&M-Corp. Chris.	96

Nickname: Tigers
Colors: Reflex Blue & Orange
Arena: Wiley Gym
   Capacity: 2,100; Year Built: 1964
SID: Lee Pearson

SCHREINER
Kerrville, TX 78028 III

2001-02 RESULTS (4-20)
71	Southwest Tex. St.	108
93	Houston Baptist ■	98
75	Colorado Col.	65

81	Benedictine (Ill.) †	87
79	Ozarks (Ark.)	93
58	Austin	63
68	Houston Baptist	106
79	Tex.-Pan American	107
75	Dallas	68
76	Texas-Dallas ■	82
90	Texas Lutheran ■	108
78	Mary Hardin-Baylor ■	95
93	Concordia-Austin ■	108
69	Sul Ross St.	89
81	Howard Payne	96
105	Hardin-Simmons ■	90
94	McMurry ■	104
108	Hardin-Simmons	91
66	McMurry	100
59	Mary Hardin-Baylor	106
65	Concordia-Austin	102
75	Sul Ross St. ■	90
93	Howard Payne ■	99
65	Texas Lutheran	89

Nickname: Mountaineers
Colors: Maroon & White
SID: Stacey Patsko

SCRANTON
Scranton, PA 18510 III

Coach: Carl Danzig, Baker 1987
2001-02 RESULTS (12-13)
68	Salem St. †	71
103	Springfield †	104
82	Connecticut Col.	77
83	Catholic	90
87	Moravian	84
73	Elizabethtown	88
72	Delaware Valley	55
81	Drew ■	50
57	Kean	73
47	Lafayette	90
81	Pitt.-Bradford ■	83
84	Hunter ■	70
61	FDU-Madison	66
68	King's (Pa.) ■	62
72	DeSales ■	71
86	Wilkes	65
59	Lycoming ■	58
61	Drew	60
76	Delaware Valley ■	58
68	King's (Pa.)	79
79	FDU-Madison ■	65
78	DeSales	91
74	Lycoming	77
67	Wilkes ■	80
67	Lycoming	70

Nickname: Royals
Colors: Purple & White
Arena: John Long Center
   Capacity: 2,800; Year Built: 1968
SID: Kevin Southard

SEATTLE
Seattle, WA 98122-4340.,........II

Coach: Joe Callero, Central Wash. 1986
2001-02 RESULTS (6-23)
76	Northwest (Wash.)	84
49	Seattle Pacific ■	64
59	Evergreen St.	71
51	Cal St. Bakersfield †	70
40	Northwest Mo. St. †	76
70	Northwest (Wash.)	51
75	Western Ore.	61
71	Humboldt St. ■	74
57	Northwest Nazarene	62
79	Pacific Lutheran	91
60	Lewis-Clark St. †	72
51	Tex. A&M-Commerce †	72
84	Western Wash.	86
67	Seattle Pacific	72
47	St. Martin's ■	59
83	Central Wash. ■	73

73	Northwest Nazarene ■	82
53	Alas. Anchorage	73
48	Alas. Fairbanks	54
67	Humboldt St.	82
57	Western Ore.	61
46	Seattle Pacific ■	72
61	Western Wash. ■	76
50	Central Wash.	61
57	St. Martin's	53
74	Mich.-Dearborn †	67
52	Briar Cliff	62
69	Alas. Fairbanks ■	74
79	Alas. Anchorage ■	68

Nickname: Redhawks
Colors: Scarlet & White
SID: To be named

SEATTLE PACIFIC
Seattle, WA 98119-1997 II

Coach: Ken Bone, Seattle Pacific 1983
2001-02 RESULTS (24-5)
67	Indianapolis ■	68
87	Lock Haven ■	59
64	Seattle	49
103	Northwest (Wash.) ■	66
86	Hawaii Pacific	56
101	Central Wash.	100
73	St. Martin's	46
68	Henderson St. †	63
76	Ashland †	63
78	Tex. A&M-Commerce ■	62
80	Lewis-Clark St.	64
85	Northwest Nazarene	64
72	Seattle ■	67
96	Western Wash. ■	89
81	Alas. Fairbanks ■	56
95	Alas. Anchorage ■	64
78	Humboldt St.	84
73	Western Ore.	57
74	St. Martin's ■	59
84	Central Wash. ■	59
72	Seattle	46
86	Northwest Nazarene	83
80	Western Wash.	88
95	Alas. Anchorage ■	86
97	Alas. Fairbanks ■	62
74	Western Ore. ■	77
81	Humboldt St. ■	78
82	BYU-Hawaii †	57
82	Humboldt St. †	89

Nickname: Falcons
Colors: Maroon & White
Arena: Brougham Pavilion
   Capacity: 2,650; Year Built: 1953
SID: Frank MacDonald

SETON HALL
South Orange, NJ 07079 I

Coach: Louis Orr, Syracuse 1980
2001-02 RESULTS (12-18)
87	San Francisco	79
79	Duke ■	80
74	Chaminade	62
62	Kansas †	80
72	Monmouth ■	51
78	Rider	66
78	St. Peter's ■	63
95	Fairleigh Dickinson ■	73
68	La Salle ■	71
64	Michigan St.	68
70	Iona †	73
66	Fordham †	57
66	Boston College ■	81
80	Virginia Tech	72
70	Syracuse	85
67	Rutgers ■	54
58	Georgetown	84
81	West Virginia ■	67
51	Notre Dame	60
63	St. John's (N.Y.) ■	61

61	Notre Dame ■	63
65	Pittsburgh	70
85	West Virginia	79
77	Georgetown ■	84
65	Illinois ■	75
71	Syracuse ■	73
60	Rutgers	66
66	Pittsburgh ■	73
78	Connecticut	90
58	St. John's (N.Y.) †	64

Nickname: Pirates
Colors: Blue & White
Arena: Continental Airlines Arena
   Capacity: 20,029; Year Built: 1981
SID: Marie Wozniak

SEWANEE
Sewanee, TN 37383-1000.......III

Coach: Joe Thoni, Sewanee 1979
2001-02 RESULTS (11-14)
91	Kenyon ■	71
60	Piedmont ■	55
87	Emory ■	70
49	Rose-Hulman	66
61	DePauw	80
45	Centre	67
77	Emory	88
43	Birmingham-So.	77
56	Huntingdon ■	48
74	Hendrix ■	47
61	Rhodes ■	59
87	Oglethorpe ■	81
63	Millsaps	72
65	Southwestern (Tex.) ■	60
59	Trinity (Tex.) ■	68
67	Maryville (Tenn.) ■	66
52	Centre	69
58	Hendrix	67
62	Rhodes	65
80	Oglethorpe ■	56
59	Millsaps ■	58
56	Southwestern (Tex.)	57
63	Trinity (Tex.)	73
69	Rose-Hulman ■	72
70	DePauw ■	87

Nickname: Tigers
Colors: Purple & White
Arena: Juhan Gymnasium
   Capacity: 1,000; Year Built: 1955
SID: Larry Dagenhart

SHAW
Raleigh, NC 27601 II

Coach: Joel Hopkins, N.C. Central 1999
2001-02 RESULTS (28-5)
86	Kennesaw St. ■	77
100	N.C. Central ■	80
75	West Ga. †	67
95	North Greenville †	66
85	Clark Atlanta	61
73	Presbyterian	78
104	Alderson-Broaddus ■	75
69	Quincy	65
71	Tampa †	68
90	Elizabeth City St.	65
107	St. Augustine's ■	86
86	Bowie St.	77
84	Virginia St.	75
69	Winston-Salem ■	76
96	St. Paul's ■	76
90	Fayetteville St.	92
82	Livingstone ■	62
78	Virginia Union	63
85	Elizabeth City St. ■	70
87	St. Paul's	76
87	Bowie St.	94
122	Virginia Union ■	81
102	Johnson Smith ■	99
99	Virginia St. ■	81
87	N.J. Inst. of Tech. ■	71

101	N.C. Central †	75
80	Winston-Salem †	65
82	Johnson Smith †	68
62	Winston-Salem †	61
69	Carson-Newman	68
102	West Ga. †	84
92	Ky. Wesleyan †	101

Nickname: Bears
Colors: Maroon & White
Arena: Spaulding Gym
   Capacity: 1,000; Year Built: 1946
SID: To be named

SHENANDOAH
Winchester, VA 22601 III

Coach: Robert Harris, Shenandoah 1991
2001-02 RESULTS (15-12)
124	Valley Forge Chrst. ■	53
108	Salisbury ■	106
71	Liberty	88
68	East. Mennonite	73
78	Southern Va.	68
92	Frostburg St.	81
86	Southern Va. ■	93
60	East Tenn. St.	110
83	Elizabethtown	99
64	Cabrini	74
57	Chris. Newport	62
100	Averett ■	80
74	Ferrum	69
79	N.C. Wesleyan	84
81	Chowan ■	72
67	Methodist	74
72	Greensboro	63
73	Chris. Newport ■	58
74	Averett	45
68	Ferrum	75
64	N.C. Wesleyan ■	69
82	Chowan	67
91	Villa Julie ■	78
75	Greensboro ■	73
88	Methodist ■	66
63	Greensboro ■	62
68	Chris. Newport †	90

Nickname: Hornets
Colors: Red, White & Midnight Blue
Arena: Shingleton Gymnasium
   Capacity: 680; Year Built: 1969
SID: Scott Musa

SHEPHERD
Shepherdstown, WV 25443-3210 II

Coach: Ken Tyler, William & Mary 1987
2001-02 RESULTS (10-17)
48	Dist. Columbia	83
46	Marshall	96
65	Columbia Union ■	52
82	Davis & Elkins ■	71
86	Mt. Aloysius ■	57
54	St. Augustine's	79
85	Bowie St.	98
83	Wheeling Jesuit	66
79	West Liberty St.	83
61	Salem Int'l ■	87
61	Fairmont St.	59
66	Alderson-Broaddus ■	70
57	West Va. Tech	72
66	Charleston (W.Va.)	79
84	Bluefield St. ■	74
74	Concord	64
83	West Virginia St.	86
77	Ohio Valley ■	63
63	Glenville St. ■	71
85	Dist. Columbia ■	81
80	Davis & Elkins	67
75	West Va. Wesleyan	78
75	Glenville St.	77
60	Columbia Union	75

81	Alderson-Broaddus	90
56	West Va. Wesleyan ■	68
62	Fairmont St.	78

Nickname: Rams
Colors: Blue & Gold
Arena: Butcher Athletic Center
Capacity: 3,500; Year Built: 1989
SID: Chip Ransom

SHIPPENSBURG
Shippensburg, PA 17257 II

Coach: Dave Springer, Ohio 1982
2001-02 RESULTS (9-17)

42	Clarion	72
78	Felician ■	67
74	West Liberty St. ■	64
64	East Stroudsburg	55
81	Millersville ■	77
80	Dickinson ■	72
67	Mansfield ■	74
73	Bloomsburg	83
72	Hillsdale	83
40	Northern Mich. †	60
83	East Stroudsburg ■	51
62	Kutztown ■	64
65	Cheyney	82
51	West Chester	77
57	Indiana (Pa.) ■	92
66	Edinboro	74
68	Calif. (Pa.)	91
73	Slippery Rock ■	74
46	Lock Haven	56
79	Clarion ■	74
56	Indiana (Pa.)	63
56	Calif. (Pa.) ■	76
91	Lock Haven ■	83
75	Edinboro	83
54	Pitt.-Johnstown	57
65	Slippery Rock	62

Nickname: Red Raiders
Colors: Red & Blue
Arena: Heiges Field House
Capacity: 2,768; Year Built: 1970
SID: John Alosi

SIENA
Loudonville, NY 12211-1462 I

Coach: Rob Lanier, St. Bonaventure 1990
2001-02 RESULTS (17-19)

54	Providence	79
62	Austin Peay †	44
64	Oklahoma St. †	82
91	Northwestern St. †	99
69	Fordham	78
60	Albany (N.Y.) ■	48
66	Cleveland St.	83
61	Toledo ■	64
69	Marist	77
77	Niagara ■	65
68	Hartford ■	52
74	St. Bonaventure ■	78
60	Rice	71
59	Xavier	68
79	Iona	70
64	Rider ■	63
82	Loyola (Md.) ■	76
73	St. Peter's ■	59
64	Manhattan ■	69
68	Canisius	76
79	Iona ■	71
73	Niagara	74
63	Canisius ■	43
70	Manhattan	75
68	Loyola (Md.) ■	58
72	Fairfield	79
73	St. Peter's	55
57	Fairfield ■	60
56	Rider	62
57	Marist ■	60

77	St. Peter's †	66
82	Marist †	76
83	Fairfield †	63
92	Niagara †	77
81	Alcorn St. †	77
70	Maryland †	85

Nickname: Saints
Colors: Green & Gold
Arena: Pepsi Arena
Capacity: 15,500; Year Built: 1990
SID: Jason Rich

SIMPSON
Indianola, IA 50125 III

Coach: Bruce Wilson, Simpson 1976
2001-02 RESULTS (14-12)

70	Manchester †	65
57	Heidelberg †	62
70	Neb. Wesleyan	77
73	Gust. Adolphus †	87
76	Upper Iowa	73
78	Graceland (Iowa) ■	62
60	Wartburg ■	63
68	Buena Vista ■	80
74	Wis.-River Falls ■	82
50	South Dakota	79
82	Central (Iowa)	75
60	Luther	58
74	Cornell College	76
78	Coe ■	71
75	Loras ■	54
73	Dubuque ■	57
64	Luther ■	40
83	Buena Vista	88
71	Wartburg	79
79	Central (Iowa) ■	67
80	Upper Iowa ■	62
89	Coe ■	70
78	Cornell College ■	60
71	Dubuque	35
69	Loras	97
76	Cornell College ■	79

Nickname: Storm
Colors: Red & Gold
Arena: Cowles Fieldhouse
Capacity: 3,000; Year Built: 1976
SID: Matt Turk

SKIDMORE
Saratoga Springs, NY 12866 ...III

Coach: John Quattrocchi, Albany (N.Y.) 1973
2001-02 RESULTS (6-19)

66	Norwich †	64
70	Plattsburgh St.	80
64	Middlebury ■	73
74	CCNY	78
75	Plattsburgh St. ■	67
81	St. Joseph (Vt.) ■	72
69	Hartwick	74
64	Utica	65
75	Manhattanville ■	71
65	Centenary (N.J.) ■	55
52	Union (N.Y.)	70
74	St. Lawrence	80
67	Clarkson	90
57	Hobart ■	86
82	Hamilton ■	95
63	Oswego St. ■	74
84	Vassar	87
47	Rensselaer ■	63
67	Hamilton	80
65	Hobart	96
55	Clarkson ■	65
66	St. Lawrence ■	82
68	Union (N.Y.) ■	75
54	Rensselaer	60
52	Vassar	46

Nickname: Thoroughbreds
Colors: Green, White & Gold

Arena: Sports & Recreation Center
Capacity: 1,500; Year Built: 1982
SID: Bill Jones

SLIPPERY ROCK
Slippery Rock, PA 16057 II

Coach: Anthony Jones, Illinois St. 1981
2001-02 RESULTS (7-19)

67	Youngstown St.	99
78	Geneva ■	85
64	Goldey-Beacom	53
75	Kutztown	73
48	East Stroudsburg	61
56	St. Vincent	72
81	Glenville St. ■	71
69	La Roche	68
48	Millersville	70
59	West Chester ■	69
47	Cheyney ■	63
49	Lock Haven ■	61
43	Bloomsburg ■	65
73	Mansfield ■	67
70	Calif. (Pa.)	85
60	Indiana (Pa.) ■	75
74	Shippensburg	73
55	Clarion ■	77
48	Lock Haven	64
66	Edinboro	80
56	Calif. (Pa.) ■	67
50	Indiana (Pa.)	67
60	Clarion	74
68	Pitt.-Johnstown ■	60
64	Edinboro ■	75
62	Shippensburg ■	65

Nickname: The Rock
Colors: Green & White
Arena: Morrow Field House
Capacity: 3,000; Year Built: 1962
SID: Bob McComas

SONOMA ST.
Rohnert Park, CA 94928-3609 ..II

Coach: Pat Fuscaldo, San Fran. St. 1983
2001-02 RESULTS (11-16)

76	Central Wash. †	87
79	Dominican (Cal.) †	61
79	Cal St. Monterey Bay ■	61
91	Humboldt St. ■	98
92	Grand Canyon	84
74	UC San Diego	65
90	Cal St. Chico ■	60
73	UC Davis ■	70
72	San Fran. St.	77
64	Humboldt St.	76
71	Cal St. Stanislaus ■	53
68	Cal St. Bakersfield ■	75
57	Cal St. Dom. Hills ■	64
52	Cal St. Los Angeles	70
52	Cal St. San B'dino	67
54	Cal Poly Pomona	59
64	San Fran. St.	66
72	Grand Canyon ■	76
76	UC San Diego ■	69
51	UC Davis	77
102	Cal St. Chico	89
53	Cal St. Bakersfield	72
70	Cal St. Stanislaus	65
72	Cal St. Los Angeles ■	69
62	Cal St. Dom. Hills ■	72
62	Cal Poly Pomona ■	67
56	Cal St. San B'dino ■	69

Nickname: Cossacks
Colors: Navy, Blue & White
Arena: Cossack Gymnasium
Capacity: 1,800; Year Built: 1968
SID: Mitch Cox

SOUTH ALA.
Mobile, AL 36688 I

Coach: Bob Weltlich, Ohio St. 1967
2001-02 RESULTS (7-21)

38	Louisville	92
70	Marist	80
64	Valdosta St. ■	56
71	Southeastern La. ■	43
66	Mississippi St.	73
66	Southern Miss. ■	76
68	Bethune-Cookman ■	55
70	Georgia ■	79
58	Auburn	73
66	Gardner-Webb ■	71
59	Middle Tenn. ■	51
61	Western Ky. ■	58
54	La.-Lafayette	75
63	New Mexico St.	80
68	Arkansas St. ■	74
44	New Orleans ■	62
65	Ark.-Little Rock	72
56	Florida Int'l	66
76	Georgia Southwestern ■	67
68	La.-Lafayette ■	73
74	New Mexico St. ■	78
58	Denver	76
73	North Texas	77
60	Denver ■	64
67	New Orleans	78
104	Bethune-Cookman	99
72	North Texas ■	78
47	Middle Tenn. †	48

Nickname: Jaguars
Colors: Red, White and Blue
Arena: Mitchell Center
Capacity: 10,000; Year Built: 1999
SID: Matt Smith

SOUTH CAROLINA
Columbia, SC 29208 I

Coach: Dave Odom, Guilford 1965
2001-02 RESULTS (22-15)

74	Chaminade †	61
56	Duke †	81
77	UCLA †	89
83	East Tenn. St. ■	66
64	Wofford	49
66	Colorado St. ■	58
67	Providence ■	48
68	Georgetown ■	70
81	Clemson	59
69	South Carolina St. ■	50
73	Citadel ■	57
86	Charleston So. ■	41
88	Mercer ■	52
60	Florida	69
50	Kentucky ■	51
62	Arkansas	60
51	Vanderbilt ■	60
94	Tennessee	60
53	Mississippi	71
80	Georgia ■	67
74	Kentucky	91
63	Florida ■	72
72	Tennessee ■	54
51	Alabama ■	52
66	Vanderbilt	43
66	LSU ■	53
46	Auburn	50
75	Georgia	82
57	Mississippi St. ■	64
69	Mississippi †	67
70	Kentucky †	57
57	Alabama †	65
74	Virginia	67
75	UNLV ■	65
82	Ball St. ■	47
66	Syracuse †	59
62	Memphis †	72

Nickname: Gamecocks
Colors: Garnet & Black
Arena: The Carolina Center
   Capacity: 18,000; Year Built: 2002
SID: Brian Binette

SOUTH CAROLINA ST.
Orangeburg, SC 29117-0001....I

Coach: Cy Alexander, Catawba 1975

2001-02 RESULTS (15-16)

65	Tennessee Tech	79
48	Colorado St. †	66
61	Mercer †	72
69	Hawaii-Hilo	87
63	Delaware St. ■	78
63	Howard ■	58
75	Wake Forest	115
89	Coastal Caro.	81
73	Kansas	106
50	South Carolina	69
91	West Virginia St. †	62
71	Winthrop	58
81	Citadel ■	89
78	Bethune-Cookman	75
72	Florida A&M	69
75	Hampton ■	81
75	Norfolk St.	51
67	Md.-East. Shore	70
54	Coppin St.	50
81	Morgan St. ■	73
71	N.C. A&T	76
61	Delaware St.	55
72	Howard	81
59	Bethune-Cookman ■	61
73	Florida A&M ■	72
73	Hampton	87
86	Norfolk St.	82
72	Md.-East. Shore ■	69
59	N.C. A&T ■	58
63	N.C. A&T †	61
70	Hampton †	80

Nickname: Bulldogs
Colors: Garnet & Blue
Arena: SHM Memorial Center
   Capacity: 3,200; Year Built: 1968
SID: Bill Hamilton

S.C.-AIKEN
Aiken, SC 29801 II

Coach: Mike Roberts, Elon 1977

2001-02 RESULTS (12-16)

78	St. Andrews	57
77	Newberry ■	65
67	Presbyterian ■	66
67	UNC Pembroke	76
68	Augusta St. ■	72
70	Carson-Newman	87
61	Carson-Newman ■	67
56	St. Leo ■	51
77	Anderson (S.C.) ■	86
70	Clayton St. ■	72
75	Francis Marion	72
59	Armstrong Atlantic	56
65	S.C.-Spartanburg ■	66
59	Kennesaw St.	71
65	Columbus St. ■	78
63	North Fla.	80
71	Lander	67
77	North Fla. ■	71
70	Columbus St.	72
64	Lander ■	62
62	GC&SU ■	61
65	UNC Pembroke ■	78
49	S.C.-Spartanburg	58
61	Kennesaw St. ■	64
72	Francis Marion ■	86
65	Augusta St.	61
92	North Fla. †	91
61	Clayton St. †	77

Nickname: Pacers
Colors: Cardinal & White
Arena: The Courthouse
   Capacity: 2,500; Year Built: 1977
SID: Brad Fields

S.C.-SPARTANBURG
Spartanburg, SC 29303-4999...II

Coach: Gary Nottingham, Glenville St.
1979

2001-02 RESULTS (11-16)

77	North Greenville ■	75
53	Limestone ■	66
67	Newberry ■	60
41	Tusculum	53
79	Columbus St. ■	83
62	Presbyterian	59
57	Lander	64
40	Tusculum ■	41
52	East Caro.	64
53	Armstrong Atlantic	60
59	Clayton St. ■	64
68	Lander ■	65
61	S.C.-Aiken ■	65
56	UNC Pembroke	66
64	Armstrong Atlantic ■	76
72	Francis Marion	49
67	Kennesaw St.	69
75	GC&SU ■	74
55	Augusta St.	62
82	Francis Marion ■	83
61	North Fla.	67
57	Augusta St. ■	51
66	Clayton St.	71
58	S.C.-Aiken ■	49
81	UNC Pembroke ■	74
58	GC&SU	49
60	Armstrong Atlantic †	68

Nickname: Rifles
Colors: Green, White & Black
Arena: G.B. Hodge Center
   Capacity: 1,535; Year Built: 1973
SID: Bill English

SOUTH DAKOTA
Vermillion, SD 57069-2390.......II

Coach: Dave Boots, Augsburg 1979

2001-02 RESULTS (19-8)

98	Mo. Western St. ■	85
96	Minn.-Morris	69
100	Mt. Senario ■	36
94	Southwest St. †	87
104	Western St. (Colo.) †	78
81	St. Cloud St.	97
80	Minn. St.-Mankato	72
75	Bellevue ■	40
76	Dakota Wesleyan ■	57
79	Simpson ■	50
90	Augustana (S.D.) ■	73
75	South Dakota St. ■	85
67	Northern Colo.	63
70	Neb.-Omaha	77
78	North Dakota ■	65
69	North Dakota St. ■	63
103	Morningside	75
71	South Dakota St.	81
71	Augustana (S.D.)	78
82	Neb.-Omaha ■	77
98	Northern Colo. ■	87
86	North Dakota St.	73
75	North Dakota	87
106	Morningside ■	39
94	Minn. St.-Mankato ■	53
60	St. Cloud St. ■	73
90	St. Cloud St.	95

Nickname: Coyotes
Colors: Vermillion & White
Arena: Dakotadome
   Capacity: 10,000; Year Built: 1979
SID: Dan Genzler

SOUTH DAKOTA ST.
Brookings, SD 57007................II

Coach: Scott Nagy, Delta St. 1988

2001-02 RESULTS (24-6)

66	Winona St.	71
103	Dakota Wesleyan ■	61
86	Michigan Tech †	89
89	Minn.-Duluth	72
83	Concordia-St. Paul	75
95	Northern St. ■	81
94	North Dakota ■	77
97	North Dakota St. ■	82
90	Sioux Falls ■	68
127	Minn.-Morris ■	60
101	Morningside	52
85	South Dakota	75
79	St. Cloud St. ■	56
97	Minn. St.-Mankato ■	66
96	Augustana (S.D.) ■	83
78	Neb.-Omaha ■	74
85	Northern Colo.	97
81	South Dakota ■	71
99	Morningside ■	60
87	Minn. St.-Mankato	76
90	St. Cloud St.	82
94	Augustana (S.D.)	76
83	Northern Colo. ■	71
87	Neb.-Omaha	76
83	North Dakota St.	91
78	North Dakota	96
91	St. Cloud St. ■	77
100	North Dakota ■	92
96	Neb.-Omaha ■	76
86	Metro St. ■	87

Nickname: Jackrabbits
Colors: Yellow & Blue
Arena: Frost Arena
   Capacity: 9,000; Year Built: 1973
SID: Ron Lenz

SOUTH FLA.
Tampa, FL 33620 I

Coach: Seth Greenberg,
Fairleigh Dickinson 1978

2001-02 RESULTS (19-13)

104	Fordham ■	84
82	Robert Morris	55
79	Hofstra †	60
69	Pittsburgh †	63
86	Prairie View ■	63
79	California ■	59
79	Northern Ill.	74
73	Florida ■	92
68	Syracuse	80
59	Bucknell ■	56
82	Ill.-Chicago ■	78
74	Florida St. ■	78
117	TCU ■	108
74	Southern Miss. ■	54
70	DePaul	63
62	Memphis	81
78	Charlotte ■	81
68	Tulane	54
68	Cincinnati ■	78
84	UCF	79
77	Louisville	96
81	UAB ■	65
76	Tulane ■	65
75	Houston	91
88	TCU	74
59	Memphis ■	71
78	UAB	83
88	Houston ■	57
75	Southern Miss.	92
65	UAB †	62
57	Cincinnati †	79
92	Ball St.	98

Nickname: Bulls
Colors: Green & Gold
Arena: Sun Dome

Capacity: 10,411; Year Built: 1979
SID: Michael Hogan

SOUTHAMPTON
Southampton, NY 11968 II

Coach: Charles Peck, St. John's (N.Y.)
1983

2001-02 RESULTS (17-12)

63	Southern Conn. St.	85
76	Caldwell	93
75	NYIT	77
84	Queens (N.Y.) ■	82
92	Mercy	87
101	C.W. Post ■	87
73	Molloy	71
62	St. Thomas Aquinas ■	56
81	St. Rose	102
86	Green Mountain †	66
68	Philadelphia U. ■	90
86	Bridgeport ■	78
98	Dowling ■	102
105	Concordia (N.Y.)	96
67	Adelphi	81
62	NYIT ■	82
92	Queens (N.Y.)	89
92	Mercy ■	82
91	C.W. Post	77
85	Molloy ■	66
61	Bridgeport	77
104	Dowling	99
107	Concordia (N.Y.) ■	96
65	Adelphi ■	80
91	St. Thomas Aquinas ■	80
67	Philadelphia U.	78
71	NYIT †	83
88	Philadelphia U.	66
113	St. Rose †	101

Nickname: Colonials
Colors: Blue & Gold
Arena: Southampton Gym
   Capacity: 1,500; Year Built: 1964
SID: Cindy Corwith

SOUTHEAST MO. ST.
Cape Girardeau, MO 63701-4799 I

Coach: Gary Garner, Missouri 1965

2001-02 RESULTS (6-22)

51	Birmingham-So. ■	62
63	Southwest Mo. St.	73
74	Ark.-Little Rock	83
58	Western Ill. ■	71
71	Vanderbilt	76
75	North Ala. ■	68
70	Mississippi Val. ■	82
62	St. Louis	88
80	Southern Ill.	92
77	Lincoln (Mo.) ■	68
75	Western Ill.	82
74	Eastern Ill.	84
82	Tennessee St. ■	94
95	Eastern Ky. ■	75
53	Morehead St.	59
73	Tenn.-Martin	89
72	Murray St.	85
62	Tennessee Tech ■	75
67	Austin Peay ■	68
65	Tennessee St.	72
67	Tennessee Tech	82
75	Morehead St.	91
81	Eastern Ky.	74
78	Tenn.-Martin ■	51
86	Murray St. ■	92
102	Eastern Ill. ■	87
47	Austin Peay	80
56	Tennessee Tech	73

Nickname: Indians
Colors: Red & White
Arena: Show Me Center

Capacity: 7,000; Year Built: 1987
SID: Ron Hines

SOUTHEASTERN LA.

Hammond, LA 70402 I

Coach: Billy Kennedy, Southeastern La. 1986

2001-02 RESULTS (7-20)

71	Sam Houston St.	70
89	Louisiana Col. ■	56
46	Memphis	65
43	South Ala.	71
54	Texas A&M	55
47	New Orleans ■	58
42	Stephen F. Austin ■	55
60	Texas-Arlington ■	69
63	McNeese St.	68
59	Dartmouth †	62
49	St. Mary's (Cal.) †	68
54	Texas-San Antonio	75
60	Southwest Tex. St.	55
54	La.-Monroe	64
63	Northwestern St. ■	72
63	Lamar	59
56	Nicholls St. ■	40
58	McNeese St. ■	60
66	Texas-Arlington	73
65	Stephen F. Austin	61
70	Sam Houston St. ■	69
51	Lamar ■	55
57	La.-Monroe	66
52	Northwestern St.	62
62	Southwest Tex. St. ■	64
50	Texas-San Antonio ■	64
39	Nicholls St.	61

Nickname: Lions
Colors: Green & Gold
Arena: University Center
   Capacity: 7,500; Year Built: 1982
SID: Dart Volz

SOUTHEASTERN OKLA.

Durant, OK 74701-0609 II

Coach: Tony Robinson, Southeastern Okla. 1976

2001-02 RESULTS (10-16)

56	Southern Ark.	54
71	Mo. Southern St. ■	77
67	Tarleton St. ■	53
74	Arkansas Tech ■	63
58	Harding	74
68	Tex. A&M-Commerce	61
63	Southern Ark. ■	73
75	Arkansas Tech	73
47	Incarnate Word †	76
58	Tex. A&M-Kingsville	56
85	Abilene Christian ■	68
102	Angelo St. ■	80
58	Eastern N.M.	75
76	West Tex. A&M	82
52	Northeastern St.	66
73	Central Okla. ■	69
49	East Central	61
85	Midwestern St. ■	76
62	Southwestern Okla. ■	82
55	Cameron	62
61	Northeastern St. ■	73
59	Central Okla.	95
58	East Central ■	67
56	Midwestern St.	65
72	Southwestern Okla.	89
73	Cameron ■	70

Nickname: Savages
Colors: Blue & Gold
Arena: Bloomer Sullivan Gym
   Capacity: 2,000; Year Built: 1956
SID: Dave Wester

SOUTHERN ARK.

Magnolia, AR 71754-0000 II

Coach: Brian Daugherty, Southern Ark. 1994

2001-02 RESULTS (16-10)

83	LeMoyne-Owen	70
54	Southeastern Okla. ■	56
69	LeMoyne-Owen †	60
69	Miles †	54
79	William Carey ■	64
87	Montevallo †	75
77	West Fla.	91
73	Southeastern Okla.	63
89	Jarvis Christian ■	75
86	Central Ark. ■	70
56	Henderson St.	76
83	Harding ■	79
98	Christian Bros. ■	72
64	Delta St.	77
79	Ouachita Baptist ■	75
71	Arkansas Tech	74
73	Ark.-Monticello ■	75
67	Central Ark.	57
60	Henderson St. ■	63
92	Harding	78
65	Christian Bros.	64
73	Delta St. ■	78
63	Ouachita Baptist	70
84	Arkansas Tech ■	74
90	Ark.-Monticello	87
66	West Ga. †	72

Nickname: Muleriders
Colors: Royal Blue & Old Gold
Arena: W.T. Watson Athletic Center
   Capacity: 2,600; Year Built: 1962
SID: Landon Stevens

SOUTHERN CALIFORNIA

Los Angeles, CA 90089-0602 I

Coach: Henry Bibby, UCLA 1972

2001-02 RESULTS (22-10)

68	Wyoming ■	55
58	Fresno St.	65
73	UC Santa Barb. ■	62
60	Bradley	50
82	Rhode Island ■	54
77	Pepperdine †	78
86	Long Beach St.	68
59	Miami (Ohio) ■	55
71	San Diego	67
81	Loyola Marymount	67
87	Washington	65
78	Washington St.	63
85	Washington St. ■	64
94	Washington ■	74
81	UCLA ■	77
80	Arizona	97
81	Arizona St.	73
91	California ■	92
90	Stanford ■	82
64	Oregon St.	51
69	Oregon	73
65	UCLA	67
83	Arizona St. ■	61
94	Arizona ■	89
77	Stanford	58
64	California	83
65	Oregon ■	67
79	Oregon St. ■	45
103	Stanford †	78
89	Oregon †	78
71	Arizona †	81
89	UNC Wilmington †	93

Nickname: Trojans
Colors: Cardinal & Gold
Arena: Los Angeles Sports Arena
   Capacity: 16,161; Year Built: 1959
SID: Tim Tessalone

SOUTHERN COLO.

Pueblo, CO 81001-4901 II

Coach: Joe Folda, Northern Colo. 1966

2001-02 RESULTS (11-15)

70	Caldwell ■	47
65	Minn.-Duluth	55
70	Western Wash.	98
69	St. Martin's †	86
67	Northern Colo.	66
80	Alas. Fairbanks ■	71
62	Fla. Southern	71
74	Fort Hays St.	90
72	Neb.-Kearney	83
93	Colo. Christian ■	94
71	Regis (Colo.) ■	79
80	Colorado Mines	70
75	Chadron St.	88
76	Metro St. ■	85
64	Mesa St.	82
61	Western St. (Colo.)	71
73	N.M. Highlands ■	69
53	Fort Lewis ■	71
73	UC-Colo. Spgs.	54
85	Adams St. ■	59
73	Mesa St. ■	76
89	Western St. (Colo.) ■	59
83	N.M. Highlands	72
71	Fort Lewis	85
78	UC-Colo. Spgs. ■	60
65	Adams St.	78

Nickname: Thunderwolves
Colors: Red & Blue
Arena: Massari Arena
   Capacity: 5,000; Year Built: 1971
SID: To be named

SOUTHERN CONN. ST.

New Haven, CT 06515 II

Coach: Art Leary, Quinnipiac 1971

2001-02 RESULTS (14-13)

85	Southampton ■	63
83	Southern N.H. ■	78
71	Bloomfield †	78
89	Farmingdale St. †	68
65	American Int'l ■	68
69	Franklin Pierce	76
62	Assumption	73
75	Bryant ■	66
36	Mass.-Lowell	69
74	Assumption ■	81
85	Pace	99
78	St. Rose ■	66
50	Franklin Pierce ■	82
75	Southern N.H.	72
68	Mass.-Lowell ■	71
66	American Int'l	53
73	Bryant	71
66	Stonehill	50
67	Bentley ■	79
80	Merrimack ■	61
77	New Haven ■	71
76	Pace ■	72
80	St. Rose	83
72	St. Michael's	65
45	St. Anselm ■	103
93	Le Moyne ■	81
51	American Int'l	73

Nickname: Owls
Colors: Blue & White
Arena: James W. Moore Fieldhouse
   Capacity: 2,800; Year Built: 1973
SID: Richard Leddy

SOUTHERN ILL.

Carbondale, IL 62901-6620 I

Coach: Bruce Weber, Wis.-Milwaukee 1978

2001-02 RESULTS (28-8)

82	Belmont ■	71
69	St. Louis	64
66	Iowa St. †	57
78	Hartford †	46
72	Illinois †	75
76	Ill.-Chicago ■	68
72	Indiana ■	60
73	George Mason	66
74	Cal St. Northridge	60
62	Colorado St.	80
92	Southeast Mo. St. ■	80
67	Murray St.	63
82	Evansville	72
79	Illinois St. ■	58
84	Southwest Mo. St. ■	74
79	Wichita St.	88
83	Northern Iowa ■	58
55	Bradley	49
91	Indiana St. ■	73
79	Drake	64
64	Northern Iowa	69
101	Evansville ■	62
79	Creighton	77
78	Wichita St. ■	58
66	Drake ■	57
71	Southwest Mo. St.	78
70	Illinois St.	84
65	Creighton ■	62
84	Indiana St.	74
84	Bradley ■	73
66	Bradley †	44
86	Southwest Mo. St. †	63
76	Creighton †	84
76	Texas Tech †	68
77	Georgia †	75
59	Connecticut †	71

Nickname: Salukis
Colors: Maroon & White
Arena: The SIU Arena
   Capacity: 10,014; Year Built: 1964
SID: Fred Huff

SIU-EDWARDSVILLE

Edwardsville, IL 62026-1129 II

Coach: Jack Margenthaler, Houston 1965

2001-02 RESULTS (7-19)

76	Monmouth (Ill.) ■	71
65	Delta St.	68
72	Bellarmine ■	83
53	Ky. Wesleyan ■	82
80	Mo.-St. Louis	70
81	Quincy	79
60	Lewis	84
64	Wis.-Parkside	70
84	St. Edward's †	79
72	Incarnate Word	73
79	Truman	67
67	Wayne St. (Mich.) ■	60
71	Indianapolis ■	74
62	Northern Ky.	90
65	Ky. Wesleyan	109
96	Southern Ind.	102
82	Quincy ■	78
92	Wis.-Parkside ■	95
86	St. Joseph's (Ind.) ■	90
55	Northern Ky.	90
81	Bellarmine	94
73	Southern Ind. ■	86
66	Mo.-St. Louis ■	70
57	Lewis ■	70
72	St. Joseph's (Ind.)	81
68	Indianapolis	93

Nickname: Cougars
Colors: Red & White
Arena: Sam Vadalabene Center
   Capacity: 4,000; Year Built: 1984
SID: Eric Hess

SCHEDULES/RESULTS

SOUTHERN IND.
Evansville, IN 47712-3534.......II

Coach: Rick Herdes, Graceland 1980

2001-02 RESULTS (22-8)
109	Tex. A&M-Commerce †	72
97	Wingate †	113
112	Grand Valley St. †	86
53	Mo.-St. Louis	69
97	Quincy	88
82	Lewis ■	75
69	Wis.-Parkside ■	70
91	Indianapolis	90
82	Northern Ky.	83
97	Oakland City ■	52
103	Abilene Christian ■	69
101	Brescia	72
94	Ky. Wesleyan ■	88
104	Wilberforce ■	60
98	Quincy ■	80
102	SIU-Edwardsville ■	96
79	Wis.-Parkside	68
87	St. Joseph's (Ind.)	92
99	Northern Ky. ■	90
116	Bellarmine ■	94
92	Olivet Nazarene ■	71
72	Mo.-St. Louis ■	63
86	SIU-Edwardsville	73
68	Lewis	81
102	St. Joseph's (Ind.) ■	88
86	Indianapolis ■	68
103	Bellarmine	56
68	Ky. Wesleyan	96
82	Indianapolis †	79
77	Ky. Wesleyan †	80

Nickname: Screaming Eagles
Colors: Red, White & Blue
Arena: Physical Activities Center
   Capacity: 3,300; Year Built: 1980
SID: Ray Simmons

SOUTHERN ME.
Gorham, ME 04038 III

Coach: Dan Costigan, Maine 1985

2001-02 RESULTS (10-16)
67	Husson ■	76
76	St. Joseph's (Me.) ■	85
78	Bates ■	76
59	Bowdoin ■	61
108	New England	70
80	Western Conn. St. ■	64
80	Colby ■	71
75	Keene St.	104
80	Salem St. ■	89
70	New Jersey City †	81
83	Haverford †	79
79	Mass.-Dartmouth	88
81	Rhode Island Col. ■	52
88	Eastern Conn. St. ■	99
79	Plymouth St. ■	89
68	Western Conn. St.	80
70	Mass.-Boston ■	66
124	Thomas	78
86	Keene St. ■	88
92	St. Joseph's (Me.)	88
58	Mass.-Dartmouth ■	77
71	Plymouth St.	72
84	Rhode Island Col.	47
72	Mass.-Boston	85
60	Eastern Conn. St.	70
67	Mass.-Dartmouth	78

Nickname: Huskies
Colors: Crimson, Navy Blue & White
Arena: Warren G. Hill Gymnasium
   Capacity: 1,400; Year Built: 1963
SID: B.L. Efring

SOUTHERN METHODIST
Dallas, TX 75275 I

Coach: Mike Dement, East Caro. 1976

2001-02 RESULTS (15-14)
74	Savannah St. ■	54
81	Navy ■	64
75	Texas Tech ■	78
90	Baylor	92
72	La Salle †	63
69	Iowa	86
74	North Texas	66
62	Tennessee ■	79
82	Oral Roberts ■	64
62	TCU	74
80	Boise St. ■	67
55	UTEP ■	46
74	Louisiana Tech	71
68	San Jose St.	66
74	Hawaii	83
76	Rice ■	49
87	Tulsa ■	95
70	Fresno St.	78
71	Nevada	57
66	Louisiana Tech ■	70
76	Hawaii ■	85
84	San Jose St. ■	55
69	Tulsa	87
63	Rice	61
77	Nevada ■	74
78	Fresno St. ■	86
63	UTEP	61
83	Boise St.	80
66	Nevada †	72

Nickname: Mustangs
Colors: Red & Blue
Arena: Moody Coliseum
   Capacity: 8,998; Year Built: 1956
SID: Brad Sutton

SOUTHERN MISS.
Hattiesburg, MS 39402 I

Coach: James Green, Mississippi 1983

2001-02 RESULTS (10-17)
83	Jackson St. ■	58
59	West Virginia †	66
50	Pacific (Cal.) †	65
66	Alcorn St. ■	60
61	Arkansas St.	85
76	South Ala.	66
73	Morris Brown ■	47
64	Millsaps ■	51
50	Western Ky. ■	74
55	Auburn	64
53	Memphis	75
54	South Fla.	74
50	UAB ■	36
61	Tulane ■	70
64	Memphis ■	73
66	Houston	74
61	TCU	75
67	St. Louis ■	46
61	Tulane	66
60	Houston ■	68
58	Marquette ■	72
58	East Caro.	61
37	Cincinnati	89
60	Ark.-Little Rock	53
81	TCU ■	68
56	UAB	66
92	South Fla. ■	75

Nickname: Golden Eagles
Colors: Black & Gold
Arena: Reed Green Coliseum
   Capacity: 8,095; Year Built: 1965
SID: Mike Montoro

SOUTHERN N.H.
Manchester, NH 03106-1045 ...II

Coach: Stan Spirou, Keene St. 1974

2001-02 RESULTS (17-11)
94	Teikyo Post †	84
77	Bridgeport	61
78	Southern Conn. St.	83
86	Pace ■	79
54	Mass.-Lowell ■	71
86	Franklin Pierce	65
81	New Haven ■	65
82	St. Anselm	72
73	St. Rose ■	85
89	Le Moyne	81
82	St. Michael's	76
50	Pace	72
72	Southern Conn. St. ■	75
67	St. Rose	77
64	St. Anselm ■	96
78	Le Moyne ■	58
99	St. Michael's ■	89
77	Assumption ■	68
78	American Int'l	77
86	Bryant ■	78
96	Merrimack ■	80
84	Bentley	85
83	Stonehill	70
75	Franklin Pierce ■	72
58	Mass.-Lowell	75
98	New Haven	102
104	St. Michael's ■	74
74	Bentley	88

Nickname: Penmen
Colors: Blue & Gold
Arena: SNHU Fieldhouse
   Capacity: 2,000; Year Built: 1980
SID: Tom McDermott

SOUTHERN U.
Baton Rouge, LA 70813 I

Coach: Ben Jobe, Fisk 1956

2001-02 RESULTS (7-20)
69	LSU	97
45	West Ala. ■	54
69	Centenary (La.) ■	99
67	Missouri	117
71	Southwest Mo. St.	98
71	Idaho St. †	76
74	Colorado	106
73	Texas Southern	92
75	Prairie View	89
78	San Francisco ■	93
106	Grambling	87
60	Jackson St. ■	68
66	Ark.-Pine Bluff	61
77	Mississippi Val.	84
68	Alabama A&M ■	82
57	Alabama St. ■	67
69	Alcorn St. ■	86
80	Morris Brown	74
80	Grambling	81
91	Jackson St.	81
90	Ark.-Pine Bluff ■	86
88	Mississippi Val. ■	73
82	Alabama A&M	80
57	Alabama St.	61
73	Alcorn St.	87
95	Prairie View ■	98
64	Texas Southern ■	72

Nickname: Jaguars
Colors: Columbia Blue & Gold
Arena: Clark Activity Center
   Capacity: 7,500; Year Built: 1976
SID: Kevin Manns

SOUTHERN UTAH
Cedar City, UT 84720 I

Coach: Bill Evans, Southern Utah 1972

2001-02 RESULTS (11-16)
86	Fort Lewis ■	69
63	Stanford	81
71	Idaho St.	73
67	Adams St.	57
63	Oregon St.	73
61	Sacramento St.	72
64	UC Riverside ■	66
68	Idaho St. ■	51
49	Boise St.	67
47	Utah	71
64	Weber St.	70
58	Brigham Young	79
67	IUPUI	80
57	Oakland	58
78	Valparaiso ■	62
68	Western Ill.	63
69	Chicago St. ■	49
71	Oral Roberts	70
54	UMKC	49
60	Oakland ■	84
61	IUPUI ■	53
70	Western Ill.	81
64	Valparaiso	71
57	Chicago St.	35
71	UMKC ■	72
82	Oral Roberts ■	75
57	UMKC †	70

Nickname: Thunderbirds
Colors: Scarlet & White
Arena: Centrum
   Capacity: 5,300; Year Built: 1985
SID: Neil Gardner

SOUTHERN VT.
Bennington, VT 05201-9983.....III

Coach: Ryan Marks, Southern California 1993

2001-02 RESULTS (15-12)
76	St. John Fisher	84
78	Keuka †	73
72	Rensselaer ■	69
91	Elms ■	81
104	Castleton St. ■	75
82	St. Joseph (Vt.) ■	73
81	Daniel Webster ■	51
96	Middlebury ■	89
69	Williams	77
44	Cortland St. †	57
94	Mass. Liberal Arts ■	92
70	Johnson & Wales	73
62	Trinity (Conn.) ■	75
60	Norwich	56
91	Emmanuel (Mass.) ■	73
74	Rivier	75
73	Keene St.	111
85	Emerson	89
69	Western New Eng. ■	63
62	Albertus Magnus	80
93	Norwich ■	68
76	Rivier	94
90	Suffolk ■	86
91	Western New Eng.	61
62	Daniel Webster	67
92	Rivier	85
71	Suffolk †	95

Nickname: Mountaineers
Colors: Green, White & Gold
Arena: Field House
   Capacity: 300; Year Built: 1991
SID: To be named

SOUTHWEST BAPTIST
Bolivar, MO 65613 II

Coach: Darin Archer, Southwest Baptist 1991

2001-02 RESULTS (12-15)
100	Ozark Christian ■	62
85	St. Edward's †	79
72	Angelo St.	83
75	Harding	77
75	Drury	68
110	Okla. Panhandle ■	84
110	Harris-Stowe ■	87
80	Missouri Valley ■	77
84	Truman ■	83
62	Mo. Southern St.	86
74	Mo.-Rolla	79
80	Washburn ■	90
88	Central Mo. St.	89
76	Emporia St.	83

67	Northwest Mo. St. ■	82
64	Pittsburg St.	80
79	Mo. Western St. ■	77
58	Truman	56
74	Mo. Southern St. ■	99
79	Mo.-Rolla ■	63
52	Washburn	89
77	Central Mo. St. ■	63
79	Emporia St. ■	69
92	Northwest Mo. St. ■	99
61	Pittsburg St.	84
52	Mo. Western St.	83
60	Mo. Southern St.	63

Nickname: Bearcats
Colors: Purple & White
Arena: Davison Field House
Capacity: 2,500; Year Built: 1963
SID: Darin Archer

SOUTHWEST MO. ST.
Springfield, MO 65804 I

Coach: Barry Hinson, Oklahoma St. 1983
2001-02 RESULTS (17-15)
77	North Texas	79
73	Southeast Mo. St. ■	63
63	UMKC	69
71	New Orleans ■	55
73	Tulsa	90
98	Southern U. ■	71
71	Texas-San Antonio ■	72
76	Texas A&M ■	65
83	Purdue †	84
80	Ill.-Chicago †	86
60	Richmond †	67
93	Evansville	82
53	St. Louis ■	50
82	Wichita St. ■	61
74	Southern Ill.	84
60	Bradley ■	64
72	Creighton ■	76
80	Northern Iowa	78
60	Illinois St.	61
76	Evansville ■	55
59	Indiana St.	53
74	Creighton	80
68	Illinois St. ■	63
65	Drake ■	51
63	Wichita St.	71
78	Southern Ill. ■	71
68	Northern Iowa ■	62
51	Bradley	49
61	Drake	68
70	Indiana St. ■	58
72	Wichita St. †	59
63	Southern Ill. †	86

Nickname: Bears
Colors: Maroon & White
Arena: Hammons Student Center
Capacity: 8,846; Year Built: 1976
SID: Mark Stillwell

SOUTHWEST ST.
Marshall, MN 56258 II

Coach: Greg Stemen, Valley City St. 1988
2001-02 RESULTS (21-8)
83	Viterbo ■	63
67	Wis.-Stout ■	58
88	Minn. St.-Mankato	84
87	South Dakota †	94
74	Augustana (S.D.)	71
54	Minn.-Duluth	74
63	Bemidji St.	66
82	Mt. Marty ■	72
62	St. Cloud St.	83
101	Minn.-Morris ■	59
62	Northern St. ■	72
73	Concordia-St. Paul	53
64	Winona St.	55

71	Wayne St. (Neb.)	66
91	Minn.-Crookston ■	68
75	Minn. St. Moorhead ■	65
84	Bemidji St.	81
64	Minn.-Duluth ■	65
65	Northern St.	59
94	Minn.-Morris	56
91	Winona St. ■	88
91	Concordia-St. Paul ■	51
59	Wayne St. (Neb.) ■	46
98	Trinity Bible (N.D.) ■	44
67	Minn. St. Moorhead	74
83	Minn.-Crookston	69
84	Minn. St. Moorhead ■	56
77	Northern St. †	70
57	Minn.-Duluth †	59

Nickname: Mustangs
Colors: Brown & Gold
Arena: R/A Facility
Capacity: 4,000; Year Built: 1996
SID: Kelly Loft

SOUTHWEST TEX. ST.
San Marcos, TX 78666-4615 I

Coach: Dennis Nutt, TCU 1986
2001-02 RESULTS (12-16)
108	Schreiner ■	71
67	Tex.-Pan American	73
99	Tex. A&M-Corp. Chris.	89
88	TCU	91
64	Stephen F. Austin	75
68	Arkansas	90
66	McNeese St.	76
62	Houston	89
70	Sam Houston St. ■	67
77	Lamar ■	78
87	Nicholls St. ■	66
55	Southeastern La.	60
73	Tex.-Pan American ■	77
71	McNeese St. ■	76
63	Northwestern St.	90
57	La.-Monroe	70
67	Stephen F. Austin ■	72
100	Texas-Arlington ■	84
82	Sam Houston St.	96
91	Lamar	84
85	Northwestern St. ■	69
60	La.-Monroe ■	51
81	Texas-San Antonio	68
64	Southeastern La.	62
72	Nicholls St.	59
59	Texas-Arlington	63
70	Texas-San Antonio ■	59
83	Texas-San Antonio	99

Nickname: Bobcats
Colors: Maroon & Gold
Arena: Strahan Coliseum
Capacity: 7,200; Year Built: 1979
SID: Tony Brubaker

SOUTHWESTERN (TEX.)
Georgetown, TX 78627-0770 ...III

Coach: Bill Raleigh, Muhlenberg 1988
2001-02 RESULTS (10-15)
66	Howard Payne ■	81
62	Dallas ■	72
62	Claremont-M-S †	72
60	Pomona-Pitzer †	61
100	Rhodes ■	69
61	Hendrix ■	53
62	Dallas	56
83	Texas-Dallas ■	73
55	Wooster ■	76
65	Millsaps	74
81	Oglethorpe	67
53	Trinity (Tex.) ■	52
77	DePauw ■	85
50	Rose-Hulman ■	53
60	Sewanee	65
61	Centre	72

76	Millsaps ■	72
72	Oglethorpe ■	52
56	Trinity (Tex.)	60
54	DePauw	81
64	Rose-Hulman	70
57	Sewanee ■	56
75	Centre ■	78
61	Rhodes	71
85	Hendrix	52

Nickname: Pirates
Colors: Black & Yellow
Arena: Corbin J. Robertson Center
Capacity: 1,800; Year Built: 1995
SID: Jim Shelton

SOUTHWESTERN OKLA.
Weatherford, OK 73096 II

Coach: George Hauser, Central Okla. 1960
2001-02 RESULTS (18-10)
83	Adams St.	91
83	Western St. (Colo.) †	90
70	Incarnate Word	81
115	Paul Quinn †	75
94	West Tex. A&M ■	89
73	Eastern N.M. ■	71
87	Arkansas Tech ■	76
73	Arkansas Tech	92
77	Tarleton St.	87
72	Tex. A&M-Commerce ■	69
79	Tex. A&M-Kingsville ■	72
84	Angelo St.	88
82	Abilene Christian	77
85	Cameron	60
89	Midwestern St. ■	68
66	Northeastern St.	87
96	Central Okla. ■	90
82	Southeastern Okla.	62
84	East Central	57
83	Midwestern St.	78
58	Cameron ■	50
59	Northeastern St. ■	64
108	Central Okla.	104
75	Rockhurst †	81
89	Southeastern Okla. ■	72
65	East Central ■	58
75	Angelo St. ■	72
59	Tarleton St. †	73

Nickname: Bulldogs
Colors: Navy Blue & White
Arena: Rankin Williams Fieldhouse
Capacity: 2,400; Year Built: 1957
SID: Matt Bush

SPRINGFIELD
Springfield, MA 01109-3797 ...III

Coach: Charlie Brock, Springfield 1976
2001-02 RESULTS (18-9)
61	Frank. & Marsh.	85
104	Scranton †	103
61	Curry	60
92	Keene St. ■	88
80	Tufts ■	74
80	Westfield St. †	63
69	Western New Eng.	49
66	Endicott ■	60
71	Marymount (Va.) ■	67
81	Middlebury	74
60	WPI ■	50
65	Trinity (Conn.)	75
56	MIT	66
72	Wentworth Inst. ■	60
60	Coast Guard ■	59
42	Babson	64
76	Clark (Mass.)	100
61	Wheaton (Mass.) ■	80
79	WPI	62
74	MIT ■	64
73	Williams	86
65	Coast Guard	52

64	Babson ■	50
66	Clark (Mass.) ■	77
80	Wheaton (Mass.)	74
59	Coast Guard ■	48
56	Babson †	72

Nickname: The Pride
Colors: Maroon & White
Arena: Blake Arena
Capacity: 2,000; Year Built: 1981
SID: John White

STANFORD
Stanford, CA 94305-2060 I

Coach: Mike Montgomery, Long Beach St. 1968
2001-02 RESULTS (20-10)
81	New Mexico	66
81	Southern Utah ■	63
78	Purdue †	62
75	Texas †	83
94	Long Beach St. ■	77
97	Belmont ■	63
87	Portland St. ■	63
76	Brigham Young †	81
75	Michigan St. †	64
82	California	62
54	California	68
67	Oregon St.	50
79	Oregon	87
83	Washington St. ■	50
105	Washington ■	60
86	UCLA	76
82	Southern California	90
90	Arizona St. ■	81
82	Arizona ■	88
90	Oregon	87
77	Oregon St. ■	55
91	Washington	65
76	Washington St.	63
58	Southern California ■	77
92	UCLA ■	95
76	Arizona	71
81	Arizona St.	76
78	Southern California †	103
84	Western Ky. †	68
63	Kansas †	86

Nickname: Cardinal
Colors: Cardinal & White
Arena: Maples Pavilion
Capacity: 7,391; Year Built: 1968
SID: Bob Vazquez

STATEN ISLAND
Staten Island, NY 10314 III

Coach: Anthony Petosa, Staten Island 1986
2001-02 RESULTS (22-7)
69	New Jersey City †	50
63	Alvernia	61
83	Farmingdale St.	74
57	Manhattanville ■	67
69	NYCCT	60
88	Ramapo	82
77	Kean ■	74
80	St. Joseph's (Brkln)	50
72	Brooklyn ■	58
77	FDU-Madison	74
59	Randolph-Macon	76
81	Rensselaer †	67
63	Montclair St.	77
79	Medgar Evers ■	74
65	York (N.Y.) ■	62
79	John Jay ■	71
73	Hunter	70
75	CCNY ■	74
92	Baruch	84
59	Lehman	62
74	NYCCT ■	80
73	Brooklyn	49
71	Medgar Evers ■	73

(York listing continued)

57	York (N.Y.)	52
92	Purchase St. ■	56
75	CCNY †	61
66	Baruch †	64
59	Medgar Evers †	57
72	Clark (Mass.) ■	101

Nickname: Dolphins
Colors: Maroon & Columbia Blue
Arena: Sports & Recreation Center
Capacity: 1,200; Year Built: 1995
SID: Jason Fein

STEPHEN F. AUSTIN
Nacogdoches, TX 75962 I

Coach: Danny Kaspar, North Texas 1978

2001-02 RESULTS (13-15)

56	Lamar ■	57
61	Arizona St.	92
59	Jackson St.	68
71	Texas Lutheran ■	52
90	Rice ■	86
75	Southwest Tex. St. ■	64
51	Centenary (La.)	62
76	Texas Southern ■	50
55	Southeastern La.	42
72	Nicholls St.	59
57	Oral Roberts	78
73	Northwestern St.	66
72	La.-Monroe	85
45	Sam Houston St. ■	49
52	Texas-Arlington	55
72	Southwest Tex. St.	67
75	Texas-San Antonio	84
72	Nicholls St. ■	56
61	Southeastern La. ■	65
95	Texas-Arlington ■	87
49	McNeese St. ■	65
62	Lamar	65
61	Sam Houston St.	71
66	Northwestern St. ■	58
52	La.-Monroe ■	51
73	Texas-San Antonio ■	62
37	McNeese St. ■	62
36	Lamar	53

Nickname: Lumberjacks
Colors: Purple & White
Arena: William Johnson Coliseum
Capacity: 7,200; Year Built: 1974
SID: Rob Meyers

STETSON
De Land, FL 32720 I

Coach: Derek Waugh, Furman 1993

2001-02 RESULTS (10-16)

87	Webber ■	57
58	Col. of Charleston	74
82	Birmingham-So.	69
71	Fla. Atlantic	82
57	Jacksonville	67
104	Western Caro. ■	102
106	Belmont ■	95
47	Texas Tech	101
66	Florida	94
69	UCF	75
67	Samford ■	89
89	Jacksonville St. ■	83
73	Georgia St.	89
82	Campbell	91
68	Troy St.	94
76	Mercer ■	71
68	Jacksonville ■	58
65	Troy St.	68
58	Mercer	55
72	Campbell ■	69
79	Georgia St. ■	94
78	Jacksonville St.	90
50	Samford	57
82	Belmont	79
65	UCF ■	78
74	Fla. Atlantic ■	77

(Hatters listing continued)

Nickname: Hatters
Colors: Green & White
Arena: Edmunds Center
Capacity: 5,000; Year Built: 1974
SID: Jamie Bataille

STEVENS TECH
Hoboken, NJ 07030-5991 III

Coach: Stephen Hayn, Stony Brook 1991

2001-02 RESULTS (8-18)

69	DeSales	85
64	FDU-Madison ■	67
61	Old Westbury	86
70	Vassar †	75
78	Rivier †	70
58	Yeshiva	70
49	Merchant Marine	79
49	Maritime (N.Y.) ■	50
44	Rensselaer	69
53	Mt. St. Mary (N.Y.)	84
69	John Jay	73
66	Manhattanville	68
83	Mt. St. Vincent	79
68	Old Westbury ■	66
52	Merchant Marine ■	60
62	New Jersey City ■	77
65	Maritime (N.Y.)	52
80	St. Joseph's (L.I.)	73
77	Mt. St. Mary (N.Y.) ■	75
48	New York U.	57
73	Mt. St. Vincent ■	58
63	Richard Stockton	76
61	Manhattanville ■	60
63	Yeshiva	70
50	St. Joseph's (L.I.)	63
54	Yeshiva	62

Nickname: Ducks
Colors: Red & Gray
Arena: Canavan Arena
Capacity: 1,500; Year Built: 1994
SID: Terry Small

STILLMAN
Tuscaloosa, AL 35403 III

Coach: Shawn Parks, Paine 1994

2001-02 RESULTS (11-14)

45	Miles	66
63	Dillard	81
50	Xavier (La.)	69
68	West Ala. ■	61
50	Paine ■	46
55	Dillard ■	72
51	West Ala.	55
67	Miles ■	76
54	Xavier (La.) ■	61
77	Maryville (Tenn.)	100
87	Talladega ■	88
81	La Grange	79
72	Talladega ■	106
63	Fisk	66
76	Concordia (Ala.) ■	74
80	Piedmont ■	60
76	Rust	82
56	Maryville (Tenn.) ■	73
71	La Grange ■	60
90	Concordia (Ala.) ■	85
81	Oakwood	65
84	Oakwood	69
82	Fisk ■	73
97	Piedmont	89
66	Rust ■	70

Nickname: Tigers
Colors: Navy Blue & Old Gold
Arena: Birthright
Capacity: 1,000; Year Built: 1954
SID: Wesley Peterson

STONEHILL
Easton, MA 02357 II

Coach: Kevin O'Brien, Tufts 1979

2001-02 RESULTS (4-22)

81	Becker	54
56	Bentley ■	101
66	St. Michael's ■	64
54	St. Anselm	75
89	Le Moyne ■	92
53	Bryant	80
51	New Haven ■	66
65	Bridgewater St. ■	50
58	NYIT	69
57	Merrimack	51
48	American Int'l ■	59
54	Assumption ■	69
61	St. Michael's	95
66	St. Anselm ■	88
70	Le Moyne	74
52	Merrimack ■	79
71	Bentley	91
50	Southern Conn. St. ■	66
73	Pace ■	77
57	St. Rose	75
57	Mass.-Lowell	71
61	Franklin Pierce	69
70	Southern N.H. ■	83
67	American Int'l	82
46	Bryant ■	58
67	Assumption	86

Nickname: Chieftains
Colors: Purple & White
Arena: Merkert Gymnasium
Capacity: 2,200; Year Built: 1973
SID: Jim Seavey

STONY BROOK
Stony Brook, NY 11794.............I

Coach: Nick Macarchuk, Fairfield 1963

2001-02 RESULTS (6-22)

55	St. John's (N.Y.)	72
71	Sacred Heart	76
62	Yale †	82
51	Binghamton †	53
37	Rutgers	76
59	Harvard	64
64	Cleveland St. ■	56
67	Hofstra	76
54	Villanova	76
60	Army	71
60	Brown	87
52	Binghamton ■	60
60	Vermont	91
68	Maine ■	65
65	Northeastern	91
54	Boston U.	90
66	Binghamton	62
68	New Hampshire ■	75
67	Vermont ■	72
70	Hartford	76
54	Albany (N.Y.) ■	65
57	New Hampshire	67
57	Maine	53
73	Hartford ■	80
85	Northeastern ■	70
62	Boston U. ■	64
48	Albany (N.Y.)	47
59	Vermont †	74

Nickname: Seawolves
Colors: Scarlet & Gray
Arena: USB Sports Complex
Capacity: 4,100; Year Built: 1990
SID: Rob Emmerich

SUFFOLK
Boston, MA 02114 III

Coach: Dennis McHugh, Salem St. 1990

2001-02 RESULTS (17-11)

79	Roger Williams †	74
74	Ramapo †	97
65	MIT	66
64	Tufts ■	71
77	Mass.-Boston ■	65
60	Bowdoin	72
91	Bates †	81
79	Brandeis ■	75
78	Wesleyan (Conn.)	96
65	Babson	79
81	Rivier ■	62
91	Emmanuel (Mass.)	73
83	Albertus Magnus	78
80	Norwich ■	68
71	Emerson	83
94	Johnson & Wales	80
95	Daniel Webster	68
73	Salve Regina	80
83	Western New Eng.	70
97	Johnson & Wales ■	81
76	Emerson	80
86	Southern Vt.	90
110	Albertus Magnus ■	97
94	Emmanuel (Mass.) ■	74
89	Emmanuel (Mass.) ■	61
95	Southern Vt. †	71
76	Johnson & Wales †	71
77	Clark (Mass.)	84

Nickname: Rams
Colors: Blue & Gold
Arena: Regan Gymnasium
Capacity: 150; Year Built: 1991
SID: Lou Connelly

SUL ROSS ST.
Alpine, TX 79832 III

Coach: Roger Grant

2001-02 RESULTS (12-13)

59	Tex. A&M-Corp. Chris.	93
60	Tex.-Pan American	99
80	Lubbock Chrst. ■	69
77	East Tex. Baptist	86
81	LeTourneau	110
66	Texas Wesleyan	83
72	Howard Payne	83
101	S'western Adventist †	86
84	Hillsdale Free Will †	60
75	Ozarks (Ark.) ■	81
72	Austin	70
88	Hardin-Simmons	95
84	McMurry	99
89	Schreiner	69
76	Texas Lutheran ■	65
76	Texas Wesleyan ■	70
71	Mary Hardin-Baylor	80
64	Concordia-Austin	79
95	Howard Payne ■	61
75	Mary Hardin-Baylor ■	70
75	Concordia-Austin ■	61
92	Hardin-Simmons ■	71
64	McMurry ■	80
90	Schreiner ■	75
67	Texas Lutheran	85

Nickname: Lobos
Colors: Scarlet & Gray
SID: To be named

SUSQUEHANNA
Selinsgrove, PA 17870-1025 III

Coach: Frank Marcinek, Penn St. 1981

2001-02 RESULTS (14-12)

91	Ursinus ■	65
64	King's (Pa.) ■	66
81	Dickinson ■	72
59	Lycoming	78
94	Baptist Bible (Pa.)	77
62	Lebanon Valley ■	67
79	Elizabethtown	107
61	Union (N.Y.) †	59
67	Marietta †	84

72	Rochester Inst. †	66
82	Wilkes	98
74	Juniata	68
77	Albright	65
74	Messiah	64
73	Widener ■	75
81	Moravian	68
71	Elizabethtown ■	95
105	York (Pa.) ■	100
62	Lebanon Valley	73
91	Albright ■	56
80	Juniata	72
84	Mt. Aloysius ■	71
65	Messiah ■	74
79	Moravian	76
71	Widener	89
77	Elizabethtown	80

Nickname: Crusaders
Colors: Orange & Maroon
Arena: O.W. Houts Gymnasium
Capacity: 1,800; Year Built: 1976
SID: Jim Miller

SWARTHMORE
Swarthmore, PA 19081-1397 ...III

Coach: Lee Wimberly, Stanford 1968

2001-02 RESULTS (6-19)

77	Tufts ■	60
70	Wash. & Lee †	63
56	Gwynedd-Mercy	66
55	Rensselaer	74
60	Union (N.Y.)	73
67	McDaniel	73
71	Washington (Md.) ■	66
40	Lehigh	75
53	Catholic	88
55	N.C. Wesleyan †	67
59	Dickinson	73
55	Phila. Sciences	54
66	Ursinus ■	73
47	Muhlenberg	63
56	Moravian	72
60	Haverford	70
51	Gettysburg ■	69
57	Drew ■	60
75	Washington (Md.)	86
48	Frank. & Marsh.	62
84	Phila. Bible ■	76
56	Johns Hopkins	69
68	Ursinus	79
44	Muhlenberg ■	75
59	Haverford ■	53

Nickname: Garnet Tide
Colors: Garnet, Gray & White
Arena: Tarble Pavillion
Capacity: 1,800; Year Built: 1978
SID: Mark Duzenski

SYRACUSE
Syracuse, NY 13244 ...I

Coach: Jim Boeheim, Syracuse 1966

2001-02 RESULTS (23-13)

78	Manhattan ■	58
74	DePaul	60
103	Binghamton ■	56
69	Michigan St. †	58
74	Wake Forest †	67
70	Colgate	51
76	Cornell ■	58
91	Albany (N.Y.)	65
91	Hofstra	65
68	North Carolina St. ■	82
80	Georgia Tech †	96
80	South Fla. ■	68
83	Buffalo ■	62
87	Rutgers ■	66
73	Providence	66
85	Seton Hall ■	70
75	West Virginia	69
56	Notre Dame ■	51
62	Tennessee	66
57	Pittsburgh	72
81	Virginia Tech ■	69
60	Georgetown	75
74	Rutgers	82
76	West Virginia ■	64
63	Pittsburgh ■	75
68	Notre Dame	65
73	Seton Hall	71
69	Georgetown ■	75
61	Villanova	67
65	Boston College ■	69
64	Villanova †	78
76	St. Bonaventure ■	66
66	Butler ■	65
62	Richmond	46
59	South Carolina †	66
54	Temple †	65

Nickname: Orangemen
Colors: Orange
Arena: Carrier Dome
Capacity: 33,000; Year Built: 1980
SID: Pete Moore

TAMPA
Tampa, FL 33606-1490 ...II

Coach: Richard Schmidt, Western Ky. 1964

2001-02 RESULTS (26-3)

68	P.R.-Cayey ■	44
84	Webber ■	56
94	P.R.-Bayamon ■	58
89	P.R.-Rio Piedras ■	61
89	P.R.-Mayaguez ■	66
88	Point Park ■	69
83	Queens (N.C.) ■	81
92	Mobile †	68
68	Shaw †	71
79	Molloy ■	54
107	Monmouth (Ill.) ■	81
75	Rollins	65
74	Barry ■	68
56	Lynn	51
78	St. Leo ■	60
82	Florida Tech	58
81	Fla. Southern	79
68	Eckerd	48
63	Barry	52
60	Lynn ■	57
69	St. Leo	49
88	Florida Tech ■	67
76	Fla. Southern	84
66	Eckerd ■	54
71	Rollins	63
75	Florida Tech †	61
84	Rollins †	63
62	Fla. Southern †	45
69	West Ga. ■	77

Nickname: Spartans
Colors: Scarlet, Gold & Black
Arena: Martinez Sports Center
Capacity: 3,432; Year Built: 1984
SID: Gil Swalls

TARLETON ST.
Stephenville, TX 76401 ...II

Coach: Lonn Reisman, Pittsburg St. 1977

2001-02 RESULTS (25-8)

73	Wingate †	83
78	Tex. A&M-Commerce †	87
73	NYIT †	58
86	Texas Col. ■	62
58	Mary Hardin-Baylor ■	50
53	Southeastern Okla.	67
68	East Central	58
106	S'western Adventist ■	40
83	National Christian ■	23
81	St. Edward's ■	51
83	Hillsdale Free Will ■	41
76	Cameron	53
87	Southwestern Okla. ■	77
65	Midwestern St.	63
74	St. Edward's	58
90	Central Okla. ■	54
53	Northeastern St. ■	58
65	Eastern N.M.	48
72	West Tex. A&M ■	54
82	Tex. A&M-Commerce	63
69	Tex. A&M-Kingsville	71
61	Abilene Christian	59
90	Angelo St. ■	60
76	Angelo St.	75
97	Abilene Christian ■	50
69	West Tex. A&M	73
87	Eastern N.M.	80
72	Tex. A&M-Kingsville ■	64
76	Tex. A&M-Commerce ■	57
76	Midwestern St. ■	60
73	Southwestern Okla. †	59
50	Northeastern †	66
59	Incarnate Word †	72

Nickname: Texans
Colors: Purple & White
Arena: Wisdom Gymnasium
Capacity: 3,212; Year Built: 1970
SID: Stan Wagnon

TEMPLE
Philadelphia, PA 19122 ...I

Coach: John Chaney, Bethune-Cookman 1955

2001-02 RESULTS (19-15)

64	Florida †	72
74	Maryland †	82
72	Charlotte ■	64
75	Penn St. ■	63
70	Wisconsin	67
57	Duke	82
66	Villanova †	70
67	Alabama †	70
54	Memphis ■	64
58	DePaul ■	60
62	Pennsylvania ■	68
86	Fordham	75
85	Duquesne	48
60	Rhode Island ■	42
74	St. Bonaventure	93
53	Massachusetts	63
68	Richmond ■	75
61	North Carolina St.	80
91	Fordham ■	74
82	St. Joseph's ■	72
71	Rhode Island	42
80	George Washington	58
67	La Salle	71
64	Massachusetts ■	47
67	Xavier ■	56
75	St. Bonaventure ■	71
75	Dayton	70
87	St. Joseph's †	84
66	La Salle †	72
81	Fresno St.	75
65	Louisville	62
63	Villanova ■	57
77	Memphis †	78
65	Syracuse †	54

Nickname: Owls
Colors: Cherry & White
Arena: Liacouras Center
Capacity: 10,206; Year Built: 1997
SID: Chet Zukowski

TENNESSEE
Knoxville, TN 37996 ...I

Coach: Buzz Peterson, North Carolina 1986

2001-02 RESULTS (15-16)

100	Florida ■	104
72	Tennessee Tech ■	63
74	Marquette †	85
74	Alas. Anchorage	54
55	St. John's (N.Y.) †	69
97	Appalachian St. ■	66
79	Southern Methodist	62
69	Memphis	71
72	Radford ■	66
72	Louisville	73
72	West Virginia ■	74
62	Wisconsin	65
82	Mississippi ■	76
70	Georgia	73
91	Mississippi St.	92
66	Syracuse ■	62
74	Middle Tenn. ■	56
60	South Carolina ■	94
82	Auburn	59
61	LSU	58
67	Vanderbilt	65
76	Kentucky	74
54	South Carolina	72
64	Arkansas ■	53
82	Alabama	95
61	Kentucky	64
62	Vanderbilt ■	67
62	Florida	68
71	Georgia ■	63
68	Arkansas †	61
72	Alabama †	91

Nickname: Volunteers
Colors: Orange & White
Arena: Thompson-Boling Arena
Capacity: 24,535; Year Built: 1987
AD: Douglas A. Dickey
SID: Craig Pinkerton

TENNESSEE ST.
Nashville, TN 37209-1561 ...I

Coach: Nolan Richardson III, Langston 1990

2001-02 RESULTS (11-17)

88	Trevecca Nazarene ■	77
101	Evansville	78
73	Kansas St.	79
54	Wright St.	66
63	Louisville	81
86	Fisk ■	72
71	Oral Roberts	87
79	Middle Tenn.	88
72	Murray St.	103
83	UNLV	101
60	Houston	91
72	Morehead St.	92
69	Eastern Ky.	68
94	Southeast Mo. St.	82
79	Tenn.-Martin ■	91
97	Lipscomb ■	82
68	Austin Peay	81
68	Tennessee Tech ■	77
91	Morehead St. ■	72
72	Southeast Mo. St. ■	65
94	Eastern Ill.	76
84	Murray St. ■	87
78	Tenn.-Martin	84
66	Eastern Ky. ■	63
78	Austin Peay ■	67
66	Tennessee Tech	81
84	Eastern Ill.	88
82	Morehead St.	91

Nickname: Tigers
Colors: Blue & White
Arena: Howard Gentry Complex
Capacity: 10,500; Year Built: 1980
SID: Kindell Stephens

TENNESSEE TECH
Cookeville, TN 38505-0001 ...I

Coach: Jeff Lebo, North Carolina 1989

2001-02 RESULTS (27-7)

63	Tennessee	72
79	South Carolina St. ■	65

87	Bluefield Col. ■	49
87	Loyola (Ill.) ■	76
86	Eastern Mich.	79
109	Reinhardt ■	49
80	New Mexico	87
66	Louisville	70
83	North Texas	89
64	Air Force	44
90	Eastern Ky.	61
81	Morehead St.	78
78	Murray St. ■	59
92	King (Tenn.) ■	57
74	Austin Peay	67
83	Tenn.-Martin ■	75
75	Southeast Mo. St.	62
77	Tennessee St.	68
97	Eastern Ill.	92
82	Southeast Mo. St. ■	67
71	Eastern Ky. ■	48
56	Murray St.	75
75	Tenn.-Martin	68
75	Morehead St. ■	68
86	Austin Peay	84
81	Tennessee St. ■	66
85	Eastern Ill.	68
73	Southeast Mo. St. ■	56
86	Austin Peay †	77
69	Murray St. †	70
64	Georgia St. ■	62
68	Dayton	59
80	Yale	61
73	Memphis	79

Nickname: Golden Eagles
Colors: Purple & Gold
Arena: Eblen Center
  Capacity: 10,150; Year Built: 1977
SID: Rob Schabert

TENN.-MARTIN
Martin, TN 38238-5021 I

Coach: Bret Campbell, Valdosta St. 1983

2001-02 RESULTS (15-14)

63	Missouri	89
99	Yale †	87
86	Lipscomb ■	79
109	St. Mary's (Mich.) ■	38
81	Bethel (Tenn.) ■	57
76	Middle Tenn. ■	71
54	Northern Ariz. ■	51
72	Mississippi †	83
60	Winthrop	86
89	West Virginia St. †	69
58	Memphis	88
76	Murray St.	90
108	Berry ■	74
71	Austin Peay	65
91	Tennessee St.	79
89	Southeast Mo. St. ■	73
81	Eastern Ill. ■	79
75	Tennessee Tech	83
100	Eastern Ky.	108
88	Morehead St.	89
68	Austin Peay ■	69
74	Murray St. ■	92
84	Tennessee St. ■	78
68	Tennessee Tech ■	75
51	Southeast Mo. St.	78
68	Eastern Ill.	62
72	Morehead St. ■	84
82	Eastern Ky. ■	77
69	Austin Peay	72

Nickname: Skyhawks
Colors: Orange, White & Royal Blue
Arena: Skyhawk Arena
  Capacity: 6,700; Year Built: 1978
SID: Joe Lofaro

TEXAS
Austin, TX 78712 I

Coach: Rick Barnes, Lenoir-Rhyne 1977

2001-02 RESULTS (22-12)

74	Arizona ■	88
78	Oregon St. †	68
64	Gonzaga †	67
71	Indiana †	77
83	Stanford †	75
89	Tex. A&M-Corp. Chris. ■	64
79	Washington St. ■	52
96	Jacksonville ■	90
80	McNeese St. ■	67
87	UNLV	78
61	Utah	71
81	Tex.-Pan American ■	69
70	Oklahoma St.	61
68	Providence ■	48
102	Baylor ■	78
74	Texas Tech	71
77	Nebraska ■	66
74	Texas A&M	80
69	Baylor	63
70	Kansas St.	71
84	Oklahoma ■	85
66	Texas A&M	52
104	Colorado ■	95
103	Kansas ■	110
72	Missouri	70
80	Oklahoma St.	85
78	Oklahoma	96
96	Texas Tech ■	71
79	Iowa St.	76
89	Missouri †	85
51	Oklahoma †	67
70	Boston College †	57
68	Mississippi St. †	64
70	Oregon †	72

Nickname: Longhorns
Colors: Burnt Orange & White
Arena: Frank Erwin Center
  Capacity: 16,079; Year Built: 1977
AD: DeLoss Dodds
SID: Scott McConnell

TEXAS A&M
College Station, TX 77843-1228 I

Coach: Melvin Watkins, Charlotte 1977

2001-02 RESULTS (9-22)

87	George Washington ■	63
77	Lamar	74
91	Tex. A&M-Kingsville ■	70
71	Long Beach St. ■	56
78	Loyola Marymount ■	80
55	Southeastern La. ■	54
55	Miami (Fla.) ■	64
56	Tulsa †	90
65	Southwest Mo. St.	76
82	Ill.-Chicago †	86
71	Purdue †	64
61	La.-Monroe †	76
62	North Carolina	96
63	Centenary (La.)	73
63	Oklahoma	89
70	Texas Tech ■	72
50	Missouri	74
63	Baylor ■	60
80	Texas	74
74	Kansas ■	86
52	Iowa St.	50
45	Baylor	97
52	Texas ■	66
64	Oklahoma ■	68
38	Kansas St.	69
66	Oklahoma St. ■	71
72	Nebraska ■	82
53	Texas Tech	74
77	Colorado ■	92
51	Oklahoma St.	66
71	Texas Tech †	80

Nickname: Aggies
Colors: Maroon & White
Arena: Reed Arena
  Capacity: 12,500; Year Built: 1998
AD: Wally W. Groff
SID: Colin Killian

TEX. A&M-COMMERCE
Commerce, TX 75429-3011 II

Coach: Sam Walker, Sam Houston St. 1991

2001-02 RESULTS (10-19)

72	Southern Ind. †	109
87	Tarleton St. †	78
58	Neb.-Omaha †	90
115	Paul Quinn †	89
58	Incarnate Word	78
67	St. Mary's (Tex.) ■	56
51	Northeastern St.	72
71	Central Okla.	102
57	Ouachita Baptist	77
72	East Central ■	65
61	Southeastern Okla. ■	68
62	Seattle Pacific	78
72	Seattle †	51
91	Ouachita Baptist ■	73
69	Southwestern Okla.	72
58	Cameron	63
47	Tex. A&M-Kingsville	67
54	Midwestern St.	57
74	Abilene Christian	76
71	Angelo St.	83
63	Tarleton St.	82
75	Eastern N.M.	70
54	West Tex. A&M	75
76	West Tex. A&M ■	79
71	Eastern N.M. ■	70
97	Angelo St. ■	84
85	Abilene Christian ■	75
87	Tex. A&M-Kingsville ■	89
57	Tarleton St.	76

Nickname: Lions
Colors: Blue & Gold
Arena: A&M-C Field House
  Capacity: 5,000; Year Built: 1950
SID: Bill Powers

TEX. A&M-CORP. CHRIS.
Corpus Christi, TX 78412 I

2001-02 RESULTS (12-15)

93	Sul Ross St. ■	59
89	Southwest Tex. St. ■	99
66	Loyola (Ill.)	86
56	Illinois	80
64	Texas	89
56	UTEP	82
67	Lamar ■	69
80	San Francisco ■	75
81	Denver ■	79
92	Wayland Baptist ■	83
102	Arkansas St. ■	98
69	Sacramento St.	82
63	San Francisco	65
79	San Diego St. ■	82
81	Centenary (La.)	80
61	UMKC	67
86	Gardner-Webb ■	78
68	New Orleans ■	82
87	Tex.-Pan American ■	80
79	Lipscomb	81
76	Gardner-Webb	86
68	Denver	78
105	Tex.-Pan American ■	110
77	Savannah St.	62
75	Lipscomb ■	61
77	Centenary (La.)	73
96	Savannah St. ■	66

Nickname: Islanders
Colors: Blue, Green & Silver
Arena: Circle K Court
  Capacity: 3,500; Year Built: 1953
SID: John Gilger

TEX. A&M-KINGSVILLE
Kingsville, TX 78363 II

Coach: Pete Peterson, Southwestern Kansas 1979

2001-02 RESULTS (15-13)

93	Texas Lutheran ■	87
70	Texas A&M	91
106	Central Okla.	86
69	Northeastern St.	77
61	St. Mary's (Tex.)	80
69	East Central ■	65
59	Incarnate Word	66
90	St. Edward's †	86
56	Southeastern Okla. ■	58
60	Cameron	70
72	Southwestern Okla.	79
67	Tex. A&M-Commerce ■	47
70	Midwestern St. ■	60
92	North Texas	100
54	Angelo St.	69
59	Abilene Christian	41
65	St. Mary's (Tex.) ■	64
71	Tarleton St.	69
59	West Tex. A&M	70
73	Eastern N.M.	77
79	Eastern N.M. ■	70
80	West Tex. A&M ■	76
103	Abilene Christian ■	59
100	Angelo St. ■	74
89	Tex. A&M-Commerce	87
64	Tarleton St.	72
71	East Central ■	68
53	Northeastern St.	65

Nickname: Javelinas
Colors: Blue & Gold
Arena: Steinke PE Center
  Capacity: 4,000; Year Built: 1970
SID: Fred Nuesch

TCU
Fort Worth, TX 76129-0001 I

Coach: Billy Tubbs, Lamar 1958

2001-02 RESULTS (16-15)

93	Northwestern St. ■	79
100	Ark.-Monticello †	57
95	UTEP †	73
77	Oklahoma St. †	95
90	La.-Monroe	94
91	Southwest Tex. St. ■	88
86	Texas Tech	99
82	Creighton ■	77
93	Lenoir-Rhyne ■	55
91	Texas-San Antonio	85
74	Southern Methodist ■	62
110	Appalachian St. ■	76
85	North Texas ■	92
92	Baylor ■	81
108	South Fla.	117
93	Memphis ■	98
85	Louisville	93
71	Houston	82
82	Tulane ■	87
72	Marquette	83
75	Southern Miss. ■	61
71	UAB ■	77
72	Memphis	83
92	DePaul ■	69
87	Houston ■	69
78	UAB	68
74	South Fla. ■	88
68	Southern Miss.	81
106	Tulane	87
66	East Caro. ■	63
86	Louisville †	110

Nickname: Horned Frogs
Colors: Purple & White
Arena: Daniel-Meyer Coliseum
  Capacity: 7,166; Year Built: 1961
SID: Steve Fink

TEXAS LUTHERAN
Seguin, TX 78155-5999 II

Coach: Tom Oswald, Tex.-San Antonio 1996

2001-02 RESULTS (13-12)
82	Thiel †	81
71	Capital	95
87	Tex. A&M-Kingsville	93
52	Stephen F. Austin	71
60	Austin	57
76	Ozarks (Ark.)	70
58	Savannah A&D ■	71
63	Incarnate Word ■	77
74	Wooster ■	71
58	Texas-Dallas ■	78
71	Dallas ■	77
108	Schreiner	90
74	Concordia-Austin ■	86
68	Mary Hardin-Baylor ■	63
66	Howard Payne	86
65	Sul Ross St.	76
80	McMurry ■	67
74	Hardin-Simmons ■	53
68	McMurry	83
86	Hardin-Simmons	75
89	Concordia-Austin	81
76	Mary Hardin-Baylor	87
98	Howard Payne ■	91
85	Sul Ross St. ■	67
89	Schreiner	65

Nickname: Bulldogs
Colors: Black & Gold
Arena: Memorial Gym
   Capacity: 1,500; Year Built: 1952
SID: Tim Clark

TEXAS SOUTHERN
Houston, TX 77004 I

Coach: Ronnie Courtney

2001-02 RESULTS (11-17)
51	New Mexico	97
63	Tex.-Pan American	96
58	Lamar	87
40	Marquette	76
65	Northern Ill. †	87
79	Houston ■	82
50	Stephen F. Austin	76
92	Southern U. ■	73
83	Alcorn St. ■	88
55	Oklahoma †	97
57	Jackson St.	66
55	Grambling	66
72	Mississippi Val. ■	69
74	Ark.-Pine Bluff ■	60
76	Alabama St.	71
56	Alabama A&M	73
76	Prairie View	80
93	Prairie View ■	90
71	Jackson St. ■	74
87	Grambling ■	68
61	Mississippi Val.	90
73	Ark.-Pine Bluff	70
64	Alabama St. ■	49
100	Alabama A&M ■	99
86	Alcorn St.	93
72	Southern U.	64
68	Mississippi Val. ■	61
65	Alcorn St. †	87

Nickname: Tigers
Colors: Maroon & Gray
Arena: Health & Physical Education Arena
   Capacity: 8,100; Year Built: 1988
SID: Bambi Hall

TEXAS TECH
Lubbock, TX 79409-3021 I

Coach: Bob Knight, Ohio St. 1962

2001-02 RESULTS (23-9)
75	William & Mary ■	55
81	San Diego St. ■	71
78	Southern Methodist	75
65	Sam Houston St. ■	69
81	UTEP ■	56
81	New Mexico St.	80
99	TCU ■	86
71	Houston	64
89	La.-Lafayette ■	72
101	Stetson ■	47
80	Minnesota ■	60
90	Wyoming ■	84
74	Kansas St. ■	49
72	Texas A&M	70
72	Oklahoma	98
71	Texas ■	74
94	Oklahoma St. ■	70
92	Oklahoma	79
69	Nebraska	80
69	Iowa St. ■	43
62	Oklahoma St.	64
81	Kansas	108
90	Baylor ■	65
97	Colorado ■	79
91	Missouri ■	68
74	Texas A&M ■	53
71	Texas	96
91	Baylor	89
80	Texas A&M †	71
73	Oklahoma St. †	51
50	Kansas †	90
68	Southern Ill. †	76

Nickname: Red Raiders
Colors: Scarlet & Black
Arena: United Spirit Arena
   Capacity: 15,050; Year Built: 1999
SID: Randy Farley

TEXAS WESLEYAN
Fort Worth, TX 76105 II

Coach: Terry Waldrop

2001-02 RESULTS (7-6)
69	Austin	76
81	Mary Hardin-Baylor †	73
84	Howard Payne ■	74
83	Sul Ross St. ■	66
83	Concordia-Austin ■	93
79	Hardin-Simmons ■	72
87	McMurry	98
86	McMurry ■	100
77	Austin ■	60
97	Hardin-Simmons	88
70	Sul Ross St.	76
84	Howard Payne	81
82	Dallas †	88

Nickname: Rams
Colors: Blue & Gold
Arena: Sid W. Richardson Gymnasium
   Capacity: 2,500
SID: James Yule

TEXAS-ARLINGTON
Arlington, TX 76013 I

Coach: Eddie McCarter, UAB 1975

2001-02 RESULTS (12-15)
71	New Mexico St. ■	88
64	Baylor	88
89	Wichita St.	102
61	Bradley	60
62	Oral Roberts	115
69	Southeastern La.	60
87	Nicholls St.	59
103	Hardin-Simmons ■	45
83	Oral Roberts ■	77
65	Northwestern St. ■	79
79	La.-Monroe	87
75	Sam Houston St. ■	72
80	Lamar	61
55	Stephen F. Austin ■	52

61	McNeese St.	67
95	Texas-San Antonio	91
84	Southwest Tex. St.	100
73	Southeastern La. ■	66
81	Nicholls St. ■	58
84	Texas-San Antonio	92
87	Stephen F. Austin	95
74	McNeese St. ■	81
94	Sam Houston St.	102
85	Lamar	94
70	La.-Monroe ■	81
65	Northwestern St.	70
63	Southwest Tex. St.	59

Nickname: Mavericks
Colors: Royal Blue & White
Arena: Texas Hall
   Capacity: 4,200; Year Built: 1965
SID: Mickey Seward

TEXAS-DALLAS
Richardson, TX 75083-0688 III

2001-02 RESULTS (9-10)
61	Dallas	56
75	Concordia-Austin ■	66
61	Mary Hardin-Baylor ■	59
85	Howard Payne	88
54	Trinity (Tex.) ■	66
73	Southwestern (Tex.)	83
69	Marian (Wis.) ■	70
77	Anderson (Ind.) ■	70
78	Texas Lutheran	58
82	Schreiner	76
76	Austin	81
62	Ozarks (Ark.)	65
77	Mississippi Col. ■	67
57	East Tex. Baptist	70
75	Dallas ■	84
86	East Tex. Baptist ■	65
66	Austin ■	69
75	Ozarks (Ark.) ■	69
56	Mississippi Col.	76

Nickname: Comets
Colors: Forest Green & Orange
SID: To be named

UTEP
El Paso, TX 79968 I

Coach: Jason Rabedeaux, UC Davis 1988

2001-02 RESULTS (10-22)
88	Ark.-Monticello ■	55
66	Northwestern St. †	60
73	TCU †	95
60	Providence †	69
56	Texas Tech	81
71	New Mexico St.	73
74	Washington ■	62
82	Tex. A&M-Corp. Chris. ■	56
58	Charlotte	86
89	Mississippi Val. ■	82
58	Mississippi	68
63	Louisiana Tech	77
46	Southern Methodist	55
68	Hawaii ■	70
66	San Jose St. ■	65
61	Tulsa ■	66
59	Rice	73
93	Nevada ■	64
77	Fresno St. ■	80
72	Boise St. ■	51
80	Alcorn St. ■	76
62	San Jose St.	67
60	Hawaii	75
68	Rice ■	75
76	Tulsa	88
64	Fresno St.	72
65	Nevada	80
85	New Mexico St. ■	81
72	Boise St.	81
61	Southern Methodist ■	63

68	Louisiana Tech ■	86
72	Boise St. †	73

Nickname: Miners
Colors: Dark Blue, Orange & Silver
Arena: Don Haskins Center
   Capacity: 11,500; Year Built: 1977
SID: Jeff Darby

TEX.-PAN AMERICAN
Edinburg, TX 78541 I

Coach: Bob Hoffman, Oklahoma Bapt. 1979

2001-02 RESULTS (20-10)
99	Sul Ross St. ■	60
73	Southwest Tex. St. ■	67
97	Texas Col. ■	79
96	Texas Southern ■	63
66	Northern Iowa	74
72	Minnesota	89
82	Portland	80
67	Washington St.	70
69	Lamar	58
66	Middle Tenn. ■	64
91	Niagara †	85
67	Oral Roberts †	58
72	Baylor †	66
81	Rice	64
101	LeTourneau ■	56
107	Schreiner ■	79
69	Texas	81
77	Southwest Tex. St.	73
58	Air Force ■	52
96	Lipscomb ■	70
94	Gardner-Webb ■	84
64	Wright St.	83
80	Tex. A&M-Corp. Chris. ■	87
58	Centenary (La.)	61
52	Middle Tenn.	70
110	Tex. A&M-Corp. Chris. ■	105
100	New Mexico St. ■	86
79	Lipscomb	62
79	Gardner-Webb	86
67	Centenary (La.) ■	85

Nickname: Broncs
Colors: Forest Green, Burnt Orange & White
Arena: UTPA Fieldhouse
   Capacity: 4,000; Year Built: 1969
SID: Dave Geringer

TEXAS-SAN ANTONIO
San Antonio, TX 78249-0691 I

Coach: Tim Carter, Kansas 1979

2001-02 RESULTS (19-10)
73	Maine †	56
71	Florida Int'l	65
63	Nebraska	81
88	Illinois St. †	82
81	Idaho St. †	72
72	Southwest Mo. St.	71
85	TCU	91
74	Lamar ■	67
90	Sam Houston St. ■	74
55	McNeese St.	71
75	Southeastern La. ■	54
93	Nicholls St. ■	65
81	McNeese St. ■	73
70	La.-Monroe	72
86	Northwestern St.	88
91	Texas-Arlington ■	95
84	Stephen F. Austin ■	75
78	Lamar	75
82	Sam Houston St.	75
92	Texas-Arlington	84
81	La.-Monroe ■	74
77	Northwestern St. ■	67
68	Southwest Tex. St. ■	81
73	Nicholls St.	51
64	Southeastern La.	50
62	Stephen F. Austin	73
59	Southwest Tex. St.	70

99 Southwest Tex. St. ■ 83
62 La.-Monroe 64

Nickname: Roadrunners
Colors: Orange, Navy Blue & White
Arena: Convocation Center
  Capacity: 5,100; Year Built: 1971
SID: Rick Nixon

THIEL
Greenville, PA 16125 III

Coach: Karel Jelinek, Hamilton 1990
2001-02 RESULTS (11-15)
81 Texas Lutheran † 82
76 St. Olaf † 93
66 Mount Union ■ 68
78 Baldwin-Wallace 86
86 Allegheny ■ 88
86 Pitt.-Bradford ■ 91
73 Pitt.-Greensburg 78
71 Carnegie Mellon 69
81 La Roche 95
58 Penn St.-Behrend ■ 52
76 Ohio Northern † 72
66 Wooster 80
81 Lake Erie ■ 82
97 Hiram ■ 70
81 Hilbert ■ 51
67 Wash. & Jeff. 61
79 Grove City 67
71 Westminster (Pa.) ■ 63
73 Bethany (W.Va.) ■ 83
56 Waynesburg 68
88 Wash. & Jeff. ■ 81
64 Grove City 63
58 Westminster (Pa.) 60
59 Bethany (W.Va.) ■ 75
95 Waynesburg ■ 91
62 Grove City ■ 77

Nickname: Tomcats
Colors: Navy Blue & Old Gold
Arena: Rissell-Beeghly Gymnasium
  Capacity: 1,000; Year Built: 1968
SID: Kevin Fenstermacher

THOMAS MORE
Crestview Hills, KY 41017-3495 III

Coach: Terry Connor, Thomas More 1992
2001-02 RESULTS (5-20)
63 Shawnee St. ■ 84
87 Ind.-East ■ 61
50 Northern Ky. 95
73 Huntington 95
67 Manchester ■ 70
85 Anderson (Ind.) ■ 88
55 Maryville (Tenn.) ■ 81
58 Ind.-Southeast 92
64 Wittenberg ■ 98
70 Pacific Lutheran † 97
60 Colorado Col. † 58
90 Linfield † 121
72 Mt. St. Joseph ■ 69
85 Franklin 93
90 Bluffton 93
55 Hanover ■ 63
88 Centre ■ 97
78 Manchester 85
85 Anderson (Ind.) 104
72 Defiance 107
82 Franklin ■ 94
63 Mt. St. Joseph 70
52 Hanover 82
88 Bluffton ■ 80
68 Transylvania ■ 63

Nickname: Saints
Colors: Royal Blue, White & Silver
Arena: Connor Convocation Center
  Capacity: 1,500; Year Built: 1989
SID: Jason Eichelberger

TOLEDO
Toledo, OH 43606 I

Coach: Stan Joplin, Toledo 1979
2001-02 RESULTS (16-14)
50 Dayton 69
69 IPFW ■ 60
64 George Mason 67
76 St. Bonaventure ■ 82
64 Siena 61
79 Youngstown St. ■ 65
55 Cincinnati 68
40 Detroit 63
68 Oakland 93
73 Western Mich. ■ 64
85 Eastern Mich. 60
59 Ball St. 68
89 Northern Ill. ■ 80
57 Bowling Green 76
61 Central Mich. 75
77 Marshall ■ 67
91 Northern Ill. 95
52 Kent St. 79
58 Central Mich. 42
54 Miami (Ohio) 64
77 Akron ■ 72
63 Ball St. 81
66 Bowling Green ■ 62
54 Buffalo ■ 42
72 Western Mich. ■ 68
69 Ohio 68
74 Eastern Mich. ■ 68
89 Eastern Mich. ■ 53
62 Central Mich. † 54
61 Kent St. † 86

Nickname: Rockets
Colors: Blue & Gold
Arena: John F. Savage Hall
  Capacity: 9,000; Year Built: 1976
SID: Steve Easton

TOWSON
Towson, MD 21252-0001 I

Coach: Michael Hunt, Furman 1985
2001-02 RESULTS (11-18)
53 Coppin St. † 51
54 UMBC † 73
40 Georgetown 91
46 LSU 83
60 Rider ■ 58
68 Va. Commonwealth 91
67 Morgan St. 62
78 Md.-East. Shore 93
57 Howard † 77
67 UMBC 77
37 UNC Wilmington 76
64 Delaware St. ■ 57
42 George Mason 71
68 Drexel ■ 62
53 Old Dominion 66
52 George Mason ■ 64
59 Delaware 53
75 James Madison 86
46 UNC Wilmington ■ 56
60 Hofstra ■ 62
45 William & Mary 62
67 Old Dominion 55
61 William & Mary ■ 58
61 Delaware ■ 57
49 Va. Commonwealth ■ 72
71 James Madison ■ 83
81 Drexel 65
61 Hofstra 60
52 Hofstra † 72

Nickname: Tigers
Colors: Gold, White & Black
Arena: Towson Center
  Capacity: 5,000; Year Built: 1976
SID: Peter Schlehr

TRINITY (CONN.)
Hartford, CT 06106 III

Coach: Stan Ogrodnik, Providence 1963
2001-02 RESULTS (19-6)
75 Adrian † 82
91 NYCCT † 83
87 Eastern Conn. St. 75
74 Western Conn. St. ■ 66
65 Coast Guard 55
72 Elms 44
79 Ursinus ■ 60
56 Pomona-Pitzer † 64
72 Occidental 65
75 Springfield ■ 65
75 Southern Vt. 62
79 Middlebury ■ 65
75 Williams 85
88 Tufts ■ 87
105 Bates ■ 96
75 Clark (Mass.) ■ 108
110 Amherst 107
71 Connecticut Col. ■ 68
72 Wesleyan (Conn.) 65
81 Colby ■ 60
82 Bowdoin ■ 57
74 Wesleyan (Conn.) ■ 71
78 Amherst 85
75 Colby-Sawyer ■ 47
61 Brockport St. 80

Nickname: Bantams
Colors: Blue & Gold
Arena: Oosting Gym
  Capacity: 2,000; Year Built: 1963
SID: David Kingsley

TRINITY (TEX.)
San Antonio, TX 78212-7200 ...III

Coach: Pat Cunningham, Kalamazoo 1974
2001-02 RESULTS (18-7)
80 Whitman † 81
90 Middlebury † 49
88 Roanoke ■ 60
79 Otterbein ■ 81
78 Hendrix ■ 62
61 Rhodes ■ 68
66 Texas-Dallas 54
63 Dallas 47
85 Oglethorpe ■ 64
52 Millsaps 62
52 Southwestern (Tex.) 53
62 Midwestern St. ■ 64
55 Rose-Hulman ■ 51
66 DePauw ■ 56
86 Centre 80
68 Sewanee 59
67 Oglethorpe ■ 51
75 Millsaps ■ 60
60 Southwestern (Tex.) ■ 56
53 Rose-Hulman 34
66 DePauw 68
55 Centre 48
73 Sewanee ■ 63
51 Hendrix 47
83 Rhodes 56

Nickname: Tigers
Colors: Maroon & White
Arena: Earl C. Sams Gymnasium
  Capacity: 1,850; Year Built: 1992
SID: Justin Parker

TROY ST.
Troy, AL 36082 I

Coach: Don Maestri, Southern Miss. 1968
2001-02 RESULTS (18-10)
60 Kansas St. 64
77 Marshall 72
73 Maine 71
70 Jacksonville St. ■ 52
65 Samford ■ 68
56 Utah 87
98 Nicholls St. ■ 86
88 Campbell ■ 81
63 San Diego † 70
100 Hampton † 91
67 Georgia St. 84
80 Belmont 75
85 UCF ■ 74
107 Fla. Atlantic ■ 100
94 Stetson 68
71 Jacksonville 74
71 Mercer ■ 65
68 Stetson ■ 65
76 Jacksonville 61
66 Fla. Atlantic 67
64 UCF 58
65 Belmont ■ 64
71 Mercer 72
81 Campbell ■ 71
88 Georgia St. ■ 102
64 Samford ■ 52
79 Jacksonville St. † 60
62 Jacksonville St. † 69

Nickname: Trojans
Colors: Cardinal & Black
Arena: Trojan Arena
  Capacity: 4,000; Year Built: 1964
SID: Joel Lamp

TRUMAN
Kirksville, MO 63501-4221 II

Coach: Jack Schrader, Arizona St. 1975
2001-02 RESULTS (3-23)
72 Wayne St. (Neb.) † 78
60 Minn. St.-Mankato 92
52 Mo.-St. Louis ■ 66
74 Quincy ■ 79
80 Drury ■ 75
60 Lincoln (Mo.) 84
79 Culver-Stockton ■ 77
67 SIU-Edwardsville 79
83 Southwest Baptist 84
73 Washburn ■ 83
61 Central Mo. St. 73
65 Northwest Mo. St. 74
75 Emporia St. ■ 79
75 Mo. Western St. ■ 82
68 Pittsburg St. 93
60 Mo.-Rolla ■ 68
62 Mo. Southern St. 77
56 Southwest Baptist ■ 58
64 Washburn 79
58 Central Mo. St. ■ 54
50 Northwest Mo. St. ■ 79
61 Emporia St. 71
60 Mo. Western St. 83
56 Pittsburg St. ■ 64
72 Mo.-Rolla 75
77 Mo. Southern St. ■ 101

Nickname: Bulldogs
Colors: Purple & White
Arena: Pershing
  Capacity: 3,000; Year Built: 1959
SID: Melissa Ware

TUFTS
Medford, MA 02155 III

Coach: Robert Sheldon, St. Lawrence 1977

2001-02 RESULTS (12-13)
60	Swarthmore	77
75	Haverford	53
100	Salem St. ■	96
71	Suffolk	64
74	Springfield	80
63	Babson	76
84	MIT ■	77
68	Wheaton (Mass.) ■	60
81	Cazenovia †	86
73	Ursinus †	71
99	Curry ■	78
78	Mass.-Boston	58
92	Brandeis ■	80
75	Mass.-Dartmouth ■	95
111	Bates ■	104
87	Trinity (Conn.)	88
71	Amherst	86
85	Keene St. ■	88
75	Colby	60
79	Bowdoin	98
69	Williams ■	85
103	Middlebury ■	88
65	Wesleyan (Conn.) ■	72
84	Connecticut Col. ■	89
57	Williams	81

Nickname: Jumbos
Colors: Brown & Blue
Arena: Cousens Gym
  Capacity: 1,000; Year Built: 1932
SID: Paul Sweeney

TULANE
New Orleans, LA 70118-0000...I

Coach: Shawn Finney, Fairmont St. 1985

2001-02 RESULTS (14-15)
87	Loyola (La.) ■	47
92	Centenary (La.) ■	76
89	Norfolk St. ■	67
76	Va. Commonwealth	72
65	Florida	81
74	New Orleans ■	63
87	Vanderbilt ■	77
77	Lipscomb ■	64
79	Georgia Tech	69
66	Mississippi St. ■	77
67	Kentucky †	101
73	DePaul	63
66	Houston ■	69
70	Memphis ■	78
70	Southern Miss.	61
87	TCU	82
54	South Fla. ■	68
63	UAB	80
66	Marquette ■	68
66	Southern Miss. ■	61
72	Memphis	78
65	South Fla.	76
83	UAB ■	72
81	Houston	85
54	Charlotte	96
87	TCU ■	106
59	St. Louis †	67
50	St. Louis †	47
69	Charlotte †	78

Nickname: Green Wave
Colors: Olive Green & Sky Blue
Arena: Avron B. Fogelman Arena
  Capacity: 3,600; Year Built: 1933
SID: John Sudsbury

TULSA
Tulsa, OK 74104-3189 I

Coach: John Phillips, Oklahoma St. 1973

2001-02 RESULTS (27-7)
104	Grambling ■	61
88	Morris Brown ■	41
75	Arkansas ■	79
73	Oral Roberts	66
90	Southwest Mo. St. ■	73
82	Wichita St.	76
90	Texas A&M †	56
80	Buffalo †	75
92	Montana †	82
88	BYU-Hawaii	67
85	Kansas †	93
76	Nevada	66
85	Fresno St.	86
66	UTEP ■	61
80	Boise St. ■	60
71	Louisiana Tech	68
95	Southern Methodist	87
78	San Jose St. ■	54
82	Hawaii ■	90
79	Rice ■	60
78	Fresno St. ■	63
73	Nevada ■	68
70	Boise St.	56
88	UTEP	76
87	Southern Methodist ■	69
72	Louisiana Tech ■	63
85	Hawaii	86
82	San Jose St.	72
67	Rice	62
72	Boise St. ■	53
81	Fresno St. ■	65
59	Hawaii ■	73
71	Marquette †	69
82	Kentucky †	87

Nickname: Golden Hurricane
Colors: Old Gold, Royal Blue,Crimson
Arena: Donald W. Reynolds Center
  Capacity: 8,355; Year Built: 1998
SID: Don Tomkalski

TUSCULUM
Greeneville, TN 37743 II

Coach: Griff Mills, DePauw 1988

2001-02 RESULTS (15-13)
50	Concord ■	45
53	S.C.-Spartanburg ■	41
36	North Greenville	49
58	Concord	62
62	Lincoln Memorial	78
57	North Greenville	68
61	Milligan ■	44
56	Erskine	50
41	S.C.-Spartanburg	40
45	Liberty	46
65	Lincoln Memorial ■	70
55	Presbyterian ■	50
61	Catawba ■	71
54	Lenoir-Rhyne	66
72	Newberry ■	50
50	Carson-Newman	64
64	Mars Hill	51
57	Wingate ■	61
52	Milligan	45
66	Presbyterian	57
46	Catawba	53
74	Lenoir-Rhyne ■	64
68	Newberry	63
52	Carson-Newman ■	62
67	Mars Hill ■	54
68	Wingate	64
46	Lenoir-Rhyne ■	44
51	Carson-Newman †	88

Nickname: Pioneers
Colors: Black & Orange
Arena: Alpine Arena
  Capacity: 2,000; Year Built: 1998
SID: Dom Donnelly

TUSKEGEE
Tuskegee, AL 36088 II

Coach: Oliver Jones, Albany St. (Ga.) 1965

2001-02 RESULTS (7-20)
59	Alabama A&M	75
90	Columbus St.	113
77	Columbus St. ■	82
53	Miles	76
67	LeMoyne-Owen	80
82	Xavier (La.) ■	79
63	Paine	64
77	North Ala. ■	83
78	Columbus St. ■	87
73	GC&SU †	76
99	Clark Atlanta	85
56	West Ala.	61
52	Fort Valley St.	55
74	Lane ■	58
64	Kentucky St. ■	78
54	Albany St. (Ga.)	63
59	Morehouse ■	88
68	Paine	77
77	Miles ■	60
74	LeMoyne-Owen ■	61
80	Clark Atlanta ■	71
74	Fort Valley St. ■	82
92	Lane	109
79	Kentucky St.	82
71	Albany St. (Ga.) ■	70
52	Morehouse	76
93	Clark Atlanta	105

Nickname: Golden Tigers
Colors: Crimson & Old Gold
Arena: James Center Arena
  Capacity: 5,000; Year Built: 1987
SID: Arnold Houston

UCLA
Los Angeles, CA 90095-1405 I

Coach: Steve Lavin, Chapman 1988

2001-02 RESULTS (21-12)
71	Houston †	60
73	Ball St. †	91
89	South Carolina †	77
78	Pepperdine ■	85
65	UC Riverside ■	50
79	Alabama †	57
75	UC Irvine ■	74
85	Washington	79
79	Washington St.	74
64	Columbia ■	55
98	Georgetown ■	91
74	Washington ■	62
81	Washington St. ■	69
77	Southern California	81
87	Kansas ■	77
82	Arizona St.	79
86	Arizona	96
76	Stanford ■	86
64	California ■	57
62	Oregon	91
70	Oregon St. ■	48
67	Southern California ■	65
57	Villanova	58
77	Arizona ■	76
68	Arizona St. ■	69
51	California	69
95	Stanford	92
65	Oregon St. ■	57
62	Oregon ■	65
61	California †	67
80	Mississippi †	58
105	Cincinnati †	101
73	Missouri †	82

Nickname: Bruins
Colors: Blue & Gold
Arena: Pauley Pavilion
  Capacity: 12,819; Year Built: 1965
SID: Marc Dellins

UNION (N.Y.)
Schenectady, NY 12308 III

Coach: Bob Montana, Brockport St. 1972

2001-02 RESULTS (21-8)
68	Williams	86
77	Haverford ■	67
73	Swarthmore ■	60
62	Hartwick ■	58
61	Utica ■	49
75	Nichols ■	59
59	Susquehanna †	61
81	Cazenovia †	75
93	Ursinus ■	81
62	Cazenovia ■	64
70	Skidmore ■	52
55	Clarkson ■	61
68	St. Lawrence ■	83
58	Middlebury ■	64
83	Hamilton ■	79
77	Hobart ■	71
83	Rensselaer ■	76
61	Vassar ■	58
70	Hobart	69
84	Hamilton	80
71	St. Lawrence ■	74
70	Clarkson ■	59
75	Skidmore	68
74	Vassar	66
61	Rensselaer	58
80	Hamilton ■	66
70	St. Lawrence ■	63
75	Lasell ■	73
50	Babson	63

Nickname: Dutchmen
Colors: Garnet
Arena: Memorial Field House
  Capacity: 3,000; Year Built: 1950
SID: George Cuttita

UPPER IOWA
Fayette, IA 52142-1857 III

Coach: Dave Martin, Upper Iowa 1990

2001-02 RESULTS (12-14)
101	St. Joseph (Conn.) †	68
88	Concordia (Ill.)	68
94	Iowa Wesleyan	109
73	Simpson ■	76
75	Cardinal Stritch †	100
83	St. Scholastica †	80
77	Cornell College	71
71	Coe	73
87	Mt. Mercy ■	68
73	Loras ■	81
80	Dubuque ■	67
67	Central (Iowa) ■	53
77	Luther	66
60	Wartburg	79
80	Buena Vista	98
67	Central (Iowa)	88
54	Coe ■	78
72	Cornell College ■	79
81	Dubuque	87
77	Loras	66
62	Simpson	80
65	Luther ■	51
72	Clarke	69
83	Buena Vista ■	68
72	Wartburg ■	76
53	Wartburg	63

Nickname: Peacocks
Colors: Blue & White
Arena: Dorman Memorial Gym
  Capacity: 2,000; Year Built: 1963
SID: Brian Thiessen

URSINUS
Collegeville, PA 19426-1000 III

Coach: Kevin Small, St. Joseph's 1991

2001-02 RESULTS (8-16)

65	Susquehanna	91
97	Lincoln (Pa.) †	105
60	Phila. Sciences ■	80
66	Lebanon Valley ■	68
65	Gwynedd-Mercy	71
69	Dickinson ■	60
67	Haverford ■	55
60	Trinity (Conn.)	79
81	Union (N.Y.)	93
71	Tufts †	73
46	Frank. & Marsh.	52
81	Washington (Md.)	84
71	Drew ■	69
73	Swarthmore	66
85	Hunter	87
85	Muhlenberg ■	82
63	Johns Hopkins	95
78	Haverford	84
73	McDaniel ■	59
92	Washington (Md.) ■	80
79	Swarthmore ■	68
66	Gettysburg	67
77	Muhlenberg	80
56	Frank. & Marsh.	70

Nickname: Bears
Colors: Red, Old Gold & Black
Arena: D.L. Helfferich Hall
Capacity: 2,500; Year Built: 1972
SID: Bill Stiles

UTAH
Salt Lake City, UT 84112-9008...I

Coach: Rick Majerus, Marquette 1970

2001-02 RESULTS (21-9)

74	St. Francis (Ill.) ■	55
64	Boise St. ■	49
65	Utah St. ■	78
61	Alabama	76
81	Pepperdine ■	74
62	Arizona St.	71
87	Troy St. ■	56
70	Weber St.	59
71	Southern Utah ■	47
75	Idaho St. ■	58
71	Texas ■	61
63	Whitworth ■	57
41	St. Mary's (Cal.)	35
86	UNLV ■	63
76	San Diego St. ■	70
63	Air Force	57
81	New Mexico ■	51
71	Brigham Young ■	66
67	Colorado St. ■	62
46	Wyoming	54
70	San Diego St.	53
64	UNLV	72
59	Air Force ■	51
66	New Mexico ■	65
61	Brigham Young	63
72	Colorado St.	62
56	Wyoming	57
69	Colorado St. †	66
70	UNLV	76
56	Indiana †	75

Nickname: Utes
Colors: Crimson & White
Arena: Jon M. Huntsman Center
Capacity: 15,000; Year Built: 1969
SID: Mike Lageschulte

UTAH ST.
Logan, UT 84322-7400 I

Coach: Stew Morrill, Gonzaga 1974

2001-02 RESULTS (23-8)

66	Montana St.	51
78	Utah	65
64	Idaho St. ■	59
90	Brigham Young ■	81
60	Montana St. ■	55

64	Weber St.	67
99	Western St. (Colo.) ■	43
73	Cal St. Northridge ■	56
81	Pacific (Cal.)	71
74	Centenary (La.) ■	59
74	Idaho St. ■	56
58	Cal Poly	61
60	UC Santa Barb.	56
66	UC Irvine ■	67
70	Long Beach St. ■	66
68	UC Riverside	42
51	Cal St. Fullerton	65
57	Idaho	46
72	UC Santa Barb. ■	64
85	Cal Poly ■	53
60	Long Beach St.	53
62	UC Irvine	61
60	Cal St. Fullerton ■	45
59	UC Riverside ■	42
65	Idaho ■	56
51	Pacific (Cal.)	55
54	Cal St. Northridge	62
61	Idaho †	41
69	Pacific (Cal.) †	65
56	UC Santa Barb. †	60
69	Montana St. ■	77

Nickname: Aggies
Colors: Navy Blue & White
Arena: Dee Glen Smith Spectrum
Capacity: 10,270; Year Built: 1970
SID: Doug Hoffman

UTICA
Utica, NY 13502-4892 III

Coach: Andrew Goodemote,
Albany (N.Y.) 1990

2001-02 RESULTS (9-15)

100	Lehman †	101
53	St. Joseph (Vt.) †	58
82	Utica/Rome ■	69
57	Hamilton ■	69
49	Union (N.Y.)	61
66	Hobart ■	71
65	Skidmore ■	64
60	Clarkson ■	68
68	Rochester Inst.	81
47	Nazareth	53
83	Cazenovia	87
67	Hartwick ■	71
75	Ithaca ■	68
58	St. John Fisher ■	69
62	Alfred ■	65
63	Elmira	56
72	Ithaca	71
71	Hartwick	69
60	Alfred	72
52	St. John Fisher	60
58	Elmira ■	67
86	Nazareth ■	48
81	Rochester Inst. ■	72
90	Keuka ■	52

Nickname: Pioneers
Colors: Blue & Orange
Arena: Clark Athletic Center
Capacity: 2,200; Year Built: 1970
SID: Ryan Hyland

UTICA/ROME
Utica, NY 13504-3050 III

Coach: Kevin Grimmer, Hamilton 1981

2001-02 RESULTS (10-15)

81	St. Joseph (Vt.) ■	69
80	Lehman	59
78	St. Joseph's (Brkln)	77
69	Utica	82
66	Geneseo St. ■	87
75	Medaille	60
58	Buffalo St.	69
59	Gallaudet †	66
48	George Fox †	50

67	Potsdam St.	83
78	Brockport St.	91
80	New Paltz St. ■	67
73	Oneonta St.	88
75	Oswego St. ■	87
71	Geneseo St.	74
67	St. Joseph (Vt.) ■	59
90	Castleton St.	80
74	Cortland St.	58
78	Fredonia St. ■	64
55	Brockport St. ■	81
75	Oswego St.	73
88	Buffalo St. ■	91
60	Cortland St.	78
68	Plattsburgh St.	81
66	Potsdam St. ■	75

Nickname: Wildcats
Colors: Royal Blue & Grey
Arena: Campus Center Gym
Capacity: 1,400; Year Built: 1987
SID: Kevin Grimmer

VALDOSTA ST.
Valdosta, GA 31698................II

Coach: Jim Yarbrough, Florida St. 1987

2001-02 RESULTS (24-8)

95	P.R.-Cayey ■	58
71	Georgia St.	82
95	Carver Bible ■	32
76	Southern Wesleyan	53
56	South Ala.	64
76	Tenn. Wesleyan ■	39
81	Selma ■	54
79	North Ala.	63
84	Southern Wesleyan ■	46
74	Albany St. (Ga.)	50
76	Florida Tech ■	61
75	Florida Tech	59
71	West Ala. ■	52
76	West Ga.	65
76	Lincoln Memorial	75
69	Ala.-Huntsville	53
54	Montevallo ■	73
46	West Fla.	55
81	North Ala. ■	73
71	West Ala.	74
54	Albany St. (Ga.) ■	50
77	West Ga.	93
73	Lincoln Memorial ■	52
77	Ala.-Huntsville ■	64
71	Montevallo	70
70	West Fla. ■	50
95	Harding †	73
66	Delta St. †	50
69	West Ga. †	72
62	Paine †	57
80	Henderson St. †	54
69	West Ga. †	81

Nickname: Blazers
Colors: Red & Black
Arena: The Complex
Capacity: 5,350; Year Built: 1982
SID: Steve Roberts

VALPARAISO
Valparaiso, IN 46383-6493 I

Coach: Homer Drew, William Jewell
1966

2001-02 RESULTS (25-8)

69	Purdue ■	73
72	Belmont	74
71	Indiana St.	54
82	Wis.-Milwaukee ■	69
70	Northern Ill.	50
80	Youngstown St. ■	50
70	Charlotte	63
68	Rhode Island	43
98	Goshen ■	54
77	New Mexico St. †	94
71	Columbia †	55

87	Buffalo †	80
76	West Virginia †	57
70	Arizona	74
73	Kansas	81
78	Western Ill.	68
62	Southern Utah	78
78	Chicago St.	66
87	Oral Roberts ■	67
78	UMKC ■	60
74	IUPUI	73
86	Oakland	77
84	Western Ill. ■	60
100	Chicago St.	63
71	Southern Utah ■	64
76	UMKC	63
74	Oral Roberts	77
79	Oakland ■	72
95	IUPUI ■	75
81	Chicago St. †	50
71	UMKC †	58
88	IUPUI †	55
68	Kentucky †	83

Nickname: Crusaders
Colors: Brown & Gold
Arena: Athletics-Recreation Center
Capacity: 5,000; Year Built: 1984
SID: Bill Rogers

VANDERBILT
Nashville, TN 37212 I

Coach: Kevin Stallings, Purdue 1982

2001-02 RESULTS (17-15)

96	Liberty ■	61
71	Connecticut	84
100	Hampton †	85
67	Monmouth †	81
69	Chattanooga †	57
69	Cal Poly ■	64
80	Western Ky. ■	75
76	Southeast Mo. St. ■	71
77	Centenary (La.) ■	75
77	Tulane	87
85	American ■	57
86	East Tenn. St. ■	77
83	Morehead St. ■	73
69	Georgia	82
79	Alabama	92
85	Florida	95
73	Auburn ■	67
60	South Carolina	51
86	Georgia ■	84
61	Mississippi	73
65	Tennessee ■	67
68	LSU ■	63
54	Florida	80
59	Kentucky	67
43	South Carolina ■	66
43	Mississippi St. ■	66
67	Tennessee	62
86	Kentucky ■	73
67	Arkansas	81
62	LSU †	69
59	Houston ■	50
68	Louisiana Tech	83

Nickname: Commodores
Colors: Black & Gold
Arena: Memorial Gymnasium
Capacity: 14,168; Year Built: 1952
SID: Brent Ross

VASSAR
Poughkeepsie, NY 12604-0750III

Coach: Mike Dutton, New Hampshire
1981

2001-02 RESULTS (9-15)

77	Becker ■	50
69	Mass. Liberal Arts ■	63
47	NYCCT	46
55	New Paltz St.	71
75	Stevens Tech †	70

68	Amherst	79
67	John Jay ■	69
63	Manhattanville	59
65	D'Youville ■	60
50	Hobart	79
67	Hamilton	56
67	Rensselaer	70
76	St. Lawrence ■	69
52	Clarkson	80
68	Mt. St. Mary (N.Y.)	79
87	Skidmore	84
58	Union (N.Y.)	61
58	Clarkson	68
55	St. Lawrence	69
59	Hamilton ■	86
61	Hobart ■	73
68	Rensselaer ■	69
66	Union (N.Y.) ■	74
46	Skidmore	52

Nickname: Brewers
Colors: Burgundy & Gray
Arena: Athletic & Fitness Facility
Capacity: 850; Year Built: 2000
SID: Casey Hager

VERMONT
Burlington, VT 05405.........I

Coach: Tom Brennan, Georgia 1971
2001-02 RESULTS (21-8)

58	Brown †	82
77	Bucknell †	60
73	Dartmouth	54
69	Cleveland St. ■	72
77	Duquesne	82
83	Lehigh	75
85	Sacred Heart	62
74	Harvard ■	54
69	Florida Int'l	64
91	Ohio †	79
71	Albany (N.Y.) ■	43
91	Stony Brook ■	60
74	Boston U.	65
80	Northeastern	77
79	Maine ■	65
81	New Hampshire ■	68
102	Northeastern ■	87
65	Hartford	78
72	Stony Brook	67
62	Michigan	75
89	Boston U. ■	85
83	Binghamton	80
45	Albany (N.Y.)	61
86	Binghamton ■	71
49	Maine	52
93	New Hampshire	77
75	Hartford ■	66
74	Stony Brook †	59
59	Maine †	61

Nickname: Catamounts
Colors: Green & Gold
Arena: Roy L. Patrick Gymnasium
Capacity: 3,200; Year Built: 1963
SID: Gordon Woodworth

VILLA JULIE
Stevenson, MD 21153-9999.....III

Coach: Brett Adams, York (Pa.) 1989
2001-02 RESULTS (8-16)

74	Juniata	87
78	Penn St.-Altoona †	68
82	Gallaudet	76
72	Bridgewater (Va.) ■	87
74	Maryland Bible ■	61
99	Chowan	94
60	Catholic ■	80
62	Goucher ■	65
85	Marymount (Va.) ■	90
57	DeSales	82
86	Washington (Md.) ■	77
84	Kean ■	75

61	Juniata ■	80
59	Johns Hopkins ■	87
85	McDaniel	66
80	Mary Washington	103
92	Marywood	79
87	Washington (Md.) ■	92
76	Frostburg St.	93
71	Misericordia	95
64	St. Mary's (Md.) ■	85
72	Messiah	73
62	Mary Washington ■	70
78	Shenandoah	91

Nickname: Mustangs
Colors: Green, Black & White
Arena: Villa Julie Activity Center
Capacity: 1,200; Year Built: 1997
SID: Mike Buchanan

VILLANOVA
Villanova, PA 19085-1674.........I

Coach: Jay Wright, Bucknell 1983
2001-02 RESULTS (19-13)

82	Grambling ■	68
59	Dayton ■	57
58	La Salle ■	61
69	Bucknell ■	45
74	Pennsylvania	75
70	Temple †	66
76	Stony Brook ■	54
104	VMI ■	91
67	Delaware St. ■	44
76	Providence ■	57
74	Notre Dame	72
81	Boston College ■	88
65	Connecticut ■	70
77	Virginia Tech	75
63	St. John's (N.Y.)	65
58	Miami (Fla.)	76
102	St. Joseph's	73
84	Virginia Tech ■	77
59	Pittsburgh ■	71
56	Miami (Fla.) ■	65
58	UCLA ■	57
40	Connecticut	46
83	Georgetown ■	72
64	Providence	72
67	Boston College	69
67	Syracuse ■	61
77	St. John's (N.Y.) ■	62
78	Syracuse †	64
70	Connecticut †	72
84	Manhattan ■	69
67	Louisiana Tech ■	64
57	Temple	63

Nickname: Wildcats
Colors: Blue & White
Arena: Pavilion
Capacity: 6,500; Year Built: 1986
SID: Mike Sheridan

VIRGINIA
Charlottesville, VA 22904-4821..I

Coach: Pete Gillen, Fairfield 1968
2001-02 RESULTS (17-12)

105	Wagner ■	74
85	East Tenn. St. ■	62
115	Howard ■	66
69	Virginia Tech ■	61
77	Auburn †	72
74	Charleston So. ■	54
61	Georgetown	55
76	Rutgers ■	68
112	Grambling ■	67
74	North Carolina St. ■	81
52	Clemson	68
71	North Carolina	67
86	Wake Forest ■	74
91	Florida St. ■	74
69	Georgia Tech	65
93	VMI	59

81	Duke	94
87	Maryland ■	91
77	Missouri	81
68	North Carolina St.	85
85	Clemson ■	71
73	North Carolina	63
70	Wake Forest	92
59	Florida St.	66
80	Georgia Tech ■	82
87	Duke ■	84
92	Maryland	112
72	North Carolina St. †	92
67	South Carolina ■	74

Nickname: Cavaliers
Colors: Orange & Blue
Arena: University Hall
Capacity: 8,392; Year Built: 1965
SID: Rich Murray

VA. COMMONWEALTH
Richmond, VA 23284-3013........I

Coach: Mack McCarthy, Virginia Tech 1974
2001-02 RESULTS (21-11)

73	Northwestern †	78
71	Rutgers †	58
82	Prairie View †	66
79	East Tenn. St. ■	71
72	Tulane ■	76
66	N.C. A&T ■	53
65	Richmond	54
91	Towson ■	68
88	Fla. Atlantic	84
82	UAB ■	76
75	Gardner-Webb ■	68
83	Wagner	88
73	Drexel	84
82	James Madison ■	75
62	Hofstra	77
81	William & Mary	92
68	Delaware ■	57
79	Old Dominion	77
75	George Mason ■	59
74	UNC Wilmington ■	68
70	Delaware	75
77	Drexel ■	65
69	Hofstra ■	67
65	James Madison	67
73	Old Dominion ■	66
62	Towson	49
80	George Mason	83
62	UNC Wilmington	73
68	William & Mary ■	60
58	Old Dominion †	54
70	Hofstra †	54
51	UNC Wilmington †	66

Nickname: Rams
Colors: Black & Gold
Arena: Stuart C. Siegel Center
Capacity: 7,500; Year Built: 1999
SID: Josh Lehman

VMI
Lexington, VA 24450-0304........I

Coach: Bart Bellairs, Warren Wilson 1979
2001-02 RESULTS (10-18)

76	Mary Washington ■	51
87	Morehead St.	98
73	Virginia Tech	74
57	Kentucky	99
98	St. Mary's (Md.) ■	72
90	Charleston So. ■	69
77	East. Mennonite ■	51
91	Villanova	104
82	Richmond	80
84	James Madison †	94
80	Western Caro.	90
60	Ga. Southern	100
74	UNC Greensboro ■	80

90	East Tenn. St.	101
68	Davidson	79
55	Col. of Charleston ■	63
93	Appalachian St.	91
59	Virginia	93
76	Furman ■	68
77	East Tenn. St. ■	96
68	Wofford	78
88	Appalachian St. ■	81
97	Western Caro.	91
64	Chattanooga	91
71	UNC Greensboro	74
55	Citadel ■	75
81	Davidson ■	77
70	Citadel †	80

Nickname: Keydets
Colors: Red, White, Yellow
Arena: Cameron Hall
Capacity: 5,029; Year Built: 1981
SID: Wade Branner

VIRGINIA ST.
Petersburg, VA 23806-0001......II

Coach: Robert Booker, Claflin 1964
2001-02 RESULTS (6-20)

88	Barton ■	77
58	N.C. Central	52
69	Lander	75
72	Charleston (W.Va.)	91
65	Salem Int'l ■	81
63	Barton	76
88	Livingstone	77
78	Charleston (W.Va.) ■	95
78	Bowie St.	88
77	Elizabeth City St. †	81
75	Shaw ■	84
74	Virginia Union †	55
78	Winston-Salem ■	86
91	Pitt.-Johnstown	80
63	St. Augustine's ■	85
68	St. Paul's ■	64
75	Johnson Smith	89
77	Pitt.-Johnstown	84
74	Virginia Union	86
72	Bowie St. ■	81
66	St. Augustine's ■	84
85	Elizabeth City St.	94
81	Shaw	99
58	Fayetteville St. ■	61
76	St. Paul's	88
55	N.C. Central †	62

Nickname: Trojans
Colors: Orange & Navy Blue
Arena: Daniel Gymnasium
Capacity: 3,454; Year Built: 1965
SID: Paul Williams

VIRGINIA TECH
Blacksburg, VA 24061..............I

Coach: Ricky Stokes, Virginia 1984
2001-02 RESULTS (10-18)

82	Mt. St. Mary's ■	59
86	Rhode Island ■	63
46	Old Dominion	55
90	East Caro. ■	62
79	Northeastern ■	56
61	Virginia	69
74	VMI ■	73
63	Murray St. †	66
78	Wis.-Milwaukee †	80
51	Western Mich. ■	55
63	Radford ■	56
49	Florida St.	78
74	Connecticut ■	86
72	Seton Hall ■	80
60	Connecticut	95
68	Miami (Fla.) ■	77
75	Villanova ■	77
68	Boston College	77
69	Syracuse	81

77 Villanova ... 84
63 St. John's (N.Y.) ■ ... 72
76 Boston College ■ ... 73
69 Providence ... 77
78 West Virginia ... 63
63 St. John's (N.Y.) ... 73
69 Providence ■ ... 64
63 Rutgers ■ ... 49
77 Miami (Fla.) ... 83

Nickname: Hokies
Colors: Burnt Orange & Maroon
Arena: Cassell Coliseum
Capacity: 10,052; Year Built: 1961
SID: Bill Dyer

VIRGINIA UNION

Richmond, VA 23220-1790 ... II

Coach: Dave Robbins, Catawba 1966

2001-02 RESULTS (12-14)

69 Livingstone ... 66
56 Johnson Smith ... 70
71 Winston-Salem ■ ... 79
64 Johnson Smith † ... 57
80 Livingstone ■ ... 65
68 Queens (N.Y.) ■ ... 52
69 Pitt.-Johnstown ■ ... 51
55 Calif. (Pa.) ■ ... 68
87 Voorhees ... 68
86 Livingstone ... 74
59 Fayetteville St. ... 66
71 Dist. Columbia ■ ... 72
58 St. Paul's † ... 41
74 St. Paul's ... 82
55 Virginia St. † ... 74
75 Bowie St. ... 90
77 Elizabeth City St. ■ ... 70
63 Shaw ■ ... 78
63 St. Augustine's ■ ... 54
77 Bowie St. ■ ... 78
86 Virginia St. ■ ... 74
81 Shaw ... 122
73 Dist. Columbia ... 78
79 N.C. Central ■ ... 59
65 Elizabeth City St. ... 69
79 St. Augustine's † ... 83

Nickname: Panthers
Colors: Steel & Maroon
Arena: Arthur Ashe Athletic Center
Capacity: 6,000; Year Built: 1982
SID: Paul Williams

VA. WESLEYAN

Norfolk, VA 23502-5599 ... III

Coach: David Macedo, Wilkes 1996

2001-02 RESULTS (16-10)

76 Clark (Mass.) † ... 82
79 Neumann † ... 73
51 Chris. Newport ... 75
70 East. Mennonite ... 55
68 Roanoke ■ ... 66
55 Wash. & Lee ■ ... 57
71 Salisbury ... 74
82 Wesley † ... 59
82 Lycoming ... 85
80 Lynchburg ■ ... 64
93 Emory & Henry ... 76
55 Guilford ... 58
69 Bridgewater (Va.) ■ ... 47
67 Randolph-Macon ... 80
60 Hampden-Sydney ... 57
67 Wash. & Lee ... 50
62 Roanoke ... 74
81 Apprentice ... 85
71 Guilford ■ ... 68
91 Emory & Henry ■ ... 81
90 Lynchburg ... 69
65 Randolph-Macon ■ ... 64
69 East. Mennonite ■ ... 45
76 Bridgewater (Va.) ... 71

78 Hampden-Sydney ■ ... 70
77 Emory & Henry † ... 79

Nickname: Blue Marlins
Colors: Navy Blue & Silver
Arena: Baffen Center
Capacity: 3,000; Year Built: 2001
SID: Rebecca Brutlag

WABASH

Crawfordsville, IN 47933 ... III

Coach: Mac Petty, Tennessee 1968

2001-02 RESULTS (15-11)

78 Walsh † ... 76
65 Hampden-Sydney ... 105
75 Hanover ■ ... 84
66 DePauw ■ ... 78
91 Kenyon ■ ... 65
69 Wittenberg ... 90
75 Denison ■ ... 62
76 Franklin ... 84
68 Olivet ■ ... 71
86 MacMurray ■ ... 65
92 Hiram ■ ... 58
71 Allegheny ■ ... 72
80 North Park ■ ... 77
69 Wooster ■ ... 72
72 Earlham ... 63
69 Oberlin ... 78
77 Wittenberg ■ ... 65
65 Kenyon ... 63
51 Ohio Wesleyan ■ ... 48
79 Denison ... 68
63 Earlham ■ ... 68
76 Wooster ... 62
81 Ohio Wesleyan ... 72
60 Oberlin ■ ... 49
89 Denison ■ ... 53
80 Wooster † ... 83

Nickname: Little Giants
Colors: Scarlet
Arena: Chadwick Court
Capacity: 1,800; Year Built: 1917
SID: Brent Harris

WAGNER

Staten Island, NY 10301-4495 ... I

Coach: Dereck Whittenburg, North Carolina St. 1984

2001-02 RESULTS (19-10)

74 Virginia ... 105
80 Lehigh ... 73
100 Brown ... 103
78 Fairleigh Dickinson ... 69
65 Monmouth ... 69
88 Iona ■ ... 73
61 Rutgers ... 77
88 Va. Commonwealth ■ ... 83
69 American ... 58
81 St. Francis (Pa.) ■ ... 80
89 Robert Morris ■ ... 63
71 Central Conn. St. ... 77
77 Quinnipiac ■ ... 75
69 Monmouth ■ ... 61
82 Sacred Heart ... 80
80 St. Francis (Pa.) ... 67
85 Quinnipiac ... 87
95 Sacred Heart ■ ... 74
102 Mt. St. Mary's ■ ... 70
97 Long Island ... 87
92 Long Island ■ ... 81
99 St. Francis (N.Y.) ■ ... 88
69 Central Conn. St. ■ ... 83
86 UMBC ■ ... 69
83 St. Francis (N.Y.) ... 71
69 UMBC ... 81
88 Mt. St. Mary's ... 58
78 Quinnipiac ■ ... 87
67 Richmond ... 74

Nickname: Seahawks
Colors: Green & White
Arena: Spiro Sports Center
Capacity: 2,100; Year Built: 1999
SID: Bob Balut

WAKE FOREST

Winston-Salem, NC 27109 ... I

Coach: Skip Prosser, Merchant Marine 1972

2001-02 RESULTS (21-13)

87 Navy ... 65
96 Clemson ■ ... 55
79 UNC Wilmington ■ ... 78
76 Arkansas ... 71
87 Elon ■ ... 67
62 Fresno St. † ... 61
67 Syracuse † ... 74
85 Minnesota ■ ... 79
76 Kansas ... 83
115 South Carolina St. ■ ... 75
93 Florida St. ■ ... 72
89 St. Francis (Pa.) ■ ... 60
60 St. John's (N.Y.) ... 72
64 Marquette ■ ... 59
67 Richmond ■ ... 52
84 North Carolina ... 62
74 Virginia ... 86
80 Duke ... 103
63 Maryland ■ ... 85
87 Georgia Tech ■ ... 74
82 North Carolina St. ... 81
89 Florida St. ... 80
90 North Carolina ■ ... 66
94 Cincinnati ■ ... 103
115 Clemson ... 118
92 Virginia ■ ... 70
61 Duke ■ ... 90
89 Maryland ... 90
77 Georgia Tech ... 90
83 North Carolina St. ■ ... 71
92 Georgia Tech † ... 83
64 Duke † ... 79
83 Pepperdine † ... 74
87 Oregon † ... 92

Nickname: Demon Deacons
Colors: Old Gold & Black
Arena: Lawrence Joel Coliseum
Capacity: 14,665; Year Built: 1989
SID: Dean Buchan

WARTBURG

Waverly, IA 50677-1003 ... III

Coach: Dick Peth, Iowa 1981

2001-02 RESULTS (20-8)

79 Faith Bapt. Bible ■ ... 59
82 Wis.-La Crosse ■ ... 81
65 Buena Vista ■ ... 74
63 Simpson ... 60
98 Central (Iowa) ... 85
77 Iowa Wesleyan ... 61
73 Hamilton † ... 84
59 Transylvania † ... 53
58 Elmhurst ... 83
65 Buffalo St. † ... 73
77 Cornell College ■ ... 65
69 Coe ■ ... 68
69 Loras ... 65
82 Dubuque ... 61
79 Upper Iowa ■ ... 60
71 Luther ■ ... 57
68 Central (Iowa) ■ ... 63
79 Simpson ■ ... 71
59 Coe ... 80
77 Cornell College ... 56
76 Buena Vista ... 86
88 Dubuque ■ ... 68
64 Loras ■ ... 76
64 Luther ... 63

76 Upper Iowa ... 72
63 Upper Iowa ■ ... 53
61 Cornell College ■ ... 56
73 Buena Vista ... 85

Nickname: Knights
Colors: Orange & Black
Arena: Knights Gym
Capacity: 1,800; Year Built: 1949
SID: Duane Schroeder

WASHBURN

Topeka, KS 66621 ... II

Coach: Bob Chipman, Kansas St. 1973

2001-02 RESULTS (20-8)

93 Benedictine (Kan.) ■ ... 59
96 Baker ■ ... 64
69 Rockhurst ... 64
86 Mid-America Naz. ■ ... 77
74 Cameron † ... 63
91 Central Okla. † ... 77
76 Lock Haven ■ ... 57
73 Metro St. ■ ... 74
92 Mo. Western St. ■ ... 95
83 Truman ... 73
86 Mo. Southern St. ■ ... 74
90 Southwest Baptist ... 80
59 Mo.-Rolla ... 53
65 Northwest Mo. St. ■ ... 67
85 Central Mo. St. ... 61
80 Emporia St. ■ ... 64
89 Pittsburg St. ■ ... 75
71 Mo. Western St. ... 73
79 Truman ■ ... 64
74 Mo. Southern St. ... 83
89 Southwest Baptist ■ ... 52
94 Mo.-Rolla ■ ... 64
57 Northwest Mo. St. ... 72
83 Central Mo. St. ■ ... 65
80 Emporia St. ... 75
69 Pittsburg St. ... 90
80 Pittsburg St. ■ ... 73
60 Mo. Western St. ... 75

Nickname: Ichabods
Colors: Yale Blue & White
Arena: Lee Arena
Capacity: 4,298; Year Built: 1984
SID: Gene Cassell

WASHINGTON

Seattle, WA 98195 ... I

Coach: Bob Bender, Duke 1980

2001-02 RESULTS (11-18)

82 Alas. Fairbanks ... 70
81 Bowling Green † ... 74
64 Butler † ... 67
69 Santa Clara ■ ... 49
77 UNLV ■ ... 64
98 San Diego ... 94
62 UTEP ... 74
75 New Mexico St. ... 74
47 Gonzaga ■ ... 67
79 UCLA ■ ... 85
65 Southern California ■ ... 87
70 St. Louis ... 71
62 UCLA ... 74
74 Southern California ... 94
81 Arizona St. ■ ... 68
69 Arizona ■ ... 74
50 California ... 62
60 Stanford ... 105
97 Oregon ■ ... 92
53 Oregon St. ■ ... 68
79 Washington St. ... 81
82 Arizona ... 91
74 Arizona St. ... 86
65 Stanford ■ ... 91
75 California ■ ... 60
68 Oregon St. ... 63
84 Oregon ... 90

82 Washington St. ■ 75
64 Oregon † 86
Nickname: Huskies
Colors: Purple & Gold
Arena: Bank of America Arena
Capacity: 10,000; Year Built: 1927
SID: Dan Lepse

WASH. & JEFF.
Washington, PA 15301-4801 ...III

Coach: Tom Reiter, Wisconsin 1975
2001-02 RESULTS (6-19)
80 Carnegie Mellon † 83
64 Allegheny † 72
121 Kenyon ■ 120
79 Pitt.-Greensburg 92
57 Penn St.-Behrend ■ 50
80 Frostburg St. ■ 90
87 Cincinnati Bible 82
47 Davidson 91
93 York (Pa.) 97
59 Grove City † 78
75 Oberlin 76
66 Carnegie Mellon ■ 94
61 Thiel 67
66 Bethany (W.Va.) 90
59 Grove City ■ 74
86 Waynesburg ■ 79
83 La Roche 73
48 Westminster (Pa.) 66
81 Thiel 88
78 Bethany (W.Va.) ■ 82
58 Grove City 80
64 La Roche 80
71 Waynesburg 86
65 Westminster (Pa.) ■ 63
77 Waynesburg 79
Nickname: Presidents
Colors: Red & Black
Arena: Henry Memorial Center
Capacity: 2,800; Year Built: 1970
SID: Scott McGuinness

WASH. & LEE
Lexington, VA 24450 III

Coach: Jeff Lafave, Southern Conn. St. 1999
2001-02 RESULTS (7-18)
71 Haverford † 43
63 Swarthmore † 70
65 Wesley ■ 70
56 Greensboro ■ 53
55 William & Mary 70
64 Randolph-Macon 82
57 Va. Wesleyan 55
55 Bridgewater (Va.) 77
55 Guilford ■ 64
56 Roanoke 71
76 East. Mennonite 73
71 Lynchburg 75
51 Hampden-Sydney ■ 78
51 Guilford 65
50 Va. Wesleyan ■ 67
39 Randolph-Macon ■ 62
75 Emory & Henry 76
69 Roanoke ■ 76
62 Emory & Henry ■ 60
63 Hampden-Sydney 80
66 Lynchburg 59
61 Mary Washington ■ 53
68 East. Mennonite 86
53 Bridgewater (Va.) ■ 73
36 Randolph-Macon † 69
Nickname: Generals
Colors: Royal Blue & White
Arena: Warner Center
Capacity: 2,500; Year Built: 1972
SID: Brian Laubscher

WASHINGTON (MD.)
Chestertown, MD 21620-1197 .III

Coach: Rob Nugent, Mass. Lib. Arts 1997
2001-02 RESULTS (10-14)
76 Case Reserve † 69
47 Greensboro † 68
71 Salisbury ■ 86
63 Mary Washington 79
57 Gettysburg 73
66 Swarthmore 71
67 Marymount (Va.) ■ 71
92 Gallaudet 87
82 Maryland Bible ■ 55
77 Villa Julie 86
68 Maritime (N.Y.) † 54
76 Johns Hopkins ■ 84
84 Ursinus 81
58 Muhlenberg 75
75 Haverford ■ 72
66 Wesley 76
71 Frank. & Marsh. 80
92 Villa Julie 87
86 Swarthmore ■ 75
70 Dickinson 79
80 Ursinus 92
81 Muhlenberg ■ 82
76 Haverford 69
88 McDaniel 80
Nickname: Shoremen
Colors: Maroon & Black
Arena: Frank C. Russell Gymnasium at Cain Athletic Center
Capacity: 1,200; Year Built: 1957
SID: Phil Ticknor

WASHINGTON (MO.)
St. Louis, MO 63130-4899 III

Coach: Mark Edwards, Washington (Mo.) 1969
2001-02 RESULTS (25-2)
99 Middlebury ■ 68
77 Whitman ■ 60
98 Hardin-Simmons ■ 44
90 Berea † 64
55 Hanover 63
100 Coe ■ 80
97 Wis. Lutheran ■ 66
88 Webster 58
81 Ill. Wesleyan ■ 58
78 MacMurray 55
71 Blackburn 55
65 Chicago ■ 62
96 Emory 91
97 Case Reserve 92
72 New York U. ■ 58
102 Brandeis ■ 55
65 Rochester ■ 48
76 Carnegie Mellon ■ 72
71 Carnegie Mellon 66
65 Rochester 63
82 Case Reserve ■ 49
93 Emory ■ 47
95 Brandeis 71
77 New York U. 43
64 Chicago 62
71 Maryville (Tenn.) ■ 57
87 DePauw † 90
Nickname: Bears
Colors: Red & Green
Arena: Washington Field House
Capacity: 3,000; Year Built: 1928
SID: Keith Jenkins

WASHINGTON ST.
Pullman, WA 99164-1602 I

Coach: Paul Graham, North Texas 1974

2001-02 RESULTS (6-21)
75 Colorado St. ■ 79
103 Prairie View ■ 55
71 Montana 75
91 Ark.-Pine Bluff ■ 75
81 Idaho ■ 55
70 Tex.-Pan American ■ 67
52 Texas 79
44 Gonzaga 67
74 UCLA ■ 79
63 Southern California ■ 78
64 Southern California 85
69 UCLA 81
85 Arizona 92
71 Arizona St. ■ 81
50 Stanford 83
57 California 90
72 Oregon St. 74
86 Oregon ■ 94
81 Washington 79
45 Arizona St. 96
68 Arizona 85
56 California ■ 77
63 Stanford ■ 76
77 Oregon 115
55 Oregon St. 91
75 Washington ■ 82
102 Centenary (La.) ■ 80
Nickname: Cougars
Colors: Crimson & Gray
Arena: Friel Court
Capacity: 12,058; Year Built: 1973
SID: Rod Commons

WAYNE ST. (MICH.)
Detroit, MI 48202-3489 II

Coach: Ron Hammye, Bowling Green 1978
2001-02 RESULTS (15-12)
74 Northwood † 82
75 Saginaw Valley 68
70 Augusta St. † 48
60 Lynn 63
80 Saginaw Valley ■ 69
78 Northwood ■ 62
94 Mich.-Dearborn ■ 52
80 Madonna ■ 44
81 Concordia (Mich.) ■ 58
59 Grand Valley St. 69
60 SIU-Edwardsville 67
77 Grand Valley St. ■ 62
92 Ferris St. ■ 79
73 Lake Superior St. 63
70 Michigan Tech 71
75 Northern Mich. 42
78 Gannon ■ 84
90 Mercyhurst ■ 77
75 Ashland 58
84 Findlay 88
68 Hillsdale 65
60 Mercyhurst 66
70 Gannon 56
68 Findlay ■ 71
60 Ashland ■ 64
62 Hillsdale ■ 69
70 Michigan Tech † 78
Nickname: Warriors
Colors: Green & Gold
Arena: Matthaei Building
Capacity: 2,000; Year Built: 1966
SID: Eva McGillivray

WAYNE ST. (NEB.)
Wayne, NE 68787-1172 II

Coach: Rico Burkett, North Dakota 1993
2001-02 RESULTS (8-19)
78 Truman † 72
68 Wis.-Parkside † 80
83 Mt. Marty ■ 68
67 Neb.-Kearney ■ 79

89 York (Neb.) ■ 62
75 Bemidji St. 77
49 Minn.-Duluth 70
70 Neb.-Omaha ■ 81
62 Augustana (S.D.) ■ 73
67 Northern St. 77
92 Minn.-Morris ■ 81
58 Winona St. 63
65 Concordia-St. Paul 67
66 Southwest St. 71
72 Minn. St. Moorhead ■ 69
79 Minn.-Crookston 74
61 Minn.-Duluth ■ 66
68 Bemidji St. 77
70 Minn.-Morris 71
65 Northern St. 90
71 Concordia-St. Paul ■ 48
72 Winona St. ■ 85
71 Briar Cliff 59
46 Southwest St. 59
71 Minn.-Crookston 84
48 Minn. St. Moorhead 76
62 Minn.-Duluth 79
Nickname: Wildcats
Colors: Black & Gold
Arena: Rice Auditorium
Capacity: 2,500; Year Built: 1960
SID: Jeremy Phillips

WAYNESBURG
Waynesburg, PA 15370 III

Coach: Rudy Marisa, Penn St. 1956
2001-02 RESULTS (18-9)
87 Widener † 100
74 Marietta † 76
91 Pitt.-Greensburg ■ 79
74 La Roche 68
79 Mt. Aloysius ■ 61
99 Davis & Elkins ■ 74
75 Wilmington (Ohio) 68
68 Penn St.-Behrend 67
81 Rutgers-Camden † 75
78 DeSales 88
86 Medaille 81
116 Ohio-Eastern 111
60 Grove City 78
81 Westminster (Pa.) ■ 70
76 Penn St.-Altoona 61
71 Bethany (W.Va.) 82
79 Wash. & Jeff. 86
68 Thiel ■ 56
64 Grove City 75
89 Frostburg St. 87
68 Westminster (Pa.) 60
89 Bethany (W.Va.) ■ 88
87 Penn St.-Altoona ■ 66
86 Wash. & Jeff. ■ 71
91 Thiel 95
79 Wash. & Jeff. ■ 77
78 Bethany (W.Va.) 88
Nickname: Yellow Jackets
Colors: Orange & Black
Arena: Marisa Field House
Capacity: 1,500; Year Built: 1985
SID: Justin Zackal

WEBER ST.
Ogden, UT 84408-2701 I

Coach: Joe Cravens, Texas-Arlington 1977
2001-02 RESULTS (18-11)
70 Illinois St. 74
103 Concordia (Ore.) ■ 77
75 LSU † 74
73 Wisconsin 69
72 Colorado St. † 69
90 Western Mont. ■ 62
47 Brigham Young 65
67 Utah St. ■ 64
59 Utah ■ 70

87	Savannah St. ■	56
70	Southern Utah ■	64
68	Bradley †	46
63	Chattanooga	71
62	Montana St. ■	64
73	Montana ■	80
78	Northern Ariz. ■	66
86	Sacramento St. ■	83
90	Montana	71
68	Montana St.	79
89	Eastern Wash. ■	78
90	Portland St. ■	85
65	Idaho St.	46
76	Sacramento St.	72
79	Northern Ariz.	85
77	Portland St.	83
66	Eastern Wash.	68
88	Idaho St. ■	82
84	Portland St. †	62
57	Eastern Wash. †	62

Nickname: Wildcats
Colors: Purple & White
Arena: Dee Events Center
Capacity: 12,000; Year Built: 1977
SID: Brad Larsen

WEBSTER
Webster Groves, MO 63119 III

Coach: David Kaneshiro, Beloit 1995
2001-02 RESULTS (13-13)

53	Hanover †	58
56	Anderson (Ind.) †	83
63	Eureka †	53
63	Lake Forest	70
77	Wis. Lutheran ■	84
58	Washington (Mo.) ■	88
99	Concordia (Mo.) ■	76
70	Aurora	80
69	Concordia (Ill.)	81
68	Austin Peay	90
63	Millikin ■	75
75	MacMurray ■	91
76	Greenville ■	75
80	Maryville (Mo.)	77
72	Fontbonne ■	69
76	Westminster (Mo.)	79
66	Blackburn	58
78	Principia ■	65
75	MacMurray	72
86	Greenville	81
52	Maryville (Mo.) ■	51
77	Fontbonne	85
91	Westminster (Mo.) ■	74
59	Blackburn ■	56
96	Principia	88
45	Maryville (Tenn.)	70

Nickname: Gorlocks
Colors: Gold, Navy Blue & White
Arena: Grant Gym
Capacity: 800; Year Built: 1992
SID: Ryan Barke

WENTWORTH INST.
Boston, MA 02115 III

Coach: Harry McShane, Northeastern 1983
2001-02 RESULTS (5-20)

71	Mass. Liberal Arts †	74
65	Becker †	52
43	Coast Guard	74
70	Emerson ■	82
55	Bridgewater St. ■	66
83	WPI	71
66	Bethany (Cal.) †	73
68	Cal St. Monterey Bay	89
37	MIT ■	66
54	Colby-Sawyer ■	85
53	Bates	84
60	Springfield	72
88	New England	93

79	Salve Regina ■	84
49	Endicott	61
91	New England Col. ■	57
59	Mass.-Boston ■	61
59	Gordon	77
58	Roger Williams ■	61
78	Curry ■	83
65	Anna Maria ■	61
63	Eastern Nazarene ■	74
84	Newbury ■	61
75	Nichols	84
66	Fisher ■	81

Nickname: Leopards
Colors: Black & Gold
Arena: Tansey Gymnasium
Capacity: 1,000; Year Built: 1970
SID: Bill Gorman

WESLEY
Dover, DE 19901-3875 III

Coach: James Wentworth, Pfeiffer 1960
2001-02 RESULTS (10-16)

80	Ferrum †	67
63	Roanoke	85
70	Wash. & Lee	65
85	Lancaster Bible ■	52
61	Frank. & Marsh.	84
62	Arcadia	53
57	Cabrini	79
76	Alvernia ■	89
59	Va. Wesleyan †	82
75	Chowan	74
78	Eastern ■	86
66	Phila. Bible	64
68	Misericordia ■	85
72	Marywood	65
77	Gwynedd-Mercy	69
76	Arcadia	81
70	Neumann ■	80
76	Washington (Md.) ■	66
63	Cabrini ■	69
63	Alvernia	78
67	Eastern	71
89	Marywood ■	81
64	Gwynedd-Mercy ■	83
63	Misericordia	70
71	Neumann	86
50	Alvernia	88

Nickname: Wolverines
Colors: Navy Blue & White
Arena: Wesley Gymnasium
Capacity: 800
SID: Jason Bowen

WESLEYAN (CONN.)
Middletown, CT 06459 III

Coach: Gerry McDowell, Colby 1976
2001-02 RESULTS (15-10)

105	New England †	72
83	Maine Maritime †	54
83	Clark (Mass.) ■	80
97	Western New Eng. ■	82
102	Eastern Conn. St. ■	87
83	Colby-Sawyer †	91
88	Maine Maritime †	76
96	Suffolk ■	78
98	Albertus Magnus	64
63	Cal St. Monterey Bay	69
94	Oneonta St. †	71
57	Williams ■	65
74	Amherst	85
87	Bowdoin ■	79
89	Colby	84
65	Connecticut Col. ■	80
105	Emmanuel (Mass.)	72
66	Williams	71
87	Middlebury	100
59	Amherst ■	73
65	Trinity (Conn.) ■	72
72	Tufts	65

77	Bates	74
75	Connecticut Col.	61
71	Trinity (Conn.)	74

Nickname: Cardinals
Colors: Red & Black
Arena: Alumni Athletic Building
Capacity: 1,500; Year Built: 1931
SID: Brian Katten

WEST ALA.
Livingston, AL 35470 II

Coach: Rick Reedy, Flagler 1977
2001-02 RESULTS (11-15)

81	Selma †	47
69	Livingstone †	50
54	Southern U.	45
61	Stillman	68
67	Christian Bros.	78
71	Lane	80
55	Stillman ■	51
59	Lincoln Memorial	72
40	Western Ky.	103
52	Valdosta St.	71
64	West Fla.	78
61	Tuskegee ■	56
63	North Ala. ■	80
60	Montevallo	68
73	Ala.-Huntsville ■	84
70	Christian Bros. ■	68
73	West Ga.	78
73	Lincoln Memorial ■	82
69	Lane ■	88
74	Valdosta St. ■	71
89	West Fla.	100
88	Selma ■	74
73	North Ala.	66
75	Montevallo ■	69
71	Ala.-Huntsville	60
56	West Ga. ■	80

Nickname: Tigers
Colors: Red, White & Black
Arena: Pruitt Hall
Capacity: 1,500; Year Built: 1962
SID: Jason Hughes

WEST CHESTER
West Chester, PA 19383 II

Coach: Dick DeLaney, West Chester 1969
2001-02 RESULTS (18-9)

79	Goldey-Beacom ■	56
74	American Int'l ■	70
65	Philadelphia U.	71
68	Dist. Columbia	70
71	Indiana (Pa.)	84
96	Calif. (Pa.)	87
76	Lock Haven	67
54	Clarion	70
80	St. Vincent †	70
60	Assumption	70
69	Slippery Rock	59
71	Edinboro	57
67	Mansfield	55
77	Shippensburg ■	51
63	Kutztown	54
51	Millersville	65
74	Cheyney ■	72
73	Bloomsburg ■	65
55	Dist. Columbia	81
89	Mansfield ■	78
70	East Stroudsburg	62
63	Kutztown	49
48	Cheyney	63
91	Millersville ■	80
66	East Stroudsburg ■	56
81	Bloomsburg	70
54	Bloomsburg ■	60

Nickname: Golden Rams
Colors: Purple & Gold
Arena: Hollinger Field House

Capacity: 2,500; Year Built: 1949
SID: Tom DiCamillo

WEST FLA.
Pensacola, FL 32514 II

Coach: Don Hogan, South Ala. 1981
2001-02 RESULTS (16-12)

61	Murray St.	100
64	Morehouse ■	66
66	Fort Valley St.	64
90	Selma ■	69
48	Henderson St. †	73
77	Miles †	78
68	Ala.-Huntsville ■	58
75	Fort Valley St. ■	58
91	Southern Ark. ■	77
81	Loyola (La.) ■	63
102	Concordia (N.Y.) †	66
99	Green Mountain †	64
82	West Ga.	97
78	West Ala.	64
95	Montevallo ■	80
73	Edward Waters	84
97	Lincoln Memorial ■	85
62	North Ala.	72
55	Valdosta St.	46
68	Ala.-Huntsville	62
76	West Ga.	78
100	West Ala. ■	89
81	Montevallo	89
90	Lincoln Memorial	91
83	North Ala. ■	76
50	Valdosta St.	70
60	Henderson St. †	56
68	West Ga. †	72

Nickname: Argonauts
Colors: Blue & Green
Arena: UWF Field House
Capacity: 3,000; Year Built: 1969
SID: Cara Lynn Teague

WEST GA.
Carrollton, GA 30118 II

Coach: Ed Murphy, Hardin-Simmons 1964
2001-02 RESULTS (24-9)

79	Augusta St.	86
99	Clayton St. ■	83
67	Shaw †	75
81	Kennesaw St.	70
78	Columbus St.	79
87	Shorter †	72
101	Columbus St. ■	98
83	Augusta St. ■	80
92	Morehouse †	77
82	Albany St. (Ga.) †	77
97	West Fla. ■	82
96	Lincoln Memorial ■	70
65	Valdosta St.	76
71	Ala.-Huntsville ■	72
80	North Ala.	71
100	Montevallo ■	85
78	West Ala. ■	73
78	Clayton St.	62
78	West Fla.	76
76	Lincoln Memorial	96
93	Valdosta St. ■	77
65	Ala.-Huntsville	68
75	North Ala. ■	72
70	Montevallo	74
92	Talladega ■	90
80	West Ala.	56
72	Southern Ark. †	66
72	West Fla. †	68
72	Valdosta St. †	69
76	Delta St. †	71
77	Tampa	69
81	Valdosta St. †	69
84	Shaw †	102

Nickname: Braves
Colors: Blue & Red

Arena: HPE Building
  Capacity: 2,800; Year Built: 1965
SID: Mitch Gray

WEST LIBERTY ST.
West Liberty, WV 26074 II

Coach: Dan Petri, West Liberty St. 1968

2001-02 RESULTS (14-14)

66	Philadelphia U. †	63
64	Shippensburg	74
86	West Va. Tech ■	65
88	Ohio-Eastern †	69
79	Wheeling Jesuit	81
71	Point Park ■	76
86	Lincoln Memorial †	93
94	Wilberforce †	88
84	Alderson-Broaddus ■	92
83	Shepherd ■	79
69	Davis & Elkins	75
78	West Va. Wesleyan	88
96	Salem Int'l ■	87
82	Ohio Valley	68
80	Fairmont St. ■	75
78	Wheeling Jesuit	89
97	Glenville St.	95
65	Charleston (W.Va.) ■	87
79	Point Park	88
71	Concord	83
105	Bluefield St.	96
83	West Virginia St. ■	78
75	Salem Int'l	93
104	Ohio Valley ■	53
74	Fairmont St.	76
87	Wheeling Jesuit ■	77
80	West Virginia St. ■	77
66	Salem Int'l †	91

Nickname: Hilltoppers
Colors: Gold & Black
Arena: ASRC
  Capacity: 1,200; Year Built: 2000
SID: Lynn Ullom

WEST TEX. A&M
Canyon, TX 79016-0999 II

Coach: Rick Cooper, Wayland Bapt. 1981

2001-02 RESULTS (16-10)

89	Okla. Panhandle ■	64
84	N.M. Highlands	79
80	Mary Hardin-Baylor †	65
82	Texas Col. †	55
89	Southwestern Okla.	94
59	Cameron	63
91	National Christian ■	30
87	Midwestern St.	81
95	Okla. Panhandle ■	60
77	N.M. Highlands ■	72
51	Northeastern St.	74
68	Central Okla.	85
81	East Central ■	66
82	Southeastern Okla. ■	76
54	Tarleton St.	72
80	Angelo St. ■	82
80	Abilene Christian ■	58
73	Eastern N.M.	82
70	Tex. A&M-Kingsville ■	59
75	Tex. A&M-Commerce	54
79	Tex. A&M-Commerce ■	76
76	Tex. A&M-Kingsville	80
73	Tarleton St. ■	69
77	Eastern N.M. ■	81
82	Abilene Christian	70
62	Angelo St.	88

Nickname: Buffaloes
Colors: Maroon & White
Arena: WTAMU Fieldhouse
  Capacity: 2,557; Year Built: 1951
SID: Paul Sweetgall

WEST VIRGINIA
Morgantown, WV 26507 I

Coach: Gale Catlett, West Virginia 1963

2001-02 RESULTS (8-20)

83	UNC Asheville ■	57
66	Southern Miss. †	59
88	New Mexico	85
105	Ark.-Monticello ■	73
75	James Madison	91
74	Florida Int'l ■	61
102	Robert Morris ■	86
61	Duquesne ■	68
74	Tennessee	72
57	Valparaiso †	76
65	Pepperdine †	97
53	St. John's (N.Y.)	72
64	Notre Dame ■	67
69	Syracuse ■	75
66	Rutgers	79
67	Seton Hall ■	81
79	Marshall †	81
59	Rutgers ■	77
89	Providence ■	81
77	Georgetown	84
64	Syracuse	76
79	Seton Hall	85
63	Virginia Tech ■	78
75	Pittsburgh ■	85
76	Notre Dame	89
73	Connecticut	95
77	Georgetown ■	87
65	Pittsburgh	92

Nickname: Mountaineers
Colors: Old Gold & Blue
Arena: WVU Coliseum
  Capacity: 14,000; Year Built: 1970
SID: Bryan Messerly

WEST VIRGINIA ST.
Institute, WV 25112-1000 II

Coach: Bryan Poore, West Virginia St. 1987

2001-02 RESULTS (9-18)

72	Mercyhurst	77
80	Bloomfield †	87
87	Concord †	74
85	Mount Olive †	90
77	Concord	80
88	Col. of West Va. †	98
62	South Carolina St. †	91
62	Tenn.-Martin †	89
115	Southern Va.	104
106	Bluefield St. ■	99
80	Charleston (W.Va.) ■	89
86	West Va. Tech	84
70	Wheeling Jesuit	73
74	West Va. Wesleyan ■	78
69	Glenville St. ■	76
79	Alderson-Broaddus	81
85	Davis & Elkins	58
86	Shepherd ■	83
59	Ohio Valley	48
82	Salem Int'l ■	92
66	Fairmont St. ■	67
78	West Liberty St.	83
72	Charleston (W.Va.)	114
70	Concord ■	74
104	Bluefield St.	89
111	West Va. Tech ■	103
77	West Liberty St.	80

Nickname: Yellow Jackets
Colors: Old Gold & Black
Arena: Fleming Hall
  Capacity: 1,800; Year Built: 1942
SID: Sean McAndrews

WEST VA. TECH
Montgomery, WV 25136 II

Coach: Steve Tucker, Mississippi Col. 1980

2001-02 RESULTS (7-20)

108	Ohio-Ironton †	78
75	Salem Int'l	99
79	Queens (N.C.)	90
70	Concord	75
65	West Liberty St.	86
90	Southern Va.	73
58	Winston-Salem ■	82
81	N.C. Central	75
61	Carson-Newman ■	79
81	Charleston (W.Va.)	82
84	West Virginia St.	86
72	Shepherd ■	57
72	Davis & Elkins	74
68	West Va. Wesleyan	74
68	Glenville St. ■	87
110	Bluefield St. ■	90
65	Wheeling Jesuit	83
67	Columbia Union	78
63	Ohio Valley	71
55	Salem Int'l ■	76
58	Fairmont St.	64
55	Alderson-Broaddus ■	77
72	Charleston (W.Va.) ■	85
82	Bluefield St. ■	71
68	Concord ■	64
103	West Virginia St.	111
69	Charleston (W.Va.)	77

Nickname: Golden Bears
Colors: Blue & Gold
Arena: Tech Fieldhouse
  Capacity: 3,000; Year Built: 1968
SID: Chad Gabrich

WEST VA. WESLEYAN
Buckhannon, WV 26201 II

Coach: Charlie Miller, West Va. Wesleyan 1966

2001-02 RESULTS (21-8)

81	Davis & Elkins †	62
94	Glenville St.	81
64	Millersville	44
88	Rio Grande ■	71
77	Ashland ■	94
66	Pitt.-Johnstown	64
106	Wheeling Jesuit ■	77
80	Northern Mich. †	84
71	Hillsdale	86
70	Salem Int'l	85
94	Ohio Valley	57
84	Fairmont St. ■	68
88	West Liberty St. ■	78
109	Davis & Elkins	114
78	West Virginia St.	74
94	Bluefield St.	63
90	Concord	74
74	West Va. Tech ■	68
100	Charleston (W.Va.)	79
74	Alderson-Broaddus ■	61
92	Glenville St.	82
78	Shepherd ■	75
75	Glenville St. ■	74
96	Alderson-Broaddus	102
82	Davis & Elkins ■	63
68	Shepherd	56
82	Wheeling Jesuit †	76
64	Charleston (W.Va.) ■	66
59	Belmont Abbey †	76

Nickname: Bobcats
Colors: Orange & Black
Arena: Rockefeller Center
  Capacity: 3,400; Year Built: 1974
SID: Beth Mecouch

WESTERN CARO.
Cullowhee, NC 28723 I

Coach: Steve Shurina, St. John's (N.Y.) 1988

2001-02 RESULTS (12-16)

66	Tenn. Wesleyan ■	58
73	Coastal Caro.	79
133	Toccoa Falls Inst. ■	58
94	Emmanuel (Ga.) ■	61
66	UNC Asheville ■	72
102	Stetson	104
79	Florida St.	69
77	Guilford ■	73
66	Kansas St.	64
73	Wichita St.	102
59	Eastern Mich.	72
90	VMI	80
71	Davidson ■	74
77	Furman ■	67
97	Citadel ■	105
79	Appalachian St.	71
87	UNC Greensboro ■	77
67	Ga. Southern	96
70	Davidson	66
62	Appalachian St. ■	66
75	UNC Greensboro	80
76	East Tenn. St. ■	86
91	VMI ■	97
64	Col. of Charleston ■	81
77	East Tenn. St.	91
77	Wofford	71
71	Chattanooga	91
61	Furman †	65

Nickname: Catamounts
Colors: Purple & Gold
Arena: Ramsey Center
  Capacity: 7,826; Year Built: 1986
SID: Mike Cawood

WESTERN CONN. ST.
Danbury, CT 06810 III

Coach: Bob Campbell, Connecticut 1972

2001-02 RESULTS (21-7)

46	Muskingum †	81
68	Lynchburg †	63
79	Albertus Magnus	61
66	Trinity (Conn.)	74
64	Southern Me.	80
75	Westfield St. ■	74
91	Mass.-Dartmouth	104
77	Hunter ■	67
86	Baruch ■	67
95	Medgar Evers ■	89
93	Plymouth St.	91
78	Keene St.	87
67	Mass.-Boston ■	59
94	Rhode Island Col. ■	51
89	Newbury	55
80	Southern Me. ■	68
72	Eastern Conn. St. ■	76
78	Mass.-Dartmouth ■	72
89	Lasell	60
102	Plymouth St. ■	76
84	Rhode Island Col.	61
90	Keene St. ■	83
82	Eastern Conn. St.	68
95	Mass.-Boston	73
84	Mass.-Dartmouth †	64
86	Keene St.	83
92	Salem St. ■	89
77	Amherst	82

Nickname: Colonials
Colors: Navy Blue, Copper & White
Arena: Stephen Feldman Arena
  Capacity: 2,100; Year Built: 1994
SID: Scott Ames

WESTERN ILL.
Macomb, IL 61455 I

Coach: Jim Kerwin, Tulane 1964
2001-02 RESULTS (12-16)

106	Cardinal Stritch ■	52
71	Eastern Ky.	62
69	Bradley ■	84
80	Drake ■	74
71	Southeast Mo. St.	58
53	Nebraska	72
72	Eastern Ill. ■	81
62	Illinois	98
70	Eastern Ky. ■	57
77	Hampton ■	74
84	Youngstown St. ■	79
82	Southeast Mo. St. ■	75
68	Valparaiso	78
98	St. Ambrose ■	63
82	Chicago St.	77
63	Southern Utah	68
51	UMKC ■	63
82	Oral Roberts ■	95
75	Oakland	93
58	IUPUI	59
60	Valparaiso ■	84
81	Southern Utah ■	70
93	Chicago St. ■	69
67	Oral Roberts	84
52	UMKC	64
77	IUPUI ■	81
82	Oakland ■	86
75	Oral Roberts †	86

Nickname: Leathernecks
Colors: Purple & Gold
Arena: Western Hall
  Capacity: 5,139; Year Built: 1964
SID: Doug Smiley

WESTERN KY.
Bowling Green, KY 42101-35761

Coach: Dennis Felton, Howard 1985
2001-02 RESULTS (28-4)

64	Kentucky	52
73	George Washington †	48
90	Evansville ■	64
101	Murray St. ■	77
91	Creighton	94
75	Vanderbilt	80
78	Akron	68
77	Austin Peay	75
103	West Ala. ■	40
95	Creighton ■	61
74	Southern Miss.	50
90	New Orleans	76
58	South Ala.	61
65	Florida Int'l	54
75	Austin Peay ■	73
63	La.-Lafayette ■	62
83	New Mexico St. ■	67
55	Middle Tenn.	45
86	Denver	59
95	Ark.-Little Rock ■	85
45	Arkansas St. ■	42
66	Florida Int'l ■	64
92	Morris Brown ■	53
83	Ark.-Little Rock	79
50	Arkansas St.	46
100	North Texas ■	76
100	Kentucky St. ■	63
65	Middle Tenn. ■	61
82	North Texas	68
73	New Mexico St. †	72
76	La.-Lafayette †	70
68	Stanford †	84

Nickname: Hilltoppers
Colors: Red & White
Arena: E.A. Diddle Arena
  Capacity: 8,100; Year Built: 1963
SID: Paul Just

WESTERN MICH.
Kalamazoo, MI 49008 I

Coach: Robert McCullum,
Birmingham So. 1976
2001-02 RESULTS (17-13)

64	Long Beach St. †	71
48	Oregon	91
63	Alabama St. †	43
81	Wis.-Milwaukee ■	80
79	Michigan ■	73
83	Morgan St. ■	63
62	Detroit	67
55	Virginia Tech	51
59	Wis.-Milwaukee	51
73	Marshall ■	77
94	Oakland	100
69	Miami (Ohio) ■	63
64	Toledo ■	73
68	Ohio	86
81	Central Mich. ■	67
62	IUPUI ■	61
72	Kent St.	75
61	Ball St.	74
95	Ohio ■	65
66	Bowling Green ■	78
67	Central Mich.	70
101	Eastern Mich. ■	94
60	Buffalo	59
94	Akron	89
97	Northern Ill.	87
80	Ball St. ■	65
68	Toledo	72
71	Eastern Mich.	52
86	Northern Ill. ■	85
83	Akron ■	90

Nickname: Broncos
Colors: Brown & Gold
Arena: University Arena
  Capacity: 5,649; Year Built: 1957
SID: Scott Kuykendall

WESTERN NEW ENG.
Springfield, MA 01119 III

Coach: Doug Pearson, Bridgeport 1967
2001-02 RESULTS (16-10)

91	Rhode Island Col. †	75
87	Oneonta St. †	77
82	Wesleyan (Conn.)	97
78	Fitchburg St.	84
80	Mass. Liberal Arts ■	72
60	Amherst ■	75
49	Springfield ■	69
71	WPI	56
79	Salve Regina ■	87
77	Elms	60
79	Emerson ■	69
78	Rivier	82
83	Westfield St.	78
75	Johnson & Wales	66
71	Norwich ■	68
84	Daniel Webster ■	57
80	Rivier ■	54
63	Southern Vt.	69
70	Suffolk ■	83
80	Albertus Magnus	58
97	Daniel Webster	68
94	Emmanuel (Mass.) ■	74
61	Southern Vt. ■	91
82	Norwich ■	49
75	Daniel Webster ■	62
69	Johnson & Wales ■	83

Nickname: Golden Bears
Colors: Royal Blue & Gold
Arena: Alumni Healthful Living Center
  Capacity: 2,000; Year Built: 1993
SID: Ken Cerino

WESTERN N.M.
Silver City, NM 88061 II

Coach: Troy Hudson, Northern Ariz. 1979
2001-02 RESULTS (1-23)

74	N.M. Highlands ■	86
61	Eastern N.M. †	75
76	Okla. Panhandle	85
88	Fort Lewis	103
69	Adams St.	73
59	N.M. Highlands	66
56	Hawaii-Hilo	92
52	Hawaii-Hilo	70
57	Chaminade	72
60	Hawaii Pacific ■	68
67	Hawaii Pacific ■	73
74	BYU-Hawaii ■	76
74	Mont. St.-Billings ■	76
67	Mont. St.-Billings ■	72
81	Chaminade ■	83
89	Chaminade ■	92
64	Hawaii-Hilo ■	90
67	New Mexico St.	98
62	BYU-Hawaii	94
69	BYU-Hawaii	80
71	Hawaii Pacific	78
101	Okla. Panhandle ■	95
83	Mont. St.-Billings	106
58	Mont. St.-Billings	96

Nickname: Mustangs
Colors: Purple & Gold
Arena: Mustang Field House
  Capacity: 2,000; Year Built: 1448
SID: Alan Kirsch

WESTERN ORE.
Monmouth, OR 97361-1394 II

Coach: Tom Kelly, Utah 1980
2001-02 RESULTS (10-17)

55	Northwest Mo. St.	70
51	Morningside †	48
67	Western Baptist ■	73
63	Northwest Mo. St. ■	77
55	Cal St. Bakersfield ■	76
72	Warner Pacific ■	71
77	Western Baptist	78
61	Seattle	75
79	Northwest Nazarene	70
78	UC Davis ■	85
79	Puget Sound ■	73
78	Humboldt St.	104
68	Alas. Anchorage ■	87
86	Alas. Fairbanks ■	75
71	St. Martin's	74
70	Central Wash.	79
112	Western Wash. ■	110
57	Seattle Pacific †	73
70	Northwest Nazarene ■	73
61	Seattle	57
68	Humboldt St.	80
82	Alas. Fairbanks	66
105	Alas. Anchorage	110
77	Central Wash. ■	97
83	St. Martin's ■	81
77	Seattle Pacific	74
65	Western Wash.	76

Nickname: Wolves
Colors: Crimson Red & White
Arena: Physical Education Building
  Capacity: 2,473; Year Built: 1972
SID: Russ Blunck

WESTERN ST.
Gunnison, CO 81231 II

Coach: Steve Phillips, Western St. 1978
2001-02 RESULTS (6-20)

67	St. Mary's (Tex.) †	72
90	Southwestern Okla. †	83

77	Northern Colo.	92
74	Augustana (S.D.)	109
78	South Dakota †	104
67	Colorado Mines	70
68	Chadron St.	95
49	Metro St. ■	77
43	Utah St.	99
75	Chaminade ■	89
60	Neb.-Kearney	82
41	Fort Hays St.	81
83	Colo. Christian ■	61
88	Regis (Colo.) ■	78
61	UC-Colo. Spgs.	67
71	Southern Colo. ■	61
82	Mesa St.	94
70	Adams St.	75
71	Fort Lewis	100
91	N.M. Highlands ■	94
74	UC-Colo. Spgs.	76
59	Southern Colo.	89
69	Mesa St. ■	87
80	Adams St. ■	66
85	Fort Lewis ■	97
104	N.M. Highlands	88

Nickname: Mountaineers
Colors: Crimson & Slate
Arena: Paul Wright Gymnasium
  Capacity: 2,250; Year Built: 1951
SID: Chris Chase

WESTERN WASH.
Bellingham, WA 98225 II

Coach: Brad Jackson, Washington St. 1975
2001-02 RESULTS (21-6)

101	Alas. Fairbanks ■	59
91	Cascade ■	94
98	Southern Colo. ■	70
94	Minn. St. Moorhead ■	97
113	Northwest (Wash.) ■	68
93	Evergreen St. ■	79
78	St. Martin's	53
84	Central Wash.	81
70	Northeastern St. †	71
85	Bellarmine †	65
82	Warner Pacific ■	61
72	Colorado Mines ■	44
86	Seattle ■	84
104	Northwest Nazarene ■	76
89	Seattle Pacific	96
87	Alas. Anchorage ■	67
110	Western Ore.	112
86	Humboldt St.	100
88	Central Wash. ■	85
70	St. Martin's ■	60
77	Northwest Nazarene	71
76	Seattle	61
88	Seattle Pacific ■	80
80	Alas. Fairbanks	71
71	Alas. Anchorage	70
76	Humboldt St. ■	66
76	Western Ore. ■	65

Nickname: Vikings
Colors: Blue, Silver & White
Arena: Sam Carver Gymnasium
  Capacity: 2,534; Year Built: 1961
SID: Paul Madison

WESTFIELD ST.
Westfield, MA 01086-1630......III

Coach: Rich Sutter, St. Bonaventure 1984
2001-02 RESULTS (11-14)

76	Ithaca †	84
55	Eastern Conn. St.	78
89	Elms ■	77
54	Medgar Evers †	58
73	NYCCT †	56
74	Western Conn. St.	75
63	Springfield †	80

64	Amherst †	75
73	Lasell	61
75	Albertus Magnus	63
65	Bridgewater St. ■	53
76	Worcester St.	58
82	Salem St. ■	71
78	Western New Eng. ■	83
69	Fitchburg St.	71
42	Framingham St.	54
77	Mass. Liberal Arts ■	82
63	Bridgewater St.	70
69	Worcester St.	83
76	Salem St.	86
100	Becker ■	83
90	Fitchburg St. ■	61
74	Framingham St.	54
108	Mass. Liberal Arts	78
71	Framingham St. ■	76

Nickname: Owls
Colors: Blue & White
Arena: Parenzo Gym
　Capacity: 400; Year Built: 1956
SID: Mickey Curtis

WESTMINSTER (MO.)
Fulton, MO 65251-1299 III

Coach: Matt Mitchell, Arkansas 1987
2001-02 RESULTS (13-12)
60	Williams Baptist †	80
96	North Cent. (Minn.) †	103
97	Sanford Brown ■	36
68	Manhattan Chrst.	66
87	Calvary Bible	60
70	Lincoln Chrst. ■	67
66	Potsdam St. †	56
63	Cal St. Monterey Bay †	78
81	Eureka	68
79	Greenville	77
62	Blackburn ■	63
56	Principia	68
68	MacMurray ■	69
90	Lincoln Chrst.	91
79	Webster ■	76
72	Maryville (Mo.) ■	76
85	Fontbonne ■	95
120	Messenger ■	59
104	Greenville ■	90
64	Blackburn	74
88	Principia ■	74
55	MacMurray	73
74	Webster	91
76	Maryville (Mo.) ■	67
65	Fontbonne	61

Nickname: Blue Jays
Colors: Blue & White
Arena: Westminster Gym
　Capacity: 1,200; Year Built: 1928
SID: Sean Wright

WESTMINSTER (PA.)
New Wilmington, PA 16172 II

Coach: Jim Dafler, Capital 1971
2001-02 RESULTS (10-15)
74	Notre Dame (Ohio) ■	62
54	Geneva ■	63
60	Muskingum †	66
84	Alma †	77
52	Mount Union	85
67	Tiffin ■	72
82	Mt. Aloysius ■	67
77	Medaille ■	46
80	Pitt.-Greensburg ■	59
74	Berea †	83
92	Concordia (Ill.) †	78
67	Penn St.-Behrend	77
58	Wooster	67
72	Geneva	80
71	Mt. Aloysius	68
77	Bethany (W.Va.) ■	78
70	Waynesburg	81

63	Thiel	71
101	Grove City ■	111
66	Wash. & Jeff. ■	48
68	Bethany (W.Va.)	85
60	Waynesburg ■	68
60	Thiel	58
76	Grove City	69
63	Wash. & Jeff.	65

Nickname: Titans
Colors: Navy Blue & White
Arena: Buzz Ridl Gymnasium
　Capacity: 2,300; Year Built: 1950
SID: Joe Onderko

WHEATON (ILL.)
Wheaton, IL 60187-5593 III

Coach: Bill Harris, Gordon 1970
2001-02 RESULTS (16-9)
85	Cardinal Stritch ■	65
77	Wittenberg ■	72
67	Chicago ■	63
69	Calvin ■	63
81	Concordia (Ill.) ■	69
79	Illinois Tech ■	50
82	Northwestern (Minn.) ■	51
88	Greenville ■	72
73	San Jose Christian	59
59	Cal St. Monterey Bay	63
91	Bethany (Cal.)	81
71	Augustana (Ill.) ■	85
61	Carthage ■	71
81	North Park ■	91
80	Elmhurst ■	77
55	Ill. Wesleyan ■	60
84	Millikin ■	69
80	Augustana (Ill.) ■	73
67	North Central	77
86	Millikin	96
87	Elmhurst ■	80
74	Ill. Wesleyan	85
72	Carthage	83
73	North Park ■	64
76	North Central ■	67

Nickname: Thunder
Colors: Orange & Blue
Arena: King Arena
　Capacity: 2,650; Year Built: 2000
SID: Brett Marhanka

WHEATON (MASS.)
Norton, MA 02766 III

Coach: Brian Walmsley, Bentley 1988
2001-02 RESULTS (13-14)
71	Albertus Magnus ■	67
55	Bates ■	67
56	Brandeis	94
62	Endicott ■	63
106	Emerson	71
71	Bridgewater St.	66
83	Salve Regina ■	77
68	Roger Williams	53
60	Tufts	68
53	Fitchburg St.	59
68	Coast Guard ■	64
70	Clark (Mass.) ■	87
53	WPI	62
94	Eastern Conn. St. ■	87
75	MIT ■	73
70	Babson ■	83
80	Springfield	61
64	Coast Guard	67
69	Clark (Mass.)	76
73	WPI ■	52
88	Mount Ida ■	61
73	MIT	78
63	Babson	82
74	Springfield ■	80
67	MIT	66
100	Clark (Mass.)	92
42	Babson †	44

Nickname: Lyons
Colors: Royal & White
Arena: Emerson Gymnasium
　Capacity: 850; Year Built: 1991
SID: Scott Dietz

WHEELING JESUIT
Wheeling, WV 26003-6295 II

Coach: Jay DeFruscio, Ursinus 1982
2001-02 RESULTS (16-12)
54	New Haven †	67
90	Ohio St. Lima †	77
98	Davis & Elkins	71
100	Bethany (W.Va.) ■	108
81	West Liberty St. ■	79
77	West Va. Wesleyan	106
120	Bluefield St. ■	98
85	Bowie St. ■	83
66	Shepherd ■	83
84	Glenville St.	86
76	Alderson-Broaddus	91
73	West Virginia St. ■	70
67	Salem Int'l	73
95	Ohio St.-Newark ■	66
83	Fairmont St. ■	69
98	Ohio Valley	84
89	West Liberty St. ■	78
90	Ohio-Eastern	71
83	West Va. Tech ■	65
88	Bluefield St.	84
84	Concord	87
86	Charleston (W.Va.) ■	95
74	Salem Int'l	69
71	Fairmont St.	88
78	Ohio Valley ■	58
77	West Liberty St.	87
87	Concord	66
76	West Va. Wesleyan †	82

Nickname: Cardinals
Colors: Red & Gold
Arena: Alma McDonough Center
　Capacity: 2,200; Year Built: 1990
SID: Susie Levitt

WHITMAN
Walla Walla, WA 99362 III

Coach: Skip Molitor, Gonzaga 1974
2001-02 RESULTS (10-15)
81	Trinity (Tex.) †	80
60	Washington (Mo.)	77
68	Eastern Ore.	70
113	Walla Walla ■	103
69	Montana St.-Northern ■	85
84	Linfield	95
61	Carroll (Mont.)	77
95	Pacific Union	56
54	Dominican (Cal.)	75
81	Bethany (Cal.)	76
64	Willamette	76
64	Lewis & Clark	78
83	Pacific Lutheran ■	72
74	Puget Sound ■	85
53	Whitworth ■	64
82	Pacific (Ore.) ■	72
88	George Fox ■	67
81	Puget Sound	96
72	Pacific Lutheran	61
64	Lewis & Clark ■	77
61	Willamette ■	68
68	Whitworth	102
91	Linfield ■	77
82	George Fox	60
82	Pacific (Ore.)	100

Nickname: Missionaries
Colors: Blue & Gold
Arena: Sherwood Center
　Capacity: 2,000; Year Built: 1968
SID: Dave Holden

WHITTIER
Whittier, CA 90608-0634 III

Coach: Rock Carter, Whittier 1989
2001-02 RESULTS (9-16)
53	Colorado Col.	62
55	Neb. Wesleyan †	57
80	Chapman ■	62
84	West Coast Chrst. †	51
98	Lewis & Clark †	114
69	Redlands	70
98	LIFE Bible ■	34
99	Hope Int'l ■	71
89	La Sierra ■	65
71	Muhlenberg ■	72
52	Chapman ■	74
76	Redlands ■	62
58	Pomona-Pitzer ■	73
59	La Verne ■	84
63	Cal Lutheran ■	82
83	Occidental ■	90
83	Caltech ■	41
63	Claremont-M-S ■	64
93	Redlands ■	84
57	Pomona-Pitzer ■	60
78	La Verne	85
61	Cal Lutheran ■	72
62	Occidental	67
73	Caltech ■	44
52	Claremont-M-S	84

Nickname: Poets
Colors: Purple & Gold
Arena: Graham Activity Center
　Capacity: 2,200; Year Built: 1979
SID: Rock Carter

WHITWORTH
Spokane, WA 99251-2501 III

Coach: Jim Hayford, Azusa Pacific 1989
2001-02 RESULTS (20-7)
94	Walla Walla ■	73
82	Drew †	43
85	North Park †	67
87	Linfield	89
89	Walla Walla	71
97	Eastern Ore. ■	43
51	Spring Hill †	49
45	Cal St. Bakersfield	60
72	Great Falls ■	54
57	Utah	63
86	Lewis & Clark	72
60	Willamette	63
92	Puget Sound ■	85
94	Pacific Lutheran ■	60
64	Whitman	53
83	George Fox ■	73
72	Pacific (Ore.) ■	50
67	Pacific Lutheran	82
89	Puget Sound	82
55	Willamette ■	58
79	Lewis & Clark ■	74
102	Whitman	68
90	Linfield ■	84
58	Pacific (Ore.)	50
100	George Fox	98
64	Willamette	49
86	Lewis & Clark	101

Nickname: Pirates
Colors: Crimson & Black
Arena: Whitworth Field House
　Capacity: 1,600; Year Built: 1960
SID: Steve Flegel

WICHITA ST.
Wichita, KS 67260 I

Coach: Mark Turgeon, Kansas 1987
2001-02 RESULTS (15-15)
47	Delaware †	62
82	Radford †	81

68	Mississippi †	80
97	Ga. Southern ■	77
102	Texas-Arlington ■	89
59	Oklahoma St.	61
65	Kansas St.	56
76	Tulsa ■	82
65	Jacksonville ■	67
102	Western Caro. ■	73
78	Chicago St.	56
70	Bradley ■	64
61	Southwest Mo. St.	82
71	Illinois St.	81
88	Southern Ill. ■	79
81	Drake	65
64	Indiana St.	63
81	Evansville ■	63
55	Creighton ■	67
49	Bradley	66
64	Drake	80
87	Indiana St. ■	84
58	Southern Ill.	78
71	Southwest Mo. St. ■	63
75	Northern Iowa	83
67	Creighton	69
77	Illinois St. ■	66
81	Evansville	83
86	Northern Iowa ■	74
59	Southwest Mo. St. †	72

Nickname: Shockers
Colors: Yellow & Black
Arena: Levitt Arena
  Capacity: 10,559; Year Built: 1955
SID: Larry Rankin

WIDENER
Chester, PA 19013-5792 III

Coach: Dave Duda, Spring Garden 1988
2001-02 RESULTS (19-8)

100	Waynesburg †	87
81	Frostburg St.	71
66	Neumann ■	81
92	Cabrini	95
83	Lincoln (Pa.) †	79
74	Neumann †	83
83	Elizabethtown ■	95
64	Juniata	46
94	Gwynedd-Mercy ■	75
77	Arcadia ■	45
79	Messiah ■	71
96	Centenary (N.J.)	76
80	Lebanon Valley	73
77	Muhlenberg	91
80	Moravian ■	57
75	Susquehanna	73
100	Albright	70
92	Lincoln (Pa.) ■	80
64	Juniata ■	54
79	Elizabethtown	77
73	Lebanon Valley ■	78
80	Messiah	83
82	Moravian	73
99	Albright ■	61
89	Susquehanna	71
77	Lebanon Valley ■	61
73	Elizabethtown	85

Nickname: Pioneers
Colors: Widener Blue & Gold
Arena: Schwartz Center
  Capacity: 1,500; Year Built: 1971
SID: Susan Fumagalli

WILKES
Wilkes-Barre, PA 18766 III

Coach: Jerry Rickrode, Skidmore 1985
2001-02 RESULTS (15-11)

88	Neumann ■	70
72	Clark (Mass.) ■	84
89	Albright	74
82	Moravian ■	88

76	FDU-Madison ■	54
48	Lycoming	65
62	York (N.Y.) †	58
77	D'Youville †	86
86	St. Mary's (Md.)	59
96	Baptist Bible (Pa.) ■	56
98	Susquehanna	82
87	DeSales ■	62
72	Drew	76
66	Delaware Valley	53
65	Scranton ■	86
59	King's (Pa.) ■	70
69	FDU-Madison	87
91	Lincoln (Pa.)	89
93	Lycoming ■	95
75	Drew ■	63
96	Lincoln (Pa.) ■	75
86	DeSales	80
74	Delaware Valley ■	69
73	King's (Pa.)	92
80	Scranton	67
84	King's (Pa.)	89

Nickname: Colonels
Colors: Navy & Gold
Arena: Arnaud Marts Sports Center
  Capacity: 3,500; Year Built: 1988
SID: John Seitzinger

WILLAMETTE
Salem, OR 97301-3931 III

Coach: Gordie James, Cal Poly Pomona 1964
2001-02 RESULTS (18-8)

85	Northwest Chrst. †	70
72	Western Baptist	81
73	Oregon Tech †	93
59	Southern Ore.	56
66	UC Santa Cruz	59
58	Holy Names †	55
89	George Fox	69
72	Pacific Lutheran	61
68	Warner Pacific	65
60	Holy Names ■	54
76	Whitman ■	64
63	Whitworth ■	60
72	Linfield	77
73	Pacific (Ore.) ■	54
54	Lewis & Clark	69
48	Oregon	71
100	Puget Sound ■	84
68	Pacific (Ore.)	63
85	Linfield ■	80
58	Whitworth	55
68	Whitman	61
81	Pacific Lutheran ■	49
56	George Fox ■	44
67	Lewis & Clark	78
76	Puget Sound	82
49	Whitworth ■	64

Nickname: Bearcats
Colors: Cardinal & Old Gold
Arena: Cone Fieldhouse
  Capacity: 2,600; Year Built: 1974
SID: Cliff Voliva

WILLIAM & MARY
Williamsburg, VA 23187 I

Coach: Rick Boyages, Bowdoin 1985
2001-02 RESULTS (10-19)

55	Texas Tech	75
55	Northern Iowa †	76
57	High Point	63
71	Charleston So.	60
62	Citadel	67
70	Wash. & Lee ■	55
58	Purdue	75
74	Akron †	62
75	Maryland	103
71	George Mason	80
59	Delaware ■	53

56	Drexel ■	58
92	Va. Commonwealth ■	81
56	UNC Wilmington ■	58
59	Hofstra	68
77	James Madison ■	59
52	Old Dominion	68
61	Drexel	78
62	Towson ■	45
63	James Madison	58
59	Hampton ■	64
58	Towson	61
58	UNC Wilmington	66
61	Hofstra ■	57
54	George Mason ■	51
72	Delaware	82
53	Old Dominion	81
60	Va. Commonwealth	68
67	James Madison †	78

Nickname: Tribe
Colors: Green, Gold, Silver
Arena: William and Mary Hall
  Capacity: 8,600; Year Built: 1970
SID: Dan Wakely

WM. PATERSON
Wayne, NJ 07470-2152 III

Coach: Jose Rebimbas, Seton Hall 1990
2001-02 RESULTS (19-10)

71	Catholic ■	68
65	Ramapo ■	94
66	New Jersey City	74
51	Montclair St.	54
56	Richard Stockton ■	60
83	Centenary (N.J.) ■	48
84	Rutgers-Camden ■	67
59	Col. of New Jersey	77
64	Lehman	55
70	Adrian †	60
53	Grove City	60
62	York (N.Y.) ■	53
69	Brockport St. ■	78
57	Rowan	56
59	Rutgers-Newark ■	67
78	Kean	75
58	Richard Stockton	56
75	Montclair St.	61
80	New Jersey City ■	70
74	Ramapo	70
64	Col. of New Jersey ■	44
68	Rutgers-Camden	69
75	Rowan ■	73
62	Kean ■	52
65	Rutgers-Newark	54
60	New Jersey City	44
66	Montclair St.	42
55	Richard Stockton ■	49
43	Cabrini	47

Nickname: Pioneers
Colors: Orange & Black
Arena: Rec Center
  Capacity: 4,000; Year Built: 1984
SID: Joe Martinelli

WILLIAMS
Williamstown, MA 01267 III

Coach: David Paulsen, Williams 1987
2001-02 RESULTS (22-6)

102	Rivier	59
90	Anna Maria †	52
86	Union (N.Y.) ■	68
62	Rensselaer	47
72	St. Joseph (Vt.) ■	35
80	Clark (Mass.) ■	78
82	Mass. Liberal Arts ■	63
85	Averett	58
77	Southern Vt. ■	69
76	Misericordia ■	53
65	Wesleyan (Conn.)	57
70	Amherst	72
76	Hamilton	79

74	Amherst ■	45
85	Trinity (Conn.) ■	75
81	Colby	65
54	Bowdoin	84
69	Clarkson ■	55
71	Wesleyan (Conn.) ■	66
72	Connecticut Col.	62
86	Springfield ■	73
85	Tufts	69
83	Bates	87
88	Middlebury ■	63
81	Tufts ■	57
62	Amherst †	69
121	Cazenovia ■	49
51	Rochester	66

Nickname: Ephs
Colors: Purple & Gold
Arena: Chandler Gymnasium
  Capacity: 2,900; Year Built: 1988
SID: Dick Quinn

WILMINGTON (OHIO)
Wilmington, OH 45177 III

Coach: Scott Stemple, Ohio Northern 1985
2001-02 RESULTS (6-19)

56	Eastern Ky.	91
52	Earlham	77
56	John Carroll	68
54	Ohio Northern	82
67	Mount Union ■	63
73	Oberlin	62
92	Baldwin-Wallace ■	85
72	Muskingum	75
77	Shawnee St. ■	97
68	Waynesburg ■	75
66	Penn St.-Behrend ■	71
70	Marietta ■	84
47	Capital ■	63
60	Heidelberg	73
75	Otterbein ■	93
59	Mount Union	78
63	Ohio Northern ■	61
84	Baldwin-Wallace	83
76	Muskingum ■	75
63	Marietta	76
61	Capital	67
74	Heidelberg ■	76
54	Otterbein	79
72	John Carroll ■	81
59	Heidelberg	73

Nickname: Quakers
Colors: Green & White
Arena: Hermann Court
  Capacity: 3,000; Year Built: 1966
SID: Bill Salyer

WINGATE
Wingate, NC 28174 II

Coach: Parker Laketa, Kansas St. 1986
2001-02 RESULTS (26-7)

83	Tarleton St. †	73
113	Southern Ind. †	97
82	Lynn †	90
92	St. Andrews	83
73	Armstrong Atlantic ■	59
69	Belmont Abbey	70
88	St. Paul's	64
107	Pfeiffer ■	74
87	N.C. Central ■	83
53	Coker ■	48
100	UNC Pembroke ■	82
81	Northern Ky. ■	73
91	Elizabeth City St. ■	70
76	Carson-Newman ■	74
95	Presbyterian	89
96	Newberry	74
97	Catawba	102
105	Mars Hill ■	84
92	Lenoir-Rhyne	74
61	Tusculum	57

79	North Greenville ■	67
75	Carson-Newman	87
99	Presbyterian	87
95	Newberry ■	64
91	Catawba ■	76
77	Mars Hill	62
67	Lenoir-Rhyne ■	47
83	Anderson (S.C.)	72
64	Tusculum	68
80	Mars Hill ■	72
76	Presbyterian †	75
62	Carson-Newman †	76
75	Winston-Salem †	90

Nickname: Bulldogs
Colors: Navy Blue & Old Gold
Arena: Cuddy Arena
  Capacity: 2,300; Year Built: 1986
SID: David Sherwood

WINONA ST.
Winona, MN 55987-5838 II

Coach: Mike Leaf, St. Mary's (Minn.) 1983
2001-02 RESULTS (14-13)

71	South Dakota St. ■	66
77	Midland Lutheran †	58
65	Neb.-Omaha	82
94	St. Mary's (Minn.) ■	64
73	Minn. St.-Mankato ■	84
96	Minn.-Morris	72
71	Northern St.	77
58	Wis.-Parkside	71
58	Lewis	84
77	Viterbo	72
75	Concordia-St. Paul ■	55
63	Wayne St. (Neb.) ■	58
55	Southwest St.	64
73	Minn.-Crookston	77
73	Minn. St. Moorhead	64
60	Bemidji St. ■	47
65	Minn.-Duluth ■	71
55	Northern St. ■	75
89	Minn.-Morris ■	78
83	Concordia-St. Paul	67
88	Southwest St.	91
85	Wayne St. (Neb.)	72
53	Minn. St. Moorhead ■	55
89	Minn.-Crookston ■	73
65	Minn.-Duluth	77
85	Bemidji St.	65
69	Bemidji St.	70

Nickname: Warriors
Colors: Purple & White
Arena: McCown Gymnasium
  Capacity: 3,500; Year Built: 1973
SID: Michael Herzberg

WINSTON-SALEM
Winston-Salem, NC 27110 II

Coach: Phillip Stitt, North Carolina 1979
2001-02 RESULTS (22-7)

79	Virginia Union	71
83	Bowie St.	90
69	Columbia Union	43
67	Columbia Union ■	63
78	St. Andrews †	51
89	Catawba	84
82	Benedict	70
82	West Va. Tech	58
106	Elizabeth City St. ■	90
87	Concord ■	68
82	Lincoln (Mo.) ■	87
88	St. Augustine's ■	83
81	Livingstone	65
76	Shaw	69
91	St. Paul's ■	77
71	Johnson Smith	86
86	Virginia St.	78
71	Johnson Smith ■	84
72	Fayetteville St. ■	51

70	N.C. Central ■	72
95	St. Augustine's †	83
73	Benedict ■	57
85	Livingstone	64
80	Fayetteville St.	74
77	N.C. Central	67
84	Elizabeth City St. †	64
65	Shaw †	80
90	Wingate †	75
61	Shaw †	62

Nickname: Rams
Colors: Scarlet & White
Arena: C.E. Gaines Center
  Capacity: 2,500; Year Built: 1978
SID: Adrian Ferguson

WINTHROP
Rock Hill, SC 29733 I

Coach: Gregg Marshall, Randolph-Macon 1985
2001-02 RESULTS (19-12)

60	Lander ■	58
54	Ohio St.	78
65	Nebraska	73
67	Birmingham-So. ■	53
58	Niagara †	63
55	Hartford †	58
65	Marshall ■	71
66	Clemson	61
86	Tenn.-Martin ■	60
58	South Carolina St. ■	71
66	George Mason †	86
48	Radford	69
76	Elon ■	64
75	Randolph-Macon ■	69
81	Liberty	48
83	High Point	75
63	Charleston So. ■	66
73	UNC Asheville	66
81	High Point ■	71
68	Coastal Caro.	49
64	Elon	71
63	Birmingham-So.	56
64	Radford ■	72
69	Liberty ■	62
57	Charleston So.	55
100	Coastal Caro. ■	74
77	UNC Asheville ■	62
66	Liberty †	59
77	Elon †	66
70	High Point †	48
37	Duke †	84

Nickname: Eagles
Colors: Garnet & Gold
Arena: Winthrop Coliseum
  Capacity: 6,100; Year Built: 1982
SID: Jack Frost

WISCONSIN
Madison, WI 53711 I

Coach: Bo Ryan, Wilkes 1969
2001-02 RESULTS (19-13)

69	UNLV	74
78	Hawaii-Hilo	62
69	Weber St. †	73
57	Hawaii †	60
61	Georgia Tech	62
70	Wis.-Green Bay ■	57
67	Temple ■	70
77	Ohio	71
48	Xavier	57
68	Furman ■	60
86	Marquette ■	73
81	Wis.-Milwaukee	79
65	Tennessee ■	62
57	Iowa	69
72	Illinois ■	66
49	Penn St.	51
64	Michigan St.	63
73	Minnesota ■	64

77	Purdue ■	66
48	Illinois	80
66	Penn St. ■	63
60	Northwestern	69
53	Michigan	64
94	Ohio St. ■	92
73	Northwestern	44
64	Indiana	65
67	Minnesota	62
64	Iowa ■	56
74	Michigan ■	54
56	Iowa †	58
80	St. John's (N.Y.) †	70
57	Maryland †	87

Nickname: Badgers
Colors: Cardinal & White
Arena: Kohl Center
  Capacity: 17,142; Year Built: 1998
SID: Justin Doherty

WIS. LUTHERAN
Milwaukee, WI 53226 III

Coach: Skip Noon, Martin Luther 1986
2001-02 RESULTS (14-11)

95	Greenville ■	88
82	Wis.-Superior ■	76
80	Clarke	83
82	Anderson (Ind.)	98
87	Ind.-Northwest †	61
71	Wis.-Whitewater ■	86
84	Webster	77
66	Washington (Mo.)	97
67	Edgewood ■	58
91	Lakeland ■	76
62	Marian (Wis.) ■	66
85	Concordia (Ill.) ■	71
55	Spring Arbor †	80
74	UC Santa Cruz †	82
68	Embry-Riddle †	90
93	Milwaukee Engr.	72
84	Concordia (Wis.)	67
65	Maranatha Baptist ■	60
75	Edgewood	70
68	Lakeland	92
70	Marian (Wis.)	68
69	Milwaukee Engr. ■	64
77	Concordia (Wis.) ■	76
67	Maranatha Baptist	73
48	Concordia (Wis.) ■	72

Nickname: Warriors
Colors: Forest Green & White
Arena: The REX
  Capacity: 2,500; Year Built: 1992
SID: Cheryl Pasbrig

WIS.-EAU CLAIRE
Eau Claire, WI 54702-4004 III

Coach: Terry Gibbons, Wis.-Oshkosh 1983
2001-02 RESULTS (11-14)

93	Northland ■	38
61	Augsburg ■	75
116	Turabo †	62
96	P.R. Metropolitana †	63
100	Mt. Senario ■	49
69	Wis.-La Crosse	72
56	Wis.-Superior	52
59	Wis.-Whitewater	74
74	Wis.-Stout ■	80
95	Milwaukee Engr.	61
93	St. Scholastica ■	60
79	North Central ■	70
62	Wis.-Stevens Point ■	72
76	Northland	58
65	Wis.-Platteville	60
53	Wis.-River Falls ■	62
69	Wis.-Oshkosh	77
67	Wis.-Whitewater ■	72
51	Wis.-Superior	68
58	Wis.-La Crosse ■	70

69	Wis.-Stout	67
79	Wis.-Stevens Point	85
64	Wis.-River Falls	66
67	Wis.-Platteville ■	80
59	Wis.-Oshkosh ■	84

Nickname: Blugolds
Colors: Navy Blue & Old Gold
Arena: W.L. Zorn Arena
  Capacity: 2,450; Year Built: 1952
SID: Tim Petermann

WIS.-GREEN BAY
Green Bay, WI 54311-7001 I

Coach: Mike Heideman, Wis.-La Crosse 1971
2001-02 RESULTS (9-21)

47	UMKC ■	48
55	Kansas St.	68
79	Northern Iowa ■	83
78	Chicago St. ■	62
57	Wisconsin	70
83	St. Bonaventure	93
106	Eastern Mich. ■	76
54	UMKC	67
69	Evansville	77
75	Boston U. ■	79
77	Lipscomb ■	44
51	Wis.-Milwaukee	63
66	Ill.-Chicago ■	75
68	Loyola (Ill.) ■	72
41	Butler	64
73	Wright St.	96
40	Detroit ■	52
61	Cleveland St. ■	50
53	Youngstown St. ■	50
74	Loyola (Ill.)	84
67	Ill.-Chicago	75
65	Detroit	61
74	Butler ■	77
70	Wright St. ■	71
55	Youngstown St.	69
74	Cleveland St.	66
66	Wis.-Milwaukee ■	76
86	Youngstown St. †	65
49	Butler †	48
57	Loyola (Ill.) †	63

Nickname: Phoenix
Colors: Green, White & Red
Arena: Brown County Arena
  Capacity: 5,600; Year Built: 1958
SID: Brian Nicol

WIS.-LA CROSSE
La Crosse, WI 54601 III

Coach: Stu Engen, Augsburg 1986
2001-02 RESULTS (17-9)

73	Grand View †	64
81	Wartburg	82
74	Mount St. Clare ■	67
65	Luther	63
127	Grinnell ■	124
58	Viterbo	47
72	Wis.-Eau Claire ■	69
65	Wis.-Stout ■	60
146	Grinnell	136
75	Wis.-Stevens Point	86
58	St. Cloud St.	82
87	Trinity Int'l ■	45
62	Wis.-Platteville	59
71	Wis.-River Falls ■	63
73	Wis.-Oshkosh	69
76	Wis.-Superior ■	83
79	Wis.-Whitewater	81
63	Wis.-Stout	78
70	Wis.-Eau Claire	58
84	Wis.-Stevens Point ■	72
80	Wis.-River Falls	74
92	Wis.-Platteville ■	60
87	Wis.-Superior	72
66	Wis.-Oshkosh ■	74

65 Wis.-Whitewater ■ ...80
82 Wis.-River Falls ■ ...91

Nickname: Eagles
Colors: Maroon & Gray
Arena: Mitchell Hall
  Capacity: 2,880; Year Built: 1964
SID: David Johnson

WIS.-MILWAUKEE
Milwaukee, WI 53211 I

Coach: Bruce Pearl, Boston College 1982
2001-02 RESULTS (16-13)
77 Concordia-St. Paul ■ ...63
80 Western Mich. ...81
69 Valparaiso ...82
62 Iowa St. ...71
87 Neb.-Omaha † ...68
84 Chicago St. ■ ...47
75 Louisville ...90
80 Virginia Tech † ...78
51 Western Mich. ■ ...59
91 Wis.-Parkside ■ ...58
79 Wisconsin ■ ...81
87 Colorado ...93
77 Youngstown St. ...55
63 Wis.-Green Bay ■ ...51
87 Loyola (Ill.) ■ ...91
75 Ill.-Chicago ■ ...49
86 Wright St. ■ ...80
73 Butler ...72
78 Cleveland St. ■ ...69
66 Detroit ■ ...48
58 Butler ■ ...59
80 Loyola (Ill.) ...70
71 Ill.-Chicago ...73
96 Youngstown St. ■ ...76
94 Wright St. ...68
67 Cleveland St. ...69
61 Detroit ...94
76 Wis.-Green Bay ■ ...66
63 Ill.-Chicago † ...75

Nickname: Panthers
Colors: Black & Gold
Arena: Klotsche Center
  Capacity: 5,000; Year Built: 1977
SID: Kevin O'Connor

WIS.-OSHKOSH
Oshkosh, WI 54901-8617 III

Coach: Ted Van Dellen, Wis.-Oshkosh 1978
2001-02 RESULTS (24-6)
79 Lawrence ■ ...69
92 Marian (Wis.) ■ ...50
54 Edgewood ■ ...50
81 St. Norbert ...66
63 Wis.-Superior ...58
78 Wis.-Platteville ...80
68 Wis.-River Falls ■ ...78
62 Transylvania † ...44
93 Hamilton † ...84
99 Northland ■ ...43
101 Finlandia ■ ...56
89 Wis.-Whitewater ■ ...80
73 Wis.-Stout ...68
69 Wis.-La Crosse ...73
63 Wis.-Stevens Point ...54
77 Wis.-Eau Claire ■ ...69
65 Wis.-River Falls ...60
72 Wis.-Platteville ■ ...75
70 Wis.-Superior ...56
66 Wis.-Stout ■ ...64
71 Wis.-Whitewater ...70
73 Wis.-Stevens Point ■ ...74
74 Wis.-La Crosse ...66
84 Wis.-Eau Claire ...59
73 Wis.-Superior ■ ...56
86 Wis.-River Falls ■ ...80
70 Wis.-Whitewater ...69

71 Ripon ■ ...56
88 St. Thomas (Minn.) ...85
71 Lewis & Clark † ...79

Nickname: Titans
Colors: Black, Gold & White
Arena: Kolf Sports Center
  Capacity: 5,800; Year Built: 1971
SID: Kennan Timm

WIS.-PARKSIDE
Kenosha, WI 53141-2000 II

Coach: Jeff Rutter, Winona St. 1988
2001-02 RESULTS (14-14)
86 Minn. St.-Mankato ...76
80 Wayne St. (Neb.) † ...68
76 Indianapolis ■ ...73
67 Northern Ky. ■ ...54
69 Ky. Wesleyan ...82
70 Southern Ind. ...69
78 Quincy ■ ...77
70 SIU-Edwardsville ...64
73 Lakeland ...63
71 Winona St. ■ ...58
58 Wis.-Milwaukee ...91
54 Edgewood ...60
65 St. Joseph's (Ind.) ■ ...55
55 Northern Ky. ...70
53 Bellarmine ...71
68 Southern Ind. ■ ...79
57 Mo.-St. Louis ■ ...60
95 SIU-Edwardsville ...92
68 Lewis ...75
80 St. Joseph's (Ind.) ...66
54 Indianapolis ...67
59 Bellarmine ...72
79 Ky. Wesleyan ■ ...90
58 Mo.-St. Louis ...76
110 Quincy ...105
57 Lewis ■ ...65
93 Northern Ky. † ...87
58 Lewis † ...70

Nickname: Rangers
Colors: Green, White & Black
Arena: Sports & Activities Center
  Capacity: 2,120; Year Built: 1969
SID: Steve Kratochvil

WIS.-PLATTEVILLE
Platteville, WI 53818-3099 III

Coach: Todd Landrum, Ohio Northern 1973
2001-02 RESULTS (14-12)
79 Coe ■ ...71
79 St. John's (Minn.) ...71
70 Dubuque ...46
83 Clarke ...67
91 Marycrest Int'l ■ ...54
58 Wis.-Stout ...87
80 Wis.-Oshkosh ■ ...78
63 Wis.-Superior ...60
50 Wis.-Whitewater ■ ...63
70 St. Xavier ...82
75 Mass.-Dartmouth † ...71
65 King's (Pa.) † ...71
59 Wis.-La Crosse ■ ...62
71 Wis.-Stevens Point ...78
60 Wis.-Eau Claire ■ ...65
73 Edgewood ...68
66 Wis.-River Falls ...62
80 Wis.-Superior ■ ...71
75 Wis.-Oshkosh ...72
58 Wis.-Stout ...51
74 Wis.-Whitewater ...82
66 Wis.-Stevens Point ■ ...73
60 Wis.-La Crosse ...92
80 Wis.-Eau Claire ...67
67 Wis.-River Falls ■ ...78
57 Wis.-Stevens Point ...72

Nickname: Pioneers
Colors: Blue & Orange

Arena: Williams Fieldhouse
  Capacity: 2,300; Year Built: 1962
SID: Paul Erickson

WIS.-RIVER FALLS
River Falls, WI 54022 III

Coach: Rick Bowen, Indiana 1966
2001-02 RESULTS (17-9)
94 Bethel (Ind.) ...97
72 Lake Forest ...59
68 St. Thomas (Minn.) ...66
62 Wis.-Whitewater ...65
84 Northwestern (Minn.) ■ ...73
78 Wis.-Oshkosh ...68
61 Wis.-Superior ...50
82 Simpson ...74
80 Viterbo ■ ...70
71 Loras ■ ...60
60 Luther ...36
79 Wis.-Stout ■ ...61
63 Wis.-La Crosse ...71
79 Wis.-Stevens Point ■ ...94
62 Wis.-Eau Claire ...53
62 Wis.-Platteville ...66
60 Wis.-Oshkosh ...65
82 Wis.-Whitewater ■ ...75
84 Wis.-Superior ...77
74 Wis.-La Crosse ...80
70 Wis.-Stout ...68
66 Wis.-Eau Claire ■ ...64
74 Wis.-Stevens Point ...77
78 Wis.-Platteville ...67
91 Wis.-La Crosse ...82
80 Wis.-Oshkosh ...86

Nickname: Falcons
Colors: Red & White
Arena: Karges Center
  Capacity: 2,000; Year Built: 1958
SID: Jim Thies

WIS.-STEVENS POINT
Stevens Point, WI 54481 III

Coach: Jack Bennett, Ripon 1971
2001-02 RESULTS (21-6)
90 Trinity Int'l ■ ...28
81 Coe ...62
80 Viterbo ...73
62 Edgewood † ...47
67 Marian (Wis.) † ...54
83 Carroll (Wis.) ...62
77 St. Francis (Ill.) ...61
71 Wis.-Whitewater ■ ...72
61 Wis.-Stout ...72
86 Wis.-La Crosse ■ ...75
109 Mt. Senario ■ ...44
90 St. Francis (Ill.) ...58
72 Wis.-Eau Claire ...62
78 Wis.-Platteville ...71
94 Wis.-River Falls ...79
54 Wis.-Oshkosh ■ ...63
72 Wis.-Superior ...70
87 Wis.-Stout ■ ...95
91 Wis.-Whitewater ...80
72 Wis.-La Crosse ...84
73 Wis.-Platteville ...66
85 Wis.-Eau Claire ■ ...79
74 Wis.-Oshkosh ...73
77 Wis.-River Falls ...74
83 Wis.-Superior ...56
72 Wis.-Platteville ■ ...57
73 Wis.-Whitewater ■ ...80

Nickname: Pointers
Colors: Purple & Gold
Arena: Quandt Fieldhouse
  Capacity: 3,281; Year Built: 1969
SID: Jim Strick

WIS.-STOUT
Menomonie, WI 54751-0790...III

Coach: Ed Andrist, Wis.-Stout 1976
2001-02 RESULTS (12-13)
74 Mary ■ ...75
72 St. John's (Minn.) ...65
58 Southwest St. ...67
73 Huron ...55
48 Northwest Mo. St. † ...85
105 Northland ■ ...48
87 Wis.-Platteville ■ ...58
60 Wis.-La Crosse ...65
72 Wis.-Stevens Point ■ ...61
80 Wis.-Eau Claire ...74
71 Viterbo ■ ...53
61 Wis.-River Falls ...79
68 Wis.-Oshkosh ■ ...73
52 Wis.-Superior ...55
85 Wis.-Whitewater ■ ...72
79 Northwestern (Minn.) ...60
95 Wis.-Stevens Point ...87
78 Wis.-La Crosse ■ ...63
51 Wis.-Platteville ...58
67 Wis.-Eau Claire ■ ...69
64 Wis.-Oshkosh ...66
68 Wis.-River Falls ■ ...70
82 Wis.-Whitewater ...89
70 Wis.-Superior ■ ...61
77 Wis.-Whitewater ...85

Nickname: Blue Devils
Colors: Navy & White
Arena: Johnson Fieldhouse
  Capacity: 1,900; Year Built: 1965
SID: Layne Pitt

WIS.-SUPERIOR
Superior, WI 54880-4500 III

Coach: Jeff Kaminsky, Grand Valley St. 1985
2001-02 RESULTS (11-15)
76 Rockford † ...66
76 Wis. Lutheran ...82
95 Northland ...50
72 St. Scholastica ...56
58 Wis.-Oshkosh ■ ...63
52 Wis.-Eau Claire ...56
60 Wis.-Platteville ■ ...63
50 Wis.-River Falls ...61
72 Concordia-M'head ■ ...71
65 MacMurray † ...61
97 Olivet † ...64
59 Wis.-Whitewater ...69
105 Northland ■ ...61
55 Wis.-Stout ...52
83 Wis.-La Crosse ...76
70 Wis.-Stevens Point ■ ...72
71 Wis.-Platteville ...80
68 Wis.-Eau Claire ■ ...51
56 Wis.-Oshkosh ...70
77 Wis.-River Falls ■ ...84
65 Wis.-Whitewater ■ ...85
98 Finlandia ...54
72 Wis.-La Crosse ...87
61 Wis.-Stout ...70
56 Wis.-Stevens Point ...83
56 Wis.-Oshkosh ...73

Nickname: Yellowjackets
Colors: Gold, Black, & White
Arena: Gates Fieldhouse
  Capacity: 2,500; Year Built: 1966
SID: Chris Vito

WIS.-WHITEWATER
Whitewater, WI 53190 III

Coach: Pat Miller
2001-02 RESULTS (21-7)
59 Elmhurst ■ ...50
80 St. Xavier ...90

77	Purdue-Calumet ■	69
86	Wis. Lutheran	71
65	Wis.-River Falls ■	62
72	Wis.-Stevens Point	71
74	Wis.-Eau Claire ■	59
63	Wis.-Platteville	50
95	Carroll (Wis.)	66
74	Ohio Wesleyan †	65
73	Albion	69
80	Wis.-Oshkosh ■	89
69	Wis.-Superior ■	59
72	Wis.-Stout	85
87	Maranatha Baptist ■	61
81	Wis.-La Crosse ■	79
72	Wis.-Eau Claire	67
80	Wis.-Stevens Point ■	91
75	Wis.-River Falls	82
82	Wis.-Platteville ■	74
85	Wis.-Superior	65
70	Wis.-Oshkosh ■	71
89	Wis.-Stout ■	82
87	Concordia (Wis.)	67
80	Wis.-La Crosse	65
85	Wis.-Stout	77
80	Wis.-Stevens Point	73
69	Wis.-Oshkosh	70

Nickname: Warhawks
Colors: Purple & White
Arena: Williams Center
Capacity: 3,000; Year Built: 1967
SID: Tom Fick

WITTENBERG
Springfield, OH 45504 III

Coach: Bill Brown, Wittenberg 1973
2001-02 RESULTS (26-4)

69	Mt. Vernon Naz. †	66
72	Wheaton (Ill.)	77
85	Case Reserve ■	45
108	Cedarville	66
96	Denison	60
90	Wabash ■	69
72	Allegheny	66
82	Urbana	62
98	Thomas More	64
81	Illinois Col. ■	58
65	Marian (Ind.) ■	62
64	Otterbein ■	73
103	Oberlin	53
86	Kenyon ■	53
91	Hiram	51
70	Ohio Wesleyan ■	68
100	Denison	69
65	Wabash	77
75	Wooster ■	70
70	Earlham	38
86	Allegheny ■	61
67	Ohio Wesleyan	64
103	Hiram ■	60
81	Earlham ■	60
68	Wooster	66
78	Earlham	51
75	Ohio Wesleyan	69
58	Wooster ■	57
75	Franklin	44
76	DePauw	89

Nickname: Tigers
Colors: Red & White
Arena: Health, PE & Rec Center
Capacity: 3,000; Year Built: 1982
SID: Ryan Maurer

WOFFORD
Spartanburg, SC 29303-3663 I

Coach: Richard Johnson, Citadel 1976
2001-02 RESULTS (11-18)

61	Memphis	88
56	Sacramento St. †	46
94	Toccoa Falls Inst. ■	42
82	Clemson	85
77	Florida A&M ■	72
49	South Carolina ■	64
46	Nebraska	65
42	North Carolina St.	80
103	Emmanuel (Ga.) ■	64
87	Virginia Intermont ■	59
77	Reinhardt ■	55
70	Georgia Tech	79
66	Col. of Charleston ■	64
59	Furman ■	49
73	Citadel ■	64
61	Col. of Charleston ■	73
77	Chattanooga	79
73	Ga. Southern	86
58	East Tenn. St.	71
76	UNC Greensboro ■	81
61	Davidson	72
78	VMI ■	68
45	Chattanooga ■	70
76	Ga. Southern ■	67
69	Appalachian St.	85
48	Furman	55
71	Western Caro. ■	77
63	Citadel	72
41	UNC Greensboro †	70

Nickname: Terriers
Colors: Old Gold & Black
Arena: Benjamin Johnson Arena
Capacity: 3,500; Year Built: 1981
SID: Mark Cohen

WOOSTER
Wooster, OH 44691 III

Coach: Steve Moore, Wittenberg 1974
2001-02 RESULTS (21-7)

94	Pitt.-Bradford ■	86
66	St. Thomas (Minn.) ■	76
74	Edinboro	57
55	Capital ■	62
88	Earlham	79
73	Ohio Wesleyan ■	63
92	Kenyon ■	59
71	Texas Lutheran	74
76	Southwestern (Tex.)	55
94	Case Reserve	43
80	Thiel ■	66
83	Denison	71
67	Westminster (Pa.) ■	58
78	Oberlin ■	58
72	Wabash	69
82	Allegheny ■	70
86	Earlham ■	70
76	Ohio Wesleyan	55
70	Wittenberg	75
88	Hiram	69
96	Kenyon	59
91	Allegheny	63
62	Wabash ■	76
93	Hiram	60
66	Wittenberg ■	68
82	Allegheny ■	72
83	Wabash †	80
57	Wittenberg	58

Nickname: Fighting Scots
Colors: Black & Old Gold
Arena: Timken Gymnasium
Capacity: 3,400; Year Built: 1968
SID: Hugh Howard

WPI
Worcester, MA 01609 III

Coach: Chris Bartley, Mass.-Lowell 1994
2001-02 RESULTS (5-20)

48	Framingham St.	69
82	Curry	75
69	Daniel Webster ■	53
47	Salve Regina ■	68
58	Brandeis	76
74	Anna Maria ■	69
71	Wentworth Inst. ■	83
54	Emerson ■	65
56	Western New Eng. ■	71
50	Springfield	60
62	Mount Ida	53
62	Wheaton (Mass.) ■	53
52	Roger Williams ■	70
41	Babson	69
57	Clark (Mass.) ■	78
46	Coast Guard ■	58
49	MIT	51
62	Springfield ■	79
51	Endicott	57
52	Wheaton (Mass.)	73
31	Babson	62
55	Clark (Mass.)	87
59	Coast Guard	72
59	MIT ■	63
38	Babson	69

Nickname: Engineers
Colors: Crimson & Gray
Arena: Harrington Auditorium
Capacity: 3,000; Year Built: 1967
SID: Steve Raczynski

WORCESTER ST.
Worcester, MA 01602-2597 III

Coach: Dave Lindberg, Worcester St. 1991
2001-02 RESULTS (8-18)

63	Plymouth St. †	73
65	Johnson & Wales †	70
42	Mass.-Dartmouth ■	69
64	Anna Maria ■	61
59	Nichols	64
51	Eastern Nazarene ■	53
51	Eastern Conn. St.	73
67	Me.-Fort Kent †	68
65	Becker †	51
47	Amherst	74
59	Clark (Mass.) ■	90
74	Montclair St.	84
49	York (N.Y.) †	70
65	Fitchburg St.	67
58	Westfield St. ■	76
71	Framingham St.	76
79	Mass. Liberal Arts	53
66	Bridgewater St. ■	57
80	Salem St.	83
52	Fitchburg St. ■	66
83	Westfield St.	69
66	Framingham St. ■	63
77	Mass. Liberal Arts ■	74
57	Bridgewater St.	55
67	Salem St. ■	70
69	Bridgewater St. ■	72

Nickname: Lancers
Colors: Royal Blue & Gold
Arena: Lancer Gymnasium
Capacity: 1,200; Year Built: 1953
SID: Bruce Baker

WRIGHT ST.
Dayton, OH 45435-0001 I

Coach: Ed Schilling, Miami (Ohio) 1988
2001-02 RESULTS (17-11)

83	St. Francis (Pa.)	67
54	Cincinnati	83
75	IPFW ■	62
66	Tennessee St. ■	54
61	Miami (Ohio)	67
72	Morehead St.	80
77	High Point	55
74	Oakland ■	54
76	Santa Clara ■	62
94	Prairie View ■	61
90	Butler	87
80	Youngstown St.	87
74	Detroit	75
68	Cleveland St. ■	64
80	Wis.-Milwaukee ■	86
96	Wis.-Green Bay ■	73
83	Tex.-Pan American ■	64
65	Loyola (Ill.)	60
66	Ill.-Chicago	68
76	Youngstown St.	69
57	Butler	72
87	Cleveland St. ■	72
64	Detroit ■	69
68	Wis.-Milwaukee	94
71	Wis.-Green Bay	70
63	Ill.-Chicago ■	62
80	Loyola (Ill.) ■	74
64	Loyola (Ill.) †	90

Nickname: Raiders
Colors: Green & Gold
Arena: Ervin J. Nutter Center
Capacity: 11,019; Year Built: 1990
SID: Robert J. Noss

WYOMING
Laramie, WY 82071 I

Coach: Steve McClain, Chadron St. 1984
2001-02 RESULTS (22-9)

55	Southern California	68
94	Ark.-Pine Bluff ■	74
98	Eastern Ky. ■	78
71	Denver	68
57	Detroit	73
86	Cal St. Fullerton ■	71
86	Cal St. Northridge ■	64
74	Boise St.	77
82	Montana St. †	69
72	Indiana St. ■	58
85	Alas. Anchorage ■	67
104	Portland St.	58
84	Texas Tech	90
69	UNLV	59
95	Colorado St. ■	72
88	San Diego St.	85
79	New Mexico	67
83	Air Force ■	76
70	Brigham Young	85
54	Utah	46
72	Colorado St.	69
82	UNLV ■	78
64	San Diego St. ■	68
51	Air Force	48
65	New Mexico	74
76	Brigham Young ■	60
57	Utah ■	56
69	Air Force †	67
69	San Diego St. †	70
74	Gonzaga †	66
60	Arizona †	68

Nickname: Cowboys
Colors: Brown & Wyoming Prairie Gold
Arena: Arena-Auditorium
Capacity: 15,000; Year Built: 1982
SID: Tim Harkins

XAVIER
Cincinnati, OH 45207-7530 I

Coach: Thad Matta, Butler 1990
2001-02 RESULTS (26-6)

72	Coastal Caro. ■	41
60	Missouri †	72
87	Miami (Ohio)	58
87	San Francisco	72
66	Purdue	70
108	Long Island ■	57
57	Wisconsin	48
55	Cincinnati ■	75
62	Kent St. ■	56
72	Creighton	65
68	Siena ■	59
66	Dayton	59
88	Fordham ■	58
72	Richmond ■	62
71	George Washington	63

SCHEDULES/RESULTS

71 La Salle ...67
67 Rhode Island ...49
75 Dayton ...59
79 Duquesne ■ ...65
67 Richmond ...64
79 St. Bonaventure ...80
89 George Washington ■ ...75
84 St. Joseph's ■ ...77
56 Temple ...67
80 Duquesne ...66
68 La Salle ■ ...53
72 Massachusetts ■ ...52
65 Massachusetts † ...59
66 Dayton † ...59
73 Richmond † ...60
70 Hawaii † ...58
65 Oklahoma † ...78

Nickname: Musketeers
Colors: Blue, Gray & White
Arena: Cintas Center
Capacity: 10,250; Year Built: 2000
SID: Tom Eiser

YALE
New Haven, CT 06520-8216 I

Coach: James Jones, Albany (N.Y.) 1986
2001-02 RESULTS (21-11)
62 Air Force † ...68
87 Tenn.-Martin † ...99
87 Penn St. ...74
82 Stony Brook † ...62
102 George Washington ...116
77 Sacred Heart ■ ...64
83 Army ■ ...73
75 Colgate ...87
90 Long Island ...54
73 Albany (N.Y.) ■ ...61
77 Rhode Island ■ ...66
69 Gardner-Webb † ...79
82 Macalester † ...90
68 Clemson ...65
65 Columbia ■ ...54
79 Cornell ■ ...74
82 Brown ■ ...87
80 Brown ...77
73 Dartmouth ...55
66 Harvard ...57
83 Pennsylvania ■ ...78
60 Princeton ■ ...50
80 Cornell ...65
76 Columbia ...56
46 Princeton ...59
63 Pennsylvania ...72
77 Harvard ■ ...72

88 Dartmouth ■ ...59
76 Princeton † ...60
58 Pennsylvania † ...77
67 Rutgers ...65
61 Tennessee Tech ■ ...80

Nickname: Elis, Bulldogs
Colors: Yale Blue & White
Arena: John J. Lee Ampitheater
Capacity: 3,100; Year Built: 1932
SID: Tim Bennett

YESHIVA
New York, NY 10033-3201 III

Coach: Jonathan Halpert, Yeshiva 1966
2001-02 RESULTS (14-12)
75 Lasell † ...83
92 Thomas † ...58
68 Old Westbury ...80
66 Mt. St. Mary (N.Y.) ■ ...48
67 Manhattanville ...72
70 Stevens Tech ...58
61 Maritime (N.Y.) ■ ...53
48 Baruch ...68
42 Rowan ■ ...57
94 Mt. St. Vincent ■ ...75
76 St. Joseph's (L.I.) ■ ...69
53 Merchant Marine ...67
81 Ramapo ■ ...101
61 CCNY ...68
81 Polytechnic (N.Y.) ■ ...46
64 Mt. St. Mary (N.Y.) ...70
56 St. Joseph's (L.I.) ...69
77 Brooklyn ...59
95 Manhattanville ■ ...70
69 Merchant Marine ■ ...78
54 Maritime (N.Y.) ...53
70 Stevens Tech ...63
75 Old Westbury ■ ...67
81 Mt. St. Vincent ...75
62 Stevens Tech ■ ...54
54 Manhattanville ...61

Nickname: Maccabees
Colors: Royal Blue & White
Arena: Max Stern Athletic Center
Capacity: 1,100; Year Built: 1985
SID: To be named

YORK (N.Y.)
Jamaica, NY 11451 ...III

Coach: Ronald St. John, York (N.Y.) 1980

2001-02 RESULTS (13-14)
74 Roanoke ■ ...88
54 Ferrum † ...62
79 St. Joseph's (L.I.) ■ ...70
58 Medgar Evers ...77
68 New Paltz St. ...62
63 Ramapo ...85
67 Brooklyn ■ ...65
58 Wilkes † ...62
52 Rochester Inst. ...64
63 Rutgers-Newark ...57
65 Savannah A&D † ...72
70 Worcester St. † ...49
53 Wm. Paterson ...62
76 NYCCT ...56
62 Staten Island ...65
60 Lehman ■ ...54
71 John Jay ...67
85 Hunter ...81
53 Old Westbury ■ ...51
52 CCNY ...75
55 Baruch ■ ...64
52 Medgar Evers ...54
78 Brooklyn ...66
82 NYCCT ...62
52 Staten Island ■ ...57
71 Lehman † ...55
65 Medgar Evers † ...68

Nickname: Cardinals
Colors: Red & White
Arena: Health & P.E. Complex
Capacity: 1,200; Year Built: 1990
SID: Darrin Ford

YORK (PA.)
York, PA 17405-7199 ...III

Coach: Jeff Gamber, Millersville 1968
2001-02 RESULTS (21-6)
94 Hiram ■ ...69
90 Bethany (W.Va.) ■ ...84
88 Keuka † ...63
68 Rochester ...73
69 Catholic ■ ...72
88 St. Mary's (Md.) ...77
84 McDaniel ...73
70 Dickinson ■ ...66
57 Gettysburg ■ ...67
88 Juniata ...87
97 Wash. & Jeff. ...93
93 Merchant Marine ■ ...80
92 Gallaudet ...58
73 Mary Washington ...63
94 Goucher ■ ...72
91 Salisbury ...81

82 Marymount (Va.) ■ ...77
82 St. Mary's (Md.) ■ ...65
100 Susquehanna ...105
78 Catholic ...94
95 Mary Washington ■ ...71
99 Gallaudet ...96
66 Salisbury ■ ...61
85 Goucher ...78
98 Marymount (Va.) ...82
91 Gallaudet ■ ...78
100 Marymount (Va.) ■ ...103

Nickname: Spartans
Colors: Kelly Green & White
Arena: Wolf Gym
Capacity: 1,200; Year Built: 1964
SID: Scott Guise

YOUNGSTOWN ST.
Youngstown, OH 44555-0001 ...I

Coach: John Robic, Denison 1986
2001-02 RESULTS (5-23)
64 Evansville ...87
99 Slippery Rock ■ ...67
69 DePaul ...107
50 Valparaiso ...80
72 Chicago St. ...81
65 Toledo ...79
75 Kent St. ...70
80 Robert Morris ...87
53 UMKC ...68
79 Western Ill. ...84
55 Wis.-Milwaukee ■ ...77
87 Wright St. ■ ...80
58 Cleveland St. ...71
50 Butler ■ ...68
51 Detroit ■ ...66
63 Loyola (Ill.) ...72
69 Ill.-Chicago ...85
50 Wis.-Green Bay ...53
69 Wright St. ...76
55 Loyola (Ill.) ■ ...75
57 Ill.-Chicago ■ ...63
76 Wis.-Milwaukee ...96
48 Cleveland St. ■ ...58
50 Butler ...75
52 Detroit ...63
69 Wis.-Green Bay ■ ...55
78 IPFW ■ ...71
65 Wis.-Green Bay † ...86

Nickname: Penguins
Colors: Red & White
Arena: Beeghley Center
Capacity: 6,500; Year Built: 1972
SID: Trevor Parks

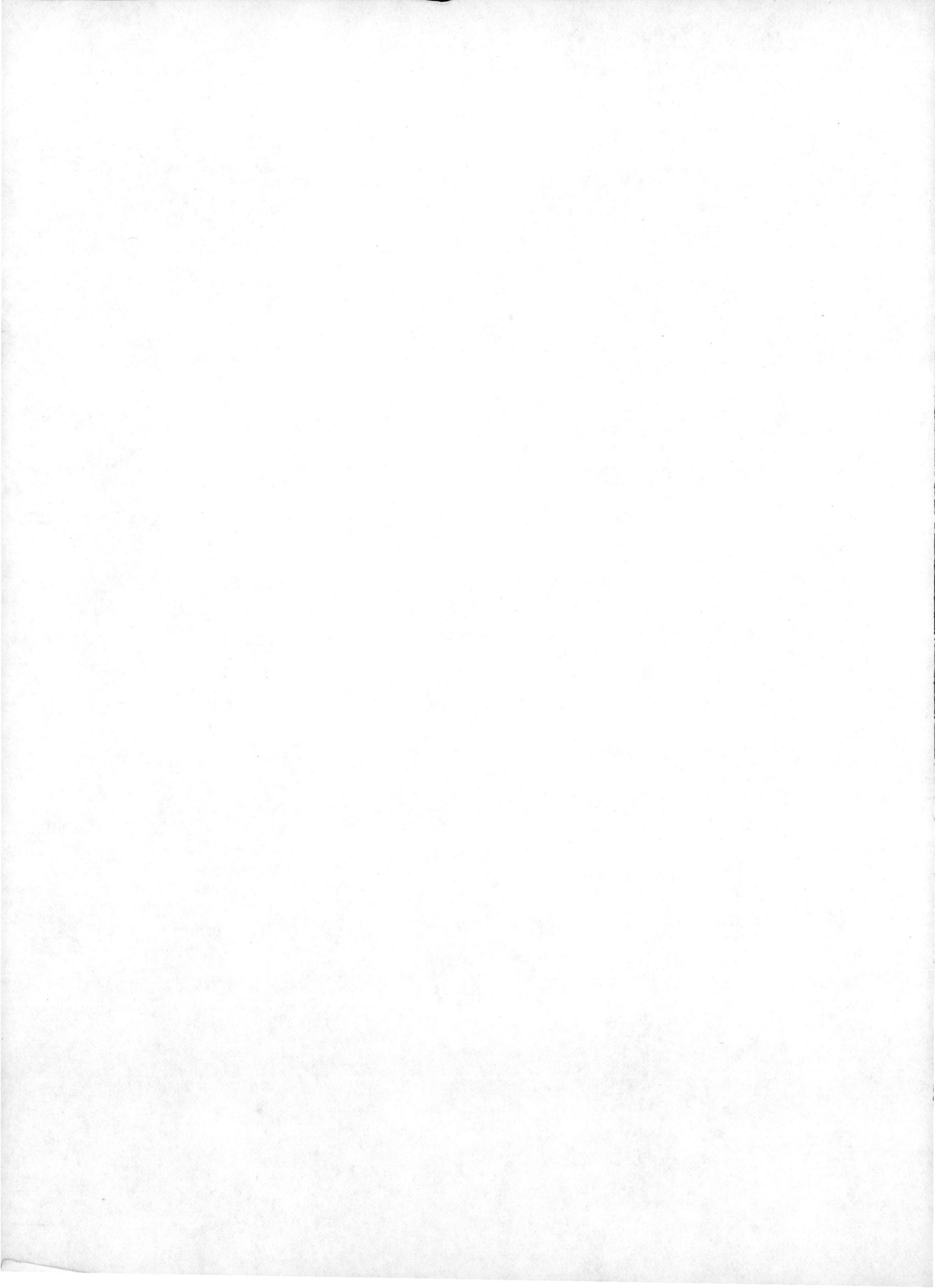